Ethical Health Care

Ethical Health Care

Patricia Illingworth

Wendy E. Parmet
Northeastern University

PEARSON
Prentice
Hall

Upper Saddle River, New Jersey 07458

Library of Congress Cataloging-in-Publication Data

Illingworth, Patricia.
   Ethical health care / Patricia Illingworth, Wendy E. Parmet.
       p. cm.
   Includes bibliographical references and index.
   ISBN 0-13-045301-3
1. Medical ethics.   2. Public health—Moral and ethical aspects.
3. Bioethics.   I. Parmet, Wendy E.   II. Title.
   R724.I544 2005
   174.2—dc22

                                                        2005005091

VP/Editorial Director: Charlyce Jones Owen
Editorial Assistant: Carla Worner
Marketing Assistant: Jennifer Lang
Production Liaison: Fran Russello
Manufacturing Buyer: Christina Helder
Cover Design: Bruce Kenselaar
Composition/Full-Service Project Management:
   Karen Berry/Pine Tree Composition, Inc.
Printer/Binder: The Courier Companies
Cover Printer: Coral Graphics

Credits and acknowledgments borrowed from other sources and reproduced, with permission, in this textbook appear on pages 599–602.

Pearson Education LTD., London
Pearson Education Singapore, Pte. Ltd
Pearson Education Canada, Ltd.
Pearson Education–Japan
Pearson Education Australia PTY, Limited

Pearson Education North Asia Ltd
Pearson Educación de Mexico, S.A. de C.V.
Pearson Education Malaysia, Pte. Ltd
Pearson Education, Upper Saddle River, New Jersey

10 9 8 7 6 5 4 3 2 1
ISBN 0-13-045301-3

To Ron, Daniel, and Anna Lanoue

and

To Harold and Zoe

Contents

Preface

One of the valuable lessons we have learned from editing this textbook is that our own work has been influenced by the work of others, including our mentors, intellectual leaders, colleagues, collaborators, students, and, of course, each other. We are grateful to these "teachers" for the reflection and work they have undertaken in the area of bioethics and public health. We have learned a great deal from them and look forward to continuing the dialogue.

We are deeply grateful to Deborah Hendricks, Jessica Wolland, Bronwyn Page, Nela Suka, Andrew Scott, and many Northeastern University Law students, including Heather Engman, Laurie Martindale, and Samuel Leadholm, for their expert research assistance. We also owe a debt of gratitude to Jan McNew for assuming the herculean task of manuscript preparation and for executing it with such care and grace. We also thank Andrew Sullivan for helping us check citations. Without the help of these associates, this book would not have come to fruition. We thank them and appreciate their commitment to the standards of excellence that we envisioned for the book.

Daniel Wikler provided us with helpful comments on the manuscript. We very much appreciate his willingness to share his time and insights with us. We are also grateful to Northeastern University and our colleagues in the Department of Philosophy and the School of Law for providing us with the time we needed to focus our efforts on preparing this book. Special thanks go to Stephen Nathanson and Emily Speiler for their commitment to facilitating faculty research in general and this project in particular. Thanks also to the staff of Northeastern University Law Library for their expert help.

We also would like to thank Ross Miller and Wendy Yurash from Prentice Hall for their commitment to the book and the vision of bioethics that it reflects. Many thanks also to John J. Paris, Boston College; James Stacey Taylor, Louisiana

State University; and Timothy J. Madigan, University of Rochester, for their thoughtful comments and suggestions. Finally, Karen Berry did a wonderful job editing our work.

Please note that we have sometimes edited lengthy cases and documents to facilitate reading; we have not used ellipses to indicate deleted material.

Patricia Illingworth
Wendy E. Parmet

Chapter One

Bioethics:
Expanding Our Horizons

A. Shifting Paradigms

Concern about the social and ethical implications of health care practices and bio-medical advances is everywhere. From discussions about partial-birth abortion to debates about stem cell research, one cannot escape controversies about the moral quandaries that arise at the forefront of modern medicine. In this book we will explore these traditional bioethical issues as well as some new ones. We will do so in a manner that is different from (and we hope more fruitful than) the approaches typically taken.

Until now, discussions about the ethical implications of health care have typically taken place from a vantage point that emphasizes the role of individual health care providers and their relationship to individual patients. These discussions, framed within the paradigm known as bioethics, generally isolate the relationship between health care providers, especially physicians, and patients—separating them from the institutions, communities, and social contexts in which they interact. Not only does this isolation give patients and providers a false sense of control over patient welfare, it fails to portray realistically the nature and complexity of the dilemmas that arise within the health care context. For in fact, the issues bioethicists have traditionally analyzed are far more complex and far more connected to larger, social forces than is generally acknowledged. Moreover, the health of individuals—which is after all the goal of medical care—is far more dependent upon the well-being of the community in which they reside than traditional bioethical discussions acknowledge. In other words, the health of individuals is at least partially dependent on the health of communities, thus falling within the purview of public health.

In recent years, bioethics as a discipline has attempted to respond to these concerns by broadening its reach and working more closely with other disciplines—

particularly law, medicine, and religion. Nonetheless, bioethical inquiry has remained, for the most part, focused on individuals. The ethical issues that arise when we consider the health of communities, and the relationship between individual health decisions and social forces, remain largely unintegrated into the discourse, creating a false divide between the health interests of individuals and that of the public, between bioethics and social justice. The results, all too often, are policies that optimize neither the health of individuals nor the well-being of their communities.

If our discussions about health care and ethics are to inform our policies and strongly support the health and freedom of all individuals and communities, we need to widen the debate and transform the paradigm. Bioethical issues must include the topics and perspectives that are typically relegated to discussions of public health, health economics, social policy, and the law. In turn, those social issues must be enriched by the understandings and discussions typically conducted by bioethics. In other words, population-based considerations must be included in the bioethics dialogue.

To begin this task of broadening the debate and redefining bioethics we need to reexamine the assumptions upon which the discipline of bioethics has been predicated. We must look also to other disciplines—particularly public health with its emphasis upon population well-being—to consider different perspectives. And, as we reexamine the issues that confront both bioethics and public health, we must remember to include the insights garnered from the other disciplines. Most important, at each step of the journey, we must continue the dialogue and engage more voices in the quest for human health and well-being.

B. The Bioethical Perspective

The discipline of bioethics developed in the late twentieth century. As with the earlier field of medical ethics, its primary focus has been on the doctor–patient relationship. But bioethics differs from traditional medical ethics, with its emphasis on developing norms for physicians, by looking at questions that arise outside of the clinical context (such as questions relating to research) and adapting a wider interdisciplinary perspective. In this respect bioethics has pioneered interdisciplinary work. Until quite recently, it has drawn most often from philosophical ethics, principles of justice, case law, and Judeo-Christian religious perspectives. Given the interdisciplinary bent of bioethics, the task of incorporating an even broader public-health perspective should not be a daunting one. The current crisis that health care faces between, on the one hand, improving access to care and, on the other hand, stemming the ever rising cost of care may be just what is needed to facilitate this shift.

Following contemporary Anglo-American philosophy, which emphasizes solving problems, such as the mind–body problem or skepticism about the external world, bioethics has focused on concrete problems. This approach can also be traced to the nature of medicine and the queries that are raised by physicians. Physicians work within the parameters of the human body and their goal is to cure specific illnesses. Faced with an ethical problem, in a dialogue with a bioethicist, physicians bring their expertise in medicine to the discussion and ethicists bring their knowledge of the normative world. Following the paradigm of practical ethics, ethicists then apply the principles and theories of a long philosophical tradition to complex medical fact patterns. Early in the history of bioethics, the discussions between physicians and "philosophical enthusiasts" often resembled "turf wars" in which the focus of the debate was over what part of the issue was medical and within the physician's expertise, and what part normative and within the purview of the ethicist.

To understand the ethical perspectives used by bioethicists, we need to know some of the key characteristics of ethical judgments. First, the ethical judgments with which we will be concerned are about people and our interaction with them. Some scholars also believe that bioethics should include within its scope nonhuman animals. Although we agree in principle, space considerations make it impossible for us to address this important topic in this volume. Second, ethics usually concerns conduct. That is, when we make ethical judgments we are usually evaluating actions. Third, ethical judgments are typically universal. An ethical judgment that is true for one person in a particular situation is also true for anyone else in the same situation. If it is wrong for your friend to break a promise made to a dying relative, it is also wrong for you to do likewise. Thus the ethical point of view is strongly committed to impartiality. Fourth, ethics is prescriptive. Ethical judgments are concerned not only with describing conduct but also modifying it and prescribing action.

Bioethicists use ethical theories and principles as tools to help them identify and resolve ethical dilemmas. Because these theories figure prominently in traditional bioethics and will appear in some of the readings we include in this volume, it is important for us to review some of them. Applied ethics draws on several kinds of theories. Most prominent are deontological and teleological theories. Deontological theories focus on actions and whether or not they conform to a rule. If the question at hand is "Should I tell this patient the truth about her cancer or should I lie?" the deontologist is interested in determining whether or not there is a rule prohibiting deception, and, of course, there is. Indeed, lying is considered morally wrong by almost all ethical systems.

Typically, rights theories are viewed as deontological. People with rights can make a legitimate claim on others to either provide them with something (a positive right) or to refrain from interfering with them (a negative right). In either case, others incur a corresponding duty to the rights' holder. For a rights theorist, the morally relevant question is, "Does this particular conduct violate a right?" If it does, then it is considered unethical. Ronald Dworkin, an important contemporary rights theorist, calls rights "trumps."[1] Put differently, when someone holds a right, that right trumps all considerations of utility.

Perhaps the most significant deontological moral theory to be used in contemporary bioethics is that of Immanuel Kant. Kant was an influential eighteenth-century German philosopher. Most of his important work on ethics appeared in a short volume entitled *Foundations of the Metaphysics of Morals,* which was published in 1786.[2] Kant, unlike John Stuart Mill and the utilitarians, did not believe that the morality of an action can be found in its consequences. Instead, he believed that the moral worth of an action could be determined by looking at whether the action conformed to moral law, a universally valid maxim of action. To ensure that the maxim that serves as the basis of action is in concert with the dictates of morality, Kant believed that the actor should determine if his or her maxim could be universalized. A maxim would qualify as universal, and in turn, as moral law, if a person could will that it apply both to his or her own case and morally similar cases. Kant also referred to the moral law as the categorical imperative. Kant formulated a second version of the categorical imperative, "respect for persons," that appears widely throughout medical ethics. According to Kant, we ought to "treat every person as an end and never solely as a means."[3] When we treat people as ends in themselves and not as means to ends, ours or anyone else, we treat them with respect and dignity.

Finally, for Kant, an agent's intentions are also morally important. Agents who act for the sake of duty are morally praiseworthy whereas those who act to achieve some end or their own self-interest do not act morally. In this respect the dictates of morality are categorical; they are not optional. Critics to the Kantian approach object to its absolutism on the grounds that it fails to be responsive to the factual intricacies of context.

Teleological moral theories regard the consequences of actions as morally important. To find out whether or not an action is morally right, teleological theories look not at the action itself, but at what the action produces. Utilitarianism is a specific kind of teleology that asks people to evaluate the consequences of actions on the basis of whether or not these actions maximize the general happiness. John Stuart Mill articulated the general happiness principle, according to which we have an obligation to maximize the general happiness,[4] each to count for one and none to count for more than one.[5] By insisting that no one count for more than one, utilitarianism introduces impartiality into the utilitarian calculation since it requires that no one's interests, including those of the person doing the calculation, count as more important than the interests of any other person. Mill defined happiness as "pleasure and the absence of pain."[6] Some contemporary utilitarians, called preference utilitarians, think that happiness should be identified with preference satisfaction.[7]

Although utilitarianism is a powerful and useful theory in bioethics, it has been associated with a number of problems. In its singular pursuit of the total greatest amount of happiness, utilitarianism appears to ignore basic human rights. If, for example, a utilitarian calculates that the general happiness would be best served by killing several homeless people for the purpose of harvesting their organs for the benefit of other socially worthwhile people, then the theory would seem to implore us to do just that. But not only is it morally counterintuitive to kill innocent people for the benefit of others, to do so involves a violation of the right to be left alone.

Yet, sometimes, utilitarianism is charged with being too morally demanding. In one formulation, known as Act Utilitarianism (AU) it requires us to maximize happiness each and every time we act. If, for example, we find that we have $100 available to spend, utilitarians require us to use the funds to maximize the general happiness. Instead of spending the money on our own pleasure or that of our family and friends, perhaps dinner and a movie, the utilitarian calculus would probably ask us to donate the money to relief of suffering in the developing world.[8] Surely, it is unrealistic to think that people could ever meet such an exacting moral standard.

Finally, utilitarianism is complicated. It requires people to make complex calculations about the long- and short-term consequences of actions and their alternatives. This can be not only intellectually challenging, but also time consuming. Many ethical decisions, including those that arise in a health care context, must be made quickly and under conditions of uncertainty about the consequences of one's actions. The emergency room (ER) leaves little time for elaborate calculations!

Utilitarians respond to these objections with an important modification to the theory. According to rule utilitarianism (RU), utilitarians can use utilitarian calculations to establish rules. They reason that certain rules can safely be adopted because the probabilities are that they will maximize the general happiness. More often than not, utility will be maximized if we tell the truth. Use of rules will decrease the disutility caused by errors in calculations. It allows us to sidestep egregious and counterintuitive violations to human rights because chances are we would have a rule against, for example, killing the innocent. It does not require agents to make complicated calculations because they would simply have to refer to the rules. Finally, it does not demand sainthood. Instead of always having to maximize happiness, rule utilitarians only have to follow a limited set of rules.

Although RU can meet the objections marshaled against AU, it seems not to be able to respond adequately to one important objection. Namely, the great appeal of AU is that it is sensitive to the specific facts at hand. Sometimes it may seem morally right to lie, for example, to save the lives of many people. AU has the flexibility to allow us to be sensitive to the context in this way. RU insists that we defer to the rule. Thus the objection to RU is that it reduces utilitarianism to a form of deontological theory and, in turn, carries with it many of the same limitations.

Moral theories are valuable tools in part because they do more or less correspond to the moral dispositions that people appear to have. When there is a symmetry between moral theory and moral disposition, people are more likely to act on the theory; that is, to act morally. In discussions about ethical issues, people often fall into one of these two theoretical camps. Either they believe that it is always wrong to violate moral rules and that it is the rightness of actions that count or they think that what counts is whether or not actions produce harmful or beneficial consequences. When there are disagreements about ethical matters it can be helpful to try to identify whether or not the disagreement hinges on a disagreement about what counts as morally fundamental, actions or consequences and rules or happiness. The advantage of using moral theories, however, is that they provide consistent results in cases that are morally similar and in this way ensure for universality of moral judgments. In this respect, then, moral theories serve the same purposes that precedent serves in the law.

But there is more to bioethics than moral theories. In particular, some bioethicists prefer to use moral principles. The principles most often used in bioethics are those of beneficence and autonomy. The principle of beneficence states that there first is a duty to do no harm, then duties to prevent harm, remove harm, and promote the good.[9] The principle of non-malfeasance or "do no harm," is crucial to the practice of medicine and to medical ethics. For example, the Hippocratic Oath repeatedly encourages physicians to act for the benefit of the patient and to do no harm. "I will apply dietetic measures for the benefit of the sick according to my ability and judgment; I will keep them from harm and injustice."[10]

Applying the principle of beneficence can be challenging because it is not always easy to identify what will constitute a "harm" or "benefit" in a particular instance. Do we, for example, benefit people when we provide lifesaving care that they do not want? Perhaps unwanted lifesaving care qualifies more as a benefit than a harm. Alternatively, care that prolongs a life that consists only in pain and suffering, even if that care is sought, might be difficult to describe as a benefit. Furthermore, when determining whether a particular action is a benefit, whose perspective should prevail? In the case of the doctor–patient relationship, should it be the doctor's or the patient's? These are examples of some of the questions that bioethicists face when they invoke the principle of beneficence.

It is not unusual for the principle of beneficence to come into conflict with what is perhaps the single most important principle in contemporary bioethics, the principle of autonomy. According to the principle of autonomy, we have a duty to respect the choices made by other people. In the medical context this translates into respecting patient choices. But how should we define *autonomy*? How we define this important concept will in part determine the scope of individual freedom to which people are entitled. Clearly there is opportunity for conflict between autonomy and beneficence. Consider the example of providing lifesaving care to patients who do not want it. Should a physician act on the principle of autonomy and respect the patient's decision to forgo lifesaving care or defer to beneficence and the principle "do something"? Part of the challenge of bioethics is to try to resolve conflicts of this kind.

Although utilitarianism, principle-based theories, and Kant's moral law are the main moral tools of bioethics, they are not the only ones. Some of the recent theories to surface in contemporary bioethics are feminist bioethics, the ethics of care, and communitarianism. A brief word about each of these is in order. The ethics of care is most often associated with the work of Carol Gilligan, in particular with her ground-breaking book, *In a Different Voice: Psychological Theory and Women's Development*.[11] Gilligan believes that morality can be approached in two ways, from an objective, rational, individualistic, and autonomy-based approach or from an approach that stresses obligations and responsibilities that arise out of our relationships with others. Moreover, she believes that these approaches are more or less gender based, represented by men and women respectively. Another important proponent of the ethics of care is Nel Noddings, who believes that ethical caring is in some important ways constituted by the experience of motherhood.[12]

But it would be a mistake to identify the ethics of care too closely with feminist bioethics. Feminist bioethicists are a varied group, distinguished by the theoretical and political perspectives that inform their work as well as by the topics they consider. Nonetheless, as Susan Wolf points out, it is probably accurate to say that a common thread among them is a concern with issues that confront women in the medical system and the harm that they may experience within it.[13] For example, some of the topics that might be of concern to feminist bioethicists are the disproportionate number of certain medical procedures in specific geographic areas, such as hysterectomies and C-sections, the moral and social implications of reproductive technologies, the exclusion of women from research, and further afar the cultural practice of female circumcision, also known as female genital mutilation. As we consider some of the traditional topics of bioethics, ask yourself whether or not some of the issues under consideration are likely to impact women differently than men and whether a deep understanding of the issue requires a distinctly feminist vantage point.

There is one additional theory we should consider, namely communitarianism. Although communitarianism can be thought of as a political theory, like other political theories, such as liberalism, it generates a particular set of obligations and duties that are in many ways in contradistinction to those of liberal political theory. While liberalism places great emphasis on individuals and respect for individual rights, communitarianism shifts the emphasis to the community and the values that support it. This is not to say that individuals are ignored, but rather that they are viewed within a social context.

C. Questions of Justice

Bioethics not only considers cases with the help of moral principles and theories that inform decision making about how people ought to be treated, but also explores how scarce resources ought to be distributed among people. For the latter task, we need to turn to principles of distributive justice to tell us what it is that people are owed. Principles of justice can guide the distribution of burdens and benefits among people. There are a number of contexts in which principles of justice may be invoked, but there are two main contexts that we will encounter in this book. In the first, as a community we must decide how to distribute the "good" of health care, whether, for example, on the basis of market principles or egalitarianism. Principles of justice also help us consider the criteria by which resources should be distributed among patients (for example, scarce resources such as organs and medicines). Principles of justice are also used when these same questions arise in a global context. In Chapter 6 we look at whether there is an obligation to provide, in addition to health care, the social preconditions required for health to people living in developing countries.

The general principle of distributive justice states that we should treat like cases alike and unlike cases differently. There are, however, a number of different theories of distributive justice that have been advanced. Here we will consider those that have been important in discussions about health care. The first, egalitarianism, takes the view that people are equally valuable and states that burdens and benefits ought to be distributed equally among members of a community. Considered in the context of health care, this principle of distribution would seem to suggest that we give equal shares of health care to every member of the community. But it needs to be asked whether it makes sense to distribute health care equally when there does not seem to be equal need.

Utilitarians offer another approach to questions about what constitutes a just distribution of burdens and benefits. This approach dictates that a just distribution is one that will maximize good outcomes. For example, we might take a drug like Tenofovir™, an important drug for the treatment of AIDS, and look at the consequence of distributing it broadly to all of those who need it in the developing world or narrowly to those who can pay for it. Utilitarianism may ignore, for example, rights to private property in determining just distributions unless, of course, it could be shown that such distributions will maximize good outcomes. In the case of Tenofovir™, it is at least arguable that respecting the intellectual property rights of pharmaceutical companies would not have good outcomes because of the harms to those in developing countries who could not afford these drugs.

In contrast, libertarians, such as Robert Nozick, believe that people have fundamental rights to private property, including their talents and skills.[14] Justice is achieved if everyone is entitled to what they have. If the state limits property rights, perhaps through a system of taxation, it would, according to Nozick, violate justice. Of course, in this view, it would follow that the state would be wrong to institute taxation in order to ensure access to health care. Such taxation would wrongly deprive people of their property. This approach views "rights" very narrowly as negative rights; that is, as rights in which others must refrain from interfering with liberty. However, in contrast with a libertarian approach, some scholars have identified positive rights, in which people are given something, such as health care. These are discussed more fully in Chapter 6.

There are also desert-based theories of justice, according to which burdens and benefits are to be distributed on the basis of what people deserve. These theories differ primarily in what they take to be the relevant category of desert. Some people believe that merit is crucial, others effort, and still others, contribution, to be assessed by the social value of the contribution.

In order to be persuasive, any theory of justice needs to provide a theoretical foundation on which to build and support its theory. Social contract theory, used historically by a number of political theorists, such as Locke, Hobbes, and Rousseau, attempts to provide just such a justification. The underlying philosophical idea is that people living in a presocial world or state of nature agree to give up certain freedoms in exchange for the protection and security of a political society. In effect, the presence of the agreement or contact legitimizes the coercive measures used by government.

Perhaps the most important recent social contract theorist to develop a theory of the just distribution of burdens and benefits is John Rawls. In *A Theory of Justice*, Rawls argues that under conditions of pure procedural justice or justice as fairness, hypothetical, self-interested rational persons, under a veil of ignorance, would choose two principles to guide the distribution of burdens and benefits.[15] In the first, the principle of equal liberty, each person has an equal right to the most extensive liberties compatible with similar liberties for all. In the second, the difference principle, social and economic inequalities should be arranged so that they are both (a) to the greatest benefit of the least advantaged persons, and (b) attached to offices and positions open to all under conditions of equality of opportunity. In other words, Rawls believed that people would not choose equality at any price; they would not choose equality if it meant that everyone would be made worse off. But even here, inequality would have to benefit the worst off members of the community. Nonetheless, Rawls' first principle, the principle of equal liberties, is basically egalitarian as is 2(b).

D. The History of Public Health

For the most part, bioethics has focused on issues relating to the provision and allocation of medical care, including questions that arise about the research undertaken to develop such care. These critical issues will be explored in depth in the chapters that follow.

But a focus limited to medical care is problematic for three reasons. First, as we shall discuss below, although medical care can make an enormous difference in an individual's health, it probably plays a relatively small role in determining the health of a broad population. Therefore, if bioethics' mandate is to provide an ethical analysis of those activities that affect and relate to health and illness, it should look beyond medical care to the field of public health, which studies the health of populations.

Second, medical care does not operate in isolation. Although medicine and related fields have their own important professional norms, which we will discuss in Chapter 4, they practice in a broader social, legal, and economic context. The insights of these other disciplines are therefore essential to understanding health care and its impact on a population's health. In this respect, epidemiology, the branch of public health that studies the relationship between diseases and populations, can be of great help. It can provide bioethics with a greater understanding of the population-wide impact of particular health care practices and policies, including those undertaken as a result of ethical inquiry. Undoubtedly that is important information for a utilitarian who is concerned about the general consequences of an action. But it is also imperative for ethicists who think about issues of social justice.

Finally, the discipline of public health asserts a set of values and perspectives that can complement those traditionally employed by bioethics. The next section will more fully discuss this so-called population perspective. Here, we provide some background about public health, its meaning, its history, and the context it can add to bioethics.

Public health is both a discipline and a goal. As the latter, it has existed as long as there have been human communities. Therefore, it is not surprising that George Rosen began his classic history of public health with a discussion of urban planning in ancient India and Egypt:

> Throughout human history, the major problems of health that men have faced have been concerned with community life, for instance, the control of transmissible disease, the control and improvement of the physical environment (sanitation), the provision

of water and food of good quality and in sufficient supply, the provision of medical care, and the relief of disability and destitution. The relative emphasis placed on each of these problems has varied from time to time, but they are all closely related.[16]

Contemporary public health traces its roots to the sanitarian movement of the early and mid-nineteenth century. At that time, much of the world was plagued with virulent epidemics of cholera, yellow fever, and other infectious diseases. People who were concerned about these epidemics decried the filthy conditions that had come to characterize the urban centers of the early industrial age. These "sanitarians" believed that as garbage decayed, it gave off a substance known as "miasma," which caused illness. The response of the sanitarians was to call for "sanitary reform" and the establishment of sewage systems and clean water supplies.

The sanitarian position was bolstered in the mid-nineteenth century by the work of early epidemiologists (originally individuals who study the causes of epidemics) such as John Snow, who used empirical observation to demonstrate the association between particular water pumps and cholera cases.[17] Snow's study was an early example of epidemiology, which today has become the chief tool of public health.

Despite the work of Snow and others, the sanitarian position was challenged in the mid-nineteenth century by contagionists. They believed that disease was caused by animate living organisms that were spread by those who were already ill. Contagionists advocated the increased use of traditional public health measures such as quarantining cargo and isolating sick individuals. Although the theory of contagionism antedated the work of Pasteur, Lister, and others, their development of the "germ theory" of disease in the late nineteenth century appeared to provide substantial support for the contagionist position.[18]

Ironically, the sanitarian movement had its greatest successes just as it was being eclipsed by the germ theory. The late nineteenth century saw the inauguration of the American Public Health Association and the establishment of standing boards of health in many cities and states in the United States and Europe.[19] (Previously these boards were established during epidemics and then permitted to disband when the crisis abated.) The era also saw the creation of municipal sewage systems, pure food acts, and eventually the establishment of housing codes.

As a result of these efforts, deaths from infectious disease declined enormously between 1880 and 1920. For example, Hoffman reports that between 1851 and 1860 the rate of typhoid fever in Chicago was 85.2 per 100,000. By 1911–1920 the rate had fallen to 5.2 per 100,000.[20] Similar dramatic declines occurred in the incidence of cholera, diphtheria, croup, measles, and small pox.[21] Not surprisingly, these declines led to a major increase in life expectancy. In 1866 the life expectancy in New York was 25; by 1903 it had increased to 42 years.[22] All of this occurred prior to the advent of antibiotics or many effective medical interventions.

The acceptance of the germ theory, however, helped to undermine the prestige and influence of the sanitarians and the public health movement more generally. Although the germ theory did not initially give medicine much of an ability to treat disease (the development of antibiotics was still far off), it did give it a new ability to diagnose conditions. It also led to developments that made surgery and childbirth safer, helping again to add to the efficacy and prestige of medicine. Moreover, the germ theory itself appeared to discredit the intellectual foundations of the sanitarian movement.

As the epidemics of infectious disease waned (in large part due to the misinformed but actually sensible suggestions of the sanitarians) and the basic building blocks of public health became firmly established (at least in the industrialized world), the demand for public health action began to diminish. Although public health as a discipline continued to develop throughout the twentieth century, it was never again able to capture the authority it had asserted at the end of the nineteenth century. With clean water and wholesome food taken for granted, individuals and even communities could begin to associate their own health care with access to medical care, forgetting the critical, but omnipresent role, played by public endeavors.[23]

The increasing predominance of medical care in public consciousness is evident by contrasting expenditures on medical services and public health activities. For example, in 1995, total spending on health care in the United States was $988.5 billion.[24] In contrast, the total expenditure by government for public health activities was only $31.4 billion and most of that amount was for personal health care services for populations served by public health agencies.[25] Relatively little was spent on such "core" public health functions as disease surveillance (which is critical to detecting new or emerging infections), health education, and health promotion. Of course, many public health activities are undertaken by institutions—public or private—that are not traditionally thought of as public health agencies. Consider, for example, the Environmental Protection Agency, which serves to protect public health by regulating the quality of air and water.

Today, the dominance of medical services for our understanding of health is clear. Popular political discussion about health focuses almost exclusively on access to medical care or the quality of medical services. Public health issues routinely take a back seat. Only when a crisis hits, such as the emergence of a new infectious disease such as SARS (Severe Acute Respiratory Syndrome), do matters of public health come to the forefront of public consciousness. But once the crisis fades, attention to public health rapidly fades.

Popular culture also highlights medical care to the derision of public health. The media, for example, vividly portray the lifesaving feats of ER doctors, seldom reminding us that, at least for populations as a whole, life and death depend more on background activities known as public health than on the dramatic, high-tech interventions that occur in modern medical centers. Thus as we watch the doctors on the TV show *E.R.* save the victims of another crash, we seldom stop to think about all of the lives that have been saved by making cars and roads safer. Lives saved by public health are far less visible, and far less dramatic, than lives saved in the surgical amphitheater.

But for all of the wonders of modern medicine, it remains undisputed that for the population as a whole, medical care plays a relatively small role in preventing mortality. There is a clear consensus that the giant strides that occurred in life expectancy in the past hundred and fifty years derived more from social and economic changes and public health activities than from the improvement in medical services. Even today, when medical care is more efficacious than ever, it continues to play a comparatively small role in population health. Thus the incidence of tobacco smoking in a population plays a far greater role in determining the population's experience of cancer deaths than does the accessibility or competence of dramatic new cancer treatments.

In addition, public health's study of population health shows us that accessibility and efficacy of medical care itself is influenced by a web of social and cultural factors that are often overlooked. Numerous recent studies, for example, have shown that African Americans are often treated differently by their health care providers than are white Americans.[26] Gender differences also appear to be significant.[27] Moreover, social policies, such as the decision to promote managed care as a form of health care organization, can have a significant impact on the decisions that individual practitioners make about the treatment of individual patients.

Epidemiology establishes that the health of individuals cannot be seen as simply the result of individual medical encounters. Instead, if we wish to promote the well-being of individuals, we need to protect the health of the communities in which they reside, and we need to understand how the social, economic, and cultural forces in those communities affect the individual's own health and the medical care he or she receives. From this it follows that issues of justice are relevant to public health. But the relationship between public health and bioethics is reciprocal. If we care about the ethical implications of health care, we need to analyze not only the ethics of the patient–provider encounter, but the ethical dilemmas that confront public-health protection or the lack thereof.

E. The Population Perspective

In 1988 the Institute of Medicine defined public health as "what we, as a society, do collectively to assure the conditions in which people can be healthy."[28] This definition implies several critical features about public health that will be relevant to our subsequent discussion. First, the definition makes clear that public health assumes that the advancement of a population's health is a positive value. In this respect, public health can be understood (and has been criticized for being) implicitly *utilitarian*. It is utilitarian in so far as it focuses on outcomes. To public health the measuring rod of an action or intervention is its impact on health. In addition, public health is utilitarian because it focuses upon the impact of an action on a group or population of individuals. However, in contrast to utilitarianism, public health does not always focus on the largest possible group (the greatest number) but on particular groups or populations that may vary widely from case to case, depending upon the issue at hand. In addition, while utilitarians assume that overall utility is derived from the aggregation of individual preference or desires, public health presupposes that health is *the* appropriate goal. As a result, public health tends to place less weight on subjective preferences than does utilitarianism.

Public health's focus on populations is undoubtedly its most defining feature and the one that distinguishes the field from most other health care professions. In contrast to clinical medicine, public health is not concerned with the health of a particular individual, or patient, but with the health of a group, or population. This perspective, similar in several respects to communitarianism, asserts a fundamental moral interdependency among individuals and the importance of a group, community, or population as the subject of moral concern. This belief in the importance of the group derives from the history and experiences of public health, including especially humanity's experiences with infectious diseases, which demonstrate the frequent interdependency of human beings with respect to health. In effect, public health's experiences have shown that we can often better understand and protect the health of a group by looking at factors that operate at the group rather than individual level. So, for example, instead of asking why a particular patient has a disease, such as HIV, a public health analyst will ask what are the factors in a particular society or group that determine its rate of HIV. This population perspective can lead to a very different picture of the cause of illness and a very different set of prescriptions for intervention than would follow from a physician's clinical examination of individual patients. For example, in the case discussed above, public health's population perspective may take note of the conditions of migrant workers that foster unsafe sexual practices, whereas the physician may simply ask if a single patient practiced unprotected sex. Or, to take another example, public health may ask how cigarette-marketing practices affect lung-cancer rates, while physicians may simply ask if an individual smoked prior to contracting lung cancer. In either case, public health is more apt to endorse broad social interventions, many of which will involve law, than are clinicians. Indeed, public health's emphasis on collective interventions is made clear by the Institute of Medicine's claim that public health is what we *"as a society, do collectively* to assure the conditions in which people can be healthy."[29]

Although a set of ethical perspectives can be discerned in the discipline of public health, it is also important to remember that public health does not purport or envision itself to be a discipline focused on ethics. Instead, it is an interdisciplinary endeavor, heavily influenced by and reliant upon the social and biological sciences. Its methodologies are primarily empirical and statistical, rather than deductive. As a result, public health's guidance on particular issues will change over time, as new empirical data are obtained and analyzed.

Public health's focus on populations and its reliance on empirical data have much to offer bioethics. An infusion of public health's population perspective can remind bioethics of the social and environmental determinants of health as well as the importance of keeping an eye on the population impact of particular policy prescriptions. In addition, epidemiology and empirical research can provide important grounding and context for bioethical analysis.

On the other hand, although we will want to draw upon public health's population perspective in our discussion of bioethical issues, we should probably pause before we adopt that perspective wholeheartedly. In its past, public health has often been too quick to discount the liberty or well-being of individuals, all in the name of improved health outcomes for the population. Sometimes, perhaps often, that sacrifice has been unnecessary. As the late Jonathan Mann suggested, individual rights and well-being are more likely to support community health than jeopardize it.[30] Population health is usually the poorest in communities where individuals lack basic rights and necessities.

Ultimately, we need to recognize the richness of the interactions between public health and medical care, the population perspective and an individualistic focus. Only by considering the ways in which public-health perspectives and policies affect individual medical encounters, and the ways in which individual medical encounters relate to public health, can we fully appreciate the ethical issues that surround the quest for individual and community well-being.

Notes

1. Ronald Dworkin, *Taking Rights Seriously* (Cambridge, Mass.: Harvard University Press, 1977), xi.
2. Immanuel Kant, *Foundations of the Metaphysics of Morals*, trans. Lewis White Beck (Indianapolis: Bobbs-Merril, 1959).
3. *Id.,* at 47.
4. John Stuart Mill, *Utilitarianism,* ed. O. Piest (Indianapolis: The Bobbs-Merrill Company, Inc., 1957), 76.
5. Ibid. quoting Jeremy Bentham.
6. Ibid. at 10.
7. R. M. Hare, "A Utilitarian Approach," in *A Companion to Bioethics,* eds. Helga Kuhse and Peter Singer (Oxford and Malden, Mass.: Blackwell Publishers, 1998), 80–85.
8. Peter Singer, *One World: The Ethics of Globalization* (New Haven and London: Yale University Press, 2002).
9. William Frankena, *Ethics,* 2nd ed. (Englewood Cliffs, N.J.: Prentice Hall, 1973), 45–47.
10. Ludwig Edelstein, "The Hippocratic Oath: Text, Translation and Interpretation," *Bulletin of the History of Medicine, Supp.* 1 (1943): 3.
11. Carol Gilligan, *In a Different Voice: Psychological Theory and Women's Development* (Cambridge, Mass.: Harvard University Press, 1982).
12. Nel Noddings, *Caring: A Feminine Approach to Ethics and Moral Education* (Berkeley: University of California Press, 1984), 16.
13. Susan M. Wolf, "Introduction: Gender and Feminism in Bioethics," in *Feminism and Bioethics: Beyond Reproduction,* ed. Susan M. Wolf (New York: Oxford University Press, 1996), 21–22.
14. Robert Nozick, *Anarchy, State, and Utopia* (New York: Basic Books, 1973). See also Stephen Nathanson, *Economic Justice* (Upper Saddle River, N.J.: Prentice Hall, 1998).
15. John A. Rawls, *A Theory of Justice* (Cambridge, Mass.: Belknap Press, 1971).
16. George Rosen, *A History of Public Health* (New York: MD Publications, 1958), 25.

17. Rosen, 285–287.
18. Ibid. 287–315.
19. Ibid. 245–250.
20. Frederick Hoffman, "American Mortality Progress During the Last Half Century," in *A Half Century of Public Health.* Ed. M. P. Ravenel (New York: American Public Health Association, 1921), 110.
21. Ibid.
22. Herman Biggs, "Preventive Medicine: Its Achievement, Scope and Possibilities," *Medical Records* 65 (1904): 8–954.
23. Wendy E. Parmet, "From *Slaughter-House* to *Lochner:* The Rise and Fall of the Constitutionalization of Public Health," *American Journal of Legal History* 40 (1996): 476, 492–501.
24. Health Care Financing Administration, Office of the Actuary: National Health Statistics Group, 1997.
25. Ibid.
26. Rene Bowser, "Racial Profiling in Health Care: An Institutional Analysis of Medical Treatment Disparities," *Michigan Journal of Race & Law* 7 (2001): 79–133.
27. Frederick Schneiders Research for The Henry J. Kaiser Family Foundation, *Perceptions of How Race and Ethnic Background Affect Medical Care,* October 1999.
28. Institute of Medicine, Committee for the Study of the Future of Public Health, *The Future of Public Health* (Washington, D.C.: National Academy Press 1988), 19.
29. Institute of Medicine, at 19.
30. Jonathan Mann "Medicine and Public Health, Ethics and Human Rights," *The Hastings Center Report* 27 (May–June 1997), 6–13.

Recommended Readings

Berlin, Isaiah. "Two Concepts of Liberty." In *Liberalism and Its Critics,* edited by Michael Sandel. New York: New York University Press, 1984.

Brock, Dan W. "Broadening the Bioethics Agenda." *Kennedy Institute of Ethics Journal* 10 (2000): 21–38.

Callahan, Daniel. "Ends and Means: The Goods of Health Care." In *Ethical Dimensions of Health Policy,* edited by Marian Davis, Carolyn Clancy, and Larry Churchill. New York: Oxford University Press, 2002: 3–18.

Coggon, D., Rose, G., and Barker, D. J. P. *Epidemiology for the Uninitiated,* 4th ed. London: BMJ Publishing Group, 1997.

Dworkin, Ronald. *Taking Rights Seriously.* Cambridge, Mass.: Harvard University Press, 1977.

Frankena, Williams. *Ethics,* 2nd ed. Englewood Cliffs, N.J.: Prentice Hall, 1973.

Gostin, Lawrence O. *Public Health Law: Power, Duty, Restraint.* Berkeley: University of California Press, 2000.

Holmes, Helen Bequaert. "When Health Means Wealth, Can Bioethicists Respond?" *Health Care Analysis* 9 (2001): 213–218.

Institute of Medicine, Committee for the Study of the Future of Public Health. *The Future of Public Health.* Washington, D.C.: National Academy Press, 1988.

Institute of Medicine, U.S. Board on Health Promotion and Disease Prevention. *The Future of the Public's Health in the 21st Century.* Washington, D.C.: National Academy Press, 2003.

Kuhse, Helga, and Singer, Peter, eds. *A Companion to Bioethics.* Oxford and Malden, Mass.: Blackwell Publishers Ltd., 1998.

McNeil, William H. *Plagues and Peoples.* Garden City, N.Y.: Anchor Press, 1976.

Mill, John Stuart. *Utilitarianism.* Edited by Oskar Piest. Indianapolis, Indiana: Bobbs Merrill Educational Publishing, 1957.

Nathanson, Stephen. *Economic Justice.* Upper Saddle River, N.J.: Prentice Hall, 1998.

Nozick, Robert. *Anarchy, State and Utopia.* New York: Basic Books, 1973.

O'Neill, Onora. "Practical Principles and Practical Judgment." *Hastings Center Report* 31 (2001): 15–23.

Parmet, Wendy E. "From *Slaughter-House* to *Lochner:* The Rise and Fall of the Constitutionalization of Public Health." *American Journal of Legal History* 40 (1996): 492–501.

Rawls, John. *A Theory of Justice.* Cambridge, Mass.: Harvard University Press, 1971.

Roberts, Marc J. and Reich, Michael R. "Ethical Analysis in Public Health." *Lancet* 359 (2002): 1055–1059.

Rosen, George. *A History of Public Health.* New York: M.D. Publications, 1958.

Ross, William D. *The Right and the Good.* Oxford: Clarendon Press, 1930.

Schlesinger, Mark. "A Loss of Faith: The Sources of Reduced Political Legitimacy for the American Medical Profession." *The Milbank Quarterly* 80 (2002): 185–235.

Taylor, Charles. *Philosophical Arguments.* Cambridge: Harvard University Press, 1995.

Tong, Rosemarie. "Teaching Bioethics in the New Millennium: Holding Theories Accountable to Actual Practices and Real People." *Journal of Medicine and Philosophy* 27 (2002): 417–432.

Walzer, Michael. *Spheres of Justice.* New York: Basic Books, 1983.

Chapter Two

The Building Blocks of Health

A. What Is Health?

Often in discussions of health and bioethics, we assume what is meant by *health*. For example, bioethicists debate the ethics of respecting a patient's choice, even when that choice appears to jeopardize her health. This debate presupposes that the patient's health exists as an objective phenomenon independent of her evaluation of it and apart from her social context. It assumes that health is a state of being in the natural world, one that is clearly identifiable and positive in its connotation. Likewise, bioethical discussions often presuppose that health is the antithesis of illness and disease and that those two are also natural and objective categories.

In fact, health, illness, and disease are complex and contested concepts. Their meaning at any time will be determined by a variety of factors, including the biology of human beings, the social context, an individual's subjective assessments, and the purpose for which we use the terms.

Recognizing the inherent complexity of the concept of health is important for the study of health care ethics. Most obviously, it helps us to identify what issues fall within the purview of health care ethics (is gun regulation a bioethical issue?). In addition, the way in which we view health (the degree to which it is biologic, subjective, or socially constructed) may affect our analysis of the rights and objectives of the parties involved in the health care system. For example, *the right to health* will have a very different content depending on how narrowly or broadly we construe *health*. The *right to health* may mean only the right to medical treatments to relieve clearly presented biologic infirmities, or it may encompass psychological and social services that will enable an individual to flourish and meet her own goals and expectations, as is suggested by the World Health Organization's (WHO) claim that health is a "state of complete physical, mental and social well-being."[1]

This broad social understanding is echoed in the first reading by René Dubos, who offers a subjective definition claiming that health is a "measure of each person's ability to do what he wants to do and become what he wants to become." Dubos' broad views contrast greatly with more traditional medical definitions that tend to view health as the absence of disease. For example, in the *Merriam Webster Medical Dictionary* "health" is defined as "the condition of an organism or one of its parts in which it performs its vital functions normally."[2] Although Daniel Callahan, in the second reading, does not explicitly endorse such a narrow biomedical definition, he does argue against adopting a broad, comprehensive definition of health. To Callahan, a broad definition undermines our ability to distinguish health concerns from other issues. In effect, we trivialize health when we see everything as a health issue. Thus he defines *health* as "a state of physical well-being," out of fear that we will otherwise find ourselves unable to draw lines of responsibility. Clearly, if maximizing good health were among our utilitarian duties, those duties would be more manageable if health were defined narrowly.

This is certainly one way to derive a definition of *health*. It sidesteps any epistemological queries about the nature of health, ignoring them and opting more or less for a functional definition. Although such an approach has the merit of simplicity and clarity, it is important to keep in mind that such definitions reflect underlying policy agendas. Alternatively, it might make greater sense to distinguish policy questions from what constitutes health and to allow questions about the allocation and provision of health care to follow from the definition of health, not the reverse.

The question of what constitutes health can have profound implications not only for ethicists and policymakers, but for patients and their families. For example, the conduct of impulsive and unruly children may be identified as a disease (ADHD), and they may be placed on powerful drugs or the children's behavior may be seen as merely their temperament or a response to their environment. If the latter view is adopted, medication and medical treatment may not be the solution. Likewise, an adult's shyness may qualify as social phobia and Paxil® may be prescribed. Or, again it may merely be understood as one variation of human behavior. In these cases, and many others, the question of whether such conditions represent a lack of health raises not only important ethical, epistemological, and policy issues but pragmatic questions for real people.

Health and Creative Adaptation

René Dubos

Anyone who has ever undergone a routine medical checkup knows that body functions are commonly described by cryptic abbreviations like EKG and technical terms like serum triglyceride. Health is expressed in numbers such as 120/80 and 98.6, which are interpreted as being inside or outside the range of normal. All too often, however, the measurements extracted from a test tube of blood or a sample of urine are normal while the patient continues to insist that something is wrong. The explanation of the discrepancy is that these measurements indicate only biological fitness, which is appropriate to animals in the wild but insufficient to describe the health of human beings.

For human beings, health transcends biological fitness. It is primarily a measure of each person's ability to do what he wants to do and become what he wants to become. Good health implies an individual's success in functioning within his particular set of values, and as such it is extremely relative. The bookish scholar in a library has a concept of health that is different from that of the financier who worries about coronary occlusion and peptic ulcer during a business lunch.

Animals in their natural habitats appear healthy and free of disease for the simple reason that any animal seriously handicapped by genetic abnormalities, old age, or disease is likely to be abandoned by the other members of its group and to fall victim to starvation or predators. The health of wild animals depends on their ability to adapt biologically to their environment, an ability based on anatomical and physiological mechanisms developed during evolution and encoded in their genes. In the human species, also, the state of health reflects a person's success in adapting to environmental challenges, but the interplay between human beings and their environment involves many factors not encountered in animal life.

Animals rarely leave the environment in which they evolved, an environment for which they are biologically suited. In contrast, human beings have settled over practically all the earth even though they essentially retain the genetic legacy acquired in the region of their biological origin, probably the warm grasslands of East Africa. Human beings are biologically semitropical animals, yet they now live in all climatic zones. In order to colonize the earth, they have been compelled to fashion habitats that enable them to function and multiply in environments where they are biological misfits. They could not have survived long even in the temperate zones were it not for adaptations that protected them against cold weather and allowed them to avoid food shortages during many months every year. Except for a few small bands of people, such as the aborigines of Australia, the human species since at least the late Stone Age has not lived without altering its surroundings. Wherever it exists, human life has modified nature profoundly, often with unpredictable consequences for biological health and the quality of the environment.

Human beings also long for new experiences—as symbolized by the episode of the apple in the Garden of Eden. For the sake of adventure, they commonly expose themselves to situations to which they are biologically or socially ill-adapted.

Because of the pressures generated by new ways of life, most social and technological changes have, throughout history, been marked by an increase in the prevalence of disease. Epidemics of plague during the Renaissance were the result of an increase in intercontinental travel.

The migration of people from rural areas into crowded, urban tenements during the first phase of the Industrial Revolution certainly played a role in the rampant spread of tuberculosis and other infectious diseases. In our own time, prosperity and modern technologies account at least in part for the increase in the so-called diseases of civilization, such as heart disease, stroke, and probably cancer.

The effects of the environment on health are further complicated by the human propensity to turn events into symbols and to react to the symbols as if they were physical challenges. Thus an individual's responses to a particular environment reflect not only its physical and chemical characteristics but also the experiences that the individual associates with that environment. Memories and emotions can metamorphose the most trivial as well as the most sublime events and can cause unexpected physiological reactions.

Similarly, anticipation, whether conscious or unconscious, can profoundly affect an individual's response to a stimulus. The sight of a food associated with the memory of a disgusting event may cause nausea. A sudden drop in the stock market or the end of a love affair can exacerbate a latent peptic ulcer or reawaken a tuberculous infection. The hope or fear of a situation that has not yet occurred may cause irregular heartbeats. The symbol of any real or imagined experience commonly becomes as effective as the experience itself in evoking physiological responses that govern health or disease.

Health in human societies, thus, has far more complex determinants than has the health of animals in the wild. However, the sociocultural view of human health also has a biological basis in the fact that *Homo sapiens* is the least specialized of animal species. Unlike animals, whose physical capabilities are rather narrowly defined, human beings can walk, run, creep, climb, and swim. They can live at sea level, at an altitude of 15,000 feet in the Peruvian Andes, or at 1,000 feet below sea level near the Dead Sea. Some people prefer the sun and others prefer the shade. All can derive nourishment—if they wish—from a completely carnivorous or herbivorous diet, or from a combination of both. Ever since the Stone Age, human beings have developed cultural mechanisms that enhance still further the adaptability provided by their low level of anatomical and physiological specialization.

The dramatic events of the 20th Century demonstrate that human beings are still as adaptable, biologically and socially, as they were when they evolved from hunter-gatherers to pastoralists and farmers and then to industrialists and city dwellers. Millions of normal people have survived the frightful ordeals of life in the trenches of World War I or of exposure to the sophisticated weaponry of more recent military conflicts. Thousands have managed to function even in the bestial atmosphere of concentration camps.

The most polluted, traumatic, and crowded cities of the world have great appeal for people of all races and all ages. Some of the most rapid increases in population occur under living conditions biologically so detestable that they seem incompatible with life. Humankind seems capable of adjusting to environmental pollution, inadequate diets, intense crowding, as well as to monotonous, ugly, and stressful surroundings.

These adjustments, however, are bought at a high price. The smoke and fumes in the air around us; the filth in our streams, lakes, and oceans; the mountains of wastes that spoil landscapes and cityscapes; the noise, glaring lights, and other unnatural stimuli that shatter our nerves—all these environmental insults contribute to the pattern of diseases peculiar to modern civilization. Authorities once believed that disorders of the cardiovascular system, various forms of cancer, and chronic and degenerative diseases in general are more prevalent simply because more people are surviving long enough to fall victim to such disorders. But the truth is that the increase in chronic and degenerative diseases is due in large part to the environmental and behavioral changes associated with industrialization and urbanization.

Unfortunately, humankind can never overcome the diseases of civilization by becoming biologically adapted to pollution or other environmental insults, because many changes in the human organism that appear adaptive on first sight are destructive in the long run. Air pollution, for example, elicits from the lung an overproduction of mucus that at first protects delicate lung tissues from pollutants. Eventually, however, the protective response gives way to chronic pulmonary disease. Continued exposure to loud noises gradually reduces one's perception of them but impairment of the hearing apparatus also limits the ability to hear musical tones and the finer qualities of the human voice. Life in extremely crowded environments generates psychological attitudes that block out excessive environmental stimuli, but these attitudes can impoverish human relationships. Such mutilations of the physical and mental being should not be regarded as adaptation but rather as undesirable mechanisms of tolerance.

Deeper biological reasons than these prevent humankind from genetically adapting to the diseases of civilization. The most important reason is that insults from the modern environment generally do not dramatically impair health during the first decades of life. Since susceptibility to environmentally induced disease does not interfere with reproductive ability, natural selection cannot work against it. If a certain air pollutant causes cancer, for example, the chances are great that people sensitive to the carcinogen will have children before the disease becomes incapacitating. As a consequence, the children will be as susceptible to the cancer-producing agent as their parents were.

Even if we could adapt to automobile fumes, the noise of jackhammers, or the traumatic experience of rush hour in the subway, adaptation through genetic changes proceeds slowly and many, many generations would be required for the changes to be significant for society as a whole.

In practice, then, the only biological adjustment we can make to deleterious environmental factors is not true adaptation but a form of tolerance achieved at the cost of impaired functioning. We must learn to design environments suited to human health, and where we fail we must deal with environmental insults either by developing ways of life that protect us from them or by treating the diseases they cause.

More than a century ago, the French physiologist Claude Bernard asserted that, in higher animals as well as in human beings, survival and health depend upon the ability of the organism to maintain its internal environment in an approximately constant state, despite exposure to endless and often large variations in the external environment. The composition of our body fluids, for example, remains remarkably constant regardless of the kind of food we eat. Recognizing a fundamental truth long before it could be scientifically demonstrated, Bernard boldly claimed in a famous phrase that "the constancy of the *milieu intérieur* [internal environment] is the essential condition for free and independent life."

In his most explicit statement of this concept, Bernard wrote: "The constancy of the *milieu intérieur* presupposes a perfection of the organism such that the external variations are at each instant compensated and brought into balance. . . . All the vital mechanisms, however varied they might be, always have one purpose, that of maintaining the integrity of the conditions for life within the internal environment."

The view that the maintenance of life depends upon the stability of the *milieu intérieur* is unquestionably one of the grandest concepts of biology and was immediately recognized as such by many scholars. As early as 1868, for example, philosopher and psychologist William James, who was then a young student at Harvard Medical School, devoted an editorial in the *North*

American Review to Bernard's theory. Not until the first decades of the 20th Century, however, did insights into physiology and biochemistry enable us to identify some of the mechanisms that the body employs to correct departures from the ideal state and to maintain itself in a state of dynamic equilibrium. Walter B. Cannon, the Harvard physiologist who adapted x-rays to the study of the digestive system, introduced the word *homeostasis* to denote this equilibrium.

As Cannon showed by physiological experimentation, the phrase "homeostatic processes" describes the multifarious physiological and metabolic reactions that continuously adjust the internal composition of the body within safe limits. The limits are precisely defined for each organism. The cybernetic nature of this adjustment was recognized by the theoretical physicist Norbert Wiener, one of Cannon's contemporaries. In Wiener's words, "The apparent equilibrium of life is an active equilibrium in which each deviation from the norm brings on a reaction in the opposite direction, which is of the nature of what we call negative feedback." This cybernetic statement of homeostasis is of course quite consonant with Claude Bernard's views of the stability of the *milieu intérieur*.

Cannon was so impressed by the perfection of the mechanisms involved in the maintenance of homeostasis that he barely mentioned illness in his book. He seemed to imply that homeostatic negative feedback always manages to return the organism to normal and thus assures the maintenance of health. But in reality, perfect homeostatic reactions are probably the exception rather than the rule. Indeed, as the following examples show, attempts at homeostasis are often excessive or misdirected.

In traumatic shock, the blood pressure plummets and the blood vessels constrict to counteract the drop. But this vasoconstriction is as dangerous as the falling pressure because it deprives organs such as the kidney of their essential blood supply. In heart failure, when the heart is too weak to pump adequate amounts of blood, the volume of fluid in the blood vessels increases in an effort to fill the heart, but ultimately this hypervolemia leads to cardiac arrest by way of both excessive vascular pressures and overdilated heart chambers. In infections, an inflammatory reaction helps to fix or destroy the aggressive agent, but when it is allowed to continue, inflammation will damage tissues and organs.

In many situations, homeostatic mechanisms have indirect and delayed consequences that are responsible for chronic disorders. The production of scar tissue, or fibrosis, is a homeostatic response that heals wounds and helps to check the spread of infection, but fibrosis destroys the liver in alcoholic cirrhosis, freezes the joints in rheumatoid arthritis, and stifles breathing in a diseased lung. Dangers are also inherent in behavioral homeostasis when reactions such as anger and excitement give way to obsessions, maniacal episodes, and other forms of pathological behavior in response to incidents that may be minor.

The ultimate value of homeostatic reactions cannot be judged, therefore, until all of the consequences of such changes have been recognized. All too often the wisdom of the body is a shortsighted wisdom.

Homeostatic mechanisms are the outcome of evolutionary adaptations, but because they emerged in response to the environmental challenges of the Paleolithic period some 750,000 years ago, they are better suited to the conditions of the past than to those of the present.

Evolutionary fitness is always fitness for the past. Homeostatic reactions that were statistically favorable under the conditions of Stone Age life are frequently unfavorable under present conditions. For example, the immune response protected the primitive hunter from wounds and infections but works against the modern surgeon's boldness in transplanting vital organs.

Purely homeostatic processes are largely unconscious. Similarly, a large percentage of responses to environmental forces are determined by instincts that operate outside consciousness and free will. Instincts come ready-made, so to speak, and enable the organism to deal decisively and often successfully with life situations similar to those experienced by the species during its evolutionary past.

But precisely because instincts are so pointed and mechanical, they are of little use in new circumstances. We have no instinct to warn us of the dangers inherent in odorless chemical fumes, invisible radiation beams, or subliminal forms of brainwashing. Instincts do not enable us to deal successfully with the unforeseeable complexities of human life.

Whereas instincts stand for biological security in a static world, awareness, knowledge, and motivation account for the adventurous liberty and creativity of the human spirit. In the words of educator John Dewey, "The brain is primarily the organ of a certain kind of behavior, not of knowing the world." To the extent that the brain can make choices, it can direct adaptive responses. Since the evolved wisdom of the body is blind and often faulty, we must substitute for it a wisdom based on knowledge of present conditions and on anticipation of future consequences.

In the final analysis, we can make choices concerning our behavior and surroundings, choices that will prevent or minimize undesirable changes in the *milieu interiéur*. Manipulation of the external environment inevitably affects mental characteristics and the constituents of some body tissues, as well as the quality of social relationships. Thought processes also play an important role in shaping the internal environment since they can profoundly alter hormonal secretions and consequently physiological mechanisms.

The activities of the thyroid and adrenal glands, for example, are markedly influenced by the mental state. And modern science has recently confirmed the claims of Indian Yogis that they can control at will their heartbeat and other physiological processes.

Obviously, following one's instincts passively is easier than directing one's creative responses; hence the unfaltering behavior of most animals in the wilderness in contrast to the worried expression on human faces at a time of decision. But to be human means being creative and making choices that often require painful effort—mental even more than physical.

Human health transcends purely biological health because it depends primarily on those conscious and deliberate choices by which we select our mode of life and adapt, creatively, to its experiences. Many have affirmed the human ability to create our own selves and shape our own lives. As George Orwell and Albert Camus independently observed, by the age of 50 we have the faces we deserve.

The concept of health as a creative adaptive process that requires choices and conscious participation by the whole organism seems at odds with the dominant trends of modern scientific medicine. Like other aspects of Western science, modern medicine emphasizes the analytical approach to knowledge, an attitude reflected in the diagnosis and treatment of a specific disease. Most other forms of medicine, by contrast, deal with the patient as part of the total environment. This fundamental difference in attitude is evident in a comparison of Western and traditional Chinese medicine.

Ever since the 17th Century, medical science has been shaped largely by Cartesian analytical philosophy. Its ideal is to subdivide every anatomic structure, physiological function, and biochemical process into smaller and smaller subunits so that each can be studied in greater and greater detail. The most sophisticated and successful application of this analytical approach is the reduction of medical problems to phenomena of molecular biology.

In contrast, traditional Chinese medicine seems to be more concerned with the interplay between the components of biological systems than with the description of these individual components. It studies, for example, the way the liver relates to other parts of the body rather than the anatomical or physiological characteristics of the liver as an isolated organ. It also pays much attention to the relationships between the living organism and its environment—the place, the seasons, the weather, the time of day, the social milieu. To a large extent, all systems of medicine except those based on modern Western science derive from and emphasize an integration of the body, the mind, and the environment.

There is no doubt, of course, that the Western analytical approach has yielded phenomenal achievements in preventive and therapeutic medicine during the past half century. But it is also true that some of the greatest triumphs of Western medicine emerged not from reductionist analysis but from an integrated view of disease and of man's relation to his total environment.

Edward Jenner had no concept of the viral basis of smallpox or of the process of immunity when he introduced the technique of vaccination. Essentially the same can be said of Louis Pasteur when he generalized Jenner's approach and developed vaccines against bacterial diseases, such as anthrax, and against rabies. Max von Pettenkofer almost eliminated typhoid fever from Munich and made it the healthiest city of 19th Century Europe simply by bringing clean water from the mountains, carting away refuse and garbage, diluting the sewage downstream in the Isar, and planting trees and flowers.

Many people assume that the successful medical and public health practices of the past were just lucky accidents. In reality, they were based on a method of reasoning that was scientific but that differed from ours in content. In most cases, they involved an implicit awareness that living organisms respond to environmental challenges by active processes that have adaptive value. Vaccination as applied by Jenner and further developed by Pasteur reflected their belief that exposure to a small amount of "virus" (the word originally meant a poison) or to a weakened form of it could increase the resistance of the human organism to the disease-causing agent. Pettenkofer believed that a clean and pleasant environment could render the human organism more resistant to a variety of stresses. Although the successful health practices of the past were not entirely derived from laboratory experimentation, they were nonetheless rational because they were derived from an awareness of the interplay between the whole organism and the total environment.

An approach to medicine that is based on concepts of organismic and social adaptation is certainly compatible with scientific developments. In fact, such an attitude leads to the conclusion that the scientific medicine of our time is not scientific enough because it neglects, and at times completely ignores, the multifarious environmental and emotional factors that affect the human organism in health and in disease, and to which the organism can consciously respond in an adaptive, creative way.

Certain people can effectively control their external environment and the organic and mental functions of their internal environment. Despite severe stress, they apparently can govern the adaptive processes that enable them to cope with their biological deficiencies and with other social and medical problems. An obese person, for example, can discipline himself to diet in the face of many pressures to overeat.

Most people, however, require help and guidance in difficult situations; they can be aided by therapeutic procedures that range from the technologies of scientific medicine to the mental support provided by a member of the health profession, the presence of a trusted person, contact with an appropriate social group, or faith in a certain procedure or in a religious symbol.

All forms of organic and mental disease inevitably interfere with the ability of patients to live as they would like: to take the social roles that appeal to them and to reach the goals they formulate for themselves. Such an interference amounts to a loss of freedom. Patients go to a healer—any member of the health profession—in the hope of recovering this lost freedom. Even when there is no treatment known to cure the disease, the healer can often help the patient to function in a fairly normal way, either by the use of drugs and other forms of medical technology, or by advice based on knowledge of human nature.

Recovery from disease may follow two different courses. The organism may return to the exact condition in which it was before the illness, or it may undergo lasting changes that go beyond mere reversal of damage and result in a new adaptive state. The first type of healing, which is rare, corresponds to the classical homeostatic *reactions* of the body; the second constitutes the creative adaptive *responses* of the whole organism.

I have used the word *reaction* for homeostatic healing processes and *response* for creative healing processes. The difference in wording conveys my belief that homeostatic reactions are determined to a large extent by unconscious physiological and biochemical mechanisms of the body, whereas creative responses tend to be goal-oriented and to involve the conscious participation of the organism as a whole.

To heal does not necessarily imply to cure. It can simply mean helping people to achieve a way of life compatible with their individual aspirations—to restore their freedom to make choices—even in the presence of continuing disease.

For further information:

Bernard, Claude. *Lectures on the Phenomena of Life Common to Animals and Plants.* Vol. 1. Charles C Thomas Publishers, 1974.

Cannon, Walter. *The Wisdom of the Body.* W. W. Norton & Co., 1939.

Dubos, René. *Man, Medicine and Environment.* Praeger Publishers, 1968.

Dubos, René. *Man Adapting.* Yale University Press, 1965.

Dubos, René. *Mirage of Health.* Harper & Row Publishers, 1971.

Dubos, René, and Maya Pines. *Health and Disease.* Time-Life Books, 1965.

The WHO Definition of Health

Daniel Callahan

There is not much that can be called fun and games in medicine, perhaps because unlike other sports it is the only one in which everyone, participant and spectator, eventually gets killed playing. In the meantime, one of the grandest games is that version of king-of-the-hill where the aim of all players is to upset the World Health Organization (WHO) definition of "health." That definition, in case anyone could possibly forget it, is,

"Health is a state of complete physical, mental, and social well-being and not merely the absence of disease or infirmity." Fair game, indeed. Yet somehow, defying all comers, the WHO definition endures, though literally every other aspirant to the crown has managed to knock it off the hill at least once. One possible reason for its presence is that it provides such an irresistible straw man; few there are who can resist attacking it in the opening paragraphs of papers designed to move on to more profound reflections.

But there is another possible reason which deserves some exploration, however unsettling the implications. It may just be that the WHO definition has more than a grain of truth in it, of a kind which is as profoundly frustrating as it is enticingly attractive. At the very least it is a definition which implies that there is some intrinsic relationship between the good of the body and the good of the self. The attractiveness of this relationship is obvious: it thwarts any movement toward a dualism of self and body, a dualism which in any event immediately breaks down when one drops a brick on one's toe; and it impels the analyst to work toward a conception of health which in the end is resistant to clear and distinct categories, closer to the felt experience. All that, naturally, is very frustrating. It seems simply impossible to devise a concept of health which is rich enough to be nutritious and yet not so rich as to be indigestible.

One common objection to the WHO definition is, in effect, an assault upon any and all attempts to specify the meaning of very general concepts. Who can possibly define words as vague as "health," a venture as foolish as trying to define "peace," "justice," "happiness," and other systematically ambiguous notions? To this objection the "pragmatic" clinicians (as they often call themselves) add that, anyway, it is utterly unnecessary to know what "health" means in order to treat a patient running a high temperature. Not only that, it is also a harmful distraction to clutter medical judgment with philosophical puzzles.

Unfortunately for this line of argument, it is impossible to talk or think at all without employing general concepts; without them, cognition and language are impossible. More damagingly, it is rarely difficult to discover, with a bit of probing, that even the most "pragmatic" judgment (whatever *that* is) presupposes some general values and orientations, all of which can

be translated into definitions of terms as general as "health" and "happiness." A failure to discern the operative underlying values, the conceptions of reality upon which they are based, and the definitions they entail, sets the stage for unexamined conduct and, beyond that, positive harm both to patients and to medicine in general.

But if these objections to any and all attempts to specify the meaning of "health" are common enough, the most specific complaint about the WHO definition is that its very generality, and particularly its association of health and general well-being as a positive ideal, has given rise to a variety of evils. Among them are the cultural tendency to define all social problems, from war to crime in the streets, as "health" problems; the blurring of lines of responsibility between and among the professions, and between the medical profession and the political order; the implicit denial of human freedom which results when failures to achieve social well-being are defined as forms of "sickness," somehow to be treated by medical means; and the general debasement of language which ensues upon the casual habit of labeling everyone from Adolf Hitler to student radicals to the brat next door as "sick." In short, the problem with the WHO definition is not that it represents an attempt to propose a general definition, but that it is simply a bad one.

That is a valid line of objection, provided one can spell out in some detail just how the definition can or does entail some harmful consequences. Two lines of attack are possible against putatively hazardous social definitions of significant general concepts. One is by pointing out that the definition does not encompass all that a concept has commonly been taken to mean, either historically or at present, that it is a partial definition only. The task then is to come up with a fuller definition, one less subject to misuse. But there is still another way of objecting to socially significant definitions, and that is by pointing out some baneful effects of definitions generally accepted as adequate. Many of the objections to the WHO definition fall in the latter category, building upon the important insight that definitions of crucially important terms with a wide public use have ethical, social, and political implications; defining general terms is not an abstract exercise but a way of shaping the world metaphysically and structuring the world politically.

Wittgenstein's aphorism, "don't look for the meaning, look for the use," is pertinent here. The ethical problem in defining the concept of "health" is to determine what the implications are of the various uses to which a concept of "health" can be put. We might well agree that there are some uses of "health" which will produce socially harmful results. To carry Wittgenstein a step further, "don't look for the uses, look for the abuses." We might, then, examine some of the real or possible abuses to which the WHO definition leads, recognizing all the while that what we may term an "abuse" will itself rest upon some perceived *positive* good or value.

Historical Origin & Context

Before that task is undertaken, however, it is helpful to understand the historical origin and social context of the WHO definition. If abuses of that definition have developed, their seeds may be looked for in its earliest manifestations.

The World Health Organization came into existence between 1946 and 1948 as one of the first major activities of the United Nations. As an outcome of earlier work, an Interim Commission to establish the WHO sponsored an International Health Conference in New York in June and July of 1946. At that Conference, representatives of 61 nations signed the Constitution of the WHO, the very first clause of which presented the now famous definition of "health." The animating spirit behind the formation of the WHO was the belief that the improvement of world health would make an important contribution to world peace; health and peace were seen as inseparable. Just why this belief gained ground is not clear from the historical record of the WHO. While there have been many historical explanations of the ori-

gin of World War II, a lack of world health has not been prominent among them; nor, for that matter, did the early supporters of the WHO claim that the Second World War or any other war might have been averted had there been better health. More to the point, perhaps, was the conviction that health was intimately related to economic and cultural welfare; in turn, that welfare, so it was assumed, had a direct bearing on future peace. No less important was a fervent faith in the possibilities of medical science to achieve world health, enhanced by the development of powerful antibiotics and pesticides during the war.

A number of memorandums submitted to a spring 1946 Technical Preparatory Committee meeting of the WHO capture the flavor of the period. The Yugoslavian memorandum noted that "health is a prerequisite to freedom from want, to social security and happiness." France stated that "there cannot be any material security, social security, or well-being for individuals or nations without health . . . the full responsibility of a free man can only be assumed by healthy individuals . . . the spread of proper notions of hygiene among populations tends to improve the level of health and hence to increase their working power and raise their standard of living. . . ." The United States contended that "international cooperation and joint action in the furtherance of all matters pertaining to health will raise the standards of living, will promote the freedom, the dignity, and the happiness of all peoples of the world."

In addition to those themes, perhaps the most significant initiative taken by the organizers of the WHO was to include mental health as part of its working definition. In its memorandum, Great Britain stated that "it should be clear that health includes mental health," but it was Dr. Brock Chisholm, soon to become the first director of the WHO, who personified what Dr. Chisholm himself called the "visionary" view of health. During the meeting of the Technical Preparatory Committee he argued that: "The world is sick and the ills are due to the perversion of man; his inability to live with himself. The microbe is not the enemy; science is sufficiently advanced to cope with it were it not for the barriers of superstition, ignorance, religious intolerance, misery and poverty. . . . These psychological evils must be understood in order that a remedy might be prescribed, and the scope of the task before the Committee therefore knows no bounds."

In Dr. Chisholm's statement, put very succinctly, are all of those elements of the WHO definition which led eventually to its criticism: defining all the problems of the world as "sickness," affirming that science would be sufficient to cope with the causes of physical disease, asserting that only anachronistic attitudes stood in the way of a cure of both physical and psychological ills, and declaring that the cause of health can tolerate no limitations. To say that Dr. Chisholm's "vision" was grandiose is to understate the matter. Even allowing for hyperbole, it is clear that the stage was being set for a conception of "health" which would encompass literally every element and item of human happiness. One can hardly be surprised, given such a vision, that our ways of talking about "health" have become all but meaningless. Even though I believe the definition is not without its important insights, it is well to observe why, in part, we are so muddled at present about "health."

Health and Happiness

Let us examine some of the principal objections to the WHO definition in more detail. One of them is that, by including the notion of "social well-being" under its rubric, it turns the enduring problem of human happiness into one more medical problem, to be dealt with by scientific means. That is surely an objectionable feature, if only because there exists no evidence whatever that medicine has anything more than a partial grasp of the sources of human misery. Despite Dr. Chisholm's optimism, medicine has not even found ways of dealing with more than a fraction of the whole range of physical diseases; campaigns, after all, are still being mounted against

cancer and heart disease. Nor is there any special reason to think that future forays against those and other common diseases will bear rapid fruits. People will continue to die of disease for a long time to come, probably forever.

But perhaps, then, in the psychological and psychiatric sciences some progress has been made against what Dr. Chisholm called the "psychological ills," which lead to wars, hostility, and aggression? To be sure, there are many interesting psychological theories to be found about these "ills," and a few techniques which can, with some individuals, reduce or eliminate antisocial behavior. But so far as I can see, despite the mental health movement and the rise of the psychological sciences, war and human hostility are as much with us as ever. Quite apart from philosophical objections to the WHO definition, there was no empirical basis for the unbounded optimism which lay behind it at the time of its inception, and little has happened since to lend its limitless aspiration any firm support.

Common sense alone makes evident the fact that the absence of "disease or infirmity" by no means guarantees "social well-being." In one sense, those who drafted the WHO definition seem well aware of that. Isn't the whole point of their definition to show the inadequacy of negative definitions? But in another sense, it may be doubted that they really did grasp that point. For the third principle enunciated in the WHO Constitution says that, "the health of all peoples is fundamental to the attainment of peace and security. . . ." Why is it fundamental, at least to peace? The worst wars of the 20th century have been waged by countries with very high standards of health, by nations with superior life-expectancies for individuals and with comparatively low infant mortality rates. The greatest present threats to world peace come in great part (though not entirely) from developed countries, those which have combatted disease and illness most effectively. There seems to be no historical correlation whatever between health and peace, and that is true even if one includes "mental health."

How are human beings to achieve happiness? That is the final and fundamental question. Obviously illness, whether mental or physical, makes happiness less possible in most cases. But that is only because they are only one symptom of a more basic restriction, that of human finitude, which sees infinite human desires constantly thwarted by the limitations of reality. "Complete" well-being might, conceivably, be attainable, but under one condition only: that people ceased expecting much from life. That does not seem about to happen. On the contrary, medical and psychological progress have been more than outstripped by rising demands and expectations. What is so odd about that, if it is indeed true that human desires are infinite? Whatever the answer to the question of human happiness, there is no particular reason to believe that medicine can do anything more than make a modest, finite contribution.

Another objection to the WHO definition is that, by implication, it makes the medical profession the gate-keeper for happiness and social well-being. Or if not exactly the gate-keeper (since political and economic support will be needed from sources other than medical), then the final magic-healer of human misery. Pushed far enough, the whole idea is absurd, and it is not neccessary to believe that the organizers of the WHO would, if pressed, have been willing to go quite that far. But even if one pushes the pretension a little way, considerable fantasy results. The mental health movement is the best example, casting the psychological professional in the role of high priest.

At its humble best, that movement can do considerable good; people do suffer from psychological disabilities and there are some effective ways of helping them. But it would be sheer folly to believe that all, or even the most important, social evils stem from bad mental health: political injustice, economic scarcity, food shortages, unfavorable physical environments, have a far greater historical claim as sources of a failure to achieve "social well-being." To retort that all or most of these troubles can, nonetheless, be seen finally as symptoms of bad mental health is, at best, self-serving and, at worst, just plain foolish.

A significant part of the objection that the WHO definition places, at least by implication, too much power and authority in the hands of the medical profession, need not be based on a fear of that power as such. There is no reason to think that the world would be any worse off if health professionals made all decisions than if any other group did; and no reason to think it would be any better off. That is not a very important point. More significant is that cultural development which, in its skepticism about "traditional" ways of solving social problems, would seek a technological and specifically a medical solution for human ills of all kinds. There is at least a hint in early WHO discussions that, since politicians and diplomats have failed in maintaining world peace, a more expert group should take over, armed with the scientific skills necessary to set things right; it is science which is best able to vanquish that old Enlightenment bogeyman, "superstition." More concretely, such an ideology has the practical effect of blurring the lines of appropriate authority and responsibility. If all problems—political, economic and social—reduce to matters of "health," then there cease to be any ways to determine who should be responsible for what.

The Tyranny of Health

The problem of responsibility has at least two faces. One is that of a tendency to turn all problems of "social well-being" over to the medical professional, most pronounced in the instance of the incarceration of a large group of criminals in mental institutions rather than prisons. The abuses, both medical and legal, of that practice are, fortunately, now beginning to receive the attention they deserve, even if little corrective action has yet been taken. (Counterbalancing that development, however, are others, where some are seeking more "effective" ways of bringing science to bear on criminal behavior.)

The other face of the problem of responsibility is that of the way in which those who are sick, or purportedly sick, are to be evaluated in terms of their freedom and responsibility. Siegler and Osmond [*Hastings Center Studies,* vol. I, no. 3, 1973, pp. 41–58] discuss the "sick role," a leading feature of which is the ascription of blamelessness, of non-responsibility, to those who contract illness. There is no reason to object to this kind of ascription in many instances—one can hardly blame someone for contracting kidney disease—but, obviously enough, matters get out of hand when all physical, mental, and communal disorders are put under the heading of "sickness," and all sufferers (all of us, in the end) placed in the blameless "sick role." Not only are the concepts of "sickness" and "illness" drained of all content, it also becomes impossible to ascribe any freedom or responsibility to those caught up in the throes of sickness. The whole world is sick, and no one is responsible any longer for anything. That is determinism gone mad, a rather odd outcome of a development which began with attempts to bring unbenighted "reason" and free self-determination to bear for the release of the helpless captives of superstition and ignorance.

The final and most telling objection to the WHO definition has less to do with the definition itself than with one of its natural historical consequences. Thomas Szasz has been the most eloquent (and most single-minded) critic of that sleight-of-hand which has seen the concept of health moved from the medical to the moral arena. What can no longer be done in the name of "morality" can now be done in the name of "health": human beings labeled, incarcerated, and dismissed for their failure to toe the line of "normalcy" and "sanity."

At first glance, this analysis of the present situation might seem to be totally at odds with the tendency to put everyone in the blame-free "sick role." Actually, there is a fine, probably indistinguishable, line separating these two positions. For as soon as one treats all human disorders—war, crime, social unrest—as forms of illness,

then one turns health into a normative concept, that which human beings must and ought to have if they are to live in peace with themselves and others. Health is no longer an optional matter, but the golden key to the relief of human misery. We *must* be well or we will all perish. "Health" can and must be imposed; there can be no room for the luxury of freedom when so much is at stake. Of course the matter is rarely put so bluntly, but it is to Szasz's great credit that he has discerned what actually happens when "health" is allowed to gain the cultural clout which morality once had. (That he carries the whole business too far in his embracing of the most extreme moral individualism is another story, which cannot be dealt with here.) Something is seriously amiss when the "right" to have healthy children is turned into a further right for children not to be born defective, and from there into an obligation not to bring unhealthy children into the world as a way of respecting the right of those children to health! Nor is everything altogether lucid when abortion decisions are made a matter of "medical judgment" (see *Roe vs. Wade*); when decisions to provide psychoactive drugs for the relief of the ordinary stress of living are defined as no less "medical judgment"; when patients are not allowed to die with dignity because of medical indications that they can, come what may, be kept alive; when prisoners, without their consent, are subjected to aversive conditioning to improve their mental health.

Abuses of Language

In running through the litany of criticisms which have been directed at the WHO definition of "health," and what seem to have been some of its long-term implications and consequences, I might well be accused of beating a dead horse. My only defense is to assert, first, that the spirit of the WHO definition is by no means dead either in medicine or society. In fact, because of the usual cultural lag which requires many years for new ideas to gain wide social currency, it is only now coming into its own on a broad scale. (Everyone now talks about everybody and everything, from Watergate to Billy Graham to trash in the streets, as "sick.") Second, I believe that we are now in the midst of a nascent (if not actual) crisis about how "health" ought properly to be understood, with much dependent upon what conception of health emerges in the near future.

If the ideology which underlies the WHO definition has proved to contain many muddled and hazardous ingredients, it is not at all evident what should take its place. The virtue of the WHO definition is that it tried to place health in the broadest human context. Yet the assumption behind the main criticisms of the WHO definition seem perfectly valid. Those assumptions can be characterized as follows: 1) health is only a part of life, and the achievement of health only a part of the achievement of happiness; 2) medicine's role, however important, is limited; it can neither solve nor even cope with the great majority of social, political, and cultural problems; 3) human freedom and responsibility must be recognized, and any tendency to place all deviant, devilish, or displeasing human beings into the blameless sick-role must be resisted; 4) while it is good for human beings to be healthy, medicine is not morality; except in very limited contexts (plagues and epidemics) "medical judgment" should not be allowed to become moral judgment; to be healthy is not to be righteous; 5) it is important to keep clear and distinct the different roles of different professions, with a clearly circumscribed role for medicine, limited to those domains of life where the contribution of medicine is appropriate. Medicine can save some lives; it cannot save the life of society.

These assumptions, and the criticisms of the WHO definition which spring from them, have some important implications for the use of the words "health," "illness," "sick," and the like. It will be counted an abuse of language if the word "sick" is applied to all individual and communal problems, if all unacceptable conduct is spoken of in the language of medical pathologies, if moral issues and moral judgments are translated into the language of "health," if the lines of authority, responsibility, and expertise are so blurred that the health profession is allowed to pre-empt the rights and responsibilities of others by re-defining them in its own professional language.

Abuses of that kind have no possibility of being curbed in the absence of a definition of health which does not contain some intrinsic elements of limitation—that is, unless there is a definition which, when abused, is self-evidently *seen* as abused by those who know what health means. Unfortunately, it is in the nature of general definitions that they do not circumscribe their own meaning (or even explain it) and contain no built-in safeguards against misuse, e.g., our "peace with honor" in Southeast Asia—"peace," "honor"? Moreover, for a certain class of concepts—peace, honor, happiness, for example—it is difficult, to keep them free in ordinary usage from a normative content. In our own usage, it would make no sense to talk of them in a way which implied they are not desirable or are merely neutral: by well-ingrained social custom (resting no doubt on some basic features of human nature) health, peace, and happiness are both desired and desirable—good. For those and other reasons, it is perfectly plausible to say the cultural task of defining terms, and settling on appropriate and inappropriate usages, is far more than a matter of getting our dictionary entries right. It is nothing less than a way of deciding what should be valued, how life should be understood, and what principles should guide individual and social conduct.

Health is not just a term to be defined. Intuitively, if we have lived at all, it is something we seek and value. We may not set the highest value on health—other goods may be valued as well—but it would strike me as incomprehensible should someone say that health was a matter of utter indifference to him; we would well doubt either his sanity or his maturity. The cultural problem, then, may be put this way. The acceptable range of uses of the term "health" should, at the minimum, capture the normative element in the concept as traditionally understood while, at the maximum, incorporate the insight (stemming from criticisms of the WHO definition) that the term "health" is abused if it becomes synonymous with virtue, social tranquility, and ultimate happiness. Since there are no instruction manuals available on how one would go about reaching a goal of that sort, I will offer no advice on the subject. I have the horrible suspicion, as a matter of fact, that people either have a decent intuitive sense on such matters (reflected in the way they use language) or they do not; and if they do not, little can be done to instruct them. One is left with the pious hope that, somehow, over a long period of time, things will change.

In Defense of WHO

Now that simply might be the end of the story, assuming some agreement can be reached that the WHO definition of "health" is plainly bad, full of snares, delusions, and false norms. But I am left uncomfortable with such a flat, simple conclusion. The nagging point about the definition is that, in badly put ways, it was probably on to something. It certainly recognized, however inchoately, that it is difficult to talk meaningfully of health solely in terms of "the absence of disease or infirmity." As a purely logical point, one must ask about what positive state of affairs disease and infirmity are an absence of—absent from what? One is left with the tautological proposition that health is the absence of nonhealth, a less than illuminating revelation. Could it not be said, though, that at least intuitively everyone knows what health is by means of the experiential contrast posed by states of illness and disease; that is, even if I cannot define health in any positive sense, I can surely know when I am sick (pain, high fever, etc.) and compare that condition with my previous states which contained no such conditions? Thus one could, in some recognizable sense, speak of illness as a de-

viation from a norm, even if it is not possible to specify that norm with any clarity.

But there are some problems with this approach, for all of its commonsense appeal. Sociologically, it is well known that what may be accounted sickness in one culture may not be so interpreted in another; one culture's (person's) deviation from the norm may not necessarily be another culture's (person's) deviation. In this as in other matters, commonsense intuition may be nothing but a reflection of different cultural and personal evaluations. In addition, there can be and usually are serious disputes about how great a deviation from the (unspecified) norm is necessary before the terms "sickness" and "illnesses" become appropriate. Am I to be put in the sick role because of my nagging case of itching athlete's foot, or must my toes start dropping off before I can so qualify? All general concepts have their borderline cases, and normally they need pose no real problems for the applicability of the concepts for the run of instances. But where "health" and "illness" are concerned, the number of borderline cases can be enormous, affected by age, attitudinal and cultural factors. Worse still, the fact that people can be afflicted by disease (even fatally afflicted) well before the manifestation of any overt symptoms is enough to discredit the adequacy of intuitions based on how one happens to feel at any given moment.

A number of these problems might be resolved by distinguishing between health as a norm and as an ideal. As a norm, it could be possible to speak in terms of deviation from some statistical standards, particularly if these standards were couched not only in terms of organic function but also in terms of behavioral functioning. Thus someone would be called "healthy" if his heart, lungs, kidneys (etc.) functioned at a certain level of efficiency and efficacy, if he was not suffering physical pain, and if his body was free of those pathological conditions which even if undetected or undetectable could impair organic function and eventually cause pain. There could still be dispute about what should count as a "patho-logical" condition, but at least it would be possible to draw up a large checklist of items subject to "scientific measurement"; then, having gone through that checklist in a physical exam, and passing all the tests, one could be pronounced "healthy." Neat, clean, simple.

All of this might be possible in a static culture, which ours is not. The problem is that any notion of a statistical norm will be superintended by some kind of ideal. Why, in the first place, should anyone care at all how his organs are functioning, much less how well they do so? There must be some reason for that, a reason which goes beyond theoretical interest in statistical distributions. Could it possibly be because certain departures from the norm carry with them unpleasant states, which few are likely to call "good": pain, discrimination, unhappiness? I would guess so. In the second place, why should society have any interest whatever in the way the organs of its citizens function? There must also be some reason for that, very possibly the insight that the organ functioning of individuals has some aggregate social implications. In our culture at least (and in every other culture I have ever heard of) it is simply impossible, finally, to draw any sharp distinction between conceptions of the human good and what are accounted significant and negatively evaluated deviations from statistical norms.

That is the whole point of saying, in defense of the WHO definition of health, that it discerned the intimate connection between the good of the body and the good of the self, not only the individual self but the social community of selves. No individual and no society would (save for speculative, scientific reasons only) have any interest whatever in the condition of human organs and bodies were it not for the obvious fact that those conditions can have an enormous impact on the whole of human life. People do, it has been noticed, die; and they die because something has gone wrong with their bodies.

This can be annoying, especially if one would, at the moment of death, prefer to be busy doing other things. Consider two commonplace occurrences. The first I have alluded to already: dropping a heavy brick on one's foot. So far as I know, there is no culture where the pain which that event occasions is considered a good in itself. Why is that? Because (I presume) the pain which results can not only make it difficult or impossible to walk for a time but also because the pain, if intense enough, makes it impossible to think about anything else (or think at all) or to relate to anything or anyone other than the pain. For a time, I am "not myself" and that simply because my body is making such excessive demands on my attention that nothing is possible to me except to howl. I cannot, in sum, dissociate my "body" from my "self" in that situation; my self is my body and my body is my pain.

The other occurrence is no less commonplace. It is the assertion the old often make to the young, however great the psychological, economic, or other miseries of the latter: "at least you've got your health." They are saying in so many words that, if one is healthy, then there is some room for hope, some possibility of human recovery; and even more they are saying that, without good health, nothing is possible, however favorable the other conditions of life may be. Again, it is impossible to dissociate good of body and good of self. Put more formally, if health is not a sufficient condition for happiness, it is a necessary condition. At that very fundamental level, then, any sharp distinction between the good of bodies and the good of persons dissolves.

Are we not forced, therefore, to say that, if the complete absence of health (i.e., death) means the complete absence of self, then any diminishment of health must represent, correspondingly, a diminishment of self? That does not follow, for unless a disease or infirmity is severe, it may represent only a minor annoyance, diminishing our selfhood not a whit. And while it will not do to be overly sentimental about such things, it is probably the case that disease or infirmity can, in some cases, increase one's sense of selfhood (which is no reason to urge disease upon people for its possibly psychological benefits). The frequent reports of those who have recovered from a serious illness that it made them appreciate life in a far more intense way than they previously had are not to be dismissed (though one wishes an easier way could be found).

Modest Conclusions

Two conclusions may be drawn. The first is that some minimal level of health is necessary if there is to be any possibility of human happiness. Only in exceptional circumstances can the good of self be long maintained in the absence of the good of the body. The second conclusion, however, is that one can be healthy without being in a state of "complete physical, mental, and social well-being." That conclusion can be justified in two ways: (a) because some degree of disease and infirmity is perfectly compatible with mental and social well-being; and (b) because it is doubtful that there ever was, or ever could be, more than a transient state of "complete physical, mental, and social well-being," for individuals or societies; that's just not the way life is or could be. Its attractiveness as an ideal is vitiated by its practical impossibility of realization. Worse than that, it positively misleads, for health becomes a goal of such all-consuming importance that it

simply begs to be thwarted in its realization. The demands which the word "complete" entail set the stage for the worst false consciousness of all: the demand that life deliver perfection. Practically speaking, this demand has led, in the field of health, to a constant escalation of expectation and requirement, never ending, never satisfied.

What, then, would be a good definition of "health"? I was afraid someone was going to ask me that question. I suggest we settle on the following: "Health is a state of physical well-being." That state need not be "complete," but it must be at least adequate, i.e., without significant impairment of function. It also need not encompass "mental" well-being; one can be healthy yet anxious, well yet depressed. And it surely ought not to encompass "social well-being," except insofar as that well-being will be impaired by the presence of large-scale, serious physical infirmities. Of course my definition is vague, but it would take some very fancy semantic footwork for it to be socially misused; that brat next door could not be called "sick" except when he is running a fever. This definition would not, though, preclude all social use of the language of "pathology" for other than physical disease. The image of a physically well body is a powerful one and, used carefully, it can be suggestive of the kind of wholeness and adequacy of function one might hope to see in other areas of life.

B. What Makes Us Healthy?

Undoubtedly, one component of an ethical health care system is that it promotes human health. While ethicists may debate the prominence that health promotion should play and the other interests that must be considered, all would concur that the advancement of human health is an important goal.

But how do we advance human health? As we have already seen, the meaning of *health* itself is contested. If we view health narrowly, in purely physiologic terms, health may be best promoted through one set of prescriptions. If we view health more broadly, as Dubos does (see Section A of this chapter), health may best be promoted through another, very different, approach. Yet, even if we could agree upon the nature and meaning of *health*, it may not always be clear as to how it can be achieved. Clinical medicine may offer one perspective. Alternative medicine may offer another. Epidemiology offers yet another.

It is common in Western thought, and in bioethics, to ascribe two predominant causes for health or its absence, illness. The first is biology. In the nineteenth century, with the advent of the germ theory, scientists came to understand the role that microorganisms play in undermining human health. In the twentieth century, our understanding of biological causation increased. Scientists began to appreciate the role that other factors, especially genetics, play in human health. Understanding those factors and learning how to prevent or respond to them is the domain of clinical medicine. As a result, it is common to assume, especially in bioethical discussions, that medicine itself is a primary causal mechanism of health.

Clinical medicine has unquestionably played an important role in the advancement and promotion of human health. One only has to name once-feared scourges such as polio and diphtheria to remember the critical role that medicine can play. And this role, of course, is not limited to the conquest of infectious diseases. In recent decades, the mortality rate from cardiac disease has declined dramatically in this country. Much of this decline has been attributed to the enormous strides that have been made in the detection and treatment of coronary heart disease.[3]

But neither biology nor medicine's interventions in biology are the only causes of health. Increasingly our culture has come to consider and appreciate the role that individual decisions play in determining health. In a famous study in 1993, J. Michael McGinnis and William H. Foege reviewed the causes of death in the United States in 1990 and found that individual "life style choices," especially relating to tobacco, alcohol, poor diet, and unsafe sex, were among the leading causes of death in the United States.[4] More recently Ali H. Mokdad and colleagues applied McGinnis and Foege's methodology to mortality statistics for 2000.[5] They found that about "half of all deaths that occurred in 2000 could be attributed to a limited number of largely preventable behaviors and exposures."[6] "[M]ost striking" was the finding that an estimated 400,000 deaths occurred due to poor diet and physical inactivity.[7] In a sense these findings, and others uncovered by epidemiologists in the last three decades, suggest that the life choices individuals make are often responsible for their health.

Nevertheless, the assertion that individuals should be viewed as responsible for their own health is itself the result of a value judgment. As Scott Yoder has written, "Determinations of responsibility for health are as much decision as discovery."[8] And they are decisions that have profound consequences for the assignment of rights and liabilities. Thus we may find that physicians, insurers, and governments have very different responsibilities if we decide that an illness, such as obesity, is caused by individual actions such as poor eating habits rather than by social choices, such as a society heavily reliant upon fast food.

The epidemiologist Geoffrey Rose presents a very different critique of the assignment of causation to individuals. According to Rose, the search for the cause of illness in a particular individual may reveal why that individual in a given population is especially prone to a disease, but it does not explain why the population as a whole has the background rate of disease that it has, nor does it explain the majority of cases in a society. In effect, by looking only at people who are at "high risk" for a disease within a given society, we overlook the great majority of cases that may occur in people who are only at "average risk." Only by comparing the rates of disease between populations, and analyzing the factors that operate at a population level, Rose claims, can we understand the etiology of most cases. Hence if we focus on the behaviors of individuals who engage in especially risky behavior, we will fail to appreciate those factors that operate more broadly and cause illness in more people, including those who do not engage in obviously risky behavior.

Taking up Rose's invitation to focus on the causes of disease for a population as a whole, social epidemiologists have studied the social factors that promote health or illness. In *Long Live Community: Social Capital as Public Health,* Ichiro Kawachi, Bruce P. Kennedy, and Kimberly Lochner argue that the social cohesion of a community helps support the health of its members. Notice that even though these authors implicitly use a narrow, biologically based understanding of health, they believe that its presence is tied to a far wider web of social factors. What implications does this view have for the assignment of rights and responsibilities with respect to health care?

One of the most glaring and persistent disparities in health outcomes in this country has been along racial lines. Much of this disparity can be attributed to socioeconomic differentials.[9] Many scholars, however, also contend that racism itself is causative of some of the disparity.[10]

These different perspectives on the causes of health and illness have profound implications for bioethics. If, for example, biology is the cause of ill health, and medical intervention its cure, then bioethics rightly focuses on the encounters of clinical medicine. On the other hand, if individual activities are predominantly responsible for health care outcomes, then perhaps the major ethical issues confronting health care are actually those that address the rights that individuals have to make unhealthy choices and the role that governments and social institutions play in influencing those choices. Likewise, if social determinants, be it inequality, racism, or lack of social cohesion, are critical to understanding a population's health status, then the field of bioethics must broaden even more. Issues of racism, poverty, and social disintegration become as critical to health as are the rights and activities that occur in the intensive care unit.

Of course, it is exceedingly likely that all of the causal mechanisms discussed, and many others, play a role in determining human health. Therefore, in order to ensure that our endeavors to promote or create health are undertaken ethically, our perspective must be broad. We must consider the doctor at the bedside as well as the society's tolerance for racial inequality.

Sick Individuals and Sick Populations

Geoffrey Rose

The Determinants of Individual Cases

In teaching epidemiology to medical students, I have often encouraged them to consider a question which I first heard enunciated by Roy Acheson: 'Why did *this* patient get *this* disease at *this* time?'. It is an excellent starting-point, because students and doctors feel a natural concern for the problems of the individual. Indeed, the central ethos of medicine is seen as an acceptance of responsibility for sick individuals.

It is an integral part of good doctoring to ask not only, 'What is the diagnosis, and what is the treatment?' but also, 'Why did this happen, and could it have been prevented?'. Such thinking shapes the approach to nearly all clinical and laboratory research into the causes and mechanisms of illness. Hypertension research, for example, is almost wholly pre-occupied with the characteristics which distinguish individuals at the hypertensive and normotensive ends of the blood pressure distribution. Research into diabetes looks for genetic, nutritional and metabolic reasons to explain why some people get diabetes and others do not. The constant aim in such work is to answer Acheson's question, 'Why did *this* patient get this disease at this time?'.

The same concern has continued to shape the thinking of all of us who came to epidemiology from a background in clinical practice. The whole basis of the case-control method is to discover how sick and healthy individuals differ. Equally the basis of many cohort studies is the search for 'risk factors', which identify certain individuals as being more susceptible to disease; and from this we proceed to test whether these risk factors are also causes, capable of explaining why some individuals get sick while others remain healthy, and applicable as a guide to prevention.

To confine attention in this way to within-population comparisons has caused much confusion (particularly in the clinical world) in the definition of normality. Laboratory 'ranges of normal' are based on what is common within the local population. Individuals with 'normal blood pressure' are those who do not stand out from their local contemporaries; and so on. What is common is all right, we presume.

Applied to aetiology, the individual-centred approach leads to the use of relative risk as the basic representation of aetiological force: that is, 'the risk in exposed individuals relative to risk in non-exposed individuals'. Indeed, the concept of relative risk has almost excluded any other approach to quantifying causal importance. It may generally be the best measure of aetiological force, but it is no measure at all of aetiological outcome or of public health importance.

Unfortunately this approach to the search for causes, and the measuring of their potency, has to assume a heterogeneity of exposure within the study population. If everyone smoked 20 cigarettes a day, then clinical, case-control and cohort studies alike would lead us to conclude that lung cancer was a genetic disease; and in one sense that would be true, since if everyone is exposed to the necessary agent, then the distribution of cases is wholly determined by individual susceptibility.

Within Scotland and other mountainous parts of Britain there is no discernible relation between local cardiovascular death rates and the softness of the public water supply.[1] The reason is apparent if one extends the enquiry to the whole of the UK. In Scotland, everyone's water is soft; and the possibly adverse effect becomes recognizable only when study is extended to other regions which have a much wider range of exposure (r = −0.67). Even more clearly, a case-control study of this question within Scotland would have been futile. Everyone is exposed, and other factors operate to determine the varying risk.

Epidemiology is often defined in terms of study of the determinants of the distribution of the disease; but we should not forget that the more widespread is a particular cause, the less it explains the distribution of cases. The hardest cause to identify is the one that is universally present, for then it has no influence on the distribution of disease.

The Determinants of Population Incidence Rate

I find it increasingly helpful to distinguish two kinds of aetiological question. The first seeks the causes of cases, and the second seeks the causes of incidence. 'Why do some individuals have hypertension?' is a quite different question from 'Why do some populations have much hypertension, whilst in others it is rare?'. The questions require different kinds of study, and they have different answers.

[Consider] the systolic blood pressure distributions of middle-aged men in two populations—Kenyan nomads[2] and London civil servants.[3] The familiar question, 'Why do some individuals have higher blood pressure than others?' could be equally well asked in either of these settings, since in each the individual blood pressures vary (proportionately) to about the same extent; and the answers might well be much the same in each instance (that is, mainly genetic variation, with a lesser component from environmental and behavioural differences). We might achieve a complete understanding of why individuals vary, and yet quite miss the most important public health question, namely, 'Why is hypertension absent in the Kenyans and common in London?'. The answer to that question has to do with the determinants of the population mean; for what distinguishes the two groups is nothing to do with the characteristics of individuals, it is rather a shift of the whole distribution—a mass influ-

ence acting on the population as a whole. To find the determinants of prevalence and incidence rates, we need to study characteristics of populations, not characteristics of individuals.

A more extreme example is provided by the population distributions of serum cholesterol levels[4] in East Finland, where coronary heart disease is very common, and Japan, where the incidence rate is low: the two distributions barely overlap. Each country has men with relative hypercholesterolaemia (although their definitions of the range of 'normal' would no doubt disagree), and one could research into the genetic and other causes of these unusual individuals; but if we want to discover why Finland has such a high incidence of coronary heart disease we need to look for those characteristics of the national diet which have so elevated the whole cholesterol distribution. Within populations it has proved almost impossible to demonstrate any relation between an individual's diet and his serum cholesterol level; and the same applies to the relation of individual diet to blood pressure and to overweight. But at the level of populations it is a different story: it has proved easy to show strong associations between population mean values for saturated fat intake *versus* serum cholesterol level and coronary heart disease incidence, sodium intake *versus* blood pressure, or energy intake *versus* overweight. The determinants of incidence are not necessarily the same as the causes of cases.

How Do the Causes of Cases Relate to the Causes of Incidence?

This is largely a matter of whether exposure varies similarly within a population and between populations (or over a period of time within the same population). Softness of water supply may be a determinant of cardiovascular mortality, but it is unlikely to be identifiable as a risk factor for individuals, because exposure tends to be locally uniform. Dietary fat is, I believe, the main determinant of a population's incidence rate for coronary heart disease; but it quite fails to identify high-risk individuals.

In the case of cigarettes and lung cancer it so happened that the study populations contained about equal numbers of smokers and non-smokers, and in such a situation case/control and cohort studies were able to identify what was also the main determinant of population differences and time trends.

There is a broad tendency for genetic factors to dominate individual susceptibility, but to explain rather little of population differences in incidence. Genetic heterogeneity, it seems, is mostly much greater within than between populations. This is the contrary situation to that seen for environmental factors. Thus migrants, whatever the colour of their skin, tend to acquire the disease rates of their country of adoption.

Most non-infectious diseases are still of largely unknown cause. If you take a textbook of medicine and look at the list of contents you will still find, despite all our aetiological research, that most are still of basically unknown aetiology. We know quite a lot about the personal characteristics of individuals who are susceptible to them; but for a remarkably large number of our major non-infectious diseases we still do not know the determinants of the incidence rate.

Over a period of time we find that most diseases are in a state of flux. For example, duodenal ulcer in Britain at the turn of the century was an uncommon condition affecting mainly young women. During the first half of the century the incidence rate rose steadily and it became very common, but now the disease seems to be disappearing; and yet we have no clues to the determinants of these striking changes in incidence rates. One could repeat that story for many conditions.

There is hardly a disease whose incidence rate does not vary widely, either over time or between populations at the same time. This means that these causes of incidence rate, unknown though they are, are not inevitable. It is possible to live without them, and if we knew what they

were it might be possible to control them. But to identify the causal agent by the traditional case-control and cohort methods will be unsuccessful if there are not sufficient differences in exposure within the study population at the time of the study. In those circumstances all that these traditional methods do is to find markers of individual susceptibility. The clues must be sought from differences between populations or from changes within populations over time.

Prevention

These two approaches to aetiology—the individual and the population-based—have their counterparts in prevention. In the first, preventive strategy seeks to identify high-risk susceptible individuals and to offer them some individual protection. In contrast, the 'population strategy' seeks to control the determinants of incidence in the population as a whole.

The 'High-Risk' Strategy

This is the traditional and natural medical approach to prevention. If a doctor accepts that he is responsible for an individual who is sick today, then it is a short step to accept responsibility also for the individual who may well be sick tomorrow. Thus screening is used to detect certain individuals who hitherto thought they were well but who must now understand that they are in effect patients. This is the process, for example, in the detection and treatment of symptomless hypertension, the transition from healthy subject to patient being ratified by the giving and receiving of tablets. (Anyone who takes medicines is by definition a patient.)

What the 'high-risk' strategy seeks to achieve is something like a truncation of the risk distribution. This general concept applies to all special preventive action in high-risk individuals—in at-risk pregnancies, in small babies, or in any other particularly susceptible group. It is a strategy with some clear and important advantages (Table 1).

Table 1   Prevention by the 'high-risk strategy': advantages

1. Intervention appropriate to individual
2. Subject motivation
3. Physician motivation
4. Cost-effective use of resources
5. Benefit: risk ratio favourable

Its first advantage is that it leads to intervention which is appropriate to the individual. A smoker who has a cough or who is found to have impaired ventilatory function has a special reason for stopping smoking. The doctor will see it as making sense to advise salt restriction in the hypertensive. In such instances the intervention makes sense because that individual already has a problem which that particular measure may possibly ameliorate. If we consider screening a population to discover those with high serum cholesterol levels and advising them on dietary change, then that intervention is appropriate to those people in particular: they have a diet-related metabolic problem.

The 'high-risk' strategy produces interventions that are appropriate to the particular individuals advised to take them. Consequently it has the advantage of enhanced subject motivation. In our randomized controlled trial of smoking cessation in London civil servants we first screened some 20 000 men and from them selected about 1500 who were smokers with, in addition, markers of specially high risk for cardiorespiratory disease. They were recalled and a random half received anti-smoking counselling. The results, in terms of smoking cessation, were excellent because those men knew they had a special reason to stop. They had been picked out from others in their offices because, although everyone knows that smoking is a bad thing, they had a special reason why it was particularly unwise for them.

There is, of course, another and less reputable reason why screening enhances subject motivation, and that is the mystique of a scientific investigation. A ventilatory function test is a powerful enhancer of motivation to stop smoking: an instrument which the subject does not quite understand, that looks rather impressive, has produced evidence that he is a special person with a special problem. The electrocardiogram is an even more powerful motivator, if you are unscrupulous enough to use it in prevention. A man may feel entirely well, but if those little squiggles on the paper tell the doctor that he has got trouble, then he must accept that he has now become a patient. That is a powerful persuader. (I suspect it is also a powerful cause of lying awake in the night and thinking about it.)

For rather similar reasons the 'high-risk' approach also motivates physicians. Doctors, quite rightly, are uncomfortable about intervening in a situation where their help was not asked for. Before imposing advice on somebody who was getting on all right without them, they like to feel that there is a proper and special justification in that particular case.

The 'high-risk' approach offers a more cost-effective use of limited resources. One of the things we have learned in health education at the individual level is that once-only advice is a waste of time. To get results we may need a considerable investment of counselling time and follow-up. It is costly in use of time and effort and resources, and therefore it is more effective to concentrate limited medical services and time where the need—and therefore also the benefit—is likely to be greatest.

A final advantage of the 'high-risk' approach is that it offers a more favourable ratio of benefits to risks. If intervention must carry some adverse effects or costs, and if the risk and cost are much the same for everybody, then the ratio of the costs to the benefits will be more favourable where the benefits are larger.

Unfortunately the 'high-risk' strategy of prevention also has some serious disadvantages and limitations (Table 2).

The first centres around the difficulties and costs of screening. Supposing that we were to embark, as some had advocated, on a policy of screening for high cholesterol levels and giving dietary advice to those individuals at special risk. The disease process we are trying to prevent (atherosclerosis and its complications) begins early in life, so we should have to initiate screening perhaps at the age of ten. However, the abnormality we seek to detect is not a stable lifetime characteristic, so we must advocate repeated screening at suitable intervals.

In all screening one meets problems with uptake, and the tendency for the response to be greater amongst those sections of the population who are often least at risk of the disease. Often there is an even greater problem: screening detects certain individuals who will receive special advice, but at the same time it cannot help also discovering much larger numbers of 'borderliners', that is, people whose results mark them as at increased risk but for whom we do not have an appropriate treatment to reduce their risk.

The second disadvantage of the 'high-risk' strategy is that it is palliative and temporary, not radical. It does not seek to alter the underlying causes of the disease but to identify individuals who are particularly susceptible to those causes. Presumably in every generation there will be such susceptibles; and if prevention and control

Table 2 Prevention by the 'high-risk strategy': disadvantages

1. Difficulties and costs of screening
2. Palliative and temporary—not radical
3. Limited potential for (a) individual
   (b) population
4. Behaviourally inappropriate

efforts were confined to these high-risk individuals, then that approach would need to be sustained year after year and generation after generation. It does not deal with the root of the problem, but seeks to protect those who are vulnerable to it; and they will always be around.

The potential for this approach is limited—sometimes more than we could have expected—both for the individual and for the population. There are two reasons for this. The first is that our power to predict future disease is usually very weak. Most individuals with risk factors will remain well, at least for some years; contrariwise, unexpected illness may happen to someone who has just received an 'all clear' report from a screening examination. One of the limitations of the relative risk statistic is that it gives no idea of the absolute level of danger. Thus the Framingham Study has impressed us all with its powerful discrimination between high and low risk groups, but when we see the degree of overlap in serum cholesterol level between future cases and those who remained healthy, it is not surprising that an individual's future is so often misassessed.[5]

Often the best predictor of future major disease is the presence of existing minor disease. A low ventilatory function today is the best predictor of its future rate of decline. A high blood pressure today is the best predictor of its future rate of rise. Early coronary heart disease is better than all the conventional risk factors as a predictor of future fatal disease. However, even if screening includes such tests for early disease, our experience in the Heart Disease Prevention Project (Table 3)[6] still points to a very weak ability to predict the future of any particular individual.

This point came home to me only recently. I have long congratulated myself on my low levels of coronary risk factors, and I joked to my friends that if I were to die suddenly, I should be very surprised. I even speculated on what other disease—perhaps colon cancer—would be the commonest cause of death for a man in the lowest group of

Table 3   Five-year incidence of myocardial infarction in the UK Heart Disease Prevention Project

Entry characteristic	% of men	% of MI cases	MI incidence rate %
Risk factors alone	15	32	7
'Ischaemia'	16	41	11
'Ischaemia' + risk factors	2	12	22
All men	100	100	4

cardiovascular risk. The painful truth is that for such an individual in a Western population the commonest cause of death—by far—is coronary heart disease! Everyone, in fact, is a high-risk individual for this uniquely mass disease.

There is another, related reason why the predictive basis of the 'high-risk' strategy of prevention is weak. It is well illustrated by some data from Alberman[7] which relate the occurrence of Down's syndrome births to maternal age (Table 4). Mothers under 30 years are individually at minimal risk; but because they are so numerous, they generate half the cases. High-risk individuals aged 40 and above generate only 13% of the cases.

The lesson from this example is that *a large number of people at a small risk may give rise to more cases of disease than the small number who are at a high risk.* This situation seems to be common, and it limits the utility of the 'high-risk' approach to prevention.

A further disadvantage of the 'high-risk' strategy is that it is behaviourally inappropriate. Eating, smoking, exercise and all our other life-style characteristics are constrained by social norms. If we try to eat differently from our friends it will not only be inconvenient, but we risk being regarded as cranks or hypochondriacs. If a man's work environment encourages heavy drinking, then advice that he is damaging his liver is unlikely to have any effect. No-one who has attempted any sort of health education effort in individuals needs to be told that it is difficult for such people to step out of line with their peers.

Table 4   Incidence of Down's syndrome according to maternal age[7]

Maternal age (years)	Risk of Down's syndrome per 1000 births	Total births in age group (as % of all ages)	% of total Down's syndrome occurring in age group
<30	0.7	78	51
30–34	1.3	16	20
35–39	3.7	5	16
40–44	13.1	0.95	11
≥45	34.6	0.05	2
All ages	1.5	100	100

This is what the 'high-risk' preventive strategy requires them to do.

The Population Strategy

This is the attempt to control the determinants of incidence, to lower the mean level of risk factors, to shift the whole distribution of exposure in a favourable direction. In its traditional 'public health' form it has involved mass environmental control methods; in its modern form it is attempting (less successfully) to alter some of society's norms of behaviour.

The advantages are powerful (Table 5). The first is that it is radical. It attempts to remove the underlying causes that make the disease common. It has a large potential—often larger than one would have expected—for the population as a whole. From Framingham data one can compute that a 10 mm Hg lowering of the blood pressure distribution as a whole would correspond to about a 30% reduction in the total attributable mortality.

The approach is behaviourally appropriate. If non-smoking eventually becomes 'normal', then it will be much less necessary to keep on persuading individuals. Once a social norm of behaviour has become accepted and (as in the case of diet) once the supply industries have adapted themselves to the new pattern, then the maintenance of that situation no longer requires effort from individuals. The health education phase aimed at changing individuals is, we hope, a temporary necessity, pending changes in the norms of what is socially acceptable.

Unfortunately the population strategy of prevention has also some weighty drawbacks (Table 6). It offers only a small benefit to each individual, since most of them were going to be all right anyway, at least for many years. This leads to the *Prevention Paradox*:[8] 'A preventive measure which brings much benefit to the population offers little to each participating individual'. This has been the history of public health—of immunization, the wearing of seat belts and now the attempt to change various life-style characteristics. Of enormous potential importance to the population as a whole, these measures offer very little—particularly in the short term—to each individual; and thus there is poor motivation of the subject. We should not be surprised that health education tends to be relatively ineffective for individuals and in the short term. Mostly people act for substantial and immediate rewards, and the medical motivation for health education is inherently weak. Their health next year is not likely to be much better if they accept our advice or if they reject it. Much more powerful as motivators for health education are the social rewards of enhanced self-esteem and social approval.

There is also in the population approach only poor motivation of physicians. Many medical practitioners who embarked with enthusiasm on anti-smoking education have become disheartened because their success rate was no more than 5 or 10%: in clinical practice one's expectation of results is higher. Grateful patients are few in

Table 5   Prevention by the 'population strategy': advantages

1. Radical
2. Large potential for population
3. Behaviourally appropriate

Table 6   Prevention by the 'population strategy': disadvantages

1. Small benefit to individual ('Prevention Paradox')
2. Poor motivation of subject
3. Poor motivation of physician
4. Benefit: risk ratio worrisome

preventive medicine, where success is marked by a non-event. The skills of behavioural advice are different and unfamiliar, and professional esteem is lowered by a lack of skill. Harder to overcome than any of these, however, is the enormous difficulty for medical personnel to see health as a population issue and not merely as a problem for individuals.

In mass prevention each individual has usually only a small expectation of benefit, and this small benefit can easily be outweighed by a small risk.[8] This happened in the World Health Organization clofibrate trial,[9] where a cholesterol-lowering drug seems to have killed more than it saved, even though the fatal complication rate was only about 1/1000/year. Such low-order risks, which can be vitally important to the balance sheet of mass preventive plans, may be hard or impossible to detect. This makes it important to distinguish two approaches. The first is the restoration of biological normality by the removal of an abnormal exposure (e.g. stopping smoking, controlling air pollution, moderating some of our recently-acquired dietary deviations); here there can be some presumption of safety. This is not true for the other kind of preventive approach, which leaves intact the underlying causes of incidence and seeks instead to interpose some new, supposedly protective intervention (e.g. immunization, drugs, jogging). Here the onus is on the activists to produce adequate evidence of safety.

Conclusions

Case-centred epidemiology identifies individual susceptibility, but it may fail to identify the underlying causes of incidence. The 'high-risk' strategy of prevention is an interim expedient, needed in order to protect susceptible individuals, but only for so long as the underlying causes of incidence remain unknown or uncontrollable; if causes can be removed, susceptibility ceases to matter.

Realistically, many diseases will long continue to call for both approaches, and fortunately competition between them is usually unnecessary. Nevertheless, the priority of concern should always be the discovery and control of the causes of incidence.

References

1. Pocock SJ, Shaper AG, Cook DG *et al.* British Regional Heart Study: geographic variations in cardiovascular mortality and the role of water quality. *Br Med J* 1980;**283**:1243–9.
2. Shaper AG. Blood pressure studies in East Africa. In: The Epidemiology of Hypertension. J Stamler, R Stamler, TN Pullman (eds). New York, Grune and Stratten, 1967. pp. 139–45.
3. Reid DD, Brett GZ, Hamilton PJS *et al.* Cardiorespiratory disease and diabetes among middle-aged male civil servants. *Lancet* 1974; **1**:469–73.
4. Keys A. Coronary heart disease in seven countries. American Heart Association Monograph Number 29. American Heart Association, New York, 1970.
5. Kannel WB, Garcia MJ, McNamara PM *et al.* Serum lipid precursors of coronary heart disease. *Human Pathol* 1971;**2**:129–51.
6. Heller RF, Chinn S, Tunstall Pedoe HD *et al.* How well can we predict coronary heart disease? Findings in the United Kingdom Heart Disease Prevention Project. *Br Med J* 1984;**288**:1409–11.
7. Alberman E, Berry C. Prenatal diagnosis and the specialist in community medicine. *Community Med* 1979;**1**:89–96.
8. Rose G. Strategy of prevention: lessons from cardiovascular disease. *Br Med J* 1981;**282**:1847–51.
9. Committee of Principal Investigators. A co-operative trial in the primary prevention of ischaemic heart disease. *Br Heart J* 1978;**40**:1069–118.

Long Live Community
Social Capital as Public Health

Ichiro Kawachi, Bruce P. Kennedy, and Kimberly Lochner

Americans now understand that their health is at risk if they smoke, overeat, and fail to exercise. But a growing body of evidence suggests that public health also depends on a less widely understood influence—social cohesion. And while many Americans have stopped smoking, gone on diets, and put on jogging shoes, American society has become, if anything, less cohesive.

Consider what happened in Roseto, a small Italian-American community in eastern Pennsylvania. During the 1950s, when the town first caught the attention of medical researchers Stewart Wolf and J.G. Bruhn, Roseto posed something of a mystery. Death rates in the small town of about 1,600 people were substantially lower than in neighboring communities. In particular, the rate of heart attacks was about 40 percent lower than expected and could not be explained by the prevalence of factors known to increase the risk of the disease. Citizens of Roseto smoked at the same rate as neighboring towns, they were just as overweight and sedentary, and their diet consisted of about the same amount of animal fat. But the one feature that stood out was the close-knit relations among residents in the community. The town had been originally settled by immigrants during the 1880s, who all came from the same village in rural Italy. The researchers noticed the social cohesiveness and ethos of egalitarianism that characterized the community:

> Proper behavior by those Rosetans who have achieved material wealth or occupational prestige requires attention to the delicate balance between ostentation and reserve, ambition and restraint, modesty and dignity. . . . The local priest emphasized that when preoccupation with earning money exceeded the unmarked boundary it became a basis

for social rejection. . . . Rosetan culture thus provided a set of checks and balances to ensure that neither success nor failure got out of hand. . . . During the first five years of our study it was difficult to distinguish, on the basis of dress or behavior, the wealthy from the impecunious in Roseto. . . . Despite the affluence of many, there was no atmosphere of "keeping up with the Joneses" in Roseto.

But as young people began to move away to seek jobs in neighboring towns and the community entered the mainstream of American life, the social taboos against conspicuous consumption began to weaken, as did the community bonds that once maintained the town's egalitarian values. About a decade into the study, the researchers noted:

> For many years the more affluent Rosetans restrained their inclination toward material indulgence and maintained in their town the image of a relatively classless society. When a few began to display their wealth, however, many others followed. By 1965 families had begun to join country clubs, drive expensive automobiles, take luxury cruises, and make flights to Las Vegas.

The unforeseen consequence of improved material well-being and, probably more important, rising socioeconomic disparities was that the incidence of heart attack in Roseto caught up with neighboring towns within a span of a decade.

The notion that social cohesion is related to the health of a population is hardly new. One hundred years ago, Emile Durkheim demonstrated that suicide rates were higher among populations that were less cohesive. In 1979, after a nine-year study of 6,928 adults living in Alameda County, California, epidemiologists

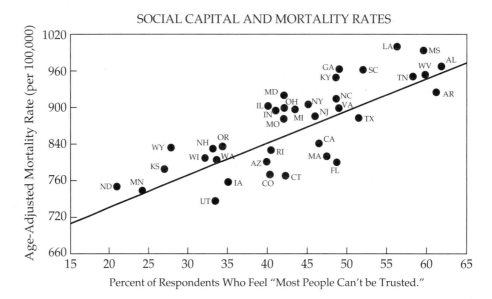

SOCIAL CAPITAL AND MORTALITY RATES

Source: National Opinion Research Center

Lisa Berkman and S. Leonard Syme reported that people with few social ties were two to three times more likely to die of all causes than were those with more extensive contacts. This relationship persisted even after controlling for such characteristics as age and health practices, including cigarette smoking, drinking, exercise, and the use of medical services. The basic findings of the Alameda County Study have since been confirmed in more than a half dozen epidemiological studies in different communities.

These findings have ominous implications if the political scientist Robert Putnam is right that social capital is declining in America [see "The Strange Disappearance of Civic America," *TAP,* Winter 1996]. Putnam's memorable metaphor for this change is bowling league membership, which has declined while bowling overall has increased. By social capital Putnam means the invisible glue that holds society together—the social networks, norms, and trust that enable groups of individuals to cooperate in pursuing shared objectives. On the basis of research in Italy

and elsewhere, Putnam argues that social capital is a major contributing factor in economic growth [see "The Prosperous Community: Social Capital and Public Life," *TAP,* Spring 1993]. In fact, as the public health research shows, the harm from weakening social cohesion may not only be civic and economic—it may also be physical.

It Does Hurt to Be Alone

To explore this question, we set out to test the relationship between social capital and public health at the state level. In fact, there are quite marked geographical variations in civic trust and association membership across the United States, and when these indicators of social capital are arrayed against regional differences in mortality and morbidity, the resulting correlations are striking. The chart "Social Capital and Mortality Rates" (above) shows the relationship between the level of civic trust and the age-adjusted rate of death from all causes for the 39 states for which data were available in the National Opinion Research Center's General Social Surveys. The lower the trust between citizens—as indicated by the proportion of respondents in each state who believed that "most people cannot be trusted"— the higher is the average mortality rate.

A similar relationship with mortality prevails for the per capita membership of state residents in voluntary associations. These relationships between social cohesion and mortality hold among both whites and African Americans, as well as among men and women, and they persist after statistical adjustment for state variations in median household income and proportion of households living below the federal poverty threshold.

The figure [below], "Social Trust and Quality of Life," displays the correlation between level of civic trust and a measure of self-reported well-being. The National Center for Chronic Disease Prevention and Health Promotion employed the Behavioral Risk Factor Surveillance System (BRFSS) to ascertain the proportion of residents in each state reporting that their health was only fair or poor as opposed to good or excellent. (The BRFSS is a representative, random telephone survey that sampled more than 350,000 community-dwelling American adults between 1993 and 1996.) Again, there is a striking correlation between social capital and quality of life.

But does "bowling alone" really increase the likelihood that you'll get sick? Putnam's reference to the decline in bowling leagues evinced skepticism from some critics. Katha Pollitt, for example, pointed out that the popularity of bowling leagues emerged from a particular period in American blue-collar culture that permitted husbands plenty of boys' nights out (think of the memorable first glimpses of Marlon Brando in *A Streetcar Named Desire*). Other critics have pointed out that declining bowling league memberships may be offset by increased participation of other kinds, such as coaching and playing in youth soccer leagues.

Nonetheless, bowling league membership turns out to correlate rather well with who lives or dies (see "Bowling League Membership and Mortality," [next page]). To paraphrase John Donne, no man

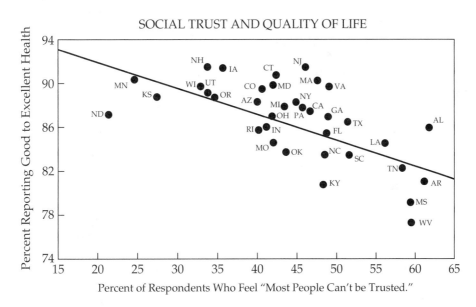

SOCIAL TRUST AND QUALITY OF LIFE

Source: National Center for Chronic Disease Prevention and Health Promotion

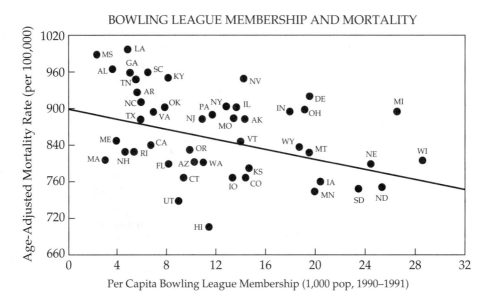

BOWLING LEAGUE MEMBERSHIP AND MORTALITY

Source: American Bowling Congress Annual Report

or woman is an island entire of itself—therefore we should never send to ask for whom the ball rolls.

Inequality and Public Health

Another feature of a society that may influence both its cohesiveness and its members' health is the level of economic inequality. In many countries, notably America, income and wealth are becoming more concentrated. According to a Census Bureau report released last year, the share of total income going to the top fifth of American households increased from 40.5 percent to 46.9 percent between 1968 and 1994. By contrast, the shares of the bottom 80 percent either declined or stagnated. The biggest income gains went to the top 5 percent of households, whose share of the economic pie increased from 16.6 percent to 21 percent. In 1994, the average income among the top 5 percent of households was more than 19 times that of the bottom 20 percent.

Might this polarization of incomes be loosening the social cement? In a forthcoming article in the *American Journal of Public Health,* we argue that this is the case. "Income Inequality (Robin Hood Index) and Social Trust" ([next page]) shows the rising trend in income inequality plotted against the steady decline in civic trust, as tracked by the General Social Surveys. The measure of income inequality we used is the Robin Hood Index, which equals the proportion of aggregate income that would have to be redistributed from households with disproportionate earnings to those earning less, if incomes were to be level. The higher the Robin Hood Index, the bigger the income gap. As "Income Inequality and Social Trust" shows, the larger the income gap, the lower is citizens' trust in each other. Nearly identical results are obtained when we plot income disparity against per capita participation in voluntary associations.

Comparing public health and income distribution across countries lends further credence to

INCOME INEQUALITY (ROBIN HOOD INDEX) AND SOCIAL TRUST

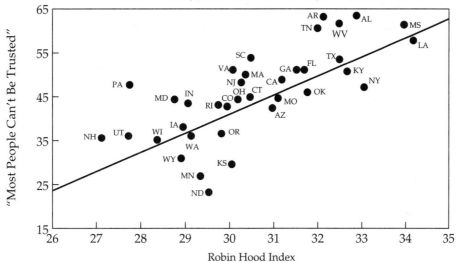

Source: National Opinion Research Center

the notion that income distribution plays a greater role in the quality of public health than more traditional indices do. In his recent book, *Unhealthy Societies: The Afflictions of Inequality,* economic historian Richard Wilkinson argues forcefully that the life expectancy in developed countries cannot be explained by differences in their absolute standard of living as measured, for example, by per capita income. Rather, a population's health depends more on the level of economic inequality.

The United States, despite having one of the highest living standards in the world (the real gross domestic product [GDP] per capita was $24,680 in 1993), has a lower life expectancy (76.1 years in 1993) than less affluent but more egalitarian countries like the Netherlands (GDP, $17,340; life expectancy, 77.5 years); Israel (GDP, $15,130; life expectancy, 76.6 years); or Spain (GDP, $13,660; life expectancy, 77.7 years). In fact, societies with the smallest income differences between rich and poor, such as Sweden and Japan,

tend to enjoy the highest life expectancy (78.3 and 79.6 years, respectively). An egalitarian distribution of wealth and income seems to imply a more cohesive, harmonious society. The quality of social relations, Wilkinson concludes, is the prime determinant of a country's human welfare and quality of life.

What does this imply for our future quality of life in this country? Is what has been happening to American society simply a case of Roseto writ large? Two studies published simultaneously in the April 20, 1996, issue of the *British Medical Journal,* including one we conducted, found that differences in income distribution across the 50 states were highly correlated with mortality rates, including deaths from heart disease, homicides, and infant mortality. To be sure, overall life expectancy in the United States has been steadily improving due to advances in medical treatment and the prevention of disease through lifestyle changes. But mortality might have declined more if income inequality had not risen. Our model suggests that for every percent increase in income inequality, the overall death rate is 2 to 3 percent higher than it needed to have been. By any definition, this is an important public health problem.

In recent years, unfortunately, government policy has tended to reinforce growing inequality, which is unsurprising in view of the disproportionate political weight that the well-off carry [see Sidney Verba, Kay Lehman Schlozman, and Henry E. Brady, "The Big Tilt: Participatory Inequality in America," *TAP*, May–June 1997]. The danger is a self-perpetuating cycle of growing income inequality, growing political inequality, and diminishing social capital. And because health too is at stake, it is no exaggeration to say that breaking that cycle will affect the body politic in every sense.

C. The Economics of Health Care

Decisions about health care, those made at the bedside, in Congress, in the courts, or in state legislatures, are not made in a vacuum. A variety of factors influence these decisions, not the least of which is the cost of health care. Health care is expensive in the United States, and it looks as if the future will only bring increasing costs. In the year 2000, expenditures on medical care and other direct services (not including public health costs) reached 1.3 trillion.[11] By 2008 this figure is expected to reach 2.3 trillion dollars, roughly 15.5 percent of the GDP.[12] Despite the amount that is spent on health care in the United States, 43 million Americans are without health insurance.[13] Other countries spend less on health care, but often provide some form of universal health care to their citizens. In 1998, France spent 9.3 percent of its GDP on health care, Britain 6.8 percent, and Canada 9.3 percent.[14] Although each spent less on health care than the United States, they all provided some form of universal access to health care.

Although Americans do not have universal health insurance, they do rely on a variety of different mechanisms to finance their medical care. Most Americans (66.6 percent) receive their health care insurance through their employers or the employers of their spouse, parent or partner.[15] This practice became widespread during World War II, when employers responded to a freeze on wages by offering employees health insurance and other benefits in place of increased wages. Today the practice continues in part because the cost of insurance provided by employers is not subject to the federal income tax. As a result, the tax system effectively subsidizes employer-provided insurance. The elderly, those over 65, and many though not most of the poor receive their health care through government-funded programs, the poor through Medicaid and the elderly through Medicare.[16] Most of the remainder of the population is uninsured, though some have private insurance.

The health care that Americans receive is also determined by the kind of health plan they have and the extent of the benefits provided by their plan. For most Americans, those who receive their health care through employers, the decision about what health care they will receive will be determined by employers, labor representatives, and the law. Today health care plans fall into two main categories, those that are managed and those that are not. In some ways "managed" is a misleading term because all health care is managed; the question is by whom. In the United

States, care that is prepaid and managed by someone other than the patient and physician dyad, a health maintenance organization (HMO) administrator, or cost containment mechanism such as capitation is called "managed care." When the health care that a patient receives is paid for retrospectively and on a fee for service basis, leaving the decisions about care in the hands of the patient and physician, informed by the professional practice standard, the reimbursement mechanism is known as "fee for service."

By 2001, 93 percent of Americans who were enrolled in employer-based health plans were enrolled in some form of managed care plan.[17] Recently there has been a shift among subscribers from highly managed plans, such as HMOs, to more loosely managed ones such as preferred provider organizations (PPOs).[18] Some have suggested that this shift is a result of the backlash against managed care as evidenced by a rise in state mandates and a temporary period of slowing health care expenditures.[19]

Health care is also an important money-generating industry. Although this has not always been the case, today our health care system is organized according to a marketplace ideology. In the year 2000, 64 percent of HMO enrollment was in for-profit plans.[20] Many people believe that this market place ethos influences the nature of care in the United States. Although for-profit managed care organizations can provide excellent care, it is important to keep in mind that for these organizations, the "health" of the organization is at least as important as the health of the people they serve. Likewise because they too have to compete in the market place, nonprofit institutions must also consider their economic well-being. As you read various topics in this book, keep in mind that the cost of health care is on everyone's mind and is often a consideration in decisions about what care to give patients.

The idiosyncrasies of health care economics were famously explored by economist Kenneth Arrow in the landmark essay *Uncertainty and the Welfare Economics of Medical Care*.[21] Arrow argued that the medical marketplace was characterized by great asymmetries of information. Physicians knew much more than their patients. In the face of uncertainty, patients could, for example, trust their physicians to act in their interest because of their physicians' values. Arrow's thoughts about health economics were, perhaps, most applicable when he wrote his article—reimbursement was then generally on a fee for service basis. It is worth reflecting on whether the same "nonmarket social institutions" can compensate for the asymmetries that exist today.

In the readings, John K. Iglehart provides an important overview of the American health care system and how health expenditures are tallied. Notice that the fastest-growing expenditure is prescription drugs. It is difficult to navigate the health care landscape without understanding business models as well as medical ones. Finally, in *Rationing Health Care and the Need for Credible Scarcity: Why Americans Can't Say No,* Wendy K. Mariner discusses some of the difficulties proposals to ration health care may face. She believes that the need to ration health care may strike many Americans as overstated because it is difficult to make a case for actual scarcity of medical resources. That is, many Americans may view rationing as arbitrary. As you read Mariner's essay, consider whether some of the concerns she identifies would be addressed by a nationalized health care system, such as the Canadian model, or through a process of deliberation and consent. Clearly, the United States has adopted a private, for-profit system, one that also turns out to be expensive. How would a contractarian like John Rawls evaluate our health care system? A libertarian such as Robert Nozick?

The American Health Care System—Expenditures

JOHN K. IGLEHART

The United States operates a health care system that is unique among nations. It is the most expensive of systems, outstripping by over half again the health care expenditures of any other country.[1] The number of people without insurance continues to increase, however, reaching 43.4 million, or 16.1 percent of the population, in 1997—the highest level in a decade.[2] By many technical standards, U.S. medical care is the best in the world,[3] but leaders in the field declared recently at a national round table that there is an "urgent need to improve health care quality."[4] The stringency of managed care and a low inflation rate have slowed the growth of medical spending appreciably, but a new government study projects that health care expenditures will soon begin escalating again and will double over the next decade.[5] In short, the American system is a work in progress, driven by a disparate array of interests with two goals that are often in conflict: providing health care to the sick, and generating income for the persons and organizations that assume the financial risk. In this report, I will take stock of this dynamic sector, which now represents one-seventh of the economy, by tracking it in the most American of ways—following the money from its collection to its expenditure.

Almost five years has elapsed since the ambitious efforts of the Clinton administration to reform the health care system fell to defeat without even reaching the floor of the House or Senate for a vote. Since then, with the enthusiastic approval of the Republican-controlled Congress and the acceptance of the Clinton administration, large numbers of private-sector employees and beneficiaries of publicly financed insurance programs have enrolled in managed-care plans. Those covered by such plans now make up an estimated 75 percent of all persons with private health insurance.

In strictly monetary terms, two trends dominate. One is the decline in the growth of health care expenditures in the past five years. In 1997, the growth rate was the slowest in the more than 35 years for which there are data on medical spending.[6] The second trend is the growth in the government's share of the nation's health care bill.

Spending by federal, state, and local governments rose in 1997 to $507 billion, or 46 percent of the total, an increase from 40 percent in 1990. Private resources financed 54 percent of personal health services ($585 billion) in 1997, down from 60 percent in 1990.[6]

The magnitude of public expenditures in any health care system is important because it indicates the amount of attention governments are likely to pay to the system and thus the influence they bring to bear on its configuration. Rhetoric notwithstanding, the government's role in the financing and regulation of health care has grown inexorably under both Republicans and Democrats ever since the enactment of Medicare and Medicaid in 1965. As the health economist Victor Fuchs puts it, "No matter how committed the country is in general to the idea of free markets and capitalism, government plays a substantial role in health care."[7]

The Role of Economic Systems

Nevertheless, the U.S. economy is driven primarily by market-based capitalism. A market-based system consists of a collection of decision-making units called households and another collection of businesses and other larger organizations. This structure is important to recognize because, as Fuchs asserts, "The households own all the productive resources in the society."[8] Thus, although funds for personal health services flow from three basic sources—employers, governments, and individuals—all of these resources are initially extracted from households as payroll deductions from the wages of working adults, as taxes and other surcharges, and as direct payments to providers and suppliers. In reality, government and employers are only intermediaries in the process. A fourth source is, as Uwe Reinhardt has described it, "an informal, albeit unreliable, catastrophic health insurance program operated by hospitals and many physicians . . . who extract the premium for that insurance through higher charges to paying patients."[9]

The Role of Employers

Collectively, private employers and employees are the most important purchasers of health care through the insurance premiums they pay together for coverage. Of the $585 billion that private payers expended for medical services in 1997, about 60 percent ($348 billion) was spent by employers and employees to purchase health insurance.[6] The premiums that finance coverage are paid in part by the employee through the explicit deduction of regular (usually weekly or monthly) amounts from the gross wages stated on the employee's paycheck. The remainder (usually 80 percent or more) is ostensibly paid by employers and not deducted from the employee's pay. There is a sharp division of opinion over who actually foots the bill for the employer-paid portion. The question is important because as employers steer their workers into insurance arrangements that employers select, very few employees (17 percent in the most recent estimate[10]) have a choice of plans.

Most employees have long believed that the employer's portion comes out of the employer's profits. Most employers share that view, believing that their premium payments are a cost of doing business and, as such, cut into the profitability of the firm. Economists and the Congressional Budget Office, on the other hand, are convinced by theory and empirical evidence that this portion, too, is actually shifted back to employees in the form of lower take-home pay.[11,12] In a recent book, the economist Mark Pauly asserted that "higher medical costs do not harm employers or owners but do reduce money wages for workers . . . Lower costs benefit workers, not employers; they add to take-home pay, not profits."[13]

By exempting from federal and state taxes the income earned by employees that is used to pay insurance premiums, the government encourages employers to provide coverage to workers. Employers' costs are treated as a deductible business expense. The exclusion from income taxes and Social Security payroll deductions creates a substantial tax subsidy for employment-based insurance. In 1999, according to the Clinton administration, this exemption will reduce federal revenues by an estimated $76 billion. If this were a federal health program, it would be the third most expensive one after Medicare and Medicaid.[14] Families with higher incomes benefit disproportionately because they are in higher tax brackets. This subsidy provides little or no benefit to people who are uninsured or who purchase their own health insurance. This regressive tax structure was an unintended consequence of the policy, but employers strongly oppose its elimination. Recently, Congress extended the tax benefit to self-employed people in a phased-in provision that will take full effect in 2003.

The Role of Government

One of the key characteristics of all modern economies is that as they prosper, they spend more money for health care. For example, high-income countries (those with per capita annual incomes above $8,500) accounted for 89 percent of global health expenditures in 1994, even though they comprised only 16 percent of the global population and represented just 7 percent of the estimated number of disability-adjusted years of life worldwide (1.4 trillion) that were lost to disease.[15] Although all nations purchase more health care as they prosper—so that about 80 percent of the variation among countries in per capita health care spending is explained by the per capita income of a country—the United States is once again an exception. Its annual bill for personal health services ($3,925 per person in 1997) is about $1,000 per person above the level that its per capita income would seemingly predict. Three reasons are that physicians in the United States are paid more than those in other countries for each unit of service,[16] a day in the hospital for similar patients is considerably more expensive in the United States, and medical technology diffuses more rapidly and is generally used to treat more patients than in other countries. In a survey of 50 health economists in 1995, 81 percent agreed with the following statement: "The primary reason for the increase in the health sector's share of [the gross domestic product] over the past 30 years is technological change in medicine."[17]

Federal and state expenditures for medical care are collected as taxes of one type or another and redistributed as income to providers and suppliers, who bill for services rendered and goods delivered. The dynamics of this system have begun to change, however, as more payments for health care are fixed and set prospectively. The federal government pays the physicians it employs and other employees of publicly operated health care facilities. States also employ physicians directly and operate public health care facilities. Public monies are allocated for health care through a variety of agencies after being appropriated by federal and state legislative bodies or collected in earmarked accounts such as social-insurance trust funds (e.g., Medicare).

One important component of national health care spending is the transfer of money from the federal to the state governments. Such transfers evolved after World War II, and their total value tripled during the 1960s. By 1995, the number of intergovernmental grants for education, health, transportation, and other purposes had risen to 633, with outlays totaling $226 billion.[18] Democrats and Republicans differ about how federal aid to states should be structured. In general, Republicans favor block grants to states—that is, grants with few strings attached—because their party supports shifting power from Washington, D.C., to the states. Democrats generally prefer categorical grants—that is, those that stipulate with greater specificity how the money should be spent.

The largest program involving the intergovernmental transfer of funds is Medicaid, which accounted for 39 percent of all federal grant outlays in 1995. In 1997, Medicaid financed acute care and long-term care services for 41.3 million aged, blind, and disabled people with low incomes, as well as poor mothers and children, at a cost of $160 billion.[6] Of that amount, the federal share was $95 billion and the state and local share $65 billion. The federal funds are appropriated annually, with the amounts determined by a formula based on each state's per capita income. Medicaid spending grew by only 3.8 percent in 1997, the smallest annual increase in the history of the program. In large part, Medicaid's slow growth stemmed from the effects of welfare-reform legislation (the Personal Responsibility and Work Opportunity Reconciliation Act of 1996), which led to an unprecedented decline in welfare caseloads[19,20] and low unemployment rates.

The largest federal health program, Medicare, is funded from four different sources: mandatory contributions by employers and employees, general tax revenues, beneficiaries' premiums, and deductibles and copayments paid by patients (or supplemental health insurance). Medicare beneficiaries include people over 65 years of age, the disabled, and those with end-stage renal disease. Medicare's Hospital Insurance Trust Fund (Part A of the program) is grounded in the principle of social insurance. That is, workers make mandatory contributions to a dedicated trust fund during their working years, with the promise of receiving benefits after they retire. By law, the nation's employers and some 151 million employees are required to pay equal amounts of a payroll tax that totals 2.9 percent of earned income. Self-employed workers pay the entire 2.9 percent of their net income into the trust fund. In 1997, these payroll taxes totaled $115 billion and made up 88 percent of the income of the trust fund; the remainder came from interest earned on the monies in the trust fund and miscellaneous sources. Approximately 22 percent of the 38 million people who are eligible for Medicare hospital insurance received hospital services in 1997.

Medicare Part B finances care by physicians and outpatient, home health, and other services; it is called the Supplementary Medical Insurance Program. The funds come largely from general tax revenues appropriated by Congress ($60 bil-

lion, or about 73 percent of the total Part B income, in 1997), rather than from a mandatory tax collected for that specific purpose. Part B funds are often erroneously called a "trust fund." Medicare beneficiaries who enroll in Part B are required to pay monthly premiums (in 1998, the premium was $43.80). Enrollment is voluntary, but virtually all people who are eligible sign up. Premiums are not related to income. Thus, in Medicare, unlike Medicaid, the rich and the poor are treated the same. In 1997, premiums accounted for $19 billion, or about 24 percent of Part B income. The remainder of its funding came from interest income on revenues.

Medicare has low administrative costs, as compared with those of managed-care companies or private insurers. Benefit payments represent 99 percent of outlays for Medicare Part A; administrative expenses, including funds to support fiscal intermediaries (generally private insurance companies), make up only 1 percent of the total.[21] More than 98 percent of the Part B outlays are for benefit payments; less than 2 percent are for administration.

The Contributions of Individual Citizens

The share of national health expenditures paid for directly by individual citizens declined for 11 straight years until 1997, when it grew markedly faster than private health insurance premiums.[6] Out-of-pocket spending is generally defined as including expenditures for coinsurance and deductibles required by insurers, as well as direct payments for services not covered by a third party. Premium amounts contributed by employees are generally not considered as out-of-pocket expenditures. Out-of-pocket spending amounted to $188 billion in 1997, or 17.2 percent of all national health expenditures. The general decline in direct consumer spending has been attributed in large part to the growth in health maintenance organizations (HMOs), which traditionally offer broad benefits with only modest out-of-pocket payments. In the past few years, however, most HMO enrollees have had increased cost-sharing requirements, as employers and health plan managers have sought to constrain spending even further.[22] In general, out-of-pocket payments are still considerably less in an HMO than with indemnity insurance.

The overall declines in per capita out-of-pocket spending mask the financial difficulties of many poor people and families.[23] A recent study estimated that Medicare beneficiaries over 65 years of age with incomes below the federal poverty level (in 1997 the level was $7,755 for individuals and $9,780 for couples) who were also eligible for Medicaid assistance (which usually covers the monthly Part B premium) still spent 35 percent of their incomes on out-of-pocket health care costs.[24] Medicare beneficiaries with incomes below the federal poverty level who did not receive Medicaid assistance spent, on average, half their incomes on out-of-pocket health care costs.

The Flow of Health Care Expenditures

In 1997, national health expenditures totaled $1,092 billion, according to the Health Care Financing Administration (HCFA), which tracks expenditures.[6] Health care spending consumed 13.5 percent of the gross domestic product in 1997, which was a slight drop from the previous year. Health care spending increased only 4.8 percent in 1997—the slowest annual growth rate in more than 35 years. Personal health expenditures accounted for 89 percent of health care spending, or $969 billion. HCFA's analysts recently projected that, beginning in 1998, national health spending would again begin to grow faster than the rest of the economy. By 2002, the agency projected that national health expenditures would total $2.1 trillion—an estimated 16.6 percent of the gross domestic product.[5] This analysis was based on two assumptions that are certain to be challenged by employers and the managed-care industry: that "the higher anticipated growth in real per capita national health spending will be driven almost entirely by rising expenditures in the private rather than the public sector," and that savings from managed care will be a one-time phenomenon, rather than a long-term trend.

Before the emergence of managed care, it was largely physicians, acting individually on behalf of their patients, who decided how most health care dollars were spent. They billed for their services, and third-party insurers usually reimbursed them without asking any questions, because the ultimate payers—employers—demanded no greater accounting. Now, many employers have changed from passive payers[25,26] to aggressive purchasers[27] and are exerting more influence on payment rates, on where patients are cared for, and on the content of care. Through selective contracting with physicians, stringent review of the use of services, practice protocols, and payment on a fixed, per capita basis, managed-care plans have pressured doctors to furnish fewer services and to improve the coordination and management of care, thereby altering the way in which many physicians treat patients.[28] In striving to balance the conflicts that arise in caring for patients within these constraints, physicians have become "double agents."[29,30] The ideological tie that long linked many physicians and private executives—a belief in capitalism and free enterprise—has been weakened by the aggressive intervention of business into the practice of medicine through managed care.

The Shifting Pattern of Expenditures

Hospital spending continues to consume the largest portion of the health care dollar ($371 billion in 1997, or 38 percent of spending on personal health services), but in large part as a consequence of the pressure applied by managed-care plans, growth in such spending has slowed appreciably.[31] The mix of services offered by most hospitals has shifted away from inpatient stays toward greater use of outpatient and postdischarge services (such as home health care and skilled-nursing facilities). Medicare and Medicaid funded half of all hospital expenditures in 1997, private insurance paid for another third, and consumers paid directly for only 3 percent of all hospital services.[6] The remainder was funded by the Departments of Defense and Veterans Affairs, state and local subsidies to hospitals, and private philanthropy.

The number of hospital days per 1000 HMO enrollees has declined steadily since 1985. Occupancy rates in community hospitals fell from 64 percent in 1990 to 60 percent in 1997; relatively few hospitals have closed, but many have merged. Hospital spending grew by only 2.9 percent in 1997, making it the slowest-growing component in HCFA's expenditure survey. Nonetheless, most hospitals maintained profit margins that were greater than in almost any earlier period.[32] Many hospitals increased their profit margins by reducing their expenses, expanding their capacity to provide outpatient services, and diversifying into postdischarge care.

Expenditures for physicians' services represented another 19.9 percent of the health care dollar in 1997, or $217.6 billion. This figure represented an increase in spending of 4.4 percent over 1996, continuing a trend of single-digit growth that began in 1992. Largely as a result of the efforts of managed-care organizations to constrain medical spending, the annual growth in mean net income for all physicians declined from an average of 7.2 percent during the period from 1986 through 1992 to 1.7 percent in 1993 through 1996.[6]

According to a new analysis of data collected by the National Institutes of Health (NIH), spending on research and development has increased steadily in recent years, both in absolute terms and as a percentage of total health care spending.[33] In 1995, the total was $35.8 billion. This represented 3.5 percent of total health expenditures, as compared with 3.2 percent in 1986. Over the decade from 1986 through 1995, the share of health-related research and development supported by private industry increased from 42 percent to 52 percent, largely as a consequence of increased spending by pharmaceutical companies.

Recently, Congress has indicated that it is prepared to double the NIH's annual appropriation over the next 5 to 10 years; the only question is how fast. Congress approved an appropriation of $15.6 billion for the NIH for fiscal 1999, an increase of almost $2 billion over the previous year and almost double the increase sought by the Clinton administration. The current situation is a far cry from the bleak assessment of the agency's future provided by the NIH director, Dr. Harold Varmus, in his Shattuck Lecture of 1995.[34]

Congress supports medical research not only because legislators are enthusiastic about its potential, but also because funding research is far less expensive than providing health care coverage for the uninsured.[35] In addition, NIH research benefits the thriving biotechnology industry by providing its raw material. Congress has taken a far different view of research on health services, as reflected in the budget of the Agency for Health Care Policy and Research (AHCPR). Several years ago, in response to a small but vocal group of spinal surgeons who opposed the results of a study of low-back pain sponsored by the AHCPR, the Republican-controlled Congress flirted with the idea of abolishing the agency.[36] Having survived that near-death experience, the AHCPR received an appropriation of $171 million in fiscal 1999, an increase of $24 million over the previous year, but considerably less than the funds provided for only one small component of the NIH—the National Human Genome Research Institute, which received $237 million.

Prescription drugs are the fastest-growing component of personal health expenditures, amounting to $78.9 billion in 1997.[6] This trend is troubling to employers, health plans, physicians, and policy makers alike.[37,38] In recent years, spending for prescription drugs has increased at double-digit rates: 10.6 percent in 1995, 13.2 percent in 1996, and 14.1 percent in 1997.[6] The federal Office of Personnel Management announced recently that in 1999 insurance premiums will increase by an average of 10.2 percent for the 8.7 million federal employees, retirees, dependents, and others covered by the Federal Employees Health Benefits Program, the largest premium hike in a decade.[39] The Office of Personnel Management attributed the increase in part to the rising costs of prescription drugs (which have increased 17 percent annually in recent years). There are several explanations for this acceleration in costs, including broader insurance coverage of prescription drugs, growth in the number of drugs dispensed, more approvals of expensive new drugs by the Food and Drug Administration, and direct advertising of pharmaceutical products to consumers. The use of some new drugs reduces hospital costs, but not enough to offset the increase in expenditures for drugs.

Conclusions

America's trillion-dollar health care system is vast—indeed, larger than the budgets of most nations—and it serves as a perpetual job-creating enterprise, providing employment to some 9 million people. Expenditures for health care are perceived in a variety of ways by different interest groups. Many health care purchasers view them as one of the few uncontrollable costs and have taken unprecedented steps to rein in costs through the constraints imposed by managed-care companies. Patients with employer-sponsored health insurance, who want the best medical care but are fearful of the costs, have sought refuge in managed-care plans, sometimes with mixed results. Physicians may also see health care expenditures as the means to earn a living, or, as Reinhardt has put it, "the allocation of lifestyles to providers."[40]

But in spite of all the money spent for medical care, education, and research, no one—whether patient, provider, or purchaser—seems satisfied with the status quo.

References

1. OECD health data 1998: a comparative analysis of 29 countries. Paris: Organisation for Economic Cooperation and Development, 1998 (CD-ROM).
2. Bureau of the Census. Current population reports. Health insurance coverage, 1997 and 1998. Washington, D.C.: Government Printing Office, 1997, 1998.
3. Berwick DM. As good as it should get: making health care better in the new millennium. Washington, D.C.: National Coalition on Health Care, 1998.
4. Chassin MR, Galvin RW. The urgent need to improve health care quality. JAMA 1998;280:1000–5.
5. Smith S, Freeland M, Heffler S, McKusick D, Health Expenditures Projection Team. The next ten years of health spending: what does the future hold? Health Aff (Millwood) 1998;17(5):128–40.
6. Levit K, Cowan C, Braden B, Stiller J, Sensenig A, Lazenby H. National health expenditures in 1997: more slow growth. Health Aff (Millwood) 1998;17(6):99–110.
7. Fuchs VR. The challenges to health policy in modern economies. The 1997 syarahan perdana. (The Prime Minister of Malaysia Fellowship Exchange Program Lecture.) Kuala Lumpur, Malaysia, September 23, 1997.
8. Fuchs VR. Health care and the United States economic system: an essay in abnormal physiology. Milbank Mem Fund Q 1972;50(2):211–44.
9. Reinhardt UE. Wanted: a clearly articulated social ethic for American health care. JAMA 1997;278:1446–7.
10. Long SH, Marquis SM. How widespread is managed competition? Data bulletin results from community tracking study. Washington, D.C.: Center for Studying Health System Change, 1998:12.
11. Krueger AB, Reinhardt UE. The economics of employer versus individual mandates. Health Aff (Millwood) 1994;13(2):34–53.
12. Congressional Budget Office, Hamilton DR. Economic implications of rising health care costs. Washington, D.C.: Government Printing Office, 1992.

13. Pauly MV. Health benefits at work: an economic and political analysis of employment-based health insurance. Ann Arbor: University of Michigan Press, 1997.

14. Budget of the United States Government: analytical perspectives of the United States: fiscal 1999. Washington, D.C.: Executive Office of the President, 1998.

15. Schieber G, Maeda A. A curmudgeon's guide to financing health care in developing countries. In: Innovations in health care financing: proceedings of a World Bank conference. World Bank discussion paper no. 365. Washington, D.C.: World Bank, 1997.

16. Fuchs VR, Hahn JS. How does Canada do it? A comparison of expenditures for physicians' services in the United States and Canada. N Engl J Med 1990;323:884–90.

17. Fuchs VR. Economics, values and health care reform. Am Econ Rev 1996;86(1):1–24.

18. Advisory Commission on Intergovernmental Relations. Characteristics of federal grant-in-aid programs to state and local governments: grants funded FY 1995. Washington, D.C.: Advisory Commission on Intergovernmental Relations.

19. Ellwood MR, Ku L. Welfare and immigration reforms: unintended side effects for Medicaid. Health Aff(Millwood) 1998;17(3):137–51.

20. The Kaiser Commission on Medicaid and the Uninsured. The decline in Medicaid spending growth in 1996: why did it happen? Menlo Park, Calif.: Henry J. Kaiser Family Foundation, 1998.

21. Federal Hospital Insurance Trust Fund. 1998 Annual report of the Board of Trustees. U.S. House Document 105–245, 105th Congress, 2d session. Washington, D.C.: Government Printing Office, 1998.

22. Gabel J. Ten ways HMOs have changed during the 1990s. Health Aff(Millwood) 1997;16(1):134–45.

23. Shearer G. Hidden from view: the growing burden of health care costs. Washington, D.C.: Consumers Union, 1998.

24. Gross DJ, Gibson MJ, Caplan CF, et al. Out of pocket health spending by Medicare beneficiaries age 65 and older: 1997 projections. Washington, D.C.: AARP Public Policy Institute, 1997.

25. Iglehart JK. Health care and American business. N Engl J Med 1982;306:120–4.

26. Sapolsky HM, Altman D, Greene R, Moore JD. Corporate attitudes toward health care costs. Milbank Mem Fund Q 1981;59:561–85.

27. Bodenheimer T, Sullivan K. How large employers are shaping the health care marketplace. N Engl J Med 1998;338:1003–7.

28. Report to the Congress: context for a changing Medicare program. Washington, D.C.: Medicare Payment Advisory Commission, 1998.

29. Angell M. The doctor as double agent. Kennedy Inst Ethics J 1993;3:279–86.

30. Shortell SM, Waters TM, Clarke KW, Budetti PP. Physicians as double agents: maintaining trust in an era of multiple accountabilities. JAMA 1998;280:1102–8.

31. Robinson JC. HMO market penetration and hospital cost inflation in California. JAMA 1991;266:2719–23.

32. Guterman S. The Balanced Budget Act of 1997: will hospitals take a hit on their PPS margins? Health Aff (Millwood) 1998;17(1):159–66.

33. Neumann PJ, Sandberg EA. Trends in health care R & D and technology innovation. Health Aff (Millwood) 1998;17(6):111–9.

34. Varmus H. Biomedical research enters the steady state. N Engl J Med 1995;333:811–5.

35. Greenberg DS. Fighting cancer in the wrong arena. Washington Post. October 12, 1998:A21.

36. Iglehart JK. Politics and public health. N Engl J Med 1996;334:203–7.

37. Tanouye E. Drug dependency: U.S. has developed an expensive habit; now, how to pay for it. Wall Street Journal. November 16, 1998:A1.

38. Lagnado L. The uncovered: drug costs can leave elderly a grim choice: pills or other needs. Wall Street Journal. November 17, 1998:A1.

39. Barr S. Federal workers face largest health insurance hike since 1989. Washington Post. September 13, 1998:A2.

40. Reinhardt UE. Resource allocation in health care: the allocation of lifestyles to providers. Milbank Q 1987;65(2):153–76.

Rationing Health Care and the Need for Credible Scarcity: Why Americans Can't Say No

WENDY K. MARINER

Introduction

Most Americans recognize a need to control health care spending, but few outside academic circles are willing to talk about rationing care. During the 1994 debate over health care reform, all of those involved seemed careful to avoid what might be a fear of rationing in this country. Albert Jonsen wrote that although he was not aware of any polls that demonstrated that Americans "fear" rationing, he "certainly recognize[d] dislike of the concept of rationing health care."[1] This does not mean that there is no rationing in America. Rudolf Klein has noted that an outsider eavesdropping on the US health care debate would be astonished at the "American delusion that health care is not rationed in the United States."[2]

Health care rationing in the United States is primarily rationing by price (health care goes to those who can pay the price asked); this type of rationing is often invisible or ignored.[3] When health care rationing is recognized, it is often viewed as withholding care from those in need, especially those unable to pay.[4] Dictionaries define "ration" as "to put on a fixed allowance"[5] or to restrict to limited allotments, as in wartime.[6] The association of rationing with wartime restrictions on the battlefield or at home means that the word often connotes deprivation, usually of something people need and want, but for a limited time and for a noble cause.[7] When the idea of rationing is applied to health care resources in general, and apart from wartime restrictions, it should not be sur-

prising that the focus is primarily on deprivation and not on any noble cause.

The concept of rationing used in discussions about health care is an "equitable distribution of scarce resources."[8,9] If rationing is intended to permit everyone to have a fair share of scarce resources, why is it not enthusiastically embraced by everyone? After all, as David Eddy remarked at the Medical Necessity Symposium held in Washington, DC, in April 1995, who wants an inequitable distribution of scarce resources?

If rationing is the allocation of scarce resources, then, in deciding whether or what it is necessary to ration, the threshold question is, Are the resources scarce? If not, there is no need to ration because there is plenty for all. If the answer is yes, however, there is, in fact, rationing. It is no longer a question of whether but how.[8,10] Resources will be distributed, one way or another. If there is not enough to satisfy everyone, the only remaining issue is how to ration: What method should be used to divide up the scarce resources?

Most rationing arguments have concerned what method should be used and, especially, what counts as an equitable distribution of scarce resources.[11] It is easy to understand why people could disagree on rationing criteria. Indeed, such disagreements are so intractable that it often appears that no consensus can be reached. But it may be that, by focusing on rationing methods, the debate has overlooked an alternative explanation for resistance to the idea of rationing: the threshold requirement of scarcity.

It is possible that most Americans simply do not believe that rationing is necessary because they do not believe that health care resources are scarce, especially in this era of excess hospital capacity and underemployed medical specialists. The hypothesis just offered is complicated by the prevalent belief that everyone is entitled to live as long as possible and to be as healthy as possible and that a long, healthy life is ordinarily attainable, given enough health care. The combination of these two beliefs may account for the negative connotation of rationing as deprivation of apparently available care to which people are entitled. Few people will tolerate external limits on care that they consider essential for themselves or their loved ones if those limits are seen not as the result of scarcity but as someone else's refusal to spend money for readily available care. This hypothesis may explain why many people view limits on their own health insurance coverage, for example, as an unfair denial of necessary care, not as necessary rationing. If true, it will be extremely difficult to limit either the use of health care or the money spent on health care as long as the supply of health care resources is perceived to be unlimited and as long as those who attempt to impose limits can be viewed as making hidden and self-interested decisions about how much money to spend. In short, an equitable distribution of health care may be impossible without a credible scarcity of resources.

What Resources Are Scarce in Health Care?

Very few health care goods or services are inherently limited by scarcity of supply in nature. The most obvious examples are organs for transplantation. A few pharmaceuticals and biologics are in limited supply because they are derived from natural elements that are themselves rare or hard to find in nature, such as derivatives of rain forest plants. When synthetic chemical substitutes can be created, the natural limit disappears. The vast majority of drugs and devices do not require naturally limited components, however, and are not naturally scarce resources. In fact, most medical technologies are not scarce. Historical examples include iron lungs for polio (followed by initially limited supplies of polio vaccine) and kidney dialysis machines.[12] Limitations on supplies are a function of the amount of money spent to produce technologies. If more money is spent, larger quantities can be (and have been) produced.

The same is true for the people who deliver health care services: the physicians, nurses, dentists, technicians, and others who counsel, test, and treat patients. The United States has enough people to deliver health care services to everyone in the country. When we heard about a shortage of nurses, for example, it was not because there were not enough people in the country to serve as nurses. It was either because not enough people had been trained to provide nursing services or because not enough money was being paid as salary to persuade people to train or work as nurses. The raw materials—people—exist. It is money that turns human resources into health care providers—money to pay for training and the services nurses deliver—just as money turns raw materials into products.

If there is no natural limit on health care providers or most technologies (including goods and services), why are health care services so often considered scarce resources? The obvious reason is that there is a limit on the amount of money people are willing to spend to "make" and use technology and providers. In theory, we could spend 100% of our gross domestic product on health care services. We do not, of course, because we could not survive without food, clothing, and shelter, and we also want education, police protection, vacations, and a host of necessary or merely desirable things. Thus, we allocate our money, devoting only a portion to health care. If the pot of money allocated to health care will not buy everything we need or want, that pot in turn is rationed among people and services. At the level of patient care, it looks as if health care services are being rationed, when in fact it is the money to buy health care services that is limited.

For example, Oregon limited the amount of money it made available for medical care for Medicaid recipients and allocated that money to services for specific conditions (diagnosis-treatment pairs) that were ranked to indicate priority. Liver transplants for cirrhosis attributable to alcoholism were originally ranked too low to be eligible for Medicaid payment. From the perspective of Medicaid beneficiaries who needed such transplants, it looked as if health care was being rationed. There was no shortage of transplantation facilities, however, and no unusual shortage of livers for transplantation. After protests that the ranking was biased or unprincipled, the legislature moved that diagnosis-treatment pair up in the ranking so that it would be covered. In essence, Oregon reallocated its Medicaid pot of money to buy more liver transplants.

If, as economists believe, money is merely a means of valuing capital, labor, and raw materials, then how we allocate our money reflects how we value different resources. Therefore, financial limits on specific resources are the functional equivalent of natural limits on those resources. Of course, natural limits impose absolute scarcity, whereas the financial limits we set create artificial or relative shortages. Nonetheless, financial limits are inevitable. Indeed, this is the rationale behind sensible arguments that health care resources ought to be distributed more equitably: because we cannot spend all (or even nearly all) of our money on health care, health care resources are effectively limited. Despite the truth in such arguments, it is not clear that this logic has been wholly embraced by consumers. Indeed, it appears that the degree to which financial limits are accepted as functional equivalents of natural scarcity depends on whose money is at issue.

Rationing and Allocation

Scholars of rationing tend to prefer the concept of resource allocation to rationing to describe how resources are distributed.[13] Resource allocation at the level of global decision making, called macroallocation, is commonly distinguished from decisions about which individuals get what services.[14] Macroallocation decisions determine how much money is allocated to health care in this country. Rationing, strictly construed, occurs when a patient is (or is not) selected to receive a treatment that is in limited supply. Bioethicists and economists correctly point out that macroallocation decisions determine how much of a given resource ultimately is made available to ration among individual patients.[15]

There is little disagreement among scholars that allocation decisions are being made every day in this country.[8–11,16] Macroallocation decisions at the federal and state government levels result, usually implicitly, from decisions about how much of the government's budget to spend on health care programs as opposed to defense, education, road repair, environmental protection, park services, the arts, and other social goals. The market also serves as a mechanism for making macroallocation decisions about private resources.

Between macroallocation decisions and rationing care to individual patients, thousands of organizations, primarily health insurers, allocate their resources in ways that affect access to care by individual patients. Although such institutional decisions are also commonly referred to as macroallocation decisions, they are actually microallocation decisions. This is because these decisions are made at the level of the individual firm or company (such as a health insurance company, health maintenance organization, or managed care network), not the national or state level. Moreover, these decisions allocate the firm's resources among several uses, such as salaries, administrative expenses, health care services, and profit; they do not choose specific services for individual patients. Microallocation decisions by companies should be distinguished both from macroallocation decisions and from physicians' decisions to recommend for or against a specific treatment for an individual patient. The amount of money available to put in a company's health care pot is determined largely at the macroallocation level as the result of market competition and, often, of government decisions; a company does not engage in national macroallocation decisions.

The allocation methods commonly discussed for macroallocation do not easily fit microallocation decisions. Macroallocation criteria have been discussed in terms of principles of social justice, that is, deciding how much to allocate to health care as opposed to other social goods. Here, the debate often centers on whether people are entitled to any particular level of resources or to particular resources for specific health needs by virtue of either an individual moral right or a societal responsibility to provide for the common good.[8,11,17,18] Such abstractions rarely play a role in decisions by private organizations about how to spend their money.

Many insurers ration care to their subscribers by approving or denying services or payment in specific cases. But true rationing or patient selection decisions are not allocation decisions, even though they may affect institutional budgets. Rationing methods include medical need, likelihood of medical benefit, degree of benefit or predicted quality of life, social and psychological resources to enhance recovery, age, social worth, economic productivity, vital responsibilities (favoring patients on whom others depend), maximizing the number of lives saved, minimizing the resources used per patient, lottery or random selection, first come/first served, and willingness to pay.[14,19-21] Because these methods focus so specifically on which patient should receive which treatment, they do not capture the type of institutional resource allocation decision that makes it necessary to limit the number of patients receiving the treat-

ment. While rationing decisions presume scarcity of a resource, microallocation decisions create artificial resource scarcity.

Perhaps microallocation decisions have been lumped with macroallocation decisions because they are both primarily financial decisions (decisions about how much money to allocate to health care). But the reasons for such decisions, as well as how the decisions are made, differ significantly depending on whether the decision maker is a government or a private organization.

In this country, there is no single pot of money allocated to health care. There are many different pots that are added up to obtain a sum called national health care expenditures. The federal government has several pots. It spends money to help train physicians, to fund health care technology research, and to pay for Medicare and Medicaid services and other programs like health care for the military and veterans and family planning services. State governments also have a few pots of money to buy Medicaid services, to pay for care for some of those without health insurance, and to fund public health programs. Private insurers, including indemnity companies, health maintenance organizations, and new integrated service networks, each have a pot of money (from premiums) to pay for services for their subscribers. Employers with self-insured employee group health plans have their own pots of money for health services. Most individuals have a small pot of money to buy health insurance and to pay for services that are not covered by health insurance. About 40 million people do not have access to an employer, insurance, or government pot and may have too little money to buy the health care they need.[22]

All governments, organizations, and individuals with a pot are able to decide how to spend their money. Indeed, the configuration of health care goods and services in the United States is a product of a multitude of decisions about how much to spend on research, administration, salaries, profit, and delivery of specific health care goods and services. This is the way in which money is allocated for health care in the United States. How the money is spent determines what health care is available to whom.

The federal government and state and local governments are responsible for about 43% of personal health care expenditures ($337 billion in 1993).[23] The balance of personal health expenditures ($445.5 billion in 1993) includes payments by private health insurers, self-insured employers, and individual patients.[23] The fact that such a large proportion of health expenditures represents private decisions means that there is no preimposed national limit on how much money will be spent for health care. Even if government imposes limits on its own health care pots, it does not limit all of the money in the country that can or will be spent for health care. Without any overall budgetary limit at the macroallocation level, patients may perceive health care funding and, therefore, health care resources as unlimited.

A private health insurance plan may view its own budget as fixed and, therefore, the resources it can provide as scarce. Yet its subscribers may not see it this way. A health plan can increase its budget or reallocate its funds, reducing overhead to provide more direct patient services, for example. The budgets of private health plans are not subject to limits at the macroallocation level (except indirectly, to the degree that market competition constrains premium prices). Most of their funds are derived from premiums sold in the insurance market, primarily on the basis of price. This means that private health insurance is rationed by price to those willing to pay. Of course, willingness to pay is, in part, a function of ability to pay.

If the amount of money allocated to health care is substantially determined by private market decisions, there does not appear to be any justification for rationing. After all, the amount of money in any single health care pot can be increased or decreased at any time. Thus, the

health care resources available to patients are not fixed or scarce but can be increased or decreased. In a market system, limits on the amount of money spent for health care can be or appear arbitrary or unfair.

Many Americans do not believe that the market is a fair way to distribute many health care services. Ethicists, philosophers, and economists have long argued about whether any or all health care services ought to be considered special (necessities of life to which all individuals are entitled) or whether they are merely economic goods (to which no moral entitlement attaches) that can be distributed through the market.[11,17,24,25] In spite of lucid arguments on all sides and the absence of any general legal right to health care, however, polls report that a majority of Americans favor increasing health insurance to cover the uninsured, primarily because everyone should be entitled to basic or essential health care services, variously defined.[26] For many, the market may be an acceptable allocation mechanism for things like cosmetic surgery and private hospital rooms but not for emergency care, immunizations, and lifesaving surgery and drugs. The latter types of services are considered important enough that they ought to be distributed equitably, which usually means according to medical need and without regard to ability to pay.[11] However, because market purchases of health insurance and services do not adhere to any ethical principle of resource allocation, the market cannot achieve a particular desired distribution of essential health care services. This may leave people with the sense that limitations on health care are the result of unfair price rationing that deprives people of essential care without justification.

Rationing by Insurers

The demise of federal health care reform has left most decisions about how to spend money for patient care in the hands of the private sector.

Even government programs like Medicare and Medicaid are beginning to shift their beneficiaries into private managed care plans, partly to improve patient care but primarily to save money.[27] Government has determined that it cannot afford to put much more money in its health care pots and hopes to make more efficient use of what it has by enrolling Medicare and Medicaid beneficiaries in private managed care plans. This delegates to private companies the power to make decisions about how to spend government funds (paid to insurers as premiums) for their beneficiaries. There are some federal or state guidelines on what the money should be spent for, but increasingly private companies will decide what specific types of care individual patients receive.

Ideally, in an increasingly competitive health care market, health plans will use their money wisely and flexibly to suit their patient populations and control costs. However, most knowledgeable analysts doubt that strategies such as managed care and improved prevention programs will succeed in reducing spending enough to avoid more limitations on care in the long run.[28–30] Because each organization is free to make its own decisions about how to spend its money, it can apply its own criteria to ration health care services among those who depend on it for care.

What criteria do private insurers and employers use to allocate their money and, in turn, ration health care services to patients? Little is known because such decisions are private. There is, however, some evidence that different insurers already make inconsistent decisions about providing care. The US General Accounting Office studied the decisions of six insurance carriers who administered Medicare Part B reimbursement claims for 74 costly or frequently used procedures in 1992 and 1993 and found a significant degree of inconsistency in the rates at which the carriers denied claims based on lack of medical necessity.[31] For example, for every 1000 angioplasty procedures approved, one carrier denied 182 claims, another denied 29, and another denied none. The primary explanation for this variation was whether and how the carriers screened for medical necessity.[32] Other factors included the carriers' different interpretations of what was covered by Medicare. If there is this much inconsistency in the way in which private insurers carry out the same statutory program, it would not be surprising if private insurers differ even more substantially in the way in which they carry out their own individual health plans.

In the absence of any consensus on what criteria to use for rationing, there is bound to be inconsistency and unfairness in rationing. Everyone with a pot of money for health care may use different criteria for rationing. Where the criteria are private and not subject to public scrutiny, patients may mistrust those who make rationing decisions. They may fear they are being denied care so that the money can be used to profit the organization. For example, after complaints that women giving birth were being rushed out of the hospital 12 to 24 hours after delivery by managed care plans, Maryland passed legislation requiring a minimum 48-hour hospital maternity stay, and New Jersey and Massachusetts are considering similar legislation.[33] Reports that the 16 largest for-profit health maintenance organizations have enjoyed an average increase in profits of 40% since 1993 may fuel fears that patients may be denied treatment in order to reward corporate executives with large salaries and bonuses.[34,35]

Vitalism and Mistrust of Rationing

Another reason for public mistrust of rationing is the peculiarly American belief in a form of vitalism: the idea that a long and healthy life is especially desirable and that each individual is morally entitled to live as long as possible and to be as healthy as possible.[36] George Annas has described this as the belief that death is optional.[37] Rene Dubos and Daniel Callahan have critiqued the American fascination with health, noting that there is no inherent limit on our desire for health.[38,39]

This vitalism encourages the notion that everything that can be done ought to be done to keep people alive as long as possible, regardless of cost. And a great deal is possible. Medical technology can keep people alive, if not always conscious, for a very long time. Without any significant external limitation on its availability, life-prolonging care can be used as long as patients desire it. Some patients have begun to set limits on care that merely prolongs the dying process.[40] Others have become so wary of aggressive medicine at the end of life that they have called for legislation to permit physicians to help them commit suicide.[41] But these seem to be exceptions that prove the general rule that most Americans want access to most medical services. Even if they wish to refuse a certain kind of care, patients still want it offered to them. They want to be the ones to reject it. Patients who are sick typically want whatever treatment their physicians recommend (and often get it), regardless of whether their health insurance policy covers it.[42,43] If necessary, they hold bake sales to raise money to pay out of pocket for the treatment. Thus, the only boundary to the use of health care is patient demand, which itself may be almost unlimited.

If this is a correct, albeit simplified, depiction of American attitudes toward health care, it reinforces public resistance to externally imposed limits on care. For example, when the media report that a woman is dying of advanced breast cancer and her insurer will not pay for high dose chemotherapy and autologous bone marrow transplantation because it considers the procedure experimental or unsuitable for her, the insurer is widely viewed as depriving the woman of a chance at life to which she is entitled. Insurers may argue that the insurance policy expressly excludes such procedures and that the woman agreed to its limits.[44] Such arguments, even when correct, do little to assuage feelings that the insurer is depriving people of care to which they should be entitled. This feeling is exacerbated by the suspicion that the insurer could pay for the treatment if it chose, that it has enough money to buy services that are readily available. Thus, what looks to the insurer as sensible budgeting may appear to the patient as unnecessary and unfair rationing.

Private insurers may attempt to allocate their money to provide the most cost-effective or cost-beneficial care to their insured population as a whole. When statistical lives are considered, cost-benefit analysis makes sense. Consider congressional proposals this year to require federal environmental and consumer protection agencies to demonstrate that the benefits (in terms of years of life saved) of their regulations exceed their costs. There is little doubt that safety regulations have saved thousands of lives and that many people would die if those regulations were repealed on the grounds that the cost per life saved is too expensive. This is a way of rationing preventive services on the basis of cost. We are less rational when individual, identified lives are at stake.[45] People who show no interest in mining safety precautions offer enormous support (and funding) to rescue a single child trapped in a mine, even though making the mines safer could prevent many more deaths at far less cost per life saved.

The same disparity in public empathy for individuals in danger and faceless groups is evident in health care. Many people recognize that it makes more economic sense to immunize children against infectious diseases than to pay for a liver transplant in a very elderly patient whose cancer has metastasized to the lungs. Yet, when the patient is your father or mother or husband or wife—or you—rational cost-benefit analysis rarely controls the decision. Few people are willing to place a dollar limitation on their own lives or the lives of their loved ones. Most people feel entitled to at least be offered the transplant, even if they choose to reject it.

The desire to save identified lives and the belief that health and longevity are supremely valuable reinforce each other. When combined with the intuition that health care resources and the money to buy them are readily available, they may explain why individuals resist limitations on health care, even if they might agree that health care resources are not being used efficiently. People may view financial limits on health care—limits imposed by health plans that refuse to pay for existing technology—as suspect. Patients are subjected to rationing, but they know that the technology is not scarce. Rather, someone, usually an insurer, is refusing to pay for something they (and their physicians) believe they are entitled to have (but cannot afford) in order to save money. Moreover, the patients will not necessarily receive the benefit of the money saved. There is no guarantee that the money saved from not paying for the transplant will be used to pay for children's immunizations, for example. The public also knows that any patient who raises the money to pay for it can have the transplant. So, if people believe that they should live as long as possible, that there are health care services that will enable them to do so, and that the only thing that stands between them and a long, healthy life is money, and they believe that their health plan (or government) is placing artificial limits on the money it is willing to spend, they are not likely to accept rationing of health care services.

Rationing by Limiting Supply

It is possible that Americans could change their attitudes about the value of health and health care and eventually accept the idea that longevity should not be the ultimate goal of human existence, that some goals are more important than personal health. Callahan, for example, has argued that society must change the way it views health because the country cannot afford to meet an infinite demand for health care.[38] Public recognition of the costs—both human and economic—of health care may ultimately produce such a change. But this change is likely to take several generations, if it occurs at all. In the meantime, the costs of health care continue to consume an increasing proportion of the gross domestic product. The country cannot afford to wait for a change in personal values if it intends to invest in goods like education and defense in addition to health care. More immediate action is needed.

It is possible that well-managed health care plans can weed out some of the waste in the health care system and use resources more efficiently. But, as Henry Aaron and William Schwartz have argued, it is unrealistic to expect such measures to save enough money to keep national health care expenditures from rising to unacceptable levels.[46] New technologies can save some money, but most do not. Many new technologies are used in addition to existing technology (e.g., to reduce diagnostic uncertainty) and serve to increase costs. Other technologies are only marginally more beneficial than existing technology, yet cost more. In the absence of any natural limit to either health care resources or our desire to use them, efficient management may slow but not stop the overall long-term increase in spending. Thus, more and more money will have to be put into all of the health care pots or the money in the pots will have to be rationed more restrictively. As each group makes its own decisions about how to spend its health care money pot, many decisions appear arbitrary and unfair.

There is little doubt that access to some kinds of health care will have to be restricted more in the future unless health care spending is brought under control. Indeed, most commentators believe that health care rationing is either already here or inevitable.[10,11,29,30,47] For this reason, many argue for open and explicit criteria for allocating health care resources or rationing, especially to avoid unethical allocation that can result from hidden or implicit decisions.[47-49] Yet it may be impossible to reach agreement on criteria for rationing if the need for rationing itself is not credible. It is unlikely that people will accept the need for rationing their own care without seeing unmistakable scarcity in health care resources, scarcity that they find credible because it is real.

As Daniels has noted, physicians find rationing decisions difficult—and both physicians and patients may perceive them as unfair—because they cannot point to a just macroallocation scheme that justifies denying care to patients.[50] Current health care financing mechanisms do not result in a just allocation of resources at the macroallocation or microallocation level. And no allocation criteria are likely to be accepted unless there is credible scarcity at both levels.

There is really only one way to limit the use of resources, and that is by limiting the supply of those resources. The only way to prevent the use of health care resources is to not have them available. If resources are physically available, both physicians and patients will insist on using them. Telling physicians or patients that using existing resources is not cost-beneficial or even cost-effective will not be convincing most of the time. People will not tolerate rationing unless they are persuaded that the thing being rationed is scarce. If there is only one organ available for transplant, people can accept the fact that it goes to another patient who needs it more urgently, because it is a scarce resource that is rationed fairly. However, if a patient's health plan refuses to pay for an expensive drug like tissue plasminogen activator (tPA), the patient is not likely to believe he or she has been treated fairly. The patient knows that other patients who belong to a more generous health plan or who can raise the money to buy tPA will get it; the drug is not naturally scarce, and it is not allocated according to need. Thus, if health care services are to be rationed, they must

be made scarce. Then it may be possible to apply ethical criteria for allocating scarce resources in an equitable manner.

Making health care services scarce means limiting their supply at the level of macroallocation. In the absence of limits on overall supply, limits at the microallocation level are not likely to be credible. People may perceive a health plan's coverage and payment decisions as artificially depriving them of necessary services that the plan could make available if it chose, and they may demand that the plan provide more care. To be credible, the supply available to health plans must itself be limited, not by self-imposed plan budgets but by the absence of resources.

The more complicated question of how supply might be limited and fairly allocated—as by direct regulatory controls on health care resources or global budgeting at the national or state level—must be deferred to a later time. The purpose of this article is merely to present the argument that such limits are an essential prerequisite to public acceptance of the need to ration health care resources equitably. If this hypothesis is true, then limiting the supply of health care resources may persuade or force people to set equitable national limits that recognize the relative importance of health in comparison with education, housing, and other valuable social investments and even to reduce health care spending by abiding by such limits. Then perhaps we can get to the important work of creating methods for the equitable distribution of these resources. Limiting supply at the macroallocation level is only the first step of a four-step process toward equitable distribution of health care. The next two steps are to allocate national health care resources among health plans (or groups of patients) in an equitable manner, and to ensure that health plans allocate their own resources so as to provide fair and adequate health care to their participants. The final step is to implement equitable criteria for rationing (in the strict sense of patient selection) health care among individual patients.

Conclusion

Americans can't say no to health care. Despite persuasive arguments that rationing is not only inevitable but being practiced in this country and general acceptance of the need to control health care costs, Americans refuse to accept limitations on their own health care. Two peculiarly American attributes may account for this apparent contradiction. The first is the health care system, with its complex array of public and private health insurance financing mechanisms that do not limit the total health care resources generally available. In the absence of any global limitation on health care resources, patients may perceive that such resources are not scarce and, therefore, not in need of rationing. The second attribute is the belief that everyone is entitled to a long life of unlimited good health. Even if people recognize that some health care money is wasted and that some services are too expensive, they can still believe that there is no natural limit on the health care to which they are entitled.

In such circumstances, why should anyone accept rationing? The rationing that does occur in public and private insurance coverage and payment decisions appears to be unprincipled and unjust, consisting of denials of care to save money for someone other than the patient. Apart from mandated benefits, private insurers are free to set their own policies about what care they pay for, so patients who are refused coverage have no assurance that their sacrifices serve any noble purpose or are even necessary. This is not to suggest that patients are to blame for the inequities in access to health care. On the contrary, patients may be responding quite rationally to the uneven distribution of care in this country. It is hard to argue that any individual patient should sacrifice his own medical care for the good of society when the same is not expected of everyone else.

It is unlikely that Americans will come to any consensus about how to reduce health care expenditures or allocate health care resources fairly if they are not faced with a shortage of resources. A just distribution of health care resources is not likely to be pursued until there is scarcity in health care. Today's ad hoc limits on the amount of money in the multitude of health care pots do not create credible scarcity. Real scarcity may be necessary before Americans are willing to say no.

References

1. Jonsen AR. Fear of rationing. Health Manage Q. 1992;14:6–9.
2. Klein R. Dilemmas and decisions. Health Manage Q. 1992;14:2–5.
3. Mechanic D. Rationing health care: public policy and the medical marketplace. Hastings Center Rep. 1976;6:34–37.
4. Reinhardt UE. On the economics and ethics of rationing health care. Decisions Imaging Economics. 1992;5:10–16.
5. Oxford English Dictionary. Compact ed., New York, NY: Oxford University Press Inc; 1971; 2:2420.
6. The American Heritage Dictionary of the English Language. Boston, Mass: Houghton Mifflin Co; 1978:1083.
7. Rhodes R, Miller C, Schwartz M. Transplant recipient selection: peacetime vs. wartime triage. Cambridge Q Healthcare Ethics. 1992;1:327–331.
8. Calabresi G, Bobbit P. Tragic Choices. New York, NY: Norton; 1978.
9. Churchill LR. Rationing Health Care in America: Perceptions and Principles of Justice. Notre Dame, Ind: University of Notre Dame Press; 1987.
10. Friedman E. Doctors and rationing: the end of the honor system. Primary Care. 1986;13:349–364.
11. Securing Access to Health Care: Report on the Ethical Implications of Differences in the Availability of Health Services. Washington, DC: President's Commission for the Study of Ethical

Problems in Medicine and Biomedical and Behavioral Research; 1983;1.

12. Mehlman MJ. Rationing expensive lifesaving medical treatments. Wis Law Rev. 1985;2:239–303.

13. Kilner JF. Allocation of health-care resources. In: Reich WT, ed. Encyclopedia of Bioethics. New York, NY: Simon & Schuster; 1995;4:1067–1084.

14. Kilner JF. Who Lives? Who Dies? Ethical Criteria in Patient Selection. New Haven, Conn: Yale University Press; 1990.

15. Buchanan A. Health-care delivery and resource allocation. In: Veatch RM, ed. Medical Ethics. Boston, Mass: Jones & Bartlett; 1989:291–327.

16. Blank RE. Rationing Medicine. New York, NY: Columbia University Press; 1988.

17. Daniels N. Just Health Care. New York, NY: Cambridge University Press; 1985.

18. Fried C. Equality and rights in medical care. Hastings Center Rep. 1976;6:29–34.

19. Rescher N. The allocation of exotic medical lifesaving therapy. Ethics. 1969;79:173–186.

20. Basson MD. Choosing among candidates for scarce medical resources. J Med Philosophy. 1979;4:313–333.

21. Annas GJ. The prostitute, the playboy, and the poet: rationing schemes for organ transplantation. Am J Public Health. 1985;75:187–189.

22. Income, Poverty, and Valuation of Non-Cash Benefits: 1993. Washington, DC: US Bureau of the Census; 1995.

23. Levit KR, Sensenig AL, Cowan CA, et al. National health expenditures, 1993. Health Care Financing Rev. 1994;16:247–294.

24. Outka G. Social justice and equal access to health care. J Religious Ethics. 1974;2:11–32.

25. Englehardt HT Jr. The Foundations of Bioethics. New York, NY: Oxford University Press Inc; 1986.

26. Blendon RJ, Brodie M, Benson J. What should be done now that national health system reform is dead? JAMA. 1995;273:243–244.

27. McMillan A. Trends in Medicare health maintenance organization enrollment: 1986-93. Health Care Financing Rev. 1993;15:135–146.

28. Schwartz WB, Mendelson DN. Why managed care cannot contain hospital costs—without rationing. Health Aff. Summer 1992:101–107.

29. Aaron H, Schwartz WB. Rationing health care: the choice before us. Science. 1990;247:418–422.

30. Evans R. Health care technology and the inevitability of resource allocation and rationing decisions. JAMA. 1983;249:2047–2052, 2208–2219.

31. Medicare Part B. Inconsistent Denial Rates for Medical Necessity across Six Carriers. Washington, DC: US General Accounting Office; 1994. GAO/T-PEMD-94-17.

32. Medicare Part B, Regional Variation in Denial Rates for Medical Necessity. Washington, DC: US General Accounting Office; 1994. GAO/PEMD-95-10.

33. Nordheimer J. Broad coalition fights insurer limits on hospital maternity stays. New York Times. June 6, 1995:B1, B5.

34. The HMO picture: more consolidation, more growth, more government business. Med Benefits. 1995;12:7.

35. Freudenheim M. Penny-pinching H.M.O.s showed their generosity in executive paychecks. New York Times. April 11, 1995:D1, D4.

36. Barsky AJ. Worried Sick: Our Troubled Quest for Wellness. Boston, Mass: Little Brown & Co Inc; 1988.

37. Annas GJ. Rationing medical care. In: Standard of Care: The Law of American Bioethics. New York, NY: Oxford University Press; 1993:211–217.

38. Callahan D. What Kind of Life: The Limits of Medical Progress. New York, NY: Simon & Schuster; 1990.

39. Dubos R. Mirage of Health: Utopias, Progress and Biological Change. New York, NY: Harper Colophon Books; 1979.

40. Annas GJ, Miller FH. The empire of death: how culture and economics affect informed consent in the U.S., the U.K., and Japan. Am J Law Med. 1994;20:357–394.

41. Compassion in Dying v. Washington, 49 F.3d 586 (9th Cir. 1995).

42. Eddy DM. Clinical decision making: from theory to practice—connecting value and costs—whom do we ask and what do we ask them? JAMA. 1990;264:1737–1739.

43. Mariner WK. Patients' rights after health care reform: who decides what is medically necessary? Am J Public Health. 1994;84:1515–1520.

44. Hall MA, Anderson GF. Health insurers' assessment of medical necessity. University Pa Law Rev. 1992;140:1637–1712.

45. Friedman E. Rationing and the identified life. Hospitals. 1984;58:65–74.

46. Schwartz WB, Aaron HJ. Serious and Unstable Condition: Financing America's Health Care. Washington, DC: Brookings Institution; 1991.

47. Callahan DC. Setting Limits: Medical Goals in an Aging Society. New York, NY: Simon & Schuster; 1987.

48. Fox RC, Swazey JP. The Courage to Fail. 2nd ed. Chicago, Ill: University of Chicago Press; 1978.

49. Wikler D. Ethics and rationing: "whether," "how," or "how much?" J Am Geriatr Soc. 1992; 40:398–403.

50. Daniels N. Why saying no to patients in the United States is so hard—cost containment, justice and provider autonomy. N Engl J Med. 1986;314:1380–1383.

Notes

1. "Preamble to the Constitution of the World Health Organization, World Health Organization: Basic Documents, 26th ed. (Geneva: World Health Organization, 1976): 1.

2. *Merriam Webster Medical Dictionary* (Springfield, Mass.: Merriam Webster Co., 2002): 332.

3. W. E. Parmet, "The Impact of Law on Coronary Heart Disease: Some Preliminary Observation on the Relationship of Law to 'Normalized' Conditions," *Journal of Law, Medicine & Ethics* 30:4 (2002): 608–622.

4. J. Michael McGinnis and William H. Foege, "Actual Causes of Death in the United States," *Journal of the American Medical Association* 270: 18 (1993): 2207–2213.

5. Ali H. Mokdad et al., "Actual Causes of Death in the United States, 2000," *Journal of the American Medical Association* 291: 10(2004): 1238–1245.

6. Ibid. 1242.

7. Ibid.

8. Scott D. Yoder, "Individual Responsibility for Health," *Hastings Center Report* 32: 2 (2002): 22–31.

9. Department of Health and Human Services, Healthy People 2000, 2000, at 40–43.

10. Nancy Krieger and Stephen Sidney, "Racial Discrimination and Blood Pressure," *American Journal of Public Health* 86 (1996): 1273, 1278.

11. Katherine Levit et al., "Inflation Spurs Spending in 2000," *Health Affairs* 21:1 (2002): 172.

12. U.S. Census Bureau, *Current Population Survey*, March 1999.

13. Charles N. Kahn III and Ronald F. Pollack, "Building a Consensus for Expanding Health Coverage," *Health Affairs* 20: 1 (Jan./Feb. 2001): 40.

14. Organization for Co-operation and Development, *Health Data 2001* at *www.oecd.org/home.*

15. Kaiser Family Foundation, *Chartbook: Trends and Indicators in the Changing Health Care Marketplace* (2002): 16.

16. John Holohan and John Kim, "Why Does the Number of Uninsured Americans Continue to Grow?" *Health Affairs* (July–Aug. 2000): 188.

17. Kaiser, 17.

18. Ibid.
19. Ibid. at 1.
20. Ibid. at 17.
21. Kenneth Arrow, "Uncertainty and the Welfare Economics of Medical Care," *The American Economic Review* 53 (5) (1963): 851–883.

Recommended Readings

Adler, Nancy E, and Newman, Katherine. "Socioeconomic Disparities in Health: Pathways and Policies; Inequality in Education, Income, and Occupation Exacerbates the Gaps Between the Health 'Haves' and 'Have Nots'." *Health Affairs*, March–April 2002.

Arrow, Kenneth J. "Uncertainty and the Welfare Economics of Medical Care." *The American Economic Review* 53 (1963): 851–883.

Berk, Marc, and Alan Monheit. "The Concentration of Health Care Expenditures, Revisited." *Health Affairs* 20 (2001): 9–18.

Bodenheimer, Thomas, Kevin Grumbach. *Understanding Health Policy.* New York: Lange Medical Books, 2002.

Boorse, Christopher. "On the Distinction between Disease and Illness." In *Medicine and Moral Philosophy,* edited by Marshall Cohen, Thomas Nagel, Thomas Scanlon. Princeton, N.J.: Princeton University Press, 1981: 3–22.

Chase, Chevy, and Marmot, Michael. "The Influence of Income on Health: Views of an Epidemiologist." *Health Affairs* 21, no. 2 (2002): 31–46.

Daniels, Norman. *Just Health Care.* Cambridge–New York: Cambridge University Press, 1985.

Daniels, Norman. "Why Saying 'No' to Patients in the U.S. Is So Hard: Cost-Containment, Justice and Provider Autonomy." *The New England Journal of Medicine* 314 (1986): 1381–1383.

Diderichsen, Finn, et. al. "The Social Basis of Disparities in Health," In *Social Epidemiology,* eds. Kawachi, Ichiro and Berkman, Lisa. New York: Oxford University Press, 2000, 13–23.

Elliot, Carl. "A New Way to Be Mad." *The Atlantic Monthly* 286 (2000): 72–84.

Frumkin, Howard. "Urban Sprawl and Public Health." *Public Health Reports* 117 (2002): 201–217.

Fuchs, Victor R. "Ethics and Economics: Antagonists or Allies in Making Health Policy? *Western Journal of Medicine* 168 (1998): 1572–1573.

Fuchs, Victor R. "What Every Philosopher Should Know about Health Economics." *Health Economics* 140 (1996): 186–195.

Gorski, Peter A. "Caring Relationships: An Investment in Health." *Public Health Reports* 115 (2000): 144–150.

Iglehart, John K. "Changing Health Insurance Trends." *The New England Journal of Medicine* 347 (2002): 956–962.

Kaiser Family Foundation. *Chartbook: Trends and Indicators in the Changing Health Care Marketplace,* California, 2002.

Kawachi, Ichario, and Berkman, Lisa. *Social Epidemiology.* New York: Oxford University Press, 2000.

McGinnis, J. Michael, and Foege, William H. "Actual Causes of Death in the United States." *Journal of the American Medical Association* 270, no. 18 (1993), 2207–2213.

Moss, Nancy. "Socioeconomic Disparities in Health in the US: an Agenda for Action." *Social Science & Medicine* 51, no. 11 (2000): 1627–1638.

Purdy, Laura. "A Feminist View of Health." In *Feminism and Bioethics,* edited by Susan M. Wolf. New York: Oxford University Press, 1996: 163–183.

Reinhardt, Uwe. "Economics." *Journal of the American Medical Association* 275 (1996): 1802–1803.

Rose, Geoffrey. "The Population Strategy of Prevention." In *The Strategy of Preventive Medicine.* New York: Oxford University Press, 1992: 95–129.

Swanson, Lynne. "Cochlear Implants: The Head-On Collision between Medical Technology and the Right to Be Deaf." *Canadian Medical Association Journal* 157 (1997): 929–932.

Ubel, Peter A. *Pricing Life.* Cambridge, Mass.: MIT Press, 2000.

Chapter Three

The Health of Individuals

A. What and Why Autonomy?

The concept of autonomy has been an important one for bioethics. Indeed the need to ensure respect for patient autonomy may have galvanized bioethics as a field in the first place—especially from the perspective of many philosophers.

The concern with individual autonomy stems from a moral interest in respecting persons understood as self-determining agents. In Chapter 1 we saw expressions of this interest in both deontological and teleological ethics. Persons are unique insofar as they have the capacity to make choices, ideally to do so in a way that reflects who they are and what their life plans are. Individuals are also unique insofar as they have different preferences, interests, and goals. Given their uniqueness, their ability to make choices, and the value they place on making their own choices, ethics recognizes the need to respect those choices. Because most people have the capacity to be self-determining, individuals, institutions, and the community are under an obligation, though with specific limits, to foster that self-determination.

John Stuart Mill, perhaps more than any other philosopher, supported and celebrated individual autonomy. As a utilitarian, much of Mill's support for individuality had to do with the benefits to be bestowed upon both individuals and society when individuality is promoted. "In proportion to the development of his individuality, each person becomes more valuable to himself, and is therefore capable of being more valuable to others."[1] In support of autonomy, Mill was committed to leaving as many choices up to individuals as possible.

Kant considered acting according to the categorical imperative as an expression of autonomy. When agents act on the categorical imperative they act on self-prescribed principles, although such principles are categorical for all rational agents. Acting, categorically, for the sake of duty expresses their autonomy. That is, in some sense moral agents will the law to which they are subject. In another sense, Kant believed that treating agents as ends in themselves respects their autonomy.

But what is it to be self-determining? Does any preference that individuals signal, any desire they have, qualify as an autonomous one that needs to be respected? In the medical context this question can have practical importance. Patients can be rushed to the emergency room after attempting suicide and indicate a wish to refuse life-saving care, and health care providers, bound by considerations for patient autonomy, may feel compelled to honor those choices even if they result in harm to the patient. But a little reflection, including self-reflection, suggests that not all of the desires that we have are desires that we endorse or would stand behind. Gerald Dworkin believes that autonomy is connected with the capacity of people to reflect upon what motivates them and with their ability to alter their preferences where needed or desired. He also believes that autonomy is uniquely important in the health care context in a way that it is not, for example, in the context of architecture, the building of a house. The significance of autonomy in health care, Dworkin believes, has to do in part with the importance of health in people's lives.

Many people raise objections to the preoccupation of bioethics with autonomy. Feminist bioethicists argue, for example, that the focus on individual autonomy over the obligations that arise out of relationships reflects a male gender bias.

David J. Rothman argues, in his critical review of patient autonomy, that the deference of American bioethics to individual autonomy during the 1960s, 1970s, and 1980s is much more the work of the legal profession and its concern with civil rights than the inspiration of philosophers. Rothman traces the history of autonomy within bioethics, beginning with issues surrounding the right to end treatment, through its second stage, when it played an important role in the movement for physician-assisted suicide and later by pharmaceutical manufacturers in support of the shift to direct-to-consumer advertising. Although Rothman may be right that the practice of bioethics has been heavily influenced by the legal system's increasing recognition of patient rights, it is important to keep in mind the distinction between legal rights and ethical ones. While legal rights are protected by law, moral rights enjoy no such protection. In general, they are founded on some kind of moral account of human nature or the relationship between people and the community. Although moral rights are not enforceable legally, they nonetheless carry a certain moral weightiness that can be persuasive.

As Rothman suggests, much of what will constitute autonomy in the medical context has been determined in the courts. Compare the views of Rothman with those of Dworkin. Is autonomy important merely because the courts have made it so, or is autonomy important because, as Dworkin seems to maintain, it helps individuals to construct meaning in their lives?

Absolutely essential to the exercise of autonomy in the clinical context is the right and ability of patients to consent to treatment and to do so on the basis of adequate information. But what will count as adequate information is a complex matter. To ensure informed consent, a criterion needs to be identified to determine what information health care providers must give. Prior to the important case of *Canterbury v. Spence*,[2] a physician-based standard was common. Put simply, physicians had a duty to disclose the information that a similarly situated physician would disclose. In other words, physicians were expected to provide patients with the information that other physicians disclosed to their patients. Although the standard ensured that patients receive more information than strict paternalism would dictate (allowing the physician to treat without securing informed consent), it was a long way off from ensuring that individual patients would have the information they needed to be self-determining. *Canterbury* (and similar cases) introduced what has come to be known as the "reasonable patient standard" according to which a physician has a duty to disclose what a reasonable patient would find significant in making a medical decision. The court stated,

> True consent to what happens to one's self is the informed exercise of a choice, and that entails an opportunity to evaluate knowledgeably the options available and the risks attendant upon each. The average patient has little or no understanding of the medical arts, and ordinarily has only his physician to whom he can look for enlightenment with which to reach an intelligent decision.[3]

In an interesting twist, the Supreme Court of California decided in *Truman v. Thomas* that physicians are obligated to disclose not only what patients find significant about having a particular procedure but also what they would find significant about *not* having the procedure.[4] Neither the *Truman* court nor the *Canterbury* court, however, required physicians to tell individual patients what they would subjectively want to know. Does that rejection of the individual patient standard thwart the courts' attempt to respect autonomy? Do the complexities of a busy medical practice justify this departure from a possible individual patient standard? Is the departure justified by the courts' fear that the individual patient standard would permit patients to testify about their own preferences, testimony that would be difficult to challenge?

Patient autonomy has also surfaced as an important issue in cases having to do with the right to refuse treatment. In *Shine v. Vega,* Catherine Shine was placed in four-point restraints and forcibly intubated when she refused the recommended treatment of ER doctors for her asthmatic attack. The defendant doctors appealed to the so-called therapeutic privilege of doctors to treat without patient consent in the case of emergencies. The court did not agree. Do you believe that as a matter of ethics the court was correct in affirming Shine's autonomy? Does the therapeutic privilege risk providing physicians with a means for disregarding autonomy too casually? Would you feel differently if the facts made it more evident that Shine would have died without the intubation?

Respect for autonomy generally assumes that a patient is competent and can make informed decisions. What should we do when a patient has either ceased being competent, because of illness, or has never been competent, because of age or mental disability? In those cases, does it still make sense to respect the patient's choice? As the reading by George J. Annas discusses, in the 1970s and 80s, a consensus developed that at least in the case of previously competent individuals, their choices should be followed.

Sometimes a patient's preferences are known because they have left an advanced directive, such as a living will or health care proxy. But often that is not the case. The recent case of Terri Schiavo illustrates the difficulty of such situations.

Schiavo was a young woman diagnosed as in a persistent vegetative state after her heart stopped briefly due to a potassium deficiency that may have been caused by an eating disorder. After she had been on a feeding tube for several years, her husband asked a state court for an order to remove the tube, claiming that Schiavo had stated before her incapacitation that she would not want to live in such a manner. The Florida courts granted the husband's request.

Schiavo's parents questioned whether she had ever expressed such views as well as her husband's motives and the diagnosis. Deeply religious, they argued that respect for life demanded that she not be left to die. They turned first to the state legislature and then Congress, each of which enacted laws aimed at blocking the removal of her tube. Ultimately both state and federal courts affirmed the original court order.

The Schiavio case raises numerous questions. Should autonomy be the guiding principle when an individual has not left any advanced directive? Or should courts in such a case give more weight to the views of family members? If so, what should be done when families disagree? Should the matter be left to state courts? Or should legislatures intervene?

In addition, we may ask whether removal of the feeding tube evidenced disrespect for people with disabilities. Does respect for individuals with disabilities require us to respect their wishes, even to die? Or does it require us to try to enhance the quality of their lives? Finally, we may want to think about why we focus on such admittedly compelling cases while far more people have their lives cut short by other preventable forms of death. Would a public health perspective point us away from cases such Shiavo and to the question of how we can prevent young people from facing the situation she faced (for example, would better access to treatment for eating disorders have prevented this situation in the first place?)? You may want to reconsider how we can balance concerns for autonomy, life, and public health when we discuss the rationing and allocation of medical resources in Chapters 4–6.

A refusal to respect a patient's choices (assuming we know what they are) in order to protect her life can be considered paternalistic. Paternalistic limitations on patient choice exist beyond the drama of cases such as Schiavo. For example, the Food and Drug Administration (FDA) prohibits the sale of medications that are not "safe and effective." Because scientific evidence did not establish its efficacy, in the 1970s the FDA prohibited the sale of laetrile, a derivative of apricot pits, that many people believed could cure cancer. What justifies prohibiting competent adults from deciding to take medications that have not been proven effective?

Advocates for such regulation point to many factors. For example, individuals may not have enough information to make truly informed choices about cancer treatments. But those arguments would suggest that the government should intervene by requiring that information be made available. The Food, Drug and Cosmetic Act does more than that. It allows the FDA to prohibit the sale of laetrile.

Scholars of public regulation, who study market failures, however, offer additional justifications for this apparent instance of paternalism. For example, governments may be justified in regulating markets in which there are "natural monopolies" precluding the process of competition.[5] In addition, sometimes (as in the case of a factory that pollutes) the price of a manufactured good may not reflect its true cost to society. Again, regulation may be justified to limit the activity that the market would otherwise not properly guide.[6] And, as is often the case with health care (recall our discussion of the work of Kenneth Arrow in Chapter 2) disparities of information may be viewed as a market failure that justifies regulations.[7] Does this explain the informed consent cases? But the problems of information are not simply a matter of providing enough information, for sometimes too much information can lead to as much confusion as too little.

In *The Tragedy of the Commons,* Garrett Hardin offers a provocative and disturbing defense of regulation in the context of reproduction. Looking at the example of sheep farmers who graze their sheep in a commons, Hardin argues that the decisions that individuals make, when they are left to decide by themselves, may not always be optimal for either themselves or the group. In a world without regulation, each farmer may choose, and indeed should choose, to overgraze his or her sheep. But if each individual makes that choice, the commons will be depleted of grass. Notice how Hardin's arguments echo public health's focus on populations as opposed to individuals. Policies that may have one effect when applied to individuals alone may have a very different and less positive one, at least from a public health perspective, when applied to a group. Can the problem of the commons be solved by dissolving the commons and privatizing it? Can such a solution work with respect to a public-health commons?

What all of these different justifications share is the belief that sometimes it is simply not efficient, or even rational, to rely upon individual decision making. For example, if there were no FDA, each of us and our health care providers would have to devote time and resources to figure out which drugs are safe and effective. That may enable some of us (those who wish to take laetrile) to make an autonomous choice. But it would also burden many of us with the time-consuming and expensive task of figuring out just what is safe and effective. And, since we can't all be experts, we may still make mistakes. Therefore, in order for most of us to achieve most efficiently what we would like (to not take an ineffective and potentially harmful drug) we may rely on the FDA to study pharmaceuticals and take ineffective drugs off the market, relieving us and our doctors of the burdens or risk of using them. That limits the autonomy of some of us but enables many of us to achieve our goal more efficiently. Is that a sufficient justification for prohibiting laetrile? For limiting other individual choices about health care?

The market justifications for regulation, however convincing they may or may not be, still do not constitute a true affirmation of paternalism because they try to maximize the choices of individuals as a group (general utility) even if they limit the choices of some individuals. Does the history of public health and the traditional role of the state in protecting public health, exercising what is known as the police power, provide a justification for a purer form of paternalism? According to Dan E. Beauchamp, "[p]ublic health...reminds us that we are not only individuals, we are also a community and a body politic...we have shared commitments to one another and promises to keep."[8] Does the community have a right to have a say in matters that affect me, because I was raised by the community and what happens to me will affect the community? Do you find this justification convincing with respect to the prohibition on laetrile?

Autonomy and Informed Consent

Gerald Dworkin

"Why do you assume you have the right to decide for someone else? Don't you agree it's a terrifying right, one that rarely leads to good? You should be careful. No one's entitled to it, not even doctors."

"But doctors are entitled to the right—doctors above all," exclaimed Dontsova with deep conviction. By now she was really angry. "Without that right there'd be no such thing as medicine!"

Solzhenitsyn, Cancer Ward

The slave doctor prescribes what mere experience suggests—and when he has given his orders, like a tyrant, he rushes off. But the other doctor, who is a freeman, attends and practices upon freemen—he enters into a discourse with the patient and with his friends—and he will not prescribe for him until he has first convinced him; at last, when he has brought the patient more and more under his persuasive influences and set him on the road to health, he attempts to effect a cure.

Plato, The Laws

In ethics, as in the law, there is often agreement concerning what to do in a particular case, or about the importance of a moral principle, co-existing with disagreement about why we should act in a certain manner, or on the nature or basis of the moral principle. Similarly, moral theories may agree about specific cases of lying while giving different accounts of why a lie is or is not justified. Becoming clearer about the sources of our principles or judgments is of both practical and theoretical importance. For agreement in particular judgments may conceal the possibility of disagreement in cases not yet encountered. Understanding the deeper sources of our judgments allows us to anticipate such divergences between ourselves and others. At the theoretical level, understanding the bases of our principles and judgments provides one mode of testing our moral theories. For the task of a theory is not to match our judgments but to account for those that are sound and criticize those that are faulty. A good theory unifies and explains its data and generates new judgments that are tested against our moral experience.

In this essay I shall consider the doctrine of informed consent, as it appears in the context of health care, and the various concepts that have been put forward as a basis for it. In particular I shall focus on the concept of autonomy, attempting to clarify its nature, distinguish it from other concepts, and defend its claim to be at the center of the justificatory basis for informed consent.

Justifications for Informed Consent

It is clear from examination of the legal and philosophical literature on informed consent that its defense has involved appeals to very different kinds of considerations. I give here a sample of typical assertions of such claims. Many of them come from the legal, rather than philosophical, literature. This is natural since the doctrine is a creature of law. But my interest in the doctrine is as a moral not a legal view. I make this distinction, not because moral and legal contexts are sharply separated, but to remind the reader that the law has specific features (such as the need to make a decision) that do not allow one to argue directly from a legal justification to more general normative conclusions.

> In our view, the patient's right of self-decision shapes the boundaries of the duty to reveal . . . And to safeguard the patient's interest in achieving his own determination on treatment, the law must itself set the standard for adequate disclosure.[1]

> The constitutional right of privacy includes the right of a mature competent adult to refuse to accept medical recommendations that may prolong one's life and which, to a third person at least, appear to be in his best interests.[2]

Anglo-American law starts with the premise of thorough-going self-determination. It follows that each man is considered to be master of his own body, and he may, if he be of sound mind, expressly prohibit the performance of lifesaving surgery.[3]

The requirement of informed consent has two parts, both of which must be met before a medical intervention is permissible: first, that sufficient information be disclosed to the patient so that he can arrive at an intelligent opinion, and second, that the patient agrees to the intervention being performed. The latter facet in particular reflects the concern, traditional in western societies, that the autonomy of the person be respected . . . autonomy is centrally associated with the notion of individual responsibility. The freedom to make decisions for oneself carries with it the obligation to answer for the consequences of those decisions.[4]

The purpose of requiring the patient's consent to treatment is to protect his physical and psychic integrity against unwanted invasions, and to permit the patient to act as an autonomous, self-determining being.[5]

The very foundation of the doctrine (of informed consent) is every man's right to forego treatment or even cure if it entails what for him are intolerable consequences or risks, however warped or perverted his sense of values may be in the eyes of the medical profession, or even of the community, so long as any distortion falls short of what the law regards as incompetency. Individual freedom here is guaranteed only if people are given the right to make choices which would generally be regarded as foolish ones.[6]

The principle of an informed consent is a statement of the fidelity between the man who performs medical procedures and the man on whom they are performed . . . The principle of an informed consent is the canon of loyalty joining men together in medical practice and investigation.[7]

. . . there does seem to exist a positive right of informed consent which exists both in therapeutic and experimental settings . . . From whence derives this right? It arises from the right each of us possesses to be treated as a person.[8]

Although the requirement of informed consent is not traditional in Hippocratic medicine, it is possible to justify such a requirement on patient-benefitting grounds. Indeed, if we recognize that judgments about what is beneficial to a particular patient will vary from patient to patient depending upon the particular norms and values of that person, a strong case can be made that informing patients of treatment alternatives so that they can participate in or even control the decision-making process will increase the likelihood that patient-benefits will be maximized.[9]

I have not listed a class of justifications that also appears in the literature. In these an appeal is made to the good consequences for others that would follow from adhering to the doctrine of informed consent. This functional analysis, exemplified by the work of Jay Katz, relies on the encouragement of rational decisionmaking, the protection of the experimental process, increasing society's awareness of the research process, and so forth. I am not denying that such reasons can play a part in the justification of informed consent but I wish to focus on defenses that refer to some property of the individual whose consent is being sought, because I believe, but will not argue here, these operate at a more fundamental level than the appeal to more general consequences.

Autonomy, Privacy, and Liberty: Distinctions

Our brief survey shows that informed consent is justified in terms of privacy, self-determination, loyalty, autonomy, freedom, integrity, dignity, and benefits. Individuals have the right to be treated as persons, as masters of their own body, as responsible for their decisions, as makers of choices. Though frequently these are regarded as equivalent notions it should be fairly obvious that they are quite different values.

Privacy and Autonomy

To take the most glaring case, consider the values of privacy and autonomy. Privacy consists of the ability of an individual to maintain control of the information about himself that is available to others. It is intimately linked with the idea of being scrutinized by others, although, with the invention of various devices for intercepting communications, it extends to what we say, think, or do. Thus, typical interferences with privacy include observations of our bodies, behavior, and interactions with others. The more control we have over knowledge about ourselves, the more privacy we maintain.

Without going into the analysis of autonomy I shall present below it is clear that while privacy may be related to autonomy in a number of ways it is not identical with it. The relationship between the two concepts may be empirical; i.e., it may be claimed that a condition for the development of our autonomy includes considerable respect for our privacy. The relationship may be conceptual; i.e., it may be argued that to deny people privacy is to deny them the respect for personhood that is closely linked with their autonomy.

But a few examples should show that the concepts are distinct. One way of interfering with your autonomy is to deceive you. This interference with information is, however, just the opposite kind from that involved in interference with privacy. What is controlled is the information coming to you, not the information coming from you. I do not know something about you that you might wish to conceal. I conceal something from you that you might wish to know. Thus, autonomy but not privacy is diminished.

Similarly, privacy may be interfered with but not autonomy. If someone taps your phone conversations without your knowledge he interferes with your privacy. But your decisions, your actions, your values, are in no way changed or altered from what they might be otherwise. You are as self-determining as ever.

The intellectual disorder that arises from confusing these two notions may be observed in the Supreme Court decision in Griswold v. Connecticut that ruled that prohibition of the use of contraceptives was a violation of the constitutional right of privacy. Whatever the misdeeds of the state of Connecticut in this matter it did not involve any attempt to get acquainted with the personal lives of its citizens. It did involve attempting to interfere with the procreative decisions of citizens, and hence raised issues of autonomy and liberty—but these are quite different issues. One reason for the confusion of these concepts is that violations of autonomy and of privacy exhibit a common failure to respect another person as an independent moral agent. But they do so in different ways and ought not to be assimilated. In particular the doctrine of informed consent cannot rest on a notion of privacy. For it is the information flow to the patient that is at issue, not the patient's control over information about himself.

Liberty and Autonomy

While the distinction between autonomy and privacy is clear the identification of liberty and autonomy is much more plausible and tempting. In this section I will argue that the two notions ought to be distinguished and the concept that most effectively grounds the doctrine of informed consent is autonomy.

I suggest we think of liberty (or freedom, which I use as a synonym) as the ability of a person to do what he wishes and to have significant options that are not closed or made less eligible by the actions of other agents or the workings of social institutions. Historically there have been two influential traditions that have explicated the idea of liberty in contrasting terms. On one view, associated with the names of Hobbes and Mill, liberty is the absence of interference with a person's actions. Coercion and force are the main enemies of liberty. Another tradition, that of Rousseau and T. H. Green, understands liberty as being more than simply the absence of interference, as including the presence of a range of alternatives and opportunities. But whether the emphasis is on restrictions or opportunities the core notion of liberty is the ability of a person to effectuate his decisions in action.

If, for example, a doctor forces a Jehovah's Witness to have a blood transfusion against his will, this is a direct interference with the liberty of the patient. But since this is also clearly a denial of the patient's autonomy, understood as a power of self-determination, the thought arises that autonomy and liberty are the same.

An example from Locke shows us that they are not. Consider a person who is put into a prison cell and told that all the doors are locked. The guards go through the motions of locking the doors but in fact one of the locks is defective and the prisoner could simply open the door and leave the cell. Because he is not aware of this he, quite reasonably, remains in his cell. The prisoner is, in fact, free to leave the cell. His liberty has not, although he does not know this, been limited. His autonomy has been limited. His view of the alternatives open to him has been manipulated by the guards in such a fashion that he will not choose to leave. This example shows that self-determination can be limited without limiting liberty.

It might be suggested that although we can interfere with autonomy but not liberty, the converse does not hold; that all interference with liberty is necessarily interference with autonomy. For if we prevent a person from doing what he wishes, do we not interfere with the ability of a person to choose what he shall do, to fashion his life? Although this seems plausible I believe it is false. We accept the claim because we are used to focusing on cases where a person wishes to be free from interference, resents having his liberty taken away. Consider, however, the classical case of Odysseus.

Not wanting to be lured onto the rocks by the siren, Odysseus commands his men to tie him to the mast and refuse all later orders he might give to be set free. He wants to have his liberty limited so that he and his men will survive. While his behavior at the time he hears the sirens is not free—he struggles against his bonds and orders his men to free him—there is another aspect of his conduct that must be understood if we are to evaluate his situation correctly. He has a preference about his preferences, a desire not to act

upon certain desires. He views the desire to steer his ship towards the sirens, and the rocks, as an alien desire. In limiting his liberty in accordance with his wishes we promote, not hinder, his efforts to define the contours of his life. We promote his autonomy by denying him liberty.

Liberty is a concept that applies to the desires and preferences a person has for particular states of affairs. It focuses on what a person wants to do at the level of action. But this level ignores a crucial feature of persons—their capacity to reflect upon and adopt attitudes towards their desires, wishes, and values. It also ignores the ways that their desires and preferences were acquired. If it matters to persons not only what they value and believe but also the process by which they came to these states then only a fuller appreciation of their higher-order preferences will illuminate self-determination.

If one looks at the structure of the arguments for and against informed consent one has a better explanation of that structure by assuming that autonomy, not liberty, is the central value in the doctor-patient relationship. If we consider the main argument for denying the necessity of informed consent, that of therapeutic privilege, we see that this is a paternalistic argument. It is grounded on the idea that we ought to advance the patient's welfare even if this involves denying him the knowledge needed to make consent informed.

Attempts to define the concept of paternalism in the medical context view paternalism as the denial of liberty. One philosopher characterizes paternalism as "interference with a person's freedom of action or freedom of information, or the deliberate dissemination of misinformation."[10]

This definition implies that if a doctor does not misinform or fail to reveal information to a patient but tells the patient more than he wants to know the doctor does not act in a paternalistic fashion. But when a doctor insists upon telling a patient what he does not want to know, for his own good, this is a clear case of paternalism.

Or to consider a different kind of case, a husband might hide his sleeping pills fearing his wife's suicidal tendencies; again an act of paternalism, but not one that interferes with either freedom or the flow of information.

Only if one views paternalism as the denial of autonomy, as the substitution of one person's judgment for another, do these cases become paternalistic. The doctor who tells the patient more than he wants to know and the husband who hides the pills both substitute their judgment for another person's. There is a usurpation of decisionmaking. I am not, at this point, arguing this is right or wrong. I am only claiming that if autonomy is the value against which paternalism offends we have an explanation of why certain acts are paternalistic—an explanation that is lacking in the view that it is liberty that is at stake.

Autonomy is a richer notion than liberty, which is conceived either as mere absence of interference or as the presence of alternatives. It is tied up with the idea of being a subject, of being more than a passive spectator of one's desires and feelings. Some of the flavor of this idea is presented by Isaiah Berlin.

> I wish my life and decision to depend on myself, not on external forces of whatever kind. I wish to be the instrument of my own, not of other men's acts of will. I wish to be a subject, not an object; to be moved by reasons, by conscious purposes, which are my own, not by causes which affect me, as it were, from outside. I wish to be somebody, not anybody; a doer—deciding not being decided for, self-directed and not acted upon by external nature or by other men . . . I wish, above all, to be conscious of myself as a thinking, willing, active being, bearing responsibility for his choices and able to explain them by reference to his own ideas and purposes.[11]

It is this notion that I want to develop more carefully and that provides the soundest basis for explaining and justifying the doctrine of informed consent.

The Concept of Autonomy

The central idea that underlies the concept of autonomy is indicated by the etomology of the term: *autos* (self) and *nomos* (rule or law). The term was first applied to the Greek city state. A city had *autonomia* when its citizens made their own laws, as opposed to being under the control of some conquering power. There is then a natural extension to persons as being autonomous when their decisions and actions are their own.

It is characteristic of persons, and seems to be a distinctively human ability, that they are able to reflect upon and adopt attitudes towards their desires, intentions, life plans. One may not just desire to smoke but also desire that one not have that desire. One may be motivated by jealousy and anger and also desire that one's motivations be different.

A person may identify with the influences that motivate him, view himself as the kind of person who wishes to be moved in particular ways. Or he may resent being motivated in certain ways, be alienated from those influences, prefer to be the kind of person who has different values and preferences. I am defining autonomy as the capacity to reflect upon one's motivational structure and to make changes in that structure. Thus, autonomy is not simply a reflective capacity but includes some ability to alter one's preferences and to make them effective in action. Indeed to make them effective partly because one has reflected upon them and adopted them as one's own.

Autonomy is a second-order capacity to reflect critically upon one's first-order preferences and desires, and the ability to either identify with these or to change them in light of higher-order preferences and values. By exercising such a capacity we define our nature, give meaning and coherence to our lives, and take responsibility for the kind of person we are.

Liberty, power, and privacy are not equivalent to autonomy but they may be necessary conditions for individuals to develop their own aims and interests, and to make their values effective in the living of their lives.

It is an implication of my view that there is no specific content to the decisions an autonomous person takes. Someone who wishes to be the kind of person who does whatever the doctor orders is as autonomous as the person who wants to evaluate those orders for himself. This view differs from others in the literature. Wolff, for example, says (in the context of the citizen and the state) "[t]he autonomous man . . . may do what another tells him, but not because he has been told to do it. . . . By accepting as final the commands of the others he forfeits his autonomy."[12] But this conception of autonomy not only has the consequence that no government is legitimate but also that such values as loyalty, objectivity, commitment, and love are inconsistent with being autonomous.

Although I do not believe there is a direct logical link between acting autonomously and being critical and independent in judging and acting, it is plausible to suppose there are psychological connections. It is likely that those who practice in their life a critical reflection on their values will tend to be suspicious of modes of thought that rely on the uncritical acceptance of authority, tradition, and custom.

It should also not be thought that those who autonomously choose to follow the commands of others can thereby escape responsibility for their actions. A person is responsible for ceding his independence to another. What does affect responsibility is interference with a person's autonomy when the person is not in a position to realize this is occurring, or to do much about it if he does. If my will is overborne or undermined, then the responsibility for what I have done shifts to those who have interfered with my autonomy.

The Value of Autonomy in Informed Consent

I have argued so far that the concept of autonomy plays a major role in arguments about the requirement of informed consent but I have not yet said very much about why the promotion of autonomy is something to be desired and valued. This question is made more difficult by the particular conception of autonomy I have presented. For a conception of autonomy that has no particular content, that allows for the possibility of a patient granting complete authority to a doctor, seems too formal to be of great value. I shall argue now that it is precisely because autonomy has this relatively weak and formal character that it can play a fundamental role in moral theory.

Let me begin by considering at the most general level what is involved in that form of practical reasoning we single out as moral reasoning. Every moral theory has some conception of equality among moral agents, some conception according to which we are to regard others as equal to ourselves. For the utilitarian, equality is represented in the theory by the claim that in calculating utility the interests of each person are to count equally. For the natural rights theorist, all persons are assumed to have equal rights. For the Kantian, I may act only in that way that I am prepared to will all others act. For the religious moralist we are all children of God.

Corresponding to these notions of equality are various devices for preserving this fundamental equality in the process of moral reasoning. According to the utilitarian an action is justified when an impartial observer would view the action as maximizing the total amount of utility in the given community. For the rights theorist and the Kantian a justification must be acceptable to each of the individuals affected. A similar motive underlies the Golden Rule that is found in most major religious theories.

Underlying the various techniques of moral justification is a prohibition against treating others in such a way that they cannot share the purposes of those who are so treating them. And behind this is a conception of the nature of persons as independent sources of moral agency. It is as distinct loci of consciousness, of purposive action, as distinct selves, that others must be respected and taken into account when each of us decides what he shall do. It is because other persons are creators of their own lives, are shapers of their own values, are the originators of projects and plans, that their interests must be taken into account, their rights respected, their projects valued.

What makes an individual the particular person he is reflects his pursuit of autonomy, his construction of meaning in his life. One can see, therefore, a number of reasons why autonomy is a relatively contentless notion. People can give meaning to their lives in innumerable ways. There is no particular way of giving shape or meaning to a life. This, of course, is compatible with certain lives being more admirable than others. In addition, any feature that is going to ground an equality of respect must be a feature that persons share, that they have in common. Any particular way of filling in the content of a life plan is not likely to be shared. Morality is owed to everyone. More intimate relationships such as friend or lover must respond to the particular qualities of another, to lives shaped in specific fashion. Moral respect is owed to all because all have (assuming we are dealing with normal persons, not defective or incompetent in serious ways) the capacity for autonomous development.

Now it is true that while all (normal) persons have such a capacity it is not the case that all have an equal capacity. Like any other capacity—say, the ability to identify with the pain of others—it is a product of one's biological and environmental circumstances. Our conception of a moral agent is of a creature who possesses this capacity above some significant threshold. That some persons will be very much above this level is not important, morally speaking, although it may be important for some purposes.

This first part of my argument has been directed to showing that a weak notion of autonomy is connected to central parts of ethical reasoning. It is also linked to important metaphysical and attitudinal features of moral agents. Our idea of who we are, of our self-identity, is linked to our ability to find and refine ourselves. The exercise of the capacity of autonomy is what makes my life mine. And, if I am to recognize others as equal persons, there is a requirement that I give weight to the way they define and value the world in deciding how I should act.

One argument, then, for the value of autonomy is that we have a conception of persons that is deeply rooted in our world view, and that this conception is worthy of respect and admiration. A full analysis of why the capacity for autonomy is worthy of respect would require a general theory of value (worth) and of morality (respect). I have neither but I shall make some comments about the value of autonomy.

Arguments for the value of anything may claim either that something is good because it leads to something else that is good (instrumental value) or because it is good for its own sake (intrinsic value). Autonomy has value along both dimensions.

On instrumental grounds being able to shape one's own choices and values makes it more likely that one's life will be satisfying than if others, even benevolent others, do the shaping. This is the traditional liberal argument that people are better judges of their own interests than others. Though debate goes on about the limits to which this is true, as a rough generalization it is highly probable.

There is also the fact that quite aside from what results from determining one's life, people get satisfaction out of doing so. We should not overlook the extent to which the process of thinking about, reflecting upon, choosing among preferences is a source of satisfaction to individuals.

But there is value connected with being self-determining that is not a matter either of bringing about good results or the pleasures of the process itself. This is the intrinsic desirability of exercising the capacity for self-determination. We desire to be recognized by others as the kind of creature capable of determining our own destiny. Our own sense of self-respect is tied to the respect of others—and this is not just a matter of psychology. Second, notions of creativity, of risk-taking, of adherence to principle, of responsibility are all linked conceptually to the possibility of autonomous action. These desirable features of a good life are not possible (logically) for nonautonomous creatures. In general, autonomy is linked to activity, to making rather than being, to those higher forms of consciousness that are distinctive of human potential.

It should not be denied that in addition to the instrumental gains of exercising autonomy there are also instrumental losses. With responsibility comes blame and punishment. With the possibility of adherence to principle comes the possibility of cowardice and betrayal. It is not part of my thesis that more autonomy is always better than less. I have only been trying to understand why autonomy has value when it does.

The Special Role of Autonomy in Health Care

I turn now to the question of whether autonomy plays some special role in the health-care context. We know that there are various professional relationships that attach significance to the autonomy of the client. A psychiatrist may point out the destructive aspects of a marriage but ought not to pressure his patient to terminate it. Architects must walk the fine line between respecting the wishes of the client and attempting to educate and refine his taste in houses. Is autonomy more important in the doctor-patient relationship than in these other cases? I believe there is something special about the health-care context that emerges from an accurate conception of the doctor's role.

It is a truism that a doctor cares for the health of the body. It is also a truism that persons are embodied creatures; meaning not merely that we have bodies but that we are bodies. From these truisms it follows that the care of our bodies is linked with our identity as persons. Whatever goals or values we have are tied up with the fate of our bodies. Health is, as Rawls puts it,

a primary good, a good that any person wishes to preserve and promote whatever the more specific details of his life plans. The function of medical care has been put most succinctly by Charles Fried.

> [T]he doctor's prime and basic function is not so much the prevention of death (which is not in his power) but the preservation of life capacities for the realization of a reasonable, realistic life plan. As in particular cases conflicts arise and decisions must be made between various capacities and between the risk of death and the impairment of various capacities, the doctor must see himself as the servant, not of life in the abstract, but of the life plans of his patients.[13]

Decisions about what form of treatment to undergo, the probabilities of cure and of side effects, judgments about how the body will look to others after various forms of surgery, whether to spend one's last days in a hospital or at home—these are not technical, medical judgments. To suppose that these are matters of expertise, decisions to be taken by experts, represents a denial of autonomy that is particularly damaging for two reasons.

First, one's body is irreplaceable and inescapable. If my architect doesn't listen to me and this results in a house I do not like, I can always move. I cannot move from my body. In addition since my body is me, failure to respect my wishes concerning my body is a particularly insulting denial of autonomy. Of course the opposite side of this coin is also true. If the denial of autonomy is justified in terms of promoting the benefit of my body then paternalism would seem to have the strongest claim in the medical context. This brings us to the issue of possible exceptions to respecting the autonomy of patients.

Possible Exceptions to Respecting Patients' Autonomy

Thus far I have argued that autonomy plays a major role in explaining the doctrine of informed consent and I have given reasons for the importance we attach to autonomy. But nothing I have said commits me to the view that respect for autonomy is, or ought to be, absolute. There are certainly other values that are of fundamental moral importance and of crucial significance to any person. These include dignity, health, well-being, integrity, security. It is possible that in order to promote any of these values it may be necessary to sacrifice some autonomy. It is also possible that promotion of autonomy in the long run requires sacrificing autonomy in the short run. Finally there are cases in which a person is already in a nonautonomous state or one of diministed autonomy and the principle ceases to have application or at least its application is more problematic than in normal cases. These seem to me the grounds for considering exceptions to the doctrine of informed consent—conflicting values and reduced autonomy—and I want to indicate the framework of moral justification that I think is appropriate for discussing the limits to principles we judge to be, at first approximation, the correct ones. I shall not argue for this framework—indeed it is not clear that such a basic outlook can be argued for—but simply present it in the hope that it will strike the reader as plausible and attractive.

Moral reasoning is a branch of practical reasoning, i.e., reasoning about what to do as opposed to how things are. Unlike other kinds of practical reasoning, e.g., prudential thought about what will promote my long-range welfare, it is tied to the existence and recognition of other persons. Just as prudential reasoning is constrained by the recognition that there is a future self whose interests must be taken into account, moral reasoning is constrained by the recognition that there are other persons whose interests are no less important to them than mine are to me. Moral reasoning is the attempt to give reasons for action that are acceptable to other independent and equal moral agents. We seek general principles for the regulation of behavior that are such that they can command the agreement of other informed, rational, and free agents. The test of a proposed principle or action is that it would be found acceptable not just to the person who proposes it but to all those whom the action affects. Justification is to others; moral motivation, the connection of morality with our will, is supplied not by sympathy alone but by our need to act in such a fashion that our actions are both understandable to ourselves and acceptable to others.

This view is a species of meta-ethical theory traditionally labeled as contractualist. It is a meta-ethical view because it says nothing directly about the content of the moral principles that are justified contractually. It is possible that the principles that are capable of being agreed to will be similar to those of utilitarians or Kantians or natural law theorists. But it is the agreement to the principles that grounds them and not the reasons for the agreement. Whatever its other merits on purely philosophical grounds such a contractualist scheme of justification is particularly appropriate for our problem—the exceptions to the doctrine of informed consent. On this view the exceptions must be capable of being justified to those whose consent will not be sought or honored. Naturally, to present this justification in the very context in which the issue arises would be self-defeating. If, for example, one believes that presenting a patient with the true facts of his diagnosis would be psychologically damaging one could hardly justify this failure to inform by stating to the patient that he would be harmed by telling him the truth of his condition. The justification, if there is one, must lie in a general agreement that is *ex ante*, which occurs or could occur before we are faced with the situation to which the exception applies. We have to deliberate about and agree upon the merits of exceptions to a principle (whether there are any and how broad they should be) in abstraction from the particular set of facts. This is not to say, of course, that a doctor faced with a real case is barred from thinking about the issue. It is to say that his thought ought to reflect, in the logic and the range of considerations he considers relevant, the position of persons who are to settle upon rules prior to their being faced with specific moral conflicts.

Exceptions to the Requirement of Informed Consent

The candidates for exceptions to informed consent can be grouped under the headings of emergency, incompetence, waiver, and therapeutic privilege.[14] The first two are relatively unproblematic in principle although they may pose problems in practice of determining when they apply. Waiver is, I shall argue, not an infringement of autonomy at all. Therapeutic privilege is the exception that most directly infringes autonomy and raises the greatest problem for justifying an exception.

It is surely rational for autonomous persons to agree that life-saving treatment may be rendered without the consent of the patient in "emergency" situations. An emergency situation is one in which the patient is unable to give consent or to receive information. If a patient should object to this treatment afterwards there is a clear justification that can be presented to him. "I acted to preserve your possibility of future autonomous action," says the doctor, "and I did so in conditions such that you could not give your consent, and in which to wait until you could would be impossible."

Note here that it is not just that important benefits for the patient are produced but that there is no reason to suppose the patient did not want the benefits *and* there was no possibility of getting consent. We have a great benefit (life) secured without any loss of autonomy. For us not to agree to such a bargain is irrational.

The possibility of broadening the concept of an emergency then arises. Suppose that it is not life but, say, limb that is at stake and consent is not impossible but costly (where cost might be defined in terms of the time necessary to get agreement). Let us suppose we have a person with a detached hand that could be reattached by immediate microsurgery. And let us suppose that the person only speaks Serbo-Croatian and the time necessary to get a translator would make the operation ineffective. Again the *ex ante* justification seems clear. Our interest in our limbs is an important one; the violation of autonomy, while greater than in the previous case (because it is possible to get consent), is minor.

Proceeding in this manner—by varying the nature of the harm to be averted as well as the costs of obtaining informed consent—we should be able to get a fix on the limits of the emergency exception. It seems plausible, for example, that there will be cases where we will insist upon consent but not upon full information (which is time-consuming and which may not be effective in conditions of great stress and pain). I do not insist that this scheme will give unique solutions. There may be hypothetical cases in which reasonable people will disagree about what rule they would agree to in advance of an emergency. Those may be precisely the cases that we leave to other institutions, such as courts, to decide on a case-by-case basis after the fact.

It is sometimes said of emergency cases that the patient has "implicitly" or "tacitly" agreed to the treatment, and hence there is no violation of autonomy. This way of talking is misleading. It suggests that there is really some consent that has taken place but one just has to know where to look for it. In fact, neither explicitly nor implicitly has any agreement taken place; if there is no loss of autonomy in these situations by not getting consent it is because autonomy has already been lost and not because the patient has really consented. My argument does not rely on any supposed agreement but on a set of principles that are justified because they are capable of securing agreement by rational agents under certain circumstances.

In the typical emergency situation, where the patient is unconscious and cannot give consent, the patient is also incompetent. The case of a psychotic patient or a senile patient or an infant are also cases where consent is impossible but here it is not a temporary problem. Again, on the level of theory, the situation does not seem too difficult. Here the problems are ones of definition, of drawing the line, of determining who ought to be authorized to consent for the patient, and what criteria should that authorized patient use. The theoretical justification is identical to the emergency case. Given that we all know we are subject to various incompetencies and that decisions may have to be made with great impact on our life chances, it is reasonable for us to "insure" against loss by authorizing health care when we are not able to do so. The case of incompetency is one in which our autonomy has already been impaired, lost, or not developed so there is no denial of autonomy on the part of the doctor. It is true there are other harms that may be inflicted on us. We may be kept alive in conditions that are insults to our dignity or privacy, and once aware of this we may want to establish limits to the treatment that is permissible without our explicit consent. But to deny any exception to the securing of informed consent, even in cases where we are not competent, would be self-defeating.

The next exception, that of waiver, is conceptually quite a distinct category. Like self-defense in the law, it ought to be considered a justification, not an excuse. It is not like the previous cases of emergency or incompetence in that one fails to get informed consent; it is that one ought not to try. If a patient has knowingly and freely requested of the doctor that he not be informed or consulted about his course of treatment then to seek to obtain informed consent would itself be a violation of autonomy. Again the difficulty is a practical one—determining that the waiver is not simply psychological denial or a process of infantilization or of giving in to the pressures of the doctor. Leaving these difficult problems aside, as I argued earlier, autonomy includes the possibility of a decision to give up one's independent determination about what one should do. While this decision may be foolish or unwise it can hardly be

interfered with on the grounds of autonomy. If one denies the legitimacy of waiver this will be on the grounds that it is better for the patient not to act in this manner. And this brings us to the issue of paternalism and the last category—therapeutic privilege.

Therapeutic privilege may be conceived as the opposite side of the coin of waiver. In waiver the patient decides that certain information will be harmful or cause distress and that he would be better off not having it. In therapeutic privilege the doctor decides that securing informed consent would be harmful to the patient and that he is better off not having it. It is a privilege since it allows exemption from a duty; it is therapeutic since it is intended for the benefit of the patient. This exception raises the clearest conflict between the value of autonomy and what is considered the best interests of the patient.

Using the framework of seeking general agreement by all the relevant parties, the issue becomes what powers to ignore our consent can we agree to grant health professionals when they claim that seeking such consent would be harmful to us. It is useful to consider a spectrum of positions ranging from weak to strong powers.

The weakest position is that autonomy may be denied only in the interests of the autonomy of the patient. This exception would allow a doctor to withhold information only when a special harm would (be likely to) follow from the disclosure of information, namely, that harm that would result in the patient's being unable or being less able to make an autonomous decision about his treatment. This justification is invoked in *Canterbury v. Spence,* when the court claimed the failure to disclose was justified because "it is recognized that patients occasionally become so ill or emotionally distraught on disclosure as to foreclose a rational decision."[15] Such an exception is maximally coherent with the principle of informed consent since it claims that the disclosure would in fact undercut the worth of the consent. Of course the fact that a doctor claims this harm would occur does not make it true, and there remains the problem of designing institutions to make the ratio of true claims as high as possible and to provide remedies for those denied their autonomy when the claim is unwarranted by the available evidence. Nevertheless this exception seems to be one we can all accept since it is justified in terms of the promotion of the value fostered by the principle to which it is an exception.

There is the much broader version of harm invoked by therapeutic privilege that is also present in another line of reasoning in Canterbury. On this view failure to disclose was justified because "risk disclosure poses such a threat of detriment to the patient as to become unfeasible or contraindicated from a medical point of view."[16] Here one can distinguish two ways in which such information might be contraindicated. In one case the disclosure has a direct harmful effect on the emotional state of the patient. He is distraught when he learns he has cancer or Hodgkin's disease. In the other kind of case the harm operates primarily via its effect on the treatment decision made by the patient. The doctor believes that disclosure would lead the patient to choose a form of treatment that is not optimal or perhaps even detrimental. Note that this is not equivalent to asserting the patient cannot make a rational or autonomous decision; it is a claim that the decision is wrong or mistaken.

What would be the results of allowing doctors to have the power to deny our autonomy when they believed that harm in one of these two forms would result? According to the mode of justification that I have been using such powers must be publicly recognized and acknowledged. Granting such authority to doctors must undermine the atmosphere of trust between doctor and patient, for the doctor could not for long simply remain silent but would have to mislead and, in many cases, lie. We would all be in a state of uncertainty about the meaning and truth of the communications from doctor to patient.

Given the possibility of explicit waiver, given the state of dependency to which illness reduces us in any case, given the erosion of trust produced by such an exception, and given the difficulty of effective restraints on the use of such powers, the resulting loss of autonomy created by the wide exception of therapeutic privilege is too great to secure general agreement among all those concerned. Competent patients have the right to the information necessary to make those evaluative, non-technical decisions about their bodies that autonomy requires.

Let me end by mentioning one final distinction. One may view the requirement of informed consent as connected to autonomy in either of two ways. In the first it is related as cause and effect. We suppose the requirement is, as a matter of fact, likely to promote the autonomy of patients. I believe the evidence is in favor of this proposition but it is an empirical claim subject to refutation. There is another way of viewing the connection, which sees the attempt to secure consent as itself being an expression of respect for the autonomy of the patient. On this view the connection is a necessary one. One way of showing respect for a person is by seeking his willing acceptance of a plan of treatment. Seeking consent is an expression of respect for autonomy in the way that apology is an expression of regret. To fail to seek consent, as in the case of therapeutic privilege, is necessarily an insult to autonomy even though motivated by pure benevolence.

Notes

1. *Canterbury v. Spence*, 464 F.2d (D.C. Cir.) at 786.
2. In re *Yetter*, 62 Pa. D&C 2d 619 at 623.
3. *Nathanson v. Kline*, 186 Kan. 393 at 406.
4. A. M. Capron, Informed Consent in Catastrophic Disease Research & Treatment, *University of Pennsylvania Law Review* 123 (December, 1974), p. 365.
5. A. Meisel, The "Exceptions" to the Informed Consent Doctrine: Striking a Balance Between Com-

peting Values in Medical Decision-making, *Wisconsin Law Review,* Vol. 1979, no. 2, p. 420:

6. F. Harper and F. James, *The Law of Torts,* supp. 68, p. 61.

7. I. Ramsey, *The Patient as Person* (Yale University Press, 1970), p. 5.

8. B. Freeman, A Moral Theory of Consent, *Hastings Center Report* (August, 1975), p. 32.

9. R. Veatch, Three Theories of Informed Consent: Philosophical Foundations and Policy Implications, *The Belmont Report* (DHEW Publication No. (OS) 78-0014), pp. 26–28.

10. A. Buchanan, Medical Paternalism, *Philosophy and Public Affairs* 7, no. 4 (Summer, 1978), p. 372.

11. I. Berlin, *Two Concepts of Liberty* (Oxford: Clarendon Press, 1969), p. 123.

12. R. P. Wolff, *In Defense of Anarchism* (New York: Harper & Row, 1970), p. 14.

13. C. Fried, *Medical Experimentation: Personal Integrity and Social Policy* (Elsevier, 1974), p. 98.

14. I am indebted to Meisel, *op. cit.,* for his classification of the exceptions to informed consent.

15. *Canterbury v. Spence,* at 789.

16. Ibid.

The Origins and Consequences of Patient Autonomy: A 25-Year Retrospective

David J. Rothman

I

This essay explores the evolution of the tension between the principles of autonomy and beneficence in American health care over the past several decades, or more specifically, the tension between doctors and patients around medical decision making. Inevitably, to address this subject demands an exploration of the interconnections between social change and medical change, with the arrows of influence clearly running in both directions. Let us, therefore, first address the impact of social forces on medical developments, which are the most critical and determinative to understanding this tension, and then run the analysis from medicine back to society. This setting of priorities is appropriate for the critical changes in medicine in its relationship to patients have been imposed on it by external forces. The dynamics of change are located not within medicine but within society.

In retrospect it is clear that the social movements of the 1960s and 70s set the tone and the goals for much of the reform agenda for the closing decades of the 20th century, and probably, for the foreseeable future as well. Civil rights, women's rights, gay rights, children's rights, and the center of our attention here, patient rights, all rose to prominence in the 60s and 70s, and all shared a similar mind set. It was characterized, in the first instance, by a profound suspicion and distrust of constituted authority—whether in familial, educational, community, political, or medical institutions. The movements shared an unwillingness to accede to the discretionary authority of whites, men, husbands, parents, clinical investigators, mental hospital superintendents, elected officials, and of course, doctors, especially when they were males practicing obstetrics, gynecology, or psychiatry. All movements subscribed to a fierce anti-paternalism, a dogged rejection of the principles of beneficence, a persistent determination to let constituents speak for themselves and define their own interests. Autonomy and consent became the bywords. In this way, they broke with the reform traditions in each of their respective areas, in essence, leaving Progressive and New Deal orientations for new models (Gaylin et al., 1978).

Setting patient rights and the drive to autonomy in the context of other rights movements is not just to mark a chronological coincidence. Rather, without the inspiration of and the models provided by the other rights movements, it is impossible to imagine an autonomy and patient rights movement. To focus on one critical aspect of this debt: it was a signal and distinguishing characteristic of all the rights movements that they were led by lawyers. While such a characteristic seems commonplace today, in fact it represented a marked departure for social reform. The ranks of Progressive reformers, for example, were filled with settlement house workers and social scientists, but not lawyers. (If anything, the lawyer was the enemy who represented vested interests; it was conservative judges, after all, who struck down the Progressive protective legislation on child labor, workmen's hours and wages, and women's labor.) The 1960s movements, by contrast, were spearheaded by lawyers, and in many ways, their orientation, strategy, and presumptions deeply influenced the reform goals.

The impact of lawyers on the emergence of a commitment to autonomy is far more critical than the term "bioethics" commonly suggests, or allows. In fact, bioethics itself as a term is misleading in giving disproportionate weight to the discipline of philosophy, when the case could easily be made that the most effective leadership, in terms of defining goals and securing practical results, came from the law. One example basic to the principle of autonomy is its emphasis on informed consent. Much, albeit not all, of the reason for this emphasis reflects the influence of lawyers on the movement. The idea, after all, was born in a court, owes practically nothing to traditional medical ethics, and to this day, seems to be a less than adequate formulation of the doctor-patient relationship to many physicians (Faden and Beauchamp, 1986). And consent fits tightly with the other critical features of the autonomy paradigm: the formality in medical decision making, the increased dependence on state and federal regulations, the novel focus within health care institutions on rules and an unprecedented insistence on written, signed documents, as in the case of advanced directives and DNR orders (Rothman, 1991).

The crucial impact of a lawyerly mindset is evidenced in the preeminence of the ideal of autonomy and the redefinition of beneficence as paternalism. The shift in language and in goal was part of a larger effort to redress the balance of power between doctor and patient. And to the degree to which this was successful, and it was on the whole successful, the change owes more to lawyers than to philosophers. In sum, without civil rights and the other rights movements, lawyers would not have left corporate office and the courtroom, and would never have seen a hospital or a doctor except in a malpractice suit—and a powerful patient rights movement would not have occurred.

Perhaps the best testimony to the validity of this argument comes from recent attacks both on the concept of autonomy and informed consent and, by implication, the role of lawyers in patient rights. The most acerbic of them has just been written, curiously but in this context, altogether predictably, by a lawyer. I have in mind the recent book by Carl Schneider, *The Practice of Autonomy* (Schneider, 1998). Schneider argues that Americans have gone overboard in their dedication to the values of patient autonomy. They have seemingly replaced the tyranny of physician beneficence with a tyranny of patient autonomy.

Lawyers' devotion to self-determination by patients have imposed unreasonable and ultimately wrongheaded duties and obligations on them. Although the principle should remain central to medical decision making, Schneider believes that it has become "mandatory," "wooden," "simplistic," and "extravagant." It presumes, as lawyers would, a "hyper-rational" patient who, in disembodied, abstract, coldly analytic, and bloodless fashion, calculates the advantages and disadvantages of one or another medical strategy, juxtaposes personal values against anticipated outcomes, and reaches a decision.

But such is not the way of patients, Schneider argues. Quoting from poll data, sociological surveys, and patient memoirs, he assembles examples of patients who did not want to make their own decisions, who, devastated by their disease, sought guidance from doctors, and yes, were ready to take their advice on particular decisions. He also describes, in very effective fashion, all the barriers to giving truly informed consent when suffering from major illness, medicated, and lying in a hospital bed.

There are many weaknesses in Schneider's arguments. His critique is most interesting not for its substance—which is deeply flawed—but as an illustration of how established the new paradigm of autonomy is. To be an iconoclast one must now attack the hard, legalistic, unemotional aspects of patient autonomy and to attempt to assert the soft side, the image of the patient as compromised, in need of help, dependent, and relying upon the knowledgeable and concerned doctor. We have surely come a long way when the man who is determined to "go against the grain" has to resurrect a child-like patient.

Let us note one other indication of just how legal-driven the patient autonomy movement was. The event that signals the movement's arrival, that announces and promotes a fundamental shift in the doctor-patient, or hospital-patient relationship, the point after which there was no going back to the old models of paternalism, comes from the legal forum in the guise of the Karen Ann Quinlan decision. In its aftermath came not only a new insistence on legal forms (to this day, lawyers oversee the signing of more advanced directives than doctors) but a shift in attitude to a "we": "they" patient mentality, as in: don't let them, that is doctors and hospitals, do to me what they did to Karen Ann. Arguably, if one had to choose just one document to represent the triumph of the autonomy movement, that document would be a court decision, and it would be the Quinlan decision (Filene, 1998).

II

However fascinating the impact of origins on subsequent development, the still more intriguing and complicated questions involve an assessment of impact. First, what difference has the movement for patient autonomy made, both within its immediate boundaries—the practice of medicine—and in its broader scope—the organization of the broader society? Second, what can we say about the future prospects of the movement? Is it on the wane? Is it flourishing? Where is it taking us?

In terms of clinical encounters, there can be no doubt that the doctor-patient relationship has undergone a revolution, and historians do not invoke that term lightly. It should be clear that this is by no means complete. But if one focuses on patients who are educated, middle class or above, younger, women, and with chronic disease (which now includes AIDS as well as various forms of cancer), then the newer designations, consumers and providers, far better capture the nature of the relationship.

At first, the change was in many ways a matter of style with a limited amount of substance in terms of decision-making. The consumer of the 1970s and the 1980s carried herself differently, certainly in manner, and did exert some impact, if circumscribed, on the major, yes-no medical decisions. So greetings changed (if I'm Mary than you are not Dr. Jones but Tom). And sooner rather than later, the sex of the doctor changed (as women began to dominate the rolls in ob-gyn), and the practice, difficult now to imagine, of anaesthetizing the patient, biopsing the breast tumor, and removing it in its entirety should cancerous cells be found, came to end, with legislation in some states accelerating the process.

The transformation continued, so that by the 1990s, the consumer had his or her say on a far greater range of treatment decisions. Some of the shift reflects the continuation of the older trend. But even more of it must be understood in terms of a second stage in the patient autonomy movement and the still broader social impact on medicine. The critical elements are the extraordinary information revolution which we are now experiencing. They include the computer, the web, the dot.coms and the search engines. This is not to say that printed matter, or for its part, televison advertising, is irrelevant. It is estimated that 50 consumer magazines exclusively devoted to health care appear each month, and that does not include the miles of print about health care included in other magazines. As for books, one need only glance over the section headings in the chain bookstores and count the rows of shelves to appreciate that the "health section" is enormous, and every disease has numerous volumes devoted to it. In the 1930s, one of the best selling volumes for patients was entitled, What to Do Until the Doctor Comes. The 1970s counterpart might have been called, What to Do After the Doctor Comes. The newest version would have to be entitled, What To Tell Your Doctor, or better yet, your nephrologist, neonatologist, or right valve specializing cardiologist.

No matter how printed volumes have proliferated, they cannot stand up against the web and the net. Go to Yahoo's Health page and you will find that for "All Diseases and Conditions," there are 7295 sites (as of March, 2000). All cancers had 561, breast cancer, 148, substance abuse 213, MS 105, genetic disorders, 96, and so on. Go to WebMD and you will find 1,267 leads for mental health, 636 for cancer, 53 for respiratory conditions. Click onto one of the disease categories and you will find "disease clubs" with message boards and chat clubs—and experts ready to do Q&A, clinical guidelines for diagnosis and treatment, the major associations, referral centers, resource centers including support groups, and herbal remedies. Everything is there, which is both the strength and weaknesses of the sites. There are, however, countless groups trying to prioritize and referee the information, which might lead to a reassertion of physician authority, but more likely, will be putting expertise more and more at the command of the consumer (Winker et al., 2000).

In the arena of patient rights, WebMD has 4,453 references. The first is a collection of articles on the Patients' Bill of Rights, the second is entitled: "Do You Know Your Medical Rights, including what informed consent is and why you should consider an advance directive." The fifth is a reference for Patient and Doctor bills of rights with a special note: "Written for women but suitable for all audiences." The seventh has a transcript of a live chat with an outstanding ethicist, Edward Beiser of Brown University, and on and on.

Does it all truly matter? Of course it does. We know this anecdotally even if more quantitative data is still forthcoming. Many of us could share stories of friends who themselves or their wives or children, contracted serious disease and in the course of days, not months, used the web to learn more than the generalist, and often even more than the specialist about the results of clinical trials for the disease in the US, Europe, Japan and Australia. The change makes the 1973 Our Bodies, Ourselves (Boston Women's Health Collective, 1973) seem antiquated, and the first AIDS clinical trial registries run by gay men's health organizations, antediluvian. It is not too much to say that the balance of power in the examining room has shifted in the 1990s not so much because of lawyers, but because of web masters.

The central theme in the second stage of patient rights may well be "control." To be sure, control was what Quinlan and mastectomy procedures were ultimately all about and it was relevant to the first stage of the patient rights movement. But the import of the concept has only increased over time, taking the desire for control into new territories. And the new territories were by no means anticipated by many of those who promoted the original patient rights movement, and may well represent places that they did not want to go. But whether one invokes the idea of unintended consequences, or recalls the adage of beware of what you ask for because you may get it, patient autonomy is now opening up new and complex issues.

The movement for physician assisted suicide is an excellent case in point. Resisted by many physicians and their organizations—and by others, as well—it points clearly to the preeminence of control issues in this new stage of patient rights. To be sure, it is not astonishing that a movement so shaped by the Quinlan case should insist two decades later on the right to PAS. But the support for it, for better or for worse, highlights the enlarged agenda for patient autonomy. As framed by proponents, the issue is not whether PAS will encourage euthanasia (with enlarged physician authority) or whether PAS will adversely affect minorities or vulnerable populations (such as nursing home residents), but whether they, accustomed to controlling their lives, will get to control their death. Of course there is fantasy here and elements of denial, but there is also an assertion of power, power by patient over doctor, and an insistence on self-determination (*Minnesotal Law Review*, 1988).

Let us consider yet another characteristic of this second stage of patient autonomy, again one that may be inconsistent with the first goals of the movement. It is doubtful whether patient rights proponents in the 60s and 70s anticipated extending the reach of pharmaceutical companies, of unleashing a dramatic and on the whole successful campaign to sell drugs by circumventing the physician and appealing directly to the consumer. But the debate over the desirability of direct advertising to the consumer by pharmaceutical companies is framed by the language of patient rights. And to a degree, those concerned about the power of advertising are hoisted on the petard of patient rights.

The growing resemblance in terms of drug company advertisements of daily newspapers like the New York Times and Wall Street Journal with the New England Journal of Medicine was never more apparent than in the recent withdrawal of the drug for the treatment of type-2 diabetes, Rezulin, from the market because of liver toxicity. Full page ads put the news of Rezulin's withdrawal in huge type and then went on to tell consumers: "Ask your doctor about [in the case of Smith Kline and Bristol Meyers] Avandia. Together you can decide whether Avandia is right for you." In fact, direct to consumer advertising of pharmaceuticals has increased to the point where it represents almost one billion of advertising expenditure (against 4 billion directed to doctors). In the Rezulin case, it would be hard for the newspaper reading public to miss the news of the FDA action. But how far down the road of consumer rights do we want to go with consumers asking doctors for Avandia (on the basis of nothing more than a one page ad), or for that matter, for Zocor, or Viagra (Terzian, 1999).

According to Alan Holmer, president of a pharmaceutical industry trade group, very far. He happily cites a survey that more than 53 million Americans have asked their physicians about a drug they saw advertised, and that DTC advertising led 21.2 million consumers to talk to their doctors about an illness or condition that they have never before mentioned. He argues that compliance with consumer-requested drugs may be higher, that many conditions, including depression, high cholesterol, high blood pressure, and diabetes itself, are undertreated. But his most impassioned rhetoric is to the effect that "pharmaceutical companies have both a right and responsibility to inform people about their products," and that through DTC advertising, "the patient has been empowered with information." Indeed, he goes on: "participatory health care—consumers assuming more responsibility for their own health—is changing the nature of the patient-physician relationship." Clearly, the pharmaceutical companies are at once reacting to a new patient rights paradigm, and just as clearly, promoting it. When commerce joins with ideology, we have a powerful engine for promoting change (Holmer, 1999).

Moreover, one physician's response to the Holmer argument (in a JAMA pro-con debate) focused on the historical reasons why physicians had a monopoly over prescribing, the dangers of misleading advertising, and the embarrassing fact that physicians often do respond to patient demands, sometimes consistent with good medical practice, but sometimes not. The core of the argument against DTC is that doctors have too little professional integrity, a point not likely to reduce consumer pressures. The physician concedes that the consumer advocates champion DTC advertising because it "shifts control over prescription decisions from physicians to patients, giving patients greater command over health care." But then how to counter such a concession? He does it lamely. "In reality, the principal effect of DTC marketing is to create consumer demand, changing the physician-patient relationship to a physician-consumer relationship." Which is precisely what has been happening since the 1970s (Hollon, 1999).

To choose one final example of the manifestation of stage two patient autonomy, look at the extraordinary resistence to the spread of managed care. Again, qualifications are very much in order. Physicians also resisted it because of the limitations it placed on both their income and their authority. But patients were even more outraged, making managed care perhaps the most maligned and unpopular innovation in the recent history of medicine. Indeed, it is more than a curiosity that a nationally legislated Patient Rights bill may emerge from this confrontation. The Gallup organization periodically questions the public on the

"honesty and ethical standards" of various people and professions as well as on their trust in a variety of institutions. In fact, doctors do not fare badly at all. In terms of honesty, 58 percent of the public gives them very high or high marks, a figure which has not changed much over time. The percentage is very much below nurses (73 percent), druggists (69 percent) and veterinarians (58 percent), but higher than clergy (56 percent), and much much higher than journalists (24 percent), Senators (17 percent), lawyers (13 percent), Congressman (11 percent) and HMO managers (10 percent). (The bottom of the list, of course is car salesmen at 8 percent) (Newport, 2000).

We still do not know how Congress will finally resolve the provisions for such a bill. But the salient issues are quite different than those that arose in the 70s—not only because fee-for-service did not provoke many of these issues but because patients are truly into the nitty gritty of health care. Patient autonomy now means the right to experimental drug protocols, external review for complaints, full disclosure of treatment options—the sorts of things that active consumers would want to have, quite apart from improving their status in an HMO.

III

Let us close with a brief effort to estimate the influence back on society from the patient rights movement. What has it contributed to the common weal? It is not an easy question to address except by being highly impressionist—how separate out this one influence from all others? But two points may be suggested. First, the patient rights movement may well have encouraged a more general suspicion of expertise. If we can question our doctors, who is immune from our queries? If we can master the intricacies of probabilistic thinking about outcomes, and ones that are deeply personal, in the area of medicine, why not in other areas? In this sense, the patient rights movement is highly democratizing, removing, as it were, the hallow around the expert and giving encouragement to the laymen. It may also be anti-regulatory, in the sense of fostering the idea that government is not needed to police and protect citizens from harms. Let us choose our health food supplements without interference from the FDA; we can manage quite well without the heavy hand of Washington. Indeed, we can function quite well without the heavy hand of the Institutional Review Board governing human experimentation.

Second, the patient rights movement undoubtedly has had a negative impact on efforts to allocate medical resources more equitably, namely, on efforts to implement anything approximating national health insurance. Trained to inquire and demand, active patients are not about to allow a government plan, or an HMO plan, to deny them access to proven or quasi-proven effective therapies. What ultimately killed the Clinton health care initiative was the fact that it was defined as a rationing plan. And what is likely to kill any sustained future effort to control health care costs—an obvious prerequisite for national health insurance—is the same abhorrence of rationing. From the consumer perspective, having mastered the literature, there is no denying the fruits of knowledge, whatever the larger consequences to others in the society (Rothman, 1997).

None of this should lead us back to a simplistic communitarianism, or drive an anti-patient rights movement. At a time when managed care is still in ascendancy and the pros and cons of various medical interventions very much in question, engaged consumers are more vital than ever. But even their best friends must concede that the tension between individual assertions of self-interest are going to stand in the way of necessary collective action, with health care delivery as the best case in point.

All that one can ultimately say is that we have arrived at a central dilemma in American society, of which medicine is one, but only one, man-

ifestation. In the end, as with so many other things, for better or for worse, Americans are getting the health care system they deserve.

References

Boston Women's Health Book Collective (1973) *Our Bodies, Ourselves; A Book for and by Women.* New York: Simon and Schuster.

Faden, R. and Beauchamp, T. (1986) *A History and Theory of Informed Consent* (chapters 2, 4 and 8). New York: Oxford University Press.

Filene, P. (1998) *In the Arms of Others: A Cultural History of the Right-to-Die in America.* Chicago: Ivan R. Dee Publishers.

Gaylin, W. et al. (1978) *Doing Good: The Limits of Benevolence* (chapter 3). New York: Pantheon Books.

Hollon, M. (1999) Direct-to-Consumer Marketing of Prescription Drugs: Creating Consumer Demand. *JAMA* 281(4), 382–384.

Holmer, A. (1999) Direct-to-Consumer Prescription Drug Advertising Builds Bridges between Patients and Physicians. *JAMA* 281(4), 380–382.

Minnesota Law Review 82(4), April 1988. See especially articles by Robert A. Burt, Patricia A. King and Leslie E. Wolf, and Susan M. Wolf.

Newport, Frank (Ed.) (2000) *Honesty/Ethics in Professions.* www.gallup.com/poll/indicators/indhnsty_ethcs.asp

Rothman, D. (1997) *Beginnings Count: The Technological Imperative in American Health Care.* New York: Oxford University Press.

Rothman, D. (1991) *Strangers at the Bedside: A History of how Law and Bioethics Transformed Medical Decision Making.* New York: Basic Books.

Schneider, C. (1998) *The Practice of Autonomy: Patients, Doctors, and Medical Decisions.* New York: Oxford University Press.

Terzian, T. (1999) Direct-to-Consumer Prescription Drug Advertising. *American Journal of Law and Medicine* 25, 149–167.

Winker, Margaret et.al. (2000) Guidelines for Medical and Health Information Sites on the Internet: Principles Governing AMA Web Sites. *JAMA* 283(12), 1600–1606.

Ian Shine, Administrator,[1] vs.
Jose Vega & another[2]
Massachusetts Supreme Judicial Court
Suffolk, January 8, 1999–April 29, 1999

MARSHALL, J. In this wrongful death case, we must resolve the conflict between the right of a competent adult to refuse medical treatment and the interest of a physician in preserving life without fear of liability. In 1990, an invasive procedure, intubation,[3] was forcibly performed on Catherine Shine (Catherine),[4] a life-long asthmatic in the midst of a severe asthma attack. Dr. Jose Vega, an emergency physician at Massachusetts General Hospital (MGH), initiated the intubation without Catherine's consent and over her repeated and vigorous objections. In 1993, Dr. Ian Shine, Catherine's father and the administrator of her estate, brought a multi-count complaint against Dr. Vega and MGH seeking damages for tortious conduct and the wrongful death of his daughter. He alleged that Catherine was traumatized by this painful experience, and that it led to her death two years later. On that occasion, Catherine again suffered a severe asthma attack but refused to go to a hospital because, it was claimed, she had developed an intense fear of hospitals. Her father alleged that Catherine's delay in seeking medical help was a substantial factor in causing her death.

I

At approximately 7 A.M. on Sunday, March 18, 1990, twenty-nine year old Catherine Shine arrived at the MGH emergency room seeking medical help for an asthma attack. Catherine had been asthmatic throughout most of her life, a condition she controlled through prescription medication. The daughter of a physician, Catherine had educated herself about her condition and was well informed about her illness. Her asthmatic attacks were characterized by rapid onset, followed by a rapid remission. She had never required intubation in the past.

Earlier that morning, Catherine had suffered a severe asthma attack at her sister Anna's apartment. Despite believing that her condition was improving after using her prescription inhaler, Catherine agreed with Anna's suggestion to go to MGH, but on the condition that she be administered only oxygen. After Anna received assurances from an MGH representative that Catherine would be treated with just oxygen, Catherine entered the MGH emergency department, accompanied by Anna.

Catherine initially was given a nebulizer, a mask placed over her mouth which delivered oxygen and medication. She complained to Anna that the medication was giving her a headache, removed the mask and indicated that she wished to leave the hospital. Catherine's behavior alarmed the nurse who was treating her. An arterial blood gas test, measuring the levels of oxygen and carbon dioxide in her blood, was drawn at approximately 7:15 A.M. The results, obtained at approximately 7:30 A.M., showed that Catherine was "very sick." Dr. Vega, the only emergency room attending physician on staff at MGH that morning, examined Catherine and concluded that she required intubation. Catherine resisted, and Dr. Vega initially agreed to try more conservative treatment with the oxygen mask. Catherine continued to disagree with the medical staff concerning her treatment.

Anna, frustrated by what she felt was a medical staff unwilling to listen to her sister, telephoned their father, Dr. Shine, who was in England. Dr. Shine had treated Catherine when she was a child and was familiar with Catherine's condition. Dr. Shine spoke to an MGH physician and told him[5] that Catherine was intelligent and "very well-informed" about her illness, and he urged the physician to listen to Catherine and to try to obtain her consent for any treatment. Dr. Vega testified that he told Dr. Shine that Catherine was in "the midst of an extremely severe asthma attack," and that he unsuccessfully had tried to avoid intubation. Dr. Vega testified that Dr. Shine asked him to wait until he flew to Boston before intubating Catherine. He also testified that he had made a "conscious decision" not to tell Catherine that her father had opposed intubation.

Anna returned to Catherine's room to find her in a "heated" argument with the MGH staff. Catherine's condition had improved somewhat, and she was able to talk and to breathe more easily. At approximately 7:40 A.M., during a moment when the doctors left Catherine and Anna alone together, Catherine told Anna to "run." They ran down the corridor to the emergency room exit doors, where they were forcibly apprehended by a physician and a security guard. Catherine was "walked back" to her room where Dr. Vega immediately ordered that she be placed in four-point restraints, in part because she had refused treatment and attempted to leave the emergency room.[6] Catherine and Anna were forcibly separated. Dr. Vega initiated the process of having Catherine intubated. At approximately 8 A.M., the results of a second blood gas test became available, showing that Catherine's condition had improved somewhat. Dr. Vega testified that the results, even if he had read them (he had not),

would not have changed his decision to intubate Catherine. At approximately 8:25 A.M., the intubation procedure commenced, approximately forty-five minutes after Catherine had been strapped in four-point restraints. Catherine never consented to this treatment. Dr. Vega testified that he never discussed with Catherine the risks and benefits of intubation. Neither Anna, who was still at the hospital, nor Dr. Shine was asked to consent to the intubation. Catherine was released from MGH the following day.

Catherine's family testified that she was traumatized by these events. She had nightmares, cried constantly, and was unable to return to work for several months. For the first time in her life, they said, she was obsessed about her medication and what she ate. Catherine became suspicious of physicians, and repeatedly "swore" she would never go to a hospital again. In July, 1992, Catherine suffered another severe asthma attack while at home with her fiancé and her brother. She did not want to go to a hospital. After she became unconscious, her brother called an ambulance. Despite two days of medical treatment at South Shore Hospital, she died.

II

Dr. Shine's central claim both at trial and on appeal is that Dr. Vega and MGH wrongfully restrained and intubated Catherine without her consent. He sought to show that Catherine's mental abilities at the relevant times were not impaired, and that she was not facing a life-threatening emergency when she was restrained and intubated.[7] The defense took the position that Dr. Vega was confronted with a life-threatening emergency, and Catherine's consent was not necessary.[8] On appeal they argue that a medical emergency operates as a limitation on the "abstract right" of a patient to refuse treatment, and that in this situation a doctor may override a patient's right to refuse treatment.[9] . . .

B

In *Norwood Hosp. v. Munoz,* 409 Mass. 116, 121 (1991), we considered in what circumstances a "competent individual may refuse medical treatment which is necessary to save that individual's life." We described in that case both the common law and constitutional bases for our recognition of the "right of a competent individual to refuse medical treatment." *Id.* at 122. See *Brophy v. New England Sinai Hosp., Inc.,* 398 Mass. 417, 430 (1986); *Superintendent of Belchertown State Sch. v. Saikewicz,* 373 Mass. 728, 739, 742 (1977) (right to refuse medical treatment is rooted in common-law jurisprudence and guaranteed through constitutional right to privacy); *Matter of Spring,* 380 Mass. 629, 634 (1980). We recognized that "[e]very competent adult has a right 'to [forgo] treatment, or even cure, if it entails what for [her] are intolerable consequences or risks however unwise [her] sense of values may be in the eyes of the medical profession.' " *Harnish v. Children's Hosp. Med. Ctr., supra* at 154, quoting *Wilkinson v. Vesey,* 110 R.I. 606, 624 (1972).

In *Norwood Hosp. v. Munoz, supra* at 122–123, we also described how the "right to bodily integrity" had developed through the doctrine of informed consent. See *Harnish v. Children's Hosp. Med. Ctr., supra.* Under that doctrine, "a physician has the duty to disclose to a competent adult 'sufficient information to enable the patient to make an informed judgment whether to give or withhold consent to a medical or surgical procedure.' " *Norwood Hosp. v. Munoz, supra* at 123, quoting *Harnish v. Children's Hosp. Med. Ctr., supra* at 154–155. We again stressed that it is "for the individual to decide whether a particular medical treatment is in [her] best interests," "whether that decision is wise or unwise," and that a patient's right to refuse medical treatment, after having been informed by her physician of the risks involved, is not undermined because the treatment involves "life-saving procedures."

Norwood Hosp. v. Munoz, supra, quoting *Lane v. Candura,* 6 Mass. App. Ct. 377, 383 (1978).

Dr. Vega and MGH concede that Catherine exercised her right to refuse medical treatment and never consented to intubation. But, they argue, Dr. Vega could override Catherine's wishes as long as he acted "appropriately and consistent with the standard of accepted medical practice" and "to save and preserve her life in an emergency situation." It was not necessary, they argue, to instruct the jury on a competent patient's right to refuse medical treatment because it was, in their words, "largely irrelevant" to the critical liability question—whether Catherine faced a life-threatening situation.

The emergency exception to the informed consent doctrine has been widely recognized and its component elements broadly described.[10] In *Matter of Spring,* 380 Mass. 629, 634 (1980), we held that "a competent person has a general right to refuse medical treatment in appropriate circumstances, to be determined by balance the individual interest against countervailing State interests, particularly the State interest in the preservation of life." We went on to say that "[u]nless there is an emergency or an overriding State interest, medical treatment of a competent patient without his consent is said to be a battery." *Id.* at 638. We did not elaborate on the requirements of the emergency exception to the informed consent doctrine because that issue was not presented. In *Canterbury v. Spence,* 464 F.2d 772 (D.C. Cir. 1972), a seminal case, the court explained that the emergency exception

"comes into play when the patient is unconscious or otherwise incapable of consenting, and harm from a failure to treat is imminent and outweighs any harm threatened by the proposed treatment. When a genuine emergency of that sort arises, it is settled that the impracticality of conferring with the patient dispenses with need for it. Even in situations of that character the physician should, as current law requires, attempt to secure a relative's consent if possible. But if time is too short to accommodate discussion, obviously the physician should proceed with the treatment."

Id. at 788–789. Consistent with other courts that have considered the issue, we recognize that the emergency-treatment exception cannot entirely subsume a patient's fundamental right to refuse medical treatment. The privilege does not and cannot override the refusal of treatment by a patient who is capable of providing consent. If the patient is competent, an emergency physician must obtain her consent before providing treatment, even if the physician is persuaded that without the treatment, the patient's life is threatened. . . . If the patient's consent cannot be obtained because the patient is unconscious or otherwise incapable of consenting, the emergency physician should seek the consent of a family member if time and circumstances permit. . . . If, and only if, the patient is unconscious or otherwise incapable of giving consent, and either time or circumstances do not permit the physician to obtain the consent of a family member, may the physician presume that the patient, if competent, would consent to life-saving medical treatment. . . . The "impracticality of conferring" with the patient or her family is an essential aspect of the emergency exception to the requirement that a physician obtain a patient's informed consent before proceeding with treatment. We are aware of no other court that has sanctioned the sweeping emergency privilege the defendants advocated here.

In the often chaotic setting of an emergency room, physicians and medical staff frequently must make split-second, life-saving decisions. Emergency medical personnel may not have the time necessary to obtain the consent of a family member when a patient is incapable of consenting without jeopardizing the well-being of the patient. But a competent patient's refusal to consent to medical treatment cannot be overridden because the patient faces a life-threatening situation.

To determine whether an "emergency" existed sufficient to insulate Dr. Vega and MGH from all tort liability, the jury should have been required to decide whether Catherine was capable of consenting to treatment, and, if not, whether the consent of a family member could have been obtained. It is up to the jury to determine whether the treating physician took sufficient steps, given all of the circumstances, to obtain either the patient's informed consent, or the consent of a family member. In this case the judge's charge foreclosed the jury from making those necessary determinations. The instructions were repeated several times by the judge. She asked the jury to consider first whether Catherine's life was threatened. If the jury answered that question affirmatively, the jury, in essence, were instructed to go no further. The jury instructions concerning assault and battery and false imprisonment were erroneous for the same reason: they were premised on the theory that, despite Catherine's refusal of treatment, the defendants were absolved of all liability if the jury determined that Catherine faced a life-threatening situation. On this record, there is no basis on which to conclude that the error was not prejudicial. A new trial is required.

IV

The judgment is vacated and the case is remanded to the Superior Court for a new trial.

So ordered.

Notes

1. Of the estate of Catherine Shine.
2. Massachusetts General Hospital.
3. Intubation is a procedure by which a tube is inserted through either the nose or the mouth into the windpipe. The tube enables oxygen to be delivered directly into the lungs, typically by means of a ventilator.
4. We use Catherine's first name to distinguish her from her sister, Anna Shine (Anna).

5. There was conflicting testimony concerning which MGH physician spoke to Dr. Shine, and whether the conversation occurred before or after Catherine was restrained. Dr. Shine testified that he spoke to an emergency room physician but that he did not believe it was Dr. Vega. Dr. Vega testified that he spoke to Dr. Shine that morning. For purposes of our decision, the conflicts are not material.

6. Dr. Vega testified that Catherine's patient chart contained the reason for her forcible restraint: "Patient became more confused and combative, refusing treatment and suddenly ran down the hallway and nearly out of the [emergency ward] and brought back."

7. Expert witnesses for Dr. Shine testified that the intubation procedure was not an appropriate treatment for Catherine, that MGH medical staff failed properly to evaluate Catherine's competency to consent to treatment, and that failure to comply with unwanted treatment does not necessarily indicate lack of competence. The plaintiff's experts also testified that the situation was not an emergency, that Catherine was able to make rational decisions, and that intubation should be used only if absolutely necessary because the patient may develop fear of future intubation. There was also expert testimony that Catherine's treatment at MGH was below the appropriate standard of care because no determination of her competence was made, and that, if she was incompetent, the treating physician should have but did not seek consent from her family.

8. Several experts testified on behalf of the defendants that the actions of the MGH staff were ap-propriate, that if Catherine had been given only oxygen, as she requested, she likely would have died, and that Catherine's treatment at MGH was not the type of experience that could produce posttraumatic stress disorder.

9. In a nonemergency setting, the right of an incompetent patient to consent to or to refuse medical treatment is protected by a judicial, "substituted-judgment" proceeding. *Rogers v. Commissioner of the Dep't of Mental Health,* 390 Mass. 489, 504 (1983). The medical best interest of the patient is not the touchstone of a substituted judgment decision. Rather, the determination is " 'that which would be made by the incompetent person, if that person were competent' . . . and giving 'the fullest possible expression to the character and circumstances of that individual.' " *Id.* at 500, quoting *Superintendent of Belchertown State Sch. v. Saikewicz,* 373 Mass. 728, 747, 752–753 (1977).

10. The requirements of the exception or privilege are:

> "(a) the patient must be unconscious or without capacity to make a decision, while no one legally authorized to act as agent for the patient is available; (b) time must be of the essence, in the sense that it must reasonably appear that delay until such time as an effective consent could be obtained would subject the patient to a risk of a serious bodily injury or death which prompt action would avoid; and [c] under the circumstances, a reasonable person would consent, and the probabilities are that the patient would consent." W.L. Prosser & W.P. Keeton, Torts § 18, at 117 (5th ed. 1984).

"Culture of Life" Politics at the Bedside—
The Case of Terri Schiavo

GEORGE J. ANNAS, J.D., M.P.H.

For the first time in the history of the United States, Congress met in a special emergency session on Sunday, March 20, to pass legislation aimed at the medical care of one patient—Terri Schiavo. President George W. Bush encouraged the legislation and flew back to Washington, D.C., from his vacation in Crawford, Texas, so that he could be on hand to sign it immediately. In a statement issued three days earlier, he said: "The case of Terri Schiavo raises complex issues. . . . Those who live at the mercy of others deserve our special care and concern. It should be our goal as a nation to build a culture of life, where all Americans are valued, welcomed, and protected—and that culture of life must extend to individuals with disabilities."[1]

The "culture of life" is a not-terribly-subtle reference to the antiabortion movement in the United States, which received significant encouragement in last year's presidential election. The movement may now view itself as strong enough to generate new laws to prevent human embryos from being created for research and to require that incompetent patients be kept alive with artificially delivered fluids and nutrition.

How did the U.S. Congress conclude that it was appropriate to attempt to reopen a case that had finally been concluded after more than seven years of litigation involving almost 20 judges? Has the country's culture changed so dramatically as to require a fundamental change in the law? Or do patients who cannot continue to live without artificially delivered fluids and nutrition pose previously unrecognized or novel questions of law and ethics?

The case of Terri Schiavo, a Florida woman who was in a persistent vegetative state and who

died on March 31, was being played out as a public spectacle and a tragedy for her and her husband, Michael Schiavo. Mr. Schiavo's private feud with his wife's parents over the continued use of a feeding tube was taken to the media, the courts, the Florida legislature, Florida Governor Jeb Bush, the U.S. Congress, and President Bush. Since Ms. Schiavo was in a medical and legal situation almost identical to those of two of the most well-known patients in medical jurisprudence, Karen Ann Quinlan and Nancy Cruzan, there must be something about cases like theirs that defies simple solutions, whether medical or legal. In this sense, the case of Terri Schiavo provides an opportunity to examine issues that most lawyers, bio-ethicists, and physicians believed were well settled—if not since the 1976 New Jersey Supreme Court decision in the case of Karen Quinlan, then at least since the 1990 U.S. Supreme Court decision in the case of Nancy Cruzan. Before reviewing Terri Schiavo's case, it is well worth reviewing the legal background information that was ignored by Congress and the President.

The Case of Karen Quinlan

In 1976, the case of Karen Quinlan made international headlines when her parents sought the assistance of a judge to discontinue the use of a ventilator in their daughter, who was in a persistent vegetative state.[2] Ms. Quinlan's physicians had refused her parents' request to remove the ventilator because, they said, they feared that they might be held civilly or even criminally liable for her death. The New Jersey Supreme Court ruled that competent persons have a right to refuse life-sustaining treatment and that this right should not be lost when a person becomes incompetent. Since the court believed that the physicians were unwilling to withdraw the ventilator because of the fear of legal liability, not precepts of medical ethics, it devised a mechanism to grant the physicians prospective legal immunity for taking this action. Specifically, the New Jersey Supreme Court ruled that after a prognosis, confirmed by a hospital ethics committee, that there is "no reasonable possibility of a patient returning to a cognitive, sapient state," life-sustaining treatment can be removed and no one involved, including the physicians, can be held civilly or criminally responsible for the death.[2]

The publicity surrounding the Quinlan case motivated two independent developments: it encouraged states to enact "living will" legislation that provided legal immunity to physicians who honored patients' written "advance directives" specifying how they would want to be treated if they ever became incompetent; and it encouraged hospitals to establish ethics committees that could attempt to resolve similar treatment disputes without going to court.

The Case of Nancy Cruzan

Although *Quinlan* was widely followed, the New Jersey Supreme Court could make law only for New Jersey. When the U.S. Supreme Court decided the case of Nancy Cruzan in 1990, it made constitutional law for the entire country. Nancy Cruzan was a young woman in a persistent vegetative state caused by an accident; she was in physical circumstances essentially identical to those of Karen Quinlan, except that she was not dependent on a ventilator but rather, like Terri Schiavo, required only tube feeding to continue to live.[3] The Missouri Supreme Court had ruled that the tube feeding could be discontinued on the basis of Nancy's right of self-determination, but that only Nancy herself should be able to make this decision. Since she could not do so, tube feeding could be stopped only if those speaking for her, including her parents, could produce "clear and convincing" evidence that she would refuse tube feeding if she could speak for herself.[4]

The U.S. Supreme Court, in a five-to-four decision, agreed, saying that the state of Missouri had the authority to adopt this high standard of evidence (although no state was required to do so) because of the finality of a decision to terminate treatment.[3] In the words of the chief justice, Missouri was entitled to "err on the side of life." Six of the nine justices explicitly found that no legal distinction could be made between artificially delivered fluids and nutrition and other medical interventions, such as ventilator support; none of the other three justices found a constitutionally relevant distinction. This issue is not controversial as a matter of constitutional law: Americans have (and have always had) the legal right to refuse any medical intervention, including artificially delivered fluids and nutrition.

Supreme Court Justice Sandra Day O'Connor, in a concurring opinion (her vote decided the case), recognized that young people (such as Karen Quinlan, Nancy Cruzan, and now Terri Schiavo—all of whom were in their 20s at the time of their catastrophic injuries) do not generally put explicit treatment instructions in writing. She suggested that had Cruzan simply said something like "if I'm not able to make medical treatment decisions myself, I want my mother to make them," such a statement should be a constitutionally protected delegation of the authority to decide about her treatment.[3] O'Connor's opinion was the reason that the Cruzan case energized a movement—encouraging people to use the appropriate documents, such as health care proxy forms or assignments of durable power of attorney, to designate someone (usually called a health care proxy, or simply an agent) to make decisions for them if they are unable to make them themselves. All states authorize this delegation, and most states explicitly grant decision-making authority to a close relative—almost always to the spouse first—if the patient has not made a designation. Such laws are all to the good.

The Schiavo Case in the Courts

Terri Schiavo had a cardiac arrest, perhaps because of a potassium imbalance, in 1990 (the year *Cruzan* was decided), when she was 27 years old. Until her death in 2005, she had lived in a persistent vegetative state in nursing homes, with constant care, being nourished and hydrated through tubes. In 1998, Michael Schiavo petitioned the court to decide whether to discontinue the tube feeding. Unlike *Quinlan* and *Cruzan*, however, the Schiavo case involved a family dispute: Ms. Schiavo's parents objected. A judge found that there was clear and convincing evidence that Terri Schiavo was in a permanent or persistent vegetative state and that, if she could make her own decision, she would choose to discontinue life-prolonging procedures. An appeals court affirmed the first judge's decision, and the Florida Supreme Court declined to review it.

Schiavo's parents returned to court, claiming that they had newly discovered evidence. After an additional appeal, the parents were permitted to challenge the original court findings on the basis of new evidence related to a new treatment that they believed might restore cognitive function. Five physicians were asked to examine Ms. Schiavo—two chosen by the husband, two by the parents, and one by the court. On the basis of their examinations and conclusions, the trial judge was persuaded by the three experts who agreed that Schiavo was in a persistent vegetative state. The appeals court affirmed the original decision of the trial court judge:

> Despite the irrefutable evidence that [Schiavo's] cerebral cortex has sustained irreparable injuries, we understand why a parent who had raised and nurtured a child from conception would hold out hope that some level of cognitive function remained. If Mrs. Schiavo were our own daughter, we could not hold to such faith.
>
> But in the end this case is not about the aspirations that loving parents have for their children. It is about Theresa Schiavo's right to make her own

decision, independent of her parents and independent of her husband. . . . It may be unfortunate that when families cannot agree, the best forum we can offer for this private, personal decision is a public courtroom and the best decision-maker we can provide is a judge with no prior knowledge of the ward, but the law currently provides no better solution that adequately protects the interests of promoting the value of life.[5]

The Supreme Court of Florida again refused to hear an appeal.

Subsequently, the parents, with the vocal and organized support of conservative religious organizations, went to the state legislature seeking legislation requiring the reinsertion of Ms. Schiavo's feeding tube, which had been removed on the basis of the court decisions.[6,7] The legislature passed a new law (2003-418), often referred to as "Terri's Law," which gave Governor Jeb Bush the authority to order the feeding tube reinserted, and he did so. The law applied only to a patient who met the following criteria on October 15, 2003—in other words, only to Terri Schiavo:

(a) That patient has no written advance directive;
(b) The court has found that patient to be in a persistent vegetative state;
(c) That patient has had nutrition and hydration withheld; and
(d) A member of that patient's family has challenged the withholding of nutrition and hydration.

The constitutionality of this law was immediately challenged. In the fall of 2004, the Florida Supreme Court ruled that the law was unconstitutional because it violates the separation of powers—the division of the government into three branches (executive, legislative, and judicial), each with its own powers and responsibilities.[8] The doctrine states simply that no branch may encroach on the powers of another, and no branch may delegate to another branch its constitutionally assigned power. Specifically, the court held that for the legislature to pass a law that permits the executive to "interfere with the final judicial determination in a case" is "without question an invasion of the authority of the judicial branch."[8] In addition, the court found the law unconstitutional for an independent reason, because it "delegates legislative power to the governor" by giving the governor "unbridled discretion" to make a decision about a citizen's constitutional rights. In the court's words:

> If the Legislature with the assent of the Governor can do what was attempted here, the judicial branch would be subordinated to the final directive of the other branches. Also subordinated would be the rights of individuals, including the well established privacy right to self determination.... Vested rights could be stripped away based on popular clamor.[8]

In January 2005, the U.S. Supreme Court refused to hear an appeal brought by Governor Bush. Thereafter, the trial court judge ordered that the feeding tube be removed in 30 days (at 1 p.m., Friday, March 18) unless a higher court again intervened. The presiding judge, George W. Greer of the Pinellas County Circuit Court, was thereafter picketed and threatened with death; he has had to be accompanied by armed guards at all times.

Ms. Schiavo's parents, again with the aid of a variety of religious fundamentalist and "right to life" organizations, sought review in the appeals courts, a new statute in the state legislature, and finally, congressional intervention. Both the trial judge and the appeals courts refused to reopen the case on the basis of claims of new evidence (including the statement from Pope John Paul II regarding fluids and nutrition[9]) or the failure to appoint an independent lawyer for her at the original hearing. In Florida, the state legislature considered, and the House passed, new legislation aimed at restoring the feeding tube, but the Florida Senate—recognizing, I think, that this new legislation would be unconstitutional for the same reason as the previous legislation was—ultimately refused to approve the bill. Thereupon, an event unique in American politics occurred: after more than a week of discussion, and after formally declaring their Easter recess without action, Con-

gress reconvened two days after the feeding tube was removed to consider emergency legislation designed to apply only to Terri Schiavo.

Congress at the Bedside

Under rules that permitted a few senators to act if no senator objected, the U.S. Senate adopted a bill entitled "For the relief of the parents of Theresa Marie Schiavo" on March 20, 2005. The House, a majority of whose members had to be present to vote, debated the same measure from 9 p.m. to midnight on the same day and passed it by a four-to-one margin shortly after midnight on March 21. The President then signed it into law. In substance, the new law (S. 686) provides that "the U.S. District Court for the Middle District of Florida shall have jurisdiction" to hear a suit "for the alleged violation of any right of Theresa Marie Schiavo under the Constitution or laws of the United States relating to the withholding or withdrawal of food, fluids, or medical treatment necessary to sustain her life." The parents "have standing" to bring the lawsuit (the federal court had previously refused to hear the case on the basis that the parents had no standing to bring it), and the court is instructed to "determine de novo any claim of a violation of any right of Theresa Marie Schiavo . . . notwithstanding any prior State court determination . . ."— that is, to pretend that no court has made any prior ruling in the case. The act is to provide no "precedent with respect to future legislation."

The brief debate on this bill in the House of Representatives (there were no hearings in either chamber and no debate at all in the U.S. Senate) was notable primarily for its uninformed and frenzied rhetoric. It was covered live by C-SPAN. The primary sponsor of the measure, Congressman Thomas DeLay (R-Tex.), for example, asserted that "She's not a vegetable, just handicapped like many millions of people walking around today. This has nothing to do with politics, and it's disgusting for people to say that it does." Others echoed the sentiments of Senate majority leader and physician Bill Frist (R-Tenn.), who said that immediate action was imperative because "Terri Schiavo is being denied life-saving fluids and nutrition as we speak."

Other physician-members of the House chimed in. Congressman Dave Weldon (R-Fla.) remarked that, on the basis of his 16 years of medical practice, he was able to conclude that Terri Schiavo is "not in a persistent vegetative state." Congressman Phil Gingrey (R-Ga.) agreed, saying "she's very much alive." Another physician, Congressman Joe Schwarz (R-Mich.), who was a head and neck surgeon for 27 years, opined that "she does have some cognitive ability" and asked, "How many other patients are there with feeding tubes? Should they be removed too?" Another physician-congressman, Tom Price (R-Ga.), thought the law was reasonable because there was "no living will in place" and the family and experts disagreed. The only physician who was troubled by Congress's public diagnosis and treatment of Terri Schiavo was James McDermott (D-Wash.), who chided his physician-colleagues for the poor medical practice of making a diagnosis without examining the patient.

Although he deferred to the medical expertise of his congressional colleagues with M.D. degrees, Congressman Barney Frank (D-Mass.) pointed out that the chamber was not filled with physicians. Frank said of the March 20 proceedings: "We're not doctors, we just play them on C-SPAN." The mantras of the debate were that in a life-or-death decision, we should err on the "side of life," that action should be taken to "prevent death by starvation" and ensure the "right to life," and that Congress should "protect the rights of disabled people."

The following day, U.S. District Court Judge James D. Whittemore issued a careful opinion denying the request of the parents for a temporary restraining order that would require the reinsertion of the feeding tube.[10] The judge concluded that the parents had failed to demonstrate "a substantial likelihood of success on the merits" of the case—a prerequisite for a temporary restraining order. Specifically, Judge Whittemore found that, as to the various due-process claims made, the case had been "exhaustively litigated"; that, throughout, all parties had been "represented by able counsel"; and that it was not clear how having an additional lawyer "appointed by the court [for Ms. Schiavo] would have reduced the risk of erroneous rulings." As to the allegation that the patient's First Amendment rights to practice her religion had been violated by the state, the court held that there were no state actions involved at all, "because neither Defendant Schiavo nor Defendant Hospice are state actors."

Whittemore's decision was reasonable and consistent with settled law, and was, not surprisingly, upheld on appeal. The case of Terri Schiavo resulted in no changes in the law, nor were any good arguments made that legal changes were necessary. The religious right and Congressional Republicans may nonetheless attempt to use this decision to their advantage. Despite the fact that Congress itself sent the case to federal court for determination, some Republicans have already begun to cite the ruling as yet another example of "legislating" by the courts. For they liken the action permitted—the withdrawal of a feeding tube—to unfavored activities, such as abortion and same-sex marriage, that courts have allowed to occur. All three activities, they argue, represent attacks on the "culture of life" and necessitate that the President appoint federal court judges who value life over liberty.

Proxy Decision Makers, Persistent Vegetative States, and Death

A vast majority of Americans would not want to be maintained in a persistent vegetative state by means of a feeding tube, like Terri Schiavo and Nancy Cruzan.[11] The intense publicity generated by this case will cause many to discuss this issue with their families and, I hope, to sign an advance directive. Such a directive, in the form of a living will or the designation of a health care proxy, would prevent court involvement in virtually all cases—although it might not have solved the problem in the Schiavo case, because the family members disagreed about Terri Schiavo's medical condition and the acceptability of removing the tube in any circumstances.

Despite the impression that may have been created by these three cases, and especially by the grandstanding in Congress, conflicts involving medical decision making for incompetent patients near the end of life are no longer primarily legal in nature, if they ever were. The law has been remarkably stable since *Quinlan* (which itself restated existing law): competent adults have the right to refuse any medical treatment, including life-sustaining treatment (which includes artificially delivered fluids and nutrition). Incompetent adults retain an interest in self-determination. Competent adults can execute an advance directive stating their wishes and designate a person to act on their behalf, and physicians can honor these wishes. Physicians and health care agents should make treatment decisions consistent with what they believe the patient would want (the subjective standard). If the patient's desires cannot be ascertained, then treatment decisions should be based on the patient's best interests (what a reasonable person would most likely want in the same circumstances). This has, I believe, always been the law in the United States.[12]

Of course, legal forms or formalities cannot solve nonlegal problems. Decision making near the end of life is difficult and can exacerbate unresolved family feuds that then are played out at the patient's bedside and even in the media. Nonetheless, it is reasonable and responsible for all persons to designate health care agents to make treatment decisions for them when they are unable to make their own. After this recent congressional intervention, it also makes sense to specifically state one's wishes with respect to artificial fluids and hydration—and that one wants no politicians, even physician-politicians, involved in the process.

Most Americans will agree with a resolution that was overwhelmingly adopted by the California Medical Association on the same day that Congress passed the Schiavo law: "Resolved: That the California Medical Association expresses its outrage at Congress' interference with these medical decisions."

If there is disagreement between the physician and the family, or among family members, the involvement of outside experts, including consultants, ethics committees, risk managers, lawyers, and even courts, may become inevitable—at least if the patient survives long enough to permit such involvement. It is the long-lasting nature of the persistent vegetative state that results in its persistence in the courtrooms of the United States. There is (and should be) no special law regarding the refusal of treatment that is tailored to specific diseases or prognoses, and the persistent vegetative state is no exception.[13,14] Nor do feeding tubes have rights: people do. "Erring on the side of life" in this context often results in violating a person's body and human dignity in a way few would want for themselves. In such situations, erring on the side of liberty—specifically, the patient's right to decide on treatment—is more consistent with American values and our constitutional traditions. As the Massachusetts Supreme Judicial Court said in a 1977 case that raised the same legal question: "The constitutional right to privacy, as we conceive it, is an expression of the sanctity of individual free choice and self-determination as fundamental constituents of life. The value of life as so perceived is lessened not by a decision to refuse treatment, but by the failure to allow a competent human being the right of choice."[15]

From the Department of Health Law, Bioethics, and Human Rights, Boston University School of Public Health, Boston.

1. President's statement on Terri Schiavo. March 17, 2005. (Accessed March 31, 2005, at http://www.whitehouse.gov/news/releases/2005/03/20050317-7.html.)
2. In re Quinlan, 70 N.J.10, 355 A2d 647 (1976).
3. Cruzan v. Director, Missouri Dept. of Health, 497 U.S. 261 (1990).
4. Cruzan v. Harmon, 760 S.W.2d 408 (Mo. 1988).
5. In re Guardianship of Schiavo, 851 So. 2d 182 (Fla. 2d Dist. Ct.App. 2003).

6. Goodnough A. Victory in Florida feeding case emboldens the religious right. New York Times. October 24, 2005:A1.

7. Kirkpatrick DD, Stolberg SG. How family's cause reached the halls of Congress: networks of Christians rallied to case of Florida woman. New York Times. March 22, 2005:Al.

8. Bush v. Schiavo, 885 So.2d 321 (Fla. 2004).

9. Shannon TA, Walter JJ. Implications of the papal allocution on feeding tubes. Hastings Cent Rep 2004;34(4):18–20.

10. Schiavo ex rel. Schindler v. Schiavo, No. 8:05-CV-530-T-27TBM (M.D. Fla. Mar. 22, 2005) (slip opinion).

11. Eisenberg D. Lessons of the Schiavo battle. Time. April 4, 2005:23.

12. Annas GJ. The rights of hospital patients. New York: Discus Books, 1975:81–4.

13. *Idem.* The health care proxy and the living will. N Engl J Med 1991;324:1210–3.

14. The Multi-Society Task Force on PVS. Medical aspects of the persistent vegetative state. N Engl J Med 1994;330:1572–9. [Erratum, N Engl J Med 1995;333:130.]

15. Superintendent of Belchertown State School v. Saikewicz, 373 Mass. 728, 742, 370 N.E.2d 417 (Mass. 1977).

The Tragedy of the Commons

*The population problem has no technical solution;
it requires a fundamental extension in morality.*

Garrett Hardin

At the end of a thoughtful article on the future of nuclear war, Wiesner and York[1] concluded that: "Both sides in the arms race are . . . confronted by the dilemma of steadily increasing military power and steadily decreasing national security. *It is our considered professional judgment that this dilemma has no technical solution.* If the great powers continue to look for solutions in the area of science and technology only, the result will be to worsen the situation."

I would like to focus your attention not on the subject of the article (national security in a nuclear world) but on the kind of conclusion they reached, namely that there is no technical solution to the problem. An implicit and almost universal assumption of discussions published in professional and semipopular scientific journals is that the problem under discussion has a technical solution. A technical solution may be defined as one that requires a change only in the techniques of the natural sciences, demanding little or nothing in the way of change in human values or ideas of morality.

In our day (though not in earlier times) technical solutions are always welcome. Because of previous failures in prophecy, it takes courage to assert that a desired technical solution is not possible. Wiesner and York exhibited this courage; publishing in a science journal, they insisted that the solution to the problem was not to be found in the natural sciences. They cautiously qualified their statement with the phrase, "It is our considered professional judgment. . . ." Whether they were right or not is not the concern of the present article. Rather, the concern here is with the important concept of a class of human problems which can be called "no technical solution problems," and, more specifically, with the identification and discussion of one of these.

It is easy to show that the class is not a null class. Recall the game of tick-tack-toe. Consider the problem, "How can I win the game of tick-tack-toe?" It is well known that I cannot, if I assume (in keeping with the conventions of game theory) that my opponent understands the game perfectly. Put another way, there is no "technical solution" to the problem. I can win only by giving a radical meaning to the word "win." I can hit my opponent over the head; or I can drug him; or I can falsify the records. Every way in which I "win" involves, in some sense, an abandonment of the game, as we intuitively understand it. (I can also, of course, openly abandon the game—refuse to play it. This is what most adults do.)

The class of "No technical solution problems" has members. My thesis is that the "population problem," as conventionally conceived, is a member of this class. How it is conventionally conceived needs some comment. It is fair to say that most people who anguish over the population problem are trying to find a way to avoid the evils of over-population without relinquishing any of the privileges they now enjoy. They think that farming the seas or developing new strains of wheat will solve the problem—technologically. I try to show here that the solution they seek cannot be found. The population problem cannot be solved in a technical way, any more than can the problem of winning the game of tick-tack-toe.

What Shall We Maximize?

Population, as Malthus said, naturally tends to grow "geometrically," or, as we would now say, exponentially. In a finite world this means that the per capita share of the world's goods must steadily decrease. Is ours a finite world?

A fair defense can be put forward for the view that the world is infinite; or that we do not know that it is not. But, in terms of the practical problems that we must face in the next few generations with the foreseeable technology, it is clear that we will greatly increase human misery if we do not, during the immediate future, assume that the world available to the terrestrial human population is finite. "Space" is no escape[2].

A finite world can support only a finite population; therefore, population growth must eventually equal zero. (The case of perpetual wide fluctuations above and below zero is a trivial variant that need not be discussed.) When this condition is met, what will be the situation of mankind? Specifically, can Bentham's goal of "the greatest good for the greatest number" be realized?

No—for two reasons, each sufficient by itself. The first is a theoretical one. It is not mathematically possible to maximize for two (or more) variables at the same time. This was clearly stated by von Neumann and Morgenstern[3], but the principle is implicit in the theory of partial differential equations, dating back at least to D'Alembert (1717–1783).

The second reason springs directly from biological facts. To live, any organism must have a source of energy (for example, food). This energy is utilized for two purposes: mere maintenance and work. For man, maintenance of life requires about 1600 kilo-calories a day ("maintenance calories"). Anything that he does over and above merely staying alive will be defined as work, and is supported by "work calories" which he takes in. Work calories are used not only for what we call work in common speech; they are also required for all forms of enjoyment, from swimming and automobile racing to playing music and writing poetry. If our goal is to maximize population it is obvious what we must do: We must make the work calories per person approach as close to zero as possible. No gourmet meals, no vacations, no sports, no music, no literature, no art. . . . I think that everyone will grant, without argument or proof, that maximizing population does not maximize goods. Bentham's goal is impossible.

In reaching this conclusion I have made the usual assumption that it is the acquisition of energy that is the problem. The appearance of atomic energy has led some to question this assumption. However, given an infinite source of energy, population growth still produces an inescapable problem. The problem of the acquisition of energy is replaced by the problem of its dissipation, as J. H. Fremlin has so wittily shown[4]. The arithmetic signs in the analysis are, as it were, reversed; but Bentham's goal is still unobtainable.

The optimum population is, then, less than the maximum. The difficulty of defining the optimum is enormous; so far as I know, no one has seriously tackled this problem. Reaching an acceptable and stable solution will surely require more than one generation of hard analytical work—and much persuasion.

We want the maximum good per person; but what is good? To one person it is wilderness, to another it is ski lodges for thousands. To one it is estuaries to nourish ducks for hunters to shoot; to another it is factory land. Comparing one good with another is, we usually say, impossible because goods are incommensurable. Incommensurables cannot be compared.

Theoretically this may be true; but in real life incommensurables *are* commensurable. Only a criterion of judgment and a system of weighting are needed. In nature the criterion is survival. Is it better for a species to be small and hideable, or large and powerful? Natural selection commensurates the incommensurables. The compromise achieved depends on a natural weighting of the values of the variables.

Man must imitate this process. There is no doubt that in fact he already does, but unconsciously. It is when the hidden decisions are made explicit that the arguments begin. The problem for the years ahead is to work out an acceptable theory of weighting. Synergistic effects, nonlinear variation, and difficulties in discounting the future make the intellectual problem difficult, but not (in principle) insoluble.

Has any cultural group solved this practical problem at the present time, even on an intuitive level? One simple fact proves that none has: there is no prosperous population in the world today that has, and has had for some time, a growth rate of zero. Any people that has intuitively identified its optimum point will soon reach it, after which its growth rate becomes and remains zero.

Of course, a positive growth rate might be taken as evidence that a population is below its optimum. However, by any reasonable standards, the most rapidly growing populations on earth today are (in general) the most miserable. This association (which need not be invariable) casts doubt on the optimistic assumption that the positive growth rate of a population is evidence that it has yet to reach its optimum.

We can make little progress in working toward optimum poulation size until we explicitly exorcize the spirit of Adam Smith in the field of practical demography. In economic affairs, *The Wealth of Nations* (1776) popularized the "invisible hand," the idea that an individual who "intends only his own gain," is, as it were, "led by an invisible hand to promote . . . the public interest"[5]. Adam Smith did not assert that this was invariably true, and perhaps neither did any of his followers. But he contributed to a dominant tendency of thought that has ever since interfered with positive action based on rational analysis, namely, the tendency to assume that decisions reached individually will, in fact, be the best decisions for an entire society. If this assumption is correct it justifies the continuance of our present policy of laissez-faire in reproduction. If it is correct we can assume that men will control their individual fecundity so as to produce the optimum population. If the assumption is not correct, we need to reexamine our individual freedoms to see which ones are defensible.

Tragedy of Freedom in a Commons

The rebuttal to the invisible hand in population control is to be found in a scenario first sketched in a little-known pamphlet[6] in 1833 by a mathematical amateur named William Forster Lloyd (1794–1852). We may well call it "the tragedy of the commons," using the word "tragedy" as the philosopher Whitehead used it[7]: "The essence of dramatic tragedy is not unhappiness. It resides in the solemnity of the remorseless working of things." He their goes on to say, "This inevitableness of destiny can only be illustrated in terms of human life by incidents which in fact involve unhappiness. For it is only by them that the futility of escape can be made evident in the drama."

The tragedy of the commons develops in this way. Picture a pasture open to all. It is to be expected that each herdsman will try to keep as many cattle as possible on the commons. Such an arrangement may work reasonably satisfactorily for centuries because tribal wars, poaching, and disease keep the numbers of both man and beast well below the carrying capacity of the land. Finally, however, comes the day of reckoning, that is, the day when the long-desired goal of social stability becomes a reality. At this point, the inherent logic of the commons remorselessly generates tragedy.

As a rational being, each herdsman seeks to maximize his gain. Explicitly or implicitly, more or less consciously, he asks, "What is the utility *to me* of adding one more animal to my herd?" This utility has one negative and one positive component.

1) The positive component is a function of the increment of one animal. Since the herdsman receives all the proceeds from the sale of the additional animal, the positive utility is nearly +1.

2) The negative component is a function of the additional overgrazing created by one more animal. Since, however, the effects of overgrazing are shared by all the herdsmen, the negative utility for any particular decision-making herdsman is only a fraction of −1.

Adding together the component partial utilities, the rational herdsman concludes that the only sensible course for him to pursue is to add another animal to his herd. And another; and another. . . . But this is the conclusion reached by each and every rational herdsman sharing a commons. Therein is the tragedy. Each man is locked into a system that compels him to increase his herd without limit—in a world that is limited. Ruin is the destination toward which all men rush, each pursuing his own best interest in a society that believes in the freedom of the commons. Freedom in a commons brings ruin to all.

Some would say that this is a platitude. Would that it were! In a sense, it was learned thousands of years ago, but natural selection favors the forces of psychological denial[8]. The individual benefits as an individual from his ability to deny the truth even though society as a whole, of which he is a part, suffers. Education can counteract the natural tendency to do the wrong thing, but the inexorable succession of generations requires that the basis for this knowledge be constantly refreshed.

A simple incident that occurred a few years ago in Leominster, Massachusetts, shows how perishable the knowledge is. During the Christmas shopping season the parking meters downtown were covered with plastic bags that bore tags reading: "Do not open until after Christmas. Free parking courtesy of the mayor and city council." In other words, facing the prospect of an increased demand for already scarce space, the city fathers reinstituted the system of the commons. (Cynically, we suspect that they gained more votes than they lost by this retrogressive act.)

In an approximate way, the logic of the commons has been understood for a long time, perhaps since the discovery of agriculture or the invention of private property in real estate. But it is understood mostly only in special cases which are not sufficiently generalized. Even at this late date, cattlemen leasing national land on the western ranges demonstrate no more than an ambivalent understanding, in constantly pressuring federal authorities to increase the head count to the point where overgrazing produces erosion and weed-dominance. Likewise, the oceans of the world continue to suffer from the survival of the philosophy of the commons. Maritime nations still respond automatically to the shibboleth of the "freedom of the seas." Professing to believe in the "inexhaustible resources of the oceans," they bring species after species of fish and whales closer to extinction[9].

The National Parks present another instance of the working out of the tragedy of the commons. At present, they are open to all, without limit. The parks themselves are limited in extent—there is only one Yosemite Valley—whereas population seems to grow without limit. The values that visitors seek in the parks are steadily eroded. Plainly, we must soon cease to treat the parks as commons or they will be of no value to anyone.

What shall we do? We have several options. We might sell them off as private property. We might keep them as public property, but allocate the right to enter them. The allocation might be on the basis of wealth, by the use of an auction system. It might be on the basis of merit, as defined by some agreed-upon standards. It might be by lottery. Or it might be on a first-come, first-served basis, administered to long queues. These, I think, are all the reasonable possibilities. They are all objectionable. But we must choose—or acquiesce in the destruction of the commons that we call our National Parks.

Pollution

In a reverse way, the tragedy of the commons reappears in problems of pollution. Here it is not a question of taking something out of the commons, but of putting something in—sewage, or chemical, radioactive, and heat wastes into water; noxious and dangerous fumes into the air; and distracting and unpleasant advertising signs into the line of sight. The calculations of utility are much the same as

before. The rational man finds that his share of the cost of the wastes he discharges into the commons is less than the cost of purifying his wastes before releasing them. Since this is true for everyone, we are locked into a system of "fouling our own nest," so long as we behave only as independent, rational, free-enterprisers.

The tragedy of the commons as a food basket is averted by private property, or something formally like it. But the air and waters surrounding us cannot readily be fenced, and so the tragedy of the commons as a cesspool must be prevented by different means, by coercive laws or taxing devices that make it cheaper for the polluter to treat his pollutants than to discharge them untreated. We have not progressed as far with the solution of this problem as we have with the first. Indeed, our particular concept of private property, which deters us from exhausting the positive resources of the earth, favors pollution. The owner of a factory on the bank of a stream—whose property extends to the middle of the stream—often has difficulty seeing why it is not his natural right to muddy the waters flowing past his door. The law, always behind the times, requires elaborate stitching and fitting to adapt it to this newly perceived aspect of the commons.

The pollution problem is a consequence of population. It did not much matter how a lonely American frontiersman disposed of his waste. "Flowing water purifies itself every 10 miles," my grandfather used to say, and the myth was near enough to the truth when he was a boy, for there were not too many people. But as population became denser, the natural chemical and biological recycling processes became overloaded, calling for a redefinition of property rights.

How to Legislate Temperance?

Analysis of the pollution problem as a function of population density uncovers a not generally recognized principle of morality, namely: *the morality of an act is a function of the state of the system at the time it is performed*[10]. Using the commons as a cesspool does not harm the general public under frontier conditions, because there is no public; the same behavior in a metropolis is unbearable. A hundred and fifty years ago a plainsman could kill an American bison, cut out only the tongue for his dinner, and discard the rest of the animal. He was not in any important sense being wasteful. Today, with only a few thousand bison left, we would be appalled at such behavior.

In passing, it is worth nothing that the morality of an act cannot be determined from a photograph. One does not know whether a man killing an elephant or setting fire to the grassland is harming others until one knows the total system in which his act appears. "One picture is worth a thousand words," said an ancient Chinese; but it may take 10,000 words to validate it. It is as tempting to ecologists as it is to reformers in general to try to persuade others by way of the photographic shortcut. But the essense of an argument cannot be photographed: it must be presented rationally—in words.

That morality is system-sensitive escaped the attention of most codifiers of ethics in the past. "Thou shalt not . . . " is the form of traditional ethical directives which make no allowance for particular circumstances. The laws of our society follow the pattern of ancient ethics, and therefore are poorly suited to governing a complex, crowded, changeable world. Our epicyclic solution is to augment statutory law with administrative law. Since it is practically impossible to spell out all the conditions under which it is safe to burn trash in the back yard or to run an automobile without smog-control, by law we delegate the details to bureaus. The result is administrative law, which is rightly feared for an ancient reason—*Quis custodiet ipsos custodes?*— "Who shall watch the watchers themselves?" John Adams said that we must have "a government of laws and not men." Bureau administrators, trying to evaluate the morality of acts in the total system, are singularly liable to corruption, producing a government by men, not laws.

Prohibition is easy to legislate (though not necessarily to enforce); but how do we legis-

late temperance? Experience indicates that it can be accomplished best through the mediation of administrative law. We limit possibilities unnecessarily if we suppose that the sentiment of *Quis custodiet* denies us the use of administrative law. We should rather retain the phrase as a perpetual reminder of fearful dangers we cannot avoid. The great challenge facing us now is to invent the corrective feedbacks that are needed to keep custodians honest. We must find ways to legitimate the needed authority of both the custodians and the corrective feedbacks.

Freedom to Breed Is Intolerable

The tragedy of the commons is involved in population problems in another way. In a world governed solely by the principle of "dog eat dog"—if indeed there ever was such a world—how many children a family had would not be a matter of public concern. Parents who bred too exuberantly would leave fewer descendants, not more, because they would be unable to care adequately for their children. David Lack and others have found that such a negative feedback demonstrably controls the fecundity of birds[11]. But men are not birds, and have not acted like them for millenniums, at least.

If each human family were dependent only on its own resources; *if* the children of improvident parents starved to death; *if*, thus, overbreeding brought its own "punishment" to the germ line—*then* there would be no public interest in controlling the breeding of families. But our society is deeply committed to the welfare state[12], and hence is confronted with another aspect of the tragedy of the commons.

In a welfare state, how shall we deal with the family, the religion, the race, or the class (or indeed any distinguishable and cohesive group) that adopts overbreeding as a policy to secure its own aggrandizement[13]? To couple the concept of freedom to breed with the belief that everyone born has an equal right to the commons is to lock the world into a tragic course of action.

Unfortunately this is just the course of action that is being pursued by the United Nations. In late 1967, some 30 nations agreed to the following[14]:

> The Universal Declaration of Human Rights describes the family as the natural and fundamental unit of society. It follows that any choice and decision with regard to the size of the family must irrevocably rest with the family itself, and cannot be made by anyone else.

It is painful to have to deny categorically the validity of this right; denying it, one feels as uncomfortable as a resident of Salem, Massachusetts, who denied the reality of witches in the 17th century. At the present time, in liberal quarters, something like a taboo acts to inhibit criticism of the United Nations. There is a feeling that the United Nations is "our last and best hope," that we shouldn't find fault with it; we shouldn't play into the hands of the archconservatives. However, let us not forget what Robert Louis Stevenson said: "The truth that is suppressed by friends is the readiest weapon of the enemy." If we love the truth we must openly deny the validity of the Universal Declaration of Human Rights, even though it is promoted by the United Nations. We should also join with Kingsley Davis[15] in attempting to get Planned Parenthood-World Population to see the error of its ways in embracing the same tragic ideal.

Conscience Is Self-Eliminating

It is a mistake to think that we can control the breeding of mankind in the long run by an appeal to conscience. Charles Galton Darwin made this point when he spoke on the centennial of the publication of his grandfather's great book. The argument is straightforward and Darwinian.

People vary. Confronted with appeals to limit breeding, some people will undoubtedly respond to the plea more than others. Those who have more children will produce a larger fraction of the next generation than those with more

susceptible consciences. The difference will be accentuated, generation by generation.

In C. G. Darwin's words: "It may well be that it would take hundreds of generations for the progenitive instinct to develop in this way, but if it should do so, nature would have taken her revenge, and the variety *Homo contracipiens* would become extinct and would be replaced by the variety *Homo progenitivus*"[16].

The argument assumes that conscience or the desire for children (no matter which) is hereditary—but hereditary only in the most general formal sense. The result will be the same whether the attitude is transmitted through germ cells, or exosomatically, to use A. J. Lotka's term. (If one denies the latter possibility as well as the former, then what's the point of education?) The argument has here been stated in the context of the population problem, but it applies equally well to any instance in which society appeals to an individual exploiting a commons to restrain himself for the general good—by means of his conscience. To make such an appeal is to set up a selective system that works toward the elimination of conscience from the race.

Pathogenic Effects of Conscience

The long-term disadvantage of an appeal to conscience should be enough to condemn it; but has serious short-term disadvantages as well. If we ask a man who is exploiting a commons to desist "in the name of conscience," what are we saying to him? What does he hear?—not only at the moment but also in the wee small hours of the night when, half asleep, he remembers not merely the words we used but also the nonverbal communication cues we gave him unawares? Sooner or later, consciously or subconsciously, he senses that he has received two communications, and that they are contradictory: (i) (intended communication) "If you don't do as we ask, we will openly condemn you for not acting like a responsible citizen"; (ii) (the unintended communication) "If you *do* behave as we ask, we will secretly condemn you for a simpleton who can be shamed into standing aside while the rest of us exploit the commons."

Everyman then is caught in what Bateson has called a "double bind." Bateson and his co-workers have made a plausible case for viewing the double bind as an important causative factor in the genesis of schizophrenia[17]. The double bind may not always be so damaging, but it always endangers the mental health of anyone to whom it is applied. "A bad conscience," said Nietzsche, "is a kind of illness."

To conjure up a conscience in others is tempting to anyone who wishes to extend his control beyond the legal limits. Leaders at the highest level succumb to this temptation. Has any President during the past generation failed to call on labor unions to moderate voluntarily their demands for higher wages, or to steel companies to honor voluntary guidelines on prices? I can recall none. The rhetoric used on such occasions is designed to produce feelings of guilt in noncooperators.

For centuries it was assumed without proof that guilt was a valuable, perhaps even an indispensable, ingredient of the civilized life. Now, in this post-Freudian world, we doubt it.

Paul Goodman speaks from the modern point of view when he says: "No good has ever come from feeling guilty, neither intelligence, policy, nor compassion. The guilty do not pay attention to the object but only to themselves, and not even to their own interests, which might make sense, but to their anxieties"[18].

One does not have to be a professional psychiatrist to see the consequences of anxiety. We in the Western world are just emerging from a dreadful two-centuries-long Dark Ages of Eros that was sustained partly by prohibition laws, but perhaps more effectively by the anxiety-generating mechanisms of education. Alex Comfort has told the story well in *The Anxiety Makers*[19]; it is not a pretty one.

Since proof is difficult, we may even concede that the results of anxiety may sometimes, from certain points of view, be desirable. The larger question we should ask is whether, as a matter of policy, we should ever encourage the use of a technique the tendency (if not the intention) of which is psychologically pathogenic. We hear much talk these days of responsible parenthood; the coupled words are incorporated into the titles of some organizations devoted to birth control. Some people have proposed massive propaganda campaigns to instill responsibility into the nation's (or the world's) breeders. But what is the meaning of the word responsibility in this context? Is it not merely a synonym for the word conscience? When we use the word responsibility in the absence of substantial sanctions are we not trying to browbeat a free man in a commons into acting against his own interest? Responsibility is a verbal counterfeit for a substantial *quid pro quo*. It is an attempt to get something for nothing.

If the word responsibility is to be used at all, I suggest that it be in the sense Charles Frankel uses it[20]. "Responsibility," says this philosopher, "is the product of definite social arrangements." Notice that Frankel calls for social arrangements—not propaganda.

Mutual Coercion Mutually Agreed Upon

The social arrangements that produce responsibility are arrangements that create coercion, of some sort. Consider bank-robbing. The man who takes money from a bank acts as if the bank were a commons. How do we prevent such action? Certainly not by trying to control his behavior solely by a verbal appeal to his sense of responsibility. Rather than rely on propaganda we follow Frankel's lead and insist that a bank is not a commons; we seek the definite social arrangements that will keep it from becoming a commons. That we thereby infringe on the freedom of would-be robbers we neither deny nor regret.

The morality of bank-robbing is particularly easy to understand because we accept complete prohibition of this activity. We are willing to say

"Thou shalt not rob banks," without providing for exceptions. But temperance also can be created by coercion. Taxing is a good coercive device. To keep downtown shoppers temperate in their use of parking space we introduce parking meters for short periods, and traffic fines for longer ones. We need not actually forbid a citizen to park as long as he wants to; we need merely make it increasingly expensive for him to do so. Not prohibition, but carefully biased options are what we offer him. A Madison Avenue man might call this persuasion; I prefer the greater candor of the word coercion.

Coercion is a dirty word to most liberals now, but it need not forever be so. As with the four-letter words, its dirtiness can be cleansed away by exposure to the light, by saying it over and over without apology or embarrassment. To many, the word coercion implies arbitrary decisions of distant and irresponsible bureaucrats; but this is not a necessary part of its meaning. The only kind of coercion I recommend is mutual coercion, mutually agreed upon by the majority of the people affected.

To say that we mutually agree to coercion is not to say that we are required to enjoy it, or even to pretend we enjoy it. Who enjoys taxes? We all grumble about them. But we accept compulsory taxes because we recognize that voluntary taxes would favor the conscienceless. We institute and (grumblingly) support taxes and other coercive devices to escape the horror of the commons.

An alternative to the commons need not be perfectly just to be preferable. With real estate and other material goods, the alternative we have chosen is the institution of private property coupled with legal inheritance. Is this system perfectly just? As a genetically trained biologist I deny that it is. It seems to me that, if there are to be differences in individual inheritance, legal possession should be perfectly correlated with biological inheritance—that those who are biologically more fit to be the custodians of property and power should legally inherit more. But

genetic recombination continually makes a mockery of the doctrine of "like father, like son" implicit in our laws of legal inheritance. An idiot can inherit millions, and a trust fund can keep his estate intact. We must admit that our legal system of private property plus inheritance is unjust—but we put up with it because we are not convinced, at the moment, that anyone has invented a better system. The alternative of the commons is too horrifying to contemplate. Injustice is preferable to total ruin.

It is one of the peculiarities of the warfare between reform and the status quo that it is thoughtlessly governed by a double standard. Whenever a reform measure is proposed it is often defeated when its opponents triumphantly discover a flaw in it. As Kingsley Davis has pointed out[21], worshippers of the status quo sometimes imply that no reform is possible without unanimous agreement, an implication contrary to historical fact. As nearly as I can make out, automatic rejection of proposed reforms is based on one of two unconscious assumptions: (i) that the status quo is perfect; or (ii) that the choice we face is between reform and no action; if the proposed reform is imperfect, we presumably should take no action at all, while we wait for a perfect proposal.

But we can never do nothing. That which we have done for thousands of years is also action. It also produces evils. Once we are aware that the status quo is action, we can then compare its discoverable advantages and disadvantages with the predicted advantages and disadvantages of the proposed reform, discounting as best we can for our lack of experience. On the basis of such a comparison, we can make a rational decision which will not involve the unworkable assumption that only perfect systems are tolerable.

Recognition of Necessity

Perhaps the simplest summary of this analysis of man's population problems is this: the commons, if justifiable at all, is justifiable only under conditions of low-population density. As the human population has increased, the commons has had to be abandoned in one aspect after another.

First we abandoned the commons in food gathering, enclosing farm land and restricting pastures and hunting and fishing areas. These restrictions are still not complete throughout the world.

Somewhat later we saw that the commons as a place for waste disposal would also have to be abandoned. Restrictions on the disposal of domestic sewage are widely accepted in the Western world; we are still struggling to close the commons to pollution by automobiles, factories, insecticide sprayers, fertilizing operations, and atomic energy installations.

In a still more embryonic state is our recognition of the evils of the commons in matters of pleasure. There is almost no restriction on the propagation of sound waves in the public medium. The shopping public is assaulted with mindless music, without its consent. Our government is paying out billions of dollars to create supersonic transport which will disturb 50,000 people for every one person who is whisked from coast to coast 3 hours faster. Advertisers muddy the airwaves of radio and television and pollute the view of travelers. We are a long way from out-lawing the commons in matters of pleasure. Is this because our Puritan inheritance makes us view pleasure as something of a sin, and pain (that is, the pollution of advertising) as the sign of virtue?

Every new enclosure of the commons involves the infringement of somebody's personal liberty. Infringements made in the distant past are accepted because no contemporary complains of a loss. It is the newly proposed infringements that we vigorously oppose; cries of "rights" and "freedom" fill the air. But what does "freedom" mean? When men mutually agreed to pass laws against robbing, mankind became more free, not less so. Individuals locked into the logic of the commons are free only to bring on universal ruin; once they see the necessity of mutual coercion, they become free to pursue other goals. I believe it was Hegel who said, "Freedom is the recognition of necessity."

The most important aspect of necessity that we must now recognize, is the necessity of abandoning the commons in breeding. No technical solution can rescue us from the misery of overpopulation. Freedom to breed will bring ruin to all. At the moment, to avoid hard decisions many of us are tempted to propagandize for conscience and responsible parenthood. The temptation must be resisted, because an appeal to independently acting consciences selects for the disappearance of all conscience in the long run, and an increase in anxiety in the short.

The only way we can preserve and nurture other and more precious freedoms is by relinquishing the freedom to breed, and that very soon. "Freedom is the recognition of necessity"—and it is the role of education to reveal to all the necessity of abandoning the freedom to breed. Only so, can we put an end to this aspect of the tragedy of the commons.

References

1. J. B. Wiesner and H. F. York, *Sci. Amer.* 211 (No. 4), 27 (1964).
2. G. Hardin, *J. Hered.* 50, 68 (1959); S. von Hoernor, *Science* 137, 18 (1962).
3. J. von Neumann and O. Morgenstern, *Theory of Games and Economic Behavior* (Princeton Univ. Press, Princeton, N.J., 1947), p. 11.
4. J. H. Fremlin, *New Sci.*, No. 415 (1964), p. 285.
5. A. Smith, *The Wealth of Nations* (Modern Library, New York, 1937), p. 423.
6. W. F. Lloyd, *Two Lectures on the Checks to Population* (Oxford Univ. Press, Oxford, England, 1833), reprinted (in part) in *Population, Evolution, and Birth Control*, G. Hardin, Ed. (Freeman, San Francisco, 1964), p. 37.
7. A. N. Whitehead, *Science and the Modern World* (Mentor, New York, 1948), p. 17.
8. G. Hardin, Ed. *Population, Evolution, and Birth Control* (Freeman, San Francisco, 1964), p. 56.

9. S. McVay, *Sci. Amer.* 216 (No. 8), 13 (1966).

10. J. Fletcher, *Situation Ethics* (Westminster, Philadelphia, 1966).

11. D. Lack, *The Natural Regulation of Animal Numbers* (Clarendon Press, Oxford, 1954).

12. H. Girvetz, *From Wealth to Welfare* (Stanford Univ. Press, Stanford, Calif., 1950).

13. G. Hardin, *Perspec. Biol. Med.* 6, 366 (1963).

14. U. Thant, *Int. Planned Parenthood News*, No. 168 (February 1968), p. 3.

15. K. Davis, *Science* 158, 730 (1967).

16. S. Tax, Ed., *Evolution after Darwin* (Univ. of Chicago Press, Chicago, 1960), vol. 2, p. 469.

17. G. Bateson, D. D. Jackson, J. Haley, J. Weakland, *Behav. Sci.* 1, 251 (1956).

18. P. Goodman, *New York Rev. Books* 10(8), 22 (23 May 1968).

19. A. Comfort, *The Anxiety Makers* (Nelson, London, 1967).

20. C. Frankel, *The Case for Modern Man* (Harper, New York, 1955), p. 203.

21. J. D. Roslansky, *Genetics and the Future of Man* (Appleton-Century-Crofts, New York, 1966), p. 177.

B. Individual Responsibility for the Health of Others

Autonomous persons are often viewed as self-determining. Because autonomy is prized, it has received special protection in our society. But even as ardent an advocate of autonomy as John Stuart Mill wouldn't claim that people are free to harm others. Under Mill's harm principle, individual conduct that harms other people may be subject to interference.[9] Hence, a person's right to an organ, for example, does not imply the right to take the organ of another without his or her consent. To do so would, of course, also violate the Kantian imperative against treating persons only as a means to an end. Surely, any social contract, hypothetical or otherwise, would include a prohibition against unconsented to intrusions of bodily integrity. Respect for an individual's autonomous health care choices does not entail permitting the individual to harm others.

It has long been recognized in law that government may limit the liberty of individuals to protect the welfare of the community (recall arguments for these limits discussed in the previous section). This principle, limiting individual liberty, was famously articulated by the Supreme Court in *Jacobson v. Massachusetts* when the Court upheld a law requiring an individual to be vaccinated against smallpox during an outbreak of the disease. Likewise, bans against indoor smoking have been justified on the ground that such smoke is injurious to others. How far does this principle extend?

Questions about limitations on autonomy, stemming from a duty to protect others, also arise in the context of positing a duty of pregnant women to protect their fetuses. It can be argued that mothers who put the health of their fetuses at risk through conduct such as smoking, drinking, narcotic use and perhaps high-risk sexual activity are morally wrong because they fail to protect their fetuses. Do pregnant women have a duty to their fetuses and do these fetuses have a corresponding claim on their "mothers" to refrain from engaging in conduct that puts the fetus

at risk? Even if we were to acknowledge that pregnant women have some responsibility to their fetuses, it is still important to explore the extent of the obligation and
whether the state also has an obligation to act in the fetus' interest even when doing
so is at odds with the mother's wishes. Are your views about the mother's obligation influenced by the fact that the fetus is not in a position to avoid the harm? Is
this different from the smoker's case? In either case, how confident need we be
about the claim that the individual's actions will harm another? And how much
harm must be at risk?

In two cases that we include here, In re *A.C.* and *Ferguson v. City of Charleston*,
we confront two different contexts in which the mother's desires appear to be at
odds with the fetus' health. In re *A.C.* a pregnant woman near death from cancer
appears to decide not to try to save the life of her fetus when she declines to consent to a cesarean section. Despite this, the surgery was performed. As you will
see from the opinion of the court of appeals, it is not clear that the surgeon's choice
in favor of the fetus was the morally right one. As you read the case, consider the
difficulty the judges had in determining the mother's authentic choice. Do you
agree with the final decision that the mother's wishes should prevail or do you
think that a balance should be struck between the mother's interests and the fetus'?
Was it easier for the appeals court to affirm the mother's autonomy given the fact
that the fetus had long died, and there was no life to save by the time it had decided
the case? What does the case say about the ability of courts to decide such issues
"at the bedside"?

In the *Ferguson* case we look at what steps may be taken to protect fetuses
from mothers who ingest illegal and potentially harmful substances, such as crack-
cocaine. In the case at hand, the Medical University of South Carolina cooperated
with the city in devising a hospital protocol for testing pregnant women suspected
of illicit drug use and, when illicit drugs were found in the newborn, using the diagnostic test on the mother for the purpose of prosecuting her. The Supreme Court
held that the hospital performed an unreasonable search and seizure in violation of
the Fourth Amendment when it tested pregnant women without their consent.
From an ethical point of view, consider whether testing high-risk mothers for the
presence of drug use is too great an intrusion into their autonomy, privacy, and liberty. If so, what steps could be ethically sanctioned as a means of protecting these
at-risk infants? Should the fact that an early study states that there is no convincing evidence of the harms of prenatal cocaine use given the inability to distinguish
them from exposure to other potential prenatal toxins influence the policy options?[10]
To what extent does the fact that the policy primarily was applied to poor, African
American women affect our understanding of the issues?

The obligation not to harm others would, at first glance, seem to require individuals in many cases, such as *Jacobson*, to take actions to protect others. But the
issue is not so clear-cut. Once we recognize that all of the people within a given interaction are autonomous, we may arrive at a rather counterintuitive conclusion.
Strict deference to individual autonomy, coupled with the harm principle, may lead

to the conclusion that individuals are surely responsible for themselves and may have no responsibility for others. For many, this may seem a harsh perspective when it is applied to the medical context. Although conceptually we can make sense of "rugged individuals," it is difficult to make much sense of a "rugged patient." The question about what obligations we have for the health of others has arisen in a number of different contexts.

In the late 1980s and early 1990s, when HIV/AIDS surfaced first within the gay community, the question was posed whether those who tested positive for HIV/AIDS had a duty to disclose their HIV status to potential sexual partners. Others asked whether there was also a duty to be tested for HIV. Perhaps surprisingly, many members of the gay community, and most gay organizations, maintained that within anonymous sexual encounters, the transmission of HIV/AIDS is primarily a harm to self.[11] According to this reasoning, when gay men knowingly engage in conduct that is at high risk for HIV (unprotected anal sex), they consent to the risk of HIV transmission. Given this and the practical likelihood that not all participants in anonymous sexual encounters will disclose honestly their HIV status if they know it, many organizations adopted what David Chambers calls the "Code of the Condom."[12] Basically this code states that provided gay men use condoms when they have anal sex, they are under no obligation to either be tested or to inform partners of their HIV status. Although this position can be defended on utilitarian grounds, as Patricia Illingworth does, it can also be supported on the view that individuals are under no moral obligation to protect others from harms to which they apparently consent.[13]

Others, however, including Amitai Etzioni and Ronald Bayer, believe that there is a moral obligation to inform partners if one tests positive for HIV. Etzioni, a communitarian, argues that this is a social obligation. In the reading Bayer, who is influenced by public health perspectives, contends that infected individuals have a responsibility to protect the uninfected. Indeed the deontological principle of beneficence advises us to minimize harms to others. Surely, when applied to the issue at hand, the principle of beneficence requires partners to disclose their HIV status. But it would be interesting to know whether those who support disclosure would do so even if it led to an increase in the number of people who contract the disease. Those who support the Code of the Condom do so at least partially because they believe that implementing this policy will reduce the rate of transmission of HIV. Some also believe, as Illingworth notes, that to disclose HIV status to partners who do not seek such information and who have consented to the minor risk inherent in protected anal sex is paternalistic and a violation of the principle "to one who consents, no harm is done."[14] Perhaps, the question of what duty one owes a sexual partner depends, at least partially, on the nature of the relationship. In a recent study, Robert Klitzman and Ronald Bayer have found that people feel a different sense of obligation about disclosure depending on the nature of the relationship.[15] Do these findings support feminist bioethics' emphasis on the importance of personal relationships?

Supreme Court of the United States.
Henning Jacobson
v.
Commonwealth of Massachusetts.
No. 70.

Argued December 6, 1904.
Decided February 20, 1905.

Mr. Justice **Harlan** delivered the opinion of the court:

This case involves the validity, under the Constitution of the United States, of certain provisions in the statutes of Massachusetts relating to vaccination.

The Revised Laws of that commonwealth, chap. 75, § 137, provide that 'the board of health of a city or town, if, in its opinion, it is necessary for the public health or safety, shall require and enforce the vaccination and revaccination of all the inhabitants thereof, and shall provide them with the means of free vaccination. Whoever, being over twenty-one years of age and not under guardianship, refuses or neglects to comply with such requirement shall forfeit $5.'

An exception is made in favor of 'children who present a certificate, signed by a registered physician, that they are unfit subjects for vaccination.' § 139.

Proceeding under the above statutes, the board of health of the city of Cambridge, Massachusetts, on the 27th day of February, 1902, adopted the following regulation: 'Whereas, smallpox has been prevalent to some extent in the city of Cambridge, and still continues to increase; and whereas, it is necessary for the speedy extermination of the disease that all persons not protected by vaccination should be vaccinated; and whereas, in the opinion of the board, the public health and safety require the vaccination or revaccination of all the inhabitants of Cambridge; be it ordered, that all the inhabitants of the city who have not been successfully vaccinated since March 1st, 1897, be vaccinated or revaccinated.'

Subsequently, the board adopted an additional regulation empowering a named physician to enforce the vaccination of persons as directed by the board at its special meeting of February 27th.

The above regulations being in force, the plaintiff in error, Jacobson, was proceeded against by a criminal complaint in one of the inferior courts of Massachusetts. The complaint charged that on the 17th day of July, 1902, the board of health of Cambridge, being of the opinion that it was necessary for the public health and safety, required the vaccination and revaccination of all the inhabitants thereof who had not been successfully vaccinated since the 1st day of March, 1897, and provided them with the means of free vaccination; and that the defendant, being over twenty-one years of age and not under guardianship, refused and neglected to comply with such requirement.

The defendant, having been arraigned, pleaded not guilty. The government put in evidence the above regulations adopted by the board of health, and made proof tending to show that its chairman informed the defendant that, by refusing to be vaccinated, he would incur the penalty provided by the statute, and would be prosecuted therefor; that he offered to vaccinate the defendant without expense to him; and that the offer was declined, and defendant refused to be vaccinated.

The defendant, standing upon his offers of proof, and introducing no evidence, asked numerous instructions to the jury, among which were the following:

That § 137 of chapter 75 of the Revised Laws of Massachusetts was in derogation of the rights secured to the defendant by the preamble to the Constitution of the United States, and tended to subvert and defeat the purposes of the Constitution as declared in its preamble;

That the section referred to was in derogation of the rights secured to the defendant by the 14th Amendment of the Constitution of the United States, and especially of the clauses of that amendment providing that no state shall make or enforce any law abridging the privileges or immunities of citizens of the United States, nor deprive any person of life, liberty, or property without due process of law, nor deny to any person within its jurisdiction the equal protection of the laws; and

That said section was opposed to the spirit of the Constitution.

Each of defendant's prayers for instructions was rejected, and he duly excepted. The defendant requested the court, but the court refused, to instruct the jury to return a verdict of not guilty. And the court instructed the jury, in substance, that, if they believed the evidence introduced by the commonwealth, and were satisfied beyond a reasonable doubt that the defendant was guilty of the offense charged in the complaint, they would be warranted in finding a verdict of guilty. A verdict of guilty was thereupon returned.

We have no need in this case to go beyond the plain, obvious meaning of the words in those provisions of the Constitution which, it is contended, must control our decision.

We assume for the purposes of the present inquiry, that the provisions of the statute require, at least as a general rule, that adults not under the guardianship and remaining within the limits of the city of Cambridge must submit to the regulation adopted by the board of health. Is the statute, so construed, therefore, inconsistent with the liberty which the Constitution of the United States secures to every person against deprivation by the state?

The authority of the state to enact this statute is to be referred to what is commonly called the police power,—a power which the state did not surrender when becoming a member of the Union under the Constitution. Although this court has refrained from any attempt to define the limits of that power, yet it has distinctly recognized the authority of a state to enact quarantine laws and 'health laws of every description;' indeed, all laws that relate to matters completely within its territory and which do not by their necessary operation affect the people of other states. According to settled principles, the police power of a state must be held to embrace, at least, such reasonable regulations established directly by legislative enactment as will protect the public health and the public safety. It is equally true that the state may invest local bodies called into existence for purposes of local administration with authority in some appropriate way to safeguard the public health and the public safety. The mode or manner in which those results are to be accomplished is within the discretion of the state, subject, of course, so far as Federal power is concerned, only to the condition that no rule prescribed by a state, nor any regulation adopted by a local governmental agency acting under the sanction of state legislation, shall contravene the Constitution of the United States, nor infringe any right granted or secured by that instrument. A local enactment or regulation, even if based on the acknowledged police powers of a state, must always yield in case of conflict with the exercise by the general government of any power it possesses under the Constitution, or with any right which that instrument gives or secures.

We come, then, to inquire whether any right given or secured by the Constitution is invaded by the statute as interpreted by the state court. The defendant insists that his liberty is invaded when the state subjects him to fine or imprisonment for neglecting or refusing to submit to vaccination; that a compulsory vaccination law is unreasonable, arbitrary, and oppressive, and, therefore, hostile to the inherent right of every freeman to care for his own body and health in such way as to him seems best; and that the execution of such a law against one who objects to vaccination, no matter for what reason, is nothing short of an assault upon his person. But the liberty secured by the Constitution of the United States to every person within its jurisdiction does not import an absolute right in each person to be, at all times and in all circumstances, wholly freed from restraint. There are manifold restraints to which every person is necessarily subject for the common good. On any other basis organized society could not exist with safety to its members. Society based on the rule that each one is a law unto himself would soon be confronted with disorder and anarchy. Real liberty for all could not exist under the operation of a principle which recognizes the right of each individual person to use his own, whether in respect of his person or his property, regardless of the injury that may be done to oth-

ers. This court has more than once recognized it as a fundamental principle that 'persons and property are subjected to all kinds of restraints and burdens in order to secure the general comfort, health, and prosperity of the state; of the perfect right of the legislature to do which no question ever was, or upon acknowledged general principles ever can be, made, so far as natural persons are concerned.' In the Constitution of Massachusetts adopted in 1780 it was laid down as a fundamental principle of the social compact that the whole people covenants with each citizen, and each citizen with the whole people, that all shall be governed by certain laws for 'the common good,' and that government is instituted 'for the common good, for the protection, safety, prosperity, and happiness of the people, and not for the profit, honor, or private interests of any one man, family, or class of men.' The good and welfare of the commonwealth, of which the legislature is primarily the judge, is the basis on which the police power rests in Massachusetts.

Applying these principles to the present case, it is to be observed that the legislature of Massachusetts required the inhabitants of a city or town to be vaccinated only when, in the opinion of the board of health, that was necessary for the public health or the public safety. The authority to determine for all what ought to be done in such an emergency must have been lodged somewhere or in some body; and surely it was appropriate for the legislature to refer that question, in the first instance, to a board of health composed of persons residing in the locality affected, and appointed, presumably, because of their fitness to determine such questions. To invest such a body with authority over such matters was not an unusual, nor an unreasonable or arbitrary, requirement. Upon the principle of self-defense, of paramount necessity, a community has the right to protect itself against an epidemic of disease which threatens the safety of its members. It is to be observed that when the regulation in question was adopted smallpox, according to the recitals in the regulation adopted by the board of health, was prevalent to some extent in the city of Cambridge, and the disease was increasing. If such was the situation,—and nothing is asserted or appears in the record to the contrary,—if we are to attach, any value whatever to the knowledge which, it is safe to affirm, in common to all civilized peoples touching smallpox and the methods most usually employed to eradicate that disease, it cannot be adjudged that the present regulation of the board of health was not necessary in order to protect the public health and secure the public safety. Smallpox being prevalent and increasing at Cambridge, the court would usurp the functions of another branch of government if it adjudged, as matter of law, that the mode adopted under the sanction of the state, to protect the people at large was arbitrary, and not justified by the necessities of the case. We say necessities of the case, because it might be that an acknowledged power of a local community to protect itself against an epidemic threatening the safety of all might be exercised in particular circumstances and in reference to particular persons in such an arbitrary, unreasonable manner, or might go so far beyond what was reasonably required for the safety of the public, as to authorize or compel the courts to interfere for the protection of such persons. If the mode adopted by the commonwealth of Massachusetts for the protection of its local communities against smallpox proved to be distressing, inconvenient, or objectionable to some,—if nothing more could be reasonably affirmed of the statute in question,—the answer is that it was the duty of the constituted authorities primarily to keep in view the welfare, comfort, and safety of the many, and not permit the interests of the many to be subordinated to the wishes or convenience of the few. There is, of course, a sphere within which the individual may assert the supremacy of his own will, and rightfully dispute the authority of any human government,—especially of any free government existing under a written constitution, to interfere with the exercise of that will. But it is equally true that in every well-ordered society charged with the duty of conserving the safety of its members the rights of the individual in respect of his liberty may at times, under the pressure of great dangers, be subjected to such restraint, to be enforced by reasonable regulations, as the safety of the general public may demand. An American citizen arriving at an American port on a vessel in which, during the voyage, there had been cases of yellow fever or Asiatic cholera, he, although apparently free from disease himself, may yet, in some circumstances, be held in quarantine against his will on board of such vessel or in a quarantine station, until it be ascertained by inspection, conducted with due diligence, that the danger of the spread of the disease among the community at large has disappeared. The liberty secured by the 14th Amendment, this court has said, consists, in part, in the right of a person 'to live and work where he will' and yet he may be compelled, by force if need be, against his will and without regard to his personal wishes or his pecuniary interests, or even his religious or political convictions, to take his place in the ranks of the army of his country, and risk the chance of being shot down in its defense. It is not, therefore, true that the power of the public to guard itself against imminent danger depends in every case involving the control of one's body upon his willingness to submit to reasonable regulations established by the constituted authorities, under the sanction of the state, for the purpose of protecting the public collectively against such danger.

Upon what sound principles as to the relations existing between the different departments of government can the court review this action of the legislature? If there is any such power in the judiciary to review legislative action in respect of a matter affecting the general welfare, it can only be when that which the legislature has done comes within the rule that, if a statute purporting to have been enacted to protect the public health, the public morals, or the public safety, has no real or substantial relation to those objects, or is, beyond all question, a plain, palpable invasion of rights secured by the fundamental law, it is the duty of the courts to so adjudge, and thereby give effect to the Constitution.

Whatever may be thought of the expediency of this statute, it cannot be affirmed to be, beyond question, in palpable conflict with the Constitution. Nor, in view of the methods employed to stamp out the disease of smallpox, can anyone confidently assert that the means prescribed by the state to that end has no real or substantial relation to the protection of the public health and the public safety. Such an assertion would not be consistent with the experience of this and other countries whose authorities have dealt with the disease of smallpox. And the principle of vaccination as a means to prevent the spread of smallpox has been enforced in many states by statutes making the vaccination of children a condition of their right to enter or remain in public schools.

The fact that the belief is not universal is not controlling, for there is scarcely any belief that is accepted by everyone. The possibility that the belief may be wrong, and that science may yet show it to be wrong, is not conclusive; for the legislature has the right to pass laws which, according to the common belief of the people, are adapted to prevent the spread of contagious diseases.

Since, then, vaccination, as a means of protecting a community against smallpox, finds strong support in the experience of this and other countries, no court, much less a jury, is justified in disregarding the action of the legislature simply because in its or their opinion that particular method was—perhaps, or possibly—not the best either for children or adults.

We are not prepared to hold that a minority, residing or remaining in any city or town where smallpox is prevalent, and enjoying the general protection afforded by an organized local government, may thus defy the will of its constituted authorities, acting in good faith for all, under the legislative sanction of the state. If such be the privilege of a minority, then a like privilege would belong to each individual of the community, and the spectacle would be presented of the welfare and safety of an entire population being subordinated to the notions of a single individual who chooses to remain a part of that population. We are unwilling to hold it to be an element in the liberty secured by the Constitution of the United States that one person, or a minority of persons, residing in any community and enjoying the benefits of its local government, should have the power thus to dominate the majority when supported in their action by the authority of the state. While this court should guard with firmness every right appertaining to life, liberty, or property as secured to the individual by the supreme law of the land, it is of the last importance that it should not invade the domain of local authority except when it is plainly necessary to do so in order to enforce that law. The safety and the health of the people of Massachusetts are, in the first instance, for that commonwealth to guard and protect. They are matters that do not ordinarily concern the national government. So far as they can be reached by any government, they depend, primarily, upon such action as the state, in its wisdom, may take; and we do not perceive that this legislation has invaded any right secured by the Federal Constitution.

Before closing this opinion we deem it appropriate, in order to prevent misapprehension as to our views, to observe—perhaps to repeat a thought already sufficiently expressed, namely—that the police power of a state, whether exercised directly by the legislature, or by a local body acting under its authority, may be exerted in such circumstances, or by regulations so arbitrary and oppressive in particular cases, as to justify the interference of the courts to prevent wrong and oppression. Until otherwise informed by the highest court of Massachusetts, we are not inclined to hold that the statute establishes the absolute rule that an adult must be vaccinated if it be apparent or can be shown with reasonable certainty that he is not at the time a fit subject of vaccination, or that vaccination, by reason of his then condition, would seriously impair his health, or probably cause his death. No such case is here presented. It is the cause of an adult who, for aught that appears, was himself in perfect health and a fit subject of vaccination, and yet, while remaining in the community, refused to obey the statute and the regulation adopted in execution of its provisions for the protection of the public health and the public safety, confessedly endangered by the presence of a dangerous disease.

We now decide only that the statute covers the present case, and that nothing clearly appears that would justify this court in holding it to be unconstitutional and inoperative in its application to the plaintiff in error.

The judgment of the court below must be affirmed. It is so ordered.

In re A.C., Appellant
No. 87-609
District of Columbia Court of Appeals

September 22, 1988, Argued
April 26, 1990, Decided

On Hearing En Banc

TERRY, Associate Judge:

This case comes before the court for the second time. In *In re A.C.*, 533 A.2d 611 (D.C. 1987), a three-judge motions division denied a motion to stay an order of the trial court which had authorized a hospital to perform a caesarean section on a dying woman in an effort to save the life of her unborn child. The operation was performed, but both the mother and the child died. A few months later, the court ordered the case heard en banc and vacated the opinion of the motions division. *In re A.C.*, 539 A.2d 203 (D.C.

1988). Although the motions division recognized that, as a practical matter, it "decided the entire matter when [it] denied the stay," 533 A.2d at 613, the en banc court has nevertheless heard the full case on the merits.

We are confronted here with two profoundly difficult and complex issues. First, we must determine who has the right to decide the course of medical treatment for a patient who, although near death, is pregnant with a viable fetus. Second, we must establish how that decision should be made if the patient cannot make it for herself—more specifically, how a court should proceed when faced with a pregnant patient, *in extremis*, who is apparently incapable of making an informed decision regarding medical care for herself and her fetus. We hold that in virtually all cases the question of what is to be done is to be decided by the patient—the pregnant woman—on behalf of herself and the fetus. If the patient is incompetent or otherwise unable to give an informed consent to a proposed course of medical treatment, then her decision must be ascertained through the procedure known as substituted judgment. Because the trial court did not follow that procedure, we vacate its order and remand the case for further proceedings.[2]

I

This case came before the trial court when George Washington University Hospital petitioned the emergency judge in chambers for declaratory relief as to how it should treat its patient, A.C., who was close to death from cancer and was twenty-six and one-half weeks pregnant with a viable fetus. After a hearing lasting approximately three hours, which was held at the hospital (though not in A.C.'s room), the court ordered that a caesarean section be performed on A.C. to deliver the fetus. Counsel for A.C. immediately sought a stay in this court, which was unanimously denied by a hastily assembled division of three judges. *In re A.C.*, 533 A.2d 611 (D.C. 1987). The caesarean was performed, and a baby girl, L.M.C., was delivered. Tragically, the child died within two and one-half hours, and the mother died two days later.

Counsel for A.C. now maintain that A.C. was competent and that she made an informed choice not to have the caesarean performed. Given this view of the facts, they argue that it was error for the trial court to weigh the state's interest in preserving the potential life of a viable fetus against A.C.'s interest in having her decision respected. They argue further that, even if the substituted judgment procedure had been followed, the evidence would necessarily show that A.C. would not have wanted the caesarean section. Under either analysis, according to these arguments, the trial court erred in subordinating A.C.'s right to bodily integrity in favor of the state's interest in potential life. Counsel for the hospital and for L.M.C. contend, on the other hand, that A.C. was incompetent to make her own medical decisions and that, under the substituted judgment procedure, the evidence clearly established that A.C. would have consented to the caesarean. In the alternative, counsel for L.M.C. argues that even if L.M.C.'s interests and those of the state were in conflict with A.C.'s wishes, it was proper for the trial court to balance their interests and resolve the conflict in favor of surgical intervention.

We do not accept any of these arguments because the evidence, realistically viewed, does not support them.

II

A.C. was first diagnosed as suffering from cancer at the age of thirteen. In the ensuing years she underwent major surgery several times, together with multiple radiation treatments and chemotherapy. A.C. married when she was twenty-seven, during a period of remission, and soon thereafter she became pregnant. She was excited about her pregnancy and very much wanted the child. Because of her medical history, she was referred in her fifteenth week of pregnancy to the high-risk pregnancy clinic at George Washington University Hospital.

On Tuesday, June 9, 1987, when A.C. was approximately twenty-five weeks pregnant, she went to the hospital for a scheduled check-up. Because she was experiencing pain in her back and shortness of breath, an x-ray was taken, revealing an apparently inoperable tumor which nearly filled her right lung. On Thursday, June 11, A.C. was admitted to the hospital as a patient. By Friday her condition had temporarily improved, and when asked if she really wanted to have her baby, she replied that she did.

Over the weekend A.C.'s condition worsened considerably. Accordingly, on Monday, June 15, members of the medical staff treating A.C. assembled, along with her family, in A.C.'s room. The doctors then informed her that her illness was terminal, and A.C. agreed to palliative treatment designed to extend her life until at least her twenty-eighth week of pregnancy. The "potential outcome [for] the fetus," according to the doctors, would be much better at twenty-eight weeks than at twenty-six weeks if it were necessary to "intervene." A.C. knew that the palliative treatment she had chosen presented some increased risk to the fetus, but she opted for this course both to prolong her life for at least another two weeks and to maintain her own comfort. When asked if she still wanted to have the baby, A.C. was somewhat equivocal, saying "something to the effect of 'I don't know, I think so.'" As the day moved toward evening, A.C.'s condition grew still worse, and at about 7:00 or 8:00 p.m. she consented to intubation to facilitate her breathing.

The next morning, June 16, the trial court convened a hearing at the hospital in response to the hospital's request for a declaratory judgment. The court appointed counsel for both A.C. and the fetus, and the District of Columbia was permitted to intervene for the fetus as *parens patriae*. The court heard testimony on the facts as we have summarized them, and further testimony that at twenty-six and a half weeks the fetus was viable, *i.e.*, capable of sustained life outside of the mother, given artificial aid. A neonatologist, Dr. Maureen Edwards, testified that the chances of survival for a twenty-six-week fetus delivered at the hospital might be as high as eighty percent, but that this particular fetus, because of the mother's medical history, had only a fifty to sixty percent chance of survival. Dr. Edwards estimated that the risk of substantial impairment for the fetus, if it were delivered promptly, would be less than twenty per-

cent. However, she noted that the fetus' condition was worsening appreciably at a rapid rate, and another doctor—Dr. Alan Weingold, an obstetrician who was one of A.C.'s treating physicians—stated that any delay in delivering the child by caesarean section lessened its chances of survival.

Regarding A.C.'s ability to respond to questioning and her prognosis, Dr. Louis Hamner, another treating obstetrician, testified that A.C. would probably die within twenty-four hours "if absolutely nothing else is done. . . . As far as her ability to interact, she has been heavily sedated in order to maintain her ventilatory function. She will open her eyes sometimes when you are in the room, but as far as her being able to . . . carry on a meaningful-type conversation . . . at this point, I don't think that is reasonable." When asked whether reducing her medication to "permit recovery of enough cognitive function on her part that we could get any sense from her as to what her preference would be as to therapy," Dr. Hamner replied, "I don't think so. I think her respiratory status has deteriorated to the point where she is [expending] an enormous amount of energy just to keep the heart going." Dr. Weingold, asked the same question, gave a similar answer: that A.C.'s few remaining hours of life "will be shortened by attempting to raise her level of consciousness because that is what is keeping her, in a sense, physiologically compliant with the respirator. If you remove that, then I think that will shorten her survival."

There was no evidence before the court showing that A.C. consented to, or even contemplated, a caesarean section before her twenty-eight week of pregnancy. There was, in fact, considerable dispute as to whether she would have consented to an immediate caesarean delivery at the time the hearing was held. A.C.'s mother opposed surgical intervention, testifying that A.C. wanted "to live long enough to hold that baby" and that she expected to do so, "even though she knew she was terminal." Dr. Hamner testified that, given A.C.'s medical problems, he did not think she would have chosen to deliver a child with a substantial degree of impairment. Asked whether A.C. had been "confronted with the question of what to do if there were a choice that ultimately had to be made between her own life expectancy and that of her fetus," he replied that the question "was addressed [but] at a later gestational age. We had talked about the possibility at twenty-eight weeks, if she had to be intubated, if this was a terminal event, would we intervene, and the expression was yes, that we would, because we felt at twenty-eight weeks we had much more to offer as far as taking care of the child." Finally, Dr. Hamner stated that "the department as a whole" concluded that "we should abide by the wishes of the family." Dr. Lawrence Lessin, an oncologist and another of A.C.'s treating physicians, testified that in meetings with A.C. he had heard nothing to indicate that, if faced with the decision, she would have refused permission for a caesarean section. Dr. Weingold opposed the operation because he believed A.C. had not seriously considered that she might not survive the birth of her baby. Dr. Weingold made explicit what was implicit in Dr. Hamner's testimony: that "in dealing with her, a message that was sent to her was that the earliest we would feel comfortable in intervening, should there be indication as to either maternal or fetal grounds, would be twenty-eight weeks."

After hearing this testimony and the arguments of counsel, the trial court made oral findings of fact. It found, first, that A.C. would probably die, according to uncontroverted medical testimony, "within the next twenty-four to forty-eight hours"; second, that A.C. was "pregnant with a twenty-six and a half week viable fetus who, based upon uncontroverted medical testimony, has approximately a fifty to sixty percent chance to survive if a caesarean section is performed as soon as possible"; third, that because the fetus was viable, "the state has [an] important and legiti-

mate interest in protecting the potentiality of human life"; and fourth, that there had been some testimony that the operation "may very well hasten the death of [A.C.]," but that there had also been testimony that delay would greatly increase the risk to the fetus and that "the prognosis is not great for the fetus to be delivered post-mortem. . . ." Most significantly, the court found:

> The court is of the view that it does not clearly know what [A.C.'s] present views are with respect to the issue of whether or not the child should live or die. She's presently unconscious. As late as Friday of last week, she wanted the baby to live. As late as yesterday, she did not know for sure.

Having made these findings of fact and conclusions of law, the court ordered that a caesarean section be performed to deliver A.C.'s child.

The court's decision was then relayed to A.C., who had regained consciousness. When the hearing reconvened later in the day, Dr. Hamner told the court:

> I explained to her essentially what was going on. . . . I said it's been deemed we should intervene on behalf of the baby by caesarean section and it would give it the only possible chance of it living. Would you agree to this procedure? *She said yes.* I said, do you realize that you may not survive the surgical procedure? *She said yes.* And I repeated the two questions to her again [and] asked her did she understand. *She said yes.* [Emphasis added.]

When the court suggested moving the hearing to A.C.'s bedside, Dr. Hamner discouraged the court from doing so, but he and Dr. Weingold, together with A.C.'s mother and husband, went to A.C.'s room to confirm her consent to the procedure. What happened then was recounted to the court a few minutes later:

THE COURT: Will you bring us up to date? Did you have a conversation with [A.C.]?

DR. WEINGOLD: I did not. I observed the conversation between Dr. Hamner and [A.C.]. Dr.

Hamner went into the room to attempt to verify his previous discussion with the patient, with the patient's husband at her right hand and her mother at her left hand. He, to my satisfaction, clearly communicated with [A.C.]. She understood.

THE COURT: You could hear what the parties were saying to one another?

DR. WEINGOLD: She does not make sound because of the tube in her windpipe. She nods and she mouths words. One can see what she's saying rather readily. She asked whether she would survive the operation. She asked [Dr.] Hamner if he would perform the operation. He told her he would only perform it if she authorized it but it would be done in any case. She understood that. She then seemed to pause for a few moments and then very clearly mouthed words several times, *I don't want it done. I don't want it done.* Quite clear to me.

I would obviously state the obvious and that is this is an environment in which, from my perspective as a physician, this would not be an informed consent one way or the other. She's under tremendous stress with the family on both sides, but I'm satisfied that I heard clearly what she said.

THE COURT: Dr. Hamner, did you wish to elaborate?

DR. HAMNER: That's accurate. I noticed she was much more alert than she had been earlier in the day and was responding to the nurses in the room as well as to all the physicians and went through the same sequence Dr. Weingold noted.

Dr. Weingold later qualified his opinion as to A.C.'s ability to give an informed consent, stating that he thought the environment for an informed consent was non-existent because A.C. was in intensive care, flanked by a weeping husband and mother. He added:

I think she's in contact with reality, clearly understood who Dr. Hamner was. Because of her attachment to him [she] wanted him to perform the surgery. Understood he would not unless she consented and did not consent.

That is, in my mind, very clear evidence that she is responding, understanding, and is capable of making such decisions.

Dr. Hamner stated that the sedation had "worn off enough for her to wake up to this state" and that "the level of drugs in her body is much different from several hours ago." Consequently, despite A.C.'s continued sedation, Dr. Weingold said that she was "quite reactive," and Dr. Hamner concurred.

After hearing this new evidence, the court found that it was "still not clear what her intent is" and again ordered that a caesarean section be performed. A.C.'s counsel sought a stay in this court, which was denied. The operation took place, but the baby lived for only a few hours, and A.C. succumbed to cancer two days later.

IV

Our analysis of this case begins with the tenet common to all medical treatment cases: that any person has the right to make an informed choice, if competent to do so, to accept or forego medical treatment. The doctrine of informed consent, based on this principle and rooted in the concept of bodily integrity, is ingrained in our common law. Under the doctrine of informed consent, a physician must inform the patient, "at a minimum," of "the nature of the proposed treatment, any alternative treatment procedures, and the nature and degree of risks and benefits inherent in undergoing and in abstaining from the proposed treatment." To protect the right of every person to bodily integrity, courts uniformly hold that a surgeon who performs an operation without the patient's consent may be guilty of a battery, or that if the surgeon obtains an insufficiently informed consent, he or she may be liable for negligence. Furthermore, the right to informed consent "also encompasses a right to informed refusal."

In the same vein, courts do not compel one person to permit a significant intrusion upon his or her bodily integrity for the benefit of another person's health. In *McFall* the court refused to order Shimp to donate bone marrow which was necessary to save the life of his cousin, McFall:

> The common law has consistently held to a rule which provides that one human being is under no legal compulsion to give aid or to take action to save another human being or to rescue. . . . For our law to *compel* defendant to submit to an intrusion of his body would change every concept and principle upon which our society is founded. To do so would defeat the sanctity of the individual, and would impose a rule which would know no limits, and one could not imagine where the line would be drawn.

Even though Shimp's refusal would mean death for McFall, the court would not order Shimp to allow his body to be invaded. It has been suggested that fetal cases are different because a woman who "has chosen to lend her body to bring [a] child into the world" has an enhanced duty to assure the welfare of the fetus, sufficient even to require her to undergo caesarean surgery. Surely, however, a fetus cannot have rights in this respect superior to those of a person who has already been born.

Courts have generally held that a patient is competent to make his or her own medical choices when that patient is capable of "the informed exercise of a choice, and that entails an opportunity to evaluate knowledgeably the options available and the risks attendant upon each." Thus competency in a case such as this turns on the patient's ability to function as a decision-maker, acting in accordance with her preferences and values.

This court has recognized as well that, above and beyond common law protections, the right to accept or forego medical treatment is of constitutional magnitude.

Decisions of the Supreme Court, while not explicitly recognizing a right to bodily integrity, seem to assume that individuals have the right, depending on the circumstances, to accept or refuse medical treatment or other bodily invasion. In *Winston v. Lee, supra,* a robbery suspect challenged the state's right to compel him to submit to surgery for the removal of a bullet which was lodged in a muscle in his chest. The Court noted that the proposed surgery, which would require a general anesthetic, "would be an 'extensive' intrusion on respondent's personal privacy and bodily integrity" and a "virtually total divestment of respondent's ordinary control over surgical probing beneath his skin," 470 U.S. at 764-765, 105 S.Ct. at 1619 (citation omitted), and held that, without the patient-suspect's consent, the surgery was constitutionally impermissible. Nevertheless, even in recognizing a right to refuse medical treatment or state-imposed surgery, neither *Winston* nor any other Supreme Court decision holds that this right of refusal is absolute.

This court and others, while recognizing the right to accept or reject medical treatment, have consistently held that the right is not absolute. In some cases, especially those involving life-or-death situations or incompetent patients, the courts have recognized four countervailing interests that may involve the state as *parens patriae:* preserving life, preventing suicide, maintaining the ethical integrity of the medical profession, and protecting third parties. Neither the prevention of suicide nor the integrity of the medical profession has any bearing on this case. Further, the state's interest in preserving life must be truly compelling to justify overriding a competent person's right to refuse medical treatment. This is equally true for incompetent patients, who have just as much right as competent patients to have their decisions made while competent respected, even in a substituted judgment framework.

In those rare cases in which a patient's right to decide her own course of treatment has been judicially overridden, courts have usually acted to vindicate the state's interest in protecting third parties, even if in fetal state.

What we distill from the cases discussed in this section is that every person has the right, under the common law and the Constitution, to accept or refuse medical treatment. This right of bodily integrity belongs equally to persons who are competent and persons who are not. Further, it matters not what the quality of a patient's life may be; the right of bodily integrity is not extinguished simply because someone is ill, or even at death's door. To protect that right against intrusion by others—family members, doctors, hospitals, or anyone else, however well-intentioned—we hold that a court must determine the patient's wishes by any means available, and must abide by those wishes unless there are truly extraordinary or compelling reasons to override them. When the patient is incompetent, or when the court is unable to determine competency, the substituted judgment procedure must be followed.

From the record before us, we simply cannot tell whether A.C. was ever competent, after being sedated, to make an informed decision one way or the other regarding the proposed caesarean section. The trial court never made any finding about A.C.'s competency to decide. Undoubtedly, during most of the proceedings below, A.C. was incompetent to make a treatment decision; that is, she was unable to give an informed consent based on her assessment of the risks and benefits of the contemplated surgery. The court knew from the evidence that A.C. was sedated and unconscious, and thus it could reasonably have found her incompetent to render an informed consent; however, it made no such finding. On the other hand, there was no clear evidence that A.C. was competent to render an informed consent after the trial court's initial order was communicated to her.

We think it is incumbent on any trial judge in a case like this, unless it is impossible to do so, to ascertain whether a patient is competent to make her own medical decisions. Whenever possible, the judge should personally attempt to speak with the patient and ascertain her wishes directly, rather than relying exclusively on hearsay evidence, even from doctors. It is improper to presume that a patient is incompetent. We have no reason to believe that, if competent, A.C. would or would not have refused consent to a caesarean. We hold, however, that without a competent refusal from A.C. to go forward with the surgery, and without a finding through substituted judgment that A.C. would not have consented to the surgery, it was error for the trial court to proceed to a balancing analysis, weighing the rights of A.C. against the interests of the state.

There are two additional arguments against overriding A.C.'s objections to caesarean surgery. First, as the American Public Health Association cogently states in its *amicus curiae* brief:

> Rather than protecting the health of women and children, court-ordered caesareans erode the element of trust that permits a pregnant woman to communicate to her physician—without fear of reprisal—all information relevant to her proper diagnosis and treatment. An even more serious consequence of court-ordered intervention is that it drives women at high risk of complications during pregnancy and childbirth out of the health care system to avoid coerced treatment.

Second, and even more compellingly, any judicial proceeding in a case such as this will ordinarily take place—like the one before us here—under time constraints so pressing that it is difficult or impossible for the mother to communicate adequately with counsel, or for counsel to organize an effective factual and legal presentation in defense of her liberty and privacy interests and bodily integrity. Any intrusion implicating such basic values ought not to be lightly undertaken when the mother not only is precluded from conducting pre-trial discovery but also is in no position to prepare meaningfully for trial. As one commentator has noted:

The procedural shortcomings rampant in these cases are not mere technical deficiencies. They undermine the authority of the decisions themselves, posing serious questions as to whether judges can, in the absence of genuine notice, adequate representation, explicit standards of proof, and right of appeal, realistically frame principled and useful legal responses to the dilemmas with which they are being confronted.

In this case A.C.'s court-appointed attorney was unable even to meet with his client before the hearing. By the time the case was heard, A.C.'s condition did not allow her to be present, nor was it reasonably possible for the judge to hear from her directly. The factual record, moreover, was significantly flawed because A.C.'s medical records were not before the court and because Dr. Jeffrey Moscow, the physician who had been treating A.C. for many years, was not even contacted and hence did not testify. Finally, the time for legal preparation was so minimal that neither the court nor counsel mentioned the doctrine of substituted judgment, which—with benefit of briefs, oral arguments, and above all, time—we now deem critical to the outcome of this case. We cannot be at all certain that the trial judge would have reached the same decision if the testimony of Dr. Moscow and the abundant legal scholarship filed in this court had been meaningfully available to him, and if there had been enough time for him to consider and reflect on these matters as a judge optimally should do.

B. Substituted Judgment

In the previous section we discussed the right of an individual to accept or reject medical treatment. We concluded that if a patient is competent and has made an informed decision regarding the course of her medical treatment, that decision will control in virtually all cases. Sometimes, however, as our analysis presupposes here, a once competent patient will be unable to render an informed decision. In such a case, we hold that the court must make a substi-

tuted judgment on behalf of the patient, based on all the evidence. This means that the duty of the court, "as surrogate for the incompetent, is to determine as best it can what choice that individual, if competent, would make with respect to medical procedures."

Under the substituted judgment procedure, the court as decision-maker must "substitute itself as nearly as may be for the incompetent, and . . . act upon the same motives and considerations as would have moved her. . . ." Most cases involving substituted judgment, have arisen in the "right to die" context, and the courts have generally concluded that giving effect to the perceived decision of the incompetent is the proper course, even though doing so will result in the incompetent's death.

We have found no reported opinion applying the substituted judgment procedure to the case of an incompetent pregnant patient whose own life may be shortened by a caesarean section, and whose unborn child's chances of survival may hang on the court's decision. Despite this precedential void, we conclude that substituted judgment is the best procedure to follow in such a case because it most clearly respects the right of the patient to bodily integrity.

We begin with the proposition that the substituted judgment inquiry is primarily a subjective one: as nearly as possible, the court must ascertain what the patient would do if competent. Due process strongly suggests (and may even require) that counsel or a guardian *ad litem* should be appointed for the patient unless the situation is so urgent that there is no time to do so.

Because it is the patient's decisional rights which the substituted judgment inquiry seeks to protect, courts are in accord that the greatest weight should be given to the previously expressed wishes of the patient. This includes prior statements, either written or oral, even though the treatment alternatives at hand may not have been addressed. The court should also consider previous decisions of the patient concerning medical treatment, especially when there may be a discernibly consistent pattern of conduct or of thought.

Thus in a case such as this it would be highly relevant that A.C. had consented to intrusive and dangerous surgeries in the past, and that she chose to become pregnant and to protect her pregnancy by seeking treatment at the hospital's high-risk pregnancy clinic. It would also be relevant that she accepted a plan of treatment which contemplated caesarean intervention at the twenty-eighth week of pregnancy, even though the possibility of a caesarean during the twenty-sixth week was apparently unforeseen. On the other hand, A.C. agreed to a plan of palliative treatment which posed a greater danger to the fetus than would have been necessary if she were unconcerned about her own continuing care. Further, when A.C. was informed of the fatal nature of her illness, she was equivocal about her desire to have the baby.

Courts in substituted judgment cases have also acknowledged the importance of probing the patient's value system as an aid in discerning what the patient would choose. We agree with this approach. Most people do not foresee what calamities may befall them; much less do they consider, or even think about, treatment alternatives in varying situations. The court in a substituted judgment case, therefore, should pay special attention to the known values and goals of the incapacitated patient, and should strive, if possible, to extrapolate from those values and goals what the patient's decision would be.

Although treating physicians may be an invaluable source of such information about a patient, the family will often be the best source. Family members or other loved ones will usually be in the best position to say what the patient would do if competent. The court should be mindful, however, that while in the majority of cases family members will have the best interests of the patient in mind, sometimes family members will rely on their own judgments or predilections rather than serving as conduits for expressing the patient's wishes. This is why the court should endeavor, whenever possible, to make an in-person appraisal "of the patient's personal desires and ability for rational choice. In this way the court can always know, to the extent possible, that the judgment is that of the individual concerned and not that of those who believe, however well-intentioned, that they speak for the person whose life is in the balance."

In short, to determine the subjective desires of the patient, the court must consider the totality of the evidence, focusing particularly on written or oral directions concerning treatment to family, friends, and health-care professionals. The court should also take into account the patient's past decisions regarding medical treatment, and attempt to ascertain from what is known about the patient's value system, goals, and desires what the patient would decide if competent.

After considering the patient's prior statements, if any, the previous medical decisions of the patient, and the values held by the patient, the court may still be unsure what course the patient would choose. In such circumstances the court may supplement its knowledge about the patient by determining what most persons would likely do in a similar situation. When the patient is pregnant, however, she may not be concerned exclusively with her own welfare. Thus it is proper for the court, in a case such as this, to weigh (along with all the other factors) the mother's prognosis, the viability of the fetus, the probable result of treatment or non-treatment for both mother and fetus, and the mother's likely interest in avoiding impairment for her child together with her own instincts for survival.

Additionally, the court should consider the context in which prior declarations, treatment decisions, and expressions of personal values were made, including whether statements were made casually or after contemplation, or in accordance with deeply held beliefs. Finally, in making a substituted judgment, the court should become as informed about the patient's condition, prognosis, and treatment options as one would expect any patient to become before making a treatment decision. Obviously, the weight accorded to all of these factors will vary from case to case.

C. The Trial Court's Ruling

After reviewing the transcript of the hearing and the court's oral findings, it is clear to us that the trial court did not follow the substituted judgment procedure. On the contrary, the court's specific finding before its decision was communicated to A.C. was as follows:

> The court is of the view that it does not clearly know what [A.C.'s] present views are with respect to the issue of whether or not the child should live or die. She's presently unconscious. As late as Friday of last week, she wanted the baby to live. As late as yesterday, she did not know for sure.

The court did not go on, as it should have done, to make a finding as to what A.C. would have chosen to do if she were competent. Instead, the court undertook to balance the state's and L.M.C.'s interests in surgical intervention against A.C.'s perceived interest in not having the caesarean performed.

After A.C. was informed of the court's decision, she consented to the caesarean; moments later, however, she withdrew her consent. The trial court did not then make a finding as to whether A.C. was competent to make the medical decision or whether she had made an informed decision one way or the other. Nor did the court then make a substituted judgment for A.C. Instead, the court said that it was "still not clear what her intent is" and again ordered the caesarean.

It is that order which we must now set aside. What a trial court must do in a case such as this is to determine, if possible, whether the patient is capable of making an informed decision about the course of her medical treatment. If she is, and if she makes such a decision, her wishes will control in virtually all cases. If the court finds that the patient is incapable of making an informed consent (and thus incompetent), then the court must make a substituted judgment. This means

that the court must ascertain as best it can what the patient would do if faced with the particular treatment question. Again, in virtually all cases the decision of the patient, albeit discerned through the mechanism of substituted judgment, will control. We do not quite foreclose the possibility that a conflicting state interest may be so compelling that the patient's wishes must yield, but we anticipate that such cases will be extremely rare and truly exceptional. This is not such a case.

BELSON, Associate Judge, concurring in part and dissenting in part: I agree with much of the majority opinion, but I disagree with its ultimate ruling that the trial court's order must be set aside, and with the narrow view it takes of the state's interest in preserving life and the unborn child's interest in life.

I think it appropriate to state my disagreement with the very limited view the majority opinion takes of the circumstances in which the interests of a viable unborn child can afford such compelling reasons. The state's interest in preserving human life and the viable unborn child's interest in survival are entitled, I think, to more weight than I find them assigned by the majority when it states that "in virtually all cases the decision of the patient . . . will control." I would hold that in those instances, fortunately rare, in which the viable unborn child's interest in living and the state's parallel interest in protecting human life come into conflict with the mother's decision to forgo a procedure such as a caesarean section, a balancing should be struck in which the unborn child's and the state's interests are entitled to substantial weight.

Notes

2. We observe nevertheless that it would be far better if judges were not called to patients' bedsides and required to make quick decisions on issues of life and death. Because judgment in such a case involves complex medical and ethical issues as well as the application of legal principles, we would urge the establishment—through legislation or oth-

erwise—of another tribunal to make these decisions, with limited opportunity for judicial review.

We also emphasize that our decision today is the result of considerable deliberation and that we have enjoyed two luxuries unavailable to the trial court: ample time to decide the case, and extensive briefs and oral argument from the parties and several *amici.* The trial judge had no such advantage. He was called in during the worst of emergencies, with little time for reflection, to make a decision which under the best of circumstances is extraordinarily difficult. Although we conclude that his decision must be set aside, we nevertheless commend him for the painstaking and conscientious manner in which he performed the task before him.

Supreme Court of the United States
Crystal M. Ferguson, et al., Petitioners,
v.
City of Charleston, et al.
No. 99-936.

Argued Oct. 4, 2000.
Decided March 21, 2001.

Justice Stevens delivered the opinion of the Court.

In this case, we must decide whether a state hospital's performance of a diagnostic test to obtain evidence of a patient's criminal conduct for law enforcement purposes is an unreasonable search if the patient has not consented to the procedure. More narrowly, the question is whether the interest in using the threat of criminal sanctions to deter pregnant women from using cocaine can justify a departure from the general rule that an official nonconsensual search is unconstitutional if not authorized by a valid warrant.

I

In the fall of 1988, staff members at the public hospital operated in the city of Charleston by the Medical University of South Carolina (MUSC) became concerned about an apparent increase in the use of cocaine by patients who were receiving prenatal treatment. In response to this perceived increase, as of April 1989, MUSC began to order drug screens to be performed on urine samples from maternity patients who were suspected of using cocaine. If a patient tested positive, she was then referred by MUSC staff to the county substance abuse commission for counseling and treatment. However, despite the referrals, the incidence of cocaine use among the patients at MUSC did not appear to change.

Some four months later, Nurse Shirley Brown, the case manager for the MUSC obstetrics department, heard a news broadcast reporting that the police in Greenville, South Carolina, were arresting pregnant users of cocaine on the theory that such use harmed the fetus and was therefore child abuse. Nurse Brown discussed the story with MUSC's general counsel, Joseph C. Good, Jr., who then contacted Charleston Solicitor Charles Condon in order to offer MUSC's cooperation in prosecuting mothers whose children tested positive for drugs at birth.

After receiving Good's letter, Solicitor Condon took the first steps in developing the policy at issue in this case. He organized the initial meetings, decided who would participate, and issued the invitations, in which he described his plan to prosecute women who tested positive for cocaine while pregnant. The task force that Condon formed included representatives of MUSC, the police, the County Substance Abuse Commission and the Department of Social Services. Their deliberations led to MUSC's adoption of a 12-page document entitled "POLICY M-7," dealing with the subject of "Management of Drug Abuse During Pregnancy."

The first three pages of Policy M-7 set forth the procedure to be followed by the hospital staff to "identify/assist pregnant patients suspected of drug abuse." The first section, entitled the "Identification of Drug Abusers," provided that a patient should be tested for cocaine through a urine drug screen if she met one or more of nine criteria. It also stated that a chain of custody should be followed when obtaining and testing urine samples, presumably to make sure that the results could be used in subsequent criminal proceedings. The policy also provided for education and referral to a substance abuse clinic for patients who tested positive. Most important, it added the threat of law enforcement intervention that "provided the necessary 'leverage' to make the [p]olicy effective." threat was, as respondents candidly acknowledge, essential to the program's success in getting women into treatment and keeping them there.

II

Petitioners are 10 women who received obstetrical care at MUSC and who were arrested after testing positive for cocaine. Respondents include the city of Charleston, law enforcement officials who helped develop and enforce the policy, and representatives of MUSC.

The Court of Appeals for the Fourth Circuit held that the searches were reasonable as a matter of law under our line of cases recognizing that "special needs" may, in certain exceptional circumstances, justify a search policy designed to serve non-law-enforcement ends. On the understanding "that MUSC personnel conducted the urine drug screens for medical purposes wholly independent of an intent to aid law enforcement efforts," the majority applied the balancing test used in *Treasury Employees v. Von Raab,* and *Vernonia School Dist. 47J v. Acton,* and concluded that the interest in curtailing the pregnancy complications and medical costs associated with maternal cocaine use outweighed what the majority termed a minimal intrusion on the privacy of the patients.

We granted certiorari to review the appellate court's holding on the "special needs" issue. We conclude that the judgment should be reversed and the case remanded for a decision on the consent issue.

III

Because the hospital seeks to justify its authority to conduct drug tests and to turn the results over to law enforcement agents without the knowledge or consent of the patients, this case differs from the four previous cases in which we have considered whether comparable drug tests "fit within the closely guarded category of constitutionally permissible suspicionless searches." In three of those cases, we sustained drug tests for railway employees involved in train accidents, for United States Customs Service employees seeking promotion to certain sensitive positions, and for high school students participating in interscholastic sports. In the fourth case, we struck down such testing for candidates for designated state offices as unreasonable.

In each of those cases, we employed a balancing test that weighed the intrusion on the individual's interest in privacy against the "special needs" that supported the program. As an initial matter, we note that the invasion of privacy in this case is far more substantial than in those cases. In the previous four cases, there was no misunderstanding about the purpose of the test or the potential use of the test results, and there were protections against the dissemination of the results to third parties. The use of an adverse test result to disqualify one from eligibility for a particular benefit, such as a promotion or an opportunity to participate in an extracurricular activity, involves a less serious intrusion on privacy than the unauthorized dissemination of such results to third parties. The reasonable expectation of privacy enjoyed by the typical patient undergoing diagnostic tests in a hospital is that the results of those tests will not be shared with nonmedical personnel without her consent. In none of our prior cases was there any intrusion upon that kind of expectation.

The critical difference between those four drug-testing cases and this one, however, lies in the nature of the "special need" asserted as justification for the warrantless searches. In each of those earlier cases, the "special need" that was advanced as a justification for the absence of a warrant or individualized suspicion was one divorced from the State's general interest in law enforcement. In this case, however, the central and indispensable feature of the policy from its inception was the use of law enforcement to coerce the patients into substance abuse treatment. This fact distinguishes this case from circumstances in which physicians or psychologists, in the course of ordinary medical procedures aimed at helping the patient herself, come across information that under rules of law or ethics is subject to reporting requirements, which no one has challenged here.

Respondents argue in essence that their ultimate purpose—namely, protecting the health of both mother and child—is a beneficent one. In *Chandler,* however, we did not simply accept the State's invocation of a "special need." Instead, we carried out a "close review" of the scheme at issue before concluding that the need in question was not "special," as that term has been defined in our cases. In this case, a review of the M-7 policy plainly reveals that the purpose actually served by the MUSC searches "is ultimately indistinguishable from the general interest in crime control."

In looking to the programmatic purpose, we consider all the available evidence in order to determine the relevant primary purpose. In this case, "it . . . is clear from the record that an initial and continuing focus of the policy was on the arrest and prosecution of drug-abusing mothers. . . ." Tellingly, the document codifying the policy incorporates the police's operational guidelines. It devotes its attention to the chain of custody, the range of possible criminal charges, and the logistics of police notification and arrests. Nowhere, however, does the document discuss different courses of medical treatment for either mother or infant, aside from treatment for the mother's addiction.

Moreover, throughout the development and application of the policy, the Charleston prosecutors and police were extensively involved in the day-to-day administration of the policy. Police and prosecutors decided who would receive the reports of positive drug screens and what information would be included with those reports. Law enforcement officials also helped determine the procedures to be followed when performing the screens. In the course of the policy's administration, they had access to Nurse Brown's medical files on the women who tested positive, routinely attended the substance abuse team's meetings, and regularly received copies of team documents discussing the women's progress. Police took pains to coordinate the timing and circumstances of the arrests with MUSC staff, and, in particular, Nurse Brown.

While the ultimate goal of the program may well have been to get the women in question into substance abuse treatment and off of drugs, the immediate objective of the searches was to generate evidence *for law enforcement purposes* in order to reach that goal. The threat of law enforcement may ultimately have been intended as a means to an end, but the direct and primary purpose of MUSC's policy was to ensure the use of those means. In our opinion, this distinction is critical. Because law enforcement involvement always serves some broader social purpose or objective, under respondents' view, virtually any nonconsensual suspicionless search could be immunized under the special needs doctrine by defining the search solely in terms of its ultimate, rather than immediate, purpose. Such an approach is inconsistent with the Fourth Amendment. Given the primary purpose of the Charleston program, which was to use the threat of arrest and prosecution in order to force women into treatment, and given the extensive involvement of law enforcement officials at every stage of the policy, this case simply does not fit within the closely guarded category of "special needs."

The fact that positive test results were turned over to the police does not merely provide a basis for distinguishing our prior cases applying the "special needs" balancing approach to the determination of drug use. It also provides an affirmative reason for enforcing the strictures of the Fourth Amendment. While state hospital employees, like other citizens, may have a duty to provide the police with evidence of criminal conduct that they inadvertently acquire in the course of routine treatment, when they undertake to obtain such evidence from their patients *for the specific purpose of incriminating those patients*, they have

a special obligation to make sure that the patients are fully informed about their constitutional rights, as standards of knowing waiver require.

As respondents have repeatedly insisted, their motive was benign rather than punitive. Such a motive, however, cannot justify a departure from Fourth Amendment protections, given the pervasive involvement of law enforcement with the development and application of the MUSC policy. The stark and unique fact that characterizes this case is that Policy M-7 was designed to obtain evidence of criminal conduct by the tested patients that would be turned over to the police and that could be admissible in subsequent criminal prosecutions. While respondents are correct that drug abuse both was and is a serious problem, "the gravity of the threat alone cannot be dispositive of questions concerning what means law enforcement officers may employ to pursue a given purpose." The Fourth Amendment's general prohibition against nonconsensual, warrantless, and suspicionless searches necessarily applies to such a policy.

Accordingly, the judgment of the Court of Appeals is reversed, and the case is remanded for further proceedings consistent with this opinion.

It is so ordered.

HIV Sufferers Have a Responsibility

Amitai Etzioni

A major drive to find a cure for AIDS was announced last week by Donna Shalala, President Clinton's Secretary of Health and Human Services. Researchers from the private sector, gay activists and government officials were teamed

up to accelerate the search for an effective treatment. Yet even highly optimistic observers do not expect a cure to be found before the end of this century. Still, as the Shalala announcement's exclusive focus on cure highlights, it is not acceptable to explore publicly the measures that could curb the spread of the disease by slowing the transmission of HIV, the virus that causes it. Indeed, before you can say What about prevention? the politically correct choir chimes in: You cannot call it a plague! You are feeding the fires of homophobia! Gay basher!

Case in point: a panel of seven experts fielded questions from 4,000 personnel managers at a conference in Las Vegas. "Suppose you work for medical records. You find out that Joe Doe, who is driving the company's 18-wheeler, is back on the bottle. Will you violate confidentiality and inform his supervisor?" The panel stated unanimously, "I'll find a way." Next question: "Joe Smith is HIV positive; he is intimate with the top designer of the company but did not tell; will you?" "No way," the panel agreed in unison.

We need to break the silence. It is not antigay but fully compassionate to argue that a massive prevention drive is a viable way to save numerous lives in the very next years. We must lay a moral claim on those who are likely to be afflicted with HIV (gays, drug addicts who exchange needles and anyone who received a blood transfusion before 1985) and urge them as a social obligation to come forward to be tested. If the test is positive, they should inform their previous sexual contacts and warn all potential new ones. The principle is elementary, albeit openly put: the more responsibly HIV sufferers act, the fewer dead they will leave in their trail.

HIV testing and contact tracing amount to "a cruel hoax," claims a gay representative from the West Coast. "There are not enough beds to take care of known AIDS patients. Why identify more?" Actually, testing is cruel only in a world where captains of sinking ships do not warn passengers because the captains cannot get off. We must marshal the moral courage to tell those infected with HIV: It is truly tragic that currently we have no way to save your life, but surely you recognize your duty to try to help save the lives of others.

"Warning others is unnecessary because everybody should act safely all the time anyhow," argues Rob Teir, a gay activist in Washington. But human nature is such, strong data show, that most people cannot bring themselves to act safely all the time. A fair warning that they are about to enter a highly dangerous situation may spur people to take special precautions. The moral duty of those already afflicted, though, must be clearly articulated: being intimate without prior disclosure is like serving arsenic in a cake. And not informing previous contacts (or not helping public authorities trace them without disclosing your name) leaves the victims, unwittingly, to transmit the fatal disease to uncounted others.

Testing and contact tracing may lead to a person's being deprived of a job, health insurance, housing and privacy, many civil libertarians fear. These are valid and grave concerns. But we can find ways to protect civil rights without sacrificing public health. A major AIDS-prevention campaign ought to be accompanied by intensive public education about the ways the illness is not transmitted, by additional safeguards on data banks and by greater penalties for those who abuse HIV victims. It may be harsh to say, but the fact that an individual may suffer as a result of doing what is right does not make doing so less of an imperative. Note also that while society suffers a tremendous loss of talent and youth and is stuck with a gargantuan bill, the first victims of non-disclosure are the loved ones of those already afflicted with HIV, even—in the case of infected women—their children.

"Not cost effective," intone the bean counters. Let's count. Take, for example, a suggestion by the highly regarded Centers for Disease Control and Prevention that hospitals be required to ask patients whose blood is already being tested whether they would consent to having it tested for HIV as well. The test costs $60 or less and routinely identifies many who were unaware they had the virus. If those who are thus identified were to transmit the disease to only one less person on average, the suggested tests would pay for themselves much more readily than a coronary bypass, PSA tests and half the pills we pop. And society could continue to enjoy the lifelong earnings and social contributions of those whose lives would be saved.

There are other excuses and rationalizations. But it is time for some plain talk: if AIDS were any other disease—say, hepatitis B or tuberculosis—we would have no trouble (and indeed we have had none) introducing the necessary preventive measures. Moreover, we should make it clear that doing all you can to prevent the spread of AIDS or any other fatal disease is part and parcel of an unambiguous commandment: Thou shalt not kill.

AIDS Prevention—Sexual Ethics and Responsibility

RONALD BAYER

Do people infected with the human immunodeficiency virus (HIV) have special responsibilities to their sexual partners? If so, what do these responsibilities involve? Merely raising these questions directly has tended, until recently, to disquiet many people involved in AIDS-prevention efforts.

From the onset of the AIDS epidemic in 1981, it became increasingly clear that questions of sexual ethics could not be avoided. Here was a new fatal disease, spread in the context of sexual relations that are typically consensual. The questions posed by AIDS were not fundamentally different from those raised by other sexually transmitted diseases. But the lethality of HIV infection added an urgency that made refusing to consider such matters more problematic.

The following questions had to be answered: Is there a moral obligation on the part of someone infected with HIV to use condoms when engaging in penetrative sex? If condoms are used, is there an additional obligation to inform one's partner that one is infected? Does this obligation change if the sexual acts in question are thought to involve a relatively low risk, or risks that are a matter of dispute? Does it matter whether the sexual contact occurs in the context of an ongoing relationship, one that is thought to be monogamous, a casual relationship, or an anonymous encounter? Does it matter if the infected person is a man or a woman or the sexual encounter gay or heterosexual? Is there an obligation to inform past sexual partners about one's HIV infection, and if so, partners from how long ago? Is the obligation to use condoms or to disclose infection obviated if there is a real or assumed threat of violence? Does the anticipation of rejection justify a failure to use condoms or to disclose one's HIV status? Does concern about possible secondary disclosure justify keeping silent about one's infection? What obligations do health departments and AIDS service organizations have to foster an ethic of personal responsibility? Should concern about stigmatizing people affect that obligation?

In the early years of the epidemic, the very idea of responsibility raised by these questions was viewed as alien and threatening. It was a concept more common to the moral and religious right, which had shown a profound indifference to the plight of those with AIDS. The emphasis on personal responsibility was often associated with condemnation of those whose sexual or drug-using behavior had exposed them to HIV, as well as with calls for invasions of privacy and deprivations of liberty. It seemed, finally, to echo the moralistic disapproval of sexual pleasure in general and of homosexuality more specifically.

Pragmatic, philosophical, and political objections to the concept of responsibility were raised. On a pragmatic level, it was claimed that a public health policy focusing on the responsibility of people with HIV to behave in ways that protected the uninfected—either by using condoms or by disclosing the fact of their infection—would, paradoxically, increase the risk of HIV transmission. Misled by false expectations, people would fail to protect themselves. Some did not know they were infected. Others knew they were at high risk but sought to avoid HIV testing. Finally, it was believed that some would lie about whether they were infected. Given these prospects, it made sense to stress self-protection rather than self-disclosure. Each person had to be responsible for condom use,[1] and this obligation was shared equally by the infected and the uninfected. Because each sexual partner was responsible for his or her own health, neither was ultimately responsible for the health of the other.

Even some health departments sought to promote condom use because it was the only way of ensuring self-protection. In an AIDS-prevention advertisement produced by the New York City Health Department, in the style of pop art, a man and woman are shown embracing and thinking, "I hope he [she] doesn't have AIDS!" To this, the voice of the Health Department responds, "You can't live on hope." The text of the advertisement continues:

"You hope this guy is finally the right guy.

You hope this time she just might be the right one.

And you both hope the other one is not infected with the AIDS virus.

Of course, you could ask. But your partner might not know.

That's because it's possible to carry the AIDS virus for many years without showing any symptoms.

The only way to prevent getting infected is to protect yourself. Start using condoms.

Every time. Ask him to use them. If he says no, so can you."

When the question of disclosure was considered in the first decade of the epidemic, it was commonly discussed in terms of the psychological burdens associated with secrecy rather than the sexual partner's right to be informed.

From a philosophical perspective, it was asserted that since HIV was primarily transmitted in the context of consensual sex, each person bore the responsibility of self-protection. Mohr wrote, "The disease's mode of contagion argues that those at risk are those whose actions contribute to their own risk of infection."[2] Relying on the legal maxim "to one who consents, no harm is done,"[3] Illingworth concluded that people who did not protect themselves had no claim against those who infected them.

Haunting the philosophical perspective on the dangerous concept of sexual responsibility was the specter of criminalization. If the protection of others was a moral duty and the consequence of disregarding that duty was a lethal infection, would it not be logical to impose criminal sanctions for unsafe sex? Many state legislatures enacted statutes imposing criminal penalties on those whose actions could result in HIV transmission, and they sometimes refused to distinguish between those who did use condoms and those who did not.[4]

A final, political objection was made to the claim that those with HIV infection had a special responsibility not to transmit the virus. In the face of indifference, hostility, and stigma, it was considered crucial to articulate an ideology of solidarity, one that rejected as divisive all efforts to distinguish the infected from the uninfected. Such distinctions, it was feared, would lead to "viral apartheid." Solidarity was endangered to the extent that the infected were held to have special duties—protecting the uninfected, even recognizing their right to choose not to have penetrative sex with them—and to the extent that the uninfected had a special need to remain uninfected. Cohesiveness could best be grounded in the concepts of universal vulnerability to HIV and the universal importance of safe sexual practices.

It is important not to overstate the extent to which the principle of self-protection rendered impossible any discussion of the responsibility of people with HIV infection. Some philosophers underscored the obligation to notify sexual partners about one's HIV status by drawing on the doctrine of informed consent.[5] And while virtually always rejecting the idea that there was a duty to disclose one's HIV status, many AIDS service organizations urged universal condom use.[6] Public health departments and the Centers for Disease Control and Prevention paid considerable attention to issues of partner notification and explicitly sought to define strategies to protect the unsuspecting sexual contacts of persons with HIV. "Privilege to disclose" legislation in many states made it possible for physicians to breach confidentiality to warn unsuspecting sexual partners.[7]

Nevertheless, self-protection was accorded a central conceptual role in AIDS-prevention efforts, especially by community-based organizations and health departments sensitive to the fears of those most at risk. In a 1995 review of preventive efforts among drug users, Des Jarlais noted that "most programs that have urged intravenous drug users to use condoms thus far have focused on the self-protective efforts of condom use. Appealing to altruistic feelings of protecting others from HIV infection may be an untapped source of motivation for increasing condom use" (Des Jarlais D: personal communication).

How deeply rooted the ideology of self-protection had become and how difficult developing programs that appealed to "altruistic feelings" might be was starkly revealed in New York City in 1993. To mark the occasion of the city's 50,000th AIDS case, efforts were made to launch a prevention campaign that would focus on protecting others as well as oneself. Those efforts were aborted when AIDS specialists inside the health department denounced the proposal as "victim blaming."

The emerging recognition of the limitations of self-protection reflects a growing awareness that new epidemiologic trends demand a new approach to prevention. Self-protection has little to offer the increasing number of women infected through heterosexual contact, who often cannot protect themselves. Patterns of new infections among young gay men suggest that, at least in part, they are vulnerable to infection from an older generation in which the prevalence of HIV infection is high.

Although a growing literature in the late 1980s and early 1990s detailed the patterns of self-disclosure of HIV status to sexual partners,[8-13] the debate about responsibility was largely inaudible. In 1995, however, *The New York Times* published a piece in which the gay journalist Michelangelo Signorile wrote, "If I am positive, I have a responsibility: not to put others at risk and to understand that not all HIV-negative people are equipped to deal with the responsibility of safer sex."[14] AIDS service organizations, he charged, had failed to address this matter. Signorile's challenge was echoed by Gabriel Rotello, a gay columnist for *New York Newsday*: "The focus on self-protection allows some who are HIV-positive to reason that if an infected partner is willing to take risks, that's the partner's choice. And if that choice results in infection, it's the partner's fault."[15]

Even more striking were the observations in 1995 by Dr. Lawrence Mass, a cofounder of Gay Men's Health Crisis (GMHC), New York's largest community-based organization devoted to AIDS prevention:

> "When I wrote the earliest version of GMHC's Medical Answers about AIDS . . . I was maximally concerned about civil liberties. Today, I remain so, but with behavior modification looking as if it will remain the sole form of prevention for years to come, I am even more aware of and concerned about personal and moral responsibility."[16]

The endorsement of personal responsibility by prominent and vocal people should not be taken to mean that the world of AIDS prevention has done an about-face. Nevertheless, it represents a profoundly important challenge, one that would require fundamentally reformulating the messages conveyed in counseling and public efforts at education about AIDS.

Acknowledging that personal responsibility has a central role in AIDS prevention raises a number of complex questions. Some proponents of this concept view it primarily as an alternative strategy of motivating people to use condoms. Others underscore the concomitant obligation to disclose one's HIV infection. After all, condoms sometimes fail. Even AIDS-prevention groups refer to sexual intercourse with the use of condoms as being "safer" rather than "safe." Should not uninfected persons be given the opportunity to decide whether to take the risk, however small, entailed by engaging in protected sex with an infected partner?

What are the implications, if people infected with HIV are obligated both to wear condoms during penetrative sex and to disclose their status to their partners? Should those who have been told that a partner is not infected agree to intercourse without a condom? Should such arrangements between partners be thought of as "negotiated safety" or "negotiated danger"?[17] Most important, should AIDS-prevention programs link the concept of candor with that of trust by suggesting that condoms may not be needed by monogamous, uninfected couples?

Alarmed at the extent to which infected people may not know that they are infected or may not be willing to share the fact, some have recommended that intercourse always be protected, even in ongoing relationships. For them, the very concept of trust—even between husband and wife—"disempowers"[18] partners by making the routine use of condoms unacceptable to those who deem their relationship completely monogamous. Sobo notes, "Unsafe sex within a so-called faithful union helps a woman to maintain her state of denial and her belief that her partnership is one of love, trust and fidelity. . . . AIDS risk denial is tied to monogamy ideals. . . ."[19] From that perspective, some, not surprisingly, have argued that romantic feelings are an impediment to effective AIDS prevention.[20] And so, in view of the risks faced by those who follow the romantic maxim "Love conquers all," it has been suggested that safety can be found only in the warning, "Let the buyer beware"—a warning appropriate to commercial exchanges.

Is such a perspective compatible with lasting relationships, heterosexual or gay? Can efforts to prevent AIDS subvert the expectation of trust within intimate relationships and still remain socially and psychologically credible? It may be appealing to assert that AIDS-prevention efforts should have it both ways, encouraging an ethic of responsibility as well as a posture of self-defense. But can candor be fostered when the continued need for vigilance and self-protection is underscored?

There are no simple answers that address the needs both for trust and candor in intimate relationships and for security in the era of AIDS. Systematic behavioral research is essential, as is searching inquiry into the ethical and psychological underpinnings of intimate relationships.

Nonetheless, these questions make it clear that matters of sexual ethics are not moralistic diversions. They are at the heart of AIDS prevention.

This week is the 15th anniversary of the first report of AIDS by the Centers for Disease Control. All public and community-based programs of HIV prevention should mark this occasion by confronting openly the challenge of sexual responsibility, a challenge that too many have addressed for too long in at best an oblique and morally cramped fashion.

References

1. Cochran SD, Mays VM. Sex, lies, and HIV. N Engl J Med 1990;322:774–5.
2. Mohr RD. Gay life, state coercion. Raritan 1986;6:38–62.
3. Illingworth P. AIDS and the good society. London: Routledge, 1990.
4. Bayer R, Fairchild-Carrino A. AIDS and the limits of control: public health orders, quarantine, and recalcitrant behavior. Am J Public Health 1993;83:1471–6.
5. Yeo M. Sexual ethics and AIDS: a liberal view. In: Overall C, Zion WP, eds. Perspectives on AIDS: ethical and social issues. Toronto: Oxford University Press, 1991:75–90.
6. Chambers DL. Gay men, AIDS, and the code of the condom. Harvard Civil Rights/Civil Liberties Law Rev 1994;29:353–85.
7. Bayer R, Toomey KE. HIV prevention and the two faces of partner notification. Am J Public Health 1992;82:1158–62.
8. Kegeles SM, Catania JA, Coates TJ. Intentions to communicate positive HIV-antibody status to sex partners. JAMA 1988;259:216–7.
9. Marks G, Richardson JL, Maldonado N. Self-disclosure of HIV infection to sexual partners. Am J Public Health 1991;81:1321–2.
10. Marks G, Richardson JL, Ruiz MS, Maldonado N. HIV-infected men's practices in notifying past sexual partners of infection risk. Public Health Rep 1992;107:100–5.
11. Perry SW, Card CA, Moffatt M Jr, Ashman T, Fishman B, Jacobsberg LB. Self-disclosure of HIV infection to sexual partners after repeated counseling. AIDS Educ Prev 1994;6:403–11.
12. Simoni JM, Mason HR, Marks G, Ruiz MS, Reed D, Richardson JL. Women's self-disclosure of HIV infection: rates, reasons, and reactions. J Consult Clin Psychol 1995;63:474–8.
13. Mason HR, Marks G, Simoni JM, Ruiz MS, Richardson JL. Culturally sanctioned secrets? Latino men's nondisclosure of HIV infection to family, friends, and lovers. Health Psychol 1995;14:6–12.
14. Signorile M. HIV-positive and careless. New York Times. February 26, 1995;4:15.
15. Rotello G. [Letter to the editor]. The Nation. April 17, 1995:510.
16. Mass L. [Letter to the editor]. The Nation. April 17, 1995:540.
17. Ekstrand M, Stall R, Kegeles S, Hays R, DeMayo M, Coates T. Safer sex among gay men: what is the ultimate goal? AIDS 1993;7:281–2.
18. Willig C. I wouldn't have married the guy if I'd have to do that: heterosexual adults' constructions of condom use and their implications for sexual practice. J Community Appl Psychol 1995;4:74–87.
19. Sobo EJ. Choosing unsafe sex: AIDS-risk denial among disadvantaged women. Philadelphia: University of Pennsylvania Press, 1995.
20. Pilkington CJ, Kern W, Indest D. Is safer sex necessary with a "safe" partner? Condom use and romantic feelings. J Sex Res 1994;31:203–10.

C. The Implications of Autonomy

As we have explored in the last section, one of the issues raised by the obligation to respect autonomy is the degree to which individuals should be responsible for the health of others. If individuals are entitled to make choices affecting their own health, then one may wonder whether others must necessarily act to protect their choices. Likewise, the recognition of individual autonomy over health care decisions may prompt us to ask whether the community at large should be obligated to bear the costs of the choices individuals have made. Or, once we see individuals as autonomous decision makers, are we entitled to hold them responsible for the consequences of their own choices?

The idea that individuals should be held accountable for the health consequences of their decisions has important ramifications for both public health policy and health care financing. Recall the discussions in Chapter 2 of the many factors that contribute to health and illness. Social and environmental factors, genetics, and even chance play a role in determining the rates of illness and whether an individual becomes ill. Nevertheless, in recent decades, as autonomy has become more valued, public health and medicine have also relied increasingly upon an individualistic perspective that focuses on how individual choices influence an individual's health. As Geoffrey Rose discussed (Chapter 2), this "high-risk" approach differs significantly from a "population strategy." Beverly Rockhill joins this debate by discussing the role that individual risk factors should play in efforts to prevent breast cancer. While acknowledging that a focus on individual risks may lead us to neglect population-wide causes of the disease, Rockhill argues that at least for breast cancer, an individualistic approach remains the best hope for preventing illness. Should the criteria for determining which approach to take be the fruitfulness of the approach to a health outcome?

Public health's focus on individual risk and individual choices, however, increases the likelihood of stigmatizing conditions and blaming the victim. Consider, for example, the case of lung cancer and smoking. Public health campaigns have long sought to educate individuals about the dangers of cigarette smoking. Today there are few adults (or even children) who do not know that "cigarettes cause cancer." In many ways, that lesson is positive, both because it gives individuals the information they need to make an informed choice (hence, enhancing their autonomy) and because some individuals will respond by not smoking (thereby improving public health and overall utility). On the other hand, if we come to see smoking as a choice, does it then follow that individuals who become ill as a result of their smoking have no one but themselves to blame? Certainly the tobacco companies have argued that smokers have "assumed the risk" of smoking. But if so, does that mean that insurers should not pay for or even that physicians need not treat the patients who "asked for it?" And does it mean that tobacco companies have no obligation to alter their marketing practices which help make smoking seem like an attractive choice? The difficulties in assigning causal responsibility to individuals for their illnesses and what that may mean for a wide variety of policy issues are explored in the reading by Gerald Dworkin.

The question whether health care policies should take into account individuals' behaviors has repeatedly arisen in the context of organ transplants. A few years ago, the famous New York Yankee baseball player Mickey Mantle was dying of liver failure. Although he had a long history of alcoholism, he was given a liver transplant, which unfortunately did not prevent his rapid death. The fact that he was given a scarce organ, despite his history of alcoholism, prompted a fierce debate.[16] (Many also questioned whether his celebrity put him to the head of the queue.)[17] Eike-Henner Kluge argues that individuals who make "medically inappropriate lifestyle choices" should not be given the same access to scarce medical resources as those who refrain from conduct that puts their health at risk.

The practice of financing health care by insurance can be justified by the fact that individuals generally have little control over whether they will become sick and need expensive care. As long as we see illness as something that can happen to any of us, we seem to be willing to pool our funds with others to ensure that if any in the group should be the unlikely one to need expensive care, the money will be there. However, once we start to see our health status and needs as matters within the control of individuals, the whole idea of insuring health care costs begins to seem problematic. (We would not, after all, ensure another's expensive vacation tastes.) And, of course, it seems especially problematic to pay for the consequences of an individual's choice when the costs associated with those consequences are extraordinarily expensive. Thus nonsmokers ask why they must pay the health care costs of smokers, and those who drive Volvos ask why they must pay for the health care costs of those who ride motorcycles without helmets.

Still, the question must be asked whether individuals truly have sufficient control over their health care outcomes to treat them as if they were responsible for those outcomes. But if individuals did have sufficient control, would public health be improved by holding individuals responsible for their own health? Or would such a policy fray the fabric of health insurance? Would it violate norms of justice? And if any of the above were true, do they suggest some other reason for limiting autonomy?

The Privatization of Risk

BEVERLY ROCKHILL

The privatization, or individualization, of risk factor knowledge has been largely responsible for a rising tide of criticism of epidemiology and preventive medicine.[1-10] This criticism is based on the perception that epidemiologists and other public health researchers, while churning out a seemingly endless torrent of relative risks associated with numerous risk factors, have failed to provide prescriptions for effective public health strategies. The current debate about the practice of epidemiology often seems polarized into 2 sides, those who support and those who attack "risk factor" epidemiology. Some critics of risk factor epidemiology have rather simplistically disallowed the real gains in knowledge about the health effects of behaviors and other lifestyle factors that have come from years of careful research.

An aim of this commentary is to reinvigorate some of Geoffrey Rose's central arguments[11] and show that this current debate may miss a key point: a risk factor is a probabilistic concept that applies to an aggregate of individuals, not to a specific individual. Risk factor knowledge compels those in public health to seek actions that shift population distributions of these factors. I will also discuss how breast cancer may be unique in terms of "public" health concerns: for this disease, a policy promoting private decision making about risk, while likely ineffective from a population standpoint, may be the only feasible primary prevention option.

The Move toward Individual Risk

The phenomenon of risk privatization, so pervasive in modern epidemiology, reflects the value system now underlying much of public health and preventive medicine in the United States. This system gives primacy to personal autonomy and action and seeks to induce personal behavior change rather than to promote social interventions that often must confront powerful opposing interests.[12] Through numerous and varied channels, including physician counseling, the near-ubiquitous health reports in the lay media, scientific sources, and myriad health-related Web sites, individuals are informed of their individual risk of major diseases on the basis of their personal risk factor profile. These individual risk estimates may pertain to relatively short time periods (5 or 10 years) or to a "lifetime," and they are usually obtained from simple epidemiologic models.

The privatization of risk has important public health implications. Traditionally, risk quantification in public health has taken its shape in large numbers, in statistics regarding average incidence, number needed to treat or screen, and average life expectancy.[1] There are few rules for translating the intrinsically aggregate-level continuous concept of risk into language useful for individuals concerned with dichotomous outcomes and dichotomous decisions about prevention strategies (e.g., use of chemoprevention). Because risk privatization makes risk, and the

ability to alter risk, an intrinsic property of the individual,[13] it raises important questions regarding assignation of disease responsibility. There are also important consequences of this individualization for disease prevention. Risk individualization denies the prevention paradox and implies that most epidemiologic risk models are accurate in predicting the future of a specific individual.

Risk Factors Are Poor Screening Tools at the Individual Level

With the shift from infectious disease to chronic disease research that occurred around the middle of the 20th century, the risk factor paradigm gained ascendancy among epidemiologists. (The term *risk factor* was coined by Framingham researchers in 1961.[14]) Risk factor logic introduced the notion of probability as a fundamental component of disease causation theories. Risk factors represented the numerous specific causes of disease, but the notion of "cause" was now different from that of the germ theory model that had underlain decades of study of infectious disease. Many of the risk factors hypothesized to be causally related to heart disease and various cancers have only modest associations at the population level. They are neither necessarily nor sufficiently causal at the individual level by definition as well as by empirical observation. Consequently, the vast majority of chronic disease risk factors, being both unnecessary and insufficient to cause disease, have proved to be quite poor at discriminating at the individual level between those who eventually develop disease (over a certain time period) and those who do not.

This poor discriminatory accuracy of risk factors can be demonstrated statistically. For most diseases studied by epidemiologists, the large majority of individuals will remain disease free over the considered time period, and thus the average estimated "individual" disease risk will be low, often around 0. The relatively few individuals who will develop disease will not receive unusually high estimates of individual risk. This is a quantitative illustration of Rose's point that for most diseases, the large majority of cases arise from the mass of the population with risk factor values (here, "individual" risk estimates) around the average.[11]

The concordance statistic, an index of predictive discrimination of statistical models based on the rank correlation between predicted and observed outcomes.[15] is a widely applicable measure of discriminatory accuracy at the individual level. Potential values of the concordance statistic range from 0.5 to 1.0. The value of the statistic represents the probability that, for a randomly selected diseased individual and a randomly selected nondiseased individual, the diseased individual has the higher estimated disease probability. A concordance statistic of 0.5 for a risk model means that the model performs no better than chance at ranking diseased and nondiseased individuals in terms of estimated probabilities: 50% of the time the diseased person will have the higher estimated probability, while 50% of the time the nondiseased person will. A concordance statistic of 1.0 means that the model performs perfectly at ranking diseased and nondiseased individuals.

Many epidemiologic risk equations produce concordance statistics that are far below 1.0: often they are between 0.50 and 0.70. This is especially true when the risk factors used in the model are associated with only modest relative risks, as is often the case in breast cancer risk models. A risk factor (or set of factors) must be very strongly associated with disease if it is to serve as a worthwhile screening tool, that is, if it is to discriminate well between diseased and nondiseased individuals as reflected by measures of sensitivity and specificity. A given risk factor (or set of factors, where the unexposed group consists of those unexposed to all factors) must have a large relative risk (>20.0) to serve as a useful screening tool.[16]

The Causes of Cases and the Causes of Incidence

In his influential writings about chronic disease risk factors, particularly those for coronary heart disease. Geoffrey Rose developed the theme of the distinction between the causes of disease incidence and the causes of individual cases.[14,17–19] Why did lung cancer incidence rise dramatically in the United States and Britain beginning in the 1930s? Why does breast cancer incidence vary positively with socioeconomic status, and why are incidence rates rising dramatically—to levels found in industrialized societies—in developing countries around the world? Why did coronary heart disease mortality decline in the United States beginning in the early 1960s, and why did the rate of this decline differ by socioeconomic status? These questions about the causes of incidence can be answered by turning to knowledge of the risk factors for the specific diseases and examining the changing distributions of these factors over time and in different population subgroups. However, knowledge that a factor is strongly associated with disease risk can seldom answer the question "Why did this individual get this disease now?" This incapability is both a mathematical reality—following from the modest, probabilistic nature of risk factor—disease associations—and a philosophical argument.[20,21]

Concern about the causes of individual cases vs the causes of population incidence has traditionally been the distinction separating clinical medicine from public health. Knowledge that a factor is associated with increased risk of disease obviously does not translate into the premise that a case of disease will be prevented if a specific individual eliminates exposure; disease pathogenesis at the individual level is a very complex process, as I will elaborate. The misleading message that an individual will prevent a particular disease by altering a particular behavior or exposure (and its converse, than an individual will develop a particular disease if such behavior is not changed) has unfortunately been widely conveyed. Rather, risk factor findings, by necessity couched in probabilistic language, call for aggregate-level policies: if exposure can be eliminated for (say) 1000 individuals, 5 cases (for example) will be averted over a 10-year time period. "Cause" and "prevention," as they pertain to probabilistic risk factor logic, are concepts that apply to an aggregate of individuals, not to a specific individual. Thus, knowledge of proximate risk factors should propel those in public health away from a focus on the individual and compel them to seek ways of shifting population distributions of these factors, by seeking to understand their social, economic, and political determinants.

The "Individual Risk" Approach to Breast Cancer Prevention

Despite the potential pitfalls of relying on assessment of, communication of, and intervention on individual risk to prevent disease, this approach is now prominent with regard to breast cancer prevention. This is probably because, unlike the situation with most other major chronic diseases, *public* health solutions to the problem of breast cancer prevention may be unavailable.

Breast cancer has a unique status among major chronic diseases as a disease of privilege, of women's liberation from their traditional childbearing role.[22] Breast cancer incidence is strongly and positively related to the nutritional status of girls and women.[22,23] Young girls in well-nourished (and now often overnourished) societies experience the onset of menses earlier than young girls who are less well fed, and early menarche is an established risk factor for breast cancer because it signifies higher lifetime exposure to endogenous ovarian hormones. Further, obesity during the postmenopausal period also increases breast cancer risk,[24] through increasing lifetime exposure to estrogens: adipose tissue is the primary site of postmenopausal estrogen production.[25] Breast cancer risk is also strongly and positively related to the degree of women's freedom to choose to reproduce far below traditional and evolutionary levels.[22,23] Nulliparity or low parity, and a late age at first birth are associated with increased risk of breast cancer, possibly through their detrimental effects on the protective process of breast cell differentiation.[26,27] Attempts to shift social and reproductive norms (e.g., to increase age at menarche or lower age at first birth) to reduce the breast cancer burden would be considered unethical or culturally undesirable in most developed and developing societies: such attempts to alleviate the public health problem of breast cancer could bring with them a net *loss* of public health.

Further, although several "modifiable" lifestyle factors, including postmenopausal hormone use and alcohol consumption, have been linked to modestly increased risk of breast cancer[28–32] it may be unethical to consider population-based strategies aimed at eliminating or greatly reducing exposure to these factors. On the basis of empiric evidence, both exposures appear to convey a net public health benefit among women: modest alcohol consumption and postmenopausal hormone use are both associated with lower (population) risk of cardiovascular disease,[28,30,33,34] the leading cause of death among older women, and postmenopausal hormones are also associated with reduced risk of osteoporosis[30] and age-related cognitive decline and dementia.[35] Women can also take a chemopreventive agent such as tamoxifen, which has recently been shown to reduce at least short-term breast cancer risk.[36] However, tamoxifen is associated with increased risk of endometrial cancer and deep vein thrombosis/pulmonary embolism, along with more common, though comparatively minor, side effects, and therefore is not recommended for widespread use. Finally, the most extreme choice, prophylactic mastectomy, appears to be highly effective in terms of prevention,[37] but owing to the drastic nature of this option it has so far been reserved for women with strong family histories of the disease or *BRCAI/BRCA2* mutations. I argue that this dilemma, whereby population-based strategies to reduce the burden of one disease, breast cancer, could have net negative effects on overall public health, has helped prompt attempts at preventing cases on an individual-by-individual basis.

Women and their clinicians are increasingly encouraged to use risk estimates derived from statistical risk factor models such as that of Gail et al.[38] (now available to all citizens in the form of the "risk disk," distributed at no cost by the National Cancer Institute and by Zeneca Pharmaceuticals, the maker of tamoxifen) to aid their personal decision making regarding potential prevention options. Women 35 years and older with an estimated 5-year risk of breast cancer of 1.67% according to this risk factor equation are eligible, according to Food and Drug Administration (FDA) guidelines, to consider using tamoxifen prophylactically against breast cancer.

An important question regarding Gail et al.'s model is its accuracy at the probability cutoff 1.67%.[39] What proportion of women who will develop breast cancer in the near future will have an estimated probability from Gail et al.'s model "high enough" (i.e., above 1.67%) to consider tamoxifen? What proportion of the vast majority of women who will remain free of breast cancer in the near future might nonetheless consider tamoxifen? It is likely that this latter number will be high.[39]

The strategy of preventing breast cancer with tamoxifen, or any other chemopreventive agent, illustrates the prevention paradox[14] well. Many women must engage in the preventive action to prevent disease in only a few. For instance, among 100 women with an estimated 5-year risk of 0.04, approximately 4 women will develop breast cancer over 5 years (assuming the model predictions are well calibrated). If tamoxifen reduces 5-year risk of breast cancer by approximately 50%,[36] 2 of these 4 women will have their breast cancer prevented while 2 women will still develop breast cancer. The remaining 96 women, who will remain free of breast cancer without tamoxifen, will be exposed to increased risk of the adverse outcomes associated with this agent.[40] There is support[40] for the notion that there will be a net *loss* of public health if tamoxifen is used for chemoprevention in all women who are eligible according to FDA guidelines. This reality supports Rose's argument that widespread use of pharmacologic agents for disease prevention is inappropriate.[14] Preventive measures that are implemented in broad segments of the population must be supported by strong evidence indicating their safety in all these segments. Because the "individual" average benefit to each person is small, it can be easily outweighed by the small "individual risk" that accompanies virtually every pharmacologic agent.

Another way of describing the above situation of chemoprevention is in terms of individual risk: each of the 100 women has her "individual" 5-year risk of breast cancer reduced from 0.04 to 0.02. However, this statement is practically meaningless. It disguises the reality that risk refers to a state of *population* health located outside of any one particular individual; it is an aggregate-level concept.

Conclusion

The privatization, or individualization, of the concept of risk raises important practical questions about disease prevention strategies. Most risk factor–disease associations in chronic disease epidemiology are modest (with some notable exceptions, such as smoking and lung cancer and certain occupational exposures and various cancers), and most epidemiologic risk models have correspondingly poor discriminatory accuracy at the individual level. Epidemiologists' ceaseless search for new risk factors, including genes, and the churning out of an endless torrent of relative risks are driven in part by this reality. However, it is likely that the ability to predict the futures of individuals will always remain out of reach, despite ever increasing knowledge about alleged independent factors or genes that may elevate disease risk in exposed groups.

While the disease of breast cancer may be unique in terms of "public" health concerns, in that no beneficial population-wide prevention strategies are readily apparent, it ironically demonstrates the logic of population-wide approaches. Suggested primary prevention strategies, including chemoprevention or avoidance of postmenopausal hormones, that are directed at supposedly "high-risk" women will not have a large impact on disease burden *unless* the strategy becomes widespread. That is, unless a large proportion of women participate in such strategies, few cases of disease will actually be prevented.

"Public" health today increasingly means education about "personal" risk for a variety of diseases. There is a growing belief in our society that individuals can, and should, exert fundamental control over their future by rationally acting to lower personal risk of a variety of diseases. This focus on individual risk calculation and communication can have positive consequences, such as promotion of healthy lifestyles in segments of the population able to obtain, and voluntarily act on, accurate health risk information. However, there are substantial negative consequences as well. Most important, there is little precedent for relying on communication about individual risk to meaningfully reduce chronic disease burden. Even a cursory reading of the history of chronic disease trends will demon-

strate that favorable population-wide changes in risk factors, and resulting decreases in disease incidence, have rarely resulted from individual risk calculations made simultaneously by key "high-risk" individuals in the population.

There are potential dangers in designating the individual the *sole* locus of "risk" and thus the locus of responsibility for "risk reduction." One danger is the amplification of existing socioeconomic health inequities, as individuals in lower socioeconomic strata are less likely to have regular contact with the health care system, to comprehend the arithmetic behind risk information, and to have the psychologic, social, and economic resources needed to voluntarily alter the factors contributing to their "personal" risk.

Another possible negative effect is the assignation of personal responsibility for illness. Ironically, while there has often been a moralistic tendency to blame individuals for their own poor health outcomes,[14] supposedly "progressive" public health research is now being used, inappropriately, to justify such individual accountability. The labeling of these risk factors as the "causes" of individual cases of disease, and the implication that responsible individuals who avoid such risk factors will prevent their own case of disease, represent strong denials of the inability of statistics and medical science to predict the futures of individuals. Further, the equating of risk factors with the causes of individual cases fosters an indifference to the social determinants of risk factor distributions and thus contributes to ineffectual insease prevention policies at the population level.

References

1. Burris S. The invisibility of public health: population-level measures in a politics of market individualism. *Am J Public Health.* 1997;87: 1607–1610.
2. Beaglehole R. Bonita R. *Public Health at the Crossroads: Achievements and Prospects.* Cambridge, UK: Cambridge University Press; 1997.

3. Wing S. Limits of epidemiology. *Med Global Survival.* 1994;1: 74–86.

4. Susser M. Does risk factor epidemiology put epidemiology at risk? Peering into the future, *J Epidemiol Community Health.* 1998;52:608–611.

5. Schwartz S, Susser E, Susser M. A future for epidemiology? *Annu Rev Public Health,* 1999; 20:15–33.

6. Rothman K, Adami H-O, Trichopoulos D. Should the mission of epidemiology include the eradication of poverty? *Lancet.* 1998; 352:810–813.

7. Pearce N. Traditional epidemiology, modern epidemiology, and public health. *Am J Public Health.* 1996;86:678–683.

8. Krieger N. Epidemiology and the web of causation: has anyone seen the spider? *Soc Sci Med.* 1994;39:887–903.

9. Aronowitz R. *Making Sense of Illness.* New York, NY: Cambridge University Press; 1998.

10. Marmot MG. Improvement of social environment to improve health. *Lancet.* 1998; 351:57–60.

11. Rose G. *The Strategy of Preventive Medicine.* New York, NY: Oxford University Press: 1992.

12. Mechanic D. The social context of health and disease and choices among health interventions. In: Brandt A, Rozin P, eds. *Morality and Health.* New York, NY: Routledge: 1997:79–100.

13. Gifford S. The meaning of lumps: a case study of the ambiguities of risk. In: Janes C. Stall R. Gifford S, eds. *Anthropology and Epidemiology.* Boston, Mass: D Reidel Publishing Co; 1986: 213–246.

14. Kannel W, Dawber T, Kagan A, Revotskie N, Stokes JI. Factors of risk in the development of coronary heart disease: six-year follow-up experience—the Framingham study. *Ann Intern Med.* 1961:55:33–50.

15. Harrell FE Jr, Lee K, Mark D. Multivariable prognostic models; issues in developing models, evaluating assumptions and adequacy, and measuring and reducing errors. *Stat Med.* 1996; 15:361–387.

16. Wald N. When can a risk factor be used as a worthwhile screening test? *BMJ.* 1999;319: 1562–1565.

17. Rose G. Strategy of prevention: lessons from cardiovascular disease. *Br Med J (Clin Res Ed).* 1981;282:1847–1851.

18. Rose G. The population mean predicts the number of deviant individuals. *BMJ.* 1990;301: 1031–1034.

19. Rose G. Sick individuals and sick populations. *Int J Epidemiol.* 1985;14:32–38.

20. Bateson G. *Mind and Nature: A Necessary Unity.* New York, NY: EP Dutton; 1979.

21. Toulmin S. On the nature of the physician's understanding. *J Med Philosophy.* 1976;1:32–40.

22. Willett W, Rockhill B, Hankinson S, Hunter D, Colditz G. Nongenetic risk factors in the causation of breast cancer. In: Harris J. Lippman M, Morrow M. Osborne C, eds. *Diseases of the Breast.* 2nd ed. Philadelphia, Pa: Lippincott Williams and Wilkins; 2000:175–221.

23. Harris JR, Lippman ME, Veronsei U, Willett WC. Breast cancer. *N Engl J Med.* 1992;327:319–328.

24. Hunter DJ. Willett WC. Diet, body size, and breast cancer. *Epidemiol Rev.* 1993;15:110–132.

25. Siiteri PK. Adipose tissue as a source of hormones. *Am J Clin Nutr.* 1987;45(suppl):277–282.

26. Russo J. Russo IH. Biologic and molecular basis of mammary carcinogenesis. *Lab Invest.* 1987;57: 112–137.

27. Russo J. Gusterson BA, Rogers AE, Russo IH, Wellings SR, van Zwieten MJ. Biology of disease: comparison study of human and rat mammary tumorigenesis. *Lab Invest.* 1990;62:244–278.

28. Grodstein F, Stampfer MJ, Colditz GA, et al. Postmenopausal hormone therapy and mortality. *N Engl J Med.* 1997;336:1769–1775.

29. Longnecker MP. Alcoholic beverage consumption in relation to risk of breast cancer: meta-analysis and review. *Cancer Causes Control.* 1994;5: 73–82.

30. Grady D, Rubin SM, Petirti DB, et al. Hormone therapy to prevent disease and prolong life in postmenopausal women. *Ann Intern Med.* 1992;117:1016–1036.

31. Smith-Warner SA, Spiegelman D, Yaun S-S, et al. Alcohol and breast cancer in women: a pooled analysis of cohort studies. *JAMA.* 1998;279: 535–540.

32. Collaborative Group on Hormonal Factors in Breast Cancer. Breast cancer and hormone replacement therapy: collaborative reanalysis of data from 51 epidemiologic studies of 52,705

women with breast cancer and 108,411 women without breast cancer. *Lancet.* 1997;350:1047–1059.

33. Thun M, Peto R, Lopez A, et al. Alcohol consumption and mortality among middle-aged and elderly US adults. *N Engl J Med.* 1997;337:1705–1714.

34. Rimm E, Williams P, Fosher K, Criqui M, Stampfer M. Moderate alcohol intake and lower risk of coronary heart disease: meta-analysis of effects on lipids and haemostatic factors. *BMJ.* 1999;319:1523–1528.

35. Yaffe K, Sawaya G, Lieberburg I. Grady D. Estrogen therapy in postmenopausal women. *JAMA.* 1998;279:688–695.

36. Fisher B, Costantino JP, Wickerham DL, et al. Tamoxifen for prevention of breast cancer: report of the National Surgical Adjuvant Breast and Bowel Project P-1. *J Natl Cancer Inst.* 1998;90:1371–1388.

37. Hartmann L, Schaid D, Woods J, et al. Efficacy of bilateral prophylactic mastectomy in women with a family history of breast cancer. *N Engl J Med.* 1999;340:77–84.

38. Gail MH, Brinton LA, Byar DP, et al. Projecting individualized probabilities of developing breast cancer for White females who are being examined annually. *J Natl Cancer Inst.* 1989;81:1879–1886.

39. Rockhill B, Colditz G, Kaye J. Re: Tamoxifen prevention of breast cancer: an instance of the fingerpost [letter]. *J Natl Cancer Inst.* 2000;92:657A–657.

40. Gail M, Costantino J, Bryant J, et al. Weighing the risks and benefits of tamoxifen treatment for preventing breast cancer. *J Natl Cancer Inst.* 1999;91:1829–1846.

Taking Risks, Assessing Responsibility

GERALD DWORKIN

In discussions about the voluntary assumption of health risks, there are four key terms—"voluntary," "responsibility," "risk," and "health." I shall not be concerned at all here with definitions of health and I shall be concerned only incidentally with the concept of risk. My main task is to examine various ideas of responsibility, particularly as that concept has been discussed by philosophers, and to relate the philosophical material to the issue of formulating health policy.

Two sets of questions are at issue—normative and conceptual. The latter are questions of causation, the types of things for which one can be responsible, and so forth. The former are questions about the principles of responsibility; disputes about what actions or consequences of actions people ought to be held responsible for and what the legitimate consequences of that responsibility ought to be. These two questions are harder to distinguish clearly in the area of responsibility than in any other area of moral philosophy. The very concept of responsibility itself is often used both to claim some connection (factual) between a person and some state of affairs and to claim that the person is in some way accountable for bringing about that state of affairs. Hence an account of the logic of the concept will be tied very closely to our views of what the correct principles are for ascribing responsibility.

To indicate the many senses in which "responsible" can be used, H.L.A. Hart made up the following story:

> As captain of the ship, X was responsible for the safety of his passengers and crew. But on his last voyage he got drunk every night and was responsible for the loss of the ship with all aboard. It was rumored that he was insane, but the doctors considered that he was responsible for his actions. Throughout the voyage he behaved quite irresponsibly, and various incidents in his career showed that he was not a responsible person. He always maintained that the exceptional winter storms were responsible for the loss of the ship, but in the legal proceedings brought against him he was found criminally responsible for his negligent conduct, and in separate civil proceedings he was held legally responsible for the loss of life and property. He is still alive and he is morally responsible for the deaths of many women and children.[1]

No doubt, all these uses of the term are linked together. It is no accident that the same term appears in these different claims. But the connections are indirect. Rather than force them all into a straitjacket of a single concept it is preferable to classify the uses, following Hart, into three broad categories.

Role-Responsibility

In Hart's story the captain was responsible for the safety of the ship. I was responsible for preparing this essay. A teacher is responsible for preparing his classes, giving students adequate notice of examinations, and assigning grades. Parents are responsible for their children's welfare. Doctors are responsible for the confidentiality of their patients' records. In each of these cases there is a distinctive place in social life, which carries with it certain duties and/or obligations. These are the responsibilities of the role.

But the responsibilities go beyond specific duties and obligations. They define a sphere of concern, which usually cannot be delimited in finite, specifiable ways. In the case of the captain, it may be his specific duty to check the weather reports for storms or ice. But one would not specify as a particular duty that he should watch out for psychotics who might damage the ship. Yet this does come under his general responsibility for the safety of the ship.

The roles mentioned above are roles in the sociological sense—positions defined by explicit criteria. But both Hart and I are using "role" much more broadly. If I knock you down with my car, I am responsible for getting you medical care. This is my role-responsibility. But there is no role of "knocking-down-pedestrian." Any sphere of concern that I have as a result of what I am or what I do is a role-responsibility. It is the area that I have to look out for.

Conversely, not all the duties that one has as part of one's role are responsibilities. I may have a duty, as a professor, not to give a final in class during the last week of the term, but that is not one of my responsibilities. It is too discrete, too short-lived.

Are all role-responsibilities voluntarily assumed? Obviously the answer is no if we are referring to specific duties. A doctor cannot disregard confidentiality on the grounds that he or she never agreed to such a duty. It comes with the role. But it may be argued at least that the role is voluntary.

But what about the role of son or daughter, and its corresponding responsibilities for aged parents? Here neither the specific duties nor the role itself seem to be voluntary. Similarly, in the car-pedestrian example, the accident may in no way be my fault. You may have stepped off the curb without looking. Nevertheless I have a responsibility to see that you get care, and it is a responsibility that belongs to me rather than any other pedestrians or motorists who happen to be present at the scene of the accident. One may have responsibilities, then, simply because of what one is or what one does—where neither of these is voluntary.

Causal-Responsibility

When a father comes home, finds the kitchen a mess, and asks "Who is responsible for this mess?" he is not asking whose duty it is to make a mess. He is asking who brought the mess about, who caused its appearance. When a judge tries to decide whether the icy road or the driver's drunkenness was responsible for the accident, she is trying to determine what factors caused the accident.

It would seem that deciding questions of responsibility in this sense is a purely factual matter. After all, questions of causation are questions about the way the world operates, empirical questions. But matters are not so simple. There will often be many causal contributors to an event, in the sense of events that were necessary for the given event to occur. Often we are interested in selecting from among them *the* cause. But what *the* cause is will reflect our interests, the normal state of affairs, what conditions we can alter, our background knowledge, and so forth. Consider why the arson investigator reports the presence at the scene of a mysterious fire of a trail of gasoline, and not oxygen.

Consider the social reformer who argues that poverty is the cause of crime, or the defendant who claims it was the egg-shell skull of the victim of his assault that caused the victim's death, or the debate about the cause of the Civil War. In all these cases there is a need to select or decide the importance of various factors, and the relationship of this decision to policies, values, purposes, prior knowledge, etc. These judgments of responsibility are precisely that—judgments. They select some factors from a range of candidates and claim these are the significant, illuminating, morally noteworthy ones to fix the responsibility.

One of the interests in deciding this issue may be that of determining who or what is to blame for a given situation, or who is to be held liable for some damage. This brings us to the next category.

Liability-Responsibility

To say that the defendant was responsible for the accident, or that Truman was responsible for the deaths of Japanese civilians at Hiroshima, or that all the conspirators were responsible for the assassination attempt is not just to assign causal responsibility. It is to claim that certain judgments or actions are warranted as a response to some faulty aspect of the person's conduct. What exactly that response is will depend on the specific context in which the action is assessed. In the case of legal liability it will usually be some punishment or civil liability. With respect to moral responsibility it will usually be some judgment of wrong-doing or some form of blame, or some duty to make amends or compensate for injury. But other consequences may flow from liability-responsibility. For example, one may not be entitled to complain of certain injuries if one is ultimately responsible for them. Provoking others makes one partly responsible for what happens to oneself, and hence one's grounds for complaint are undercut. Or, again, if one goes out mountain-climbing having been warned of the avalanche conditions prevalent, one may not have the right to call on the rescue-teams to help in the event of disaster.

Two distinct elements are involved in this ascription of responsibility. One is that the harm is in some way the product of some faulty aspect of the person or his or her conduct; the other is that certain consequences do or ought to flow from this first judgment. I shall refer to the first aspect as culpability and the second as liability. These two are logically independent of one another. In cases of strict liability in the law, such as holding the owner of a tavern liable for selling liquor to somebody under age even if the person has (phony) ID, we may attach consequences to conduct even while conceding there is no culpability. Conversely, we may believe somebody culpable but not attach consequences, such as the first offender whom we decide to give "another chance." Judgments of culpability are for the record; they establish fault and assign blame. They look to the past. Judgments of liability are for action; they are demands on the person to do something or on others to act toward him in certain ways. They look to the future.

The relationships between role-responsibility, causal-responsibility, and liability-responsibility are complex and it is not necessary to discuss them here in detail. But, roughly speaking, each category serves as a foundation for reasoning about the next. One's role-responsibilities determine one's liabilities and obligations. They also serve to determine causal influences. It is the gardener's failure to water the lawn that caused the marigolds to die, not mine—although neither of us watered the lawn. In turn, what one causes determines for what one can be held accountable and for what one is liable. But of course the step from causation to blame is never direct and is always open to rebuttal through the ideas of excuse and justification. We make excuses when we admit that we caused some harm but maintain that the action was not fully voluntary; we were drunk or coerced or negligent or too tired to pay attention. We say we were justified when we admit we caused harm but claim that in the circumstances it was self-defense, or he had it coming to him, or we had a right to do it.

Finally we come to the question of what one is responsible for; what kinds of things one can be held accountable for. A short answer would be—anything. But for our purposes it is sufficient to note the following items. One is responsible for what one does, where this includes both actions and behavior. One is also responsible for continuing behavior after one has initiated it. In addition to what one does one may be responsible for the consequences of what one does; what follows causally from one's actions or behavior.

Here one has to distinguish among three classes of consequences. First, and most broadly, there are all the *possible* consequences of one's acts. All the events that are more likely to come about as a result of what one did. This is the category of risk-creation. That the risk does not produce harm may not absolve one from responsibility for creation of the risk. The drunken driver may not hit anyone but he is responsible for endangering the lives of others just the same. In fact we tend to assign liability, at least with respect to punishment, taking into account whether risks result in harm or not. The drunken driver who kills a pedestrian is liable for manslaughter. The drunken driver who is fortunate enough to not hit anybody is guilty of a far less serious offense in the eyes of the law, although no good moral or legal reason exists for such a differentiation in degree of punishment.

The next set of consequences for which one can be held responsible are the *actual* consequences of one's acts. On this view no matter how long and attenuated the chain of causation if some harm eventuates for which one was, in some measure, causally responsible and at fault then one is culpable or liable. This might be called the "for want of a nail. . ." principle of responsibility. One rather subtle point is that even on this view it is not sufficient that one be at fault and that one cause harm; there must be the appropriate connection between the two. Consider Robert Keeton's hypothetical example.

> The defendant, proprietor of a restaurant, placed a large unlabelled can of rat poison beside cans of flour on a shelf near a stove in a restaurant kitchen. The victim, while in the kitchen making a delivery to the restaurant, was killed by an explosion of the poison.[2]

Here the defendant was at fault, negligent in putting the poison where it could be mistaken for flour, and his placing the poison there caused harm, but assuming that there was no reason to know poison is explosive, the harm that he caused was not the harm that he was at fault in risking.

This brings us to the next class of consequences for which one might be responsible; those which are foreseen or reasonably foreseeable. On this view we are not responsible for those harms that result from our conduct unless we were aware of the possibility that they might occur or we were negligent in not thinking about their possibility. If the chain of causation is too long, or if there are intervening factors that are purely fortuitous (freaky), then we are not, or ought not, to be held responsible.

One might think that limiting the consequences to the foreseeable would narrow the scope of one's responsibilities as far as possible. But another view, which has ancient theological sanction and has taken on renewed vigor in some more recent philosophical writings, holds that we are particularly responsible for the subset of the class of foreseeable consequences that we intend. We are still responsible for what we foresee but do not intend, but our responsibility could be less in such cases, because of the distinction between what we merely foresee and what we intend. We are primarily responsible, in this view, for what we invest with our purposes, for what we aim at rather than what we simply cause to happen.

The Consequences of Assigning Blame

Having assembled this apparatus I want to apply it to the question of individual responsibility for voluntary health risks and the issue of formulating social policy based on claims about the individual's responsibility. I am less interested in providing an answer to social policy questions than in indicating what moral, empirical, and conceptual premises must be supplied to justify the various arguments.

The claim that individuals are personally responsible for their health is ambiguous. Perhaps most often it is a claim about the role-responsibility of the individual. That is, it is an assertion about the sphere of concern for which the individual is responsible. It is a claim that one of the areas for which one is required to look out, to discharge duties, to take charge, is one's health.

More accurately, it is a claim that one is responsible for behaving in various ways that are causally connected to one's health status. One must engage in that wide variety of behaviors associated with maintaining and improving one's health. These behaviors can include keeping informed about new developments in medicine, monitoring one's body in specific ways, warding off threats, taking precautions, engaging in certain activities, omitting others, and so forth. They are all different ways of keeping in touch with one's sphere of concern and obligation.

It is worth noting some special features about this claim. First, if this is a case of role-responsibility it is not like the more typical cases that one confronts. It is not the kind of role that is so prominent in F.H. Bradley's view of "My Station and its Duties," that is, a role within an institution defined by rules, statuses, expectations, and sanctions. One has this responsibility just by virtue of being a living organism, with certain abilities and capacities.

Second, this is one of those role-responsibilities that is not required to be voluntarily assumed. Presumably we are required to look out for our health whether or not we want to, decide to, or intend to. And unlike the case of being responsible for one's children, no prior voluntary act can be cited as the reason why one must accept this responsibility.

Third, there is not available (at this level of assignment of responsibility) the appeal to the interests, rights, or welfare of other people. It is uncontroversial that our sphere of responsibility extends to avoiding the creation of certain risks and dangers to others. It is more controversial, but still intuitively clear to many, that our responsibility extends to rendering aid to others in various situations of grave danger (at least where there is relatively little risk to ourselves). But it is much more doubtful to many that our responsibilities (obligations and duties) extend to avoiding risks and harms to ourselves.

Fourth, there are difficulties about knowing where the boundaries of one's role-responsibility lie. How much time and energy do I have to devote to my health? What about conflicts with other role-responsibilities I have, for example, the Supreme Court justice who refused to retire although his doctor warned that continued service would aggravate an already serious heart condition? What sacrifices are required of me? If I live with somebody who smokes, do I have to move out? If I live in New Jersey, do I have to move to Utah? Some of these questions bear on the question of how voluntary the behaviors are that lead to poor health, and I shall return to this issue later.

The claim about the individual's responsibility for his health can also be interpreted as causal-responsibility. When Robert Veatch says,

> If individuals are responsible to some degree for their health . . . , why should they not also be responsible for the costs involved?[3]

the use of responsible in the premise is different from its use in the conclusion, and neither use is that of role-responsibility. In the premise he is making an assertion about causal responsibility; in the conclusion one about liability-responsibility. In the premise there is a claim about the degree to which the behavior and life styles of individuals causally affect their health status. It is a largely empirical claim about the relationship between the behaviors of the individual and good or bad health.

But as we saw earlier, the question of causal determinant is a judgment, and one that is affected by our interests, our view of the normal and expected course of events, the extent to which variables are subject to human manipulation, and so on. We might expect therefore that ideological disputes will arise as to the issue of causal-responsibility. Is it the person who smokes or the manufacturer of cigarettes who causes the eventual lung cancer? Or is it the growers of tobacco? Or is it the advertising of cigarettes? Or

the stresses of the social system that lead people to seek sources of relief?

It is easy enough to identify the choice of a man to smoke as a necessary condition for the development of his particular lung cancer but there were lots of other necessary conditions that we do not cite as causes, including the fact that he was born at all. Selecting his smoking behavior reflects a particular view about causal-responsibility or about liability-responsibility.

To make a claim about the culpability of individuals for their poor health status is to claim three things: that the individual was in some way at fault in behavior; that the faulty behavior produced the lowered health status; that the faultiness of the behavior created the damage to health. We have already discussed the second condition, that of causal attribution, and the third is merely there for philosophical accuracy and rules out bizarre cases such as Jones who smokes too much, and therefore because of his short-windedness is not able to outrun the rabid dog who bites him, thereby killing him.

The fault condition is the most controversial. And as with any fault attributions there are numerous ways of trying to defeat it. One can argue that the behavior is not (fully) voluntary. Individuals accept employment in hazardous occupations because their market skills are so limited that they have no real choice. People eat the wrong things because they do not have the time and information to make wiser choices. People drink too much because of genetic predispositions or because they are unhappy and cannot find other ways of relieving their distress. People smoke because they are manipulated into such behavior by advertising or peer pressure. All these are basically excusing conditions. They attempt to show that the behavior does not originate in the defective character of the individual but in circumstances external to that character.

A second way of defeating fault is by claiming justification for the behavior. Being a test-pilot is a highly risky occupation but one could argue that society needs people to take such risks, and therefore persons in such occupations are not at fault in accepting health risks. Or one could argue that it is reasonable for people with high blood pressure not to take their medication since the side effects are so awful. Or that mountain-climbers are not at fault in engaging in high-risk behavior because individuals have a right to define themselves as persons who take risks as a part of a certain ideal of human excellence.

Both excuses and justifications assume an initial burden of proof to show that what appears to be defective behavior is really not, either because it is not defective or because its defects are not linked to the agent. A more drastic way of denying fault is to reject the burden of proof. On this view my health is my concern, and as such is not capable of being faulty since there is no standard against which it might be measured and found lacking. Since there is no obligation to preserve one's health, any more than to preserve one's wealth, the whole idea of fault is inappropriate.

From Culpability to Liability

For practical purposes the last notion of responsibility, liability-responsibility, is the most important responsibility claim. The current controversy in health policy arises because we need to decide how to distribute the costs that may arise out of risky behavior. To focus most sharply on this issue I propose the following strategy. With respect to a certain class of behaviors, let us accept the behavior as voluntary and directly linked to an increase in the risk of damaging one's health. Let us assume, moreover, that avoiding the behavior is not difficult, and that satisfactions from engaging in the behavior are not very significant. Further let us assume there is no obvious social justification for the behavior. Finally, and perhaps most unrealistically, let us assume that the causal link between the actual damage that occurs and the risky behavior is straightforward and easy to as-

certain. (I believe the behavior of motorists who do not fasten their seat belts meets all the above requirements, but the truth of that belief is in no way necessary to my argument.) Given these assumptions, what normative conclusions follow and what additional premises are required to make the inference?

I suppose the most drastic inference would be that those who provide medical care ought to refuse to do so for those individuals and those health problems that are appropriately connected. This means that doctors would be required to refuse treatment for patients, perhaps long-standing patients, who are able and willing to pay for such services. Such a policy has the following features in its favor. It might (this is an empirical question) serve as a strong deterrent to those risky modes of behavior. It would probably release some medical resources to be allocated in other ways. There is little else to be said in its favor and much to be said against. Whatever burdens it might be reasonable to impose on those who have damaged their health voluntarily, leaving them in pain and suffering cannot be appropriate. Notice that we do not contemplate imposing such a burden on those (criminals) who have voluntarily harmed others.

The strongest position that has any plausibility would hold that voluntary assumption of health risks is morally relevant when we have to make a choice among patients due to harsh scarcity of resources. Thus, if the last bed in the ICU could be used either for someone who was injured in an automobile accident because she did not fasten her seat-belt, or for someone who was struck by a drunken driver while crossing the street, it is relevant to take into account the fact that the former voluntarily contributed to her situation whereas the latter did not.

This policy is clearly not motivated by consequentialist considerations. Any deterrent effect will be very small in light of the rarity of such occurrences. The view must be that the "bad" patient has forfeited some consideration to equal treatment. But how is this to be argued? The obvious analogy is with the case of the criminal who has forfeited his right not to be injured. But the disanalogies between the two situations are obvious. In the latter cases there is deliberate intent to create an unequal situation between two parties with the knowledge that this has been forbidden by the society. Because the individual is, in Kantian terms, acting on a maxim that involves distinguishing himself morally from others (by taking liberties that he denies to others) we are entitled to deprive him of certain rights. But the "bad" patient might be perfectly willing to generalize his conduct. He is not asking for an exception to be made for himself. Therefore we have been given no argument for why he has forfeited his right to equal consideration in treatment.

There is the further difficulty that making such judgments involves a comparison with the "good" patient. But the "good" patient may be taking comparable risks and simply be fortunate enough to have his current health-damage arise from nonvoluntary origins. Should the alleviation of human suffering depend on such contingencies?

The next set of policies to emerge from our assumptions has to do with assigning responsibility for the costs of treatment. Shouldn't individuals who have voluntarily assumed health risks be responsible (liable) for the costs of their care? This policy could take a number of different forms. Those who are currently subsidized by the state for their health care (the indigent, the aged) might be denied such subsidy. Those who take part in a national health insurance program might have to pay higher premiums. Those who engage in risky behavior might have to pay a tax that would be used to finance health care and research related to the appropriate health damage. Now, since these are very different policies, with different mechanisms, different consequences, different symbolic significance, one would have to examine each in de-

tail to ascertain the relevant considerations in favor of each. But I would like to look very generally at what is required to bridge the gap from our assumption that an individual is voluntarily taking health risks to the normative claim that, therefore, he ought to be responsible (liable) for the financial burdens.

Is it the case that people ought to be liable for the burdens that are foreseeable consequences of their voluntary behavior? More particularly, ought people be liable for the monetary costs of restoring them to a status quo, when they have voluntarily deviated from the status quo?

Consider what must be assumed even in this very pure case. For one thing, it does not seem to be enough that the behavior is voluntary; bearing the costs must be voluntary as well. Take the case of the man who engages in risky behavior but at the same time puts aside money each week in the bank to meet the costs of damage to his health. If the bank fails and he loses his money, is he still responsible for bearing the costs? Here the fact that he is a burden on the community is not something he intended or could reasonably foresee.

This point is relevant to a national health scheme. For if membership in such a plan is mandatory, then it is not up to the "bad" patient whether or not to burden others with his health costs. So the jump from responsibility (causality) to responsibility (liability) is not immediate.

What is it about the voluntary character of the risk that makes some such jump plausible? At least the following elements appear relevant. First, a utilitarian argument. Since the hazard is within the control of the agent, it is avoidable. Therefore, holding the agent responsible for the costs of such risks acts as an incentive to hold the risks down. Second, efficiency. Although there may be other ways of reducing risk, having the agent exercise choice may be the cheapest. Third, fairness. People ought to bear the costs of their activities. This is on the assumption that income is in other respects justly distributed and that there are not other reasons for subsidizing their activities. Finally, and here I am following some unpublished work of Thomas Scanlon, we may view the moral importance of the fact that risks are chosen as the appropriate compromise between our wish to be able to make claims upon others for help (when we find ourselves in a position where we cannot meet our own needs) and the need to draw limits upon the claims made by others.

Under the very strong assumptions we have been operating on, a reasonable case can be made that individuals should be financially liable for their health care. But once one begins to weaken the assumptions and to look at the other effects such a policy would have, the argument becomes much more dubious. A list of the difficulties would include the following: the mixed character of the voluntariness of many behaviors. The existing unfairness of the income distribution. The difficulty in differentiating between the moderate and the heavy drinker when it comes to taxing unhealthy substances such as alcohol. The possibility of genetic differences between those who smoke and get cancer and those who smoke and do not. The ability to monitor certain

activities and not others. The difficulty in determining the relative causal role of voluntary vs. nonvoluntary factors in the genesis of illness.

My guess is that the jump from culpability to liability in the area of voluntary health risks will be very much like the one in the area of criminal punishment. Basic considerations of justice will show that it is not *unfair* to treat certain individuals more harshly than others, and the role of choice will be essential to showing this. But whether we *ought* to do so will depend upon very complex issues of how much good we can accomplish and how this can be weighed against other injustices and bad consequences that arise out of the institutions required to implement the policies.

References

1. Herbert L. A. Hart, "Postscript: Responsibility and Retribution," in *Punishment and Responsibility* (New York: Oxford University Press, 1968), p. 211.
2. Robert Keeton, *Legal Cause in the Law of Torts* (Columbus: Ohio State University Press, 1963), p. 6.
3. Robert M. Veatch, "Voluntary Risks to Health," *Journal of the American Medical Association* 243: 1 (January 4, 1980), 50–55.

Drawing the Ethical Line between Organ Transplantation and Lifestyle Abuse

EIKE-HENNER KLUGE

Recent articles about organ transplantation discussed whether age is in itself an ethically acceptable reason to refuse a patient organ transplantation.[1-2] When organs are scarce, the primary criteria for selective allocation should

be medical in nature: need, tissue compatibility and physiologic fit are among the most commonly mentioned considerations. Criteria such as the patient's social- and family-support mechanisms, and psychologic ability to handle the transplant, are mentioned less frequently but they are often used and are generally considered acceptable.

However, one criterion is rarely discussed. Lifestyle considerations are an appropriate reason to refuse someone a donated organ, just as they provide an appropriate basis for refusing access to other scarce health care resources.

Canadians believe that everyone has the moral right of equal access to health care. This is not a politically given right but an ethical right based on the principle of equality and justice. Society must provide equitable opportunity for health care to all its members. A society that does not do so is unjust.

The proof is simple. A just society will try to ensure that everyone is treated equitably and justly. In a just society, everyone must be able to compete on an equal footing for the opportunities the society offers. Since health is a primary determinant of someone's ability to compete equally with others, society must provide health services for those who require them: everyone must have a socially guaranteed right of equitable access to health care.[3]

However, no right is absolute. All are conditioned by the presumptions that lie behind them and that form part of the conditions under which the rights can be claimed. The right to free speech is conditioned by the presumption that this speech will be truthful and will not unjustly endanger the life or welfare of others. Similarly, the right to confidentiality is not absolute, not even in the medical setting—it is always conditioned by the rights of others not to be harmed by the failure to breach confidentiality. That is why the CMA's ethical guidelines state that under certain circumstances confidentiality not only can, but must, be breached.[4]

One of the most important presumptions underlying the right of equal access to health care is that no one has control over the need for care; in this respect, everyone is equal. A just society tries to redress the balance for those whose health is impaired because otherwise they would be punished for an accident of fate.

This presumption about lack of control over health is generally true. We have no control over our genetic inheritance, and therefore over our genetic inheritance, and therefore over our susceptibility to disease, the way our organs function, or the way our bodies react to foods, chemicals, allergens, and so on. As well, we usually have little, if any, control over accidents that result in injury and require medical treatment.

However, this is not true when medically inappropriate lifestyle choices are made. When we adopt an unhealthy lifestyle, we adopt a way of life that we know will lead to injury and result in the need for health care—something we could have avoided. When people make lifestyle choices, they are taking actions that will place an otherwise avoidable strain on available health care resources.

When people who have made such choices claim that they have the same right to care as anyone else, they are wrong: their own needs were controllable and foreseeable. Therefore, their claim to equal rights contradicts the basic presumption that underlies the right of access to care.

Smoking is a good example. People become smokers by choice, not by uncontrollable accident, inherent need or genetic predisposition. Furthermore, the dangers of smoking are too well advertised not to be known. It may be difficult to quit smoking but it is not impossible, and it is certainly possible never to start in the first place. Therefore, to smoke is to create an artificial and preventable health need. That is irresponsible, and to insist that smokers be treated like nonsmokers is to unjustly treat irresponsible people the same as responsible people.[5]

This fact is not undermined by society's decision to allow the sale of tobacco products. Society also insists on placing health warnings on them, thus following the principle of the least intrusive alternative: it respects the right to autonomy and is unwilling to infringe individual freedom, but wants to ensure that people know the price of exercising that freedom. The profits from the sale of tobacco should go to assist those who are victims of second-hand smoke, not to those who are creating their own need for health care.

Some people have argued that alcohol abuse is different because alcoholism is a genetically determined disease and people should not be punished for a disease over which they have no control.[6]

They are wrong. Alcohol is not like a pheromone—people can and do resist it. If there is a genetic component to alcohol abuse, it's one that merely predisposes. It does not determine.

We have control over our predispositions. One way is by being responsible and not putting ourselves into situations in which predispositions become actualized. This is not impossible with alcoholism, which is actualized gradually. There are plenty of well-known warning signs. Potential alcoholics can escape alcoholism, and many do.

There is nothing wrong with society allowing the sale and consumption of alcohol. It is permitted on the tacit understanding that alcohol will be used responsibly, and this is clearly stated in the advertising campaigns of governments and manufacturers alike. In the case of nonalcoholics, "responsibly" means using alcohol moderately; for those who have the predisposition to become full-blown alcoholics, it means not using alcohol at all.

Alcohol abusers who need health care, and especially a liver transplant, have impaired their health by acting irresponsibly, thus creating a preventable need. To treat them the same as people who have acted responsibly is to ignore this ethically relevant difference. It is to say: "Don't bother acting responsibly. We'll take care of you, no matter what." This would undermine the ethics of health promotion and lead to an unjust act when it comes to deciding who has a morally greater claim.[7]

By creating their need, alcohol abusers are exacerbating the current organ shortage and depriving those who have no control over their need of a vital resource.[7] If others die because alcohol abusers have received the available livers, the blame will lie not only with alcohol abusers but also with those who insist on treating alcoholics the same as responsible persons.

Smoking and alcoholism are the best-known examples, but this reasoning also applies to other self-induced health care needs. Health care resources are scarce, and will become scarcer. To continue to treat irresponsible patients the same as responsible ones is to violate the principle of equality and justice. Some hospitals have already recognized this ethical truth and have adjusted their programs accordingly. For instance, Canadian Health Care Management Dispatch DP 53.2 (1990) states that University Hospital in London, Ont., has written guidelines for allocating donated livers. Drinkers have been placed at the bottom of the list.

Perhaps it is time for others to follow suit.

References

1. Brooks J: The heart of the matter: Dalton Camp and his controversial transplant. *Can Med Assoc J* 1993; 149: 996–997, 1000–1002
2. Kluge E-H: Age and organ transplantation. *Can Med Assoc J* 1993; 149: 1003
3. Daniels N: *Just Health Care.* Cambridge U Pr, Cambridge, 1985, 32–35
4. CMA Position: Acquired Immunodeficiency Syndrome. *Can Med Assoc J* 1989; 140: 64A,B
5. Veatch R: Who should pay for smokers' health care? *Hastings Cent Rep* 1974; 4: 8–9
6. Cohen C, Benjamin M: Alcoholics and liver transplantation. *JAMA* 1991; 265: 1299–1301
7. Moss AH, Siegler M: Should alcoholics compete equally for liver transplantation? *JAMA* 1991; 265: 1295–1298

Notes

1. John Stuart Mill, *On Liberty* (Oxford: Oxford University Press, 1975), 78.
2. 464 F. 2d. 772 (D.C. Cir. 1972).
3. Ibid. at 780 (notes omitted).
4. 27 Cal.3d 285, 165 Cal. Rptr. 308, 611 P. 2d 902 (1980).
5. Robert Baldwin and Martin Case, *Understanding Regulation: Theory, Strategy and Practice* (New York: Oxford University Press, 1999), 9–17.
6. Ibid.
7. Ibid.
8. Dan E. Beauchamp, "Community: The Neglected Tradition of Public Health," in *New Ethics for the Public's Health,* eds. Dan E. Beauchamp and Bonnie Steinbock (New York: Oxford University Press, 1999) 57–67.
9. John Stuart Mill, "On Liberty" in *John Stuart Mill Three Essays,* ed. Richard Wollheim (Oxford: Oxford University Press 1975), 100.
10. Deborah Frank, "Growth, Development, and Behavior in Early Childhood Following Prenatal Cocaine Exposure: A Systematic Review," *Journal of the American Medical Association* 285(12) (2001): 1163–1625.
11. Udo Schuklenk, "AIDS: Individual and 'Public' Interests," in *A Companion to Bioethics,* eds. Helga Kuhse and Peter Singer (Oxford: Blackwell, 1998), 346–365; Patricia Illingworth, *AIDS and the Good Society* (London and New York: Routledge, 1990), 22–55.
12. David L. Chambers "Gay Men, AIDS, and the Code of the Condom," *Harvard Civil Rights Law Review* 29(1993): 353.
13. Illingworth, 22–55.
14. Ibid.
15. Robert Klitzman and Ronald Bayers, *Mortal Secrets* (Baltimore and London: Johns Hopkins University Press, 2003), 30–72.
16. Lisa Scott, "Mantle's Transplant Raises Questions," *Modern Healthcare* (June 12, 1995): 3.
17. Delthia Ricks, "Do Rich and Famous Get Preference for Transplants?," *Orlando Sentinel,* June 9, 1995, A1.

Recommended Readings

Baldwin, Robert and Cave, Martin. *Understanding Regulation: Theory, Strategy, and Practice.* New York: Oxford University Press, 1999.

Bayer, Ronald. *Private Acts, Social Consequences.* New York: The Free Press, 1989.

Brody, Howard. "The Multiple Facets of Futility." *Journal of Clinical* Ethics 5(1994): 142–144.

Bursztajn, Harold et al. "Depression, Self-Love, Time, and the 'Right' to Suicide." *General Hospital Psychiatry* 8(1986): 91–95.

Cohen, Joshua. "Patient Autonomy and Social Fairness." *Cambridge Quartely of Healthcare Ethics* 9(2000): 391–399.

Crawford, Robert. "You Are Dangerous to Your Health." *Social Policy* 8(1978): 11.

Darby, Amy. "The Individual, Health Hazardous Lifestyles, Disease and Liability." *DePaul Journal of Health Care* Law 7(1999): 787–818.

Dworkin, Gerald. *The Theory and Practice of Autonomy.* New York: Cambridge University Press, 1988.

Dworkin, Gerald. "Paternalism," in *Philosophy of Law,* eds. Feinburg, Joel, and Coleman, Jules. Belmont, Calif.: Thompson Wadsworth, 2004: 293–303.

Engelhardt, Tristram, Jr. "The Many Faces of Autonomy." *Health Care Analysis* 9(2001): 283–297.

Gundermann, Richard. "Illness as Failure." *Hastings Center Report* 30(2000): 7–28.

Hiatt, Howard H. "Protecting the Medical Commons: Who Is Responsible?" *New England Journal of Medicine* 293(1975): 235–241.

Katz, Jay. *The Silent World of Doctor and Patient.* New York: The Free Press, 1984.

Kelly, Katherine. "The Assumption of Risk Defence and the Sexual Transmission of AIDS: A Proposal for the Application of Comparative Knowledge." *University of Pennsylvania Law Review* 143(1995) 1121–1189.

Klitzman, Robert, and Bayer, Ronald. *Mortal Secrets.* Baltimore & London: Johns Hopkins University Press, 2003.

Minkler, Meredith. "Promoting Responsibility for Health: Contexts and Controversies." In *Promoting Health Behavior: How Much Freedom? Whose Responsibility?* Ed. Daniel Callahan. Washington, D.C.: Georgetown University Press, 2000: 1–22.

Morreim, E. Haavi. "Lifestyles of the Risky and Infamous: From Managed Care to Managed Lives." *Hastings Center Report* 25(1995): 5.

Nahas, Brigitte M. "Comment: Drug Tests, Arrests and Fetuses: A Comment on the U.S. Supreme Court's Narrow Opinion in *Ferguson v. City of Charleston,*" *Cardozo Women's Law Journal* 8(2001) 105–142.

Robertson, John, Kahn, Jeffrey, and Wagner, John. "Conception to Obtain Hematopoietic Stem Cells." *The Hastings Center Report* 32(2002): 34–40.

Schneewind, Jerome B. *The Invention of Autonomy.* New York: Cambridge University Press, 1998.

Schwartz, Robert. "Lifestyle, Health Status and Distributive Justice." *Health Matrix* 3(1993): 195.

Tauber, Alfred. "Historical and Philosophical Reflections on Patient Autonomy." *Health Care Analysis* 9(2001): 299–319.

Truog, Robert, Brett, Alan, and Frader, Joel. "The Problem with Futility." *New England Journal of Medicine* 326(1992): 1560–4.

Veatch, Robert M. *Transplantation Ethics.* Washington, D.C.: Georgetown University Press, 2000.

Wikler, Daniel. "Persuasion and Coercion for Health: Ethical Issues in Government Efforts to Change Life-Styles." *Milbank Memorial Fund Quarterly: Health and Society* 56(1978): 303–338.

Cases

Bouvia v. Superior Court, 179 Cal.App.3d 1127, 225 Cal. Rptr. 297 (Cal. Ct. App. 1986).
Canterbury v. Spence, 464 F. 2d 772 (D.C. Cir. 1972).
Truman v. Thomas, 27 Cal.3d 285, 611 P.2d 902, 165 Cal. Rptr. 308 (Cal. 1980).
United States v. Rutherford, 442 U.S. 544 (1979).

Chapter Four

The Ethical Obligations of Health Care Providers

A. The Ethical Obligations of Physicians and Other Providers

The delivery of health care today generally requires the participation of numerous disciplines: physicians, nurses, x-ray technicians, social workers, and so on. Nevertheless, there can be little doubt that physicians remain the dominant members of the interdisciplinary team that provides health care. Moreover, their relationship with their patients remain critical to any discussion of health care ethics.

Despite the almost mythic image the patient-physician relationship has come to have in our culture, the relationship actually begins as a simple contract (either explicit or implicit) between doctor and patient. Prior to incurring any responsibilities toward a particular patient, physicians must have established a relationship between themselves and their patients. The Hippocratic Oath (fifth century B.C.), for example, assumes a relationship prior to imposing on the physician the duty to do no harm. Principle VI of the Principles of Medical Ethics of the American Medical Association states, "A physician shall in the provision of appropriate patient care, except in emergencies, be free to choose whom to serve."[1]

Common law has traditionally also required the formation of a relationship prior to the imposition of duties. In *Childs v. Weis*, the court found that physician Weis was not responsible for the death of Daisy Childs's infant, who died 12 hours after birth, because, despite the fact that he was called when she arrived at the emergency room in labor and possibly hemorrhaging, Dr. Weis had never established a relationship with Ms. Childs.[2] The court stated, "[Since] it is unquestionably the law that the relationship of physician and patient is dependent upon contract, either express or implied, a physician is not to be held liable for arbitrarily refusing to respond to a call of a person even urgently in need of medical care."[3]

At the same time, many states have enacted Good Samaritan laws that protect physicians and other providers from civil liability should they provide someone with medical aid under emergency conditions. In this way, although physicians are under no legal duty to treat someone with whom they do not have an existing patient-provider relationship, public policy encourages them to render emergency aid. Moreover, although physicians may not be under a legal duty to treat, historically there has been an ethical presupposition that they would treat the poor. Albert Jonsen refers to this as the duty of gratuitous care for the sick poor.[4] Nonetheless he also points out, that as health insurance became common, the duty of charity medicine disappeared. Indeed, today with the rise of luxury practices or boutique medicine, many physicians appear to assume few or no obligations to the poor.

Although physicians do not have a legal obligation to treat the sick in the absence of a contract agreeing to treat, once the relationship is established, their obligations to their patients change considerably. The relationship between patient and physician has a number of dimensions. It is first and foremost a relationship that delivers medical care to patients, in order, when possible, to heal them. To this end physicians have a duty of competence, which is explored more in Section B.

Physicians are also professionals. As such, their relationship with their patients and the community is marked by a commitment to professional values. Although the principle putting the patient first has been part of medical codes as far back as the Hippocratic Oath, it also finds expression in the legal and ethical obligations of fiduciaries. Fiduciary law is based on the law of trusts.[5] In the trust relationship one person holds the property of another for the benefit of the beneficiary.[6] In paradigmatic fiduciary relationships such as this one, it is difficult for the beneficiary (entruster) to monitor what the trustee does.

Because of the inability of the "entruster" (person doing the trusting) to supervise the trustee (person trusted), fiduciaries usually have special duties to avoid self-dealing and conflicts of interest. The presence of a power imbalance, often created by a disparity in information within professional relationships, can trigger these higher duties. Unlike other professionals, doctors do not have general fiduciary obligations, but more specific ones. Fiduciary law has been applied to physicians with respect to (1) the duty not to abandon patients, (2) the duty to maintain confidence, and (3) the duty to obtain informed consent to treatment.[7] In addition, although courts are not unanimous on the subject, in *Moore v. Regents of the University of California* the court recognized in connection with a fiduciary duty an obligation to disclose personal interests unrelated to the patient's health, such as research and economic interests, that may affect a doctor's decision making.[8] Moreover, although physicians have limited legal fiduciary duties, they may also, as Mark Rodwin states, "often act as traditional fiduciaries and espouse a fiduciary ethic."[9]

The selection we have chosen by Matthew Wynia and others, entitled *Medical Professionalism in Society*, places the discussion of professional values in a historical and contemporary context. Wynia and colleagues believe that there are three core elements of professionalism: (1) devotion to medical services, (2) public profession of the values of medicine, and (3) negotiation and advocacy of professional values. Although each of these obligations is important for medical professionals, the first, devotion to medical services, is foundational. According to these authors, "Physicians should cultivate in themselves and in their peers a devotion to health care values by placing the goals of individual and public health ahead of other goals. That is, physicians must be devoted to the work of providing health care." Are the patient-physician relationship and the professional values that protect it important enough to justify the possible costs involved? When in Chapter 5 we consider the obligations of organizations, we shall look at arguments that suggest that physicians who focus exclusively on the interest of their patients lose sight of their duties of social justice.

In the last twenty years, the values traditionally associated with the patient-physician relationship have been implicitly criticized by ethicists who have focused on and have tried to distinguish the ethical perspectives of other health care professions. The critique and contribution offered by those who have discussed the ethics of nursing and the ethical foundation of the nurse-patient relationship is especially worth noting.

Two facts are critical to understanding discussions of nursing ethics. First, despite the important role that nurses often play in patient care and treatment, nurses have historically served as subordinate professionals, who act under at least the nominal oversight and directive of physicians. Indeed, even nurse practitioners and nurse midwives, who are licensed in most states to practice with a significant degree of independence, remain dependent by law on their relationship with a physician. Second, although the number of female physicians has grown dramatically in recent years, so that today approximately 50 percent of new physicians are women, nursing remains a disproportionately female profession.

The historic view of nursing as a women's profession subordinate to medicine has led many nursing ethicists to turn to feminism to develop an ethical perspective for nursing distinct from that traditionally associated with medicine. The selection we have chosen from Dena S. Davis is representative of this literature.

Davis, like many other ethicists, believes that the foundation for nursing ethics can be derived from the work of Carol Gilligan,[10] who famously claimed that females tend to analyze ethical issues in a more relational and contextual mode than do males, who tend to view ethical issues abstractly in terms of rights. Although Davis believes that the differences Gilligan described between the moral development of males and females cannot be strictly tied to gender, she does contend that Gilligan's articulation of a relational and contextual ethics can help to describe the ethics of nursing, which she calls an "ethic of care" that is distinguished from an ethics for medicine that is grounded in "individuation" and "autonomy."

Helga Kuhse argues that an ethic of care is an insufficient foundation for nursing ethics. Kuhse concedes that care is an important part of nursing, but she claims that nursing ethics must also include principles and theories of justice, lest it be incapable of explaining itself and being condemned to an inferior position vis à vis medical ethics.

As you read the selections by Davis and Kuhse, ask yourself what they mean by "care" and whether their portrayal of medical ethics is complete. From their discussions of medical ethics, you might conclude that it relies totally on abstraction and that the nature and particularities of the relationship between physician and patient is irrelevant. In fact, many bioethicists would contend that for physicians, as well as other health professionals who deal directly with patients, the key to a successful and ethical relationship lies not with adherence to abstract rules but in the development of trust.

A patient's trust in his or her health care provider may be necessary for the patient to achieve the relationship's therapeutic benefits. Some of the studies demonstrating the positive impact of placebos on health outcomes have been interpreted to illustrate the therapeutic benefits of the doctor-patient relationship itself.[11] According to K. B. Thomas, writing in *The Lancet*, "The placebo effect in general practice is the power of the doctor alone to make the patient feel better."[12] Others have argued that many of the benefits ascribed to the placebo effect of the doctor-patient relationship may more accurately be attributed to the general effects of caring.[13] Perhaps then the relationship of physicians to patients may depend more than we think on the traits we associate with nursing. Perhaps also the fiduciary duty of physicians to their patients and the relations it facilitates not only substitutes for patient monitoring of their physicians but also has a healing effect. If so, then diluting the fiduciary ethic may result in worse health outcomes for patients.

Nevertheless professionalism and the fiduciary ethic implicit in it may be threatened by a variety of sources. The principles of autonomy explored in Chapter 3, plus the economic pressures upon the health care system (discussed in Chapter 2), may undermine the ability of providers to act as fiduciaries, or even the value of their doing so. Likewise, concerns for social justice and public health, further explored in subsequent chapters, may make the provider as fiduciary appear to be an anachronism of a bygone day. As you read the sections that follow, ask yourself what values are fostered by viewing the provider as a fiduciary and whether those values are viable and necessary in today's world.

The Hippocratic Oath

I swear by Apollo Physician and Asclepius and Hygieia and Panaceia and all the gods and goddesses, making them my witnesses, that I will fulfil according to my ability and judgment this oath and this covenant:

To hold him who has taught me this art as equal to my parents and to live my life in partnership with him, and if he is in need of money to give him a share of mine, and to regard his offspring as equal to my brothers in male lineage and to teach them this art—if they desire to learn it—without fee and covenant; to give a share of precepts and oral instruction and all the other learning to my sons and to the sons of him who has instructed me and to pupils who have signed the covenant and have taken an oath according to the medical law, but to no one else.

I will apply dietetic measures for the benefit of the sick according to my ability and judgment; I will keep them from harm and injustice.

I will neither give a deadly drug to anybody if asked for it, nor will I make a suggestion to this effect. Similarly I will not give to a woman an abortive remedy. In purity and holiness I will guard my life and my art.

I will not use the knife, not even on sufferers from stone, but will withdraw in favor of such men as are engaged in this work.

Whatever houses I may visit, I will come for the benefit of the sick, remaining free of all intentional injustice, of all mischief and in particular of sexual relations with both female and male persons, be they free or slaves.

What I may see or hear in the course of the treatment or even outside of the treatment in regard to the life of men, which on no account one must spread abroad, I will keep to myself holding such things shameful to be spoken about.

If I fulfil this oath and do not violate it, may it be granted to me to enjoy life and art, being honored with fame among all men for all time to come; if I transgress it and swear falsely, may the opposite of all this be my lot.

Medical Professionalism in Society

Matthew K. Wynia, Stephen R. Latham, Audiey C. Kao,
Jessica W. Berg, and Linda L. Emanuel

Today, at the dawn of a new century, genuine medical professionalism is in peril. Increasingly, physicians encounter perverse financial incentives, fierce market competition, and the erosion of patients' trust,[1–7] yet most physicians are ill equipped to deal with these threats.[8,9] The role of professionalism has been so little discussed that it has virtually disappeared in the battle between those who favor market competition in a trillion-dollar industry and those who seek greater government regulation.[8] Physicians, feeling trapped between these camps, are turning to unionization and other tactics.[10]

In the first half of this century, medical professionalism was generally understood according to the structural-functional approach of Talcott Parsons and his school.[11–13] This approach catalogued the distinctive characteristics of professions and then attempted to discern the social function of each. For instance, professional cooperation, rather than competition, was seen as serving the public good by increasing the speed of dissemination of new information. Parsons also believed that professionals were predisposed to public service because they were less interested in amassing wealth than in achieving recognition among their colleagues for doing good work.[11]

Although their work was illuminating in many ways, the structural functionalists failed to consider the moral foundations of professionalism, and this failure resulted in a confusing conflation. Distinctive characteristics rather than moral premises were used to define professionalism. For example, self-regulation, which is a distinctive characteristic necessitated by the nature of professional work, was understood instead as the essence of professionalism. In the absence of an explicit moral base, critics could readily claim that self-regulation by physicians was nothing but a cover for the monopolization of trade.

In the 1960s, a critical academic literature seized on this weakness, combined it with empirical evidence of professional self-interest, and asserted that professional ethics were a cynical ploy.[14–18] As Freidson noted, "When the leaders of the profession invoke ethics and the values of professionalism, [the] critics declare it a self-serving ideology that masks the reality of naked self-interest."[19] Practical attacks on professionalism gained strength from these criticisms. Throughout the 1970s and 1980s, claims that physicians were exploiting their trade monopoly led to the use of antitrust legislation against physicians.[20]

By the 1990s, many academics were reaffirming the importance of professional self-reg-

ulation, especially in health care.[19,21] Sociologists who study the professions have become less cynically focused on power. They have acknowledged that professional self-regulation, although susceptible to abuse, serves necessary social functions.[19,22] Still, the earlier attacks on professionalism left this term with no coherent meaning. Lacking systematic knowledge about professionalism, many people use the term to refer to ill-defined, sometimes self-serving, concepts.[23–25] A clarification of genuine medical professionalism is necessary if the current unraveling is to be reversed.[8,26–28]

Professionalism in Society

Medical professionalism is more than merely an activity that straddles market competition and government regulation. Likewise, it is much more than a technical necessity for delivering a needed good or service, and it cannot be reduced to a "deal" negotiated with society. We think of professionalism as an activity that involves both the distribution of a commodity and the fair allocation of a social good but that is uniquely defined according to moral relationships.[29] Professionalism is a structurally stabilizing, morally protective force in society. Along with private-sector and public or government activities, it is a cornerstone of a stable society.

Dramatic failures of medical professionalism to provide moral protection have occurred in recent memory, each failure marking a time of social disarray or worse. Apartheid in South Africa overpowered core health care values,[30] as did the Soviet Union's misuse of psychiatric diagnoses.[31] The perversion of medical values, and the complicity of physicians and other health care practitioners in this perversion, were an integral part of Nazism.[32–34]

The social role of professionalism as a stabilizing force is not unique to the medical profession. Complex societies in different times and places have had in common a need for meritocratic, dedicated subgroups that function to keep private interests and government power in balance through attention to greater social goods. For instance, de Tocqueville remarked that American lawyers of his time served as a stabilizing force in American society, tempering the excesses of government and private industry.[35] Similarly, the protected Mandarin class in pre-Communist China served this role for many years, criticizing both the state and the private sector in order to protect vulnerable social goods.[36]

Professions protect not only vulnerable persons but also vulnerable social values. Many values are vulnerable: individuals and societies may abandon the sick, ignore due process in judging the guilt or innocence of a person accused of a crime, provide inadequate support for education, propagate information that suits those in power while stifling different perspectives, and so on. Values are so vulnerable that it is hard to think of any society that has not at times lapsed in protecting them. Good civilizations, however, limit and reverse such lapses, in part by entrusting designated groups of people—physicians, lawyers, teachers, journalists, and others—to safeguard the values. When professionalism in these core social activities becomes unsteady, it marks the emergence of societal problems.

That the need for professionalism is more than technical does not undermine the legitimacy of the technical argument.[19] In medical matters, neither patients as consumers nor government regulators have sufficient training, experience, or time to assess every health care product and service; the services purchased are too complex, rapidly changing, and difficult to correlate with measurable outcomes. Lay medical education can alter the scope of needed professional oversight, and this is desirable in many cases. But illness will always limit the ability of patients to "shop around" when important purchasing choices must be made.[3] Professional groups, through the establishment of standards, educa-

tion, and peer review, can go a long way toward supplying quality assurance.[37]

In making a full case for professionalism, we do not wish to overstate the claim. In particular, we note that respect for human worth, trustworthiness, and the protection of important values are not the exclusive province of professionals; neither is competence. But they are particular obligations of professionals. We also remain mindful that professionals, no less than entrepreneurs or government officials, can misuse their power and have done so. The danger that power will be misused is inherent in any system that assigns authority to a group of people to police themselves. A full understanding of what professionalism entails provides some protection against this danger.

A Model of Professionalism

Three core elements of professionalism, each different in nature, are necessary for it to work properly. First, professionalism requires a moral commitment to the ethic of medical service, which we will call devotion to medical service and its values. This devotion leads naturally to a public, normative act: public profession of this ethic. Public profession of the ethic serves both to maintain professionals' devotion to medical service and to assert its values in societal discussions. These discussions lead naturally to engagement in a political process of negotiation, in which professionals advocate for health care values in the context of other important, perhaps competing, societal values.

Devotion to Medical Service

Physicians should cultivate in themselves and in their peers a devotion to health care values by placing the goals of individual and public health ahead of other goals. That is, physicians must be devoted to the work of providing health care.

Physicians who value individual and public health more than other social goods remain motivated to work hard even when the financial rewards for such work are not great. They criticize and police one another even when such actions have personal, social, and financial costs. They offer high-quality services whether or not patients are capable of judging their quality. They continue to provide health care even when, as during an epidemic, they risk their own health. And they maintain their obligations to care for financially disadvantaged patients.[38–40] Today, the ascendance of marketplace values puts health care for the poor at particular risk.[3,41,42] Physicians should influence the organizations in which they practice to adopt policies that address the care of impoverished persons. Similarly, physicians must resist incentives that place the trust between patient and doctor and even patient care at risk.[5,43,44] Devotion to medical service is so important that physicians must avoid even the appearance that they are primarily devoted to their own interests rather than to the interests of others. Dramatic rises in physicians' incomes over the past four decades have fostered the trust-destroying belief, whether true or not, that physicians as a group are greedy and take advantage of patients.[17,45–49]

Public Profession of Values

Physicians should speak out about their values. The word "profession" means, from the Latin, "speaking forth." Public avowal of values has been a distinctive feature of the professions from before medieval times.

Although acting on one's professional devotion to medical service is a form of public profession of values, it is not enough. The unique nature of the relationship between patient and physician requires an explicit and professionally protected moral base so that there can be legitimate shared expectations, even in circumstances, such as emergencies, in which individual rela-

tionships have not had time to mature. The patient-physician relationship is based on shared experiences of vulnerability and the potential for health or illness and on a resultant respect for the inestimable value of human life and health.[50] Furthermore, health care values focus on the public as well as the individual. As Samuel Johnson noted, "A decent provision for the poor is the true test of civilization."[51] Health care values reflect this assertion. Through public profession of health care values, patients and the public hear about these values as well as the standards that result from them. They hear that physicians' commitment to such important standards as never exploiting patients' inherent vulnerability and not abandoning patients is timeless. They hear that other, specific aspects of health care values are delineated in a continuous dynamic process with society, to which physicians bring their training, professional virtues, interprofessional relations, and above all, experiences in caring for patients. Finally, public profession of values—for example, by participating in "white-coat ceremonies," posting ethics codes in waiting areas, and contributing to and espousing the standards of a professional association—demands commitment.[52,53] A public, collective commitment to fulfill legitimate expectations implies an acceptance of accountability for one's professional actions, as well as an acceptance of the shared standards of the profession, which may sometimes conflict with personal beliefs.

Negotiation Regarding Professional Values and Other Social Values

Public profession of values inevitably requires professionals to engage with the public in negotiating social priorities that balance medical values with other societal values. This political process of negotiation should lead to what is sometimes referred to as a social contract between physicians and the public.[54]

The process of negotiation not only clarifies legitimate public and professional expectations but can also prevent counterproductive paternalistic behavior on the part of professionals. Individually, the process fosters patient-centered care by including each patient's health goals in decision making. Collectively, it can help accommodate a suitable social disposition toward medical care. The process of negotiation can make clear professionals' obligations to meet public needs, reminding the profession that it cannot have everything its own way and simultaneously demanding appropriate advocacy. Tension may develop between what society wants of physicians and physicians' devotion to health care values. For example, portions of society today favor intense market competition among physicians as a way to lower the costs of care. But such competition encourages the development of trade secrets among physicians, such as proprietary practice guidelines,[55] and impedes the collegial interaction and information sharing that are needed to provide high-quality care. The challenge for physicians is to be accountable to the public and its changing values while protecting core health care values.

An Archetypal Model of Professionalism

We propose that an ideal archetypal model[19,56] of medical professionalism entails the three elements of devotion, profession, and negotiation. The model is ideal in that it is not descriptive of the reality today or in any other era. It is archetypal because it is intended to describe only core elements of professionalism. The purpose of the model is to provide a normative guide.

Each element may fail, may be misapplied, or may not be in balance with the other two. A failure of devotion to the ethic of medical service leads to self-protective behavior on the part of physicians, as occurred, for instance, in the difficult transition to managed care and at the start of the AIDS epidemic. Failure to profess health care values publicly may lead to uninformed, misinformed, or piecemeal public policies. And failure to negotiate an acceptable social contract

leads the public to establish other contracts in order to obtain what it needs and wants. As one example, "alternative" practitioners and therapies become more attractive to the public when they provide something desirable that the profession has ignored in individual or social negotiations. Yet negotiation does not mean simply giving the public what it wants. An overemphasis on satisfying public demands, without attention to core health care values, will ultimately leave both professionals and society unprotected. In addition, professionalism may be misused if physicians become devoted, as individuals or groups, to values derived from other sources, such as business values. Finally, an exaggerated devotion to an ethic that is determined solely by professionals may lead to paternalism or to the refusal to consider other important perspectives.

A Spectrum of Professional Activism

With this model of professionalism as devotion, profession, and negotiation, exactly how, in a practical sense, should physicians act on behalf of patients, the public, and health care values? What types of activity constitute professional advocacy?

The advocacy activities of individual professionals should fall along a spectrum, with more extreme actions requiring more stringent justifications.[57] At one end of the spectrum is routine advocacy for patients and public health. Routine advocacy constitutes physicians' regular daily activity. Physicians working in health care delivery organizations—coordinating care, working to improve practice guidelines, and so on—should advocate health care values rather than government or corporate values, speaking on behalf of patients and health care. Occasionally, this type of advocacy may be personally risky. For instance, physicians who appeal adverse coverage decisions on behalf of their patients may put at risk their standing with health plans.

If advocacy fails, physicians have an obligation to express internal dissent with regard to activities or policies that undermine core health care values. This responsibility is what distinguishes genuine professionals from "company docs." Although internal dissent is not always clearly distinct from routine advocacy, it is a negative form of activism that may go against an internal hierarchy. Internal dissent may require courage and skill to achieve a positive outcome, but it generally requires minimal moral justification.

Public dissent is next on the spectrum and should be used with more care. It may raise tensions and backfire, causing harm. For instance, the dissenter may be demoted or fired, thereby perhaps harming patients' care, or a point of dissent may become more difficult to resolve because publicity can provoke denial or defensiveness. Public dissent is warranted only when internal dissent has demonstrably failed to remedy a harmful situation, when outside pressure is likely to be required to achieve change, when public silence allows the harmful situation to continue, and when the potential harms to patients from public dissent are relatively small. For example, the proposed closing of a clinic may justify efforts to galvanize community support through public dissent.

With direct professional disobedience, the fourth form of activism on the spectrum, professionals act against authorities, publicly disobeying rules or laws that are antithetical to health care. Direct professional disobedience has a clear potential to harm patients, the profession, and professionals themselves. It should therefore be reserved for situations in which both internal and public dissent have failed, direct disobedience is likely to be effective in remedying the problem, the problem is very serious (preferably, its seriousness can be documented empirically), and the action entails as little harm as possible.[58] Surreptitious disobedience, such as secretly "gaming" a billing code to obtain coverage for services, is not justifiable as a form of direct professional disobedience, since it is neither public nor aimed at achieving systemic change.[59] In contrast, delivering free care despite a policy to the contrary, urging colleagues not to comply with California's Proposition 187 (which called on physicians not to treat illegal immigrants), and openly breaking a contractual "gag rule" are examples of justifiable disobedience.[60,61]

Indirect professional disobedience is the disobeying of otherwise unobjectionable rules in order to call attention to a wrong.[58] Indirect actions become appealing when it is not helpful to disobey directly. For example, physicians may not be effective in protesting a health plan's underprovision for the uninsured by directly caring for them—providing charity care is a normal part of professionalism and in an open system it may even facilitate the injustice. But an indirect action, such as collectively refusing to honor a dress code, might call attention to the situation. Although the danger of harm from such an action may seem remote, indirect disobedience can be more harmful than direct disobedience, because in the latter the action itself preserves patient care. Protestors may also overestimate the effectiveness of their campaigns.[58] To be justified, the disobedient act should, at a minimum, be clearly linked with the offensive situation, be seen as reasonable by the public, be unlikely to result in greater harm to patients or others, and be likely to result in lasting positive change.

Finally, a principled exit from medical practice within a health care system is justifiable in catastrophic circumstances. Patients will frequently be harmed by a physician's exit, so it must be justifiable on the following moral grounds. The harm to be prevented must be obvious and large; advocacy, dissent, and disobedience must have been tried; and there must be a good prospect that health care overall will be substantially better served if the professional makes a principled exit than if he or she continues to exert a strong voice for change within the organization. Because a principled exit is sometimes easier than disobedience, particular care should be taken to avoid distorted versions of it. A self-righteous exit helps no one in need (and actually does harm by eliminating a potential source of advocacy) and primarily serves the dissenter's self-image. This type of exit is an act of self-righteousness or even cowardice masquerading as professionalism. In the right circumstances, however, an exit may be both honorable and courageous. In one very unusual circumstance, professional disobedience and exit were chosen simultaneously by a group of physicians as the only way to maintain the moral base of medical practice: Dutch physicians in World War II turned in their licenses but continued to practice underground, to avoid practicing under Nazi rule.[34] The extreme nature of this example illustrates the burden of proof that those who wish to exit must meet before claiming that such an action is necessary to maintain professionalism.

Conclusions

We believe there is an essential role for professionalism in society that market-driven and government-controlled health care alone cannot provide, and we propose three core elements of medical professionalism: devotion to service, profession of values, and negotiation within society. Each element can be misapplied, but in balance they offer normative guidance. The model calls on physicians to engage in professional activities along a spectrum of advocacy, thereby helping to preserve the decency and stability that are essential to civilized society.

References

1. Grumbach K, Osmond D, Vranizan K, Jaffe D, Bindman AB. Primary care physicians' experience of financial incentives in managed-care systems. N Engl J Med 1998;339:1516–21.
2. Angell M. The doctor as double agent. Kennedy Inst Ethics J 1993;3:279–86.
3. Kassirer JP. Managed care and the morality of the marketplace. N Engl J Med 1995;333:50–2.
4. Feldman DS, Novack DH, Gracely E. Effects of managed care on physician-patient relationships, quality of care, and the ethical practice of medicine. Arch Intern Med 1998;158:1626–32.
5. Kao AC, Green DC, Zaslavsky AM, Koplan JP, Cleary PD. The relationship between method of physician payment and patient trust. JAMA 1998;280:1708–14.
6. Blumenthal D. Effects of market reforms on doctors and their patients. Health Aff (Millwood) 1996;15(2):170–84.
7. Anders G. Health against wealth: HMOs and the breakdown of medical trust. Boston: Houghton Mifflin, 1996.
8. Sullivan WM. What is left of professionalism after managed care? Hastings Cent Rep 1999;29:7–13.
9. Donelan K, Blendon RJ, Lundberg GD, et al. The new medical marketplace: physicians' views. Health Aff (Millwood) 1997;16(5):139–48.
10. Klein S. AMA to establish national collective bargaining unit. American Medical News. July 5, 1999;42:1, 34–5.
11. Parsons T. The professions and social structure. Social Forces 1939;17:457–67.
12. Parsons T. Essays in sociological theory. London: Free Press, 1954.
13. Vollmer HM, Mills DL. Professionalization. Englewood Cliffs, N.J.: Prentice-Hall, 1966.
14. Freidson E. Professional dominance: the social structure of medical care. Chicago: Aldine, 1970.
15. Krause EA. Death of the guilds: professions, states, and the advance of capitalism, 1930 to the present. New Haven, Conn.: Yale University Press, 1996.
16. Larson MS. The rise of professionalism: a sociological analysis. Berkeley: University of California Press, 1977.
17. Starr P. The social transformation of American medicine. New York: Basic Books, 1982.
18. Buchanan A. Is there a medical profession in the house? In: Spece R, Shimm D, Buchanan A, eds. Conflicts of interest in clinical practice and research. New York: Oxford University Press, 1996:105–36.
19. Freidson E. Professionalism reborn: theory, prophecy, and policy. Chicago: University of Chicago Press, 1994.
20. Curry R. Medicine for sale. Knoxville, Tenn.: Grand Rounds Press, 1992.
21. Gordon R, Simon S. The redemption of professionalism? In: Nelson R, Trubeck D, Solomon R,

eds. Lawyers' ideals/lawyers' practices: transformations in the American legal system. Ithaca, N.Y.: Cornell University Press, 1992:230–57.

22. Reuschemeyer D. Comparing legal professions cross-nationally: from a professions-centered approach to a state-centered approach. Am Bar Found Res J 1986(Summer):415–46.

23. Swick HM, Szenas P, Danoff D, Whitcomb ME. Teaching professionalism in undergraduate medical education. JAMA 1999;282:830–2.

24. Reynolds PP. Reaffirming professionalism through the education community. Ann Intern Med 1994;120:609–14.

25. Cruess RL, Cruess SR. Teaching medicine as a profession in the service of healing. Acad Med 1997;72:941–52.

26. Cruess RL, Cruess SR, Johnston SE. Renewing professionalism: an opportunity for medicine. Acad Med 1999;74:878–84.

27. Blumenthal D. The vital role of professionalism in health care reform. Health Aff (Millwood) 1994;13(1):252–6.

28. Emanuel L. Bringing market medicine to professional account. JAMA 1997;277:1004–5.

29. Pellegrino ED, Relman AS. Professional medical associations: ethical and practical guidelines. JAMA 1999;282:984–6.

30. Silove D. Doctors and the state: lessons from the Biko case. Soc Sci Med 1990;30:417–29.

31. Pellegrino ED. Guarding the integrity of medical ethics: some lessons from Soviet Russia. JAMA 1995;273:1622–3.

32. Pellegrino ED. The Nazi doctors and Nuremberg: some moral lessons revisited. Ann Intern Med 1997;127:307–8.

33. Grodin MA, Annas GJ. Legacies of Nuremberg: medical ethics and human rights. JAMA 1996;276:1682–3.

34. Alexander L. Medical science under dictatorship. N Engl J Med 1949;241:39–47.

35. de Tocqueville A. Democracy in America. In: Mayer JP, translator. Garden City, N.Y.: Doubleday, 1969.

36. Dworkin R. Decline of the Mandarin class. Baltimore Sun. September 8, 1998: 11A.

37. Orentlicher D. The influence of a professional association on physician behavior. Albany Law Rev 1994;57:582–605.

38. Council on Ethical and Judicial Affairs, American Medical Association. Caring for the poor. JAMA 1993;269:2533–7.

39. Lundberg GD, Bodine L. Fifty hours for the poor. JAMA 1987;258:3157.

40. Pellegrino ED. Altruism, self-interest, and medical ethics. JAMA 1987;258:1939–40.

41. Cunningham PJ, Grossman JM, St Peter RF, Lesser CS. Managed care and physicians' provision of charity care. JAMA 1999;281:1087–92.

42. Cunningham PJ. Pressures on safety net access: the level of managed care penetration and uninsurance rate in a community. Health Serv Res 1999;34(1):255–70.

43. Gray BH. Trust and trustworthy care in the managed care era. Health Aff (Millwood) 1997;16(1):34–49.

44. Kerr EA, Hays RD, Mittman BS, Siu AL, Leake B, Brook RH. Primary care physicians' satisfaction with quality of care in California capitated medical groups. JAMA 1997;278:308–12.

45. Jaklevic MC. Doc income still rising—AMA data. Mod Healthcare 1998;28(13):3.

46. Rodwin MA. Medicine, money, and morals: physicians' conflicts of interest. New York: Oxford University Press, 1993.

47. James C. "Hope" series returns with darker view of doctors. New York Times. September 23, 1999:B1, B9.

48. Cauthen DB. Luxurious cars: should physicians flaunt their wealth? JAMA 1989;262:1631.

49. Reinhardt UE. Resource allocation in health care: the allocation of lifestyles to providers. Milbank Q 1987;65:153–76.

50. Pellegrino ED, Thomasma DC. A philosophical basis of medical practice. Oxford, England: Oxford University Press, 1981.

51. Boswell J. Life of Johnson. Oxford, England: Oxford University Press, 1904.

52. Pellegrino ED. The medical profession as a moral community. Bull N Y Acad Med 1990;66:221–32.

53. Orr RD, Pang N, Pellegrino ED, Siegler M. Use of the Hippocratic Oath: a review of twentieth century practice and a content analysis of oaths administered in medical schools in the U.S. and Canada in 1993. J Clin Ethics 1997;8:377–88.

54. Veatch RM. A theory of medical ethics. New York: Basic Books, 1981.

55. Brody H, Bonham VL Jr. Gag rules and trade secrets in managed care contracts: ethical and legal concerns. Arch Intern Med 1997;157:2037–43.

56. Weber M. Economy and society: an outline of interpretive sociology. New York: Bedminister Press, 1968.

57. Emanuel L. Professionalism and accountability in managed care. In: American Board of Internal Medicine Report of the 1996 Summer Conference. Philadelphia: American Board of Internal Medicine, 1996:67–72.

58. Cohen C. Militant morality: civil disobedience and bioethics. Hastings Cent Rep 1989;19(6):23–5.

59. Morreim EH. Balancing act: the new medical ethics of medicine's new economics. Washington, D.C.: Georgetown University Press, 1995.

60. Ziv TA, Lo B. Denial of care to illegal immigrants: Proposition 187 in California. N Engl J Med 1995;332:1095–8.

61. Woolhandler S, Himmelstein DU. Extreme risk—the new corporate proposition for physicians. N Engl J Med 1995;333:1706–8.

Nursing: An Ethic of Caring

DENA S. DAVIS

The profession of nursing is in turmoil as it seeks to redefine its identity. I believe that the ideas of Carol Gilligan concerning moral development, as presented in her book, *In a Different Voice* (9), have much to say to nurses as they struggle to "come of age." To my knowledge, Gilligan's ideas have not yet been applied to the riddle of the nurse's identity. My task in this paper is to present these ideas, to explain why I believe they have much to say to nurses about their profession, and to sketch out some directions in which the dialogue between nurses and ethicists might proceed. Since I am not a nurse or a practitioner of ethics in the mode for which Gilligan is arguing (I am a scholar and teacher of biomedical ethics, and tend toward a heavily rights-oriented approach), I will do no more than make the introduction, hoping thereby to act as a catalyst and thus stimulate some helpful discussions within the nursing profession.

The essay begins with a discussion of the present state of self-understanding within the nursing profession. From there it moves to a description of Gilligan's work. The next portion of the paper extracts, from her gender-oriented language, the different modes of ethical thinking she describes. When clearly apprehended, these differences suggest ways in which nurses could apply Gilligan's observations and arguments. The paper closes with some reasons why I believe this mode of "doing" ethics is particularly appropriate to nursing practice.

The nursing community finds itself at a crucial point in its history. Long thought of as "handmaidens" of doctors, nurses are now arguing for their status as a "profession," distinct from but equal to medicine. However, within the nursing community, there is great controversy, even confusion, over how that new profession is to be defined and in what direction it should develop. Larry Churchill (3), for example, points to three common but distorted descriptions of nurses' roles: nurses as doctors' handmaidens, nurses as "minor-league" doctors, and nurses as surrogate mothers. These issues of definition and direction contain strong components of ethical inquiry, for at least three related reasons.

First, one group of theorists concentrates on the *relationship* between patient and practitioner as the focal concept for distinguishing and defining the profession. The patient-practitioner relationship often is expressed in terms of values and moral imperatives. Thus, Leah Curtin (5) asks, "What is nursing?" and replies:

> The distinction between nursing and other health professions, particularly between nursing and medicine, may be clearer if we emphasize the philosophical rather than the functional differences. Other than the legal title RN, what makes a nurse a nurse? Certainly, it cannot be the functions nurses perform, for there is little relationship among the functions of a nursing administrator, a nursing educator, a nursing clinical specialist, a public health nurse, and so forth. Yet, they are all nurses. Perhaps . . . it is the point of view, the philosophy, that nurses bring to the health-care endeavor that identifies a nurse. The point of view brought to health care by physicians is primarily directed toward discovering the cause of disease and applying scientific principles to the alleviation or cure of disease. The pharmacist, the physical therapist, and other health-care providers are similarly concerned with specific and circumscribed needs of patients or clients. The point of view nurses bring to health care is not so circumscribed. *Nurses view patients in their wholeness, in their integrity as persons.* Here I am not using "person" in the sense of body alone, but rather as an intangible union of those physiological, sociological, and subjective elements that comprise the human *Dasein* ("the totality of human life"). *Thus nursing is essentially a moral art, that is, its primary moral conviction shapes its fundamental nature.* [Italics mine.]

The moral art that is nursing, she continues, expresses itself as caring.

> Nurses, as practitioners of a moral art, are committed to care for, as well as to the care of, other human beings. This commitment is a particularly intense form of the general moral imperative to care for one another, and its roots are found deep within the grounds of the nurse-patient relationship.

Churchill seems to share Curtin's view when he comments that "to become like doctors may mean to focus on pathologies and blunt the caring sensitivities that have made nurses such essential and highly prized people in patient care."

Second, as nurses participate in discussions of bioethics, they find that when seen from a nursing perspective, many situations require a different ethical analysis than when seen from the viewpoint of medicine or administration. Describing ethics rounds with intensive-care nurses, Anne J. Davis (6) noted that "the nature of the issues that arose in the discussion was substantially different from that of those we had heard in the ethics rounds led by physicians. Underlying the ethical problems to a large extent was the nurse's social position in the hospital organization and the potential problem of multiple loyalties."

Unresolved ethical conflicts over such concerns as when to stop treatment and what to tell patients, and so on, contribute to the high degree of stress and "burn-out" that many nurses experience. This stress is often intensified because usually it is the nurse who spends the most time with the patient whose care is the object of controversy. For example, a few years ago at a university hospital, a neonate who had no mental function after repeated intracranial bleeding was kept on life-support equipment for nearly a year, at the insistence of his parents. In this difficult situation the nurses suffered most, because day after day they cared for the "baby." Furthermore, they were in the neonatal intensive care unit at least eight hours a day, and had the unfortunate infant before them constantly; doctors, however, "rotated" in and out, alternating attendance in the unit with teaching and research duties. The nurse's ethical problems are compounded because very often she has no channel through which she can make an effective statement of her concerns. An undergraduate nursing student told Davis: "The doctor comes in and briefly looks over things, writes orders, and leaves. I am obligated to care for a patient in this ethically laden situation without benefit of any discussion. I find this the single most difficult aspect of taking care of patients in critical-care settings." I find that the nurses and nursing students enrolled in my bioethics classes are eager for any help the class can offer, but pessimistic and frustrated about their opportunities to put their learning into practice. Francesca Lumpp (11) calls this "double jeopardy"; the nurse faces conflict between her own moral position and that of her patient, and also possible conflict with other authorities—including physicians, hospital adminstrators, and so on. Curtin notes that "it is immoral to instill in a nurse through courses in ethics a deeper sense of her obligations and commitments, while perpetuating a system that prevents their fulfillment."

Third, like all professions, nursing has its own code of ethics, which continually must be explored, revised, and tested. According to Flaherty (8), acceptance of a code of ethics is one of the five characteristics of the professional nurse. In developing such a code, its adherents must explore a good many questions: Do we need separate ethical codes for the different health-care professions? Are any points of conduct peculiar to nurses? Does the nurse take her ethical perspective primarily from her relationship to her health-care colleagues or from her relationship to the patient?

If Curtin is correct in the distinction she makes between nursing and medicine, it may be that the nurse also should adopt different forms of ethical thinking. I believe it would be rewarding to compare the differences in ethical perspective between medicine and nursing with Gilligan's differences between male and female patterns of moral development.

Gilligan argues that women tend to see human relationships from a different perspective than men; they emphasize relationality, caring, and connectedness, while men emphasize rights, hierarchies, and the boundaries between persons. Because Piaget, Kohlberg, and the other students of moral development used only males as research subjects, women appear morally "immature" when tested against these norms. A woman's concern for the relationship within which a moral conflict is embedded, for example, makes her less likely to embrace the ideals of disinterested fairness and nonintervention, which are important characteristics of Kohlberg's "higher" moral stages. As Gilligan explains:

> When one begins with the study of women and derives developmental constructs from their lives, the outline of a moral conception different from that described by Freud, Piaget, or Kohlberg begins to emerge and informs a different description of development. In this conception, the moral problem arises from conflicting responsibilities rather than from competing rights and requires for its resolution a mode of thinking that is contextual and narrative rather than formal and abstract. This conception of morality, as concerned with the activity of care, centers moral development around the understanding of responsibility and relationships, just as the conception of morality as fairness ties moral development to the understanding of rights and rules.
>
> Thus it becomes clear why a morality of rights and noninterference may appear frightening to women in its potential justification of indifference and unconcern. At the same time, it becomes clear why, from a male perspective, a morality of responsibility appears inconclusive and diffuse, given its insistent contextual relativism . . . i.e., a morality that insists on judging the rightness or wrongness of an act by looking at the context or situation in which it is embedded. The psychology of women that has been consistently described as distinctive in its greater orientation toward relationships and interdependence implies a more contextual mode of judgment and a different moral understanding.

Given the differences in women's conceptions of self and morality, women bring to the life cycle a different point of view and order human experience in terms of different priorities.

Later we must confront Gilligan's use of gender as the defining distinction between these two "styles" of thinking about ethical problems. For now, let us accept her use of gender until we have examined the contrasts she delineates.

Basic to Gilligan's work is the idea that "male" ethics is concerned primarily with individuation, universalizability, hierarchical standing, and noninterference. Often the concern is with "turf" or position—the area within which one can claim rights of noninterference. When the issue is one of justice, the focus is likely to be on the impersonal value of universalizability—treating "like as like"—with the implication that people really can be dealt with impersonally, at least on the philosophical level. Much weight is given to universalizability: Can an ethical stance be universalized to fit all similar situations?

In our day, such an impersonal ethic is likely to focus sharply on the notion of autonomy. Most recently, John Rawls presented probably the classic example of an impersonal ethic. The reader can best apprehend his explicit use of game theory, and more importantly his insistence that "justice is fairness," by starting behind a "veil of ignorance." This state, in which one ignores all one's personal characteristics, including history, loved ones, and so on, presents a caricature of the sort of "male" ethic Gilligan describes. Such an ethic "takes rights seriously," in Dworkin's (7) phrase. It succeeds in respecting certain "turf," and in strengthening the lines of separation which are necessary to protect autonomy and individuation, and to guarantee a certain minimum level of political liberty and material goods to all. In contrast to such a "male" ethic, Gilligan presents an ethic which concentrates on the personal relationships within which ethical problems are embedded. Against a morality of rights, she holds up a morality of responsibility; against an emphasis on separation, an emphasis on connection; against the primary consideration of the individual, the consideration of the relationship.

In this conception, the moral problem arises from conflicting responsibilities rather than from competing rights and requires for its resolution a mode of thinking that is contextual and narrative rather than formal and abstract. This conception of morality, as concerned with the activity of care, centers moral development around the understanding of responsibility and relationships, just as the conception of morality as fairness ties moral development to the understanding of rights and rules.

What might a more "female" ethic look like? Nel Noddings (12) claims that it would be an ethic of *attachment* rather than *detachment*, in which one gives primary consideration to the nuances and history of the caring relationship within which the ethical issue arises. This ethic is concerned more with our responsibilities to give care to people, and less with people as carriers of rights which we fear to trample. It is less wedded to universalizability as one of the prime indices of an adequate ethic, and is more comfortable with a situational ethic that rejects impersonal universalizability as insufficiently sensitive to the precious reality of individual persons. For example, Kohlberg's well-known ethical problem about whether or not Heinz should steal a drug that will cure his wife's cancer (but that he cannot afford) assumes that this is a case of comparing values—property *versus* life—and that the child on his way to a mature morality can discern that life has a higher priority than property, despite rules against stealing. Another, more "female," way to look at the problem, however, is to express concern for the breakdown of community to which this dilemma points. Why is the druggist impervious to Heinz's pleas to sell the drug at a price which he *can* afford? Why does the community allow this situation to exist? How will Heinz's theft of the drug affect his relationship with his wife? Can the dilemma (or, better, *multilemma*) can be resolved in such a way that not only will a life be saved, but relationships within marriage and community will grow and be strengthened? (It is worth noting that the answer Kohlberg wants to elicit, that Heinz should steal the drug, is static in its consequences: the wife lives, yes, but the next person who cannot afford the drug will be in the same dilemma.)

Recently I have begun to reflect on the way in which I use cases in classroom teaching. Usually I introduce ethical models by engaging students in discussion about some dilemma. Typically, students will respond to a "hard case" by refusing to stick within the confines of the case as presented; they will demand more information, make up details to embellish the bare facts, and so on. As a practitioner of what Gilligan would identify as a "male" theory of ethics, I have tended to interpret these demands for more information as the students' refusal to confront an unappetizing conclusion—in short, as showing a lack of academic rigor. The message I am giving them is that the best way to "do" ethics is in isolation from any real situation. Furthermore, I note with bemusement that one standard introductory lecture is organized around two ethical dilemmas involving truth-telling; and, in both cases, it is essential for the argument that the person in the center of the dilemma be without any living family. In short, to make these cases "work," it is necessary to cut off the object of concern from the most profound human relationships.

To this point, I have accepted the perspective of Gilligan and Noddings that these two "modes" of ethical thought can be appropriately tied to gender. Although both writers deny that the pattern is completely consistent, neither Gilligan nor Noddings is concerned to find other terms in which to express their theories—terms not oriented toward gender. Thus Noddings tells us:

> This approach through law and principle is not, I suggest, the approach of the mother. It is the approach of the detached one, of the father. The view to be expressed here is a feminine view. This does not imply that all women will accept it or that men

will reject it; indeed, there is no reason why men should not embrace it. It is feminine in the deep classical sense—rooted in receptivity, relatedness, and responsiveness. It does not imply either that logic is to be discarded or that logic is alien to women. It represents an alternative to present views, one that begins with the moral attitude of longing for goodness and not with moral reasoning. It may indeed be the case that such an approach is more typical of women than of men, but this is an empirical question I shall not attempt to answer.

And we hear from Gilligan:

> The different voice I describe is characterized not by gender but by theme. Its association with women is an empirical observation, and it is primarily through women's voices that I trace its development. But this association is not absolute, and the contrasts between male and female voices are presented here to highlight a distinction between two modes of thought and to focus a problem of interpretation rather than to represent a generalization about either sex.

Gilligan and Noddings are content to leave the problem here, probably because both are working out of an interest in moral development theory, and are concerned to show how differences in developmental experience may point to different ways of perceiving moral issues. Their approach is primarily *descriptive*.

Turning from a descriptive to a more activist approach, women in general, at this point in the movement for greater equality and professional opportunity, must decide whether to adopt a more "male" approach to the ethical implications of so many interpersonal relations, or whether to attempt to change the workplace to reflect more "female" values. Until this decade, in the absence of a feminist critique of marketplace values, it was taken more or less for granted that "male" values were the mature, efficient, professional values. When women deviated from those norms, they put at risk their hard-won toehold in the professional world. So women exhort each other to "dress for success" and "power lunch," to learn the "games your mother never taught you." And to return to our theme, nurses are tempted to advance their professionalism by becoming more and more like doctors. The equation is seductive: if "female" approaches are synonomous with nonprofessionalism, then by all means become professional (and win the respect of self and others) by adopting "male" values. However, this is to state the problem in a way that is already becoming outdated, and makes two questionable assumptions: first, that nursing is a female, and medicine a male, profession; second, that the differences Gilligan delineates are indeed best conceptualized in terms of gender. The first assumption is no longer true. In some schools of medicine today the number of female students approaches 50 per cent; while nursing does not show the same influx of male "immigrants," their numbers are fast growing. The second assumption requires our careful attention.

As we saw above, Gilligan argues that the voices she describes are characterized not by gender but by "theme." Had Piaget, Kohlberg and others conducted their research into moral development along more evenhanded lines, it might have seen long before now that important differences broke along "fault lines" which correlated with a number of different factors, only one of them (perhaps) gender. Psychology having developed in a male-oriented way, we now have to provide correctives, and in that process we find ourselves using gender terms to express our ideas and advance our arguments. However, we need to make three important points. First, the *strongest* claim that could possibly be made is that "male" and "female" ethical thinking exists on a continuum, with more women on one side and more men on the other. Second, even if this strong claim is empirically correct, the reasons adduced for that are clearly societal. As more men share in parenting, as more children spend time in childcare centers, as more men choose to work in such centers and in elementary schools, these forces will change. Even now,

among those of us who grew up in the mother-centered homes of the 1950s, we can discern differences along the lines Gilligan describes, but as a function of household personalities and forces, rather than of gender.

Third, we need, however clumsily, to find new terminology with which to express Gilligan's findings, lest their importance be lost in semantics. It is simply too awkward to be explaining continually that "female" and "male" don't really refer to gender, but to "modes of thought." After many tries, I have tentatively concluded that it is impossible to come up with a pair of terms which will point to some real qualities without carrying unwanted baggage, but let me suggest "narrative" and "rights-based" as terms to go on with.

If we can put together what has been said thus far about the character of the nursing profession in contrast to that of medicine, with the different "themes" of "narrative" versus "rights-based" ways of approaching ethics, I would assert that the nursing profession attracts, at least ideally, primarily those with a narrative approach, while medicine appeals more to those who approach ethics in a rights-based fashion. As the profession of nursing becomes more widely respected, and as the two professions become increasingly free of gender expectations—in other words, as people choose nursing or medicine because of their actual rather than conventional character—this distinction will become even sharper. Now this can be seen not as a criticism of either profession, or as a statement about the predominant gender in the two groups, but as a positive recognition that, just as different professions carry with them different responsibilities, so they also may imply different cognitive and ethical perspectives.

Much of the current frustration of consumers with the medical profession arises at least partially because we focus too much on doctors, and too little on the other members of the health care team. We tend to turn to the doctor with all our questions and concerns, and feel dissatisfied when we are directed to a nurse instead. However, the task we ask medicine to perform is probably too varied and demanding to be fulfilled by a single person, least of all a doctor, given medicine's organ-oriented, disease-oriented approach. David Barnard (1), arguing for "meaning-centered" medicine, describes the patient who "presents" with a symptom as having all of these questions: "What does my symptom mean? What does it mean to me to experience this symptom? What is the meaning of the diagnostic or therapeutic procedures proposed to me, or which I am experiencing? What is the meaning of my life, in light of my illness?" He points out that the personal meaning of illness to the individual may be largely invisible to the health professional: it may involve questions of social and sexual interaction, family roles, job productivity, and so on. "The diabetic's embarrassment and squeamishness about diet or syringes carry further connotations of increased dependency and the possible foreshortening of life ambitions. The person with ulcerative colitis struggles not only with the logistics of diarrhea, but with literal and symbolic loss of control, connotations of immaturity, and being soiled. The person with arthritis struggles with immobility, swelling, and pain; but also with changing images of body and self."

Barnard argues that a meaning-centered medical ethics requires that "physicians (1) *acknowledge* the patient's need for meaning in the illness experience; (2) *learn* the symbol system and world view within which the patient assigns meaning to life events; (3) *negotiate* conflicts in meaning that stem from the different assumptive worlds and/or cultures of doctor and patient; (4) *support* the patient's continuing efforts to integrate the facts and implications of illness into new life meanings." To implement these obligations, Barnard suggests a rich list of skills physicians will have to learn—for example, "mastery of the arts of nonverbal communication, and sensitivity to patterns of language use among the cultures whose members present for care."

Barnard teaches at the Institute for Medical Humanities at the University of Texas, where pa-

tients come from a variety of backgrounds, so he is aware of the magnitude of the challenge his paper presents. To me, at least in the context of a tertiary care hospital, it seems unlikely that physicians will be able to fulfill the four tasks he has laid out. Probably the best we can hope for, from most physicians, is that they respond to the first requirement, and acknowledge the patient's need for meaning; then they can go on to respect the ways in which other members of the caring professions—including not only nurses but administrators, technicians, chaplains, and so on—help the patient (and the patient's family) fulfill the rest of the agenda. By *acknowledge* and *respect* I mean much more than lip-service. Decisions normally considered those of the physician alone, such as type of medication, length of hospitalization, and so on, might be affected.

While it is never a good idea to assign roles too rigidly to members of the health care team, it does seem reasonable to expect that nurses will be the prime providers of Barnard's kind of meaning-centered care. It is nurses who spend the most time with patients, especially time *alone* with patients. It is nurses who have the training to be nurse-educators; it is nurses who, standing at the center of the great web of relationships that makes up a health-care system, can best perceive what kind of experience the patient is having, and can detect what needs are going unmet. Here one might be concerned that this assignment may be interpreted as "letting doctors off the hook," and therefore as relieving them from responsibility toward authentic personal involvement with the patient. However, think of the success we have had in recent years with "teams" such as Institutional Review Boards, in which no one is expected to provide a completely rounded approach to ethical issues; rather, we rely for our final judgment on a rich mix of members who bring a diversity of experience, knowledge, and perspectives. Inevitably hospital care, including care of outpatients, is provided by a group of individuals; my suggestion capitalizes on this necessity.

There is an added reason why narrative ethics is more appropriate to the nursing profession, and why rights-based ethic befits medicine. There is a sharp difference in the balance of power between the two parties in the nurse-patient and the doctor-patient relationship. At present, despite the rise of "consumerism" and contract notions of medicine, doctors wield an enormous amount of power, especially over patients who are poor, weak, old, or otherwise vulnerable. This is true both in terms of their functions—to prescribe, to admit and discharge, to operate—and in terms of how they are perceived in contrast to the patient—healthy, sure of themselves, upper class and competent, as opposed to sick, baffled, pathetic and helpless. The offices, clinics, and hospitals in which the practice of medicine usually is conducted are still set up to make it easy for the doctor to avoid careful, caring, time-consuming interaction with the client. Furthermore, the tradition of medicine is so strongly paternalistic that paternalism will be relinquished only slowly, despite the move away from paternalism in *writing* about medical ethics (4). The fact that it is beneficence that prompts paternalism does not necessarily lessen the wariness with which the modern patient may approach a doctor. James Childress (2) points to four developments which "lessen trust in the professional's interpretation and application of the principle of beneficence": pluralism in values; decline of close, intimate contact among doctors, patients and families; decline of contact between doctor and "whole person," who is now "parcelled out to various specialists"; and the growth of large, impersonal hospitals and clinics. Childress comments:

> Even where there is estrangement, trust may still be possible. It may have a different content, and it may be combined with increased control. As reconceived in a pluralistic setting, trust may be confidence in and reliance upon health-care professionals to respect persons and their rights. . . . If consensus exists in a pluralistic setting, it is primarily about

rules and procedures. . . . In such a setting, trust may presuppose commitment to secondary virtues and to procedures. . . . It may involve respect more than care. Trust may express itself as confidence in and reliance upon others to adhere to moral limits that derive from respect for persons and their rights.

Summary

Taking all these elements together, it makes sense to nurture in medicine an ethic which focuses on individuation, respect for autonomy, and rights, in order to protect the weaker party in an unbalanced relationship. In contrast, the nursing profession, which in its current state of development needs to find ways in which to define itself as increasingly "professional" without leaving behind the traditional values of *care* and *comfort*, may discover in a contextual or narrative ethic the foundation for its identity. It ought to go without saying that this is not a plea for a return to the self-effacing, self-sacrificing tradition of nursing with all of its anti-professional connotations. Rather, nurses—both as human beings and as members of their profession—need to take with great seriousness their ethical obligations of *care* and comfort toward themselves, as well as toward their patients.

References

1. Barnard D. Meaning-centered medicine: medical ethics and the study of religion. Presented at the American Academy of Religion, 9 Dec 1984.
2. Childress J. Who should decide?: Paternalism in health care. New York: Oxford University Press, 1982.
3. Churchill L. Ethical issues of a profession in transition. Am Jrnl Nursing 1977;77:873–75.
4. Clements C, Sider R. Medical ethics' assault upon medical values. JAMA 1983;250:2011–15.
5. Curtin L. Ethical issues in nursing practice and education. In: Ethical issues in nursing and nursing education. National League for Nursing, Pub. #16-1822, 1980:25–26.

6. Davis AJ. Ethics rounds with intensive care nurses. Nursing Clinics of North America 1979;14:45–55.

7. Dworkin R. Taking rights seriously. Cambridge: Harvard University Press, 1977.

8. Flaherty MJ. Nursing's contract with society. In: Curtin L, Flaherty MJ, eds. Nursing ethics: theories and pragmatics. Bowie, Maryland: Robert J. Brady Co., 1982.

9. Gilligan C. In a different voice. Cambridge: Harvard University Press, 1982.

10. Horner M. Toward an understanding of achievement-related conflicts in women. Journal of Social Issues 1972;28:157–75.

11. Lumpp F. The role of the nurse in the bioethical decision-making process. Nursing Clinics of North America 1979;14:13–21.

12. Noddings N. Caring: a feminine approach to ethics and moral education. Berkeley: University of California Press, 1982.

Clinical Ethics and Nursing: "Yes" to Caring, but "No" to a Female Ethics of Care

HELGA KUHSE

I. Introduction: Ethics, Principles, Women and Nurses

Is ethics gendered? Do women and men approach ethics differently? The answer of many thinkers has been "yes".

Rousseau thought that abstract truths and general principles are "beyond a woman's grasp . . .; woman observes, man reasons".[1] Schopenhauer bluntly proclaimed: ". . . the fundamental fault of the female character is that it has *no sense of justice*". This "weakness in their reasoning faculty", Schopenhauer continued, "also explains why women show more sympathy for the unfortunate than men".[2] Finally, to give just one more example, Freud believed that "for women the level of what is ethically normal is different from what it is in men". Women, he wrote, "show less sense of justice than men".[3]

On these views, then, men and women not only approach ethics differently, but insofar as women were thought to lack a head for abstract principles, and a sense of justice, their ethical approach was also regarded as somewhat defective and inferior to that of men. At the same time, and rather paradoxically, women's traits and moral dispositions were often seen as somewhat purer, and more worthy, than those of men. For Rousseau, for example, women who had developed the distinctively feminine traits of gentleness, tenderness, compassion, self-sacrifice and mental passivity, were only a "little lower than the angels";[4] and the poet Lord Tennyson called women the "interpreters between gods and men".[5]

Nursing has always been a predominantly female profession and there was, and probably still is, a widespread belief that nursing, like few other professions, allows women to develop and express their specific feminine virtues. As one writer put it as recently as 1980:

> [N]urses were . . . angels! Angels of mercy! They were with him constantly, these women figures.

They were gentle and good. They fixed his pillows. They came when he called for help. They said: "This will make you feel better" and "There, isn't that better?" They touched him with their hands, flesh to flesh. His succor. His life savers. His lifelines.[6]

Mary Wollstonecraft, a contemporary of Rousseau's, saw a firm link between the feminine virtues of gentleness and docility, and the subjection of women. She charged that Rousseau and some other "specious reasoners", consistently recommended "gentleness, docility and a spaniel-like affection . . . as the cardinal virtues of the sex", but ultimately regarded women as "gentle, domestic brutes", incapable of the kind of reason that distinguishes human beings from the beast. "The nature of reason", she said, "must be the same in all".[7]

Many modern feminists still accept Wollstonecraft's basic point that there is but one ethics for women and men. There is, however, also another school of thought which holds that traditional male thinkers, while wrong on much else, were right on at least one point: that women and men do approach ethics differently. This school of thought rejects the idea that women are *incapable* of abstract, principled thinking; rather, and much more fundamentally, it claims that principled ethical thinking is not the only valid (or best) approach to ethics. There is, according to this view, an alternative "female" approach to ethics which is based not on abstract "male" ethical principles or wide generalisations, but on "care", that is, on receptivity and responsiveness to the needs of others.

Nurses have taken a keen interest in these female approaches to ethics. Drawing on the views expounded by Carol Gilligan[8] and Nel Noddings,[9] nurses claim that a female "ethics of care" better captures their moral experiences than a traditional male "ethics of justice".[10] The latter approach, a prominent proponent of a nursing ethics of care proclaims, regards principles as more important than people; nurse-caring, on the other hand, is patient-centered: "it ties us to

the people we serve and not to the rules through which we serve them".[11]

The claim that women and men approach ethics differently is not the focus of my paper, although I will briefly return to it at the end of my discussion. I will be addressing the second issue, that is, the claim that nurses should adopt a female ethics of care because this is preferable to the justice approach. Since different writers have distinct ideas about what constitutes a (nursing) ethics of care, all I can do in this paper is introduce and then briefly discuss one common central theme: that a female ethics of care has no use for, and does not need, universal principles or rules.

As my discussion will show, I very much doubt that such an ethics will serve either patients or nurses well. Rather, nurses who decide to conduct their professional lives in accordance with an ethics of care are likely to find themselves in a position where they, like generations of nurses and women before them, may be praised for their caring feminine traits and dispositions, but will be unable to assert their moral claims, or to speak on behalf of those for whom they care.

Let me begin my critique by taking a closer look at the notion of "care".

II. Caring as a Moral Disposition[12]

"Care" is a rich and highly ambiguous notion. Caring for another person—the notion that will occupy us in the present context—has connotations of concern, compassion, worry, anxiety, and of burden; there are also connotations of inclination, fondness and affection; connotations of carefulness, that is, of attention to detail, of responding sensitively to the situation of the other; and there are connotations of looking after, or providing for, the other.[13]

For the purposes of understanding and evaluating an ethics that has care as its central concept, it would be important to know which understanding of "care" its exponents have in mind. Unfortunately the nursing literature is not of any great help. Nurses use the term "care" in many different and potentially contradictory ways.[14] As Howard Curzer notes, proposals include "presence", "empathy plus expression of feeling", "truth-telling and touch", "showing concern", and "enabling or assisting".[15] Underlying these different understandings is some general agreement that "care" must involve more than mere caring behaviour; there must also be some empathy, attachment or connectedness, in the sense of "caring about" the patient.

What precisely "caring for/caring about" amounts to is, however, none too clear. Definitions and explanations are imprecise, obscure and sometimes even mystical. One prominent writer in the field, Sally Gadow, for example, defines "care"

> as an end in itself. While it may serve as a means of reaching a further state, it is always and above all a state that itself can be fully inhabited. While it may serve as a vessel for reaching a remote shore, it is at the same time and above all a vessel in which one can live even when—especially when—there is no destination in sight or in mind.[16]

Similarly Jean Watson. Watson holds that true "transpersonal caring" entails that

> the nurse is able to form a union with the other on a level that transcends the physical . . . [where] there is a freeing of both persons from their separation and isolation . . .[17]

Other writers speak of nurse-caring as "a feeling of dedication to the extent that it motivates and energizes action to influence life constructively and positively by increasing intimacy and mutual self-actualization";[18] an "interactive process", which is achieved by "a conscious and intuitive opening of self to another, by purposeful trusting and sharing energy, experiences, ideas, techniques and knowledge";[19] or as "the creative, intuitive or cognitive helping process for individuals and groups based upon philosophic, phenomenologic, and objective and subjective experiential feelings and acts of assisting others".[20]

Writers in the field generally recognize that the notion of "care" is as yet inadequately understood, and that there is as yet no satisfactory ethics of care that can serve as a foundation for nursing.

Despite these inconsistencies and obscurities, and my doubts about the feasibility of building an ethical theory on the concept of care alone, there is value in focusing on care as an important, but often neglected, component of ethics.

A sympathetic reading of the nursing literature will reveal a number of common threads. As also in Nel Noddings' approach,[21] there is emphasis on relationship, on attachment, openness, and on attentiveness and responsiveness to the needs of the cared-for. "Caring" is thus not so much a matter of actions, task, or processes, as a mode of being, a virtue, or a stance or attitude towards the object of one's attention. In other words, in attempting to articulate an ethics of care, writers are not so much trying to answer the traditional ethical question of right action: "What should I do?"; but rather the question: "How should I, the carer, meet the cared-for". I shall refer to this understanding of care as "dispositional care".

Dispositional care presupposes not only commitment and motivation, but also openness and receptivity to the needs of the other—a state that Nel Noddings calls "engrossment". Engrossment entails a putting aside of the self so that the carer can perceive, and then sensitively respond to, the particular and unique experiences and needs of the other.

The ideas of dispositional care and of engrossment are far from unproblematical. Various criticisms have been raised against current articulations of them—that they are, for example, based on an impractical ideal, that they employ a notion of care that, while suited to characterise personal relationships of great intimacy and depth, is ill-suited for the nurse-patient encounter, or that they are potentially exploitative of women.[22] While these criticisms cannot easily be dismissed, I take it as given that there is *some* sense in which our attitudes or dispositions matter and that a caring disposition or stance, loosely understood as sensitive openness and responsiveness to the needs of particular others, will contribute to better patient care. It emphasises the importance of receptivity and responsiveness, as well as the uniqueness of particular persons and situations. Health-care professionals who are "dispositional carers" are more likely to be receptive to the needs of patients, where these patients are recognised as *particular others,* that is, as individuals, with special needs, beliefs, desires and wants—rather than, say, as "the cancer" in Ward 4. This entails that dispositional care is not only an appropriate part of nursing ethics, but of medical ethics as well.

When dispositional care is lacking, patients' needs may not be met. This view gets some support from a recently published observational study reporting on the interaction of nurses and doctors with dying patients. The non-participant observer reported one case, where nurses failed to notice that a dying patient was thirsty, that the patient could not reach the drink that was placed before her, and that she could not sit up unaided and would fall back when no support was provided. While many factors other than the lack of dispositional care could also explain why this patient's needs were not met, the case description suggests that the nurses, rather than simply being callous, were not receptive and sensitive enough to recognize that this particular patient needed additional help.[23]

As Lawrence Blum has observed, moral philosophy's traditional preoccupation with action-guiding rules and principles, and focus on such notions as universalizability and impartiality, have masked the importance of what he calls "moral perception and particularity"—that is, the important role that is played by our ability to recognise the morally salient features of a situation. For all the moral principles in the world (and our willingness to employ them) will not help if we lack the kind of "moral perception" necessary to tell us when to employ them.[24]

To sum up, then, it seems that Blum and proponents of a nursing ethics of care are right when they say that such traits as perceptivity, sensitivity and responsiveness are morally significant. Blum is also right, it seems to me, when he says that philosophy's traditional preoccupation with sometimes blunt rules and principles, and with universalizability and impartiality, has resulted in less than adequate attention being paid to this aspect of ethics. Proponents of a care approach do, however, often want to go much further than that. They are saying that care alone should be playing a role—that there is no place, or only a very limited place, in an ethics of care for abstract universal principles or rules.

III. The Rejection of Principles

Caring is a good thing and everyone, not just nurses, should be more caring. If dispositional care can thus quite properly be regarded as a significant part of ethics, it is, however, not the whole of ethics. Ethics is also, and some would say, primarily, about the justification of actions. This aspect of ethics becomes particularly important in contexts, such as nursing and medicine, where there is frequent moral disagreement about the rightness or wrongness of actions: whether a dying patient should, for example, be kept alive, or allowed to die; told the truth, or be protected from it for her own good.

Proponents of female ethics of care do, however, display a distaste for reasoned argument and justification. In her book *Caring,* Nel Noddings explicitly rejects abstract principles and the requirement of universalizabililty as an appropriate part of ethics. Ethics, she suggests, is not a matter of impartial and abstract principles and rules, but of relationships—of care for family, friends, and the "proximate stranger".[25] But, as Hilde Nelson notes, care is "blind and indiscriminate".[26] It cannot by itself tell us what to do.

The following "personal narrative" by a nurse, Randy Spreen Parker, will illustrate what can happen when the rejection of principles is taken to its logical conclusion.[27] The narrator describes herself as a "seasoned critical care nurse", who had abandoned "[t]he language of rights, duties and obligations" (which she experienced as "alien" and "detached from the experience" of nursing) to "learn the lines of a different script—a script that was written in a universal, relational language"—the language of care.

Parker had cared in what appears to have been an admirable fashion for an aphasic patient, Mike, who had difficulties in speaking and understanding.

Mike was a diabetic. Due to poor blood circulation, it was necessary to perform a hip-disarticulation—a radical amputation of the leg at the hip. He was left with a deteriorating "gaping cavernous wound that extended from his rib cage to his pelvis". The wound needed dressing changes every three hours. This was excruciatingly painful, since Mike, who also had a lung problem, could not be given adequate pain medication.

When it became clear to both patient and nurse that "further medical interventions served no meaningful purpose", Parker spoke to the attending physician and head nurse and told them that she "did not feel" that Mike (who had difficulty speaking coherently) wanted to continue life-sustaining treatment.

Parker asked to remain Mike's primary nurse and to care for him, but, she explained, she could not participate in any further dressing changes or resuscitation measures.

> I tried to explain my rationale but found myself fumbling for the right words. How could I translate my own moral experience into traditional moral language? The scripts were different. After several meetings with the attending physician and other nurse managers, I was removed from intensive care and placed on a medical-surgical unit.

Over the next week, Mike was resuscitated several times, before he died "in pain, frightened and alone".[28]

Parker's realization that her "moral experience" of caring and "traditional moral language" have radically different scripts is of course quite correct. Moral experience is private, traditional moral language is not. One person's raw moral experience holds no persuasive powers for others, and should also be regarded critically by the person herself. After all, at times our feelings and experiences may seriously mislead us. They need testing against some standard that lies outside the experience itself.

When it comes to the justification of particular actions, we need to give reasoned arguments for our views. In the clinical context, such arguments will typically rely on certain universal principles, such as respect for autonomy or a health care professional's *prima facie* duty to act in the patient's best interests. To eschew all moral principles is to withdraw from moral discourse and to retreat into an essentially dumb world of one's own.

Of course, the assumption is that caring, in its sensitive attention to the particularities of the situation can give the right answer. But this is not so. Sensitivity and particularity alone can not guide action. We always must decide which particularities of a situation, which elements of the personal histories of those involved, are of moral significance and which are not.

To decide what she should do, the agent must first "abstract" some particularities of the situation—those that she regards as morally significant—as her action guide. These abstractions—for example that Mike was suffering and wanted to die, that there was no hope, and so on—are the kind of stuff that principles are made of. Once stated in principled form (for example: "Patients who are hopelessly ill, who are suffering and want to die, should be allowed to die") these abstractions can be tested, and accepted or rejected, as the case may be. Without principles of some sort—and it is of course an open question what these principles should be—there can be no ethical discourse, no justification—only particularities and unguided feelings; neither will have any persuasive powers for others, nor should they have persuasive power for us.

Caring advocates' distaste for principles follows, of course, from the requirement that the carer should be fully attentive to the circumstances of each individual person, and the nuances of her particular and unique situation. The assumption is that abstraction presupposes sameness, where there is, in fact, uniqueness.

Nel Noddings provides an extensive critique of abstract principles by distinguishing the "approach of the father" from that "of the mother":

> The first moves immediately to abstraction where . . . thinking can take place clearly and logically in isolation from the complicating factors of particular persons, places, and circumstances; the second moves to concretization where . . . feelings can be modified by the introduction of facts, the feelings of others, and personal histories.[29]

Noddings is correct when she suggests that additional facts, feelings, and personal histories will, and should, often make a difference to our moral evaluation of a situation. Nonetheless, the dichotomy she draws between an "ethics of care" and an "ethics of principle" in terms of the distinction between "concretization" and "abstraction" is a false one.

In the passage just quoted, the contrast between "abstraction" and "concretization" seems to rest, at least in part, on the distinction between "thinking in isolation from complicating factors" and "thinking modified by the introduction of facts . . .". But could ethical thinking *ever* proceed in isolation from concrete facts and particular circumstances? Even Kant, rigidly holding that one must never lie, even to a would-be-murderer, needs to refer to the facts: do you really know whether the man's intended victim is in the house? How sure do you have to be that he is there, for the statement "I don't know where he is" to count as a lie?[30]

By the same token, even those who take Noddings' "mother's approach" will have to abstract some details from the infintely many that describe a given situation. Noddings' reference to "feelings" and "personal histories" is already an abstraction of particular aspects of the situation: apparently a person's height, or hair colour can (always? usually?) be left out. But even then, it is simply not possible to take all the feelings, or each aspect of every personal history into account. This means that the question is not *whether* context is relevant, but rather *which* elements of that context ought to be "abstracted" from the overall context as significant for ethical decision-making.[31]

What the morally relevant factors are is perhaps the most central and vexing question in traditional ethics. Those who approach ethics from the perspective of the justice tradition will focus on aspects relevant to the application of certain principles or rules; those who approach ethics from a consequentialist perspective will focus on certain goals—for example, how much pleasure or pain a given action will produce, or how well it satisfies the preferences of all those affected by the action; and those who approach ethics from the care perspective will focus on aspects related to the maintenance of relationships, that is, on care for family, friends, and the "proximate stranger".

This brings us to the next question: Is an ethics that focuses on our responsibilities to those with whom we stand in direct relationships adequate?

Nel Noddings regards concern for those distant from us—for example, those starving in Africa, those who are not our patients, or those who do not belong to our species—as a form of "romantic rationalism".[32] But this response will not do. It entails that a whole range of important ethical issues that go beyond personal human relationships and the lived experience of human care, such as the distribution and redistribution of wealth or the distribution of scarce health care resources, could not be challenged from within the care perspective.[33]

If women and nurses excessively devalue reasoned argument, if they dismiss ethical principles and norms and hold that notions of impartiality and universalizability have no place in a female ethics of care, then they will be left without the theoretical tools necessary to condemn some actions or practices, and to defend others. Bereft of a universal ethical language, women will be unable to participate in ethical discourse. They will not be able to speak on behalf of the patients for whom they care, nor will they be able to defend their own legitimate claims[34]—and the motto of the first Canadian school of nursing: "I see and I am silent" would have continuing relevance for nurses.[35]

IV. Conclusion

I began my paper by asking whether women and men approach ethics differently. I myself am dubious about the claim that ethics is gendered and that women are inherently more caring than men. Rather, I am more persuaded by the general idea that social practices and roles give rise to particular moral experiences and visions of "the good". Women have traditionally tended the home, nurtured children, supported husbands, and nursed the sick. Men, on the other hand, have traditionally played more public roles. Their activities did not primarily involve care for "concrete others" but rather dealings with strangers or "abstract others".[36]

Broad ethical principles and rules, notions of rights and justice have an appropriate role to play in the public sphere. Insofar as the public sphere is the realm of strangers, we cannot know the personal histories and particular circumstances of all those affected by our decisions, nor can we care for them in a personal way. But we can, and must, ensure that their rights and claims are protected, and that they are treated fairly.

Care, on the other hand, has a more central role to play in the private sphere, where people can respond to each other as "concrete" others, and where the maintenance of relationships requires sensitivity and responsiveness to the particularities of the situation and the needs and desires of those concerned.

Now, if it is the case that traditional ethical theories are based on the experiences of men in the public sphere, then we should not be too surprised to find that the insights of women, derived from their experience in the private sphere have often been ignored.[37] Nursing straddles the public and the private. It is a public enterprise, but "care" is quite properly recognised as the—largely—appropriate mode for the one-to-one encounter between nurses and patients. Patients as a whole would not be well-served if they were regarded as "abstract" individuals, as merely the bearers of certain rights or claims. Such an approach would leave many of their needs unmet. While "care" is thus necessary for good patient care, it is not—as I have suggested above—an adequate foundational concept for a nursing ethics of care. Ethics, and women and nurses, need justice as well.

I started by quoting a number of traditional thinkers. Let me close with a quote from one other philosopher. "Clearly", Aristotle maintained,

> . . . moral virtue belongs to all . . . but the temperance of a man and of a woman, or the courage and justice of a man and of a woman are not . . . the same . . . "Silence is a woman's glory", but this is not equally the glory of man.[38]

One way to prove him wrong, is to reject a female (nursing) ethics of care.

Notes

1. Jean-Jacques Rousseau: *Emile,* trans. Barbara Foxley, London: Dent, 1966, pp. 349, 350.
2. Arthur Schopenhauer: "On Women" in Mary Mahowald (ed): *Philosophy of Woman—An Anthology of Classic and Current Concepts,* Indianapolis: Indiana, 1983, p. 231 (emphasis in original).
3. Sigmund Freud: "Some Psychical Consequences of the Anatomical Distinction Between the Sexes", in *The Standard Edition of the Complete Psychological Works of Sigmund Freud,* trans. and ed. James Strachey, London: The Hogarth Press, 1961. Vol. XIX, pp. 257–58. (I owe this reference to Carol

Gilligan: *In a Different Voice*, Cambridge, Mass.: Harvard University Press, 1982, p. 7.)

4. Jean-Jacques Rousseau: *Emile*, op. cit., p. 359.

5. Alfred Lord Tennyson: "The Princess". (The poem can be found in various anthologies.)

6. Martha Lear: *Heartsounds*, New York: Simon and Schuster, 1980, pp. 38–39.

7. Mary Wollstonecraft: *A Vindication of the Rights of Women*, New York: Norton, 1967, pp. 50, 68, 69.

8. Carol Gilligan: *In a Different Voice*, Cambridge: Harvard University Press, 1982.

9. Nel Noddings: *Caring—A Feminine Approach to Ethics and Moral Education*, Berkeley: University of California Press, 1984.

10. See, for example, the articles in the collection by Jean Watson and Marilyn A. Ray (eds.): *The Ethics of Care and the Ethics of Cure: Synthesis in Chronicity*, New York: National League for Nursing, 1988; Mary Carolyn Cooper: "Gilligan's Different Voice: A Perspective for Nursing", *Journal of Professional Nursing*, Vol. 5, No. 1, 1989, pp. 10–16; Sara T. Fry: "Toward a theory of nursing ethics", *Advances in Nursing Science*, Vol. 11, No. 4, pp. 9–22; Randy Spreen Parker: "Nurses' stories: The search for a relational ethics of care", *Advances in Nursing Science*, Sept. 1990, pp. 32–40; Dena S. Davis: "Nursing: An Ethics of Caring", *Hum. Med.*, 1985, Vol. 2, No. 1, pp. 19–25.

11. Jean Watson: "An Introduction: An Ethics of Caring/Curing/Nursing" *qua* Nursing: in Jean Watson and Marilyn A. Ray (eds.): *The Ethics of Care . . .*, op cit., p. 2. Jean Watson is here citing Nel Noddings: *Caring . . .*, op. cit., no page number given.

12. This section contains some passages drawn from Helga Kuhse: "Against the Stream: Why Nurses Should Say 'No' to a female Ethics of Care", forthcoming in *Revue Internationale de Philosophique*.

13. On the richness of the notion of "caring", see Nel Noddings: *Caring . . .*, op. cit., pp. 9–16.

14. For a thorough critique of Sara Fry's concept of care (in "The role of caring in a theory of nursing", *Hypatia*. Vol. 4, No. 2, 1989, pp. 88–103) see Howard J. Curzer: "Fry's Concept of Care in Nursing Ethics, *Hypatia*, Vol. 8, No. 3, 1993. pp. 174–183.

15. Howard J. Curzer: "Fry's Concept of Care . . .", ibid., p. 175.

16. Sally Gadow: "Covenant Without Cure: Letting Go and Holding On in Chronic Illness", in (eds.) Jean Watson and Marilyn A. Ray (eds.): *The Ethics of Care and the Ethics of Cure . . .*, op. cit., p. 5–6.

17. Jean Watson: *Nursing—Human Science and Human Care: A Theory of Nursing*, Norwalk, Conn.: Appleton-Century Crofts, 1985, p. 66.

18. E.O. Bevis: "Caring: A Life Force", in (ed.) M. Leininger: *Caring: An Essential Human Need*, Thorofare, NJ: Slack, 1981, p. 50.

19. B. Blattner: *Holistic Nursing*, Englewood Cliffs, NJ: Prentice Hall, 1981, p. 70.

20. M. Leininger: "Caring: A Central Focus of Nursing and Health Care Services", *Nursing and Health Care*, October 1980, p. 143, as cited by Hilde L. Nelson: "Against Caring", *The Journal of Clinical Ethics*, Vol. 3, No. 1, Spring 1992, p. 9.

21. Nel Noddings: *Caring . . .*, op. cit.

22. See, for example, Stan van Hooft: "Caring and professional commitment". *The Australian Journal of Advanced Nursing*, Vol. 4, No. 4, 1987, pp. 29–38; Helga Kuhse: "Caring is not enough: reflections on a nursing ethics of care", *The Australian Journal of Advanced Nursing*, Vol. 11, No. 1, 1993, pp. 32–42. Catharine A. MacKinnon: *Feminism Unmodified: Discourses on Life and Law*, Cambridge: Harvard University Press, 1987. Janice G. Raymond: "Reproductive Gifts and Gift Giving: The Altruistic Woman", *Hastings Center Report*, November/December 1990, pp. 7–11.

23. Mina Mills, Huw T.O. Davies, William A. Macrae: "Care of dying patients in hospital", *British Medical Journal*, Vol. 309, Sept. 3, 1994, pp. 583–586.

24. Lawrence Blum: "Moral Perception and Particularity", *Ethics*, Vol. 101, July 1991, pp. 701–725.

25. Nel Noddings: *Caring . . .*, op. cit.

26. Hilde L. Nelson: "Against Caring", *The Journal of Clinical Ethics*, Vol. 3, No. 1, 1992, p. 9.

27. A similar description of this case also appears in Helga Kuhse: "Against the Stream . . .", op. cit.

28. Randy Spreen Parker: "Nurses' Stories . . .", op. cit., pp. 31–34.

29. Nel Noddings: *Caring . . .*, op. cit., pp. 36–37.

30. See I. Kant: "On a supposed right to tell lies from benevolent motives" in *Kant's Critique of Practi-*

cal Reason and Other Works on the Theory of Ethics, trans. Thomas Kingsmill Abbott, London: Longman's, Green & Co., 1909, pp. 361–365.

31. This point is also made by George Sher: "Other Voices, Other Rooms", in (eds.) Eva Federe Kittay and Diana Meyers: *Women and Moral Theory,* United States of America: Rowman and Littlefields Publishers, 1987, p. 180.

32. Nel Noddings: *Caring . . . ,* op. cit., p. 3.

33. See also Claudia Card: "Caring and Evil", *Hypatia,* Vol. 5, No. 1, Spring 1990, pp. 101–108.

34. See also L.M. Purdy: "Feminist Healing Ethics" in *Hypatia,* Vol. 4, No. 2, Summer 1989, pp. 9–12.

35. John O. Goden: "Editorials—No Longer Silent", *Humane Medicine,* Vol. 4, No. 1, May 1988, p. 1.

36. Jean Grimshaw: "The Idea of a Female Ethic" in Peter Singer: *Companion to Ethics,* Oxford: Blackwell, 1991, pp. 496–499.

37. See also Jean Grimshaw: "The Idea of a Female Ethic", op. cit.

38. Aristotle: *Politics,* Book I, Chapter 13.

B. The Obligations of Physicians to Provide Quality Care

There can be little doubt that physicians continue to play a significant role in the health care system. Although many other professionals, from nurses to emergency medical technicians (EMTs), provide essential health care services to patients, physicians remain the dominant health care professionals, in many instances the ones who are ultimately responsible for the patient's care. Under the law in many states, there are a number of health care services, from surgery to the diagnosis of complex conditions, that only they can perform.

Yet, as our health care system has changed, the ethical obligations and responsibilities that are placed upon physicians and their colleagues in other health care professions have become less clear. The old codes, discussed in Section A, may no longer suffice in a time in which patient autonomy is valued and the paternalism and insularity of the medical profession is questioned. Moreover, the old codes and the values they place on the patient-physician relationship may appear to be unrealistically romantic in a time when health care is financed by third parties and increasingly delivered by complex, impersonal institutions.

In this section and the ones that follow, we look at the complex and conflicting obligations that physicians have to their patients in light of the contemporary health care system. To what extent do traditional norms of physician responsibility provide valuable guidance? To what extent does patient autonomy suffice as an alternative guiding principle? Or, under current conditions, should other principles or perspectives be controlling?

We begin by considering what may appear to be the most obvious ethical precept: the obligation to provide quality care. It goes without saying that a physician is obligated to provide competent care for the patient. Indeed, physicians are licensed by the state and thus are privileged to perform services that others may not by law provide, precisely because they are expected to have skills and knowledge that others lack. As the Supreme Court said over a hundred years ago when it upheld the constitutionality of the licensing requirement in *West Virginia v. Dent,*

> Few professions require more careful preparation by one who seeks to enter it than that of medicine. It has to deal with all those subtle and mysterious influences upon which health and life depend, and requires not only a knowledge of the properties of vegetable and mineral substances, but of the human body in all its complicated parts, and their relation to each other, as well as their influence upon the mind. The physician must be able to detect readily the presence of disease, and prescribe appropriate remedies for its removal. Every one may have occasion to consult him, but comparatively few can judge of the qualifications of learning and skill which he possesses. Reliance must be placed upon the assurance given by his license, issued by an authority competent to judge in that respect, that he possesses the requisite qualifications.[14]

On the other hand, it is clear that physicians cannot, either practically or ethically, be expected to be miracle workers and cure all of their patients. Some illnesses simply cannot be cured. Even with the best of medical care, all patients will die inevitably. We cannot expect physicians always to "cure" their patients.

Because of this somber reality, neither law nor ethics requires physicians to provide patients with cures. The guiding principle in the Hippocratic Oath, reprinted in Section A, is that physicians shall use their "ability and judgment" to benefit the patients and keep them from "harm and injustice." This principle has been thought to reflect the basic paternalism of physicians since it judges benefits to the patient from the perspective of the physician, not the patient. Likewise, the law expects individual physicians to do only what others in their profession in general do. Thus in most states, physicians are only required by law to render care of a quality that a reasonable physician offers. In effect, medical custom constitutes the legal standard of care. Even so limited, the obligation to provide quality care may come into conflict with other goals and principles, such as public health, overall utility, or patient autonomy.

The famous legal case *Helling v. Carey,* included in the readings, explores the conflict between relying upon a customary standard of care and the advancement of public health. In *Helling* the physician did not offer his patient a glaucoma test. Given her age, this decision was within the bounds of customary practice. Nevertheless, departing from traditional legal doctrine, the court concluded that the physician could be held liable for malpractice because the custom itself did not adequately protect the public's health. But, we may ask, how confident can we be that the court is better able than the medical profession to decide whether public health will be advanced by performing glaucoma screening tests on a younger population? In fact, many critics have argued that the *Helling* court neglected the costs (economic and emotional) of false positives.

Even if the *Helling* court was correct about the utility of the standard of care it promoted, should such norms be imposed by courts in malpractice cases? Or is the threat of increased malpractice liability a barrier to improving quality of care? In its controversial report *To Err Is Human: Building a Safer Health System,* the Institute of Medicine contended that the quality of medical care over all might be improved if we focused less on the duties of individual physicians, the so-called bad apples, and more on the systems and structures around which care is organized.[15] Interestingly, the Institute suggested that such an approach might require an alteration or lessening of legal liability, on the theory that physicians and institutions would be less willing to review their practices and institute new approaches to reduce medically caused adverse events if they were subject to liability. Would a reduction of legal liability lead to a diminution of a provider's fiduciary responsibility? Would it leave patients who are injured by physician errors insufficiently compensated? Or could a "no fault" system compensate injured patients without implying physician fault?

A physician's obligation to provide quality care, as measured by medical custom, may also conflict with respect for a patient's autonomy. At a basic level, the obligation to provide quality care means that a physician must treat the patient in a manner that medical custom (or, as in *Helling*, some higher objective standard) advises will lead to the best health outcome. That raises the question, What happens when medical standards conflict with a patient's own choices or desires? For example, what is the physician's obligation when the patient requests a treatment that is medically contraindicated? Must a physician prescribe an antibiotic for a virus if the patient wants it, even though the antibiotic is totally ineffective against the virus? What if the antibiotic presents risks for the patient? Should the physician still prescribe the medication and honor the patient's wishes, or should the physician rely upon medical standards and refuse to "do harm"?

Consider here the so-called futility debate, which was prominent in the late 1980s and early 1990s and was epitomized by the case of Helga Wanglie. As Marcia Angell and Steven H. Miles explain in their companion, and conflicting, articles on the case, Helga Wanglie was an 86-year-old woman in a persistent vegetative state. Her physicians and the hospital she was in concluded that further treatment would be futile in the sense that she could not be restored to consciousness and the treatments she was receiving would not benefit her. Her family disagreed, believing that her life should be sustained as long as possible.

According to Miles, Wanglie's physicians had an ethical responsibility, based on an "ethic of stewardship" to resist the family's request and seek review of the determination to end treatment. Interestingly, Miles does not claim that the physicians could, after review, deny treatment simply because it would be ineffective or harmful to the patient. Rather he rests his argument on the view that physicians have a duty "to people who have pooled their resources to insure their collective access to appropriate health care." In other words, physicians have a duty to safeguard the resources of the community. Is this appropriate? If the Wanglie family had paid for her care out of their own pockets, and not with insurance, would Miles have then supported the continuation of so-called futile care? And would the procedures he suggests adequately protect the interests of patients who desire care that physicians find futile, or perhaps more correctly, wasteful?

Marcia Angell, in her commentary, strongly disagrees with Miles. To Angell, patient autonomy must prevail, and when a patient, such as Wanglie, cannot speak for herself and has not left advanced directives, the family's wishes should be followed. For physicians to impose their perceptions of inappropriate treatment, Angell claims, would be "callous" and could not be done on a principled basis. But what about a situation in which a patient or family requests a treatment that medical science posits will be totally ineffective (a leg amputation to cure severe asthma)? Would Angell argue for respect for patient autonomy in that case or is she really only arguing that physicians should respect a patient's judgment as to the ethical, rather than scientific, value or worth of a particular treatment?

Angell's assertion that patient autonomy should trump the physicians' perspective in so-called futility cases assumes that we can know the patient's preferences and take them at face value. In many cases, such as Wanglie, when a patient is incompetent and has left no advanced directive (such as a living will or health care proxy), that seems questionable. But even when a patient is conscious and competent, we may want to question whether the expressed preferences of ill patients can always be taken at face value. (Recall here our discussion of *Bouvia* in Chapter 3.) According to Edmund Pellegrino, sickness and dependency compromise "the actual expression of autonomy to some degree."[16] As a result, Pellegrino argues that a physician must not be a morally neutral agent, carrying out the patient's expressed desires without question. Instead, the physician must exercise his or her own autonomy and act as a "beneficent agent" acting on behalf of a patient. What would such a beneficent agent do in the *Wanglie* case?

No issue raises this conflict more profoundly than does physician-assisted suicide. In the last decade, the question of whether physicians should be permitted to assist patients in committing suicide has been at the forefront of bioethics, perhaps displacing earlier debates about the so-called right-to-die. One state, Oregon, enacted a statute, the Oregon Death with Dignity Act, permitting the practice in limited circumstances.[17] The implementation of this Act was threatened by the United States Attorney General, who argued that physicians prescribing under the Act would violate federal drug control laws. The federal Court of Appeals for the Ninth Circuit disagreed, emphasizing in its opinion that states traditionally define the parameters of medical practice.[18]

In other states, voters have rejected referenda designed to legalize the practice. Meanwhile, physician-assisted suicide has been effectively legalized in the Netherlands as well as Switzerland.[19] Some insight into the reasons patients give for seeking physician-assisted suicide may be helpful in determining whether physicians should aid them. A recent study involving a questionnaire distributed to 545 hospice nurses and social workers in Oregon indicated that a "very important reason" why patients requested physician-assisted suicide was out of a desire to control the circumstance of death.[20] Does this strike you as a good reason for supporting the practice? Alternatively, perhaps the desire to control the time of death is an expression of a neurotic wish and is more accurately characterized as "controlling" than autonomous. Should it matter what a person's reasons are when we decide whether to grant the request?

Some commentators argue that respect for patient autonomy requires the acceptance of physician-assisted suicide. If we respect the right of patients to choose their treatments and to terminate them at will, then why should we not follow their directives when they request medicines that will be used to kill them? Are there any differences between following patients' wishes to end treatment (as in *Bouvia*) and following their wishes when they seek to commit suicide? Not according to David Orentlicher who argues that there is little moral difference between permitting a patient to reject or terminate a treatment necessary for life and permitting the patient to choose a procedure that will enable the patient to kill herself.[21] In both cases, the patient is making a life-ending choice. And in both cases, the patient is calling upon the physician to play a role in that choice.

Nevertheless, physician-assisted suicide, and perhaps even the discontinuation of life-sustaining treatments in cases such as *Bouvia*, may be seen as inherently contradictory to the idea of beneficence and corrosive to the integrity of the medical profession as a profession. But why does beneficence prohibit assisting suicide when patients are in pain and cannot be fully comforted by other means?

Although many debates about physician-assisted suicide focus on the nature of the patient-physician relationship, other issues are also critical. The relationship, after all, does not exist in a vacuum. And physician-assisted suicide is not being discussed in a utopian health care system. In the United States it is being discussed in the context of a system in which many individuals lack health insurance and there are enormous demands upon physicians and other providers to reduce costs. Do these factors play a role in creating the "demand" for assisted suicide? Critics argue that they do, suggesting that the high cost of health care may influence people to seek a quick and inexpensive end to their illnesses. Likewise, opponents question whether physicians in an era of managed care and limited resources may unduly or subtly pressure patients with long, expensive illnesses into committing suicide. Would that be troubling from a utilitarian perspective? If so, why?

Many in the disability rights community argue that the movement for assisted suicide stems from the disrespect and limited options given to people with disabilities. In his article, Jerome E. Bickenbach claims that in our society people who are disabled and dependent upon others are made to feel as if their lives are worthless and they are a burden on others. Under such circumstances, suicide seems like the socially desirable option. Legalization of assisted suicide, he fears, would only accelerate that trend and negate any pressures upon society to increase respect and resources for people with painful and/or disabling conditions.

All of these issues, and others, were presented before the United States Supreme Court in *Washington v. Glucksberg*.[22] The plaintiffs in that case were several people with terminal diseases from the state of Washington. They argued that the state's ban on physician-assisted suicide was unconstitutional because it deprived them of a fundamental right to commit suicide with the assistance of a physician.

In the so-called philosopher's brief, a group of distinguished philosophers and bioethicists supported that position, arguing that respect for individual autonomy and liberty required the recognition of a constitutional right.[23] A unanimous Supreme Court disagreed.

In the majority opinion, Chief Justice Rehnquist focused on the nature of constitutional rights. He wrote that because the putative right to assisted suicide is not mentioned in the Constitution, it can only be recognized by the Court if there was a long history of its recognition in Anglo-American law. Because he could not find such a history, he argued that the state could choose to ban assisted suicide as long as the ban was "rational," which it was because it helped to protect vulnerable citizens as well as the medical profession itself. Do you find such justifications sufficient to justify the state's limitation upon autonomy?

In their concurring opinions, other justices focused more on the ethics of physician-assisted suicide itself. Justice Stevens, for example, began by discounting the primacy of autonomy, arguing that the community has a legitimate moral interest in an individual's suicide. But, he continued, "for some patients, it would be a physician's refusal to dispense medication to ease their suffering and make their death tolerable and dignified that would be inconsistent with the healing role." Nevertheless, Justice Stevens concurred with the Court's majority both because the state has a compelling interest in protecting the vulnerable and because "there remains room for vigorous debate about the outcome of particular cases that are not necessarily resolved by the opinions announced today." Likewise, Justice O'Connor cautioned that the majority's opinion should be read narrowly and that the issue might remain open if a patient were to come before the Court with evidence that assisted suicide was the only way to prevent unremitting pain.

The *Glucksberg* case resolved (for now) the question of whether the right to assisted suicide broadly framed is a fundamental one under our Constitution, but the case did not answer the ethical question. Indeed, *Glucksberg* showed some of the distinctions between constitutional law and ethics. The Court held that there was no constitutional right to physician-assisted suicide, but that did not mean that states could not choose to permit the practice. Nor did it answer the question of whether they should do so or whether it is ethical for a physician to undertake the practice. That debate continues.

Supreme Court of Washington, En Banc.
Morrison P. Helling and Barbara Helling, his wife, Petitioners,
v.
Thomas F. Carey and Robert C. Laughlin, Respondents. No. 42775.

March 14, 1974.

HUNTER, Associate Justice. This case arises from a malpractice action instituted by the plaintiff (petitioner), Barbara Helling.

The plaintiff suffers from primary open angle glaucoma. Primary open angle glaucoma is essentially a condition of the eye in which there is an interference in the ease with which the nourishing fluids can flow out of the eye. Such a condition results in pressure gradually rising above the normal level to such an extent that damage is produced to the optic nerve and its fibers with resultant loss in vision. The first loss usually occurs in the periphery of the field of vision. The disease usually has few symptoms and, in the absence of a pressure test, is often undetected until the damage has become extensive and irreversible.

The defendants (respondents), Dr. Thomas F. Carey and Dr. Robert C. Laughlin, are partners who practice the medical specialty of ophthalmology. Ophthalmology involves the diagnosis and treatment of defects and diseases of the eye.

The plaintiff first consulted the defendants for myopia, nearsightedness, in 1959. At that time she was fitted with contact lenses. She next con-

sulted the defendants in September, 1963, concerning irritation caused by the contact lenses. Additional consultations occurred in October, 1963; February, 1967; September, 1967; October, 1967; May, 1968; July, 1968; August, 1968; September, 1968; and October, 1968. Until the October 1968 consultation, the defendants considered the plaintiff's visual problems to be related solely to complications associated with her contact lenses. On that occasion, the defendant, Dr. Carey, tested the plaintiff's eye pressure and field of vision for the first time. This test indicated that the plaintiff had glaucoma. The plaintiff, who was then 32 years of age, had essentially lost her peripheral vision and her central vision was reduced to approximately 5 degrees vertical by 10 degrees horizontal.

Thereafter, in August of 1969, after consulting other physicians, the plaintiff filed a complaint against the defendants alleging, among other things, that she sustained severe and permanent damage to her eyes as a proximate result of the defendants' negligence. During trial, the testimony of the medical experts for both the plaintiff and the defendants established that the standards of the profession for that specialty in the same or similar circumstances do not require routine pressure tests for glaucoma upon patients under 40 years of age. The reason the pressure test for glaucoma is not given as a regular practice to patients under the age of 40 is that the disease rarely occurs in this age group. Testimony indicated, however, that the standards of the profession do require pressure tests if the patient's complaints and symptoms reveal to the physician that glaucoma should be suspected.

The trial court entered judgment for the defendants following a defense verdict. The plaintiff thereupon appealed to the Court of Appeals, which affirmed the judgment of the trial court. The plaintiff then petitioned this Court for review, which we granted.

In her petition for review, the plaintiff's primary contention is that under the facts of this case the trial judge erred in giving certain instructions to the jury and refusing her proposed instructions defining the standard of care which the law imposes upon an ophthalmologist. As a result, the plaintiff contends, in effect, that she was unable to argue her theory of the case to the jury that the standard of care for the specialty of ophthalmology was inadequate to protect the plaintiff from the incidence of glaucoma, and that the defendants, by reason of their special ability, knowledge and information, were negligent in failing to give the pressure test to the plaintiff at an earlier point in time which, if given, would have detected her condition and enabled the defendants to have averted the resulting substantial loss in her vision.

We find this to be a unique case. The testimony of the medical experts is undisputed concerning the standards of the profession for the specialty of ophthalmology. It is not a question in this case of the defendants having any greater special ability, knowledge and information than other ophthalmologists which would require the defendants to comply with a higher duty of care than that 'degree of care

and skill which is expected of the average practitioner in the class to which he belongs, acting in the same or similar circumstances.' The issue is whether the defendants' compliance with the standard of the profession of ophthalmology, which does not require the giving of a routine pressure test to persons under 40 years of age, should insulate them from liability under the facts in this case where the plaintiff has lost a substantial amount of her vision due to the failure of the defendants to timely give the pressure test to the plaintiff.

The defendants argue that the standard of the profession, which does not require the giving of a routine pressure test to persons under the age of 40, is adequate to insulate the defendants from liability for negligence because the risk of glaucoma is so rare in this age group. The testimony of the defendant, Dr. Carey, however, is revealing as follows:

Q. Now, when was it, actually, the first time any complaint was made to you by her of any field or visual field problem? A. Really, the first time that she really complained of a visual field problem was the August 30th date. (1968) Q. And how soon before the diagnosis was that? A. That was 30 days. We made it on October 1st. Q. And in your opinion, how long, as you now have the whole history and analysis and the diagnosis, how long had she had this glaucoma? A. I would think she probably had it ten years or longer. Q. Now, Doctor, there's been some reference to the matter of taking pressure checks of persons over 40. What is the incidence of glaucoma, the statistics, with persons under 40? A. In the instance of glaucoma under the age of 40, is less than 100 to one per cent. The younger you get, the less the incidence. It is thought to be in the neighborhood of one in 25,000 people or less. Q. How about the incidence of glaucoma in people over 40? A. Incidence of glaucoma over 40 gets into the two to three per cent category, and hence, that's where there is this great big difference and that's why the standards around the world has been to check pressures from 40 on.

The incidence of glaucoma in one out of 25,000 persons under the age of 40 may appear quite minimal. However, that one person, the plaintiff in this instance, is entitled to the same protection, as afforded persons over 40, essential for timely detection of the evidence of glaucoma where it can be arrested to avoid the grave and devastating result of this disease. The test is a simple pressure test, relatively inexpensive. There is no judgment factor involved, and there is no doubt that by giving the test the evidence of glaucoma can be detected. The giving of the test is harmless if the physical condition of the eye permits. The testimony indicates that although the condition of the plaintiff's eyes might have at times prevented the defendants from administering the pressure test, there is an absence of evidence in the record that the test could not have been timely given.

Under the facts of this case reasonable prudence required the timely giving of the pressure test to this plaintiff. The precaution of giving this test to detect the incidence of glaucoma to patients under 40 years of age is so imperative that irrespective of its disregard by the standards of the opthalmology profession, it is the duty of the courts to say what is required to protect patients under 40 from the damaging results of glaucoma.

We therefore hold, as a matter of law, that the reasonable standard that should have been followed under the undisputed facts of this case was the timely giving of this simple, harmless pressure test to this plaintiff and that, in failing to do so, the defendants were negligent, which proximately resulted in the blindness sustained by the plaintiff for which the defendants are liable.

The judgment of the trial court and the decision of the Court of Appeals is reversed, and the case is remanded for a new trial on the issue of damages only.

UTTER, Associate Justice (concurring).

I concur in the result reached by the majority. I believe a greater duty of care could be imposed on the defendants than was established by their profession. The duty could be imposed when a disease, such as glaucoma, can be detected by a simple, well-known harmless test whose results are definitive and the disease can be successfully arrested by early detection, but where the effects of the disease are irreversible if undetected over a substantial period of time.

The difficulty with this approach is that we as judges, by using a negligence analysis, seem to be imposing a stigma of moral blame upon the doctors who, in this case, used all the precautions commonly prescribed by their profession in diagnosis and treatment. Lacking their training in this highly sophisticated profession, it seems illogical for this court to say they failed to exercise a reasonable standard of care. It seem to me we are, in reality, imposing liability, because, in choosing between an innocent plaintiff and a doctor, who acted reasonably according to his specialty but who could have prevented the full effects of this disease by administering a simple, harmless test and treatment, the plaintiff should not have to bear the risk of loss. As such, imposition of liability approaches that of strict liability.

Sounding Board

Informed Demand for "Non-Beneficial" Medical Treatment

STEVEN H. MILES

An 85-year-old woman was taken from a nursing home to Hennepin County Medical Center on January 1, 1990, for emergency treatment of dyspnea from chronic bronchiectasis. The patient, Mrs. Helga Wanglie, required emergency intubation and was placed on a respirator. She occasionally acknowledged discomfort and recognized her family but could not communicate clearly. In May, after attempts to wean her from the respirator failed, she was discharged to a chronic care hospital. One week later, her heart stopped during a weaning attempt; she was resuscitated and taken to another hospital for intensive care. She remained unconscious, and a physician suggested that it would be appropriate to consider withdrawing life support. In response, the family transferred her back to the medical center on May 31. Two weeks later, physicians concluded that she was in a persistent vegetative state as a result of severe anoxic encephalopathy. She was maintained on a respirator, with repeated courses of antibiotics, frequent airway suctioning, tube feedings, an air flotation bed, and biochemical monitoring.

In June and July of 1990, physicians suggested that life-sustaining treatment be withdrawn since it was not benefiting the patient. Her husband, daughter, and son insisted on continued treatment. They stated their view that physicians should not play God, that the patient would not be better off dead, that removing life support showed moral decay in our civilization, and that a miracle could occur. Her husband told a physician that his wife had never stated her preferences concerning life-sustaining treatment. He believed that the cardiac arrest would not have occurred if

she had not been transferred from Hennepin County Medical Center in May. The family reluctantly accepted a do-not-resuscitate order based on the improbability of Mrs. Wanglie's surviving a cardiac arrest. In June, an ethics committee consultant recommended continued counseling for the family. The family declined counseling, including the counsel of their own pastor, and in late July asked that the respirator not be discussed again. In August, nurses expressed their consensus that continued life support did not seem appropriate, and I, as the newly appointed ethics consultant, counseled them.

In October 1990, a new attending physician consulted with specialists and confirmed the permanence of the patient's cerebral and pulmonary conditions. He concluded that she was at the end of her life and that the respirator was "non-beneficial," in that it could not heal her lungs, palliate her suffering, or enable this unconscious and permanently respirator-dependent woman to experience the benefit of the life afforded by respirator support. Because the respirator could prolong life, it was not characterized as "futile."[1] In November, the physician, with my concurrence, told the family that he was not willing to continue to prescribe the respirator. The husband, an attorney, rejected proposals to transfer the patient to another facility or to seek a court order mandating this unusual treatment. The hospital told the family that it would ask a court to decide whether members of its staff were obligated to continue treatment. A second conference two weeks later, after the family had hired an attorney, confirmed these positions, and the husband asserted that the patient had consistently said she wanted respirator support for such a condition.

In December, the medical director and hospital administrator asked the Hennepin County Board of Commissioners (the medical center's board of directors) to allow the hospital to go to court to resolve the dispute. In January, the county board gave permission by a 4-to-3 vote. Neither the hospital nor the county had a financial interest in terminating treatment. Medicare largely financed the $200,000 for the first hospitalization at Hennepin County; a private insurer would pay the $500,000 bill for the second. From February through May of 1991, the family and its attorney unsuccessfully searched for another health care facility that would admit Mrs. Wanglie. Facilities with empty beds cited her poor potential for rehabilitation.

The hospital chose a two-step legal procedure, first asking for the appointment of an independent conservator to decide whether the respirator was beneficial to the patient and second, if the conservator found it was not, for a second hearing on whether it was obliged to provide the respirator. The husband crossfiled, requesting to be appointed conservator. After a hearing in late May, the trial court on July 1, 1991, appointed the husband, as best able to represent the patient's interests. It noted that no request to stop treatment had been made and declined to speculate on the legality of such an order.[2] The hospital said that it would continue to provide the respirator in the light of continuing uncertainty about its legal obligation to provide it. Three days later, despite aggressive care, the patient died of multisystem organ failure resulting from septicemia. The family declined an autopsy and stated that the patient had received excellent care.

Discussion

This sad story illustrates the problem of what to do when a family demands medical treat-

ment that the attending physician concludes cannot benefit the patient. Only 600 elderly people are treated with respirators for more than six months in the United States each year.[3] Presumably, most of these people are actually or potentially conscious. It is common practice to discontinue the use of a respirator before death when it can no longer benefit a patient.[4,5]

We do not know Mrs. Wanglie's treatment preferences. A large majority of elderly people prefer not to receive prolonged respirator support for irreversible unconsciousness.[6] Studies show that an older person's designated family proxy overestimates that person's preference for life-sustaining treatment in a hypothetical coma.[7–9] The implications of this research for clinical decision making have not been cogently analyzed.

A patient's request for a treatment does not necessarily oblige a provider or the health care system. Patients may not demand that physicians injure them (for example, by mutilation), or provide plausible but inappropriate therapies (for example, amphetamines for weight reduction), or therapies that have no value (such as laetrile for cancer). Physicians are not obliged to violate their personal moral views on medical care so long as patients' rights are served. Minnesota's Living Will law says that physicians are "legally bound to act consistently within my wishes within limits of reasonable medical practice" in acting on requests and refusals of treatment.[10] Minnesota's Bill of Patients' Rights says that patients "have the right to appropriate medical . . . care based on individual needs . . . [which is] limited where the service is not reimbursable."[11] Mrs. Wanglie also had aortic insufficiency. Had this condition worsened, a surgeon's refusal to perform a life-prolonging valve replacement as medically inappropriate would hardly occasion public controversy. As the Minneapolis

Star Tribune said in an editorial on the eve of the trial,

> The hospital's plea is born of realism, not hubris. . . . It advances the claim that physicians should not be slaves to technology—any more than patients should be its prisoners. They should be free to deliver, and act on, an honest and time-honored message: "Sorry, there's nothing more we can do."[12]

Disputes between physicians and patients about treatment plans are often handled by transferring patients to the care of other providers. In this case, every provider contacted by the hospital or the family refused to treat this patient with a respirator. These refusals occurred before and after this case became a matter of public controversy and despite the availability of third-party reimbursement. We believe they represent a medical consensus that respirator support is inappropriate in such a case.

The handling of this case is compatible with current practices regarding informed consent, respect for patients' autonomy, and the right to health care. Doctors should inform patients of all medically reasonable treatments, even those available from other providers. Patients can refuse any prescribed treatment or choose among any medical alternatives that physicians are willing to prescribe. Respect for autonomy does not empower patients to oblige physicians to prescribe treatments in ways that are fruitless or inappropriate. Previous "right to die" cases address the different situation of a patient's right to choose to be free of a prescribed therapy. This case is more about the nature of the patient's entitlement to treatment than about the patient's choice in using that entitlement.

The proposal that this family's preference for this unusual and costly treatment, which is commonly regarded as inappropriate, establishes a right to such treatment is ironic, given that preference does not create a right to other needed, efficacious, and widely desired treatments in the United States. We could not afford a universal health care system based on patients' demands. Such a system would irrationally allocate health care to socially powerful people with strong preferences for immediate treatment to the disadvantage of those with less power or less immediate needs.

After the conclusion was reached that the respirator was not benefiting the patient, the decision to seek a review of the duty to provide it was based on an ethic of "stewardship." Even though the insurer played no part in this case, physicians' discretion to prescribe requires responsible handling of requests for inappropriate treatment. Physicians exercise this stewardship by counseling against or denying such treatment or by submitting such requests to external review. This stewardship is not aimed at protecting the assets of insurance companies but rests on fairness to people who have pooled their resources to insure their collective access to appropriate health care. Several citizens complained to Hennepin County Medical Center that Mrs. Wanglie was receiving expensive treatment paid for by people who had not consented to underwrite a level of medical care whose appropriateness was defined by family demands.

Procedures for addressing this kind of dispute are at an early stage of development. Though the American Medical Association [13] and the Society of Critical Care Medicine [14] also support some decisions to withhold requested treatment, the medical center's reasoning most closely follows the guidelines of the American Thoracic Society. [15] The statements of these professional organizations do not clarify when or how a physician may legally withdraw or withhold demanded life-sustaining treatments. The request for a conservator to review the medical conclusion before considering the medical obligation was often misconstrued as implying that the husband was incompetent or ill motivated. The medical center intended to emphasize the desirability of an independent review of its medical conclusion before its obligation to provide the respirator was reviewed by the court. I believe that the grieving husband was simply mistaken about whether the respirator was benefiting his wife. A direct request to remove the respirator seems to center procedural oversight on the soundness of the medical decision making rather than on the nature of the patient's need. Clearly, the gravity of these decisions merits openness, due process, and meticulous accountability. The relative merits of various procedures need further study.

Ultimately, procedures for addressing requests for futile, marginally effective, or inappropriate therapies require a statutory framework, case law, professional standards, a social consensus, and the exercise of professional responsibility. Appropriate ends for medicine are defined by public and professional consensus. Laws can, and do, say that patients may choose only among medically appropriate options, but legislatures are ill suited to define medical appropriateness. Similarly, health-facility policies on this issue will be difficult to design and will focus on due process rather than on specific clinical situations. Public or private payers will ration according to cost and overall efficacy, a rationing that will become more onerous as therapies are misapplied in individual cases. I believe there is a social consensus that intensive care for a person as "overmastered" by disease as this woman was is inappropriate.

Each case must be evaluated individually. In this case, the husband's request seemed entirely inconsistent with what medical care could do for his wife, the standards of the community, and his fair share of resources that many people pooled for their collective medical care. This case is about limits to what can be achieved at the end of life.

References

1. Tomlinson T, Brody H. Futility and the ethics of resuscitation. JAMA 1990; 264:1276–80.
2. In re Helga Wanglie, Fourth Judicial District (Dist. Ct., Probate Ct. Div.) PX-91-283. Minnesota, Hennepin County.
3. Office of Technology Assessment Task Force. Life-sustaining technologies and the elderly. Washington. D.C.: Government Printing Office, 1987.
4. Smedira NG, Evans BH, Grais LS, et al. Withholding and withdrawal of life support from the critically ill. N Engl J Med 1990;322:309–15.
5. Lantos JD, Singer PA, Walker RM, et al. The illusion of futility in clinical practice. Am J Med 1989;87:81–4.
6. Emanuel LL, Barry MJ, Stoeckle JD, Ettelson LM, Emanuel EJ. Advance directives for medical care—a case for greater use. N Engl J Med 1991; 324:889–95.
7. Zweibel NR, Cassel CK. Treatment choices at the end of life: a comparison of decisions by older patients and their physician-selected proxies. Gerontologist 1989;29:615–21.
8. Tomlinson T, Howe K, Notman M, Rossmiller D. An empirical study of proxy consent for elderly persons. Gerontologist 1990; 30:54–64.
9. Danis M, Southerland LI, Garrett JM, et al. A prospective study of advance directives for life-sustaining care. N Engl J Med 1991:324:882–8.
10. Minnesota Statutes. Adult Health Care Decisions Act. 145b.04.
11. Minnesota Statutes. Patients and residents of health care facilities; Bill of rights. 144 651:Subd. 6.
12. Helga Wanglie's life. Minneapolis Star Tribune. May 26, 1991:18A.
13. Council on Ethical and Judicial Affairs. American Medical Association. Guidelines for the appropriate use of do-not-resuscitate orders. JAMA 1991; 265:1868–71.
14. Task Force on Ethics of the Society of Critical Care Medicine. Consensus report on the ethics of foregoing life-sustaining treatments in the critically ill. Crit Care Med 1990: 18:1435–9.
15. American Thoracic Society. Withholding and withdrawing life-sustaining therapy. Am Rev Respir Dis (in press).

The Case of Helga Wanglie
A New Kind of "Right to Die" Case

MARCIA ANGELL

Helga Wanglie, an 86-year-old Minneapolis woman, died of sepsis on July 4 after being in a persistent vegetative state for over a year. She was the focus of an extremely important controversy over the right to die that culminated in a court decision just three days before her death.[1] The controversy pitted her husband and children, who wanted her life maintained on a respirator, against doctors at the Hennepin County Medical Center, who wanted her removed from the respirator because they regarded the treatment as inappropriate. The judge decided in favor of Mr. Wanglie, and Helga Wanglie died still supported by the respirator.

The Wanglie case differed in a crucial way from earlier right-to-die cases, beginning with the case of Karen Quinlan 16 years ago. In the earlier cases, the families wished to withhold life-sustaining treatment and the institutions had misgivings. Here it was the reverse; the family wanted to continue life-sustaining treatment, not to stop it, and the institution argued for the right to die. Mr. Wanglie believed that life should be maintained as long as possible, no matter what the circumstances, and he asserted that his wife shared this belief.

In one sense, the court's opinion in the Wanglie case would seem to be at odds with most of the earlier opinions in that it resulted in continued treatment of a patient in a persistent vegetative state. In another sense, however, the opinion was quite consistent, because it affirmed the right of the family to make decisions about

life-sustaining treatment when the patient was no longer able to do so. By granting guardianship of Mrs. Wanglie to her husband, the judge indicated that the most important consideration was who made the decision, not what the decision was. I believe that this was wise; any other decision by the court would have been inimical to patient autonomy and would have undermined the consensus on the right to die that has been carefully crafted since the Quinlan case.

What are the elements of that consensus and how should they be applied to the Wanglie case and others like it? There is general agreement that competent adults may refuse any recommended medical care. This right, based on principles of self-determination, has repeatedly been buttressed by the courts. When patients are no longer mentally competent, families are to act in accordance with what the patient would wish (a principle known as substituted judgment).[2–4] Disputes have arisen, however, when the patient had not, while competent, clearly expressed his or her preferences. This was the situation in the Wanglie case, as it was thought to be in the Cruzan case.[5]

To avoid these disputes, there is a growing movement to encourage all adults to prepare a document that would provide guidance, if necessary, for their families and doctors.[6] Such documents include living wills, durable powers of attorney, and other instruments that have been specially devised for the purpose. Congress recently mandated that as of December 1991, all health care facilities must provide an opportunity for patients to prepare such a document on admission.

We are still left with the problem of deciding for those who have nevertheless provided no guidance, including those who were unable to do so, such as children or profoundly retarded adults. In these cases as well, families usually make decisions on behalf of the patient, but since the patient's wishes are unknown, the consensus holds that the family's decision must be consistent with the patient's best interests.[2–4] A decision consistent with best interests is usually defined as a choice that reasonable adults might make if faced with the problem. This is a vague but useful standard that, by definition, restricts the range of permissible decisions. It can, however, allow for more than one possible choice. For example, the decision to withdraw the respirator from Karen Quinlan was thought by the New Jersey Supreme Court to be consistent with her best interests, but her father was given the latitude to decide either way.[7]

The well-publicized legal disputes involving the right to die—such as the Quinlan case, the Brophy case in Massachusetts,[8] and the Cruzan case in Missouri—have reached the courts either because the institution believed it improper to withhold life-sustaining treatment at the family's request or because the institution wanted legal immunity before doing so. Until the Wanglie case, there was only one well-publicized case of the reverse situation—that is, of a family wishing to persist in treatment over the objections of the institution. This was the poignant case of Baby L, described last year in the *Journal*.[9] The case involved a two-year-old child, profoundly retarded and completely immobile, who required repeated cardiopulmonary resuscitation for survival. Baby L's mother insisted that this be done as often as necessary, despite the fact that there was no hope of recovery. Representatives of the hospital challenged her decision in court on the grounds that the continued treatment caused great suffering to the child and thus violated its best interests. Before the court reached a decision, however, the mother transferred the child to a hospital that agreed to continue the treatment, and the case became legally moot.

Unlike the case of Baby L, the Wanglie case did not involve a course that would cause the patient great suffering. Because she was in a persistent vegetative state, Mrs. Wanglie was incapable of suffering. Therefore, a compelling case could not be made that her best interests were being violated by continued use of the respirator. Instead, representatives of the institution invoked Mrs. Wanglie's best interests to make a weaker case: that the use of the respirator failed to serve Mrs. Wanglie's best interests and should therefore not be continued. It was suggested that a victory for Mr. Wanglie would mean that patients or their families could demand whatever treatment they wished, regardless of its efficacy. Many commentators also emphasized the enormous expense of maintaining a patient on life support when those resources are needed to care for people who would clearly benefit. Elsewhere in this issue, Steven H. Miles, M.D., the ethics committee consultant at the Hennepin County Medical Center who was the petitioner in the Wanglie case, presents the arguments of the institution.[10] They are strong arguments that deserve to be examined, but I believe that they are on balance not persuasive.

It is generally agreed, as Miles points out, that patients or their surrogates do not have the right to demand any medical treatment they choose.[11,12] For example, a patient cannot insist that his doctor give him penicillin for a head cold. Patients' rights on this score are limited to refusing treatment or to choosing among effective ones. In the case of Helga Wanglie, the institution saw the respirator as "non-beneficial" because it would not restore her to consciousness. In the family's view, however, merely maintaining life was a worthy goal, and the respirator was not only effective toward that end, but essential.

Public opinion polls indicate that most people would not want their lives maintained in a persistent vegetative state. Many consider life in this state to be an indignity, and care givers often find caring for such patients demoralizing. It is important, however, to acknowledge that not everyone agrees with this view and it is a highly personal issue. For the decision to rest with the family is the most sensitive and workable approach, and it is the generally accepted one. Furthermore, a system in which life-sustaining treatment is discontinued over the objections of those who love the patient, on a case-by-case basis, would be callous. It can be argued on medical grounds that the definition of brain death should be legally extended to include a persistent vegetative state, but unless that is done universally we have no principled basis on which to override a family's decision in this kind of case. It is dismaying, of course, that resources are spent sustaining the lives of patients who will never be sentient, but we as a society would be on the slipperiest of slopes if we permitted ourselves to withdraw life support from a patient simply because it would save money.

Since the Quinlan case it has gradually been accepted that the particular decision is less important than a clear understanding of who should make it and the Wanglie case underscores this approach. When self-determination is impossible or an unambiguous proxy decision is unavailable, the consensus is that the family should make the decision. To be meaningful, this approach requires that we be willing to accept decisions with which we disagree. Only if a decision appears to violate the best interests of a patient who left no guidance or could provide none, as in the case of Baby L, should it be challenged by the institution. Thus, the sources of decisions about refusing medical treatment are, in order of precedence, the patient, the patient's prior directives or designated proxy, and the patient's family. Decisions from each of these sources should reflect the following standards, respectively: immediate self-determination, self-determination exercised earlier, and the best in-

terests of the patient. Institutions lie outside this hierarchy of decision making and should intervene by going to court only if they believe a decision violates these standards. Although I am sympathetic with the view of the doctors at the Hennepin County Medical Center, I agree with the court that they were wrong to try to impose it on the Wanglie family.

References

1. In re Helga Wanglie, Fourth Judicial District (Dist. Ct., Probate Ct. Div.) PX-91-283. Minnesota, Hennepin County.
2. Society for the Right to Die. The physician and the hopelessly ill patient: legal, medical and ethical guidelines. New York: Society for the Right to Die, 1985.
3. Guidelines on the termination of life-sustaining treatment and the care of the dying: a report by the Hastings Center. Briarcliff Manor, N.Y.: Hastings Center, 1987.
4. President's Commission for the Study of Ethical Problems in Medicine and Biomedical and Behavioral Research. Deciding to forego life-sustaining treatment: a report on the ethical, medical, and legal issues in treatment decisions. Washington, D.C.: Government Printing Office, 1983.
5. Cruzan v. Harmon, 760 S.W.2d 408 (1988).
6. Annas GJ. The health care proxy and the living will. N Engl J Med 1991; 324:1210–3.
7. In re Quinlan, 70 NJ 10, 355 A.2d 647 (1976).
8. Brophy v. New England Sinai Hospital, Inc., (Mass. Probate County Ct., Oct. 21, Nov. 29, 1985) 85E0009-G1.
9. Paris JJ, Crone RK, Reardon F. Physicians' refusal of requested treatment: the case of Baby L. N Engl J Med 1990; 322:1012–5.
10. Miles SH. Informed demand for "non-beneficial" medical treatment. N Engl J Med 1991; 325:512–5.
11. Brett AS, McCullough LB. When patients request specific interventions: defining the limits of the physician's obligation. N Engl J Med 1986 315:1347–51.
12. Blackhall LJ. Must we always use CPR? N Engl J Med 1987:317:1281–5.

Disability and Life-Ending Decisions

JEROME E. BICKENBACH

The debate over physician-assisted suicide is usually carried out in terms of the rights to autonomy and self-determination. The submissions of two disability advocacy groups, in the United States decisions of *Washington v. Gluckman* and *Vacco* v. *Quill* and the Canadian decision in *Rodriguez* v. *British Columbia,* suggest that this approach is too facile. The fact of the social devaluation of the life of persons with disabilities, as a matter of both attitude and practice, demands that the governing moral principle ought to be equality, and in particular equality of autonomy. In a world in which physical and mental disability are systematically understood as decreasing the quality of life, the decision of a person with a severe disability to commit suicide, or seek assistance to do so, is morally coerced by the fact of socially limited options. There may be exceptional cases in which this is not so, but the law must be designed for the unexceptional and typical case, even if doing so limits the autonomy of the exceptional few.

* * *

Physician-Assisted Suicide and Equality

Sue Rodriguez was a forty-two-year-old woman living in British Columbia, Canada. She was married and the mother of an eight-year-old son. She suffered from amyotrophic lateral sclerosis, better known as Lou Gehrig's disease. Her condition was rapidly deteriorating, and doctors told her she had between two and fourteen months to live. She was told that soon she would lose the ability to swallow, speak, walk, and move her body without assistance, and not long after that

she would lose her capacity to breathe without a respirator or eat without a gastrotomy. A well-educated, articulate, and strong-willed woman, Sue Rodriguez decided that she wished to determine the time and manner of her death. As long as she had the capacity to enjoy life, she did not wish to die. But when her quality of life slipped below what was tolerable for her, she wished to terminate her life. But at that point, she realized, she would be physically unable to commit suicide without assistance.

Section 241(b) of Canada's *Criminal Code* prohibits anyone from counseling, aiding or abetting a person to commit suicide.[1] In 1993, Sue Rodriguez petitioned the British Columbia Supreme Court that section 241(b) violated the Canadian Charter of Rights and Freedoms and sought a court order allowing a qualified medical practitioner to set up the technological means by which she might, by her own hand and at the time of her choosing, end her life.[2] She argued that she had the constitutionally guaranteed right to the inherent dignity of a human person, the right to control her body, and the right to be free from government interference in making fundamental personal decisions concerning the final stages of her life. She lost at trial and on appeal. But, buoyed by a powerful dissent at the Court of Appeal, Sue Rodriguez brought her case before the Supreme Court of Canada. In due course, that court also dismissed her appeal in a five-to-four decision.[3] A few months later, a physician illegally assisted Ms. Rodriguez to end her life.

Like the United States Supreme Court decision in *Washington* v. *Glucksberg,* the Rodriguez case raises the legal issue of whether the prohibition of physician-assisted suicide impinges upon the liberty interests of individuals who wish to commit suicide, but cannot do so.[4] And on that question, the majority judgments are very similar: The state has legitimate interests in prohibiting assisted suicide, and doing so accords with, in Chief Justice Rehnquist's words, "a consistent and almost universal tradition that has long rejected the asserted right." The state also has an unqualified interest in the preservation of human life, in protecting integrity and ethics of the medical profession, in protecting vulnerable groups, and, finally, in prohibiting a practice which, if allowed, might lead first to voluntary and perhaps also involuntary euthanasia. Finally, the majority in *Rodriquez* agreed with the United States Supreme Court in *Quill* v. *Vacco,* that assisting in the termination of life is categorically different from withholding life-sustaining treatment for which consent has been refused.[5]

Still, the *Rodriguez* judgment differs from the two United States judgments in one crucial respect: Sue Rodriquez did not rest her case on liberty alone; she also argued that the ban against physician-assisted suicide violated her right to equality by discriminating against her on the basis of her disabilities. Her argument—which was developed in a long and carefully written dissent by Chief Justice Lamer—came to this: Persons with disabilities who are or will become unable to end their lives without assistance are discriminated against by the prohibition of assisted suicide since, unlike persons capable of causing their own deaths, they are deprived of the option of choosing suicide. In neither country is suicide illegal, and public attitudes on the practice are mixed. There is, therefore, a case to be made that being legally prevented from pursuing a legal option, on the basis of physical disability, is discriminatory.

Rodriguez was joined in this argument by the country's largest disability advocacy group, then known as the Coalition of Provincial Organizations of the Handicap (COPOH).[6] COPOH argued that disabled persons have been historically victimized by stereotypical attitudes about their abilities and worth, coupled with a paternalism that has undercut their right to self-determination. Denying people with disabilities the option of suicide is an example of this unequal treatment, and must be resisted as demeaning and discriminatory. It is also true, the COPOH submission quickly added, that persons with disabilities are vulnerable to abuse. Indeed the same social attitudes that deny them full autonomy also devalue their lives. In such a hostile social environment, persons with disabilities may come to believe that their lives are worthless and burdensome to others and, as a result, contemplate suicide. While this is certainly possible, COPOH argued that clear legal safeguards for physician-assisted suicide can protect the vulnerable while reinforcing the right of persons with disabilities to control over their bodies.

In the United States, by contrast, the amici curiae brief of the disability advocacy group Not Dead Yet argued that assisted suicide is the most lethal form of discrimination against people with disabilities, inasmuch as it is the "ultimate expression of society's fear and revulsion regarding disability."[7] Given the pervasive prejudice against people with disabilities and their devaluation by prevailing practices such as the denial of adequate healthcare and suicide-prevention services, safeguards are not the answer. "[S]afeguards cannot be established to prevent abuses resulting in the wrongful death of numerous disabled persons, old and young." Indeed, the only true safeguard against abuse "is that assisted suicide remain illegal and socially condemned for all citizens equally."

That COPOH and Not Dead Yet should come to such different conclusions is noteworthy, since they were in perfect agreement about everything else. Both groups chose to center their legal argument on equality. They agreed about the entrenched social inequality of persons with disabilities. They agreed that a history of neglect, stigmatization, and paternalism, especially among medical professionals, has robbed persons with disabilities of their dignity, self-respect, and autonomy. They agreed that the lives of persons with disability have been systematically devalued. Yet, for these two advocacy organizations, the demand for equality drove them in diametrically opposite directions.

In fact, this opposition is more apparent than real, or rather more strategic than substantial. As an advocacy group representing the interests of persons with disabilities, COPOH was in an awkward position. In its factum it argued that there is a real danger that "negative stereotypes and attitudes which exist about the lack of value and quality inherent in the life of a person with disability" may be the primary cause of the suicidal wish. Yet, in light of Sue Rodriguez's self-confident and single-minded determination to exert control over her own death, COPOH would have lost credibility if it had argued that she had succumbed to these subtle pressures or that she was a victim of social devaluation. Not Dead Yet was not similarly constrained and could argue, more powerfully and more consistently, that for people with disabilities as a group, the "lethal discrimination" of assisted suicide represents a social evil far more serious than the denial of unfettered autonomy in end-of-life decisions.

At the same time, Not Dead Yet can be taken to task for its paternalistic overemphasis of the vulnerability of persons with disabilities. The group's brief marshals evidence that the prevailing view of persons with disabilities is that they have a low quality of life; so low in certain instances that the life is simply not worth living. This view informs policies for allocating medical resources (including suicide-prevention services) and court decisions concerning withholding treatment and other end-of-life decisions. In this environment, they argued, when a person with a disability expresses the decision to die, it is too readily accepted by nondisabled people who are quick to believe that the request is rational. Indeed, social attitudes and practices have such a powerful influence over their decisions that,

even absent outright coercion and manipulation, the decision by a person with a disability to die will not be autonomous: "as long as people with disabilities are treated as unwelcome and costly burdens on society, assisted suicide is not voluntary but is a forced 'choice.'"

The deterministic excesses of the Not Dead Yet argument should also be discounted as strategic. It was important to put to rest the simplistic view that people can make life-or-death decisions wholly unaffected by background social beliefs and practices about the value of their lives. Nonetheless, it is surely true that even in a cultural medium in which ill health and disability are assumed always to lower quality of life, and in which this is reflected in social attitudes, policies, and laws, one can still imagine a person with a disability making the autonomous decision to commit suicide. And Sue Rodriguez had the qualities of such an individual. She had been able to secure her sense of self and develop her self-esteem long before becoming ill. Her disease was rapidly and tragically debilitating, though it had no effect on her mental capacity. Most of all, she had support from relatives and friends who, throughout her ordeal, saw her not as a "disabled person," but as Sue Rodriguez taking control over her life.

That being said, even if Sue Rodriguez herself was neither vulnerable nor the victim of social attitudes about the low value of her life, her case is arguably exceptional. The weight of the evidence warrants caution about generalizing from her case. In any event, the law must be written for everyone, not just the exceptional person. It is a commonplace in political theory that an institutional constraint on autonomy may well be justified if, in general and in the long run, it protects people who are vulnerable, though on occasion it produces undesirable, even right-infringing, results for the exceptional few. Ignoring this point is the principal flaw in COPOH's position. Once that obstacle is removed, the submissions of COPOH and Not Dead Yet converge to produce a single, equality-based argument against physician-assisted suicide, an argument which takes seriously the concerns of persons with disabilities.

Inequality of Autonomy

Recentering the debate over physician-assisted suicide in terms of equality reveals issues that are of special concern to persons with disabilities. What the equality focus reveals is that, setting aside debates about the moral difference between physician-assisted suicide and "passive" practices such as the consensual removal of life-sustaining treatment, or general concerns about what the practice might do to the profession of medicine, the central question is whether the practice should be legalized in a social context characterized by *inequality of autonomy*.[8]

The common argument made by COPOH and Not Dead Yet is that persons with disabilities are vulnerable and lack full autonomy in end-of-life decision-making because of the prevailing view that their lives are not truly livable. To sustain this argument, however, what needs to be shown is that, as a rule (and exceptions like Sue Rodriguez notwithstanding), it is more likely than not that for a person with disabilities the decision to kill oneself, or seek assistance to do so, is a coerced, manipulated, or forced decision.

At this juncture, an important distinction has to be drawn. There are two, very different, ways of making out the claim that a decision has been forced or coerced.[9] The first of these gathers evidence of direct or indirect psychological pressures that come to bear on the decision-maker and argues that the nature and extent of the pressure was such that the person's will was overborne, and the "decision" was forced. Much of the evidence provided by both advocacy groups was of this sort. There is also a body of research on social attitudes about disability and its adverse psychological impact that adds some support to this view.[10] In short, this first approach characterizes coercion as a purely psychological phenomenon (an overborne will or psychological compulsion), a phenomenon that, given the variety of human natures and circumstances, would have to be plausibly demonstrated in each case.

Despite its initial plausibility, in this context the psychological approach to coercion is flawed because it miscasts the significance of the social attitudes and practices it cites as evidence of psychological pressure. This approach to coercion views adverse social attitudes and practices as neutral and immutable forces that, though causally linked to the psychological pressure, cannot be held morally accountable for it. It ignores the fact that there were morally responsible, human decisions that brought about the pressure in the first place.

In other words, the prevailing social attitude that a life with disabilities is devalued itself devalues life. The life is devalued by the social perception of disability and the social consequences of that perception. Whatever the effect of disabilities on quality of life—and there is no reason to assume it is inevitably adverse—it remains true that prejudicial social responses to disability also lower quality of life. And for this reason, a just legal system would respond to the injustice of a person suffering from disadvantages that flow, not from disabilities, but from attitudes about them.

But social attitudes also translate into social practice. To take one kind of example, quality-of-life assessment tools used in health outcome research and planning presume that the existence of a severe disability compromises quality of life.[11] International epidemiological measures of disease burden, such as the Quality of Life Adjusted Year (QALY) and Disability-Adjusted Life Year (DALY), are used by agencies like the World Bank and the World Health Organization to assess the cost-effectiveness of health interventions, in terms of the cost per unit of disease burden averted.[12] These and other quasi-scientific measures also incorporate the view that disease and its consequences lower quality of life, not as a matter of social attitude, but of purported fact.

In a political environment in which economic considerations are dominant, these instruments create policy consequences that directly affect the resources available to persons with disabilities. They are also invoked to support economic judgments that it is not cost-effective to provide resources to those whose quality of life is, and will likely remain, too low.[13]

The first point, then, is that attitudes and practices that devalue the lives of persons with disabilities constitute far more than psychological pressure; they themselves lower quality of life. Consider as well the findings of psychologist Carol Gill that the desire among terminal patients to die may be motivated by the realization that death is the only escape from an intolerable institutional setting, or inadequate medical or palliative care. Her research also suggests that the suicidal urge may be viewed as the only effective means at the individual's disposal of sparing the family the financial and emotional strain of a lingering illness.[14] These are real pressures, and the decisions that are made in light of them are rational enough. But these pressures arise from discriminatory social responses to disabilities, not from the disabilities themselves.

And this leads to the second point. When an individual chooses death as the only way of escaping from an intolerable situation, it is perverse and unfair to say that this is an expression of self-determination or autonomy. Such a choice is voluntary in the sense that the person made the choice, consciously and knowingly. We would be concerned if the individual made the choice unconsciously, or unknowingly. But we should also be concerned if the choice was made only because there were no other viable options.

The second sense of "coercion," therefore, applies to choices that are forced by the artificial absence of viable alternatives and options, choices constrained as a result of social attitudes and practices. The distinction between the psychological and what might be called the moral sense of "coercion" is reflected in the domain of law. In legal terms, coercion as a defense to criminal or civil liability can be understood either as an excuse (in which an overborne and nonculpable will is said to have produced an involuntary, pseudochoice) or as a justification (in which unfair circumstances have limited options and forced a unwanted choice).[15] Of course, the constraints on options directly produced by human mortality and the limits of human knowledge or skill are not the constraints that characterize a coerced decision in this second sense. What is salient to the moral conception of coercion is that the range of options has been unfairly, arbitrarily, or unjustifiably limited, not by hard facts and physical laws, but by human beliefs, decisions, actions, and policies.

In this sense of coercion, the constraint of choice created by social attitudes and practices concerning disability is appropriately characterized as an infringement on equality of respect and concern. If, because of a mental or physical disability, one individual is confronted by a more limited range of options concerning his or her remaining life than another, then the decision setting is discriminatory. Straightforwardly, one person has a different set of opportunities than another, and that difference is neither immutable nor morally justifiable.

In this sense of "coercion," we can say with far more confidence that the unexceptional people with disability are vulnerable to forced decisions about wishing their own death or seeking assistance to die. Sue Rodriguez may still be an exception. She may have been immune from moral coercion, and her opportunities constrained only by the functional limitations of her disabilities, the prognosis of the disease, and limitations of human knowledge and skill. If so, then her autonomy is infringed by the prohibition against assisted suicide. But if hers is the rare case, the exception, then violating her autonomy may well be the price that must be paid to secure the legitimate state interest of protecting those persons with disabilities who are coerced by unfair limitations imposed on their options.

Viewed in this way, as an issue of equality in the first instance, the three cases take on another dimension. Recasting the evidence presented by COPOH and Not Dead Yet as evidence of moral rather than psychological coercion and conceptualizing vulnerability as an unjustifiable limitation of options available to a person with disabilities in a decision setting in which suicide is one option, the equality argument in favor of a ban on physician-assisted suicide falls into place. Using the framework provided by the Americans with Disabilities Act of 1990[16] (which has direct analogues in Canadian equality jurisprudence),[17] the laws banning physician-assisted suicide constitute a "reasonable accommodation" to the social devaluation of the lives of persons with disabilities.

In antidiscrimination jurisprudence, an accommodation is any adjustment to social practices that eliminates or lessens the adverse effect on persons with disabilities of the way the social world is organized and structured. Providing a ramp for the benefit of persons in wheelchairs is an accommodation to the constructed environment inasmuch as it makes possible equal access to buildings. Similarly, a flexible work schedule for a person with chronic fatigue syndrome is an accommodation to the conditions of employment that make it possible for the person to work during those periods when the health condition has abated and the person has enough energy to do the job.

An accommodation is "reasonable" when it does not cause an "undue hardship" to whomever is required to implement the change. There are various reasons why an accommodation might be unreasonable in this sense. If an employer cannot afford it, or if health and safety regulations would be violated, then the alternation may be judged to cause undue hardship. If the rights of others, those with and those without disabilities, are infringed or limited by the accommodation, that too may make the accommodation unreasonable.

Is the limitation of Sue Rodriguez's autonomy an undue hardship? This is not an easy question to answer. Accommodations invariably infringe someone's autonomy, so the issue is not whether there is infringement, but whether it is justifiable. Doubtless, the degree of hardship experienced by Ms. Rodriguez, and, indeed, (if this were measurable) the diminution of her quality of life that resulted, were considerable. But how is that commensurable with the legitimate state interest of protecting vulnerable individuals against moral coercion?

Undoubtedly, it was this difficult question that persuaded COPOH, and at least one member of the Canadian Supreme Court, to seek the apparent compromise of a liberalized law constrained by safeguards. What is typically meant by safeguards in the case of physician-assisted suicide are procedural techniques for ensuring that the potential suicide is competent, has made the decision freely and voluntarily, is in a terminal state or in great and unrelievable pain, is physically incapable of performing the act of suicide, and has adequate opportunity to change his or her mind. COPOH argued that perhaps as well the law should require a mandatory visit from a trained advocate who would inform the person of his or her rights and entitlements. As we saw, Not Dead Yet in its submissions finessed the question of safeguards entirely by making the sweeping claim that, in the cultural environment in which people with disabilities live, autonomy for end-of-life decisions is simply not possible.

Though safeguards are a tempting compromise, Not Dead Yet was probably wise not to enter into a discussion of them. If the point of safeguards is to ensure that exceptional cases, the Sue Rodriguezes of the world, are not denied autonomy, then the only relevant safeguard would be a reliable determination of competency and a free and voluntary decision. It is wholly irrelevant what a person's physical condition is. If autonomy is to be preserved even in the face of a life-ending decision, then there is no reason, indeed we have no right, to inquire into the motivation for the decision. Why should the right to physician-assisted suicide depend on whether one is physically able to perform the act? Why does it matter that one is in pain, or in a terminal state, or has any medical condition whatsoever? We learn from John Stuart Mill that the value and importance of self-determination is not contingent on what is decided or done. Respecting autonomy does not mean respecting the right of people to arrive at correct decisions that are in their self-interest and consistent with their welfare; it means respecting their right to make whatever decision they wish.

To its credit, Not Dead Yet realizes this, and makes the point, as a final submission, that if the court ignores all of its preceding arguments and finds a constitutional right to assisted suicide, then it should apply that right to "every citizen, regardless of their health status. . . ." Though a rhetorical flourish, the submission is not without a point. It is telling that in all of the hundreds of pages in these three courts decisions, there is never any suggestion that the right to physician-assisted suicide should extend to people who do not have a severe disability. Implicit in the judgments themselves, in other words, is precisely the prevailing prejudicial social attitude that having a disability is a sensible reason for committing suicide.

Perhaps proponents of physician-assisted suicide would be steadfast in their view even if it meant that qualified doctors could patrol school grounds waiting for despondent but mentally competent seventeen-year-olds who, having failed geography or been unable to find a date for the prom, might want to use their assisted-suicide services. Why indeed do we have the right to demand that the seventeen-year-olds continue to live; are we not forcing them to die later of accident, disease, or old age? We have no less an authority than Ronald Dworkin who, in an often quoted passage, claims that "making someone die in a way that others approve, but he believes a horrifying contradiction of his life, is a devastating, odious form tyranny."[18]

But if proponents refuse to embrace autonomy in this blunt and unalloyed form, then the argument for physician-assisted suicide shifts its center of gravity. If respecting autonomy itself is not enough, then proponents must return to the view that some lives are not worth living; that is, that people can be justified in wanting to have themselves killed. This move constitutes the first, sliding step down a slope that Not Dead Yet describes in its submission: If some lives, because of their low quality, are justifiably ended by means of assisted suicide, what point is there in insisting upon mental competency?

We already have legal evidence of how the slide will proceed. In an English case, *Airedale N.H.S. Trust* v. *Bland*, the father of a seventeen-year-old who sustained massive head injuries in an accident asked the court to allow physicians to discontinue life-sustaining treatment.[19] The court agreed, arguing that being in persistent vegetative state the boy had no further interest in being kept alive. The father said he was convinced that his son, were he competent, would not "want to be left like that."[20] And in Canada, Mr. Latimer killed his twelve-year-old daughter because cystic fibrosis had left her impaired, not only severely mentally and physically disabled, but also in a constant state of pain. The case is still making its way through the courts, but both at trial and before the Court of Appeal, Mr. Latimer argued in defense that he was merely assisting his daughter in relieving her pain, something she would have requested were she competent.[21]

If anything, the equality-based argument against physician-assisted suicide is stronger in the case of people who are not mentally competent. It is common to argue that, quite independently of the presence of pain, physical debilitation, or shortened lifespan, the most profound assault on quality to life is the diminution of autonomy itself, brought about by the mental incapacity to recognize and appreciate options and choices.[22] As a result, the social devaluation of life is far more evident among people with developmental disabilities and other forms of mental and psychiatric impairments than those who, like Ms. Rodriguez, are mentally unaffected by illness or disability. When autonomy itself is disabled, surrogate decision-makers like Mr. Bland and Mr. Latimer can more easily make the argument that continued life is "not in the best interest of the patient." The options thought available to a person who is mentally incompetent are, as a consequence, far more constrained; indeed, often the choice is not even theirs to make.

Conclusion

The debate over physician-assisted suicide has typically been carried out in terms of the rights to autonomy and self-determination. What the disability community has argued, time and again, is that this approach is too facile. The fact of the social devaluation of the life of persons with disabilities, as a matter of both attitude and practice, demands that the governing moral principle ought to be equality, and in particular equality of autonomy. In a world in which physical and mental disability were not systematically viewed as grounds for judging a life to be of less value, or indeed of no value, and in which the decisions about life and death did not have to be made in the context of moral coercion, then we might judge physician-assisted suicide entirely on the grounds of autonomy and self-determination. But ours is not that world.

Notes

1. *Revised Statutes of Canada*, 1985, c. C-46.
2. Part B, *Constitution Act*, 1982.
3. *Rodriguez* v. *British Columbia (Attorney General)* 107 D.L.R. (4th) 342 (1993). All subsequent quotes from this case come from this report.
4. See appendix A at the end of this volume.

5. See appendix A at the end of this volume.
6. This and all subsequent references to COPOH's arguments come from COPOH's Intervener Factum (Court File No. 23476) and the affidavit of Francine Arsenault, submitted 10 May 1993.
7. This and all subsequent references to the arguments of Not Dead Yet come from the Amici Curiae Brief of Not Dead Yet and American Disabled for Attendant Programs Today in Support of Petitioners in *Vacco* v. *Quill*, the Supreme Court of the United States, No. 95–1858, October Term, 1995. *Vacco* v. *Quill*, 117 Sup. Ct 2293 (1997).
8. See the review of standard arguments pro and con in Robert F. Weir, "The Morality of Physician-Assisted Suicide," *Law, Medicine and Health Care* 20: 116–126 (1992).
9. I am following a distinction developed in considerable detail in Alan Wertheimer's book *Coercion* (Princeton, NJ: Princeton University Press, 1989).
10. I discuss this literature in my *Physical Disability and Social Policy* (Toronto: University of Toronto Press, 1993), chapter 5.
11. See Ian McDowell and Claire Newell, *Measuring Health* (New York: Oxford University Press, 1987), chapter 6; and Dan Brock's review of the notion and the standard measuring instruments in "Quality of Life Measures in Health Care and Medical Ethics' in Martha C. Nussbaum and Amartya Sen, eds., *The Quality of Life* (Oxford: Clarendon Press, 1993), pp. 94–132.
12. For a discussion of QALYs see Alan Williams, "The Value of QALYS," *Health and Social Service Journal* (1985): 3–15. For DALYs, their development and use internationally, see Christopher J. L. Murray and Alan D. Lopez, eds., *The Global Burden of Disease* (Boston, MA: Harvard University Press, 1996).
13. For a general discussion of this and related points see David Orentlicher "Destructuring Disability: Rationing of Health Care and Unfair Discrimination against the Sick" *Harvard Civil Rights/Civil Liberties Law Review* 13: 49–89 (1996).
14. C. J. Gill "Suicide Intervention for People With Disabilities: A Lesson in Inequality," *Issues in Law and Medicine* 8: 37–56 (1992).

15. See Paul H. Robinson, *Criminal Law Defenses*, vol. 1, (St. Paul, MN: West Publishing Co., 1984) chapter 2.
16. 42 U.S.C. section 12111.
17. See *Law Society of British Columbia et al. v. Andrews* 1 S.C.R. 143 (1989).
18. Ronald Dworkin, *Life's Dominion* (New York: Knopf, 1993), p. 217.
19. I All ER 821 (1992).
20. On the clinical side, G. R. Scofield has argued that consent for ending life-sustaining treatment ought not to be necessary if the quality of life is too low. See "Is Consent Useful When Resuscitation Isn't?" *Hastings Center Report* 21: 28–30 (1991).
21. *R. v. Latimer* 128 Sask. R. 19 (1995) (Saskatchewan Court of Appeal).
22. See the discussion by Brock, *supra* note 11, 105–16.

Supreme Court of the United States
Washington, et al., Petitioners,
v. Harold Glucksberg et al.
No. 96–110.

Argued Jan. 8, 1997.
Decided June 26, 1997.

Chief Justice REHNQUIST delivered the opinion of the Court.

The question presented in this case is whether Washington's prohibition against "caus[ing]" or "aid[ing]" a suicide offends the Fourteenth Amendment to the United States Constitution. We hold that it does not.

It has always been a crime to assist a suicide in the State of Washington. In 1854, Washington's first Territorial Legislature outlawed "assisting another in the commission of self-murder." Today, Washington law provides: "A person is guilty of promoting a suicide attempt when he knowingly causes or aids another person to attempt suicide." Wash. Rev.Code § 9A.36.060(1) (1994). "Promoting a suicide attempt" is a felony,

punishable by up to five years' imprisonment and up to a $10,000 fine. §§ 9A.36.060(2) and 9A.20.021(1)(c). At the same time, Washington's Natural Death Act, enacted in 1979, states that the "withholding or withdrawal of life-sustaining treatment" at a patient's direction "shall not, for any purpose, constitute a suicide." Wash. Rev. Code § 70.122.070(1).[2]

Petitioners in this case are the State of Washington and its Attorney General. Respondents Harold Glucksberg, M. D., Abigail Halperin, M. D., Thomas A. Preston, M. D., and Peter Shalit, M. D., are physicians who practice in Washington. These doctors occasionally treat terminally ill, suffering patients, and declare that they would assist these patients in ending their lives if not for Washington's assisted-suicide ban. In January 1994, respondents, along with three gravely ill, pseudonymous plaintiffs who have since died and Compassion in Dying, a nonprofit organization that counsels people considering physician-assisted suicide, sued in the United States District Court, seeking a declaration that Wash.Rev.Code § 9A.36.060(1) (1994) is, on its face, unconstitutional.

The plaintiffs asserted "the existence of a liberty interest protected by the Fourteenth Amendment which extends to a personal choice by a mentally competent, terminally ill adult to commit physician-assisted suicide."

We begin, as we do in all due process cases, by examining our Nation's history, legal traditions, and practices. In almost every State—indeed, in almost every western democracy—it is a crime to assist a suicide. The States' assisted-suicide bans are not innovations. Rather, they are longstanding expressions of the States' commitment to the protection and preservation of all human life. *Cruzan, supra,* at 280, 110 S.Ct., at 2852. ("[T]he States—indeed, all civilized nations—demonstrate their commitment to life by treating homicide as a serious crime. Moreover, the majority of States in this country have laws imposing criminal penalties on one who assists another to commit suicide.") Indeed, opposition to and condemnation of suicide—and, therefore, of assisting suicide—are consistent and enduring themes of our philosophical, legal, and cultural heritages.

More specifically, for over 700 years, the Anglo-American common-law tradition has punished or otherwise disapproved of both suicide and assisting suicide.

For the most part, the early American Colonies adopted the common-law approach. For example, the legislators of the Providence Plantations, which would later become Rhode Island, declared, in 1647, that "[s]elf-murder is by all agreed to be the most unnatural, and it is by this present Assembly declared, to be that,

wherein he that doth it, kills himself out of a premeditated hatred against his own life or other humor: . . . his goods and chattels are the king's custom, but not his debts nor lands; but in case he be an infant, a lunatic, mad or distracted man, he forfeits nothing." Virginia also required ignominious burial for suicides, and their estates were forfeit to the Crown.

Over time, however, the American Colonies abolished these harsh common-law penalties.

However, the movement away from the common law's harsh sanctions did not represent an acceptance of suicide; rather, as this change reflected the growing consensus that it was unfair to punish the suicide's family for his wrongdoing. Nonetheless, although States moved away from Blackstone's treatment of suicide, courts continued to condemn it as a grave public wrong.

That suicide remained a grievous, though nonfelonious, wrong is confirmed by the fact that colonial and early state legislatures and courts did not retreat from prohibiting assisting suicide. And the prohibitions against assisting suicide never contained exceptions for those who were near death. Rather, "[t]he life of those to whom life ha[d] become a burden—of those who [were] hopelessly diseased or fatally wounded—nay, even the lives of criminals condemned to death, [were] under the protection of the law, equally as the lives of those who [were] in the full tide of life's enjoyment, and anxious to continue to live."

Though deeply rooted, the States' assisted-suicide bans have in recent years been reexamined and, generally, reaffirmed. Because of advances in medicine and technology, Americans today are increasingly likely to die in institutions, from chronic illnesses. Public concern and democratic action are therefore sharply focused on how best to protect dignity and independence at the end of life, with the result that there have been many significant changes in state laws and in the attitudes these laws reflect.

The Washington statute at issue in this case, Wash. Rev.Code § 9A.36.060 (1994), was enacted in 1975 as part of a revision of that State's criminal code. Four years later, Washington passed its Natural Death Act, which specifically stated that the "withholding or withdrawal of life-sustaining treatment . . . shall not, for any purpose, constitute a suicide" and that "[n]othing in this chapter shall be construed to condone, authorize, or approve mercy killing. . . ." Natural Death Act, 1979 Wash. Laws, ch. 112, § 8(1), p. 11 (codified at Wash. Rev.Code § § 70.122.070(1), 70.122.100 (1994)). In 1991, Washington voters rejected a ballot initiative which, had it passed, would have permitted a form of physician-assisted suicide. Washington then added a provision to the Natural Death Act expressly excluding physician-assisted suicide.

Attitudes toward suicide itself have changed since, but our laws have consistently condemned, and continue to prohibit, assisting suicide. Despite changes in medical technology and notwithstanding an increased emphasis on the importance of end-of-life decisionmaking, we have not retreated from this prohibition. Against this backdrop of history, tradition, and practice, we now turn to respondents' constitutional claim.

II

The Due Process Clause guarantees more than fair process, and the "liberty" it protects includes more than the absence of physical restraint. The Clause also provides heightened protection against government interference with certain fundamental rights and liberty interests. We have assumed, and strongly suggested, that the Due Process Clause protects the traditional right to refuse unwanted lifesaving medical treatment.

But we "ha[ve] always been reluctant to expand the concept of substantive due process because guideposts for responsible decisionmaking in this unchartered area are scarce and open-ended." *Collins*, 503 U.S., at 125, 112 S.Ct., at 1068. By extending constitutional protection to an asserted right or liberty interest, we, to a great ex-

tent, place the matter outside the arena of public debate and legislative action. We must therefore "exercise the utmost care whenever we are asked to break new ground in this field," *ibid.*, lest the liberty protected by the Due Process Clause be subtly transformed into the policy preferences of the Members of this Court.

Our established method of substantive-due-process analysis has two primary features: First, we have regularly observed that the Due Process Clause specially protects those fundamental rights and liberties which are, objectively, "deeply rooted in this Nation's history and tradition," and "implicit in the concept of ordered liberty," such that "neither liberty nor justice would exist if they were sacrificed." Second, we have required in substantive-due-process cases a "careful description" of the asserted fundamental liberty interest. Our Nation's history, legal traditions, and practices thus provide the crucial "guideposts for responsible decisionmaking" that direct and restrain our exposition of the Due Process Clause.

Turning to the claim at issue here, the Court of Appeals stated that "[p]roperly analyzed, the first issue to be resolved is whether there is a liberty interest in determining the time and manner of one's death," or, in other words, "[i]s there a right to die?," *id.*, at 799. Similarly, respondents assert a "liberty to choose how to die" and a right to "control of one's final days," and describe the asserted liberty as "the right to choose a humane, dignified death," and "the liberty to shape death." The Washington statute at issue in this case prohibits "aid[ing] another person to attempt suicide," and, thus, the question before us is whether the "liberty" specially protected by the Due Process Clause includes a right to commit suicide which itself includes a right to assistance in doing so.

We now inquire whether this asserted right has any place in our Nation's traditions. Here, as discussed *supra*, at 2262–2267, we are confronted with a consistent and almost universal tradition that has long rejected the asserted right, and continues explicitly to reject it today, even for terminally ill, mentally competent adults. To hold for respondents, we would have to reverse centuries of legal doctrine and practice, and strike down the considered policy choice of almost every State.

Respondents contend, however, that the liberty interest they assert *is* consistent with this Court's substantive-due-process line of cases, if not with this Nation's history and practice. Pointing to *Casey* and *Cruzan*, respondents read our jurisprudence in this area as reflecting a general tradition of "self-sovereignty," and as teaching that the "liberty" protected by the Due Process Clause includes "basic and intimate exercises of personal autonomy." According to respondents, our liberty jurisprudence, and the broad, individualistic principles it reflects, protects the "liberty of competent, terminally ill adults to make end-of-life decisions free of undue government interference." The question presented in this case, however, is whether the protections of the Due Process Clause include a right to commit suicide with another's assistance. With this "careful description" of respondents' claim in mind, we turn to *Casey* and *Cruzan*.

In *Cruzan*, we considered whether Nancy Beth Cruzan, who had been severely injured in an automobile accident and was in a persistive vegetative state, "ha[d] a right under the United States Constitution which would require the hospital to withdraw life-sustaining treatment" at her parents' request. We concluded that "the common-law doctrine of informed consent is viewed as generally encompassing the right of a competent individual to refuse medical treatment." Next, we reviewed our own cases on the subject, and stated that "[t]he principle that a competent person has a constitutionally protected liberty interest in refusing unwanted medical treatment may be inferred from our prior decisions." Therefore, "for purposes of [that] case, we assume[d] that the United States Constitution would grant a competent person a con-

stitutionally protected right to refuse lifesaving hydration and nutrition."

Respondents contend that in *Cruzan* we "acknowledged that competent, dying persons have the right to direct the removal of life-sustaining medical treatment and thus hasten death," and that "the constitutional principle behind recognizing the patient's liberty to direct the withdrawal of artificial life support applies at least as strongly to the choice to hasten impending death by consuming lethal medication."

The right assumed in *Cruzan*, however, was not simply deduced from abstract concepts of personal autonomy. Given the common-law rule that forced medication was a battery, and the long legal tradition protecting the decision to refuse unwanted medical treatment, our assumption was entirely consistent with this Nation's history and constitutional traditions. The decision to commit suicide with the assistance of another may be just as personal and profound as the decision to refuse unwanted medical treatment, but it has never enjoyed similar legal protection. Indeed, the two acts are widely and reasonably regarded as quite distinct. In *Cruzan* itself, we recognized that most States outlawed assisted suicide—and even more do today—and we certainly gave no intimation that the right to refuse unwanted medical treatment could be somehow transmuted into a right to assistance in committing suicide.

Respondents also rely on *Casey*. There, the Court's opinion concluded that "the essential holding of *Roe v. Wade* should be retained and once again reaffirmed." In reaching this conclusion, the opinion discussed in some detail this Court's substantive-due-process tradition of interpreting the Due Process Clause to protect certain fundamental rights and "personal decisions" and noted that many of those rights and liberties "involv[e] the most intimate and personal choices a person may make in a lifetime." *Id.,* at 851, 112 S.Ct., at 2807.

That many of the rights and liberties protected by the Due Process Clause sound in personal autonomy does not warrant the sweeping conclusion that any and all important, intimate, and personal decisions are so protected, and *Casey* did not suggest otherwise.

The history of the law's treatment of assisted suicide in this country has been and continues to be one of the rejection of nearly all efforts to permit it. That being the case, our decisions lead us to conclude that the asserted "right" to assistance in committing suicide is not a fundamental liberty interest protected by the Due Process Clause. The Constitution also requires, however, that Washington's assisted-suicide ban be rationally related to legitimate government interests. See *Heller v. Doe*, 509 U.S. 312, 319-320, 113 S.Ct. 2637, 2642-2643, 125 L.Ed.2d 257 (1993); *Flores*, 507 U.S., at 305, 113 S.Ct., at 1448-1449. This requirement is unquestionably met here. As the court below recognized, 79 F.3d, at 816-817,[20] Washington's assisted-suicide ban implicates a number of state interests.

First, Washington has an "unqualified interest in the preservation of human life." The State's prohibition on assisted suicide, like all homicide laws, both reflects and advances its commitment to this interest. This interest is symbolic and aspirational as well as practical:

> While suicide is no longer prohibited or penalized, the ban against assisted suicide and euthanasia shores up the notion of limits in human relationships. It reflects the gravity with which we view the decision to take one's own life or the life of another, and our reluctance to encourage or promote these decisions.

Respondents admit that "[t]he State has a real interest in preserving the lives of those who can still contribute to society and have the potential to enjoy life." The Court of Appeals also recognized Washington's interest in protecting life, but held that the "weight" of this interest depends on the "medical condition and the wishes of the person whose life is at stake." Washington, however, has rejected this sliding-scale approach and, through its assisted-suicide ban, insists that all

persons' lives, from beginning to end, regardless of physical or mental condition, are under the full protection of the law. As we have previously affirmed, the States "may properly decline to make judgments about the 'quality' of life that a particular individual may enjoy."

Relatedly, all admit that suicide is a serious public-health problem, especially among persons in otherwise vulnerable groups. The State has an interest in preventing suicide, and in studying, identifying, and treating its causes.

Those who attempt suicide—terminally ill or not—often suffer from depression or other mental disorders. Research indicates, however, that many people who request physician-assisted suicide withdraw that request if their depression and pain are treated. The New York Task Force, however, expressed its concern that, because depression is difficult to diagnose, physicians and medical professionals often fail to respond adequately to seriously ill patients' needs. Thus, legal physician-assisted suicide could make it more difficult for the State to protect depressed or mentally ill persons, or those who are suffering from untreated pain, from suicidal impulses.

The State also has an interest in protecting the integrity and ethics of the medical profession. In contrast to the Court of Appeals' conclusion that "the integrity of the medical profession would [not] be threatened in any way by [physician-assisted suicide]," the American Medical Association, like many other medical and physicians' groups, has concluded that "[p]hysician-assisted suicide is fundamentally incompatible with the physician's role as healer." And physician-assisted suicide could, it is argued, undermine the trust that is essential to the doctor-patient relationship by blurring the time-honored line between healing and harming.

Next, the State has an interest in protecting vulnerable groups—including the poor, the elderly, and disabled persons—from abuse, neglect, and mistakes. The Court of Appeals dismissed the State's concern that disadvantaged persons might be pressured into physician-assisted suicide as "ludicrous on its face." We have recognized, however, the real risk of subtle coercion and undue influence in end-of-life situations. *Cruzan,* 497 U.S., at 281. Similarly, the New York Task Force warned that "[l]egalizing physician-assisted suicide would pose profound risks to many individuals who are ill and vulnerable. . . . The risk of harm is greatest for the many individuals in our society whose autonomy and well-being are already compromised by poverty, lack of access to good medical care, advanced age, or membership in a stigmatized social group." If physician-assisted suicide were permitted, many might resort to it to spare their families the substantial financial burden of end-of-life health-care costs.

The State's interest here goes beyond protecting the vulnerable from coercion; it extends to protecting disabled and terminally ill people from prejudice, negative and inaccurate stereotypes, and "societal indifference." The State's assisted-suicide ban reflects and reinforces its policy that the lives of terminally ill, disabled, and elderly people must be no less valued than the lives of the young and healthy, and that a seriously disabled person's suicidal impulses should be interpreted and treated the same way as anyone else's.

Finally, the State may fear that permitting assisted suicide will start it down the path to voluntary and perhaps even involuntary euthanasia. The Court of Appeals struck down Washington's assisted-suicide ban only "as applied to competent, terminally ill adults who wish to hasten their deaths by obtaining medication prescribed by their doctors." Washington insists, however, that the impact of the court's decision will not and cannot be so limited. If suicide is protected as a matter of constitutional right, it is argued, "every man and woman in the United States must enjoy it." The Court of Appeals' decision, and its expansive reasoning, provide ample support for the State's concerns. The court noted, for example, that the "decision of a duly appointed surrogate decision maker is for

all legal purposes the decision of the patient himself," that "in some instances, the patient may be unable to self-administer the drugs and . . . administration by the physician . . . may be the only way the patient may be able to receive them" and that not only physicians, but also family members and loved ones, will inevitably participate in assisting suicide. Thus, it turns out that what is couched as a limited right to "physician-assisted suicide" is likely, in effect, a much broader license, which could prove extremely difficult to police and contain. Washington's ban on assisting suicide prevents such erosion.

This concern is further supported by evidence about the practice of euthanasia in the Netherlands. The Dutch government's own study revealed that in 1990, there were 2,300 cases of voluntary euthanasia (defined as "the deliberate termination of another's life at his request"), 400 cases of assisted suicide, and more than 1,000 cases of euthanasia without an explicit request. In addition to these latter 1,000 cases, the study found an additional 4,941 cases where physicians administered lethal morphine overdoses without the patients' explicit consent. This study suggests that, despite the existence of various reporting procedures, euthanasia in the Netherlands has not been limited to competent, terminally ill adults who are enduring physical suffering, and that regulation of the practice may not have prevented abuses in cases involving vulnerable persons, including severely disabled neonates and elderly persons suffering from dementia. The New York Task Force, citing the Dutch experience, observed that "assisted suicide and euthanasia are closely linked," New York Task Force 145, and concluded that the "risk of . . . abuse is neither speculative nor distant." Washington, like most other States, reasonably ensures against this risk by banning, rather than regulating, assisting suicide.

We need not weigh exactly the relative strengths of these various interests. They are unquestionably important and legitimate, and Washington's ban on assisted suicide is at least

reasonably related to their promotion and protection. We therefore hold that Wash. Rev.Code §
9A.36.060(1) (1994) does not violate the Fourteenth Amendment, either on its face or "as applied to competent, terminally ill adults who
wish to hasten their deaths by obtaining medication prescribed by their doctors."

* * *

Throughout the Nation, Americans are engaged
in an earnest and profound debate about the
morality, legality, and practicality of physician-
assisted suicide. Our holding permits this debate
to continue, as it should in a democratic society.
The decision of the en banc Court of Appeals is
reversed, and the case is remanded for further
proceedings consistent with this opinion.

It is so ordered.

Notes

2. Under Washington's Natural Death Act, "adult
persons have the fundamental right to control the
decisions relating to the rendering of their own
health care, including the decision to have life-
sustaining treatment withheld or withdrawn in
instances of a terminal condition or permanent
unconscious condition." Wash. Rev.Code §
70.122.010 (1994). In Washington, "[a]ny adult
person may execute a directive directing the withholding or withdrawal of life-sustaining treatment in a terminal condition or permanent
unconscious condition," § 70.122.030, and a
physician who, in accordance with such a directive, participates in the withholding or withdrawal of life-sustaining treatment is immune
from civil, criminal, or professional liability,
§ 70.122.051.

20. The court identified and discussed six state interests: (1) preserving life; (2) preventing suicide;
(3) avoiding the involvement of third parties and
use of arbitrary, unfair, or undue influence; (4)
protecting family members and loved ones; (5)
protecting the integrity of the medical profession;
and (6) avoiding future movement toward euthanasia and other abuses.

C. The Obligation of Confidentiality

Among the many traditional duties of physicians to patients is the obligation to
keep a patient's confidences. The Hippocratic Oath states, "What I may see or
hear in the course of the treatment or even outside of the treatment in regard to
the life of men, which on no account one must spread abroad, I will keep to myself holding such things shameful to be spoken about." Contemporary professional oaths echo that statement. The American Medical Association's statement
of "Fundamental Elements of the Patient-Physician Relationship" states that "[t]he
patient has the right to confidentiality. The physician should not reveal confidential communications or information without the consent of the patient, unless provided for by law or by the need to protect the welfare of the individual or
the public interest."[24]

Despite its ancient lineage, the rationale and parameters of the duty to keep
confidences are surprisingly complex and problematic. While it is easy to argue
that physicians (or other health care providers) should not idly gossip about their
patients (because gossip itself is seldom appropriate), or that they should not sell
a patient's confidences for their own profit, it is harder to explain why confidentiality should trump other legitimate interests.

Sometimes, the provider's obligation to respect a patient's confidences is
understood in terms of the nature of the relationship between a physician and

patient. As discussed in Section A of this chapter, a physician can be understood to be a type of fiduciary who is obligated to act in the interests of the patient. In this relationship, patients are especially vulnerable and must often reveal information that they normally would keep secret. For the physician to disclose the information to others, especially without good cause, could be seen as a betrayal of the relationship, much as a spouse betrays her partner by telling the world her partner's private problems. This rationale has influenced courts, such as the federal court writing in *Hammonds v. Aetna Casualty & Surety Co.*,[25] which held that a patient may recover damages for breach of fiduciary when a physician discloses confidential information without consent or good cause. Other courts have held that a physician violates an implied contract with the patient when the physician breaches the duty of confidentiality.[26] Both rationales predicate the right to confidentiality on the bedrock of the physician-patient relationship. Such a foundation may not extend to medical information that is uncovered outside of that relationship, such as occurs when life insurers take blood tests of their prospective customers or when employers look over the insurance claims of their employees.

Another widely held rationale for medical privacy connects it to respect for autonomy and an individual's right to self-determination. In promulgating regulations governing the disclosure of identifiable medical information (the so-called HIPAA regulations named after the Health Insurance Portability and Accountability Act, which authorized the regulations), the Department of Health and Human Services suggested that medical privacy is a "fundamental right." According to the agency, medical privacy is connected with or an aspect of respect for an individual's autonomy and self-determination and protected, at least by some degree, by constitutional law.[27] From this perspective, the information we give to our physicians, or the information they learn about us, is an aspect of our identity and critical to the way the world perceives us. Is this argument convincing?

According to Jeffrey Reiman, "privacy is a social ritual by means of which an individual's moral title to his existence is conferred."[28] Because medical information is often especially intimate and revealing, confidentiality in this arena may be seen as particularly critical to an individual's ability to be an author of his or her own life's plan. In *Whalen v. Roe*, the United States Supreme Court seemed to share that sentiment, but ultimately, it upheld a New York law that required physicians and pharmacists to inform the state about controlled substances prescribed for patients. What justification did the Court give for failing to protect the constitutionally rooted privacy interest?

Perhaps in permitting the state to demand the disclosure of prescription records, the Court was simply determining that an individual's right to autonomy must be balanced against other interests. Or, the Court may have been suggesting that interests in confidentiality qua confidentiality are not actually first order goods. Instead, they are worthy of protection only because they are generally necessary to serve other interests. Because the state in *Whalen* promised to safeguard the confidentiality of the records it obtained (once it had demanded the breach of the physician-patient relationship), individuals would not be readily harmed by the handing over of the information to the state. Hence, there was no violation of the constitutional right.

This vision of medical confidentiality as a second order good, one that is worthy of protection only because it enables other goods to be obtained, has deep roots in American policy and ethical debates. Often, the arguments for medical confidentiality are framed in highly pragmatic terms, where the ultimate good to be obtained is public health. People are thought more likely to seek and comply with medical treatment if they are assured that the information they reveal will be kept confidential. Hence, state laws have long provided confidentiality assurances for serological testing for venereal diseases. Likewise, in 1988 the Presidential Commission on HIV, iterating the views of many public health experts, called upon states to enact laws that would assure the confidentiality of HIV tests.[29] As the Commission saw it, without that assurance, individuals might avoid testing and counseling and create a greater risk of spreading their infection.

Once confidentiality is viewed in this pragmatic or utilitarian way, however, the door is readily opened to balancing the communal benefits gained by protecting confidentiality to those lost by dispensing with it. Thus rejecting the argument that HIV tests must always be consensual and confidential, Amitai Etzioni argues for mandatory HIV screening of infants, even though such tests inevitably reveal information about the mother's HIV status. And more broadly, Helena Gail Rubenstein, who like Etzioni writes from a communitarian perspective, argues that because individuals in our society benefit from the successes of medical research and public health policies, they should be seen as bearing an obligation to disclose relevant medical information to researchers. Likewise, despite the paeans to privacy in the preamble of the HIPAA regulations, the final regulations provide for a laundry list of situations in which confidentiality may be violated.[30] These include

- Disclosures that occur in the course of treatment (such as when a doctor asks a colleague about a difficult case);
- Disclosures to public health officials as required by law (such as when state law requires a physician to notify the state about cases of a reportable disease); and
- Disclosures to law enforcement or state officials as required by law (such as occurs under child abuse reporting laws).

More generally, the regulations permit physicians to predicate treatment upon a patient's willingness to waive confidentiality to his or her insurer. In effect, the regulations recognize that public health will sometimes be benefited but sometimes harmed by protecting confidentiality. Perhaps, too, the regulations reflect the fact that the economic underpinnings of our health care system make notions of a private relationship difficult to sustain. But if that is so, what is left of the idea of confidentiality and the protections for it that the preamble promises?

Perhaps the most dramatic situation in which the patient's right to privacy is pitted against the well-being of others occurs in the so-called duty to warn cases, which are, in effect, the common law analog to the mandatory reporting statutes advocated by Etzioni. The seminal case is *Tarasoff v. Regents of the University of California.* In *Tarasoff*, the patient, Prosenjit Poddar, told his psychologist, Dr. Lawrence Moore, about his desire and intention to kill Tatiana Tarasoff. Although Moore did not actually maintain strict confidentiality (he called the campus police), he did not inform or warn Tarasoff about Poddar's plans. After she was killed, Tarasoff's family sued Moore and his employer, the University of California, for failing to warn her about the danger she faced.

For the majority of the California Supreme Court, the chief issue in the case was whether Moore had a duty to Tarasoff, an identifiable person with whom he did not have a physician-patient relationship. Viewing the physician-patient relationship as a special relationship that gives rise to duties beyond its own boundaries, the Court held that the psychologist, who it treated as akin to a physician, had a duty to warn identifiable individuals about harms caused by a patient. To the dissent, this duty undermined the physician's duty of confidentiality and threatened to weaken public health over all as it might discourage potentially violent patients from seeking psychiatric care. Notice that both the majority and dissent focused more on the good of the community than on the patient's own interest in either treatment or confidentiality. Is that simply because Poddar was a murderer and we do not care very much about his interests? Or does it suggest more generally that physicians have duties to the community at large? If so, what is the nature and scope of those duties? And how do we balance those duties against the physician's duty to treat and provide care for the patient?

In *Tarasoff* the duty to others, and the incursion upon confidentiality, was relatively narrow because they were limited to the situation in which the physician had knowledge about a specific intended victim. In *Garamella v. New York Medical College*,[31] the court considered the extension of *Tarasoff* to a situation in which the victim, a sexually abused child, was not specifically identified in advance by the perpetrator, the child's psychiatrist. Neverthless, given the particular circumstances of the case, including the fact that the physician defendant was also the perpetrator's supervising analyst and that the physician and patient were in a training relationship, rather than a traditional physician-patient relationship, the court still found that the physician had a duty of care to the child.

The *Garamella* case, even more so than *Tarasoff*, raises the same question posed by mandatory disclosure laws: Do physicians have duties to the community at large and, if so, can those duties be reconciled with respect for confidentiality? As you read the materials that follow, ask yourself not only why medical confidentiality is an important value, but whether it is a relic of a bygone era. Should it be protected in our interconnected, interdependent information age?

Supreme Court of the United States
Robert P. Whalen, as Commissioner of Health of New York, Appellant,
v.
Richard Roe, an infant by Robert Roe, his parent, et al.
No. 75-839.

Argued Oct. 13, 1976.
Decided Feb. 22, 1977.

Mr. Justice STEVENS delivered the opinion of the Court.

The constitutional question presented is whether the State of New York may record, in a centralized computer file, the names and addresses of all persons who have obtained, pursuant to a doctor's prescription, certain drugs for which there is both a lawful and an unlawful market.

Many drugs have both legitimate and illegitimate uses. In response to a concern that such drugs were being diverted into unlawful channels, in 1970 the New York Legislature created a special commission to evaluate the State's drug-control laws. The commission found the existing laws deficient in several respects. There was no effective way to prevent the use of stolen or revised prescriptions, to prevent unscrupulous pharmacists from repeatedly refilling prescriptions, to prevent users from obtaining prescriptions from more than one doctor, or to prevent doctors from over-prescribing, either by autho-rizing an excessive amount in one prescription or by giving one patient multiple prescriptions.

The new New York statute classified potentially harmful drugs in five schedules. Drugs, such as heroin, which are highly abused and have no recognized medical use, are in Schedule I; they cannot be prescribed. Schedules II through V include drugs which have a progressively lower potential for abuse but also have a recognized medical use. Our concern is limited to Schedule II which includes the most dangerous of the legitimate drugs.

With an exception for emergencies, the Act requires that all prescriptions for Schedule II drugs be prepared by the physician in triplicate on an official form. The completed form identifies the prescribing physician; the dispensing pharmacy; the drug and dosage; and the name, address, and age of the patient. One copy of the form is retained by the physician, the second by the pharmacist, and the third is forwarded to the New York State Department of Health in Albany. A prescription made on an official form may not exceed a 30- day supply, and may not be refilled.

The District Court found that about 100,000 Schedule II prescription forms are delivered to a receiving room at the Department of Health in Albany each month. They are sorted, coded, and logged and then taken to another room where the data on the forms is recorded on magnetic tapes for processing by a computer. Thereafter, the forms are returned to the receiving room to be retained in a vault for a five-year period and then destroyed as required by the statute. The receiving room is surrounded by a locked wire fence and protected by an alarm system. The computer tapes containing the prescription data are kept in a locked cabinet. When the tapes are used, the computer is run "off-line," which means that no terminal outside of the computer room can read or record any information. Public disclosure of the identity of patients is expressly prohibited by the statute and by a Department of Health regulation. Willful violation of these prohibitions is a crime punishable by up to one year in prison and a $2,000 fine. At the time of trial there were 17 Department of Health employees with access to the files; in addition, there were 24 investigators with authority to investigate cases of overdispensing which might be identified by the computer. Twenty months after the effective date of the Act, the computerized data had only been used in two investigations involving alleged overuse by specific patients.

A few days before the Act became effective, this litigation was commenced by a group of patients regularly receiving prescriptions for Schedule II drugs, by doctors who prescribe such drugs, and by two associations of physicians. After various preliminary proceedings, a three-judge District Court conducted a one-day trial. Appellees offered evidence tending to prove that persons in need of treatment with Schedule II drugs will from time to time decline such treatment because of their fear that the misuse of the computerized data will cause them to be stigmatized as "drug addicts."

II

Appellees contend that the statute invades a constitutionally protected "zone of privacy." The cases sometimes characterized as protecting "privacy" have in fact involved at least two different kinds of interests. One is the individual interest in avoiding disclosure of personal matters, and another is the interest in independence in making certain kinds of important decisions. Appellees argue that both of these interests are impaired by this statute. The mere existence in readily available form of the information about patients' use of Schedule II drugs creates a genuine concern that the information will become publicly known and that it will adversely affect their reputations. This concern makes some patients reluctant to use, and some doctors reluctant to prescribe, such drugs even when their use is medically indicated. It follows, they argue, that the making of decisions about matters vital to the care of their health is inevitably affected by the statute. Thus, the statute threatens to impair both their interest in the nondisclosure of private information and also their interest in making important decisions independently.

We are persuaded, however, that the New York program does not, on its face, pose a sufficiently grievous threat to either interest to establish a constitutional violation.

Public disclosure of patient information can come about in three ways. Health Department employees may violate the statute by failing, either deliberately or negligently, to maintain proper security. A patient or a doctor may be accused of a violation and the stored data may be offered in evidence in a judicial proceeding. Or, thirdly, a doctor, a pharmacist, or the patient may voluntarily reveal information on a prescription form.

The third possibility existed under the prior law and is entirely unrelated to the existence of the computerized data bank. Neither of the other two possibilities provides a proper ground for attacking the statute as invalid on its face. There is no support in the record, or in the experience of the two States that New York has emulated, for an assumption that the security provisions of the statute will be administered improperly. And the remote possibility that judicial supervision of the evidentiary use of particular items of stored information will provide inadequate protection against unwarranted disclosures is surely not a sufficient reason for invalidating the entire patient-identification program.

Even without public disclosure, it is, of course, true that private information must be disclosed to the authorized employees of the New York Department of Health. Such disclosures, however, are not significantly different from those that were required under the prior law. Nor are they meaningfully distinguishable from a host of other unpleasant invasions of privacy that are associated with many facets of health care. Unquestionably, some individuals' concern for their own privacy may lead them to avoid or to postpone needed medical attention. Nevertheless, disclosures of private medical information to doctors, to hospital personnel, to insurance companies, and to public health agencies are often an essential part of modern medical practice even when the disclosure may reflect unfavorably on the character of the patient. Requiring such disclosures to representatives of the State having responsibility for the health of the community, does not automatically amount to an impermissible invasion of privacy.

Appellees also argue, however, that even if unwarranted disclosures do not actually occur, the knowledge that the information is readily available in a computerized file creates a genuine concern that causes some persons to decline needed medication. The record supports the conclusion that some use of Schedule II drugs has been discouraged by that concern; it also is clear, however, that about 100,000 prescriptions for

such drugs were being filled each month prior to the entry of the District Court's injunction. Clearly, therefore, the statute did not deprive the public of access to the drugs.

Nor can it be said that any individual has been deprived of the right to decide independently, with the advice of his physician, to acquire and to use needed medication. Although the State no doubt could prohibit entirely the use of particular Schedule II drugs, it has not done so. This case is therefore unlike those in which the Court held that a total prohibition of certain conduct was an impermissible deprivation of liberty. Nor does the State require access to these drugs to be conditioned on the consent of any state official or other third party. Within dosage limits which appellees do not challenge, the decision to prescribe, or to use, is left entirely to the physician and the patient.

We hold that neither the immediate nor the threatened impact of the patient-identification requirements in the New York State Controlled Substances Act of 1972 on either the reputation or the independence of patients for whom Schedule II drugs are medically indicated is sufficient to constitute an invasion of any right or liberty protected by the Fourteenth Amendment.

III

The appellee doctors argue separately that the statute impairs their right to practice medicine free of unwarranted state interference. If the doctors' claim has any reference to the impact of the 1972 statute on their own procedures, it is clearly frivolous. For even the prior statute required the doctor to prepare a written prescription identifying the name and address of the patient and the dosage of the prescribed drug. To the extent that their claim has reference to the possibility that the patients' concern about disclosure may induce them to refuse needed medication, the doctors' claim is derivative from, and therefore no stronger than, the patients'. Our rejection of their claim therefore disposes of the doctors' as well.

IV

A final word about issues we have not decided. We are not unaware of the threat to privacy implicit in the accumulation of vast amounts of personal information in computerized data banks or other massive government files. The collection of taxes, the distribution of welfare and social security benefits, the supervision of public health, the direction of our Armed Forces, and the enforcement of the criminal laws all require the orderly preservation of great quantities of information, much of which is personal in character and potentially embarrassing or harmful if disclosed. The right to collect and use such data for public purposes is typically accompanied by a concomitant statutory or regulatory duty to avoid unwarranted disclosures. Recognizing that in some circumstances that duty arguably has its roots in the Constitution, nevertheless New York's statutory scheme, and its implementing administrative procedures, evidence a proper concern with, and protection of, the individual's interest in privacy. We therefore need not, and do not, decide any question which might be presented by the unwarranted disclosure of accumulated private data whether intentional or unintentional or by a system that did not contain comparable security provisions. We simply hold that this record does not establish an invasion of any right or liberty protected by the Fourteenth Amendment.

Reversed.

HIV Testing of Infants: Privacy and Public Health

AMITAI ETZIONI

Imagine for a moment that a serious illness threatens the life of a newborn infant. However, the law of the land prevents the infant from obtaining the treatment that could save his or her life. If this sounds far-fetched, it is not very far from describing the current situation regarding testing for human immunodeficiency virus (HIV) among infants and the conveying of the results of that test to an infant's parents.

By October 1998 Congress expects the results of a study it charged the Institute of Medicine (IOM) to conduct. The question is whether forty-nine states and the District of Columbia should be expected to enact laws like the one now in effect only in New York State. The New York law requires that the results of testing infants for HIV antibodies be disclosed to their mothers. This paper examines the policy, moral, and legal issues raised by testing and disclosure.[1]

A Brief Overview of the Facts

As of 1987 the Centers for Disease Control and Prevention (CDC), in conjunction with local health authorities in forty-four states and the District of Columbia, has arranged and paid for "blind" testing of all newborn infants for the presence of HIV antibodies.[2] The CDC used the resulting data to assess the level of HIV in the populations involved (both the infants and their mothers).

In 1993 New York State Assembly woman Nettie Mayersohn introduced a bill that would mandate unblinding the results of these HIV tests, which entails informing the mothers of the results. The bill followed reports from the New York State Department of Health estimating that as many as 60 percent of the infants who tested positive were leaving hospitals unidentified and untreated.[3] It should be noted that, technically speaking, standard HIV antibody tests (the ELISA and Western Blot) do not determine a newborn's HIV status but indicate the presence of the mother's HIV antibodies in the newborn's blood. The testing of infants thus reveals that the mother is infected with HIV, release of which information is widely considered a violation of the mother's privacy and autonomy.

It also is firmly established that a significant number of the infants whose mothers are infected will become infected with HIV and ultimately develop acquired immunodeficiency syndrome (AIDS).[4] These infants likely will die after a prolonged and vicious illness. It is estimated that approximately 25 percent of infants born to HIV-positive mothers contract HIV from their mothers during pregnancy or birth; the other 75 percent of newborns may clear their systems of HIV antibodies and remain HIV-negative, under conditions to be discussed shortly.[5]

The fate of both groups is deeply affected by treatments administered by their mothers and by health care personnel. If the 75 percent of newborns who eventually clear their systems of their mothers HIV antibodies, and thus are HIV-negative, are breastfed, a given percentage of them will acquire HIV from their mothers in this manner. The World Health Organization (WHO) reports that "up to one-third of HIV-infected infants are infected through breastfeeding."[6] These infants' illnesses and deaths could be prevented if their mothers were warned not to breastfeed and heeded this warning.

Moreover, there is significant evidence that the lives of the 25 percent of infants born with HIV could be greatly improved and prolonged if mothers and health care personnel were informed of the condition of the infants. These infants could be treated with AZT (and possibly newer drugs), which would reduce their viral loads, providing many corollary benefits?[7] The U.S. Public Health Service recommends that if AZT treatment is not begun before or during delivery, such therapy should be "initiated as soon as possible after birth, preferably within 12–24 hours," and should continue for six weeks.[8] Doctors also could help to prevent opportunistic infections such as tuberculosis, varicella, meningitis, mycobacterium avium complex, thrush, and particularly pneumocystis carinii pneumonia (PCP). All of these treatments presume that mothers and health care personnel are aware that the infants are endangered.

Most importantly, a 1997 study conducted by the AIDS Institute and the New York State Department of Health indicates that "initiation of ARV [antiretroviral] prophylaxis in the newborn period (within 48 hours of birth) may be associated with an intermediate decline in transmission." Among the persons in the initial cohort studied, postpartum administration of ARV prophylaxis resulted in a rate of transmission from mothers to their infants of 8.9 percent, a significant improvement over the 26.5 percent rate when no prophylaxis is provided.[9] Although additional studies need to be conducted, these results indicate that AZT given within forty-eight hours of birth saves lives by preventing transmission.

As these and other facts about the beneficial effects of postnatal treatment became known, public support for unblinding tests increased. In June 1996 Nettie Mayersohn's legislation was passed in New York State, despite strong and prolonged objections by the American Civil Liberties Union (ACLU), the Gay Men's Health Crisis (GMHC), and the New York chapter of the National Organization for Women (NOW), among others.[10]

As is often the case, opponents raised both principled and practical objections to this legislation. Principled objections focused on the violations of the rights of the mothers caused by the involuntary disclosure of the test results. The New York ACLU argued that "the testing of newborns is an underhanded way of testing mothers and circumventing their rights to consent to the test."[11] Jeffrey Reynolds, deputy director of the Long Island Association for AIDS Care, stated that newborn testing amounts to mandatory testing by proxy, and without informed consent or counseling requirements, for all pregnant women in New York."[12] HIV Law Project Director Terry McGovern has argued that "information is often not kept confidential. . . . I can't tell you how many heartbreaking cases we see where women are thrown out by their families, where children are thrown out of schools."[13] Given these strong objections, other states so far have not followed New York's example.

On the federal level, in 1995 Rep. Tom Coburn (R-OK) and Rep. Gary Ackerman (D-NY) introduced draft legislation that would require all states to follow the New York State pattern or lose the sizable federal funds they receive under the Ryan White CARE Act. However, this bill raised strong objections from many of the same groups that objected to it in New York. In response to this initial opposition, the federal law that was enacted in 1996 reflected a compromise according to which all states are required to meet certain goals for pediatric AIDS prevention within five years.[14] States that do not meet these goals would have to implement unblinded mandatory newborn testing for all mothers who did not receive a prenatal HIV test, or lose their Ryan White funds.[15] The IOM was charged with the task of conducting a study of the states testing procedures and the results obtained. Thus, through this bill Congress delayed any ruling on the unblinding of infant tests for a period of close to five years. The next round of debate for these issues will arise when the IOM report is delivered to the Department of Health and Human Services (HHS) and Congress, anticipated in late 1998.

The Public Policy Debate

An Alternative: Voluntary Testing of Pregnant Women

Parties that are opposed to unblinded testing argue that voluntary testing of pregnant women, as part of prenatal care or a special program, would achieve the same public health goals. The ACLU, the GMHC, and the CDC have adopted this position.[16] This stance is supported by the results of a 1994 study that found that if AZT treatment is administered during pregnancy and delivery to pregnant women who have HIV, and to the infant for six weeks after birth, the risk of infection for their infants would be reduced by two-thirds, from 25 percent to 8 percent.[17] The CDC issued guidelines in 1995 calling for the voluntary HIV testing of all pregnant women.[18] Although, as a result, there have been some reduction in these cases, the CDC reported in June 1997 that the total number of pediatric AIDS cases grew to 7,902.[19]

Voluntary testing of mothers during prenatal care would preempt the ethical and legalistic objections that when infants are tested and mothers are informed without their prior consent, their privacy is violated. Moreover, if the proper funds are allocated, health care personnel could provide mothers with counseling before the test is administered and help them to cope with the results. Furthermore, many health care professionals argue for prenatal as opposed to postnatal testing because prenatal treatment is most effective.[20]

The proper analysis, I suggest, would assume that testing pregnant women, counseling them, and encouraging them to take proper medications and care is beneficial. For this to occur, (1) considerable resources must be allocated; (2) physicians, other health care personnel, hospitals, and clinics must be required to include HIV testing and counseling in their prenatal care programs; and (3) efforts must be made to find the mothers who do not seek prenatal care. However, this benefit does not obviate the need for infant testing, for the following reasons.

First, many pregnant women, including those most likely to develop HIV, do not present themselves for prenatal care, despite considerable efforts to get them to do so. Second, only a proportion of those pregnant women who do seek prenatal care consent to be tested for HIV. Third, pregnant women who have tested negative may develop HIV after they have been tested but before delivery. (Research suggests that the greatest risk of infection for the infant occurs during birth.)[21] Furthermore, if a pregnant woman was infected just before the test, the results may not indicate her infection and would produce a false negative result. This problem is referred to as the "window" problem.

These arguments are supported by the fact that voluntary counseling and testing programs have failed to identify numerous HIV carriers. A study in New York that gathered data from July through September 1993 determined that only 53 percent of infected infants were identified through prenatal testing and counseling.[22]

It is theoretically possible that if more and more resources are invested in locating, counseling, and testing pregnant women, eventually only a very few (one hopes none) would transmit the disease to their children. The best way to establish that this day has arrived is to test the infants. But efforts to reach such a day do not require canceling infant tests or keeping them blind. Indeed, these measures are important until such a goal is finally achieved.

Arguments in favor of unblinded testing in addition to testing the mother are as follows. First, the costs of testing the infants are minimal because blood is already drawn from the infants and subjected to a battery of tests for diseases, including syphilis, phenylketonuria (PKU),

branched-chain ketonuria, homocystinuria, galactosemia, hypothyroidism, biotinidase deficiency, and sickle-cell anemia.[23] The additional costs associated with conducting an ELISA test are estimated to be only a few dollars.[24] A Western Blot test must be conducted to confirm positive ELISA results, which would add to the cost, but of course it would only be needed for those infants found to be HIV-positive through the ELISA—a minority of those tested.

Second, continued infant testing serves epidemiological purposes because these tests provide a highly reliable source of data. In effect, all babies delivered in the health care system can be tested, which offers the possibility of taking random samples or stratification if desired. On the other hand, pregnant women self-select for testing; hence, their tests provide less-reliable information.

Third, and most importantly, a significant number of pregnant women, many of whom are most at risk, will not be located so that one can ask them to agree to be tested; even if located and tested, many will not take the needed medications. Testing infants enables health care providers to identify these mothers and provide them and their children with potentially life-saving treatments and counseling, particularly regarding the dangers of breastfeeding. In short, whether or not one favors testing pregnant women, there does not seem to be a compelling reason not to test the infants. The additional costs of testing infants are small, and the benefits are considerable.

Negative Unanticipated Consequences?

Opponents of unblinded mandatory testing of infants argue that such a program will scare women away from the health care system, thereby forcing them to avoid prenatal care and hospital deliveries.[25] The ACLU argues that "mandatory testing of pregnant women and newborns would have detrimental public health consequences, most significantly by deterring women, especially low income women, from seeking prenatal care. . . . Without trust there is rarely compliance, especially when a woman is confronting not only the possibility that her child has an incurable disease, but the certainty that she does as well.[26] The GMHC concurs: "[M]andatory or coercive proposals, which offer no guarantee of services and which ignore the need to involve the mother in the care of her child, neither reduce the possibility of HIV transmission nor increase the likelihood that infants or their mothers will receive the care they need."[27]

These claims have been countered by the Association to Benefit Children (ABC), a foster-care provider in New York City. After years of work, they have observed that "an HIV positive result typically meant that a mother took strengthened interest in managing her health and that of her child."[28] Observations by both sides on this point are anecdotal; until systematic data are generated, it seems that this particular argument cannot be used any more to oppose unblinding than to support it.

Consensual Disclosure?

The main public policy debate so far has focused on the options discussed above. However, another option comes to mind and in effect has been tried: seeking the mothers consent to be informed about the test results. This approach appears to have the best of both worlds: Practically all mothers could be reached at delivery (which is not the case for prenatal counseling), and consensual disclosure does not violate privacy.

The costs of this approach are much higher than the costs of unblinding the test would be, because under this approach all mothers would need to be counseled (before they can be asked

to consent), instead of only those whose test results are positive (if no a priori consent is required).

Ethically, consent under the given conditions is far from compelling-indeed, is unlikely to be considered ethical by a typical bioethics committee. First of all, many of the treating professionals are of a much higher socioeconomic status than the mothers are and constitute strong authority figures. Marcia Angell, executive editor of the New England Journal of Medicine, notes that "many people can be coerced into submitting to harmful experiments, especially if they are poor and uneducated."[29] Although the context of her remark was overseas AZT experiments involving pregnant women, the same principle applies in this discussion. Even many white, middle-class mothers find it difficult to object to suggestions made by their physicians. Most importantly, the consent has to be sought as a pregnant woman is in labor, a point at which it might be considered unethical to ask her to consider agreeing to a test that might establish that she is HIV-positive and might have infected her child. Counseling under such conditions would be difficult, at best.

Although requests for consent to disclose might be delayed until after delivery, they must be made very shortly thereafter, to avoid breastfeeding and to start medication if necessary, and because mothers stays in the hospital are rather short these days. (All mothers must be asked for consent, because a system of asking only those whose infants test positive would soon become known and would be tantamount to disclosure without consent.)

Last but not least, the treatment of the mothers who refuse consent must be faced. The fact that their number might be small, which is far from being well established, does not resolve the ethical dilemmas. The life and well-being of each infant, and the privacy and autonomy of each mother, must be treated in their own right.

Consensual disclosure (if issues of cost are not allowed to prevail) does have some advantages over nonconsensual disclosure, but the difference is much smaller than it at first may seem, given that consent under these conditions is rather dubious. (One might say that dubious consent is better than none, but note that consent will have to be gained from all mothers, whereas disclosure needs to be made only to those who tested positive and were not reached during prenatal testing.) Finally, the ethical issue of facing the mothers who would rather not be informed cannot be avoided in either case.

Ethical and Legal Issues

Many strongly oppose the unblinding of the test on the grounds that it violates the mothers legal right to privacy. Persons other than the mother find out about her condition without her consent, especially medical personnel.[30] For HIV, there are specific laws requiring that persons be asked to grant written informed consent before they submit to an HIV test and providing for the strict confidentiality of HIV test results.[31] A law that requires mandatory testing of newborns and disclosure of the results would override all such considerations.

Violation of rights other than that of privacy are also said to follow, as a result of discrimination: stigma; the loss of jobs, health and life insurance, and housing; and even domestic abuse or the loss of one's family. The ACLU argues that "these women are susceptible to the same kinds of discrimination faced by others if it becomes known that they are infected with HIV."[32] AIDS Project Los Angeles and the San Francisco AIDS Foundation point out that "there have been numerous court cases involving HIV-positive individuals who have lost their health insurance, their job, or both. The reality is that we cannot legislate away the stigmatization that people with HIV experience."[33] In addition, Karen Rothenberg and Stephen Paskey believe that

"HIV-infected women are particularly vulnerable to the risk of domestic violence.[34] If the test remains blind, such consequences cannot follow from it because nobody can identify the subjects who test positive. They are merely nameless numbers in statistical tables. To deal with these challenges, one must consider the place of the rights at issue in our total network of values.

The Ranking of Values

In ranking the rights and values involved, one may draw on abstract ethical theories, such as weighing autonomy against beneficence. Here instead I draw mainly on the core values of the democratic society in which these issues must be worked out.[35] As I see it, these values provide clear guidance in the case at hand. Our core values and the legal code that expresses them generally rank the loss of life over that of limb, and both higher than the loss of property. Other concerns are less clearly ranked but usually do not take precedence over life, or knowingly allowing a major illness to fester when it can be treated. The Tuskegee experiment is a case in point; the fact that those who participated were not informed about their conditions and provided with the available treatment is considered one of the great ethical failures of U.S. public health policy. Angell has defended this analogy strongly and very well.[36]

In terms of the law, this "ranking" of values is evident in court cases involving the well-being of children. Although parents have the right to give informed consent for treatment on behalf of their children, the parents' right to determine the course of treatment for children is limited.[37] Leonardo Renna states that "a parent may not deprive a child of life-saving treatment" and adds that courts have consistently allowed the state to intervene when a child's health is in danger.[38]

If the issue before us is viewed from this standpoint, one set of facts stands out: If infant tests remain blind, this will directly contribute to the death of a significant proportion of infants born to mothers who have HIV. These infants will not receive beneficial treatments early, and their mothers might breastfeed them out of ignorance. The data cited earlier underscore the importance of early AZT treatment as a means of saving lives and ameliorating severe suffering for HIV-positive infants.[39]

Apart from the failure to avert infant deaths when they could be prevented (certainly a most grievous concern), infants who are not treated are also condemned to severe illness. AIDS, of course, differs from sudden infant death syndrome and many other illnesses in that AIDS entails a long, debilitating period of suffering for both the infant and his or her family. A newborn is subject to many devastating opportunistic infections, which painfully kill the child over the course of many months or even years. Furthermore, infants with HIV also suffer from "recurrent severe bacterial infections, cancer, specific encephalopathy, and wasting syndrome."[40] Even if keeping the information from the mothers would not cause the immediate death of a significant number of infants, the severity of the illness to which they will be exposed if their mothers are kept uninformed is in itself a major concern.

Mothers' Suffering

Opponents of unblinded infant testing are correct in paying attention to the psychological and sociological effects of having one's privacy violated. But one must also heed the suffering inflicted on the infants mothers if they are not informed about positive test results. One far from atypical account runs as follows. A baby girl was born to a mother at Mt. Sinai Hospital in New York City on the morning of 31 January 1991. The doctor assured the mother that her baby was normal and healthy. Nine months later the mother rushed her child to the same hospital. Her child

was having seizures and had stopped breathing. To the mother's astonishment, she learned that her child was HIV-positive and was suffering from meningitis, a pneumococcal infection brought on by an HIV-weakened immune system, which eventually left the child blind, deaf, brain-damaged, and paralyzed. The mother was amazed to discover two anguishing facts: first, that this debilitating infection could have been prevented if her child had been diagnosed and treated soon after birth, and second, that her child was actually tested for HIV as a newborn in the hospital, but the results were withheld from her "to protect her own privacy."[41]

Similar scenarios have been repeated many times across the country for more than ten years.[42] Mothers who take their infants home without being informed of their HIV status may have a child that gradually develops a variety of misdiagnosed illnesses that may seem like a severe flu, pneumonia, or diarrhea. After continued treatment of these children for these various illnesses, their mothers discover the true nature of their child's problem and his or her prospects. The guilt these mothers may feel about having inadvertently contributed to the disease and possible death of their child must be a very serious concern, as is their anger at the medical community for denying them information that could have prevented the suffering and possible death. One further wonders if such mothers do not have a legal, or at least an ethical, claim against those who did not inform them of their child's severe, though treatable, condition.

Aside from sparing the mother some measure of mental suffering, mothers may benefit in other ways from unblinded tests. As explained earlier, a positive newborn test result indicates the mother's HIV status. If the tests are unblinded, the mother may obtain medical treatment for herself. Given the favorable results obtained through newly developed pharmaceuticals, the medical benefit of knowing one's HIV status, provided that care is available, is undisputed. Furthermore, the mother's treatment indirectly benefits the infant, who depends on her for care.[43] Additionally, "identification of a mother's seropositive status helps her make informed decisions about her future family plans."[44] She can make informed decisions as to future pregnancies and appropriate care if she plans to have additional children. She also may make early arrangements for the care of the children who may survive her. Finally, the knowledge of her HIV status gives the mother the opportunity to take precautions against further transmission of HIV to her sexual partner(s).

Violation of Privacy

It should be noted that privacy is not an absolute value and does not trump all other rights or concerns for the common good. As Alan Westin writes, "[A]n individual's desire for privacy can never be absolute, 'since participation in society is an equally powerful desire'."[45] Even civil libertarians recognize that the police have a right to search someone's home if there is specific evidence that a murder weapon is hidden in it. It thus is not sufficient to argue that unblinding violates privacy and then rest one's case. One must weigh the harm done by violations of and losses to the mother, infant, and community when there is no disclosure against the harm that is done by violating privacy.

In judging this question, one must take into account that, even if newborn test results remain blind, privacy will not be preserved for long. As Renna observes, "[T]he reality is that [an HIV-positive mother] is likely to learn of her newborn's HIV status in short order. . . . Without treatment, the probability that an HIV-infected infant will develop an opportunistic infection within the first year is great. . . . She not only will be forced to deal with the sudden revelation of her and her infant's status, but will be forced to

deal with her infant's serious HIV-related illness (and possibly her own), as well as the realization that this illness might have been preventable."[46] In short, the HIV status of both the baby and the mother will be revealed whether the newborn is tested or not, and the issue of discrimination and other ill effects of disclosures will not long be delayed. (The mother herself is likely to develop more visible symptoms over time.)

Violation of Autonomy

Some have argued that, in addition to privacy concerns, the autonomy of mothers is violated when they are informed about the results of a test that they did not seek and provided with information that they did not wish to have. Violation of autonomy can be seen even when mothers are merely asked to consider whether they wish to know, because the mothers may be perturbed by having to make such considerations.

Here one could embark on a valuable discussion of what autonomy encompasses—the difference between a right to know versus a right not to know, and related issues. The main issue here, though, is not whether autonomy is being infringed upon and to what extent, but whether another consideration justifies whatever diminution of autonomy is entailed. The moral equation, it seems to me, is similar to the equation that we faced when the standing of privacy was examined: Given that there is a significant probability of causing a death if autonomy is fully honored, and given that the intrusion is limited to sharing information (best done in the context of counseling), it seems that life should take precedence. Indeed, a case could be made that health care personnel have a moral obligation to proceed.

If this is a valid argument, the same holds only more strongly for a mother. Even if one would completely respect her autonomy, if not informed she is likely to cause irreparable harm to a defenseless infant. Even strong libertarians concede that one's various rights do not entail a right to cause serious damage to, let alone endanger the life of, others. And our laws and ethics fully support taking the much more drastic step of removing children from their parents when they abuse or even merely neglect them. Informing mothers about action that must be taken when life might be endangered seems in comparison a rather temperate step.

Discrimination

Discrimination is certainly a matter of grave concern. In effect, many of the mothers involved are already subject to discrimination. Two-thirds of mothers whose children tested positive are poor and members of minority groups.[47] The greatest percentage of these mothers contracted HIV through injection drug use (41 percent).[48] However, it should be noted that laws against discrimination based upon a person's HIV status already have been toughened in several states.[49] For example, in New York a person disclosing confidential HIV information may be fined heavily or prosecuted.[50] Additional penalties for unauthorized disclosure might well be called for and are being contemplated for unauthorized disclosure of medical records in general.

One must not overlook the fact, however, that unblinding entails informing the mother and not public health authorities; it does not involve inclusion in public records (as when a crime is alleged to have taken place, long before conviction), and it does not involve informing employers or neighbors (as in Megan's laws regarding disclosure of sexual predators in a neighborhood). If the mother and the health care professionals who attend to her and the infant keep the information confidential, as required by law, professional code, and elementary ethics, there are no obvious ways she will suffer discrimination.

When all is said and done, it seems that unblinding the HIV tests of infants and a concur-

rent disclosure of the results to their mothers and those entrusted with their health care is strongly justified. Indeed, it should be noted that in other medical research projects, when it has been discovered early in the process that certain treatments are highly beneficial, the studies have been stopped and the results shared with one and all. The same urgency applies here.

Notes

1. R.J. Simonds, "Prophylaxis against Pneumocystis Carinii Pneumonia among Children with Perinatally Acquired Immunodeficiency Virus Infection in the United States," New England Journal of Medicine (23 March 1995): 786; U.S. Centers for Disease Control, "Guidelines for Prophylaxis against Pneumocystis Carinii Pneumonia for Children Infected with Human Immunodeficiency Virus," Morbidity and Mortality Weekly Report (15 March 1991): 40; L. Renna, "New York State's Proposal to Unblind HIV Testing for Newborns: A Necessary Step in Addressing a Critical Problem," Brooklyn Law Review 60 (1994): 407, 415; L.K. Altman, "AIDS is Now the Leading Killer of Americans from 24 to 44," New York Times, 31 January 1995, C7; and C. Crawford, "An Argument for Universal Pediatric HIV Testing, Counseling, and Treatment," Cardozo Women's Law Journal 3 (1996): 31, 39–41.
2. Report of the Subcommittee on Newborn Screening of the New York State AIDS Advisory Council (Albany: 10 February 1994), Appendix F.
3. New York State Department of Health statistics.
4. S. Arpadi and W.B. Caspe, "HIV Testing," Pediatrics (July 1991): S8; and M.H. Burroughs and P.J. Edelson, "Medical Care of the HIV-Infected Child," Pediatric Clinics of North America (February 1991): 47.
5. Estimates of the number of infants infected perinatally range from as low as 20 percent to as high as 30 percent. C. Wilfert et al., "Evaluation and Medical Treatment of the HIV-Exposed Infant," Pediatrics (June 1997): 909–917.

6. These figures reflect worldwide vertical HIV transmission rates. World Health Organization, "HIV and Infant Feeding: An Interim Statement," World Health (13 March 1997): 30.

7. Renna, New York State's Proposal," 418.

8. U.S. Centers for Disease Control and Prevention, Public Health Service Task Force Recommendations for the Use of Aniretroviral Drugs in Pregnant Women Infected with HIV-I for Maternal Health and for Reducing Perinatal HIV-I Transmission in the United States," Morbidity and Mortality Weekly Report (30 January 1998): 22.

9. G.S. Birkhead et al., "Pathogenesis and Prevention of Vertical HIV Transmission" (Paper presented at the second meeting of the Institute of Medicine's Perinatal Transmission of HIV Committee, Washington, D.C., 11–12 February 1998).

10. J. Dwyer, "A Silence That Kills Children," Newsday (City Edition), 15 April 1994, 2; N. Hentoff, "The New Tuskegee Experiment: Infected Has a Right to Be Told—No Matter What the ACLU Says," Village Voice, 1 October 1996, 8.

11. American Civil Liberties Union, "New York to Require All Mother[s] Be Tested for AIDS," ACLU News Wire, 6 June 1996.

12. J.L. Reynolds, "Keep Policy on Newborns' HIV Test," Newsday (Nassau and Suffolk Edition), 6 January 1994, 105.

13. CNN, transcript of News," 1 May 1996, 8:07 p.m. (Transcript no. 1504-3).

14. By 2000 states must reduce their number of pediatric AIDS cases by 50 percent or, through counseling, test 95 percent of pregnant women for HIV. Office of Rep. Tom Coburn (R-OK), personal communication, 4 September 1997.

15. Ibid.; and "U.S. House Bill Passed Requiring HIV Test for Infants," AIDS Weekly Plus, 13 May 1996, 17.

16. See M. Chapman, CDC Still Plays Politics while Babies Die," Human Events, 10 January 1997; CDC, CDC Draft Guidelines for HIV Counseling and Voluntary Testing for Pregnant Women (Atlanta: CDC, 21 February 1995); ACLU, ACLU Position Statement on Prenatal and Newborn HIV Testing (New York: ACLU, 1996); and Gay Men's Health Crisis, New York State Legislative Agenda (New York: GMHC, 1996), 7.

17. Wilfert et al., Evaluation and Medical Treatment of the HIV-Exposed Infant." The study only reflects treatment for women meeting very specific conditions with regard to their HIV infection.

18. CDC, IU.S. Public Health Service Recommendations for Human Immunodeficiency Virus Counseling and Voluntary Testing for Pregnant Women," Morbidity and Mortality Weekly Report (7 July 1995): 1–15.

19. "AIDS Drug Revolution Excludes the Young," New York Times, 8 September 1997, A14.

20. "HIV Testing Project Draws Complaints," New York Times, 16 June 1997, AS.

21. One analyst estimates that "30 percent to 50 percent of HIV-infected infants have detectable levels of virus in their blood within 48 hours of birth. Of the remainder, more than 90 percent have detectable virus within two weeks of birth. These facts suggest that most infected infants acquire infection around the time of delivery." C. Wilfert, "Preventing Vertical Transmission: A Wise Investment," HIV Newsline (August 1997): 85.

22. Renna, "New York State's Proposal," 430–431.

23. N. Hentoff, "Privacy That Kills," Washington Post, 8 April 1995, A19; and Crawford, "An Argument for Universal Pediatric HIV Testing, Counseling, and Treatment," 33–34.

24. G.S. Birkhead, New York State Department of Health, AIDS Institute, remarks at the second meeting of the IOM's Perinatal Transmission of HIV Committee, Washington, D.C., 11–12 February 1998.

25. ACLU, ACLU Position Statement on Prenatal and Newborn HIV Testing; and N. Lowenstein, "Mandatory Screening of Newborns for HIV: An Idea Whose Time Has Not Yet Come," Cardozo Women's Law Journal 30 (1996): 43, 46–47.

26. ACLU, ACLU Position Statement on Prenatal and Newborn HIV Testing.

27. GMHC, New York State Legislative Agenda, 7.

28. Crawford, "An Argument for Universal Pediatric HIV Testing, Counseling, and Treatment," 35; and Gretchen Buckenhold, executive director, Association to Benefit Children, personal communication, January 1998.

29. M. Angell, "Tuskegee Revisited," Wall Street Journal, 28 October 1997, A22.

30. Lowenstein, "Mandatory Screening of Newborns for HIV," 43–44; and ACLU, ACLU Position Statement on Prenatal and Newborn HIV Testing.

31. Lowenstein, "Mandatory Screening of Newborns," 44. In New York disclosure is permitted to the attending health care providers, third-party payers or insurance companies authorized by the protected person, and certain employees of correctional facilities. Renna, "New York State's Proposal," 424.

32. ACLU, ACLU Position Statement on Prenatal and Newborn HIV Testing.

33. S. Kwong and R. Allgaier, "Letters to the Editor, Recorder, 9 August 1996, 5.

34. KJ. Rothenberg and SJ. Paskey, "The Risk of Domestic Violence and Women with HIV Infection: Implications of Partner Notification, Public Policy, and the Law." American Journal of Public Health (November 1995): 1570.

35. I am well aware that these values themselves require further examination. See A. Etzioni. The New Golden Rule: Community and Morality, in a Democratic Society (New York: Basic Books, 1996), chap. 8.

36. M. Angell, The Ethics of Clinical Research in the Third World," New England Journal of Medicine (18 September 1997): 847–849; and Angell, Tuskegee Revisited."

37. S. Sangree, "Control of Childbearing by HIV-Positive Women: Some Responses to Emerging Legal Policies," Buffalo Law Review 309 (1993): 374; and Renna, "New York State's Proposal," 426.

38. Renna, "New York State's Proposal," 426.

39. Ibid., 418; and Birkhead et al., "Pathogenesis and Prevention of Vertical HIV Transmission."

40. M. Mayaux et al., "Neonatal Characteristics in Rapidly Progressive Perinatally Acquired HIV-1 Disease," Journal of the American Medical Association (28 February 1996): 606–610.

41. Story adapted from J. Dwyer, "Breakthroughs Damn HIV Rule," Newsday (City Edition), 17 June 1994, A02.

42. J. Dwyer, "They Want to Know: Law Kept Women in Dark That Their Babies Had HIV," Newsday (City Edition), 13 June 1994, A02;J. Dwyer, "A Silence That Kills Children," Newsday (City Edition), 15 April 1994, A02; and J. Dwyer, "AIDS Rule Not Kid Proof," New York Daily News, 12 October 1995, 4.

43. Renna, "New York State's Proposal," 434.

44. Ibid., 435.

45. As quoted by R.P. Bezanson, "The Right to Privacy Revisited: Privacy, News, and Social Change, 1890–1990," California Law Review 80 (1992): 1133, 1147.

46. Renna, "New York State's Proposal," 441.

47. "AIDS among Children—United States, 1996," American Health Association Journal of School Health (May 1997): 175.

48. Ibid.

49. Renna, "New York State's Proposal," 441.

50. Ibid., 424.

If I Am Only for Myself, What Am I?
A Communitarian Look at the Privacy Stalemate

HELENA GAIL RUBINSTEIN

I. Introduction

There is little quarrel that access by medical and health policy researchers to medical records and claims data has spurred advances in quality and access to medical treatment. Nevertheless, dissatisfaction lingers with the regime used to regulate access to that information. The American regulatory regime on medical record access has politely been characterized as "fragmented"[1] and less politely as a "black hole."[2] U.S. Senator Edward M. Kennedy asserts, "[t]oday, video rental records have greater protection than sensitive medical information."[3] At the center of this dissatisfaction is the question of how much say an individual should have in letting others—even those with legitimate need—look at and use an individual's records. . . .

II. Foundations of the Privacy Debate

Although privacy has been largely a nonlegal concept throughout American history,[20] American law began to address it in the nineteenth century, at the point where the forces of industrialization and urbanization began to challenge it as never before.[21] In a seminal article, Samuel D. Warren and Louis D. Brandeis, defining privacy as "the right of the individual to be let alone,"[22] argued that the individual should enjoy, cognizable in the law, freedom from unwanted publicity.[23] As the twentieth century progressed, the privacy right of the individual was championed in such areas as reproductive law[24] and criminal law.[25] In the realm of health law, one can argue that privacy has always been valued, because the Hippocratic oath required physicians to keep private what they learned through their physician-patient relationship.[26]

However, while the privacy of medical relationships is deeply rooted in tradition, philosophy and ethics, the law is inconsistent in respecting this relationship. For example, although many regard the privacy of medical records as a "right," it is one that the U.S. Supreme Court has been reluctant to recognize. In *Whalen v Roe*,[27] the Supreme Court overrode privacy objections to uphold a New York statute requiring pharmacists to transmit a copy of prescriptions for certain dangerous drugs to a state registry. The state offered law enforcement and public health justifications for the statute.[28] Patients contended that the statute violated their right to privacy by creating a risk that information about their use of medications might be known publicly and might therefore adversely affect their reputations.[29] Patients also alleged that the statute had a chilling effect on their freedom to choose appropriate medications.[30]

The court was particularly unsympathetic to the patients' privacy arguments noting:

[These disclosures are not] meaningfully distinguishable from a host of other unpleasant invasions of privacy that are associated with many facets of health care. Unquestionably, some individuals' concern for their own privacy may lead them to avoid or to postpone needed medical attention. Nevertheless, disclosures of private medical information to doctors, to hospital personnel, to insurance companies and to public health agencies are often an essential part of modern medical practice even when the disclosure may reflect unfavorably on the character of the patient. Requiring such disclosures to representatives of the State having responsibility for the health of the community does not automatically amount to an impermissible invasion of privacy.[31]

Notwithstanding the Supreme Court's failure to recognize a right to privacy in medical information, restrictions on the disclosure and use of identifiable medical data are firmly rooted in a patchwork of federal and state laws.[32] Although state laws historically stipulated that medical records were the sole property of the health care provider,[33] most state laws also required health care professionals to maintain the confidentiality of a patient's personal information.[34] Thus, if a patient discloses personal information to a health care professional believing it is private, the professional may be liable in tort for disclosure without the patient's consent.[35]

More significant to the current debate is that state laws do not protect confidential medical information that is disclosed with the consent of the patient.[36] A substantial quantity of medical record and claims data enter the public domain through the use of blanket consent forms.[37] As a condition to apply for insurance or assert claims, patients must routinely sign blanket consent forms authorizing discretionary disclosure by the recipient for any lawful purpose.[38] "These contractual arrangements [typically] permit disclosure between and within healthcare systems and payer organizations."[39] Additionally, the forms often permit release of information to others not directly involved in the provider-patient relationship.[40]

Although courts have upheld the validity of general releases,[41] it is arguable whether the consent documented by these forms is either voluntary or informed.[42] It is undisputed that the widespread use of the general release form has partially fueled the huge growth in the collection and sale of health data.[43] This in turn has fueled calls for the systemic reform of health care information access.

* * *

Today, employers have or may obtain a great deal of medical information pertaining to an employee. Many employers choose to self-insure under the Employee Retirement Income Security Act of 1974.[55] Through such mechanisms as claims processing, claims auditing and utilization review, employers come into greater contact with employees' private medical information.[56] A self-insuring employer armed with information about high-cost employees can rewrite the company health plan to exclude high-cost illnesses.[57] The Americans with Disabilities Act (ADA) offers no relief in this circumstance because "[d]iscrimination in health benefits is permissible under the ADA so long as it is based on valid actuarial principles and is not a subterfuge for disability discrimination."[58]

Further exacerbating the problem is the rise of managed care and the paradigm shift in medicine from physician autonomy to oversight, and from personal judgment and anecdotal information to evidence-based medicine, utilization review and clinical practice guidelines. Managed care derives its life blood from data; data is to managed care as air is to human beings.[59] Conclusions are likely to be more valid and generalizeable when based on a broader number of individual experiences. But in an era in which "[m]edical treatments often still rely on notions transmitted from masters to apprentices (during medical training)," efforts to evaluate and improve treatments appear to the public like interference in the physician-patient relationship, leaving both parties unnerved and distrustful.[60] Although medical and health policy research are performed to improve the efficacy and efficiency of "cost[-]containment efforts, outcomes studies, disease management projects, and many other functions that characterize today's delivery system,"[61] research indicates a growing concern that outcomes will be used to examine utilization and eliminate benefits, as many perceive managed care has already done.[62] The irony of this concern is that data can demonstrate whether MCOs are providing quality care.[63]

Finally, the computerization of medical records is seen as a great threat to privacy, although it also has the capacity to provide protections for the data.

> Computers are a mixed blessing, because the ease with which they can make data widely available poses new risks to individual privacy. Compared to paper-based records, electronic information is more easily manipulated and linked . . . [and] also raises the specter of a huge national database of identifiable, comprehensive health information.[64]

The possibility of an individual or entity linking health data with another nonhealth database creates concern, because "[t]hese consolidated personal data may be used by employers, private investigators, or others who may have a non-beneficent interest in an individual's personal health or lifestyle."[65] In a study conducted by the California Health Care Foundation, fifty-four percent of all adults interviewed opined that "the shift from paper recordkeeping systems to electronic or computer-based systems makes it more difficult to keep personal medical information private and confidential."[66] This difficulty is due more to the risk of electronic piracy than data disclosure.

However, paper records are far from secure. Unlike computers that can encrypt identifying information or hide certain information fields from view, paper records are fully identifiable and available to a wide number of individuals in a hospital or health practitioner's office. Further, computers can contain password protections and audit trails, limiting and identifying those who view the data, thereby deterring in-

appropriate viewing. Paper records contain no such protections.

* * *

V. A Proposal for a Communitarian Framework

At first glance, the arguments advanced by privacy advocates seem convincing. The anecdotal evidence of data misuse, central to the argument that consumers should have near absolute control over the disclosure of their medical information,[148] plays into Americans' fear of big government. Yet privacy advocates are rarely called on to justify the potential cost of their orthodoxy to the broader community. Viewed from the health care consumer's perspective, the claims of the data user community are not insubstantial. As never before, consumers of health care hold the medical community accountable for low-cost and effective treatment.[149] Assessment of physician performance has undergone a paradigm shift, from anecdotal evidence to data-driven guidelines. In this new environment, "[s]carcely a day goes by in Washington's health policy community without some recitation of the demand for evidence-based assessments of clinical practice, report cards"[150] and other expressions of information-based assessment tools. In response to the demands of consumer advocates, the bodies that accredit health care organizations now provide Internet access to data on the performance of accredited organizations, thereby facilitating informed purchasing choices.[151] Health policy analysts and clinical researchers who utilize medical records and insurance claims data to evaluate the quality and cost effectiveness of medical care provide information that health care purchasers need to make informed decisions. Legislation that impedes the flow of data to health researchers will threaten the very research that is popular with health care consumers, such as studies examining the health risks of cigarette smoking, obesity and occupational exposure to chemicals.[152]

As privacy advocates and data users continue to position themselves in the final months before HIPPA's deadline for congressional action, fundamental normative differences between the two sides will continue to haunt efforts at reaching a politically viable solution. Data users and privacy advocates frame the debate in different ways. Recognizing the potential for abuse as more and more data is computerized, the National Research Council, a panel of esteemed scientists, views the problem as one of protecting data security, defined as "a condition in which information is shared or released in a controlled manner."[153] Privacy advocates see the issue not as one of data security but of data control. Alan Westin defines privacy as the "degree of control" individuals have over the dissemination of information about themselves.[154] The American Civil Liberties Union of Massachusetts defines privacy in the health data context as "the right of the individual patient to control access to her own medical record."[155] To privacy advocates, control is an integral issue because "the amount of information revealed about the self is related to the amount of control the person feels in a given situation."[156] Thus, the effort to achieve societal consensus on the appropriate way to regulate the use of health data is hampered by "dramatically opposing views about who in society should control the flow and uses of data."[157]

Privacy, which is intertwined with the concept of control over what is disseminated about oneself, is an expression of autonomy. The principle of autonomy is the lightning rod for a line of cases establishing patient control in the medical setting. Cases establishing the requirement that a patient consent before being administered any medical treatment[158] follow Justice Cardozo's assertion in *Schloendorff v. Society of New York Hospital*[159] that "[e]very human being of adult years and sound mind has a right to determine what shall be done with his own body."[160] This principal was applied to give patients the right to forgo life-sustaining medical care,[161] and then to

give surrogates that right on behalf of incompetent patients.[162] But while autonomy is an appropriate framework for evaluating questions concerning the treatment of one's body, it is not the appropriate framework for evaluating rules to regulate the use of health data. Privacy advocates would have Congress focus on autonomy principles when regulating access to medical data. Some would urge that patient "consent be obtained every time information changes hands."[163] Absent such consent, privacy advocate Beverly Woodward laments that medical and public health research renders the individual a mere means to an end because it is "impractical" to do otherwise.[164]

The difficulty in conditioning the use of health data to the consent of the subject only begins with the impracticality of quickly obtaining the large number of consents needed for the typical research protocol.[165] One analyst sees in consent requirements the "potential for chaos," creating an "insurmountable" administrative burden.[166] Requiring consent as a precursor to data use would preclude health plans from using information in their databases to identify individuals who could be at risk, thereby preventing the plans from offering the disease management programs to at risk individuals.[167] Further, if patients are given the right to decide who may use their data for purposes of medical and health policy research, researchers studying diseases that first afflict or disproportionately afflict a vulnerable population may find fewer individuals willing to supply their data than would those researchers studying illnesses afflicting a broader population.[168] Requiring consent for each use of medical records will result in biased studies, thus delaying if not foreclosing the possibility of research and disease detection as well as possible cures or treatments.

The Mayo Clinic studied the effect of changes to Minnesota's privacy law that limit the availability of data for medical research.[169] The Clinic found that women were more likely to refuse authorization than men; persons under the age of sixty were more likely to refuse than older people; and people with certain underlying illnesses, such as mental disorders, breast cancer and reproductive problems, were more likely to refuse authorization.[170] The study concluded that individuals who refused to give authorization were systematically different from others, and their exclusion from research protocols would skew studies.[171] The Mayo Clinic's Melton argues that restrictions in Minnesota's law pose an obvious threat to patient-oriented investigations, such as observational outcome studies based on existing medical record data that require personal identifiers to link initial interventions with ultimate results.[172] Moreover, those who "opt out" by refusing consent may lose more than they gain. Women and minorities traditionally have not been the subject of medical research; new procedures and therapies are tested primarily on men.[173] Only when these drugs and procedures come to market do we learn how they work on women or minorities, in a process known as "post-market surveillance."[174] This process makes all women research subjects, because a particular drug or process is assumed safe though it can only be proved effective and safe after a large enough sample of women have used it.

Health data research is also critical for evaluating the long-term side effects of drugs, doctors' success rates, the safety of medical devices or procedures, the rates of nosocomial or iatrogenic infections, the cost effectiveness of alternative medical practices and the usefulness of diagnostic tests.[175] Without data neither the health plan report cards desired by consumer advocates nor the yearly evaluations of the best hospitals and health plans could be produced. In short, data provides public accountability.

Despite the vast benefits obtained when medical records are made available to medical and health policy researchers, privacy advocate Woodward responds that citizens' participation in the production of medical research is an op-

tional service, not a public duty.[176] Woodward is correct to observe that participation in physically invasive medical research, such as clinical trials, is an optional service, and under an autonomy-based framework, her analysis could apply to the use of health data for research purposes. Indeed, in a rights-based social construct in which the primacy of the individual is achieved by taking an instrumental view of society, individual rights neither imply nor extract from the individual any correlative obligation toward society. Under a right-based construct, an individual's "obligation to sustain a society . . . is seen as derivative, as laid on us conditionally, through our consent, or through its being to our advantage. In a rights-based construct, individual rights trump responsibility for the common good."[177] Indeed, John Rawls suggests that

> [e]ach person possesses an inviolability founded on justice that even the welfare of society as a whole cannot override. For this reason justice denies that the loss of freedom for some is made right by a greater good shared by others.[178]

In proclaiming the primacy of the "right" over the "good," Rawls has argued that individuals are entitled to construct and pursue their unique philosophical understanding of the good, observing that "a person's good is determined by what is for him the most rational long-term plan of life given reasonably favorable circumstances."[179] Under this analysis, community is subordinate to and derives its meaning from the individual. Rawls's construct of the primacy of the individual would not prevent individuals from pursuing the betterment of the community as their end, however, the "community must find its virtue as one contender among others. . . ."[180]

However, the primacy of the individual has had deleterious effects on the subordinated community. Michael Sandel has observed a resulting erosion of our concern for the civic republic, in which

[f]reedom was understood as taking a share in democratic institutions rather than as a matter of "personal rights," and "the possibility of civic virtue was a live concern" to be set off against those rights. That view was gradually overridden by forces that nationalized and individualized our political understandings. The result is that we now inhabit a "procedural republic" where rights are "defined not as a function of democracy but in opposition to democracy" and our image as choosers "unbound by obligations antecedent to rights" negates attachments and commitments based on other ethical considerations.[181]

Communitarians reject the primacy of the individual, and invite members of the community to move beyond self-interest in favor of a vision of society defined by community ties and a search for the communal good. The individual lives as a member of a community; indeed, "[I]t is impossible to think of human beings except as part of ongoing communities, defined by reciprocal bonds of obligation, common traditions, and institutions."[182] For communitarians, the community is *the* end, not, as in the liberalist vision of society, *an* end, "one contender among others within the framework defined by justice."[183] A sense of community can involve "some divergence of interest . . . between individual and community."[184] It is the very act of sacrifice, the willingness to sacrifice individual interests in favor of the common good, that defines community membership. Indeed, one "cannot think about a meaningful sense of community without thinking of some sense of sacrifice."[185] Through sacrifices for the communal good, the community may enjoy a result greater than the sum of each individual's sacrifice. Medical and health policy progress requires sacrifice from every individual who hopes to benefit from that progress.

Inherent in the privacy advocates' rejection of the public duty paradigm is a refusal to recognize, in exchange for the vast improvements in medical care, a correlative responsibility on the part of the individual, as a potential consumer of health care services, toward the community.

As individuals rely on their right to be let alone, they shift the burden on others in the community to accept the responsibility for providing the data needed to advance medical and health policy information. Their individualist vision threatens the entire community, because when particular segments of the community opt out of participation as data subjects, the resulting value of the research is questionable, and many worthwhile protocols could be abandoned on that basis. Thus, a policy that requires consent before each use of health data might have unintended and undesirable consequences for our medical care and health policy.[186]

If the law has ceded to individuals dominion over their body, as it has with informed consent and right to terminate treatment cases,[187] the law has taken a different stand when individual choice would have wider societal implications, as, for example, in physician-assisted suicide. In such cases, the autonomy principal fails and individual choice is reduced in consideration of the potential consequences to the community.[188] Privacy concerns are subsumed to the community benefit in cases of communicable disease, where notification is required by law.[189] Communities are notified when a sexual predator takes up residence in the area.[190] The balance in these cases resides with the community, not the individual. And for this reason, the autonomy principle is inapposite to a consideration of the use of health data for medical and health policy research without the prior consent of the data subjects.

One of the biggest challenges in reaching consensus on the instant issue is caused by our culture. We live in a social environment of increasing distrust and hostility.[191] Further, other aspects of our culture ensure that the privacy issue is addressed in a venue that almost guarantees that the issue's costs and benefits cannot be thought through carefully by the American citizenry. As Jane Mansbridge observes, "[I]n a highly decentralized unit, such as a town meeting or a family, members know that they cannot have what they are unwilling to pay for."[192] But our society is highly centralized. Citizens rely on thirty second sound-bites instead of personal contact with politicians to inform their political decisions. The wholesale nature of contemporary politics has eliminated the dialogue between the governor and the governed, leaving citizens uninformed and unchallenged as to the real costs and benefits of any policy initiative. Further, possibly as an artifact of the continuing erosion of the civic republic, membership in voluntary associations has decreased.[193] If, as Mansbridge observes, the decline in those with membership experience has meant that "fewer citizens . . . have the experience of learning to moderate their demands for the common good,"[194] then fewer individuals are prepared to recognize that they are not "autonomous rights bearers,"[195] but citizens in a community, having correlative rights and responsibilities. Fewer challenge themselves, nor are they challenged to view societal problems from multiple perspectives. Further, they do not become engaged "in the weighing that hard decisions require."[196] This realization becomes critical to an evaluation of the polling data supplied by privacy advocates in support of their position.

Relinquishing control over health data may be the cost of the advances in medicine and health policy that we as a society desire. If an agreement can be reached on this basis, then society's obligation toward the individual is to ensure that there is "proportionality between social ends and the extent to which individuals may be called upon to suffer disadvantage in pursuit of those ends."[197] Specifically, data users must be accountable to individuals who suffer discrimination resulting from a breach of the data subject's confidentiality. And our legislatures and courts must adopt laws that meaningfully enable those who suffer discrimination to press their case and that discourage those who currently engage in discriminatory practices from continuing to do so.[198]

Encryption, extension of the Common Rule to nongovernment funded research[199] and sanctions against those who misuse data have been proposed as methods to constrain the actions of data users and protect the confidentiality of data subjects. Some of these mechanisms are acceptable to data users; others, such as a blanket extension of the Common Rule, are viewed by some as overkill, although less onerous than having to obtain successive individual consents.[200] Phyllis Freeman and Anthony Robbins have suggested that one way to move beyond the privacy stalemate is to differentiate among data users based on their utility to the community.[201] This approach has broad appeal.[202] Many would likely agree that while one analysis should apply to a researcher attempting to demonstrate that a particular health payment system encourages higher utilization of health benefits, a different analysis should apply to marketers trying to influence consumer buying habits. Further, different incentives and prohibitions exist in different industries. One health economist, whose work relies on research, informed a state legislative committee that any researcher who behaved inappropriately with respect to data "would be permanently branded in the research/health policy community, and banished."[203] When the sole incentive is financial gain, as in the case of organizations that warehouse data and indiscriminately sell it to all comers,[204] incentives may drive behavior in a different direction. Therefore, it is important to draw distinctions among users in crafting rules regulating the use of personal health data.

However, care must be taken in drawing those distinctions. Privacy advocates seize on the CVS drugstore chain's decision to release identified patient data to a marketing firm that, in turn, used the data to remind CVS customers to renew their prescriptions as a prime example of what is wrong with the current system.[205] Their point is not frivolous. Next to Big Brother, polling data indicates that individuals are most upset that big business has access to their health data.[206] But it is a point that some observers of the privacy debate, including communitarians,[207] concede too quickly. Although CVS stands to gain financially if patients renew their prescriptions, customers who do not take their medication as prescribed have much to lose. Failure to take high blood pressure medication can lead to heart attack, kidney failure, stroke and other metabolic disorders. It may be more constructive from a public health standpoint to require organizations like CVS to prohibit their marketing partners from making secondary use of prescription data than to prohibit CVS from reminding their customers to renew prescribed medication.[208]

The obsession of some privacy advocates with the possibility that encrypted or anonymized data will be turned into identifiable data and be publicly released injects a red herring into the privacy debate. Even though it may be possible, in theory, for a medical or health policy researcher to identify a data subject from anonymized data, institutional norms already create a substantial disincentive for the researchers to do so. . . .

If privacy implicates issues of the self, research implicates issues of the community. The individual does not live alone on the planet. And given that both the individual and the community have interests, those interests must be balanced carefully to give a measure of security to each. Each side in the privacy debate will have to compromise to achieve a workable regulatory scheme.

Just as technology's limitations would make this symposium topic unimaginable twenty years ago, the speed at which technology advances in the information age may make some of the conclusions seem quaint twenty years hence. However, the fundamental question posed by this Article about whether the community should handcuff vital research in order to protect the autonomy interests of some of its members is timeless. Approximately two thousand years ago, Rabbi Hillel[214] posed three questions that are particularly relevant to the successful resolution of this issue. He asked first, If I am only for others, who am I? This question challenges individuals to look after their own welfare. In bringing concerns about data misuse

to the forefront, privacy advocates have ensured that data security procedures will be strengthened. Whatever regulations are ultimately promulgated will require data users to maintain the utmost caution when working with the data in order to maintain the privacy and dignity of the data subjects. He next asked, If I am only for myself, what am I? This question challenges individuals to recognize their responsibility to the common good. This Article argues that citizens must accept their dual role as both consumers of medical benefits and providers of data. Members of a community should not accept all of its benefits while refusing to contribute to its support. Along this principle, individuals should not assert their "right to be let alone" when it is time to contribute to the collective good, but ask for and accept the help of the collective when receiving medical care. Privacy advocates must demonstrate flexibility and understanding to prevent restrictions on disclosure from threatening the utilization of medical records and claims data for the public good. And finally, he asked, If not now, when? For several years, privacy advocates, health policy analysts, encryption specialists and others interested in the outcome of this question have watched legislatures unsuccessfully debate this thorny issue. By replacing rights language with reciprocal duties language, legislation can be enacted to satisfy the needs and concerns of privacy advocates and the health research community alike.

Notes

1. *See* William W. Lowrance, *Department of Health and Human Services, Privacy and Health Research: A Report to the Secretary of Health and Human Services* § 6 (May 1997). (visited Apr. 9, 1999) <http://www.aspe.os.dhhs.gov/datacncl/PHR6.htm>.

2. *See* Richard C. Turkington, Medical Record Confidentiality, Law, Scientific Research and Data Collection in the Information Age, 25 J.L. *Med. & Ethics* 113, 115 (1997).

3. Senator Edward M. Kennedy, Statement on the Introduction of the Medical Information Privacy and Security Act (Mar. 10, 1999).

20. See David H. Flaherty, *The Right to Privacy One Hundred Years Later: On the Utility of Constitutional Rights to Privacy and Data Protection*, 41 Case W. L. Rev. 831, 832 (1991).

21. See David Seipp, *The Right to Privacy in American History* 102–13 (1978); Note, The Right to Privacy in Nineteenth Century America, 94 Harv. L. Rev. 1892, 1892–96 (1981).

22. Samuel D. Warren & Louis D. Brandeis, The Right to Privacy, 4 *Harv. L. Rev.* 193, 193, 205 (1890). Justice Brandeis dissenting in *Olmstead v. United States*, a wiretapping case, stated that "[the makers of our Constitution] conferred, as against the government, the right to be let alone —the most comprehensive of rights and the right most valued by civilized men." 277 U.S. 438, 478 (1928).

23. See *Warren & Brandeis, supra* note 22, at 206.

24. See *Roe v. Wade*, 410 U.S. 113 (1973) (enlarging the right of individuals to privacy in reproductive matters to include abortions); Eisenstadt v. Baird, 405 U.S. 438 (1972) (holding that the right of privacy inheres in individuals, not marital relationships alone); Griswold v. Connecticut, 381 U.S. 479 (1965) (establishing a privacy right of married persons to control reproductive decisions).

25. The Fourth Amendment to the U.S. Constitution guarantees "the right of the people to be secure in their persons, houses, papers and effects." U.S. Const. amend. IV. However, the Fourth Amendment, and cases thereunder, did not establish a broad right to privacy. It only prevented government officials from *unlawfully* intruding into an individual's home or personal property, and left private citizens to do so at will.

26. The evidentiary privilege that prohibits physicians from giving testimony adverse to the interests of their patients is a modern embodiment of this principle.

27. 429 U.S. 589 (1976).

28. See *id.* at 598–99.

29. See *id.* at 599–600.

30. See *id.* at 600.

31. *Id.* at 602. Contrary to the challengers' arguments, the court concluded that the statute did not in fact reduce the demand for medications subject to the statute or dissuade physicians from prescribing them. *See id.* at 603. Interestingly enough, the very argument offered by the challengers and rejected by the U.S. Supreme Court features prominently in the arguments that privacy advocates make to Congress in seeking restrictive comprehensive privacy legislation. See, e.g., Statement of Harding, *supra* note 11.

32. See Lawrence O. Gostin et al., *Legislative Survey of State Confidentially Laws, with Special Emphasis on HIV and Immunization* (1996) (visited Apr. 14, 1999) <http://www.epic.org/privacy/medical/cdc_survey.html> (discussing the variation in public health laws that exist from state to state). Records maintained by federal agencies, such as the Veteran's Administration Health System, are subject to the Privacy Act of 1974, a comprehensive statute regulating all aspects of federal records maintenance. See Lawrence O. Gostin, Privacy and Security of Personal Information in a New Health Care System, 270 *JAMA* 2487, 2489 (1993). The Department of Health and Human Services (HHS) conditions participation in the Medicare and Medicaid programs by requiring that participating institutions maintain the confidentiality of patient records. See 42 C.F.R. § 482.24(b)(3) (1999). Another federal law protects the confidentiality of persons who attend substance abuse programs. See 42 U.S.C. § 290dd-2 (1998).

33. See Dana C. McWay, *Legal Aspects of Health Information Management* 85–89 (1996); see also *McGarry v. J.A. Mercier Co.*, 262 N.W. 296, 297 (Mich. 1935) (finding that unless an agreement to the contrary exists, x-ray negatives are the property of the physician who made them incident to treating a patient). For this reason, it is generally accepted that providers are free to utilize nonidentifiable medical record information or anonymized medical record data as they see fit.

34. State laws governing the confidentiality of medical records, however, also contain exceptions permitting disclosure in cases where the public interest outweighs the patient's privacy interests. See William H. Roach, Jr. & Aspen Health Law Center, *Medical Records and the Law* 127–35, 177–98 (2d ed. 1994). These exceptions, which vary from state to state, require the disclosure of confidential

medical information in certain cases. See *id.* at 127–35. State laws sometimes also make confidential medical information available to researchers without patient consent. See *id.* at 138–39. *Cf.* L. Joseph Melton III, The Threat to Medical-Records Research, 337 *New Eng. J. Med.* 1466, 1467 (1997) (describing barriers to nonconsensual medical records research under Minnesota law).

35. See Gostin, *supra* note 32, at 2489–90.

36. See Turkington, *supra* note 2, at 115, 119. Richard Turkington noted that blanket consent forms permitting the disclosure of confidential information are considered legal despite the lack of "the most rudimentary features of informed consent." *Id.*

37. See *id.* at 115. Turkington described the movement as "[t]he black hole of confidentiality for the private sector health records." *Id.*

38. See *id.*

39. *Id.*

40. See *id.* Data provided to the Medical Information Bureau (MIB) is used by insurance companies to evaluate applications for coverage and to develop marketing lists targeting persons known to suffer certain ailments. See *id.* This data is made available to MIB through the general release. See *id.*

41. See, e.g., Jones v. Prudential Ins. Co., 388 A.2d 476 (D.C. 1978).

42. See Turkington, *supra* note 2, at 115.

43. For example, MIB stores personal medical information provided by more than 680 life and health insurers, and provides that information to health, life and disability insurers considering an individual's application for coverage. See National Academy of Sciences, *For The Record: Protecting Electronic Health Information* 32 (1997). IMS Health Inc., a Westport, Connecticut-based corporation, collects and processes 72 billion pharmaceutical records provided by doctors, hospitals, pharmacies and nursing homes. See Sam Loewenberg, The Politics of Medical Privacy, *Legal Times,* Mar. 22, 1999, at 4.

44. Barbara Flood. The Emotionality of Privacy, 23 *Am. Soc'y for Information Sci.* 7 (1997). Indeed, what motivated Samuel Warren to take up the issue was the fact that Warren, a Boston Brahmin, found his social life become grist for the mills of the tabloid press, a fact he found to be most dis-

agreeable. See Robert C. Post, The Social Foundations of Privacy: Community & Self in the Common Law Tort, 77 *Calif. L. Rev.* 957, 958–59 (1989).

45. See Robert J. Blendon et al., Data Watch: Who Has the Best Health Care System? A Second Look, 14 *Health Aff.* 220.; see also Equifax-Harris Consumer Privacy Survey (1994) (finding public distrust to be rising, and noting a steady rise over the previous 15 years); Joseph S. Nye, Jr., Introduction: The Decline of Confidence in Government, in *Why People Don't Trust Government* 1, 1–2 (Joseph S. Nye, Jr. et al. eds., Harvard Univ. Press, 1997).

46. See Richard Morin & Dan Balz, Reality Check, The Politics of Mistrust: Americans Losing Trust in Each Other and Institutions, *Wash. Post,* Jan. 28, 1996, at A1.

47. *Id.* at A6.

48. See Melton, *supra* note 34, at 1466.

49. George J. Annas, Privacy Rules for DNA Databanks, 270 *JAMA* 2346, 2346 (1993).

50. See, e.g., Dorothy Nelkin & Laurence Tancredi, *Dangerous Diagnostics: The Social Power of Biologic Information* 6–7 (1989).

51. Mark A. Rothstein, The Law of Medical and Genetic Privacy in the Workplace, in *Genetic Secrets: Protecting Privacy and Confidentiality in the Genetic Era* 281 (Mark A. Rothstein ed., 1997).

52. *Id.* at 281–82.

53. See *id.* at 282.

54. See Etzioni, *supra* note 13, at 144; see also Sheri Alpert, Smart Cards, Smarter Policy: Medical Records, Privacy, and Health Care Reform, *Hastings Ctr. Rep.,* Nov.-Dec., at 13, 15 (1993) (citing an Office of Technology Assessment study that found many employers were not willing to hire employees with preexisting medical conditions).

55. 29 U.S.C. §§ 1001–1461 (1994).

56. In *Doe v. Southeastern Pa. Transp. Auth.,* 72 F.3d 1133 (3d Cir. 1995), an employee whose prescription for zidovudine, together with his identity, appeared in a utilization report, sued after learning that his supervisor shared the information of his HIV status with others in the company. See *id.* at 1135–37. Although he won at the trial court level, on appeal, his award of $125,000 was overturned, when the court held that an employer's interests

in the pharmacy information outweighed the "minimal intrusion" into the employee's privacy. See *id.* at 1135, 1143.

57. See McGann v. H & H Music Co. et al., 946 F.2d 401 (5th Cir. 1991); see also Rothstein, *supra* note 51, at 310–11.

58. Rothstein, *supra* note 51, at 295.

59. Observing the changing paradigm in health care and its need for data, Janlori Goldman writes "Nearly every facet of health care—including health care delivery, payment, medication prescribing, outcomes analysis, research, and marketing—is undergoing dramatic changes as our society moves toward managed care and the development of integrated health data networks." Goldman, *supra* note 6, at 48.

60. See Etzioni, *supra* note 13, at 153; see also Stephen C. Shoenbaum, Towards Fewer Procedures and Better Outcomes, 269 *JAMA* 794, 796 (1993) (observing that "[i]t should be disturbing to us as a profession that we have so few outcomes data and use so few in our practices").

61. See Lise Rybowski, *Protecting the Confidentiality of Health Information* (National Health Policy Forum, The George Washington University, July 1998).

62. Indeed, such information has been used by health maintenance organizations (HMOs) for cost-control purposes and not patient care. See Privacy? At Most HMOs You Don't Have Any, *USA Today*, July 13, 1998, at 12A. HMOs insist, however, that free access to such private information is needed "to identify physicians performing expensive treatments" and to keep track of patients who have obtained "unneeded medical care." See *id.* Additionally, HMOs do use private patient information in their quality assurance programs and in monitoring health care progress. See Karen Ignagni, Do Not Retard Progress, *USA Today*, July 13, 1998, at 12A (explaining that health plans also use private patient information to improve care, for example, by reminding women to have mammograms).

63. See Ellyn E. Spragins, What Are They Hiding? HMOs are getting more secretive about quality, *Newsweek*, Mar. 1, 1999, at 74, 74.

64. See Rybowski, *supra* note 61, at 3.

65. Etzioni, *supra* note 13, at 143.

66. California Health Care Foundation, *Medical Privacy and Confidentiality Survey Summary and Overview* (visited Jan. 28, 1999) <http://www.chcf.org/confernce/survey.pdf>.

148. See Goldman, *supra* note 6, at 50.

149. See Regina E. Herzlinger, *Market Driven Health Care: Who Wins, Who Loses in the Transformation of America's Largest Service Industry* 7–8 (1997) (arguing that informed and assertive consumers of health services demand efficient high quality care as never before).

150. Donald W. Morin, Health Information Policy: On Preparing For the Next War, 17 *Health Aff.*, Nov.-Dec. 1998, at 9, 10.

151. See, e.g., *Quality Check* (visited May 24, 1999) <http://www.jcaho.org/qualitycheck> (information on Joint Commission for the Accreditation of Healthcare Organization accredited institutions), Accreditation (visited May 24, 1999) <http://www.ncqa.org/pages/policy/accreditation/mco/acred497.htm> (information on National Committee for Quality Assurance accredited institutions).

152. *Patient Confidentiality, Hearings Before the Subcomm. on Health of the House Comm. on Ways and Means* (Mar. 24, 1998) (statement of Sherine E. Gabriel, M.D., M.Sc., physician and researcher at the Mayo Clinic) (visited May 10, 1999) <http://www.house.gov/ways_means/health/testmony/3-24-98/3-24gabr.htm> [hereinafter Statement of Gabriel].

153. Freeman & Robbins, *supra* note 67, at 61.

154. See Jo Anne Czecowski Bruce, *Privacy and Confidentiality of Health Care Information* 1 (1984) (quoting Alan F. Westin, *Privacy and Freedom* 7 (1970)).

155. *Id.*

156. Flood, *supra* note 44.

157. *Id.*

158. See, e.g., *Canterbury v. Spence*, 464 F.2d 772 (D.C. Cir. 1972); *Chouinard v. Marjani*, 575 A.2d 238 (Conn. App. Ct. 1990).

159. 105 N.E. 92 (N.Y. 1914).

160. *Id.* at 93.

161. See, e.g., *Bouvia v. Superior Court*, 225 Cal. Rptr. 297 (Cal. App. 1986).

162. See, e.g., *In re Westchester County Medical Center on Behalf of O'Connor*, 531 N.E.2d 607 (N.Y. 1988) (holding that a hospital is authorized to insert a

feeding tube into an incompetent patient unless there is clear and convincing proof that the patient had made a firm commitment to decline such assistance when competent); *Cruzan v. Director, Missouri Dep't of Health,* 497 U.S. 261 (1990) (holding that the U.S. Constitution does not forbid a state from requiring clear and convincing evidence of an incompetent's wishes before withdrawing life-sustaining treatment and that due process does not require a state to accept the substituted judgment of close family members absent substantial proof that their views reflect those of the patient).

163. Rybowski, *supra* note 61, at 10.

164. Woodward, *supra* note 102, at 92.

165. See Statement of Feldblum, *supra* note 98.

166. See Morin, *supra* note 150, at 13.

167. See Ignagni, *supra* note 62, at 12A.

168. See e.g., Randy Shilts, *And The Band Played On: Politics, People, and the AIDS Epidemic* (1987) (arguing that government footdragging left researchers of the acquired immune deficiency syndrome without adequate funding, and silence by the mainstream press left Americans uninformed until the disease was found in more mainstream populations).

169. See Melton, *supra* note 34, at 1466.

170. See *id.* at 1469.

171. See *id.* at 1467–69. By systematically different, Joseph Melton refers to the fact that those who opt out are not doing so randomly, but are of discrete age, sex and health status, and hence were opting out in particular patterns. This is a concern to any study that seeks validity and generalizability, because the result of a study where discrete populations have opted out likely could not be applied to the general public, and hence the research would be of limited value. See, e.g., Charles H. Hennekens & Julie E. Buring, *Epidemiology in Medicine* 37–38 (1987).

172. *Id.*

173. See, e.g., Rebecca Dresser, Wanted: Single, White Male for Medical Research, *Hastings Ctr. Rep.,* Jan.-Feb. 1992, at 24 (analyzing the arguments against including women as research subjects).

174. See 21 C.F.R. § 5.60 (1999). This term comes from the FDA regulatory process. After a drug has been

tested, it is released. However, its release is conditional because the FDA continues to collect data about the drug's performance once it is disseminated to the general population. See *id.*

175. See Statement of Gabriel, *supra* note 152.

176. See Woodward, *supra* note 102, at 94. She cites Hans Jonas for this proposition. However, Jonas's work, Philosophical Reflections on Experimenting with Human Subjects, 98 *Daedelus* 219 (1969) may be inapposite to the instant consideration. In 1969, when his work was published, Americans were still coming to terms with the ghastly human subject experiments performed during the Holocaust on captive populations, and were learning about other inappropriate experiments performed on vulnerable populations in the United States.

177. William R. Lund, Politics, Virtue, and the Right To do Wrong: Assessing the Communitarian Critique of Rights, *J. Soc. Phil.,* Winter 1997, at 101, 103 (explaining the communitarian view of liberalism). For a strong defense of rights theory, see Ronald Dworkin, *Taking Rights Seriously* (1977).

178. John Rawls, *A Theory of Justice* 3–4 (1971) (providing a view of society premised on the concept that individual rights override communal ends).

179. *Id.* at 92–93.

180. Michael Sandel, *Liberalism and the Limits of Justice* 64 (2d ed. 1982).

181. Lund, *supra* note 177, at 103 (citing Michael Sandel, Morality and the Liberal Ideal, *New Republic,* May 7, 1984, at 15).

182. 3 Joel Feinberg, *The Moral Limits of the Criminal Law* 47 (1986).

183. Sandel, *supra* note 180, at 64.

184. Frederick Schauer, Community, Citizenship, and the Search For National Identity, 84 *Mich. L. Rev.* 1504, 1504 (1986).

185. *Id.*

186. See, e.g. Carol Gentry, Breaches of Medical Records A Tough Condition to Treat, *Wall St. J.,* May 5, 1999, at NE1 (describing Maine's attempt to implement a medical records confidentiality law). Among the unintended consequences resulting from the law were that hospitals would not tell family members that their loved ones were in the hospital or provide information on

their condition, florists could not deliver flowers, clergymen were unable to visit congregants and pharmacists would not release prescription medications to anyone but the intended patient, even if that patient was bedridden. See *id.* Shortly after the law took effect, the state legislature reconsidered the legislation and postponed its effective date. See *id.* Senator Bennett's bill addresses some of these deficiencies; it affirmatively authorizes the release of patients' names, general location and general condition to any person unless the patient has previously objected to the release of such information. See S. 881 § 204(b).

187. See *supra* notes 158–62 and accompanying text.

188. Donald L. Beschle, The Role Of Courts In The Debate On Assisted Suicide: A Communitarian Approach, 9 *Notre Dame J. L., Ethics, & Pub. Pol'y* 367, 389 (1995).

189. See Roach & Aspen Health Law Center, *supra* note 34, at 147–48.

190. See, e.g., Alaska Stat. 18.065.087 (1998), which authorizes the Department of Public Safety to maintain a central registry of sex offenders and to make the following information about those offenders available to the public: name, address, photograph, place of employment, date of birth, crime for which convicted, date of conviction, place and court of conviction and length of sentence. This information is posted on the Internet at *Sex Offender Registration Report* (visited May 24, 1999) <http://www.dps.state.ak.us/sorcr>.

191. See Jane Mansbridge, Social and Cultural Causes of Dissatisfaction with U.S. Government, in *Why People Don't Trust Government* 134, 134 (Joseph S. Nye, Jr. et al. eds.).

192. *Id.*

193. See *id.* at 145–46.

194. *Id.* at 146.

195. See Beschle, *supra* note 188, at 405.

196. See Mansbridge, *supra* note 1921, at 152.

197. Beschle, *supra* note 188, at 405.

198. See Rosa Eckstein, Comment, Towards a Communitarian Theory of Responsibility: Bearing the Burden for the Unintended, 45 *Univ. Miami L. Rev.* 843, 855, 864–878, 907–09 (1991) (arguing that a rejection of liberalist jurisprudence in em-

ployment discrimination in favor of a communitarian definition of responsibility will enable plaintiffs to prevail more often, by shifting the inquiry away from intent, which is by nature individualistic, toward an inquiry that includes an examination of the structural problems that may contribute to the discriminatory environment).

199. It has been suggested by privacy advocates and some members of Congress that the Common Rule be extended to privately funded research involving the use of health data. See Loewenberg, *supra* note 43, at 4. It has alternatively been suggested that alternative arrangements between data providers and data users, such as confidentiality policies or confidentiality agreements, may provide adequate protection with less burden. *Id.* at 5. The author believes that each of these positions has merit and should be given full consideration before Congress.

200. See *id.* at 4–5.

201. See Freeman & Robbins, *supra* note 67, at 60, 73.

202. Indeed, Amitai Etzioni, widely regarded as the father of communitarian thinking, uses a similar framework in his recent article on resolving the privacy stalemate. See Etzioni, *supra* note 13, at 15. Etzioni suggests that those who are directly responsible for treating patients should have broad access to identified health information while those who seek to use data simply for profit, such as marketing interests, should have little or no access. See *id.* at 19, 20. Health researchers fall somewhere in the middle. *See id.* Etzioni proposes a system under which each individual would be issued a Unique Personal Identifier (UPI) number. See *id.* at 20–21. Data given to researchers would be encrypted, in most cases only with the UPI. See *id.* This, he believes, would answer the objection of the research community that arbitrarily encrypted data precludes researchers from tracking patients' health conditions over time. See *id.* Researcher access to additional patient identification data would only be available on a showing of critical need and would be edited to preclude further identification of the subject. See *id.* This paper does not endorse Etzioni's approach. Health researchers work within an ethical framework that is similar to those who

provide patient care. To the extent that researchers need any further incentive to protect the confidentiality of research subjects, it can be found in the sanctions language of each of the major privacy bills. Etzioni's proposal would unjustifiably penalize the health research community for indiscretions committed by unscrupulous individuals and other communities of data users by increasing the cost of access to data. Moreover, the practicability of the UPI system is doubtful in the face of opposition from civil liberties interests that have traditionally argued against the issuance of national identification cards.

203. Letter from Richard Zeckhauser, Frank P. Ramsey Professor of Political Economy, John F. Kennedy School of Government, Harvard University, to Massachusetts State Representative Harriet Chandler, Chair of the Joint Committee on Health Care 1 (Mar. 15, 1977) (on file with the author).

204. See Gentry, *supra* note 186, at NE1 (discussing the experience of a Massachusetts physician who was questioned about items in his medical record by an attorney who obtained the record from a data clearinghouse).

205. Goldman told a congressional subcommittee about the story of an "Orlando woman who had

her doctor perform some routine tests, and received a letter weeks later from a drug company touting a treatment for her high cholesterol." Statement of Goldman, *supra* note 94.

206. Although significant law enforcement interests exist for obtaining this information, allowing the government access to medical records data poses significant risks of government misuse. See, e.g., Christopher Matthews, Kennedy & Nixon 302, 302 (1996) (discussing the Nixon administration's decision to obtain medical records information unlawfully). These difficult questions are beyond the scope of this Article.

207. See, e.g., Etzioni, *supra* note 13.

208. Another approach may be to provide pharmacy customers with the opportunity to state whether they wish to receive patient education materials when they fill their prescriptions. Those customers who affirmatively decline would not receive letters such as those mailed by CVS's marketing partner.

214. Rabbi Hillel lived from the end of the first century B.C.E. to some point in the first century C.E. toward the end of the Second Temple Period. see Yitzhak Buxbaum, *The Life and Teachings of Hillel* 268–70 (1994).

Vitaly Tarasoff et al., Plaintiffs and Appellants,

v.

The Regents of the University of California et al., Defendants and Respondents Supreme Court of California

July 1, 1976

Opinion by

TOBRINER

Opinion

On October 27, 1969, Prosenjit Poddar killed Tatiana Tarasoff. Plaintiffs, Tatiana's parents, allege that two months earlier Poddar confided his intention to kill Tatiana to Dr. Lawrence Moore, a psychologist employed by the Cowell Memorial Hospital at the University of California at Berkeley. They allege that on Moore's request, the campus police briefly detained Poddar, but released him when he appeared rational. They further claim that Dr. Harvey Powelson, Moore's superior, then directed that no further action be taken to detain Poddar. No one warned plaintiffs of Tatiana's peril.

Concluding that these facts set forth causes of action against neither therapists and policemen involved, nor against the Regents of the University of California as their employer, the superior court sustained defendants' demurrers to plain-tiffs' second amended complaints without leave to amend. This appeal ensued.

Plaintiffs' complaints predicate liability on two grounds: defendants' failure to warn plaintiffs of the impending danger and their failure to bring about Poddar's confinement pursuant to the Lanterman-Petris-Short Act (Welf. & Inst. Code, § 5000 *ff.*) Defendants, in turn, assert that they owed no duty of reasonable care to Tatiana and that they are immune from suit under the California Tort Claims Act of 1963 (Gov. Code, § 810 *ff.*).

We shall explain that defendant therapists cannot escape liability merely because Tatiana herself was not their patient. When a therapist determines, or pursuant to the standards of his profession should determine, that his patient presents a serious danger of violence to another, he incurs an obligation to use reasonable care to protect the intended victim against such danger. The discharge of this duty may require the therapist to take one or more of various steps, depending upon the nature of the case. Thus it may call for him to warn the intended victim or others likely to apprise the victim of the danger, to notify the police, or to take whatever other steps are reasonably necessary under the circumstances.

In the case at bar, plaintiffs admit that defendant therapists notified the police, but argue on appeal that the therapists failed to exercise reasonable care to protect Tatiana in that they did not confine Poddar and did not warn Tatiana or others likely to apprise her of the danger. Defendant therapists, however, are public employees. Consequently, to the extent that plaintiffs seek to predicate liability upon the therapists' failure to bring about Poddar's confinement, the therapists can claim immunity under Government Code section 856. No specific statutory provision, however, shields them from liability based upon failure to warn Tatiana or others likely to apprise her of the danger, and Government Code section 820.2 does not protect such failure as an exercise of discretion.

Plaintiffs therefore can amend their complaints to allege that, regardless of the therapists' unsuccessful attempt to confine Poddar, since they knew that Poddar was at large and dangerous, their failure to warn Tatiana or others likely to apprise her of the danger constituted a breach of the therapists' duty to exercise reasonable care to protect Tatiana.

Plaintiffs, however, plead no relationship between Poddar and the police defendants which would impose upon them any duty to Tatiana, and plaintiffs suggest no other basis for such a duty. Plaintiffs have, therefore, failed to show that the trial court erred in sustaining the demurrer of the police defendants without leave to amend.

1. Plaintiffs' Complaints

Plaintiffs, Tatiana's mother and father, filed separate but virtually identical second amended complaints. The issue before us on this appeal is whether those complaints now state, or can be amended to state, causes of action against defendants. We therefore begin by setting forth the pertinent allegations of the complaints.

Plaintiffs' first cause of action, entitled "Failure to Detain a Dangerous Patient," alleges that on August 20, 1969, Poddar was a voluntary outpatient receiving therapy at Cowell Memorial Hospital. Poddar informed Moore, his therapist, that he was going to kill an unnamed girl, readily identifiable as Tatiana, when she returned home from spending the summer in Brazil. Moore, with the concurrence of Dr. Gold, who had initially examined Poddar, and Dr. Yandell, assistant to the director of the department of psychiatry, decided that Poddar should be committed for observation in a mental hospital. Moore orally notified Officers Atkinson and Teel of the campus police that he would request commitment. He then sent a letter to Police Chief William Beall requesting the assistance of the police department in securing Poddar's confinement.

Officers Atkinson, Brownrigg, and Halleran took Poddar into custody, but, satisfied that Poddar was rational, released him on his promise to stay away from Tatiana. Powelson, director of the department of psychiatry at Cowell Memorial Hospital, then asked the police to return Moore's letter, directed that all copies of the letter and notes that Moore had taken as therapist be destroyed, and "ordered no action to place Prosenjit Poddar in 72-hour treatment and evaluation facility."

Plaintiffs' second cause of action, entitled "Failure to Warn On a Dangerous Patient," incorporates the allegations of the first cause of action, but adds the assertion that defendants negligently permitted Poddar to be released from police custody without "notifying the parents of Tatiana Tarasoff that their daughter was in grave danger from Posenjit Poddar." Poddar persuaded Tatiana's brother to share an apartment with him near Tatiana's residence; shortly after her return from Brazil, Poddar went to her residence and killed her.

We direct our attention to the issue of whether plaintiffs' second cause of action can be amended to state a basis for recovery.

2. *Plaintiffs Can State a Cause of Action Against Defendant Therapists for Negligent Failure to Protect Tatiana*

The second cause of action can be amended to allege that Tatiana's death proximately resulted from defendants' negligent failure to warn Tatiana or others likely to apprise her of her danger. Plaintiffs contend that as amended, such allegations of negligence and proximate causation, with resulting damages, establish a cause of action. Defendants, however, contend that in the circumstances of the present case they owed no duty of care to Tatiana or her parents and that, in the absence of such duty, they were free to act in careless disregard of Tatiana's life and safety.

In analyzing this issue, we bear in mind that legal duties are not discoverable facts of nature, but merely conclusory expressions that, in cases of a particular type, liability should be imposed for damage done. As stated in *Dillon* v. *Legg* (1968) 68 Cal.2d 728, 734 [69 Cal.Rptr. 72, 441 P.2d 912, 29 A.L.R.3d 1316]: "The assertion that liability must . . . be denied because defendant bears no 'duty' to plaintiff 'begs the essential question—whether the plaintiff's interests are entitled to legal protection against the defendant's conduct. . . . [Duty] is not sacrosanct in itself, but only an expression of the sum total of those considerations of policy which lead the law to say that the particular plaintiff is entitled to protection.' (Prosser, Law of Torts [3d ed. 1964] at pp. 332–333.)"

In the landmark case of *Rowland* v. *Christian* (1968) 69 Cal.2d 108 [70 Cal.Rptr. 97, 443 P.2d 561, 32 A.L.R.3d 496], Justice Peters recognized that liability should be imposed "for injury occasioned to another by his want of ordinary care or skill" as expressed in section 1714 of the Civil Code. Thus, Justice Peters, quoting from *Heaven* v. *Pender* (1883) 11 Q.B.D. 503, 509 stated: "'whenever one person is by circumstances placed in such a position with regard to another . . . that if he did not use ordinary care and skill in his own conduct . . . he would cause danger of injury to the person or property of the other, a duty arises to use ordinary care and skill to avoid such danger.'"

We depart from "this fundamental principle" only upon the "balancing of a number of considerations"; major ones "are the foreseeability of harm to the plaintiff, the degree of certainty that the plaintiff suffered injury, the closeness of the connection between the defendant's conduct and the injury suffered, the moral blame attached to the defendant's conduct, the policy of preventing future harm, the extent of the burden to the defendant and consequences to the community of imposing a duty to exercise care with resulting liability for breach, and the availability, cost and prevalence of insurance for the risk involved."

The most important of these considerations in establishing duty is foreseeability. As a general principle, a "defendant owes a duty of care to all persons who are foreseeably endangered by his conduct, with respect to all risks which make the conduct unreasonably dangerous." (*Rodriguez* v. *Bethlehem Steel Corp.* (1974) 12 Cal.3d 382, 399 [115 Cal.Rptr. 765, 525 P.2d 669]). As we shall explain, however, when the avoidance of foreseeable harm requires a defendant to control the conduct of another person, or to warn of such conduct, the common law has traditionally imposed liability only if the defendant bears some special relationship to the dangerous person or to the potential victim. Since the relationship between a therapist and his patient satisfies this requirement, we need not here decide whether foreseeability alone is sufficient to create a duty to exercise reasonable care to protect a potential victim of another's conduct.

Although, as we have stated above, under the common law, as a general rule, one person owed no duty to control the conduct of another (*Richards* v. *Stanley* (1954) 43 Cal.2d 60, 65 [271 P.2d 23]); nor to warn those endangered by such conduct (Rest.2d Torts, *supra*, § 314, com. c.; Prosser, Law of Torts (4th ed. 1971) § 56, p. 341), the courts have carved out an exception to this rule in cases in which the defendant stands in some special relationship to either the person whose conduct needs to be controlled or in a relationship to the foreseeable victim of that conduct (see Rest.2d Torts, *supra*, §§ 315–320). Applying this exception to the present case, we note that a relationship of defendant therapists to either Tatiana or Poddar will suffice to establish a duty of care; as explained in section 315 of the Restatement Second of Torts, a duty of care may arise from either "(a) a special relation . . . between the actor and the third person which imposes a duty upon the actor to control the third person's conduct, or (b) a special relation . . . between the actor and the other which gives to the other a right of protection."

Although plaintiffs' pleadings assert no special relation between Tatiana and defendant therapists, they establish as between Poddar and defendant therapists the special relation that arises between a patient and his doctor or psychotherapist. Such a relationship may support affirmative duties for the benefit of third persons. Thus, for example, a hospital must exercise reasonable care to control the behavior of a patient which may endanger other persons. A doctor must also warn a patient if the patient's condition or medication renders certain conduct, such as driving a car, dangerous to others.

Although the California decisions that recognize this duty have involved cases in which the defendant stood in a special relationship *both* to the victim and to the person whose conduct created the danger, we do not think that the duty should logically be constricted to such situations. Decisions of other jurisdictions hold that the single relationship of a doctor to his patient is sufficient to support the duty to exercise reasonable care to protect others against dangers emanating from the patient's illness. The courts hold that a doctor is liable to persons infected by his patient if he negligently fails to diagnose a contagious disease (*Hofmann* v. *Blackmon* (Fla.App. 1970) 241 So.2d 752), or, having diagnosed the illness, fails

to warn members of the patient's family (*Wojcik* v. *Aluminum Co. of America* (1959) 18 Misc.2d 740 [183 N.Y.S.2d 351, 357–358]).

Defendants contend, however, that imposition of a duty to exercise reasonable care to protect third persons is unworkable because therapists cannot accurately predict whether or not a patient will resort to violence. In support of this argument amicus representing the American Psychiatric Association and other professional societies cites numerous articles which indicate that therapists, in the present state of the art, are unable reliably to predict violent acts; their forecasts, amicus claims, tend consistently to overpredict violence, and indeed are more often wrong than right. Since predictions of violence are often erroneous, amicus concludes, the courts should not render rulings that predicate the liability of therapists upon the validity of such predictions.

The role of the psychiatrist, who is indeed a practitioner of medicine, and that of the psychologist who performs an allied function, are like that of the physician who must conform to the standards of the profession and who must often make diagnoses and predictions based upon such evaluations. Thus the judgment of the therapist in diagnosing emotional disorders and in predicting whether a patient presents a serious danger of violence is comparable to the judgment which doctors and professionals must regularly render under accepted rules of responsibility.

We recognize the difficulty that a therapist encounters in attempting to forecast whether a patient presents a serious danger of violence. Obviously, we do not require that the therapist, in making that determination, render a perfect performance; the therapist need only exercise "that reasonable degree of skill, knowledge, and care ordinarily possessed and exercised by members of [that professional specialty] under similar circumstances." (*Bardessono* v. *Michels* (1970) 3 Cal.3d 780, 788 [91 Cal.Rptr. 760, 478 P.2d 480, 45 A.L.R.3d 717]). Within the broad range of reasonable practice and treatment in which professional opinion and judgment may differ, the therapist is free to exercise his or her own best judgment without liability; proof, aided by hindsight, that he or she judged wrongly is insufficient to establish negligence.

In the instant case, however, the pleadings do not raise any question as to failure of defendant therapists to predict that Poddar presented a serious danger of violence. On the contrary, the present complaints allege that defendant therapists did in fact predict that Poddar would kill, but were negligent in failing to warn.

Amicus contends, however, that even when a therapist does in fact predict that a patient poses a serious danger of violence to others, the therapist should be absolved of any responsibility for failing to act to protect the potential victim. In our view, however, once a therapist does in fact determine, or under applicable professional standards reasonably should have determined, that a patient poses a serious danger of violence to others, he bears a duty to exercise reasonable care to protect the foreseeable victim of that danger. While the discharge of this duty of due care will necessarily vary with the facts of each case, in each instance the adequacy of the therapist's conduct must be measured against the traditional negligence standard of the rendition of reasonable care under the circumstances. (Accord *Cobbs v. Grant* (1972) 8 Cal.3d 229, 243 [104 Cal.Rptr. 505, 502 P.2d 1].) As explained in Fleming and Maximov, *The Patient or His Victim: The Therapist's Dilemma* (1974) 62 Cal.L.Rev. 1025, 1067: ". . . the ultimate question of resolving the tension between the conflicting interests of patient and potential victim is one of social policy, not professional expertise. . . . In sum, the therapist owes a legal duty not only to his patient, but also to his patient's would-be victim and is subject in both respects to scrutiny by judge and jury."

The risk that unnecessary warnings may be given is a reasonable price to pay for the lives of possible victims that may be saved. We would hesitate to hold that the therapist who is aware

that his patient expects to attempt to assassinate the President of the United States would not be obligated to warn the authorities because the therapist cannot predict with accuracy that his patient will commit the crime.

Defendants further argue that free and open communication is essential to psychotherapy (see *In re Lifschutz* (1970) 2 Cal.3d 415, 431-434 [85 Cal.Rptr. 829, 467 P.2d 557, 44 A.L.R.3d 1]); that "Unless a patient . . . is assured that . . . information [revealed by him] can and will be held in utmost confidence, he will be reluctant to make the full disclosure upon which diagnosis and treatment . . . depends." (Sen. Com. on Judiciary, comment on Evid. Code, § 1014.) The giving of a warning, defendants contend, constitutes a breach of trust which entails the revelation of confidential communications.

We recognize the public interest in supporting effective treatment of mental illness and in protecting the rights of patients to privacy (see *In re Lifschutz, supra,* 2 Cal.3d at p. 432), and the consequent public importance of safeguarding the confidential character of psychotherapeutic communication. Against this interest, however, we must weigh the public interest in safety from violent assault. The Legislature has undertaken the difficult task of balancing the countervailing concerns. In Evidence Code section 1014, it established a broad rule of privilege to protect confidential communications between patient and psychotherapist. In Evidence Code section 1024, the Legislature created a specific and limited exception to the psychotherapist-patient privilege: "There is no privilege . . . if the psychotherapist has reasonable cause to believe that the patient is in such mental or emotional condition as to be dangerous to himself or to the person or property of another and that disclosure of the communication is necessary to prevent the threatened danger."

We realize that the open and confidential character of psychotherapeutic dialogue encourages patients to express threats of violence, few of which are ever executed. Certainly a therapist should not be encouraged routinely to reveal such threats; such disclosures could seriously disrupt the patient's relationship with his therapist and with the persons threatened. To the contrary, the therapist's obligations to his patient require that he not disclose a confidence unless such disclosure is necessary to avert danger to others, and even then that he do so discreetly, and in a fashion that would preserve the privacy of his patient to the fullest extent compatible with the prevention of the threatened danger. (See Fleming & Maximov, *The Patient or His Victim: The Therapist's Dilemma* (1974) 62 Cal.L.Rev. 1025, 1065–1066.)

The revelation of a communication under the above circumstances is not a breach of trust or a violation of professional ethics; as stated in the Principles of Medical Ethics of the American Medical Association (1957), section 9: "A physician may not reveal the confidence entrusted to him in the course of medical attendance . . . *unless he is required to do so by law or unless it becomes necessary in order to protect the welfare of the individual or of the community.*" (Italics added.) We conclude that the public policy favoring protection of the confidential character of patient-psychotherapist communications must yield to the extent to which disclosure is essential to avert danger to others. The protective privilege ends where the public peril begins.

Our current crowded and computerized society compels the interdependence of its members. In this risk-infested society we can hardly tolerate the further exposure to danger that would result from a concealed knowledge of the therapist that his patient was lethal. If the exercise of reasonable care to protect the threatened victim requires the therapist to warn the endangered party or those who can reasonably be expected to notify him, we see no sufficient societal interest that would protect and justify concealment. The containment of such risks lies in the public interest. For the foregoing reasons, we find that plaintiffs' complaints can be amended to state a cause of action against defendants Moore, Pow-

elson, Gold, and Yandell and against the Regents as their employer, for breach of a duty to exercise reasonable care to protect Tatiana.

Turning now to the police defendants, we conclude that they do not have any such special relationship to either Tatiana or to Poddar sufficient to impose upon such defendants a duty to warn respecting Poddar's violent intentions. (See *Hartzler* v. *City of San Jose* (1975) 46 Cal.App.3d 6, 9-10 [120 Cal.Rptr. 5]; *Antique Arts Corp.* v. *City of Torrance* (1974) 39 Cal.App.3d 588, 593 [114 Cal.Rptr. 332].) Plaintiffs suggest no theory, and plead no facts that give rise to any duty to warn on the part of the police defendants absent such a special relationship. They have thus failed to demonstrate that the trial court erred in denying leave to amend as to the police defendants. (See *Cooper* v. *Leslie Salt Co.* (1969) 70 Cal.2d 627, 636 [75 Cal.Rptr. 766, 451 P.2d 406]; *Filice* v. *Boccardo* (1962) 210 Cal. App.2d 843, 847 [26 Cal.Rptr. 789].)

Conclusion

For the reasons stated, we conclude that plaintiffs can amend their complaints to state a cause of action against defendant therapists by asserting that the therapists in fact determined that Poddar presented a serious danger of violence to Tatiana, or pursuant to the standards of their profession should have so determined, but nevertheless failed to exercise reasonable care to protect her from that danger. To the extent, however, that plaintiffs base their claim that defendant therapists breached that duty because they failed to procure Poddar's confinement, the therapists find immunity in Government Code section 856. Further, as to the police defendants we conclude that plaintiffs have failed to show that the trial court erred in sustaining their demurrer without leave to amend.

The judgment of the superior court in favor of defendants Atkinson, Beall, Brownrigg, Hallernan, and Teel is affirmed. The judgment of the superior court in favor of defendants Gold, Moore, Powelson, Yandell, and the Regents of the University of California is reversed, and the cause remanded for further proceedings consistent with the views expressed herein.

Mosk, J., Concurring and Dissenting. I concur in the result in this instance only because the complaints allege that defendant therapists did in fact predict that Poddar would kill and were therefore negligent in failing to warn of that danger. Thus the issue here is very narrow: we are not concerned with whether the therapists, pursuant to the standards of their profession, "should have" predicted potential violence; they allegedly did so in actuality. Under these limited circumstances I agree that a cause of action can be stated.

Whether plaintiffs can ultimately prevail is problematical at best. As the complaints admit, the therapists *did* notify the police that Poddar was planning to kill a girl identifiable as Tatiana. While I doubt that more should be required, this issue may be raised in defense and its determination is a question of fact.

I cannot concur, however, in the majority's rule that a therapist may be held liable for failing to predict his patient's tendency to violence if other practitioners, pursuant to the "standards of the profession," would have done so. The question is, what standards? Defendants and a responsible amicus curiae, supported by an impressive body of literature discussed at length in our recent opinion in *People* v. *Burnick* (1975) 14 Cal. 3d 306 [121 Cal. Rptr. 488, 535 P.2d 352], demonstrate that psychiatric predictions of violence are inherently unreliable.

In *Burnick*, at pages 325–326, we observed: "In the light of recent studies it is no longer heresy to question the reliability of psychiatric predictions. Psychiatrists themselves would be the first to admit that however desirable an infallible crystal ball might be, it is not among the tools of their profession. It must be conceded that psychiatrists still experience considerable difficulty in confidently and accurately *diagnosing* mental illness. Yet those difficulties are multiplied manyfold when psychiatrists venture from diagnosis to

prognosis and undertake to predict the consequences of such illness: "A diagnosis of mental illness tells us nothing about whether the person so diagnosed is or is not dangerous. Some mental patients are dangerous, some are not. Perhaps the psychiatrist is an expert at deciding whether a person is mentally ill, but is he an expert at predicting which of the persons so diagnosed are dangerous? Sane people, too, are dangerous, and it may legitimately be inquired whether there is anything in the education, training or experience of psychiatrists which renders them particularly adept at predicting dangerous behavior. Predictions of dangerous behavior, no matter who makes them, are incredibly inaccurate, and there is a growing consensus that psychiatrists are not uniquely qualified to predict dangerous behavior and are, in fact, less accurate in their predictions than other professionals." (*Murel v. Baltimore City Criminal Court* (1972) . . . 407 U.S. 355, 364–365, fn. 2 [32 L.Ed.2d 791, 796–797, 92 S.Ct. 2091] (Douglas, J., dissenting from dismissal of certiorari).)" (Fns. omitted.)

Obviously the two cases are not factually identical, but the similarity in issues is striking: in *Burnick* we were likewise called upon to appraise the ability of psychiatrists to predict dangerousness, and while we declined to bar all such testimony (id., at pp. 327–328) we found it so inherently untrustworthy that we would permit confinement even in a so-called civil proceeding only upon proof beyond a reasonable doubt.

I would restructure the rule designed by the majority to eliminate all reference to conformity to standards of the profession in predicting violence. If a psychiatrist does in fact predict violence, then a duty to warn arises. The majority's expansion of that rule will take us from the world of reality into the wonderland of clairvoyance.

Clark, J. Until today's majority opinion, both legal and medical authorities have agreed that confidentiality is essential to effectively treat the mentally ill, and that imposing a duty on doctors to disclose patient threats to potential victims would greatly impair treatment. Further, recognizing that effective treatment and society's safety are necessarily intertwined, the Legislature has already decided effective and confidential treatment is preferred over imposition of a duty to warn.

The issue whether effective treatment for the mentally ill should be sacrificed to a system of warnings is, in my opinion, properly one for the Legislature, and we are bound by its judgment. Moreover, even in the absence of clear legislative direction, we must reach the same conclusion because imposing the majority's new duty is certain to result in a net increase in violence.

The majority rejects the balance achieved by the Legislature's Lanterman-Petris-Short Act. (Welf. & Inst. Code, § 5000 et seq., hereafter the act.) In addition, the majority fails to recognize that, even absent the act, overwhelming policy considerations mandate against sacrificing fundamental patient interests without gaining a corresponding increase in public benefit.

Common Law Analysis

Entirely apart from the statutory provisions, the same result must be reached upon considering both general tort principles and the public policies favoring effective treatment, reduction of violence, and justified commitment.

Generally, a person owes no duty to control the conduct of another. (*Richards* v. *Stanley* (1954) 43 Cal.2d 60, 65 [271 P.2d 23]; *Wright* v. *Arcade School Dist.* (1964) 230 Cal.App.2d 272, 277 [40 Cal.Rptr. 812]; Rest.2d Torts (1965) § 315.) Exceptions are recognized only in limited situations where (1) a special relationship exists between the defendant and injured party, or (2) a special relationship exists between defendant and the active wrongdoer, imposing a duty on defendant to control the wrongdoer's conduct. The majority does not contend the first exception is appropriate to this case.

Policy generally determines duty. (*Dillon* v. *Legg* (1968) 68 Cal.2d 728, 734 [69 Cal.Rptr. 72,

441 P.2d 912, 29 A.L.R.3d 1316].) Principal policy considerations include foreseeability of harm, certainty of the plaintiff's injury, proximity of the defendant's conduct to the plaintiff's injury, moral blame attributable to defendant's conduct, prevention of future harm, burden on the defendant, and consequences to the community. (*Rowland* v. *Christian* (1968) 69 Cal.2d 108, 113 [70 Cal.Rptr. 97, 443 P.2d 561, 32 A.L.R.3d 496].)

Overwhelming policy considerations weigh against imposing a duty on psychotherapists to warn a potential victim against harm. While offering virtually no benefit to society, such a duty will frustrate psychiatric treatment, invade fundamental patient rights and increase violence.

The importance of psychiatric treatment and its need for confidentiality have been recognized by this court. (*In re Lifschutz* (1970) 2 Cal.3d 415, 421–422 [85 Cal.Rptr. 829, 467 P.2d 557, 44 A.L.R.3d 1].) "It is clearly recognized that the very practice of psychiatry vitally depends upon the reputation in the community that the psychiatrist will not tell." (Slovenko, *Psychiatry and a Second Look at the Medical Privilege* (1960) 6 Wayne L.Rev. 175, 188.)

Assurance of confidentiality is important for three reasons.

Deterrence from Treatment

First, without substantial assurance of confidentiality, those requiring treatment will be deterred from seeking assistance. (See Sen. Judiciary Com. comment accompanying § 1014 of Evid. Code; Slovenko, *supra,* 6 Wayne L.Rev. 175, 187–188; Goldstein & Katz, *Psychiatrist-Patient Privilege: The GAP Proposal and the Connecticut Statute* (1962) 36 Conn.Bar J. 175, 178.) It remains an unfortunate fact in our society that people seeking psychiatric guidance tend to become stigmatized. Apprehension of such stigma—apparently increased by the propensity of people considering treatment to see themselves in the worst possible light—creates a well-recognized reluctance to seek aid. (Fisher, *The Psychotherapeutic Professions and the Law of Privileged Communications* (1964) 10 Wayne L.Rev. 609, 617; Slovenko, *supra*, 6 Wayne L.Rev. 175, 188; see also Rappeport, *Psychiatrist-Patient Privilege* (1963) 23 Md.L.J. 39, 46–47.) This reluctance is alleviated by the psychiatrist's assurance of confidentiality.

Full Disclosure

Second, the guarantee of confidentiality is essential in eliciting the full disclosure necessary for effective treatment. (*In re Lifschutz, supra*, 2 Cal.3d 415, 431.) The psychiatric patient approaches treatment with conscious and unconscious inhibitions against revealing his innermost thoughts. "Every person, however well-motivated, has to overcome resistances to therapeutic exploration. These resistances seek support from every possible source and the possibility of disclosure would easily be employed in the service of resistance." (Goldstein & Katz, *supra*, 36 Conn. Bar J. 175, 179.) Until a patient can trust his psychiatrist not to violate their confidential relationship, "the unconscious psychological control mechanism of repression will prevent the recall of past experiences." (Butler, *Psychotherapy and Griswold: Is Confidentiality a Privilege or a Right?* (1971) 3 Conn.L.Rev. 599, 604.)

Successful Treatment

Third, even if the patient fully discloses his thoughts, assurance that the confidential relationship will not be breached is necessary to maintain his trust in his psychiatrist—the very means by which treatment is effected. "[The] essence of much psychotherapy is the contribution of trust in the external world and ultimately in the self, modelled upon the trusting relationship established during therapy." (Dawidoff, *The Malpractice of Psychiatrists*, 1966 Duke L.J. 696, 704.) Patients will be helped only if they can form a trusting relationship with the psychiatrist. (*Id.*,

at p. 704, fn. 34; Burham, *Separation Anxiety* (1965) 13 Arch.Gen.Psych. 346, 356; Heller, *supra*, 30 Temp.L.Q. 401, 406.) All authorities appear to agree that if the trust relationship cannot be developed because of collusive communication between the psychiatrist and others, treatment will be frustrated. (See, e.g., Slovenko (1973) Psychiatry and Law, p. 61; Cross, *Privileged Communications Between Participants in Group Psychotherapy* (1970) Law & Soc. Order, 191, 199; Hollender, *The Psychiatrist and the Release of Patient Information* (1960) 116 Am.J.Psych. 828, 829.)

Given the importance of confidentiality to the practice of psychiatry, it becomes clear the duty to warn imposed by the majority will cripple the use and effectiveness of psychiatry. Many people, potentially violent—yet susceptible to treatment—will be deterred from seeking it; those seeking it will be inhibited from making revelations necessary to effective treatment; and, forcing the psychiatrist to violate the patient's trust will destroy the interpersonal relationship by which treatment is effected.

Violence and Civil Commitment

By imposing a duty to warn, the majority contributes to the danger to society of violence by the mentally ill and greatly increases the risk of civil commitment—the total deprivation of liberty—of those who should not be confined. The impairment of treatment and risk of improper commitment resulting from the new duty to warn will not be limited to a few patients but will extend to a large number of the mentally ill. Although under existing psychiatric procedures only a relatively few receiving treatment will ever present a risk of violence, the number making threats is huge, and it is the latter group—not just the former—whose treatment will be impaired and whose risk of commitment will be increased.

Both the legal and psychiatric communities recognize that the process of determining potential violence in a patient is far from exact, being fraught with complexity and uncertainty. (E.g.,

People v. *Burnick* (1975) 14 Cal.3d 306, 326 [121 Cal.Rptr. 488, 535 p.2d 352].) In fact, precision has not even been attained in predicting who of those having already committed violent acts will again become violent, a task recognized to be of much simpler proportions. (Kozol, Boucher & Garofalo, *supra,* 18 Crime & Delinq. 371, 384.)

This predictive uncertainty means that the number of disclosures will necessarily be large. As noted above, psychiatric patients are encouraged to discuss all thoughts of violence, and they often express such thoughts. However, unlike this court, the psychiatrist does not enjoy the benefit of overwhelming hindsight in seeing which few, if any, of his patients will ultimately become violent. Now, confronted by the majority's new duty, the psychiatrist must instantaneously calculate potential violence from each patient on each visit. The difficulties researchers have encountered in accurately predicting violence will be heightened for the practicing psychiatrist dealing for brief periods in his office with heretofore nonviolent patients. And, given the decision not to warn or commit must always be made at the psychiatrist's civil peril, one can expect most doubts will be resolved in favor of the psychiatrist protecting himself.

Neither alternative open to the psychiatrist seeking to protect himself is in the public interest. The warning itself is an impairment of the psychiatrist's ability to treat, depriving many patients of adequate treatment. It is to be expected that after disclosing their threats, a significant number of patients, who would not become violent if treated according to existing practices, will engage in violent conduct as a result of unsuccessful treatment. In short, the majority's duty to warn will not only impair treatment of many who would never become violent but worse, will result in a net increase in violence.

The second alternative open to the psychiatrist is to commit his patient rather than to warn. Even in the absence of threat of civil liability, the doubts of psychiatrists as to the seriousness of patient threats have led psychiatrists to overcommit to mental institutions. This overcommitment has been authoritatively documented in both legal and psychiatric studies. (Ennis & Litwack, *Psychiatry and the Presumption of Expertise: Flipping Coins in the Courtroom, supra,* 62 Cal.L.Rev. 693, 711 et seq.) This practice is so prevalent that it has been estimated that "as many as twenty harmless persons are incarcerated for every one who will commit a violent act." (Steadman & Cocozza, *Stimulus/Response: We Can't Predict Who Is Dangerous* (Jan. 1975) 8 Psych. Today 32, 35.)

Given the incentive to commit created by the majority's duty, this already serious situation will be worsened, contrary to Chief Justice Wright's admonition "that liberty is no less precious because forfeited in a civil proceeding than when taken as a consequence of a criminal conviction." (*In re Gary W.* (1971) 5 Cal.3d 296, 307 [96 Cal.Rptr. 1, 486 p.2d 1201].)

Conclusion

In adopting the act, the Legislature fully recognized the concerns that must govern our decision today—adequate treatment for the mentally ill, safety of our society, and our devotion to individual liberty, making overcommitment of the mentally ill abhorrent. (§ 5001.) Again, the Legislature balanced these concerns in favor of nondisclosure (§ 5328), thereby promoting effective treatment, reducing temptation for overcommitment, and ensuring greater safety for our society. Psychiatric and legal expertise on the subject requires the same judgment.

The tragedy of Tatiana Tarasoff has led the majority to disregard the clear legislative mandate of the Lanterman-Petris-Short Act. Worse, the majority impedes medical treatment, resulting in increased violence from—and deprivation of liberty to—the mentally ill.

We should accept legislative and medical judgment, relying upon effective treatment rather than on indiscriminate warning.

The judgment should be affirmed.

D. The Physician-Patient Relationship in the Era of Managed Care

The doctor-patient relationship is in the midst of change primarily because of the shift from fee-for-service reimbursement to managed medical care (Chapter 2). Managed care can be defined in a number of ways. Most importantly for our purposes, it is a reimbursement mechanism that shifts the management of care from the physician and patient to physician and third party payer (insurer). When care is managed, the insurer plays a more active role in determining what care patients will receive, where it will be done, who will do it, and what they are willing to pay for it. Managed care organizations use a number of cost-containment mechanisms to achieve cost-effective care, including some that affect the doctor-patient relationship by shifting the financial risk of patient care from the insurer to the physician.

Many cost containment mechanisms, such as the use of gatekeeper physicians (primary care physicians who control patient access to resources) and capitation (fixed monthly payment to physicians for plan members), have an impact on how physicians can care for patients. Susan Dorr Goold explains that whether or not a reimbursement mechanism adversely affects the doctor-patient relationship depends on the context and the amount of money at issue. According to Dorr Goold, "The intrusiveness of incentives for physicians depends both on the size and strength of the incentives, that is on what percentage of income and what dollar amount is 'at risk' (and how important that amount is to the physician), and on its linkage to individual patient decisions—how much a physician could lose in a single decision."[32]

When faced with aggressive managed care cost-containment mechanisms, many physicians have opted to advocate for their patients by manipulating reimbursement rules. Matthew Wynia et al found that roughly 40 percent of physicians deceive third party payers in order to access benefits for their patients.[33] Others have speculated that this deception is fueled by physician desires to meet their fiduciary obligations.[34] Still others have given some anecdotal evidence that physicians may "withhold the truth about rationing from patients."[35]

The problem raised by many managed care cost-containment mechanisms is that they put physicians in a classic conflict of interest situation by compensating them when they withhold beneficial treatment from patients. (Of course, fee-for-service reimbursement systems may create the opposite conflict, giving physicians an incentive to provide unnecessary treatments.) This conflict cannot only adversely affect patient care but can hurt the relationship between doctor and patient. Given what we know about trust, patients appear to need to believe that their physicians will act only in their interest in order to trust their physicians. According to Mechanic and Meyer, "Most patients regardless of their health insurance arrangements, want to believe that their interests are primary and that their doctors would do everything possible to serve them as needed. Commitment to the patient and patient advocacy are common themes in patients' concepts of trust."[36] The concern about managed care is that once patients recognize that their health care providers have obligations and interests that are inconsistent with their welfare, they will no longer be able to trust them. According to Mechanic and Schlesinger, "Patients' trust depends on their perceptions that physicians are free to act in their best interest."[37] Honesty and candor are also important for the cultivation of trust. Thus deception of the kind observed by Wynia and colleagues can put trust between doctor and patient at risk. In her paper, *Bluffing, Puffing, and Spinning in Managed-Care Organizations,* Patricia Illingworth argues that managed care organizations, like other business organizations, have a "caveat emptor" approach to truth-telling. She argues that such an approach is unethical in the medical context, which should be governed by the higher ethics of fiduciaries. Moreover, Illingworth argues that a climate of deception within managed-care medicine may have the unfortunate result of leading to patient deception, which would undermine physicians' ability to make timely and accurate diagnoses. In this way, it threatens to hurt patients' physical well-being.

Others have argued that although a successful relationship between doctor and patient requires trust (see Section A of this chapter), trust is inconsistent with patient knowledge of managed care incentives. Hence, patient trust in physicians can be preserved only if we refrain from disclosing the nature of the incentives to patients. For example, David Mechanic argues for implicit rationing—that is rationing that is insulated from both patient and public view.[38] Surely given the importance placed on patient autonomy and self-determination, we must ask if it is ethical to keep such rationing from patients. Can patients be self-determining if they do not know that they will be denied some beneficial care because of economic considerations?

In practice, it is difficult for many people to believe that patients really do consent to the health plans that they are enrolled in, not only because most Americans purchase their health plans from their employers, who typically offer but one plan, but also because adequate information about the terms of plans is not always available. Moreover, it is not clear in the present world of managed care that plan members and their physicians can really be confident that money not spent on their care will be spent for other patients or other morally important goods. In the article included in the readings, Norman G. Levinsky writes, "It certainly is not self-evident that resources saved by limiting health care will be allocated to other equally worthy programs, such as preventive medicine, health maintenance, or improved nutrition and housing for the needy." He also worries that given the nature of medical decision making, anything other than patient advocacy will lead to additional ethical problems, such as discrimination against the elderly. Levinsky concludes that the doctor's master must continue to be the patient. Thus, he advocates for the professional values that we discussed in Section A of this chapter. Yet, perhaps as Paris and Post argue, within the current health care landscape individual patients in managed care plans must use their moral imaginations to "leap" beyond their own interests narrowly construed to the interest of all plan participants. This is part of what is involved in being a member of a moral community and considering the "common good." Do you think this argument is convincing even with respect to for-profit managed care organizations? Are the interests of populations being served or those of corporate shareholders?

Bluffing, Puffing and Spinning in Managed-Care Organizations

PATRICIA ILLINGWORTH

I. Introduction

Physicians lying to patients, patients lying to physicians, both lying to managed care organizations (MCOs) and MCOs lying to them. Can medical care be delivered in this context? Many people believe that business organizations endorse a model of truth-telling different from the one used in other contexts, and perhaps different from the one that exists in medicine. According to some scholars, bluffing and puffing are commonplace in business and are thought to be morally sound.

The question of whether or not MCOs and the physicians who are contractually associated with them have a duty to tell the truth has been raised directly by those concerned with whether physicians must give patients information about rationing decisions (Levinsky, 1998) and, indirectly, by those who question the legal and ethical legitimacy of gag clauses (Martin and Bjerknes, 1996; Hall, 1993). Answers to these questions are important not only for what they tell us about the duties of MCOs and physicians (to bluff or not), but also for their ability to tell us whether patients will also have to lie to get fair access to care. If duties of veracity are not strictly adhered to by MCOs and the physicians who contract with them, then patients are likely to become increasingly savvy consumers of health-care and begin to do likewise. As a matter of fact, recent media suggests that patients are arming themselves to do just that ('Health and medicine: A special report,' 1998). Little attention has yet been

paid to the question of whether patients have a duty to tell the truth and whether it is even desirable to encourage them to do so in a context in which MCOs and providers routinely deceive others.[1] Although regulation can be imposed on MCOs and providers, for example, to prohibit the use of gag orders and disclose financial incentives, these measures will have limited success if the underlying ethic in the health care system is one in which bluffing, puffing and spinning dominate.

Those who advocate the privatization of medicine, including the emphasis on profit maximization, must reckon with the likelihood that if the ethic of bluffing secures a foothold in medicine, as it apparently has in the wider business world, it is likely to do so in ways other than with respect to the rationing decisions of physicians and MCOs. Rationing decisions are rarely discussed directly in the doctor-patient relationship. Instead, they are veiled from the patient (Levinsky, 1998). In this way the ethic of bluffing, often associated with business, insinuates itself into medicine. If the ethic of bluffing and puffing permeates the organizational side of managed-care medicine, physicians and patients will be forced to make use of the same ethic. What is less clear, however, is that each of these constituencies stands to gain and lose the same with respect to their use of bluffing. Truth probably serves different functions in medicine and business such that although it can arguably be sacrificed in one, it cannot be sacrificed in the other. In this essay, I adopt the warranty theory of truth and argue that MCOs and physicians have warranted truth. Thus when they deceive subscribers/patients, they do so wrongly. I also argue that in the presence of widespread deception, it is likely that patients will lie and that when they do, they put their health at risk. Thus deception in managed-medical care is morally wrong because it violates the ethics of organizations and the ethics of medicine.

II. Bluffing and the Warranty Theory of Truth

Deception has a variety of faces, which we value differently depending on factors such as the intent of the speaker, context, and subject matter. "Bluffing," "puffing" and "spinning" are terms that we use on a daily basis and thus they have an ordinary-language meaning. They are also terms of art. "Puffing" is a quasi-legal term, which has to do with sellers embellishing the qualities of their products (*Black's Law Dictionary*, 1990). When a salesperson proclaims "This is the best four-wheel drive on the market" he is puffing and not making a statement of fact. "Bluffing" as I use it here is based in the field of business ethics, where it is used loosely to refer to deception that occurs in a context in which the parties have consented to have the usual guarantee of truth lifted. For example, in real estate negotiations, the seller may stipulate an unreasonably high asking price knowing full well that, in this way, and following negotiation, he will get the price he wants and expects, though is unwilling to reveal to the buyer. By withholding information he is able to maintain the illusion that he will not budge from his asking price. "Spin," a term used in public relations, refers to putting a positive light on something which is potentially damaging to an organization (Ewen, 1996). But spin occurs in everyday contexts as well. When an investment goes sour, stockbrokers, accountants and other "spin doctors" are quick to highlight the tax advantages. In what follows, I will primarily focus on bluffing as it appears in the business-ethics literature. Although perhaps counter-intuitively, I will use the term "deception" as a morally neutral term to refer to the different ways people refrain from telling the truth.

Deception is more widespread than many of us would like to acknowledge. Thus it was not surprising when President Clinton acknowledged that while under oath he made misleading, though perhaps legally accurate, statements about his relationship with Ms. Lewinsky. Although many people were simply angry or disappointed with the President, others also acknowledged that sex is a subject about which people lie (*The New York Times*, 1998). And still others believed that although people regularly lie about sex, they ought not to do so while under oath—that is, after they have warranted truth-telling. Business, like politics, is a context in which the rules about truth telling are more relaxed and the primary oath is that of *caveat emptor*. Thus context is important for how we value a bit of deception. Although not unheard of, someone who lies in the confessional still inspires puzzlement. Yet a similar response might be forthcoming when someone tells the truth while in the midst of negotiation with a used-car salesman.

Not atypical is Albert Carr, who supports the view that bluffing in business is ethical. He begins his defense of bluffing with a quotation from Henry Taylor, "falsehood ceases to be falsehood when it is understood on all sides that the truth is not expected" (Carr, 1997, p. 451). Carr believes that this is an accurate description of bluffing in poker, diplomacy and business (Carr, 1997). He gives the following account of his view of business bluffing:

> Most executives . . . are almost compelled, in the interests of their companies or themselves, to practice some form of deception when negotiating with customers, dealers, labor unions, government officials, or even other departments of their companies. By conscious misstatements, concealment of perti-

nent facts, or exaggeration—in short, by bluffing—they seek to persuade others to agree with them. I think it is fair to say that if the individual executive refuses to bluff from time to time—if he feels obligated to tell the truth, the whole truth and nothing but the truth—he is ignoring opportunities permitted under the rules and is at a heavy disadvantage in his business dealings (Carr, 1997, p. 451).

So bluffing is a fact of business life and business people would be at a disadvantage were they unable to bluff (Horowitz, 1981). It is ethical, according to Carr, because no one expects otherwise. "The game calls for distrust of the other fellow. It ignores the claim of friendship. Cunning deceptions and concealment of one's strength and intentions, not kindness and open-heartedness, are vital in poker" (Carr, 1997, p. 451). Just as people do not judge the game of poker badly when it uses its own special brand of ethics, so they should not judge business badly for its unique brand of ethics. Thus for Carr bluffing in business is morally neutral.

Thomas Carson, another business ethicist, compares business bluffing to negotiations when it is to the advantage of negotiators not to reveal their minimum bargaining position (Carson, 1997). He suggests a new definition of "lying" which I call the "warranty theory of truth." It goes as follows: "A lie is a false statement which the 'speaker' does not believe to be true made in a context in which the speaker warrants the truth of what he says" (Carson, 1997, p. 458). Carson summarizes his view in the following way. "To lie . . . is to invite trust and encourage others to believe what one says by warranting the truth of what one says and at the same time to betray that trust by making false statements which one does not believe to be true . . ." (Carson, 1997, p. 458). And according to Paul Ekman, "It is not just the liar that must be considered in defining a lie, but the liar's target as well. In a lie the target has not asked to be misled, nor has the liar given any prior notification of an intention to do so" (Ekman, 1992, p. 27).

At the heart of this view is the idea that if truth is not warranted, then it is not expected. If people are on notice that a particular context is one in which the commitment to truth telling has been relaxed, yet they nonetheless participate, then they consent. In Ekman's words they authorize the deception. This authorization transforms lying into mere bluffing and, in this way, takes the moral sting out of it. Thus consent is the relevant moral notion here. One of the implications of promising to tell the truth is that one thereby encourages others to do likewise, to tell the initial speaker the truth. Promises of truth-telling create a context in which the truth can be told. In view of this, people who promise to tell the truth and then renege on their promise, by lying, will nonetheless enjoy the truth-telling their promise has encouraged. They are free riders of a sort. But just as promising to tell the truth gives rise to truth-telling, so habitual failure to tell the truth achieves the opposite. Sometimes the promise or warranty is not explicit but implicit in the context. Thus in an intimate relationship if one party generally tells the truth, it is a betrayal of trust for the other party to lie.

III. Deception by Managed Care Organizations: Business as Usual

Bluffing, puffing and spinning play a pivotal role in corporate life and thus they have a presence in MCOs. Annual and quarterly reports that are required to meet security regulations are carefully designed to underplay corporate weaknesses and to highlight corporate strengths while at the same time meeting SEC disclosure requirements. Advertisements make frequent use of puffing. Until recently, MCOs subscribed to the use of gag orders in their contracts with providers—devices that certainly had the consequence of obfuscating the truth. Today, although there are not explicit gag clauses, MCOs undertake practices such as economic credentialing of health providers and capitation which create the likelihood of physicians feeling compelled to practice in a gagged manner by avoiding high-cost medical treatment alternatives with uninformed patients (Levinsky, 1998).

MCOs indirectly interfere with their subscribers securing information by, for example, reducing the amount of reimbursable time physicians have with their patients. But MCOs also manipulate information with respect to the grounds they use when they refuse treatment to patients. Treatment is usually denied on the basis that it is (1) not covered, (2) medically unnecessary, and/or (3) experimental. Mark Hiepler, a plaintiff's attorney in MCO cases, says of HMOs, "They do not want to specifically exclude anything, so they put in words like 'experimental' or 'investigational' or 'medically necessary' that have no meaning, and can't be defined, to provide a label for anything they don't want to pay for" (Reuben, 1996, p. 55).

One reason MCOs may not want to specifically exclude anything is because doing so would lend itself to comparison with other MCOs and this, in turn, to informed shopping. For example, reasonable people, especially in the early days of managed care, would not have assumed that "medically necessary" care was a term of exclusion (Mariner, 1995). Terms such as "medically necessary" and "experimental" are notoriously vague and open to interpretation. Vague terms are problematic because they fail to give notice and place too much discretion in the hands of those who decide if the requisite conditions exist to satisfy them. Using vague language of this kind allows MCOs to put a positive spin on the practice of denying benefits.

MCOs use puffing techniques in their advertisements. Like most corporations, MCOs try to persuade consumers to purchase their services through promotional materials. To this end, they represent themselves as patient-centered, as home to excellent and caring physicians, and as providers of the right care at the right time. Some important common law is developing in which

the action lies in misrepresentation and breach of warranty by the MCO. In these cases MCOs make misrepresentations in their advertisements to their subscribers about the quality of their services, or their primary goals in delivering services (e.g., profit vs. care).[2] Although the courts distinguish between mere puffing, which is permissible, and misrepresentation, which is impermissible, both are probably forms of deception.[3] There is, then, extensive evidence that MCOs, like other business organizations, employ deceptive mechanisms, such as puffing and spinning, on a regular basis.

IV. Physician Deception

Physicians who work with MCOs must, on the one hand, meet their fiduciary duties to patients, and, on the other hand, meet their contractual duties to MCOs. Specifically, they have fiduciary duties to provide materially beneficial care, yet, for example, they may have a contractual duty to follow cost-driven, managed-care practice guidelines. One way for them to try to deal with this conflict in duties is to deceive both patients and MCOs. Haavi Morreim has discussed the possibility of physicians gaming the system at some length (Morreim, 1995). According to her, gaming occurs when physicians attempt ". . . to bypass the rules while still appearing to honor them and thereby to secure resources that were not . . . intended for this patient" (Morreim, 1995, p. 70). Thus gaming is an indirect way to access resources.

Physicians who game the MCO can exaggerate the seriousness of a patient's condition to rationalize the ordering of tests or, gain a clinically indicated, but otherwise MCO-considered not "medically necessary" hospital admission. Diagnostic uncertainty is another way that the physician can deceive MCOs. Physicians can specify that tests are being ordered to rule out an illness instead of as part of a routine screening in a plan that pays for the former but not the latter. In this way, they put the most favorable-to-the-patient spin on the test. From the perspective of the marketplace, this kind of exaggeration may qualify as mere puffing of the patient's condition. Norman Levinsky believes that many decisions to ration patient care are surreptitiously motivated by the self-interested desires of hospital administrators and physicians in collaboration with third-party payers to maintain patient numbers and physician incomes (Levinsky, 1998).

There is good evidence that physicians are willing to use deception. In a recent survey undertaken by Victor G. Freeman, seventy percent of physicians surveyed by Georgetown University Medical Center indicated that they would condone lying to an insurer. According to the results of the survey, the sanctioning of dishonesty was proportionately greater in areas with higher rates of managed care ('Liar, liar: The Pinocchio dilemma,' 1997). This confirms earlier research undertaken by Novack et al., which showed that physicians are willing to lie especially when confronted with conflicting moral values or threats to patient confidentiality and to a third party to benefit patients (Novack et al., 1998).

In the past, prior to managed care, physicians were often suspected of beneficent deception with patients; they kept information from patients about the seriousness of their illness for the sake of the patient (Spire, 1998). Physicians can deceive patients through willful blindness about their specific health benefits, resulting in refusal to refer them to costly specialists and limiting patient choice of providers even beyond that already limited by the MCO. They can also obscure the financial incentives they are working under.

V. Warranting the Truth

According to the warranty theory of truth, people do not lie unless they make a false statement, which they know to be false in a context in which they have warranted to tell the truth. Thus in order to determine whether the deception of physicians and MCOs qualifies as mere bluffing or as lying, we need to ask if physicians and MCOs have warranted the truth. If they have warranted the truth, yet fail to tell the truth, then their deception will count as lying.

As fiduciaries, physicians are under duties of trust with respect to patients. Although they don't say, "I do hereby warrant truth," an implicit warranty can be inferred on the basis of contextual clues. Fiduciary law has been applied to physicians with respect to a number of duties, among which is the duty to obtain informed consent (Rodwin, 1993). In addition, the court in *Moore v. the Regents of the University of California* (1990) recognized that connected with the fiduciary duty to obtain informed consent is a duty to disclose any personal interest unrelated to the patient's health, such as research and economic interests that may affect the physician's judgment. And in *Wickline v. State of California* (1986), an important managed-care case, the court said that given a physician's fiduciary duty to patients, the physician must give priority to the patient's needs over the needs of others, including the physician him- or herself. In view of these fiduciary duties, and the implicit warranty of truth telling that can be inferred from them, physicians who deceive patients, perhaps about rationing decisions, would qualify as having lied even on the warranty theory's relaxed notion of what it is to lie. An argument can also be made that MCOs have warranted the truth to subscribers.

MCOs that secure their subscribers through employers appear to have warranted truth because of the Employee Retirement Income Security Act (ERISA). More generally, they warrant truth through their close association with physicians who are, themselves, fiduciaries (ERISA, 1974). As organizations that provide health care in addition to insurance, and primarily through physicians, who are fiduciaries, MCOs may have, in the eyes of patients, assumed some of the same fiduciary duties as physicians. Moreover, some MCOs will qualify as fiduciaries under ERISA (ERISA, 1974, Section 3(21)(A), Section 1002(21)(A)). ERISA imposes a number of duties of fiduciaries, including a duty to refrain from making materially false or misleading statements to plan participants (*Varity Corp. v. Howe,* 1996). In one case, an MCO was held to have violated its ERISA fiduciary duties because it had made certain misleading statements about physician incentives (*Drolet v. Healthsource,* 1997). Whether or not an MCO will be found to be an ERISA fiduciary depends largely on the extent of discretionary power and control they exercise.[4] ERISA fiduciaries must discharge their duties "solely in the interest of the participants and beneficiaries" (ERISA, 1974, Section 404(a)(1)).

MCOs use promotional materials that promise subscribers wonderful health-care with a trusting, caring physician. In these materials, MCOs highlight their association with physicians, who have traditionally been trusted by patients, and thus piggyback on that trust. Needless to say, these advertisements never mention the MCOs' goal of profit maximization. Subscribers who receive their health care through their employment may also transfer to their MCO the trust they have for their employer. Moreover, employers who provide their employees with health plans through self-insured mechanisms may also incur certain ERISA-based fiduciary obligations to their employees.

Together these activities portray MCOs as having warranted truth. A strong case can be made that both MCOs and physicians have warranted the truth. Thus, according to the warranty theory of truth, when they use deception they do so unethically; they lie. Lying is wrong here because it violates the warranty theory of truth, and it creates a context in which the truth cannot be told. If MCOs and physicians lie to each other and to patients, they create a climate in which patients have little choice but to lie as well. Fostering patient deception in this way compounds the wrong inherent in violating the warranty theory of truth.

VI. Patient Deception: Damned if They Do, Damned if They Don't

There is widespread evidence that under managed care, patients are more active and better-prepared consumers of their medical care than they were in the past. It is also clear that patients have lower levels of trust for physicians who are associated with capitated reimbursement mechanisms (Kao *et al.*, 1998) and they are gathering information that could be useful for deceiving their physicians and MCOs ('Health and medicine: A special report,' 1998). Patients can be deceptive about their symptoms. They can malinger—i.e., pretend to have symptoms that they do not have—with an eye to securing referrals to specialists or expensive tests and medications. They can exaggerate and distort the seriousness of their condition with the same end in mind or trump up symptoms (chest pain, headaches, etc.).

In order for patients to deceive effectively, they need to know enough about symptoms, diagnosis and treatments to make their deception plausible. According to a *New York Times* article, "[w]ith the rise of managed care, patients have become increasingly distrustful of their doctors, and so they are busily arming themselves with information from newspapers, books, the Internet. . ." (Stolberg, 1997, p. E3). This article does not specify whether patients are arming themselves in order to critically evaluate their doctors' orders or in order to deceive them. Both are consistent with the effort of patients to gather information. David Rothman states that ". . . [N]o trend has promoted patient activism as much as managed care. Now a loss of trust has turned into acute suspicion, because you're no longer certain whether your physician is interested in your well being, or his reimbursement schedule. Better educated is better prepared and will be better served" (Stolberg, 1997, p. E3).

Patient activism has been facilitated by recent changes to the rules governing the advertising of drugs directly to the consumer of those drugs, the patient. In August 1997, the Food and Drug Administration liberalized its guidelines for direct-to-consumer advertising for drugs to permit television advertising. This makes it easier for pharmaceutical companies to target patients directly and, in turn, supplements patients' information about drugs. This advertising is credited with increasing pharmaceutical sales and with driving patients to the doctor's office with unrealistic expectations and a desire for expensive drugs (Tanouye, 1998).

The Internet has proven to be a valuable source of information for patients. According to a recent survey conducted by both the Institute for the Future and Princeton Survey Research Associates, roughly two-thirds of the people who use the Web do so to obtain medical information and referrals (Hafner, 1998). In a poll of physicians, 67 percent of those surveyed said that patients came in with information they had found on the Web (Gediman and Lieberman, 1996). Although many physicians are skeptical about the validity of the information patients obtain from the Internet, many also recognize that patients are better informed about some illnesses than are some treating physicians. Physicians, for example, must have general knowledge about hundreds of different diseases and conditions while patients become specialists about the condition they have (Gediman and Lieberman, 1996). Clearly, there is a revolution toward a new kind of patient activism, egged on by managed care.

At most, this establishes that some patients have the wherewithal to deceive their physicians. That is, they have the informational savvy to deceive them if they decide to and sufficient distrust to increase the likelihood that they will do so. Psychiatrists are familiar with the many different ways in which patients deceive their physicians. Munchausen syndrome, malingering and imposters are illustrative of the kinds of patient deception they encounter (Gediman and Lieberman, 1996). In a recent report in *The Journal of the American Medical Association* it was noted that on-line support groups have proven to be a haven for people who pretend to have an illness in order to secure sympathy and nurturing (Stephenson, 1998). Moreover, the report underscores that on-line information ". . . makes it easy for people faking an illness to get details about their supposed condition" (Stephenson, 1998, p. 1297). Although it isn't clear from the report whether or not the Internet has brought with it more patient deception, it does explicitly say that it is easier for patients to lie now than in the past. The crux of the problem is that as the fiduciary component of the doctor-patient relationship is eroded and transformed by the ethics of "business as usual," we can expect the behavior of patients to change accordingly.

Patients are probably in the least strategically good position to deceive their providers because when they do they undermine their own care. Prior to the advent of managed care, one would assume that patients had little incentive to lie outside of the forensic context, where, for example, what they say to a physician employed as an expert witness could be used against them in a court of law. Typically, patients could trust their physicians and it was in their interest to tell the truth for purposes of accurate diagnosis and treatment. Managed medical care, however, seems to have collapsed the distinction between medicine and forensic medicine. Today many patients trust neither their physicians (Stolberg, 1997) nor their MCOs (Mechanic, 1996), and they especially do not trust them with respect to information over which they are already anxious, namely, information about their health. Among the justifications that can be given for lying, having been lied to stands out as common and persuasive (Bok, 1978). Psychologically there is an easing of standards of truthfulness once people have been lied to, such that they have fewer reservations about lying. Morally, rightly or wrongly, once people have been lied to they may invoke the principle of a lie for a lie (Bok, 1978). Thus, the presence of puffing and spinning in the managed-care context serves as an invitation to patients to lie.

Consider deception from the perspective of patients. Patients who refuse to deceive their physicians and MCOs may have to pay for medical services that they would not have had to pay for if they had successfully deceived their physicians. Many patients cannot afford to pay out of pocket for these services, and thus they will have to do without them. Thus, if these patients don't deceive their physicians they put their health at risk. This, no doubt, increases the likelihood that in the present context they will turn to deceptive mechanisms. Patients may believe that they will increase their chances of securing medical care if they deceive their physicians. It is difficult, if not impossible in some cases, for physicians to make accurate and timely diagnoses when patients deceive them about symptoms, etc. Thus patients find themselves trapped between the proverbial rock and hard place—damned if they do and damned if they don't. From their point of view, they may have nothing to gain from truth telling, but something to gain from deception.

David Mechanic has discussed some of the losses to patients when there is a breakdown in trust. Trust ensures a high quality of communication between doctor and patient. This, in turn, makes it more likely that patients will discuss personal information about stigmatized conditions, cooperate with treatment and adopt health-promoting behavior (Mechanic, 1996). Norman Levinsky, in a discussion about deceiving patients about rationing decisions, points out that patients are thereby deprived of the right to contest the decision to ration care in their own case— and as a social policy. Patients have too much to lose through deception. Finally, patients may be too sick to deceive effectively. Successful deception requires a good memory. Many illnesses involve memory impairment. Deception requires a level of effort that many very sick patients may not have. When physicians and MCOs lie, they increase the likelihood that patients will lie. But when patients lie they put their health at risk. Arguably, then, the presence of deception in MCOs puts patients at increased risk of harm.

VII. *Assumption of the Risk*

It might be argued that since patients engage in deception themselves, they are in no position to object to the harms that befall them. In other words, although patients are harmed, they assume the risk associated with their own deception. But assumption of the risk requires that patients voluntarily assume the risk. Patients don't choose to be sick and they often don't have much choice about their health-care plans. From the perspective of patients, they stand to lose their health, and even their lives, if they do not deceive their providers. Moreover, the presence of a context in which deception is widespread increases the likelihood that patients will deceive their physicians and in this way undermine their own care. Given these conditions, it would be difficult to construe either patient deception as voluntarily engaged in, or the harms associated with it as voluntarily assumed.

It will be difficult to decrease the incidence of deception and to reinstate an atmosphere of mutual trust. Business ethicists like Carr and Carson believe that bluffing is widespread in business. Like other business organizations. MCOs make liberal use of deceptive mechanisms. Unlike other business organizations, however, they do so in a context that has a long fiduciary history, in which the main participants do not anticipate deception and cannot in any case consent to the deception. Physicians are under pressure to lie. And it is clear that many patients do not trust MCOs. In view of the widespread distrust in managed care organizations, it is reasonable to expect that lying will continue.

Nonetheless, the fact that it continues and even increases does not make it ethically desirable. Thus a lie is a lie and not a bluff.

The warranty theory of truth may be right on target when it asserts that one needs to have warranted truth in order for some falsehood to count as a lie. In this way, the theory highlights the moral significance of context. Medical care depends on patients telling the truth and what the warranty theory makes vivid is that it is difficult for patients to tell the truth when other significant constituencies lie. It might be argued that patients have self-interested reasons to tell the truth—namely, their health. But in the world of managed medical care many patients cannot rely on their health plans, or unfortunately their physicians, to be forthcoming with the necessary resources. Hence apparent self-interest may direct them to deceive their providers.

I take this to be a significant argument against the general view that health care should be treated solely as a business and, specifically, against managed medical care, which too often reduces medicine to profit considerations. If deception is endemic to business and, as I have speculated, widespread within MCOs, but cannot be justified even on the warranty theory's relaxed conception of deception, then this is an argument against managed medical care because the latter cultivates a climate in which deception is rampant. It follows from my analysis that if we accept the warranty theory of truth and assume that MCOs and physicians have warranted the truth, then their deception would be unethical because they have promised to do otherwise. I also showed that deception is unethical because of the indirect harm it causes patients. Healthcare is a necessity and patients have little choice over how it is delivered. As organizational ethicists work at constructing ethics codes for healthcare organizations, they need to keep in mind that both the spoken and unspoken values of a system need to be challenged. Bluffing, puffing and spinning are an accepted part of business and they may well be an inevitable part of managed medical care.

Notes

1. Although Martin Benjamin's work is useful on questions concerning the foundation of patients' obligations to their physicians, it speaks only briefly to the question that concerns this paper—having to do with what patients ought to do when medical professionals and providers engage in deception. Benjamin's position is consistent with contract law, namely, that breach of obligation by one party releases the other party from having to meet their obligations. See Benjamin, 1985.

2. See *McClellan v. Health Maintenance Org. of Pennsylvania*, 1992, finding ostensible agency based on advertisements by the HMO and claiming that it carefully screened primary care physicians.

3. This point underscores the crux of the problem. Puffing is an acceptable and legally permissible part of business. Yet in the medical context it is highly problematic in part because this context has a long tradition of fiduciary relationships and because the success of the doctor-patient relationship depends on truth.

4. "[A] person is a fiduciary with respect to a plan to the extent: The person exercises any discretionary authority or discretionary control respecting management of such plan or exercises any authority or control respecting management disposition of its assets" (ERISA 3(21)(a) of ERISA, 29 U.S.C. Section 1002(21)(a)).

References

Benjamin, M. (1985). 'Lay obligations in professional relations,' *The Journal of Medicine and Philosophy* 10, 85–103.

Black's Law Dictionary (6th edition) (1990). West Publishing Co., St. Paul, p. 1233.

Bok, S. (1978). 'Lying to liars' in *Lying*, Quartet Books Limited, London, 123–133.

Carr. A.Z. (1997). 'Is business bluffing ethical?' in T.L. Beauchamp and N.E. Bowie (eds.), *Ethical Theory and Business* (5th edition), Prentice Hall, New Jersey, pp. 451–456.

Carson. T. (1997). 'Second thoughts about bluffing,' in T.L. Beauchamp and N.E. Bowie (eds.), *Ethical Theory and Business* (5th edition), Prentice Hall, New Jersey, pp. 456–462.

Drolet v. Healthsource, 968 F. Supp. 757 (1997).

Ekman, P. (1992). *Telling Lies*, W.W. Norton and Company Inc., New York.

The Employment Retirement Income Security Act of 1974 (ERISA) (1974). 88 Stat. 832, 29 U.S.C., pp. 1001–1461.

Ewen. S. (1996). *PR! A Social History of Spin.* Basic Books, New York.

Gediman. H.K., and Lieberman, J.S. (1996). *The Many Faces of Deceit.* Jason Aronson Inc., New Jersey.

Hafner, K. (1998). 'Can the Internet cure the common cold?' *The New York Times*, July 9.

Hall, M.A. (1993). 'Informed consent to rationing decisions.' *The Milbank Quarterly* 71(4), 645–667.

'Health and medicine: A special report' (1998). *The Wall Street Journal*, October 19.

Horowitz, B. (1981). 'When should executives lie?' *Industrial Week.* November 16.

Kao, A.C., Green, D., Zaslavsky, A., Koplan, J.P., and Cleary, P.D. (1998). 'The relationship between method of physician payment and patient trust.' *Journal of the American Medical Association* 280(19), 1708–1713.

Levinsky, N.G. (1998). 'Truth or consequences.' *The New England Journal of Medicine* 38, 913–915.

'Liar, liar: The Pinocchio dilemma' (1997). *Modern Physician* (August), 6.

Mariner, W. (1995). 'Business vs. medical ethics: Conflicting standards for managed care,' *Journal of Law, Medicine and Ethics* 23, 236–246.

Martin, J.A., and Bjerknes, L.K. (1996). 'The legal and ethical implications of gag clauses in physician contracts.' *The American Journal of Law & Medicine* 22, 433–476.

McClellan v. Health Maintenance Org. of Pennsylvania, 604 A. 2d 1053, Pa. Super. Ct. (1992).

Mechanic, D. (1996). 'Changing medical organizations and the erosion of trust.' *The Milbank Quarterly* 74(2), 171–189.

Moore v. the Regents of the University of California, 51 Cal. 3d 120 (1990).

Morreim, E.H. (1995). *Balancing Act*, Georgetown University Press, Washington, D.C. *The New York Times* (1998). August 28.

Novack, D.H., *et al.* (1998). 'Physicians' attitudes toward using deception to resolve difficult ethical problems.' *Journal of the American Medical Association* 261(20), 2980–2985.

Reuben, R.C. (1996). 'In pursuit of health,' *ABA Journal* 82, 55–60.

Rodwin, M. (1993). *Medicine, Money and Morals.* Oxford University Press. New York.

Spire, H. (1998). *The Power of Hope,* Yale University Press. New Haven. Connecticut. pp. 111–118.

Stephenson, J. (1998). 'Patient pretenders weave tangled "web" of deceit,' *Journal of the American Medical Association* 280(15), 1297.

Stolberg, C.G. (1997). 'Now prescribing just what the patient ordered.' *The New York Times*, August 10, E3.

Tanouye, E. (1998). 'Doctors and patients: The fine print,' *The Wall Street Journal*, October 19, R6.

Varity Corp, v. Howe, 116 S.Ct. 1065. 1073 (1996).

Wickline v. State of California, 192 Cal. App. 3d, 1630 (1986).

The Doctor's Master

Norman G. Levinsky

There is increasing pressure on doctors to serve two masters. Physicians in practice are being enjoined to consider society's needs as well as each patient's needs in deciding what type and amount of medical care to deliver. Not surprisingly, many government leaders and health planners take this position. More remarkably, important elements of the medical profession are promoting this view.

I would argue the contrary, that physicians are required to do everything that they believe may benefit each patient without regard to costs or other societal considerations. In caring for an individual patient, the doctor must act solely as that patient's advocate, against the apparent interests of society as a whole, if necessary. An analogy can be drawn with the role of a lawyer defending a client against a criminal charge. The attorney is obligated to use all ethical means to defend the client, regardless of the cost of prolonged legal proceedings or even of the possibility that a guilty person may be acquitted through skillful advocacy. Similarly, in the practice of medicine, physicians are obligated to do all that they can for their patients without regard to any costs to society.

Society benefits if it expects its medical practitioners to follow this principle. As Fried[1] has eloquently argued, in any decent, advanced society there are rights in health care, in that "one is entitled to be treated decently, humanely, personally and honestly in the course of medical care. . . ." In such a just society "the physician who withholds care that it is in his power to give because he judges it is wasteful to provide it to a particular person breaks faith with his patient." A similar position has been stated by Hiatt[2]: "A

physician or other provider must do all that is permitted on behalf of his patient. . . . The patient and the physician want no less, and society should settle for no less." A just society must have a group of professionals whose sole responsibility as health-care practitioners is to their patients as individuals.

The issue is not whether physicians must do everything technically possible for each patient. Rather it is that they should decide how much to do according to what they believe best for that patient, without regard for what is best for society or what it costs. I do not argue, as some have,[3] that doctors are obligated to prolong life under all circumstances or that they are required to use their expertise to confer technological immortality on dehumanized bodies. Actual practice is infinitely complex and varied. Caring and experienced doctors will differ about what to do in individual cases. In my opinion, ethical physicians may discontinue life-extending treatment if their decisions are based solely on what they and the patient or his or her surrogate believe to be the patient's best interests. (The legal issues surrounding such decisions are beyond the scope of this paper.) They are not entitled to discontinue treatment on the basis of other considerations, such as cost. This distinction may become blurred if physicians are pressed to balance the needs of their patients with societal needs. The practitioner may make decisions for economic reasons but rationalize them as in the best interest of the individual patient. This phenomenon may be occurring in Britain, where physicians "seem to seek medical justification for decisions forced on them by resource limits. Doctors gradually redefine standards of care so that they can escape the constant recognition that financial limits compel them to do less than their best."[4]

A similar danger lurks if physicians attempt to conserve resources by using probabilities of success or failure to make decisions about the care of individual patients. Estimates of the probable outcome of a clinical condition in a given patient are almost invariably based on "soft data": uncontrolled studies, reports of cases of dubious comparability, or the physician's anecdotal clinical experience—all further devalued by rapidly changing diagnostic and therapeutic techniques. The standard errors of such estimates are undefined but undoubtedly large. Yet leading physicians[5,6] advise doctors to practice probabilistic medicine—i.e., to withhold expensive treatment if the probability of success is low. How is the practitioner to define "low" in everyday practice—2, 5, 10, or 20 per cent likelihood of survival with a good quality of life? Even if the dividing line were defined and the requisite precision in estimating outcome could be achieved, the role of the doctor as patient advocate would be subverted by probabilistic practice. This point should not be blurred by using the phrase "hopelessly ill."[3] If there is no hope for a patient, then there is no problem for the doctor in discontinuing treatment. In practice, doctors can rarely be certain who is hopelessly ill. This problem is not resolved by redefining the phrase to exclude consideration of the "rare report of a patient with a similar condition who survived. . ."[5] in deciding whether to continue aggressive treatment. Physicians cannot discharge their responsibility to their individual patients if they try to conserve societal resources by discontinuing treatment on statistical grounds.

An example may indicate the possibilities for disregarding the best interests of a patient in an attempt to conserve societal resources by probabilistic practice. A gerontologist has suggested that we may rapidly be approaching a time when the majority of people will live until the end of a maximal life span to the point of "natural death" at about 85 years of age.[7] Even if the argument is correct as applied to populations, what is the individual doctor to do when caring for a desperately ill 85-year-old patient? Should advanced treatment be withheld, because "high-level medical technology applied at the end of a natural life span epitomizes the absurd"?[7] In terms of probability, the practitioner may be correct in predicting that the patient will not respond to treatment, but how is the physician to know that this person was not destined for a life span of 90 years? On what grounds can the physician withhold maximal treatment?

Another consideration weighs against any dilution of the mandate to doctors to consider solely the needs of their individual patients. Societal decisions about the proper allocation of resources are highly subjective and open to bias. For example, Avorn[8] has argued that cost-benefit analyses in geriatric care tend to turn age discrimination into health policy, because they depend on techniques for quantifying benefits that have a built-in bias against expenditures on health care for the elderly. A large part of the recent increase in overall health-care costs is due to the growing expense of care for older people. Negative attitudes toward aging and the elderly may influence our willingness to meet these costs. Society may encourage physicians to withhold expensive care on the basis of age, even if such care is likely to benefit the individual patient greatly. In Great Britain, persons over age 55 who have end-stage renal disease are steered away from long-term dialysis.[4]

None of the foregoing implies that in caring for individual patients doctors should disregard the escalating cost of medical care. Physicians can help control costs by choosing the most economical ways to deliver optimal care to their patients. They can use the least expensive setting, ambulatory or inpatient, in which first-class care can be given. They can eliminate redundant or useless diagnostic procedures ordered because of habit, deficient knowledge, personal financial gain, or the practice of "defensive medicine" to avoid malpractice judgments.

However, it is society, not the individual practitioner, that must make the decision to limit the availability of effective but expensive types of medical care. Heart and liver transplantation are current cases in point. These are extraordinarily expensive procedures that may prolong a life of "good quality" for some people. Society, through its elected officials, is entitled to decide that the resources required for such programs are better used for other purposes. However, a physician who thinks that his or her patient may benefit from a transplant must make that patient aware of this opinion and assist the patient in obtaining the organ.

The continuous increase in the costs of medical care is a difficult social issue. However, it is not self-evident that expenditures for health care should be limited to any arbitrary percentage of the gross national product, such as the current 11 per cent figure. Moreover, if physicians and others make concerted and effective attempts to eliminate health-care expenditures that do not truly benefit patients, it is not a given fact that the proportion of the national wealth devoted to health care will increase indefinitely. It certainly is not self-evident that resources saved by limiting health care will be allocated to other equally worthy programs, such as preventive medicine, health maintenance, or improved nutrition and housing for the needy. In the United States, the societal decision to limit potentially life-saving health care will not easily be made or enforced, nor should it be, in my opinion. Officials who press for the rationing of medical resources must be prepared for a public outcry, since unlimited availability of useful medical care has been perceived as a right in American society. Governor Lamm of Colorado was recently the target of such a response. Concerned that society cannot afford

technological advances such as heart transplants, he quoted favorably a philosopher who believes that it is our societal duty to die. If society decides to ration health care, political leaders must accept responsibility. David Owen, who is both a political leader in Britain and a physician, believes that "it is right for doctors to demand that politicians openly acknowledge the limitations within which medical practice has to operate."[9] I agree and would add that doctors are entitled to lobby vigorously in the political arena for the resources needed for high-quality health care.

Through its democratic processes, American society may well choose to ration medical resources. In that event, physicians as citizens and experts will have a key role in implementing the decision. Their advice will be needed in allocating limited resources to provide the greatest good for the greatest number. As experience in other countries has shown,[4] it may be difficult for doctors to separate their role as citizens and expert advisors from their role in the practice of medicine as unyielding advocates for the health needs of their individual patients. They must strive relentlessly to do so. When practicing medicine, doctors cannot serve two masters. It is to the advantage both of our society and of the individuals it comprises that physicians retain their historic single-mindedness. The doctor's master must be the patient.

References

1. Fried C. Rights and health care—beyond equity and efficiency. N Engl J Med 1975; 293;241–5.
2. Hiatt HH. Protecting the medical commons: who is responsible? N Engl J Med 1975: 293:235–41.
3. Epstein FH. The role of the physician in the prolongation of life. In: Ingelfinger FJ, Ebert RV, Finland M, Relman AS. eds. Controversy in internal medicine II. Philadelphia: WB Saunders, 1974: 103–9.
4. Aaron HJ, Schwartz WB, The painful prescription: rationing hospital care. Washington. D.C.: Brookings Institution, 1984.

5. Wanzer SH, Adelstein SJ, Cranford RE, et al. The physician's responsibility toward hopelessly ill patients. N Engl J Med 1984: 310: 955–9.

6. Leaf A. The doctor's dilemma—and society's too. N Engl J Med 1984; 310:711–21.

7. Fries JF. Aging, natural death, and the compression of morbidity, N Engl J Med 1980; 303:130–5.

8. Avorn J. Benefit and cost analysis in geriatric care: turning age discrimination into health policy. N Engl J Med 1984; 310:129–301.

9. Owen D. Medicine, morality and the market. Can Med Assoc J 1984; 130:134–5.

Managed Care, Cost Control, and the Common Good

JOHN J. PARIS AND STEPHEN G. POST

The Clinton administration's revised rules regulating but not prohibiting the common practice in managed care of linking physician compensation with cost cutting and control of services demonstrates the complexity of ethical issues in managed care.[1] As originally proposed, the federal guidelines on payment for Medicare and Medicaid services would have precluded any interrelationship between payment to physicians and delivery of services.[2] Such a restriction would have gutted the primary mechanism in managed care plans to curb the unacceptably high cost of healthcare delivery: making physicians directly responsible for cost control by placing them at direct financial risk. At first blush such a linkage seems to involve an obvious and irreconcilable conflict of interest. How can a physician be responsible for the well-being of a patient while at the same time aware that a proportion of his or her income is linked to the provision of cost-conscious care?

This conflict has led many of the leading commentators in medicine and bioethics to denounce such arrangements as unethical.[3] Support for that position is found in the AMA's Council on Ethical and Judicial Affairs statement that while physicians have a concern for society's resources, they "must remain primarily dedicated to the health care needs of their individual patients."[4] The council believes this consideration is so overriding that "[r]egardless of any allocation guidelines or gatekeeper directives, physicians must advocate for any care they believe will materially benefit their patients."

Here the council echoes Edmund Pellegrino's position that the physician is and must remain primarily an "advocate of the patient."[5] Pellegrino expanded on this statement and its implications in a commentary on potential conflicts of interest in managed care settings: "When conflicts or doubts arise, the physician's first responsibility is to the genuine needs and welfare of his or her patient—not the system, the plan, or its other members."[6] Pellegrino's sentiments are not novel. They were articulated a decade ago in a now oft-cited essay by Norman Levinsky, who argued that physicians are to serve single-mindedly as the patient's advocate "without regard to costs or other social obligations."[7]

These voices, which lament that our actions fall short of the ideal, are correct in their concern that when the physician does not have the means to do all that is in the patient's interests something of significance is lost. That sense of compunction, however, is not sufficiently nuanced; it must be balanced by a sense of equity and fairness in the distribution of resources. And it must be mindful of the constraints imposed by available resources.

A devotion to the patient's goals indifferent to all other concerns, including the physician's self-interest and comfort, reflects the highest aspirations of the profession. But this mission of selfless service in the cause of the patient presupposes a situation that no longer prevails: a private patient-physician relationship in which the treatment proposals are within the financial means of the patient and the patient assumes the responsibility, both personal and financial, for the choices made. That simple era, in which most of what medicine could provide was contained in the physician's little black bag, and in which 80% of patients paid for their treatment out of pocket, lasted through the 1950s.

Over the past three decades vastly advanced technology, third-party payment, and a near-exclusive focus on patient autonomy has transformed medicine into an institution with no apparent limits on what could be demanded and what would be attempted. The furthest reach of this out-of-control system is seen in the now-infamous Baby K case, where, at a mother's insistence, an anencephalic infant was resuscitated, ventilated, and maintained with intensive care measures for some two and one-half years.[8] Although the physicians caring for Baby K opposed such aggressive treatment as "inappropriate" and "contrary to the standard of care," a federal district court ordered them to provide it. That order was upheld by Fourth Circuit Court of Appeals as mandated by a federal "anti-dumping" statute that required hospitals to "stabilize" any patient presenting with a medical emergency before a transfer could be effected.[9]

By the time of the Supreme Court's denial of certiorari in that case, the insurer, Kaiser Permanente, had paid $410,000 for the care of Baby K. Medicaid had paid an additional $100,000 for her nursing home coverage. Such an unrestrained approach to the delivery of care, Daniel Callahan notes, leads to a cultural dilemma: there is no room for professional standards and, if left unchecked, the process will soon lead to bankruptcy.[10]

The fiscal issue, if not a concern for treatment guidelines and professional standards, now controls the political agenda with regard to healthcare. It also forces us to reconsider the approach that reduces all ethical interest in healthcare to the individual patient-physician dyad.[11] Despite Levinsky's recent admonition that any "proposed limits must be evaluated in terms of their effects on the well-being of individual patients,"[12] the ethical focus now is, and of necessity must be, much broader than the impact of treatment decisions on individual patients. Our task is to understand what brought about the present transformation of medicine and then to determine the ethical contours of its new environment.

The rapidly shifting context of healthcare delivery is not a mystery. The change is, as Ezekiel Emanuel notes, "a response to many problems within the American health care system, in particular to uncontrolled costs."[13] Our refusal as a society to embrace a single-payer national health plan or any other scheme for capitated healthcare costs led inevitably, as Thurow had predicted in his 1984 essay on the relationship of economics and healthcare,[14] to the marketplace as the mechanism for making difficult choices, choices that, in Kassirer's words, "nobody wants to make."[15]

Given our apparent inability to reach a common social judgment about the moral validity of such choices—our inability to find any alternative to personal autonomy and patient self-determination as the norm for "good" medicine—Thurow's default, the market, came into play. Now a third party—the insurer, or more specifically, the purchaser of the insurance coverage, not the patient or physician—determines what is to be provided.

A market-based system necessarily utilizes market forces to assure constraint and efficiency: financial incentives. Financial incentives such as capitation, salary "withholds," and bonus arrangements are designed precisely to place the physician at financial risk for providing marginal or superfluous treatments. Such risk, as Emanuel notes, is "the most effective—if not the only—way to ensure that physicians seriously evaluate services and refrain from providing those that are unnecessary or marginal."

What is surprising about regulations attempting to prohibit such practices is its failure to realize, as the Physician Payment Review Commission's study unambiguously demonstrated, that almost all managed care plans use financial incentives and the majority of them believe it is the single most effective cost control technique.[16]

The need for such incentives follows from Reinhold Niebuhr's insight that when self-interest is at stake, exhortations to moral goodwill fall on deaf ears.[17] Niebuhr, largely under the influence of Sigmund Freud, was keenly aware of the extent to which rational appeals to the moral right are always somewhat irrational. They are, at least to some extent, if not entirely, shaped by self-interest. Pure reason, in such circumstances is, as it were, a thin veneer disguising self-interest. Given this condition of "fallen human nature," Niebuhr believed that individuals in all but the most intimate of circumstances are incapable of self-transcendence. Thus the only way to effect change in their behavior is with "a measure of coercion"—coercion involving their perceived self-interest.

The ethical principle at stake with regard to "financial incentives" is not whether these incentives present a potential conflict of interest (all financial incentives, including fee-for-service, involve that danger), but whether they serve a public good. Do they help control spiraling costs? Do they eliminate marginal or useless interventions? Are they effective in guaranteeing a more equitable access to common resources? These are questions of societal as opposed to individual claims about equity and fairness. They involve what Aquinas calls the "general justice" of the system as a whole.[18] Applied to managed care, general justice requires a concern not only for the particular patient but for the well-being of all those affected by the plan: patients, physicians, payers, providers—most particularly, all the other participants in the plan.

An emphasis on distributive justice and collective control of resources held in common is an even more demanding imperative than a concern for the well-being of an individual patient, for without it we would all suffer what Garret Hardin labels "the tragedy of the commons."[19] There will be nothing left for anyone. The personalistic communitarianism that is proposed, to use Maritain's phrase,[20] is not a subordination of the good of the individual to that of the group. Rather it signals a recognition that the dignity of each human person is achieved in community with others. As John Donne poetically put it, "No man is an island." The actions of each one inevitably affect others.

A concern for the implications of that interrelatedness leads us to organize our lives within some shared vision. Sustaining that vision requires that our actions be disciplined by the virtues necessary to maintain a community of common interest. The alternative, as Hobbes put it, is a state of nature where isolated self-interest leads to life that is poor, solitary, nasty, brutish, and short. Or to one that is dominated by a sovereign Leviathan.[21]

Today's managed care environment requires the reinvigoration of what Cicero describes as a *res publica*, i.e., "an assemblage of people in large numbers associated in agreement with respect to justice and a partnership for the common good."[22] The presupposition of such an arrangement is

Aristotle's insight that human beings are social or political entities whose good by nature is necessarily bound up with the good of the polis.[23]

Almost two centuries ago, Alexis de Tocqueville observed that Americans seem to substitute a strategic ethics of enlightened self-interest (the contractarian tradition) for the strong moral sense of impartial benevolence that defines res publica ideals.[24] Commitment to the common good, inclusive of all citizens equally considered, and therefore a contrast to utilitarian distinctions according to "social worth," requires distributive fairness. The common good can be constructed on other-regarding sentiments, but if such idealism is impossible, appeals to long-term self-interest might suffice, e.g., if emergency rooms are used as the point of entry for patients who might otherwise have been treated preventively, *my* healthcare premiums will go up.

The hope would be that American physicians will extend their benevolent sentiments to encompass all citizens in need, reflect seriously on the principle of fair distribution, and make unnecessary Niebuhrian "measures of coercion." But perhaps due to idiosyncrasies of American cultural and professional history, "measures of coercion" now seem necessary. Either take the common good seriously, or suffer certain economic consequences.

Here it is worth recovering as analogy the classic definition of "extraordinary care" developed among the Catholic moralists over the past four hundred years.[25] That definition took seriously the impact costly treatment might have on the family commons. A treatment was not considered morally obligatory if it meant that a family would be thrown into poverty.

In the family sphere, genuine other-regarding impulses sustain a *res publica* writ small. But with regard to the stranger in need of healthcare, these impulses are weak at best. Human beings, if Niebuhr is correct, have difficulty expanding their benevolent impulses concentrically to include everyone within the moral domain. Moral philosophy and religious traditions with their concepts of a golden rule attempt to universalize their highly particularistic benevolent impulses.

A managed care system requires an act of moral imagination, i.e., a leap beyond this particular patient subscriber to *all* subscribers. It requires this imagination not only of subscribers themselves, but of physicians. Presuming carefully constrained salaries for managed care executives and a nonprofit system in place, this leap from the one to the many is beneficence at its best, i.e., interwoven with the demands of justice. If some modest "measures of coercion" are needed to fuel the imagination, that may be a result worth the social price.

This approach has direct implications for the way autonomy is understood. Autonomy's most important meaning is not negative or the right to be left alone, but positive—the ability to determine and shape one's life in an active and creative way. Negative freedom, as Isaiah Berlin notes, may sometimes be absolute, e.g., the right to be free from torture.[26] Positive freedom or the right of self-determination is, of necessity, constrained. Even for that most ardent supporter of personal liberty, John Stewart Mill, one's freedom ends when it adversely affects the liberty of another.[27]

Clancy and Brody apply Mill's insight to managed care settings: "the physician who devotes expensive and marginally beneficial resources to the care of patient A, might through that act be harming patients X, Y, and Z, who could have benefited much more substantially had those same resources been made available elsewhere."[28] This realization forces a shift from a myopic focus on "the good of the individual patient" to the broader social ethic of "how does the excessive and marginal treatment of a particular patient affect the other members of this healthcare plan—healthy and ill alike?"

This issue led E. Haavi Morreim to coin the term "contributive justice," i.e., a concern for the legitimate expectations of those whose contributions create the common resource pool.[29] This concern has seemed almost specious for the past three decades. A seemingly inexhaustible source of funding for healthcare led us to applaud every advance and conquest in medicine. As Norman Daniels has observed, under an open-ended payment system it was very hard to say "No."[30] The insurer did not complain about the expense and there was no reason to believe that the resources not used for a particular patient would directly benefit others with medical needs.

All that has changed. A capitated managed care system is inevitably concerned with exhausting limited funding. If excessive utilization by the few—or even the low per-person but high aggregate cost of valued but low-yield medical services such as prostate antigen screening—deplete the common treasury, there is nothing left to meet the legitimate expectations of other participants. Unlike a world of unlimited resources, the members of a health plan are not isolated, nor are they indifferent to the actions of all others. Should the behavior of some threaten the fiscal solvency of the plan, Donne's warning will be true for all: "Don't ask for whom the bell tolls, it tolls for thee."[31]

In this new social arrangement, the patient–physician relationship does not constitute the totality of the real. Nor, as Morreim notes, are the others—"courts, risk managers, society at large, insurers, or other economic agents"—intruders.[32] They are essential components and interested parties in the social body they constitute. Each is a moral agent concerned not only for its immediate self-interest but also with the preservation and well-being of the corporate entity.

This is the basis of the broader ethical concern each now has. Within this moral community of shared interest, no entity—patient, physician, insurer, regulator, or administrator—can be legitimately indifferent to the harm his or her actions impose on others. Each has a responsibility nei-

ther to make excessive claims nor to impose unfair burdens on the others.

Who then should make the decisions within such a system? David Eddy, in an insightful essay, "Connecting Value and Costs," believes that "the determination of whether the value of a health activity is worth its cost should be made by the people who will both actually receive the value (experience the benefits and harms) and pay the costs."[33] In comparing values and costs, he observes that this debate is not between groups holding different philosophic or economic viewpoints; it is a debate within each of us concerning whether the cost is worth it. Sometimes the answer is "no," even when the individual in need disagrees.

Eddy asks whether this is heresy with regard to healthcare. "No," he replies, "it is a moral assessment of value and cost." It is an assessment not only for the individual patient for whom value is all and cost is nothing, but for the entire community of those who contribute financial resources to the common pool. Their health claims, after all, depend on that pool. They are thus anything but indifferent to its depletion.

A capitated delivery system means an end to healthcare delivery as we know it. No longer may a parent demand a million dollars worth of treatment for an infant who could never enjoy a conscious moment, as did Baby K's mother, with a shrug of the shoulders and the reply: "You know what—my baby is worth it." Worth it to her? Of course. She faced no direct correlation of value and cost. Worth it to those who pay the bill through their increased premiums or to those who find their healthcare needs restricted by such an expenditure in a capitated resource pool? The answer is not even doubtful. In an Oregon-type calibration, such treatment would not even be ranked.

This new era of healthcare delivery requires a decided shift in how decisions are made.[34] The emphasis can no longer be exclusively on patient autonomy or even the physician's personal responsibility for the well-being of an individual patient "indifferent to cost or other social considerations."[35] We agree with Clancy and Brody that "the most fair and defensible principle would be to try to match treatments with those patients most likely to benefit and to begin to discourage or withhold expensive treatments when patients whose chance of benefit is very slim or nearly zero can be identified."[36] If even further restrictions on services is required to provide affordable healthcare coverage, outcomes data, as well as membership participation in the assessment of value versus cost, would be the most appropriate mechanism to determine what will be provided.

Notes

1. Health Care Financing Administration. Final rule: requirements for physician incentive plans in pre-paid health care organizations. *Federal Register* 1996; 61(252):69034–49.

2. Omnibus Budget Reconciliation Act of 1986 Section 9313 (c). PL99-509 (April 1, 1989).

3. Woolhandler S, Himmelstein DU. Extreme-risk: the corporate proposition for physicians. *New England Journal of Medicine* 1995;333:1706–8; Emanuel EJ, Dubler NN. Preserving the physician-patient relationship in the era of managed care. *JAMA* 1995;273:323–9; Pellegrino ED. Interests, obligations, and justice: some notes toward an ethic of managed care. *Journal of Clinical Ethics* 1995; 6:312–7; Kassirer JP. Managed care and the morality of the marketplace. *New England Journal of Medicine* 1995;333:50–2.

4. American Medical Association, Council on Ethical and Judicial Affairs. Ethical issues in managed care. *JAMA* 1995;273:330–5.

5. Pellegrino ED. Rationing health care: the ethics of medical gatekeeping. *Journal of Contemporary Health Law and Policy* 1986;2:23–45.

6. See note 3, Pellegrino 1995.

7. Levinsky N. The doctor's master. *New England Journal of Medicine* 1984;311:1573–5.

8. Paris JJ, Miles SH, Kohrman A, Reardon F. Guidelines on the care of anencephalic infants: a response to Baby K. *Journal of Perinatology* 1995; 15:318–24.

9. In the matter of Baby K, 16F.3rd 590 (4th Cir., 1994).

10. Callahan D. Necessity, futility and the good society. *Journal of the American Geriatric Society* 1994;42:866–7.

11. Sharpe VA, Faden AI. Appropriateness in patient care: a new conceptual framework. *Milbank Quarterly* 1996;74:115–38.

12. Levinsky NG. Social, institutional, and economic barriers to the exercise of patients' rights. *New England Journal of Medicine* 1996;334:532–4.

13. Emanuel EJ. Medical ethics in the era of managed care: the need for institutional structures instead of principles for individual cases. *Journal of Clinical Ethics* 1995;6:335–8.

14. Thurow L. Learning to say "No." *New England Journal of Medicine* 1984;311:1569–72.

15. Kassirer JP. Managed care and the morality of the marketplace. *New England Journal of Medicine* 1995;333:50–2.

16. Physician Payment Review Commission. *Arrangements Between Managed Care Plans and Physicians*. Washington, D.C.: PPRC, 1995.

17. Niebuhr R. *Moral Man and Immoral Society*. New York: Scribners, 1960.

18. Thomas Aquinas, *Summa Theologiae* II-II. Q.58, art. 6.

19. Hardin G. The tragedy of the commons. *Science* 1968;152:1243–8.

20. Maritain J. *The Person and the Common Good*. Notre Dame, Ind.: University of Notre Dame, 1946.

21. Hobbes T. *Leviathan*, I; Schneider HW, intro. Indianapolis: Bobbs-Merrill, 1958: Parts I and II.

22. Cicero. *De res publica*. Cambridge. Mass.: Harvard University Press, 1970: 1,25,39 LCL 213.

23. Aristotle. *Nicomachean Ethics*. In: McKeon R. ed., *The Basic Works of Aristotle*. New York: Random House, 1941: 1097b,1. 10.

24. de Tocqueville A. *Democracy in America*. New York: Random House, 1994.

25. Kelly G. The duty of using artificial means of preserving life. *Theological Studies* 1950;11:430–9.

26. Berlin I. Two concepts of liberty. In: Berlin I. *Four Essays on Liberty.* Oxford: Clarendon Press, 1969.

27. Mill JS. *On Liberty.* London: John W. Parker & Son, 1859:21–3.

28. Clancy CM, Brody H. Managed care: Jekyll or Hyde? *JAMA* 1995;273:338–9.

29. Morreim EH. Moral justice and legal justice in managed care: the assent of contributive justice. *Journal of Law, Medicine & Ethics* 1995;23:247–65.

30. Daniels N. Why saying no to patients in the U.S. is so hard. *New England Journal of Medicine* 1986;314:1380–3.

31. Donne J. Devotions on emergent occasions. No. 17 (1624).

32. Morreim EH. The new medical ethics of medicine's new economics. In Engelhardt HT, Spicker SF, eds. *Balancing Act.* Dordrecht: Kluwer, 1991:184–93.

33. Eddy DM. Connecting value and costs. *JAMA* 1990;264:1737–9.

34. LORAN Commission. The LORAN commission: a report to the community. In: Blank RH, ed. *Biomedical Policy.* New York: Columbia University Press, 1992:64–86.

35. Halevy A, Brody BA. A multi-institution collaborative policy on medical futility. *JAMA* 1996; 276:572–4.

36. See note 28, Clancy, Brody 1995.

Notes

1. American Medical Association, *Council on Ethical and Judicial Affairs: Principles of Medical Ethics in Codes of Professional Responsibility: Ethics Standards in Business, Health and Law,* ed. Rena A. Gorlin, 4th ed. (Washington, D.C.: Bureau of National Affairs, 1999), 341.

2. 440 S.W. 2d 104 (Tex. Civ. App. 1969).

3. Ibid., 107.

4. Albert Jonsen, *The Birth of Bioethics* (New York: Oxford University Press, 1998), 10.

5. Marc Rodwin, *Medicine, Money & Morals: Physicians' Conflicts of Interest* (New York: Oxford University Press, 1993), 181–184.

6. Ibid.

7. Ibid.

8. *Moore v. Regents of the University of California,* 51 Cal. 3d, 120, 271 Cal. Rptr. 146, 793 P. 2d 479 (1990).

9. Rodwin, 210.

10. Carol Gilligan, *In a Different Voice: Psychological Theory and Women's Development* (Cambridge, Mass.: Harvard University Press, 1982).

11. Alan G. Johnson, "Surgery as a Placebo," *The Lancet* 344:8930(1994): 1140–1142.

12. K. B. Thomas, "The Placebo in General Practice," *The Lancet* 344:8929(1994): 1066–1067.

13. Julian Hart and Paul Dieppa, "Caring Effects," *The Lancet* 347(1996): 1606–1608.

14. 129 U.S. 114 (1888).

15. Institute of Medicine, *To Err Is Human: Building a Safer Health System,* ed. Linda T. Kohn et al. (Washington, D.C.: National Academy Press, 2000).

16. Edmund D. Pellagrino, "Patient and Physician Autonomy: Conflicting Rights and Obligations in the Physician-Patient Relationship," in *The Virtues in Medical Practice* (New York and Oxford: Oxford University Press, 1993), 31–50.

17. Oregon Death with Dignity Act, Oreg. Rev. Stat. 127. 800-897 127.

18. *State of Oregon v. Ashcroft,* 2004 U.S. APP. LEXIS 10349 (9th Cir. May 26, 2004).

19. Helena Bachmann, "One-Way Ticket," *Time International* (Oct. 14, 2002), 40.
20. Linda Ganzimi, Theresa Harvath, et al., "Experiences of Oregon Nurses and Social Workers with Hospice Patients Who Requested Assistance with Suicide," *New England Journal of Medicine* 347(8)2002: 582–588.
21. David Orentlicher, *In Matters of Life and Death: Making Moral Theory Work in Medical Ethics and the Law* (Princeton, N.J.: Princeton University Press 2001), 24–52.
22. 521 U.S. 702 (1997).
23. Brief for Ronald Dworkin, Thomas Nagel, et al. as Amici Curiae, in Support of the Respondents, *Washington v. Glucksberg*, 521 U.S. 702 (1997).
24. Council on Ethical and Judicial Affairs, American Medical Association.
25. 237 F. Supp. 96 (N.D. Ohio. 1965).
26. *Doe v. Roe*, 93 Misc. 2d 201 (N.Y.S.Ct. 1977).
27. 45 CFR. Pts. 160,164.
28. Jeffrey Reiman, "Privacy, Intimacy, and Personhood," *Philosophy and Public Affairs* 6 (1976): 26, 39.
29. Report of the Presidential Commission on the Human Immunodeficiency Virus Epidemic (Washington, D.C: Government Printing Office, 1988): 126–127.
30. 45 CFR 160, 164.
31. 23 F. Supp. 2d 167 (D. Conn. 1998), *sum. judgment granted in part and denied in part*, 23 F. Supp. 2d 153 (D. Conn. 1998).
32. Susan Dorr Goold, "Money and Trust: Relationships between Patients, Physicians, and Health Plans," *Journal of Health Politics, Policy, and Law* 23:4(1998): 687–695.
33. Matthew K. Wynia et al., "Physician Manipulation of Reimbursement Rules for Patients: Between a Rock and a Hard Place," *Journal of the American Medical Association* 283:14(2000): 1858–1865.
34. M. Gregg Bloche, "Fidelity and Deceit at the Bedside," *Journal of the American Medical Association* 283:14(2000): 1881–1884.
35. Norman Levinsky, "Truth or Consequences," *New England Journal of Medicine* 338:13(1998): 915.
36. David Mechanic and Sharon Meyer, "Concepts of Trust Among Patients with Serious Illness," *Social Science* 51:5(2000): 657.
37. David Mechanic and Mark Schlesinger, "The Impact of Managed Care on Patients' Trust in Medical Care and Their Physicians," *Journal of the American Medical Association* 271:21(1996): 1996.
38. David Mechanic, "Models of Rationing: Professional Judgment and the Rationing of Medical Care," *University of Pennsylvania Law Review* 140(1992): 1713–1754.

Recommended Readings

Ainslie, Donald C. "Questioning Bioethics: AIDS, Sexual Ethics, and the Duty to Warn." *Hastings Center Report* 29(5)(1999): 26–35.
Amundsen, D. W. "The Physician's Obligation to Prolong Life: A Medical Duty without Classical Roots." *Hastings Center Report* 8(4) (August 1978): 23–30.

Angell, Marcia. "Medicine: The Endangered Patient-centered Ethic." *Hastings Center Report* 17(1987): 12–13.

Angell, Marcia. "The Doctor as Double Agent." *Kennedy Institute of Ethics Journal* 3(1993): 279–286.

Battin, Margaret P. *Ethical Issues in Suicide.* Upper Saddle River, N.J.: Prentice Hall, 1995.

Bloche, M. Gregg. "Fidelity and Deceit at the Bedside." *Journal of the American Medical Association* 283(2000): 1881–1884.

Boozang, Kathleen M. "The Therapeutic Placebo: The Case for Patient Deception." *Florida Law Review* 54(2002): 687–746.

Branch, William T., "Is the Therapeutic Nature of the Patient-Physician Relationship Being Undermined? A Primary Care Physician's Perspective." *Archives of Internal Medicine* 160(2000): 2257–2260.

Brett, Allan S. "The Case Against Persuasive Advertising by Health Maintenance Organizations." *New England Journal of Medicine* 32(1992): 1353–1357.

Clark, Robert. "Agency Costs Versus Fiduciary Duties." In *Principals and Agents: The Structure of Business.* Edited by Pratt, John and Zeckhauser, Richard. Boston: Harvard University Press, 1985: 71–79.

Daniels, Norman. "Duty to Treat or Right to Refuse?" *Hastings Center Report* 22(1991): 36–46.

Davis, J. K. "The Concept of Precedent Autonomy." *Bioethics* 16(2)(2002): 114–133.

Dworkin, Ronald. *Life's Dominion: An Argument About Abortion, Euthanasia, and Individual Freedom.* New York: Knopf, 1993.

Emanuel, Ezekiel J. "Euthanasia and Physician-Assisted Suicide: A Review of the Empirical Data from the United States." *Archives of Internal Medicine* 162(2002): 142–152.

Emanuel, Ezekiel, and Dubler, Nancy Neveloff. "Preserving the Physician-Patient Relationship in the Era of Managed Care," *Journal of the American Medical Association* 273(1995): 323–329.

Fleck, Leonard M., and Squier, Harriet. "Facing the Ethical Challenges of Managed Care." *Family Practice Management* (October 1995): 49–55.

Freidson, Eliot. *Professionalism The Third Logic.* Chicago: The University of Chicago Press, 2001.

Ganzini, Linda et al. "Oregon Physicians' Attitudes About and Experiences with End-of-Life Care Since Passage of the Oregon Death with Dignity Act." *Journal of the American Medical Association* 285(2001): 2353–2369.

Gatter, Ken M. "Genetic Information and the Importance of Context: Implications for the Social Meaning of Genetic Information and Individual Identity." *Saint Louis Law Journal* 47(2003): 423–459.

Givelber, Daniel J. et al. "*Tarasoff,* Myth and Reality: An Empirical Study of Private Law in Action." *Wisconsin Law Review* (1984): 443–497.

Goldman, Janlori. "Protecting Privacy to Improve Health Care." *Health Affairs* 17(6)(1998): 47–60.

Goold, Susan. "Money and Trust: Relationships between Patients, Physicians, and Health Plans." *Journal of Health Politics, Policy, and Law* 23(1998): 687–695.

Gostin Lawrence O., and Hodge, James G., Jr. "Piercing the Veil of Secrecy in HIV/AIDS and Other Sexually Transmitted Diseases: Theories of Privacy and Disclosure in Partner Notification." *Duke Journal Gender Law & Policy* 5(1998): 9–93.

Gray, Bradford. "Trust and Trustworthy Care in the Managed Care Era." *Health Affairs* 16(1979): 34–49.

Hall, Mark A. "Law, Medicine and Trust." *Stanford Law Review* 55(2002): 463–527.

Hall, Mark, Dugan, Elizabeth, Balkrishnan, Rajesh, and Bradley, Donald. "How Disclosing HMO Physician Incentives Affects Trust." *Health Affairs* 21(2002): 197–206.

Harman, Jane. "Topics for Our Times: New Health Care Data—New Horizons for Public Health." *American Journal of Public Health* 81(7)(1998): 1019–1021.

Hart, Julian Tudor, and Dieppe, Paul. "Caring Effects," *The Lancet* 347(1996): 1606–1608.

Harvard Medical Practice Study to the State of New York. *Patients, Doctors, and Lawyers: Medical Injury, Malpractice Litigation, and Patient Compensation in New York*. Cambridge, Mass.: Harvard University Press, 1990.

Jansen, Lynn A., and Friedman Ross, Lainie. "Patient Confidentiality and the Surrogate's Right to Know." *Journal of Law, Medicine & Ethics* 28(2)(2000): 137–143.

Kao, Audiey, Green, Diane, Zaslavsky, Alan, Koplan, Jeffrey, and Cleary, Paul. "The Relationship between Method of Physician Payment and Patient Trust." *Journal of the American Medical Association* 280(1998): 1708–1714.

Kao, Audley, Green, Diane, Davis, Neil, Koplan, Jeffery, and Cleary, Paul. "Patients' Trust in Their Physicians: Effects of Choice, Continuity, and Payment Method." *Journal of General Internal Medicine* 13(1998): 681–686.

Kohn, Linda T. et al. *To Err Is Human: Building a Safer Health System*. Washington, D.C.: National Academy Press, 2000.

McKinlay, John B., and Marceau, Lisa D. "The End of the Golden Age of Doctoring." *International Journal of Health Services* 32(2002): 379–416.

Mechanic, David. "The Functions and Limitations of Trust in the Provision of Medical Care." *Journal of Health Politics, Policy and Law* 23(1998): 661–686.

Mechanic, David. "Models of Rationing: Professional Judgment and the Rationing of Medical Care." *University of Pennsylvania Law Review* 140(1992): 1713–1754.

Mechanic, David, and Meyer, Sharon. "Concepts of Trust among Patients with Serious Illness." *Social Science and Medicine* 51(2000): 657–668.

Miller, Tracy E., and Sage, William M. "Disclosing Physician Financial Incentives." *Journal of the American Medical Association* 281(1999): 1424–1430.

Moreno, Jonathan, ed. *Arguing Euthanasia: The Controversy Over Mercy Killing, Assisted Suicide and the "Right to Die."* New York: Simon and Schuster, 1995.

Morreim, E. Haavi. *Balancing Act: The New Medical Ethics of Medicine's New Economics*. Washington, D.C.: Georgetown University Press, 1995.

Orentlicher, David. *Matters of Life and Death: Making Moral Theory Work in Medical Ethics and Law*. Princeton, N.J.: Princeton University Press, 2001.

Orenlichter, David, and Caplan, Arthur. "The Pain Relief Promotion Act of 1999: A Serious Threat to Palliative Care," *Journal of the American Medical Association* 283(2000): 255–258.

Parker, L. S. "Information (al) Matters: Bioethics and the Boundaries of the Public and the Private." *Social Philosophy Policy* 19(2002): 83–112.

Pellegrino, Edmund D. "Trust and Distrust in Professional Ethics," in *Ethics Trust, and the Professions: Philosophical and Cultural Aspects,* edited by Edmund D. Pellegrino, Robert M. Veatch, and John P. Langan. Washington, D.C.: Georgetown University Press, 1991: 69–89.

Peters, Philip G., Jr. "The Quiet Demise to Custom: Malpractice Law at the Millennium." *Washington and Lee Law Review* 57(2000): 163–205.

Reiman, Jeffrey H. "Privacy, Intimacy, and Personhood." *Philosophy and Public Affairs* 6(1976): 26–44.

Resnick, David. "Physician-Assisted Suicide: The Culture of Medicine and the Undertreatment of Pain." In *Physician-Assisted Suicide: What Are the Issues?* Eds. Kopelman, Loretta M., and DeVille, Kenneth A. Dordrecht, Boston, London: Kluwer, 2002, 127–148.

Rhodes, Rosamond, and Strain, James J. "Trust and Transforming Medical Institutions." *Cambridge Quarterly of Healthcare Ethics* 9(2000): 205–217.

Rodwin, Marc. *Medicine, Money and Morals: Physicians' Conflicts of Interest.* New York: Oxford University Press, 1993.

Rogers, W. A. "Is There a Moral Duty for Doctors to Trust Patients?" *Journal of Medical Ethics* 28(2)(2002): 77–80.

Sabin, James E. "The Second Phase of Priority Setting: Fairness as a Problem of Love and the Heart: A Clinician's Perspective on Priority Setting." *British Medical Journal* 317(1998): 1002–1004.

Schattner, A., and Tal, M. "Truth Telling and Patient Autonomy: The Patient's Point of View." *American Journal of Medicine* 113(1)(July 2002): 66–69.

Seay, G. "Do Physicians Have an Inviolable Duty Not to Kill?" *Journal of Medicine and Philosophy* 26(1)(2001): 75–91.

Shapiro, Arthur, and Shapiro, Elaine. "Patient-Provider Relationships and the Placebo Effect." In *Behavioral Health.* Edited by Joseph D. Matarazzo and Alan Herd. New York: John Wiley and Sons, 1984.

Shortell, Stephen M. et al. "Physicians as Double Agents: Maintaining Trust in an Era of Multiple Accountabilities." *Journal of the American Medical Association* 280(1998): 1102–1108.

Sullivan, Amy D. "Legalized Physician-Assisted Suicide in Oregon, 1998–2000," *New England Journal of Medicine* 344(2001): 605–607.

Sullivan, M. "The New Subjective Medicine: Taking the Patient's Point of View on Health Care and Health." *Social Science and Medicine* 56(7)(2003): 1595–1604.

Sullivan, Mark D., and Younger, Stuart J. "Depression, Competence and the Right to Refuse Life-Saving Treatment." *American Journal of Psychiatry* 151(1994): 971–978.

Summary of HIPAA Privacy Rule, Health Privacy Project, Institute for Health Care Research and Privacy, Georgetown University (September 13, 2002), http://www.healthprivacy.org/urs_doc/RegSummary2002.pdf (accessed 6/24/03).

Thomas, K. B. "The Placebo in General Practice." *The Lancet* 344(1994): 1066–1067.

van der Feltz Cornelis, C. M. "The Impact of Factitious Disorder on the Physician-Patient Relationship: An Epistemological Model." *Medicine, Health Care, and Philosophy* 5(3)(2002): 253–261.

Wolf, Susan M. "Physician-Assisted Suicide, Abortion, and Treatment Refusal: Using Gender to Analyze the Difference." In *Physician-Assisted Suicide: Ethical Positions, Medical Practices, and Public Policy Options,* Weir, Robert, ed. Bloomington, Ind.: Indiana University Press, 1997.

Wynia, Matthew, Cummins, Deborah, VanGeest, Jonathan, and Wilson, Ira. "Physician Manipulation of Reimbursement Rules for Patients: Between a Rock and a Hard Place." *Journal of the American Medical Association* 283(2000): 1858–1865.

Cases

Childs v. Weis, 440 S.W. 2d 104 (Tex. Civ. App. 1969).

Garamella v. New York Medical College, 23 F. Supp.2d 167; 23 F. Supp. 2d 153 (D. Conn. 1998).

Kentucky Association of Health Plans, Inc. v. Miller, 538 U.S. 329 (2003).

MacDonald v. Clinger, 84 A.D. 2d 482, 446 N.Y.S. 2d 801, (Sup. Ct. N.Y. App. Div. 1982).

Moore v. Regents of the University of California, 51 Cal. 3d 120, 793 P.2d 479, 271 Cal. Rptr. 146 (1990).

Pegram v. Herdrich, 530 U.S. 211 (2000).

Rush Prudential HMO, Inc. v. Moran, 536 U.S. 355 (2002).

State of Oregon v. Ashcrof, 368 F.3d 1118 (9th Cir. 2004).

Wickline v. State of California, 192 Cal. App. 3d 1630, 239 Cal. Rptr. 810 (1986).

Chapter Five

The Ethical Obligations of Health Care Institutions

A. The Ethical Obligations of Hospitals

Although it is traditional to focus bioethical discussions upon the interactions of patients and physicians, their relationship seldom occurs in a vacuum. As Chapter 4 pointed out, the policies of insurers and employers, not to mention government regulators and courts, profoundly affect the physician-patient relationship. But these are not the only institutions that play a leading role. In fact, health care takes place in the context of a wide array of institutional relationships. Hospitals, physician groups, out-patient clinics, ambulatory surgical and birthing centers, pharmaceutical companies, drug store chains, university medical centers, and many other institutional players deliver health care and influence its delivery.

In recent decades, hospitals have been particularly important institutional actors. Before the closing decades of the nineteenth century, hospitals were usually small, charitable institutions where the poor and lonely went to be cared for and to die. With the advent of antisepsis and anesthesia around the end of the nineteenth century, hospitals developed into institutions that middle class, paying patients sought to go for their health care needs and physicians sought to use for their training and practice.[1] By the middle of the twentieth century, private insurance programs, such as the Blue Cross/Blue Shield plans and later managed care organizations, developed to pay for hospital care for their members, while starting in the 1960s, government programs, such as Medicare and Medicaid, paid for the care of senior citizens and many, but never all, of the poor. Eventually, hospitals became the site for the care of the very sickest of patients.

When hospitals were charities providing care only to the indigent, their mere existence could be seen as an act of altruism to the community (even if the care given was often terrible). The law supported that view by granting hospitals so-called charitable immunity that prevented patients from recovering damages from hospitals for any injuries that may have resulted from negligence at the hospital.[2] Hospitals were also freed from liability on the premise that they were merely "hotels," buildings in which doctors practiced their profession. It was the physician, the professional, who bore the legal and perhaps moral responsibility for patient care.

As hospitals came to play a more important role in patient care, and to charge patients and their insurers for hospital services, questions arose about their obligations to patients. By the middle of the twentieth century, courts began to rethink hospital immunity. In 1957 the Supreme Court of New York noted that

> [T]oday's hospital is quite different from its predecessor of long ago; it receives wide community support, employs a large number of people and necessarily operates its plant in businesslike fashion.
>
> . . .
>
> The conception that the hospital does not undertake to treat the patient, does not undertake to act through its doctors and nurses, but undertakes instead simply to procure them to act upon their own responsibility, no longer reflects the fact. Present-day hospitals, as their manner of operation plainly demonstrates, do far more than furnish facilities for treatment. They regularly employ on a salary basis a large staff of physicians, nurses and internes, as well as administrative and manual workers, and they charge patients for medical care and treatment, collecting for such services, if necessary, by legal action.[3]

As a result, the court found that hospitals should be treated like any other employer and institution, responsible for the wrongdoing of its employees.

Whether hospitals should be further obligated by law to ensure patient care remained for some time an open question. The case *of Darling v. Charleston Memorial Hospital*, which is included in the materials, is often cited as the seminal case for finding that hospitals themselves have a duty of care to their patients. What are the reasons for this duty? Is it based simply upon the empirical reality that hospitals act as if they provide patient care and patients believe that they do? Is that a sufficient reason to reach a normative conclusion? Or, is the duty based upon a utilitarian determination that hospitals are usually in the best position to reduce injuries to patients? More than individual doctors, they can institute procedures, train staff, and buy the equipment that may be essential to prevent unnecessary injuries. Consider the reading from Lucian L. Leape and Donald M. Berwick, in which they argue that improvements in patient safety cannot depend upon the vigilance of individual providers alone. Instead injury prevention requires a "culture of safety" that can best be implemented at the institutional or organizational level, where designs of systems and processes for safety can occur. What responsibilities does their argument imply for institutions such as hospitals?

Inevitability the hospital's legal and perhaps ethical obligation to provide quality patient care may conflict with the obligation of a physician to do the same.

After all, we have traditionally assumed that the physician is the professional who is first and foremost responsible for patient care. But if the hospital is also responsible, does that mean that it may direct the physician on what course of treatment is to be followed? Does a physician then have an obligation to comply with the practices and procedures that the hospital has put into place to reduce injuries even if the physician believes they are unwarranted or harmful for a particular patient? Does the assumption of the hospital's responsibility invariably diminish the physician's?

Perhaps the most vexing set of questions about the ethical responsibilities of a hospital, however, concern its obligations to provide care to patients who lack insurance. As was discussed in Section A of Chapter 3, the patient-physician relationship is generally understood to be a voluntary one. For the most part, physicians do not have obligations (at least any more than any other fellow human being has) to individuals who are not their patients. Thus while we may believe that it is good and noble for a physician to treat those who cannot pay for treatment, free service is generally not considered either legally or morally obligatory.

Can the same be said about hospitals? In many states, courts, relying upon different theories, have held that hospital emergency rooms are obligated to provide at least some care to all patients who present to the ER with an emergency. For many years hospitals could meet this legal obligation because private insurers and Medicare provided relatively generous reimbursement rates, enabling hospitals to use those funds to "cross subsidize" the care of the uninsured. But when health care costs began to escalate dramatically in the 1980s, payers instituted a variety of mechanisms, including prospective payment and capitation, designed to cut their costs and make hospitals treat insured patients more efficiently. The result was less money available to treat the uninsured. In response, some hospitals began to "dump" patients, transferring them without treatment to other emergency rooms.

Media stories about patient dumping provoked an outcry by the public and a response from Congress. The result was the Emergency Medical Treatment and Active Labor Act[4] (EMTALA), which requires all hospitals that participate in the federal Medicare program (which means almost all hospitals) to provide an "appropriate medical screening" of anyone who shows up at an emergency room and to treat such a person until he or she is stabilized. Importantly, EMTALA does not require that hospitals provide care once the patient is stabilized. Do hospitals have an ethical obligation to continue to treat patients who present at an emergency room once they are stable? For example, if a patient comes to an emergency room with a heart attack, must the hospital provide the long-term care that may be required to return the patient to full cardiovascular health?

More fundamentally, EMTALA raises the question of how we can reconcile demands for efficiency with ethical obligations to patients. Can we expect hospitals to operate efficiently with a firm focus on the bottom line and at the same time provide high quality of care to patients who lack any or adequate insurance? Do the demands for uncompensated care inevitably undermine the ability of hospitals to provide a high quality of care? If so, what should hospitals be obligated to do, provide high quality of care to a few, well-insured patients or perhaps lesser care to more patients? Or should hospitals simply focus on reducing costs so that governments and employers will not face escalating health care bills? What does justice require? What are the public health consequences of a hospital system that does not provide emergency care? Of one that is bankrupt?

Ethicists have also debated whether it makes any sense at all to ask these ethical questions about hospitals, which are, after all, complex institutions forced to operate in a relatively unforgiving marketplace. Some ethicists argue that we can speak about hospitals as if they were moral actors and that nonprofit hospitals, that are generally tax-exempt, have particular obligations as charitable institutions to act in the public good. For example, Daniel Wikler contends that nonprofit hospitals can and ought to be "virtuous."[5] Because they have this moral obligation, which for-profit institutions may lack, Wikler argues that there is a value to maintain a large role for charitable institutions in the health care marketplace.

Market theorists such as Regina E. Herzlinger and William S. Krasker disagree and argue that the evidence does not support the proposition that nonprofit hospitals behave more ethically than for-profit institutions.[6] Moreover, they suggest that we should not expect hospitals to fulfill the public's need whether or not they are organized as charities. According to such theorists, if hospitals were required to provide free care, it would undermine efficiency and lead to an increase in health care costs, which may make it harder for people to get insurance in the first place. Instead, these scholars claim that the needs of the uninsured should be taken care of by the state.

This position has influenced one state court. In the controversial but rarely followed case of *Utah County v. Intermountain Health Care, Inc.*, the Utah Supreme Court reviewed the actions of two nonprofit hospitals and determined that they were not serving the interests of their community and did not deserve the charitable exemption from state property taxes. Left unexplored by the court was whether community interests would be better served by granting the tax exemption and requiring the hospitals to truly act as charities or by denying them tax benefits and forcing them to compete with for-profit institutions.

Also unexplored by the court was whether we should expect all hospitals, even those that are for-profit institutions and pay taxes, to service the uninsured. Do hospitals, which have relied for so long on public funding and support, have an ethical obligation that other actors in the market, such as clothing retailers, do not have? Or, are the needs of the uninsured matters that should be handled by the state, and should hospitals, or other private institutions, be regarded simply as actors in the marketplace rather than as ethical agents? We will revisit this question in Section C of this chapter, when we consider the obligations of pharmaceutical organizations.

Supreme Court of Illinois.
Dorrence Kenneth Darling, II, Appellee,
v.
Charleston Community Memorial Hospital, Appellant.
No. 38790.

Sept. 29, 1965.
Rehearing Denied Nov. 18, 1965.

SCHAEFER, Justice.

This action was brought on behalf of Dorrence Darling II, a minor (hereafter plaintiff), by his father and next friend, to recover damages for allegedly negligent medical and hospital treatment which necessitated the amputation of his right leg below the knee. The action was commenced against the Charleston Community Memorial Hospital and Dr. John R. Alexander, but prior to trial the action was dismissed as to Dr. Alexander, pursuant to a covenant not to sue. The jury returned a verdict against the hospital in the sum of $150,000. This amount was reduced by $40,000, the amount of the settlement with the doctor. The judgment in favor of the plaintiff in the sum of $110,000 was affirmed on appeal by the Appellate Court for the Fourth District, which granted a certificate of importance. 50 Ill.App. 2d 253, 200 N.E.2d 149.

On November 5, 1960, the plaintiff, who was 18 years old, broke his leg while playing in a college footballgame. He was taken to the emergency room at the defendant hospital where Dr.

Alexander, who was on emergency call that day, treated him. Dr. Alexander, with the assistance of hospital personnel, applied traction and placed the leg in a plaster cast. A heat cradle was applied to dry the cast. Not long after the application of the cast plaintiff was in great pain and his toes, which protruded from the cast, became swollen and dark in color. They eventually became cold and insensitive. On the evening of November 6, Dr. Alexander "notched" the cast around the toes, and on the afternoon of the next day he cut the cast approximately three inches up from the foot. On November 8 he split the sides of the cast with a Stryker saw; in the course of cutting the cast the plaintiff's leg was cut on both sides. Blood and other seepage were observed by the nurses and others, and there was a stench in the room, which one witness said was the worst he had smelled since World War II. The plaintiff remained in Charleston Hospital until November 19, when he was transferred to Barnes Hospital in St. Louis and placed under the care of Dr. Fred Reynolds, head of orthopedic surgery at Washington University School of

Medicine and Barnes Hospital. Dr. Reynolds found that the fractured leg contained a considerable amount of dead tissue which in his opinion resulted from interference with the circulation of blood in the limb caused by swelling or hemorrhaging of the leg against the construction of the cast. Dr. Reynolds performed several operations in a futile attempt to save the leg but ultimately it had to be amputated eight inches below the knee.

The evidence before the jury is set forth at length in the opinion of the Appellate Court and need not be stated in detail here. The plaintiff contends that it established that the defendant was negligent in permitting Dr. Alexander to do orthopedic work of the kind required in this case, and not requiring him to review his operative procedures to bring them up to date; in failing, through its medical staff, to exercise adequate supervision over the case, especially since Dr. Alexander had been placed on emergency duty by the hospital, and in not requiring consultation, particularly after complications had developed. Plaintiff contends also that in a case which developed as this one did, it was the duty of the nurses to watch the protruding toes constantly for changes of color, temperature and movement, and to check circulation every ten to twenty minutes, whereas the proof showed that these things were done only a few times a day. Plaintiff argues that it was the duty of the hospital staff to see that these procedures were followed, and that either the nurses were derelict in failing to report developments in the case to the hospital administrator, he was derelict in bringing them to the attention of the medical staff, or the staff was negligent in failing to take action. Defendant is a licensed and accredited hospital, and the plaintiff contends that the licensing regulations, accreditation standards, and its own bylaws define the hospital's duty, and that an infraction of them imposes liability for the resulting injury.

The defendant's position is stated in the following excerpts from its brief: "It is a fundamental rule of law that only an individual properly educated and licensed, and not a corporation, may practice medicine. * * * Accordingly, a hospital is powerless under the law to forbid or command any act by a physician or surgeon in the practice of his profession. * * * A hospital is not an insurer of the patient's recovery, but only owes the patient the duty to exercise such reasonable care as his known condition requires and that degree of care, skill and diligence used by hospitals generally in that community. * * * Where the evidence shows that the hospital care was in accordance with standard practice obtaining in similar hospitals, and Plaintiff produces no evidence to the contrary, the jury cannot conclude that the opposite is true even if they disbelieve the hospital witnesses. * * * A hospital is not liable for the torts of its nurse committed while the nurse was but executing the orders of the patient's physician, unless such order is so obviously negligent as to lead any reasonable person to anticipate that substantial injury would result to the patient from the execution of such order. * * * The extent of the duty of a hospital with respect to actual medical care of a professional nature such as is furnished by a physician is to use reasonable care in selecting medical doctors. When such care in the selection of the staff is accomplished, and nothing indicates that a physician so selected is incompetent or that such incompetence should have been discovered, more cannot be expected from the hospital administration."

The basic dispute, as posed by the parties, centers upon the duty that rested upon the defendant hospital.

As has been seen, the defendant argues in this court that its duty is to be determined by the care customarily offered by hospitals generally in its community. Strictly speaking, the question is not one of duty, for "* * * in negligence cases, the duty is always the same, to conform to the legal standard of reasonable conduct in the light of the apparent risk. What the defendant must do, or must not do, is a question of the standard of conduct required to satisfy the duty." (Prosser on Torts, 3rd ed. at 331.) "By the great weight of modern American authority a custom either to take or to omit a precaution is generally admissible as bearing on what is proper conduct under the circumstances, but is not conclusive." (2 Harper and James, The Law of Torts, sec. 17.3, at 977–978.) Custom is relevant in determining the standard of care because it illustrates what is feasible, it suggests a body of knowledge of which the defendant should be aware, and it warns of the possibility of far-reaching consequences if a higher standard is required. (Morris, Custom and Negligence, 42 Colum.L.Rev. 1147 (1942); 2 Wigmore, Evidence, 3rd ed. secs. 459, 461.) But custom should never be conclusive.

In the present case the regulations, standards, and bylaws which the plaintiff introduced into evidence, performed much the same function as did evidence of custom. This evidence aided the jury in deciding what was feasible and what the defendant knew or should have known. It did not conclusively determine the standard of care and the jury was not instructed that it did.

"The conception that the hospital does not undertake to treat the patient, does not undertake to act through its doctors and nurses, but undertakes instead simply to procure them to act upon their own responsibility, no longer reflects the fact. Present-day hospitals, as their manner of operation plainly demonstrates, do far more than furnish facilities for treatment. They regularly employ on a salary basis a large staff of physicians, nurses and internes, as well as administrative and manual workers, and they charge patients for medical care and treatment, collecting for such services, if necessary, by legal action. Certainly, the person who avails himself of 'hospital facilities' expects that the hospital will attempt to cure him, not that its nurses or other employes will act on their own responsibility." (Fuld, J., in Bing v. Thunig (1957), 2 N.Y.2d 656, 163 N.Y.S.2d 3, 11, 143 N.E.2d 3, 8.) The Standards for Hospital Accreditation, the state licensing regulations and the defendant's bylaws demonstrate that the medical profession and other responsible authorities regard it as both desirable and feasible that a hospital assume certain responsibilities for the care of the patient.

We now turn to an application of these considerations to this case.

We believe that the jury verdict is supportable. On the basis of the evidence before it the jury could reasonably have concluded that the nurses did not test for circulation in the leg as frequently as necessary, that skilled nurses would have promptly recognized the conditions that signalled a dangerous impairment of circulation in the plaintiff's leg, and would have known that the condition would become irreversible in a matter of hours. At that point it became the nurses' duty to inform the attending physician, and if he failed to act, to advise the hospital authorities so that appropriate action might be taken. As to consultation, there is no dispute that the hospital failed to review Dr. Alexander's work or require a consultation; the only issue is whether its failure to do so was negligence. On the evidence before it the jury could reasonably have found that it was.

Judgment affirmed.

Safe Health Care: Are We Up to It?

We Have to Be

LUCIAN L. LEAPE AND DONALD M. BERWICK

In the eight months since we put out the call for papers for this special issue of the *BMJ* devoted to medical errors, the landscape has changed considerably. In Britain the Bristol Inquiry has continued to focus professional and public attention on patient safety in a manner unprecedented both for its depth and for the extent of professional involvement.[1] In the United States the recent publication of the report *To Err is Human* by the Institute of Medicine of the National Academy of Sciences[2] received extraordinary media coverage as well as prompt responses to its recommendations from the President and Congress.[3]

The error prevention "movement" has clearly accelerated. As the papers in this issue bear witness, major changes are occurring in the way we think about and carry out our daily work. For practising physicians, some of the ideas and practices described here may be mind bending, or at least mind stretching. But most of the insights and solutions will, we think, have resonance for all those who strive to provide safe care for patients. All physicians, after all, have had the unwelcome experience of becoming what Wu calls "the second victim," being involved in an error or patient injury and feeling the attendant sense of guilt or remorse as responsible professionals.[4] Familiar, too, are Helmreich's findings that doctors, like pilots, tend to overestimate their ability to function flawlessly under adverse conditions, such as under the pressures of time, fatigue, or high anxiety.[5]

Some of the solutions reported here are as simple as teaching emergency room doctors to read x ray films[6]; others require substantial capital investment.[7] The new world of automation described by Bates and by Gaba seems ever closer,[8,9] and, although every new technology will in-

evitably introduce new forms of error, it is high time for medicine to enter the computer age. We should now hope that the death knell has at last been sounded for the handwritten paper prescription; and the paper medical record, a dinosaur long overdue for extinction, may at last be on route to replacement by far more useful and reliable automated systems.

But, several of these authors warn us, making the more fundamental and lasting changes that will have a major impact on patient safety is much more difficult than simply installing new technologies. There are no "quick fixes." We must re-examine all that we do and redesign our many and complex systems to make them less vulnerable to human error.[10,11] The necessary changes are as much cultural as technical. Creating a culture of safety requires attention not only to the design of our tasks and processes, but to the conditions under which we work—hours, schedules and work loads; how we interact with one another; and, perhaps most importantly, how we train every member of the healthcare team to participate in the quest for safer patient care.

We have already learnt a great deal from the early experiences of error reduction in healthcare organisations. Firstly, we have discovered an immense reservoir of creativity and motivation among healthcare workers of all kinds. When given the opportunity to help, when the barriers of shame and punishment are removed, doctors, nurses, pharmacists, and others eagerly work to improve safety, implementing best practices or developing new ones.

Secondly, we have learnt again that leadership is an essential ingredient of success in the search for safety, as it is throughout the enterprise of quality improvement. In the absence of commitment from professional and organisational leaders, efforts will be fragmentary and uncoordinated and will have only minor effects. We need leadership at all levels. While local "champions"—individual doctors, pharmacists, or nurses—can, by their enthusiasm, motivate others to make improvements, major systems changes require direction and support from the top—leaders who communicate their own commitment by insisting on safety as an explicit organisational goal backed by adequate resources. The test, as Reinertsen tells us, is that senior managers feel personally responsible for each error.[12]

Thirdly, we have learnt that the problem of medical error is not fundamentally due to lack of knowledge. Though clearly we have much more to learn about how to make our systems safe, we already know far more than we put into practice. Simple measures of known effectiveness, such as unit dosing, marking the correct side before surgery on paired organs, and 24 hour availability of pharmacists and emergency physicians, are often ignored. Health care alone refuses to accept what other hazardous industries recognised long ago: safe performance cannot be expected from workers who are sleep deprived, who work double or triple shifts, or whose job designs involve multiple competing urgent priorities. Based on currently available knowledge, constructive, effective changes to improve patient safety can begin at once.

If we can mobilise our resources and make safety our priority, health care can make tremendous strides in the next few years. But today's culture of blame and guilt too often shackles us. Achieving the culture we need—one of learning, trust, curiosity, systems thinking, and executive responsibility—will be immensely difficult. Harder still, we must now accomplish this cultural change under the spotlight of a newly aroused public that, given our track record, is understandably doubtful that health care can, on its own, do what needs to be done. Indeed, the public's doubt in our commitment may be all too

well founded. In truth, no other hazardous industry has achieved safety without substantial external pressure. Safe industries are, by and large, highly regulated. Health care's track record of failure to act on over three decades of accumulating evidence of medical errors offers plenty of ammunition to those who claim that we may need to be forced to do what is, at bottom, right.

The need is obvious, and the mandate is clear. Will we respond adequately and fast enough? Will hospitals and healthcare organisations get serious enough, soon enough, about patient safety? Will they make the changes that are needed, and will they be willing to hold themselves accountable for achieving improvements? Can we accept the legitimacy of the public's right to know when serious accidents occur, and can we honour the public's legitimate expectation that we will admit our mistakes, investigate them, and make the changes necessary to prevent them in the future? As we enter the new century, a key lesson from the old is that everyone benefits from transparency. Both the safety of our patients and the satisfaction of our workers require an open and non-punitive environment where information is freely shared and responsibility broadly accepted.

Are we ready to change? Or will we procrastinate and dissemble—to lament later when the inevitable regulatory backlash occurs? It may seem to some that the race for patient safety has just begun, but the patience of the public we serve is already wearing thin. They are asking us to promise something reasonable, but more than we have ever promised before: that they will not be harmed by the care that is supposed to help them. We owe them nothing less, and that debt is now due.

Notes

1. www.bristol-inquiry.org.uk/brisphase2.htm; accessed 6 March 2000.
2. Kohn LT, Corrigan JM, Donaldson MS, eds. *To err is human. Building a safer health system.* Washington, DC: National Academy Press. 1999.

3. Charatan F. Clinton acts to reduce medical mistakes. *BMJ* 2000;320:597.

4. Wu A. Medical error: the second victim. *BMJ* 2000;320:726–7.

5. Helmreich RL. On error management: lessons from aviation. *BMJ* 2000;320:781–5.

6. Espinosa JA, Nolan TW. Reducing errors made by emergency physicians in interpreting radiographs: longitudinal study. *BMJ* 2000;320:737–40.

7. Nightingale PG, Adu D, Richards NT, Peters M. Implementation of rules based computerised bedside prescribing and administration: intervention study. *BMJ* 2000;320:750–3.

8. Bates DW. Using information technology to reduce rates of medication errors in hospitals. *BMJ* 2000;320:788–91.

9. Gaba DM. Anaesthesiology as a model for patient safety in health care. *BMJ* 2000;320:785–8.

10. Reason J. Human error: models and management. *BMJ* 2000;320:768–70.

11. Nolan TW. System changes to improve patient safety. *BMJ* 2000;320:771–3.

12. Reinertsen JL. Let's talk about error. *BMJ* 2000;320:730.

Supreme Court of Utah.
Utah County, By and Through the County Board of Equalization of Utah County, Plaintiff,
v.
Intermountain Health Care, Inc., and Tax Commission of the State of Utah, Defendants.
No. 17699.

June 26, 1985.

DURHAM, Justice: Utah County seeks review of a decision of the Utah State Tax Commission reversing a ruling of the Utah County Board of Equalization. The Tax Commission exempted Utah Valley Hospital, owned and operated by Intermountain Health Care (IHC), and American Fork Hospital, leased and operated by IHC, from *ad valorem* property taxes. At issue is whether such a tax exemption is constitutionally permissible. We hold that, on the facts in this record, it is not, and we reverse.

IHC is a nonprofit corporation that owns and operates or leases and operates twenty-one hospitals throughout the intermountain area, including Utah Valley Hospital and American Fork Hospital. IHC also owns other subsidiaries, including at least one for-profit entity. It is supervised by a board of trustees who serve without pay. It has no stock, and no dividends or pecuniary profits are paid to its trustees or incorporators. Upon dissolution of the corporation, no part of its assets can inure to the benefit of any private person.

IHC's policy with respect to all of its hospitals is to make charges to patients for hospital services whenever it is possible to do so. Hospital charges are paid either by patients, by private insurance companies such as Blue Cross and Blue Shield, or by governmental programs such as Medicare and Medicaid. IHC and its individual hospitals also are the recipients of private bequests, endowments, and contributions in amounts not established in the record.

Utah County seeks the resolution of two issues: (1) whether U.C.A., 1953, §§ 59-2-30 (1974) and 59-2-31 (1974), which exempt from taxation hospitals meeting certain requirements, constitute an unconstitutional expansion of the charitable exemption in article XIII, section 2 of the Utah Constitution; and (2) whether Utah Valley Hospital and American Fork Hospital are exempt from taxation under article XIII, section 2 of the Utah Constitution.

Utah County does not seriously dispute that the two hospitals in this case comply with sections 59-2-30 and 59-2-31, but contends instead that these statutes unlawfully expand the charitable exemption granted by article XIII, section 2 of the Utah Constitution (1895, amended 1982), which provides in pertinent part:

> The property of the state, cities, counties, towns, school districts, municipal corporations and public libraries, lots with the buildings thereon used exclusively for either religious worship or charitable purposes, . . . shall be exempt from taxation.

The power of state and local governments to levy property taxes has traditionally been limited by constitutional and statutory provisions such as those at issue in this case that exempt certain property from taxation. These exemptions confer an indirect subsidy and are usually justified as the *quid pro quo* for charitable entities undertaking functions and services that the state would otherwise be required to perform. A concurrent rationale, used by some courts, is the assertion that the exemptions are granted not only because charitable entities relieve government of a burden, but also because their activities enhance beneficial community values or goals. Under this theory, the benefits received by the community are believed to offset the revenue lost by reason of the exemption.

A consideration of the reasons for exemption provisions is important in determining the proper standards under which they should be reviewed.

> A liberal construction of exemption provisions results in the loss of a major source of municipal revenue and places a greater burden on nonexempt taxpayers, thus, these provisions have generally been strictly construed. For the same reasons parties seeking an exemption bear the burden of proving their entitlement to it. The doctrine of strict construction and the difficulties taxpayers have in bearing the burden of proof explain why taxation has been the rule and exemption has been the exception. In some jurisdictions, however, the doctrine of strict construction has been eroding. Courts in these jurisdictions pay "lip service" to the doctrine but fail to apply it to exemption provisions.

Comment, *Real Estate Tax Exemption for Federally Subsidized Housing Corporations,* 64 Minn.L.Rev. 1094, 1096-97 (1980) (footnotes omitted).

An entity may be granted a charitable tax exemption for its property under the Utah Constitution only if it meets the definition of a "charity" or if its property is used exclusively for "charitable" purposes. Essential to this definition is the element of gift to the community.

> Charity is the *contribution* or *dedication* of something of value . . . to the common good. . . . By exempting property used for charitable purposes, the constitutional convention sought to encourage individual or group sacrifice for the welfare of the community. An essential element of charity is an *act of giving.*

Given the complexities of institutional organization, financing, and impact on modern community life, there are a number of factors which must be weighed in determining whether a particular institution is in fact using its property "exclusively for . . . charitable purposes." Utah Const. art. XIII, § 2 (1895, amended 1982). These factors are: (1) whether the stated purpose of the entity is to provide a significant service to others without immediate expectation of material reward; (2) whether the entity is supported, and to what extent, by donations and gifts; (3) whether the recipients of the "charity" are required to pay for the assistance received, in whole or in part; (4) whether the income received from all sources (gifts, donations, and payment from recipients) produces a "profit" to the entity in the sense that the income exceeds operating and long-term maintenance expenses; (5) whether the beneficiaries of the "charity" are restricted or unrestricted and, if restricted, whether the restriction bears a reasonable relationship to the entity's charitable objectives; and (6) whether dividends or some other form of financial benefit, or assets upon dissolution, are available to private interests, and whether the entity is organized and operated so that any commercial activities are subordinate or incidental to charitable ones. These factors provide, we believe, useful guidelines for our analysis of whether a charitable purpose or gift exists in any particular case. We emphasize that each case must be decided on its own facts, and the foregoing factors are not all of equal significance, nor must an institution always qualify under all six before it will be eligible for an exemption.

Because the "care of the sick" has traditionally been an activity regarded as charitable in American law, and because the dissenting opinions rely upon decisions from other jurisdictions that in turn incorporate unexamined assumptions about the fundamental nature of hospital-based medical care, we deem it important to scrutinize the contemporary social and economic context of such care. We are convinced that traditional assumptions bear little relationship to the economics of the medical-industrial complex of the 1980's. Nonprofit hospitals were traditionally treated as tax-exempt charitable institutions because, until late in the 19th century, they were true charities providing custodial care for those who were both sick and poor. The hospitals' income was derived largely or entirely from voluntary charitable donations, not government subsidies, taxes, or patient fees. The function and status of hospitals began to change in the late 19th century; the transformation was substantially completed by the 1920's. "From charities, dependent on voluntary gifts, [hospitals] developed into market institutions financed increasingly out of payments from patients." The transformation was multidimensional: hospitals were redefined from social welfare to medical treatment institutions; their charitable foundation was replaced by a business basis; and their orientation shifted to "professionals, and their patients," away from "patrons and the poor."

The magnitude and character of the change in hospital care is suggested by a number of factors. (1) The social composition of hospital patients appears to have changed until by the early 20th century it became quite similar to the population at large. Paul Starr, *The Social Transformation of American Medicine* at 159 (1982). The change in hospital architecture (large wards were replaced with private rooms) suggests the same movement away from the poor to paying patients. *Id.* (2) The number and percentage of paying patients increased as did the percentage of revenue derived from patient fees. This revenue amounted to over 65 percent for general hospitals in the country as a whole by 1922. Public appropriations amounted to about 18 percent; endowment income amounted to 3.6 percent; and donations added 5.7 percent. *Id.* at 161. (3) The practice of not permitting physicians to charge private patients for their services in hospitals was abandoned during this period. In 1880, according to one study, no hospital permitted physician fees. By 1905, 47 of 52 New England hospitals surveyed permitted physicians to charge for services to private patients. *Id.* at 163–64. (4) Before 1880, less than 2 percent of physicians had hospital privileges; by 1933, 5 of 6 physicians had hospital privileges. *Id.* at 162, 167. (5) The number of hospitals increased, according to census figures, from 178 in 1872 to over 4,000 in 1910. *Id.* at 169. (6) Between 1890 and 1920 there was a substantial growth in for-profit hospitals, organized by physicians and corporations, as the opportunity for profit in the hospital business improved. *Id.* at 170. All of the above factors indicate a substantial change in the nature of the hospital; a part of that change was the gradual disappearance of the traditional charitable hospital for the poor.

Also of considerable significance to our review is the increasing irrelevance of the distinction between nonprofit and for-profit hospitals for purposes of discovering the element of charity in their operations. The literature indicates that two models, described below, appear to describe a large number of nonprofit hospitals as they function today.

(1) The "physicians' cooperative" model describes nonprofit hospitals that operate primarily for the benefit of the participating physicians. Physicians, pursuant to this model, enjoy power and high income through their direct or indirect control over the nonprofit hospitals to which they bring their patients. The nonprofit form is believed to facilitate the control by physicians better than the for-profit form. Pauley & Redisch, *The Not-For-Profit Hospital as a Physicians' Cooperative*, 63 Am.Econ.Rev. 87, 88–89 (1973). This model has also been called the "exploitation hypothesis" because the physician "income maximizing" system is hidden behind the nonprofit facade of the hospital. Clark, *Does the Nonprofit Form Fit the Hospital Industry?*, 93 Harv.L.Rev. 1416, 1436–37 (1980). A minor variation of the above theory is the argument that many nonprofit hospitals operate as "shelters" within which physicians operate profitable businesses, such as laboratories. Starr, *supra*, at 438.

(2) The "polycorporate enterprise" model describes the increasing number of nonprofit hospital chains. Here, power is largely in the hands of administrators, not physicians. Through the creation of holding companies, nonprofit hospitals have grown into large groups of medical enterprises, containing both for-profit and nonprofit corporate entities. Nonprofit corporations can own for-profit corporations without losing their federal nonprofit tax status as long as the profits of the for-profit corporations are used to further the nonprofit purposes of the parent organization. *Id.* at 437. (IHC owns at least one for-profit subsidiary.) The emergence of hospital organizations with both for-profit and nonprofit components has increasingly destroyed the charitable pretensions of nonprofit organizations: "The extension of the voluntary hospital into profit-making businesses and the penetration of other corporations into the hospital signal the breakdown of the traditional boundaries of voluntarism. Increasingly, the polycorporate hospitals are likely to become multihospital systems and competitors with profit-making chains, HMO's and other health care corporations." *Id.* at 438.

The foregoing discussion of the economic environment in which modern hospitals function is critical to our analysis in this case because it is an analysis which is generally not present in any of the cases relied upon by the dissenting opinions. Those cases, in our view, do not take into account the revolution in health care that has transformed a "healing profession" into an enormous and complex industry, employing millions of people and accounting for a substantial proportion of our gross national product. Dramatic advances in medical knowledge and technology have resulted in an equally dramatic rise in the cost of medical services. At the same time, elaborate and comprehensive organizations of third-party payers have evolved. Most recently, perhaps as a further evolutionary response to the unceasing rise in the cost of medical services, the provision of such services has become a highly competitive business.

Having discussed the standards for the application of Utah's constitutional exemption for property used for charitable purposes, and the economic and historic context in which we conduct this review, we now examine the record respecting the two hospitals ("the defendants") whose eligibility has been challenged by Utah County. We note that this examination focuses exclusively on what the record before us demonstrates regarding these two hospitals, and only these hospitals. The policies, practices, and structure of Intermountain Health Care, Inc., are relevant to this examination insofar as they have been shown in this case to affect the operations of these hospitals. Evidence concerning the functions and operations of other hospitals in the IHC system appears to be entirely irrelevant, as the exempt status of the property used by those hospitals is not now before us.

The stated purpose of IHC regarding the operation of both hospitals clearly meets at least part of the first criterion we have articulated for determining the existence of a charitable use. Its articles of incorporation identify as "corporate purposes," among other things, the provision of "care and treatment of the sick, afflicted, infirm, aged or injured within and/or without the State of Utah." The same section prevents any "part of the net earnings of this Corporation" to inure to the private benefit of any individual. Furthermore, under another section, the assets of the corporation upon dissolution likewise may not be distributed to benefit any private interest.

The second factor we examine is whether the hospitals are supported, and to what extent, by donations and gifts. [C]urrent operating expenses for both hospitals are covered almost entirely by revenue from patient charges. Although a substantial donation to capital was identified in the case of Utah Valley Hospital, there was no demonstration of the impact of that donation on the current support, maintenance, and operation of that hospital in the tax year in question in this lawsuit. The evidence was that both hospitals charge rates for their services comparable to rates being charged by other similar entities, and no showing was made that the donations identified resulted in charges to patients below prevailing market rates. Presumably such differentials, if they exist, could be quantified and introduced into evidence. The defendants have failed to provide such evidence, and it is they who bear the burden of showing their eligibility for exemption.

One of the most significant of the factors to be considered in review of a claimed exemption is the third we identified: whether the recipients of the services of an entity are required to pay for that assistance, in whole or in part. The Tax Commission in this case found as follows:

> The policy of [IHC's hospitals] is to collect hospital charges from patients whenever it is reasonable and possible to do so; however, no person in need of medical attention is denied care solely on the basis of a lack of funds.

The record also shows that neither of the hospitals in this case demonstrated any substantial imbalance between the value of the services it provides and the payments it receives apart from any gifts, donations, or endowments. The record shows that the vast majority of the services provided by these two hospitals are paid for by government programs, private insurance companies, or the individuals receiving care. Collection of such remuneration does not constitute giving, but is a mere reciprocal exchange of services for money. Between 1978 and 1980, the value of the services given away as charity by these two hospitals constituted less than one percent of their gross revenues. Furthermore, the record also shows that such free service as did exist was deliberately not advertised out of fear of a "deluge of people" trying to take advantage of it. Instead, every effort was made to recover payment for services rendered. Utah Valley Hospital even offered assistance to patients who claimed inability to pay to enter into bank loan agreements to finance their hospital expenses.

The defendants argue that the great expense of modern hospital care and the universal availability of insurance and government health care subsidies make the idea of a hospital solely supported by philanthropy an anachronism. We believe this argument itself exposes the weakness in the defendants' position. It is precisely because such a vast system of third-party payers has developed to meet the expense of modern hospital care that the historical distinction between for-profit and nonprofit hospitals has eroded. For-profit hospitals provide many of the same primary care services as do those hospitals organized as nonprofit entities. They do so at similar rates as those charged by defendants. The doctors and administrators of nonprofit hospitals have the same opportunity for personal remuneration for their services as do their counterparts in for-profit hospitals. *See Georgia Osteopathic Hospital, Inc. v. Alford,* 217 Ga. 663, 665, 124 S.E.2d 402, 403 (1962).

The fourth question we consider is whether the income received from all sources by these IHC hospitals is in excess of their operating and maintenance expenses. Because the vast majority of their services are paid for, the nonprofit hospitals in this case accumulate capital as do their profit-seeking counterparts. The record indicates that this accumulated capital is used for the construction of additional hospitals and other facilities throughout the IHC system and the provision of expanded services. The record before us is undeveloped on this point, but there is nothing therein to indicate that the capital accumulated by either of the defendant hospitals is

even earmarked in any way for use in their facilities or even in Utah County. In view of the fact that Intermountain Health Care owns and operates facilities, for-profit and nonprofit, throughout this state and in other states, we are particularly concerned that there is no showing on the record that surplus funds generated by one hospital in the system will not be utilized for the benefit of facilities in other counties, outside the state of Utah, or purely for administrative costs of the system itself.

A large portion of the profits of most for-profit entities is used for capital improvements and new, updated equipment, and the defendant hospitals here similarly expend their revenues in excess of operational expenses. There can be no doubt, in reviewing the references in the record by members of IHC's administrative staff, that the IHC system, as well as the two hospitals in question, has consistently generated sufficient funds in excess of operating costs to contribute to rapid and extensive growth, building, competitive employee and professional salaries and benefits, and a very sophisticated management structure. While it is true that no financial benefits or profits are available to private interests in the form of stockholder distributions or ownership advantages, the user *entity* in this case clearly generates substantial "profits" in the sense of income that exceeds expenses. This observation is not intended to imply that an institution must consume its assets in order to be eligible for tax exemption—the requirement of charitable giving may obviously be met before that point is reached. However, there is a serious question regarding the constitutional propriety of subsidies from Utah County taxpayers being used to give certain entities a substantial competitive edge in what is essentially a commercial marketplace. None of the defendants in this case made any effort to demonstrate that they would suffer any operating losses or have to discontinue any services if they are ineligible for exemption from property taxes. Justice Stewart's assertion that the taxes levied by the county would have to be passed on to patients in the form of higher charges is without any foundation in the evidence. The far more logical assumption is that *growth of the IHC system* would possibly be slowed, but there is no indication of a likelihood that current and future levels of care would be jeopardized.

The final two factors we address are whether the beneficiaries of the services of the defendants are "restricted" in any way and whether private interests are benefited by the organization or operation of the defendants. Although the policy of IHC is to impose no restrictions, there were some incidents recounted in the testimony which suggested that these institutions do not see themselves as being in the business of providing hospital care "for the poor," an activity which was certainly at the heart of the original rationale for tax exemptions for charitable hospitals. Otherwise, it appears that they meet this criterion. On the question of benefits to private interests, certainly it appears that no individuals who are employed by or administer the defendants receive any distribution of assets or income, and some, such as IHC's board of trustees members, volunteer their services. We have noted, however, that IHC owns a for-profit entity, as well as non-profit subsidiaries, and there is in addition the consideration that numerous forms of private commercial enterprise, such as pharmacies, laboratories, and contracts for medical services, are conducted as a necessary part of the defendants' hospital operations. The burden being on the taxpayer to demonstrate eligibility for the exemption, the inadequacies in the record on these questions cannot be remedied by speculation in the defendants' favor.

In summary, after reviewing the facts in this case in light of the factors we have identified, we believe that the defendants in this case confuse the element of gift to the community, which an entity must demonstrate in order to qualify as a charity under our Constitution, with the concept of community benefit, which any of countless private enterprises might provide. We have no quarrel with the assertion that Utah Valley Hospital and American Fork Hospital meet great and important needs of persons within their communities for medical care. Yet this meeting of a public need by a provision of services cannot be the sole distinguishing characteristic that leads to an automatic property tax exemption. "[T]he usefulness of an enterprise is not sufficient basis for relief from the burden of sharing essential costs of local government." *In re Marple Newtown School District,* 39 Pa.Commw. 326, 336, 395 A.2d 1023, 1028 (1978). Such a "usefulness" rule would have to be equally applied to for- profit hospitals and privately owned health care entities, which also provide medical services to their patients. We note, for example, that the increasing emphasis on competition in health care services is resulting in significant expansion of the activities and roles of health care providers generally, including hospitals, both for-profit and non-profit. Laboratory services, pharmaceutical services, "birthing" centers, and outpatient surgical units are becoming common adjuncts to traditional hospital care. It would be impossible to justify a distinction, within the constitutional boundaries of "charitable" activities, between outpatient surgical services, for example, provided on property owned by an IHC hospital and those provided on privately owned property, where both are identical and are remunerated at the same rate. As we have pointed out, there was no showing in the record that either of the hospitals in question uses billing rates which differ materially from rates charged for the same services by for-profit hospitals, or that the defendants' rates or services would change if they were required to pay county property taxes.

Neither can we find on this record that the burdens of government are substantially lessened as a result of the defendants' provision of services. The record indicates that Utah County budgets approximately $50,000 annually for the payment of hospital care for indigents. Furthermore, the evidence described two instances within a three-month period where, after a Utah County official had declined to authorize payment for a person in the emergency room, Utah Valley Hospital refused to admit the injured person on the basis of that person's inability to pay. The county official was told in these instances to either authorize payment or to "come and get" the person. Such behavior on the hospital's part is inconsistent with its argument that it functions to relieve government of a burden. Likewise, as we have pointed out, there has been no showing that the tax exemption is a significant factor in permitting these defendants to operate, thereby arguably relieving government of the burden of establishing its own medical care providers. In fact, government is already carrying a substantial share of the operating expenses of defendants, in the form of third-party payments pursuant to "entitlement" programs such as Medicare and Medicaid.

As we noted in the introduction to this opinion, the "burden" theory of tax exemptions has been traditionally based on the notion that a charitable organization should be eligible for exemption because it performs a task which the government would otherwise have to perform. The basis for the tax exemption is a *quid pro quo:* "private charities perform functions that the state would be required to undertake and tax exemption is granted as a quid pro quo for the performance of these functions and services." E. Fisch, D. Freed & E. Schacter, *Charities and Charitable Foundations* § 787, at 602 (1974) (footnote omitted). A hospital, whether nonprofit or for-profit, that provides its services to paying patients relieves no public burden because, in its absence, the government would not (or would have no duty to) provide free health care to patients able to pay for treatment. *See* Note, *Exemption of Educational, Philanthropic and Religious Institutions from State Real Property Taxes,* 64 Harv.L.Rev. 288, 290 (1950). If nonprofit hospitals, which charge fully for their services, were to be made tax ex-

empt under the "burden" theory, for-profit hospitals logically ought to be treated in the same manner since both provide the public with the same service. Indeed, it might be argued that for-profit hospitals relieve a greater portion of the public "burden" because they provide medical care without public subsidy. All hospitals use tax-supported public services, including road construction and maintenance, police protection, fire protection, water and sewer maintenance, and waste removal, to name a few. Exempt hospitals use those services at the expense of nonexempt health care providers and other taxpayers, commercial and individual. Furthermore, nonprofit hospitals that generate a surplus from their operations ought not to be tax exempt under the "burden" theory because they are not passing along the benefit of the exemption to the public unless they are charging less for services than would be required absent the tax exemption: "Even if the organization uses such surplus to expand its public benefit services, thereby remaining within the definition of nonprofitability, it does so at the expense of the beneficiaries whom it was created to serve." Ginsberg, *The Real Property Tax Exemption of Nonprofit Organizations: A Perspective,* 53 Temp.L.Q. 291, 317–18 (1980).

We cannot find, on this record, the essential element of gift to the community, either through the nonreciprocal provision of services or through the alleviation of a government burden, and consequently we hold that the defendants have not demonstrated that their property is being used exclusively for charitable purposes under the Utah Constitution.

Because we so hold, it follows that U.C.A., 1953, § 59-2-31 provides no safe harbor for defendants.

STEWART, Justice (dissenting):

Introduction

In holding the hospitals to be noncharitable, the majority opinion ignores the donation of literally tens of millions of dollars worth of private and public funds for the erection of hospital buildings and the purchase of equipment dedicated to the welfare of the public at large. Also ignored by the majority is the hospitals' expenditure of hundreds of thousands of dollars for the care of indigents and several millions of dollars for direct subsidization of hospital care to low income groups. The hospital facilities are made available to all persons, irrespective of race, religion, national origin, or ability to pay.

The Court's holding is without precedent either in Utah or elsewhere in the United States.

The effect of the majority opinion will likely be far-reaching. According to the chairman of Intermountain Health Care, Inc. (IHC), the taxation of tertiary care hospitals, which provide the most sophisticated and technologically advanced medical care, will jeopardize their existence. The immediate result of the majority's holding is that the already high cost of hospital care will be increased. If patients treated at Utah Valley Hospital and American Fork Hospital were required to pay *ad valorem* property taxes at only the 1980 level, they would pay $371,274.07 and $26,177.58, respectively, in addition to the cost of hospital services. In the case of Utah Valley Hospital, that amounts to an additional overhead cost of approximately $1,000 per day or approximately $1,000 per bed per year.

Definition of Charity

Two centuries ago, the Lord Chancellor of England declared that charity is "[a] gift to a general public use, which extends to the poor as well as to the rich," *Jones v. Williams,* 2 Amb. 651 (cited in *Matanuska-Susitna Borough v. King's Lake Camp,* Alaska, 439 P.2d 441, 446 (1968)).

The charging of fees for services rendered, and even the receipt of revenues in excess of expenses, does not make a nonprofit hospital noncharitable if the surplus is used for the charitable purposes of the organization. *E.g., Scripps Memorial Hospital v. California Employment Commission,* 24 Cal.2d 669, 151 P.2d 109 (1944).

The legal concept of charity does not require, as the majority apparently requires, that a hospital incur a deficit to qualify as a charitable institution. Charitable hospitals need not be self-liquidating.

One court has noted: "The image of a voluntary institution as a charitable organization, financing its care of patients to a substantial degree through philanthropy . . . is largely anachronistic. Philanthropy, though increasing, has not been able to match the redoubled demands for health care." *Eastern Kentucky Welfare Rights Organization v. Simon,* 506 F.2d at 1288 n. 20 (*quoting* Professor William Thomas, *Hearings on Conditions and Problems of the Nation's Nursing Homes,* Subcommittee on Longterm Care, Spec. Committee on Aging, U.S. Senate, 89th Cong. 1st Sess., Pt. 2 (Feb. 15, 1965), p. 55).

It is also permissible for charitable nonprofit hospitals to fix their rates to cover the cost of replacing capital assets, as well as to meet the costs of current operations.

It is true that the hospitals in this case receive substantial revenues from third-party payors and patients, but there is not a shred of evidence in this record, much less a finding by the Tax Commission, that one cent of the revenues is used for any purpose other than furthering the charitable purposes of providing hospital services to the sick and infirm. On the contrary, the Tax Commission's findings affirmatively establish that no person has profited from the revenues produced at either Utah Valley or American Fork Hospitals other than patients. Under time-honored legal principles, both hospitals qualify as charitable institutions.

Utah Valley Hospital's and American Fork Hospital's Gifts to the Community

An entity may be granted a charitable tax exemption for its property under the Utah Constitution only if it meets the definition of a "charity" or if its property is used exclusively for "charitable" purposes. Essential to this definition is the element of gift to the community.

"Charity is the *CONTRIBUTION* OR *DEDICATION* OF SOMETHING OF VALUE . . . TO THE COMMON GOOD . . . by exempting property used for charitable purposes, the constitutional convention sought to encourage individual or group sacrifice for the welfare of the community. An essential element of charity is an *act of giving.*" *Salt Lake County v. Tax Commission ex rel. Greater Salt Lake Recreational Facilities,* Utah, 596 P.2d 641, 643 (1979) (emphasis added). A gift to the community can be identified either by a substantial imbalance in the exchange between the charity and the recipient of its services or in the lessening of a government burden through the charity's operation. *Laborers Local No. 295,* 658 P.2d at 1198 (Oaks, J., concurring).

The Court contends that neither of the hospitals here at issue has demonstrated "any substantial imbalance between the value of the services it provides and the payments it receives" because "the vast majority of the services provided . . . are paid for by government programs, private insurance companies, or the individuals receiving care." The majority cites no authority in support of the assertion that a nonprofit hospital loses its charitable status if its patient receipts cover current operating costs. The law, as stated above, is otherwise. More importantly, there is in fact a very substantial imbalance between the *total* cost of the hospital care given and the revenues of the hospital in this case, which is so apparent from the record as to be undeniable.

A. Direct Patient Subsidies

The basic facts are not disputed. Both hospitals render wholly free patient services in substantial amounts. In addition, they subsidize the cost of hospital services to the poor, the elderly, and workers whose hospital bills are paid only in part by worker's compensation. During the years 1978–80, Utah Valley Hospital rendered wholly free services to indigents in the amount of $200,000, and in each of those years the amount increased substantially over the preceding year. During the same period, the hospital subsidized services rendered to Medicare, Medicaid, and worker's compensation patients in the amount of $3,174,024. The corresponding figures for American Fork Hospital were $39,906 in indigent care and $421,306 for subsidization of Medicare, Medicaid, and worker's compensation benefits.

However, the value of the charity extended to indigents is in fact greater than the amounts stated. The cost of the charity extended to patients who are first identified as charity patients *after* admission rather than *at* admission is charged to the "bad debts" account, along with traditional uncollectible accounts or bad debts, instead of being charged to charity. The reason for this accounting procedure is that some patients do not, or cannot (as in the case of emergency admissions), report their indigency status when they are first admitted to the hospital. After services have been rendered, the hospitals stop collection efforts once it is determined that a patient qualifies for charity. In such cases, the hospital accounting system shows the patient as a noncharity account. This accounting procedure is not unique to IHC hospitals. *See, e.g., Jackson County v. State Tax Commission,* Mo., 521 S.W.2d 378 (1975); *West Allegheny Hospital v. Board of Property Assessment,* 63 Pa.Commw. 555, 439 A.2d 1293, 1295 n. 4 (1981), *reversed,* 500 Pa. 236, 455 A.2d 1170 (1982).

In sum, the *direct* cost of patient charity given away by Utah Valley Hospital for the period in question is in excess of $3,374,024, but less than $4,942,779 (which includes bad debts). The *direct* cost of the charity given away by American Fork Hospital is in excess of $461,212, but less than $639,024 (which includes bad debts).

The majority argues that for-profit hospitals also have bad debts. That is, of course, true, but it completely evades the central point. Unlike for profit hospitals, Utah Valley and American Fork have a policy against turning away indigent patients. Therefore, that portion of the hospitals' bad debts which is attributable to indigency is bona fide charity since the charges would have been initially made to the charity account had the patient's indigency been discovered at admission. Those charges are not just ordinary business bad debts experienced by all commercial enterprises, as the majority would have it.

More importantly, the majority opinion ignores the total dollar amount of charity provided by each hospital by dismissing the hospitals' subsidization of Medicare, Medicaid, and worker's compensation patients with the assertion that for-profit hospitals do the same. Even if that be true, it does not diminish the value of the benefits of a tertiary care hospital available to them (in the case of Utah Valley Hospital) which they would not have at a for-profit hospital.

B. Capital Subsidies and Gifts

The most glaring lapse in the majority opinion, in my view, is its flat-out refusal to recognize that there would be no Utah Valley Hospital—at all—if it had not been given lock, stock, and barrel to IHC by the Church of Jesus Christ of Latter-Day Saints, which initially built the hospital. American Fork Hospital apparently was initially erected by taxpayers' money. At the City's request, IHC took over the operation of the hospital as a lessee of American Fork City to relieve the City of a governmental burden. It follows that all patients at both hospitals, whether indigent, part-paying, or fully paying patients, are direct beneficiaries of large monetary investments in land, buildings, and medical equipment. In the case of Utah Valley Hospital, the total value of the plant and equipment approximates $24,769,220. In the case of American Fork Hospital, the amount approximates $1,963,515.

In addition to the "gift to the community" of the actual physical facilities, each and every patient benefits from the fact that IHC is a nonprofit corporation whose hospitals make no profit on the value of the assets dedicated to hospital care. The majority's effort to portray IHC hospitals as

if they were operated as for-profit entities has no substance in the record whatsoever. A for-profit hospital, unlike a nonprofit hospital, must necessarily price its services to make a profit on its investment if it is to stay in business. The surplus that Utah Valley and American Fork budget for is not by any means the equivalent of profit, as the majority wrongly suggests.

In short, all patients at American Fork and Utah Valley Hospitals, whether indigent, partially subsidized, or those who pay the full amount charged, are benefited by the initial gift of the capital assets and by all subsequent donations to capital. In addition, they benefit directly by the nonprofit structure of the hospitals, which means that the hospital rates charged include nothing for profit or a return of capital invested by investors. Moreover, the direct contributions to patient care referred to above are understated by the amortized value of the capital assets donated and the amount of profit that would be charged patients had those hospitals been for-profit hospitals.

The majority's dismissal of the $4,000,000 donated to Utah Valley Hospital for the construction of additional physical facilities in 1978 demonstrates the scope of the Court's disregard of the facts. The majority simply sets that gift at naught with the comment that there "was no demonstration of the impact of that donation on the *current support, maintenance, and operation of that hospital in the tax year in question.*" (Emphasis added.) Apparently the majority holds that the $4,000,000 should be ignored because it was not shown to have been expended, at least in part, on current expenses. It is clear that that sum did not go into current operating expenses, but rather into physical assets. In all events, the amount was substantial by any measure: some twenty percent of the whole project.

Furthermore, the majority inaccurately asserts that Utah Valley charges rates comparable to other similar entities. The evidence is to the contrary. Utah Valley Hospital, with its 385 beds and expensive, sophisticated acute care equipment, charges rates comparable to the rates charged by

Payson Hospital, a small for-profit hospital that renders inexpensive types of services. That comparison indicates that Utah Valley's rates are low. Certainly the cost of operating the 80-bed, primary care Payson hospital ought to be *lower* than Utah Valley's costs. Furthermore, the majority flatly ignores the uncontradicted testimony of the chairman of IHC that "we charge significantly less for the same admission" and "[w]e charge lower prices to our patients for the same level of complexity than would a for-profit hospital."

In a similar vein, the majority asserts that there is no evidence that the gifts and donations to the hospital resulted in patient charges below "prevailing market rates," that is, rates established by for-profit hospitals. The above facts show otherwise. In addition, there are no "prevailing market rates" for tertiary care hospitals, if by that term the majority means prevailing rates of competitive for-profit hospitals. There is no for-profit tertiary care hospital in the entire state of Utah; all tertiary care hospitals are nonprofit institutions. In fact, there is no other tertiary care hospital, whether nonprofit or for-profit, in the immense, sparsely populated area served by the Utah Valley Hospital, which extends from Utah County to the Nevada-Arizona border. Indeed, the facts strongly suggest that a for-profit tertiary care hospital could not survive in the geographical market area served by Utah Valley.

In short, *all* patients at both hospitals receive substantial benefits from tens of millions of dollars that have been invested to promote the health of citizens in Utah County and in the entire central and southern parts of the state. Common sense dictates that the above realities be recognized, yet the majority refuses to recognize any value whatsoever in the gift of the capital assets or the value of having those assets free of any charge for a return on interest.

Presumably, only if the hospitals ran deficits, i.e., if the direct expenses of patient care exceeded patient income, would a hospital qualify in the majority's view as a charitable institution. Of course, the deficits would have to be made up by donations, or the hospital would shortly lapse into bankruptcy. As the cases cited above recognize, modern hospitals can hardly be run on the basis that donations must subsidize current expenses. Moreover, the majority concludes that because governmental programs, private insurance companies, and individuals pay for the vast majority of the services provided, "collection of such remuneration does not constitute giving, but is a mere reciprocal exchange of services for money." That conclusion is wrong because it ignores the fact that the hospitals' charges do not cover the full costs, both overhead and direct, of operating a hospital. In the private sector of the economy, services are rarely given at cost or less than cost, let alone for free. If on rare occasions that does occur, it is usually only as a sales promotion to stimulate further profits. In contrast, the exchange in this case is not reciprocal because rates charged by these hospitals do not cover all costs.

Of course hospital charges are made; of course those who can pay do pay, whether it be through their insurance companies, through government programs, or personally; of course expenses are generally covered by revenues. As far as I know, every single court that has considered these factors has held that they do not make a nonprofit hospital noncharitable for tax purposes. The majority's suggestion that a nonprofit hospital must have a deficit in its current accounts to qualify for charitable status is both anachronistic and a prescription for lesser quality hospital care, if not bankruptcy.

Differences Between For-Profit and Nonprofit Hospitals

A fundamental proposition which pervades the majority opinion is that there is no essential difference between for-profit and nonprofit hospital corporations.

Two fundamental differences between for-profit and nonprofit corporations are ignored by the majority. First, it is axiomatic that a for-profit hospital must conduct its business to make a profit if it is to remain in business. Second, a for-profit hospital's investment decisions as to what markets or communities to enter and what kinds of equipment to invest in are made from a basically different motive than a nonprofit hospital's. The decisions of a for-profit hospital corporation must be based upon careful calculations as to the rate of return that may be expected on invested capital. If the rate of return is not sufficient, the investment is not made. Whether the surplus is reinvested in part or paid out to investors in dividends in whole or in part, the investor receives personal monetary benefit either in the increased value of his stock or in dividends.

The record indicates that for-profit hospitals in Utah have invested to a limited extent in high-volume, low-cost services such as pediatric, psychiatric, and obstetrical-gynecological services, but not in higher-cost, lower-volume kinds of services. It may well be that competition from a for-profit hospital is beneficial to the hospital industry generally, but there is no indication in this record that for-profit hospitals have acted in any fashion other than a for-profit corporation would normally act.

Nonprofit hospitals must, of course, be concerned with generating sufficient revenue to maintain themselves, but they are not concerned with earning a return on their investment for the benefit of stockholders. Their purposes are altruistic. Any surplus must be used in a manner that aggrandizes no one, such as for the lowering of rates, the acquisition of new equipment, or the improvement of facilities. This fundamental difference was explained by Mr. William N. Jones, a trustee and chairman of the Board of Trustees of Intermountain Health Care. He testified:

> A nonprofit hospital system or hospital has a different approach to hospital care or health care, if you will, than someone who might be involved in it as a business, a business where they desire to have a fine product, and they do. I'm talking now about profit-oriented business systems or hospitals, [they] must do well as a business. We must as a nonprofit system do well in our mission which is

to provide health care. So consequent[ly] when we try to provide health care, we do not try to provide just the health care that's easy and remunerative such as obstetrics and pediatrics which are relatively not too complex, and you receive a fairly high level of income from them. On the other hand, examples of health care which are not—you are not able to really receive enough to cover them would be trauma, burns, open-heart, that kind of high level care.

Moreover, there is credible evidence that nonprofit hospitals in general are more efficient and charge less than for-profit hospitals. One study indicates that for-profit hospitals charge 17 percent more per admission to patients with health insurance and that administrative and general service costs were 13 percent higher than nonprofit hospitals. Paul Starr, *The Social Transformations of American Medicine*, 434 (1982). "National data also indicate that, for every bed-size category, for-profit hospitals have higher costs than the overall coverage for community hospitals." *Id.* Mr. Jones also testified that IHC's Board of Trustees considers itself a trustee of the health care facilities for the public. "[W]e see ourselves as owned by the community since the corporation owns itself and in effect the church gave the hospitals to the communities, and we're entrusted with the running of the hospitals. We see them as in effect owned by the communities. We have fund raising drives and strive to have the communities feel that [they are] involved."

In short, the majority's argument that the only significant difference between for-profit and nonprofit hospitals is the distribution of assets on dissolution simply ignores reality. The majority's wholly unsupported assertion that "the historical distinction between for-profit and nonprofit hospitals has eroded" is without any factual foundation in this record. The Court states:

> Because the vast majority of their services are paid for, the nonprofit hospitals in this case accumulate capital, as do their profit-seeking counterparts. The record indicates that this accumulated capital is used for the construction of additional hospitals

and other facilities throughout the IHC system and the provision of expanded services. The record before us is undeveloped on this point, but there is nothing therein to indicate that the capital accumulated by either of the defendant hospitals is even earmarked in any way for use in their facilities or even in Utah County.

Again, the Court's position is contrary to the facts. Utah Valley Hospital budgets for the projected cost of services plus an additional five to seven percent reserve for contingencies and for replacement of building and equipment and for future expansion. Nothing is budgeted for IHC expansion. Even if the five to seven percent reserve were considered the equivalent of profit, which it is not, that would not begin to compare with the amount that would be required by most commercial institutions to make a reasonable return on investment. The administrator of Utah Valley Hospital, Mr. Davis, testified that the budget at that hospital

> consists of those actual costs plus a contingency or reserve, and that includes, of course, monies or funds for either future expansion, replacement of equipment, replacement of buildings and so on. You see, we are in many ways, we are at the mercy of doctors and public and economy. For example, how do you budget the number of patients that are going to come to your hospital in a year or in advance? We find many times that we miss that sometimes regionally, sometimes nationally. Wherein we would budget for a given number of patients or income and the bottom falls out for three or four months. In that case, there is no reserve. There is no originality.

> We fight and scramble to make ends meet for the year, and those are the things that we are vulnerable to . . . I think it is safe to say in order to remain viable, in order to keep from—what's the word I want—self-liquidating ourselves, we must have something in the range of probability five or seven percent in order to stay alive. Now, that's what we shoot for. That's not what we always get. Without that, you see, we would be self-liquidating.

Utah Valley Hospital has recently acquired expensive, high technology equipment not found in any other hospital in its market area, whether for-profit or nonprofit. That technology includes a 22-bed neonatal unit, a linear accelerator to treat cancer, and a heart catheterization laboratory. It also has a number of well-recognized specialists on its staff and has recently applied to do open heart surgery because of the facilities it has been able to acquire. Whether those facilities were acquired from surplus revenues or from donations is of no consequence in my judgment.

Conclusion

In sum, I submit that the majority misapplies Article XIII, Section 2 of the Constitution and makes a radical departure from sound legal principles that are universally recognized. In part, the majority comes to the result it does because it refuses to recognize facts that are patently evident, in part because it assumes propositions of fact about this case that are unproved, and in part because it believes that nonprofit hospitals should stand on the same footing as for-profit hospitals to assure competitive equality because of changes in the nature of the hospital.

B. The Ethical Obligations of Managed Care Organizations

Although managed care first surfaced on the West Coast as a progressive and cooperative way to ensure access to care, more recently it has been used to control escalating health care costs.[7] Managed care initially received substantial government approval and support when Congress passed the Health Maintenance Organization Act of 1973. Some of the goals of the Act included financial assistance, preempting restrictive state laws, and mandating some employers to offer an HMO plan to their employees. Eventually, with the help of the Act, managed care took off.[8] Although its growth has slowed in the very recent past, managed health plans came to dominate health systems during the 1990s. The cost of health care rose dramatically during the 1980s, with health care comprising 8.8 percent of the gross domestic product (GDP) in 1980 and 13.1 percent in 1992.[9] Unhappy with the high cost of health care, payers demanded and collectively lobbied for a way to reign in escalating health care costs. Many people viewed managed care as the solution.

Managed care organizations (MCOs) are a unique hybrid of insurer and provider of health care. The goal of MCOs is to deliver health care in a cost-effective manner in response to escalating health care costs and the demands of employers and other payers to control those costs. By combining the traditionally distinct functions of insuring and providing care, MCOs are able to exercise some control over the use of expensive health care resources. In particular, they target physician behavior with economic incentives that encourage them to practice cost effective care. At the same time, they risk undertreating patients. As you consider the moral obligations of MCOs, note that although health care spending stabilized in the 1990s, it is again on the rise, leading many to speculate that managed care is unable to meet its promise to lower the cost of health care.[10]

MCOs use a number of cost containment mechanisms to control health care spending. Primarily, however, they control costs by shifting some of the financial risk of patient care to physicians. In a capitated system, for example, physicians are paid a specific per member, per month amount and are required to provide care within that amount. When a patient's care exceeds the capitated amount, as it often will with the sickest patients or those with chronic conditions, the physician is nonetheless responsible for providing care. A likely consequence of this is that physicians will not want to serve the sickest members of the community, preferring instead relatively healthy populations (this practice has been referred to as "cherry picking"). Capitation is often coupled with a gatekeeping system in which a primary care physician (PCP) is responsible for controlling patient access to health care resources, such as specialists. As we saw in Chapter 4, Section D, the drawback to cost containment mechanisms that target physician behavior is that they also affect the relationship between patient and physician and, in turn, the therapeutic potential of the relationship.

As insurers, MCOs have obligations to an entire population of members and not just to one patient. This has led James Sabin to claim that "insurers take care of stewardship," which he defines as "seeking fairness for the population."[11] On this view, insurers may deny beneficial care to some patients in order to provide it to other patients. From this perspective, insurers would seem to have moral duties of distributive justice. That is, they must distribute the resources they have in a fair and just manner, however that is defined. The problem with this characterization of MCOs is that it cannot always be said that the amount of money available to spend on patient care, known in the organizational context as the "medical loss" ratio, is a fixed amount in a closed system. In other words, patients and their physicians cannot be assured that whenever they give up some potentially beneficial health care, other patients in the system will benefit from their sacrifice.

Because managed care has involved a significant departure from the traditional doctor-patient relationship and the fiduciary ethic, we should ask whether managed medical care is itself ethical. Wendy Mariner argues that although the ethics of managed care is best understood within a framework of business and contract ethics, neither do justice to the vulnerability of patients as individuals and the higher fiduciary ethics of physicians to them. Her statement that "[a] 'deal is a deal' is not a palatable response to a dying patient who cannot afford the recommended treatment" strikes at the heart of the matter.

E. Haavi Morreim, in her article, *Moral Justice and Legal Justice in Managed Care: The Ascent of Contributive Justice,* acknowledges that MCOs are rarely "closed systems" but argues they aim to provide health care to a specific population within the funds that are available to them. According to Morreim, the ethics of contract governs the obligations of MCOs to their subscribers. However, because of the inherent vagueness of much of the benefit language imbedded in contracts, another principle, the principle of contributive justice, is needed to supplement that of contract and to guide us in interpreting benefit decisions. "Contributive justice concerns fairness to the large number of people whose financial contributions comprise the resource pool from which individual needs are then served. That pool must be managed so that the members as a whole can receive the spectrum of benefits they legitimately expect, without permitting excessive demands of a few unduly to deplete what is left for the many." As you consider the case that Morreim makes for contributive justice, ask also whether all agreements made between MCOs and subscribers are just or whether some might violate substantive justice because they provide for too little care. That is, is there a threshold level of care below which it would be unethical to go especially in a country as wealthy as the United States? Moreover, what is the moral relevance of "contribution" to the question about what reimbursement mechanism should be endorsed? As you evaluate these contractarian approaches, consider whether or not the persuasiveness of this ethical framework is undermined by the fact that, as Mariner discusses, subscribers do not always have a choice of health plans (their employers or the government pick their plans), and there is good evidence that many do not understand the terms of their plans in any case.

As more and more medical decision making occurs in the context of a managed health plan, often by the health plan itself, it is worth asking what sort of obligations MCOs have to subscriber patients. In *Pegram v. Herdrich,* this question was addressed by the Supreme Court. When Cynthia Herdrich went with abdominal pain to see her physician, Dr. Pegram, who was associated with Carl HMO, an employer plan, she was told by Dr. Pegram to wait eight days to have an ultrasound done 50 miles away at one of the HMO's facilities. In the meantime, Ms. Herdrich's appendix ruptured. Ms. Herdrich took her case to court, claiming that her HMO breached its duty based on the Employee Retirement Income Security Act of 1974 (ERISA), the federal law governing employee pensions and benefits, to act solely in the interest of beneficiaries. The Supreme Court did not agree and seemed to defend the cost-saving incentives of managed care organizations. At the same time, however, it raised the question whether the HMO had a fiduciary duty to disclose the nature of its incentives to plan participants.

Of the specific duties that might be imputed to managed care organizations, none would seem to be as pressing as the duty to inform patients about the MCO's cost containment mechanisms. Clearly a moral presupposition of contractarian and Kantian approaches to managed care is that those who agree to be managed know what it is to which they agree. Yet, recall that scholars concerned about trust worry that disclosing the financial incentives used by MCOs will erode patient trust in their physicians.

Vickran Khanna and colleagues discuss some of the complex issues around disclosure in their paper, *Disclosure of Operating Practices by Managed-Care Organizations to Consumers of Healthcare: Obligations of Informed Consent.* They argue that there are good ethical reasons for imposing a duty to disclose financial incentives and operating practices on MCOs. They also believe that considerations of respect for patient autonomy and beneficence (minimizing harms to patients) require disclosure by MCOs at the point that subscriber/patients purchase their plans. In addition, it has also been argued that disclosure will help consumers exercise other substantive rights that they have, such as the right to change their physician or appeal coverage decisions to independent boards.[12] Does it matter in your evaluation of the duty to disclose that many subscribers to health plans have but one choice of plan? Moreover, if disclosure happens but once and the choice is between physicians disclosing incentives and MCOs disclosing, might not the implications of other information for particular patients be more credible coming from physicians? Or will the imposition of this duty on physicians put patient trust at risk? As you consider the duty to disclose financial incentives and the moral reasons that underlie it, be sure to weigh the costs and benefits of the trade-off between trust and patient autonomy.

Managed care has met with widespread dissatisfaction among consumers, the public, and those working in the profession. A number of criticisms have been raised. Some have said that managed care denies patients beneficial care, that it encourages cherry picking, interferes with the doctor-patient relationship, that it undermines trust, and that it does so without being forthright. Alternatively, perhaps, as David Mechanic argues, many of the objections to managed care are unfounded. He believes that complaints, such as that patient visits are shorter under managed care and that physicians are "gagged," are for the most part without merit.[13] Moreover, MCOs are responding to the willingness of payer/employers to pay for benefits. In other words, people get what they pay for. Is it not possible that even if some of the complaints against managed care are unfounded, the burdens it can impose on patients are nonetheless unethical?

In *Rush Prudential HMO v. Moran,* the Supreme Court upheld a state law ensuring patients the right to an independent second opinion when they are denied medically necessary care.[14] Although the Supreme Court's decision appeared to be a victory for patients' rights, it does not apply to all health plans. For example, it does not apply to the self-insured plans of many large companies. Moreover, the

Supreme Court has recently made clear that employees cannot obtain damages in state court from managed care plans governed by ERISA that erroneously deny beneficial care.[15] This has renewed calls for Congress to pass a "Patients' Bill of Rights," but such legislation has been tied up over many issues for many years now. Still, ethics need not be bound by the law. Managed care organizations may have a moral duty to provide subscribers with the right to independent review even if they are not legally bound to do so.

Business vs. Medical Ethics: Conflicting Standards for Managed Care

Wendy K. Mariner

The increased competition for a share of the market of insured patients, which arose in the wake of failed comprehensive health care reform, has provoked questions about what, if any, standards will govern new "competitive" health care organizations.[1] Managed care arrangements, which typically shift to providers and patients some or all of the financial risk for patient care,[2] are of special concern because they can create incentives to withhold beneficial care from patients.[3] Of course, fee-for-service (FFS) medical practice creates incentives to provide unnecessary services, and managed care can avoid that type of harm.[4] Still, as Edmund Pellegrino has noted, "managed care, by its nature, places the good of the patient into conflict with . . . (1) the good of all the other patients served by the plan; (2) the good of the plan and the organization, themselves . . .; and (3) the self-interest of the physician."[5]

These potential conflicts have sparked a small flurry of articles and conferences that examine the "ethics" of managed care.[6] Participants in this discussion recognize the benefits of managed care, including its focus on disease prevention and health promotion (long overdue in Ameri-

can medical practice), its coordination of services based on the totality of a patient's health needs (rather than on isolated responses to specific symptoms), and its ability to hold down premiums. Yet financial incentives to limit services may undermine managed care's ability to achieve such benefits.

Carolyn Clancy and Howard Brody distinguish good managed care organizations (MCOs), which they call "Jekyll care," from "bad" organizations or "Hyde care."[7] In their view, Jekyll organizations typically are well-established, non-profit health maintenance organizations (HMOs), like Group Health Cooperative of Puget Sound and Kaiser-Permanente Foundation, that encourage coordinated care, including preventive services, in long-term personal relationships between patients and primary care providers. They find bad managed care most often in the newer, investor-owned, for-profit entities operated by insurance companies and managers.[8] With little or no experience in health care delivery, such organizations may focus on cutting costs and on ensuring an adequate return on investment to their shareholders.

The idea that some managed care is good and some bad suggests that some socially accepted standard can be defined against which to judge individual plans. But, we have no such standard yet. Indeed, disagreement persists over whether any standard is even necessary. Among those who advocate particular standards, there is implicit disagreement on whether the standard should be based on principles of economics, policy, or ethics; and if ethical principles apply, whether they should be medical ethics or business ethics.

This article explores the difficulty of adopting ethical standards for MCOs. First, it is not clear what counts as an ethical standard for an organization. The ideals of quality and efficiency are desirable goals but do not describe how they ought to be achieved. The ethical principles that promote free and fair competition are quite different from the ethical principles that preserve the integrity of the physician patient relationship and specifically those that protect patient welfare and these principles can lead to quite different outcomes. MCOs were created to achieve economic objectives that may be fundamentally incompatible with traditional principles of medical ethics. Moreover, in today's open-ended health care system, it is questionable whether American economic institutions are susceptible to purely moral suasion. Thus, even if it is possible to agree that certain ethical principles ought to apply to managed care, the market may make it impossible to live fully by those principles.

Finally, it is important not to mistake ethical managed care for an ethical national health care system. Good MCOs may be able to provide efficient, high quality care; but, in the long run, they are not likely to be able to do so and simultaneously cut costs and promote equitable access to care. If the analysis presented here is correct, then we have a choice: either abandon the goal of universal access to health care, or regulate the health care system by eliminating those marketplace standards that conflict with equitable access to care.

Economic and Political Goals for Managed Care

Ethical principles are sometimes conflated with economic and political goals. When the Clinton administration's task force was developing the Health Security Act, it invited a group of ethicists to propose principles for the plan. The group's list of fourteen principles was reduced to the following six for presentation to the public: security, savings, choice, quality, responsibility, and simplicity.[9] These may be laudable goals for health care reform, but, with the possible exception of choice and responsibility, they are not ethical principles.

The current growth of MCOs is encouraged as an alternative to comprehensive health care reform.[10] The Clinton administration's proposal provoked successful opposition from groups who argued that additional government intervention was not needed in the health insurance market because increased competition could achieve the goals of controlling costs and providing good quality care.[11] (They did not claim that competition could achieve universal access to care.) Were care, "managed" properly, it could maintain quality and lower costs (or at least limit cost increases). Thus, the goals of managed care came to be seen as the efficient use of health care resources (or controlling costs) to provide quality care.[12] The most politically appealing argument was cost control; and managed care is advocated first and foremost as a cost-control mechanism by those who oppose additional government intervention in health care financing.[13]

Today, health insurers only have a limited number of ways to save money: use resources efficiently; pay providers less; shift the risk of loss to providers; exclude costly patients from coverage; reduce covered benefits; limit services and deny treatment claims; and increase deductibles and copayments. It is certainly possible to increase efficiency, and avoid waste and duplication of services, in administering and delivering health care.[14] Still, many knowledgeable commentators believe that, in the long run, efficiency alone will not reduce costs enough to avoid limiting the amount of beneficial services needed by patients,[15] especially where the patient population includes an increasing number of older, sicker people.

The remaining cost-control methods are likely to result in reducing services available to patients or increasing patients' out-of-pocket expenditures. For example, insurers can reduce their own costs by lowering the amount they pay providers—especially hospitals and physicians—to care for patients, either by obtaining fee discounts, or by paying providers on a capitated basis (a fixed fee per subscriber) in whole or in part, so that the provider bears the risk of financial loss if the costs of care exceed the capitation fee.[16] Managed care plans may use practice guidelines, quality control committees, and financial rewards and penalties to influence physicians' treatment decisions.[17] Plans may also require patient care to be screened by primary care gatekeepers and employ or contract only with physicians who practice in a cost-saving manner and adhere to the plan's efficient treatment methods.

Historically, most insurers avoided large or unpredictable expenses by refusing to insure patients who were at risk of needing expensive services.[18] The practice of "cherry-picking," or insuring only healthy patients who are unlikely to get sick, is still an effective cost-control device.[19] Plans can also encourage patients who require expensive services to leave the plan and join another, by, for example, providing poor or inconvenient service, refusing desired care, or not responding to complaints.[20]

Health plans can limit their expenses by reducing the number and type of medical benefits covered by the plan. Where services are not expressly excluded from the contract, insurers may deny coverage on the grounds that they are not medically necessary, for example.[21] Finally, increased deductibles and copayments shift to patients a larger proportion of the cost of their care, although their contribution to insurer cost savings may be minimal.

The goals of efficiency and quality care are desirable programmatic goals for health plans, but they do not specify ethical standards for their achievement. They may also conflict with one another. Efficiency is unlikely to control costs enough to avoid hard decisions about limitations on care. Defining and measuring quality of care remains problematic.[22] In such circumstances, ethical standards to guide MCOs' actions appear especially needed.

Differences in Medical Ethics and Business Ethics

Can and should ethical standards apply to MCOs? The answer to such a question depends on what counts as an ethical standard. Traditional principles of medical ethics that govern the physician-patient relationship certainly have a role to play in the delivery of medical care, whether it is done in private FFS practice or in integrated service networks.[23] MCOs, however, do more than deliver medical care. They combine insurance, management, and care delivery. It may be argued that the organization itself does not deliver medical care; its physicians and nurses do. The organization is an economic entity, often a corporation—a legal fiction, not a person in a profession with a history of professional ethics. Thus, the ethical principles that have traditionally been thought to apply to health care practitioners do not easily fit MCOs.

Susan Wolf has rightly distinguished between physician's ethics and organizational ethics, arguing for the development of ethical standards for health care organizations.[24] That task faces several obstacles. First, it is debatable whether organizations are moral entities or capable of having ethics at all.[25] Wolf argues that health care organizations qualify as moral agents because they "specify levels of management and care delivery, formulate rules and policies, and consider moral reasons." Of course, most, if not all organizations (including Microsoft and R.J. Reynolds) formulate rules and policies and consider moral reasons for their actions. The fact that corporations make decisions based on moral reasoning does not mean that they must. These two criteria alone do not suffice to describe an institutional moral agent.

What distinguishes health care organizations from other (commercial and non-profit) enterprises is the fact that they are in the business of delivering health care (Wolf's first factor). Moreover, that health care is actually provided by individual professionals who do have ethical obligations. MCOs perform both medical and business functions, taking actions to provide or withhold care that touch the traditional sphere of medical ethics, and, at the same, acting like ordinary business enterprises with no moral obligations or, at least, obligations that have little to do with traditional medical ethics. This functional duality gives health care organizations a foot in both the medical and the business camps.

However, it is not necessary to confer moral agency on organizations in order to hold them to ethical standards of conduct. Whether or not organizations are moral entities or have moral rights or duties, their actions can be judged by moral standards and either praised or condemned.[26] Organizations can voluntarily create institutional structures and policies that require or encourage ethical behavior on the part of their personnel. Moreover, ethical standards of conduct can be legally imposed where it is socially desirable to achieve important goals.[27] The more difficult tasks will be developing the content of standards that take into account the dual business and medical functions of MCOs and ensuring that organizations can adhere to such standards in an increasingly competitive environment.

The types of standards that have been proposed for managed care entities tend to reflect different conceptions of the organization—either its medical functions or its business functions, but not both. Those who seek ethical standards to ensure the delivery of high quality care appear to conceive of the organization as an entity that has or should have moral obligations because of its medical care functions.[28] The standards they propose focus on preserving physicians' traditional (or updated) ethical commitment to patient welfare despite financial and management controls designed to restrict the cost of care. Others appear to conceive of the organization as a purely economic enterprise, a business with no moral obligations to patients.[29] The standards they discuss are not ethical principles, but management goals, such as economic efficiency, product quality, information dissemination, and fair competition. A consensus on standards is unlikely unless these conflicting views are reconciled.

Problems with Business Ethics

Business ethics in the United States deal with the ethical conduct of business in a competitive marketplace.[30] The ethical principles governing business are designed to promote fair competition. These include honesty, truthfulness, and keeping promises. More specific principles give content to these general principles. For example, businesspeople should avoid disseminating information that is false or misleading and avoid exploiting relationships for personal gain.

Fair competition assumes some measure of equality among those who do business, and seeks to assure conditions in which people are free to make voluntary choices to buy or sell goods or services. Medical ethics, in contrast, assumes significant inequality in knowledge and skill between physicians and patients. For this reason, physicians have been found to have a type of fiduciary obligation to their patients. Business organizations do not have fiduciary obligations to their customers. Their fiduciary obligations are to their shareholders, in the case of investor owned, for-profit enterprises,[31] or to the state, in the case of non-profit organizations. Investor-owned businesses are expected to preserve their assets to accomplish the organization's business purpose and to provide a financial return to investors. Non-profit organizations must also use their resources to accomplish a stated noncommercial purpose.

MCOs face difficulties when achievement of their mission to provide medical care conflicts with their obligation to preserve their assets. This is especially true in the case of for-profit MCOs, which may be under pressure to maintain stock prices and to pay dividends. Some commercial organizations have attempted to adopt socially responsible corporate policies, such as producing or using products that do not harm the environment. Often, such products are both popular and profitable, so that the company can satisfy both its customers and its shareholders. Similarly, many MCOs hope that patient satisfaction will attract new subscribers and, hence, sufficient revenues to yield a satisfactory return to investors. Investors or shareholders of an MCO, however, are rarely the same people as those enrolled in the health plan. If an MCO's financial goals conflict with its service methods, little in the field of business ethics argues for giving subscribers priority.

Stanley Reiser offers the following values to guide health care institutions: humaneness, reciprocal benefit, trust, fairness, dignity, gratitude, service, and stewardship.[32] Apart from fairness, such values are not generally included in discussions of business ethics. Richard DeGeorge describes American business values as freedom (to buy and sell), profit, fairness (including honesty and truthfulness), equal opportunity, and pragmatism or efficiency.[33] Some of Reiser's values may be incompatible with achieving the MCO's financial goals. For example, his concept of reciprocal benefit restrains institutions from actions that harm some to benefit others. MCOs, however, may have to allocate their resources in ways that explicitly harm some patients or

providers to benefit others, so to use resources efficiently to provide the most services to an entire enrollee population. The notion of service, or the obligation to use one's talents to benefit others rather than to expect rewards for labor, is similarly problematic. MCOs typically assume the opposite; they frequently use financial rewards and penalties to influence physician behavior, for example. In addition, humaneness, which encompasses compassion for people, may work against cost control, especially where compassion favors providing treatment that is not covered by a health plan. Although these values seem relevant to providing medical care (and appear to be derived from principles used in medical ethics), more sophisticated concepts are necessary if they are to be incorporated into standards that provide concrete guidance to MCOs.

Few business ethics texts even discuss organizations that deliver medical care. Most tend to focus on ethical principles for individual personal conduct, rather than the actions or policies of an organization.[34] The American College of Healthcare Executives (ACHE) has perhaps the best code of ethics for the behavior of health care executives.[35] Its preamble states that because "every management decision affects the health and well-being of both individuals and communities," health care executives "must safeguard and foster the rights, interests, and prerogatives of patients, clients or others served." Yet the code's normative responsibilities are primarily duties of honesty, such as conducting all professional activities with "honesty, integrity, respect, fairness, and good faith," being truthful and avoiding "information that is false, misleading, and deceptive or information that would create unreasonable expectation," avoiding "the exploitation of professional relationships for personal gain," and creating "institutional safeguards to prevent discriminatory organizational practices."

The ACHE Code makes clear that executives have a responsibility to the organization as well as to patients, noting that they should respect the customs of patients "consistent with the organization's philosophy." Obligations to provide health care services may be limited by available resources. Although executives are to assure "a resource allocation process that considers ethical ramifications," the code does not indicate what ethical principles might be relevant.[36] The fundamental question for managers is whether their responsibilities to the organization supersede any responsibilities to the patients served by the organization. In other words, when the organization's financial needs conflict with the needs of patients, does the manager have an ethical obligation to give patient needs priority? Unfortunately, existing codes of ethics do not answer this question. Most imply that constraints on organizational resources also constrain obligations to patients.[37]

It is possible that ethical management principles would bar organizations from excluding physicians who generate high costs by providing appropriate care to their patients. After all, if the organization's mission is to provide appropriate care to its patient population, its employed or contracting physicians cannot be faulted for achieving that mission. This would support recommendations that MCOs evaluate physician performance solely on the basis of quality of care, without regard to the quantity or cost of services generated.[38] At the same time, the organization needs to preserve itself; and if the cost of providing appropriate care became unreasonable, even a principle requiring fair treatment of physicians might not override the financial imperative of self-preservation. In the absence of any standard for determining the proportion of resources that should be devoted to patient care and what an appropriate level of care should be, existing principles are not likely to resolve such conflicts. Moreover, fair treatment of physicians and employees would not require retaining subscribers whose illnesses were costly to treat. Thus, even ethical management principles are unlikely to prevent organizations from limiting medical benefits or excluding patients in the absence of other principles defining an obligation to provide care.

Even if codes of ethics for managers contained more specific normative principles, it is not clear how effective they would be in the face of countervailing financial pressure. No formal rules regulate the conduct of business managers. The ACHE's only sanction for violations of its code is expulsion from the ACHE, which does not necessarily affect an offender's ability to work. In contrast, a violation of the American Medical Association's Principles of Medical Ethics,[39] could result in a complaint to the board of registration, which has the power to revoke a physician's license to practice medicine, even if such sanctions are rarely invoked in practice.

Ethical Obligations to Patients/Enrollees

Although patients may view their health plan as an assurance of medical care, their legal relationship to an MCO is based on contract principles developed for application in the marketplace of consumer goods. The conditions for an enforceable contract are: an exchange of promises; a fair bargaining process (no coercion); and a meeting of the minds.[40] A relationship based on contract principles is fundamentally different from one based on trust or fiduciary obligations. For example, a physician has an ethical obligation to act in the patient's best interest, while a party to a contract need only perform according to the contract. Thus, in a contractual relationship, an MCO that does not provide care that is not promised in the contract does not treat patients unjustly, even if the care is necessary and appropriate.

While physicians have a duty to treat all patients equally, no contract principle requires that all contracts be the same. Thus, two patients with the same illness who are covered by different health plans may receive quite different treatment.

In business ethics, the principle of honesty undoubtedly requires MCOs to inform prospective subscribers of the contract terms, but no principle insists that the contract contain specific benefits or be consistent with other contracts. Contract variations may violate some conceptions of justice, yet they are entirely consistent with market values and the goals of competition among health plans.

Fair competition is premised on the freedom of consumers to choose what goods and services to buy. In today's medical marketplace, consumer choice is advocated not only as a valuable freedom in itself, but also as a means to force MCOs to offer quality medical care. It is notable, therefore, that patient choice has all but disappeared from the goals of managed care.[41] If care is managed, then, by definition, the patient is not free to choose what care he or she gets. The American Heritage Dictionary, for example, defines *manage* as "to direct or control the use of; to exert control over; make submissive to one's authority, discipline, or persuasion."[42] The purpose of managing care is to eliminate choices that are wasteful, harmful, or too expensive. Patient choice is not always desirable from society's perspective, because patients sometimes make unwise choices and want unnecessary or even harmful treatment. Managed care's cost-control mechanisms are designed to eliminate certain choices or to influence patients (by means of deductibles and copayments, for example) to choose specific (usually less expensive) types of care.[43] In the ideal world, good management will result in better care for patients, but it will not encourage patient choice.

Of course, managed care was never intended to promote patient choice of care. Rather, "choice" here is the choice of which health care plan to buy or "join."[44] If patients are consumers or customers, then the product is the health plan—that package of insured services paid for by the insurer, subject to deductibles, copayments, caps, and other limits. The organization's primary relationship to its patients is that of an insurer to an insured, not of a health care provider to a patient.[45] This is underscored by the insurance terminology for patients: subscribers, enrollees, or, most recently, covered lives.

Advocates of competition among health plans have argued that rational people will choose the health plan that suits their needs.[46] They assume that, when people choose a plan, they have deliberately and necessarily chosen its doctors, nurses, practice patterns, administrative procedures, and benefits package—everything about their health care. A choice to buy a cheaper plan entails assuming the risk that some services will not be covered. For this reason, they conclude, patients must live (or die) with their choices—that is, what the health plan contract provides. This conclusion is based on false assumptions. The most obvious is that people make rational choices about their health care. Even if people could make rational choices about their health care, there are at least three practical problems with assuming that choosing a health plan satisfies the requirements of choice.

First, most patients do not choose their health plans; their employers do. The vast majority of Americans with health insurance get it through their employers.[47] The insurer's primary customers are employers, not individual patients. A recent survey found that among companies with fewer than fifty employees and with employee health insurance, 86 percent offered only one plan.[48] Sixty percent of larger firms offered no choice. The number of employers who offer plans that are closed panel HMOs or limited panel preferred provider organizations (PPOs) is increasing.[49] MCO growth rates are expected to continue over the next few years as government programs like Medicare and Medicaid encourage more beneficiaries to join managed care plans.[50] Thus, the number of patients who have not merely a limited choice of plans, but no choice of plans, is increasing.

A recent Commonwealth Fund study of 3,000 employees in Boston, Los Angeles, and Miami found that 29 percent of respondents in managed care plans did not have the choice of enrolling in a FFS plan.[51] Those without such a choice reported more dissatisfaction with their plans than those who did.[52] Almost half of the employees had changed plans in the past three years, and, of those, nearly three-fourths did so involuntarily. Employees who changed health plans were often forced to change physicians as well: 48 percent of HMO enrollees and 29 percent of PPO enrollees, compared to 12 percent of FFS patients.

If patients are not choosing the plans they join, it cannot be said that they are freely entering into a contract by which they should be bound. Of course, they could "choose" not to join the employer's plan, but for many employees, such a "choice" is unaffordable. Furthermore, people whose employers do not offer health insurance may have little or no choice of plans they can afford.

A second reason why patients do not choose their health plans in practice is that patients rarely know exactly what benefits their plans offer when they must choose them. It is the rare patient who fully understands a benefit contract or appreciates what it means to "choose" a health plan. Contracts are frequently revised and may not even be available to subscribers in final form until several months into the contract year. Information about plans is ordinarily summarized in general terms in brochures distributed to employees or prospective subscribers.[53] Summaries are clearest on how to choose a physician, where services are and are not available, and the amounts of copayments and deductibles. Benefits are usually described generically as hospital care, physicians' services, and laboratory services, for example. Typically, mention is made of the fact that the plan covers "medically necessary" services, but subscribers may not appreciate that the term *medically necessary* serves as a limitation on coverage. It is often difficult to know what particular kinds of treatment are covered until a patient gets sick and needs specific services.[54] Then, it is too late: patients are not likely to be able to change plans at that time, either because they do not get sick during the annual plan enrollment period or because any new plan they join may exclude coverage for their now preexisting illness, at least for the period in which they need treatment. Thus, much of the information necessary for a rational choice is not available when the choice must be made.

Finally, many patients do not want to be bound by their contracts. Even if patients had perfect information and actually chose their health plans, they would not necessarily want contract exclusions enforced when they get sick. "A deal is a deal" is not an palatable response to a dying patient who cannot afford the recommended treatment. People who appear to be rational consumers when they enroll in a health plan may change their minds when they need treatment. Many are surprised to find that, contrary to their expectations, their health plan does not cover the care they need or desire.[55] Even those who might have appreciated that the plan would not cover certain kinds of care (or did not want to pay for it), such as experimental treatment, may consider the contract unfair if the experiment offers their only chance for survival.

Patients may be especially likely to consider benefit denials unfair in a competitive environment where a wide variety of health plans offer different benefits; patients know that other health plans provide the desired care to their subscribers. Even where benefits are the same, different insurers may interpret them differently, resulting in inconsistent benefit determinations.[56] Many patients are likely to perceive such variation not as healthy variety in a free marketplace, but as arbitrary and unfair rationing by their health plan.[57] Given recent publicity about high profits earned by many HMOs and about multimillion dollar compensation paid to their chief executive officers, subscribers may also believe that different treatment is based on corporate greed, not on individual patient needs.[58] This is not to suggest that patients are entitled to whatever care they want, but rather that they may want it, regardless of what their health plan covers or of the likely effectiveness of the desired treatment.[59]

The circumstances in which individuals enroll in health plans today are significantly removed from the basic conditions for fair and enforceable contracts contemplated by law. Yet, in spite of deviations from the ideal, courts have not questioned the validity of such contracts. Neither have they hesitated to enforce contract exclusions (denying medical benefits to patients) when their terms were clear.[60] Although enforcement has been inconsistent, courts have most commonly refused to enforce coverage exclusions on the grounds that the contract language was ambiguous or the treatment at issue was not necessarily excluded by explicit language. Thus, it seems unlikely that patients could successfully claim that their health plans are invalid.

Of course, ethical standards may demand more than law requires. Thus, whether making patients abide by the terms of their health plans is fair or unfair depends on how fairly the plans themselves are structured. But what should count as a fair structure? What choices ought to be available to patients? Fundamentally, the search for standards of fairness is a quest for ethical principles that prescribe what kind of care patients should get. Medical ethics suggests that every patient is entitled to the best available care, but does not obligate anyone to provide that care if it is not paid for. Business ethics also does not obligate anyone to provide any particular care to anyone else, absent a contractual promise. An adequate answer requires more specific standards than either business or medical ethics offers.

Goals for Developing Standards

What might new ethical standards for MCOs look like? Several basic features appear necessary, but will require substantially more discussion, definition, and clarification than can be offered here.

First, ethical standards for MCOs should recognize the organizations' medical responsibilities as well as their business functions. The organization has responsibility—as an organization—for providing health care to individual enrollees, and this responsibility should not be delegable to individuals, even though officers and staff should remain bound by their personal ethical obligations. MCOs should be held directly accountable to enrollees for the scope and quality of patient care, because patients are not customers in the usual sense. Because the MCO's mission is to finance and provide quality medical care, its business structures, policies, and practices should facilitate and not hinder good care. Indeed, ethical standards should give priority to MCOs' medical mission.

Second, organizational standards should reflect ethical principles that apply to all human endeavors, such as fairness, honesty, and truthfulness, respect for persons, and justice. The principle of justice, which governs resource allocation, is especially relevant to MCOs because the very nature of managed care requires allocating resources for the benefit of all members of a group. MCOs must marshal sufficient resources (both human and financial) to care for an entire patient population. In this respect, MCOs differ from other commercial enterprises that do not attempt to allocate their products or services among their potential customers. While physicians may act as patient advocates, the organization's purpose is to ensure that *all* of its enrollees receive appropriate care. Obvious potential conflicts arise between being fair to a population and being fair to an individual patient. But reaching acceptable solutions is more likely when decisions are based on ethical principles of justice and respect for persons than when they are perceived to be based on financial self-interest.

Of course, reasonable people disagree on what justice requires and on what counts as a just allocation of resources.[61] A standard that allocates benefits according to patient need is as plausible as one that eliminates expensive, experimental therapies in order to provide more preventive services. Some proponents of market competition in health care also adopt a libertarian view of justice that does not require any particular distribution of services. In this view, the principles of fair contracting are sufficient to create a just allocation of resources, without regard to who receives what services or why. This latter approach, in effect, argues against any ethical standard that seeks to achieve a more equal distribution of services or benefits.

An even greater difficulty with just allocation as an ethical standard for MCOs is that it applies only to the organization itself. Although one MCO may produce a just distribution of resources across its own subscribers, it does not affect those in other plans or those without health insurance, so that the allocation of resources throughout society may remain quite unjust. One organization cannot be expected to solve the inequities of society as a whole, but society should recognize that organizations whose standards are entirely inward looking are not likely to produce a fairer health care system.

The principles of honesty and fairness suggest that MCOs should fully and completely disclose the terms and conditions of the contracts they offer, especially in a market system that depends on consumer demand. At a minimum, this requires telling current and potential enrollees (and the public) what the plan does and does not provide and the specific conditions in which services will be made available, and ensuring that patients are not coerced into a particular plan.[62] An obligation on the MCO's part for even more extensive disclosure is supported by traditional business ethics and assumptions about market transactions. Fair competition requires informed consumers. Disclosure is a competitive market method of promoting informed consumer choice.

Full disclosure is also supported, analogously, by the doctrine of informed consent.[63] If a subscriber is validly to consent to join a health plan (and to be bound by its terms), then the MCO—the entity with the relevant information—should have a duty to disclose all information relevant to the subscriber's decision. This should include detailed information on the specific treatments that are and are not covered for particular medical conditions, the criteria for making decisions about new or innovative therapies, the MCO's history of approving or denying claims for treatment, and procedures for challenging treatment denials. In addition, the MCO should disclose all financial arrangements with providers, including affiliated physicians and hospitals, and the organization's officers and employees.[64] Standard formats for presenting information should be developed to enable consumers to compare different health plans. The MCO should also ensure that its officers, employees, and health care practitioners are equally open and honest with patients. Full disclosure is intended to move the relationship between MCOs and patients closer to one of fair bargaining, so that patients can actually begin to choose.[65]

There are limits to the utility of information disclosure, however.[66] Not everyone will see or understand the information provided. More important, many consumers do not have the freedom to act on the information or to bargain at all. Their employer may offer only one plan and they may not be able to afford the plan they prefer. The current market does not include any mechanism for such consumers to pressure MCOs to change their policies.[67] Thus, full disclosure is necessary, but insufficient to foster a fair contractual relationship.

MCOs that distinguish themselves by adhering to ethical standards may find that they are penalized in the marketplace. For most commercial enterprises, customer satisfaction produces increased revenues and profits and higher stock values. Patient satisfaction, however, may be associated with more services that cost a for-profit MCO revenues and reduce stock prices. A competitive market is likely to discourage MCOs from seeking subscribers who are likely to need expensive medical care (or from contracting with their physicians). This means that a competitive market will not provide universal health insurance coverage. Some regulation may be necessary to permit MCOs to compete without abandoning their ethical standards. For example, were all companies required to enroll individuals regardless of their medical conditions (assuming a fair distribution of either high risk patients or premium adjustments, with or without financial assistance from government), MCOs would be free to compete on quality of care, including patient satisfaction. Universal coverage would undoubtedly reduce the feasible profit margin for all companies, but the pressure to sacrifice patient welfare for cost control would be substantially diminished. In such circumstances, ethical standards promoting patient welfare could enhance a company's competitive position. Thus, a regulated market that removes or reduces incentives to compete for profits is more likely to encourage the adoption of ethical standards that protect patients.

Conclusion

MCOs combine insurance, management, and health care delivery. They face conflicts, between their financial incentives and their mission (or potential ethical duty) to provide appropriate care, that are analogous to the conflicts faced by physicians in MCOs. The difference between the organizations and the physicians (and other professionals) is that neither the manager nor the organization has any significant history of ethical obligations that counter inappropriate financial incentives. Patients and physicians may wish to judge MCOs by ethical standards that were created for individual physicians and nurses, but the market in which MCOs operate does not use those standards. Those who argue that MCOs should operate like efficient businesses in the competitive marketplace are, in effect, arguing for no standards at all. A free market approach stresses organizing and delivering health care in an economically efficient, value-free way. This effectively precludes the imposition of normative values on MCOs.

In absence of standards that address MCOs' business and medical functions, we may be left with two incompatible sets of standards—one for business and one for medicine. Scholars have begun to rethink conceptions of medical ethics for physicians in MCOs. It is time to rethink business ethics for MCOs. If business ethics do not recognize an organizational commitment to patient welfare, conflicts between physicians and managers, and managers and patients, may be exacerbated, pitting financial power against patient welfare. In such circumstances, it is not cynical to fear that financial pressure may overwhelm patient welfare, leaving companies who risk too much money to provide services to patients at a competitive disadvantage or out of business.

MCOs should not have to choose between ethics and money, but they do need a different set of standards from those of ordinary commercial enterprises. The challenge is to formulate new standards that apply to organizations, not just individuals, and that recognize and reconcile their business and medical functions. If such standards are to be more than idealistic goals, however, it may be necessary to regulate the market to make it possible for organizations to put such standards into practice.

References

1. Erik Eckholm, "While Congress Remains Silent, Health Care Transforms Itself," *New York Times,* Dec. 18, 1994, at 34.

2. John K. Iglehart, "The American Health Care System—Managed Care," *N. Engl. J. Med.,* 327 (1992): 743–47.

3. Marc A. Rodwin, "Conflicts in Managed Care," *N. Engl. J. Med.,* 332 (1995): 604–07.

4. Marc A. Rodwin, *Medicine, Money & Morals: Physicians' Conflicts of Interest* (New York: Oxford University Press, 1993); and Peter Franks, Carolyn M. Clancy, and Paul A. Nutting, "Gatekeeping Revisited—Protecting Patients from Over-treatment," *N. Engl. J. Med.,* 327 (1992): 424–29.

5. Edmund D. Pellegrino, "Words *Can* Hurt You: Some Reflections on the Metaphors of Managed Care," *Journal of the American Board of Family Practice,* 7 (1994): 505–10.

6. Committee on Child Health Financing, American Academy of Pediatrics, "Guiding Principles for Managed Care Arrangements for the Health Care of Infants, Children, Adolescents, and Young Adults," *Pediatrics,* 95 (1995): 613–15; Council on Ethical and Judicial Affairs, American Medical Association, "Ethical Issues in Managed Care," *JAMA,* 271 (1994): 1668–70; Mark H. Waymack, "Health Care as a Business: The Ethic of Hippocrates versus the Ethic of Managed Care," *Business & Professional Ethics Journal,* 9, nos. 3–4 (1990): 69–78; and Susan M. Wolf, "Health Care Reform and the Future of Physician Ethics," *Hastings Center Report,* 24, no. 2 (1994): 28–41.

7. Carolyn M. Clancy and Howard Brody, "Managed Care—Jekyll or Hyde?," *JAMA,* 273 (1995): 338–39.

8. The percentage of MCOs that are for-profit companies grew from 18 percent in 1982 to 67 percent in 1988. See Karen Davis et al., *Health Care Cost Containment* (Baltimore: Johns Hopkins University Press, 1990).

9. The White House Domestic Policy Council, *The President's Health Security Plan. The Clinton Blueprint* (New York: Times Books, 1993): at 11–12.

10. As Sager has noted, managed care, in the form of employee group health organizations, was considered a radical (even socialist) innovation before and after World War II. See Alan Sager, "Reforming Managed Care: More Benefits—Fewer Costs," presented at the conference "Ethics of Managed Care: Values, Conflicts, and Resolutions," Boston University School of Public Health, Boston, Massachusetts, December 9, 1994. Group Health of Puget Sound, the Health Insurance Plan of New York, and the Kaiser-Permanente Medical Care Program have provided comprehensive care at a relatively reasonable cost to large groups of employees for at least fifty years. See John G. Smillie, *Can Physicians Manage the Quality and Costs of Medical Care? The Story of the Permanente Group* (New York: McGraw-Hill, 1991).

11. Theodore R. Marmor and Jonathan Oberlander, "A Citizen's Guide to the Healthcare Reform Debate," *Yale Journal on Regulation,* 11 (1994): 495–506.

12. Stephen M. Shortell, Robin R. Gillies, and David A. Anderson, "The New World of Managed Care: Creating Organized Delivery Systems, *Health Affairs,* 13, no. 4 (1994): 46–64; and Alain C. Enthoven, "The History and Principles of Managed Competition," *Health Affairs,* 12, supp. (1993): 24–48.

13. Paul Starr, "Look Who's Talking Health Care Reform Now," *New York Times Magazine,* Sept. 3, 1995, at 42–43.

14. R.H. Miller and Harold S. Luft, "Managed Care Plan Performance Since 1980: A Literature Analysis," *JAMA,* 271 (1995): 1512–19.

15. Congressional Budget Office, *The Effects of Managed Care and Managed Competition, CBO Memorandum* (Washington, D.C.: Congressional Budget Office, Feb. 1995); Theodore R. Marmor and Jerry L. Mashaw, "Conceptualizing, Estimating, and Reforming Fraud, Waste, and Abuse in Healthcare Spending," *Yale Journal on Regulation,* 11 (1994): 455–94; William B. Schwartz and Daniel N. Mendelson, "Eliminating Waste and Inefficiency Can Do Little to Contain Costs," *Health Affairs,* 13, no. 1 (1994): 223–35; and Henry Aaron and William B. Schwartz, "Rationing Health Care: The Choice Before Us," *Science,* 247 (1990): 418–22.

16. See Iglehart, *supra* note 2.

17. Institute of Medicine, Bradford H. Gray and Marilyn J. Field, eds., *Controlling Costs and Changing Patient Care? The Role of Utilization Management* (Washington D.C.: National Academy Press, 1989); Alan L. Hillman, Mark V. Pauly, and Joseph J. Kerstein, "How Do Financial Incentives Affect Physicians' Clinical Decisions and the Financial Performance of Health Maintenance Organizations?," *N. Engl. J. Med.*, 321 (1989): 87–92; and Rodwin, *supra* note 4.

18. Donald W. Light, "The Practice and Ethics of Risk-Rated Health Insurance," *JAMA*, 267 (1992): 2503–08.

19. Several states have considered legislation prohibiting insurers from excluding coverage of pre-existing medical conditions (completely or for a limited time period). In general, the insurance industry has opposed such legislation.

20. James Morone, "The Ironic Flaw in Health Care Competition: The Politics of Markets," in Richard J. Arnould et al., eds., *Competitive Approaches to Health Care Reform* (Washington, D.C.: Urban Institute Press, 1993): 207–22; Gerald W. Grumet, "Health Care Rationing Through Inconvenience: The Third Party's Secret Weapon," *N. Engl. J. Med.*, 321 (1989): 607–11; U.S. Inspector General, *Beneficiary Perspectives of Medicare Risk HMOs* (Washington, D.C.: Dept. of Health and Human Services, OEI-06-91-00730, 1995); and Robert Blendon, *Sick People in Managed Care Have Difficulty Getting Services and Treatment* (Princeton: Robert Wood Johnson Foundation, 1995).

21. Wendy K. Mariner, "Patients' Rights after Health Care Reform: Who Decides What is Medically Necessary?," *American Journal of Public Health*, 84 (1994): 1515–20.

22. U.S. Congress, Office of Technology Assessment, *Identifying Health Technologies That Work: Searching for Evidence* (Washington, D.C.: Government Printing Office, OTA-H-608, Sept. 1994); and Wendy K. Mariner, "Outcomes Assessment in Health Care Reform: Promise and Limitations," *American Journal of Law & Medicine*, XX (1994): 37–57.

23. Tom Beauchamp and LeRoy Walters, *Contemporary Issues in Bioethics* (Belmont: Wadsworth, 4th ed., 1994). The concept of medical ethics itself is subject to different interpretations. See Michael A. Grodin, "Introduction: The Historical and Philosophical Roots of Bioethics," in Michael A. Grodin, ed., *Meta Medical Ethics: The Philosophical Foundations of Bioethics* (Dordrecht: Kluwer, 1995): at 1–26.

24. See Wolf, *supra* note 6.

25. George J. Annas, "Transferring the Ethical Hot Potato," *Hastings Center Report*, 17, no. 1 (1987): 20–21. With respect to whether corporations in general are moral entities, compare Milton Friedman, "The Social Responsibility of Business Is to Increase its Profits," *New York Times Magazine*, Sept. 13, 1970, at 32–33, 122, 124, 126; Herbert A. Simon, *Administrative Behavior* (New York: Free Press, 1965) (arguing that corporations cannot be held morally responsible); and John Ladd, "Morality and the Ideal of Rationality in Formal Organizations," *The Monist*, 54 (1970): 488–516 (arguing for corporate responsibility). For general discussions of the debate, see Peter A. French, *Collective and Corporate Responsibility* (New York: Columbia University Press, 1984); and Hugh Curtler, ed., *Shame, Responsibility and the Corporation* (New York: Haven, 1986).

26. Richard T. DeGeorge, *Business Ethics* (New York: Macmillan, 4th ed., 1995): at 127.

27. Legal obligations have been a significant source of ethical standards for business. See Paul Steidlmeier, *People and Profits: The Ethics of Capitalism* (Englewood Cliffs: Prentice Hall, 1992): at 14; and John R. Boatright, *Ethics and the Conduct of Business* (Englewood Cliffs: Prentice Hall, 1993): at 386. Federal antitrust legislation, such as the Sherman Act and the Robinson-Patman Act, were arguably efforts to impose ethical standards of fair competition on industry, and law is often seen as the "guardian of business ethics." See Verne E. Henderson, *What's Ethical in Business* (New York: McGraw-Hill, 1992): at 7.

28. Daniel P. Sulmasy, "Physicians, Cost Control and Ethics," *Annals of Internal Medicine*, 116 (1992): 920–26; Gail Povar and John Moreno, "Hippocrates and the Health Maintenance Organization," *Annals of Internal Medicine*, 109 (1988): 419–24; Council on Ethical and Judicial Affairs,

supra note 6; Pellegrino, *supra* note 5; and Wolf, *supra* note 6.

29. Lester C. Thurow, "Medicine Versus Economics," *N. Engl. J. Med.*, 313 (1985): 611–14.

30. See, for example, DeGeorge, *supra* note 26; James P. Wilbur, *The Moral Foundations of Business Practice* (Lanham: University Press of America, 1992); Ronald M. Green, *The Ethical Manager: A New Method for Business Ethics* (New York: Macmillan, 1994); Ronald Berenbeim, *Corporate Ethics* (New York: Conference Board, 1992); Karen Paul, ed., *Business Environment and Business Ethics* (Cambridge: Ballinger, 1987); and Henderson, *supra* note 27.

31. See Boatright, *supra* note 27, at 386; and DeGeorge, *supra* note 26.

32. Stanley Joel Reiser, "The Ethical Life of Health Care Organizations," *Hastings Center Report*, 24, no. 6 (1994): 28–35.

33. See DeGeorge, *supra* note 26. Steidlmeier has summarized American business values as follows: "(1) protecting the interests of property owners by promoting efficiency, reducing costs, and thereby increasing profits; (2) encouraging respect for the rights of property owners; (3) refraining from anticompetitive activities; (4) guarding the freedom of labor, owners, and customers; (5) discouraging government interference; (6) developing personal honesty, responsibility and industriousness; and (7) encouraging private contributions to charity." See Steidlmeier, *supra* note 27.

34. See, for example, Kurt Darr, *Ethics in Health Services Management* (Baltimore: Health Professions Press, 2d ed., 1993), which is directed at developing a personal ethic for individual managers.

35. American College of Healthcare Executives, *Codes of Ethics* (1988).

36. The American College of Health Care Administrators' *Code of Ethics* requires the administrator to "strive to provide to all those entrusted to his or her care the highest quality of appropriate services possible *in light of resources or other constraints.*" See The American College of Health Care Administrators, *Code of Ethics* (1989) (emphasis added). Even the Joint Commission on Accreditation of Healthcare Organizations, which requires hospitals to have a mechanism for considering ethical issues in patient care, qualifies its requirement by providing that the hospital reasonably respond to a patient's need for treatment "within the hospital's capacity." See Joint Commission on Accreditation of Healthcare Organizations, *1995 Accreditation Manual for Hospitals, Vol. I Standards* (Oakbrook Terrace: JCAHO, 1994).

37. The Group Health Association of America has proposed some standards for managed care and health plans, but these deal with financial solvency requirements (common in insurance regulation), patient confidentiality, and some consumer protections. See John K. Iglehart, "The Struggle Between Managed Care and Fee-for-Service Practice," *N. Engl. J. Med.*, 331 (1994): 63–67.

38. See Council on Ethical and Judicial Affairs, *supra* note 6.

39. American Medical Association, *Principles of Medical Ethics* (Chicago: American Medical Association, 1980).

40. Joseph M. Perillo, *Corbin on Contracts* (St. Paul: West, vol. 1, 1993).

41. MCOs are increasingly offering preferred provider or point of service plans that permit enrollees to obtain service outside the plan's network of providers for a larger copayment or deductible. Such plans appear to be a response to enrollee demand for greater freedom to choose physicians and services.

42. *American Heritage Dictionary* (Boston: Houghton Mifflin, 1978): at 792.

43. Health plans that offer services through independent practice association (IPAs) preserve greater choice of physicians for enrollees than do staff model HMOs, for example. Historically, however, IPAs have produced smaller cost savings for health plans. See Miller and Luft, *supra* note 14.

44. Alain C. Enthoven and Richard Kronick, "A Consumer-Choice Health Plan for the 1990's: Universal Health Insurance in a System Designed to Promote Quality and Economy," *N. Engl. J. Med.*, 320 (1989): 29–37.

45. Of course, most MCOs also provide health care through providers in a widening array of

organizational structures, including staff model HMOs, group practice HMOs, networks of IPAs, or other integrated services and preferred provider organizations.

46. Paul Starr, "The Framework of Health Care Reform," *N. Engl. J. Med.*, 329 (1993): 1666–72; Enthoven and Kronick, *supra* note 44; Mark A. Hall and Gerard F. Anderson, "Health Insurers' Assessment of Medical Necessity," *University of Pennsylvania Law Review*, 140 (1992): 1637–712; Paul T. Menzel, *Strong Medicine: The Ethical Rationing of Health Care* (New York: Oxford University Press, 1990); and David Eddy, "Clinical Decision Making: From Theory to Practice—Connecting Value and Costs—Whom Do We Ask and What Do We Ask Them?," *JAMA*, 264 (1990): 1737–39.

47. Employee Benefit Research Institute, *Sources of Health Insurance and Characteristics of the Uninsured: Analysis of the March 1993 Current Population Survey* (Washington, D.C.: EBRI, Jan. 1994).

48. Joel C. Cantor, Stephen H. Long, and M. Susan Marquis, "Private Employer-Based Health Insurance in Ten States," *Health Affairs*, 14, no. 2 (1995): 199–211. Smaller employers were more likely than larger to offer a FFS plan, but such plans were more likely to cover fewer benefits and to exclude preexisting conditions. Only about half of the smaller employers offered any health insurance at all.

49. Deborah Chollet, "Employer-Based Health Insurance in a Changing Work Force," *Health Affairs*, 13, no. 1 (1994): 327–36.

50. Christopher Georges, "Medicare Drive Toward Managed-Care System Could Turn Out to Produce a Costly Success," *Wall Street Journal*, July 31, 1995, at 16; and John K. Iglehart, "Medicaid and Managed Care," *N. Engl. J. Med.*, 322 (1995): 1727–31. Some states, like Tennessee, Florida, and New York, have reported problems in moving Medicaid beneficiaries quickly into some managed care plans. See Ian Fisher, "Forced Marriage of Medicaid and Managed Care Hits Snags," *New York Times*, Aug. 28, 1995, at B1, B5; and Martin Gottlieb, "The Managed Care Cure-All Shows its Flaws and Potential," *New York Times*, Oct. 1, 1995, at 1, 16.

51. Karen Davis et al., "Choice Matters: Enrollees' Views of Their Health Plans," *Health Affairs*, 14, no. 2 (1995): 99–112.

52. The Commonwealth Fund Survey found that among respondents who reported a serious illness, 45 percent of those in FFS medicine rated their plans as excellent, compared to 33 percent of those in managed care. *Id.*

53. The Employee Retirement Income Security Act, 29 U.S.C.S. §§ 1021–25 (1995), which governs employee group health insurance plans offered by employers, requires only that employees receive a summary of the plan, not the contract itself.

54. Describing covered benefits in detail would require extensive lists because appropriate treatment often depends significantly on individual medical conditions. See Ira Mark Ellman and Mark A. Hall, "Redefining the Terms of Insurance to Accommodate Varying Consumer Risk Preferences," *American Journal of Law & Medicine*, XX (1994): 187–201.

55. Recent examples of patients who claimed their health plan should have covered various treatments are described in a series of articles by Michael A. Hiltzik, David R. Olmos, and Barbara Marsh in *The Los Angeles Times*, Aug. 27–31, 1995.

56. U.S. General Accounting Office, *Medicare Part B: Inconsistent Denial Rates for Medical Necessity Across Six Carriers* (Washington, D.C.: GAO, GAO/T-PEMD-94-17, 1994); and General Accounting Office, *Medicare Part B: Regional Variation in Denial Rates for Medical Necessity* (Washington, D.C.: GAO, GAO/PEMD-95-10, 1994).

57. Wendy K. Mariner, "Rationing Health Care and the Need for Credible Scarcity: Why Americans Can't Say No," *American Journal of Public Health*, 85 (1995): 1439–45.

58. George Anders, "HMOs Pile Up Billions in Cash, Try to Decide What to Do With It," *Wall Street Journal*, Dec. 21, 1994, at A1, A5; and Milt Freudenheim, "Penny-pinching H.M.O.'s Showed Their Generosity in Executive Paychecks," *New York Times*, Apr. 11, 1995, at D1, D4. In remarks to Congress on August 30, 1995, H. Ross Perot was reported to say, "If someone were to ask me what is my principal concern about H.M.O.'s, it's the giant concentration of power;

it's the giant salaries. . . . You know, that doesn't look good to me." See Robert Pear, "Perot Tells Senate Committee It's Time to Get Experts' Opinion on Reining in Medicare," *New York Times*, Aug. 31, 1995, at B13.

59. See Mariner, *supra* note 57.

60. See, for example, *Fuja v. Benefit Trust Life Ins. Co.*, 18 F.3d 1405 (7th Cir. 1994).

61. For summaries of different conceptions of justice with respect to allocating health care resources, see John F. Kilner, "Allocation of Health-Care Resources," in Warren Thomas Reich, ed., *Encyclopedia of Bioethics* (New York: Simon & Schuster, vol. 4, 1995): at 1067–84; and President's Commission for the Study of Ethical Problems in Medicine and Biomedical and Behavioral Research, *Securing Access to Health Care: Report on the Ethical Implications of Differences in the Availability of Health Services* (Washington, D.C.: President's Commission, 1983).

62. Anderson et. al. have recommended objective assessments of technologies and therapies and better education to ensure that patients know what they are buying. Gerald F. Anderson, Mark A. Hall, and Earl P. Steinberg, "Medical Technology Assessment and Practice Guidelines: Their Day in Court," *American Journal of Public Health*, 83 (1993): 1635–39.

63. Ruth R. Faden and Tom L. Beauchamp, *A History and Theory of Informed Consent* (New York: Oxford University Press, 1986).

64. Ironically, capitation of physicians—the financial arrangement that has prompted the most concern about ethical standards—may be the least problematic method of payment. This is because capitation permits the MCO to avoid micromanaging patient care decisions in order to control costs. When the risk of financial loss is shifted to the physician, an MCO's financial self-interest rarely conflicts with patient welfare. It is the physician who faces a potential conflict. Physicians have a longer history of personal obligations to patients defined by medical ethics. Nonetheless, because the MCO is responsible for patient care, it should have a responsibility to calculate capitation payments that adequately provide for its patients. In addition, the MCO may be obligated to create different physician payment arrangements that reduce the potential conflict of interest.

65. Several states have introduced legislation to require the disclosure of certain information by MCOs, but the industry has generally opposed such regulation. Michael A. Hiltzik and David R. Olmos, "State Widely Criticized for Regulation of HMOs," *Los Angeles Times*, Aug. 28, 1995, at A1.

66. See Rodwin, *supra* note 4, at 212–22.

67. Yarmolinsky has noted, "Patients may be the only consumers who have to seek permission from someone else in order to obtain services." See Adam Yarmolinsky, "Supporting the Patient," *N. Engl. J. Med.*, 332 (1995): 602–03. In some instances, employees may be able to persuade their employers to offer a different health plan or to have the employer negotiate with an MCO to change the terms of the plan.

Moral Justice and Legal Justice in Managed Care: The Ascent of Contributive Justice

E. HAAVI MORREIM

Several prominent cases have recently high-lighted tension between the interèsts of individuals and those of the broader population in gaining access to health care resources. The care of Helga Wanglie, an elderly woman whose family insisted on continuing life support long after she had lapsed into a persistent vegetative state (PVS), cost approximately $750,000, the majority of which was paid by a Medi-gap policy purchased from a health maintenance organization (HMO).[1] Similarly, Baby K was an anencephalic infant[2] whose mother, believing that all life is precious regardless of its quality, insisted that the hospital where her daughter was born provide mechanical ventilation, including intensive care, whenever respiratory distress threatened her life. Over the hospital's objections, courts ruled that aggressive care must be provided.[3] Much of Baby K's care was covered by her mother's HMO policy.[4] In the 1993 case of *Fox v. HealthNet,* a jury awarded $89 million to the family of a woman whose HMO had refused, as experimental, coverage for autologous bone marrow transplant in treating her advanced breast cancer.[5]

On a more mundane level, studies show that low-osmolar contrast media (a new kind of dye used for radiographic studies) can save the lives of some people at risk for allergic reactions to an older dye, and can be much more comfortable for most patients. But the new dyes are far more expensive—to the point that numerous lives could be saved elsewhere were the costlier dyes reserved only for high-risk patients.[6] Examples abound in which one test or treatment

may be somewhat superior, but only at vastly higher cost.[7]

In each of the above cases, a high level of care for a few individuals is very expensive. Yet only recently has the national bioethics conversation begun to consider that these costs, and their implications for people with competing needs and claims, pose a serious moral challenge. This article will explore how this historically weak interest in statistical, unidentified other people must now emerge as a potent force in health care ethics. In the process, we must reconsider prevailing notions of justice.

Background

Traditionally, the moral concept of *distributive* justice in health care has emphasized the needs of vulnerable individuals, not only focusing on those who lack basic access to care, but also attending to particular people who are denied access to some specific intervention. However, justice that focuses mainly on specific individuals can have adverse, though often hidden, implications for the other people who rely on the same health care system. As I will argue, our traditionally narrow focus must now be explicitly complemented with other notions of justice. *Formal* justice emphasizes that what is done for one person is owed to all others in similar circumstances. *Contractual* justice advocates enforcement of fair agreements. And a new notion, which I call *contributive* justice, observes the legitimate expectations of the many whose contributions create the common resource pool, particularly in cases where contractual language is unclear or inadequate.

Although court decisions have reflected the traditional emphasis on needy individuals, more recently they are actually leading the way in this transition to a broader focus. As discussed below, "judge-made insurance," prominent in the 1980s, generously granted benefits to patients, sometimes well beyond any plausible interpretation of insurance contracts. That trend is now giving way to a considerably greater judicial deference to contractual terms. In the process, courts are openly expressing concern about the broader implications of decisions that may advance the interests of particular individuals to the detriment of the broader group. By reflecting on this recent legal trend, it is possible to construct a balance that can honor vulnerable individuals, while at the same time preventing their needs from holding others' legitimate claims hostage. Justice as fairness to all will require a combination of all four notions of justice.

In this article, one important justice question will be addressed by stipulation. It is assumed that an affluent society such as ours should ensure access to at least some reasonable level of basic care for all citizens, though I will make no attempt to specify the content of such basic care. Once everyone is assured such access, it becomes important to look at other justice issues that arise when the claims of a few conflict with the interests of the larger group. These conflicts are my focus.

Although these issues arise throughout health care, they are especially evident in managed care organizations (MCOs) such as HMOs. It is common to claim that these systems operate within a fixed budget each year, so that money spent on one patient is directly unavailable for other patients or other uses—in other words, that MCOs represent financially "closed" systems[8] in which trade-offs among potential uses of resources are relatively clear.

The truth is somewhat more complex. Managed care runs a wide spectrum of forms, ranging from completely integrated, self-contained delivery systems, such as HMOs (the paradigm MCO), to managed fee-for-service plans in which indemnity insurers pay for services as they are rendered, but add utilization controls to ensure prudent resource use.[9]

Strictly speaking, no health system is perfectly closed, because it is always possible that expenses in a given year will exceed revenues. And, in principle, any deficits an MCO has in one year can be reclaimed by purchasing stop-loss insurance and by raising premiums the following year. Furthermore, some MCOs are currently running extravagant cash surpluses—hardly a lifeboat situation.[10]

However, several factors steer us back toward the original picture of a relatively closed financial system. First, MCOs cannot freely raise premiums from year to year as they once did. Employers and governments are demanding price restraint in an ever more competitive market. In some parts of the United States, MCOs are actually rolling back premiums.[11] Second, many MCOs already function at the limits of their budgets, while more affluent ones are likely to see their surpluses dwindle in the not too distant future. Above all, an HMO aims to provide all health care within the funds available. Unlike a traditional indemnity insurer, which simply pays bills as they are accrued, HMOs take vigorous steps to ensure that expenditures do not exceed designated budgets. Hence, virtually all HMOs place financial incentives on physicians,[12] and most also impose tight utilization controls.[13]

As a result, expenditures on one patient or group will be felt elsewhere in the system. Physicians who see their risk-pool money dwindling may be less inclined to order marginal testing; the pharmacy formulary committee may narrow its list of approved drugs or refrain from adding a promising but costly new drug; a policy permitting easy access to low-osmolar contrast media may be restricted to high-risk patients.[14] In short, whatever is spent on one patient is clearly unavailable for another; and, reciprocally, whatever is not spent for one purpose can[15] be used for other purposes.

Furthermore, MCOs ordinarily have a defined patient population for a defined period of time. For their usually year-long membership period, all patients are identified, and it is theoretically possible to track fairly precisely how much money is spent for what kinds of care, for which patients. Trade-offs of various potential expenditures within the system are clearer, and it is possible, at least in principle, to construct reasonably clear resource policies. Accordingly, I will focus on the integrated delivery of managed care, although much of what is said also applies to indemnity insurance and other financing systems.

Moral Justice

The bioethics literature's emphasis on individuals, almost to the exclusion of the wider group's interests and needs, is historically understandable. In the 1960s and 1970s, revelations about patient abuses in medical research and in the paternalism of ordinary medical care directed the emerging field of bioethics to focus on individual patients' autonomous right to receive information and to give or with-hold consent.

Further, traditional notions of physicians' fiduciary duties hold that it would be morally wrong for them to pass up even an "infinitesimally beneficial" procedure for a patient in order to save money for third parties.[16] In the standard litany, "physicians are required to do everything they believe may benefit each patient without regard to costs or other societal considerations"; [17] "asking physicians to be cost-conscious . . . would be asking them to abandon their central commitment to their patients."[18]

Even our concepts of justice focus mainly on individuals. In principle, distributive justice concerns the entire distribution of benefits and burdens throughout society. Yet in practice, discussions of distributive justice mainly concern individuals who are left out of society's benefits—the minority who still lack access to the health care system, and the individuals who need but cannot afford some specific, perhaps costly, treatment. In 1972, for instance, a national commission studying the totally implantable artificial heart concluded that although its cost would be enormous, it would be unjust not to fund it for all who needed it. Interests of other people were deemed relevant only to the selection of power source: nuclear power, with its potential risks for others, should be forgone in favor of an electric rechargeable battery.[19]

On this traditional view, competing needs and interests can permissibly figure only in situations of *commodity* scarcity. Where some particular product or device, such as an intensive care unit (ICU) bed or a transplant organ, is too scarce to meet the need, justice seeks a fair way to decide who will receive and who will not. Here, trade-offs cannot be avoided. But *fiscal* scarcity—the shortage of money itself, with its vastly more amorphous trade-offs between identified individuals and statistical groups—was virtually unrecognized as a resource problem, and certainly was not a routine consideration in discussions of justice.[20]

And not without reason. Until recently, health care was (perceived to be) funded from a bottomless artesian well of money. Payers reimbursed generously and usually without question, passing their costs along to businesses that paid tax-free premiums without much difficulty. Patients were almost completely insulated from the costs, and physicians could usually count on being paid for as many services as they delivered.[21] When money is truly no object, it is wrong to deny something to a patient in order to save some third party money.[22] If scarcity is minimal or only sporadic, justice needs only to focus on those few who are left out altogether or who are denied some particular intervention.

Further, this focus on the individual is consistent with the American insistence that the individual is precious in his own right, not valued merely for his usefulness to society. And it accords with our societal emphasis on personal freedom. In health care, that freedom has sometimes been construed as the right not only to refuse unwanted care, but also to demand whatever resources one wants.

However, it is now clear that health care is not funded from a bottomless well. For decades, costs have risen far faster than the rate of inflation. A wide range of cost-containment efforts has largely failed to stem that increase, and the prospect of adding another forty million people to the access rolls is as financially frightening as it is morally essential. Likewise, it has become clear that whatever is spent on one patient is not available for other uses. When Baby K required a ventilator, her ICU bed was not available for some other infant with prospects for a healthy and active life; and the money to pay for Baby K's care was not available for other uses. Helga Wanglie's year in PVS was paid from the same money designated for her fellow HMO members' care. This is not to say, of course, that money saved by limiting treatment for a Baby K or a Helga Wanglie would surely be put to better use. But in the managed care systems, the negative implication is assured: money spent for these purposes is assuredly not available for anyone else.

Once it is understood that money is limited and that trade-offs are inevitable even if not always obvious, it becomes necessary to consider other concepts of justice. Although distributive justice applies in principle to all benefits and burdens in society, the concept has mostly been reserved for deprived individuals. Therefore, we need to add conceptual breadth through notions of *formal* justice, *contractual* justice, and *contributive* justice.

Formal Justice

Formal justice requires that we treat like cases alike.[23] By this principle, the money used to grant exotic or costly care for one patient must also be granted to every other patient in similar circumstances—potentially escalating expenditures enormously. Some commentators would dispute this implication. The cost of treating anencephalics, for example, is unlikely to make much impact on overall budgets, because so few are born every year and so few of their parents want aggressive care.[24] In reply, the demands for exotic care are not limited to anencephalics, as Helga Wanglie illustrates. But even here, some commentators argue that the cost of so-called futile care is not high relative to the nation's total health care budget.[25]

At this point, however, two further concerns arise. First, even this limited group of patients can place a real strain on a smaller MCO's budget, or on a hospital's budget if the care is uncompensated. Second, it is very difficult to limit the definition of *similar care* to encompass just a specific diagnosis or narrow medical scenario. If Baby K and Wanglie can command unlimited support, so can anyone with advanced dementia. Or if an HMO grants bone marrow transplant for a woman with advanced breast cancer, the financial implications are not limited just to women with breast cancer, because other people have other diseases with comparably dismal prognoses. Neither are they limited to just the patients who want bone marrow transplant. Many costly new treatments are being developed for different illnesses. Ultimately, a wide variety of other patients with similarly grim prognoses, all demanding equally costly, last-ditch, unproven[26] treatments, would have a serious moral claim to be treated.[27] In the final analysis, serious deference to formal justice could potentially have an enormous impact on a health plan's overall resources.

Contractual Justice

Contractual justice concerns fair exchange, honest dealing, and keeping one's agreements in good faith.[28] A variety of contracts exists:

between physicians and their medical partners; among physicians, hospitals, and MCOs; between these providers and assorted payers; and the like. Of special interest here are contracts between patients and payers that establish what services or reimbursements a patient can expect in return for a premium payment.

Such contracts must specify each side's obligations and rights as clearly as possible. Whereas distributive justice considers what people need, contractual justice asks to what they are legally or economically entitled by way of these explicit agreements.[29] We might argue in a given instance that a patient needs or deserves more than that which he is technically entitled. But ignoring contractual limits, even out of compassion, can disserve not only the payer with whom the patient has contracted, but also all its other subscribers.[30]

If a patient's MCO or insurer clearly excludes experimental care, for instance, the patient who somehow extracts coverage for such a procedure has violated all the other patients who have refrained in good faith from asking for that care, or who have been denied it on request. The payer, in turn, has broken its implicit promise to the others; namely, that their premiums will be used only according to the organization's policies, so that it will have enough money to ensure that every subscriber will receive the health coverage to which he is entitled.[31] Additionally, when other beneficiaries' requests for similarly extraordinary treatment are denied, as they surely will be, the principle of formal justice is again offended.

Contributive Justice

What I call *contributive justice* concerns fairness to the large number of people whose financial contributions comprise the resource pool from which individual needs are then served. That pool must be managed so that the members as a whole can receive the spectrum of benefits they legitimately expect, without permitting excessive demands of a few unduly to deplete what is left for the many.

Questions of contributive justice mainly arise when contracts are unclear or incomplete. Because no contract can cover all contingencies, and contract language inevitably contains ambiguities, the administration of health care contracts will always require discretion.[32] Contributive justice holds that this discretion must consider not just the particular individuals requesting coverage; but also the answers' implications for other subscribers. The exercise of discretion should serve, by its cumulative impact and logical implications, the broader interests of the mainstream of subscribers rather than cater to idiosyncratic demands of particular segments.[33] Therefore, administrators must look to the spirit of the agreement, the basic values governing health care and resource use that contractors hoped to achieve in signing on. These are the expectations subscribers held *ex ante*, at the time they chose their policy, not what a few now wish they had, after events have defined their needs more clearly.[34]

Currently, many MCO and insurance contracts are rather vague about what constitutes "medically necessary" or "experimental" care. And sometimes coverage decisions are made not so much according to the merits of the case, as according to which patients complain the loudest or threaten a lawsuit.[35] Such concessions may help the complaining individuals, but they can also offend contributive justice if, by broader implication, they threaten to exhaust the margin of discretionary funding with large expenditures of common money for hopeless, marginal, or unintended uses.

Contributive justice can overlap with contractual justice. When a health plan administrator simply ignores clear rules so to accommodate someone's urgent or highly publicized demand, he violates contractual justice. But he also offends contributive justice. The other people in the plan might not actually experience direct deprivation of necessary care, but the resources available to them have been affected, and their good faith in the fairness of the program has been violated.

In sum, as distributive justice historically focuses on those who are left out, either from the health care system or from particular treatments, it is now time to consider the other people in that system. Formal justice states that what we do for one, we must do for others similarly situated; contractual justice requires that agreements be honored as written; and contributive justice protests when discretionary generosity for a few is bought at others' expense.

. . .

Legal Justice

In this section, we will review mainstream trends in health law before proceeding, in the next section, to examine recent developments that lead the way toward a broader view of justice.

Judge-Made Insurance Law

Much of the litigation in health insurance concerns coverage disputes and prevailing principles favor beneficiaries over insurers. Judges generally construe contractual ambiguities against the contract drafter—here, the MCO or insurer.[36] Additionally, health coverage is usually considered a contract of adhesion: a stronger party controls the terms of an agreement that the individual must simply take or leave, as presented, for a service he needs. Considerable deference is therefore accorded to the vulnerable party. Courts are also likely to favor the plaintiff if they find some flaw in the payer's procedures as when the health plan administrator has acted arbitrarily or capriciously in denying benefits[37] or has failed to investigate a claim adequately.[38]

Some cases do feature genuine ambiguities, procedural flaws, or administrative arbitrariness.[39] But not all. Numerous observers have identified a strong trend of judge-made insurance law in the past couple of decades.[40] The most prominent cases feature people with life-threatening diseases who seek a costly new treatment that represents their only hope for survival. The plaintiff requests an injunction ordering coverage for the treatment, and the judge finds some reason to grant it.

Thus, in *DiDomenico v. Employers Co-op. Industry Trust*, a patient needing liver transplant won such an injunction. Public policy favors the sanctity of life, the court reasoned, and errors should favor a plaintiff who stands to lose his life rather than a payer whose stands only to lose money.[41] In *Leonhardt v. Holden Business Forms Co.*, similar reasoning favored a patient requesting autologus bone marrow transplant for multiple myeloma.[42]

Sometimes, judges appear to go well beyond any plausible interpretation of contractual language or finding of ambiguity in order to award benefits to desperate individuals. In *Bailey v. Blue Cross/Blue Shield of Virginia*, a woman with advanced breast cancer sought high-dose chemotherapy with peripheral stem cell rescue (a form of bone marrow transplant). The insurer's policy language stated: "Autologous bone marrow transplants and other forms of stem cell rescue (in which the patient is the donor) with high dose chemotherapy and/or radiation . . . are not covered." Although the policy listed several kinds of cancer that constituted exceptions to this exclusion, it explicitly stated that breast cancer was not such an exception.[43] Nevertheless, the court found for the plaintiff on the ground that the policy was ambiguous. On other occasions, courts find that, although no ambiguity exists, some particular clause in a policy is so adverse to beneficiaries' interests that its very existence is against public policy.[44]

Across these cases, courts have presumed that public policy must favor the individual, who is often quite helpless in comparison to the large corporation whose decisions he contests. The rulings thereby reject the traditional presumption of contract law that courts should not interfere with citizens' freedom to contract and that unambiguous contracts should be enforced as written.

Instead, they emphasize individuals' lack of power to bargain over terms or to make coverage determinations; and thus they interpret contracts according to what the beneficiary might reasonably have expected or should be entitled to expect, rather than according to a literal reading of contract terms or to this particular beneficiary's actual expectations.[45]

Viewing only a needy individual against a large corporation, it is easy to find for the individual. But when formal justice is applied, the broader implications can be formidable. Extraordinary needs of a few individuals, expanded by logical extension to other similar individuals, can imperil resources needed for the larger group. Indeed, it was partly with this concern in mind that Congress chose in 1974 to revamp employee benefits law so to assure that employees who were counting on benefits, whether pensions, health care, or other, would not find themselves empty-handed in their time of need. Although it protects individuals, ERISA also recognizes that the wider group is comprised of individuals who likewise need protection.

. . .

ERISA Law and Developments

[Omitted: discussion of federal ERISA law and courts' overall willingness, albeit sometimes with reluctance, to enforce the limits of ERISA governed health plans.]

Contract Law

Whereas a number of district courts in the 1980s and early 1990s seemed eager to award benefits to individuals, circuit courts in the mid-1990s have become increasingly disposed to hold that, unless a contract is ambiguous, its plain language should control. In *Loyola University of Chicago v. Humana Insurance Co.,*[79] for example, surgeons performing coronary bypass surgery were unable to wean the patient from intraoperative heart-lung bypass equipment; they im-

planted an artificial heart as a bridge to the human heart transplant that was performed a month later. The insurer refused payment for the artificial heart on the ground that it was experimental, and denied coverage for the human heart transplant because the patient failed to secure the required utilization review approval. The Seventh Circuit court upheld: "This is a contract case and the language of the benefit plan controls. Again, Loyola and Mr. Via were certainly free to attempt these life-saving procedures, but the benefits plan does not require Humana to pay for them."[80]

The same court ruled similarly in *Fuja v. Benefit Trust Life Insurance Co.,* a case in which a woman sought autologous bone marrow transplant for her advanced breast cancer. The insurance contract excluded treatments connected with research, and the court determined that autologous bone marrow transplant for her disease constituted research. "Under the present state of the law, we are bound to interpret the language of the specific contract before us and cannot amend or expand the coverage contained therein."[81]

The Tenth Circuit echoed this theme in *McGee v. Equicor-Equitable HCA Corp.,* upholding an HMO's refusal to pay for nursing home care that had not been approved in accordance with utilization review requirements.

> We are mindful that the objective in construing a health care agreement, as with general contract terms, is to ascertain and carry out the true intention of the parties. However, we do so giving the language its common and ordinary meaning *as a reasonable person in the position of the HMO participant,* not the actual participant, would have understood the words to mean. . . . Under general contract law principles, "words cannot be written into the agreement imparting an intent wholly unexpressed when it was executed."[82]

A number of other recent cases likewise insist on faithfulness to contractual language.[83]

Interestingly, in a number of these cases, courts express sympathy for the plaintiff who is denied medical benefits or tort recovery, but expressly reject such feelings as a basis for judicial ruling. In *Loyola*: "Although it seems callous for Humana to deny coverage for a life-saving procedure and thereafter deny all subsequent hospital expenses—in essence saying to Mr. Via 'we will not cover you because you should be dead'—Humana's humanity is not the issue here. This is a contract case and the language of the benefit plan controls."[84]

In a poignant footnote, the *Fuja* court quoted a district court judge in *Harris v. Mutual of Omaha*:

Despite rumors to the contrary, those who wear judicial robes are human beings, and as persons, are inspired and motivated by compassion as anyone would be. Consequently, we often must remind ourselves that in our official capacities, we have authority only to issue rulings within the narrow parameters of the law and the facts before us. The temptation to go about, doing good where we see fit, and to make things less difficult for those who come before us, regardless of the law, is strong. But the law, without which judges are nothing, abjures such unlicensed formulation of unauthorized social policy by the judiciary.

Plaintiff Judy Harris well deserves, and in a perfect world would be entitled to, all known medical treatments to control the horrid disease from which she suffers. In ruling as this court must, no personal satisfaction is taken, but that the law was followed. The court will have to live with the haunting thought that Ms. Harris, and perhaps others insured by the Mutual of Omaha Companies under similar plans, may not ultimately receive the treatment they need and deserve.[85]

The *Fuja* court went on: "We note at the outset that cases of this nature pose most difficult policy questions of who should bear the burden of paying for expensive medical treatments that are at the time of treatment of unknown efficacy. Although we fully realize the heartache Mrs. Fuja's family has endured, as judges we are called upon to resolve the legal question presented in this appeal, i.e., interpreting the Benefit Trust insurance contract."[86]

Judges' sympathy for patients in need has been tempered not just by their interest in upholding law, but also by a recognition that patients can and should bear some responsibility for their own conduct, both in choosing health plans and in fulfilling contractual obligations once they select one. The *McGee* court pointed out that "[w]hile it is readily apparent Mr. McGee sought the best possible care for his daughter, he was still obligated to work within the defined contractual borders of the HMO he *elected* to participate in."[87] The court went on to point out that these borders may be especially important in managed care. "HMOs are not traditional insurance companies designed to indemnify participants for services they unilaterally select at any geographic location. Instead, HMOs . . . provide comprehensive prepaid medical services within a defined geographic area, and with specific exceptions, only by participating medical professionals and facilities."[88] Equicor, the defendant HMO, had made rehabilitation benefits contingent on periodic determinations by the patient's primary care physician—a requirement that Mr. McGee knew about but chose not to fulfill.

Similarly, the Third Circuit upheld an insurer's requirement that the patient pay 30 percent of his medical bill because he failed to secure advance approval for his care. The patient knew at least a full day ahead of time that he would need to enter the hospital. His wife could have obtained precertification within the time required; moreover, he presented hospital admissions staff with an outdated insurance card that lacked current precertification information.[89] Analogously, the *Loyola* court pointed out that "prior approval was indeed a condition precedent. As the plan unambiguously states, no benefits are payable without prior approval. It is undisputed that necessary records on Mr. Via's condition were not sent by Loyola until after the heart transplant and that the records were not received by Humana until after Mr. Via's death."[90]

Recent Legal Trends: Analysis

[Omitted: Discussion of courts' attempts to balance interests of individuals against the broader needs of health care subscribers and society at large.]

Balancing the Justices

Each of the four notions of justice has an important message. *Distributive* justice asks us to help individuals who have been left out of society's benefits, and reminds us that sometimes a person's health care access may be so inadequate that it is morally unfair. *Formal* justice points out that because equals must be treated equally, every benefit determination has policy implications.[107] *Contractual* justice points out that entitlements are defined by agreements: one should expect to receive all the benefits for which he has contracted, but no more. And *contributive* justice takes over where contractual clarity ends, reminding us that a generous compassion for one is inevitably bought at the expense of many whose contributions create and who in turn rely on the common resource pool. Benefits administration must honor the spirit as well as the letter of the agreement.

A tidy formula for resolving conflicts among these kinds of justice is unattainable. Many of the strongest concerns about distributive justice can be met if everyone has access to a basic level of care—a precept presumed at the outset of this paper. Honoring other forms of justice begins with the need to ensure that patients have real choices. One reason courts have been so generous in granting benefits to individual patients—sometimes in violation of contributive, formal, and contractual justice—is that patients typically have so few choices in their health care. Their employers choose their health plans[108] and the

plans limit choices of providers and treatments; often the patient's only real choice is to "take it or leave it."[109]

But just as it is difficult to hold patients to the adverse consequences of contracts over which they had no choice, conversely it is far easier to hold them to agreements that they have freely made from among adequate options, clearly described. Thus, it may be proposed that the other forms of justice hinge significantly on constructing and enforcing contracts.

Contract Construction

Universal access need not entail uniform access. For reasons discussed elsewhere, a single one-size-fits-all standard of resources for all citizens is arguably neither morally mandatory nor practically attainable.[110] Within and above a basic package, citizens need to be able to choose the kinds of services they deem most important, and to forgo those they do not need or want.

Havighurst envisions a marketplace in which various sets of guidelines articulate the levels of care from which people could choose.[111] Kalb describes three tiers from which people might choose.[112] The most basic level of care would only include measures that are demonstrated to be safe, effective, and cost-effective. A second tier might add technologies that are safe and effective but not cost-effective. Thus, if two antibiotics are equally effective for a particular condition, the basic tier might only have access to the less costly one that must be taken several times a day, while the higher tier might enjoy the convenience of the costlier, one-a-day version; the basic level might reserve costly low-osmolar contrast dyes for high-risk patients, while a higher tier might avail them to all. Above these tiers might be a third level granting access to innovative technologies that have not yet been fully evaluated. A comparable approach is proposed by Hall and Anderson.[113]

Such options can honor distributive justice by permitting individuals to choose the level of care they want, beyond whatever adequate minimum is presumed for all. When someone spends his own money to enhance his health care, he does not unfairly disadvantage others; in fact, he may actually, by contributing extra resources to the system, help to enhance care for all. Those on the third tier, who purchase access to the most innovative technologies, may speed these treatments' development and evaluation and thereby their availability to others.[114] Perhaps on that top tier we might also place heroic life support for PVS patients, like Wanglie and Baby K; although such care would then be available to those who value it, the rest of society would not be forced to pay.

Contracting procedures should of course be fair and clear: if subscribers do not know the limits of the health plans they buy, they cannot be said to have chosen those limits nor, therefore, can those limits be fairly enforced. A policy must do more than state that it does not cover experimental care, for example. It must define, as precisely as possible, what will count as experimental or preventive care, and when these are not to be covered.[115] If certain treatments are excluded because they are not cost-effective, or if providers are financially rewarded for curtailing care, these policies likewise must be laid out as clearly as possible.[116]

Contract Enforcement

Enforcing contracts fairly but rigorously is an act of respect for the contractor. It presumes that he is an adult capable of making his own decisions for his own reasons, and that he can be held responsible for what he does. If people cannot count on their contracts' being enforced, their freedom to contract is nullified, along with the choices they might have actualized through such contracts.[117]

When contractual language is clear and the subscriber has entered that contract by choice,[118] then formal and contractual justice both require that it be enforced as written: treat in the same way all who have signed the same contract, according to its terms. This means granting what is owed as well as denying what is not. Everyone is imperiled when a fellow subscriber is denied his due.

When contractual language is unclear, contributive justice requires that contracts be enforced according to the intentions of subscribers *ex ante*, not by what desperate individuals wish they would have bought *ex post*.[119] When someone wants to limit his health care expenditures by buying a package that excludes the costliest care, his good faith is violated—and eventually his budget and his health care—if that plan's administrators ignore this contractual limit by "generously" giving such technologies to other subscribers who demand them.

In sum, courts must be willing to see individuals as capable of making up their own minds and of being held to their decisions. But an important question remains, because individuals can really be more vulnerable in this very complex area of contracting than elsewhere in their lives. Even if we discard the idea that health care contracts are adhesory[120] and subject to paternalistic judicial rewriting, we must still consider what sort of deference individuals should receive, given the relative power imbalance in such situations.

Several replies can be made. First, choice and information reduce vulnerability considerably. Where the subscriber could have opted for a richer level of benefits but did not, and where comprehensive, comprehensible information was readily available, courts have been willing to enforce contracts. This is particularly the case when individuals have had their interests represented by powerful agents bargaining on their behalf.[121]

Second, although illness renders patients vulnerable in the context of receiving care, most individuals are not ill at the time of choosing health plans. They have time to educate themselves and, particularly in a system with annual open enrollment, to correct poor choices by switching plans. If all plans must provide at least a basic minimum of benefits, no choice can err too seriously.

Third, there is no good reason to require that subscribers must understand and accept, in advance, every conceivable implication of their choice. It is impossible to describe every potential contingency for every possible illness to the full understanding of every prospective subscriber; requiring it would defeat any opportunity for binding contracts in health care. Rather, what should be required is a reasonable general description of the kinds of benefits included in the plan and a careful accounting of its procedures for determining benefits and adjudicating appeals.[122]

Conclusion

Managed care, with its fixed budgets and defined populations, illustrates that health care must now be conceived in terms of trade-offs. What is done for one person has wider implications: it must be matched for others similarly situated, and the costs of such matching may harm the larger group of subscribers who rely on the plan.

Significantly, the courts are paving the way for this important transition by revitalizing contractual justice. By ensuring that individuals receive everything they are entitled to, courts protect the interests of every subscriber with those same entitlements. At the same time, by keeping individuals from claiming more than their due, courts guard the resource pool from which all subscribers' needs must be served.

Much work remains to be done, of course. Society must ensure that all citizens have access to health care, and to a reasonable variety of health plans for delivering that care. And those plans must make their priorities and limits considerably clearer than many now do. But as real options emerge, people should be expected to abide by those choices. Then, it is to be hoped, we may not feel compelled to allow the wishes or needs of a few to violate a hundred nameless other people. This, surely, lies at the heart of justice as fairness to everyone.

Acknowledgments

The author acknowledges with gratitude the very helpful comments provided on earlier drafts of this manuscript by Lance Stell, Ph.D., Clark Havighurst, J.D., Barry Furrow, J.D., Nancy King, J.D., Max Mehlman, J.D., Larry Churchill, Ph.D., and Philip Boyle, Ph.D.

References

1. On July 4, 1991, Wanglie died after more than a year in PVS, kept alive only by intensive medical life support. Although the HMO did not protest the expenditure, in fact it had no alternative because Minnesota State law forbids HMOs from placing financial limits on HMO policies. See S.H. Miles, "Interpersonal Issues in the Wanglie Case," *Kennedy Institute of Ethics Journal*, 2 (1992): at 65. See also S.H. Miles, "Informed Demand for 'Non-Beneficial' Medical Treatment," *N. Engl. J. Med.*, 325 (1991): 512–15; and M. Angell, "The Case of Helga Wanglie: A New Kind of 'Right to Die' Case," *N. Engl. J. Med.*, 325 (1991): 511–12.

2. Anencephaly is a condition in which the brain is completely absent except for the brainstem. It is defined as "congenital absence of the cranial vault, with cerebral hemispheres completely missing or reduced to small masses attached to the base of the skull." See *Dorland's Illustrated Medical Dictionary* (Philadelphia: W.B. Saunders, 26th ed., 1981). Major portions of skull and scalp are likewise missing. Because of these anomalies, the anencephalic infant will never be conscious in any way.

3. In July 1993, a federal district court relied on antidiscrimination and emergency medical treatment laws to rule that any time the infant presents at the hospital in respiratory distress, the mother's demand for aggressive care must be met. Baby K subsequently resided in a nursing home, but on several occasions developed respiratory distress requiring mechanical ventilation. In its antidiscrimination arguments, the district court invoked § 504 of the Rehabilitation Act and the Americans with Disabilities Act. The district court also invoked the Emergency Medical Treatment and Active Labor Act (EMTALA), which requires hospitals to evaluate and stabilize all patients presenting for emergency care, prior to any transfer to another facility. Although the hospital argued that aggressive treatment for Baby K was futile, since nothing can reverse anencephaly, the district court found that these laws contain no exceptions for futility. See *In the Matter of Baby K*, 832 F. Supp. 1022 (E.D. Va. 1993).

   In February 1994, the Fourth Circuit Court of Appeals upheld the district court's ruling, basing its decision exclusively on emergency medical treatment law. The court found that whenever the infant's respiratory distress could only be stabilized with the use mechanical ventilation, such treatment must be provided. Like the district court, the Fourth Circuit ruled that EMTALA grants no exceptions on grounds of futility; such exceptions must be made by Congress. See *In the Matter of Baby K*, 16 F.3d 590 (4th Cir.), *cert. denied*, 115 S. Ct. 91 (1994).

4. Baby K's hospital bills were mainly paid for by Kaiser Permanente. See D.M. Gianelli, "Doctors Argue Futility of Treating Anencephalic Baby," *American Medical News*, Mar. 21, 1994, at 5. Baby K died on April 5, 1995, of cardiac arrest. See M. Tousignant and B. Miller, "Death of 'Baby K' Leaves a Legacy of Legal Precedent," *Washington Post*, May 7, 1995, at B3.

5. Fox eventually raised the money on her own, but died shortly after completing treatment. The jury found that the HMO's denial of funds delayed her treatment long enough to be a substantial cause of her death, and therefore that the refusal constituted bad faith, breach of contract, and reckless infliction of emotional distress. See E.J. Pollock, "Jury Tells HMO to Pay Damages in Dispute over Refused Coverage," *Wall Street Journal*, Dec. 28, 1993, at B4; and M. Meyer and A. Murr, "Not My Health Care," *Newsweek*, 123, no. 2 (1994): 36–38. Rather than being appealed, the case was later settled out of court for a substantially lesser amount.

6. In a study conducted for Kaiser Permanente, Southern California Region, Dr. David Eddy determined that, if the costly low-osmolar dyes are used for everyone instead of only patients at high risk for adverse reaction, the HMO's additional cost would be about $35 million. He also calculated some hypothetical opportunity costs: this money, instead of being used to enhance comfort and to avoid forty severe but nonfatal reactions, could alternatively avoid thirty-five breast cancer deaths, or 100 deaths from cervical cancer, or thirteen sudden deaths from cardiac disease, if used for improved preventive care and the like. See D.M. Eddy, "Applying Cost-Effectiveness Analysis: The Inside Story," *JAMA*, 268 (1992): 2575–82.

7. See, for example, GUSTO Investigators, "An International Randomized Trial Comparing Four Thrombolytic Strategies for Acute Myocardial Infarction," *N. Engl. J. Med.*, 329 (1993): 673–82; GUSTO Investigators, "The Effects of Tissue-Plasminogen Activator, Streptokinase, or Both on Coronary-Artery Patency, Ventricular Function, and Survival after Acute Myocardial Infarction," *N. Engl. J. Med.*, 329 (1993): 1615–22; M.E. Farkouh, J.D. Land, and D.L. Sackett, "Thrombolytic Agents: The Science of the Art of Choosing the Better Treatment," *Annals of Internal Medicine*, 120 (1994): 886–88; K.L. Lee et al., "Holding GUSTO Up to the Light," *Annals of Internal Medicine*, 120 (1994): 876–81; P.M. Ridker et al., "A Response to 'Holding GUSTO Up to the Light'," *Annals of Internal Medicine*, 120 (1994): 882–85; and K. Terry, "Technology: The Biggest Health-Care Cost-Driver of All," *Medical Economics*, 71, no. 6 (1994): 124–37.

8. N. Daniels, "Why Saying No to Patients in the United States is so Hard," *N. Engl. J. Med.*, 314 (1986): 1380–83.

9. J.P. Weiner and G. de Lissovoy, "Razing a Tower of Babel: A Taxonomy for Managed Care and Health Insurance Plans," *Journal of Health Politics, Policy and Law*, 18 (1993): 75–103.

10. G. Anders, "HMOs Pile Up Billions in Cash, Try to Decide What to Do with It," *Wall Street Journal*, Dec. 21, 1994, at A1, A12.

11. J. Johnsson, "Price Quake Rattles Doctors, Hospitals," *American Medical News*, Oct. 24, 1994, at 1, 18; and M. Mitka, "HMO Enrollment Tops 50 Million: Low Premium Costs Fuel Rapid Expansion," *American Medical News*, Dec. 26, 1994, at 3.

12. Many MCOs withhold part of physicians' fees, salary, or capitation payment; many also add bonuses or even pay-back penalties based on resources used through the year. See A.L. Hillman, "Financial Incentives for Physician in HMOs: Is There a Conflict of Interest?," *N. Engl. J. Med.*, 317 (1987): 1743–48; A.L. Hillman, "Health Maintenance Organizations, Financial Incentives, and Physicians' Judgments," *Annals of Internal Medicine*, 112 (1990): 1891–93; and A.L. Hillman, "Managing the Physician: Rules Versus Incentives," *Health Affairs*, 10, no. 4 (1991): 138–46. More recently, many MCOs have switched to capitated arrangements that place physicians almost entirely at risk for the care provided.

13. See Hillman (1991), *supra* note 12.

14. See Eddy, *supra* note 6.

15. To say that money saved can be used for other patient care does not mean that it will be. Other, less salutary uses might be made. A for-profit HMO might return savings to stockholders in the form of earnings, and virtually any HMO may return some savings to physicians as part of its incentive system. However, the negative is assured: money spent on one patient within a financially closed system is not available for any other subscriber.

16. R.M. Veatch, *A Theory of Medical Ethics* (New York: Basic Books, 1981): at 285. For a useful summary of this line of thought, see M.A. Hall, "The Ethics of Health Care Rationing," *Public Affairs Quarterly*, 8 (1994): 33–49.

17. N.G. Levinsky, "The Doctor's Master," *N. Engl. J. Med.*, 311 (1984): at 1573.

18. R.M. Veatch, "DRGs and the Ethical Reallocation of Resources," *Hastings Center Report*, 16, no. 3

(1986): at 38. For further discussion of the traditional view, see also E.H. Morreim, *Balancing Act: The New Medical Ethics of Medicine's New Economics* (Dordrecht: Kluwer, 1991): at 45; and Hall, *supra* note 16, at 34–35.

19. T.L. Beauchamp and J.F. Childress, *Principles of Biomedical Ethics* (New York: Oxford University Press, 3rd ed., 1989): at 258–59.

20. See Morreim, *supra* note 18; and E.H. Morreim, "Fiscal Scarcity and the Inevitability of Bedside Budget Balancing," *Archives of Internal Medicine*, 149 (1989): 1012–15.

21. See Weiner and Lissovoy, *supra* note 9, at 76–77.

22. E.H. Morreim, "Redefining Quality by Reassigning Responsibility," *American Journal of Law & Medicine*, XX (1994): 79–104.

23. See Beauchamp and Childress, *supra* note 19, at 259.

24. A.M. Capron, "Medical Futility: Strike Two," *Hastings Center Report*, 24, no. 5 (1994): 42–43.

25. E.J. Emanuel and L.L. Emanuel, "The Economics of Dying: The Illusion of Cost Savings at the End of Life," *N. Engl. J. Med.*, 330 (1994): 540–44.

26. Although bone marrow transplant is often used for breast cancer, its safety and effectiveness have still not been proved. Because it is so widely available through insurers, relatively few women are willing to enter a scientific trial in which they might receive standard treatment rather than the transplant. Hence, it is very difficult to recruit enough subjects to complete scientific trials. See G. Kolata, "Women Rejecting Trials for Testing a Cancer Therapy," *New York Times*, Feb. 15, 1995, at A1, B7.

27. E.H. Morreim, "Futilitarianism, Exoticare, and Coerced Altruism: The ADA Meets Its Limits," *Seton Hall Law Review*, 25 (1995): 883–926.

28. See Morreim, *supra* note 18, at 79–81.

29. *Id.* at 74–76.

30. For an excellent discussion of the role of contract in health care and health reform, see C.C. Havighurst, *Health Care Choices: Private Contracts as Instruments of Health Reform* (Washington, D.C.: American Enterprise Institute, 1995).

31. The surgical separation of the Lakeburg siamese twins provides a poignant example. The procedure cost $1.2 million dollars, and, although In-

diana's Medicaid rules expressly forbade paying for such highly experimental treatments, an exception was made for this much publicized case. One twin died, as expected, during the surgery, and the other lived only a few months. See L.M. Fleck, "Just Caring: Health Reform and Health Care Rationing," *Journal of Medicine and Philosophy*, 19 (1994): at 438–39.

Technically, Medicaid does not represent a contract between patients and the government in the same sense as that between private payers and their beneficiaries. However, these programs closely resemble contracts for managed care or insurance, in that they promise a particular set of services to a defined population, and those who are denied their due have legal recourse.

32. Contractual vagueness is also partly a function of health plans' historical difficulty in writing their contracts in language that judges are willing to uphold. See Havighurst, *supra* note 30, at 16, 31ff., 115ff.; and M.A. Hall and G.F. Anderson, "Health Insurers' Assessment of Medical Necessity," *University of Pennsylvania Law Review*, 140 (1992): 1637–712.

Note also that even medical guidelines or practice parameters, which if made explicit could add to contracts' specificity, cannot address every conceivable medical contingency. They, too, must leave room for flexibility and for individuality of care.

33. This notion somewhat parallels Havighurst's concept of health care contracts as a convenant among subscribers. See Havighurst, *supra* note 30, at 176ff.

34. D.M. Eddy, "Connecting Value and Costs: Whom Do We Ask, and What Do We Ask Them?," *JAMA*, 264 (1990): 1737–39; and D.M. Eddy, "What Do We Do About Costs?," *JAMA*, 264 (1990a): 1161, 1165, 1169, 1170.

35. W.P. Peters and M.C. Rogers, "Variation in Approval by Insurance Companies of Coverage for Autologous Bone Marrow Transplantation for Breast Cancer," *N. Engl. J. Med.*, 330 (1994): 473–77.

36. The doctrine is called *contra proferentum*. See Havighurst, *supra* note 30, at 182ff.

37. *Leonhardt v. Holden Business Forms Co.*, 828 F. Supp. 657 (D. Minn. 1993).

38. *Id.; Wilson v. Group Hospitalization*, 791 F. Supp. 309 (D.D.C. 1992); and *Weaver v. Phoenix Home Life Mut. Ins. Co.*, 990 F.2d 154 (4th Cir. 1993).

39. G.W. Grumet, "Health Care Rationing Through Inconvenience: The Third Party's Secret Weapon," *N. Engl. J. Med.*, 321 (1989): 607–11; and D.W. Light, "Life, Death and the Insurance Companies," *N. Engl. J. Med.*, 330 (1994): 498–500.

40. For a more detailed discussion of judge-made insurance, see, for example, K.S. Abraham, "Judge-Made Law and Judge-Made Insurance: Honoring the Reasonable Expectations of the Insured," *Virginia Law Review*, 67 (1981): 1151–91; J. H. Ferguson, M. Dubinsky, and P.J. Kirsch, "Court-Ordered Reimbursement for Unproven Medical Technology: Circumventing Technology Assessment," *JAMA*, 269 (1993): 2116–21; Hall and Anderson, *supra* note 32; F. James, "The Experimental Treatment Exclusion Clause: A Tool for Silent Rationing?," *Journal of Legal Medicine*, 12 (1991): 359–418; Havighurst, *supra* note 30; P.E. Kalb, "Controlling Health Care Costs by Controlling Technology: A Private Contractual Approach," *Yale Law Journal*, 99 (1990): 1109–26; P. Huber, *Liability: The Legal Revolution and Its Consequences* (New York: Basic Books, 1988); S.W. Gottsegen, "A New Approach for the Interpretation of Insurance Contracts—*Great American Insurance Co. v. Tate Construction Co.*," *Wake Forest Law Review*, 17 (1981): 140–52; and *Great American Ins. Co. v. C.G. Tate Const.*, 279 S.E. 2d 769 (N.C. 1981).

41. *DiDomenico v. Employers Co-op. Industry Trust*, 676 F. Supp. 903, 908 (N.D. Ind. 1987).

42. *Leonhardt v. Holden Business Forms Co.*, 828 F. Supp. 657, 658 (D. Minn. 1993).

Sometimes judicial generosity seems to stem from medical confusion. In finding the plaintiff's insurance contract ambiguous, a federal district court declared in *Nesseim* that autologous bone marrow transplant is just an extension of chemotherapy. See *Nesseim v. Mail Handlers Ben. Plan*, 792 F. Supp. 674, 675 (D.S.D. 1992), *rev'd*, 995 F. 2d 804 (8th Cir. 1993). Similarly, in *Calhoun*, the court declared: "The bone marrow transplant, while necessary to avoid a disastrous side effect, is not the procedure designed to treat the cancer." See *Calhoun v. Complete Health Care, Inc.*, 860 F.

Supp. 1494, 1499 (S. C. Ala. 1994). *Pirozzi* likewise identified an ambiguity in the term *experimental* in order to award bone marrow transplant to a woman with advanced breast cancer. See *Pirozzi v. Blue Cross-Blue Shield of Va.*, 741 F. Supp. 586 (E.D. Va. 1990). See also *Wilson*, 791 F. Supp. at 309; and *Taylor v. BCBSM*, 517 N.W.2d 864 (Mich. App. 1994).

Another court asserted that autologous bone marrow transplant (ABMT) is

> a very minor portion of [the plaintiff's] overall treatment plan. . . . The record does not preclude the possibility that there may indeed be cases where HDC [high dose chemotherapy] is not accompanied by PSCR [peripheral stem cell rescue] or ABMT. They certainly are different procedures in that they are administered at different times and for different purposes. The purpose of the HDC is to kill the cancer; whereas, the purpose PSCR is to restore the immune system.

See *Bailey v. Blue Cross/Blue Shield of Va.*, 866 F. Supp. 277, 281, 282 (E.D. Va. 1994).

Such reasoning is dramatically different from medical realities. High-dose chemotherapy cannot be undertaken, given current medical technology, without a reinfusion of healthy bone marrow to restore the patient's ability to produce the vital blood cells. To regard the two as somehow distinct is rather like regarding sutures to close a surgical incision as a separable from the surgery, and potentially optional—as though the surgery is to fix the problem, while the sutures are simply to prevent potential postoperative problems.

43. *Bailey*, 866, F. Supp. at 280.
44. See *Arkansas BCBS v. Long*, 792 S.W.2d 602 (1990); and *Blue Cross and Blue Shield v. Brown*, 800 S. W.2d 724 (Ark. App. 1990) (each overrules the insurer's provision that all coverage would be forfeit if the patient left the hospital against medical advice).
45. See commentators on judge-made insurance law, *supra* note 40.
79. *Loyola University of Chicago v. Humana Ins. Co.*, 996 F.2d 895 (7th Cir. 1993).
80. *Id.* at 903.
81. *Fuja*, 18 F.3d at 1412.
82. *McGee v. Equicor-Equitable HCA Corp.*, 953 F.2d 1192 (10th Cir. 1992) (citing *Firestone Tire & Rubber Co. v. Bruch*, 489 U.S. 101 (1989)). The Tenth Circuit did require the HMO to pay for some benefits that, in fact, met their utilization requirements.
83. In *Gee*, the Utah Court of Appeals upheld an insurer's denial of coverage for removal of breast implants, holding that the policy was not ambiguous. "Insurance policies are contracts, and are interpreted under the same rules governing ordinary contracts . . . [A] policy term is not ambiguous simply because one party ascribes a different meaning to it to suit his or her own interests" (*Gee v. Utah State Retirement Bd.*, 842 P.2d 919, 920–21 (Utah App. 1992)).

Other courts have expressed similar views. "Moreover, because of the plain language of the contract, we would have no choice but to affirm the denial of coverage even if, *arguendo*, we were to review that decision *de novo*" (*Harris v. Mutual of Omaha Cos.*, 992 F.2d 706, 713 (7th Cir. 1993)).

"The plan is clear and not ambiguous . . . The contract is clear. HDC-ABMT is not covered under the 1992 Plan. Accordingly, Blue Cross/Blue Shield's decision denying coverage and OPM's review and affirmance of that decision are rational. Denial of coverage is clearly not an arbitrary and capricious decision; indeed, because of the plain language of the contract, the Court would affirm denial of coverage even if that decision were reviewed *de novo*" (*Arrington v. Group Hospitalization & Med. Serv.*, 806 F. Supp. 287, 290 (D.D.C. 1992)).

For similar cases upholding payers' denial of funding based on the plain language of the contract, see *Barnett v. Kaiser Foundation Health Plan, Inc.*, 32 F.3d 413 (9th Cir. 1994); *Goepel v. Mail Handlers Ben. Plan*, No. 93-3711, 1993 WL 384498 (D.N.J. Sept. 24, 1993); *Nesseim v. Mail Handlers Ben. Plan*, 995 F.2d 804 (8th Cir. 1993); *Farley v. Benefit Trust Life Ins. Co.*, 979 F.2d 653 (8th Cir. 1992); *Harris v. Blue Cross Blue Shield of Mo.*, 995 F.2d 877 (8th Cir. 1993); *McLeroy v. Blue Cross/Blue Shield of Ore., Inc.*, 825 F. Supp. 1064 (N.D. Ga. 1993); *Thomas v. Gulf Health Plan, Inc.*, 688 F. Supp. 590 (S.D. Ala. 1988); and *Doe v. Group Hospitalization & Med. Serv.*, 3 F.3d 80 (4th Cir. 1993).

See also: *Madden v. Kaiser Foundation Hospitals*, 552 P.2d 1178 (Cal. 1976) (holding that an employee who had chosen his HMO from among several options, negotiated on his behalf by a state agency, was bound by the arbitration clause to which he had agreed; and noting that "[o]ne who assents to a contract is bound by its provisions and cannot complain of unfamiliarity with the language"). Also see *Sarchett v. Blue Shield of Cal.*, 729 P.2d 267 (Cal. 1987) (upholding insurer's right to deny payment, based on its own judgment of medical necessity).

Two other cases upholding contracts are of interest. In *Adnan Varol, M.D. v. Blue Cross & Blue Shield* (708 F. Supp. 826 (E.D. Mich. 1989)), a district court informed a group of psychiatrists that they were expected to adhere to their contract with an insurer, even though they now disagreed with its cost-containment provisions. In *Williams v. HealthAmerica* (535 N.E.2d 717 (Ohio App. 1987)), an Ohio appellate court ruled that, although a malpractice action against an HMO physician should go to arbitration, the patient could also pursue separately a breach of contract action against that physician.

84. *Loyola University of Chicago v. Humana Ins. Co.*, 996 F.2d 895, 903 (7th Cir. 1993).

85. *Fuja* (18 F.3d at 1407–08, n.2) cites Judge Tinder in *Harris v. Mutual of Omaha*—another case in which the plaintiff's request for autologous bone marrow transplant for her advanced breast cancer was rejected on the ground that the treatment was experimental and therefore not covered by the insurance contract. The judge goes on to pose the broad question: "Perhaps the question most importantly raised about this case, and similar cases, is who should pay for the hopeful treatments that are being developed in this rapidly developing area of medical science?" (*id.* at 1408, n.2).

A similar view was expressed in *Arrington*: "The Court has sympathy for plaintiff's situation, but this consideration cannot be material to a decision on the merits of this case" (*Arrington*, 806 F. Supp. at 290).

86. *Fuja*, 18 F.3d at 1407.

87. *McGee v. Equicor-Equitable HCA Corp.*, 953 F.2d 1192, 1207 (10th Cir. 1992) (emphasis added).

88. *Id.*

89. *Nazay v. Miller*, 949 F.2d 1323, 1336 (3d Cir. 1991). The court went on to note that it is legitimate for those who pay for health care to attempt to contain their rising costs (*id.* at 1328). In this case, a corporation gave teeth to their precertification requirement by imposing a 30 percent penalty on those who failed to comply. Were this requirement overruled, the corporation "and its employees would be deprived of an important weapon in their joint battle against rising healthcare costs" (*id.* at 1338).

90. *Loyola University of Chicago v. Humana Ins. Co.*, 996 F.2d 903 (7th Cir. 1993).

In the same vein, in *Free*, a Maryland district court held that an insurer was not obligated to pay for the patient's laetrile:

> [T]he plaintiff's unfettered right to select a physician and follow his advice does not create a corresponding responsibility in the defendant to pay for every treatment so chosen. As one court noted, "it is simply not enough to show that some people, even experts, have a belief in [the] safety and effectiveness [of a particular drug]. A reasonable number of Americans will sincerely attest to the worth of almost any product or even idea.". . . Finally, the Court notes that the plaintiff, by his own admission, was well aware that laetrile and nutritional therapy are disapproved of by the majority of cancer specialists. He was equally well informed of the accepted alternative, chemotherapy.

See *Free v. Travelers Ins. Co.*, 551 F. Supp. 554, 560 (D. Md. 1982).

Similarly, in *McLeroy*, a district court in Georgia pointed out that it was "well within the bargaining rights of the parties" to determine the conditions under which special alternative services might be provided. See *McLeroy v. Blue Cross/Blue Shield of Ore., Inc.*, 825 F. Supp. 1064, 1071 (N. D. Ga. 1993).

In *Goepel*, a New Jersey district court held that the plaintiffs' written policy was clearly written, with adequate notice of policy changes, and enabled the plaintiffs to make an informed purchase. Significantly, the court also expressed an interest in the responsibilities of subscribers.

This Court is also troubled by the invitation to recognize a cause of action, not based on the fact that the policy was unclear, but rather, as plaintiffs suggest, on the premises that insureds (1) do not read the full brochure detailing policy coverage and (2) do not heed the admonition in the section on "How the Plan Changes" to review the entire policy.

See *Goepel v. Mail Handlers Ben. Plan*, No. 93-3711, 1993 WL 384498 (D.N.J. Sept. 24, 1993).

This decision was subsequently overturned by the Third Circuit, but not on grounds of its substance. Rather, the issue was jurisdictional: the preemption from state to federal court should not have been done automatically. The preemption question required further adjudication. See *Goepel v. National Postal Mail Handlers Union*, 36 F.3d 306 (3d. Cir. 1994).

107. The Fourth Circuit acknowledged this principle of formal justice quite explicitly. The plaintiff contended that, because two consulting physicians within the plan had disagreed about what length of psychiatric hospitalization should be granted, the plan was arbitrary in opting for one physician's recommendation over the other. The court rejected this argument. The charge of inconsistency applies not to this situation, but to "inconsistent applications of the Plan to members suffering from the same or similar ailments." See *Sheppard & Enoch Pratt Hosp. v. Travelers Ins. Co.*, 32 F.3d 120, 126 (4th Cir. 1994). In other words, the court identified judicially unacceptable inconsistency in terms of formal (in)justice: treating similar patients differently.

108. Eighty-four percent of businesses that provide health insurance for their employees only provide one choice—take it or leave it—and many of the remaining businesses provide only a few options. See R.J. Blendon, M. Brodie, and J. Benson, "What Should be Done Now that National Health System Reform is Dead?," *JAMA*, 273 (1995): at 243.

109. See E.H. Morreim, "Diverse and Perverse Incentives of Managed Care," *Widener Law Symposium Journal*, (1995): forthcoming.

110. E.H. Morreim, "Rationing and the Law," in M.A. Strosberg et al., eds., *Rationing America's Medical Care: The Oregon Plan and Beyond* (Washington,

D.C.: Brookings Institution, 1992): at 162–63; E.H. Morreim, *supra* note 18, at 58–60, 89–90, 143–47; and Havighurst, *supra* note 30.

111. See Havighurst, *supra* note 30, at 222ff.

112. See Kalb, *supra* note 40, at 1121–24.

113. See Hall and Anderson, *supra* note 32.

114. This notion of personal choice was heartily endorsed in *Harrell*. The Missouri Supreme Court upheld a statute granting malpractice immunity for nonprofit health services corporations including HMOs, arguing that people should have the opportunity to save money in their health care by buying into (and then being held to the terms of) less costly arrangements.

> Just as the ancient Chinese are reputed to have paid their doctors while they remained well, a person may elect to pay fixed dues in advance so that medical services may be available without additional cost when they are needed. The legislature well might feel that these arrangements were in the public interest and that those organizations that do not operate for profit should not be burdened by the additional cost of malpractice litigation . . . People are concerned both about the cost and the unpredictability of medical expenses. A plan such as Total offered would allow a person to fix the cost of physicians' services. The legislature might easily perceive that the costs of a plan would be substantially increased if the Health Services Organization were to be subject to claims originating in malpractice, that the cost of these claims would necessarily be shared by other plan members, and that malpractice liability might threaten the solvency of the plan.

See *Harrell v. Total Health Care, Inc.*, 781 S.W.2d 58, 61 (Mo. banc 1989).

115. Hall and Anderson, for instance, lay out a fairly specific set of procedures by which a health plan might adjudicate which interventions are covered and which experimental. See Hall and Anderson, *supra* note 32.

116. In the current situation, unfortunately, adequate disclosure is not always made, and deficiencies in contracting procedures are not limited to ambiguities in contractual language. Many MCOs, for instance, do not disclose their cost-containment policies, such as incentive systems that reward physicians for conservative care, or

therapeutic substitution protocols that replace brand name medications with cheaper pharmacologic equivalents. Although at present no statutory requirements for such disclosure exist, there are strong reasons based in both fiduciary law and contract law for believing that they should be made. See E.H. Morreim, "Economic Disclosure and Economic Advocacy: New Duties in the Medical Standard of Care," *Journal of Legal Medicine,* 12 (1991): 275–329; E.B. Hirshfeld, "Should Third Party Payors of Health Care Services Disclose Cost Control Mechanisms to Potential Beneficiaries?," *Seton Hall Legislative Journal,* 14 (1990): 115–50; S.F. Figa and H.M. Tag, "Redefining Full and Fair Disclosure of HMO Benefits and Limitation," *Seton Hall Legislative Journal,* 14 (1990): 151–57; L.V. Tiano, "The Legal Implications of HMO Cost Containment Measures," *Seton Hall Legislative Journal,* 14 (1990): 79–102; Chittenden, *supra* note 56; G.J. Glover and B.N. Kuhlik, "Potential Liability Associated with Restrictive Drug Policies," *Seton Hall Legislative Journal,* 14 (1990): 103–13; and Havighurst, *supra* note 30, at 27, 122, 143–47, 185, 311.

117. This point was explicitly recognized by the California Supreme Court, in *Sarchett,* when it upheld an insurer's right retrospectively to refuse payment for services, based on its own evaluation of their medical necessity. The court noted that, if physicians were empowered to dictate unilaterally which services an insurer must cover, the ultimate result would be a diminution of citizens' freedom elsewhere. If insurers cannot control what costs physicians incur, they will limit subscribers' choices among physicians.

> Sarchett had a choice between the Blue Shield plan, which offered him unlimited selection of physicians but provided for retrospective review, and alternative plans which would require him to choose from among a limited list of physicians but guaranteed payment. A holding that retrospective review is against public policy would narrow the range of choices available to the prospective subscriber, since it is unlikely that any insurer could permit the subscriber free selection of a physician if it were required to accept without question the physician's view of reasonable treatment and good medical

practice . . . [A]lthough a judicial ruling that retrospective review violates public policy would protect against retrospective denial of coverage, subscribers would pay the price in reduced insurance alternatives and increased premiums.

See *Sarchett v. Blue Shield of Cal.,* 729 P.2d 267, 274–75 (Cal. 1987).

Abraham notes that judge-made insurance can seriously constrain the freedom of individuals to choose the coverage they want. Such rulings can

> limit the insured's freedom of choice by involuntarily increasing the scope of the coverage he purchases. Any increase in a policy's package of insurance protection will often increase its price. Those who would prefer the narrower but cheaper coverage will then be forced to accept more insurance than they want in order to obtain the coverage they need. Where having insurance coverage is optional, some people will choose not to buy it at all—the increase in cost caused by the expectations principle will have priced them out of the market. Where the coverage is effectively mandatory—automobile liability or fire insurance on mortgaged real estate—insureds will have to give up other noninsurance goods in order to buy the mandated but overly broad coverage.

See Abraham, *supra* note 40, at 1188.

See also Havighurst: "By treating certain rights and duties as extracontractual (and therefore not subject to alteration by contract) and by refusing to interpret health care contracts with due regard for their cost-saving intent, the courts have effectively undermined the freedom of consumers to specify prospectively the nature and content of the services that they purchase" (Havighurst, *supra* note 30, at 6, also 28, 104, 328).

118. *Madden v. Kaiser Foundation Hosps.,* 552 P.2d 1178 (Cal. 1976).

119. See Eddy (1990), *supra* note 34; Eddy (1990a), *supra* note 34; R.E. Leahy, "Rational Health Policy and the Legal Standard of Care: A Call for Judicial Deference to Medical Practice Guidelines," *California Law Review,* 77 (1989): 1483–528; P.T. Menzel, *Strong Medicine* (New York: Oxford University Press, 1990): at 10ff.; Hall, *supra* note 16, at 39; Kalb, *supra* note 40, at 1125; Hall and Ander-

son, *supra* note 32, at 1676; and Havighurst, *supra* note 30, at 28, 159.

120. "Interpreting insurance contracts as mutual contracts rather than as contracts of adhesion would by no means require that courts abandon their equitable responsibilities. It would require, however, that they refuse to honor unreasonable expectations and refuse to find advantages where none exist. It would require, in short, the curtailment of judge-made insurance." See Kalb, *supra* note 40, at 1125.

121. *Madden*, 552 P.2d at 1178.

122. For a much richer discussion of this proposal, see Havighurst, *supra* note 30, at 176–84.

One remaining problem concerns the harms that health plans may cause when they flagrantly violate their obligations. Currently, ERISA provides a remarkable level of protection against tort litigation, even for egregious misconduct by employment-based health plans. While, on the one hand, this serves the valid goal of ensuring that the plans' resources are not depleted by flurries of litigation, on the other, it leaves mistreated members with little or no recourse. The *Corcoran* court suggested that change might be in order.

> [T]he world of employee benefit plans has hardly remained static since 1974. Fundamental changes such as the widespread institution of utilization review would seem to warrant a reevaluation of ERISA so that it can continue to serve its noble purpose of safeguarding the interests of employees.

See *Corcoran v. United Healthcare, Inc.*, 965 F.2d 1321, 1338 (5th Cir.), *cert. denied*, 113 S. Ct. 812 (1992).

Such a reevaluation, of course, must not open the doors to a flood of lawsuits that could destroy the integrity of health plans or permit the interests of lone individuals to thwart the legitimate claims of the larger group—another infringement on contributive justice. Recognizing broader damage allowances within existing ERISA litigation is one option, or, perhaps, as implied by the *Corcoran* court, the ERISA law itself may need revision.

Lori Pegram, et al., Petitioners,

v.

Cynthia Herdrich.
No. 98–1949.

Argued Feb. 23, 2000.
Decided June 12, 2000.

Justice SOUTER delivered the opinion of the Court.

I

The question in this case is whether treatment decisions made by a health maintenance organization, acting through its physician employees, are fiduciary acts within the meaning of the Employee Retirement Income Security Act of 1974 (ERISA), 88 Stat. 832, as amended, 29 U.S.C. § 1001 *et seq.* (1994 ed. and Supp. III). We hold that they are not.

Petitioners, Carle Clinic Association, P. C., Health Alliance Medical Plans, Inc., and Carle Health Insurance Management Co., Inc. (collectively Carle), function as a health maintenance organization (HMO) organized for profit. Its owners are physicians providing prepaid medical services to participants whose employers contract with Carle to provide such coverage. Respondent, Cynthia Herdrich, was covered by Carle through her husband's employer, State Farm Insurance Company.

The events in question began when a Carle physician, petitioner Lori Pegram,[1] examined Herdrich, who was experiencing pain in the midline area of her groin. Six days later, Dr. Pegram discovered a six by eight centimeter inflamed mass in Herdrich's abdomen. Despite the noticeable inflammation, Dr. Pegram did not order an ultrasound diagnostic procedure at a local hospital, but decided that Herdrich would have to wait eight more days for an ultrasound, to be performed at a facility staffed by Carle more than 50 miles away. Before the eight days were over, Herdrich's appendix ruptured, causing peritonitis.

Herdrich sued Pegram and Carle in state court for medical malpractice, and she later added two counts charging state-law fraud. Carle and Pegram responded that ERISA preempted the new counts, and removed the case to federal court, where they then sought summary judgment on the state-law fraud counts. The District Court granted their motion as to the second fraud count but granted Herdrich leave to amend the one remaining. This she did by alleging that provision of medical services under the terms of the Carle HMO organization, rewarding its physician owners for limiting medical care, entailed an inherent or anticipatory breach of an ERISA fiduciary duty, since these terms created an incentive to make decisions in the physicians' self-interest, rather than the exclusive interests of plan participants.

Herdrich sought relief under 29 U.S.C. § 1109(a), which provides that

[a]ny person who is a fiduciary with respect to a plan who breaches any of the responsibilities, obligations, or duties imposed upon fiduciaries by

this sub-chapter shall be personally liable to make good to such plan any losses to the plan resulting from each such breach, and to restore to such plan any profits of such fiduciary which have been made through use of assets of the plan by the fiduciary, and shall be subject to such other equitable or remedial relief as the court may deem appropriate, including removal of such fiduciary.

When Carle moved to dismiss the ERISA count for failure to state a claim upon which relief could be granted, the District Court granted the motion, accepting the Magistrate Judge's determination that Carle was not "involved [in these events] as" an ERISA fiduciary. App. to Pet. for Cert. 63a. The original malpractice counts were then tried to a jury, and Herdrich prevailed on both, receiving $35,000 in compensation for her injury. 154 F.3d, at 367. She then appealed the dismissal of the ERISA claim to the Court of Appeals for the Seventh Circuit, which reversed. The court held that Carle was acting as a fiduciary when its physicians made the challenged decisions and that Herdrich's allegations were sufficient to state a claim:

> "Our decision does not stand for the proposition that the existence of incentives *automatically* gives rise to a breach of fiduciary duty. Rather, we hold that incentives can *rise* to the level of a breach where, as pleaded here, the fiduciary trust between plan participants and plan fiduciaries no longer exists (i.e., where physicians delay providing necessary treatment to, or withhold administering proper care to, plan beneficiaries for the sole purpose of increasing their bonuses)." *Id.,* at 373.

II

Whether Carle is a fiduciary when it acts through its physician owners as pleaded in the ERISA count depends on some background of fact and law about HMOs, medical benefit plans, fiduciary obligation, and the meaning of Herdrich's allegations.

A

Traditionally, medical care in the United States has been provided on a "fee-for-service" basis. A physician charges so much for a general physical exam, a vaccination, a tonsillectomy, and so on. The physician bills the patient for services provided or, if there is insurance and the doctor is willing, submits the bill for the patient's care to the insurer, for payment subject to the terms of the insurance agreement. In a fee-for-service system, a physician's financial incentive is to provide more care, not less, so long as payment is forthcoming. The check on this incentive is a physician's obligation to exercise reasonable medical skill and judgment in the patient's interest.

Beginning in the late 1960's, insurers and others developed new models for health-care delivery, including HMOs. Cf. Rosenblatt 546. The defining feature of an HMO is receipt of a fixed fee for each patient enrolled under the terms of a contract to provide specified health care if needed. The HMO thus assumes the financial risk of providing the benefits promised: if a participant never gets sick, the HMO keeps the money regardless, and if a participant becomes expensively ill, the HMO is responsible for the treatment agreed upon even if its cost exceeds the participant's premiums.

Like other risk-bearing organizations, HMOs take steps to control costs. At the least, HMOs, like traditional insurers, will in some fashion make coverage determinations, scrutinizing requested services against the contractual provisions to make sure that a request for care falls within the scope of covered circumstances (pregnancy, for example), or that a given treatment falls within the scope of the care promised (surgery, for instance). They customarily issue general guidelines for their physicians about appropriate levels of care. See *id.,* at 568–570. And they commonly require utilization review (in which specific treatment decisions are reviewed by a decisionmaker other than the treating physician) and approval in advance (precertification) for many types of care, keyed to standards of medical necessity or the reasonableness of the proposed treatment. See Andresen, Is Utilization Review the Practice of Medicine?, Implications for Managed Care Administrators, 19 J. Legal Med. 431, 432 (Sept.1998). These cost-controlling measures are commonly complemented by specific financial incentives to physicians, rewarding them for decreasing utilization of health-care services, and penalizing them for what may be found to be excessive treatment, see Rosenblatt 563–565; Iglehart, Health Policy Report: The American Health Care System—Managed Care, 327 New England J. Med. 742, 742–747 (1992). Hence, in an HMO system, a physician's financial interest lies in providing less care, not more. The check on this influence (like that on the converse, fee-for-service incentive) is the professional obligation to provide covered services with a reasonable degree of skill and judgment in the patient's interest.

The adequacy of professional obligation to counter financial self-interest has been challenged no matter what the form of medical organization. HMOs became popular because fee-for-service physicians were thought to be providing unnecessary or useless services; today, many doctors and other observers argue that HMOs often ignore the individual needs of a patient in order to improve the HMOs' bottom lines. In this case, for instance, one could argue that Pegram's decision to wait before getting an ultrasound for Herdrich, and her insistence that the ultrasound be done at a distant facility owned by Carle, reflected an interest in limiting the HMO's expenses, which blinded her to the need for immediate diagnosis and treatment.

B

Herdrich focuses on the Carle scheme's provision for a "year-end distribution," n. 3, *supra*, to the HMO's physician owners. She argues that this particular incentive device of annually paying physician owners the profit resulting from

their own decisions rationing care can distinguish Carle's organization from HMOs generally, so that reviewing Carle's decisions under a fiduciary standard as pleaded in Herdrich's complaint would not open the door to like claims about other HMO structures. While the Court of Appeals agreed, we think otherwise, under the law as now written.

Although it is true that the relationship between sparing medical treatment and physician reward is not a subtle one under the Carle scheme, no HMO organization could survive without some incentive connecting physician reward with treatment rationing. The essence of an HMO is that salaries and profits are limited by the HMO's fixed membership fees. This is not to suggest that the Carle provisions are as socially desirable as some other HMO organizational schemes; they may not be. See, *e.g.,* Grumbach, Osmond, Vranigan, Jaffe, & Bindman, Primary Care Physicians' Experience of Financial Incentives in Managed–Care Systems, 339 New England J. Med. 1516 (1998) (arguing that HMOs that reward quality of care and patient satisfaction would be preferable to HMOs that reward only physician productivity). But whatever the HMO, there must be rationing and inducement to ration.

Since inducement to ration care goes to the very point of any HMO scheme, and rationing necessarily raises some risks while reducing others (ruptured appendixes are more likely; unnecessary appendectomies are less so), any legal principle purporting to draw a line between good and bad HMOs would embody, in effect, a judgment about socially acceptable medical risk. A valid conclusion of this sort would, however, necessarily turn on facts to which courts would probably not have ready access: correlations between malpractice rates and various HMO models, similar correlations involving fee-for-service models, and so on. And, of course, assuming such material could be obtained by courts in litigation like this, any standard defining the unacceptably risky HMO structure (and consequent vulnerability to claims like Herdrich's) would depend on a judgment about the appropriate level of expenditure for health care in light of the associated malpractice risk. But such complicated factfinding and such a debatable social judgment are not wisely required of courts unless for some reason resort cannot be had to the legislative process, with its preferable forum for comprehensive investigations and judgments of social value, such as optimum treatment levels and health-care expenditure.

We think, then, that courts are not in a position to derive a sound legal principle to differentiate an HMO like Carle from other HMOs. For that reason, we proceed on the assumption that the decisions listed in Herdrich's complaint cannot be subject to a claim that they violate fiduciary standards unless all such decisions by all HMOs acting through their owner or employee physicians are to be judged by the same standards and subject to the same claims.

C

We turn now from the structure of HMOs to the requirements of ERISA. A fiduciary within the meaning of ERISA must be someone acting in the capacity of manager, administrator, or financial adviser to a "plan," see 29 U.S.C. §§ 1002(21)(A)(i)–(iii), and Herdrich's ERISA count accordingly charged Carle with a breach of fiduciary duty in discharging its obligations under State Farm's medical plan. App. to Pet. for Cert. 85a-86a. ERISA's definition of an employee welfare benefit plan is ultimately circular: "any plan, fund, or program . . . to the extent that such plan, fund, or program was established . . . for the purpose of providing . . . through the purchase of insurance or otherwise . . . medical, surgical, or hospital care or benefits." § 1002(1)(A). One is thus left to the common understanding of the word "plan" as referring to a scheme decided upon in advance, see Webster's New Interna-

tional Dictionary 1879 (2d ed.1957); Jacobson & Pomfret, Form, Function, and Managed Care Torts: Achieving Fairness and Equity in ERISA Jurisprudence, 35 Houston L.Rev. 985, 1050 (1998). Here the scheme comprises a set of rules that define the rights of a beneficiary and provide for their enforcement. Rules governing collection of premiums, definition of benefits, submission of claims, and resolution of disagreements over entitlement to services are the sorts of provisions that constitute a plan. See *Hansen v. Continental Ins. Co.,* 940 F.2d 971, 977 (C.A.5 1991). Thus, when employers contract with an HMO to provide benefits to employees subject to ERISA, the provisions of documents that set up the HMO are not, as such, an ERISA plan; but the agreement between an HMO and an employer who pays the premiums may, as here, provide elements of a plan by setting out rules under which beneficiaries will be entitled to care.

D

As just noted, fiduciary obligations can apply to managing, advising, and administering an ERISA plan, the fiduciary function addressed by Herdrich's ERISA count being the exercise of "discretionary authority or discretionary responsibility in the administration of [an ERISA] plan," 29 U.S.C. § 1002(21)(A)(iii). And as we have already suggested, although Carle is not an ERISA fiduciary merely because it administers or exercises discretionary authority over its own HMO business, it may still be a fiduciary if it administers the plan.

In general terms, fiduciary responsibility under ERISA is simply stated. The statute provides that fiduciaries shall discharge their duties with respect to a plan "solely in the interest of the participants and beneficiaries," § 1104(a)(1), that is, "for the exclusive purpose of (i) providing benefits to participants and their beneficiaries; and (ii) defraying reasonable expenses of administering the plan," § 1104(a)(1)(A). These responsibilities imposed by ERISA have the familiar ring of their source in the common law of trusts. Thus, the common law (understood as including what were once the distinct rules of equity) charges fiduciaries with a duty of loyalty to guarantee beneficiaries' interests: "The most fundamental duty owed by the trustee to the beneficiaries of the trust is the duty of loyalty. . . . It is the duty of a trustee to administer the trust solely in the interest of the beneficiaries." 2A A. Scott & W. Fratcher, Trusts § 170, p. 311 (4th ed. 1987) (hereinafter Scott).

Beyond the threshold statement of responsibility, however, the analogy between ERISA fiduciary and common law trustee becomes problematic. This is so because the trustee at common law characteristically wears only his fiduciary hat when he takes action to affect a beneficiary, whereas the trustee under ERISA may wear different hats.

Speaking of the traditional trustee, Professor Scott's treatise admonishes that the trustee "is not permitted to place himself in a position where it would be for his own benefit to violate his duty to the beneficiaries." 2A Scott § 170, at 311. Under ERISA, however, a fiduciary may have financial interests adverse to beneficiaries. Employers, for example, can be ERISA fiduciaries and still take actions to the disadvantage of employee beneficiaries, when they act as employers (*e.g.,* firing a beneficiary for reasons unrelated to the ERISA plan), or even as plan sponsors (*e.g.,* modifying the terms of a plan as allowed by ERISA to provide less generous benefits). Nor is there any apparent reason in the ERISA provisions to conclude, as Herdrich argues, that this tension is permissible only for the employer or plan sponsor, to the exclusion of persons who provide services to an ERISA plan.

ERISA does require, however, that the fiduciary with two hats wear only one at a time, and wear the fiduciary hat when making fiduciary decisions. Thus, the statute does not describe fiduciaries simply as administrators of the plan, or managers or advisers. Instead it defines an administrator, for example, as a fiduciary only "to the extent" that he acts in such a capacity in relation to a plan. 29 U.S.C. § 1002(21)(A). In every case charging breach of ERISA fiduciary duty, then, the threshold question is not whether the actions of some person employed to provide services under a plan adversely affected a plan beneficiary's interest, but whether that person was acting as a fiduciary (that is, was performing a fiduciary function) when taking the action subject to complaint.

E

The allegations of Herdrich's ERISA count that identify the claimed fiduciary breach are difficult to understand. In this count, Herdrich does not point to a particular act by any Carle physician owner as a breach. She does not complain about Pegram's actions, and at oral argument her counsel confirmed that the ERISA count could have been brought, and would have been no different, if Herdrich had never had a sick day in her life.

What she does claim is that Carle, acting through its physician owners, breached its duty to act solely in the interest of beneficiaries by making decisions affecting medical treatment while influenced by the terms of the Carle HMO scheme, under which the physician owners ultimately profit from their own choices to minimize the medical services provided. She emphasizes the threat to fiduciary responsibility in the Carle scheme's feature of a year-end distribution to the physicians of profit derived from the spread between subscription income and expenses of care and administration.

The specific payout detail of the plan was, of course, a feature that the employer as plan sponsor was free to adopt without breach of any fiduciary duty under ERISA, since an employer's decisions about the content of a plan are not themselves fiduciary acts. Likewise it is clear that there was no violation of ERISA when the incorporators of the Carle HMO provided for the year-end payout. The HMO is not the ERISA plan, and the incorporation of the HMO preceded its contract with the State Farm plan.

The nub of the claim, then, is that when State Farm contracted with Carle, Carle became a fiduciary under the plan, acting through its physicians. At once, Carle as fiduciary administrator was subject to such influence from the year-end payout provision that its fiduciary capacity was necessarily compromised, and its readiness to act amounted to anticipatory breach of fiduciary obligation.

F

The pleadings must also be parsed very carefully to understand what acts by physician owners acting on Carle's behalf are alleged to be fiduciary in nature. It will help to keep two sorts of arguably administrative acts in mind. What we will call pure "eligibility decisions" turn on the plan's coverage of a particular condition or medical procedure for its treatment. "Treatment decisions," by contrast, are choices about how to go about diagnosing and treating a patient's condition: given a patient's constellation of symptoms, what is the appropriate medical response?

These decisions are often practically inextricable from one another, as *amici* on both sides agree. This is so not merely because, under a scheme like Carle's, treatment and eligibility decisions are made by the same person, the treating physician. It is so because a great many and possibly most coverage questions are not simple yes-or-no questions, like whether appendicitis is a covered condition (when there is no dispute that a patient has appendicitis), or whether acupuncture is a covered procedure for pain relief (when the claim of pain is unchallenged). The more common coverage question is a when-and-how question. Although coverage for many conditions will be clear and various treatment options will be indisputably compensable, physicians

still must decide what to do in particular cases. The issue may be, say, whether one treatment option is so superior to another under the circumstances, and needed so promptly, that a decision to proceed with it would meet the medical necessity requirement that conditions the HMO's obligation to provide or pay for that particular procedure at that time in that case. The Government in its brief alludes to a similar example when it discusses an HMO's refusal to pay for emergency care on the ground that the situation giving rise to the need for care was not an emergency, Brief for United States as *Amicus Curiae* 20–21. In practical terms, these eligibility decisions cannot be untangled from physicians' judgments about reasonable medical treatment, and in the case before us, Dr. Pegram's decision was one of that sort. She decided (wrongly, as it turned out) that Herdrich's condition did not warrant immediate action; the consequence of that medical determination was that Carle would not cover immediate care, whereas it would have done so if Dr. Pegram had made the proper diagnosis and judgment to treat. The eligibility decision and the treatment decision were inextricably mixed, as they are in countless medical administrative decisions every day.

The kinds of decisions mentioned in Herdrich's ERISA count and claimed to be fiduciary in character are just such mixed eligibility and treatment decisions: physicians' conclusions about when to use diagnostic tests; about seeking consultations and making referrals to physicians and facilities other than Carle's; about proper standards of care, the experimental character of a proposed course of treatment, the reasonableness of a certain treatment, and the emergency character of a medical condition.

We do not read the ERISA count, however, as alleging fiduciary breach with reference to a different variety of administrative decisions, those we have called pure eligibility determinations, such as whether a plan covers an undisputed case of appendicitis. Nor do we read it as claiming breach by reference to discrete administrative decisions separate from medical judgments; say, rejecting a claim for no other reason than the HMO's financial condition. The closest Herdrich's ERISA count comes to stating a claim for a pure, unmixed eligibility decision is her general allegation that Carle determines "which claims are covered under the Plan and to what extent," App. to Pet. for Cert. 86a. But this vague statement, difficult to interpret in isolation, is given content by the other elements of the complaint, all of which refer to decisions thoroughly mixed with medical judgment. Any lingering uncertainty about what Herdrich has in mind is dispelled by her brief, which explains that this allegation, like the others, targets medical necessity determinations.

III

A

Based on our understanding of the matters just discussed, we think Congress did not intend Carle or any other HMO to be treated as a fiduciary to the extent that it makes mixed eligibility decisions acting through its physicians. We begin with doubt that Congress would ever have thought of a mixed eligibility decision as fiduciary in nature. At common law, fiduciary duties characteristically attach to decisions about managing assets and distributing property to beneficiaries. Trustees buy, sell, and lease investment property, lend and borrow, and do other things to conserve and nurture assets. They pay out income, choose beneficiaries, and distribute remainders at termination. Thus, the common law trustee's most defining concern historically has been the payment of money in the interest of the beneficiary.

Mixed eligibility decisions by an HMO acting through its physicians have, however, only a limited resemblance to the usual business of traditional trustees. To be sure, the physicians (like regular trustees) draw on resources held for others and make decisions to distribute them in accordance with entitlements expressed in a written instrument (embodying the terms of an ERISA plan). It is also true that the objects of many traditional private and public trusts are ultimately the same as the ERISA plans that contract with HMOs. Private trusts provide medical care to the poor; thousands of independent hospitals are privately held and publicly accountable trusts, and charitable foundations make grants to stimulate the provision of health services. But beyond this point the resemblance rapidly wanes. Traditional trustees administer a medical trust by paying out money to buy medical care, whereas physicians making mixed eligibility decisions consume the money as well. Private trustees do not make treatment judgments, whereas treatment judgments are what physicians reaching mixed decisions do make, by definition. Indeed, the physicians through whom HMOs act make just the sorts of decisions made by licensed medical practitioners millions of times every day, in every possible medical setting: HMOs, fee-for-service proprietorships, public and private hospitals, military field hospitals, and so on. The settings bear no more resemblance to trust departments than a decision to operate turns on the factors controlling the amount of a quarterly income distribution. Thus, it is at least questionable whether Congress would have had mixed eligibility decisions in mind when it provided that decisions administering a plan were fiduciary in nature. Indeed, when Congress took up the subject of fiduciary responsibility under ERISA, it concentrated on fiduciaries' financial decisions, focusing on pension plans, the difficulty many retirees faced in getting the payments they expected, and the financial mismanagement that had too often deprived employees of their benefits. Its focus was far from the subject of Herdrich's claim.

Our doubt that Congress intended the category of fiduciary administrative functions to encompass the mixed determinations at issue here hardens into conviction when we consider the consequences that would follow from Herdrich's contrary view.

B

First, we need to ask how this fiduciary standard would affect HMOs if it applied as Herdrich claims it should be applied, not directed against any particular mixed decision that injured a patient, but against HMOs that make mixed decisions in the course of providing medical care for profit. Recovery would be warranted simply upon showing that the profit incentive to ration care would generally affect mixed decisions, in derogation of the fiduciary standard to act solely in the interest of the patient without possibility of conflict. Although Herdrich is vague about the mechanics of relief, the one point that seems clear is that she seeks the return of profit from the pockets of the Carle HMO's owners, with the money to be given to the plan for the benefit of the participants. See 29 U.S.C. § 1109(a) (return of all profits is an appropriate ERISA remedy). Since the provision for profit is what makes the HMO a proprietary organization, her remedy in effect would be nothing less than elimination of the for-profit HMO. Her remedy might entail even more than that, although we are in no position to tell whether and to what extent nonprofit HMO schemes would ultimately survive the recognition of Herdrich's theory.[11] It is enough to recognize that the Judiciary has no warrant to precipitate the upheaval that would follow a refusal to dismiss Herdrich's ERISA claim. The fact is that for over 27 years the Congress of the United States has promoted the formation of HMO practices. The Health Maintenance Organization Act of 1973, 87 Stat. 914, 42 U.S.C. § 300e *et seq.*, allowed the formation of HMOs that assume financial risks for the provision of health-

care services, and Congress has amended the Act several times, most recently in 1996. See 110 Stat. 1976, 42 U.S.C. § 300e (1994 ed., Supp. III). If Congress wishes to restrict its approval of HMO practice to certain preferred forms, it may choose to do so. But the Federal Judiciary would be acting contrary to the congressional policy of allowing HMO organizations if it were to entertain an ERISA fiduciary claim portending wholesale attacks on existing HMOs solely because of their structure, untethered to claims of concrete harm.

C

The fiduciary is, of course, obliged to act exclusively in the interest of the beneficiary, but this translates into no rule readily applicable to HMO decisions or those of any other variety of medical practice. While the incentive of the HMO physician is to give treatment sparingly, imposing a fiduciary obligation upon him would not lead to a simple default rule, say, that whenever it is reasonably possible to disagree about treatment options, the physician should treat aggressively. After all, HMOs came into being because some groups of physicians consistently provided more aggressive treatment than others in similar circumstances, with results not perceived as justified by the marginal expense and risk associated with intervention; excessive surgery is not in the patient's best interest, whether provided by fee-for-service surgeons or HMO surgeons subject to a default rule urging them to operate. Nor would it be possible to translate fiduciary duty into a standard that would allow recovery from an HMO whenever a mixed decision influenced by the HMO's financial incentive resulted in a bad outcome for the patient. It would be so easy to allege, and to find, an economic influence when sparing care did not lead to a well patient, that any such standard in practice would allow a factfinder to convert an HMO into a guarantor of recovery.

These difficulties may have led the Court of Appeals to try to confine the fiduciary breach to cases where "the sole purpose" of delaying or withholding treatment was to increase the physician's financial reward, *ibid.* But this attempt to confine mixed decision claims to their most egregious examples entails erroneous corruption of fiduciary obligation and would simply lead to further difficulties that we think fatal. While a mixed decision made solely to benefit the HMO or its physician would violate a fiduciary duty, the fiduciary standard condemns far more than that, in its requirement of "an eye single" toward beneficiaries' interests. But whether under the Court of Appeals's rule or a straight standard of undivided loyalty, the defense of any HMO would be that its physician did not act out of financial interest but for good medical reasons, the plausibility of which would require reference to standards of reasonable and customary medical practice in like circumstances. That, of course, is the traditional standard of the common law. Thus, for all practical purposes, every claim of fiduciary breach by an HMO physician making a mixed decision would boil down to a malpractice claim, and the fiduciary standard would be nothing but the malpractice standard traditionally applied in actions against physicians.

What would be the value to the plan participant of having this kind of ERISA fiduciary action? It would simply apply the law already available in state courts and federal diversity actions today, and the formulaic addition of an allegation of financial incentive would do nothing but bring the same claim into a federal court under federal-question jurisdiction. It is true that in States that do not allow malpractice actions against HMOs the fiduciary claim would offer a plaintiff a further defendant to be sued for direct liability, and in some cases the HMO might have a deeper pocket than the physician. But we have seen enough to know that ERISA was not enacted out of concern that physicians were too poor to be sued, or in order to federalize mal-

practice litigation in the name of fiduciary duty for any other reason. It is difficult, in fact, to find any advantage to participants across the board, except that allowing them to bring malpractice actions in the guise of federal fiduciary breach claims against HMOs would make them eligible for awards of attorney's fees if they won. See 29 U.S.C. § 1132(g)(1). But, again, we can be fairly sure that Congress did not create fiduciary obligations out of concern that state plaintiffs were not suing often enough, or were paying too much in legal fees.

The mischief of Herdrich's position would, indeed, go further than mere replication of state malpractice actions with HMO defendants. For not only would an HMO be liable as a fiduciary in the first instance for its own breach of fiduciary duty committed through the acts of its physician employee, but the physician employee would also be subject to liability as a fiduciary on the same basic analysis that would charge the HMO. The physician who made the mixed administrative decision would be exercising authority in the way described by ERISA and would therefore be deemed to be a fiduciary. See 29 CFR §§ 2509.75-5, Question D-1; 2509.75-8, Question D-3 (1993) (stating that an individual who exercises authority on behalf of an ERISA fiduciary in interpreting and administering a plan will be deemed a fiduciary). Hence the physician, too, would be subject to suit in federal court applying an ERISA standard of reasonable medical skill. This result, in turn, would raise a puzzling issue of preemption. On its face, federal fiduciary law applying a malpractice standard would seem to be a prescription for preemption of state malpractice law, since the new ERISA cause of action would cover the subject of a state-law malpractice claim.

We could struggle with this problem, but first it is well to ask, again, what would be gained by opening the federal courthouse doors for a fiduciary malpractice claim, save for possibly random fortuities such as more favorable scheduling, or the ancillary opportunity to seek attorney's fees. And again, we know that Congress had no such haphazard boons in prospect when it defined the ERISA fiduciary, nor such a risk to the efficiency of federal courts as a new fiduciary malpractice jurisdiction would pose in welcoming such unheard-of fiduciary litigation.

IV

We hold that mixed eligibility decisions by HMO physicians are not fiduciary decisions under ERISA. Herdrich's ERISA count fails to state an ERISA claim, and the judgment of the Court of Appeals is reversed.

It is so ordered.

Notes

1. Although Lori Pegram, a physician owner of Carle, is listed as a petitioner, it is unclear to us that she retains a direct interest in the outcome of this case.

11. Herdrich's theory might well portend the end of nonprofit HMOs as well, since those HMOs can set doctors' salaries. A claim against a nonprofit HMO could easily allege that salaries were excessively high because they were funded by limiting care, and some nonprofits actually use incentive schemes similar to that challenged here, see *Pulvers v. Kaiser Foundation Health Plan,* 99 Cal.App.3d 560, 565, 160 Cal.Rptr. 392, 393–394 (1979) (rejecting claim against nonprofit HMO based on physician incentives).

Disclosure of Operating Practices by Managed-Care Organizations to Consumers of Healthcare
Obligations of Informed Consent

VIKRAM KHANNA, HENRY SILVERMAN, AND JACK SCHWARTZ

Due to soaring healthcare costs and the political gridlock over meaningful national healthcare reform, the delivery of healthcare through managed-care organizations (MCOs) has grown dramatically. The managed-care approach to healthcare market reform, while holding out the promise of more effective case management, risks an excessive focus on organizational structures and strategies designed to reduce expenditures as rapidly as possible.

Consequently, many MCO practices have alienated healthcare consumers, whose medical welfare is at stake. These practices include frequent denials of emergency room care; rapid discharge of mothers and their newborns; considerable administrative burdens for major procedures (for example, autologous bone marrow transplants); and invoices that are not paid on time, thus exposing consumers to improper billing by physicians and other providers.[1] These alienating practices have resulted in a deluge of reform legislation in state legislatures, as consumers protest against managed-care practices and the industry's unwillingness to police itself.[2]

State legislatures are considering more than 1,000 bills annually related to managed care.[3]

In this legislative ferment, however, one crucial form of protection to consumers is often overlooked: the protection provided by disclosure of accurate, important, and understandable information. There is broad concern that consumers are not receiving adequate information about the recent changes in the healthcare system. For example, a 1996 Kaiser Family Foundation survey reported that only 27 percent of Americans even know what the term "managed care" means.[4] Unfortunately, industry-based information efforts like HEDIS (the Health Plan Employer Data and Information Set), address only a relatively narrow range of health plan services and do not provide a comprehensive picture of how a particular health plan operates. In addition, MCOs may mislead consumers with advertising that emphasizes their "utopian" features (for example, unlimited hospital days and generous coverage of office visits) without mentioning the built-in incentives and constraints that can lead to the denial of beneficial care.

More importantly, consumers need information about an MCO's operating practices that may lead to the denial of beneficial care. These practices include selective contracting with physicians; gatekeeper arrangements; imposition of utilization review, including the use of protocols and practice guidelines; and the use of financial incentives (for example, capitation, payment withholds, and bonuses) to influence physicians' practice patterns. These mechanisms of managed care not only have potentially adverse effects on physicians' autonomy, but the failure to provide detailed information about these practices to consumers confirms their already vulnerable position and induces further erosion of the physician-patient relationship. Economic issues are now so closely intertwined with clinical matters that, without disclosure of information on the operating practices of MCOs, consumers cannot be confident that they have received full information about significant issues related to their healthcare.

Basis of an Ethical Obligation to Disclose Information

Several reasons can be given to support the requirement of disclosure of an MCO's key operating practices. First and foremost, a policy of disclosure is justified by the principle of autonomy, because this information enhances patients' capacity to make their own decisions in light of their personal goals and values. Prior to the era of managed care, patients primarily needed medical information to determine for themselves how best to balance the benefits and burdens of proposed medical interventions. Economics rarely entered these deliberations, as third-party reimbursements were deliberately structured to insulate patients and physicians from considering costs at the time of decision making.

Because MCOs now use various mechanisms that may lead to limitations on care, consumers need information concerning these mechanisms prior to choosing a health plan (assuming, of course, that an individual has a genuine choice among different plans, which may not exist for some consumers). With this information, consumers would be better positioned to strike their own balance between a particular plan's benefits package and their desire to pay for it in the form of higher premiums, deductibles, and copayments. Consumers can better choose among the different plans if they are informed about each plan's limitations, restrictions, and definitions of important but ambiguous terms like "experimental treatment." According to Morreim, "there are strong reasons based in both fiduciary law and contract law for believing that [disclosure of MCO benefits and limitations] should be made."[5]

The second function of information is to provide protection—specifically, protection against limitations of potentially beneficial care. While the physician-patient relationship is fiduciary, in the sense that the physician will try to promote the patient's interests rather than exploit the patient's vulnerability, these expectations are in jeopardy when financial incentives to limit care create a major conflict of interest for physicians.[6] Consequently, patients who doubt the extent to which they can depend on their physicians' advocacy for them need information to advocate for themselves, if necessary, in often contentious dealings with MCOs. Hence, disclosure of information is supported by the principle of beneficence, as consumers themselves can advance their best interests.

Information can also empower consumers, as they can form partnerships with healthcare providers to scrutinize managed-care practices that could impair the patient-physician relationship.[7] Acting in concert with physicians, consumers can gain political leverage by influencing the governmental processes that control and regulate the behavior of MCOs. Disclosure of information would encourage dialogue among consumers, physicians, local regulators, employers, and MCOs. Disclosure would even help employees of companies that offer only a single plan, as they would have the information with which to encourage their employers to choose one of the better plans in the marketplace. Indeed, the empowering effect of information might shift the competitive balance to those MCOs that have developed a true code of institutional ethics[8] in which the patient-physician relationship is viewed as the central value rather than as a vexing cost center.

Timing of Disclosures

Disclosures could occur at two distinct points, the point of purchase or the point of care (that is, the clinical encounter). For maximum effect, disclosures should occur at the point of purchase, so that consumers can compare plans and make an informed purchasing decision at the time of enrollment. Disclosure at the point of care is too late for patients to exercise choice as consumers.

Another benefit derived from disclosure of the financial arrangements made between physicians and MCOs at the point of purchase is that it would obviate the need for physicians to perform this task. Disclosure of financial arrangements at the initial clinical encounter is ill-timed for building trust, and would more likely elicit distrust.[9] The AMA's *Code of Medical Ethics* recognizes that physicians could satisfy their obligation of disclosure to their patients by assuring that MCOs provide adequate disclosure on financial inducements to patients enrolled in the plan.[10] At the same time, general disclosures by MCOs at the point of purchase do not discharge physicians from their duty to ensure an informed consent process at the point of care that takes account of the particulars of a patient's problem and, hence, of individual treatment options and their specific implications for payment.[11] Insofar as the constraints of managed care can cause physicians to consciously alter a recommended plan of care for a specific patient (for example, by failing to mention a potentially beneficial diagnostic or treatment alternative because of plan limitations or economic incentives), the duty to ensure that consent is informed remains. Even if the particular procedure or service is thought ineligible for coverage by the plan's benefit package, consumers have a right to this information so that they can appeal the exclusion, pay out-of-pocket, or forgo the care. Physicians should not adhere to any "gag rule" about important alternatives.

Incremental Reform in the States

Since disclosure of information regarding an MCO's practices at the time of enrollment would benefit consumers in every state, a federal law providing for uniform disclosure of practices would be optimal. A federal disclosure law would also apply to all MCOs, including those administering employer-sponsored health benefit plans. Such a broad application, however, cannot presently be achieved by state law, because direct state regulation of employer-sponsored plans is blocked by the federal Employment Retirement Income Security Act (ERISA).[12] Indeed, an important original objective underlying the enactment of ERISA was to free employer-sponsored pension plans from potentially conflicting state regulations.[13] Yet ERISA also extends to other employer-sponsored benefit plans, including health plans, and thus immunizes them from most state regulatory requirements, including disclosure requirements.[14] Hence, because an ever-larger proportion of healthcare is delivered through these plans, state laws requiring disclosure by MCOs would have limited applicability.

To be sure, under ERISA, employer-sponsored benefit plans are subject to various federal requirements, including limited disclosure requirements.[15] But these regulatory disclosure requirements are inadequate. Although a health plan may risk liability under ERISA if it suppresses important information about financial incentives,[16] the benefits of an employer's healthcare plan are typically summarized without detailed disclosure of the operating practices that, in practice, can lead to the denial of beneficial care.

Federal reform efforts, however, cannot be relied on to redress the current deficiency in disclosure requirements. Indeed, Congress's most recent healthcare legislation, the Kennedy-Kassebaum Bill,[17] contains no new disclosure requirements. When attempts have been made to introduce disclosure reform, the results have been inadequate. For example, current federal regulations impose certain disclosure requirements on MCOs that provide services under Medicare or Medicaid. Specifically, these MCOs are required to disclose whether a prepaid plan has a compensation arrangement with physicians that affects the use of referral services and, if so, what type of arrangement it is.[18] This regulation, however, has the significant drawback

of requiring MCOs to make even this limited disclosure only to those beneficiaries who know that they can request the information.

Inadequacies at the federal level are unlikely to be rectified soon. The continued division of the government between a Democratic president and a Republican-controlled Congress makes it improbable that any additional major healthcare reform, let alone a bill encompassing comprehensive disclosure requirements for MCOs, will pass. It is also unlikely that Congress will significantly alter ERISA to allow states broader enforcement authority over benefit plans covered by ERISA.

Given the existence of federal laws that fall short of meeting consumers' needs and a likely impasse in Congress, disclosure by MCOs is an issue that states should address. Because of the political intimacy at the state level, physicians and consumers can exert immediate force on the formulation of policy that would not be possible at the federal level. State governments already take the primary role in regulating and licensing health plans and physicians, and, through state consumer protection statutes, many commercial aspects of healthcare transactions. States are also more likely to act quickly to implement reforms that are of their own making, and enforcement may be more effective when it is closer to the local marketplace.[19]

Despite the partial barrier of ERISA, legislative efforts by the states can still be useful.[20] Indeed, a well-designed state law requiring disclosure of MCO practices would have beneficial ripple effects throughout that state's healthcare market. As information is made available to consumers who obtain their healthcare coverage through insurance policies not subject to ERISA's provision barring state regulation, other consumers, employers, and healthcare providers will see its value and press for wider access to it. As previous experience with laws governing postpartum hospital stays illustrates, Congress itself may be persuaded to act once the states begin to address the problem separately. Congress's enactment of a 48-hour hospitalization minimum following a vaginal birth[21] came only after a flurry of comparable legislative initiatives at the state level.[22]

State disclosure laws are beginning to be debated and, in some states, enacted. In Arizona, for example, MCOs must provide "a concise description" of "any incentives or penalties that are intended to encourage plan providers to withhold services or minimize or avoid referrals to specialists."[23] In New York, MCOs must describe "the types of methodologies" used for reimbursement of providers.[24] In Wyoming, HMOs are required to inform their contractors about "withholding agreements," under which a provider's reimbursement is subject to after-the-fact coverage decisions.[25]

These particular disclosure laws, however, are too limited to meet consumers' need for information. They lack key elements of useful disclosure: a standard format that permits comparisons among MCOs and a broad-enough range of information so that particular items like "withholding agreements" are placed in an understandable context.

A recent enactment in Maryland illustrates a disclosure model that ought to be pursued. The legislation, called the Health Care Consumer Information and Education Act, requires managed-care plans to include information about the following key points in their enrollment marketing material: how they operate, how they pay healthcare providers, and how much they actually spend on direct provision of healthcare.[26] Plans also must disclose, in understandable terms, their reimbursement methodologies to the physicians with whom they contract. Hence, for the first time in Maryland, consumers will receive a clear explanation of a capitation arrangement between an MCO and a physician. Finally, under the new Maryland law, plans will also have to show, in the form of pie charts or bar graphs, the proportion of each $100 of premiums spent on direct medical care for enrollees, as contrasted with administrative expenses. While insurance companies now file selected financial information with state insurance commissioners, who make some of it available for review by the general public, depositing data with the bureaucracy is no substitute for putting understandable information directly into the hands of consumers.

An appealing aspect of the Maryland law for MCOs is that it does not require disclosure of sensitive proprietary information that might be capable of causing harm to a plan's competitive position in the marketplace, such as plan-specific payment rates to physicians, or the formulas used to calculate those rates. Rather, the disclosures simply make capitation and other financial arrangements that affect care more meaningful to consumers. The language that plans insert in marketing materials to describe their reimbursement methodologies will be drafted by a state agency, in consultation with the industry, providers, and consumers. This mechanism, suggested by plan officials, is intended to ensure standardized information and prevent use of potentially deceptive language.

Enactment of the Maryland law required formation of a broad coalition of supporters, including leading consumer groups, the attorney general, senior citizens, labor unions, community groups, and healthcare providers. These supporters pointed out the lack of information currently available to help consumers decide what plan to choose or to assess a plan's operating practices. Physicians helped the process by expressing the view that heightened access to information about a plan's operation benefits them and their patients by motivating open discussions about plans' practices, and gives healthcare professionals a chance to help their patients make more knowledgeable choices.

It is true that the Maryland law will add to the materials that consumers already receive from plans prior to enrollment, and, hence, there is a concern that not every consumer will read and absorb all of the provided information.[27] The incremental amount added by the Maryland law—a few paragraphs of straightforward text and clear charts—will, however, give consumers an opportunity to learn more about managed-care plans without imposing a substantial burden.

Conclusion

Healthcare providers, state legislators, and consumers should build coalitions in support of effective disclosure measures like those in the new Maryland law. To be sure, mandated disclosure at the state level is only a first step in properly regulating managed-care plans. Yet, because information can empower, disclosure is a critical step, and, potentially, a catalyst for national reform. Advocacy for disclosure also allows physicians to take the political steps necessary to organize effectively and build bridges with consumers. Only coalition politics can preserve a patient-centered healthcare system and prevent further erosion of the doctor-patient relationship.

Notes

1. W. Peters and M. Rogers, "Variation in Approval by Insurance Companies of Coverage for Autologous Bone Marrow Transplantation for Breast Cancer," *New England Journal of Medicine* 330 (1994): 473–77; E.B. Fein and E. Rosenthal, "Delays by HMO Leaving Patients Haunted by Bills," *New York Times,* 1 April 1996, A1.

2. L. Demkovich, "Managed Care Plans Feel Consumer, Provider Backlash," *State Health Notes* 17, no. 224 (1996): 1–2.

3. M. Rodwin, "Consumer Protection and Managed Care: Issues, Reform Proposals, and Trade-Offs," *Houston Law Review* 32 (1996): 1319–81.

4. "Managed Care a Mystery to Most Americans," *CCH Monitor* 4, no. 16 (1996): 5.

5. E.H. Morreim, "Moral Justice and Legal Justice in Managed Care: The Ascent of Contributive Justice," *Journal of Law, Medicine & Ethics* 23 (1995): 247–65.

6. M. Angell, "The Doctor as Double Agent," *Kennedy Institute of Ethics Journal* 3 (1993): 279–86.

7. D. Mechanic and M. Schlesinger, "The Impact of Managed Care on Patients' Trust in Medical Care and Their Physicians," *Journal of the American Medical Association* 275 (1996): 1693–97.

8. S.J. Reiser, "The Ethical Life of Health Care Organization," *Hastings Center Report* 24, no. 6 (1994): 28–35.

9. G.J. Annas, "Patients' Rights in Managed Care—Exit, Voice, and Choice," *New England Journal of Medicine* 337 (1997): 210–15.

10. American Medical Association Council on Ethical and Judicial Affairs, "Opinion 8.13; Referral of Patients—Disclosure of Limitations," in *Code of Medical Ethics: Current Opinions With Annotations* (Chicago, Ill.: American Medical Association, 1994), 119.

11. P.S. Applebaum, "Must We Forgo Informed Consent to Control Health Care Costs? A Response to Mark Hall," *Milbank Quarterly* 71 (1993): 669–76.

12. W.K. Mariner, "State Regulation of Managed Care and the Employee Retirement Income Security Act," *New England Journal of Medicine* 335 (1996): 1986–90.

13. *New York State Conference of Blue Cross & Blue Shield Plans v. Travelers Ins. Co.,* 115 S. Ct. 1671, 1677 (1995).

14. *U.S. Code,* vol. 29, sec. 1144 (1988).

15. *Code of Federal Regulations,* vol. 29, sec. 2520.102-3 (1996).

16. *Shea v. Esensten,* 107 F.3d 625 (8th Cir. 1997).

17. *Health Insurance Portability and Accountability Act of 1996,* Public Law 104–191.

18. *Code of Federal Regulations,* vol. 42, secs. 417.479(h)(3) and 434.70(a)(4) (1996).

19. E. Friedman, "Getting a Head Start: The States and Health Care Reform," *Journal of the American Medical Association* 271 (1994): 875–78.

20. R. Karpatkin and G. Shearer, "A Short-Term Consumer Agenda for Health Care Reform," *American Journal of Public Health* 85 (1995): 1352–35.

21. *Newborns' and Mothers' Health Protection Act of 1996,* Public Law 104–204, Title VI.

22. F.J. Hellinger, "The Expanding Scope of State Legislation," *Journal of the American Medical Association* 276 (1996): 1065–70.

23. Arizona Revised Statutes Annotated, sec. 20-1076.

24. New York Insurance Law sec. 3217-a(4).
25. Wyoming Statutes, sec. 26-34-109(a)(xxv).
26. Senate Bill 162, 1997 Session, Maryland General Assembly.

27. M.A. Rodwin, "Consumer Protection and Managed Care: Issues, Reform Proposals, and Trade-Offs," *Houston Law Review* 32 (1996): 1319–81.

C. The Ethical Obligations of Pharmaceutical Companies

Today, pharmaceutical organizations are among the most important health care institutions. There are a number of reasons for this. Drugs comprise a significant portion of medical expenditures. In 2002, $162.4 billion was spent on prescription drugs, and it is anticipated that this figure will escalate in the future.[16] Moreover, spending on prescription drugs in the United States grew 15% from 2001 to 2002.[17] In part, these increasing costs can be attributed to the availability of more effective drugs and the higher cost of drugs. Some predict that within the next few years, spending on medicine will be second only to hospitalization.[18] Spending on drugs is also expensive for individuals. Americans pay more for medicines than do people from other countries, including Canadians. Indeed many Americans travel to Canada to purchase medicine.

Drugs are not only important as an economic component of the health economy. Medicines can also save lives and enhance the quality of life that many people experience. The potential for medicine to save lives makes their high cost morally disconcerting. The pharmaceutical industry is, of course, a for-profit industry, devoted to increasing shareholder profit. In 1999, the industry had a profit of 18.6 percent on sales of 125 billion dollars.[19] Despite the industry's potential impact on individual and social welfare, its mission is not focused on social justice and welfare. Because of the importance of drugs to patients and the community, it is worth considering why drugs are as expensive as they are, especially in the United States, and whether their high cost can be morally justified.

At the same time, we will consider whether pharmaceutical organizations have any duties to patients to price drugs within a range that makes them accessible to those who need them. The pharmaceutical industry maintains, through its trade association, Pharmaceutical Research and Manufacturers of America (PhRMA), that the high price of drugs in the United States is required to pay for the expense of innovative research and development (R&D) of new drugs. In addition, PhRMA maintains that the American drug industry subsidizes R&D for the rest of the world. According to the industry, the average total spent on R&D for each new drug that comes to market, including the amount spent on failures, is 802 million dollars per drug.[20] Thus, according to the industry, the risk of R&D is built into the pricing of drugs that do make it to market. Arnold Relman and Marcia Angell raise a number of questions about this figure, but they also make the following point:

> Whatever the cost of bringing each new drug to market, the total R&D expenditures of the pharmaceutical industry—according to PhRMA, now about $30 billion for all its

members in the United States and abroad—are indeed large. But they should be compared with reported expenditures on marketing and administration, which are more than twice as much as R&D expenditures. Moreover, the most important financial fact about the major pharmaceutical firms is that, despite their expenses, they are immensely profitable. . . . And this has generally been the case for the past two decades. A business consistently this profitable cannot by any stretch of language be described as "risky" or needing special protection of its revenues.[21]

Explaining the high cost of drugs to American consumers on the basis of the high cost of R&D may also be inadequate because R&D is often subsidized by substantial government grants. Arguably, spending on research from public funds should entitle Americans to more accessible prices. Justifying the high cost of drugs on the basis of R&D should raise questions about the ethics of R&D.

Some effort has been made in recent years to make drugs more accessible to people. Under the Medicare Prescription Drug Improvement and Modernization Act of 2003, Medicare recipients are able to save between 10 and 25 percent on prescription drugs with Medicare-approved drug discount cards. By 2006, all people with Medicare will be able to enroll in plans that cover part of the cost of prescription benefits. Although the specific entitlements of the Act are complex, it promises some relief for those who have to pay for pricey drugs. However, that relief may not be generous enough given the price of drugs. Moreover, the law prohibits Medicare from negotiating better prices and, at the time of writing, it is still illegal to import less expensive drugs from Canada or other foreign markets.

The pharmaceutical industry's approach to research and development raises other important ethical questions. Decisions about what drugs to develop and what diseases to address are based on market considerations; that is, on what drugs will be most profitable. Many drugs that are developed are what are called "me too" drugs that are only slight variations of very successful drugs. Moreover, most R&D money targets profitable diseases such as cardiovascular disease and cancer. This approach leaves out the many so-called "orphan" diseases that are so rare that they do not constitute a lucrative market. Likewise there are many not-so-rare diseases in developing countries for which there is again no ready market. In her article, *The Pharmaceutical Industry—To Whom Is It Accountable?*, Marcia Angell argues not only that some form of price control should be imposed on pharmaceuticals, but also that the industry should contribute a certain amount of money to social purposes, such as HIV treatment in Sub-Saharan Africa. We will look at these questions more fully in Chapter 6, Section B, when we consider bioethics in a global context.

Many drugs that are developed have nothing to do with "life and death diseases" but are "lifestyle drugs—remedies that may one day free the world from the scourge of toe nail fungus, obesity, baldness, face wrinkles and impotence."[22] Moreover, the market for such drugs is worth billions of dollars. Unfortunately, the drugs that stand to reap the most profits are not always the drugs that are most widely needed to meet medical needs. This issue is addressed by David Healy in *Good*

Science or Good Business? Healy shows that there has been a dramatic rise in the number of people diagnosed with depression, from 50 people per million in the 1950s to 100,000 per million today. He attributes this to the fact that selective seratonin re-uptake inhibitors (SSRIs) were shown to be effective in beating depression and more widely in the treatment of "community nervousness" or "alienation." According to Healy, the effectiveness of SSRIs in the treatment of the latter conditions led to an increase in people being diagnosed with depression and, in turn, to the recent explosion in cases of depression. Many people who were not in fact depressed were treated and diagnosed as if depressed because Prozac and like drugs "work" for them. In effect, the marketing of SSRIs created the explosion of cases of depression. This is similar for other diseases, such as Paxil and shyness. Should the fact that "something" is responsive to a drug determine whether it is a disease? Put differently, should we allow the possibility of effective marketing by drug companies to determine what will count as a disease? As you consider the moral obligations of the pharmaceutical companies, ask whether they ought to refrain from marketing practices that alter people's conception of self or that medicalize "normal" human experience. Alternatively, does the principle of beneficence dictate that pharmaceuticals reduce all suffering, even suffering that is simply part of the human condition?

The effective marketing of drugs has been facilitated by the relatively recent practice of direct-to-consumer (DTC) advertising, made possible by changes in regulations by the FDA. In one sense this new practice can be seen as the fruit of an increasing respect for patient rights and a growing recognition that physicians should not have a monopoly over medical information. Nevertheless, a number of objections have been raised against DTC. Matthew Hollon, for example, argues against DTC on the grounds that it conveys misleading information about medicines to patients, drives up the cost of advertising and medical expenditures, and, in turn, leads to inappropriate consumer demand for drugs.[23] For the benefit of patients, physicians and public health, Hollon argues for stricter regulation of DTC.

Do you agree that the costs to the public of DTC are too high to permit deference to the patient autonomy it is claimed to support? Does it in fact show respect for patient autonomy?

Proliferating Internet pharmacies are in part another mechanism for coping with expensive medicines. Some of the lowest prices can be secured from international Internet pharmacies. Internet pharmacies work in a number or ways. Basically, consumers transmit prescriptions to the pharmacies (over the Internet, by telephone, by mail) and then the medicines are either picked up at a local pharmacy or mailed to the consumer. There are a number of potential problems with these pharmacies, most having to do with safety for consumers. Consumers risk purchasing expired drugs, purchasing unapproved drugs or counterfeit drugs, or purchasing drugs without a valid prescription. As increasing numbers of people purchase medicine over the Internet, the risks associated with cyber pharmacies are likely to be magnified. As you consider the various strategies Americans have created to cope with pricey medicines, ask if pharmaceutical organizations might not assume some moral obligation to control costs even at the risk of a lower profit margin.

The Pharmaceutical Industry—
To Whom Is It Accountable?

MARCIA ANGELL

The pharmaceutical industry is under mounting scrutiny because of rapidly increasing expenditures for drugs in the United States. Drug expenditures are now the fastest-growing component of health care costs, increasing at the rate of about 15 percent per year.[1,2] They account for about 8 percent of health care spending, and at their current rate of increase, they will soon surpass spending for physicians' services and, for many health maintenance organizations (HMOs), the costs of hospitalization. The increase is due both to a greater use of drugs and to higher prices for individual drugs. Patients feel drug costs keenly, because they pay much of them out of pocket. Many private insurers tightly limit drug coverage, and Medicare does not cover outpatient drugs at all.

The President and members of Congress on both sides of the aisle are considering adding some sort of drug benefit to Medicare. Discussions of this issue have drawn attention not only to the acceleration in drug expenditures, but also to the apparent capriciousness of drug pricing and other practices of the pharmaceutical industry. Americans regularly pay up to twice as much as Europeans and Canadians for the same drug.[3] Prices also vary widely within the United States, where—perversely—they are highest for those in greatest need and least able to pay. Medicare recipients with no supplementary insurance pay on average twice as much for the 10 most commonly prescribed drugs as do favored customers, such as large HMOs and the Veter-

ans Affairs system.[4,5] For example, a month's supply of Zocor (simvastatin) was reported last year to be priced at $103.87 for Medicare recipients, as compared with $42.95 for favored customers.[5] Chronically ill, older Americans may thus be hit with annual drug costs of many thousands of dollars—sums they simply cannot pay. There are frequent stories of older Americans who play out their prescriptions for as long as possible by taking reduced doses, or who share drugs with their spouses, or who simply do without, choosing food and heat over drugs.

The media have recently highlighted another inequity in drug access—the inability of people in the underdeveloped world to obtain the drugs they desperately need. Some underdeveloped countries, overwhelmed by the human immunodeficiency virus (HIV) epidemic and unable to afford brand-name antiretroviral agents, have sought exceptions to patent protections, so that they can manufacture or import generic drugs. The pharmaceutical industry, with the support of the U.S. government, has fought these efforts.[6,7] The industry has also been notably uninterested in developing drugs to treat tropical diseases that afflict millions of people with low purchasing power. A recent story in the New York Times described the reluctance of manufacturers to maintain production of drugs to treat trypanosomiasis in Africa. According to a spokesman for one of the drug companies, "The industry has never been philanthropic. It has always produced products with an aim to getting a return on investment."[8]

How do the drug companies respond to these criticisms? First, they point out that the American pharmaceutical industry has, over the past two decades, produced remarkably effective drugs—drugs that not only extend life and improve its quality, but also save money by holding chronic diseases at bay and averting hospitalizations. High prices, according to this view, simply reflect high value. As for the fact that Americans pay more for the same drugs than people in other countries, the industry maintains that it needs to make up for the depressed prices in countries that impose price controls. Similarly, it is argued that differential pricing within the United States is justified by the need to offset the steep discounts demanded by high-volume purchasers of drugs. Supporters say that someone needs to pay prices high enough to attract the investment necessary to sustain the industry's extraordinary research and development costs. They frequently remind critics that for every drug brought to market, there are innumerable false starts—drugs that never make it. Prices reflect the development costs of not just a particular drug, but all the potential drugs that enter the pipeline.

In sum, the industry contends that it leads the world in innovative drug development because it functions in a free market where returns can be commensurate with the very great risks. Yes, drug coverage should be extended to everyone, but not at the cost of price controls or other government interference that would stifle innovation. (That is why the industry opposes a Medicare drug benefit unless it is administered through the private sector.)

The case for the pharmaceutical industry sounds reasonable, but is it valid? Some of it undoubtedly is. There is no question that the past 20 years have seen the introduction of many new drugs that have changed the face of medicine and improved the lives of millions. (Whether they have resulted in net savings from averted hospitalizations is far less clear.) But much of the case for the pharmaceutical industry is exaggerated or misleading, and some of it is simply false. Let's look at the argument more closely.

How risky is the pharmaceutical business? For a small company pinning everything on a few products, it may be immensely risky. But that is not the case for the large drug companies that dominate the market. True, their research and development costs are high, as compared with those of other industries. The top 10 drug companies are reported to spend on average about 20 percent of their revenues on research and development.[9] (Many critics charge that marketing and promotional costs are misleadingly included in this figure.) But the pharmaceutical giants have so many drugs in the pipeline at any given time that they can count on being able to bring a certain number of drugs to market regularly.

It is instructive to compare the research and development costs of the large drug companies with their profits. The top 10 drug companies are reported to have profits averaging about 30 percent of revenues—a stunning margin.[4,10] Over the past few years, the pharmaceutical industry as a whole has been by far the most profitable industry in the United States.[9,11] According to a recent issue of Fortune, in 1999 the pharmaceutical industry realized on average an 18.6 percent return on revenues. Commercial banking was second, at 15.8 percent, and other industries ranged from 0.5 to 12.1 percent.[11] An industry whose profits outstrip not only those of every other industry in the United States, but often its own research and development costs, simply cannot be considered very risky.

What about the picture of the drug industry as an exemplar of the free market? That image is very far from the truth. On the contrary, the pharmaceutical industry enjoys extraordinary government protections and subsidies. Much of the early basic research that may lead to drug development is funded by the National Institutes of Health.[12] It is usually only later, when the research shows practical promise, that the drug companies become involved. The industry also enjoys great tax advantages. Not only are its research and development costs deductible, but so are its massive marketing expenses. The average tax rate of major U.S. industries from 1993 to 1996 was 27.3 percent of revenues. During the same period the pharmaceutical industry was reportedly taxed at a rate of only 16.2 percent.[13] Most important, the drug companies enjoy 17-year government-granted monopolies on their new drugs—that is, patent protection. Once a drug is patented, no one else may sell it, and the drug company is free to charge whatever the traffic will bear.

Is it correct that the U.S. pharmaceutical industry is highly innovative? Only partly. Some recently launched drugs do indeed fill important, previously unmet medical needs. But it is hard to escape the conclusion that many other new drugs add little to the therapeutic armamentarium except expense and confusion. Consider the welter of very similar drugs to lower cholesterol levels. Developing genuinely innovative drugs is difficult and chancy. It is easier to make "me-too" drugs or minor variants of established products. To be profitable, the variation need only be sufficient to secure a new patent, and the rest is marketing. Critics believe drug companies are doing far too much of that sort of thing. They also charge that many industry-sponsored clinical trials are designed more to find small advantages that can be highlighted in promotional campaigns than to find clinically meaningful effects.[14]

The industry has certainly been ingenious in finding ways to extend patents on its bestselling drugs. For example, a recent Wall Street Journal article describes a complicated business deal between Merck and Schering-Plough for the marketing of two new drug combinations, one to lower serum lipid levels and the other to relieve allergies. Each combination will pair one company's "blockbuster" drug, whose patent as a single product will soon expire, with a drug with supplementary action owned by the other company. The combination drugs will have new patents, and their profits will be shared by both companies.[15] This may be good business, but the medical soundness of fixed drug combinations as opposed to flexible combinations of separate drugs is debatable.

The marketing budgets of the drug industry are enormous—much larger than the research and development costs—although exact figures are difficult to come by, in part because marketing and administrative expenses are often folded together and in part because some of the research and development budget is for marketing research. According to its annual report, Pfizer spent 39.2 percent of its revenues on marketing and administration in 1999[16]; Pharmacia & Upjohn is reported to have spent about the same.[12] The industry depicts these huge expenditures as serving an educational function. It contends that doctors and the public learn about new and useful drugs in this way. Unfortunately, many doctors do indeed rely on drug-company representatives and promotional materials to learn about new drugs, and much of the public learns from direct-to-consumer advertising.[17] But to rely on the drug companies for unbiased evaluations of their products makes about as much sense as relying on beer companies to teach us about alcoholism. The conflict of interest is obvious. The fact is that marketing is meant to sell drugs, and the less important the drug, the more marketing it takes to sell it. Important new drugs do not need much promotion. Me-too drugs do.

How about the claim that the American pharmaceutical industry is the world's engine for drug innovation? The United States accounts for 36 percent of global pharmaceutical research and development. Europe accounts for 37 percent, and Japan for 19 percent.[18] The U.S. fraction is certainly large, but not greatly disproportionate to the country's population. Innovative products come from the pharmaceutical industries of many countries, including those that regulate drug prices, and most large companies have global markets.

The pharmaceutical industry deserves recognition for the many truly extraordinary drugs it has developed. Furthermore, it is hard to imagine any other system for developing new drugs and bringing them to market. This is clearly a job for the private sector. But, in my view, an industry so important to the public health and so heavily subsidized and protected by the government has social responsibilities that should not be totally overshadowed by its drive for profits. There needs to be a better balance between the interests of the shareholders and those of the public.

This is not the place to propose detailed reforms that might right the balance. My purpose here is primarily to describe the problems. But I would like to suggest a few steps that could be taken.

Congress should modify its enabling legislation to permit the Food and Drug Administration to require some pre-marketing trials to compare new drugs with the best available drugs, not with placebos, and to make its approval contingent on the results of those trials. In some cases, the new drug should be compared with both the best available treatment and a placebo. Requiring manufacturers to demonstrate that a new drug is substantially better than anything available would help to stem the rising tide of me-too drugs. Third-party payers might also link coverage to the quality and outcome of trials, as suggested by Ray et al.[19]

To consider other reforms, I believe we need an independent national advisory panel to study the pharmaceutical industry's practices thoroughly and then make recommendations. There have been such panels in the past, but the magnitude of the problems is greater now and a prominent panel would accordingly have more influence. The panel should consist of distinguished experts with no stake in the pharmaceutical industry. Although its recommendations would not be binding, they would stimulate and inform a public debate that would lead to reforms.

Among the most important questions belonging on the panel's agenda should be whether some form of price controls is desirable, and if so, how it might be implemented. This is an exceedingly difficult question that will require careful study and analysis, but in my opinion, some method of constraining prices will probably be needed. Just as public utilities are not permitted to charge whatever the traffic will bear, neither should drug companies. It is hard to take seriously the inevitable industry argument that price controls would stifle innovation and frighten investors when profit margins are so great and so much revenue is spent on marketing.

The panel might also consider whether some small fraction of the industry's revenues should be set aside for social purposes. I believe it should. Such funds might be used to subsidize HIV treatment in sub-Saharan Africa or the purchase of drugs by the needy. The recent decision by five drug companies to cut the price of HIV drugs in Africa was a good but small start. There have been other generous actions by drug companies, notably Merck's 1987 decision to donate millions of doses of ivermectin to treat onchocerciasis and lymphatic filariasis in underdeveloped countries.[20] These are examples that the rest of the industry might do well to emulate in an organized way. Drug companies should also allow exceptions to patent restrictions that currently prevent underdeveloped countries from manufacturing generic drugs for humanitarian purposes or importing drugs from the countries where they can be obtained most cheaply.

The pharmaceutical industry is extraordinarily privileged. It benefits enormously from publicly funded research, government-granted patents, and large tax breaks, and it reaps lavish profits. For these reasons, and because it makes products of vital importance to the public health, it should be accountable not only to its shareholders, but also to society at large.

References

1. Levit K, Cowan C, Lazenby H, et al. Health spending in 1998: signals of change. Health Aff (Millwood) 2000;19(1):124–32.
2. Murray S, Lagnado L. Drug companies face assault on prices. Wall Street Journal. May 11, 2000:B1.
3. Dose of reality: idea of having Medicare pay for elderly's drugs is roiling the industry. Wall Street Journal. February 19, 1999:1.
4. Bernstein S. Drug makers face evolving marketplace. Los Angeles Times. January 31, 1999:A1.
5. Knox RA. Drug-coverage crisis hurting elderly. Boston Globe. March 6, 1999:B1.
6. Hoffmann V. Health groups say poor nations need access to generic drugs. Boston Globe. November 27, 1999.
7. McNeil DG Jr. Patent holders fight proposal on generic AIDS drugs for poor. New York Times. May 18, 2000:A5.
8. McNeil DG Jr. Drug makers and the Third World: a case study in neglect. New York Times. May 21, 2000:1.
9. Tanouye E. Drug dependency: U.S. has developed an expensive habit: now, how to pay for it? Wall Street Journal. November 16, 1998:1.
10. The pharmaceutical industry. The Economist. February 21, 1998.
11. How the industries stack up. Fortune. April 17, 2000.
12. Gerth J, Stolberg SG. Drug makers reap profits on tax-backed research. New York Times. April 23, 2000:1.
13. Anderson C. Drug firms said to pay less in taxes. Boston Globe. December 26, 1999.
14. Langreth R. Drug marketing drives many clinical trials. Wall Street Journal. November 16, 1998.
15. Harris G. Drug makers pair up to fight key patent losses. Wall Street Journal. May 24, 2000.
16. Annual report, 1999. New York: Pfizer, 1999.
17. Avorn J, Chen M, Hartley R. Scientific versus commercial sources of influence on the prescribing behavior of physicians. Am J Med 1982;73:4–8.
18. PhRMA facts and figures. Washington, D.C.: Pharmaceutical Research and Manufacturers of America, August 1997.
19. Ray WA, Griffin MR, Avorn J. Evaluating drugs after their approval for clinical use. N Engl J Med 1993; 329: 2029–32.
20. Waldholz M. Merck, in unusual gesture, will donate drug to fight leading cause of blindness. Wall Street Journal. October 22, 1987.

Good Science or Good Business?

David Healy

When *Listening to Prozac* emerged in 1993, it was one of the few books dealing with psychiatry to become an international best-seller since Freud's and Jung's works and the only book on psychopharmacology ever to do so. The book dealt with the effects of an "antidepressant" on conditions that often looked more like states of alienation than classic depressions. For many, this was their first awareness that antidepressants were drugs distinguishable from minor tranquillizers. For others, Peter Kramer's book and the notion of cosmetic psychopharmacology that it introduced raised interesting ethical and philosophical dilemmas. But the argument here is that the attraction of the book has depended on a series of engineered transformations in the way we think about mental well-being. The "alienation" Prozac and similar therapies "treat" has very commonly been defined in terms of the interests of the medico-pharmaceutical complex, and the arguments on offer about the merits of Prozac look more like descriptions of the interests of their proponents than dependable accounts of reality.

The interface between mental health and alienation traces to the emergence of psychodynamic therapy at the turn of the century, but this new industry remained at one remove from psychiatry until the 1950s. While the therapists took charge of such problems as alienation, psychiatrists dealt with those suffering from full-blown psychoses. In the interim, there was considerable recourse to do-it-yourself pharmaco "therapy" that employed alcohol, opiates, bromides, and barbiturates to manage community nervousness (that is, nervous conditions that do not lead to hospitalization), but this use, unconstrained by a therapy establishment, gave rise to little talk of alienation among philosophers. Indeed one can wonder whether many philosophy departments would be able to function without alcohol to facilitate social intercourse.

When imipramine, the first antidepressant, was introduced, clinicians and pharmaceutical company executives could see little rationale for it. The frequency of affective disorders appeared vanishingly low and these conditions responded to antipsychotics or ECT Clinicians used the antidepressants sparingly,[1] and the very word "antidepressant" only begins to appear in dictionaries in the mid 1980s. Unlike the antipsychotics, the antidepressants had no clear niche. However, they did seem capable of making some difference to a large number of people, even if those people might have to be persuaded that they needed this difference in their lives. As early as 1958, Roland Kuhn, the discoverer of imipramine, had noted that some sexual perversions responded to imipramine and that many patients, when they recovered, felt better than well.[2] Such transformations opened up significant philosophical and ethical issues—claims now strongly suggestive of Kramer's agenda. But whereas Kramer's book became a runaway best-seller, Kuhn's speculations had minimal impact. The philosophers who were excited by the new psychotropic compounds in the 1950s and are now interested in neuroscience and Prozac were not interested in imipramine.

Market Development

The developmental trajectory for the antidepressants was largely determined by a critical external event—the thalidomide disaster. The public reaction to the birth defects caused by thalidomide, which had been taken by pregnant women to combat "morning sickness," led to the 1962 Food and Drug Act amendments, which channeled drug development toward clear diseases. Drug availability was restricted to prescription-only medicines, placing it in the hands of individuals who supposedly would make drugs available for problems stemming only from diseases rather than for those stemming from other sources. These developments radically changed psychiatry, first by putting a premium on "categorical" rather than "dimensional" models of disease, so that psychiatrists were more likely to treat diseases as conditions that patients either have or lack rather than have to some degree, and second because prescription-only status brought nervousness within the psychiatric ambit.

Initially, the straitjacket of the 1962 amendments had the outcomes intended. But if drugs are made available only for diseases, it was perhaps predictable that there would be a mass creation of disease. There has been, and these developments shape our perceptions of how alienation is being managed. In the 1950s, it was thought that only fifty people per million were depressed. Nowadays no one blinks on being told that depression affects over 100,000 per million and that it leads to more disability and economic disadvantage than any other disorder.[3] But this change plainly requires a major change in our view of what constitutes disease. If 10 to 15 percent of the population is depressed, the label "disease" does not make sense if understood in terms of the biological disruption that bacterial infections produce. What is meant can be grasped only if the "disease state" is framed in terms of temperamental factors and only if what is aimed at is a state of comparative well-being rather than cure.

Oddly enough, the widespread acceptance of our views of depression conceals the process by which they were changed. When first faced with the question of what community nervousness is, the psychiatric profession and the pharmaceutical industry understood it in terms of anxiety, and they resorted to Valium and other anxiolytics to treat it. This led to the first debates about the ethics of treating "problems of living" in this way.[4] In the West, however, the 1980s crisis surrounding benzodiazepine dependence led to the eclipse of both the minor tranquilizers and the whole notion of anxiolysis. This ushered in the antidepressant era. In contrast, in Japan, where dependence is less of a problem, the anxiolytics remain the most widely used drugs for nervousness and the antidepressant market remains small—in fact, Prozac is unavailable.

Depression as it is now understood by clinicians and at street level is therefore an extremely recent phenomenon, largely confined to the West. Its emergence coincides with the development of the selective serotonin reuptake inhibitors (SSRIs), which in the mid-1980s appeared capable of development as either anxiolytics or antidepressants.[5] Since their initial launch as antidepressants, various SSRIs have been approved for the treatment of panic disorder, social phobia, post-traumatic stress disorder, obsessive-compulsive disorder, and other anxiety-based conditions. In a number of these disorders, the SSRIs are more effective than they are in depression. Indeed, it has not been possible to show that Prozac is effective in classic depressive disorders. Worse, there is some evidence that far from reducing rates of suicide and disability

associated with depression, antidepressants may actually increase them. Prozac and related drugs are prescribed to over four million children and teenagers per annum in the United States, yet a preponderance of evidence suggests that such prescriptions are not warranted.[6]

The designation of Prozac as an antidepressant means that some efficacy in some milder depressions can be shown for this compound and it is accordingly not illegal to market it as a treatment for depression, but the fact that Prozac "works" for some people does not mean that they have classic depression. That it was marketed this way stems from business rather than scientific calculations.[7]

Changes in the way we think about problems of living are not restricted to depression. The research demonstrating that SSRIs could be useful for treating other nervous conditions has been associated with marked increases in estimates of their frequency as well.[8] Obsessive-compulsive disorder has increased a thousand-fold in apparent frequency. Panic disorder, a term coined in the mid-1960s and first appearing in diagnostic classification systems in 1980, has become one of the most widely recognized psychiatric terms at street level. Social phobia, all but invisible until the 1990s, now appears to affect the population in such epidemic proportions that the launch of Paxil as an anti-shyness agent was a media event.

These changes have very likely been brought about by the pharmaceutical industry itself, through its highly developed capacities for gathering and disseminating evidence germane to its business interests. The methods that might have this effect include convening consensus conferences and publishing the proceedings, sponsoring symposia at professional meetings, and funding special supplements to professional journals. The industry may also establish and support patient groups to lobby for treatments. The claim here-though defended elsewhere-is that these and other techniques for marketing information are sufficiently well developed that significant changes in the mentality of both clinicians and the public can be produced within a few years.[9] In effect, the industry has educated prescribers and the public to recognize many other kinds of cases as depression.

These changes are facilitated by a broader social shift. When dynamic therapies occupied the citadels of orthodoxy in psychiatry, their terminology leaked out into popular language. A variety of terms were used in ways that technically were wholly inaccurate but that nevertheless became part of the way in which we thought of ourselves and conceptualized alienation. Recently, the psychobabble prevalent during much of the century has begun to give ground to a newly minted biobabble. A rootless patois of biological terms—"low brain amines," for example—has settled into the popular consciousness, with consequences for our self conception that can only be guessed at.[10]

Possibly, Prozac's success has also depended partly on a lack of information. Prozac has been shown to "work" using clinician-based disease-specific rating scales, but when patient-based, nonspecific quality of life instruments have been used, it has not been shown to work for depression-although this information has not seen the light of day.[11] Current methods to estimate the side effects of drugs in clinical trials actually underestimate them, according to some tallies, by a sixfold factor.[12] Finally, the SSRIs have been sold on the back of a claim that the rate of suicide is 600 per every 100,000 patient years. But this is the rate for people with severe depression, for which Prozac does not work. The rate for primary care depression is on the order of 30 out of every 100,000 people. Yet in these populations, suicide rates of 189 for every 100,000 on Prozac have been reported.[13] Thus there are good grounds to believe that Prozac can trigger suicidality. The pharmaceutical companies are not investigating, however; one wonders whether they are receiving legal advice echoing that given to the tobacco companies, that any investigation of these issues may increase product liability. From this vantage point, Prozac might seem better cast

as a symbol of the alienation that large corporations can visit on people rather than as a symbol of the "treatment" of alienation that a psychotropic agent can bring about.

Lifestyles and the Disease Model

The public perception of Prozac, as shaped by *Listening to Prozac*, was that the drug had been rationally engineered, in the sense that it had been developed so as to achieve highly reproducible clinical outcomes. If it is important that a drug be rationally engineered, it seems clear that Kuhn's discovery of cosmesis, in contrast to Kramer's, could not have gone anywhere.

However, Kramer's mythic account of the development of Prozac was mistaken. It was perhaps prophetic, since neuroimaging technologies, pharmacogenetic techniques, and other novel strategies will make the development of psychotropic drugs increasingly rational in this industrial sense, but none of this applied to Prozac. While Prozac works for some people, it has not been possible to offer any guarantees as to the quality of clinical outcomes when using it. Lacking such guarantees does not matter as much in treating genuine disease, since when patients are in danger, even doing something risky is by consensus preferable to doing nothing. But poor outcomes are much less tolerable in the management of less severe conditions. Thus a disease model offers pharmaceutical companies and clinicians a valuable escape from quality standards.

A disease model offers other advantages to pharmaceutical companies. It acts powerfully to legitimate drug-taking, allowing Prozac, for example, to escape the flak that Valium drew in the 1970s. And it can function as a means of resolving problems about equitable access to health resources, since it is widely accepted that there are greater difficulties with inequities in health care than with inequities in the access to computers or digital televisions.

Prozac is of course only one of a growing number of agents that modulate lifestyles rather than cure diseases. Viagra is another good example of this trend. Viagra's designation as a lifestyle agent depends in good part on the reliability with which the intended responses can be elicited. What is interesting about Viagra is that we have had other drugs for two decades now that have comparable effects on sexual function. The SSRIs may have weak and unpredictable effects on depression, but they can reliably delay orgasm, and other antidepressants can advance it.[14] Thus we have had the capacity to "engineer" sexual performance for some time; the pharmaceutical companies have simply not marketed pills for such uses, presumably because they were uncertain about the acceptability of a "lifestyle market" for their wares.[15] Seen against this background, the promotion of Viagra marks an important turning point in the way drugs are developed.

In general, clinical therapeutics is increasingly comprised of a series of domains removed to varying degrees from the management of bacterial infections. The provision of oral contraceptives on a prescription-only basis is notionally underpinned by a disease model. Hormone replacement therapy is likewise presented as treatment for a disease. "Treatments" for baldness, age-induced skin changes, obesity, and a range of other lifestyle agents wait in the wings. All of these raise the question of what qualifies as a disease. In recent history, a disease has been thought of as an entity established by an underlying biological lesion. Previously, illnesses were anything that made the individual feel less well, a definition which potentially included halitosis. Latterly, the emergence of agents that can modify natural variations in hair loss or ejaculatory latency push us closer to making explicit one of the currently implicit but increasingly important definitions of disease, which is that it is, in practice, something that third-party payers will reimburse on.

Before 1962, tonics flourished along with treatments for halitosis and other problems of living. Cyproheptadine, an imipramine-like agent, which reliably improves appetite and sleep and less reliably cures depressions, was on sale as a tonic. The 1962 amendments required redesignation of agents like this as antidepressants rather than tonics, but in many ways they might have had greater public acceptability if classified as tonics, a usage hallowed by centuries of practice rather than as antidepressants, since as drugs they quickly became associated with risks of addiction. Would we be talking about alienation if it were over-the-counter tonics rather than prescription-only antidepressants that were involved—or if we were, would the public take our debate seriously? Could it be that much of the current debate is predicated on a combination of pseudoscientific mystique and regulatory artifact? Consider in this connection one of the dilemmas raised by Kramer: because of its prescription-only status, Prozac raises special moral problems for the physician, who is now called on to decide whether it would be a good thing to reduce the general level of melancholy in the community, with the consequent loss of spirituality or creativity that might go with that.

These dilemmas would be transformed if the power to make these decisions were returned to the consumer. We may be unwittingly alienated choosing to purchase automobiles, but we would certainly feel alienated if it were the prerogative of the automobile salesmen to decide which brand of vehicle we should get.

References

1. D. Healy, "The Three Faces of the Antidepressants," Journal of Nervous and Mental Disease 187 (1999): 174–80.
2. R. Kuhn, "The Treatment of Depressive States with 622355 (Imipramine Hydrochloride)," American Journal of Psychiatry 115 (1958): 459–64.
3. C. Murray and A. Lopez, The Global Burden of Disease (Cambridge, Mass.: Harvard University Press, 1996).
4. M. C. Smith, A Social History of the Minor Tranquillizers (Binghamton, N.Y.: Haworth Press, 1991).

5. D. Healy and D. Nutt, "Prescriptions, Licences and Evidence," Psychiatric Bulletin 22 (1998): 680–84; D. Healy, "The Marketing of 5HT," British Journal of Psychiatry 158 (1991): 737–42.

6. See ref. 5, Healy, "The Marketing of 5HT"

7. R. L. Fisher and S. Fisher, Antidepressants for Children: Is Scientific Support Necessary? (With commentary by L. Eisenberg and E. Pellegrino)." Journal of Nervous & Mental Disease 184 (1996): 98–108.

8. D. Healy, The Antidepressant Era (Cambridge, Mass.: Harvard University Press, 1997).

9. For a full defense, see ref. 8, Healy, The Antidepressant Era.

10. See E. S. Valenstein, Blaming the Brain (New York: Free Press, 1998).

11. See ref. 1, Healy, "The Three Faces of the Antidepressants."

12. S. Stecklow and L. Johannes, "Questions Arise on New Drug Testing: Drug Makers Relied on Clinical Researchers Who Now Await Trial," Wall Street Journal 15 August 1997.

13. D. Healy et al., "Suicide in the Course of the Treatment of Depression," Journal of Psychopharmacology 13 (1999): 94–99.

14. See ref. 8, Healy, The Antidepressant Era.

15. See ref. 8, Healy, The Antidepressant Era.

Notes

1. Rosemary Stevens, *In Sickness and in Wealth, American Hospitals in the Twentieth Century* (New York: Basic Books, 1989), 17–39.

2. *Schloendorff v. New York Hospital,* 211 N.Y. 125, 105 N.E. 92 (1914).

3. *Bing v. Thunig,* 2 N.Y. 2d 656, 664–65, 143 N.E. 2d 3, 7 (1957) (citations omitted).

4. 42 U.S.C. 1395dd.

5. Daniel Wikler, "The Virtuous Hospital: Do Nonprofit Institutions Have A Distinctive Moral Mission?" in *In Sickness and in Health: The Mission of Voluntary Health Care Institutions,* eds. J. David Seay and Bruce C. Valdek (New York: McGraw-Hill, 1988), 127–153.

6. Regina E. Herzlinger and William S. Krasker, "Who Profits from Nonprofits?" *Harvard Business Review* (January–February 1987): 93–106.

7. See Paul Starr, *The Social Transformation of American Medicine* (New York: Basic Books, 1982), 320–327.

8. Peter D. Jacobson. *Strangers in the Night: Law and Medicine in the Managed Care Era* (Oxford and NewYork: Oxford University Press, 2002).

9. Kaiser Family Foundation, *Chartbook: Trends and Indicators in the Changing Medical Marketplace* (2002): 6.

10. Sheila Smith et al., "The Next Ten Years of Health Spending: What Does the Future Hold?" *Health Affairs* 17:5(1998): 128–140.

11. James Sabin, "The Second Phase of Priority Setting: Fairness as a Problem of Love and the Heart: A Clinician's Perspective on Priority Setting," *British Medical Journal* 317:7164(1998): 1002.

12. Tracy Miller and William Sage, "Disclosing Physician Financial Incentives," *Journal of the American Medical Association* 281(1999): 1424–1430, 1427.

13. David Mechanic, "The Managed Care Backlash: Perceptions and Rhetoric in Healthcare Policy and the Potential for Healthcare Reform," *The Milbank Quarterly* 79:1(2001): 35–54.

14. 536 U.S. 355 (2002).

15. Aetna Health Inc. v. Davila, _____ U.S. _____ , 124 S.Ct. 2488 (2004).

16. Kaiser Family Foundation, Prescription Drug Trends, KFF October 2004, at www:kff.org/rxdrugs/loader.cfm?url=/commonsport/security/getfile/cfm&pageID=48305.

17. Ibid.

18. Arnold Relman and Marcia Angell, "How the Drug Industry Distorts Medicine and Politics: America's Other Drug Problem," *The New Republic* 30 (December 16, 2002).

19. Kaiser Family Foundation, 46.

20. Pharmaceutical Research and Manufacturers of America, "2002 Industry Profile," (Washington, D.C.: PhRMA, 2002) 8.

21. Relman and Angell, 30.

22. Ken Silverstein, "Millions for Viagra, Pennies for the Poor: Research Money Goes to Profitable Lifestyle Drugs," *The Nation* 269:3(July 19, 1999): 13.

23. Matthew F. Hollon, "Direct to Consumer Marketing of Prescription Drugs: Creating Consumer Demand," *Journal of the American Medical Association* 281:4(1999): 382–384.

Recommended Readings

Arno, Peter, and Davis, Michael H. "Why Don't We Enforce Existing Drug Price Controls? The Unrecognized and Unenforced Reasonable Pricing Requirements Imposed upon Patents Deriving in Whole or in Part from Federally Funded Research." *Tulane Law Review* 75(2001): 631–693.

Bloche, M. Gregg. "Health Policy Below the Waterline: Medical Care and the Charitable Exemption." *Minnesota Law Review* 80(1995): 299–398.

Buchanan, Allen. "Trust in Managed Care Organizations." *Kennedy Institute of Ethics Journal* 10(2000): 189–212.

Calfee, John E. "Pharmaceutical Price Controls and Patient Welfare." *The Annals of Internal Medicine* 134(2001): 1060–1064.

Clark, Robert C. "Does the Nonprofit Form Fit the Hospital Industry." *Harvard Law Review* 93 (1980): 1417–1489.

Dame, Lauren A. "The Emergency Medical Treatment and Active Labor Act: The Anomalous Right to Health Care." *Health Matrix* 8(1998): 3–28.

Davidoff, Frank. "The Heartbreak of Drug Pricing." *The Annals of Internal Medicine* 134(2001): 1068–1071.

Hall, Mark A., and Berenson, Robert A. "Ethical Practice in Managed Care: A Dose of Realism." *Annals of Internal Medicine* 128(1998): 395–402.

Herzlinger, Regina E., and Krasker, William S. "Who Profits from Nonprofits?" *Harvard Business Review* (January–February, 1987): 93–106.

Hollen, Matthew F. "Direct-to-Consumer Marketing of Prescription Drugs: Creating Consumer Demand." *Journal of the American Medical Association* 281(1999): 382–384.

Illingworth, Patricia. "Employer Leadership in the Era of Workplace Rationing." *Cambridge Quarterly of Healthcare Ethics* 10(2001): 172–183.

Jacobson, Peter D. *Strangers in the Night.* New York: Oxford University Press, 2002.

Jones, Gary E. "The Right to Health Care and the State." *The Philosophical Quarterly* 33(132)(1983): 279–287.

Kravitz, Richard. "Direct-to-Consumer Advertising of Prescription Drugs: Implications for the Patient-Physician Relationship." *Journal of the American Medical Association* 284:17(2000): 2244.

Mechanic, David. "The Managed Care Backlash: Perceptions and Rhetoric in Health Care Policy and the Potential for Health Care Reform." *The Milbank Quarterly* 79(2001): 35–54.

Morreim, E Haavi. *Holding Health Care Accountable.* New York: Oxford University Press, 2001.

Needleman, Jack. "The Role of Nonprofits in Health Care." *Journal of Health Politics, Policy and Law* 26(5)(2001): 1113–1130.

Noble, Alice A., Hymas, Andrew L., and Kane, Nancy M. "Charitable Hospital Accountability: A Review and Analysis of Legal and Policy Initiatives." *Journal of Law, Medicine and Ethics* 26(2)(1998): 116–137.

Norton, Edward C., and Staiger, Douglas O. "How Hospital Ownership Affects Access to Care for the Uninsured." *RAND Journal of Economics* 25(Spring 1994): 171–185.

Randel, Lauren, Pearson, Steven, Sabin, James, Hyams, Tracey, and Emanuel, Ezekiel. "How Managed Care Can be Ethical." *Health Affairs* 20:4 (July/August 2001): 43–56.

Relman, Arnold, and Angell, Marcia. "America's Other Drug Problem: How the Drug Industry Distorts Medicine and Politics." *The New Republic* (December 16, 2002): 2727–2741.

Salbu, Steven R. "AIDS and Drug Pricing: In Search of a Policy." *Washington University Law Quarterly* 71(1993): 691–734.

Waymack, Mark H. "Health Care as a Business: The Ethic of Hippocrates Versus the Ethic of Managed Care." *Business and Professional Ethics Journal* 9(1990): 69–78.

Wikler, Daniel. "The Virtuous Hospital: Do Non-Profit Institutions Have a Distinctive Moral Mission," in *In Sickness and in Health: The Mission of Voluntary Health Care Institutions.* Eds. J. David Seay and Bruce C. Vladek. New York: McGraw-Hill, 1988.

Wilkes, Michael S., Bell, Robert A., and Kravitz, Richard. "Direct to Consumer Advertising: Trends, Impact, and Implications." *Health Affairs* 19(2000): 110–128.

Zachry, William. "Patient Autonomy and the Regulation of Direct-to-Consumer Advertizing." *Clinical Therapeutics* 23:12(2001): 2022–2023.

Cases

Aetna Health, Inc. v. Davilia, _____ U.S. _____, 124 S.Ct. 2488 (2004).

Rush v. Prudential HMO v. Moran, 536 U.S. 355 (2002).

Chapter Six

Individuals, Society, and Health

A. The Obligations of the State

Is there a "right to health care?" It is common in public debate and political discourse to ask that question. Many lament that the United States is the only developed nation in which "there is no right to health care." They note that the Constitution of the World Health Organization (WHO) states that "[t]he enjoyment of the highest attainable standard of health is one of the fundamental rights of every human being without distinction of race, religion, political belief, economic or social condition" and that "[g]overnments have a responsibility for the health of their peoples which can be fulfilled only by the provision of adequate health and social measures."

But the question of whether there is a right to health care cannot readily be answered unless we first consider some preliminary questions. The first is what type of right. Rights theorists, following in the footsteps of Isaiah Berlin,[1] often distinguish between negative rights, which preclude others from interfering with or coercing a rights-holder, and so-called positive rights, which enable the rights-holder "to act in a particular way, or to receive or posses a particular thing."[2] Such a right implies a corresponding duty on the part of another to provide the rights-holder with that to which he or she has a claim. As we have explored in previous chapters, patients have many ethical and legal rights against individual health care providers and institutions. For example, both ethics and the law support the idea that individuals have a right to be provided with competent treatment. Likewise there is a legal right, grounded in federal statute, to be treated until stabilized in a hospital emergency room. These rights are undoubtedly rights to health care. Therefore, it is not quite true to say that there are no legal rights to health care in the United States.

We should consider that these rights to health care that exist are hardly comprehensive and they are not the sort of absolute right to medical care most people have in mind when they speak about "a right to health care." As James Childress argues, when people talk about a right to health care, they are usually speaking of a right against the state for the provision of health care.[3] This would appear to be a "positive right" that does not simply require the state to abstain from interfering in the health care activities or choices of an individual. Instead, it requires the state to ensure that individuals have the means necessary to obtain health care. Put differently, the WHO charter proclaims that states have the "responsibility" to ensure the "provision of adequate health." Likewise the Universal Declaration of Human Rights explicitly ties the right to health care to the provision of a "standard of living adequate for the health and well-being" of each individual. Under this Declaration, a state cannot simply refrain from acting, it must ensure that people have the means for obtaining health care.

Traditionally there has been reluctance in the United States to recognize such positive rights, at least broadly and as a matter of law. (Remember that there are numerous narrow, positive legal rights to health care, such as EMTALA's requirement that hospitals provide emergency care.) In *Harris v. McRae*, for example, the Supreme Court made clear that as a matter of constitutional law individuals have no right to obtain health care from the government.[4] In upholding a statute that denied Medicaid funding for nonelective abortions, the Supreme Court relied upon the distinction between the negative rights, including the right to an abortion, that it had previously upheld and the positive right the woman sought. The Court stated, "[A]lthough government may not place obstacles in the path of a woman's exercise of her freedom of choice, it need not remove those not of its own creation. Indigency falls in the latter category. The financial constraints that restrict an indigent woman's ability to enjoy the full range of constitutionally protected freedom of choice are the product not of governmental restrictions on access to abortions, but rather of her indigency."[5]

The fact that the Supreme Court does not recognize a positive constitutional right to health care, however, does not settle the ethical argument. An ethical right may exist even in the absence of its legal recognition. In recent decades many ethicists have grappled with whether there is a positive right to health care as an ethical matter. In analyzing this issue, they have had to confront two major, interrelated questions: Why should there be a right to health care as opposed to a right to other goods that humans desire? And what is the nature of such a "right"? Each question has invariably provoked a third query: What is a fair distribution of health care?

In 1983 the *President's Commission for the Study of Ethical Problems in Medicine and Biomedical and Behavioral Research* issued an influential volume on the topic. The Commission argued that health care is special because of its importance in promoting "personal well-being by preventing or relieving pain, suffering, and disability and by avoiding loss of life."[6] Without health care, many people cannot live full and rewarding lives and they will lack a broad range of opportunities. Because of the "special nature" of health care, the Commission stated that it "ought to be accessible, in a fair fashion, to all."[7] Nevertheless, the Commission concluded that it was extremely complex and difficult to determine what would constitute an equitable division of health care. As a result, the Commission decided that an equitable distribution only required an "adequate level of health care."[8] But even with that caveat, the Commission backed away from stating that there was any right to health care and argued simply that society has an "obligation" to provide all with an "adequate level of health care."[9] One may wonder, as many have, what is the distinction between finding an obligation and a positive right.

Other ethicists, including some who contributed to the Commission's work, have been bolder than the Commission and have argued that there is indeed a moral (if not legal) right to at least some level of health care. Probably the most prominent contribution to this literature is Norman Daniels' analysis. Relying upon the work of John Rawls, Daniels argues that we need to distinguish among types of health care. Sometimes health care satisfies mere preferences. There is no right to such health care services. But, at other times, health care becomes a need, because it is necessary for individuals to enjoy a normal range of life opportunities. According to Daniels, because a just society ensures an equal range of life opportunities, it must ensure that individuals have access to the health care necessary to enjoy those opportunities.[10]

Writing from a market-oriented perspective, legal scholar Richard A. Epstein agrees that health care is "special" or different from most goods allocated in the market place in important ways.[11] Yet while Epstein finds the recognition of a positive right to health care alluring, he believes that the complexities and practical problems that would accompany the recognition of any such right should prevent us from doing so. Epstein concludes that we should rely upon the market, abetted by private charity, to ensure the provision of health care.

Surprisingly few scholars go as far as Epstein in rejecting almost any role for government in the provision of health care. Nevertheless, many agree that the devil lies in the details and that while it may be easy to argue that health care is an especially valuable good, it is difficult to define the parameters of that good or determine what exactly would be guaranteed if there were a "right to health care."

In fact, precisely because many arguments about the right to health care are grounded in concerns for equality, theorists about a right to health care frequently focus their attention on questions of equity and what constitutes a just distribution of health care. For example, in the selection that is included, Norman Daniels concedes that the account of justice that relates a right to health to equality of opportunity cannot answer difficult distributional questions. Instead he posits the need for fair procedures, which include social deliberation over the allocation of scarce health care resources. In contrast, ethicist Dan Brock criticizes other discussions of health care justice for failing to take into account the special needs and claims of vulnerable populations. According to Brock, "the most plausible ethical framework for considering the claims of vulnerable populations in health resource priorization is that of priority for worse-off groups."[12]

It may be ironic, but understandable, that in a nation that spends more than any other on health care and in which millions lack health insurance, discussions about the right to health care almost inevitably turn into discussions about limiting resources and rationing. When the health care costs for an individual can easily exceed over a million dollars a year, discussion about a right to health care, or equal care, may appear absurd without the development of a principle or methodology for limiting care.

The reciprocal relationship between finding rights to health care and rationing care became especially evident in the early late 1980s when the state of Oregon proposed to expand its Medicaid program and simultaneously ration the services available. Under the plan, health care services were prioritized according to their cost-effectiveness.[13] In determining the effectiveness of different procedures, the quality of life that the procedure would likely provide a patient was considered. The state's goal, therefore, was to more broadly provide those treatments that were cost-effective but limit treatments that were expensive and offered little "improvement" in a patient's quality of life.

In many ways, the Oregon plan constituted an ethicist's dream come true. Here was a state developing a rational methodology for making "tragic choices." But despite that appeal, the plan immediately ran into problems. Most acute was the federal government's determination that the initial prioritization list violated the legal rights of people with disabilities. Although the list was later modified to meet the objections, questions remain about how to make just determinations about the value of particular treatments. In a discussion clearly influenced by John Rawls, Caitlin J. Halligan writes,

> Binding consent requires that participants in the decisionmaking process be knowledgeable about the consequences of their choices and capable of envisioning themselves in each of the predicaments that result from a decision. If the relevant decision concerns the allocation of health care resources, then participants must be able to imagine themselves suffering from each possible condition, and benefiting from—or going without—the paired treatment. But citizens will find it difficult, if not impossible to imagine themselves stricken with congenital or early-onset diseases. Likewise, persons of affluent means may find it difficult to imagine living in an area severely polluted by toxic waste, with no chance of moving to a safer locale. . . . This inability to place oneself "behind the veil" may skew public valuation of various risks and outcomes.[14]

Perhaps the most relevant coda to the Oregon plan is that it never did lead to the provision of universal care in the state. An experiment that was supposed to pave the way to ensuring every one a right to the most highly prioritized treatments ended up as yet another device for limiting care for those dependent upon public insurance. Indeed, in November 2002, voters in the state rejected a referendum that would have called upon the state to provide coverage to all state residents.[15] More broadly, while ethicists continue to debate whether there should be a right to health care and, if so, how it should be limited, millions of Americans remain without any health insurance.

Moreover, any focus on the distribution of health care services may miss the point. As the readings in Chapter 2, Section B suggest, health care (understood as the services of physicians, hospitals, allied professionals, and pharmacies) plays only a limited role in determining a population's health. As a result, it may well be that the provision of health care would not be the most effective way to ensure "[t]he enjoyment of the highest attainable standard of health" that the World Health Organization obliges states to defend.

So we should ask whether states have an ethical obligation to protect a population's health, broadly speaking. In *The Future of the Public's Health in the 21st Century*, the Institute of Medicine asserts that they do because only concerted, public efforts can ensure a population's health. The Institute writes,

> The public's health can be achieved only through collective action, not through individual endeavor. Acting alone, persons of means may procure personal medical services and many of the necessities of living. Yet no single individual, or group, can assure the conditions needed for health. Meaningful protection and assurance of the population's health require communal effort. The community as a whole has a stake in environmental protection, hygiene and sanitation, clear air and surface water, uncontaminated food and drinking water, safe roads and products and the control of infectious disease.[16]

Others have predicated public health protection upon democratic theory and its understanding of the role of the state. Almost seventy-five years ago, legal scholar James Tobey argued, "The protection and promotion of public health has long been recognized as the responsibility of the sovereign power. Government is, in fact, organized for the express purpose, among others, of conserving the public health and cannot divest itself of this important duty."[17] After reviewing public health laws in the American colonies and during the early years under the federal Constitution, Wendy E. Parmet concludes that the political philosophy of the Framers, especially as it was understood via social contract theory, "saw the duty to protect health as stemming from the social or governmental contract in which individual and state were related by mutual obligations." In essence, the protection from epidemics (a major source of death in the eighteenth century) was one of the reasons that people gave their allegiance to government. In Chapter 7 we will discuss whether the reemergence of infectious diseases today requires a renewed commitment to a public health ethic.

Traditional public health efforts are not, of course, the only determinants of health. In *Justice is Good for Our Health*, Norman Daniels and colleagues argue not that justice requires equality of health care, but that justice is a determinant of a healthy population. Thus if we want our population to be healthy, we will take strides to ensure a fairly just (in Rawlsian terms) distribution of income. While it may be appealing to invert the relationship this way, and to see public health as a justification for justice, the question must be asked why public health itself has the value the authors assert, i.e., a value that subordinates justice itself. Even if public health is a primary value, does that justify any or many infringements of other interests? Perhaps the real question is whether we can have a world where public health is valued and protected, without public health itself becoming exploited and hegemonic? We will take up those questions again in Chapter 7.

Constitution of the World Health Organization

The States Parties to this Constitution declare, in conformity with the Charter of the United Nations, that the following principles are basic to the happiness, harmonious relations and security of all peoples:

Health is a state of complete physical, mental and social well-being and not merely the absence of disease or infirmity.

The enjoyment of the highest attainable standard of health is one of the fundamental rights of every human being without distinction of race, religion, political belief, economic or social condition.

The health of all peoples is fundamental to the attainment of peace and security and is dependent upon the fullest co-operation of individuals and States.

The achievement of any State in the promotion and protection of health is of value to all.

Unequal development in different countries in the promotion of health and control of disease, especially communicable disease, is a common danger.

Healthy development of the child is of basic importance; the ability to live harmoniously in a changing total environment is essential to such development.

The extension to all peoples of the benefits of medical, psychological and related knowledge is essential to the fullest attainment of health.

Informed opinion and active co-operation on the part of the public are of the utmost importance in the improvement of the health of the people.

Governments have a responsibility for the health of their peoples which can be fulfilled only by the provision of adequate health and social measures.

Accepting these principles, and for the purpose of co-operation among themselves and with others to promote and protect the health of all peoples, the Contracting Parties agree to the present Constitution and hereby establish the World Health Organization as a specialized agency within the terms of Article 57 of the Charter of the United Nations.

Chapter I—Objective

Article 1

The objective of the World Health Organization (hereinafter called the Organization) shall be the attainment by all peoples of the highest possible level of health.

Chapter II—Functions

Article 2

In order to achieve its objective, the functions of the Organization shall be:

a. to act as the directing and co-ordinating authority on international health work;
b. to establish and maintain effective collaboration with the United Nations, specialized agencies, governmental health administrations, professional groups and such other organizations as may be deemed appropriate;
c. to assist Governments, upon request, in strengthening health services;

d. to furnish appropriate technical assistance and, in emergencies, necessary aid upon the request or acceptance of Governments;

e. to provide or assist in providing, upon the request of the United Nations, health services and facilities to special groups, such as the peoples of trust territories;

f. to establish and maintain such administrative and technical services as may be required, including epidemiological and statistical services;

g. to stimulate and advance work to eradicate epidemic, endemic and other diseases;

h. to promote, in co-operation with other specialized agencies where necessary, the prevention of accidental injuries;

i. to promote, in co-operation with other specialized agencies where necessary, the improvement of nutrition, housing, sanitation, recreation, economic or working conditions and other aspects of environmental hygiene;

j. to promote co-operation among scientific and professional groups which contribute to the advancement of health;

k. to propose conventions, agreements and regulations, and make recommendations with respect to international health matters and to perform such duties as may be assigned thereby to the Organization and are consistent with its objective;

l. to promote maternal and child health and welfare and to foster the ability to live harmoniously in a changing total environment;

m. to foster activities in the field of mental health, especially those affecting the harmony of human relations;

n. to promote and conduct research in the field of health;

o. to promote improved standards of teaching and training in the health, medical and related professions;

p. to study and report on, in co-operation with other specialized agencies where necessary, administrative and social techniques affecting public health and medical care from pre-ventive and curative points of view, including hospital services and social security;

q. to provide information, counsel and assistance in the field of health;

r. to assist in developing an informed public opinion among all peoples on matters of health;

s. to establish and revise as necessary international nomenclatures of diseases, of causes of death and of public health practices;

t. to standardize diagnostic procedures as necessary;

u. to develop, establish and promote international standards with respect to food, biological, pharmaceutical and similar products;

v. generally to take all necessary action to attain the objective of the Organization.

Chapter III—Membership and Associate Membership

Article 3

Membership in the Organization shall be open to all States.

Article 4

Members of the United Nations may become Members of the Organization by signing or otherwise accepting this Constitution in accordance with the provisions of Chapter XIX and in accordance with their constitutional processes.

Article 5

The States whose Governments have been invited to send observers to the International Health Conference held in New York, 1946, may become Members by signing or otherwise accepting this Constitution in accordance with the provisions of Chapter XIX and in accordance with their constitutional processes provided that such signature or acceptance shall be completed before the first session of the Health Assembly.

Article 6

Subject to the conditions of any agreement between the United Nations and the Organization, approved pursuant to Chapter XVI, States which do not become Members in accordance with Articles 4 and 5 may apply to become Members and shall be admitted as Members when their application has been approved by a simple majority vote of the Health Assembly.

Article 7

If a Member fails to meet its financial obligations to the Organization or in other exceptional circumstances, the Health Assembly may, on such conditions as it thinks proper, suspend the voting privileges and services to which a Member is entitled. The Health Assembly shall have the authority to restore such voting privileges and services.

Article 8

Territories or groups of territories which are not responsible for the conduct of their international relations may be admitted as Associate Members by the Health Assembly upon application made on behalf of such territory or group of territories by the Member or other authority having responsibility for their international relations. Representatives of Associate Members to the Health Assembly should be qualified by their technical competence in the field of health and should be chosen from the native population. The nature and extent of the rights and obligations of Associate Members shall be determined by the Health Assembly.

Chapter IV—Organs

Article 9

The work of the Organization shall be carried out by:

   a. The World Health Assembly (herein called the Health Assembly);

   b. The Executive Board (hereinafter called the Board);

   c. The Secretariat.

Chapter V—The World Health Assembly

Article 10

The Health Assembly shall be composed of delegates representing Members.

Article 11

Each Member shall be represented by not more than three delegates, one of whom shall be designated by the Member as chief delegate. These delegates should be chosen from among persons most qualified by their technical competence in the field of health, preferably representing the national health administration of the Member.

Article 12

Alternates and advisers may accompany delegates.

Article 13

The Health Assembly shall meet in regular annual session and in such special sessions as may be necessary. Special sessions shall be convened at the request of the Board or of a majority of the Members.

Article 14

The Health Assembly, at each annual session, shall select the country or region in which the next annual session shall be held, the Board subsequently fixing the place. The Board shall determine the place where a special session shall be held.

Article 15

The Board, after consultation with the Secretary-General of the United Nations, shall determine the date of each annual and special session.

Article 16

The Health Assembly shall elect its President and other officers at the beginning of each annual session. They shall hold office until their successors are elected.

Article 17

The Health Assembly shall adopt its own rules of procedure.

Article 18

The functions of the Health Assembly shall be:

a. to determine the policies of the Organization;
b. to name the Members entitled to designate a person to serve on the Board.

Universal Declaration of Human Rights

GENERAL ASSEMBLY OF THE UNITED NATIONS

Preamble

Whereas recognition of the inherent dignity and of the equal and inalienable rights of all members of the human family is the foundation of freedom, justice and peace in the world,

Whereas disregard and contempt for human rights have resulted in barbarous acts which have outraged the conscience of mankind, and the advent of a world in which human beings shall enjoy freedom of speech and belief and freedom from fear and want has been proclaimed as the highest aspiration of the common people,

Whereas it is essential, if man is not to be compelled to have recourse, as a last resort, to rebellion against tyranny and oppression, that human rights should be protected by the rule of law,

Whereas it is essential to promote the development of friendly relations between nations,

Whereas the peoples of the United Nations have in the Charter reaffirmed their faith in fundamental human rights, in the dignity and worth of the human person and in the equal rights of men and women and have determined to promote social progress and better standards of life in larger freedom,

Whereas Member States have pledged themselves to achieve, in cooperation with the United Nations, the promotion of universal respect for and observance of human rights and fundamental freedoms,

Whereas a common understanding of these rights and freedoms is of the greatest importance for the full realization of this pledge,

Now, therefore,

The General Assembly,

Proclaims this Universal Declaration of Human Rights as a common standard of achievement for all peoples and all nations, to the end that every individual and every organ of society, keeping this Declaration constantly in mind, shall strive by teaching and education to promote respect for these rights and freedoms and by progressive measures, national and international, to secure their universal and effective recognition and observance, both among the peoples of Member States themselves and among the peoples of territories under their jurisdiction.

Article 1

All human beings are born free and equal in dignity and rights. They are endowed with reason and conscience and should act towards one another in a spirit of brotherhood.

Article 2

Everyone is entitled to all the rights and freedoms set forth in this Declaration, without distinction of any kind, such as race, colour, sex, language, religion, political or other opinion, national or social origin, property, birth or other status. Furthermore, no distinction shall be made on the basis of the political, jurisdictional or international status of the country or territory to which a person belongs, whether it be independent, trust, non-self-governing or under any other limitation of sovereignty.

Article 3

Everyone has the right to life, liberty and security of person.

Article 4

No one shall be held in slavery or servitude; slavery and the slave trade shall be prohibited in all their forms.

Article 5

No one shall be subjected to torture or to cruel, inhuman or degrading treatment or punishment.

Article 6

Everyone has the right to recognition everywhere as a person before the law.

Article 7

All are equal before the law and are entitled without any discrimination to equal protection of the law. All are entitled to equal protection against any discrimination in violation of this Declaration and against any incitement to such discrimination.

. . .

Article 25

1. Everyone has the right to a standard of living adequate for the health and well-being of himself and of his family, including food, clothing, housing and medical care and necessary social services, and the right to security in the event of unemployment, sickness, disability, widowhood, old age or other lack of livelihood in circumstances beyond his control.
2. Motherhood and childhood are entitled to special care and assistance. All children, whether born in or out of wedlock, shall enjoy the same social protection.

. . .

Article 29

1. Everyone has duties to the community in which alone the free and full development of his personality is possible.
2. In the exercise of his rights and freedoms, everyone shall be subject only to such limitations as are determined by law solely for the purpose of securing due recognition and respect for the rights and freedoms of others and of meeting the just requirements of morality, public order and the general welfare in a democratic society.
3. These rights and freedoms may in no case be exercised contrary to the purposes and principles of the United Nations. . . .

Justice, Fair Procedures, and the Goals of Medicine

NORMAN DANIELS

In his influential works, Daniel Callahan has argued that concerns about justice do not carry us far enough in thinking about the goals of health care reform, claiming that justice is "too thin and formal a concept to give us the kind of help we need." It fails to address the dramatic way in which new technologies expand medical capabilities and the "need" for these services, and even modify our notion of normal functioning. Callahan's proposal is that we clarify our social values by focusing on what we collectively agree should be the goals of medicine.

I want to suggest a mechanism for bridging the gap between my interest in justice and Callahan's interest in goals. In particular, I will suggest how a social conversation about the goals of medicine can be advanced if we induce or require insurers and managed care organizations to adopt publicly accountable procedures for deciding when to cover new technologies and when to impose limits on other treatments.

On my view, a health care system—public health and medical services of all types—should be designed to promote normal functioning (more exactly, "species-typical" normal functioning), because doing so makes an important contribution to the protection of equality of opportunity.[1] The central idea is that disease and disability restrict the range of opportunities individuals have open to them: whereas health care protects it. Although health care is an especially important good because of its contribution to opportunity, it is not our only important good. Reasonable and fair choices must be made about how much to invest in health care and how much in other kinds of goods, like education or job creation and training, which also promote equal opportunity. Fair decisions must be made about how to meet competing needs within a limited budget to protect opportunity for the whole population.

This account of justice is more robust than Callahan admits: It has implications for access and the relative importance of different kinds of health care, and it rules out some kinds of constraints on limits to services. My goal here, however, is to concentrate on a crucial point of agreement, not disagreement, with Callahan. Recently I have argued that a principle assuring equality of opportunity, like other general principles of distributive justice, is too indeterminate to solve some key rationing problems.[2] The concern for equal opportunity tells us, for example, that we must give some priority to those with the most restricted opportunities, but it cannot give a principled account of how much priority to give. Similarly, we know that to protect opportunity in a whole population, we must sometimes favor the aggregation of modest benefits to larger numbers over significant benefits to very few. Here too we have no principled account of how to aggregate.[3] Similarly, I believe we do not know how to solve in a principled way the problem of balancing the promotion of best outcomes with the promotion of fair opportunity.

When general principles of distributive justice fail to give principled solutions, we must either look for more fine-grained principles, or we must turn to fair procedures and treat their outcomes as fair. Just as general principles of justice prove too indeterminate to solve crucial rationing problems, so too do general specifications of the "goals" of medicine. Agreeing, for example, that reducing "premature death" is a reasonable goal of medicine while eliminating all fatal disease is not[4] does not provide us with solutions to the kinds of rationing problems noted here.

We are pushed instead to emphasize fair, publicly accountable procedures. Only such procedures can establish the legitimacy of setting limits for beneficial medical services. This is especially true for public systems, where rationing often is carried out covertly and hidden in budget setting practices, and it is particularly pressing in our mixed system, where the grounds for decisionmaking may even be viewed as "trade secrets." Why should a patient or a clinician who takes her agency role seriously accept limits set by managed care organizations? For those limits to seem fair and reasonable, they would have to reflect concerns about how to meet the more important needs of other patients under resource constraints. Because most or all managed care organizations do not provide any reasons at all for their coverage decisions, even where good reasons may underlie the actual decision, they feed the suspicion of many people that decisions are largely motivated by efforts to reduce costs and improve the "bottom line," whether the organization is for-profit or not. Since some for-profit managed care organizations spend between 25 and 30 percent of every dollar on marketing, return on investments, high CEO salaries, and bloated administrative costs, limits on services are greeted with deserved skepticism.

What would a fair decisionmaking procedure involve, given that these decisions have a moral content, people may disagree about what outcomes seem fair, and the stakes are high? If we were talking about decisions in a public agency (like the Oregon Health Resources or Health Services Commissions), we might be tempted to emphasize public participation and we might be

lulled into thinking the key element was a democratic procedure, such as a majority vote among appropriate officials, including patient representatives and representatives of other interest groups. The problem with this procedure, even in public agencies, is that it may seem to result only in the aggregation of preferences. Yet we are inclined to think that moral decisions about public policy should not simply be the result of maximizing the satisfaction of preferences.[5] Good reasons matter, and deliberation about them is key. Given pluralism about values, we cannot expect that all moral reasons and reasoning will be persuasive to everyone, but if fundamental interests are at stake, we at least should seek to base our decisions on reasons that all "free and equal" citizens can accept.

We need to adapt this "deliberative democracy" approach to the context of managed care organizations. Although institutional structures may not permit us to insist on direct participation in deliberation about limit setting, we should insist that the deliberative process produce reasons that all can accept as a basis for making decisions about how to protect normal functioning for a defined population under budget constraints. If the reasons for decisions about coverage for new technologies are made explicit and are available to clinicians, patients, and would-be members, then there is the basis for a wider social conversation and deliberation about the goals of medicine. The fair procedure would also involve grievance or dispute resolution mechanisms and opportunity for revisiting decisions.

An example will help. Suppose a managed care organization decides to cover growth hormone treatment but only for children who are growth hormone deficient or who have Turner syndrome. It should state the reason for its limitations on coverage. This statement might appear, for example, in its medical director's letter to clinicians, where such policies are often published (generally without reasons or rationale).

Reasons should also be provided in support materials used to inform would-be patients or families during the informed consent process or, better, to engage in "shared decisionmaking" about the procedure.

Good reasons for limiting coverage to these categories of patients might be that there is inadequate evidence of efficacy or inadequate evidence of good risk-benefit ratios for other children. Such reasons clearly are aimed at a public good all can understand, the provision of effective and safe treatment to a defined population under resource constraints. Of course, if new evidence of broader efficacy or safety emerges, then the decision may have to be revisited if that is the only reason for the limits.

Another defensible but more controversial reason for the limited coverage might be that coverage should be restricted to treatment of disease or disability ("departures from normal functioning"), whereas being very short, with no other diagnosable condition, is not a disease or disability. This reason requires a moral argument. Not all will accept it; those who do may have a more expansive view of the tasks of medicine.[6]

Over time, through this process of reason-giving, managed care organizations would articulate a fine-grained conception of how to provide high quality care to a defined population under resource constraints. The decisions and the accompanying reasons would constitute a form of "case law." Through interaction, challenge, and deliberation among all those affected by these decisions, the decisions can be modified. Over time, if these organizations are responsive to some combination of market forces and public regulation, the social deliberation that the reason-giving enables becomes the basis for articulating acceptable goals of medicine. Through this process, we can flesh out acceptable reasons for setting limits, and organizations that appeal to these reasons will be perceived as having a legitimate decisionmaking procedure.

Acknowledgments

Research for this paper is funded by the Greenwall Foundation, the Retirement Research Foundation, the Robert Wood Johnson Foundation, the National Science Foundation, and the Harvard-Pilgrim Foundation. I am indebted for discussion of these ideas to James Sabin, M.D., my co-principal investigator for these grants, and to Susann Wilkinson, a collaborator on this research.

References

1. Norman Daniels, *Just Health Care* (New York: Cambridge University Press, 1985).
2. Norman Daniels, "Rationing Fairly: Programmatic Considerations," *Bioethics* 7, no. 2/3 (1993): 724–33; Norman Daniels, "Four Unsolved Rationing Problems," *Hastings Center Report* 24, no. 4 (1994): 27–29.
3. For an important exploration of issues surrounding aggregation, see Frances Kamm, *Morality and Mortality: Death and Whom to Save From It*, vol. 1 (Oxford: Oxford University Press, 1993), esp. chaps. 9–10. Kamm's discussion does not, however, yield an account of fine-grained principles we can use in rationing contexts.
4. See "The Goals of Medicine: Toward a Sustainable Future" (draft of February, 1996).
5. See John Rawls, *Political Liberalism* (New York: Columbia University Press, 1993), esp. lecture 6; Joshua Cohen, "Deliberation and Democratic Legitimacy," in *The Good Polity,* ed. Alan Hamlin and Phillip Petit (Oxford: Blackwells, 1989), pp. 17–34; Cass Sunstein, *The Partial Constitution* (Cambridge: Harvard University Press, 1993), esp. chaps. 1 and 6.
6. Norman Daniels, "Growth Hormone Therapy for Short Stature: Can We Support the Treatment/Enhancement Distinction?" *Growth, Genetics, & Hormones* 8 (1992, Supplement 1): 46–48; James E. Sabin and Norman Daniels, "Determining 'Medical Necessity' in Mental Health Practice," *Hastings Center Report* 24, no. 6 (1994): 5–13.

Health Care and the Constitution
Public Health and the Role of the State in the Framing Era

Wendy E. Parmet

Health and Governments: Background Understandings

Current legal analysis assumes that the relationship between individual and state is primarily negative. The Constitution imposes no obligation upon government to protect the public health. Instead, the Constitution's role is to empower government while, at the same time, limiting its ability to impinge upon individual interests. Under constitutional theory, public goals play a role only indirectly in determining whether governmental restraints upon individuals are justified by the weight of the public interest at stake. Public goals do not form the basis of public duties. Under this view, the dilemma for judicial review is how to justify limits placed upon majoritarian policies for the protection of individual rights.

This conventional view presupposes that the role of law and legal rights is to restrain governmental action. It also assumes that individual liberty is prior to law. Whatever the general merit of this conceptualization of rights and law, in the context of health care it overlooks two fundamental facts. First, if liberty is prior to states, so is mortality. Disease, injury, and threats to health constrain freedom without the help of any state, although states can surely exacerbate such dangers. Thus, there is no ideal state of nature in which the only threat to freedom is the one libertarians identify: aggression towards property. Rather, any hypothetical state of nature would

have to include dangers and threats to liberty posed by the inevitability of disease. Second, whatever the theoretical role of the law, it has always had to deal with the constraints imposed by disease and mortality. Law has always had to respond to the constraints imposed by disease. Governments typically have assumed an active role with respect to health care, acting as if their role were obligatory.

While disease is omnipresent and prior to social organization, communal life can create special hazards. The effects of trade, urbanization, and the consequent problems of sanitation and pollution show that while the organization of society can reduce the dangers of disease, it can also exacerbate them. This epidemiological phenomenon can be seen most starkly in the colonization of the New World by Europeans. As is well known, European settlement wrecked havoc on the native population by exposing it to Old World diseases. What may be less well known is that even within the white settlements of North America, it was urbanization (without adequate sanitation) accompanied by international trade that brought forth repeated epidemics of yellow fever and cholera epidemics, and, later, the enduring epidemic of tuberculosis.

The reality is that the dangers of ill health will always exist. Even in the mid-twentieth century industrialized world, during the brief calm between the polio and AIDS epidemics when communicable disease seemed anachronistic, threats such as carcinogens in air pollution suggested that health risks are part and parcel of the human condition.

To the economist, efforts to combat these risks are at least partially public goods. The benefits from public goods are indivisible among beneficiaries. A sole private purchaser of health care would give others in society a "free ride" with respect to the benefits obtained. For example, one's vaccination protects another from infection. Conversely, the costs of failing to pay for such goods may be reaped by others. If I have active tuberculosis and fail to take my medication, you may become ill. If I lack the resources to pay for my medication and neither you nor the state help me to purchase it, you may also become ill. To market theorists, such goods are legitimate objects of governmental intervention in the market. As Amartya Sen has written, "The market can indeed be a great ally of individual freedom in many fields, but the freedom to live long without succumbing to preventable morbidity and mortality calls for a broader class of social instruments."

While the theory of public goods helps explain aspects of public health law and assists in fitting it into modern economic theory, it omits a critical point. Ill health is not a mere byproduct of economic activity. It is an inevitable concomitant of human existence. As a result, wherever there is human society, there will be public health. Every society has to face the risks of disease. And because it must, every society searches to make disease, like mortality, comprehensible within the context of the society's own particular culture, theology, or science. In this sense, health care is public not only because its benefits are indivisible and threats to it arise from factors outside of the individual, but also because communal life gives individuals the cultural context in which to understand it.

Contemporary Americans who are used to thinking of illness as a personal and private matter are apt to forget that almost all societies have public policies for the control and alleviation of disease. All societies must come to terms with illness. They seek to do so in the ways understood by their society: strengthening community bonds and their statehood in the process.

Throughout history, the need to deal with disease has been an accepted role of civil society. As legal scholar James Tobey said over sixty years ago, "The protection and promotion of the public health has long been recognized as the responsibility of the sovereign power. Government is, in fact, organized for the express purpose, among others, of conserving the public health and can not divest itself of this important duty."

How governments have fulfilled that duty has varied throughout time and across societies, affected always by the wealth, scientific sophistication, and fundamental values of the culture. Because health is defined in part by a community's belief system, public health measures reflect cultural norms. In highly religious societies, the preservation and regulation of health is intermingled with theological considerations. Heavenly appeal is sought in time of plague. In Puritan New England, for example, fear of disease was met with official days of prayer and fasting. In our more secular era, governments rely on less theistic approaches, such as investment in medical research.

Throughout history, governments have performed their public health role by providing care for the indigent and by taking steps to prevent the spread of epidemics. Although many of the steps taken were not efficacious and the care provided may even have been harmful given the poor quality of medical knowledge, states acted in the only way they could, relying on the practices and theories of the day to protect the public health. The Hellenic city-states had public physicians who were paid from the public coffers and likely treated the indigent, as well as serving all, in times of plague. The Romans built aqueducts and sewers and regulated food and sanitation. Medieval Jewish communities established hospitals and paid communal midwives and physicians.

During the late Medieval and Renaissance eras, many European states developed complex laws to prevent and treat communicable diseases, especially plague. Italian city-states enacted detailed systems of mercantile quarantines, while individuals stricken, especially the poor, were isolated and treated in the listeria. In Calvinist Geneva, the City Council ran the famous hospital, which cared for the sick and poor.

In England, the nation with which our own Framers would have been most familiar, the government's role to protect public health was long established in both theory and practice. Long before the American revolution, English political theorists recognized the need for a government role in health protection. To Hobbes, life without government was one of "continual fear, and danger of violent death; and the life of man, solitary, poor, nasty, brutish and short." To the more sanguine Locke, people unite "for their mutual *Preservation* of their Lives, Liberties and Estates." These theoretical statements fit comfortably with actual public health practices in England.

Although urbanization and sophisticated systems of public health probably appeared later in England than in Italy, ordinances designed to abate nuisances in England date back to 1350. Recognition of the danger of unsanitary conditions also came surprisingly early. In the fifteenth century, the royal government established a commission on sewerage. Henry VII forbade slaughterhouses in cities or towns "leste it might engender sickness."

As elsewhere, fear of plague was an early impetus for the establishment of English public health laws. In 1518, a royal proclamation was issued to control those "contagious infections" which were "likely to continue if remedy by the sufferance of Almighty God was not provided." The proclamation, devised by Cardinal Woolsey for London, required contagion houses to be identified by marking them with straw for forty days and inmates of plague houses to carry white sticks when walking the streets. Enforcement of the proclamation was left to the justices of the peace.

Between 1544 and 1577, hospitals were established by London's leaders to provide for the diseased and disabled as well as foundling children and "idle rogues." In 1578, the Privy Council issued its first book of Plague Orders, prepared with the cooperation of the College of Physicians. The orders, directed to the justices of the peace, contained a typical feature of early public health laws: they intermingled prevention and restrictions of freedom with care and protections. They required the justices to meet every three weeks to receive updates on plague infections, to assess general taxes for the provision of care to plague victims, and to quarantine victims and their families for up to six weeks. The orders were codified in 1604 and made perpetual in 1641. Although Parliament modified the regulations continually throughout the seventeenth century, it consistently provided for isolation and the provision of care for the infected, especially the indigent.

Those actions taken to protect public health did not likely derive from feelings of altruism toward the poor or ill. The laws providing medical care were related to the poor laws, which are not remembered for their compassion. Rather, far stronger motivations such as fear and necessity may have spurred seventeenth and eighteenth century public health regulations and may explain why such laws were not seen as mere "gratuities" which could be easily repealed.

Health laws went to the heart of the governmental role. Referring to England's complex system of plague regulations, Blackstone stated that they were "of the highest importance." More fundamentally, in describing the "rights and liberties" recognized by the laws of England, Blackstone declared that: "The rights of personal security consist in a person's legal and uninterrupted enjoyment of his life, limbs, his body, his health, and his reputation." He included as among an Englishman's rights "[t]he preservation of a man's health from such practices as may prejudice or annoy it." Thus, preservation of the public's health was essential and traditional to the law's role. It was upon this understanding that colonial practices developed. . . .

Public Health Law and the Political Theory of the Framers

What is the significance of the colonial and early federalist public health laws? What do they say about the era's understanding of the role of public health and the individual's relationship to the state with respect to health? At a minimum, the pervasiveness of public health regulation suggests that the populace saw no significant problem with government exercising public health authority. Nor did they see any fundamental problem with provision of health care to the poor. Thus, at least with respect to public health, the Framers did not come from a laissez faire world and they would have had no reason to assume that a minimal state was the norm. This suggests that the Framers might not have shared the libertarian assumptions underlying current constitutional doctrine.

The question remains, however, whether the Framers merely tolerated an active role for government in the protection of public health, or whether they went further and actually assumed that government was somehow obliged to fulfill such a role. In other words, did the Framers, like Justice Rehnquist, see public health care and protection as a mere privilege which government can, but need not, provide. Or did they see it as some type of government obligation?

The answer cannot be definitively stated. The participants of the Constitutional Convention left little evidence of their views on the topic. The text of the document they produced certainly does not speak of public health, nor of an obligation on the part of the government to provide protection from dread diseases. Nevertheless, such a belief

would not only have been compatible with their own experience, it would have comported with their more general political vision. . . .

A. The Debate over the Political Theory of the Framing Era

In recent years there has been considerable debate, first in the historical and then in the legal literature, about the political views of the framing generation. In particular, the debate has focused on whether the Framers were predominantly Lockean liberals, as has been traditionally assumed, or were predominantly classical republicans in their political theory.

The view that the Framers were primarily Lockean liberals stresses the influence of John Locke and his emphasis on individual, natural rights. According to this view, the Framers followed Locke in believing that individuals and their rights are prior to government, and that the primary role of law is to protect those rights. As a result, it is argued that the Constitution is primarily about limits on government. Taken to the extreme, this view can be used to support contemporary doctrine's assumption that constitutional rights are merely negative restrictions on governmental authority. The Constitution posits no duties or affirmative responsibilities on the part of government, and assumes a laissez faire state as the baseline norm.

In contrast, those scholars who argue that the Framers were primarily republicans de-emphasize Locke's influence and stress instead the influence of classical republican theory as modified by the English country party. That so-called civic humanist tradition stressed the primacy of political life. It saw individual freedom as emerging only within the context of communal life. Public participation in the self-government of the community was essential. The danger to republican values lay in self-interestedness or corruption, which could destroy the virtue and freedom of any republic.

Given its anti-individualistic orientation and its reliance on the works of seventeenth-century English theorist Thomas Harrington, who feared maldistribution of wealth as likely to breed self-interestedness or corruption, the argument that the Framers were primarily republican has served lately as a foil for the libertarian assumptions of conventional constitutional jurisprudence and has been particularly associated with a search for affirmative or welfare rights. As a political theory which stresses the communal good and the role of public life in the attainment of individual fulfillment, classical republicanism obviously conflicts with the starkly libertarian judgments of today's constitutional doctrine. Further, republican theory's emphasis on communal concern and public caretaking seems to support a reading of the Constitution supportive of mutual caring and the primacy of public values.

This radical, if not utopian, view of the republican influence on the framing era is certainly vulnerable to dispute. Overstated, it overlooks the all too evident influence of Locke in eighteenth century American thought and the Framers' concern with the preservation of property. And it is not easily reconciled with the text of *The Federalist Papers* and its partial preoccupation with the problem of self-interest and the need to check power. Moreover, even if the Framers were card-carrying civic republicans, that hardly means that they were advocates for the Great Society or any other version of modern welfare statism. As Linda Hirschman has noted correctly, the republican revisionists have been far more successful in demonstrating the republican influence on the Framers' beliefs about political participation and self-government than they have been in connecting its influence to any substantive values or policies.

The assertion that the Framers assumed a public health obligation on the part of government depends, however, neither on the acceptance nor on the rejection of the Lockean or republican hypotheses. The assertion is surprisingly compatible with modified versions of both theories, and may even highlight the ways in which the framing generation interwove theories that, considered abstractly, appear antagonistic.

The key to understanding why eighteenth century thought may have presumed a public health obligation lies first in the recognition that the Framers were primarily practical politicians and only secondarily political theorists. The purity of their theory was less important to them than its ability to resolve the problems they faced, legitimate the government they needed, and provide a stable political order. As a result, the Framers, unlike many modern-day scholars, drew from a variety of sources: from the republican to the liberal, the classical to the Enlightenment. Protestant morality, as well as the English common law, especially their reading of Blackstone, guided their beliefs and framed their vision. As Isaac Kramnick has written, "There was a profusion and confusion of political tongues among the founders. They lived easily with that clatter; it is we, two hundred and more years later, who chafe at their inconsistency."

The Framers could borrow from many theories because they did not appear as incompatible to them as the theories do to us. Of course, the differences between liberal and republican, not to mention federalist and anti-federalist, were real and were of critical consequence to a number of issues. Theoretically, the republican and liberal strands differed over the relationship between the common good and the sum of individual goods, and which was instrumental to which. Another significant difference concerned what constituted freedom in the state of nature, which is but another way of asking whether individuals are primarily political or apolitical, communal or self-interested.

What our current preoccupation with these very real differences obscures is that in the eighteenth century, before industrialization and urbanization irrevocably altered social life, there was still much upon which all sides of the republican-liberal debate could agree. Moreover, there was a political construct—with its own shared language and assumptions—to which all sides subscribed. Social contract theory was that construct.

B. Social Contract Theory

Social contract theory is typically associated with Thomas Hobbes, John Locke, and a liberal tradition that assumes the primacy of individuals. Although liberal individualism clearly formed a significant strand of the theory, social contract theory was amorphous and elastic enough to accommodate a variety of political psychologies and ideologies. That Thomas Hobbes and John Locke, James Madison and Jean Jacques Rousseau could all speak in the language of social contract suggests that the theory did not exclude either liberals or republicans, utopians or pessimists, individualists or communitarians. It was, rather, a bridge by which the separate and often contradictory strands of eighteenth century political theory could come together.

At its most general level, the one upon which all could agree, social contract theory stressed that political legitimacy derived from the consent of the governed. Radically, the theory postulated that individuals came together from a pre-political state, first to form a social compact in which they agreed to live in society and then a governmental compact in which they granted authority to the government.

As an abstract and general theory, social contract had much to offer both republicans and liberals. To republicans, social contract theory emphasized the need for a social contract to enable passage out of the individualistic state of nature and into a civil society where the common good could be pursued. Under this view, the goal of the social contract was the fulfillment of the common good. As Samuel West stated in

1776, "Thus we see that both reason and relation perfectly agree in pointing out the nature, end, and design of government, viz., that it is to promote the welfare and happiness of the community." Unless governments fulfill these obligations and pursue the common good, they lack legitimacy.

In the eighteenth century, liberals did not disagree about the role or essential meaning of the social contract. After all, it was John Locke, that early individualist, who wrote that the legislative power "can never be suppos'd to extend farther than the common good but is obliged to secure every one's Property" and that the authority and powers of the state are "to be directed to no other end, but the *Peace, Safety,* and *public good* of the People." The preservation of property as an individual right was emphasized by Locke, and later by Madison, but property also played a critical role in the republican tradition. Before the triumph of laissez faire capitalism in the nineteenth century, liberals and republicans alike could and did speak the language of social contract, which included an assertion that governments are created to fulfill the public good.

To Americans searching for a way to legitimate their separation from England, social contract theory provided an ideal inspiration. With its emphasis on the consent of the governed and its insistence that compacts made can be broken, the theory appeared to provide a legalistic justification for American independence from England. It is thus not surprising that Jefferson relied upon the rhetoric of social contract theory in the Declaration of Independence.

Social contract theory provided more than a justification for America's independence. It also helped to legitimate state, and eventually federal, authority once independence was achieved. Although often misunderstanding the technical details of the theory, Americans after the Revolution perceived that their governmental contract had dissolved. They thus turned to social contract theory to legitimate the governmental authority they sought. State constitutions, and ultimately the federal one, were conceived as new social contracts among the people which would legitimate the authority of the state. This is most evident in the Constitution's preamble "We the People" and in its reliance on ratification by the states "in convention" rather than by the legislatures. It was this ratification of the document by conventions that led Chief Justice Marshall years later to see the Constitution as deriving its authority not from the states, but from the people as a whole.

Social contract theory further provided a basis for judging governments. Implicit in the view that the compact between the British and Americans had been broken by the time of the Declaration of Independence was the theory that governments which fail to respect the social compact are, in effect, illegitimate. Further, to fulfill compact obligations, governments must serve the common good. State constitutions of the confederation era were replete with such statements. The Virginia Constitution of 1776 is illustrative:

> That government is, or ought to be, instituted for the common benefit, protection, and security of the people, nation, or community . . . and that which government shall be found inadequate or contrary to these purposes, a majority of the community hath an indubitable, inalienable, and indefeasible right to reform, alter, or abolish it, in such manner as shall be judged most conducive to public weal.

Its words were echoed eleven years later in the Constitution's preamble: "We the People of the United States, in Order to form a more perfect Union, establish Justice, insure domestic Tranquility, provide for the common defence, promote the general Welfare, and secure the Blessings of Liberty to ourselves and our Posterity, do ordain and establish this Constitution. . . ." The same vision appears in *The Federalist Papers*, which states that "[t]he aim of every political constitution is, or ought to be, first to obtain for rulers men who possess most wisdom to discern, and most virtue to pursue, the common good of the society."

C. Public Health as a Common Good

The eighteenth century belief in government's compact obligation to fulfill the common good is consistent with the pattern of regulation and provision evident in colonial and early federalist public health regulations. More fundamentally, it suggests that the framing generation may have seen the duty to protect health as stemming from the social or governmental contract in which individual and state were related by mutual obligations.

Although social contract theorists, and the framing generation in general, spoke often about the public good, the common weal, and the general welfare, they provided remarkably little elucidation of those phrases. Social contract theory was eclectic and amorphous. While everyone might have agreed about the government's obligation to protect the public good, they often disagreed about exactly what that meant. To Locke, the concept was ultimately individualistic. Individuals agree to leave the state of nature "for the mutual *Preservation* of their Lives, Liberties and Estates, which I call by the general Name *Property*." Jefferson, echoing that language, saw preservation of "life, liberty and the pursuit of happiness" as the goal of government. Madison saw the preservation of property as among the primary reasons for having government. He may have seen that goal as largely instrumental, however, since he believed that the preservation of property was essential to maintaining the ability of government to achieve the common good.

Despite the disagreement and uncertainty over the actual meaning of "the common good," it seems likely that the preservation of public health, as exemplified by protection against epidemics, was one meaning that all would share. Tradition and practice pointed to it. Theorists such as Montesquieu supported it. So did popular political discourse. According to historian Ronald Peters, "the answer of the literature is unequivocal on this point: the only end of civil society is the common good. And the *sine qua non* of the common good is public safety—*salus populi suprem lex est.*" In an era of frequent epidemics, safety meant more than protection from foes—it likely included, or was often associated with, preservation of health.

The equation of public health with safety, and thereby with the common good, did not necessarily derive from any heightened sense of altruism. To say that the framing generation believed that the social contract obligated government to protect the public's health and to provide care to the ill is not to say that they were utopians or even humanitarians. Many in the framing generation supported slavery. They also held negative views about the indigent. Much of the care provided to the indigent ill emerged from the almshouse and poor law tradition, a tradition not known for the dignity and respect it bestowed upon the poor. It was, therefore, not altruism that caused public health to be part of the common good, but a tradition motivated by the pragmatism and pessimism derived from the insecurity of life in a preindustrial age.

In an era of frequent epidemics, when an increasing number of physicians thought disease stemmed either from accumulated filth in public places or from contagion, it likely appeared self-evident that public health protection constituted a core element of the common good. The idea commonly held today that health is a matter of individual life style choices and treatments determined privately by patients and physicians would have seemed insufficient in the eighteenth century. Government always had attempted to protect public health, and it always would.

Whether one endorsed a republican theory of communal virtue or a liberal theory of self-interest, pragmatism compelled the same conclusion. Public health was a prerequisite to public safety. It constituted a part of the common good. As a result, under social contract theory, government was not only entitled, but also obligated, to protect public health.

The different schools of thought would have framed the issue from different theoretical perspectives. Those influenced by classical republican thought accepted communal obligations and their primacy over individual rights. With such a view, in a time of repeated epidemics which could regularly kill a large percentage of the population, protection of public health fit easily within understanding of the public good. Moreover, the classical republican emphasis on self-government would also have pointed to a further relationship between the public health and the common good. As the framing generation knew only too well, self-government becomes insecure under the threat of epidemics. Colonial history, in which governments repeatedly had to adjourn in the face of epidemics, would have suggested to the Framers the dangers disease posed to self-rule. Although it occurred after the ratification of the Constitution, the collapse of civil government in Philadelphia in 1793 followed a scenario that the Framers could have imagined. Even without the total collapse of self-government, the republican ideal would have required government to care for the ill because individuals who lack health cannot participate in government. Public health, therefore, would have been a necessary part of the common good because it was a precondition to maintaining the republic wherein that good could flourish.

Lockeans would also have seen public health protection as falling within their understanding of the common good. To Locke, for example, the social contract creating civil society was formed not because the state of nature was idyllic, but because it was insecure. Without social protections, individuals pose threats to one another. Individuals enter into society "only with an intention in every one the better to preserve himself his Liberty and Property." Included within Locke's definition of an individual's property was the individual's "own *Person.*" Although the protection of property was an essential element of Lockean thought, so too was the protection of self.

In a time of frequent epidemics, the preservation of self and property almost inevitably would have been seen as requiring public efforts to prevent the spread of disease. As individuals came into contact with each other, as commerce and population grew, epidemics developed. Individuals faced death, commerce was destroyed, and property was threatened. The preservation of individual interests thus necessarily required efforts to prevent disease. Whether contagionist or sanitarian, pragmatism—not benevolence—ultimately required the care of those who could not afford to care for themselves. Without provision for the poor, including their treatment during times of illness, and steps such as inoculation designed to prevent illness, other individual interests would have remained insecure. Thus, individual preservation was inextricably linked to public health policies. If the Lockean individualist entered the social contract to preserve his or her own self and property, then the society's obligation under that contract would by necessity have included the protection of the public's health, the only way in which the individual's health could be reasonably protected.

D. Social Contract Theory and Public Health Protection

Social contract theory, in both its individualistic and republican forms, supported an assumption that the public good required the protection of health. As a result, the state was not only empowered to protect the public's health, but was obligated to do so, at least under natural, if not positive, law. A government that failed to protect health violated the terms of its compact and had no right to expect obedience. A government's authority was a function of its fulfillment of its duties.

Under social contract theory, individuals gave obedience or consent to society on the understanding that they would receive protection from it. Far from endorsing a laissez faire understanding of the relationship between individual and state, as is often mistakenly assumed, social contract theory in its eighteenth century form actually assumed a reciprocal relationship between individual rights and governmental duties.

Under this understanding of the legitimacy of the state, individual rights, such as rights of property, were necessarily curtailed by the social and governmental compacts. In society, as opposed to the state of nature, individuals did not have unlimited or absolute control over themselves or their property. Their rights were necessarily limited by social obligation. This fully accorded with the common law's understanding of property, especially the law of nuisance which limited property rights in the public interest. It also accorded with the experiences of a mercantilist society in which regulation, not free enterprise, was the norm. Most importantly, this view of rights would have been compatible with the era's public health practices, which limited and even impounded property in order to protect the public health. The framing generation would have had no reason to see a conflict between rights of property and public health protection. Even opponents of redistribution, such as Madison, would not have seen public health measures as redistributive.

To Locke and the Framers, the social compact was a way of theoretically delineating the necessary relationship between individual, society, and the state. Individual rights were curtailed not because they were not recognized or respected, but only because they were ultimately to be realized by achieving the common good which government was obligated by compact to fulfill.

As a result, the sharp distinction that exists under modern doctrine between positive and negative rights could not have existed in the framing era with respect to public health care. As many scholars have pointed out, eighteenth century thought did not generally distinguish between positive and negative rights and liberties the way we do today. Under common law, in contrast to *DeShaney,* any person who gave allegiance to a government was entitled to have her health and security protected by it. Allegiance and protection were reciprocal and even correlative.

Thus, the pattern of colonial and early federalist public health laws accords with the understanding of rights and liberties, obligations and duties, prevailing at the time of the Constitution's framing. Governments were not only empowered to protect the public health, but were expected to do so. When crises occurred, they were expected to act. Their authority to do so was unquestioned.

Individual rights of property, travel, and even access to one's home gave way before the public health power. Those restraints were not seen as violations of individual liberties, as we might see them today. Rather, they were part and parcel of the relationship under the social or governmental contract: a construct which gave society a claim upon individuals only in return for the fulfillment of its obligation to provide care and protection. Thus, when ships arrived from plague-infested ports, they could be quarantined. Homes could be impounded; privies regulated. When individuals were sick, they were cared for. When they could not afford care, it was usually provided. As members of the society, individuals lacked absolute rights; instead, they received the benefits of the epidemics or plagues that were prevented by the authority of government acting to preserve the common good.

Justice Is Good for Our Health

NORMAN DANIELS, BRUCE KENNEDY, AND ICHIRO KAWACHI

We have long known that the more affluent and better-educated members of a society tend to live longer and healthier lives: René Louis Villermé made this point as early as 1840, and it has been shown to hold for just about every human society. Recent research suggests that the correlations between income and health do not end there. We now know, for example, that countries with a greater degree of socioeconomic inequality show greater inequality in health status; also, that middle-income groups in relatively unequal societies have worse health than comparable, or even poorer, groups in more equal societies. Inequality, in short, seems to be bad for our health.

Moreover, and perhaps more surprisingly, universal access to health care does not necessarily break the link between social status and health. Our health is affected not simply by the ease with which we can see a doctor—though that surely matters—but also by our social position and the underlying inequality of our society. We cannot, of course, infer causation from these correlations between social inequality and health inequality (though we will explore some ideas about how the one might lead to the other). Suffice to say that, while the exact processes are not fully understood, the evidence suggests that there are *social determinants of health.*

These social determinants offer a distinctive angle on how to think about justice, public health, and reform of the health care system. If social factors play a large role in determining our health, then efforts to ensure greater justice in health care should not focus simply on the traditional health sector. Health is produced not merely by having access to medical prevention and treatment, but also, to a measurably greater extent, by the cumulative experience of social conditions over the course of one's life. By the time a sixty-year-old heart attack victim arrives at the emergency room, bodily insults have accumulated over a lifetime. For such a person, medical care is, figuratively speaking, "the ambulance waiting at the bottom of the cliff." Much contemporary discussion about reducing health inequalities by increasing access to medical care misses this point. We should be looking as well to improve social conditions—such as access to basic education, levels of material deprivation, a healthy workplace environment, and equality of political participation—that help to determine the health of societies.

These conditions have unfortunately been virtually ignored within the academic field of bioethics, and in public discussions about health care reform. Academic bioethics is quick to focus on exotic new technologies and the vexing questions they raise for doctors and health administrators, who must make decisions about patient care and the allocation of scarce medical resources. And we all worry about the doctor-patient relationship under managed care, as insurance companies have taken a newly aggressive role in making medical decisions. But with some significant exceptions neither academic nor popular discussion has looked "up-

stream," past the new technologies, managed care, and the organization of health insurance, to the social arrangements that determine the health achievement of societies.

We hope to fill this gap by exploring some broader issues about health and social justice. To avoid vague generalities about justice, we shall advance a line of argument inspired principally by the theory of "justice as fairness" put forth by the philosopher John Rawls. We find Rawls's theory compelling as an account of justice quite apart from its usefulness as an approach to the health care issue. But even those who do not share our ideas about justice may find our argument a helpful first step in thinking about social justice and public health.

Rawls's theory of justice as fairness was not designed to address issues of health care. He assumed a completely healthy population and argued that a just society must assure people equal basic liberties, guarantee that the right of political participation has roughly equal value for all, provide a robust form of equal opportunity, and limit inequalities to those that benefit the least advantaged. When these requirements of justice are met, Rawls argued, we can have reasonable confidence that others are showing us the respect that is essential to our sense of self-worth.

Recent empirical literature about the social determinants of health suggests that the failure to meet Rawlsian criteria for a just society is closely related to health inequality. The conjecture we propose to explore, then, is that by establishing equal liberties, robustly equal opportunity, a fair distribution of resources, and support for our self-respect—the basics of Rawlsian justice—we would go a long way toward eliminating the most important injustices in health outcomes. To be sure, social justice is valuable for reasons other than its effects on health. And social reform in the direction of greater justice would not eliminate the need to think hard about fair allocation of resources within the health care system. Still, acting to promote social justice may be a key step toward improving our health.

Social Determinants of Health

Let's take a closer look at some of the central findings in the recent literature on the social determinants of health, each of which has implications for an account of justice and health inequalities.

Cross-National Inequalities

A country's prosperity is related to its health, as measured, for example, by life expectancy: in richer countries people tend to live longer. This well-established finding suggests a natural ordering of societies along some fixed path of economic development: as a country or region develops economically, average health improves.

But the evidence suggests that things are more complicated. Figure 1 shows the relationship between the wealth of nations, as measured by per capita gross domestic product (GDPpc), and the health of nations, as measured by life expectancy. Clearly, GDPpc and life expectancy are closely associated, but only up to a point. The relationship levels off when the GDPpc reaches $8,000 to $10,000; beyond this threshold, further economic advance buys virtually no further gains in life expectancy. This leveling effect is most apparent among the advanced industrial economies (see figure 2), which largely account for the upper tail of the curve in figure 1.

Closer inspection of these two figures shows some startling discrepancies. Though Cuba and Iraq are equally poor (each has a GDPpc of about $3,100), life expectancy in Cuba exceeds that in Iraq by 17.2 years. The difference between the GDPpc for Costa Rica and the United States is enormous (about $21,000), yet Costa Rica's life expectancy exceeds that of the United States (76.6 to 76.4). In fact, despite being the richest nation

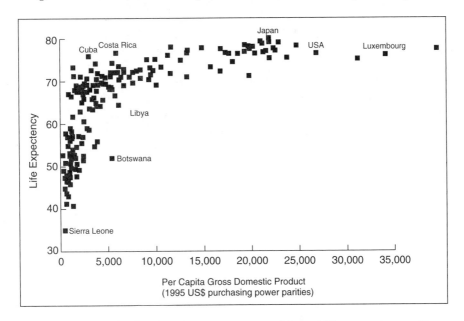

Figure 1   Relationship between country wealth and life expectancy, all nations

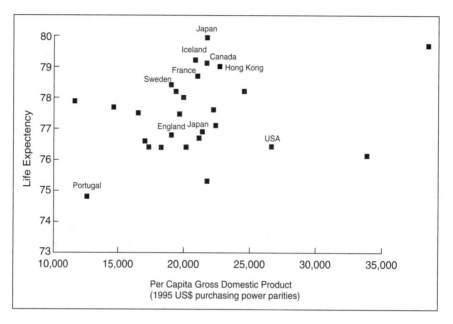

Figure 2   Wealth and life expectancy, countries with GDPpc over $10,000

on the globe, the United States performs rather poorly on major health indicators.

Taken together, these observations show that the health of nations may depend, in part, on factors other than wealth. Culture, social organization, and government policies also help determine population health, and variations in these factors may explain many of the differences in health outcomes among nations.

Relative Income

One especially important factor in explaining the health of a society is the distribution of income: the health of a population depends not just on the size of the economic pie but on how the pie is shared. Differences in health outcomes among developed nations cannot be explained simply by the absolute deprivation associated with low economic development—lack of access to the basic material conditions necessary for health such as

clean water, adequate nutrition and housing, and general sanitary living conditions. The degree of relative deprivation within a society also matters.

Numerous studies have provided support for this *relative-income hypothesis,* which states, more precisely, that inequality is strongly associated with population mortality and life expectancy across nations. To be sure, wealthier countries generally have higher average life expectancy. But rich countries, too, vary in life expectancy (see the tail of figure 1), and that variation dovetails with income distribution. Wealthy countries with more equal income distributions, such as Sweden and Japan, have higher life expectancies than does the United States, despite their having lower per capita GDP. Likewise, countries with a low GDPpc but remarkably high life expectancy, such as Costa Rica, tend to have a more equitable distribution of income.

We find a similar pattern when we compare states within the United States. Wealthier states typically have lower mortality rates. But if we control for differences in state wealth, income inequality accounts for about 25 percent of the between-state variation in age-adjusted mortality rates. Furthermore, a recent study across U.S. metropolitan areas found that areas with high income inequality had an excess of death compared to areas with low inequality. This excess was very large, equivalent in magnitude to all deaths due to heart disease.

Most of the evidence for this pattern comes from cross-sectional studies, which compare different places (countries, states, metropolitan areas) at a single point in time. But longitudinal studies, which look at a single place over time, support similar conclusions. Widening income differentials in both the United States and the United Kingdom have coincided with a slowing down of improvements in life expectancy. In many of the poorest areas of the United Kingdom, the mortality rate for several cohorts of relatively young people has increased as income inequality has widened. In the United States between 1980 and 1990, states with the highest income inequality showed slower rates of improvement in average life expectancy than did states with more equitable income distributions.

Individual SES

Finally, when we move from comparing whole societies to comparing their individual members, we find, once more, that inequality is important. At the individual level, numerous studies have documented what has come to be known as the *socioeconomic gradient:* at each step along the socioeconomic ladder, we see improved health outcomes over the rung below. This suggests that differences in health outcomes are not confined to the extremes of rich and poor but are observed across all levels of socioeconomic status (SES).

Moreover, the SES gradient does not appear to be explained by differences in access to health care. Steep gradients have been observed even among groups of individuals, such as British civil servants, who all have adequate access to health care, housing, and transport.

The slope of the gradient varies substantially across societies. Some societies show a relatively shallow gradient in mortality rates: being better off confers a health advantage, but not so large an advantage as elsewhere. Others, with comparable or even higher levels of economic development, show much steeper gradients. The slope of the gradient appears to be fixed by the level of income inequality in a society: the more unequal a society is in economic terms, the more unequal it is in health terms. Moreover, middle-income groups in a country with high income inequality typically do worse in terms of health than comparable or even poorer groups in a society with less income inequality. We find the same pattern within the United States when we examine state and metropolitan area variations in inequality and health outcomes.

Pathways

Earlier, we cautioned that correlations between inequality and health do not necessarily imply causation. Still, there are plausible and identifiable pathways through which social inequalities appear to produce health inequalities. In the United States, the states with the most unequal income distributions invest less in public education, have larger uninsured populations, and spend less on social safety nets. The facts on educational spending and educational outcomes are especially striking: controlling for median income, income inequality explains about 40 percent of the variation between states in the percentage of children in the fourth grade who are below the basic reading level. Similarly strong associations are seen for high school dropout rates. It is evident from these data that educational opportunities for children in high-income-inequality states are quite different from those in states with more egalitarian distributions.

These effects on education have an immediate impact on health, increasing the likelihood of premature death during childhood and adolescence (as evidenced by the much higher death rates for infants and children in the high-inequality states). Later in life, they appear in the SES gradient in health.

When we compare countries, we also find that differential investment in human capital—in particular, education—is a strong predictor of health. Indeed, one of the strongest predictors of life expectancy among developing countries is adult literacy, particularly the disparity between male and female adult literacy, which explains much of the variation in health achievement among these countries after accounting for GDPpc. For example, among the 125 developing countries with a GDPpc less than $10,000, the difference between male and female literacy accounts for 40 percent of the variation in life expectancy after factoring out the effect of the GDPpc. The fact that gender disparities in access to basic education drive the level of health achievement further underscores the role of broader social inequalities in patterning health inequalities. Indeed, in the United States, differences between the states in women's status—measured in terms of their economic autonomy and political participation—are strongly negatively correlated with female mortality rates: higher status is associated with lower mortality.

These societal mechanisms—for example, income inequality leading to educational inequality leading to health inequality—are tightly linked to the political processes that influence government policy. For example, income inequality appears to affect health by undermining civil society. Income inequality erodes social cohesion, as indicated by higher levels of social mistrust and reduced participation in civic organizations. Lack of social cohesion leads to lower participation in political activity (such as voting, serving in local government, volunteering for political campaigns). And lower partici-

pation, in turn, undermines the responsiveness of government institutions in addressing the needs of the worst off. States with the highest income inequality, and thus lowest levels of social capital and political participation, are less likely to invest in human capital and provide far less generous social safety nets.

In short, the case for social determinants of health is strong. What are the implications of this fact for ideas of justice?

Inequalities and Inequities

When is a health inequality between two groups "inequitable"? Margaret Whitehead and Goran Dahlgren have suggested a useful and influential answer: health inequalities count as inequities when they are avoidable, unnecessary, and unfair.

The Whitehead/Dahlgren analysis is deliberately broad. Age, gender, race, and ethnic differences in health status exist independent of the socioeconomic differences we have been discussing, and they raise distinct questions about equity. For example, should we view the lower life expectancy of men compared to women in developed countries as an inequity? If it is rooted in biological differences that we do not know how to overcome, then it is unavoidable (and therefore not an inequity). This is not an idle controversy: taking average, rather than gender-differentiated, life expectancy in developed countries as a benchmark will yield different estimates of the degree of inequity women face in some developing countries. In any case, the analysis of inequity is only as good as our understanding of what is avoidable or unnecessary.

The same point applies to judgments about fairness. Is the poorer health status of groups whose members smoke and drink heavily unfair? We may be inclined to say it is not unfair, provided that participation in such risky behaviors is truly voluntary. But if many people in a cultural group or class behave similarly, then the behavior might acquire the qualities of a social norm—in which case we might wonder just how voluntary the behavior is (and therefore how much responsibility we should ascribe to them for it). Whitehead and Dahlgren's terms leave us with an unresolved complexity of judgments about responsibility, and as a result, with disagreements about fairness and avoidability.

The poor in many countries lack access to clean water, sanitation, adequate shelter, basic education, vaccinations, and prenatal and maternal care. As a result of some, or all, of these factors, infant mortality rates for the poor exceed those for the rich. Since social policies could supply the missing determinants of infant health, these inequalities are avoidable.

Are these inequalities also unfair? Most of us would think they are, perhaps because we believe that policies that create and sustain poverty are unjust, and perhaps also because we object to social policies that compound economic poverty with lack of access to the determinants of health. The problem of justice in health care becomes more complicated, however, when we remember one of the basic findings from the literature on social determinants: we cannot eliminate health inequalities simply by eliminating poverty. Health inequalities persist even in societies that provide the poor with access to all standard public health and medical services, as well as basic income and education, and they persist as a gradient of health throughout the social hierarchy, not just between the very poorest groups and those above them.

What, then, are we to think of the health inequalities that would persist, even if poverty were eliminated? To eliminate health inequalities, should we eliminate all socioeconomic inequalities? We might believe that all socioeconomic inequalities, or at least all inequalities we did not freely choose, are unjust—but very few embrace such a radical egalitarian view. Indeed, we may well believe that some degree of socioeconomic inequality is unavoidable, or even necessary, and therefore not unjust. On issues of this kind, we should take guidance from

a well-articulated account of social justice—the one put forth by John Rawls.

Justice as Fairness

In *A Theory of Justice*, Rawls sought to show that a social contract designed to be fair to free and equal people would lead to equal basic liberties and equal opportunity and would permit inequalities only when they work to make the worst-off groups fare as well as possible. Though Rawls's account was devised for the most general questions of social justice, it also provides a set of principles for the just distribution of the social determinants of health.

Rawls did not talk about disease or health in his original account. To simplify the construction of his theory, he assumed that his contractors were fully functional over a normal life span—no one becomes ill or dies prematurely. This idealization provides a clue about how to extend this theory to the real world of illness and premature death. The goal of public health and medicine is to keep people as close to the idealization of normal functioning as possible under reasonable resource constraints. Maintaining normal functioning, in turn, makes a limited but significant contribution to protecting the range of opportunities open to individuals. So one might see the distribution of health care as governed by a norm of fair equality of opportunity.

We can now say more directly why justice, as described by Rawls's principles, is good for our health.

Let us start by considering what a just society would require with regard to the distribution of the social determinants of health. In such an ideal society, everyone is guaranteed equal basic liberties, including the right to participate in politics. In addition, there are safeguards aimed at assuring for all, whether richer or poorer, the worth or value of those rights. Since, as we argued above, there is evidence that political participation is a social determinant of health, the

Rawlsian ideal assures institutional protections that counter the usual effects of socioeconomic inequalities on participation—and thus on health.

Moreover, according to Rawls, justice requires fair equality of opportunity. This principle condemns discriminatory barriers and requires robust measures aimed at mitigating the effects of socioeconomic inequalities and other contingencies on opportunity. In addition to equitable public education, such measures would include the provision of developmentally appropriate day care and early childhood interventions intended to promote the development of capabilities independently of the advantages of family background. These measures match, or go beyond, the best models of equal-opportunity interventions currently in place, such as European efforts at day care and early childhood education. We also note that the strategic importance of education for protecting equal opportunity has implications for all levels of education, including access to graduate and professional education.

The equal opportunity principle also requires extensive public health, medical, and social support services aimed at promoting normal functioning for all. It even provides a rationale for the social costs of reasonable accommodation to incurable disabilities, as required by the Americans with Disabilities Act. Because the equal opportunity principle aims at promoting normal functioning for all as a way of protecting opportunity for all, it at once aims at improving population health and reducing health inequalities. Obviously, this focus requires provision of universal access to comprehensive health care, including public health, primary health care, and medical and social support services.

To act justly in health policy, we must have knowledge about the causal pathways through which socioeconomic (and other) inequalities work to produce differential health outcomes. Suppose we learn, for example, that workplace organization induces stress and a loss of control,

and that these tend, in turn, to promote health inequalities. We should then think of modifying those features of workplace organization in order to mitigate their negative effects on health as a public health requirement of the equal opportunity approach.

Finally, a just society restricts inequalities in income and wealth to those that benefit the least advantaged. Rawls calls this requirement the "difference principle." The inequalities allowed by this principle—in conjunction with the principles assuring equal opportunity and the value of political participation—are probably more constrained than those we observe in even the most industrialized societies. If so, just inequalities would produce a flatter gradient of health inequality than we currently observe in even the more extensive welfare systems of northern Europe.

In short, Rawlsian justice—though not devised for the case of health—regulates the distribution of the key social determinants of health, including the social bases of self-respect. There is nothing about the theory that should make us focus narrowly on medical services. Properly understood, justice as fairness tells us what justice requires in the distribution of all socially controllable determinants of health.

We still face a theoretical issue of some interest. Even if a just distribution of the determinants of health flattens health gradients further than what we observe in the most egalitarian developed countries, we must still expect a residue of health inequalities: people who are less well off in economic terms will continue to be less healthy. Should we aim to reduce further those otherwise justifiable economic inequalities because of the inequalities in health status they create?

Suppose we reduce socioeconomic inequalities and thereby reduce health inequalities—but the result is that the health of all is worsened because productivity is reduced so much that important institutions are undermined. That is not acceptable. Our commitment to reducing health inequality should not require steps that threaten to make health worse off for those with less-than-equal health status. So the theoretical issue reduces to this: would it ever be reasonable to allow some health inequality in order to produce some nonhealth benefits for those with the worst health prospects?

We know that in real life people routinely trade health risks for other benefits. They do so when they commute longer distances for a better job or take a ski vacation. Trades of this kind raise questions of fairness. For example, when is hazard pay a benefit workers gain only because their opportunities are unfairly restricted? When is it an appropriate exercise of their autonomy? Some such trades are unfair; others will be restricted only by paternalists.

Rawls gave priority to the principle of protecting equal basic liberties because he believed that once people achieve some threshold level of material well-being, they will not trade fundamental liberties for other goods. Making such a trade might deny them the liberty to pursue their most cherished ideals, including their religious beliefs, whatever they turn out to be. Can we make the same argument about trading health for other goods?

There is some plausibility to the claim that rational people should refrain from trading their health for other goods. Loss of health may preclude us from pursuing what we most value in life. We do, after all, see people willing to trade almost anything to regain health once they lose it.

Nevertheless, there is also strong reason to think this priority is not clear-cut, especially when the trade is between a risk to health and other goods that people highly value. Refusing to allow any (*ex ante*) trades of health risks for other goods, even when the background conditions on choice are otherwise fair, may seem unjustifiably paternalistic, perhaps in a way that a refusal to allow trades of basic liberties is not.

We propose a pragmatic route around this problem. Fair equality of opportunity is only approximated even in an ideally just system, because we can only mitigate, not eliminate, the effects of family and other social contingencies. For example, only if we were willing to violate widely respected parental liberties could we intrude into family life and "rescue" children from parental values that arguably interfere with equal opportunity. Similarly, though we give a general priority to equal opportunity over the difference principle, we cannot achieve complete equality in health any more than we can achieve completely equal opportunity. Justice is always rough around the edges.

Suppose, then, that the decision about trade-offs is made by the legislature in a democratic society in which everyone has a fair chance to participate. Because those principles require effective political participation across all socioeconomic groups, we can suppose that groups most directly affected by any trade-off decision have a voice in the decision. Since there is a residual health gradient, groups affected by the trade-off include not only the worst off, but those in the middle as well. A democratic process that involved deliberation about the trade-off and its effects might be the best we could do to provide a resolution of the unanswered theoretical question.

In contrast, where the fair value of political participation is not adequately assured—and we doubt it is so assured in even our most democratic societies—we have much less confidence in the fairness of a democratic decision about how to trade health against other goods. It is much more likely under actual conditions that those who benefit most from the inequalities—that is, those who are better off—also wield disproportionate political power and will influence decisions about trade-offs to serve their interests. It may still be that the use of a democratic process in nonideal conditions is the fairest resolution we can practically achieve, but it still falls well short of what an ideally just democratic process involves.

If we were to achieve a just distribution of resources, then, with the least well off being as well off as possible, there would still be health inequalities. But decisions about whether to reduce those inequalities even more are matters for democratic process. Justice itself does not command their reduction.

Policy Implications

We earlier suggested that the Whitehead/Dahlgren analysis of health inequities (inequalities that are avoidable and unfair) is useful. We then suggested that the Rawlsian account of justice as fairness provides a fuller account of what is fair and unfair in the distribution of the social determinants of health. The theory provides a more systematic way to think about which health inequalities are inequities. And it delivers the conclusion that most health inequalities that we now observe worldwide among socioeconomic and racial or ethnic groups are "inequities" that should be remedied. Even the countries with the shallowest health gradients, such as Sweden and England, have viewed their own health inequalities as unacceptable and have initiated policy measures to mitigate them. Clearly, the broader World Health Organization efforts in this direction are, probably without exception, also aimed at true inequities.

Before saying more about the kind of reforms outside the health care system that would improve our health, we want to head off a misconception. We are not suggesting that we should simply ignore medical services and health sector reform because other steps will have a bigger long-term health payoff. Even if we had a highly just distribution of the social determinants of health and of public health measures, people will still become ill and need medical services. The fair design of a health system arguably should give some extra weight to meeting actual medical needs.

To see the importance of meeting medical needs, let's distinguish between "identified victims"—people who are already ill and have known needs—and "statistical victims," whose lives would be spared illness by robust public health measures and a fairer distribution of social determinants of health. We might be tempted to judge these lives impartially, to say that statistical lives saved are just as valuable or important as identified victims. But other considerations temper our inclination to such impartial reallocation from identified to statistical victims and suggest that we give special moral weight to the urgent needs of those already ill. Medical providers may legitimately believe that the good they can control through their delivery of medical care has a greater claim on them than the good that would be brought about by more indirect measures beyond their control. More generally, many of us will be connected as family members and friends to the identified victims and will feel that we have obligations to assist them that supersede the obligations we have to more distant, statistical victims.

We do not suggest, then, that our society should immediately reallocate resources away from medicine to schools, for example, in the hope and expectation that a better-educated population will be healthier. But the arguments here suggest that some reallocations of resources to improve the social determinants are justifiable.

Domestic Policy

What sorts of social policies should governments pursue to reduce health inequalities? The menu of options ought to include policies aimed at equalizing individual life opportunities, such as investment in basic education, affordable housing, income security, and other forms of antipoverty policy. Though the connection between these social policies and health may seem somewhat remote, and they are rarely linked to issues of health in our public policy discussions, the evidence outlined earlier suggests that they should be part of the debate. The kinds of policies suggested by a social determinants perspective encompass a much broader range of instruments than would ordinarily be considered for improving the health of the population.

Consider, then, four examples of social policies that might improve health by reducing socioeconomic disparities: investment in early childhood development, nutrition programs, improvements in the quality of the work environment, and reductions in income inequality.

1. Early Life Intervention. Growing evidence points to the importance of early childhood environment in influencing the behavior, learning, and health of individuals later in the life course. Ensuring equal opportunity requires interventions as early in life as possible. Several studies have demonstrated the benefits of early supportive environments for children. In the Perry High/Scope Project, children in poor economic circumstances were provided a high-quality early childhood development program between the ages of three and five. Compared to a control group, those in the intervention group completed more schooling by age twenty-seven; were more likely to be employed, own a home, and be married with children; experienced fewer criminal problems and teenage pregnancies; and were far less likely to have mental health problems.

Compensatory education and nutrition in the early years of life seem also to yield important gains for the most disadvantaged groups. As part of the War on Poverty, the federal government introduced two small compensatory education programs: Head Start for preschoolers and Chapter I for elementary school children. Evaluations of these programs indicate that children who enroll in them learn more than those who do not. So

the programs create more equality of opportunity. Educational achievement, meanwhile, is a powerful predictor of health in later life, partly because education provides access to employment and income and partly because education has a direct influence on health behavior in adulthood, including diet, smoking, and physical activity. So the programs also lead to more health equality.

2. Nutrition. A similarly persuasive case can be made for nutritional supplementation in low-income women and children. An analysis of the National Maternal and Infant Health Survey found that participation of low-income pregnant women in the WIC program (the Special Supplemental Nutrition Program for Women, Infants, and Children) was associated with about a 40 percent reduction in the risk of subsequent infant death. A mother's nutritional state affects her infant's chance of death not just in the first year of life but also throughout the life course. Thus a woman's weight prior to pregnancy is one of the strongest predictors of her child's birth weight; in turn, low birth weight has been shown to be linked with increased risks of coronary heart disease, hypertension, and diabetes in later life. It follows that investing in policies that reduce early adverse influences may produce benefits not only in the present but also for future generations.

3. Work Environment. We alluded earlier to the finding that the health status of workers is closely linked to the quality of their work environment, specifically to the amount of control and autonomy available to workers on their jobs. Low-control work environments—such as monotonous machine-paced work (e.g., factory assembly lines) or jobs involving little opportunity for learning and utilization of new skills (e.g., supermarket cashiers)—tend to be concentrated among low-income occupations. Michael Marmot and colleagues have shown that social disparities in health arise partly as a consequence of the way labor markets sort individuals into positions of unequal authority and control. Low-control, highly demanding job conditions not only are more common in lower-status occupations but also place workers at increased risks of hypertension, cardiovascular disease, mental illness, musculoskeletal disease, and physical disability.

A growing number of case studies from around the world have concluded that it is possible to improve the level of control in workplaces by several means: increasing the variety of different tasks in the production process, encouraging work-force participation in the production process, and allowing more flexible work arrangements, such as altering the patterns of shift work to make them less disruptive of workers' lives. In some cases it may even be possible to redesign the workplace and to enhance worker autonomy without adversely affecting productivity, since absence due to sickness may diminish as a consequence of a healthier workplace.

4. Income Redistribution. Many policies suggested by the social determinants perspective tend to fall under the category of antipoverty policy. However, research on the social determinants of health warns us that antipoverty policies do not go far enough in reducing unjust health disparities. Though priority should go to reducing the plight of the worst off, the fact is that health inequalities occur as a gradient: the poor have worse health than the near-poor, but the near-poor fare worse than the lower middle class, the lower middle class do worse than the upper middle class, and so on up the economic ladder. Addressing the social gradient in health requires action above and beyond the elimination of poverty.

To address comprehensively the problem of health inequalities, governments must begin to address the issue of economic inequalities directly. Evidence we sketched earlier indicates that the extent of socioeconomic disparities—the size of the gap in incomes and assets between the top and bottom of society—is itself an important determinant of the health achievement

of society, independent of the average standard of living. Most important, economic disparities seem to influence the degree of equality in measures of political participation, including voting, campaign donations, contacting elected officials, and other forms of political activity. The more unequal the distribution of incomes and assets, the more skewed the patterns of political participation, and consequently, the greater the degree of political exclusion of disadvantaged groups.

Inequalities in political participation determine the kinds of policies passed by national and local governments. For example, Kim Hill and colleagues studied the relationship between the degree of electoral mobilization of lower-class voters and the generosity of welfare benefits provided by state governments. Even after adjusting for other factors that might predict state welfare policy—the degree of public liberalism in the state, the federal government's welfare cost-matching rate for individual states, the state unemployment rate and median income, and state taxes—robust relationships were found between the extent of political participation by lower-class voters and the degree of generosity of state welfare payments. In other words, who participates matters for political outcomes, and the resulting policies have an important impact on the opportunities for the poor to lead a healthy life.

For both of the foregoing reasons—that it yields a higher level of health achievement as well as greater political participation—the reduction of income inequality ought to be a priority of governments concerned about addressing social inequalities in health. Although discussion of strategies is beyond our scope here, a number of levers do exist by which governments could address the problem of income inequality, spanning from the radical (a commitment to sustained full employment, collective wage bargaining, and progressive taxation) to the incremental (expansion of the earned income tax credit, increased child care credit, and raising the minimum wage).

International Development

Our discussion has implications for international development theory, as well as for economic choices confronted by industrialized countries. To the extent that income distribution matters for population health status, it is not obvious that giving strict priority to economic growth is the optimal strategy for maximizing social welfare. Raising everyone's income will improve the health status of the poor—the trickle-down approach—but not as much as paying attention to the distribution of the social product would. Within the developing world, a comparison of Kerala, a state in India, with highly unequal countries such as Brazil and South Africa illustrates this point. Despite having only one-third to a quarter of the income of Brazil or South Africa (and thereby having a higher prevalence of poverty in the absolute sense), the citizens of Kerala nonetheless live longer, most likely as a result of the higher priority that the government of Kerala accords to a fair distribution of economic gains.

The real issue for developing countries is what kind of economic growth is salutary. Hence Jean Dreze and Amartya Sen distinguish between two types of successes in the rapid reduction of mortality, which they term "growth-mediated" and "support-led" processes. The former works mainly through fast economic growth, exemplified by mortality reductions in countries such as South Korea or Hong Kong. Their successes depended on the growth process being wide-based and participatory (for example, full employment policies) and on the gains from economic growth being utilized to expand social services in the public sector, particularly health care and education. Their experiences stand in stark contrast to the example of countries such as Brazil, which have similarly achieved rapid economic growth but have lagged behind in health improvements.

In contrast to growth-mediated processes, "support-led" processes—for example, in China, Costa Rica, or Kerala—operate not through fast economic growth but through governments giving high priority to the provision of social services that reduce mortality and enhance the quality of life.

Policies of either kind can succeed in promoting the health of the population. In either case, success depends on generating a more fair distribution of income. Once more, health is the byproduct of justice.

We noted earlier that academic bioethics and popular discussion of health care reform have generally tended to focus on medicine at the point of delivery and have inadequately attended to determinants of health "upstream" from the medical system itself. Empirical findings about the social determinants of health suggest that this is a serious mistake: upstream is precisely where we need to look. Put these findings together with a philosophical theory of justice that might apply to any society, and we get this striking result: In a just society, health inequalities will be minimized and population health status will be improved—in short, social justice is good for our health.

B. Obligations to Other Societies

In past chapters we explored the moral obligations and entitlements of, among others, health care providers, patients, health care organizations, and states. These queries were raised in the context of the American health care system and society. But sickness, injury, and public health problems are not unique to the United States. In fact, Americans enjoy some of the best health and health care of any nation in the world. Arguably, however, the focus on the American context, though necessary, in order to take into account the economic, policy, and organizational context of the health care delivery system is artificially imposed. Although law and health care systems may be based on national boundaries, neither health care problems nor ethics are. In this chapter, we shift our focus and contextual framework from a national one to a global one, from the claims and obligations of Americans to the claims (and obligations) of those living in developing countries, those whose needs are greatest. Although people living in developed countries suffer from many diseases, those in the developing world face health problems far more dire. At present, about 25 million people have HIV/AIDS in Africa, most in sub-Saharan Africa.[18] Many of these people will die because they do not have access to the life-saving medicines that they require in order to live. Our shift in focus can be justified on the basis of a number of moral and practical considerations.

The most important reason for the shift in focus from domestic to global is because of what some have referred to as the globalization of health. Julio Frenck and Octavio Gomez-Dantes, for example, point out that given the presence of "microbial traffic," facilitated by an unprecedented increase in world travel, it makes little sense to frame health problems in domestic and international terms.[19] In a global world, our health quite literally depends on the health of those living in other nations. This certainly was evident in the spread of the Black Death in Europe in the 1300s, a result of international trade, and most recently the rapid spread of SARS, brought from China to Vietnam, Singapore, North America, and elsewhere by international travelers. Globalization can also breed social exclusion and intolerance and, at the worst, as we saw on 9/11, terrorism. We shall look at this issue more closely in Chapter 7, Section C.

In 1978, the World Health Organization (WHO) convened an international conference on primary care in Alma-Ata, USSR. Out of this conference came an influential, international document entitled the Declaration of Alma Ata. Among the ten declarations made was a commitment that "[a] main social target of governments, international organizations and the world community in the coming decades should be the attainment by all peoples of the world by the year 2000 of a level of health that will permit them to lead a socially and economically productive life."[20] The year 2000 has come and gone and the global community has certainly not achieved "health for all." As you consider what the nature of our obligation to achieve "health for all" is, evaluate the arguments contained in the following articles. Should the failure to achieve the goals of the Declaration of Alma Ata be attributed to the weakness of the arguments in support of the duty, the overwhelming magnitude of the task, or, more simply yet, apathy on the part of the developed world?

In *Global Disparities in Health and Human Rights: A Critical Commentary*, Solomon R. Benatar provides a good overview of the disparities in health between the developed and the developing world, underscoring the need to meet the global challenge of health for all. Interestingly, he believes that the American commitment to market-driven health care "has eclipsed the need to affirm the associated social and economic rights that foster essential community values." According to Benatar, "Health care delivery is being transformed from a professional service delivered with dedication, concern, and compassion within mutually rewarding and trusting healing relationships toward the sale of a commodity in an adversarial marketplace in which professional satisfaction from patient care is being eroded. . . . Legitimation of this transition transmits a powerful message that gravely undermines the will and ability of other nations to develop and sustain equitable access to affordable healthcare."

Recall our discussion of the effect of managed care cost-containment mechanisms on the trust relationship between doctor and patient in Chapter 4, Section D. In Chapter 5, Section B, we discussed some possible moral obligations of MCOs. In view of Benatar's position, might not an argument be made for a professionally sensitive medical community on the grounds that the costs to the developing world (the neediest members of our global community) are too great otherwise? Do Benatar's objections to market-driven health care resonate as morally compelling or do they strike you as simply farfetched?

Although Peter Singer, in his influential essay, *Famine, Affluence, and Morality,* is concerned with the specific problem of famine in Bengal, he articulates and defends a moral principle that speaks as much for global responsibilities with respect to health as it does for those with respect to the provision of food world wide. Singer's principle goes as follows: "if it is in our power to prevent something bad from happening without thereby sacrificing anything of comparable moral importance, we ought, morally, to do it." This principle would seem to speak on behalf of a duty to provide health care and the social and economic conditions necessary for health to people in other societies. Certainly the disease, suffering, and death that can come from poor health qualify as something bad. Chances are that as a community we could reduce much of the suffering caused by malnutrition and the absence of medical care without losing anything of "comparable moral importance." As you consider Singer's principle and its application to the question of what we owe other societies, if anything, consider what it is that we would have to sacrifice to improve the health of other societies and whether Singer's principle is too demanding morally.

One way that the health of those in developing countries may be improved is with the provision of life-saving medicines. Perhaps pharmaceutical companies have an obligation to provide essential medicines to those who need them or to set aside their intellectual property rights in the case of essential medicines. In the following articles we look at the question about who has a duty to help the sick and suffering in the developing world and what the scope of that obligation is. Among the key issues to be discussed on this topic is whether the patents held by pharmaceutical companies which they claim are necessary in order to both undertake research and development (R&D) on innovative medicines and to recapture some of their investment, should be lifted. The reader may want to supplement the reading of this section with some of the readings from Chapter 5, Section C, on the obligations of pharmaceutical companies. Among the concerns articulated in that chapter was that the extent of public funding that goes into R&D does not seem to be reflected in the prices that consumers must pay for their medicines in the United States.

David B. Resnick, in *Developing Drugs for the Developing World: An Economic, Legal, Moral, and Political Dilemma,* argues that pharmaceutical companies have obligations to the developing world that they can meet by undertaking research on drugs that affect developing countries, discounting medicines, and implementing drug giveaways. Resnick, however, believes that developing countries have a corresponding obligation to ensure that pharmaceutical companies make a reasonable profit by respecting their patents and agreeing to international intellectual property treaties. Jillian Clare Cohen and Patricia Illingworth, drawing on some of the research done on theory of the firm, argue that there are competing views of both the nature of the firm and the moral and legal obligations that firms have. The theory of the firm that they support, the "social entity" conception, claims that "corporations have broader social duties than mere profit maximization." Given this, they express a preference for responding to the crisis in Africa and other developing countries with equity pricing, that is, pricing according to the economic profile of a country. Nonetheless, there is some evidence that the policy focus on patents and the obligations of pharmaceutical companies as the solution to the health problems facing the developing world is misleading. At the most, however, these arguments support a *moral* obligation to increase access to essential drugs and such an obligation is far less substantial than a legally enforceable right. Still, the language of ethics can serve as a powerful critique of existing practices, regulations, and law.

Attaran and Gillespie-White studied the patent status of 15 antiretroviral drugs (drugs used for the treatment of HIV/AIDS) that are used in 53 African countries and found that only a small subset of these are under patent. They claim that in Africa there is no correlation between access to antiretroviral drugs and a drug's patent status. On the basis of their study, they conclude that

> the extreme dearth of international aid finance, rather than patents, is most to blame for the lack of antiretroviral treatment in Africa. It is remarkable that the world's richest nations of North America, Western Europe, and Asia-Pacific together set aside only $74 million specifically for African AIDS in 1998—about $3 per HIV-infected African, or what it costs to build 3 miles (5 km) of rural freeway. Such sums do not come close to financing the physicians, clinics, and infrastructure needed to administer antiretroviral therapy, much less to screen patients for HIV infection, and this has the lamentable result that even in cases in which pharmaceutical companies discount or freely donate antiretroviral drugs, poor African countries still cannot afford to use them. . . . The failure of wealthy governments to provide sufficient aid to fund these highly necessary interventions violates not only basic medical ethics but possibly international human rights laws as well.[21]

If we believe that wealthy Western countries have some obligations to people living in other societies, especially those living in developing countries, we may wonder if these obligations are purely ethical or whether they can also be legal. In either case, it is worth asking about the scope of those obligations. In an article entitled *Global Life Expectancies and the Duty to Die*, Margaret Battin argues that given the disparities in life expectancy between developed and developing countries, those living in developing countries may have a duty to die.[22] Consider whether her conclusion is a *reductio ad absurdum*, ultimately showing that we have no duties to other countries, or does it actually support such a duty? Is our own early death the price those of us living in wealthy Western countries must pay for globalization?

Global Disparities in Health and Human Rights: A Critical Commentary

SOLOMON R. BENATAR

Introduction

Global challenges at the millennium's end call for deep introspection by the people of the nations that have been most privileged to benefit from scientific and economic progress and for reevaluation of the costs of such progress for those less fortunate. In this regard, we should consider how progress is linked to exploitation of people and nature and how it contributes to the widening national and global disparities in health, wealth, and human rights) that now jeopardize human health and survival. Such threats to billions of marginalized people can be addressed only through a long-term perspective acknowledging that the self-interest of wealthy and powerful nations will be optimized through the pursuit of policies that foster all human well-being. Failure to respond to such global challenges can only lead to greater poverty and deprivation, continuing conflict, escalating migration of "asylum seekers" from poor to rich countries, and the spread of new and recrudescing infectious diseases (for example, drug-resistant tuberculosis) and ecologic damage that will harm all nations individually and the world collectively.

Consider, for example, that in the 1960s the richest quintile of the world's population was 30 times richer than the poorest 20% and that this gap had increased to over 60 times by the 1990s. An analogy can be drawn between this global scenario and the problems faced in delivering health care, sustaining medical professionalism, and improving public health. Here the challenge is to find ways of providing greater equity in access to health care for individuals within constrained budgets and the means for improving population health within nations and globally. If the annual per capita expenditure of $3500 on health care in the United States (10 times the total annual per capita gross national product [GNP] of half the world's population) is not enough to ensure access to a decent level of health care for all US citizens, we must ask what implications this has for US citizens and for the structure of health care systems and health care delivery in poor countries.

I should like to offer here a synoptic (and therefore necessarily incomplete) perspective on such complex global problems. My hope is that a perspective that acknowledges the complex roots of global disparities while seeking resolutely to ensure more widespread realization of human rights can refocus attention on these issues and lead to more open scholarly debate and new commitments to finding solutions that may influence the future. Imaginative, global thinking and visionary actions specific for particular societies are the seeds for initiating and propagating qualitative and quantitative changes that could have major long-term advantages for humankind.

Man's Exploitation of Man and the Creation of Two Worlds

The Western world view has been shaped over centuries through the power of the scientific method, analytical philosophy, industrialization, urbanization, democratization, liberalism, and capitalism. The modern perspective emphasizes capitalism, the pursuit of rational economic interest, and the nation-state framework of international relations.[1,2] These scientific, industrial, and economic developments, much cherished in the Western world, have emancipated human life and fostered unprecedented human progress. However, the application of a somewhat libertarian version of liberal political philosophy,[3] with overemphasis on economic thinking (and underemphasis on social and economic rights), has also been associated with erosion of spirituality, loss of a sense of community, and division of the world (and many countries) into a small, rich core and a large, poor periphery.[4] Growing polarization between these worlds as they drift apart threatens the future of both wealthy and poor countries. The failure of socialism, as implemented under communist rule in the Soviet Union, has seemingly vindicated the "capitalist" world view. However, celebration is premature, because the crisis of liberal internationalism must now be faced, particularly in regard to the competing elements of the liberal agenda—human rights and the expansion of free trade.[2] While the liberal vision has been effectively focused on limiting excessive and arbitrary state power, it has neglected the other great enemy in today's world: violence among the poor and dispossessed and the disintegration of power leading to millions of refugees fleeing poverty and disaster.[2,5]

Human domination and subordination of others in the understandable (perhaps inevitable) pursuit of self-interest has long been clearly evident. However, more recently the scientific credibility given to a form of rationality based on economics that has fostered the growth of powerful and unaccountable multinational corporations has led to the evolution of less obvious exploitative behavior. It is less widely appreciated how these more sophisticated and more covert means of achieving shortterm economic self-interest cast a shadow over a broader moral conception of life.[1–13]

Fortunately, our consciences can be reawakened through critical thinking and social activism. For example, a 50-year program against slavery ultimately led to its delegitimation; the implications of destructive uses of nuclear power are increasingly being counteracted through endeavors to delegitimate nuclear testing and prevent the further development of weapons of mass destruction; the degradation of human dignity inflicted through colonial imperialism in Africa (and elsewhere) is being more widely appreciated; there is a deeper understanding that nazism in Germany reflected submission to authority and that such submission to authority also occurs with different implications in other countries; and the adverse effects of neocolonialism resulting from the collusion of superpowers with despotic leaders in developing countries are being exposed. Lessons learned from these adverse experiences increase awareness of the need for attention to a conception of human rights that goes beyond civil and political rights.

The International Bill of Human Rights (which includes the United Nations Charter [1945], the Universal Declaration of Human Rights [1948], and the International Covenant on Civil and Political Rights [1976], with its optional protocol) was a global expression of the rejection of human domination and exploitation of fellow humans, a dedication to the need for respecting individual human dignity, and an attempt to foster this through development of international law. Nations that refused to identify with the Universal Declaration of Human Rights (for example, the Soviet Union and South Africa) and placed what they perceived to be their own self-interest above high aspirations delayed their own progress toward peaceful democracies. The failures of socialism under communist rule and of apartheid provide powerful messages in favor of valuing human dignity and human rights. But less obvious human exploitation persisted and grew within and between even those nations that aspired to be the international guardians of human rights. Sophisticated forms of exploitation, propagated through cultural imperialism, militarism, and devastating was intimately linked to economic power struggles that shaped a globalized economy, inexorably widened the gap between rich and poor peoples and nations and prevented the widespread access to education, employment, and other opportunities required to foster the realization of human rights.

A brief overview of some demographic data and of wasted resources on armed conflict will vividly portray the consequent predicament of the world's poor. In the 1990s, 77% of the world's population lives in developing countries. The 85%:15% distribution of global GNP between industrialized and developing nations reflects respective average annual per capita GNPs of $12 510 and $710.[10] In 1986, 50% of the world's rapidly growing population lived in countries where the annual per capita GNP was less than $270.[10] Poverty is increasing in most parts of the world, and this is a major factor preventing sustainable control of population growth, which in turn threatens physical and mental health as the prerequisites for a decent human life and global survival.

In addition, modern international economic policies have resulted in the extraction of vast quantities of material and human resources from poor developing countries to rich industrialized nations.[1,4,9–15] Total developing country world debt in 1990 was $1.3 trillion (double the level in 1980), and it had grown further to $1.9 trillion by 1995.[1] The net transfer of resources from developing to industrialized nations between 1983 and 1989 was $241 billion[10]: "a kind of colonial tribute extracted by the rich nations from the poorest people on earth"[11] to service the industrial world's deficits and growth rates.[10] Thus, "the debt burden is a scandal which in numerical terms makes the international slave trade of the nineteenth century look like a petty crime."[15] Trade protectionism in industrialized countries costs developing countries a further $150 billion annually in lost export earnings.[10] Finally, the losses incurred through the "brain drain" are incalculable.

The world spends almost $1 trillion a year (according to 1990 figures) on military goods and services.[12,16] About 20% of the world's 2.5 million research scientists and engineers (50% of physicists and engineering scientists) work entirely on military research and development.[17] Approximately $340 billion worth of military arms were sold or given to developing countries between 1981 and 1988, most of which were produced by the Soviet Union or the United States.[12] The value of arms produced in developing countries (under the influence of superpowers' expansion of their military industrial complex) increased 500-fold between 1950 and 1980 (from $2 million to $1.1 billion).[12] Such militarization and the associated militarism have compromised the health of individuals and nations through many mechanisms: killing, maiming, torture, refugeeism, destruction of livelihoods, diversion of resources, crime, terrorism, black markets, poverty, starvation, environmental damage, and destabilization within developing countries.

Industrialized countries spend an average 5.4% of GNP on the military and only 0.3% on aid to developing countries. The Nordic countries admirably contribute 0.9% of their GNP to developing countries, most for social development, whereas the United States focuses most of the 0.15% of its GNP it donates on defense support for Egypt, Israel, Turkey, Pakistan, and the Philippines.[10] In 1990, British aid fell by two thirds of its 1979 value to the lowest ever, 0.27% of GNP.[15]

Despite Henry Kissinger's statement at the World Food Conference in 1974, "the profound comment of our era is that for the first time we may have the technical capacity to free mankind from the scourge of hunger"—up to 1 million people died in the Ethiopian famine,[18] the specter of Somalia and Rwanda haunts us today, and the industrialized world continues to impose austere structural adjustment programs that divert resources away from food, education, health, and welfare in poor countries to repay debts that can in reality never be repaid.[13,15]

The wealthy, productive, and fortunate in the world cannot be burdened with all of the blame for the complex series of historical developments that polarize the world. However, insight is required into the complex adverse social forces initiated and sustained over centuries,[4,10,14,19,20] which, with destabilizing effects of "independence" under adverse conditions,[21,22] distanced and further separated many developing countries from the industrialized world.[4] Regrettably, disparities between rich and poor within industrialized nations have essentially similar causes, highlighting the pervasiveness of adverse economic policies and the need to ameliorate these policies to improve social stability.[23]

Ecological Implications

Domination and subordination through exploitation of people is not the whole story. For centuries, the goals of philosophy and science had been the search for wisdom in understanding the natural order and endeavoring to live in harmony with it. Since the scientific revolution, this integrative approach to nature has shifted toward an aggressive quest to dominate nature in pursuit of economic growth that has, until recently, included little concern for its profound ecological and, hence, evolutionary consequences. "We are destroying the life support systems of this planet and threatening not only civilization as we know it, but also the survival of our species. . . . Cumulative use of fossil fuels has doubled every twenty years since 1890."[24] The world has lost 500 million acres of trees since 1972 (roughly one third the area of the continental United States). Lakes, rivers, even whole seas have been turned into sewers and industrial swamps.[25] The 1 billion people residing in industrialized countries use 10 times the resources and produce 10 times the waste per capita of the 4 billion people residing in developing countries.[24] What is needed now, as never

before, is a major shift in our way of thinking about the future.[24–26]

Africa

The African continent has been most severely affected by the temporal relationship of the powerful social forces described earlier to its economic and political development.[18,21,27–30] The desperate condition of Africa has recently been reviewed from differing but complementary perspectives.[31,32] The withdrawal of industrialized nations from even attempting to deal with the dire condition of the African continent is reflected in the writings of political scientists. "The crisis is so diffuse and of such magnitude that the United States and the world at large shrink from engaging it."[30] "In fact, history mocks the very idea of an international coalition to save Africa."[27] Economic analysts now suggest that "with the end of the Cold War, Africa has lost whatever political lustre it may once have had."[27] Southern countries are weaker individually and collectively than 15 years ago, and the debt crises have reduced their control over their own economic destinies.[33] International affairs in the 1990s are increasingly dominated by economic affairs. As the Cold War recedes, there is the danger that it will be replaced by trade wars between the three major northern economic blocks and that increased competition between southern countries may extend to armed (even nuclear) conflict.[33]

Deeply troubling questions persist and cannot be ignored. As Gill has asked in his powerful account of Africa: Whose industries benefit from continuing underdevelopment in the Third World? Whose consumers benefit from primary products that keep African producers just above the bread line? Whose bankers benefit from Third World indebtedness? Whose arms manufacturers benefit from African arms races? Whose delicate consciences are soothed by the giving of modest gifts?[18] Hancock has documented these concerns in a devastating critique of the inefficiency, inadequacies, and corruption associated with many official international development aid projects.[13]

Human Rights and International Ethics

The Universal Declaration of Human Rights has no enforcement machinery, yet as a statement of aspirations it has served as the basis for constitutions and bills of rights in many countries. Regrettably, worldwide paper support for such human rights is frequently not followed in practice.[7,8] In a discussion of such widespread violations of the declaration, a South African activist,[34] outspokenly critical of industrialized nations' morality, has suggested that the statement "All human beings are born free and equal in dignity and rights" is not a social fact either in any liberal democracy rooted in the laissez-faire principles of capitalism or in socialist countries.

> There is no equality between the peoples of the First and the Third Worlds and there is no equality between a child born in an African township and one born in a white suburb. The child in the slum is born neither within dignity nor in dignity and he or she is born with practically no rights. . . . Theologically, we are born free and equal, sociologically we are born into differential socioeconomic-emotional situations; and in the world in which we live sociology defines our reality. . . . On a global level the [Universal Declaration of Human Rights] fails because of the ethnocentric satisfaction of developed countries with their own state of freedom and their general unconcern for the freedom of others. . . . Those under their jurisdiction, as colonized or, in the sense of capitalistic exploitation, continue to be treated as lesser people, deserving of lesser rights whatever the noble articulations of the First World. . . . Self interest and expediency, and not mutual concerns for each other's freedom and dignity, govern international relations.[34]

The depressing reality of this view is intensified by the despicable attitude that two thirds of all of the people in the world are "superfluous

from the perspective of the market. By and large we do not need what they have; they can't buy what we sell."[35] Inconsistencies in human rights standards demanded of other nations by powerful nations, the lack of self-assessment regarding rights that a monitoring country itself violates, and the consequent influence on human rights elsewhere should also be noted.[36,37] Human rights are most at risk when political, military, and economic considerations become the overwhelming preoccupation of governments.[8]

These concerns should not be misinterpreted as a "collectivist" critique of Western liberal values; rather, they underscore the clash between competing elements of the liberal agenda: human rights and the expansion of free trade.[2] The financial revolution that has been associated with massive expansion of the world economy since the Second World War, together with the revolution in communications that encourages international speculation and instantaneous transfers of vast sums of money, has fostered the growth of an integrated global economy. This has allowed multinational corporations, unfettered by the democratic requirement of accountability, to wield great economic and political power. Through such processes, the combined assets of the top 300 firms in the world now constitute roughly 25% of the world's productive assets. Their formidable economic power and transnational mobility increasingly undermine the ability of national governments to provide the legal, monetary, or protective functions necessary for a well-working national economy. The trillion-dollar-a-day market for foreign exchange effectively places the valuation of any nation's currency at the pleasure of the "market" rather than at the discretion of its monetary authorities, thus disrupting the relationship between the economy and the state. Less than 10% of the trillions of dollars transacted across financial networks are for trade in goods and services. Of the 5.6 billion people in the world, about 3.6 billion have no cash or credit with which to make purchases, and more and more people are clamoring to get into the global labor pool. The naive view that these trends can only be beneficial has been contested, and some of the adverse implications of such "irresponsible forces" (both for industrialized democracies and for developing countries) have been described.[38–40]

Overemphasis on market forces and on civil and political rights has eclipsed the need to affirm the associated social and economic rights that foster essential community values.[39,41] A broader formulation of human rights must include state and corporate duties to avoid depriving, duties to protect from deprivation, and duties to aid the deprived.[42] Articulating the problems of living in the modern world and vigorously proposing possible solutions to the appalling conditions confronting humanity today must become intellectual and political priorities if human rights are to be more widely achieved.[3,9,41,43] The challenges involved in redistribution of wealth, propagation of the education and skills required to sustain development, and reparations for centuries of human and environmental exploitation are fraught with difficulty.[40,44,45] They are, however, surely essential both within nations (as in the new South Africa) and at the global level to ensure that progress since the scientific revolution is not limited to the rich at the increasing expense of the poor.[4,14,38–40,41,44–46]

Medical Practice and Health for All

The foregoing suggests an analogy between global trends and Western medical practice. Advances in medicine and technology have provided many with much celebrated relief from suffering, hope for cure, and additional years of productive and satisfying lives but, through overaggressive approaches to transplantation and use of technology, have also inflicted intense suffering on others in the quest for new knowledge.[47,48]

The progressively dominating influence of "economic rationality" (with money as the bottom line) in medical care and its bureaucratic implementation by powerful multinational drug companies, insurance companies, and managers are also impoverishing the concept of medicine as a caring profession. "Increasingly, physicians find themselves engaged in bureaucratic and political struggles that sap their time and energy, exhaust their patience for treating uninsured people, and erode their dignity."[49] Impressive scientific and medical advances with profound impacts on human well-being have, regrettably, become associated with an inequitable, costly "medical industrial complex" within the most powerful nation on earth.[50]

Market-driven health care in a powerful nation has profound symbolic and material effects on health services worldwide. Health care delivery is being transformed from a professional service delivered with dedication, concern, and compassion within mutually rewarding and trusting healing relationships[49–51] toward the sale of a commodity in an adversarial marketplace in which professional satisfaction from patient care is being eroded and increasingly replaced by rewards external to the professional service: satisfying health service bureaucrats and acquiring wealth, scientific fame, and prestige among peers. Legitimation of this transition transmits a powerful message that gravely undermines the will and ability of other nations to develop and sustain equitable access to affordable health care. Established national health systems (for example, those in Canada and the United Kingdom) are fracturing under the influence of the market model, and health care reform in the new South Africa is being largely confined within a shrinking and weakened public sector while a bloated private sector continues largely unaffected.[52]

Efforts to reverse these trends by dedicated and enlightened physicians[50,51,53–55] are supported by professional organizations in the United States[56,57] and through changes in medical education that incorporate education in the humanities into the medical curriculum.[58,59] However, health care reform in the United States, and elsewhere, remains an elusive goal. Debate must go beyond medical education and the physician/patient relationship to include consideration of macro-allocation of resources, the structure of health care systems, and ways to deliver health care that will enhance the dignity and lives of individual patients and advance population health. Recognizing international disparities in health and health care provision as the single gravest problem of medical ethics challenges physicians, lawyers, and ethicists to become involved in global aspects of justice, human rights, and health care.[67] . . .

Acknowledgments

I am grateful to Professors Heribert Adam, Kogila Moodley, H.C.J. van Rensburg, Peter Folb, and Fredrik Barth; Dr Elena Nightingale; and the anonymous reviewers for their constructive assistance and encouragement and to Harvard University for a Fellowship in the Program in Ethics and the Professions in 1994/95, during which this project was further developed.

References

1. *Our Global Neighbourhood: Report of the Global Commission on Global Governance.* Oxford, England: OUP; 1995.
2. Hoffman S. The crisis of liberal internationalism. *Foreign Policy.* 1995;98:159–177.
3. Rosenblum N, ed. *Liberalism and the Moral Life.* Cambridge, Mass: Harvard University Press; 1989.
4. Gilbert A. *An Unequal World: The Links between Rich and Poor Nations.* 2nd ed. London, England: Nelson; 1992.
5. Fuller G. The next ideology. *Foreign Policy.* 1995;98:145–157.
6. Schwartz B. *The Battle for Human Nature: Science Morality and Modern Life.* New York, NY: WW Norton & Co; 1986.
7. Vincent RJ. *Human Rights and International Relations.* Cambridge, England: Cambridge University Press; 1986.
8. Donnelly J. *Universal Human Rights in Theory and Practice.* Ithaca, NY: Cornell University Press; 1989.
9. Massey DS, Denton NA. *American Apartheid: Segregation and the Making of the Underclass.* Cambridge, Mass: Harvard University Press; 1991.
10. *Human Development Report 1991.* New York, NY: Oxford University Press Inc; 1991.
11. Summerfield D. Western economics and Third World health. *Lancet.* 1989; 2:551–552.
12. Kiefer CW. Militarism and world health. *Soc Sci Med.* 1992;34:719–724.
13. Hancock G. *Lords of Poverty.* London, England: Macmillan Publishing Co Inc; 1989.
14. Wallerstein I. America and the world: today, yesterday and tomorrow. *Theory Soc.* 1992; 21:1–28.
15. Logie D. The great exterminator of children. *BMJ* 1992;304:1423–1426.
16. Zwi AB, Ugalde A. Military expenditure and foreign aid: should they be linked? *BMJ.* 1992;304: 1421–1422.
17. *The World Armaments and Disarmament SIPRI Yearbook 1983.* London, England: Taylor & Frances Ltd; 1983.
18. Gill P. *A Year in the Death of Africa: Politics, Bureaucracy and the Famine.* London, England: Paladin Grafton Books; 1986.
19. *World Population: Fundamentals of Growth.* 2nd ed. Washington, DC: Population Reference Bureau; 1990.
20. Ransford O. *The Slave Trade: The Story of Transatlantic Slavery.* London, England: John Murray Publications; 1971.
21. Boahen AA. *African Perspectives on Colonialism.* Baltimore, Md: Johns Hopkins University Press; 1987.
22. Ray JL. *Global Politics.* 4th ed. Boston, Mass: Houghton Mifflin; 1992.
23. Wilkinson RG. *Unfair Shares: The Effect of Widening Income Differences on the Welfare of the Young.* Brighton, England: Trafford Centre for Medical Research, University of Sussex; 1994.
24. *Blue Planet: Now or Never.* Ottowa, Ontario, Canada: Blue Planet Group; 1991.
25. Last J. Redefining the unacceptable. *Lancet.* 1995;346:1642–1643.
26. Potter VR. Global bioethics facing a world in crisis. *Global Bioethics.* 1992;5:69–76.
27. Chege M. Remembering Africa. *Foreign Aff* 1992;71:146–163.

28. Davidson B. *The Black Man's Burden: Africa and the Curse of the Nation-State.* London, England: James Currey; 1992.

29. Ayittey GBN. African Rights. *Policy Rev.* 1986; 35:8–9.

30. Marcum JA. Africa: a continent adrift. *Foreign Aff* 1989;68:159–179.

31. Elmoore-Meegan M, O'Riorden T. Africa on the precipice: an ominous but not yet hopeless future. *JAMA.* 1993;270:629–631.

32. Benatar SR. Africa and the world. *S Afr Med J* 1994;84:723–726.

33. Ravenhill J. The north-south balance of power. *Int Aff.* 1990;66:731–748.

34. Meer F. The Universal Declaration of Human Rights and the Freedom Charter—similar or apart? *J Hum Rights Trust.* 1988;71–74.

35. Gardels N. The post-Atlantic capitalist order. *New Perspect Q.* Spring 1993:2–3.

36. Howard RE. Monitoring human rights: problems of consistency. *Ethics Int Aff* 1990;4:33–51.

37. Wipfler WL. Human rights violations and US foreign assistance: the Latin American connection. In: Brown G, Maclean D, eds. *Human Rights and US Foreign Policy.* Lexington, Mass: Lexington Books; 1979.

38. Kennedy P. *Preparing for the Twenty First Century.* New York, NY: Random House; 1993.

39. Teeple G. *Globalization and the Decline of Social Reform.* Atlantic Highlands, NJ: Humanities Press; 1995.

40. Heilbroner R. *Twentieth Century Capitalism.* New York, NY: WW Norton & Co; 1993.

41. Howard RE. Human rights and the search for community. *J Peace Res.* 1995;32:1–8.

42. Shue H. *Basic Rights.* Princeton, NJ: Princeton University Press; 1980.

43. Vincent RJ. The idea of rights in international ethics. In: Nardin T, Mapel DR, eds. *Traditions of International Ethics.* Cambridge, England: Cambridge University Press; 1992.

44. Young M. Sustainable investment: the economic challenge. *Impact Sci Soc.* 1992;16:111–119.

45. Moll P, Nattrass N, Loots L. eds. *Redistribution: How Can It Work in South Africa?* Cape Town, South Africa: David Phillip Publications; 1991.

46. Hosle V. The Third World as a philosophical problem. *Soc Res.* 1992;59:227–262.

47. Fox R, Swazey J. *Spare Parts: Organ Replacement in American Society.* New York, NY: Oxford University Press Inc, 1992.

48. Rothman DJ. *Strangers at the Bedside.* New York, NY: Basic Books; 1991.

49. Iglehart J. The American health care system. *N Engl J Med.* 1992;326:962–967.

50. Relman AS. Shattuck Lecture. The health care industry: where is it taking us? *N Engl J Med.* 1991;325:854–859.

51. Lundberg GD, Countdown to millennium—balancing the professionalism and business of medicine: medicine's rocking horse. *JAMA.* 1990; 263:86–87.

52. Benatar SR. Health care reform in the new South Africa. *N Engl J Med.* 1997;336:891–895.

53. Pellegrino ED. The medical profession as a moral community. *Bull N Y Acad Med.* 1990;66:221–232.

54. Pellegrino ED, Thomasma D. *For the Patient's Good: The Restoration of Beneficence in Health Care.* New York, NY: Oxford University Press Inc; 1987.

55. Bulgar RE, Reiser SJ, eds. *Integrity in Health Care Institutions: Humane Environments for Teaching, Enquiry and Healing.* Iowa City, Iowa: Iowa Press; 1990.

56. Access to health care. *Ann Intern Med.* 1990; 112:641–661.

57. Chapman A, ed. *Health Care Reform: A Human Rights Approach.* Washington, DC: Georgetown University Press; 1994.

58. White KL, Connelly JE, eds. *The Medical School's Mission and the Population's Health.* New York, NY: Springer-Verlag; 1992.

59. *Healthy America: Practitioners for 2005.* An Agenda for Action for US Medical Schools. Durham, North Carolina: Pew Health Professions Commission; 1991.

60. Attfield R. The global distribution of health care resources. *J Med Ethics.* 1990;16:153–156.

61. Gellert GA. Global health interdependence and the international physicians movement. *JAMA.* 1990;264:610–613.

62. Lanza R, ed. *Medical Science and the Advancement of World Health.* New York, NY: Praeger; 1985.

63. Holdstock P. Arms or health: a role for medical colleagues. *J R Coll Physicians Lond.* 1989;23: 185–188.

64. Grant JP. From cell to society: public health in the next millennium. Presented at the 75th Anniver-

sary Meeting of The Johns Hopkins School of Hygiene and Public Health, April 1992, Baltimore, Md.

65. Susser M. Public health as a human right: an epidemiologist's perspective on the public health. *Am J Public Health.* 1993;83:418–426.

66. Grodin MA, Annas GJ, Glantz LH. Medicine and human rights: a proposal for international action. *Hastings Cent Rep.* 1993;4:8–12.

67. Grodin MA, Annas GJ. Legacies of Nuremberg: medical ethics and human rights. *JAMA.* 1996;276:1682–1683.

Famine, Affluence, and Morality

PETER SINGER

I begin with the assumption that suffering and death from lack of food, shelter, and medical care are bad. I think most people will agree about this, although one may reach the same view by different routes. I shall not argue for this view. People can hold all sorts of eccentric positions, and perhaps from some of them it would not follow that death by starvation is in itself bad. It is difficult, perhaps impossible, to refute such positions, and so for brevity I will henceforth take this assumption as accepted. Those who disagree need read no further.

My next point is this: if it is in our power to prevent something bad from happening, without thereby sacrificing anything of comparable moral importance, we ought, morally, to do it. By "without sacrificing anything of comparable moral importance" I mean without causing anything else comparably bad to happen, or doing something that is wrong in itself, or failing to promote some moral good, comparable in significance to the bad thing that we can prevent. This principle seems almost as uncontroversial as the last one. It requires us only to prevent what is bad, and to promote what is good, and it requires this of us only when we can do it without sacrificing anything that is, from the moral point of view, comparably important. I could even, as far as the application of my argument to the Bengal emergency is concerned, qualify the point so as to make it: if it is in our power to prevent something very bad from happening, without thereby sacrificing anything morally significant, we ought, morally, to do it. An application of this principle would be as follows: if I am walking past a shallow pond and see a child drowning in it, I ought to wade in and pull the child out. This will mean getting my clothes muddy, but this is insignificant, while the death of the child would presumably be a very bad thing.

The uncontroversial appearance of the principle just stated is deceptive. If it were acted upon, even in its qualified form, our lives, our society, and our world would be fundamentally changed. For the principle takes, firstly, no account of proximity or distance. It makes no moral difference whether the person I can help is a neighbor's child ten yards from me or a Bengali whose name I shall never know, ten thousand miles away. Secondly, the principle makes no distinction between cases in which I am the only person who could possibly do anything and cases in which I am just one among millions in the same position.

I do not think I need to say much in defense of the refusal to take proximity and distance into account. The fact that a person is physically near to us, so that we have personal contact with him, may make it more likely that we *shall* assist him, but this does not show that we *ought* to help him rather than another who happens to be further away. If we accept any principle of impartiality, universalizability, equality, or whatever, we cannot discriminate against someone merely because he is far away from us (or we are far away from him). Admittedly, it is possible that we are in a better position to judge what needs to be done to help a person near to us than one far away, and perhaps also to provide the assistance we judge to be necessary. If this were the case, it would be a reason for helping those near to us first. This may once have been a justification for being more concerned with the poor in one's town than with famine victims in India. Unfortunately for those who like to keep their moral responsibilities limited, instant communication and swift transportation have changed the situation. From the moral point of view, the development of the world into a "global village" has made an important, though still unrecognized, difference to our moral situation. Expert observers and supervisors, sent out by famine relief organizations or permanently stationed in famine-prone areas, can direct our aid to a refugee in Bengal almost as effectively as we could get it to someone in our own block. There would seem, therefore, to be no possible justification for discriminating on geographical grounds.

There may be a greater need to defend the second implication of my principle—that the fact that there are millions of other people in the same position, in respect to the Bengali refugees, as I am, does not make the situation significantly different from a situation in which I am the only person who can prevent something very bad from occurring. Again, of course, I admit that there is a psychological difference between the cases; one feels less guilty about doing nothing if one can point to others, similarly placed, who have also done nothing. Yet this can make no real difference to our moral obligations.[2] Should I consider that I am less obliged to pull the drowning child out of the pond if on looking around I see other people, no further away than I am, who have also noticed the child but are doing nothing? One has only to ask this question to see the absurdity of the view that numbers lessen obligation. It is a view that is an ideal excuse for inactivity; unfortunately most of the major evils—poverty, overpopulation, pollution—are problems in which everyone is almost equally involved.

The view that numbers do make a difference can be made plausible if stated in this way: if everyone in circumstances like mine gave £5 to the Bengal Relief Fund, there would be enough to provide food, shelter, and medical care for the refugees; there is no reason why I should give more than anyone else in the same circumstances as I am; therefore I have no obligation to give more than £5. Each premise in this argument is true, and the argument looks sound. It may convince us, unless we notice that it is based on a hypothetical premise, although the conclusion is not stated hypothetically. The argument would be sound if the conclusion were: if everyone in circumstances like mine were to give £5, I would have no obligation to give more than £5. If the conclusion were so stated, however, it would be obvious that the argument has no bearing on a situation in which it is not the case that everyone else gives £5. This, of course, is the actual situation. It is more or less certain that not everyone in circumstances like mine will give £5. So there will not be enough to provide the needed food, shelter, and medical care. Therefore by giving more than £5 I will prevent more suffering than I would if I gave just £5.

It might be thought that this argument has an absurd consequence. Since the situation appears to be that very few people are likely to give substantial amounts, it follows that I and everyone else in similar circumstances ought to give as much as possible, that is, at least up to the point at which by giving more one would begin to cause serious suffering for oneself and one's dependents—perhaps even beyond this point to the point of marginal utility, at which by giving more one would cause oneself and one's dependents as much suffering as one would prevent in Bengal. If everyone does this, however, there will be more than can be used for the benefit of the refugees, and some of the sacrifice will have been unnecessary. Thus, if everyone does what he ought to do, the result will not be as good as it would be if everyone did a little less than he ought to do, or if only some do all that they ought to do.

The paradox here arises only if we assume that the actions in question—sending money to the relief funds—are performed more or less simultaneously, and are also unexpected. For if it is to be expected that everyone is going to contribute something, then clearly each is not obliged to give as much as he would have been obliged to had others not been giving too. And if everyone is not acting more or less simultaneously, then those giving later will know how much more is needed, and will have no obligation to give more than is necessary to reach this amount. To say this is not to deny the principle that people in the same circumstances have the same obligations, but to point out that the fact that others have given, or may be expected to give, is a relevant circumstance: those giving after it has become known that many others are giving and those giving before are not in the same circumstances. So the seemingly absurd consequence of the principle I have put forward can occur only if people are in error about the actual circumstances—that is, if they think they are giving when others are not, but in fact they are giving when others are. The result of everyone doing what he really ought to do cannot be worse than the result of everyone doing less than

he ought to do, although the result of everyone doing what he reasonably believes he ought to do could be.

If my argument so far has been sound, neither our distance from a preventable evil nor the number of other people who, in respect to that evil, are in the same situation as we are, lessens our obligation to mitigate or prevent that evil. I shall therefore take as established the principle I asserted earlier. As I have already said, I need to assert it only in its qualified form: if it is in our power to prevent something very bad from happening, without thereby sacrificing anything else morally significant, we ought, morally, to do it.

The outcome of this argument is that our traditional moral categories are upset. The traditional distinction between duty and charity cannot be drawn, or at least, not in the place we normally draw it. Giving money to the Bengal Relief Fund is regarded as an act of charity in our society. The bodies which collect money are known as "charities." These organizations see themselves in this way—if you send them a check, you will be thanked for your "generosity." Because giving money is regarded as an act of charity, it is not thought that there is anything wrong with not giving. The charitable man may be praised, but the man who is not charitable is not condemned. People do not feel in any way ashamed or guilty about spending money on new clothes or a new car instead of giving it to famine relief. (Indeed, the alternative does not occur to them.) This way of looking at the matter cannot be justified. When we buy new clothes not to keep ourselves warm but to look "well-dressed" we are not providing for any important need. We would not be sacrificing anything significant if we were to continue to wear our old clothes, and give the money to famine relief. By doing so, we would be preventing another person from starving. It follows from what I have said earlier that we ought to give money away, rather than spend it on clothes which we do not need to keep us warm. To do so is not charitable, or generous. Nor is it the kind of act which philosophers and theologians have called "supererogatory"—an act which it would be good to do, but not wrong not to do. On the contrary, we ought to give the money away, and it is wrong not to do so.

I am not maintaining that there are no acts which are charitable, or that there are no acts which it would be good to do but not wrong not to do. It may be possible to redraw the distinction between duty and charity in some other place. All I am arguing here is that the present way of drawing the distinction, which makes it an act of charity for a man living at the level of affluence which most people in the "developed nations" enjoy to give money to save someone else from starvation, cannot be supported. It is beyond the scope of my argument to consider whether the distinction should be redrawn or abolished altogether. There would be many other possible ways of drawing the distinction—for instance, one might decide that it is good to make other people as happy as possible, but not wrong not to do so.

Despite the limited nature of the revision in our moral conceptual scheme which I am proposing, the revision would, given the extent of both affluence and famine in the world today, have radical implications. These implications may lead to further objections, distinct from those I have already considered. I shall discuss two of these.

One objection to the position I have taken might be simply that it is too drastic a revision of our moral scheme. People do not ordinarily judge in the way I have suggested they should. Most people reserve their moral condemnation for those who violate some moral norm, such as the norm against taking another person's property. They do not condemn those who indulge in luxury instead of giving to famine relief. But given that I did not set out to present a morally neutral description of the way people make moral judgments, the way people do in fact

judge has nothing to do with the validity of my conclusion. My conclusion follows from the principle which I advanced earlier, and unless that principle is rejected, or the arguments are shown to be unsound, I think the conclusion must stand, however strange it appears. It might, nevertheless, be interesting to consider why our society, and most other societies, do judge differently from the way I have suggested they should. In a well-known article, J. O. Urmson suggests that the imperatives of duty, which tell us what we must do, as distinct from what it would be good to do but not wrong not to do, function so as to prohibit behavior that is intolerable if men are to live together in society.[3] This may explain the origin and continued existence of the present division between acts of duty and acts of charity. Moral attitudes are shaped by the needs of society, and no doubt society needs people who will observe the rules that make social existence tolerable. From the point of view of a particular society, it is essential to prevent violations of norms against killing, stealing, and so on. It is quite inessential, however, to help people outside one's own society.

If this is an explanation of our common distinction between duty and supererogation, however, it is not a justification of it. The moral point of view requires us to look beyond the interests of our own society. Previously, as I have already mentioned, this may hardly have been feasible, but it is quite feasible now. From the moral point of view, the prevention of the starvation of millions of people outside our society must be considered at least as pressing as the upholding of property norms within our society.

It has been argued by some writers, among them Sidgwick and Urmson, that we need to have a basic moral code which is not too far beyond the capacities of the ordinary man, for otherwise there will be a general breakdown of compliance with the moral code. Crudely stated, this argument suggests that if we tell people that they ought to refrain from murder and give everything they do not really need to famine relief, they will do neither, whereas if we tell them that they ought to refrain from murder and that it is good to give to famine relief but not wrong not to do so, they will at least refrain from murder. The issue here is: Where should we draw the line between conduct that is required and conduct that is good although not required, so as to get the best possible result? This would seem to be an empirical question, although a very difficult one. One objection to the Sidgwick-Urmson line of argument is that it takes insufficient account of the effect that moral standards can have on the decisions we make. Given a society in which a wealthy man who gives 5 percent of his income to famine relief is regarded as most generous, it is not surprising that a proposal that we all ought to give away half our incomes will be thought to be absurdly unrealistic. In a society which held that no man should have more than enough while others have less than they need, such a proposal might seem narrow-minded. What it is possible for a man to do and what he is likely to do are both, I think, very greatly influenced by what people around him are doing and expecting him to do. In any case, the possibility that by spreading the idea that we ought to be doing very much more than we are to relieve famine we shall bring about a general breakdown of moral behavior seems remote. If the stakes are an end to widespread starvation, it is worth the risk. Finally, it should be emphasized that these considerations are relevant only to the issue of what we should require from others, and not to what we ourselves ought to do.

The second objection to my attack on the present distinction between duty and charity is one which has from time to time been made against utilitarianism. It follows from some forms of utilitarian theory that we all ought, morally, to be working full time to increase the balance of happiness over misery. The position I have taken here would not lead to this conclusion in all circumstances, for if there were no bad occurrences that we could prevent without sacrificing something of comparable moral importance, my argument would have no application. Given the present conditions in many parts of the world, however, it does follow from my argument that we ought, morally, to be working full time to relieve great suffering of the sort that occurs as a result of famine or other disasters. Of course, mitigating circumstances can be adduced—for instance, that if we wear ourselves out through overwork, we shall be less effective than we would otherwise have been. Nevertheless, when all considerations of this sort have been taken into account, the conclusion remains: we ought to be preventing as much suffering as we can without sacrificing something else of comparable moral importance. This conclusion is one which we may be reluctant to face. I cannot see, though, why it should be regarded as a criticism of the position for which I have argued, rather than a criticism of our ordinary standards of behavior. Since most people are self-interested to some degree, very few of us are likely to do everything that we ought to do. It would, however, hardly be honest to take this as evidence that it is not the case that we ought to do it.

It may still be thought that my conclusions are so wildly out of line with what everyone else thinks and has always thought that there must be something wrong with the argument somewhere. In order to show that my conclusions, while certainly contrary to contemporary Western moral standards, would not have seemed so extraordinary at other times and in other places, I would like to quote a passage from a writer not normally thought of as a way-out radical, Thomas Aquinas.

> Now, according to the natural order instituted by divine providence, material goods are provided for the satisfaction of human needs. Therefore the division and appropriation of property, which proceeds from human law, must not hinder the satisfaction of man's necessity from such goods. Equally, whatever a man has in superabundance is

owed, of natural right, to the poor for their sustenance. So Ambrosius says, and it is also to be found in the *Decretum Gratiani:* "The bread which you withhold belongs to the hungry; the clothing you shut away, to the naked; and the money you bury in the earth is the redemption and freedom of the penniless."[4]

I now want to consider a number of points, more practical than philosophical, which are relevant to the application of the moral conclusion we have reached. These points challenge not the idea that we ought to be doing all we can to prevent starvation, but the idea that giving away a great deal of money is the best means to this end.

It is sometimes said that overseas aid should be a government responsibility, and that therefore one ought not to give to privately run charities. Giving privately, it is said, allows the government and the noncontributing members of society to escape their responsibilities.

This argument seems to assume that the more people there are who give to privately organized famine relief funds, the less likely it is that the government will take over full responsibility for such aid. This assumption is unsupported, and does not strike me as at all plausible. The opposite view—that if no one gives voluntarily, a government will assume that its citizens are uninterested in famine relief and would not wish to be forced into giving aid—seems more plausible. In any case, unless there were a definite probability that by refusing to give one would be helping to bring about massive government assistance, people who do refuse to make voluntary contributions are refusing to prevent a certain amount of suffering without being able to point to any tangible beneficial consequence of their refusal. So the onus of showing how their refusal will bring about government action is on those who refuse to give.

I do not, of course, want to dispute the contention that governments of affluent nations should be giving many times the amount of gen-

uine, no-strings-attached aid that they are giving now. I agree, too, that giving privately is not enough, and that we ought to be campaigning actively for entirely new standards for both public and private contributions to famine relief. Indeed, I would sympathize with someone who thought that campaigning was more important than giving oneself, although I doubt whether preaching what one does not practice would be very effective. Unfortunately, for many people the idea that "it's the government's responsibility" is a reason for not giving which does not appear to entail any political action either.

Another, more serious reason for not giving to famine relief funds is that until there is effective population control, relieving famine merely postpones starvation. If we save the Bengal refugees now, others, perhaps the children of these refugees, will face starvation in a few years' time. In support of this, one may cite the now well-known facts about the population explosion and the relatively limited scope for expanded production.

This point, like the previous one, is an argument against relieving suffering that is happening now, because of a belief about what might happen in the future; it is unlike the previous point in that very good evidence can be adduced in support of this belief about the future. I will not go into the evidence here. I accept that the earth cannot support indefinitely a population rising at the present rate. This certainly poses a problem for anyone who thinks it important to prevent famine. Again, however, one could accept the argument without drawing the conclusion that it absolves one from any obligation to do anything to prevent famine. The conclusion that should be drawn is that the best means of preventing famine, in the long run, is population control. It would then follow from the position reached earlier that one ought to be doing all one can to promote population control (unless one held that all forms of population control were wrong in themselves, or would have significantly bad consequences). Since there are organizations working specifically for population control, one would then support them rather than more orthodox methods of preventing famine.

A third point raised by the conclusion reached earlier relates to the question of just how much we all ought to be giving away. One possibility, which has already been mentioned, is that we ought to give until we reach the level of marginal utility—that is, the level at which, by giving more, I would cause as much suffering to myself or my dependents as I would relieve by my gift. This would mean, of course, that one would reduce oneself to very near the material circumstances of a Bengali refugee. It will be recalled that earlier I put forward both a strong and a moderate version of the principle of preventing bad occurrences. The strong version, which required us to prevent bad things from happening unless in doing so we would be sacrificing something of comparable moral significance, does seem to require reducing ourselves to the level of marginal utility. I should also say that the strong version seems to me to be the correct one. I proposed the more moderate version—that we should prevent bad occurrences unless, to do so, we had to sacrifice something morally significant—only in order to show that, even on this surely undeniable principle, a great change in our way of life is required. On the more moderate principle, it may not follow that we ought to reduce ourselves to the level of marginal utility, for one might hold that to reduce oneself and one's family to this level is to cause something significantly bad to happen. Whether this is so I shall not discuss, since, as I have said, I can see no good reason for holding the moderate version of the principle rather than the strong version. Even if we accepted the principle only in its moderate form, however, it should be clear that we would have to give away enough to ensure that the consumer society, dependent as it is on people spending on trivia rather than giving to famine relief, would slow down and perhaps disappear entirely. There are several reasons why this would be desirable in itself. The value and necessity of economic growth are now being questioned not only by conservationists, but by economists as well.[5] There is no doubt, too, that the consumer society has had a distorting effect on the goals and purposes of its members. Yet looking at the matter purely from the point of view of overseas aid, there must be a limit to the extent to which we should deliberately slow down our economy; for it might be the case that if we gave away, say, 40 percent of our Gross National Product, we would slow down the economy so much that in absolute terms we would be giving less than if we gave 25 percent of the much larger GNP that we would have if we limited our contribution to this smaller percentage.

I mention this only as an indication of the sort of factor that one would have to take into account in working out an ideal. Since Western societies generally consider 1 percent of the GNP an acceptable level for overseas aid, the matter is entirely academic. Nor does it affect the question of how much an individual should give in a society in which very few are giving substantial amounts.

It is sometimes said, though less often now than it used to be, that philosophers have no special role to play in public affairs, since most public issues depend primarily on an assessment of facts. On questions of fact, it is said, philosophers as such have no special expertise, and so it has been possible to engage in philosophy without committing oneself to any position on major public issues. No doubt there are some issues of social policy and foreign policy about which it can truly be said that a really expert assessment of the facts is required before taking sides or acting, but the issue of famine is surely not one of these. The facts about the existence of suffering are beyond dispute. Nor, I think, is it disputed that we can do something about it, either through orthodox methods of famine relief or through population control or both. This is therefore an issue on which philosophers are competent to take a position. The issue is one which faces everyone who has more money than he needs to support himself and his dependents, or who is in a position to take some sort of political action. These categories must include practically every teacher and student of philosophy in the universities of the Western world. If philosophy is to deal with matters that are relevant to both teachers and students, this is an issue that philosophers should discuss.

Discussion, though, is not enough. What is the point of relating philosophy to public (and personal) affairs if we do not take our conclusions seriously? In this instance, taking our conclusion seriously means acting upon it. The philosopher will not find it any easier than anyone else to alter his attitudes and way of life to the extent that, if I am right, is involved in doing everything that we ought to be doing. At the very least, though, one can make a start. The philosopher who does so will have to sacrifice some of the benefits of the consumer society, but he can find compensation in the satisfaction of a way of life in which theory and practice, if not yet in harmony, are at least coming together.

Postscript

The crisis in Bangladesh that spurred me to write the above article is now of historical interest only, but the world food crisis is, if anything, still more serious. The huge grain reserves that were then held by the United States have vanished. Increased oil prices have made both fertilizer and energy more expensive in developing countries, and have made it difficult for them to produce more food. At the same time, their population has continued to grow. Fortunately, as I write now, there is no major famine anywhere in the world; but poor people are still starving in several countries, and malnutrition remains very widespread. The need for assistance is, therefore, just as great as when I first wrote, and we can be sure that without it there will, again, be major famines.

The contrast between poverty and affluence that I wrote about is also as great as it was then. True, the affluent nations have experienced a recession, and are perhaps not as prosperous as they were in 1971. But the poorer nations have suffered as least as much from the recession, in reduced government aid (because if governments decide to reduce expenditure, they regard foreign aid as one of the expendable items, ahead of, for instance, defense or public construction projects) and in increased prices for goods and materials they need to buy. In any case, compared with the difference between the affluent nations and the poor nations, the whole recession was trifling; the poorest in the affluent nations remained incomparably better off than the poorest in the poor nations.

So the case for aid, on both a personal and a governmental level, remains as great now as it was in 1971, and I would not wish to change the basic argument that I put forward then.

There are, however, some matters of emphasis that I might put differently if I were to rewrite the article, and the most important of these concerns the population problem. I still think that, as I wrote then, the view that famine relief merely postpones starvation unless something is done to check population growth is not an argument against aid, it is only an argument against the *type* of aid that should be given. Those who hold this view have the same obligation to give to prevent starvation as those who do not; the difference is that they regard assisting population control schemes as a more effective way of preventing starvation in the long run. I would now, however, have given greater space to the discussion of the population problem; for I now think that there is a serious case for saying that if a country refuses to take any steps to slow the rate of its population growth, we should not give it aid. This is, of course, a very drastic step to take, and the choice it represents is a horrible choice to have to make; but if, after a dispassionate analysis of all the available information, we come to the conclusion that without population control we will not, in the long run, be able to prevent famine or other catastrophes, then it may be more humane in the long run to aid those countries that are prepared to take strong measures to reduce population growth, and to use our aid policy as a means of pressuring other countries to take similar steps.

It may be objected that such a policy involves an attempt to coerce a sovereign nation. But since we are not under an obligation to give aid unless that aid is likely to be effective in reducing starvation or malnutrition, we are not under an obligation to give aid to countries that make no effort to reduce a rate of population growth that will lead to catastrophe. Since we do not force any nation to accept our aid, simply making it clear that we will not give aid where it is not going to be effective cannot properly be regarded as a form of coercion.

I should also make it clear that the kind of aid that will slow population growth is not just assistance with the setting up of facilities for dispensing contraceptives and performing sterilizations. It is also necessary to create the conditions under which people do not wish to have so many children. This will involve, among other things, providing greater economic security for people, particularly in their old age, so that they do not need the security of a large family to provide for them. Thus, the requirements of aid designed to reduce population growth and aid designed to eliminate starvation are by no means separate; they overlap, and the latter will often be a means to the former. The obligation of the affluent is, I believe, to do both. Fortunately, there are now many people in the foreign aid field, including those in the private agencies, who are aware of this.

One other matter that I should now put forward slightly differently is that my argument does, of course, apply to assistance with development, particularly agricultural development, as well as to direct famine relief. Indeed, I think the former is usually the better long-term investment. Although this was my view when I wrote the article, the fact that I started from a famine situation, where the need was for immediate food, has led some readers to suppose that the argument is only about giving food and not about other types of aid. This is quite mistaken, and my view is that the aid should be of whatever type is most effective.

On a more philosophical level, there has been some discussion of the original article which has been helpful in clarifying the issues and pointing to the areas in which more work on the argument is needed. In particular, as John Arthur has shown in "Rights and the Duty to Bring Aid", something more needs to be said about the notion of "moral significance." The problem is that to give an account of this notion involves nothing less than a full-fledged ethical theory; and while I am myself inclined toward a utilitarian view, it was my aim in writing "Famine, Affluence, and Morality" to produce an argument which would appeal not only to utilitarians, but also to anyone who accepted the initial premises of the argument, which seemed to me likely to have a very wide acceptance. So I tried to get around the need to produce a complete ethical theory by allowing my readers to fill in their own version—within limits—of what is morally significant, and then see what the moral-consequences are. This tactic works reasonably well with those who are prepared to agree that such matters as being fashionably dressed are not really of moral significance; but Arthur is right to say that people could take the opposite view without being obviously irrational. Hence,

I do not accept Arthur's claim that the weak principle implies little or no duty of benevolence, for it will imply a significant duty of benevolence for those who admit, as I think most nonphilosophers and even off-guard philosophers will admit, that they spend considerable sums on items that by their own standards are of no moral significance. But I do agree that the weak principle is nonetheless too weak, because it makes it too easy for the duty of benevolence to be avoided.

On the other hand, I think the strong principle will stand, whether the notion of moral significance is developed along utilitarian lines, or once again left to the individual reader's own sincere judgment. In either case, I would argue against Arthur's view that we are morally entitled to give greater weight to our own interests and purposes simply because they are our own. This view seems to me contrary to the idea, now widely shared by moral philosophers, that some element of impartiality or universalizability is inherent in the very notion of a moral judgment. (For a discussion of the different formulations of this idea, and an indication of the extent to which they are in agreement, see R. M. Hare, "Rules of War and Moral Reasoning," *Philosophy & Public Affairs* I, no. 2, 1972.) Granted, in normal circumstances, it may be better for everyone if we recognize that each of us will be primarily responsible for running our own lives and only secondarily responsible for others. This, however, is not a moral ultimate, but a secondary principle that derives from considera-

tion of how a society may best order its affairs, given the limits of altruism in human beings. Such secondary principles are, I think, swept aside by the extreme evil of people starving to death.

Notes

2. In view of the special sense philosophers often give to the term, I should say that I use "obligation" simply as the abstract noun derived from "ought," so that "I have an obligation to" means no more, and no less, than "I ought to." This usage is in accordance with the definition of "ought" given by the *Shorter Oxford English Dictionary*: "the general verb to express duty or obligation." I do not think any issue of substance hangs on the way the term is used; sentences in which I use "obligation" could all be rewritten, although somewhat clumsily, as sentences in which a clause containing "ought" replaces the term "obligation."

3. J. O. Urmson, "Saints and Heroes," in *Essays in Moral Philosophy*, ed. Abraham I. Melden (Seattle: University of Washington Press, 1958), p. 214. For a related but significantly different view see also Henry Sidgwick, *The Methods of Ethics*, 7th ed. (London: Dover Press, 1907), pp. 220–1, 492–3.

4. *Summa Theologica*, 11–11, Question 66, Article 7, in *Aquinas, Selected Political Writings*, ed. A. P. d'Entrèves, trans. J. G. Dawson (Oxford: Basil Blackwell, 1948), p. 171.

5. See, for instance, John Kenneth Galbraith, *The New Industrial State* (Boston: Houghton Mifflin, 1967); and E. J. Mishan, *The Costs of Economic Growth* (New York: Praeger, 1967).

Developing Drugs for the Developing World
An Economic, Legal, Moral, and Political Dilemma

DAVID B. RESNIK

... [P]harmaceutical companies also spend over $6 billion per year on clinical trials, and they sponsor 70% of the clinical trials conducted in the US.[10] According to industry estimates, pharmaceutical companies spent $26.4 billion on research and development (R&D) in the US in the year 2000, or more than 60% of total biomedical R&D funding. According to industry estimates, pharmaceutical companies spent $14 billion on marketing in 2000.[11] The percentage of biomedical R&D funded by the industry has risen dramatically in the last two decades.[12] Although many writers have pointed out that companies spend too much money on marketing and not enough on R&D, there is no denying the fact that the world now depends heavily on drug companies to fund biomedical research. While many people regard the drug companies as villains, the plain truth is that a great deal of research would simply not be done without money from this industry.

Thus, the pharmaceutical industry is a highly visible and obvious target for anger and criticism as well as hope or even praise. Many governments in developing nations have taken or are considering taking steps to combat the industry. Some governments, such as India, Bangladesh, Thailand, and Brazil do not honor pharmaceutical product patents. India honors patents on manufacturing processes but not patents on products, which allows generic drug companies to reverse engineer and manufacture drugs without paying royalties to the companies who own patents on those drugs.[13]

As a result, the price of drugs is much cheaper in these countries. For example, the wholesale price of fluconazole is $6.38 per pill in South Africa, $8.52 in Kenya, $9.78 in the US, but $0.41 per pill in Bangladesh. Madawa Pharmaceuticals manufactures the drug in Bangladesh and pays no royalties to Pfizer.[14] According to pharmaceutical industry estimates, the industry loses about $100 million per year in India. Most of the large companies have abandoned efforts to obtain or enforce patents in India.[15]

Other tactics for making drugs more affordable include importation of 'generic' drugs and compulsory licensing. A country might honor pharmaceutical patents but allow drug distributors to import drugs from countries that do not honor those patents, thereby insuring a lower price. For example, Kenya's parliament debated a law that would allow the health minister to declare a public health crisis and void drug patents or allow importation of cheaper, 'generic' drugs.[16] Compulsory licensing is a strategy a country might use to force a drug company to license another company to manufacture a drug. Although the company would still have to pay royalties to the company that owns the patent, it could offer the drug at a cheaper price. A global trade treaty signed in 1994 allows countries to use compulsory licensing to deal with a public health crisis. South Africa has considered compulsory licensing as a way of making drugs more affordable for its citizens.[17]

Although each of these potential responses to the problem of making drugs more affordable for people in the developing world have some merit, they can establish an atmosphere that is combative rather than cooperative. As one might expect, pharmaceutical companies have objected to some of these tactics on the grounds that they violate intellectual property rights.[18] If developing nations do not honor pharmaceutical patents, companies may decide that it is not worth the trouble of developing drugs for the developing world. Indeed, it has only been recently that pharmaceutical companies have considered taking major steps to expand their markets into developing nations. From the pharmaceutical industry's perspective, developing drugs for the developing world is not a lucrative business proposition, since these nations lack buying-power. Why bother with developing drugs for the third world if those countries that need those medications cannot afford them? Why do business with a country that refuses to honor your drug patents? It would be more profitable to develop a drug designed to enhance sexual performance for Anglo-American males than to develop a medicine designed to treat or prevent malaria. There is more money to be made in developing a slightly improved lipid-lowering drug than in developing a vaccine for dysentery. One startling piece of data speaks of itself: 90% of the money spent of health R&D focuses on medical conditions responsible for only 10% of the world's burden of disease.[19]

Should developing nations just ignore the pharmaceutical companies and develop their own drugs? This is probably not a realistic option, since most of these nations lack sufficient funds to invest in pharmaceutical R&D. According to pharmaceutical industry estimates, it costs an average of $500 million to develop and test a single drug that will be sold in the US.[20] Since it often takes several different drugs to treat or prevent an infectious disease, it could cost well over a billion dollars to develop drugs

to treat one disease. Developing nations are too poor to pay this price. For better or worse, the people of developing nations need help from the pharmaceutical industry. If Pfizer, Merck, Glaxo-Wellcome, and other pharmaceutical companies do not develop drugs to combat the infectious diseases that plague developing nations, then who will? There is a real danger that people in developing nations will become 'therapeutic orphans' if the pharmaceutical companies lack the proper incentives to develop drugs for the developing world.[21]

Thus, developing drugs for the developing world is an economic, legal, political, and moral dilemma for both pharmaceutical companies and for the governments of developing nations. Pharmaceutical companies must decide 1) whether and how to invest R&D money for medications designed to treat disease epidemics that plague the developing world, and 2) how to address the problems of affordability and accessibility of medications for the developing world. Developing nations, on the other hand, must decide how best to respond to pharmaceutical companies and whether to use any of the tactics described above. I cannot hope to solve all these problems, as they involve many different political, cultural, legal, medical, and economic factors and conditions that are beyond the scope of a short essay. However, I will offer an analysis of these dilemmas that may provide some insights for industry leaders and policy makers. I will argue that large, global pharmaceutical companies have a moral obligation to develop affordable drugs for the developing world and to make these drugs accessible, and that developing nations should cooperate with these companies in achieving these goals. Pharmaceutical companies and developing nations should negotiate agreements where these countries promise strong patent protection and a productive business environment in exchange for a commitment to develop medicines that are affordable and accessible.

The Pharmaceutical Industry and Social Responsibility

Let us begin our analysis by considering the pharmaceutical industry's obligations to developing nations. One popular conception of private businesses is that they are either immoral or amoral, operating outside the bounds of morality and barely within scope of the law.[22] Without a doubt, many business practices have contributed to this attitude, such as the use of sweatshops in the textile industry, the production of vehicles that are known to be unsafe in the automotive industry, or the use of exploitative marketing in the tobacco industry. During the 20th century, many business professors and economists provided a theoretical basis for this idea by arguing that companies have one primary obligation, to make profit. By pursuing profit, companies manage their resources effectively and produce goods and services that benefit society. Laws can be useful in regulating corporate conduct, but corporations have no moral obligations over and above the requirement to comply with the law.[23] I suspect that many people regard pharmaceutical companies in the same light: pharmaceutical companies are pariahs.

Although it is undoubtedly the case that many companies frequently ignore or violate moral standards, many scholars hold that businesses do have moral responsibilities. All businesses are shaped by and depend upon social values, such as honesty, integrity, fidelity, diligence, and fairness. These values provide a social infrastructure for contractual arrangements, employer-employee relations, marketing, investing, trading, and so on. Values play a key role in creating a climate within and among companies for conducting business. Without these values in place, corruption, theft, fraud, disloyalty, and other ethical problems would make it impossible to do business. Thus, most businesses today recognize the importance of ethical conduct in business and many adopt and enforce codes of conduct.[24]

Many people would accept the idea that moral values play an important role within business, but they might argue that they play no role in the interaction between businesses and society at large. A business could adopt and enforce a code of ethics that applies to its dealings with employees, customers, stockholders, and associates yet show absolutely no respect for other social values not directly related to business. Although it is also probably the case that many businesses ignore these other values, many writers argue that businesses have social responsibilities. Businesses have these responsibilities because they exist within societies where people care about the environment, public safety, public health, and other goods. There are at least two reasons why businesses have social responsibilities. First, businesses that ignore their social responsibilities may face the public's wrath. A company that wantonly pollutes, for example, will one day have to deal with additional pollution regulations. Companies that make unsafe products may have to deal with expensive lawsuits or consumer boycotts. Thus, social responsibility makes good business sense.[25]

Second, corporations are like moral agents in that they make decisions that have important effects on human beings. In making these decisions, corporations can decide to either accept or ignore social values, such as respect for the environment, public safety, and so on. Although corporate decision-making differs from individual decision-making in many ways, e.g. corporations do not have a conscious mind that deliberates about decisions, corporations can still be held legally and morally responsible for their decisions and actions. If corporations are like moral agents, then they have some of the same duties that apply to other moral agents. In particular, corporations have obligations to avoid causing harm and to promote social welfare and justice. That is, they have social responsibilities.[26]

Since pharmaceutical companies are corporations, they also have social responsibilities.

Consider two kinds of duties that apply to pharmaceutical companies:

1. *Beneficence.* Pharmaceutical companies should promote the greatest balance of benefits/ harms for society. They should avoid doing harm and try to do good.
2. *Justice.* Pharmaceutical companies should distribute benefits and burdens equitably.

The rationale for a duty of beneficence is fairly straightforward and uncontroversial. Indeed, most countries have a variety of laws designed to regulate drug testing, manufacturing, and sales in order to prevent harms to the public and promote the development of effective drugs. In the US, the Food and Drug Administration (FDA) regulates drug testing, manufacturing, and sales.[27] Although this duty is fairly obvious, its application is usually complex and controversial, as societies must weigh benefits, harms as well as justice and basic liberties in deciding questions about approving the sale of new drugs. For example, many medications that offer some chance of a cure for patients with advanced cancer or HIV also involve many harmful side effects and one must balance benefits and harms in deciding whether to make the medications available to patients.[28]

The rationale for the duty of justice is not as obvious or straightforward, but there is a growing recognition that pharmaceutical companies should promote access to medications. For example, Brody has argued that pharmaceutical prices should not be so high that they make important medications inaccessible.[29] Spinello applies egalitarian principles to pharmaceutical pricing and argues that medication prices should promote social justice.[30] However, both authors acknowledge that the duty of justice must be balanced against the practical need to make a reasonable return on investment. A 'reasonable price' is therefore a price that allows the company to earn its money but also promotes accessibility and equity.[31]

Other writers have argued that companies should distribute the benefits and burdens of research participation equitably. For example, if a company sponsors a study using a specific population, then members of the population that participate in the study should derive some benefits from their participation. In particular, the drug should be made available to members of the population at a reasonable price. It is not fair to place members of the population at risk without a reasonable expectation of a benefit. Research protocols that recruit subjects from a population without a reasonable expectation of some benefit to that population are exploitative.[32]

How do the above considerations apply to developing drugs for the developing world? In general, these considerations imply that pharmaceutical companies have moral responsibilities to develop drugs that benefit society and to make those drugs available to participant populations at a reasonable price. These responsibilities apply to new, existing, and prospective drugs. Some pharmaceutical companies, such as Bayer Corporation, have adopted ethics and values statements that mention responsibilities to the community, customers, and the environment. Ciba-Geigy, a chemical company that merged with Sandoz (a pharmaceutical company) in 1997, adopted a vision and values statement that includes responsibilities to the environment and society.[33] However, merely recognizing that pharmaceutical companies should be socially responsible provides little guidance in determining how companies should exercise that responsibility. It does not provide specific guidance as to what a company should do, how much it should do, how many resources it should devote to a project, or even where it should focus its attention.

To get some insight into these questions consider how an individual might decide how to act socially responsible. Most major moral theories, including Kantianism, utilitarianism, and virtue ethics, hold that individuals have duties relating to beneficence and justice. However, there is also strong theoretical support that for the idea many moral duties, including the duty of beneficence, are not absolute: there are morally acceptable and desirable limits on the amount of good one may do for others. Although we should all do our part for society, we are not required to be moral saints. The conduct exemplified by Mother Theresa deserves great praise, but it is above and beyond the call of duty. Since most individuals cannot completely sacrifice themselves for the good of society, they must weigh and consider other moral obligations and commitments in light of their circumstances and conditions in order to decide how to be socially responsible. To use Kantian terminology, social responsibilities, such as the duty of beneficence, are 'imperfect duties.'[34]

For example, consider a person, let's call her Joan, who struggles with meeting her social responsibilities. She gives money to charity, provided that it fits within her budget. She will do volunteer work, provided that she has the time, talent and interests. She decides to work for Habitat for Humanity, an organization that builds houses for economically disadvantaged people, because she is good at carpentry and likes working with her hands. However, Joan decides that she can only work one weekend a month, due to her other commitments to family and work: she works during the week and takes her children to soccer games on other weekends. One of her friends asks her to work for the Red Cross during a blood drive during a Wednesday evening, so she decides to help out because she can fit it in her schedule. Several charities call her on the phone asking for money, but she refuses their request since she has already given all that she has budgeted for charity. A panhandler asks her for money but she decides not to give him any because she believes he will spend it on booze. However, she does give money to

UNICEF when some children from her church come by to collect money for this organization. Is Joan callous or irresponsible? I would say not: Joan is probably a lot like other people who must decide how to meet social responsibilities. She must weigh and consider many different factors when deciding how to act responsibly.

I think the same points apply to social responsibility considered at a corporate level. Companies, like individuals, have obligations to be socially responsible, but these obligations are not absolute. Companies should not act like moral scoundrels, but they do not need to act like moral saints. To meet their social responsibilities, corporations must weigh and consider many factors, such as their talents, abilities, resources, interests, commitments, and obligations. As far as pharmaceutical companies are concerned, the goals of developing medications for populations and promoting access to those medications would seem to be a natural fit, given their interests, talents, and so on. But this still leaves open the question of how far a company should go in meeting this responsibility. Corporations, like Joan, must consider their resources, such as time and money, as well as other obligations and commitments, when deciding how to act responsibly. Most pharmaceutical companies will have little trouble fulfilling some minimal responsibilities if they develop drugs that benefit people and make those drugs accessible. But the harder question to answer is *how far* companies should go in exercising this responsibility. Companies also have commitments to their stockholders and employees. They have obligations to make a profit and to use their economic resources effectively. For example, Bayer's values statement also mentions duties to capital investment and resource allocation. Ciba-Geigy's statement mentions commitments to financial performance and improved market shares.[35] If one agrees that profit (and other financial factors) should play a key role in business decisions, then it is morally legitimate (and perhaps even morally responsible) for a company to weigh and consider these or other financial factors when making a decision to be socially responsible.[36]

Money is not the only factor in deciding how to exercise social responsibility. Companies may also consider social, economic, legal, or political conditions, since these factors may impact the effectiveness of a particular program aimed at meeting social responsibilities. These factors may provide significant barriers to implementing social responsibility. For example, a company might decide that it is not worth the effort to supply free medications to a country if that country is in such political turmoil that distribution is futile or impossible. A company might also decide that it is not worth selling a medication at a discounted price in a country if that country does not honor the company's pharmaceutical patents. On the other hand, a company might decide to initiate a research program aimed at developing a vaccine for an infectious disease, if the company obtains financial and political support from a country that would like to have such a vaccine.

Finally, companies also need to consider geography in deciding how to exercise their social responsibility. A corporation could consider all the factors we have just discussed yet conclude that it should provide free medications in the US and Europe but ignore the developing world. Would it be acceptable (or even consistent) for a pharmaceutical company to ignore the developing world while claiming to be socially responsible?

I think there are several reasons why pharmaceutical companies have social responsibilities to the developing world. First, if a company conducts business in a country, then it has duties to act responsibly in that country. This type of social responsibility can be justified in terms of reciprocity and should not be especially controversial: if you make money in a country, you have an obligation to give something back to that country over and above taxes, goods and ser-vices. But companies can avoid this responsibility by simply not doing business in developing nations. A pharmaceutical company could market its products in the developed world in order to avoid the economic, social, political, and legal challenges of conducting business in the developing world. This brings us to a second, perhaps more important reason why pharmaceutical companies have social obligations to the developing world: companies should promote the welfare of humankind. This implies duties of beneficence and justice to all people, not just to people living in the US or Europe. Obviously, it may be difficult for small, local corporations to promote the welfare of humankind, but large, global corporations, such as Merck, Glaxo-Wellcome, or Pfizer, should be concerned with the welfare of humankind and they should therefore conduct business in developing nations and attempt to meet social responsibilities to developing nations.[37] However, even global companies may decide to avoid doing business in some countries in the developing world due to adverse financial, political, legal, or other conditions: companies do not have to expand their markets to developing nations no matter what the costs. I will return to this point later.

Many pharmaceutical companies have taken important steps to act on their social responsibilities to the developing world. First, companies are now sponsoring research on diseases that affect people in the developing world, such as tuberculosis, HIV/AIDS, and malaria. Second, some companies have decided to provide free medications to people in developing nations. For example, Merck and the Gates Foundation have pledged to give $100 million worth of medicine and money to Botswana. Bristol-Myers Squibb is providing $100 million over five years to train doctors and develop community outreach programs in sub-Saharan Africa.[38] Pfizer recently agreed to donate $50 million worth of fluconazole to be distributed in South Africa, a nation where 20% of adults are infected with HIV.[39] Although these offers have been met with a degree of skepticism and cynicism, they do represent a step on the path of social responsibility.

Thus, I conclude that global pharmaceutical companies have social responsibilities to developing nations. But how far should they go to meet these obligations? How much should they do to help? These are complex issues that depend, in part, on how developing nations respond to pharmaceutical companies. If we think of exercising social responsibility as an attempt to make a gift to a society (or societies), and we understand giving as a relationship (or agreement) between the giver and recipient, then we need to say a bit more about the recipient of the gift. Exercising social responsibility in the developing world depends, in part, on social, economic, political, and legal conditions in the developing world, since these conditions can either assist or impede a company's attempt to exercise social responsibility in its business practices. Most companies, I believe, will resist doing business in the developing world if (1) they have no guarantee of a reasonable profit; (2) they must overcome or adapt to an unproductive (bad or adverse) business climate. But what is a reasonable profit and what is an unproductive business climate? We need to address these issues before returning to the topic of social responsibility.

Reasonable Profits, Drug Prices, and Patents

As mentioned earlier, the pharmaceutical industry is very profitable, with profit margins as high as 30% in some companies. Determining what counts as 'reasonable' profit is a complex issue in business ethics. According to some commentators, there should be no limits on profit other than the free market. If a company can make a 30% profit, then this is 'fair' in the market sense of 'fairness.' Moreover, profits are morally justifiable in that they contribute to the overall social welfare. Businesses that make profits can use those funds to compensate employees or stock-

holders or make investments in new equipment, buildings, or other resources.[40] Furthermore, according to this argument, attempts to control or regulate profit margins could have drastic economic consequences for businesses that would restrict their ability to contribute to society. First, investors might avoid an industry where the government regulates profits. Second, companies will have a more difficult time with financial planning and resource allocation if there are some legal limits on profits. Third, since profits depend, in part, on prices, profit regulation must involve some form of price regulation which could lead to market inefficiencies because prices need to change quickly in response to market demands but government agencies often act slowly. Fourth, if companies face limitations on profits or prices, they may cut back on their investments in R&D and focus more on marketing.

For these as well as many other reasons, government regulation of profits under normal, free market conditions is morally questionable. However, when free markets cannot set fair prices due to monopolies, exclusive dealing, price discrimination, or collusion, then the government may regulate or scrutinize prices in order to buffer or counteract these restrictions on trade. For example, there are good reasons to regulate the prices charged by public utilities and other corporations that have a monopoly. There may also be good reasons to investigate pricing practices when one suspects that different companies have adopted agreements designed to inflate prices.[41]

On the other hand, one might accept the thrust of this argument yet maintain that companies that make healthy profits have strong moral obligations to return more of those profits to society because they are better equipped to meet obligations of beneficence and justice. Consider the analogy with an individual. A person making a high salary, one might argue, has an obligation to give more money to charity than a person making a low salary because he can afford to give more to charity. When the hat is passed in church, the wealthy businessman should make a proportionally higher tithe than the not so wealthy teacher. There is nothing inherently wrong with being wealthy (or having a high profit margin) but greater wealth implies greater responsibility.

Now there are many ways that a profitable company could return some wealth to society. The company could offer price discounts, it could give away some of its products, it could invest funds in developing drugs to treat 'orphan' diseases, or it could invest in other social programs. Regardless of how wealthy companies choose to exercise their social responsibilities, it should be clear that their decisions affect their overall profit margins because these choices will incur additional costs or expenses. Thus, a morally reasonable profit (the profit a company should be allowed to realize) might be lower than an economically reasonable profit (the profit a company can realize). If a company decides to return some wealth to society through pricing practices, then its 'morally reasonable' prices (the prices it ought to charge) could be lower than its 'economically reasonable' prices (the prices it can charge).

How does all of this apply to the pharmaceutical industry? The argument implies that companies with high profit margins should consider taking additional steps to be socially responsible, such as discounts on prices, product giveaways, etc. If a company decides to fulfill its social responsibilities through pricing policies, then the company should be willing to lower its drug prices (and therefore perhaps lower its profits) in order to make those drugs more accessible. Since it is probably not very efficient to lower the prices of all drugs in all markets, a company should probably be selective in its socially responsible pricing policies, focusing its discounts on specific drugs in specific markets. If we focus our attention on the developing world, this argument implies that global companies with high profit margins, such as Pfizer, Merck, and Glaxo-Wellcome, should be willing to forego some profits in the developing world in order to fulfill social responsibilities to the developing world. They can accomplish this task in many different ways, including price discounts or drug giveaways.

But how much money should a pharmaceutical company devote toward socially responsible projects? The answer to this question depends in part on the company's current and projected profits. By almost any standard, most large, global pharmaceutical companies are highly profitable. Global pharmaceutical companies can (and should) be able to devote hundreds of millions of dollars toward projects designed to benefit developing nations without losing a great deal of profit. However, their ability to continue realizing these profits depends on strong patent protection. Patents play a key role in profitability in the pharmaceutical industry since patents allow companies to obtain returns on their R&D investments.[42] Without this protection, companies would not make these risky investments. Pharmaceutical R&D investing is a high-risk proposition for several reasons. First, the new drug may not prove to be safe and effective and the company may decide to abandon the drug in the middle of clinical testing. Second, if the company completes its clinical trials, there is no guarantee that the FDA (or other relevant agency) will approve the new drug. Third, if the agency approves the new drug, it may not have a strong market due to competition from other drugs or lack of consumer demand. Fourth, once the drug is on the market, the agency could take it off the market to protect public health and safety. Finally, there is always the possibility that the company will face lawsuits from consumers that are harmed by the drug. Without adequate patent protection, a company might take these risks and develop its product only to have a competing company manufacture the product at a lower price. According to the pharmaceutical industry, only 30% of new drugs are profitable.[43]

Although patents offer pharmaceutical companies control over their inventions, this control is not absolute or unlimited. First, in the US (and most other countries), a patent lasts 20 years from the time of the application, which gives a drug company an approximately 10-year window to make a return on its R&D investment.[44] Once the patent expires, anyone can make the drug without infringing the patent. Second, most patent laws allow for some degree of 'copycat' inventions. A copycat invention is an invention that is very similar to a previous invention but represents a useful innovation or improvement. In the United States, companies can produce legally sanctioned generic drugs by making slight changes to the original patented drugs. (An illegal copycat would be an exact copy of the drug.) The possibility of copycat drugs creates a potential limit on a company's ability to control the market for a drug. For example, the company could invent a new blood pressure medication and dominate the market for this product until other companies develop copycat versions of the medication.[45] However, it is important to realize that the US Patent and Trade Office (PTO) does not accept all copycat drugs; it only accept those drugs that are useful improvements.

We should also note that patents only provide legal protection in the country in which they are issued: a US patent provides no legal protection in Britain. Thus, when a drug company develops a new drug, it usually applies for patent protection in the countries where it plans to sell the drug. If a country does not provide the company with patent protection, then it may lose business in that country and perhaps others. If we think of the whole world as a potential market, a company that invents a new drug and patents it in many countries may still lose a significant portion of its potential market volume if several countries do not honor the patent and export the drug around the world. This is why the pharmaceutical companies find India's patent policies so troubling: they lose the market in India as well as in other countries that import drugs

from India. Drug companies can still make a profit when their patents are not honored around the world, but they have to make their profits in countries that honor those patents. It is hard to say exactly how much money pharmaceutical companies lose as a result of the failure to recognize patents globally. Industry representatives say they lose as much as 10% of their profits this way, and it likely that drug prices would be lower if the companies could take advantage of a larger market.[46]

So what does pharmaceutical patenting have to do with reasonable profits, prices, and social responsibility? A great deal, I think. Briefly, companies can afford to do business in a country and exercise social responsibility insofar as they have a guarantee of reasonable profits. But obtaining these profits depends, in large part, on patent laws. When companies have strong patent protection, they can expect to profit from their R&D investments, and they can afford to devote more resources to socially responsible programs. If they fail to realize profits, they have less money to devote to programs designed to enhance social welfare. Thus, developing nations that fail to honor pharmaceutical patents may actually be harming themselves in the long run. In the short run, a developing country might obtain some benefit by not honoring pharmaceutical patents because it could acquire inexpensive drugs or attract 'generic' drug companies or distributors. This strategy could backfire in the long run, however, since larger, global pharmaceutical companies may decide not to do business in countries that do not honor their patents and they may decide not to invest money in R&D to develop drugs for the developing world. Why invest several billion dollars in developing a malaria vaccine if 'generic' drug companies will reverse engineer the vaccine and sell it at a very low price? If companies lack sufficient patent protection in the developing world, many patients in the developing world will remain therapeutic orphans.

Productive Business Environment

In this section I would like to address briefly another important factor in conducting business in the developing world and exercising social responsibility, the business environment. There are many different social, economic, political, and legal characteristics that contribute to a good business environment. A few of these are:[47]

1. A coherent and effective legal system.
2. Ethical business practices.
3. A stable currency.
4. A reliable banking system.
5. Free and open markets.
6. A well-educated public.
7. A middle class or consumer class.
8. A physical and social infrastructure.
9. Democratic institutions.

These characteristics played a key role in the rise of capitalism, and they can be found, to a great degree, in the developed nations, such as the US, Germany, and Britain. Very often, developing nations lack the characteristics that define a good business environment. Moreover, it may take many years for developing nations to develop some of these characteristics, such as a well-educated public, a physical and social infrastructure, or democratic institutions. It simply takes time to build bridges, roads, power lines, and telephone networks, acquire education, develop a middle class, establish democracy; to and so on. A company that refused to do business in the developing world because its business environment is less than ideal would be acting foolishly and unfairly: in order to expand their markets and their influence, companies need to take some risks and conduct business in undeveloped nations.

On the other hand, there are some acceptable limits on what a company should be willing to do to expand into a developing nation. Some business environments can be so adverse that doing business in that country is impossible or highly inefficient. Consider the difficulties involved in selling products in a society that uses the barter system, investing funds in a society where the banks do not insure savings or checking accounts, hiring employees in a society where employee theft is common, or signing contracts in a society where bribery is expected. In order to do business in the developing world and exercise their social responsibility, companies need to have a reasonable expectation that those nations are taking steps to promote the rule of law, ethical business practices, a stable currency and banking system, free and open markets, etc. Doing business in a country with an extremely poor business climate is going above and beyond the call of corporate duty. Developing nations can attract businesses by demonstrating that they are making progress toward developing a good business environment. (As an aside, even a developed nation can have a poor business environment. Many global companies have faced a variety of problems, such as corruption and an unreliable banking system, in trying to conduct business in Russia and other former Soviet Republics.)

Conclusion: Reciprocity

Let's retrace the steps of my argument. In the second section, I argued that large, global pharmaceutical companies have social responsibilities (or duties of beneficence and justice) to the developing world. There are a variety of ways that companies can exercise these responsibilities, including investing in R&D related to diseases that affect developing nations, offering discounts on drug prices, and initiating drug giveaways. However, I also argued that these social responsibilities are not absolute requirements and may be balanced against other obligations and commitments in light of economic, social, legal, and other conditions. In the third and fourth sections, I argued that the degree to which a company may exercise social responsibility in a society depends on two major factors, (1) the prospects for a reasonable profit and (2) the prospects for a good business environment. Developing nations can either help or hinder the pharmaceutical industry's efforts to exercise social responsibility through various policies and practices. To insure that companies can make a reasonable profit, developing nations should honor pharmaceutical patents. If they do not honor those patents, this will lower the industry's profits and take away money that could be devoted to projects designed to promote access to medications. To insure that companies have a good business environment, developing nations should try to promote the rule of law, ethical business practices, stable currencies, reliable banking systems, free and open markets, democracy, and other social, economic, legal, and political conditions conducive to business.

Overall, I hold that reciprocity and cooperation are the keys to developing drugs for the developing world. Pharmaceutical companies and developing nations need to work together in order to develop and market drugs to treat or prevent diseases that affect the developing world. Companies can do their part by investing in R&D for the developing world's diseases, offering drug discounts, or establishing drug giveaway programs. In return, they should expect developing nations to provide strong patent protection and to take steps to establish productive business environments. Developing nations should adhere to international agreements on intellectual property, such as the Trade-Related Aspects of Intellectual Property Rights (TRIPS) agreement. Nations that abide by TRIPS honor pharmaceutical product patents and do not allow importation of inventions from countries that violate TRIPS. TRIPS allows for some compulsory licensing to address public safety or public health crises. Developing nations should also take steps to promote a sound legal, ethical, financial, and social environment for business.

In pursuing this cooperative approach, developing nations may use a variety of other strategies to encourage pharmaceutical companies to act responsibly. For example, a nation could help reduce the cost of R&D and marketing by subsidizing R&D funding and by providing a company with a guaranteed market. If developing nations lower these costs to the company, the company will be able to develop a drug, sell it at a low price, and still make a reasonable profit. A developing nation could also help a drug company design research protocols and help the company with recruitment of subjects, informed consent, data monitoring, and other important aspects of humans subjects research. A nation could also help a company develop a drug giveaway program by providing an efficient, reliable, and fair system for distributing these medications. Finally, developing nations can also buy drugs in large quantities directly from pharmaceutical companies in order to take advantage of bulk buying. Nations could sell these drugs at a discounted price or give them away. Many countries have already pursued some of these strategies and there are many more constructive solutions than those mentioned in this essay.[48]

Although I believe strongly in the importance of reciprocal arrangements between pharmaceutical companies and developing nations, I also recognize that these agreements may not always work and that an atmosphere of animosity can easily develop. If a developing nation starts making concessions to the pharmaceutical industry and the industry does not respond through socially responsible policies and programs, then it would be reasonable for that nation to take retaliatory measures, such as compulsory licensing or importing drugs from countries that do not honor pharmaceutical patents. On the other hand, if a pharmaceutical company offers to aid a developing nation and that nation does not respond in kind, then that company would also have reasons to not make good on its commitment to that nation. I can foresee that these situations will arise and I would not admonish either side for retaliatory conduct.

However, I would still strongly urge developing nations and pharmaceutical companies to work together in addressing the urgent economic, legal, moral and political dilemma of developing drugs for the developing world.

Notes

10. Bodenheimer, T. Uneasy Alliance: Clinical Investigators and the Pharmaceutical Industry. *The New England Journal of Medicine* 2000; 342: 1539–1544.

11. Pharmaceutical Research and Manufacturing Association (PHRMA). 2000. The Pharmaceutical Industry's R&D Investment. Washington, DC. PHRMA.

12. Jaffe, A. Trends and Patterns in Research and Development Expenses in the United States. *Proceedings of the National Academy of Sciences* 1996; 93: 12658–12663.

13. McNeil, ...

14. McNeil, D. Selling Cheap Generic Drugs, India's Copycats Irk Industry. *New York Times.* 1 December 2000: F1.

15. Ibid.

16. McNeil, ...

17. Ibid.

18. Ibid.

19. Benatar, ...

20. Angell, ...

21. Reich, ...

22. DeGeorge, R. 1995. *Business Ethics,* 4th ed. Englewood Cliffs, NJ. Prentice-Hall.

23. Friedman, M. The Social Responsibility of Business is to Increase its Profits. *New York Times Magazine.* 13 September 1970: 1.

24. Murphy, P. 1998. *Eighty Exemplary Ethics Statements.* Notre Dame, Indiana. University of Notre Dame Press.

25. DeGeorge, note 22.

26. Ibid.

27. Brody, B. 1995. *Ethical Issues in Drug Testing, Approval, and Pricing.* New York. Oxford University Press.

28. Schüklenk, U. 1998. *Access to Experimental Drugs in Terminal Illness.* New York. Pharmaceutical Products Press.

29. Brody, B. Public Good and Fair Prices: Balancing Technological Innovation with Social Well Being. *Hastings Center Report* 1996; 26, 2: 5–11.

30. Spinello, R. Ethics, Pricing, and the Pharmaceutical Industry. *Journal of Business Ethics* 1992; 11: 617–626.

31. Brody, note 29; Spinello, note 30.

32. This issue of exploitation has come up many times in research involving the developing world. One of the criticisms of the HIV trials (mentioned in note 4) is that these studies would not make the new treatment reasonably available to the population. See Crouch, R. and Arras, J. AZT Trials and Tribulations. *Hastings Center Report* 1998; 28, 6: 26–34. Some writers have argued that the Human Genome Diversity Project will not offer participant populations a reasonable benefit. See Resnik, D. The Human Genome Diversity Project: Ethical Problems and Solutions. *Politics and the Life Sciences* 1999; 18, 1:15–24. See also Benatar, ...

33. Murphy, note 24.

34. See Pojman, L. 1995. *Ethics.* Belmont, CA. Wadsworth. Although most people would agree that beneficence is an imperfect duty, I would also maintain that justice is an imperfect duty if we understand the duty as including a duty to follow specific material principles of justice, such as the obligation to distribute benefits and burdens equitably. First, it is impossible for a person to follow these principles perfectly. As any parent can testify, it is impossible to distribute benefits and burdens to different children in a perfectly equitable fashion, no matter how hard one tries. Second, these principles must be weighed against one another and against other values or commitments. For example, when faced with a scarce resource in health care, such as a shortage of influenza vaccinations, it is morally acceptable to emphasize utility while de-emphasizing equity. If there is a shortage of influenza vaccines, then public health officials are justified in offering these vaccines to the patients who need them the most. For further discussion, see Beachamp, T. and Childress, J. 1996. *Principles of Biomedical Ethics,* 4th edition. New York. Oxford University Press.

35. Murphy, note 24.

36. DeGeorge, note 22.

37. Simpson, J. Ethics and Multinational Corporations vis-à-vis Developing Nations. *Journal of Business Ethics* 1982; 1, 4: 227–37.

38. Sternberg, S. AIDS Activists Discount Big Drugmakers' Gifts. *USA Today.* 11 July 2000: 9D.

39. Swarns, R. South Africa to Distribute $50 Million in Donated AIDS Drugs. *New York Times.* 2 December 2000: D1.

40. Jacobsen, R. Economic Efficiency and the Quality of Life. *Journal of Business Ethics* 1991; 10, 3: 201–209.

41. Ferrell, O. and Fraedrick, J. 1991. *Business Ethics.* Boston: Houghton Mifflin.

42. Pharmaceutical Research and Manufacturing Association (PHRMA). 2000. PHRMA Policy Paper: Strong Patent Protection is Essential. Washington, DC. PHRMA.

43. Ibid.

44. PTO. 2000. General Information Regarding Patents. Washington, DC. PTO.

45. Stolberg, G. and Gerth, J. Medicine Merchants: Holding Down the Competition. *New York Times.* 23 April 2000: A1.

46. Reich, ...

47. Samuelson, P. 1980. *Economics.* New York. McGraw-Hill.

48. Reich, ...

The Dilemma of Intellectual Property Rights for Pharmaceuticals

The Tension Between Ensuring Access of the Poor to Medicines and Committing to International Agreements[1]

JILLIAN CLARE COHEN AND PATRICIA ILLINGWORTH

'At the beginning of the 21st century, one-third of the world's population still lacks access to the essential drugs it needs for good health. In the poorest parts of Africa and Asia, over 50% of the population do not have access to the most vital drugs.'[2]

I. *Introduction*

In this paper, we put forward some possible resolutions to the issue of improving access of the poor to essential medicines. This paper responds in part to arguments put forward in an earlier volume of *Developing World Bioethics* (Volume 1, Number 1, 2001). In that volume, Resnik argued that pharmaceutical firms have social responsibilities and moral obligations to meet the health needs of the populations in developing countries. He argued further that if pharmaceutical firms provide reduced pricing or donations to developing countries, then developing countries in turn should foster an adequate business environment for these firms. That is to say, they should honour intellectual property laws for pharmaceuticals. In response, Brock in the same volume took issue with Resnik on the grounds that increased social responsibility may be inconsistent with a corporation's duties to their shareholders, but was not convinced that developing countries should respect intellectual property protection for pharmaceuticals in return for reduced pricing on pharmaceuticals. We acknowledge the murkiness that is inherent to the discussion of pharmaceutical intellectual property protection and access to medicines for the poor; and the risk that pharmaceutical firms and governments of developing countries may not be able to resolve the thorny issue of intellectual property protection to essential medicines bilaterally. We thus call for the intervention of a third party—whether it is through the financing of drugs by an international organisation, like the World Bank, to help improve access of the poor to essential medicines. While intellectual property protection for pharmaceuticals is not the single cause of the lack of access of medicines to the poor, for the purpose of this article we focus on this issue exclusively and on the World Bank's potential role in it.[3] We use the World Bank simply as a model of an international organisation that could become more central to the provision of medicines for the poorest.

The paper is organised as follows. First, we provide an overview of the Trade Related Aspects of Intellectual Property Rights (TRIPs Agreement), and its provisions which are relevant for pharmaceutical products and processes. Second, we explain how specific pharmaceutical policy tools can help developing states mitigate the worst effects of the TRIPs Agreement. Third, we provide an overview of the ethical dilemmas that intellectual property protection for pharmaceuticals presents. And fourth, we put forward solutions that could be implemented by an international organisation, like the Bank, to help overcome the divide between creating private incentives for research and development of innovative medicines, and ensuring access of the poor to critical medicines.

II. Background on the TRIPs Agreement

The TRIPs Agreement was one of the many trade agreements that were agreed upon during the Uruguay Round and included in the new international trading system, governed by the World Trade Organisation (WTO). The Agreement covers a range of intellectual property issues beyond patents, such as trade-marks, industrial designs, and copyright, applicable to any sector.[4] It provides minimum standards for intellectual property law, procedures, and remedies so rights' holders can enforce their rights effectively. The main rule of TRIPs for patents is that they should be available for any invention, whether product or process, in all fields of technology with discrimination. Inventions covered under the patent law have to meet the criteria of novelty, inventive step, and industrial applicability. The minimum obligations for pharmaceuticals are: pharmaceutical products and micro-organisms are patentable for up to twenty years from the date the inventor files for the patent application. Second, there is no discrimination permitted against patent rights for imported products. Third, exclusive marketing rights are granted until patent expiry; and, there are transitional periods for developing countries without pharmaceutical product patents.[5] The Agreement does provide a degree of freedom to member states. For example, states can deny patent protection for specific inventions (Articles 27.2 and 27.3), such as 'diagnostic, therapeutic and surgical methods for the treatment of humans or animals'; and plants and animals (other than micro-organisms) and biological processes (other than micro-biological) for their production.[6]

The Agreement also provides governments with the authority to issue a compulsory license for a pharmaceutical license without the permission of the patent owner when it can be justified in the public interest. The latter was strengthened further in the Doha Agreement on TRIPs and Public Health (November 2001). Compulsory license refers to when a judicial or government official is allowed by law to grant a license without permission from the holder on the grounds of general interest (such as public health considerations).[7] Proponents of the compulsory licensing system stress that consumer price benefits arise from effectively abrogating the market exclusivity of the patent. The TRIPs Agreement also does not prohibit the parallel importing of drug products. Parallel trade refers to the act of purchasing a drug product that is lower priced in another country and importing it to a country for resale where the same product is priced higher.

III. The Costs and Benefits of Intellectual Property Protection

The potential costs and benefits of intellectual property protection are well known and have been discussed at length elsewhere. Thus, in this section, we highlight a selection of the arguments on both sides of the debate to serve as requisite background for our ensuing discussion. The application of intellectual property rights is viewed by some as a beneficial government intervention insofar as it can possibly prevent free-riding behaviour and the attendant 'congestion problem' that is particularly acute when intellectual assets are easy to copy. (This applies to the pharmaceutical sector, as the reverse engineering of patented drugs is not technically demanding.) New knowledge potentially may suffer from overuse in the absence of intellectual property because access to it would not be costly. The overuse of knowledge could minimise the economic value of an innovation and limit incentives for others to pursue advances in knowledge.[8] Intellectual property rights thus mitigate the tendency toward free-riding behaviour by limiting who has the rights to an intellectual asset.

Furthermore, they provide an inventor with some degree of certainty that he can capture a sufficient amount of rent for his innovation effort by preventing congestion behaviour, and thus encourage the pursuit of new knowledge. This argument assumes that pharmaceutical patents provide incentives for firms to invest resources in the research and development of new drug therapies. New drug therapies are desir-

able if we assume that they can help cure or prevent diseases and improve the health of the population, which in turn, can lead to economic growth.[9] Thus, pharmaceutical patent protection should encourage firms to invest in the research and development of new drug therapies specific to the disease burden of developing states that had previously not protected pharmaceutical patents. We deem this highly unlikely, given existing trends in the research and development of pharmaceuticals.

The TRIPs Agreement imposes minimum standards for pharmaceutical patents for member states of the WTO. Compliance for most developed states, including those with relatively mature production and innovation systems, did not demand significant changes in existing standards and institutions.[10] For developing states, the pharmaceutical patent regime, for the most part, was considerably below the minimum criteria of the TRIPs Agreement. From the standpoint of innovating drug firms in the advanced economies, the TRIPs Agreement corrects deficiencies in the latter regimes that lead to copying of products and ultimately loss of rent for innovating firms. These include the absence of patents for pharmaceutical products, the issuing of compulsory licenses for products without adequately compensating the firm of an innovating product, and a weak or poorly defined system of rules to protect trade secrets, therefore facilitating the imitation and copying of products.[11]

From a public health perspective, particularly for the poorest, intellectual property protection for pharmaceuticals may maintain the uneven direction of product research and development, by limiting the type of drug therapies available to treat disease among the poor. Here is the reason why. Patents impede progress in technology by precluding other firms from cross-learning and building on the original innovation. Patents produce a loss or 'dead-weight burden' insofar as the benefits of the new knowledge to society would have been greater in the absence of a patent regime, and thus reduce the capacity for other firms to exploit the knowledge on a competitive basis.[12] Additionally, the application of pharmaceutical patents could result in the further concentration of production of pharmaceuticals in advanced economies. International drug firms will be free to export finished or semi-finished products, instead of transferring technology. Consequently, foreign direct investment may be lessened.[13]

A much anticipated cost of the TRIPs Agreement is that it gives pharmaceutical firms greater scope for price discrimination, a rational move for profit-maximising firms, but exploitative to persons in developing countries.[14] If drug prices increase, in addition to the obvious implications for public health, this could be potentially politically disastrous for many politicians in developing states who are already under pressure from their constituents to improve access to medicines and lower pharmaceutical prices.

Although the innovating pharmaceutical industry emphasises the importance of patents as an incentive for research and development, there are also powerful economic arguments that counter them. Arrow argued that the entrenched patent monopolist has weaker incentives than a 'would-be' entry firm to initiate an R&D programme that would produce substitutes, even superior quality ones, than for goods, which were already profit-generating.[15] This, in turn, results in sub-optimal outcomes for social welfare.

Prior to the TRIPs Agreement, many governments in developing countries had adopted an explicit policy preference not to honour intellectual property protection for pharmaceuticals in an effort to promote self-sufficiency in the production of basic medicines, and as in the case of India, develop a competitive local industry. Domestic producers, both private and public, could, then, supply their populations with basic medicines, at prices often considerably lower than those of the research-based pharmaceutical industry and learn by doing so.

In short, the TRIPs Agreement requires developing states to reform drug policy and thereby limit the drug portfolios of local firms. The potential impacts of this are more costly pharmaceuticals and/or limited access of the population to essential medicines. Developed states, by comparison, have tended to support pharmaceutical patent protection in order to protect revenue streams from their established innovative pharmaceutical industry and to promote investment in technological innovation.[16]

IV. Recommended Solutions to Lessen the Tension Between Local and International Imperatives

Specific pharmaceutical policy tools, such as parallel importing, compulsory licensing and price controls, could potentially mitigate the worst effects of the TRIPs Agreement on drug supplies in developing states. We do not claim that these mechanisms solve the issue of improving access of the poor to essential medicines. However, they are policy tools for governments to use in order to adjust the terms of the treaty to local economic and public health realities.

At the international level, however, possible policy options exist that could help ease the tension between ensuring access of the poorest to essential medicines and intellectual property rights. Our following suggestions do not purport to be original, but we offer new thoughts by assigning responsibility for the realisation of these suggestions to an international global policy maker, and we make use of the World Bank as an example. Each one of the ensuing recommendations is imperfect, entailing trade-offs, either for the local and international pharmaceutical industry or for developing states. However, they present possible resolutions to the increasingly complex problem of providing incentives for the development of new drug therapies and ensuring equal access of the population to these new therapies.

These are: (1) intensified loans or grants to client states for the purchase of patented medicines; (2) the cancellation of debt relief and the use of these 'extra' financial resources for pharmaceuticals currently under patent; (3) the purchase of patents from the research-based pharmaceutical industry and the licensing of production of the patented drugs to generic drug firms in client states (a split-TRIPs model); (4) the promotion of a tiered pharmaceutical pricing (equity-pricing) system.

Resolution One: Intensified Pharmaceutical Loans for Patented Drugs

An international organisation, such as the World Bank, could assume an important role in resolving the conflict surrounding the TRIPs Agreement by providing specific loans and grants to developing countries that could enable them to have the financing they need for the purchase of essential medicines that are protected under the patent treaty. To achieve this, the Bank would need to allocate more financing for pharmaceutical procurement and for the monitoring of the types of drugs that client states purchase through these special loans, to ensure that they are in compliance with intellectual property laws and that the drugs are distributed effectively to those in need.

Alternatively, the Bank could provide its client states with loans to purchase drug patents from pharmaceutical firms and license the production of specific drugs to local firms. This solution would enable public financing to reduce the prices of medicines to their marginal costs of production, and permit the research and development firms to recoup their sunk costs of research and development by ensuring that they receive payment for their products. This Resolution presents potential disadvantages to developing states as well as to the international research-based pharmaceutical industry. Unfortunately, some countries, as noted earlier, may not even have the capacity to manufacture these products. For the international research-based pharmaceutical industry, the disadvantage is clearly the reduction of rents in developing markets.

Resolution Two: Debt Cancellation to Purchase Critical Pharmaceuticals

Another possible mechanism that could contribute to abating the conflict surrounding the TRIPs Agreement is for international institutions, like the Bank, to forgive the debt of the poorest countries, and demand as conditions attached to the forgiveness of debt that the 'surplus' money is spent on priority medicines under patent for those in need.[17] This Resolution builds on the Highly-Indebted Poor Countries Initiative (HIPC I) in 1996 and HIPC II in 1999, which the Bank initiated along with the International Monetary Fund (IMF). The HIPC Trust Fund has obtained $2.5 billion in bilateral contributions and pledges from about 20 countries. To date, the Bank has transferred more than $1.3 billion to the Bank component of the Trust Fund.[18]

To ensure that the countries honour their commitment to purchase patented medicines, the debt relief assigned to drug purchases could be transferred directly to the Bank. The Bank would then be responsible for managing the procurement of essential drugs under patent and monitoring their delivery in the targeted client state. This Resolution could benefit both developing states and the pharmaceutical industry. Developing states make gains by having their debts cancelled and probably improving the access of their population to pharmaceuticals. It does not guarantee that increases in drug spending will result in measurable gains in health outcomes. Nor does this Resolution offer a long-term solution to the dilemma of ensuring rents to the research-based pharmaceutical industry and access to patented drugs to the most vulnerable. Finally, it assumes that the Bank will have sufficient human resources to take on these expanded responsibilities.

**Resolution Three: Purchase of Patents
by the Bank and Licensing of Patented Drugs
to Generic Drug Manufacturers**

The Bank could purchase patents from the research-based pharmaceutical industry and make licensing agreements with generic drug firms that may or may not be located in developing states. Using financing provided by donors, the Bank could purchase patents from the research-based pharmaceutical industry and then provide licenses to generic drug manufacturers in developing states to produce the requisite medicines and distribute them widely.[19]

This Resolution is a modification of compulsory licensing, which the TRIPs Agreement permits, whereby a government can compel a patent holder to grant licenses to domestic firms. These firms then pay the patent holder a royalty for the license. The benefit of having the Bank purchase the patent from the pharmaceutical firm is that the firm may have more trust that the Bank will deliver a sufficient level of rent. Furthermore, the Bank could exercise some measure of quality control by only agreeing to license out the patented drug to generic drug firms that meet international standards, such as Good Manufacturing Practices (GMPs).

Resolution Four: Equity Pricing

The pharmaceutical industry currently prices its pharmaceuticals by using a tiered pricing system. This type of pricing refers to market segmentation based on the economic profile of a state. We propose, like others before us, that the research-based pharmaceutical industry offers countries an equity-pricing scheme, based on the economic profile of the poorest consumer of a state. This is based on the concept of price discrimination, whereby a pharmaceutical firm sells the same product to different consumers at different prices. Prices are not based on the costs of production but on what the consumer will and can pay. The Bank, ideally, could assist the pharmaceutical in-

dustry and developing states in this type of initiative by acting as a broker between them.

Pharmaceuticals under patent could be subject to different pricing schemes depending on the purchasing power of the poorest consumer and health needs. Consumers in developed states would then find themselves subsidising the pharmaceutical needs of consumers in developing states. For developing states, equity pricing is potentially beneficial because it takes into account social and economic conditions but does not guarantee universal access. For the research-based pharmaceutical industry, equity pricing poses the risk of more intensified parallel imports between states. Parallel importing occurs when drugs are imported from a state where a pharmaceutical product is placed on the market with patent holder consent to another state, without the patent holder's consent. The use of parallel importing is permissible under the TRIPs Agreement and employed by many countries, such as those of the European Union.

V. *Some Moral Considerations*

Whether to implement one or more of these Resolutions should be made in light of ethical considerations. Although each of the Resolutions is beneficial insofar as it aims to facilitate access to needed medicines for people living in developing countries, we argue that an equity pricing system is morally preferable. This is not to say that we do not support each Resolution, for the problems that face developing countries are of such a magnitude that all of the Resolutions may need to be implemented. Before developing our argument in favour of Resolution Four, equity pricing, we will look at some of the moral problems raised by Resolutions One, Two, and Three.

Our argument is made against the background of two assumptions about the World Bank: that (1) its resources are limited in light of its mission to fight poverty in the developing world and to '. . . establish economic growth that is stable, sustainable and equitable'; and (2) that this mission is morally important.[20] This is only to say that the demand for World Bank resources far exceeds the available resources, and that some priority setting is necessary. Although we also assume that pharmaceutical organisations have limited resources, we do not *assume* that their mission is *necessarily* morally important. Nonetheless, our argument will show that once pharmaceutical organisations are acknowledged to have a de facto socially and morally important mission, then arguably they ought to shoulder greater moral responsibility for ensuring access to essential drugs.

We are concerned that Resolution One's proposal to offer additional loans to already heavily indebted countries for the purpose of purchasing essential drugs, will not significantly improve access to drugs and, in turn, reduce the suffering in developing countries. Resolution One ensures that pharmaceutical firms will receive rent on their products and, arguably, this will encourage the innovation of medicines that may help people, including those living in developing countries; although for the latter, current trends do not suggest this will be the case.

However, the prospect of such debt, often in addition to longstanding debt, may have a chilling effect on the willingness and ability of developing countries, especially the least developed, to secure loans for essential drugs for their communities. Our fear then is that Resolution One will do little in the end to relieve the suffering in developing countries.

From the perspective of justice, it is also worth asking whether, given the health and welfare crisis in developing countries and the economic robustness of the pharmaceutical industry, is it just for developing countries to be further burdened with additional debt when pharmaceutical companies might well assume greater economic responsibility? This is a concern about who ought to shoulder the burden. World Bank funds that are not directed at paying for patented drugs could be directed toward meeting other urgent social needs in the developing world. The pharmaceutical industry argues that they need to charge high prices on their patented property in order ultimately to effectively undertake R&D. However, a recent article in the *Economist* reports that the cost of R&D in the pharmaceutical industry is on the decline.[21] Moreover, as Resnik and later Schüklenk and Ashcroft point out, the developing world is not the primary source of pharmaceutical profits.[22] From a justice-based perspective, increasing the burden on developing countries, even indirectly through the World Bank, when there is another alternative, is morally problematic.

Naturally, we are also concerned that measures, such as loans, will place developing countries in the morally undesirable position of depending on others for additional loans that they may never be able to pay back and will not contribute to the development of sustainable pharmaceutical systems. We assume that this will encourage a cycle in which loan repayment figures importantly, and sound economic development becomes impossible. In the end, Resolution One may do little to alter the burden of disease in developing countries.

Resolution Two, which proposes to forgive debt contingent upon using the forgiven amount for the purchase of needed medicines, also raises moral concerns. First, although the World Bank could offer to forgive the debt contingent on the beneficiary using the forgiven amount to purchase critical drugs, many developing countries cannot now afford to repay their debts because they simply do not have the economic wherewithal to do so. If funds are unavailable to repay loans, they may likewise be unavailable to pay the high cost of patented drugs for the millions of people who need them. If so, then developing countries would ultimately be unable to make use of the opportunity afforded by Resolution Two. Thus, as with Resolution One, we assume that Resolution Two will not result in benefits for developing countries.

Second, given the wide ranging economic and social problems that many developing countries face, it is far from clear that they ought to devote the 'surplus' to pay the high prices of patented pharmaceuticals and, in this way ultimately subsidise the pharmaceutical preferences of the developed world.[23] Using loan forgiveness as an incentive to fashion a developing countries' health policy may be paternalistic.

Third, Resolution Two may also be coercive in so far as the original agreement was not made between free and equal parties. Consider the following. The fairness of a given agreement is determined in part by whether the parties to the agreement are free and equal at the time of the agreement.[24] It is not clear that any agreement between developed and developing countries or NGOs for the purpose of providing necessities to developing countries, is fully voluntary.[25] The pull of poverty, sickness, and death place the bargainers under duress. Even if, strictly speaking, the agreements are valid, they can certainly be challenged under the moral principles that ground the notion of an agreement made freely and without duress. When necessities, such as food, shelter, and medicine are at issue, it is not clear that repayment ought to be demanded in any case. If the initial loan agreement was morally compromised because one of the parties was under great duress, neither equal nor free at the time of the agreement, then the original wrong would only be compounded were the forgiveness of the loan made contingent upon purchasing drugs. In other words, the loan should be forgiven outright.

It might be argued that Resolution Two has the merit of benefiting both the research-based pharmaceutical industry and developing countries by increasing demand for pharmaceuticals, creating incentives and ensuring that developing countries get the drugs they need. Again, as with Resolution One, we are not convinced that the resources of the World Bank (and indirectly the developing countries) should pay for patented drugs.

Although Resolution Three, like One and Two, has the potential to make critical medicines more accessible to those in need in developing countries, it does so at a high cost, since it also requires the payment of 'market' price for these patents. Thus, it shares some of the same moral weakness as Resolutions One and Two.

Resolution Four proposes that an international broker, like the World Bank, negotiate an equity-pricing system with pharmaceutical firms and that the pharmaceutical industry implement such a policy. Because this Resolution prices medicine according to morally relevant factors, such as what countries are able to pay, it has distinct moral advantage. It ensures that the principle of charging what the market will bear will not impede access of the poor to needed medicines. It promises to reduce suffering in a way that Resolution One, Two, and Three do not. Presumably, most people would share the view that ability to pay for medicine should not determine whether someone enhances the quality of his or her life, or even lives or dies, recalling the extraordinary properties of medicines. Moreover, it shifts the burden of helping improve the access of the poor to medicines, to the pharmaceutical industry. We propose this with the understanding that pharmaceutical corporations have obligations to their shareholders. We argue, however, that this obligation should not be viewed as an obstacle to implementing Resolution Four—an equity-pricing system.

To this end, it will be helpful to evaluate the theoretical model that has been used to justify the corporate practice of charging what the market will bear. Although we shall call this the 'primacy of the shareholder' view, it has been referred to in a number of ways.[26] According to this principle, the primary duty of organisations is to maximise shareholder profits. Managers who sacrifice profit may be interpreted to be in breach of their legal Duty of Care to shareholders.[27]

Our discussion of shareholder primacy will be framed around the dialogue that took place between David Resnik and Dan Brock in which they discussed the concept of corporate social responsibility as it applied to pharmaceutical companies.[28] Although a number of related matters were discussed in that dialogue, we will focus only on their discussion of corporate responsibility. Resnik argued that pharmaceutical companies have social responsibilities to the developing world because they, like other moral agents, '. . . have obligations to avoid causing harm and to promote social welfare.'[29] Brock argued that corporations are unlike moral agents insofar as their responsibilities are to their shareholders.[30] Brock seems to be invoking an argument in support of role differentiation. That is, he appears to be arguing that corporations do not have the same moral obligations as individuals because they serve a different social role, one that requires shareholder primacy.

Debunking the Myth of Shareholder Primacy

Indeed, corporations do have legal responsibilities to shareholders. However, it is far from clear that these are as primary as Brock and others appear to assume. We agree with some of the objections that Brock presents against Resnik's arguments. We argue, however, that corporations have considerable social obligations to facilitate access to essential drugs in developing countries. Although these obligations may not rise to the level of legal obligations, they potentially have greater force than mere supererogatory obligations. The view articulated by Schüklenk and Ashcroft, that a social responsibility approach relies too heavily on philanthropic inclinations, may be less problematic than they suppose.[31]

The classical theory of shareholder primacy, and the one that Brock invokes, holds that there is a fiduciary relationship between directors and shareholders that puts the interests of shareholders first. Because Brock does not reference his statement about shareholder primacy, it is difficult to know what argument he has in mind. In any case, many of the most persuasive statements of this position have come from legal

cases, scholars, and the economist Milton Friedman.[32] One of the main legal arguments is based on agency law, according to which shareholders are viewed as the owners (the principals) of the corporation and managers, their agents.[33] This indeed has even deeper roots in master-servant law. Both of these maintain that the agent must act only for the principal, leaving aside other constituencies, including the manager himself. When applied to the modern corporation, however, this argument seems only remotely relevant. The modern corporation is a great departure from the principal-agent model since it is based on the separation of ownership and control of the corporation, with managers assuming a very active role and shareholders a relatively passive one.

The shareholder primacy view has also been justified on the grounds that the shareholders own the corporation, that they are the principals, and that the directors are bound to maximise their wealth. This conception of the modern corporation, called the 'property conception', was articulated by A.A. Berle in the now famous Harvard debate and re-articulated in the popular press by Friedman.[34] On this conception, maximisation of the stockholders' wealth is thought to follow from the fact that they *own* the corporation. However, even if we accept the view that stockholders *own* the corporation, there is nothing about ownership *per se* that necessarily means that the corporation must aim at shareholder profit, especially when shareholders contribute little other than money. Moreover, the common practice of extending stock options certainly weakens any claim of shareholder ownership.[35]

A relatively recent but significant modification to the reasoning in support of shareholder primacy can be found in the 'agency costs' view. According to this view, in the best of all possible worlds, it would be preferable if managers could consider the interests of all of a corporation's constituencies (all those who affect the organisation and are affected by it), including among others employees, clients, and the community.

Unfortunately it cannot, because any departure from shareholder primacy would entail giving too much discretion to managers, who after all are human and therefore too opportunistic to be given such discretion.[36] Were managers to be given such discretion they would not necessarily act in the interests of society but instead act in their own interest (the classic principal-agent problem). Mark Roe states: '. . . a stakeholder measure of managerial accountability could leave managers so much discretion that managers could easily pursue their own agenda, one that might maximize neither shareholder, employer, consumer, nor national wealth, but only their own.'[37]

In yet another view, identified as the social entity conception, the corporation is seen as a social construction, with social purposes. According to Merrick Dodd, 'Business—which is the economic organization of society—is private property only in a qualified sense, and society may properly demand that it be carried on in such a way as to safeguard the interests of those who deal with it either as employees or consumers even if the proprietary rights of its owners are thereby curtailed.'[38] Dodd believes the case for social responsibility is even stronger with respect to companies that have strong public dimensions, such as railways and public utilities. Arguably, pharmaceutical companies would fall into this category. On the social entity conception, corporations have much broader social purposes and duties than simply the maximisation of shareholder wealth.[39] From this brief overview of the three main theories of the firm, it can be seen that the theory we adopt will influence what we take to be the duties of pharmaceutical organisations.

Many people take the property conception, coupled with shareholder primacy, as a given. Nonetheless according to William Allen, the courts and legislatures have endorsed the entity view and the social obligations it supports.[40] Interestingly, one of the ways that the legal system has accomplished this is with the enactment of corporate constituency statutes. These statutes have undermined the primacy of shareholders, in support of other constituencies, such as employees and the community. In the United States, at least 29 states have adopted corporate constituency statutes.[41]

Provisions 4 and 5 of the New York statute, for example, permit directors to consider other constituencies when it acts, and to act on behalf of these other constituencies.[42] Ultimately, corporate constituency statutes realign the focus of a corporation's duty of care to include others in addition to shareholders. Thus, managers may well have a (legal) right to consider other constituencies in addition to shareholders without being in violation of their obligations to shareholders. Scholarly work on the theory of the firm—and the corporate constituency statutes that follow from it—show that shareholder primacy can no longer be taken for granted and that corporations cannot be shielded from assuming greater social responsibilities on the basis of it. In this respect, the moral intuitions of many ethicists seem to have informed and guided the law.

The American firm seems to be responding to imperatives other than shareholder primacy. If this is so, it is a mistake to shield pharmaceutical companies from increased moral responsibility for ensuring access to essential drugs for those in developing countries on the basis of shareholder primacy. Moreover, pharmaceutical companies may in theory at least, embrace the social entity view. Merck, for example, says in its first statement of values: 'Our business is preserving and improving human life.' Second, Merck claims, 'we are committed to the highest standards of ethics and integrity.'[43]

If we move away from the belief that corporations are obligated only to shareholders, we can better evaluate Resolution Four. In effect, our strategy has been to show that the *role* that was invoked to exempt pharmaceutical companies from assuming greater social responsibility to render aid, namely their duty to shareholders, is a fiction.

Pharmaceuticals for Social Justice: Equity Pricing

It is arguable that the pharmaceutical industry could assume a greater role in providing medicines to the neediest. Such action can be justified based on a number of principles, including consequentialism, the principle of beneficence and its social and legal correlate, Good Samaritan laws.[44] In what follows, we will focus on the principle that Peter Singer articulates in his paper, 'Famine, Affluence and Morality.' The principle is as follows: 'if it is in our power to prevent something bad from happening, without thereby sacrificing anything of comparable moral importance, we ought morally to do it.'[45] The application of this principle to the issue at hand is obvious, but it will be helpful to go through the analysis. Relieving pain, suffering, loss and unnecessary death are moral goods by many moral barometers—including consequentialism and the principle of beneficence. Equity pricing can relieve the suffering of many of those in developing countries who need essential drugs, by making those drugs affordable. So clearly, pharmaceuticals can satisfy the first part of Singer's principle—that is, they can prevent something bad from happening, such as suffering and death.

We examine briefly if an equity-pricing scheme could be accomplished without losing something of comparable moral value. The only loss of comparable value would be the loss of other lives. Would the lives saved through equity pricing cause the loss of other lives? We can speculate confidently that the answer is 'no.' It is worth noting that the pharmaceutical industry is the most profitable industry in the U.S.[46] Moreover, many of the drugs it manufactures are 'me too' drugs, requiring little innovation but rendering high profits. And the industry spends much more on marketing than on R & D.[47] Many of the drugs that the industry spends money on have little to do with saving lives and much more to do with improving quality of life (e.g. Viagra,

Paxil, Ritalin). When we apply Singer's Principle, we find that pharmaceutical companies ought to respond more appropriately to the health needs of the poor in developing countries, such as through an equity pricing system.

VI. Penultimate Thoughts

A study conducted by MIT in 1995 found that of the 14 drugs the pharmaceutical company had identified as the most medically important in the last 25 years, 11 were partially supported by government funds. Publicly funded science is, thus, an important component of the pharmaceutical industry's R & D.[48] Thus, the view that profits belong solely to the pharmaceutical industry because it has only invested in R & D is not always the case. The industry does invest large amounts into R & D for innovative medicines, but public entities, such as the National Institute for Health, also contribute. This is a large issue that cannot be sufficiently addressed here, but we raise it for consideration.

Public funds are directed to research that will, ideally, result in helpful medicines that contribute to the public good. This is so for many reasons, including the moral qualities of medicine. Medicines play a foundational role in supporting other community values, such as liberty, equal opportunity, and human flourishing and are critical for the good functioning of health systems. In view of this, they cannot be considered as equivalent to other consumer goods. A similar intuition underlies Dodd's view that public utilities have unique social obligations.[49] In short, we believe that of the four Resolutions, Resolution Four, which advocates equity-pricing, has a distinct moral advantage and is likely to be the most practical Resolution to apply.

VII. Conclusions

The TRIPs Agreement and pharmaceutical pricing policies present complex ethical dilemmas about ensuring access of the poor to critical medicines. The Treaty may impede efforts to improve access of the poor to medicines under patent, unless creative public policies are put forward. We have argued that there is space for a global policy maker—such as the World Bank—to assume a central and active role. We put forward four potential Resolutions: (1) intensified pharmaceutical loans and grants for patented drugs; (2) debt cancellation to purchase critical pharmaceuticals; (3) purchase of patents by the bank and the licensing of patented drugs to generic drug manufacturers; and (4) equity pricing. These Resolutions are not novel. Some are even well in progress. Indeed, there is a trend toward equity pricing. Because of considerable pressure from public health activists, pharmaceutical companies, such as Merck & Co. and GlaxoSmithKline PLC are beginning to provide drugs at marginal production costs or less in developing countries.[50] While prices are still out of reach for the poor, they at least demonstrate that equity pricing can be put in practice. We believe we have contributed to the debate about pharmaceutical intellectual property rights by integrating ethical issues and practical solutions and proposing that the pharmaceutical industry can make profits and act in a socially responsible manner.

Notes

1. The authors wish to acknowledge the very helpful comments of anonymous reviewers and the outstanding research and editing suggestions of Jessica Wolland.
2. G. H. Brundland. May 1, 2000. Speech to the WHO/Public Interest NGO Pharmaceuticals Roundtable, Third Meeting. Geneva, Switzerland.
3. For example, poor infrastructure, mismanagement, and sometimes corruption, are all variables that can potentially limit the access of the poor to essential medicines.
4. Patent protection for pharmaceuticals is exclusively examined in this paper.
5. H. Redwood. 1995. *Brazil: The Future Impact of Pharmaceutical Patents.* Felixstowe, Suffolk. Oldwicks Press.
6. Jeffrey J. Schott, ed. 2000. *The WTO after Seattle.* Washington, D.C.: Institute for International Economics.
7. Schott, *op. cit.* note 6, p. 41.
8. K.E. Maskus. September 12–14, 1997. *The International Regulation of Intellectual Property.* Paper prepared for the IESG Conference on International Trade and Investment. Nottingham. p. 3.
9. The Bank health sector strategy paper notes, 'no country can secure sustainable economic growth or poverty reduction without a healthy, well nourished, and educated population.' Bank. 1997. *Health, Nutrition, and Population Sector Strategy Paper.* Washington, D.C. Bank Group: 10.
10. C. R. Frischtak. 1993. Harmonization Versus Differentiation in Intellectual Property Rights Regimes. In *The Global Dimensions of Intellectual Property Rights in Science and Technology: A Conference.* M.B. Wallerstein, M.E. Mogee, & R.A. Schoen, eds. Washington, D.C. National Academy Press: 99.
11. Maskus, *op. cit.* note 8.
12. Maskus, *op. cit.* note 8, p. 34.
13. WHO. March 2001. Globalization, TRIPS and Access to Pharmaceuticals. In *WHO Policy Perspectives on Medicines.* Geneva. WHO.
14. J. Stiglitz. *Two Principles for the Next Round: Or How to Bring Developing Countries in From the Cold.* Paper prepared for the WTO/Bank Conference on Developing Countries in a Millennium Round, WTO Secretariat, Geneva, 20–21 September 1999. p. 34. (Stiglitz argues further that in the next round of trade negotiations, efforts should be made to explore ways to ensure that developing countries achieve 'most favoured pricing' status.)
15. K.J. Arrow. 1962. Economic Welfare and the Allocation of Resources for Invention. In *The Rate and Direction of Inventive Activity: Economic and Social Factors.* Princeton, N.J. National Bureau of Economic Research: 609–25. As quoted in: Paul A. David. 1993. Intellectual Property Institutions. In *The Global Dimensions of Intellectual Property Rights in Science and Technology: A Conference.* M.B. Wallerstein, M.E. Mogee & R.A. Schoen, eds. Washington, D.C. National Academy Press: 4.

16. C. Correa. 2000. *Integrating Public Health Concerns into Patent Legislation in Developing Countries.* Geneva: South Centre.

17. J. Sachs. February 24, 2000. Submission to the Senate Subcommittee on African Affairs. Washington.

18. For more information see: http://www.worldbank.org.hipc

19. R. Weissman. AIDS and Developing Countries: Facilitating Access to Essential Medicines. *Foreign Policy in Focus* 2001; 6.

20. http://www.worldbank.org/about/whatwedo

21. G. Carr. Survey: The Pharmaceutical Industry: Beyond the Behemoths. *The Economist* February 21, 1998: 16–18.

22. D. Resnik. Developing Drugs for the Developing World: An Economic, Legal, Moral, and Political Dilemma. *Developing World Bioethics* 2001; 1: 11–22; U. Schuklenk & R. Ashcroft. Affordable Access to Essential Medication in Developing Countries: Conflicts Between Ethical and Economic Imperatives. *Journal of Medicine and Philosophy* 2002; 27: 179–195.

23. D.J. Ncayiyana. Antiretroviral Therapy Cannot Be South Africa's First Priority. *CMAJ JAMC* 2001; 164: 1857–1858.

24. This is implicit in the kinds of considerations that are used to negate contracts (e.g. infancy, insanity, undue influence, and duress). See: A.L. Corbin. 1950. *Corbin on Contracts.* St. Paul. West Publishing Company.

25. See: *Henningsen v. Bloomfield Motors.* Supreme Court of New Jersey, 32 N.J. 358; 161 A.2d 69 (a good case on necessities).

26. It has been referred to by a number of terms, including fiduciary duty and classical view. We choose this term because it is most perspicuous for an interdisciplinary audience.

27. M. Friedman. 1997. The Social Responsibility of Business is to Increase Profits. In *Ethical Theory and Business.* T. L. Beauchamp & N.E. Bowie, eds. Upper Saddle River, NJ. Prentice Hall: 30, 56; Revised Model Business Code 8: 30(a), 1992.

28. D. Resnik, *op. cit.* note 22; D.W. Brock. Some Questions about the Moral Responsibilities of Drug Companies in Developing Countries. *Developing World Bioethics* 2001; 1: 33–37.

29. Ibid.

30. D.W. Brock, *op. cit.* note 28, p. 34.

31. Schuklenk & Ashcroft, *op. cit.* note 22, pp. 179–195.

32. A.A. Berle, Jr. Corporate Powers as Powers in Trust. *Harvard Law Review* 1932; 45: 1049–1074.

33. One reason to think that this view is wrong when applied to managers is that they are not agents in the classic sense. Modern corporations separate ownership and control of the corporation because owners frequently know little about the corporation while managers know a great deal.

34. Berle, *op. cit.* note 32; M. Dodd. For Whom Are Corporate Managers Trustees? *Harvard Law Review* 1932; XLV: 1162; Friedman, *op. cit.* note 27, p. 30.

35. Ibid. p. 1192. See also: F. Black & M. Scholes. The Pricing of Options and Corporate Liabilities. *J. Pol. Econ.* 1973; 81: 637.

36. Ibid.

37. M.J. Roe. Symposium Norms and Corporate Law: The Shareholder Wealth Maximization Norm and Industrial Organization. *U. Pa. L. Rev.* 2001; 149: 2063, 2065.

38. Dodd, *op. cit.* note 34, p. 1162.

39. Ibid. pp. 1149—150.

40. W.T. Allen. Our Schizophrenic Conception of the Business Corporation. *Cardozo Law Review* 1992; 14: 276.

41. E.W. Orts. Beyond Shareholders: Interpreting Corporate Constituency Statutes. *George Washington Law Review* 1992; 61: 14–135. See also: R. Roman. What is the Value of Other Constituency Statutes to Shareholders? [Comment]. *University of Toronto Law Journal* 1993; XLIII: 533–542.

42. New York's Corporate Constituency Statute:

    In taking action a director shall be entitled to consider without limitations . . . the effects that the corporation's actions may have . . . for any of the following: . . .

    4. the corporation's customers and creditors
    5. the ability of the corporation to provide as a going concern, goods, services, employment opportunities and employment benefits and otherwise to contribute to the communities in which it does business.

43. Merck & Co., Inc. 'Mission Statement: Our Values,' at www.merck.com.overview/philosophy

44. See for example: The Bill Emerson Food Donation Act. Public Law 104–210 (October 1, 1996), which protects donors (typically grocery stores) who donate food to non-profit organisations from liability for harm caused by the product. Although not typical of Good Samaritan laws, this Act shows that as a community we encourage organisations to render aid that they are uniquely suited to render, especially with respect to necessities.

45. P. Singer. 2001. Famine, Affluence and Morality. In *Writings on an Ethical Life*. New York. Harper Collins: 107.

46. Marcia Angell. The Pharmaceutical Industry: To Whom is It Accountable? *NEJM* 2000; 342: 1902–1904.

47. Angell, *op. cit.* note 46.

48. J. Gerth and S.G. Stolberg. Medicine Merchants: Birth of a Blockbuster; Drug Makers Reap Profits On Tax-Backed Research. *New York Times* April 23, 2000.

49. Dodd, *op. cit.* note 34, p. 1162.

50. M. Ganslandt, K.E. Maskus and E.V. Wong. Developing and Distributing Essential Medicines to Poor Countries: the DEFEND Proposal, IUI Working Paper Series 552. The Research Institute of Industrial Economics.

C. Are Health Care Ethics Culturally Specific?

Global health care ethics, though perhaps required in a global world, is a complex undertaking. We must ask what such an enterprise involves, whether it is feasible and perhaps even whether it is ethical. The impetus behind the turn toward a global health care ethics comes in part from our knowledge that health and disease are indeed global problems. Moreover, the health of developed countries is inextricably bound to the health of developing countries. This point will be highlighted in Chapter 7 when we consider the implications of increased worldwide travel for the spread of contagious diseases. Put in its simplest terms, bioethics must go global because health is a global issue.

The concern for many, however, is that global bioethics will amount to little more than developed countries imposing their values and culture on developing countries as the price for their help. In his essay, *Globalization or Westernization? Ethical Concerns in the Whole Bio-Business*, Godfrey B. Tangwa argues that there is a "danger that globalisation might end up as or, in fact, might not and never has been more than, mere Westernisation, given the history and reality of Western industrial-technological power, colonization of non-Westerners, domination and insensitivity to all things non western." Using the Kantian principle of universalizability, however, he points out that there is a distinction between morality and custom and that morality will trump custom. Moreover, Tangwa insists that although there is cultural diversity and pluralism, there are nonetheless core ethical values. Successful and ethical globalization will require (1) a dialogue about the use of technology that all parties can participate in; (2) dialogue and interaction among parties around the globe; (3) talking and listening among all parties that includes respect for different expressive customs; and (4) a willingness by all to teach and to learn.

Rosemarie Tong, in her essay *Towards a Feminist Global Bioethics: Addressing Women's Health Concerns World Wide*, also believes that although global bioethics is challenging, it is a feasible enterprise. Tong develops an argument in support of global feminist bioethics by focusing on common human needs. To this end, she turns to Martha Nussbaum's capabilities approach. According to this view, all persons require an equal opportunity to satisfy the following list of functional human capabilities: (1) life, (2) bodily health and integrity, (3) bodily integrity, (4) senses, imagination, and thought, (5) emotions, (6) practical reason, (7) affiliation, (8) other species, (9) play, and (10) control over one's environment.

Thus for Tong, global bioethics is possible even in a world of globalism and diversity, if it looks to common human needs as reflected in human capabilities. Moreover and importantly, both Tong and Nussbaum, before her, believe that we need not be dissuaded from meeting human needs in other cultures simply because women of those cultures defend their current cultural values and practices. According to Nussbaum, "The capabilities approach insists that a woman's affiliations with a certain group or culture should not be taken as normative for her unless, on due consideration, with all the capabilities at her disposal, she makes that norm her own. We should take care to extend to each individual full capabilities to pursue the items on the list and then see whether they want to avail themselves of these opportunities."[23] As you evaluate Tong's arguments, consider whether they will adequately meet the concern expressed by Godfrey Tangwa, that global bioethics is just another form of Westernization. Is the human capabilities approach culturally neutral enough to circumvent objections based on a concern with Westernization?

Few social issues have raised as much ethical rancor, especially among feminist bioethicists, as those that have surfaced around the practice of female genital cutting, also known as female genital mutilation (FGM) or female circumcision. FGM is a widespread practice in Africa, north of the equator, and in many African communities outside of Africa. Many countries, such as the United States and the United Kingdom, have prohibited the practice, especially on girls under the age of 18.[24] Here we will explore some of the questions that arise in connection with global bioethics as they relate to FGM.[25] Although we will consider these questions in a global context, it is important to realize that we needn't travel to Sierra Leone in order to confront the issues raised by FGM. The United States espouses values of pluralism and diversity, and medicine is committed to respecting patient autonomy. Many physicians have had to grapple with the question of whether or not they ought to perform FGM, when asked to do so. Thus some of the questions that arise with respect to cultural relativism and the feasibility of global bioethics arise in a domestic context as well.

Consider the paper by Loretta M. Kopelman, entitled *Female Genital Circumcision and Conventionalist Ethical Relativism*. Following Louis Pojman and Anthony Flew, Kopelman defines "conventional ethical relativism" in the following way: "To be a relativist about values is to maintain that there are no universal standards of good and bad, right and wrong." The problem is if there are no universal standards, then critiques of practices such as FGM would seem to be little more than one culture imposing their values on another culture. She believes that relativism of this kind can result in ethically sanctioning practices such as racism, slavery, and torture—a counterintuitive conclusion at best. Kopelman argues that conventional ethical relativists who take the extreme view that there are no cross-cultural moral values have the burden of proving their counterintuitive position. She contends that the moral arguments against FGM are strong and that the conventional relativist would be hard pressed to meet them.

Questions about the ethics of FGM would be relatively easy to answer if most women who undergo the procedure object to it. But this does not seem the case. Richard Shweder, for example, reports that at least one survey of 3,805 women in the Sudan, of which 89 percent were circumcised, shows that 90 percent of those circumcised believe that the practice should continue and that 96 percent said that they would circumcise their daughters.[26] In fact many women in these cultures appear to regard circumcised genitalia as beautiful and uncircumcised as "barbaric."[27] Moreover, Shweder believes that the view that FGM is injurious to women is overstated and unsubstantiated. Are Shweder's argument's persuasive? Consider them in light of the capabilities approach of Martha Nussbaum, echoed in the essay of Rosemarie Tong. According to Nussbaum, a woman's choices and affiliations are not necessarily her own unless she has been able to make use of all her capabilities. Are the views of the Sudanese women surveyed reliable indications of their wishes? Finally, as you evaluate the arguments for and against FGM, reflect also on the obstacles they suggest for the enterprise of global bioethics. Does the presence of genuine, well-intentioned disagreement over what many would regard as an "easy case" bode poorly for the future of global bioethics? Or should it be viewed as evidence of a great need for future scholarship and articulation of a new bioethical paradigm? Does the existence of human rights that seem to transcend culturally specific ethical values support the enterprise of global bioethics or are they just Western values discussed in yet different clothes? We will visit this question again in the next chapter when we discuss health and human rights.

Globalisation or Westernisation?
Ethical Concerns in the Whole Bio-Business

GODFREY B. TANGWA

Introduction

A Handshake Should Not Go Beyond the Elbow

The above African proverb is the convenient nail in conceptual space, as it were, on which I would like to hang the spirit, as distinguished from the mere letter, of what I would like to say here. I will not, of course, attempt to interpret the proverb because another proverb says that 'it is the fool who says a proverb and then proceeds to interpret it himself/herself' or, alternatively, that 'it is only to the fool that when you say a proverb you also need to interpret it'. This African proverbial approach will help me in avoiding too much bluntness which often tends to turn dialogue into confrontation. Furthermore, since Western space and time worship will surely not permit me to say all I could have said here, I would like to commend rather my figures of speech and not the speech itself to your further reflection.

Globalisation

Globalisation, as a descriptive process, has been made possible and inevitable by advances in science and technology, especially in locomotion and communication technologies. The net result of these advances has been increased contact between the various peoples and cultures that populate the world. Thanks to this state of affairs, the world is today, unlike yesterday, aptly described as a 'global village'. This villagisation of the world should have as one of its logical consequences the slow but sure transformation of the world into a 'rainbow village', by analogy with our appellation of South Africa, in our optimistic moments, as the 'Rainbow Nation'. Resistance to this aspect of the process of globalisation, exemplified in the savagery with which persons from some parts of the globe are sometimes forcibly excluded from some other parts, cannot but create a lot of tension within the process. Modern technology, in general, and locomotion and communication technologies, in particular, are, of course, inventions of the Western world which have been very effectively used, *inter alia*, in colonising and dominating peoples in other parts of the world.

Globalisation, as a prescriptive process, arises from increasing awareness of both the diversity as well as interdependence of the various parts, peoples and cultures of the world. Globalisation in this sense, is essentially a moral concept. Underlying such blueprints of globalisation as the *Biodiversity Convention* and the *Human Genome Project*, are clear ethical impulses, concerns and imperatives. But between globalisation as a descriptive process and globalisation as a prescriptive ideal, there is a difference which involves the danger that globalisation might end up as or, in fact, might not and never has been more than, mere Westernisation, given the history and reality of Western industrial-technological power, colonisation of non-Westerners, domination and insensitivity to all things non-Western.

Westernisation

The European *Industrial Revolution* of the 18th and 19th centuries drew its impetus from the slogan that 'knowledge is power' convertible into commercial value, from the idea that all knowledge is unqualifiedly good, from the belief that nature is, in principle at least, completely knowable and controllable, and from perception of the universe as something which ought to be explored, subdued, dominated and exploited. These ideas and the attitudes they created had their origins and foundation in Judaeo-Christianity and its remarkable creation myths, but they led, paradoxically, to secularisation, desacrelisation and profanation of everything in the universe—the very antithesis of the Judaeo-Christian ethic. The spirit of omnivorous discovery which the *Industrial Revolution* engendered and made possible in Europeans guided them to all parts of the globe where they discovered peoples and cultures so different from theirs that they felt reluctant to qualify them as 'human'. From then on, Europeanisation (Westernisation) of other peoples and cultures appeared naturally in their eyes as humanisation and civilisation. It is in this way that both altruistic and egoistic motives became mixed and confounded in the relationship between the technologically very advanced Western world, peoples and culture and other (technologically less advanced) worlds, peoples and cultures. Since the Industrial Revolution, technology has been propelled to great heights by Western commerce and the profit motive, by war and the will to dominate, by pure epistemological and scientific curiosity, as well as (occasionally) by the altruistic urge to improve human well-being. In this process, Western culture has developed the penchant for patenting, monopolising and commercialising any of its so-called discoveries and a knack for spreading and promoting its ideas, vision, convictions and practices under the guise of universal imperatives of either rationality or morality which ought to be binding on all human beings who are sufficiently rational and moral. I have metaphorically described Western culture as having a big mouth but small ears (Tangwa, 1996, p. 185).

Morality

In spite of the remarkable pluralism and cultural diversity of the world, core ethical values are evidently the same for all human beings, if these are carefully separated from, and not confused with, mere customs, cultural practices, preferences, idiosyncrasies and positive laws. Law and custom are evidently subordinate to morality in the sense that they are ultimately to be justified by reference to morality but not vice versa. A morally unjustifiable law or custom ought not to exist whereas a moral or ethical principle cannot be justified or unjustified by reference to either law or custom. Moreover, it is in the nature of laws and customs to differ from place to place, from culture to culture and even from time to time within the same place and culture, whereas such a situation would be intolerable in morality, properly considered. Universalisability, as Kant and other Western moralists have so rightly argued, is a necessary and indispensable condition of morality. We recognise moral rules from their unconditional imperativeness (or imperative unconditionality). This does not, of course, mean that there cannot be justifiable exceptions to moral rules but only that such putative exceptions do not reverse the rule or, in any way, affect the validity of its imperativeness and unconditionality. (Wiredu, 1995, p.39). 'Moral relativism', in my view, can, therefore, only arise from somehow conflating or confusing customs, laws and practices with morality, strictly considered. Morality can and should overrule both law, custom and practice, in fact, morality can and should overrule every other thing except its own very rationale.

A Good Will

From the subjective and practical point of view, the first and most important principle of morality is what in Lamnso' is called *shiliv she jung shi* (a *good will*, literally, a good heart). If we always act out of good will, we can never be morally blame-worthy. However, a good will is only a necessary but not a sufficient condition for moral rightness. A subjectively good will is putatively quite compatible with objective moral error. This has the consequence that one may act from a morally worthy motive and still be morally wrong—subjectively right but objectively wrong.

This apparently contradictory situation is due to human epistemological limitations. A good will excludes the possibility of knowingly and willingly doing wrong. And, if all moral evil knowingly and willingly done were to be excluded from the sum-total of evil in the world, there would surely be very little left. Kant was also quite right, at least, in considering a good will to be central to all morality. Kant derived his famous doctrine of the *categorical imperative* from the notion of a good will. In the opening sentence of his *Groundwork of the Metaphysic of Morals*, Kant declares:

> It is impossible to conceive of anything in the world, or even out of it, which can be taken as good without qualification, save only a good will.

Willing is, of course, something subjective and there is, therefore, an important subjective element or component to morality, captured in the idea and importance of *conscience*, which does not, however, exclude inter-subjectivity or the possibility of objective appraisal of what is or is not moral.

All this has the consequence that there is nothing in the world, or even out of it, which is superior to morality. And it is in this light that we can consider positive laws, customs and taboos as derivatives of, and aids to, morality, even though they are liable to be conflated and confused with it.

Bioethics

Bioethics, as an area of particular concern, is a recent specialised branch of morality, whose focus is the dilemmas, questions, worries and controversies arising from modern Western medicine, biomedical research, bioengineering, biotechnology and attendant/allied processes. Of course, science and technology, in general, have always raised ethical problems and there is a sense in which Bioethics has always been present in all human societies at all times. Professor Van Rensselaer Potter of the University of Wisconsin-Madison, USA, claims to have coined the word 'bioethics' in 1970. (Potter, 1996, p. 2). By it he intended an extension of ethics to cover not only medical ethics but environmental and agricultural ethics, in short, 'the application of ethics to all of life' (ibid). He complains that the medical profession has seized upon the term 'bioethics' and tried to restrict it to medical ethics. Thus, in a broader sense, bioethics can be considered as covering all possible ethical problems that arise or may arise, not only from or within the biological sciences, but in relation to life and living things generally. However, bioethics, in the more restricted sense, is of special concern, because of the potential of biotechnology to transform our lives and our world and because of the rapidity, novelty and magnitude of the problems that it raises.

Biodiversity

The biodiversity of the world, which is similar to its cultural and linguistic diversity, is a gift, so to speak, of evolution and certainly a value which we need only to recognise, accept, use and protect. The Darwinian theory of evolution, with its key concepts of *natural selection* through *survival of the fittest,* may go a long way in explaining biodiversity as a scientific fact, but biodiversity cannot be completely explained and remains, partly, one of the mysteries of nature. Natural gene mutation and natural selection through survival of the fittest can be considered as nature's own version of biotechnology, with an in-built safety mechanism for nature as a whole. This 'natural biotechnology', as it were, is, by its very nature, gradual and piecemeal, always allowing any ecosystem, including soil, plants, animals and humans, the chance to adjust as painlessly and imperceptibly as possible to changes. Human biotechnology, on the other hand, lacks this advantage and, therefore, ought to proceed more cautiously, always attempting in advance, as far as possible, to assess carefully its short, medium and long-term impact and consequences. Such assessment ought to include the possible cumulative effects on the socio-economic and cultural practices and way of life of all communities likely to be affected by any putative technological intervention and should, in any case, never be limited merely to considerations of marketability and profitability. Failure to do this would be tantamount to using biotechnology in a reckless and ethically unjustifiable way.

Globalisation and Westernisation

Some of the earth's most valuable wealth, in the form of remarkable variety of biological entities and forms, is to be found in the technologically relatively innocent parts of the earth. Africa, for instance, presents remarkable diversity and variety, not only ecologically and culturally, but biologically. This diversity and variety is what has shaped and coloured African social systems, ethical, religious and metaphysical ideas. The African metaphysical world-view can be aptly

described as eco-bio-communitarian (Tangwa, 196, p.192), implying the recognition and acceptance of interdependence and peaceful coexistence between the earth, plants, animals and human beings. This world-view can be contrasted with its Western counterpart which can be described as individualistic and anthropocentric. Within the African outlook, humans are more humble and more cautious, epistemologically more sceptical of their own capabilities and, therefore, practically more conciliatory and respectful of other people, animals, plants, inanimate things and the invisible/intangible forces of nature. They are, thus, also more timorous of tampering with nature and more disposed towards an attitude of *live and let live.*

If this background is not taken into consideration in 'globalising' Western technologies, then globalisation may be simply co-terminus with Westernisation. It would be like a handshake that has gone beyond the elbow. Africans are no strangers to the experience of losing a whole arm in what they went into believing to be a friendly handshake. Technology, in itself, has nothing to do with what people think or believe, how they conceive of or organise their lives. The globalisation of Western technology should not be accompanied by the globalisation of Western ways of thinking and acting, Western ways, manners and style of doing things, Western idiosyncrasies and eccentricities. Other cultures should be able to beg, borrow or buy Western technology without having to take it along with all its Western packaging, its entire surrounding value system.

If globalisation is to be meaningful and justifiable in a world populated by different cultural groups, whose respective material conditions, level of technological development, powers, ideas, experiences and attitudes differ rather widely, then it must be premised on certain pertinent presuppositions. Some of such pertinent presuppositions, in my view, would be the following: (1) While technology in itself is a good thing, the USES to which it may be put is an entirely different matter over which even the technologically innocent may have useful contributions to make; (2) Globalisation implies and is impossible without interaction and dialogue between the different components of the globe; (3) Dialogue further implies both talking and listening between the various dialoguing groups, each with its own peculiar modes, manner and style of expression; (4) In any genuine dialogue there must be the readiness and willingness on all sides, not only to *teach* but also to *learn,* even from the most taciturn of interlocutors. (Wiredu, 1997, p.41).

Conclusion

In typical African fashion and manner, let me end with a true story which may also be a significant metaphor. As an undergraduate philosophy student, I once got an over-the-long-vacation assignment to 'describe God in the conception of your own people and then critically asses such description in the light of theism'. On holidays back home, I went to seek help from an elderly traditional Nso' priest. In the course of chatting about several other unrelated issues, I asked him: 'Taa (elder), how would you describe God, the way we, Nso' people see him?' He paused briefly and responded:

'You want me to describe God?'
'Yes', I confirmed eagerly.
'Are you a fool?', he queried.

I did not answer his rhetorical question, but carefully explained about my assignment. He said nothing for a long time and soon other visitors came in and the conversation shifted to other things. I thought he had forgotten about my question by the time I greeted him and started leaving, disappointment and frustration vaguely forming in my mind. But, just as I was about to step out of the door, he told me:

'When you get back to school, ask your teacher for me whether he has nothing useful to teach you. He says you should describe God, but where have you seen God? If you describe God correctly or wrongly, how would he know when he himself has never seen God?'

I went away in silence. (Silence is very important in traditional African informal pedagogy and learning.)

It is only recently that this encounter re-occurred to me when I started reflecting on the use we make of metaphors and how, very often, we forget that they are metaphors and take them quite literally, and how this can be the cause of a lot of trouble. 'Jesus is the son of God' or 'Mary conceived him without losing her virginity' are clearly metaphors. It even appears to me that our conception of God cannot but be a metaphor which may run us into many problems if we take it too literally. Faithful adherents of all the great Western religions would, no doubt, consider these views heretical. But it really appears to me that there may be some correlation between people's conception of God and their general attitudes and behaviour. May it not be the case that people, groups, communities or cultures whose metaphor about God is too clear, definite, confident and uncompromising behave in like manner, which cannot but lead to fanatical extremism and intolerance when up against a similar but opposite attitude and behaviour from others? Consider for a moment the intractability of the perennial disputes and conflicts within and between adherents of the different great Western faiths which have given birth to the worst forms of terrorism in the world today.

May it not be a matter of significance that all African religions are somewhat vague, non-doctrinaire, non-proselytising, unsystematised and unorganised? African peoples and cultures also happen to be one of the most tolerant and accommodating on earth, with the broadest *live and let live* attitude and latitude.

It could be said that Western society today is one in which God is, more or less, dead, in spite of its monumental churches, cathedrals, mosques, synagogues etc., relics of, perhaps, a more genuinely religious epoch, which now serve mainly the function of tourist attractions. But even though God may be dead in Western society, his attributes are evidently not dead but have been appropriated by Westerners and their science and technology, their economics and philosophies, their ethics, customs and laws. Today it is much easier to defy God than to defy the Western world. One remarkable thing about Western discourse in all domains of enquiry is the relative absence of *tentativeness,* especially in discussing issues and expressing views which are likely to be controversial because others are known to hold contrary views or opinions. It is not by accident that traditional Africans generally prefer to tell a proverb, parable, simile or metaphor in answer to a very difficult or controversial issue or question. The advantage here is that, since these figures of speech and literary devices are interpretatively inexhaustible, they can easily accommodate a variety of contrary or incompatible elements.

The following questions should thus be posed: Is the Western conception and description of God as omniscient, omnipotent, omnipresent and omnibenevolent a disguised project description of Western epistemological ambitions, technological power, ubiquity and paternalistic philanthropy? Will the process of globalisation be more than another school, for the rest of us, where Western doctrinal catechetical lessons are dispensed and imbibed?

References

Potter, V.R., 1996, 'What does Bioethics Mean?' in *The AG Bioethics Forum,* Vol. 8, No. 1, pp. 2–3.

Tangwa, G. B., 1996, 'Bioethics: An African Perspective' in *BIOETHICS,* Vol. 10, No. 3, pp. 183–200.

Wiredu, K., 1995, *Conceptual Decolonisation in African Philosophy,* Ibadan, Nigeria, pp. 73.

Wiredu, K., 1997, 'African Philosophy and Inter-Cultural Dialogue' in *QUEST: Philosophical Discussions,* Vol. XI, No. 1-2, pp. 29–41.

Towards a Feminist Global Bioethics
Addressing Women's Health Concerns Worldwide

ROSEMARIE TONG

Due to technological and communication advances, we are virtually forced to recognize that not only our own people but all people are capable of feeling pain and experiencing suffering. Our media routinely flash before our eyes images of real people who are dying from AIDS in our world's rural outposts and overcrowded cities; suffering from neglect or even abuse in our world's orphanages; and huddling in our world's refugee camps. This aspect of so-called globalization invites bioethicists to develop morally sound criteria for improving people's health status and health care worldwide. Bioethics must, it seems, become more global in its scope, as justice can no longer remain blind to the fact that people live in more than their own nations. They live in the world.

But just because a global bioethics is desirable does not mean it is possible. Upon what moral foundation *can* we build a robust global bioethics? Although I do not have a complete answer to this enormously difficult question, I believe the beginnings of such an answer can be found in several approaches to bioethics. I particularly endorse those feminist approaches to bioethics that use "universal human rights" language but move beyond it to "universal human *needs*" language, thereby emphasizing the importance of people's positive as well as negative rights. If we wish to create international healthcare policies that are just, that treat all people as deserving of equal respect and consideration, we must first convince ourselves that, for all our differences, we human beings are united in our common need for freedom and well being. . . .

Towards a Global Feminist Bioethics

Given that what is good for one woman or one group of women is not necessarily good for another, both power-focused and care-focused feminist bioethicists have wondered whether women share anything in common over and beyond a few biological characteristics. In recent years feminist bioethicists have increasingly rejected not only women's sameness with men but also women's sameness to each other. At first, it might strike us as ethically counterintuitive to reject locutions such as "Policy X is (is not) in Women's best interest" or "Women want to be equal to men." After all, the idea of sameness has enabled us to develop a rich theory of human rights and the conviction that all people are created equal.

Yet, upon careful reflection, it becomes possible to see how the idea of essential human sameness can function oppressively. For example, in the course of analyzing the work of historian Kenneth Stampp, feminist philosopher Elizabeth Spelman focuses on one of his well-meaning comments, intended to break down racial barriers in the United States. In an effort to convince white men that black and white men are equal, Stampp asserted "that innately Negroes are, after all, only white men with black skins, nothing more, nothing else" (Spelman, 1988: 12). Rather than affirming Stampp's words, Spelman criticizes them as unintentionally racist. Why, she asks, is it that *black* men are "nothing more, nothing else" than white men? Why assume that black men want only to be white men? Why not assume instead that *white* men are "nothing more, nothing else" than black men—that white men want only to be black men? Could it be, asks Spelman, that white people cannot imagine black people preferring to be black?

Not wanting to fall into the trap that ensnared Stampp, feminists, including feminist bioethicists embraced the idea of difference enthusiastically. It has become routine for them to precede their analyses of any issue related to women with disclaimers such as, "Please note that I am speaking from the perspective of a white, middle-class, middle-aged, heterosexual, married with children, well-educated U.S. academic. I do not assume that what constitutes good health care for a woman like me also constitutes good health care for a woman unlike me. Nevertheless, I will share my thoughts for what they are worth." But, just how *worthy* are moral thoughts without any *prescriptive* or *normative* force? And if women's differences truly preclude there being anything the same about all women, then how can feminist bioethicists speak forcefully about women's rights, gender justice, or sexual equality? Clearly, in its extreme form, the idea of difference, like the idea of sameness, is an ethically counterproductive concept.

Fortunately, as a result of greater participation in international conferences and organizations, feminists are now rethinking the balance between women's differences and samenesses. Particularly successful was the Beijing Women's

Conference (1995). It succeeded, where earlier women's conferences faltered (Mexico, Copenhagen, Nairobi), because it was able to draw on previous groundwork through regional and global electronic networks and because it insisted on linking women's rights to human rights. Even more importantly for our purposes, the Beijing Women's Conference spent far less time on "ideological slogoneering" than on identifying "practical targets" for action that would satisfy specific groups of women's immediate needs for better health care, education and employment (Dickenson, 1997: 107–113).

Among the feminists who have contributed to developing a theory that fits the practice of a feminist global bioethics is Uma Narayan, a woman of Indian background who now lives in the United States. In her book *Dislocating Cultures: Identities, Traditions, and Third World Feminisms,* Narayan observes that Westerners should acknowledge their role in creating unfavorable representations of the so-called Other as uncivilized, primitive, barbaric, or animalistic, and for letting their negative ideas about the Other be used as conceptual ammunition to defend unjust colonial policies. However, she adds the important point that Westerners should not seek forgiveness for their past sins against people in the East by refusing to engage in any moral criticism of them now (Narayan, 1997: 127). Narayan stresses that she does not want guilt-ridden Westerners to unreflectively respect her native land as incapable of evil, but to insist with her that what was wrong about U.S. segregation and South African apartheid is what is wrong about the Indian caste system, for example. In addition, Narayan pleads that when she, Uma Narayan, condemns female genital mutilation, the sale of human organs, or sex-selective abortion, she not be dismissed by Westerners as, afterall, only a "Westernized" Indian woman, unable to speak on behalf of "authentic" Indian women, who presumably endorse every feature of their soci-

ety, no matter how morally dubious or unjust (Narayan, 1997: 146).

Narayan's conviction that Westerners, but particularly Western feminists need to apply the same moral standards to all people is not unique to her. It is a viewpoint shared by an increasing number of feminists who believe that now is the time to develop a "feminist humanism" that combines "the respect for differences characteristic of progressive movements since the 1960s with the universalistic aspirations of earlier liberatory traditions" (Holstrom, 1998: 288). For example, feminist political theorist Susan Moller Okin has argued that feminists must talk about *women's* needs generically, for, as she sees it, the category of gender is of great political importance. She stresses that without the concept of Woman, feminists have no way to make cross-cultural comparisons about male-female inequalities and to condemn them as wrong (Okin, 1995: 294).

Although all women do not experience a particular gender inequality to the same extent and degree, Okin stresses they all experience it in some way or another, for the same reasons, and with the same consequences (Okin, 1995: 294). Because virtually all societies regard women as the "second sex," as somehow existing for men's sexual pleasure and reproductive use, and as less intelligent, strong, and rational than men, women throughout the world tend to have less sexual freedom, fewer reproductive rights, and a worse socioeconomic status than men. Indeed, at all of the most recent International Women's Conferences, including the relatively unsuccessful ones, women from both developed and developing nations similarly commented that their quality of life is negatively affected by virtue of their sex. They discussed how their nations's sex, reproduction, marriage, divorce, child-custody, and family-life laws lessen their lot in life; how women and girls, far more than men and boys, are sexually vulnerable; and how less healthy, wealthy, and educated their nations' women are than their nations' men (Okin, 1998: 42). Given that throughout the world men remain the "first sex," Okin comments that women's *sameness* consists simply in women's lesser or greater *subordination* to men. Therefore, women in countries where there is more gender inequality should work together with women in countries where there is less gender inequality to achieve for *all* women the kind of freedom and well-being that men typically have. For more advantaged women to help less advantaged women is not an exercise in cultural imperialism on the part of more advantaged women, but simply their response to a call for assistance.

Okin's growing conviction that the idea of women's sameness—indeed of a common human nature—can be used to liberate rather than oppress women has been further developed by feminist philosopher and political theorist Martha Nussbaum. Nussbaum argues that a conception of the human being and human functioning is the best basis for evaluating women's position *vis á vis* men's position around the world. Just because some philosophers have conflated human nature with male nature, thus wrongly defining the quintessential human being as a *male* human being, does not mean that feminists cannot appropriate the concept of human nature effectively and use it to prove that women are no less fully human than men. This being the case, there is no basis for the claim that men and women should have different norms of human functioning, or that they should exercise the same norms in different spheres—men in the public realm and women in the private realm. What all persons need, in Nussbaum's estimation, is an equal opportunity to develop two sets of functional human capabilities—those which, if left undeveloped, render a life not human at all; and those which, if left undeveloped, render a human life less than a *good* human life. Among the latter capabilities, Nuss-

baum lists some which are of particular interest to all bioethicists: (1) "being able to live to the end of a human life of normal length, not dying prematurely or before one's life is so reduced as to be not worth living;" (2) "being able to have good health . . . adequate nourish(ment) . . . shelter . . . opportunities for sexual satisfaction and choice in matters of reproduction;" and (3) "being able to live with concern for and in relation to animals, plants, and the world of nature" (Nussbaum, 1999: 41).

To be sure, Nussbaum's complete list of functional human capabilities—(1) life (2) bodily health and integrity, (3) bodily integrity, (4) senses, imagination, and thought, (5) emotions, (6) practical reason, (7) affiliation, (8) other species, (9) play and (10) control over one's environment—is the product of her own mind. As such it is contestable on the grounds that, once again, a self-appointed Western/Westernized expert is determining what is to count and not count as a functional human capability for human beings throughout the world. But this objection is surmountable. Nussbaum's list is not a novel one. In fact, it is virtually indistinguishable from the "capabilities lists" that are produced whenever and wherever people are permitted to freely reflect upon and express their basic aspirations for themselves and their children.

According to Jürgen Habermas, for example, before we endorse the norms of a community, we must determine whether its members *genuinely* accept them. In order to make this determination, we must ask ourselves whether, under conditions of undistorted communication, virtually all of the community's members would affirm their community's norms as rational ones for themselves. If the answer to this question is "no," we should, in Habermas's estimation, conclude that at least some members of the community in question have been tricked, mystified, or otherwise manipulated into espousing and even internalizing its norms (Habermas, 1979: 75).

If Habermas is correct, and I believe he is, we should not assume that simply because an individual woman defends cultural practices or institutions that demean, denigrate, neglect or harm other women, that woman would not, upon reflection and given certain opportunities, speak out against and even rebel against such practices. Defending what she terms a "capabilities approach" to constructing a globally just ethics, Nussbaum comments:

> The capabilities approach insists that a woman's affiliation with a certain group or culture should not be taken as normative for her unless, on due consideration, with all the capabilities at her disposal, she makes that norm her own. We should take care to extend to each individual full capabilities to pursue the items on the list and then see whether they want to avail themselves of these opportunities. Usually they do, even when tradition says they should not. Martha Chen's work with [Indian] widows like Metha Bai reveals that they are already deeply critical of the cultural norms that determine their life quality. One week at a widows' conference in Bangelore was sufficient to cause these formerly secluded widows to put on forbidden colors and to apply for loans; one elderly woman, 'widowed' at the age of seventy, danced for the first time in her life, whirling wildly in the center of the floor . . . Why should women cling to a tradition, indeed, when it is usually not their voice that speaks or their interests that are served (Nussbaum, 1999: 146–147).

Conclusion

Because I recognize both the samenesses and differences among women, and for that matter, human beings, I believe that in order to speak meaningfully of a global bioethics, feminist bioethicists must perform two tasks. First, they must create safe moral spaces for dialogue in which all voices are free to speak, and in which those who do not ordinarily speak are encouraged to speak first. This would create the kind of forum in which the authority of so-called expertise demurs to the authority of lived experi-

enced. According to Jaggar, for example, it takes effort, skill, and the practice of such virtues as responsibility, self-discipline, sensitivity, respect, and trust. It also assumes "that understanding between diverse people becomes possible only when those involved *care* for each other as specific individuals" (Jaggar, 1995: 116). In this connection, Jaggar notes an article in which feminist philosophers María Lugones and Elizabeth Spelman propose that neither self-interest nor duty but friendship is the only appropriate motive for Anglo and Hispanic women, for example, to come together to iron out their differences. Lugones specifically writes that "[a] non-imperialist feminism requires that . . . you [Anglo feminists] follow us into our world out of friendship" (Spelman and Lugones, 1992: 363). Feminist bioethicists must imaginatively and "electronically," if not also physically, travel to each other's worlds. Together they must create a greater number of democratic forums such as the one created during the Beijing Women's Conference (1995) which enabled feminist bioethicists to obtain the kind of data they need to help shape health care policies, practices, and institutions that are globally, and not simply locally just.

Yet, as important as it is for feminist bioethicists to engage in genuine dialogue, it is even more important for them to actively work to eliminate the gap between the world's "Haves" and "Have-Nots," particularly because far more women and girls than men and boys populate the class of the "Have-Nots." If feminist bioethicists want to improve women's health worldwide, they must do more to educate themselves about women's health issues in both the developing and developed nations. They must also organize and participate in more conferences such as the recent Feminist Approaches to Bioethics Network Conference (2000) held in London, where over a hundred feminist bioethicists from approximately twenty-five countries gathered together to educate each other about their specific problems, concerns, and interests. Although everyone learned much about how the "Other" sees the world, on the whole, feminist bioethicists from developed nations discovered just how little they knew about the plight of women in most developing countries.

Among the lessons learned at global conferences by feminist bioethicists from the developed world are precisely how discrimination against women and girls in many developing countries often begins before birth in the form of systematic prenatal diagnosis and techniques and abortion for the purpose of sex-selection. The fact that many Indian and Chinese women, for example, willingly abort their female fetuses is, of course, not surprising. Knowing just how difficult it is to be a woman as opposed to a man in their societies, some Indian and Chinese view no life at all as preferable to life as a woman (Myntti, 1998: 143).

Discrimination against females does not, of course, end in the womb. In many developing societies it continues in particularly blatant ways throughout childhood. For example, throughout South Asia and the Arab world, girls typically receive less food and less health care than boys. As a result, girls' growth may be stunted from the combined effect of malnutrition and untreated illnesses. Already weakened, these girls grow yet weaker when they begin what will probably be but the first of many pregnancies. In developing nations where fertility is still relatively high—about four children per woman— the physical and psychological demands of child bearing and child rearing typically lead to so-called maternal-depletion syndrome, characterized by severe anemia (Myntti, 1998: 144).

Of course, like women in developed nations, women in developing nations have all sorts of health concerns. Their problems are not limited to reproductive and sexual concerns. Yet many feminist bioethicists in the developed nations have paid little attention to anything other than the fertility rates of women in many developing nations and the practice of female genital cutting (female circumcision/female genital mutilation). Not surprisingly, many thoughtful women in the developing nations have criticized this myopic tendency for two reasons.

First, women in the developing nations believe that feminists in the developed nations frequently fail to understand that the main concerns of women in the developing nations are more social and economic than sexual and reproductive in nature. For example, at a very large international women's conference in Nairobi, Kenya held in 1985, Nawal el Saadawi, an Egyptian writer, lamented that "Western women often go to countries such as Sudan and 'see' only clitoridectomy, but never notice the role of multinational corporation and their exploited labor" (Gillian, 1991: 224). As Saadawi sees it, women in developed nations frequently fail to appreciate the extent to which *they* contribute to the economic and political oppression of women (and men) in developing nations. The same U.S. woman who is willing to attend protests against clitoridectomy might not be willing to attend protests against the multinational corporation that pays its employees in developing nations meager wages. As a result of this practice, the corporation can pay its employees in developed nations generous salaries.

Second, and relatedly, women in developing nations are bothered when feminist bioethicists in developed nations do not look at the health-related problems of women in developed nations through the eyes of women in developing nations. Feminist bioethicists in the developed nations need to understand that from the point of view of many women in the developing nations, feminists in the developed nations are "spoiled." Their concerns—for example, too much elective cosmetic surgery, a rash of eating disorders, multiple pregnancies caused by IVF, and the race to create perfect babies—would evaporate were their advantaged nations willing to transfer more of their health care resources to disadvantaged nations. The money some

Western women spend on perfecting their bodies could instead be spent on corrective surgeries for the maimed and scarred victims of torture and war throughout the world. Similarly, the money some women in the developed nations spend on diet drugs, "diet doctors," and diet books could instead be spent on much needed food supplies for people in developing nations who would be glad to eat a full meal.

Clearly, if U.S. feminist bioethicists, for example, want to improve women's health status and health care worldwide, they must try harder than they have in the past to understand what women in all sorts of nations want for themselves and their daughters. What they will probably discover is that, generally, all people want the same things: health, wealth, happiness, security, family and friends, work, and so on. It is just that they want these same things differently.

Particularly instructive in this connection is a study conducted by Rosalind Petchesky and Karen Judd. They studied how low-income, urban women in seven, very different nations (Brazil, Egypt, Malaysia, Mexico, Nigeria, Philippines, and the United States) interpret what the Western world terms "women's reproductive rights." Despite the fact that the women in the study shared neither the same political and religious beliefs nor the same cultural and social traditions, all of them used the idea of "motherhood" to justify their conviction that it should be up to them to decide the size of their families since women and not men "suffer the greatest burdens, pains and responsibilities of pregnancy, child bearing and child rearing" (Petchesky and Judd, 1998: 362).

Feminist bioethicists in the developed nations, particularly in the U.S., who focus on theory must develop theoretical perspectives that better reflect the enormous strides feminist activists have made to improve the status of women's health worldwide. In other words, at least in the U.S., feminist bioethicists need to be as serious about the justice of redistribution as they have been about the justice of recognition

moving beyond a celebration of diversity to narrowing the gaps between the different lives the "Haves" and "Have-nots" of this world respectively lead.

In a recent article, philosopher Margaret P. Battin has argued that given "stark differences in life expectancy around the world, from as high as 80 in the richest nations to below 50 in the poorest," people in the developed world should consider not spending excessive amounts of money in order to prolong their lives for at most a month or two. What is more, argues Battin, the monies saved by people in the developed nations, who decline expensive life-prolonging treatment, should be redistributed to people in the developing nations in an effort to fund the basic health care measures that would increase their life expectancy (Battin, 2000: 1). Feminist bioethicists in the developed world must honestly confront whether they are really interested in creating the kind of structures and systems that would facilitate the kind of global redistribution program Battin envisions.

The picture of justice that most inspires me is not the image of justice blindfolded and holding a sword and scales, but that of the Greek goddess Nemesis—she of the "Third Eye"—continually looking for wrongdoers, for oppressors, for those who would deprive anyone, particularly the most vulnerable members of a population of what they need to lead a truly *good* human life. Unless we continually remind ourselves what is wrong about a world in which some of us live well into our 80's and 90's, while others of us die before we have had a chance to live; in which some of us go on diets and pay cosmetic surgeons to excise our excess flesh, while others of us starve or beg for food; and in which some of us have access to life-saving technologies, abundant pharmaceuticals, and every manner and fashion of care giver conceivable, while others of us drink contaminated water, breathe foul air, and lack the simplest of immunizations, feminist bioethicists will fail. They will fall tragically short of their core goal; namely, making the realm of

health care one that structures and organizes itself so as to serve women and men (as well as all
races, classes and nations) equally, for in the end
we are all the same, united as we are in our car-
nality and mortality.

References

Angier, N. (1991) Women Join the Ranks of Science
But Remain Invisible at the Top. *The New York Times*
May 21, 88.

Battin, M.P. (2000) Global Life Expectancies and the
Duty to Die. In: J.M. Humber and R.F. Almeder
(Eds.), *Is There a Duty to Die?* (pp. 1–21). Totowa,
NJ.: Humana Press.

Bordo, S. (1993) *Unbearable Weight: Feminism, Western Culture and the Body.* Berkeley: University of
California.

Clancy, C. and Massion, C. (1992) American
Women's Healthcare: A Patchwork Quilt with
Gaps. *JAMA* 14, 268.

Clark, A. (1985) Subtle Forms of Sterilization Abuse:
A Reproductive Rights Analysis. In: R. Arditti, R.
Duelli, D. Klein and S. Minden (Eds.), *Test-Tube
Women: What Future for Motherhood?* London: Pan-
dora Press.

Dickenson, D. (1997) Counting Women In: Globalization, Democratization, and the Women's Movement. In: A. McGrew (Eds.), *The Transformation of
Democracy* (pp. 97–120). Cambridge: Polity Press.

Gillian, A. (1991) Women's Equality and National Liberation. In: C.T. Mohanty, A. Russo, and L. Torres
(Eds.), *Third World Women and the Politics of Feminism* (pp. 215–236). Bloomington: Indiana University Press.

Habermas, J. (1979) *Communication and the Evolution
of Society.* Boston: Beacon Press.

Hoagland, S.L. (1991) Some Thoughts about Caring.
In: C. Card (Ed.), *Feminist Ethics* (pp. 246–264).
Lawrence: University Press of Kansas.

Hoagland, S.L. (1992) Why Lesbian Ethics? *Hypatia*
7, 195–206.

Holstrom, N. (1998) Human Nature. In: A.M. Jaggar
and I. M. Young (Eds.), *A Companion to Feminist Philosophy* (pp. 280–288). Oxford: Blackwell.

Jaggar, A.M. (1995) Abortion and a Woman's Right to
Decide. In: C.C. Gould and M.W. Wartofsky (Eds.),
Women and Philosophy: Toward a Theory of Liberation
(pp. 347–364). New York: Putnam's.

Lugones, M. and Spelman, E.V. (1992). Have We Got
a Theory for You! Feminist Theory, Cultural Impe-
rialism, and the Demand for 'The Woman's Voice.'
In: J.A. Kournay, J.P. Sterba and R. Tong (Eds.),
Feminist Philosophies (pp. 474–486). Englewood
Cliffs, NJ: Prentice-Hall.

Lynn, J. (1992) Travels in the Valley of the Shadow. In:
H. Spiro, M.G. McCrea Curner, E. Peschel, and D.
St. James (Eds.), *Empathy and the Practice of Medi-
cine* (pp. 40–53). New Haven: Yale University Press.

Merton, V. (1996) Ethical Obstacles to the Participation
of Women in Biomedical Research. In: S.M. Wolf
(Ed.), *Feminism & Bioethics: Beyond Reproduction* (pp.
216–251). New York: Oxford University Press.

Myntti, C. (1998) Women and Health. In: N.P.
Stromquist (Ed.), *Women in the Third World: An En-
cyclopedia of Contemporary Issues* (pp. 143–147). New
York: Garland Publishing, Inc.

Mullett, S. (1989) Shifting Perspectives: A New Ap-
proach to Ethics. In: L. Code. S. Mullett and C.
Overall (Eds.), *Feminist Perspectives: Philosophical
Essays on Method and Morals.* Toronto: University of
Toronto Press.

Narayan, U. (1997) *Dislocating Cultures: Identities, Traditions, and Third-world Feminisms.* New York: Routledge.

Noddings, N. (1984) *Caring: A Feminine Approach to
Ethics and Moral Education.* Berkeley, CA: University of California Press.

Nussbaum, M. (1999) *Sex and Social Justice.* New York:
Oxford University Press.

Okin, S.M. (1995) Inequalities Between Sexes in Different Cultural Contexts. In: M. Nussbaum and S.
Glover (Eds.), *Women, Culture and Development.* Oxford: Clarendon Press.

Okin, S.M. (1998) Feminism, Women's Human Rights,
and Cultural Differences. *Hypatia* **13,** 32–52.

Petchesky, R. and Judd, K. (Eds.) (1998) *Negotiating Reproductive Rights: Women's Perspectives Across Countries and Cultures.* London: Zed Books.

Rubia, J.H. (1991) Neglected Women's Health Research
Wins Funds. *The Philadelphia Inquirer* March 21, A3.

Spelman, E.V. (1998) *Inessential Woman: Problems of Exclusion in Feminist Thought.* Boston: Beacon Press.

Wendell, S. (1993) *The Rejected Body: Feminist Philosophical Reflections on Disability.* New York: Routledge.

*Report of the National Institute of Health: Opportunities
for Research on Women's Health.* Hunt Valley, Maryland: September 4–6, 1991, 19.

Female Genital Circumcision and Conventionalist Ethical Relativism

LORETTA M. KOPELMAN

Traditionally Masai girls from Kenya are circumcised at seven or eight in order to be eligible for marriage at fourteen or fifteen. Their fathers, however, are now arranging marriages for them at increasingly early ages, sometimes when they are only nine years old. A Kenya news account offers an economic explanation for this social change, saying that "fathers are motivated by greed and the desire to get their hands on the dowries they receive in exchange for their daughters as early as possible." They seek a top bride price, such as "two cows, several crates of beer and some money" before the girls are old enough to resist.[1] Masai girls want to go to school and escape marriages to men often as old as their fathers. Sometimes they run away and find sanctuary at a boarding school about an hour south of Nairobi, headed by Priscilla Nankurrai. She helps them get schooling, avoid arranged marriages, and obtain medical attention for their all-too-frequent emotional and physical scars. The girls' mothers may help them escape, although they risk beatings if discovered. A developmental consultant who is herself Masai, Naomi Kipury, says conservatives fiercely oppose schooling for girls because they believe "the girls will reject the traditions of Masai culture if they are allowed to go to school. I think some parents are trying to get their children out of school to marry them quickly and regain control. Education opens up a whole other world and they fear the girls will get lost from the community."[2]

This news account reminds us that what some of us view as child abuse, neglect, or ex-

ploitation is viewed by others as traditional family and cultural values. In many parts of the world female genital cutting, child marriages, and denying girls the same opportunities for schooling that boys receive are regarded as violations of the law. Female genital cutting, the subject of this chapter, is viewed as mutilation and abuse in many parts of the world, including the United Kingdom, France, Canada, and the United States.[3] National medical societies such as the American Medical Association and influential international agencies including UNICEF, the International Federation of Gynecology and Obstetrics, and the World Health Organization (WHO) openly condemn and try to stop these practices. Around the world, women's groups protest the practice of female genital cutting and infibulation, denying that it is just a cultural issue and arguing that these rites should be treated with the same vigor as other human rights violations.[4]

These procedures involve the removal of some, or all, of the external female genitalia, denying women orgasms and causing disease, disability, and death in women, girls, and infants in these regions. These surgical rites, usually performed on girls between infancy and puberty, are intended to promote chastity, religion, group identity, cleanliness, health, family values, and marriage. Most of the people practicing this ritual are Muslim, but it is neither required by the Koran nor practiced in the spiritual center of Islam, Saudi Arabia.[5] These rites predate the introduction of Islam into these regions.

At least 80 million living women have had some form of this mutilation, and each year 4–5 million girls have it done.[6] It is hard to collect data, however, since these rites are technically illegal in many of these countries, the unenforced remnants of colonial days. The United Nations has a special ambassador on female genital mutilation, fashion model Waris Dirie, who, like some of the little Masai girls, ran away from her home in Somalia after undergoing a form of ritual circumcision making it impossible for her to have orgasms. She believes that these practices are wrong and should be stopped but warns that well-meaning Westerners may do more harm than good by attacking African practices. She urges them to use their energies to stop these rites in their own countries.[7] The Center for Disease Control estimates that around 48,000 girls currently living in the United States are likely to undergo these rites, over half of them living in the New York City area. Parents sometimes believe it is especially important to have these procedures done in the United States, since they view it as a sex-obsessed society where it is especially necessary to control female sexuality. Like the Masai fathers, these parents fear they will lose control of their daughters if they go uncircumcised. Immigrants generally get around laws prohibiting these rites by taking their girls back home or going to practitioners within their communities.

The U.S. federal laws are relatively new, however, and immigrants may not even know about them. Senator Pat Schroeder helped frame and pass the federal law upon hearing of the plight of Fauziy Kasinga.[8] In 1994, with the help of her female relatives, she fled Togo after learning she was about to be mutilated. She was imprisoned in the United States for illegal immigration but ultimately was allowed to stay. Her case set a precedent that female genital mutilation is a form of persecution.[9] In what follows, I argue against tolerating these rites as having cultural approval in these communities. I begin by defining some terms and clarifying the problem, since "female circumcision" and "relativism" have many different meanings.

Defining Terms and Setting the Problem

Female genital cutting or circumcision is commonly classified according to three types. Type 1 circumcision is the removal of the clitoral hood or prepuce (skin around the clitoris). Type 2, or intermediary circumcision, is the removal of the entire clitoris and most or all of the labia minora. Type 3, or pharaonic circumcision, is the removal of the clitoris, labia minora, and parts of the labia majora. Infibulation refers to stitching shut the wound to the vulva from genital cutting, leaving a tiny opening so that the woman can pass urine and menstrual flow.

People who want to continue these practices resent crosscultural criticisms, seeing them as assaults on their social traditions and identity. A version of ethical relativism supports their judgment, holding that people from other cultures have no legitimate basis for such condemnation. Anthony Flew defines ethical relativism as follows: "To be a relativist about values is to maintain that there are no universal standards of good and bad, right and wrong."[10] To avoid confusion with other definitions of "ethical relativism," I will, following Louis P. Pojam,[11] call this position *conventionalist ethical relativism*. It denies the existence of any underlying universal moral principles among cultures, asserting that moral principles depend entirely on cultural notions and acceptances. It rejects all forms of objectivism (a view that social differences can have underlying similarities with universal validity).[12] David Hume disavowed conventionalist ethical relativism when he wrote, "Many of the forms of breeding are arbitrary and casual; but the thing expressed by them is still the same. A Spaniard goes out of his own house before his guest, to signify that he leaves him master of all. In other countries, the landlord walks out last, as a common mark of deference and regard."[13]

Conventionalist ethical relativism is different from, although sometimes confused with, certain noncontroversial views.[14] For example, descriptive relativism holds that notions of moral right and wrong vary among cultures (sometimes called the diversity thesis). Conventionalist ethical relativism, however, goes beyond this to claim that no crosscultural moral judgments have moral force, since something is wrong or right only by the standards of some cultural group.[15] Conventionalist ethical relativism does not stop at asserting that different rankings and interpretations of moral values or rules by different groups exist but goes on to maintain that we have no basis for saying that one is better than another. Anthropologists sometimes use the locution "ethical relativism" differently, to mean what philosophers would call "descriptive relativism." Some simply use "ethical relativism" to signal that we should be very careful about making crosscultural judgments or that it is very hard to discern underlying similarities. To add to the confusion, both philosophers and anthropologists have used the locution "cultural relativism" to refer to normative as well as descriptive views.[16]

In addition, some philosophers and anthropologists seem to advocate a weaker version of "ethical relativism," especially those attracted to postmodern views. They hold that some crosscultural judgments have moral force but show disdain for substantive and fully articulated moral theories clothed as purely rational, abstract, and universal. For example, Susan Sherwin maintains that traditional moral theorists generally support the subservience of women and concludes, "Feminist moral relativism remains absolutist on the question of the moral wrong of oppression but is relativist on other moral matters."[17] She argues that female circumcision is wrong. By maintaining that some judgments have cross-cultural moral authority, however, Sherwin is not defending conventionalist ethical relativism in the sense defined.

Female genital cutting and infibulation serve as a test case for conventionalist ethical relativism because these rites have widespread approval within the cultures that practice them and

thus on this theory are right. Yet they have widespread disapproval outside their cultures for reasons that seem compelling but on this theory lack any moral authority. Thus many discussions in ethics about female genital mutilation examine which forms of ethical relativism entail that genital cutting is a justifiable practice in societies that approve it.[18]

Despite its popularity, there is a substantial logical problem with conventionalist ethical relativism.[19] From the fact that different cultures have different moral codes or norms, it does not follow that there is no objective moral truth or standards *of any sort* underlying our different behavior. The relativists' conclusion about what is the case (there are no universal moral codes or standards of any sort) does not follow from premises about what people believe is true.[20]

In response to this logical problem the conventionalist ethical relativists might argue that our different social lives and codes offer the best evidence that there are no objective moral standards and that what is right or good is determined by social approval. Therefore, I propose to consider the evidence and argue that it does not support the plausibility of conventionalist ethical relativism or a justification for tolerance of female genital circumcision or infibulation.

Morbidity and Mortality of Female Genital Circumcision

Of the three forms of female genital mutilation, Type 1 is the least mutilating and, unlike the other types, may not preclude orgasm. Type 1 circumcision, however, is very difficult to perform without removing additional tissue.[21] Types 2 and 3 are the most popular forms of circumcision and preclude orgasms. These rituals are so widespread that they probably contribute to the belief of men and woman in these regions that sex cannot be pleasurable for women, other than knowing that they bring pleasure to their husbands.[22] More than three-quarters of the girls in the Sudan, Somalia, Ethiopia, Egypt, and other north African and southern Arabian countries undergo type 2 or type 3 circumcision, with many of the others circumcised by type 1.[23] One survey by El Dareer shows that over 98 percent of Sudanese women have had this ritual surgery, 12 percent with type 2 and 83 percent with type 3.

A series of pioneering studies conducted in the Sudan by El Dareer, in Sierra Leone by Koso-Thomas, and in Somalia by Abdalla document that female genital cutting harms girls and women in many ways, having both short- and long-term complications. Later studies confirmed their findings.[24] The operation causes immediate problems that can even be fatal. They find initial problems are pain, bleeding, infection, tetanus, and shock. The degree of harm correlates with the type of circumcision. El Dareer found that bleeding occurred in all forms of circumcision, accounting for 21.3 percent of the immediate medical problems; infections are frequent because the surgical conditions are often unhygienic. She also found that the inability to pass urine was common, constituting 21.7 percent of the immediate complications. Finally, she found that these rites cause many long-term medical complications, including difficulty in the consummation of marriage and hazardous labor and delivery. Of the women surveyed, 24.5 percent estimated that these rites cause long-term complications from urinary tract infections and 23.8 percent recognized that the rituals have caused chronic pelvic infection.[25]

As high as the rate of these reported complications are, investigator El Dareer believes that the actual rates are probably even higher for several reasons. First, there are unenforced laws against female genital cutting. Although it is nonetheless widely practiced, people are reluctant to discuss illegal activities. Second, people may be ashamed to admit that they have had complications, fearing they are to blame. Third, some women believe that female circumcision or infibulation is necessary for their health and well-being and may not fully associate these problems with the surgery. They assume that their problems would have been worse without

it. Of course, many other women, as these studies show, are well aware of the complications from these rituals.[26]

Reasons for Female Genital Cutting

Investigators have identified five primary reasons for these rites: (1) religious requirement, (2) group identity, (3) cleanliness and health, (4) virginity, family honor, and morality, and (5) marriage goals, including greater sexual pleasure for men.[27] These investigators, who are members of cultures practicing female genital mutilation, report many factual errors and inconsistent beliefs about the procedure and the goals they believe these rites serve.[28] They therefore argue that the real reasons for continuing this practice in their respective countries rest on ignorance about reproduction and sexuality and, furthermore, that these rites fail as means to fulfill established community goals.

Meets a Religious Requirement

According to these studies, the main reason given for performing female genital cutting and infibulation is that it is a religious requirement. Most of the people practicing this ritual are Muslims, but it is not a practice required by the Koran.[29] El Dareer writes that "there is nothing in the Koran to suggest that the Prophet [Mohammed] commanded that women be circumcised."[30] Female genital cutting and infibulation, moreover, is not practiced in the spiritual center of Islam, Saudi Arabia. Another reason for questioning this as a Muslim practice is that clitoridectomy and infibulation predate Islam, going back to the time of the pharaohs.[31]

Preserves Group Identity

According to the anthropologist Scheper-Hughes[32] when Christian colonialists in Kenya introduced laws opposing the practice of female circumcision in the 1930s, African leader Kenyatta expressed a view still popular today:

This operation is still regarded as the very essence of an institution which has enormous educational, social, moral, and religious implications, quite apart from the operation itself. For the present, it is impossible for a member of the [Kikuyu] tribe to imagine an initiation without clitoridectomy. . . . the abolition of *IRUA* [the ritual operation] will destroy the tribal symbol which identifies the age group and prevents the Kikuyu from perpetuating that spirit of collectivism and national solidarity which they have been able to maintain from time immemorial.[33]

In addition, the practice is of social and economic importance to many women who are paid for performing the rituals.[34]

Investigators Koso-Thomas, El Dareer, and Abdalla agree that people in these countries support female circumcision as a good practice, but only because they do not understand that it is a leading cause of sickness, or even death, for girls, mothers, and infants, and a major cause of infertility, infection, and maternal-fetal complications. They conclude that these facts are not confronted because these societies do not speak openly of such matters. Abdalla writes, "There is no longer any reason, given the present state of progress in science, to tolerate confusion and ignorance about reproduction and women's sexuality."[35] Female circumcision is intended in these cultures to honor women as male circumcision honors men, and members of cultures that practice the surgery are shocked when clitoridectomy is likened to removal of the penis.[36]

Helps to Maintain Cleanliness and Health

The belief that the practice advances health and hygiene is incompatible with stable data from surveys done in these cultures, where female genital mutilation has been linked to mortality or morbidity such as shock, infertility, infections, incontinence, maternal-fetal complications, and protracted labor. The tiny hole generally left to allow for the passage of blood and urine is a constant source of infection.[37] Koso-Thomas writes,

"As for cleanliness, the presence of these scars prevents urine and menstrual flow from escaping by the normal channels. This may lead to acute retention of urine and menstrual flow, and to a condition known as *hematocolpos*, which is highly detrimental to the health of the girl or woman concerned and causes odors more offensive than any that can occur through the natural secretions."[38] Investigators Dirie and Lindmark, completing a recent study, wrote that "the risk of medical complications after female circumcision is very high as revealed by the present study [conducted in the capital of Mogadishu]. Complications which cause the death of the young girls must be a common occurrence especially in the rural areas. . . . Dribbling urine incontinence, painful menstruations, hematocolpos, and painful intercourse are facts that Somali women have to live with—facts that strongly motivate attempts to change the practice of female circumcision."[39]

Although promoting health is given as a reason for female genital mutilation, many parents seem aware of its risks and try to reduce the morbidity and mortality by seeking good medical facilities. Some doctors and nurses perform the procedures for high fees or because they are concerned about the unhygienic techniques that traditional practitioners may use. In many parts of the world, however, these practices are illegal, and medical societies prohibit doctors and nurses from engaging in them even if it might reduce morbidity and mortality.[40]

Preserves Virginity and Family Honor and Prevents Immorality

Type 3 circumcision and infibulation is used to control women's sexual behavior by trying to keep women from having sexual intercourse before marriage or conceiving illegitimate children. In addition, many believe that types 2 and 3 circumcision are essential because uncircumcised women have excessive or even uncontrollable sexual drives. El Dareer, however, believes that this view is not consistently held in her culture, the Sudan, where women are respected and men would be shocked to apply this cultural view to members of their own families.

Beliefs that uncircumcised women have uncontrollable sexual drives, moreover, seem incompatible with the general view that sex cannot be pleasant for women, which investigators El Dareer, Koso-Thomas, and Abdalla found was held by both men and women in these cultures. Investigators also found that female circumcision and infibulation did not represent a foolproof way to promote chastity. These procedures can actually lead to promiscuity because they do not diminish desire or libido, even though they make orgasms impossible.[41] Some women continually seek experiences with new sexual partners because they are left unsatisfied in their sexual encounters.[42] Some even pretend to be virgins by getting stitched up tightly again.[43]

Furthers Marriage Goals, Including Greater Beauty for Women and Sexual Pleasure for Men

Those practicing female genital cutting not only believe that it promotes marriage goals, including greater sexual pleasure for men, but that it deprives women of nothing important, according to investigator Koso-Thomas. El Dareer and Abdalla also found widespread misconceptions that women cannot have orgasms and that sex cannot be directly pleasing to women coexisting with beliefs that these rites are needed to control women's libido and keep them from becoming "man-crazy."[44]

To survive economically, women in these cultures must marry, and they will not be acceptable marriage partners unless they have undergone this ritual surgery.[45] It is a curse, for example, to say that someone is the child of an uncircumcised woman.[46] The widely held belief that infibulation enhances women's beauty and men's sexual pleasure makes it difficult for women who wish to marry to resist this practice.[47] They view uncut female genitals as ugly.[48]

For those outside these cultures, beliefs that these rites make women more beautiful are difficult to understand, especially when surveys show that many women in these cultures attribute keloid scars, urine retention, pelvic infections, puerperal sepsis, and obstetrical problems to infibulation.[49] Even some people from within these cultures, such as Koso-Thomas, have difficulty understanding this view:

> None of the reasons put forward in favor of circumcision have any real scientific or logical basis. It is surprising that aesthetics and the maintenance of cleanliness are advanced as grounds for female circumcision. The scars could hardly be thought of as contributing to beauty. The hardened scar and stump usually seen where the clitoris should be, or in the case of the infibulated vulva, taut skin with an ugly long scar down the middle, present a horrifying picture.[50]

The investigators who conducted these studies believe that education about these misconceptions may be the most important means to stop these practices. Some activists in these cultures such as Toubia[51] and Abdalla want an immediate ban. Others encourage type 1 circumcision (removal of the clitoral hood) in order to "wean" people away from types 2 and 3 by substitution. Type 1 has the lowest association with morbidity or mortality and, barring complications, does not preclude orgasm in later life. The chance of success through this tactic is more promising and realistic, they hold, than what an outright ban would achieve; people could continue many of their traditions and rituals of welcome without causing so much harm.[52] Other activists in these countries, such as Raquiya Abdalla, object to equating type 1 circumcision in the female with male circumcision: "To me and to many others, the aim and results of any form of circumcision of women are quite different from those applying to the circumcision of men."[53] Nahid Toubia also objects because type I circumcision causes considerable, albeit unintended, harm to the clitoris.[54]

Debates over Conventionalist Ethical Relativism

Do moral judgments made by outsiders concerning these rites simply reflect their own moral codes, which carry no moral authority in another culture? For example, when international agencies such as UNICEF or WHO condemn female genital mutilation, do they just express a cluster of particular societal opinions having no moral standing in other cultures? Consider some key points of this debate over how to answer these questions.

How Do You Count Cultures?

Debates over female genital cutting and infibulation illustrate a difficulty for defenders of conventionalist ethical relativism concerning the problem of differentiating cultures. People who take the practice of female circumcision with them when they move to another nation claim that they continue to make up a distinct cultural group. Some who moved to Canada, the United States, France, and Britain, for example, resent laws that condemn the practice as child abuse, claiming interference in their culture. If ethical relativists are to appeal to cultural approval in making the final determination of what is good or bad and right or wrong, they must tell us how to distinguish one culture from another.

How exactly do we count or separate cultures? A society is not a nation-state because some social groups have distinctive identities within nations. If we do not define societies as nations, however, how do we distinguish among cultural groups, for example, well enough to say that an action is child abuse in one culture but not in another? Subcultures in nations typically overlap and have many variations. Even if we could count cultural groups well enough to say exactly how to distinguish one culture from another, how and when would this be relevant? How big or old or vital must a culture, subculture, or cult be in order to

be recognized as a society whose moral distinctions are self-contained and self-justifying?

A related problem is that there can be passionate disagreement, ambivalence, or rapid changes within a culture or group over what is approved or disapproved, as illustrated in the Masai people of Kenya. According to conventionalist ethical relativism, where there is significant disagreement within a culture there is no way to determine what is right or wrong. But what disagreement is significant? As we saw, some people in these cultures, often those with higher education, strongly disapprove of female genital cutting and infibulation and work to stop it.[55] Are they in the same culture as their friends and relatives who approve of these rituals?

It seems more accurate to say that people may belong to distinct groups that overlap and have many variations. Members of the same family may belong to different professional groups and religions, or marry into families of different racial or ethnic origins. To say that we belong to overlapping cultures, however, makes it difficult to see conventionalist ethical relativism as a helpful theory for determining what is right or wrong. To say that something is right when it has cultural approval is useless if we cannot identify distinct cultures.

Do We Share Any Methods of Assessing False Beliefs and Inconsistencies in Moral Judgments?

Critics of conventionalist ethical relativism argue that a culture's moral and religious views are often intertwined with beliefs that are open to rational and empirical evaluation, and this can be a basis of crosscultural examination and intercultural moral criticism. Defenders of female genital cutting and infibulation do not claim that this practice is a moral or religious requirement and end the discussion; they are willing to give and defend reasons for their views. For example, advocates of female genital cutting and infibulation claim that it is a means of enhancing women's health and well-being. Such claims are open to crosscultural examination because facts can be weighed to determine whether these practices promote the ends of health or really cause morbidity or mortality. Beliefs that the practice enhances fertility and promotes health, that women cannot have orgasms, and that allowing the baby's head to touch the clitoris during delivery causes death to the baby are incompatible with stable medical data.[56] Thus shared medical information and values offer an opening for genuine crosscultural discussion or criticism of the practice.

As we saw in the section discussing the morbidity and mortality associated with these rites, some moral claims can be evaluated in terms of their consistency with one another or as means to goals. These rituals are incompatible with goals to promote maternal-fetal health because they imperil mothers and infants. We need not rank values similarly with people in another culture (or our own) to have coherent discussions about casual relationships, such as what means are useful to promote the ends of maternal-fetal safety. Even if some moral or ethical (I use these terms interchangeably) judgments express unique cultural norms, then critics argue they may still be morally evaluated by another culture on the basis of their logical consistency and their coherence with stable and crossculturally accepted empirical information.

Defenders of conventionalist ethical relativism could respond that we do not *really understand* their views at all, and certainly not well enough to pick them apart. The alleged inconsistencies and mistaken beliefs we find do not have the same meaning to people raised in the culture in question. In short, some defenders of conventionalist ethical relativism argue that we cannot know enough about another culture to make any crosscultural moral judgments. We cannot really understand another society well enough to criticize it, they claim, because our feelings, concepts, or ways of reasoning are too different; our

so-called ordinary moral views about what is permissible are determined by our upbringing and environments to such a degree that they cannot be transferred to other cultures.

Philosophers point out that there are two ways to understand this objection.[57] The first is that nothing counts as understanding another culture except being raised in it. If that is what is meant, then the objection is valid in a trivial way. But it does not address the important issue of whether we can comprehend well enough to make relevant moral distinctions or engage in critical ethical discussions about the universal human right to be free of oppression.

The second, and nontrivial, way to view this objection is that we cannot understand another society well enough to justify claiming to know what is right or wrong in that society or even to raise moral questions about what enhances or diminishes life, promotes opportunities, and so on. Yet we think we can do this very well. We ordinarily view international criticism and international responses concerning human rights violations, aggression, torture, and exploitation as important ways to show that we care about the rights and welfare of other people and, in some cases, think these responses have moral authority. Travelers to other countries, moreover, quickly understand that approved practices in their own country are widely condemned elsewhere, sometimes for good reasons.

People who deny the possibility of genuine crosscultural moral judgments must account for why we think we can and should make them, or why we sometimes agree more with people from other cultures than with our own neighbors about the moral assessments of aggression, oppression, capital punishment, abortion, euthanasia, rights to health care, and so on. International meetings also seem to employ genuinely crosscultural moral judgments when they seek to distinguish good from bad uses of technology and promote better environmental safety, health policies, and so on.

Do We Share Any Goals or Values?

Although we may implement them differently, *some* common goals are shared by people from different parts of the world, for example, the desirability of promoting people's health, happiness, opportunities, and co-operation, and the wisdom of stopping war, pollution, disease, oppression, torture, and exploitation. These common values help to make us a world community. By using shared methods of reasoning and evaluation, critics argue we can discuss how these goals should be implemented. We use these shared goals, critics argue, to assess whether genital cutting is more like respect or oppression, more like enhancement or diminishment of opportunities, or more like pleasure or torture. Genuine differences among citizens of the world exist, but arguably we could not pick them out except against a background of similarities. Highlighting our differences presupposes that we share ways to do this.

Defenders of conventionalist ethical relativism argue that crosscultural moral judgments lack genuine moral authority and perpetuate the evils of absolutism, dogmatism, and cultural imperialism. People rarely admit to such transgressions, often enlisting medicine, religion, or science to arrive at an allegedly impartial, disinterested, and justified conclusion that they should "enlighten" and "educate" the "natives," "savages," or "infidels." Anthropologist Scheper-Hughes[58] and others assume that if we claim we can make moral judgments across cultures, we thereby claim that a particular culture knows best and has the right to impose its allegedly superior knowledge on other cultures.

This presupposition is incorrect because being able on some occasions to judge aspects of other cultures in a way that has moral force does not entail that one culture is always right, absolutism is legitimate, or we can impose our beliefs on others. Relativists sometimes respond that even if this is not a strict logical consequence, it is a practical result. Philosopher Susan Sherwin writes;

"Many social scientists have endorsed versions of relativism precisely out of their sense that the alternative promotes cultural dominance. They may be making a philosophical error in drawing that conclusion, but I do not think that they are making an empirical one."[59] I find even this more modest conclusion problematic, as I explain in the next section.

Does Conventionalist Ethical Relativism Promote or Avoid Oppression or Cultural Imperialism?

Defenders of ethical relativism such as Scheper-Hughes often argue that their theoretical stance is an important way to avoid cultural imperialism. I argue, in contrast, that it causes rather than avoids oppression and cultural imperialism. Conventionalist ethical relativism entails not only the affirmation that female genital cutting is right in cultures that approve it but that anything with wide social approval is right, including slavery, war, discrimination, oppression, racism, and torture. That is, if saying that an act is right means that it has cultural approval, then it follows that culturally endorsed acts of war, oppression, enslavement, aggression, exploitation, racism, or torture are right. The disapproval of other cultures, on this view, is irrelevant in determining whether acts are right or wrong. Accordingly, the disapproval of people in other cultures, even victims of war, oppression, enslavement, aggression, exploitation, racism, or torture, does not count in deciding what is right or wrong except in their own culture.

Consequently, conventionalist ethical relativism instructs us to regard as morally irrelevant the approval or objections by people in other cultures; the approval and complaints are merely an expression of their own cultural preferences and have no moral standing whatsoever in the society that is engaging in the acts in question. I have argued that this leads to abhorrent conclusions.[60] If this theoretical stance is consistently held, it leads to the conclusion that we cannot make intercultural judgments with moral force about *any* socially approved form of oppression, including wars, torture, or exploitation of other groups. As long as these activities are approved in the society that does them, they are right. Yet the world community believed that it was making important crosscultural judgments with moral force when it criticized the Communist Chinese government for crushing prodemocracy student protest rallies, apartheid in South Africa, the Soviets for using psychiatry to suppress dissent, and the slaughter of ethnic groups in the former Yugoslavia and Rwanda. In each case, representatives from the criticized society usually said something like, "You don't understand why this is morally justified in our culture even if it would not be in your society." If conventionalist ethical relativism is plausible, these responses should be as well.

Defenders of conventionalist ethical relativism may respond that cultures sometimes overlap and hence the victims' protests within or between cultures ought to count. But this response raises two further difficulties. If it means that the views of people in other cultures have moral standing and oppressors *ought* to consider the views of victims, such judgments are incompatible with conventionalist ethical relativism. They are inconsistent with this theory because they are crosscultural judgments with moral authority. Second, as we noted, unless cultures are distinct, conventionalist ethical relativism is not a useful theory for establishing what is right or wrong.

Conventionalist ethical relativists who want to defend sound social, crosscultural, and moral judgments about the value of freedom, equality of opportunity, or human rights in other cultures seem to have two choices. On the one hand, if they agree that some crosscultural norms have moral authority, they should also agree that some intercultural judgments about female genital cutting and infibulation also may have moral authority. Sherwin is a relativist taking this route,

thereby rejecting the conventionalist ethical relativism being criticized here.[61] On the other hand, if they defend this version of conventionalist ethical relativism yet make crosscultural moral judgments about the importance of values like tolerance, group benefits, and the survival of cultures, they will have to admit to an inconsistency in their arguments. For example, Scheper-Hughes advocates tolerance of other cultural value systems but fails to see that claim as being inconsistent.[62] She is saying that tolerance between cultures is *right*, yet this is a crosscultural moral judgment using a moral norm (tolerance). Similarly, relativists who say it is *wrong* to eliminate rituals that give meaning to other cultures are also inconsistent in making a judgment that presumes to have genuine crosscultural moral authority. Even the sayings sometimes used by defenders of ethical relativism (e.g., "When in Rome do as the Romans") mean that it is *morally permissible* to adopt all the cultural norms of whatever culture one finds oneself in.[63] Thus it is not consistent for defenders of conventionalist ethical relativism to make intercultural moral judgments about tolerance, group benefit, intersocietal respect, or cultural diversity.

I have argued that, given these difficulties, the burden of proof is on defenders of conventionalist ethical relativism. They must show why we cannot do something we think we sometimes ought to do and can do very well, namely, engage in intercultural moral discussion, cooperation, or criticism and give support to people whose welfare or rights are in jeopardy in other cultures. Defenders of conventionalist ethical relativism need to account for what seems to be the genuine moral authority of international professional societies that take moral stands, for example, about fighting pandemics, stopping wars, halting oppression, promoting health education, or eliminating poverty. Responses that our professional groups are themselves cultures of a sort seem plausible but are incompatible with conventionalist ethical relativism, as already discussed.

Some defenders of conventionalist ethical relativism object that eliminating important rituals from a culture risks destroying the society. Scheper-Hughes insists that these cultures cannot survive if they change such a central practice as female circumcision. This counterargument, however, is not decisive. Slavery, oppression, and exploitation are also necessary to some ways of life, yet few would defend these actions in order to preserve a society. El Dareer responds to this objection, moreover, by questioning the assumption that these cultures can survive only by continuing clitoridectomy or infibulation. These cultures, she argues, are more likely to be transformed by war, famine, disease, urbanization, and industrialization than by the cessation of this ancient ritual surgery. Further, if slavery, oppression, and exploitation are wrong, whether or not there are group benefits, then a decision to eliminate female genital multilation should not depend on a process of weighing its benefits to the group.

It is also inconsistent to hold that group benefit is so important that other cultures should not interfere with local practices. This view elevates group benefit as an overriding crosscultural value, something that these ethical relativists claim cannot be justified. If there are no crosscultural values about what is wrong or right, a defender of conventionalist ethical relativism cannot consistently make statements such as,

> one culture ought not interfere with others,
> we ought to be tolerant of other social views,
> every culture is equally valuable, or
> it is wrong to interfere with another culture.

Each claim is an intercultural moral judgement presupposing authority based on something other than a particular culture's approval.

Conclusion

Female genital cutting and infibulation cause disability, death, and disease among mothers, infants, and children. It leads to difficulty in consummating marriage, infertility, prolonged and obstructed labor, and increased morbidity and mortality. It strains the overburdened health care systems in developing countries where it is practiced with impunity. Investigators who have documented these health hazards come from these cultures but draw upon interculturally shared methods of discovery, evaluation, and explanation in concluding that female genital mutilation fails as a means to fulfill many of the cultural goals for which it is intended, other than control of female sexuality. Although many values are culturally determined and we should not impose moral judgments across cultures hastily, we sometimes seem to know enough to condemn practices such as female genital mutilation, war, pollution, oppression, injustice, and aggression. Conventionalist ethical relativism challenges this view, but a substantial burden of proof falls on upholders of this moral theory to show why criticisms of other cultures *always* lack moral authority. Because of the hazards of even type 1 circumcision, especially on children, many groups, including WHO and the AMA, want to stop all forms of ritual genital surgery on women. Unenforced bans have proven ineffective, however, since this still popular practice has been illegal in most countries for many decades.[64] Other proposals by activists in these regions focus on fines and enforcement of meaningful legislation, but education of the harms of genital cutting and infibulation may be the most important route to stop these practices.[65] Thus an effective means to stopping these practices may be to promote education.

Notes

1. Rosalind Russel, "Child Brides Rescued by Shoestring School: Masai Fathers Sell Daughters for Cows, Beer, Money," *Saturday Argus*, January 30–31, 1999, p. 13.

2. Ibid.
3. June Thompson, "Torture by Tradition," *Nursing Times* 85, no. 15 (1989): 17-18; Patricia Schroeder, "Female Genital Mutilation—A Form of Child Abuse," *New England Journal of Medicine* 331 (1994): 739–740.
4. Nah Toubia, "Female Circumcision As a Public Health Issue," *New England Journal of Medicine* 331 (1994): 712–716.
5. Asthma El Dareer, *Woman, Why Do You Weep? Circumcision and Its Consequences* (London: Zed, 1982); Daphne Williams Ntiri, "Circumcision and Health Among Rural Women of Southern Somalia as Part of a Family Life Survey," *Health Care for Women International* 14, no. 3 (1993): 215–216.
6. Ntiri, "Circumcision and Health," pp. 215–216.
7. Amy Finnerty, "The Body Politic," *New York Times Magazine,* May 9, 1999, p. 22.
8. Schroeder, "Female Genital Mutilation" pp. 739–740.
9. Sharon Lerner, "Rite or Wrong: As the U.S. Law Against Female Genital Mutilation Goes into Effect, African Immigrants Debate an Ancient Custom," *Village Voice Worldwide*; on-line http://www/villagevoice.com./inI/lerner .html Accessed March 3, 1997.
10. Anthony Flew, "Relativism," *Dictionary of Philosophy* (New York: St. Martin's, 1979), p. 281.
11. Louis P. Pojman, "Relativism," in Robert Audi, ed., *The Cambridge Dictionary of Philosophy* (Cambridge: Cambridge University Press, 1995), pp. 690–691.
12. Edward Craig, "Relativism," in Edward Craig, ed., *Routledge Encyclopedia of Philosophy* (London: Routledge, 1998), 8:189–190.
13. David Hume, *An Enquiry Concerning the Principles of Morals, 1777.* References are to section and paragraph 8:2.
14. The definition of ethical relativism used here is similar to that found in the most recent and important encyclopedias of philosophy (Craig) and two influential dictionaries of philosophy (Flew and Pojman).
15. To add to the confusion, some call ethical relativism "cultural relativism."
16. Richard Shweder, "Ethical Relativism: Is There a Defensible Version?" *Ethos* 18 (1990): 205–218.
17. Susan Sherwin, *No Longer Patient: Feminist Ethics and Health Care* (Philadelphia: Temple University Press, 1992), pp. 58, 75.
18. Sherwin, *No Longer Patient*; Loretta M. Kopelman, "Female Circumcision and Genital Mutilation," in *Encyclopedia of Applied Ethics* (1998), 2:249–259. Portions of this article were used or adapted in writing this chapter.
19. Craig, "Relativism," pp. 189–190; Flew, "Relativism," p. 281; James Rachels, *The Elements of Moral Philosophy,* 2d ed. (New York: McGraw-Hill, 1993).
20. Rachels, *Elements of Moral Philosophy.*
21. Toubia, "Female Circumcision," p. 713.
22. Ibid.; Koso-Thomas, *The Circumcision of Women* (London: Zed, 1987); Ruquiya H.D. Abdalla, *Sisters in Affliction: Circumcision and Infibulation of Women in Africa* (London: Zed, 1982).
23. El Dareer, *Woman*; Ntiri, "Circumcision and Health," pp. 215–216; Koso-Thomas, *Circumcision of Women.*
24. Loretta M. Kopelman, "Medicine's Challenge to Relativism: The Case of Female Genital Mutilation," in Ronald A. Carson and Chester R. Burns, eds., *Philosophy of Medicine and Bioethics: A Twenty-Year Retrospective and Critical Appraisal* (Dordrecht: Kluwer, 1997), pp. 221–238; Kopelman, "Female Circumcision," pp. 249–259.
25. El Dareer, *Woman*; Koso-Thomas, *Circumcision of Women*; Abdalla, *Sisters in Affliction*; June Thompson, "Torture by Tradition," *Nursing Times* 85, no. 15 (1991): 17–18.
26. Ibid.
27. El Dareer conducted her studies in the Sudan, Koso-Thomas in and around Sierra Leone, and Abdalla in Somalia.
28. El Dareer, *Woman*; Koso-Thomas, *Circumcision of Women*; Abdalla, *Sisters in Affliction*; Ntiri, "Circumcision and Health," pp. 215–216.
29. El Dareer, *Woman*; Ntiri, "Circumcision and Health," pp. 215–216.
30. El Dareer, *Woman.*
31. Ibid.; Abdalla, *Sisters in Affliction.*
32. Nancy Scheper-Hughes, "Virgin Territory: The Male Discovery of the Clitoris," *Medical Anthropology Quarterly* 5, no. 1 (1991): 25–28.
33. Ibid.

34. El Dareer, *Woman;* Koso-Thomas, *Circumcision of Women;* Abdalla, *Sisters in Affliction;* Faye Ginsberg, "What Do Women Want? Feminist Anthropology Confronts Clitoridectomy," *Medical Anthropology Quarterly* 5, no. 1 (1991): 17–19.
35. Abdalla, *Sisters in Affliction.*
36. El Dareer, *Woman.*
37. Ibid.; Koso-Thomas, *Circumcision of Women;* Abdalla, *Sisters in Affliction;* Ntiri, "Circumcision and Health," pp. 215–216.
38. Koso-Thomas, *Circumcision of Women,* p. 10.
39. M. A. Dirie and G. Lindmark, "The Risk of Medical Complication After Female Circumcision," *East African Medical Journal* 69, no. 9 (1992): 479–482.
40. Thompson, "Torture by Tradition," pp. 17–18.
41. El Dareer, *Woman.*
42. Koso-Thomas, *Circumcision of Women.*
43. El Dareer, *Woman.*
44. Lerner, "Rite or Wrong."
45. Abdalla, *Sisters in Affliction.*
46. Koso-Thomas, *Circumcision of Women.*
47. Ibid.; El Dareer, *Woman.*
48. Lerner, "Rite or Wrong."
49. Ntiri, "Circumcision and Health," pp. 215–216; Abdalla, *Sisters in Affliction.*
50. Koso-Thomas, *Circumcision of Women.*
51. Toubia, "Female Circumcision," pp. 712–716.
52. El Dareer, *Woman.*
53. Abdalla, *Sisters in Affliction.*
54. Toubia, "Female Circumcision," pp. 712–716.
55. El Dareer, *Woman;* Koso-Thomas, *Circumcision of Women;* Abdalla, *Sisters in Affliction.*
56. Koso-Thomas, *Circumcision of Women.*
57. Elliott Sober, *Core Questions in Philosophy* (New York: Macmillan, 1991); Kopelman, "Medicine's Challenge to Relativism," pp. 221–238; Kopelman, "Female Circumcision," pp. 249–259.
58. Scheper-Hughes, "Virgin Territory," pp. 25–28.
59. Sherwin, *No Longer Patient,* pp. 63–64.
60. Kopelman, "Medicine's Challenge to Relativism," pp. 221–238; Kopelman, "Female Circumcision," pp. 249–259.
61. Sherwin, *No Longer Patient.*
62. Scheper-Hughes, "Virgin Territory," pp. 25–28.
63. Ibid.
64. El Dareer, *Woman.*
65. Ibid.; Abdalla, *Sisters in Affliction;* Dirie and Lindmark, "The Risk of Medical Complication" pp. 479–482; Toubia, "Female Circumcision," pp. 712–716.

Notes

1. Isaiah Berlin, "Two Concepts of Liberty," in *Four Essays on Liberty* (London: Oxford 1969), 118.
2. Steven J. Heyman, "Constitutional Perspectives: The First Duty of Government: Protection, Liberty, and the Fourteenth Amendment," *Duke Law Journal* 1991: 507, 571.
3. James F. Childress, *Practical Reasoning in Bioethics* (Bloomington, Ind.: Indiana University Press, 1997): 237, 240–241.
4. 448 U.S. 297 (1980).
5. Ibid., 316–317.
6. President's Commission for the Study of Ethical Problems in Medicine and Biomedical and Behavioral Research, *The Ethical Implications of Differences in the Availability of Health Services, Volume One: Report* (Washington, D.C.: U.S. Government Printing Office: 1983), 16–17.
7. Ibid., 18.
8. Ibid., 20.

9. Ibid., 22.

10. Norman Daniels, *Just Health Care* (New York: Cambridge University Press, 1985).

11. Richard A. Epstein, *Mortal Peril: Our Inalienable Right to Health Care* (Reading, Mass.: Addison-Wesley: 1997), 767–82.

12. Daniel W. Brock, "Health Resource Allocation for Vulnerable Populations," in *Ethical Dimensions of Health Policy* (New York: Oxford University Press, 2002), 284.

13. Philip G. Peters, Jr., "Health Care Rationing and Disability Rights," *Indiana Law Journal* 70(1995): 491–547.

14. Caitlin J. Halligan, "Just What the Doctor Ordered: Oregon's Medicaid Process and Public Participation in Risk Regulation," *Georgetown Law Journal* 83(1995): 2697, 2723.

15. N. Christopher Marquis, "The 2002 Elections: Ballot Initiatives; Candidates Share Space with Issues Like Health Care and Marijuana Laws," *New York Times,* Nov. 6, 2002, at B-8.

16. Committee on Assuring the Health of the Public in the 21st Century, Board on Health Promotion and Disease Prevention, Institute of Medicine at the National Academies, *The Future of the Public's Health in the 21st Century* (Washington, D.C.: National Academies Press, 2003), 22.

17. James A. Tobey, "Public Healthy and the Police Power," *New York University Law Review* 4(1927): 126.

18. Amir Attaran and Lee Gillespie-White, "Do Patents for Antiretroviral Drugs Constrain Access to AIDS Treatment in Africa?" *Journal of the American Medical Association* 286(15)(2001): 1886–1892, 1886.

19. Julio Frenck and Octavio Gomez, "Globalization and the Challenges to Health Systems," *British Medical Journal* 325(2002): 95–97.

20. Declaration of Alma Ata, International Conference on Primary Health Care, USSR, Sept. 1978, Declaration V, http//www.who.int/hrp/archive/docs/almaata.html.

21. Attaran and Gillespie-White, 1886–1892 (notes omitted).

22. Margaret Battin, "Global Life Expectancies and the Duty to Die," in *Is There a Duty to Die,* eds. James M. Humber and Robert F. Almeder (Totowa, N.J.: Humana Press, 2000), 1–21.

23. Martha Nussbaum, *Sex and Social Justice* (Oxford: Oxford University Press 1999), 146–147 as quoted in Rosemarie Tong, "Towards a Feminist Global Bioethics Agenda: Addressing Women's Health Concerns Worldwide" *Health Care Analysis* (2001): 229–246.

24. 18 U.S.C. 116.

25. World Health Organization, *Female Genital Mutilation: An Overview* (Geneva, Switzerland: World Health Organization, 1998).

26. Richard Schweder, "What About Female Genital Mutilation? And Why Understanding Culture Matters in the First Place." *Daedalus* 129(2000): 209–232.

27. Ibid.

Recommended Readings

Alora, Tan, and Lumitao, Josephine M., eds. *Beyond a Western Bioethics: Voices from the Developing World.* Washington, D.C.: Georgetown University Press, 2001.

Attaran, Amir, and Gillespie-White, Lee. "Do Patents for Antiretroviral Drugs Constrain Access to AIDS Treatment in Africa?" *Journal of the American Medical Association* 286(2001): 1886–1892.

Barnard, David. "In the High Court of South Africa, Case No. 4138/98: The Global Politics of Access to Low-Cost AIDS Drugs in Poor Countries." *Kennedy Institute of Ethics Journal* 12(2002): 141–174.

Battin, Margaret. "Global Life Expectancies and the Duty to Die." In *Is There a Duty to Die?* Humber, James M., and Almeder, Robert F., eds. Totowa, N.J.: Humana Press, 2000, pp. 1–21.

Benatar, Solomon, Daar, Abdalla S., and Singer, Peter A. "Global Health Ethics: The Rationale for Mutual Caring." *International Affairs* 79(2003): 107–138.

Binswanger, Hans P. "HIV/AIDS Treatment for Millions." *Science* 292(2001): 221–223.

Brock, Dan W. "Health Resource Allocation for Vulnerable Populations." In *Ethical Dimensions of Health Policy*, Danis, Marion et al., eds. New York: Oxford University Press, 2002, pp. 283–309.

Califano, Jr., Joseph A. "Rationing Health Care: The Unnecessary Solution." *University of Pennsylvania Law Review* 140(1992): 1525–1538.

Callahan, Daniel. "Health and the Common Good: Setting Social Priorities." In *What Kind of Life: The Limits of Medical Progress.* New York: Simon and Schuster, 1990, pp. 103–134.

Cherry, Mark. "The Search for a Global Bioethics: Fraudulent Claims and False Promises." *Journal of Medicine and Philosophy* 27(2002): 683–698.

Childress, James F. *Practical Reasoning in Bioethics.* Bloomington, Ind.: Indiana University Press, 1997, pp. 237–262.

Daniels, Norman. *Just Health Care.* Cambridge, U.K.: Cambridge University Press, 1985.

Ezzell, Carol. "AIDS Drugs for Africa." *Scientific American* 283(2000): 98–103.

Frenck, Julio, and Dantes, Octavio Gomez. "Globalisation and the Challenges to Health Systems." *British Medical Journal* 325(2002): 95–97.

Halligan, Caitlin J. "Just What the Doctor Ordered: Oregon's Medicaid Process and Public Participation in Risk Regulation." *Georgetown Law Journal* 83(1995): 2697–2725.

Howson, Christopher P., Fineberg, Harvey V., and Bloom, Barry R. "The Pursuit of Global Health: The Relevance of Engagement for Developed Countries." *The Lancet* 351(1998): 586–599.

International Conference on Primary Health Care. *Declaration of Alma-Ata.* Alma-Ata, USSR, September 1978, at http://www.who.int/hpr/archive/docs/almaata.html.

James, Stephen A. "Reconciling International Human Rights and Cultural Relativism: The Case of Female Circumcision." *Bioethics* 8(1994): 1–26.

Kaul, Inge, Grunberg, Isabelle, and Stern, Marc A., eds. *Global Public Goods.* New York: Oxford University Press, 1999.

Lamm, Richard D. "Rationing of Health Care: 'Inevitable and Desirable.'" *University of Pennsylvania Law Review* 140(1992):1511–1523.

Lappe, Marc. "Values and Public Health: Value Considerations in Setting Health Policy." *Theoretical Medicine* 4(1)(1983): 71–92.

Miles, Morgan P., Munilla, Linda S., and Covin, Jeffrey G. "The Constant Gardener Revisited: The Effect of Social Blackmail on the Marketing Concept, Innovation, and Entrepreneurship." *Journal of Business Ethics* 41(2002): 287–295.

Peters, Philip G. "Health Care Rationing and Disability Rights." *Indiana Law Review* 70(1995): 119–183.

Pogge, Thomas. "Human Flourishing and Universal Justice." *Social Philosophy and Policy* 16(1999): 333–361.

President's Commission for the Study of Ethical Problems in Medicine and Biomedical and Behavioral Research. *Securing Access to Health Care: A Report on the Ethical Implications of Differences in the Availability of Health Services, Volume One.* Washington, D.C.: United States Government Printing Office, 1983.

Rawls, John. *The Law of Peoples.* Cambridge, Mass.: Harvard University Press, 1999.

Reich, Michael R. "The Global Drug Gap." *Science* 287(2000): 1979–1981.

Reich, Michael, ed. *An Assessment of US Pharmaceutical Donation: Players, Processes, and Products.* Boston, Mass.: Harvard School of Public Health, 1999.

Rhodes, Rosamond, et al. *Medicine and Social Justice: Essays on the Distribution of Health Care.* Oxford, U.K.: Oxford University Press, 2002.

Schuklenk, Udo, and Ashcroft, Richard. "Affordable Access to Essential Medication in Developing Countries: Conflicts Between Ethical and Economic Imperatives." *Journal of Medicine and Philosophy* 27:2(2001): 179–195.

Singer, Peter. *One World.* New Haven, Conn.: Yale University Press, 2002.

Tao Lai Po-Wah, Julia, ed. *Cross-Cultural Perspectives on the (Im)possibility of Global Bioethics.* Dordrecht: Kluwer Academic Publishers, 2002.

Thomas, W. John. "The Oregon Medicaid Proposal: Ethical Paralysis, Tragic Democracy, and the Fate of a Utilitarian Health Care Program." *Oregon Law Review* 72 (1993):47–156.

Tobey, James. "Public Health and the Police Power." *New York University Law Review* 4(1927): 126.

Toubia, Nahid. "Female Circumcision as a Public Health Issue." *New England Journal of Medicine* 331 (11) (1994): 712–716.

Chapter Seven

Individuals, Society, and Biomedical Science
Emerging and Reemerging Issues

A. Human Subjects in Medical Research

Almost every day we learn about new scientific breakthroughs, many of which offer the prospect of exciting new advances in humanity's quest for health and longevity. Almost as often, we hear tales of the misuse of science and warnings about the dangers of technology, unleashed. The tension—between our hopes for science and our fears of science—is an old one, at least as old as Pandora, who opened the box of knowledge and unleashed plagues around the earth. It is a tension that remains more salient today than ever.

Traditionally, in bioethics, much of the discourse about technology has been focused on the impact of research on individual human beings who are used as subjects, in the course of medical or scientific research. In these discussions, the issues relate to the way and degree to which individual well-being and autonomy may be undermined to advance the public's interest in knowledge that may lead to cures or medical benefits for many others. Less frequently, the analysis has focused not upon the impact of science on particular human subjects but on society itself, or what some call "human dignity." These discussions focus not so much on the process by which science advances, but on the very idea of scientific advancement in certain directions. The first debate, which centers on how individuals are used or abused by science, is discussed here. Section B focuses on the more substantive question, whether certain technological advancements are themselves inappropriate.

Biomedical research has long used human subjects to learn about diseases and test new treatments. Pasteur tested his new rabies vaccine on a young child exposed to rabies.[1] More generally, many of the advances that we take for granted today developed from a crude experimental empiricism that marked biomedical research in the late nineteenth and early twentieth centuries.

For many years, few questions were asked about how physicians and scientists treated their patients/subjects. That changed after World War II when some of the experiments perpetrated by the Nazi doctors on concentration camp victims came to light and formed the basis for the *Doctors' Trial,* one of the postwar trials held by the Allies at Nuremberg.[2] Following that trial, the judges issued the so-called *Nuremberg Code,* which proclaimed that the "voluntary consent of the human subject is absolutely essential" for the use of a human being in research. The *Code* also required that all experiments should be "conducted as to avoid all unnecessary physical and mental suffering and injury" and should never be undertaken if there "is an a priori reason to believe that death or disabling injury will occur."

In many ways, the *Nuremberg Code* represents one of the most absolute, deontological statements that have been offered on the subject. *Nuremberg* rejects any balancing of the individual's right to consent, or to agree to unnecessary pain or suffering, with the greater good of society. The deonotology of the *Nuremberg Code* may be contrasted with the teleology of the World Medical Association's *Declaration of Helsinki.* Although the *Declaration of Helsinki* seems to follow *Nuremberg* in stating that "considerations related to the well-being of the human subject should take precedence over the interests of science and society," it departs from *Nuremberg* in permitting surrogate consent when individuals are themselves incapable of giving informed consent. It also distinguishes between nontherapeutic research, which does not seek to provide treatment for the subject, and clinical research, which combines elements of therapy with research. Under *Helsinki,* greater leeway is given to physicians who offer therapy in conjunction with research. Is this justified by principles of beneficence? Or by concern for the greater good?

Despite the *Nuremberg Code* and the *Helsinki Declaration,* scientists throughout the world continued to use individuals, often without their full, voluntary consent, in biomedical research. One of the more infamous examples of this practice was the so-called Tuskegee Study conducted by the United States Public Health Service. In this study, the United States Public Health Service decided to study "untreated male Negro subjects" infected with syphilis to observe the course of their disease. Individuals who were enrolled were not informed about the nature of their disease or the study, nor were they given state-of-the-art treatment, even when modern antibiotics became available.[3] At times, researchers actually tried to prevent participants from obtaining treatment.[4]

Public revelations about the study in the 1970s led to a great outcry and demands for investigation and greater protection for human subjects. Eventually the federal government promulgated the "Common Rule," regulations that today govern the use of human subjects in federally funded research protocols, as well as in clinical trials pursuant to the FDA's licensing process.[5] The Common Rule modulates its demand for informed consent with a provision permitting surrogate consent when an individual cannot provide informed consent.[6] The Common Rule also places great weight on Institutional Review Boards, or IRBs, which are required to review all research protocols involving human subjects that are subject to the regulations.[7] These boards are required to be interdisciplinary and are charged with determining whether a proposed research protocol provides for informed consent, utilizes an equitable selection of subjects, protects subject privacy, and is designed in such a way that the risks are minimized and are proportional to the benefits anticipated.

Multiple, perhaps conflicting, principles and precepts coexist within the Common Rule. For example, the Common Rule relies upon informed consent, but only to a degree, as it permits surrogate consent and sometimes the use of a subject without any consent at all. It also requires that the IRB engage in an independent assessment of the cost/benefit ratio of research. Does that undermine the priority of patient autonomy, or does it safeguard it? And what rule does the IRB itself apply? By requiring a board to review independently a proposed research protocol, the Common Rule seems to adopt a procedural view of ethics, suggesting that review by the IRB can override any particular substantive conclusion as to when and under what circumstances human research may be justified. But what values and stances should the members of the IRB bring to their review? Do they represent the community or the institution for which most members work? Do they give priority to the good of the many, which may be promoted by research, or to the good of the subjects? Perhaps, most importantly, we can question whether the primarily procedural protections in the Common Rule form an adequate response to the problems illustrated by both the Nazi doctors and Tuskegee. Did these abuses occur because of a lack of informed consent and oversight or because of the deep climate of racism that encouraged researchers to devalue the humanity of the people who were used as their subjects? Does the Common Rule adequately address that problem?

The need to protect vulnerable populations from inappropriate experiments was discussed in a less dramatic setting by the Maryland Court of Appeals in the case of *Grimes v. Kennedy Krieger Institute.* The case involved a study by a well-respected research institute of low-cost techniques to abate lead in older inner-city housing. The subjects of the study were inner-city children, many of whom were minorities, who were exposed to lead during the course of the study. The study was approved by the IRB and the parents signed consent forms, although they were not told that the researchers expected that the children would have elevated levels of lead. Nor were the parents offered the "gold standard" approach to lead abatement. Indeed, the whole point of the study was to see what would happen to the children if less expensive abatement techniques were used.

Grimes v. Kennedy Krieger Institute highlights the numerous conflicts and problems inherent in research on human beings, particularly vulnerable ones. On the one hand, there was a legitimate public health reason to conduct the study. Many inner-city residents and landlords cannot afford to rid residences of lead using standard techniques. If lower-cost methods were found and proven to reduce the risk of lead poisoning, it is possible that fewer children will suffer the dire effects of lead poisoning. On the other hand, the research was clearly not therapeutic, as it was not trying to "cure" sick children. Moreover, the children, by being children, were inherently vulnerable, and their parents, generally inner-city parents who could not afford to live in lead-free residences, were also not well positioned to make fully informed and independent choices. And, as noted previously, many of the children were minorities, raising at the least the shadow of race-based mistreatment. Finally, as the court concluded, the IRB, in its review of the protocols, seemed to be representing the institution (which wanted to approve the research) rather than the subjects, who were nameless and faceless children not represented on the board. Accordingly, the Court of Appeals, in permitting the plaintiffs' lawsuit to go forward, expressed outrage at the IRB and questioned whether nontherapeutic research could ever be done on children. After you read the case, that reaction may be understandable. But would such a rule endanger more children, including poor, inner-city minority children, in the long run? How do we account for the interests of the unnamed children who might benefit from the studies that would no longer be permitted? Or is it possible that a biomedical science that ignores the needs and dignity of vulnerable groups will in the long run be unable to address their needs effectively?

Similar issues have now arisen with respect to research conducted in the developing world by Western scientists. Research on HIV in Africa presents the problems in a particularly stark light. HIV is far more prevalent in sub-Saharan Africa than in most other areas of the globe. In addition, neonatal transmission rates there are far higher and access to advanced antiviral therapies far less common. In many ways, this means that the populations of African nations are at the greatest risk for contracting HIV and are in greatest need for the development of vaccines and inexpensive ways of reducing transmission from mother to child. On the other hand, as Marcia Angell points out in *The Ethics of Clinical Research in the Third World*, there are serious ethical problems when Western researchers conduct clinical trials in the developing world. For Angell, such trials should only be considered ethical if the participants in the trial's control group are offered the Western standard of care, not the prevailing standard of care (no antivirals) given in their own community. According to Angell, the justification for giving placebos to women in Africa is "reminiscent of those for the Tuskegee study: Women in the Third World would not receive antiretroviral treatment anyway, so the investigators are simply observing what would happen to the subjects' infants if there were no study." She goes on to charge that reliance upon a "local standard of care" is simply "self-serving." "The fact remains that many studies are done in the Third World that simply could not be done in countries sponsoring the work. Clinical trials have become a big business, with many of the same imperatives." As you read Angell's article, recall the discussion of female genital mutilation in Chapter 6, Section C. How do we avoid using local standards as a pretext for exploiting the vulnerable? Can we apply a single standard of ethics around the world?

Keymanthri Moodley, from South Africa, takes up these issues directly. He agrees that great care needs to be taken when Westerners conduct clinical trials in Africa. According to Moodley, the predominant ethical guidelines for clinical research (such as the *Nuremberg Code* and the *Helsinki Declaration*) derive from and are relevant to liberal, individualistic societies. Notions like informed consent may have a very different meaning and less value in more communitarian cultures, where

"Ubuntu," or communalism, is in place. Therefore, researchers need to take into account local customs and traditions in designing research protocols. But, he argues, they also need to take care not to rely upon local customs to permit ad hoc adjustments to ethical guidelines, thereby rationalizing the aims of the researchers. Moreover, researchers must heed the requirements of justice that the burdens of research be equitably distributed and that subjects should not be chosen simply because they are convenient or easy to manipulate. In addition, justice may require that the benefits of new technologies that are developed as the result of research be shared equally with those societies that bore the burdens of the research. Thus, using Africans to test therapies that may, if proven safe and effective, only be available or affordable to Westerners seems especially problematic. In light of Tuskegee and *Grimes*, one wonders whether the same recommendations should not apply to research in this country.

Nuremberg Code

1. The voluntary consent of the human subject is absolutely essential. This means that the person involved should have legal capacity to give consent; should be so situated as to be able to exercise free power of choice, without the intervention of any element of force, fraud, deceit, duress, over-reaching, or other ulterior form of constraint or coercion; and should have sufficient knowledge and comprehension of the elements of the subject matter involved as to enable him to make an understanding and enlightened decision. This latter element requires that before the acceptance of an affirmative decision by the experimental subject there should be made known to him the nature, duration, and purpose of the experiment; the method and means by which it is to be conducted; all inconveniences and hazards reasonable to be expected; and the effects upon his health or person which may possibly come from his participation in the experiment.

    The duty and responsibility for ascertaining the quality of the consent rests upon each individual who initiates, directs or engages in the experiment. It is a personal duty and responsibility which may not be delegated to another with impunity.

2. The experiment should be such as to yield fruitful results for the good of society, unprocurable by other methods or means of study, and not random and unnecessary in nature.

3. The experiment should be so designed and based on the results of animal experimentation and a knowledge of the natural history of the disease or other problem under study that the anticipated results will justify the performance of the experiment.

4. The experiment should be so conducted as to avoid all unnecessary physical and mental suffering and injury.

5. No experiment should be conducted where there is an *a priori* reason to believe that death or disabling injury will occur; except, perhaps, in those experiments where the experimental physicians also serve as subjects.

6. The degree of risk to be taken should never exceed that determined by the humanitarian importance of the problem to be solved by the experiment.

7. Proper preparations should be made and adequate facilities provided to protect the experimental subject against even remote possibilities of injury, disability, or death.

8. The experiment should be conducted only by scientifically qualified persons. The highest degree of skill and care should be required through all stages of the experiment of those who conduct or engage in the experiment.

9. During the course of the experiment the human subject should be at liberty to bring the experiment to an end if he has reached the physical or mental state where continuation of the experiment seems to him to be impossible.

10. During the course of the experiment the scientist in charge must be prepared to terminate the experiment at any stage, if he has probable cause to believe, in the exercise of the good faith, superior skill and careful judgment required of him that a continuation of the experiment is likely to result in injury, disability, or death to the experimental subject.

World Medical Association Declaration of Helsinki

Adopted by the 18th World Medical Assembly, June 1964 and amended by the 29th World Medical Assembly, October 1975, 35th World Medical Assembly, October 1983 and the 41st World Medical Assembly, September 1989

A. Introduction

1. The World Medical Association has developed the Declaration of Helsinki as a statement of ethical principles to provide guidance to physicians and other participants in medical research involving human subjects. Medical research involving human subjects includes research on identifiable human material or identifiable data.

2. It is the duty of the physician to promote and safeguard the health of the people. The physician's knowledge and conscience are dedicated to the fulfillment of this duty.

3. The Declaration of Geneva of the World Medical Association binds the physician with the words, "The health of my patient will be my first consideration," and the International Code of Medical Ethics declares that, "A physician shall act only in the patient's interest when providing medical care which might have the effect of weakening the physical and mental condition of the patient."

4. Medical progress is based on research which ultimately must rest in part on experimentation involving human subjects.

5. In medical research on human subjects, considerations related to the well-being of the human subject should take precedence over the interests of science and society.

6. The primary purpose of medical research involving human subjects is to improve prophylactic, diagnostic and therapeutic procedures and the understanding of the aetiology and pathogenesis of disease. Even the best proven prophylactic, diagnostic, and therapeutic methods must continuously be challenged through research for their effectiveness, efficiency, accessibility and quality.

7. In current medical practice and in medical research, most prophylactic, diagnostic and therapeutic procedures involve risks and burdens.

8. Medical research is subject to ethical standards that promote respect for all human beings and protect their health and rights. Some research populations are vulnerable and need special protection. The particular needs of the economically and medically disadvantaged must be recognized. Special attention is also required for those who cannot give or refuse consent for themselves, for those who may be subject to giving consent under duress, for those who will not benefit personally from the research and for those for whom the research is combined with care.

9. Research Investigators should be aware of the ethical, legal and regulatory requirements for research on human subjects in their own countries as well as applicable international requirements. No national ethical, legal or regulatory requirement should be allowed to reduce or eliminate any of the

protections for human subjects set forth in this Declaration.

B. Basic Principles for All Medical Research

10. It is the duty of the physician in medical research to protect the life, health, privacy, and dignity of the human subject.

11. Medical research involving human subjects must conform to generally accepted scientific principles, be based on a thorough knowledge of the scientific literature, other relevant sources of information, and on adequate laboratory and, where appropriate, animal experimentation.

12. Appropriate caution must be exercised in the conduct of research which may affect the environment, and the welfare of animals used for research must be respected.

13. The design and performance of each experimental procedure involving human subjects should be clearly formulated in an experimental protocol. This protocol should be submitted for consideration, comment, guidance, and where appropriate, approval to a specially appointed ethical review committee, which must be independent of the investigator, the sponsor or any other kind of undue influence. This independent committee should be in conformity with the laws and regulations of the country in which the research experiment is performed. The committee has the right to monitor ongoing trials. The researcher has the obligation to provide monitoring information to the committee, especially any serious adverse events. The researcher should also submit to the committee, for review, information regarding funding, sponsors, institutional affiliations, other potential conflicts of interest and incentives for subjects.

14. The research protocol should always contain a statement of the ethical considerations involved and should indicate that there is compliance with the principles enunciated in this Declaration.

15. Medical research involving human subjects should be conducted only by scientifically qualified persons and under the supervision of a clinically competent medical person. The responsibility for the human subject must always rest with a medically qualified person and never rest on the subject of the research, even though the subject has given consent.

16. Every medical research project involving human subjects should be preceded by careful assessment of predictable risks and burdens in comparison with foreseeable benefits to the subject or to others. This does not preclude the participation of healthy volunteers in medical research. The design of all studies should be publicly available.

17. Physicians should abstain from engaging in research projects involving human subjects unless they are confident that the risks involved have been adequately assessed and can be satisfactorily managed. Physicians should cease any investigation if the risks are found to outweigh the potential benefits or if there is conclusive proof of positive and beneficial results.

18. Medical research involving human subjects should only be conducted if the importance of the objective outweighs the inherent risks and burdens to the subject. This is especially important when the human subjects are healthy volunteers.

19. Medical research is only justified if there is a reasonable likelihood that the populations in which the research is carried out stand to benefit from the results of the research.

20. The subjects must be volunteers and informed participants in the research project.

21. The right of research subjects to safeguard their integrity must always be respected. Every precaution should be taken to respect the privacy of the subject, the confidentiality of the patient's information and to minimize

the impact of the study on the subject's physical and mental integrity and on the personality of the subject.

22. In any research on human beings, each potential subject must be adequately informed of the aims, methods, sources of funding, any possible conflicts of interest, institutional affiliations of the researcher, the anticipated benefits and potential risks of the study and the discomfort it may entail. The subject should be informed of the right to abstain from participation in the study or to withdraw consent to participate at any time without reprisal. After ensuring that the subject has understood the information, the physician should then obtain the subject's freely-given informed consent, preferably in writing. If the consent cannot be obtained in writing, the non-written consent must be formally documented and witnessed.

23. When obtaining informed consent for the research project the physician should be particularly cautious if the subject is in a dependent relationship with the physician or may consent under duress. In that case the informed consent should be obtained by a well-informed physician who is not engaged in the investigation and who is completely independent of this relationship.

24. For a research subject who is legally incompetent, physically or mentally incapable of giving consent or is a legally incompetent minor, the investigator must obtain informed consent from the legally authorized representative in accordance with applicable law. These groups should not be included in research unless the research is necessary to promote the health of the population represented and this research cannot instead be performed on legally competent persons.

25. When a subject deemed legally incompetent, such as a minor child, is able to give assent to decisions about participation in research,

the investigator must obtain that assent in addition to the consent of the legally authorized representative.

26. Research on individuals from whom it is not possible to obtain consent, including proxy or advance consent, should be done only if the physical/mental condition that prevents obtaining informed consent is a necessary characteristic of the research population. The specific reasons for involving research subjects with a condition that renders them unable to give informed consent should be stated in the experimental protocol for consideration and approval of the review committee. The protocol should state that consent to remain in the research should be obtained as soon as possible from the individual or a legally authorized surrogate.

27. Both authors and publishers have ethical obligations. In publication of the results of research, the investigators are obliged to preserve the accuracy of the results. Negative as well as positive results should be published or otherwise publicly available. Sources of funding, institutional affiliations and any possible conflicts of interest should be declared in the publication. Reports of experimentation not in accordance with the principles laid down in this Declaration should not be accepted for publication.

C. Additional Principles for Medical Research Combined with Medical Care

28. The physician may combine medical research with medical care, only to the extent that the research is justified by its potential prophylactic, diagnostic or therapeutic value. When medical research is combined with medical care, additional standards apply to protect the patients who are research subjects.

29. The benefits, risks, burdens and effectiveness of a new method should be tested against those of the best current prophylactic, diag-

nostic, and therapeutic methods. This does not exclude the use of placebo, or no treatment, in studies where no proven prophylactic, diagnostic or therapeutic method exists.[1]

30. At the conclusion of the study, every patient entered into the study should be assured of access to the best proven prophylactic, diagnostic and therapeutic methods identified by the study.[2]

31. The physician should fully inform the patient which aspects of the care are related to the research. The refusal of a patient to participate in a study must never interfere with the patient-physician relationship.

32. In the treatment of a patient, where proven prophylactic, diagnostic and therapeutic methods do not exist or have been ineffective, the physician, with informed consent from the patient, must be free to use unproven or new prophylactic, diagnostic and therapeutic measures, if in the physician's judgement it offers hope of saving life, re-establishing health or alleviating suffering. Where possible, these measures should be made the object of research, designed to evaluate their safety and efficacy. In all cases, new information should be recorded and, where appropriate, published. The other relevant guidelines of this Declaration should be followed.

1. Note of clarification on paragraph 29 of the WMA Declaration of Helsinki:

The WMA hereby reaffirms its position that extreme care must be taken in making use of a placebo-controlled trial and that in general this methodology should only be used in the absence of existing proven therapy. However, a placebo-controlled trial may be ethically acceptable, even if proven therapy is available, under the following circumstances:

- Where for compelling and scientifically sound methodological reasons its use is necessary to determine the efficacy or safety of a prophylactic, diagnostic or therapeutic method; or
- Where a prophylactic, diagnostic or therapeutic method is being investigated for a minor condition and the patients who receive placebo will not be subject to any additional risk of serious or irreversible harm.

All other provisions of the Declaration of Helsinki must be adhered to, especially the need for appropriate ethical and scientific review.

2. Note of clarification on paragraph 30 of the WMA Declaration of Helsinki:

The WMA hereby reaffirms its position that it is necessary during the study planning process to identify post-trial access by study participants to prophylactic, diagnostic and therapeutic procedures identified as beneficial in the study or access to other appropriate care. Post-trial access arrangements or other care must be described in the study protocol so the ethical review committee may consider such arrangements during its review.

Ericka Grimes v. Kennedy Krieger Institute, Inc.
Myron Higgins, a minor, etc.,
et al. v. Kennedy Krieger Institute, Inc.
Court of Appeals of Maryland

August 16, 2001, Filed

Opinion by Cathell, J.

Prologue

We initially note that these are cases of first impression for this Court. For that matter, precious few courts in the United States have addressed the issues presented in the cases at bar. In respect to nontherapeutic research using minors, it has been noted that "consent to research has been virtually unanalyzed by courts and legislatures." Robert J. Katerberg, *Institutional Review Boards, Research on Children, and Informed Consent of Parents: Walking the Tightrope Between Encouraging Vital Experimentation and Protecting Subjects' Rights*, 24 J.C. & U.L. 545, 562, quoting National Commission for the Protection of Human Subjects of Biomedical and Behavioral Research, Report and Recommendations [National Commission]: Research Involving Children 79–80 (1977). Our research reveals this statement remains as accurate now as it was in 1977.

In these present cases, a prestigious research institute, associated with Johns Hopkins University, based on this record, created a nontherapeutic research program[2] whereby it required certain classes of homes to have only partial lead paint abatement modifications performed, and in at least some instances, including at least one of the cases at bar, arranged for the landlords to receive public funding by way of grants or loans to aid in the modifications. The research institute then encouraged, and in at least one of the cases at bar, required, the landlords to rent the premises

to families with young children. In the event young children already resided in one of the study houses, it was contemplated that a child would remain in the premises, and the child was encouraged to remain, in order for his or her blood to be periodically analyzed. In other words, the continuing presence of the children that were the subjects of the study was required in order for the study to be complete. Apparently, the children and their parents involved in the cases *sub judice* were from a lower economic strata and were, at least in one case, minorities.

The purpose of the research was to determine how effective varying degrees of lead paint abatement procedures were. Success was to be determined by periodically, over a two-year period of time, measuring the extent to which lead dust remained in, or returned to, the premises after the varying levels of abatement modifications, and, as most important to our decision, by measuring the extent to which the theretofore healthy children's blood became contaminated with lead, and comparing that contamination with levels of lead dust in the houses over the same periods of time. In respect to one of the protocols presented to the Environmental Protection Agency and/or the Johns Hopkins Joint Committee on Clinical Investigation, the Johns Hopkins Institutional Review Board (IRB), the researchers stated: "To help insure that study dwellings are occupied by families with young children, City Homes will give priority to families with young children when renting the vacant units following R & M [Repair and Maintenance] interventions."

The same researchers had completed a prior study on abatement and partial abatement methods that indicated that lead dust remained and/or returned to abated houses over a period of time. In an article reporting on that study, the very same researchers said: "Exposure to lead-bearing dust is particularly hazardous for children because hand-to-mouth activity is recognized as a major route of entry of lead into the body and because absorption of lead is inversely related to particule size." Mark R. Farfel & J. Julian Chisolm, *Health and Environmental Outcomes of Traditional and Modified Practices for Abatement of Residential Lead-Based Paint*, 80 American Journal of Public Health 1240, 1243 (1990). After publishing this report, the researchers began the present research project in which children were encouraged to reside in households where the possibility of lead dust was known to the researcher to be likely, so that the lead dust content of their blood could be compared with the level of lead dust in the houses at periodic intervals over a two-year period.

Apparently, it was anticipated that the children, who were the human subjects in the program, would, or at least might, accumulate lead in their blood from the dust, thus helping the researchers to determine the extent to which the various partial abatement methods worked. There was no complete and clear explanation in the consent agreements signed by the parents of the children that the research to be conducted was designed, at least in significant part, to measure the success of the abatement procedures by measuring the extent to which the children's blood was being contaminated. It can be argued that the researchers intended that the children be the canaries in the mines but never clearly told the parents. (It was a practice in earlier years, and perhaps even now, for subsurface miners to rely on canaries to determine whether dangerous levels of toxic gasses were accumulating in the mines. Canaries were particularly susceptible to such gasses. When the canaries began to die, the miners knew that dangerous levels of gasses were accumulating.)

The researchers and their Institutional Review Board apparently saw nothing wrong with the search protocols that anticipated the possible accumulation of lead in the blood of otherwise healthy children as a result of the experiment, or they believed that the consents of the parents of the children made the research appropriate. Institutional Review Boards (IRB) are oversight entities within the institutional family to which an entity conducting research belongs. In research experiments, an IRB can be required in some instances by either federal or state regulation, or sometimes by the conditions attached to governmental grants that are used to fund research projects.[4] Generally, their primary functions are to assess the protocols of the project to determine whether the project itself is appropriate, whether the consent procedures are adequate, whether the methods to be employed meet proper standards, whether reporting requirements are sufficient, and the assessment of various other aspects of a research project. One of the most important objectives of such review is the review of the potential safety and the health hazard impact of a research project on the human subjects of the experiment, especially on vulnerable subjects such as children. Their function is *not* to help researchers seek funding for research projects.

In the instant case, as is suggested by some commentators as being endemic to the research community as a whole, *infra*, the IRB involved here, the Johns Hopkins University Joint Committee on Clinical Investigation, in part, abdicated that responsibility, instead suggesting to the researchers a way to miscast the characteristics of the study in order to avoid the responsibility inherent in nontherapeutic research involving children. In a letter dated May 11, 1992, the Johns Hopkins University Joint Committee on Clinical Investigation (the RB for the University), charged with insuring the safety of the subjects and compliance with federal regulations, wrote to Dr. Farfel, the person in charge of the research:

> "A number of questions came up. . . . Please respond to the following points[:]
>
> 2. The next issue has to do with drawing blood from the control population, namely children growing up in modern urban housing. *Federal guidelines are really quite specific regarding using children as controls in projects in which there is no potential benefit* [to the particular children]. To call a subject a normal control is to indicate that there is no real benefit to be received [by the particular children]. . . . So, we think it would be much more acceptable to indicate that the 'control group' is being studied to determine what exposure outside the home may play in a total lead exposure; thereby, indicating that these control individuals are gaining some benefit, namely learning whether safe housing alone is sufficient to keep the blood-lead levels in acceptable bounds. We suggest that you modify . . . consent form[s] . . . accordingly." [Emphasis added.]

While the suggestion of the IRB would not make this experiment any less nontherapeutic or, thus, less regulated, this statement shows two things: (1) that the IRB had a partial misperception of the difference between therapeutic and nontherapeutic research and the IRB's role in the process and (2) that the IRB was willing to aid researchers in getting around federal regulations designed to protect children used as subjects in nontherapeutic research. An IRB's primary role is to assure the safety of human research subjects—not help researchers avoid safety or health-related requirements. The IRB, in this case, misconceived, at least partially, its own role.

The provisions or conditions imposed by the federal funding entities, pursuant to federal regulations, are conditions attached to funding. As far as we are aware, or have been informed, there are no federal or state (Maryland) statutes that mandate that all research be subject to certain conditions. Certain international "codes" or "declarations" exist (one of which is supposedly binding but has never been so held) that, at least

in theory, establish standards. We are guided, as we determine what is appropriate, by those international "codes" or "declarations," as well as by studies conducted by various governmental entities, by the treatises and other writings on the ethics of using children as research subjects, and by the duties, if any, arising out of the use of children as subjects of research.

Otherwise healthy children, in our view, should not be enticed into living in, or remaining in, potentially lead-tainted housing and intentionally subjected to a research program, which contemplates the probability, or even the possibility, of lead poisoning or even the accumulation of lower levels of lead in blood, in order for the extent of the contamination of the children's blood to be used by scientific researchers to assess the success of lead paint or lead dust abatement measures. Moreover, in our view, parents, whether improperly enticed by trinkets, food stamps, money or other items, have no more right to intentionally and unnecessarily place children in potentially hazardous nontherapeutic research surroundings, than do researchers. In such cases, parental consent, no matter how informed, is insufficient.

While the validity of the consent agreement and its nature as a contract, the existence or nonexistence of a special relationship, and whether the researchers performed their functions under that agreement pursuant to any special relationships are important issues in these cases that we will address, the very inappropriateness of the research itself cannot be overlooked. It is apparent that the protocols of research are even more important than the method of obtaining parental consent and the extent to which the parents were, or were not, informed. If the research methods, the protocols, are inappropriate then, especially when the IRB is willing to help researchers avoid compliance with applicable safety requirements for using children in nontherapeutic research, the consent of the parents, or of any consent surrogates, in our view, cannot make the research appropriate or the actions of the researchers and the Institutional Review Board proper.

The research relationship proffered to the parents of the children the researchers wanted to use as measuring tools, should never have been presented in a nontherapeutic context in the first instance. Nothing about the research was designed for treatment of the subject children. They were presumed to be healthy at the commencement of the project. As to them, the research was clearly nontherapeutic in nature. The experiment was simply a "for the greater good" project.[6] The specific children's health was put at risk, in order to develop low-cost abatement measures that would help all children, the landlords, and the general public as well.

The research project at issue here, and its apparent protocols, differs in large degree from, but presents similar problems as those in the Tuskegee Syphilis Study conducted from 1932 until 1972 (*The Tuskegee Syphilis Study*, 289 New England Journal of Medicine 730 (1973)), the intentional exposure of soldiers to radiation in the 1940s and 50s (*Jaffee v. United States*, 663 F.2d 1226 (3d Cir. 1981)), the tests involving the exposure of Navajo miners to radiation (*Begay v. United States*, 591 F. Supp. 991 (1984), aff'd, 768 F.2d 1059 (9th Cir. 1985)), and the secret administration of LSD to soldiers by the CIA and the Army in the 1950s and 60s (*United States v. Stanley*, 483 U.S. 669, 107 S. Ct. 3054, 97 L. Ed. 2d 550 (1987)). The research experiments that follow were also prior instances of research subjects being intentionally exposed to infectious or poisonous substances in the name of scientific research. They include the Tuskegee Syphilis Study, aforesaid, where patients infected with syphilis were not subsequently informed of the availability of penicillin for treatment of the illness, in order for the scientists and researchers to be able to continue research on the effects of the illness, the Jewish Hospital study, and several other post-war research projects. Then there are the notorious use of "plague bombs" by the

Japanese military in World War II where entire villages were infected in order for the results to be "studied"; and perhaps most notorious, the deliberate use of infection in a nontherapeutic project in order to study the degree of infection and the rapidity of the course of the disease in the Rose and Mrugowsky typhus experiments at Buchenwald concentration camp during World War II. These programs were somewhat alike in the vulnerability of the subjects; uneducated African American men, debilitated patients in a charity hospital, prisoners of war, inmates of concentration camps and others falling within the custody and control of the agencies conducting or approving the experiments. In the present case, children, especially young children, living in lower economic circumstances, albeit not as vulnerable as the other examples, are nonetheless, vulnerable as well.

It is clear to this Court that the scientific and medical communities cannot be permitted to assume sole authority to determine ultimately what is right and appropriate in respect to research projects involving young children free of the limitations and consequences of the application of Maryland law. The Institutional Review Boards, IRBs, are, primarily, in-house organs. In our view, they are not designed, generally, to be sufficiently objective in the sense that they are as sufficiently concerned with the ethicality of the experiments they review as they are with the success of the experiments.

Here, the IRB, whose primary function was to insure safety and compliance with applicable regulations, encouraged the researchers to misrepresent the purpose of the research in order to bring the study under the label of "therapeutic" and thus under a lower safety standard of regulation. The IRB's purpose was ethically wrong, and its understanding of the experiment's benefit incorrect.

The conflicts are inherent. This would be especially so when science and private industry collaborate in search of material gains. Moreover, the special relationship between research entities and human subjects used in the research will almost always impose duties.

In respect to examining that special relationship, we are obliged to further examine its nature and its ethical constraints. In that regard, when contested cases arise, the assessment of the legal effect of research on human subjects must always be subject to judicial evaluation. One method of making such evaluations is the initiation of appropriate actions bringing such matters to the attention of the courts, as has been done in the cases at bar. It may well be that in the end, the trial courts will determine that no damages have been incurred in the instant cases and thus the actions will fail for that reason. In that regard, we note that there are substantial factual differences in the Higgins and in the Grimes cases. But the actions, themselves, are not defective on the ground that no legal duty can, according to the trial courts, possibly exist. For the reasons discussed at length in the main body of the opinion, a legal duty normally exists between researcher and subject and in all probability exists in the cases at bar. Moreover, as we shall discuss, the consents of the parents in these cases under Maryland law constituted contracts creating duties. Additionally, under Maryland law, to the extent parental consent can ever be effective in research projects of this nature, the parents may not have been sufficiently informed and, therefore, the consents ineffective and, based on the information contained in the sparse records before this court, the research project, may have invaded the legal rights of the children subjected to it.

As a result of the atrocities performed in the name of science during the Holocaust, and other happenings in the World War II era, what is now known as The Nuremberg Code evolved. Of special interest to this Court, the Nuremberg Code, at least in significant part, was the result of legal thought and legal principles, as opposed to medical or scientific principles, and thus should be the preferred standard for assessing the legality

of scientific research on human subjects. Under it, duties to research subjects arise.

"Following the Doctors' Trial (the 'Medical Case'), which included charges of conducting lethal studies of the effects of high altitude and extreme cold, the action of poisons, and the response to various induced infections, the court issued 'The Nuremberg Code' *as a summary of the legal requirements for experimentation on humans.* The Code requires that the informed, voluntary, competent, and understanding consent of the research subject be obtained. Although this principle is placed first in the Code's ten points, the other nine points must be satisfied before it is even appropriate to ask the subject to consent.

The Nuremberg Code is the 'most complete and authoritative statement of the law of informed consent to human experimentation.' It is also 'part of international common law and may be applied, in both civil and criminal cases, by state, federal and municipal courts in the United States.' However, even though courts in the United States may use the Nuremberg Code to set criminal and civil standards of conduct, none have used it in a criminal case and only a handful have even cited it in the civil context. Even where the Nuremberg Code has been cited as authoritative, it has usually been in dissent, and no United States court has ever awarded damages to an injured experimental subject, or punished an experimenter, on the basis of a violation of the Nuremberg Code. There have, however, been very few court decisions involving human experimentation. It is therefore very difficult for a 'common law' of human experimentation to develop. This absence of judicial precedent makes codes, especially judicially-crafted codes like the Nuremberg Code, all the more important." [Footnotes omitted.] [Emphasis added.]

George J. Annas, *Mengele's Birthmark: The Nuremberg Code in United States Courts,* 7 Journal of Contemporary Health Law & Policy 17, 19–21 (Spring, 1991).

"Why wasn't the Nuremberg Code immediately adopted by United States courts as setting the minimum standard of care for human experimentation? One reason, perhaps, is that there was little opportunity. As remains true today, almost no experiments resulted in lawsuits in the 1940's, 50's, and 60's. A second reason may be that the Nazi experiments were considered so extreme as to be seen as irrelevant to the United States. This may explain why our own use of prisoners, the institutionalized retarded, and the mentally ill to test malaria treatments during World War II was generally hailed as positive, making the war 'everyone's war.' Likewise, in the late 1940's and early 1950's, the testing of new polio vaccines on institutionalized mentally retarded children was considered appropriate. Utilitarianism was the ethic of the day.... Noting that the Code applied primarily to the type of outrageous nontherapeutic experiments conducted during the war, physician groups tended to find the Code too 'legalistic' and irrelevant to their therapeutic experiments, and set about to develop an alternative code to guide medical researchers. The most successful and influential has been the World Medical Association's (WMA) Declaration of Helsinki...." *[See infra.]*

Mengele's Birthmark, supra, at 24 (footnotes omitted). In his conclusions the author noted:

"However, since American judges promulgated the [Nuremberg] Code under both natural and international law standards, it is disturbing that we have not taken it more seriously in areas where there is no question that it has direct application....

...We have yet to succeed in eradicating our birthmark that impels us to trample human rights and welfare when either society's welfare seems in jeopardy, or the promise of 'progress' is dangled before us.... Neither Alymer nor Mengele will be called to account in a world that puts expediency over ethics, and exalts progress over human rights."

Id. at 43–44 (footnotes omitted).

Karine Morin in her article, *The Standard of Disclosure in Human Subject Experimentation,* 19 Journal of Legal Medicine 157 (June 1998), after discussing the history of informed consent as it developed in medical practice, describes nontherapeutic experimental research, differentiating it from therapeutic medical treatment. She stated that "any manipulation, observation, or other study of a human being—or of anything related to that human being that might subsequently result in manipulation of that human being—done with the intent of developing new

knowledge and which differs in any form from customary medical (or other professional) practice." *Id.* at 166 (quoting from a paper by Robert Levine to the National Commission for the Protection of Human Subjects of Biomedical and Behavioral Research).

In respect to the difference between research involving treatment and nontherapeutic research, she further notes that:

"Practice represents the utilization of knowledge, while research amounts to its creation. Because experimentation takes place in the realm of the unknown, or at least the 'scientifically unproven,' several aspects distinguish it from treatment: risks may be unforeseeable; assumptions are not supported by scientific evidence and expertise is therefore more vulnerable than it is in clinical practice; a subject's consent cannot be based on anticipated benefits; and researchers and subjects may have conflicting interests."

Id. at 213 (footnotes omitted).

Morin, in respect to nontherapeutic research, also postulates that:

"It is essential to recognize that society's interest in knowledge may not coincide with an individual subject's interest; the individual subject stands to gain nothing and lose everything, including his or her right of self-determination....

...

...Some analysts contend that RB review tends to focus exclusively on consent requirements, rather than fully evaluating the merits of the research. Yet, it is important to recognize *that, even before consent becomes an issue, the scientific merits and the acceptability of risks need to be appraised.* As at least one author has argued, this aspect of the review may be jeopardized if members who have institutional allegiances are caught between the desire to promote the interests of the institution and the need to protect the subject...."

Investigator–Subject Relationship

Another notable difference between treatment and experimentation lies in the relationship between physician–patient and investigator–subject....

. . .

Other than through the difference that relates to the disclosure of information, the relationship between investigator and subject is unique in terms of the purpose for which information is gathered. . . . Data are collected to confirm or revoke a hypothesis, independently of the subject. Finally, investigators' motivations differ from those of treating physicians. The experiment is driven by the investigator's dedication to the advancement of knowledge, and often by a commitment to those who have funded the research; it is also driven by society's interest in future benefits that will flow from medical discoveries. As one author remarks, 'the price of a bad outcome is exacted from the individual who suffers the untoward reaction, whereas the benefit of the breakthrough is available to society as a whole.' "

Id. at 215–18 (emphasis added) (footnotes omitted). In arguing that a fuller disclosure should be made when consent is sought for nontherapeutic research, as opposed to therapeutic research, Morin notes:

"Furthermore, as long as courts continue to interpret the doctrine of informed consent in experimentation as it applies in the context of treatment, the uniqueness of the protection needed for human research subjects will be overlooked. Failing to recognize that subjects who volunteer for the sake of the advancement of science are differently situated from patients who stand to benefit from treatment results in an analysis that misconceives the purpose of disclosure. Beyond informing the patient as to means available to treat him or her, a subject must become a voluntary and willing participant in an endeavor that may yield no direct benefit to him or her, or worse, that may cause harm."

Id. at 220.

Just recently the research community has been subjected to question as a result of genetic experimentation on a Pennsylvania citizen. Jesse Gelsinger consented to participate in a research project at the University of Pennsylvania's Institute of Human Gene Therapy. After Gelsinger's death, the U.S. Food and Drug Administration

ordered a halt to eight human gene therapy experiments at the Institute. Additionally, other similar projects were halted elsewhere. The FDA took the action after a "discovery of a number of serious problems in the Institute's informed consent procedures and, more generally, a lapse in the researchers' ethical responsibilities to experimental subjects." Jeffrey H. Barker, *Human Experimentation and the Double Facelessness of a Merciless Epoch*, 25 New York University Review of Law and Social Change 603, 616 (1999).

Gelsinger had a different type of ornithine transcarbamylase deficiency (OTC) disease, than that addressed by the research. His particular brand of the disease was under control. There was no possibility that the research being conducted would directly benefit him. It was thus, as to him, as it was to the children in the case at bar, nontherapeutic; a way to study the affects on the subjects (in the present case, the children) in order to measure the success of the experiment. In Gelsinger's case, the research was to test the efficiency of disease vectors. In other words, weakened adenovirus (common-cold viruses) were used to deliver trillions of particles of a particular OTC gene into his artery and thus to his liver. Gelsinger experienced a massive and fatal immune system reaction to the introduction of the common-cold virus.

There were problems with the extent of the informed consent there obtained. Barker noted that:

"Is this just a case of rogue experimenters giving a bad name to all genetic research? Not at all. The program in Philadelphia is (or at least was) one of the most prestigious in the world and the researchers there were first-rate. Rather, the problems with that program are indicative of systemic problems with genetic research and informed consent as a protection of the autonomy of research subjects.

. . .

Why are there such serious problems with informed consent in some of these trials, and why is there almost total noncompliance with regulations concerning serious side effects? The answers to these questions are related. Informed consent has suffered from pressure to get results-as quickly as possible. . . . Informed consent procedures, properly followed, are troublesome, time-consuming, costly, and may even threaten proprietary information valuable to the biotech companies. The ethical face of the research subject can be obscured by such factors.

Id. at 617–20.

Because of the way the cases *sub judice* have arrived, as appeals from the granting of summary judgments, there is no complete record of the specific compensation of the researchers involved. Neither is there in the record any development of what pressures, if any, were exerted in respect to the researchers obtaining the consents of the parents and conducting the experiment. Nor, for the same reason, is there a sufficient indication as to the extent to which the Institute has joined with commercial interests, if it has, for the purposes of profit, that might potentially impact upon the researcher's motivations and potential conflicts of interest—motivations that generally are assumed, in the cases of prestigious entities such as Johns Hopkins University, to be for the public good rather then a search for profit.

We do note that the institution involved, the respondent here, like the Wendell Johnson Speech and Hearing Center, is a highly respected entity, considered to be a leader in the development of treatments, and treatment itself, for children infected with lead poisoning. With reasonable assurance, we can note that its reputation alone might normally suggest that there was no realization or understanding on the Institute's part that the protocols of the experiment were questionable, except for the letter from the RB requesting that the researchers mischaracterize the study.

Negligence

It is important for us to remember that appellants allege that KKI was negligent. Specifically, they allege that KKI, as a medical researcher, owed a duty of care to them, as subjects in the research study, based on the nature of the agreements between them and also based on the nature of the relationship between the parties. They contend specifically that KKI was negligent because KKI breached its duty to: (1) design a study that did not involve placing children at unnecessary risk; (2) inform participants in the study of results in a timely manner; and (3) to completely and accurately inform participants in the research study of all the hazards and risks involved in the study.

In order to establish a claim for negligence under Maryland law, a party must prove four elements: "(1) that the defendant was under a duty to protect the plaintiff from injury, (2) that the defendant breached that duty, (3) *that the plaintiff suffered actual injury or loss* and (4) that the loss or injury proximately resulted from the defendant's breach of the duty." (Emphasis added.) *Rosenblatt v. Exxon*, 335 Md. 58, 76, 642 A.2d 180, 188 (1994). Because this is a review of the granting of the two summary judgments based solely on the grounds that there was no legal duty to protect the children, we are primarily concerned with the first prong—whether KKI was under a duty to protect appellants from injury.

The relationship that existed between KKI and both sets of appellants in the case at bar was that of medical researcher and research study subject. Though not expressly recognized in the Maryland Code or in our prior cases as a type of relationship which creates a duty of care, evidence in the record suggests that such a relationship involving a duty or duties would ordinarily exist, and certainly could exist, based on the facts and circumstances of each of these individual cases.

The Ethical Appropriateness of the Research

The World Medical Association in its Declaration of Helsinki included a code of ethics for investigative researchers and was an attempt by the medical community to establish its own set of rules for conducting research on human subjects. The Declaration states in relevant part:

"III. Non-therapeutic biomedical research involving human subjects
(Non-clinical biomedical research)

1. *In the purely scientific application of medical research carried out on a human being, it is the duty of the physician to remain the protector of the life and health of that person on whom biomedical research is being carried out.*
2. The subjects should be volunteers—either healthy persons or patients for whom the experimental design is not related to the patient's illness.
3. The investigator or the investigating team should *discontinue the research if in his/her or their judgement it may, if continued, be harmful to the individual.*
4. *In research on man, the interest of science and society should never take precedence over considerations related to the well being of the subject."* [Emphasis added.]

Adopted in Declaration of Helsinki, World Medical Assembly (WMA) 18th Assembly (June 1964), amended by 29th WMA Tokyo, Japan (October, 1975), 35th WMA Venice, Italy (October 1983), and the 41st WMA Hong Kong (September 1989).

The determination of whether a duty exists under Maryland law is the ultimate function of various policy considerations as adopted by either the Legislature, or, if it has not spoken, as it has not in respect to this situation, by Maryland courts. In our view, otherwise healthy children should not be the subjects of nontherapeutic experimentation or research that has the potential to be harmful to the child. It is, first and foremost, the responsibility of the researcher and the research entity to see to the harmlessness of such nontherapeutic research. Consent of parents can never relieve the researcher of this duty. We do not feel that it serves proper public policy concerns to permit children to be placed in situations of potential harm, during nontherapeutic procedures, even if parents, or other surrogates, consent. Under these types of circumstances, even where consent is given, *albeit* inappropriately, policy considerations suggest that there remains a special relationship between researchers and participants to the research study, which imposes a duty of care. This is entirely consistent with the principles found in the Nuremberg Code.

Researchers cannot ever be permitted to completely immunize themselves by reliance on consents, especially when the information furnished to the subject, or the party consenting, is incomplete in a material respect. A researcher's duty is not created by, or extinguished by, the consent of a research subject or by IRB approval. The duty to a vulnerable research subject is independent of consent, although the obtaining of consent is one of the duties a researcher must perform. All of this is especially so when the subjects of research are children. Such legal duties, and legal protections, might additionally be warranted because of the likely conflict of interest between the goal of the research experimenter and the health of the human subject, especially, but not exclusively, when such research is commercialized. There is always a potential substantial conflict of interest on the part of researchers as between them and the human subjects used in their research. If participants in the study withdraw from the research study prior to its completion, then the results of the study could be rendered meaningless. There is thus an inherent reason for not conveying information to subjects as it arises, that might cause the subjects to leave the research project. That conflict dictates a stronger reason for full and continuous disclosure.

In research, the study participant's "well-being is subordinated to the dictates of a research protocol designed to advance knowledge for the sake of future patients." Jay Katz, *Human Experimentation and Human Rights,* 38 St. Louis U. L.J. 7, 8 (1993). In a recent report, the National Bioethics Advisory Commission recognized that this conflict between pursuit of scientific knowledge and the well-being of research participants requires some oversight of scientific investigators:

"However noble the investigator's intentions, when research involves human participants, the uncertainties inherent in any research study raise the prospect of unanticipated harm. In designing a research study an investigator must focus on finding or creating situations in which one can test important scientific hypotheses. *At the same time, no matter how important the research questions, it is not ethical to use human participants without appropriate protections.* Thus, there can be a conflict between the need to test hypotheses and the requirement to respect and protect individuals who participate in research. This conflict and the resulting tension that can arise within the research enterprise suggest a need for guidance and oversight."

National Bioethics Advisory Commission, *Ethical and Policy Issues in Research Involving Human Participants,* 2–3 (Dec. 19, 2000) (emphasis added). When human subjects are used in scientific research, the rights of the human subjects are afforded the protection of the courts when such subjects seek redress for any wrongs committed.

A special relationship giving rise to duties, the breach of which might constitute negligence, might also arise because, generally, the investigators are in a better position to anticipate, discover, and understand the potential risks to the health of their subjects. Practical inequalities exist between researchers, who have superior knowledge, and participants "who are often poorly placed to protect themselves from risk." *Id.* at 3. "Given the gap in knowledge between investigators and participants and the inherent conflict of interest faced by investigators, participants cannot and should not be solely responsible for their own protection." *Id.* at 3–4.

This duty requires the protection of the research subjects from unreasonable harm and requires the researcher to completely and promptly inform the subjects of potential hazards existing from time to time because of the profound trust that participants place in investigators, institu-

tions, and the research enterprise as a whole to protect them from harm. "Faced with seemingly knowledgeable and prestigious investigators engaged in a noble pursuit, participants may simply assume that research is socially important or of benefit to them individually; they may not be aware that participation could be harmful to their interests." *Id.*

As is evident from the cases discussed in this opinion, abuses with regard to the protection of human subjects in experimental research still occur in this country.

The purpose of the study in the case at bar was, in the words of Dr. Mark R. Farfel Sc.D., Director of KKI's Lead Abatement Department "to document the longevity of various lead base paint abatement strategies, factored in terms of reducing lead exposure in house dust and the children's blood lead levels." In other words, the purpose of the experiment was to determine whether there was a less expensive way than full abatement that would be cost-effective in reducing lead poisoning in children from a lower economic background. The study, by its design, placed and/or retained children in areas where they might come into contact with elevated levels of lead dust. Clearly, KKI contemplated that at least some of the children would develop elevated blood lead levels while participating in the study. At 45 C.F.R. section 46.111 *Criteria for IRB approval of research,* the regulations require IRBs to encourage the safety aspects of research rather than encouraging noncompliance with regulations: "(b) When some or all of the subjects . . . such as children . . . [are] economically or educationally disadvantaged persons, *additional* safeguards have been included . . . to protect the rights and welfare of these subjects." (Emphasis added.)

While we acknowledge that foreseeability does not necessarily create a duty, we recognize that potential harm to the children participants of this study was both foreseeable and potentially extreme. A "special relationship" also exists in circumstances where such experiments are conducted.

Parental Consent for Children to Be Subjects of Potentially Hazardous Nontherapeutic Research

The issue of whether a parent can consent to the participation of her or his child in a nontherapeutic health-related study that is known to be potentially hazardous to the health of the child raises serious questions with profound moral and ethical implications. What right does a parent have to knowingly expose a child not in need of therapy to health risks or otherwise knowingly place a child in danger, even if it can be argued it is for the greater good? The issue in these specific contested cases does not relate primarily to the authority of the parent, but to the procedures of KKI and similar entities that may be involved in such health-related studies. The issue of the parents' right to consent on behalf of the children has not been fully presented in either of these cases, but should be of concern not only to lawyers and judges, but to moralists, ethicists, and others. The consenting parents in the contested cases at bar were not the subjects of the experiment; the children were. Additionally, this practice presents the potential problems of children initiating actions in their own names upon reaching majority, if indeed, they have been damaged as a result of being used as guinea pigs in nontherapeutic scientific research. Children, it should be noted, are not in our society the equivalent of rats, hamsters, monkeys, and the like.

It is not in the best interest of a specific child, in a nontherapeutic research project, to be placed in a research environment, which might possibly be, or which proves to be, hazardous to the health of the child. We have long stressed that the "best interests of the child" is the overriding concern of this Court in matters relating to children. Whatever the interests of a parent, and whatever the interests of the general public in fostering research that might, according to a researcher's hypothesis, be for the good of all children, this Court's concern for the particular child and particular case, overarches all other interests. It is, simply, and we hope, succinctly put, not in the best interest of any healthy child to be intentionally put in a nontherapeutic situation where his or her health may be impaired, in order to test methods that may ultimately benefit all children.

To think otherwise, to turn over human and legal ethical concerns solely to the scientific community, is to risk embarking on slippery slopes, that all to often in the past, here and elsewhere, have resulted in practices we, or any community, should be ever unwilling to accept.

We have little doubt that the general motives of all concerned in these contested cases were, for the most part, proper, albeit in our view not well thought out. The protocols of the research, those of which we have been made aware, were, in any event, unacceptable in a legal context. One simply does not expose otherwise healthy children, incapable of personal assent (consent), to a nontherapeutic research environment that is known at the inception of the research, might cause the children to ingest lead dust. It is especially troublesome, when a measurement of the success of the research experiment is, in significant respect, to be determined by the extent to which the blood of the children absorbs, and is contaminated by, a substance that the researcher knows can, in sufficient amounts, whether solely from the research environment or cumulative from all sources, cause serious and long term adverse health effects. Such a practice is not legally acceptable.

When it comes to children involved in nontherapeutic research, with the potential for health risks to the subject children in Maryland, we will not defer to science to be the sole determinant of the ethicality or legality of such experiments. The reason, in our view, is apparent from the research protocols at issue in the case at bar. Moreover, in nontherapeutic research using children, we hold that the consent of a parent alone cannot make appropriate that which is innately inappropriate.

Additionally, there are conflicting views in respect to nontherapeutic research, as to whether consent, even of a person capable of consenting, can justify a research protocol that is otherwise unjustifiable.

"This 'justifying' side of consent raises some timeless and thorny questions. What if people consent to activities and results which are repugnant, or even evil? Even John Stuart Mill worried about consensual slavery. . . . Today, we wonder whether a woman's consent to appear in graphic, demeaning, or even violent pornography justifies or immunizes the pornographer. If she appears to consent to a relationship in which she is repeatedly brutalized, does her consent stymie our efforts to stop the brutality or punish the brute?

These problems make us squirm a little, just as they did Mill. We have three ways out: We can say, first, 'Yes, consent justifies whatever is consented to—you consented, so case closed;' second, 'This particular consent is deficient—you did not really consent and so the result or action is not justified;' or third. 'You consented, but your consent cannot justify this action or result.' . . .

Note the subtle yet crucial difference between these three options: In the first, consent is king, while the third option assumes a moral universe shaped and governed by extra-consensual considerations. The second option, however, reflects the tension between the other two. We might block the consented-to action, but we pay lip service to consent's justifying role by assuring ourselves that had the consent been untainted, had it been 'informed,' it would have had moral force. In fact, we pay lip service precisely because we often silently suspect that consent cannot and does not always justify. Rather than admit that the consent does not and could not justify the act, we denigrate the consent and, necessarily, the consenter as well.

This is cheating; it is a subterfuge designed to hide our unease and to allow us to profess simultaneous commitment to values that often conflict."

Garnett, *Why Informed Consent? Human Experimentation and the Ethics of Autonomy*, 36 Catholic Lawyer 455, 458–60 (1996) (footnotes omitted). The article continues:

"We should worry about the behavior of the experimenter, about our own culpability, and not about the subject's choosing capacities.

Such restrictions on consent, which aim at objective behaviors and results rather than at subjective decision-making processes, are common in the criminal law. For example, guilty pleas must usually be supported by a factual basis, and be knowing and voluntary. We recognize that defendants might quite rationally plead guilty to crimes they did not commit and that prosecutors might be willing to accept such pleas. However, because such pleas embroil the legal system in a monstrous falsehood, we refuse to accept them while admitting that they might indeed be in the defendant's correctly perceived best interests.

. . .

The Nuremberg Code explicitly recognized the need to place nonpaternalistic limits on the scope of experiments. The Code asks more of an experiment, a researcher, or society than mere consent."

Id. at 494–97. Based on the record before us, no degree of parental consent, and no degree of furnished information to the parents could make the experiment at issue here, ethically or legally permissible. It was wrong in the first instance.

Conclusion

We hold that in Maryland a parent, appropriate relative, or other applicable surrogate, cannot consent to the participation of a child or other person under legal disability in nontherapeutic research or studies in which there is any risk of injury or damage to the health of the subject.

We hold that informed consent agreements in nontherapeutic research projects, under certain circumstances can constitute contracts; and that, under certain circumstances, such research agreements can, as a matter of law, constitute "special relationships" giving rise to duties, out of the breach of which negligence actions may arise. We also hold that, normally, such special relationships are created between researchers and the human subjects used by the researchers. Additionally, we hold that governmental regulations can create duties on the part of researchers towards human subjects out of which "special relationships" can arise. Likewise, such duties and relationships are consistent with the provisions of the Nuremberg Code.

The determination as to whether a "special relationship" actually exists is to be done on a case by case basis. We hold that there was ample evidence in the cases at bar to support a fact finder's determination of the existence of duties arising out of contract, or out of a special relationship, or out of regulations and codes, or out of all of them, in each of the cases.

Notes

2. At least to the extent that commercial profit motives are not implicated, therapeutic research's purpose is to directly help or aid a patient who is suffering from a health condition the objectives of the research are designed to address—hopefully by the alleviation, or potential alleviation, of the health condition.

   Nontherapeutic research generally utilizes subjects who are not known to have the condition the objectives of the research are designed to address, and/or is not designed to directly benefit the subjects utilized in the research, but, rather, is designed to achieve beneficial results for the public at large (or, under some circumstances, for profit).

4. In respect to research conducted or supported by any federal agency, Institutional Review Boards, among other requirements, must furnish the agency with: (1) a list of IRB members, their degrees, representative capacity, experience, and employment relationships between the member and the research entity. Each IRB is required to have at least five members of varying back-grounds; there must be racial, gender, and cultural diversity. Each IRB has to contain at least one scientific member and one non-nonscientific member and one member who is not affiliated with the institution in any way. No member of an IRB can have a conflicting interest. 45 C.F.R. Subtitle A, sections 46.103 and 46.107.

6. The ultimate goal was to find the cost of the minimal level of effective lead paint or lead dust abatement costs so as to help landlords assess, hopefully positively, the commercial feasibility of attempting to abate lead dust in marginally profitable, lower rent-urban housing, in order to help preserve such housing in the Baltimore housing market. One of the aims was to evaluate low-cost methods of abatement so that some landlords would not abandon their rental units. For those landlords, complete abatement was not deemed economically feasible. The project would be able to assess whether a particular level of partial abatement caused a child's blood lead content to be elevated beyond a level deemed hazardous to the health of children.

   The tenants involved, presumably, would be from a lower rent-urban class. At least one of the consenting parents in one of these cases was on public assistance, and was described by her counsel as being a minority. The children of middle class or rich parents apparently were not involved.

The Ethics of Clinical Research
in the Third World

MARCIA ANGELL

An essential ethical condition for a randomized clinical trial comparing two treatments for a disease is that there be no good reason for thinking one is better than the other.[1,2] Usually, investigators hope and even expect that the new treatment will be better, but there should not be solid evidence one way or the other. If there is, not only would the trial be scientifically redundant, but the investigators would be guilty of knowingly giving inferior treatment to some participants in the trial. The necessity for investigators to be in this state of equipoise[2] applies to placebo-controlled trials, as well. Only when there is no known effective treatment is it ethical to compare a potential new treatment with a placebo. When effective treatment exists, a placebo may not be used. Instead, subjects in the control group of the study must receive the best known treatment. Investigators are responsible for all subjects enrolled in a trial, not just some of them, and the goals of the research are always secondary to the well-being of the participants. Those requirements are made clear in the Declaration of Helsinki of the World Health Organization (WHO), which is widely regarded as providing the fundamental guiding principles of research involving human subjects.[3] It states, "In research on man [sic], the interest of science and society should never take precedence over considerations related to the wellbeing of the subject," and "In any medical study, every patient—including those of a control group, if any—should be assured of the best proven diagnostic and therapeutic method."

One reason ethical codes are unequivocal about investigators' primary obligation to care for the human subjects of their research is the strong temptation to subordinate the subjects' welfare to the objectives of the study. That is particularly likely when the research question is extremely important and the answer would probably improve the care of future patients substantially. In those circumstances, it is sometimes argued explicitly that obtaining a rapid, unambiguous answer to the research question is the primary ethical obligation. With the most altruistic of motives, then, researchers may find themselves slipping across a line that prohibits treating human subjects as means to an end. When that line is crossed, there is very little left to protect patients from a callous disregard of their welfare for the sake of research goals. Even informed consent, important though it is, is not protection enough, because of the asymmetry in knowledge and authority between researchers and their subjects. And approval by an institutional review board, though also important, is highly variable in its responsiveness to patients' interests when they conflict with the interests of researchers.

A textbook example of unethical research is the Tuskegee Study of Untreated Syphilis.[4] In that study, which was sponsored by the U.S. Public Health Service and lasted from 1932 to 1972, 412 poor African-American men with untreated syphilis were followed and compared with 204 men free of the disease to determine the natural history of syphilis. Although there was no very good treatment available at the time the study began (heavy metals were the standard treatment), the research continued even after penicillin became widely available and was known to be highly effective against syphilis. The study was not terminated until it came to the attention of a reporter and the outrage provoked by front-page stories in the *Washington Star* and *New York Times* embarrassed the Nixon administration into calling a halt to it.[5] The ethical violations were multiple: Subjects did not provide informed consent (indeed, they were deliberately deceived); they were denied the best known treatment; and the study was continued even after highly effective treatment became available. And what were the arguments in favor of the Tuskegee study? That these poor African-American men probably would not have been treated anyway, so the investigators were merely observing what would have happened if there were no study; and that the study was important (a "never-to-be-repeated opportunity," said one physician after penicillin became available).[6] Ethical concern was even stood on its head when it was suggested that not only was the information valuable, but it was especially so for people like the subjects—an impoverished rural population with a very high rate of untreated syphilis. The only lament seemed to be that many of the subjects inadvertently received treatment by other doctors.

Some of these issues are raised by Lurie and Wolfe elsewhere in this issue of the *Journal*. They discuss the ethics of ongoing trials in the Third World of regimens to prevent the vertical transmission of human immunodeficiency virus (HIV) infection.[7] All except one of the trials employ placebo-treated control groups, despite the fact that zidovudine has already been clearly shown to cut the rate of vertical transmission greatly and is now recommended in the United States for all HIV-infected pregnant women. The justifications are reminiscent of those for the Tuskegee study: Women in the Third World would not receive antiretroviral treatment anyway, so the investigators are simply observing what would happen to the subjects' infants if there were no study. And a placebo-controlled study is the fastest, most efficient way to obtain unambiguous information that will be of greatest value in the Third World. Thus, in response to protests from Wolfe and others to the secretary of Health and Human Services, the directors of the National Institutes of Health (NIH) and the Centers for Disease Control and Prevention

(CDC)—the organizations sponsoring the studies—argued, "It is an unfortunate fact that the current standard of perinatal care for the HIV-infected pregnant women in the sites of the studies does not include any HIV prophylactic intervention at all," and the inclusion of placebo controls "will result in the most rapid, accurate, and reliable answer to the question of the value of the intervention being studied compared to the local standard of care."[8]

Also in this issue of the *Journal*, Whalen et al. report the results of a clinical trial in Uganda of various regimens of prophylaxis against tuberculosis in HIV-infected adults, most of whom had positive tuberculin skin tests.[9] This study, too, employed a placebo-treated control group, and in some ways it is analogous to the studies criticized by Lurie and Wolfe. In the United States it would probably be impossible to carry out such a study, because of long-standing official recommendations that HIV-infected persons with positive tuberculin skin tests receive prophylaxis against tuberculosis. The first was issued in 1990 by the CDC's Advisory Committee for Elimination of Tuberculosis.[10] It stated that tuberculin-test-positive persons with HIV infection "should be considered candidates for preventive therapy." Three years later, the recommendation was reiterated more strongly in a joint statement by the American Thoracic Society and the CDC, in collaboration with the Infectious Diseases Society of America and the American Academy of Pediatrics.[11] According to this statement, ". . . the identification of persons with dual infection and the administration of preventive therapy to these persons is of great importance." However, some believe that these recommendations were premature, since they were based largely on the success of prophylaxis in HIV-negative persons.[12]

Whether the study by Whalen et al. was ethical depends, in my view, entirely on the strength of the preexisting evidence. Only if there was genuine doubt about the benefits of prophylaxis would a placebo group be ethically justified. This is not the place to review the scientific evidence, some of which is discussed in the editorial of Msamanga and Fawzi elsewhere in this issue.[13] Suffice it to say that the case is debatable. Msamanga and Fawzi conclude that "future studies should not include a placebo group, since preventive therapy should be considered the standard of care." I agree. The difficult question is whether there should have been a placebo group in the first place.

Although I believe an argument can be made that a placebo-controlled trial was ethically justifiable because it was still uncertain whether prophylaxis would work, it should not be argued that it was ethical because no prophylaxis is the "local standard of care" in sub-Saharan Africa. For reasons discussed by Lurie and Wolfe, that reasoning is badly flawed.[7] As mentioned earlier, the Declaration of Helsinki requires control groups to receive the "best" current treatment, not the local one. The shift in wording between "best" and "local" may be slight, but the implications are profound. Acceptance of this ethical relativism could result in widespread exploitation of vulnerable Third World populations for research programs that could not be carried out in the sponsoring country.[14] Furthermore, it directly contradicts the Department of Health and Human Services' own regulations governing U.S.-sponsored research in foreign countries,[15] as well as joint guidelines for research in the Third World issued by WHO and the Council for International Organizations of Medical Sciences,[16] which require that human subjects receive protection at least equivalent to that in the sponsoring country. The fact that Whalen et al. offered isoniazid to the placebo group when it was found superior to placebo indicates that they were aware of their responsibility to all the subjects in the trial.

The *Journal* has taken the position that it will not publish reports of unethical research, regardless of their scientific merit.[14,17] After deliberating at length about the study by Whalen et al., the editors concluded that publication was ethically justified, although there remain differences among us. The fact that the subjects gave informed consent and the study was approved by the institutional review board at the University Hospitals of Cleveland and Case Western Reserve University and by the Ugandan National AIDS Research Subcommittee certainly supported our decision but did not allay all our misgivings. It is still important to determine whether clinical studies are consistent with preexisting, widely accepted ethical guidelines, such as the Declaration of Helsinki, and with federal regulations, since they cannot be influenced by pressures specific to a particular study.

Quite apart from the merits of the study by Whalen et al., there is a larger issue. There appears to be a general retreat from the clear principles enunciated in the Nuremberg Code and the Declaration of Helsinki as applied to research in the Third World. Why is that? Is it because the "local standard of care" is different? I don't think so. In my view, that is merely a self-serving justification after the fact. Is it because diseases and their treatments are very different in the Third World, so that information gained in the industrialized world has no relevance and we have to start from scratch? That, too, seems an unlikely explanation, although here again it is often offered as a justification. Sometimes there may be relevant differences between populations, but that cannot be assumed. Unless there are specific indications to the contrary, the safest and most reasonable position is that people everywhere are likely to respond similarly to the same treatment.

I think we have to look elsewhere for the real reasons. One of them may be a slavish adherence to the tenets of clinical trials. According to these, all trials should be randomized, double-blind, and placebo-controlled, if at all possible. That rigidity may explain the NIH's pressure on Marc Lallemant to include a placebo group in his study, as described by Lurie and Wolfe.[7] Sometimes journals are blamed for the problem, because they are thought to demand strict conformity to the standard methods. That is not true, at least not at this journal. We do not want a scientifically neat study if it is ethically flawed, but like Lurie and Wolfe we believe that in many cases it is possible, with a little ingenuity, to have both scientific and ethical rigor.

The retreat from ethical principles may also be explained by some of the exigencies of doing clinical research in an increasingly regulated and competitive environment. Research in the Third World looks relatively attractive as it becomes better funded and regulations at home become more restrictive. Despite the existence of codes requiring that human subjects receive at least the same protection abroad as at home, they are still honored partly in the breach. The fact remains that many studies are done in the Third World that simply could not be done in the countries sponsoring the work. Clinical trials have become a big business, with many of the same imperatives. To survive, it is necessary to get the work done as quickly as possible, with a minimum of obstacles. When these considerations prevail, it seems as if we have not come very far from Tuskegee after all. Those of us in the research community need to redouble our commitment to the highest ethical standards, no matter where the research is conducted, and sponsoring agencies need to enforce those standards, not undercut them.

References

1. Angell M. Patients' preferences in randomized clinical trials. N Engl J Med 1984;310:1385–7.
2. Freedman B. Equipoise and the ethics of clinical research. N Engl J Med 1987;317:14–5.
3. Declaration of Helsinki IV, 41st World Medical Assembly, Hong Kong, September 1989. In: Annas GJ, Grodin MA, eds. The Nazi doctors and the Nuremberg Code: human rights in human experimentation. New York: Oxford University Press, 1992:339–42.
4. Twenty years after: the legacy of the Tuskegee syphilis study. Hastings Cent Rep 1992;22(6):29–40.
5. Caplan AL. When evil intrudes. Hastings Cent Rep 1992;22(6):29–32.
6. The development of consent requirements in research ethics. In: Faden RR, Beauchamp TL. A history and theory of informed consent. New York: Oxford University Press, 1986:151–99.
7. Lurie P, Wolfe SM. Unethical trials of interventions to reduce perinatal transmission of the human immunodeficiency virus in developing countries. N Engl J Med 1997;337:853–6.
8. The conduct of clinical trials of maternal-infant transmission of HIV supported by the United States Department of Health and Human Services in developing countries. Washington, D.C.: Department of Health and Human Services, July 1997.
9. Whalen CC, Johnson JL, Okwera A, et al. A trial of three regimens to prevent tuberculosis in Ugandan adults infected with the human immunodeficiency virus. N Engl J Med 1997;337:801–8.
10. The use of preventive therapy for tuberculous infection in the United States: recommendations of the Advisory Committee for Elimination of Tuberculosis. MMWR Morb Mortal Wkly Rep 1990;39(RR-8):9–12.
11. Bass JB Jr, Farer LS, Hopewell PC, et al. Treatment of tuberculosis and tuberculosis infection in adults and children. Am J Respir Crit Care Med 1994;149:1359–74.
12. De Cock KM, Grant A, Porter JD. Preventive therapy for tuberculosis in HIV-infected persons: international recommendations, research, and practice. Lancet 1995;345:833–6.
13. Msamanga GI, Fawzi WW. The double burden of HIV infection and tuberculosis in sub-Saharan Africa. N Engl J Med 1997;337:849–51.
14. Angell M. Ethical imperialism? Ethics in international collaborative clinical research. N Engl J Med 1988;319:1081–3.
15. Protection of human subjects, 45 CFR § 46 (1996).
16. International ethical guidelines for biomedical research involving human subjects. Geneva: Council for International Organizations of Medical Sciences, 1993.
17. Angell M. The Nazi hypothermia experiments and unethical research today. N Engl J Med 1990;322:1462–4.

HIV Vaccine Trial Participation in South Africa—An Ethical Assessment

KEYMANTHRI MOODLEY

I. Introduction

With more than 16,000 new people infected daily throughout the world, HIV/AIDS is clearly an illness of global importance and is a major priority for the world community. An effective preventive HIV vaccine could be a powerful tool in the struggle against the expanding HIV pandemic. However, such a vaccine would have to be tested in clinical trials using human subjects in the absence of a suitable animal model. HIV vaccine trials began 10 years ago in the United States and Europe and are now increasingly being planned and implemented in developing countries (Guenter, Esparza, & Macklin, 2000, p. 37).

Recruiting volunteers for these trials is critical to the success of the endeavor, yet it is fraught with scientific, social, political and ethical concerns, especially when the target communities live in the Third World and funding is from affluent countries. The decision to participate in research is likely to be influenced by a wide range of factors. It is critical to determine what information is to be given to potential subjects or guardians to enable them to make an informed decision. A vital component of such patient information is the risk-benefit ratio that determines the ethical acceptability of clinical research. In AIDS vaccine research, however, the half of the equation that deals with risk is "virtually unknown." There is no data about the potential for risks such as "vaccine-induced immunotoxicity or antibody-induced enhancement of infection" (Tacket & Edelman, 1990, p. 356).

In anticipation of the launch of HIV vaccine trials worldwide, guidelines have been developed to protect the rights of those participating in international vaccine trials. As noted in the Declaration of Helsinki of 2000, "concern for the interest of the individual must always prevail over the interests of science and society." Accordingly individual informed consent becomes of central importance to investigators and trial sponsors in trying to develop effective vaccines, study the effective use of expensive anti-retroviral treatment, or treat participants in developing countries who become infected during the trials.

The problem inherent in any research is that one must balance the rights of the individual and group benefit, in this case not only societal good but global good. In some cases there can be a conflict between what benefits the individual and what promotes the societal good. Many of the principles of African "Communitarianism" or "*Ubuntu,*" which exists in various forms especially in rural, traditional South African communities, seem to be in stark contrast to the more individualistic principles of the West yet are beginning to be influenced by western individualism (Constitution of the Republic of South Africa 1996, Chapter 2—Bill of Rights), and this is reflected in the way research is being conducted. This will be illustrated by ethical concerns central to the HIV vaccine trials, and its relevance in the African context will be discussed. Ultimately, the idea that an appeal to "*Ubuntu*" might be our only hope of conducting ethical HIV vaccine trials that will respond to the pandemic of HIV/AIDS in South Africa will be explored.

II. Research in Developing Communities: HIV Vaccine Trials and Consent in the Third World

Some charge that developing communities around the world are sometimes seen as excellent candidates for medical research largely because people in these communities tend to be poor, malnourished, illiterate and desperate. Lurie and Wolfe wrote of earlier HIV vertical transmission trials, "Residents of impoverished, postcolonial countries, the majority of whom are people of color, must be protected from potential exploitation in research. Otherwise, the abominable state of health care in these countries can be used to justify studies that could never pass ethical muster in the sponsoring country" (Lurie & Wolfe—1997 Public Citizen's Health Research Group). In the aftermath of these controversial HIV Vertical transmission trials, HIV Vaccine Trials are now emerging as the next major ethical challenge in South African research circles. Basic ethical principles need to be applied, interpreted and specified within different cultural settings (Barry, 1988, p. 1083). The Nuremberg Code and its progeny require that participation in biomedical research be based on "freedom of *individual choice* with no element of coercion or constraint." This may prove to be a problematical standard in the Third World where *personal choice* is extremely limited, because in many African cultures the concept of personhood differs substantially from that in Western cultures. One's tribe, village or social group defines personhood. In certain African societies, selfhood cannot be extricated from a dynamic system of social relationships, both of kinship and of community as defined by the village (Barry, 1988, p. 1083). South African philosopher Augustine Shutte, in his work on *"Ubuntu,"* explains that the dominant form of contemporary European thought is materialist in character and a human community is seen as a collection of

separate individuals. He refers to this as the "mechanistic theory of society" with the individualist version of this theory underlying liberalism and capitalism: On the other hand, the African concept of personhood differs: persons exist only in relation to other persons. According to him, in all African languages, there is the local variant of the Nguni saying "umuntu ngumuntu ngabantu"—a person is a person through persons. Each individual member of the community sees the community as *themselves*, as one with them in character and identity (unpublished data). Under such circumstances, it is easier for traditional African communities to see research as an altruistic endeavor as opposed to an endeavor for personal benefit only. Similarly, in Ugandan culture, the wishes of the individual are often subordinated to those of the immediate or extended family. As such, participation of an individual in biomedical research may depend on the acquiescence or consent of another family member (Loue, Okello, & Kawuma, 1996, p. 49). The concept of family consent is not peculiar to Africa alone. It is an important concept in Japanese culture as well. As such, the principle of autonomy, as it exists in its traditional North American paradigm, is not entirely applicable to Japanese culture. Instead, Edmund Pellegrino refers to "something close to autonomy" that is respected in the context of Japanese society (Akabayashi, Fetters, & Elwyn, 1999, pp. 296–301). Similarly, ancient Chinese medical ethics, established on the foundations of Confucian ethics, emphasizes a respectful attitude towards one's patients based on an unconditional value for human life, but does not include respecting their autonomous choices (Tsai, 1999, pp. 315–321). It is thus clear that where the notion of persons as individuals is not dominant, the consent process may shift from the individual to the family or community (Christakis, 1988, p. 34).

Thus, an investigator seeking informed consent from individual persons in such settings may need to approach community elders for their consent before attempting to obtain informed consent from individual persons (Barry, 1988, p. 1083). The person acknowledged to be a "community leader" would vary from one culture to another and from one investigator to another. In some cases they would need permission to approach individuals to seek their participation. Since the consent of the individual is sought, this would not be incompatible with Western models. What would be incompatible, however, would be where no one needed to ask the individual person because the tribal leader's authorization was *sufficient* for studies carrying risk. Rather what is typically different in Africa is the need for family consent in addition to individual consent in biomedical research. One might need a waiting period before an informed consent form is signed so this could be discussed with family or elders. Yet this waiting period can often be problematic since it might involve returning to the region, costly transportation and loss of time. Furthermore, the nature of the information regarding the trial may be misrepresented and it is possible that informed consent will not be obtained. However, with no suitable alternatives, a waiting period remains an option when obtaining informed consent in Africa.

In short, it may be a problem to understand who will be giving consent (the person, family or elders) in addition to the sort of review needed in the West. Let us assume, however, that we know this. The next set of problems concerns trying to convey adequate information. During a workshop held in South Africa to discuss ethical issues in HIV vaccine trials in September 1998, Oliver Ransome, the medical ombudsman, outlined some standard prerequisites for obtaining and documenting informed consent. One should have an information sheet for potential subjects, a third party adviser, and time to reflect as well as the actual written consent. The details on the information sheet should include the overall purpose of the research "in comprehensible language." Confidentiality should be stressed and it should be clear that the subject is free to decline

or withdraw. Questions should be invited. However, in South Africa, with very high rates of illiteracy, such a sheet may be inappropriate to use. In a similar workshop in Uganda, it was established that with their currently "high rate of illiteracy, many prospective research participants would be unable to read a form and understand it" (Loue et al., 1996, p. 50). This would also have serious implications for obtaining the "written consent" referred to by Ransome.

Illiteracy coupled with language barriers in Africa make the description of AIDS-related studies difficult. When concepts like germ theory, viruses and vaccines are alien, it is indeed challenging to establish what is sufficient information for informed consent. Ron Bayer (HIV Centre, New York) also expresses concern regarding the explanation of "complicated scientific methods such as randomization, placebos, vaccine inefficiency, the fact that participation in one trial may exclude future participation in trials of more effective vaccines and discrimination linked to participation" (Bayer, 1998, p. 5).

An interesting problem with language was illustrated in the HIV Vertical Transmission Trials conducted on pregnant women in South Africa in 1997. The placebo drug used in these trials was translated as being a "spaza" drug or a "chuff-chuff" drug (Prabhakaran, 1997, p. 5). While a "chuff-chuff" drug is understood to be a "pretend" drug, the word "spaza" is a colloquial term generally meaning "half the real thing" or pretence of the real thing. In no way are they associated with the concept of inertness inherent in a placebo. As such, the use of the term "spaza" to describe a placebo is clearly misleading.

In addition to the problems of supplying adequate information for informed consent, one must also ensure that the potential subject or guardian who gives consent does so voluntarily and competently. These too present problems in the third world where research participants are usually poor, desperate and dependent. Consider problems with voluntariness. Research participants should be able to choose freely amongst alternatives and also have a right to refuse to participate. In a research setting, manipulation rather than coercion or persuasion tends to occur. In the context of decision-making in health care, informational manipulation tends to be the key form of manipulation employed. Misleading research participants, as in the case of using the word "spaza" to describe a placebo, is a form of deception that is clearly inconsistent with autonomous choice. Attractive offers such as free medication or extra money can leave persons without any meaningful choice apart from accepting the offer largely because such persons are constrained in a desperate situation. Whatever we may decide to call this, it is widely held that offers of this magnitude to a person in desperate need is inherently exploitative and is not consistent with autonomous choice.

In South Africa, it is general research practice that trial participants are paid $6 per trial visit that is intended to cover costs for transport and meals for the day. Including this amount in the informed consent document is problematic in poor communities where people would consent to such research for half this amount of money. Research methodology and statistical validity may also be adversely influenced by follow-up visits if patients are offered payment for these visits. The development of "side-effects" might be very attractive if one is aware that one will be paid for all "illness visits" to a trial site.

Looking specifically at the ethical design of an AIDS vaccine trial in Africa, Christakis warns researchers that

> it is difficult to avoid coercing subjects in most settings where clinical investigation in the developing world is conducted. African subjects with relatively little understanding of medical aspects of research participation, indisposed toward resisting the suggestions of Western doctors, perhaps operating under the mistaken notion that they are being treated, and possibly receiving some ancillary benefits from participation in the research, are very susceptible to coercion. Their vulnerability warrants greater care in procuring consent and ne-

cessitates greater sensitivity to protect this class of research subjects. (Christakis, 1988, p. 35)

Research conducted in Durban, South Africa to assess whether informed consent for HIV testing in a South African hospital was truly informed and voluntary yielded interesting results. Of the 56 women studied, 88% felt compelled to participate, even though they were assured that their participation was entirely voluntary. 28% of the women "perceived the research to be integral with the service at the hospital and agreed to the HIV test because they thought that refusal would compromise their care. This subtle coercive element may stem from the social context of a hospital where the health professionals are held in high regard." When patients have little recourse to other medical care, they may have no choice but to participate in a research study conducted at the only tertiary hospital at their disposal. It is highly probable that informed consent sought under such circumstances might be "less than voluntary." This study concluded that "subtle and unexpected elements of coercion can reside in the perceptions (real or imagined) held by patients recruited into a research project in a medical care setting" (Abdool Karrim, Abdool Karrim, Coovadia, & Susser, 1998, p. 640).

A discussion on informed consent would be incomplete without examining the important precondition of competence. In biomedical contexts a person has been viewed as competent if able to understand a therapy or research procedure, to deliberate regarding major risks and benefits, and to make a decision in light of this deliberation (Beauchamp & Childress, 1994, p. 136). The label of "incompetence" has traditionally been applied to children, the mentally retarded, people with major psychiatric illnesses and those with delirium or dementia. Such people are regarded as vulnerable research subjects because they lack capacity to give informed consent and because they depend on others to protect them (Kopelman, 1994, p. 2291). Little attention has been paid to the millions of people in developing countries, like South Africa, who due to poverty, malnutrition and lack of opportunities for education are either illiterate or uneducated. Coupled to this are the constraints of cultural belief systems especially where causation in illness is concerned. To these people, many concepts in science and medicine are alien and they often have to undergo an enormous paradigm shift in order to understand and deliberate about the complexities of Western biomedical research. This group of people also falls into the category of "vulnerable research subjects" because fear, ignorance or pressure may account for their agreement to participate. Too little protection of these subjects risks their exploitation; too much protection risks unjustified paternalism (Kopelman, 1994, p. 2292).

At the risk of the latter charge, I believe that it is highly probable that in many cases of biomedical research in the developing world, subjects, although adult and not mentally impaired or retarded, do not fulfil all the criteria for competence outlined above. Often, subjects do not understand what they have been told about a complicated and foreign research protocol and when they do not understand they are not competent to decide whether to accept or reject their involvement in such a setting. The capacities necessary for such understanding include "a memory for words, phrases, ideas and sequences of information." Furthermore, the

> chance nature of the occurrence of risks and benefits highlights the importance of the ability to understand causal relations and the likelihood of various outcomes. Finally, it may be important for patients to be able to understand not only what they are told, but also that they have a critical part to play in the decision-making process. Deficits in attention span, intelligence and memory may detract from these abilities. (Appelbaum & Grisso, 1988, p. 1636)

It is not my intention to suggest that all people from developing communities are incompetent and hence cannot give informed consent to participate in research conducted in the third world. This

would deprive such subjects of their decision-making rights and would represent a serious infringement of liberty. Rather, it is possible that a position of "limited competence" exists in many instances.

In the aftermath of the apartheid era in South Africa, many people who are completely competent still relinquish their decision-making rights to authority figures, be they doctors, researchers or both. This is accentuated when researchers and study participants belong to different racial groups and where asymmetrical power relationships, based on the previous apartheid system, exist. Enormous efforts are required on the part of the medical profession and researchers to create the level of understanding necessary to meet the criteria of competence. Coupled with this is a need for empowerment of many patients, who, as a result of decades of oppression, have never learned how to exercise their decision-making rights.

It is evident from this discussion on the procurement of informed consent from prospective participants in HIV vaccine trials that the concept is riddled with intricacies. The precise demands of the principle of autonomy are largely unsettled and remain open to interpretation and specification.

III. What Risks Will Be Faced by Participants in An HIV Vaccine Trial?

To begin with, adverse effects of the vaccine itself may occur as with other vaccines in current use, such as pain or infection at the injection site, fever or allergic reactions. A study conducted in Thailand among high-risk populations to assess willingness to participate in AIDS vaccine trials found that vaccine side effects were considered to be important barriers to trial participation (Celentano et al., 1995, p. 1079).

More specifically, with an HIV vaccine, participants are likely to be concerned about actually developing HIV disease from the vaccine. With the current use of genetically altered or killed viruses, this risk is unlikely. The current subunit vaccine candidates, which employ genetically engineered proteins from the HIV envelope—with a piece of the virus being used—are likely to allay much anxiety (Jonston, 1998, p. 1). However, participants' fears are likely to magnify as vaccine developers incorporate the use of whole killed or live attenuated virus. Already, scientists are becoming impatient to test live attenuated virus vaccines! However, leading clinicians are still hesitant regarding the safety of such vaccines. The majority opinion at present is that "there is just not enough evidence that a live-attenuated HIV-1 vaccine is safe—or effective" (McCarthy, 1997, p. 1082).

Even with current genetically engineered vaccines, while it is possible that disease will be prevented, infection might still occur. Few of the candidate HIV vaccines appear promising for preventing infection, and the expectation that HIV vaccines will in fact prevent infection is yielding, in the scientific community, to the hope that they may prevent disease (Bloom, 1998, p. 186). In reality, when the first AIDS vaccine trials were launched in the United States and Thailand in 1998, using the HIV envelope protein gp120 in a vaccine called AIDSVAX, two outcome measures were to be assessed: "infection by HIV and viral load in those infected."

Furthermore, the possibility of vaccine failure is very real and the occurrence of "breakthrough HIV infections" or disease cannot be excluded. This particular risk to the subject needs to be assessed in the context of the different types of trials that are performed. It is reasonable to assume that the risk of developing HIV infection during the course of phase 1 or 2 trials by low risk participants will be far greater than the risk taken by people entering phase 3 trials, already at high risk by virtue of lifestyle or other predisposing factors (Jenkins, Temoshok, & Virochsiri, 1995, p. 171). Where the HIV vaccine is concerned, in South Africa, phase 1 and 2 trials will have to be conducted here as these vaccines are specifically directed against the clade C virus.

Researchers will have an obligation to provide anti-retroviral treatment to subjects who be-

come infected during the course of the trials. Scientists and researchers are concerned that treatment with anti-retroviral drugs will compromise the ability of the trial to measure the efficacy of the vaccine in preventing disease (Bloom, 1998, p. 186). A critical measure of the success of an AIDS vaccine trial would be whether the vaccine lowers the "viral load" in people who get infected. Anti-retroviral treatment will also lower the viral load. If many of the participants who become infected begin taking potent anti-retroviral drugs, reduction in viral loads due to the vaccine cannot be assessed. Scientists fear that it will become impossible to design a "scientifically valid" trial if there is widespread use of anti-retroviral drugs. The head of the biotech company VaxGen, that launched the first efficacy trials of an AIDS vaccine in the United States, argued that not everyone would start treatment immediately, and because researchers would be taking blood from participants every 24 weeks or so, they should be able to make at least one viral load measurement in many untreated people who become infected (Cohen, 1998, p. 22). Delaying drug treatment until viral loads can be measured, as is implicit in the trial design by VaxGen, however, only adds to the complex ethical problems already inherent in treating participants who develop HIV infection during the trials. This delay in treatment will pose problems in the developed world where it will be ethically required that individuals in vaccine trials who have acquired HIV infection will be offered anti-retroviral therapy as soon as possible. A delay in treatment will not be tolerated in the West. The standard of care in the developing world is clearly "no treatment for HIV/AIDS." This will also obviate the ethical dilemma of delaying treatment to measure viral load.

The question of the duty to treat trial participants with anti-retroviral drugs if they develop infection during the trials remains largely unanswered. During a workshop in South Africa in 1998, the issue was skirted, stating that this issue would be left up to the host country to decide. An idea of what is likely to happen in South Africa may be extrapolated from the Thai trial funded by VaxGen, where neither the company nor the cash-strapped Thai government plans to give treatment to people who become infected (Cohen, 1998, p. 23).

Various "social harms" may burden participants in a vaccine trial. Participants might be identified as high risk for AIDS, or might be mistakenly assumed to have AIDS. A Thai study has shown that 24–49% of participants believed that their partners would refuse to have sex with them after immunization (Celentano et al., 1995, p. 1079). Discrimination based on HIV antibody status may occur in a number of settings—acceptance into the military, the job corps, the pease corps or the foreign service; the purchase of insurance; permission to immigrate or travel abroad or incarceration (Hodel, 1994, p. 256). While it is possible to distinguish between HIV positive results from a vaccine as opposed to natural infection, many potential participants and others might be unaware of this. Testing HIV positive after the vaccine will be perceived as a significant risk.

The possibility of being included in a control group in the trial, where a placebo will be used instead of the HIV vaccine, will create further problems. Researchers in Philadelphia have already reported that interest in participating in a vaccine trial dropped from 47% to 24% when the possibility of using a placebo was mentioned (Jenkins et al., 1995, p. 37).

Finally, a further risk inherent in an HIV vaccine trial is the possibility of increased risk-taking behavior by participants who mistakenly believe that they have been protected by the vaccine.

IV. What Are the Benefits, If Any, to Trial Participation?

As scientists weigh the potential benefits of conducting a trial against the potential risks, so too will individual participants and target communities weigh relevant data before deciding to participate. This risk-benefit calculus will ultimately be informed by social values. This is of special relevance to the Third World where in communities already

> burdened by violence, drugs, alcohol, unemployment, urban decay and the like, the AIDS epidemic has merely exacerbated an already arduous burden of day-to-day survival. For many inner city residents the threat of random gunfire easily exceeds the somewhat less immediate threat of HIV infection, a risk profile that is difficult for outsiders to appreciate. (Hodel, 1994, p. 255)

This sentiment is echoed by South African social anthropologist, Virginia van der Vliet:

> Increasingly, those affected are the poor in urban ghettos, illegal migrants, drug users, street children, prostitutes, or the impoverished people in Third World countries. They are not unacquainted with the savagery of life. For them, AIDS is just an additional problem, often faced with their customary fatalism. Fatalism is no protection against AIDS. (1996, pp. 77–78)

It is against this backdrop of fatalism that one needs to assess whether the development of a protective vaccine against AIDS will be perceived to be of overwhelming benefit to the Third World.

Subjects may be motivated to join a trial either on altruistic grounds or on grounds of personal benefit. A few studies have been conducted to date to assess the motivation of people to participate in trials. In one such study in Thailand, purely altruistic motives were unrelated to willingness to participate (Jenkins et al., 1995, pp. 40–41). Similarly, in another survey of 2180 Thai people, 62% found that the principal inducement to join a trial was health insurance (Celentano et al., 1995, pp. 1079–1082).

Where HIV vaccine trials are concerned, the risk-benefit ratio is situated in a rather precarious position. Participants have little to benefit personally from such trials and potentially much to lose! In a French vaccine trial, only 57 of 645 persons who had expressed initial interest by mail actually enrolled in the trial. Other surveys have found that under the relatively hypothetical condition of being asked to join a phase 2 or 3 HIV vaccine trial, levels of willingness have ranged from 37% to 84% (Jenkins et al., 1995, p. 37).

Studies that have gone beyond asking the simple question of whether participants would be willing to join a trial have found that interest dropped dramatically when specific trial features or procedures were explained. Research on intravenous drug users in the New York City area found that the percentage of "very interested" potential volunteers dropped from 50% to 17% after they received information normally contained in a consent form. Another study found that 73% of those approached in Baltimore were interested in participation, although this figure dropped to 49% after the issue of testing HIV antibody-positive as a consequence of immunologic response to the vaccine was discussed (Jenkins et al., 1995, p. 37). Both studies were conducted on people at high risk to develop HIV infection!

Interestingly, studies are also finding that willingness to participate in these trials is associated with lower levels of education. In a Thailand study of 255 participants, high school-educated respondents were more willing to participate than university graduates (Jenkins et al., 1995, p. 39). One wonders whether this choice not to participate by more educated respondents is not the result of a more accurate appreciation of the risk-benefit ratio inherent in these trials, namely the high risk-low benefit scenario.

Given full details of the risks and benefits of an HIV vaccine trial, participants will either exercise their right of refusal to participate or will agree to participate only if the benefit is maximized in terms of personal incentives, in particular, health care, in the developing world. A crucial factor to be considered is that in order for the benefits to outweigh the risks in the trial of an HIV vaccine, an individual would have to be at some risk of HIV infection. The necessity of being at risk therefore has scientific and ethical import.

V. Justice, Consent and the HIV/AIDS Pandemic

The principle of justice or fairness requires that the benefits and the burdens of research be equitably distributed among individuals or communities. No single group can be required to bear a disproportionate share of the risk or be favored with a disproportionate share of the benefits (Loue et al., 1996, p. 51). Under the principle of justice, research subjects should be chosen "for reasons directly related to the problem being studied," and not "because of their easy availability, their compromised position, or their manipulability." As a result, the "practical concerns that make an AIDS vaccine trial easier to conduct in Africa do not alone constitute sufficient justification to use Africans as subjects. Only the scientific concerns related directly to the problem of establishing the ability of a vaccine to prevent HIV infection are relevant" (Christakis, 1988, p. 36).

Where HIV/AIDS is concerned, it is evident that this disease is rampant in Africa. As a result, it may be unavoidable that a higher degree of research risk is tolerated in order to deal with the problem and this may even be socially sanctioned. However, this does not mean that Westerners should "indiscriminately benefit from research conducted in Africa if Africans are systematically subjected to excess research risks with the prospect of deriving but little benefit" (Christakis, 1988, p. 36).

Obviously, however, the entire world stands to gain from the development of an effective vaccine. In keeping with the principle of justice, those who stand to benefit from the vaccine should also bear the burden. Hence, the research risks should be fairly distributed as should the benefits. Vaccine development trials need not be restricted to the African continent. In Africa, economic constraints may prevent adequate distribution of such a vaccine. The benefits to Africans are thus "only hypothetical unless there is a financial commitment by the developed world to provide the vaccine. In this light, it would be frankly unethical to subject Africans to a disproportionate share of the research risks" (Christakis, 1988, p. 36).

CIOMS Guideline 15 on Externally Sponsored Research requires that any trial "must be responsive to the health needs of the host country. . . . Any product developed through such research (should) be made reasonably available to the inhabitants of the host community or country at completion of successful testing" (Bloom, 1998, pp. 186–187). This is also a requirement of the latest version of the Declaration of Helsinki (October 2000).

A contingency of any trial of an AIDS vaccine in Africa by Western scientists should thus be to provide access to the technology once it is developed—possibly in the form of free or subsidized vaccine (Christakis, 1988, p. 36).

In South Africa, this well established principle has been violated. In 2001, four years after the completion of trials in which shorter courses of anti-retroviral treatment for HIV infected pregnant women were found to be effective, millions of eligible women still go without treatment. Anti-retroviral treatment has been recently and selectively introduced at a few antenatal clinics only in South Africa (Dr. Mark Cotton, pediatrician, Tygerberg Hospital, South Africa—personal communication).

In a paper published in the *American Journal of Public Health*, this issue is discussed openly. The outcome of the trials performed on impoverished populations around the world was clearly not the delivery of the necessary drugs to these developing countries. Instead, the purpose was "to provide information that the host country can use to make a sound judgement about the appropriateness and financial feasibility of providing the intervention" (Annas & Grodin, 1998, p. 561). Good intent in the absence of a sound plan to provide the intervention, once proven to be effective, is no justification for the performance of such research. Annas and Grodin go on to say that

Unless the intervention being tested will actually be made available to the impoverished populations

that are being used as research subjects, developed countries are simply exploiting them in order to quickly use the knowledge gained from the clinical trials for the developed countries' own benefit. If the research reveals regimens of equal efficacy at less cost, these regimens will surely be implemented in the developed world. If the research reveals the regimens to be less efficacious, these results will be added to the scientific literature, and the developed world will not conduct these studies. (1998, p. 561)

Once again, with the proposed vaccine trials, South Africa has not clarified that it will only conduct these trials on condition that a definite plan is in place to acquire the vaccine for widespread use, if it proves to be effective. Of note, however, is the fact that South Africa has decided not to conduct trials using a clade B vaccine that has already been developed in the United States. This viral subtype is not common in sub-Saharan Africa but it is the predominant clade in North America where homosexual transmission of HIV is common. In South Africa, with a predominantly heterosexual transmission of disease, the predominant subtype is clade C. South African researchers have opted to develop an appropriate clade C vaccine for experimentation here (Makgoba, 1998, p. 10).

Yet another way in which subjects could be exploited for research and the principle of justice violated involves encouraging trial participants to continue practicing other preventative measures after the vaccine has been administered. It will be difficult to assess vaccine efficacy if they suddenly change their habits. These interventions could diminish the ability of the study to detect a difference between true vaccine recipients and controls by decreasing the incidence of HIV infection in all participants for reasons unrelated to vaccine status (Christakis, 1988, p. 34). On the other hand, failing to stress these preventative measures could result in a greater risk of contracting HIV infection, especially if the vaccine proves to be ineffective. To circumvent this problem, a larger study group would be required to detect the relatively smaller measured influence of the vaccine. As a result, more individuals will be exposed to the experimental vaccine and the cost of the trials will be higher. It will also take longer to get statistically significant results. To prevent this potential harm to participants and in all fairness to them, it is imperative that researchers continue to promote preventative measures.

VI. Trial Participation—The Tension Between Liberalism and Communitarianism

Research guidelines and principles that guide human investigation need to be interpreted and applied within different cultural settings. As Beauchamp and Childress note,

> making respect for autonomy a trump moral principle, rather than one moral principle in a system of principles, gives it an excessive value. . . In many clinical circumstances the weight of respect for autonomy is minimal, and the weight of nonmaleficence or beneficence is maximal. Similarly, in public policy, the demands of justice can easily outweigh the demands of respect for autonomy. (1994, p. 181)

There are, of course, tensions once one agrees that the principles of beneficence, non-maleficence, justice and autonomy have no one ranking. This is true in Africa when we consider morally justified research.

In South Africa, as we emerge from a history where the rights of the vulnerable and poor have been negated in the service of apartheid, the preference for a subject-oriented view, where research is concerned, is a logical choice. Our new democratic order, our Constitution and Bill of Rights bear testimony to individual rights. Yet the importance of the needs of the community cannot be ignored. Medical research is seen as one of the essential goods in a society and is therefore vital to the survival of such a society (Ackerman & Strong, 1989, pp. 166–179). Christakis comments that an African might find it "difficult to see how the interests of the subject conflict with the interests of the society except, of course, if the society is not his own." In traditional Africa, in

keeping with the concept of "*Ubuntu*," the interests of the subject and of society are necessarily congruent. People see themselves as "potential persons" who become fully human to the extent that they are included in relationships with others (Shutte—unpublished data).

Scientifically, South Africa is an ideal site for HIV vaccine research. Yet, the HIV Vaccine Trials pose a grave and significant risk to the individual who may subsequently have little to gain. Under such circumstances, statistically significant trial participation can only be ensured by an appeal to altruism—"*Ubuntu*" in the African context. In this regard, the interests of science and society are seen as one with the interests of the individual. Interdependence and connectedness is a prominent feature of traditional African society. In such a setting, trial participation and hence medical research will be possible. Appeals to "*Ubuntu*" will be difficult since liberalism and notions of personal rights are becoming entrenched in Africa. In rural Africa, an appeal to "*Ubuntu*" could succeed in harnessing trial participation. However, in the developed areas of Africa, where individualism is spreading, this will not be possible.

VII. Conclusion

Ethical principles and research guidelines try to balance individual rights with the good of the community. Ethical principles and research guidelines must be adapted and applied to the community in which the research will be done, taking account of their traditions and honoring their practices. Affluent countries cannot presuppose that they understand how the concept of informed consent should be understood. If the principles which underpin the 2000 version of the Declaration of Helsinki are strictly adhered to, constraints on the rights of the individual will be impermissible and in the Third World, this would render research unethical and hence, impossible. The global population is not homogenous, and universality "obscures and obliterates the particularity and specificity of morality which is grounded in communal traditions" (Bernstein, 1982, p. 137). It is therefore unnecessary for "every country to follow the practice of autonomy in all of its details in a fashion identical to that found in North America" (Akabayashi, Fetters, & Elwyn, 1999, p. 299). We need to "take into account local customs and traditions that should be respected and incorporated into the research process" as far as is possible (Loue et al., 1996, p. 51). Culturally relevant ethical issues need to be incorporated into existing frameworks to augment them with cultural sensitivity. However, changing the rules from time to time and from place to place to achieve the research aims of the West will be both unjustifiable and morally reprehensible.

Undoubtedly, the HIV Vaccine Trials in South Africa will pose a major ethical challenge to all involved. We must, however, be wary that in our haste to develop and test an HIV vaccine, we do not cause an ethical catastrophe that we will never be able to justify. It has taken a long time for the research community to recover from Tuskegee. May we never tread along that path again!

References

Abdool Karim, Q., Abdool Karim, S.S., Coovadia, H.M., & Susser, M. (1998). Informed consent for HIV testing in a South African hospital: Is it truly informed and truly voluntary? *American Journal of Public Health, 88*(4), 637–640.

Ackerman, T.F., & Strong, C. (1989). *A casebook of medical ethics.* New York: Oxford University Press.

Akabayashi, A., Fetters, M.D., & Elwyn, T.S. (1999). Family consent, communication, and advance directives for cancer disclosure: A Japanese case and discussion. *Journal of Medical Ethics, 25,* 296–301.

Annas, G.J., & Grodin, M.A. (1998). Human rights and maternal-fetal HIV transmission prevention trials in Africa. *American Journal of Public Health, 88*(4), 560–562.

Appelbaum, P.S., & Grisso, T. (1988). Assessing patients' capacities to consent to treatment. *The New England Journal of Medicine, 319*(25), 1635–1636.

Barry, M. (1988). Ethical considerations of human investigation in developing countries: The AIDS

dilemma. *The New England Journal of Medicine, 319*(16), 1083–1085.

Bayer, R. (1998). What is informed consent? *Workshop on ethical issues in the conduct of HIV vaccine trials.* Durban, South Africa.

Beauchamp, T.L., & Childress, J.F. (1994). *Principles of biomedical ethics* (4th ed.). New York: Oxford University Press.

Bernstein, R.J. (1986). Nietzsche or Aristotle? Reflections on Alasdair MacIntyre's *After Virtue.* In: R.J. Bernstein (Ed.), *Philosophical profiles. Essays in a pragmatic mode.* Oxford: Basil Blackwell (Polity Press).

Bloom, B.R. (1998). The highest attainable standard: Ethical issues in AIDS vaccines. *Science, 279,* 186–187.

Celentano, D.D., Beyrer, C., Natpratan, C., Eiumtrakul, S., Sussman, L., Renzullo, P.O., Khamboonruang, C., & Nelson, K.E. (1995). Willingness to participate in AIDS vaccine trials among high-risk populations in northern Thailand. *AIDS, 9,* 1079–1083.

Christakis, N.A. (1988, June/July). The ethical design of an AIDS vaccine trial in Africa. *Hastings Center Report,* 31–37.

Cohen, J. (1998). No consensus on rules for AIDS vaccine trials. *Science, 281,* 22–23.

Constitution of the Republic of South Africa. (1996). As adopted on 8 May 1996 and amended on 11 October 1996 by the Constitutional Assembly. Act 108 of 1996. Chapter 2—Bill of Rights.

Guenter, D., Esparza, J., & Macklin, R. (2000). Ethical considerations in international HIV vaccine trials: Summary of a consultative process conducted by the Joint United Nations Programme on HIV/AIDS (UNAIDS). *Journal of Medical Ethics, 26,* 37–43.

Hodel, D. (1994). HIV preventive vaccine efficacy trials in the United States: An overview of target communities' concerns. *AIDS Research and Human Retroviruses, 10*(2), 255.

Jenkins, R.A., Temoshok, L.R., & Virochsiri, K. (1995). Incentives and disincentives to participate inpProphylactic HIV vaccine research. *Journal of Acquired Immune Deficiency Syndromes and Human Retrovirology, 9,* 36–42.

Kopelman, L.M. (1994). Research policy/ III. Risk and vulnerable groups. *Encyclopedia of Bioethics* (2nd ed.). New York: Macmillan Free Press.

Loue, S., Okello, D., & Kawuma, M. (1996). Research bioethics in the Ugandan context: A program summary. *Journal of Law, Medicine & Ethics, 24,* 47–53.

Lurie, P., & Wolfe, S.M. (1997). Unethical trials of interventions to reduce perinatal transmission of the human immunodeficiency virus in developing countries. *The New England Journal of Medicine, 337*(12), 853–855.

Makgoba, W. (1998). Should South Africa embark on clade B vaccine trials? *Workshop on ethical issues in the conduct of HIV vaccine trials.* Durban, South Africa.

McCarthy, M. (1997). AIDS doctors push for live-virus vaccine trials. *The Lancet, 350,* 1082.

Prabhakaran, S. (1997, October 3–9). Mothers give support to placebo trials. *Mail & Guardian,* 5.

Ransome, O. (1998). What is informed consent? *Workshop on the ethical issues in the conduct of HIV vaccine trials.* Durban, South Africa.

Shutte, A. *Ubuntu. The African vision.* Chapter Two. Unpublished book.

Tacket, C.O., & Edelman, R. (1990). Ethical issues involving volunteers in AIDS vaccine trials. *The Journal of Infectious Diseases, 161,* 356.

Tsai, D.F. (1999). Ancient Chinese medical ethics and the four principles of biomedical ethics. *Journal of Medical Ethics, 25,* 315–321.

Van der Vliet, V. (1996). *The Politics of AIDS.* London: Bowerdean Publishing Company Limited.

World Medical Association (2000). *Declaration of Helsinki.* Ethical Principles for Medical Research Involving Research Subjects Adopted by the 18th WMA General Assembly Helsinki, Finland, June 1964 and amended by the 52nd WMA General Assembly, Edinburgh, Scotland, October 2000.

B. Science and Society

The ethical analysis of biomedical research often requires us to assess the risks and harms that might befall particular individuals affected by the research against the potential benefits that might accrue to the larger population. In some cases, however, research may not harm any identifiable individuals. Indeed, it may offer them some hypothetical benefits. But the research may be questioned because of its potential harm to society-at-large or to significant subsets of the population. Are there some sorts of research that simply should not be undertaken?

The question whether scientific knowledge is always a "good" and should be pursued wherever it may lead has long been salient to nuclear physicists. After all, discoveries about atomic energy early in the twentieth century greatly expanded our understanding of the universe and offered significant benefits to humanity. At the same time, these discoveries made possible the development of the most destructive weapons known to humankind. As Albert Einstein said, "The unleashing of power of the atom bomb has changed everything except our mode of thinking, and thus we head toward unparalleled catastrophes."[8] Was it ethical for the early atomic scientists to pursue their work? Did the ethics only change when they became directly involved, during World War II, with the development of nuclear weapons? Or did the exigencies of the war itself justify the development of nuclear bombs?

Only in recent decades have biologists and medical researchers had to face such questions. Perhaps, the issue arose initially in 1967 when Dr. Christian Barnard first transplanted the heart of a cadaver into a human being. At that time, the debate was not only about the impact of the transplant on the recipient (the subject of the experiment) but also about the impact of such transplants on humanity itself. Likewise, the advent of in vitro fertilization in the 1970s provoked a debate about whether such novel approaches to human reproduction were inherently wrong because they diminished the dignity or sanctity of human life. And concerns about the development of recombinant DNA techniques (more commonly known as "gene-splicing" or "genetic engineering") in the 1970s led researchers to agree upon a temporary voluntary moratorium for research that could lead to the development of potentially dangerous new organisms.[9]

Today, the debate continues with respect to numerous fields of biomedical research. For example, the Human Genome Project, which aimed at mapping the genetic code of homeo sapiens, provoked intense debate about the ethical and legal implications of identifying the genes within individuals and populations. In response to these concerns, the National Institutes of Health announced that 1 to 3 percent of the money spent on the Genome Project would be devoted to studies of its social and ethical implications.[10]

For the most part, the debates about the Genome Project have centered upon a critical but practical issue: How shall we deal with the knowledge we obtain? Ethicists have seldom questioned the appropriateness of the research itself but have cautioned us that care must be taken about the way we use the fruits of that research. For example, important issues have been raised about the privacy and confidentiality of genetic information. Access to an individual's genome allows scientists not only to make predictions about the individual's medical fate but also to learn the genetic destiny of the individual's relatives. In a society in which prejudice against many conditions remains prevalent and in which health insurers (and employers) discriminate against those who may be expected to incur significant health care costs in the future, it may be ethically imperative that the privacy of genetic information be especially guarded.

While the ethical discourse about the Genome Project has focused upon the use and treatment of the information garnered, ethicists have raised even more profound and fundamental questions about other areas of biomedical research. Perhaps no areas of research have generated as much controversy as the interrelated fields of cloning and embryonic stem cell research.

Cloning (or somatic cell nuclear transfer) is the process of creating a living organism from the genetic material of a single already existing organism. In other words, cloning is asexual reproduction. While cloning is common in invertebrates, debate arose in 1997 when scientists at the Roslin Institute in Scotland announced that they had cloned a sheep.[11] This was done by inserting the genetic material of one sheep (the cloned animal) in the denucleated egg of another sheep and then implanting that egg in a ewe's uterus. Responding to that development and fearing that it might pave the way for the cloning of a human being (something that recent studies suggest may be far harder to do than was thought in the 1990s),[12] the National Bioethics Advisory Commission in 1997 deliberated on the issue and concluded that "it is morally unacceptable for anyone in the public or private sector, whether in a research or clinical setting, to attempt to create a child using somatic cell nuclear transfer cloning."[13]

More recently, the President's Council on Bioethics issued a report, *Human Cloning and Human Dignity: An Ethical Inquiry*, which reviews the arguments for and against cloning. In the report, which is included in the readings, the Council notes that individuals have rights to make their own reproductive decisions and that cloning may at times be the only way that an individual can reproduce genetically. Nevertheless, the Council concludes that human reproductive cloning is inappropriate in part because it would constitute experimenting on a not-yet-existent person. The Council also argues that cloning may create problems pertaining to the identity and individuality of the cloned child. But perhaps most interestingly, the Council fears that cloning may lead to a form of eugenics that "could prove dangerous to our humanity." While recognizing that medicine often seeks to alter nature's course, the Council states that "[t]he fear of a new eugenics is not, as is sometimes alleged, a concern born of some irrational fear of the future or the unknown. . . . It is rather born of the rational recognition that once we move beyond therapy into efforts at enhancement, we are in uncharted waters without a map, without a compass, and without a clear destination that can tell us whether we are making improvements or the reverse."

Other opponents of cloning believe that it is morally wrong because when individuals engage in cloning, they "play God," undermining the mysteries of reproduction. Many critics come to this view as a result of their religious beliefs. What role should such views play in society's debates about new technology?

John Robertson, in contrast, sees reproductive cloning as a potential extension of human reproductive freedom. To Robertson, respect for individual autonomy requires recognition of the right to reproduce. For individuals who are unable to reproduce naturally, cloning may be the only way for them to exercise their right.[14] Reproductive cloning, therefore, should be accepted as are other forms of artificial reproduction because it may enhance human autonomy. Nevertheless, worried about eugenics, Robertson condemns cloning pursued to produce children with particular genetic profiles. Why does autonomy not go that far?

Many of the arguments about reproductive cloning have recently been applied to discussions of the use of cloning in embryonic stem cell research or therapy. Embryonic stem cells taken from very early embryos are special in that they are pluripotent; they have the ability to become any type of cell found in the body. Researchers have theorized that such stem cells may provide the key for treating numerous conditions, including diabetes and Parkinson's disease. Stem cells harvested from an embryo cloned from an individual seeking treatment for such a disease may be particularly useful because the cells would have the identical genetic material of the patient, thereby negating the possibility of rejection.

Proponents of so-called therapeutic cloning point to the possible enormous benefits that such techniques may hold for individuals facing painful and difficult diseases. They claim that any halt of research devalues the needs and interests of individuals with painful diseases. They also contend that an early embryo is not a unique human being and does not have interests sufficient to justify the suppression of the research. Opponents argue that cloning (and indeed the use of embryonic cells) is not necessary for the advancement of stem cell research because stem cells can be gathered from other tissue and that destroying an embryo to treat someone threatens the dignity of humans.

To some extent the debate about embryonic stem cell research and cloning replays the abortion debates about the status of embryos and whether they should be valued as individual human beings. To the degree that they are, stem cell research may be challenged within the traditional bioethics framework as jeopardizing the interests and rights of distinct human beings, the embryos. In announcing in the summer of 2001 that federal funding would not be available for research that would lead to the creation of new stem cells, but would be available for research on already existing stem cell lines, President Bush relied precisely on the argument that "life, including early life, is biologically human, genetically distinct and valuable. But one need not be prolife to be disturbed by the prospect of fetal farming or cloning to provide spare human parts."[15]

The President's decision, to allow funding for research on cells from already existing stem cell lines, may strike many as essentially political or pragmatic. According to the President, "while it is unethical to end life in medical research, it is ethical to benefit from research where life and death decisions have already been made."[16] Thus the problem with embryonic stem cell use is the fact that it requires the use and destruction of a human embryo. If that has already occurred, there is no reason not to reap the benefits that may arise from the research. Does that conclusion risk creating an incentive for otherwise unethical research? Or is it justified because research upon early embryos is not really equivalent to unethical or non-consensual research upon human beings?

While the President's discussion of embryonic stem cell research focused upon the potential impact on embryos, other opponents have raised different issues. For example, while many individuals with disabilities ardently support stem cell research as offering them a hope for a "cure," others in the disability community see such research and the money devoted to it as devaluing of their lives. In an online journal, Erik Leipoldt, Christopher Newell, and Maurice Corcoran write that

> It concerns us greatly that the embryonic stem cell research lobby appears to be using the public's innate fears of disability, and people with disabilities, for its own ends. It presents disability as a highly emotional tragedy, an anomaly, which requires no less than a medical cure. . . .
>
> People with disabilities have been there and found that worldview wanting. It has led to their lives being described as "unworthy of life," culminating in their mass sterilization in many countries and the killing of at least 200,000 of them in Nazi Germany. Today, unlawful sterilization of girls with developmental disability and genetic screening of unborn babies with disabilities with a view to their abortion happens in Australia. A predominant medical view of their condition makes people with disabilities vulnerable to a "cure-or-death" ethic.[17]

What is the relevance or weight that should be given to such arguments? Do people with disabilities have a privileged position in debates over stem cell research or cloning? If so, how do we interpret the fact that many people with disabilities appear to support such research? Is the voice of the community different from the voices of its individual members?

In the concluding reading, *Too Much of a Good Thing: How Splendid Technologies Can Go Wrong,* Daniel Callahan proposes some very different questions about medical technology. According to Callahan, technology warrants our caution not because it threatens to erode a fundamental notion of human dignity, nor because it unduly harms particular groups. Rather it is worrisome because it provides an illusion of neutrality and progress, yet it may actually do little to advance our health. Technology is glamorous and seductive, and it commands our resources, trampling the claims of many, less exciting, but ultimately more important claims, such as the underlying social and economic conditions that affect a population's health.

As you read the different selections on cloning and stem cell research, ask yourself to what extent should various inevitably speculative claims about the potential social impact of science lead us to limit scientific investigations. Should we accept a "precautionary principle," as George Annas and his colleagues recommend,[18] and say that the burden of proof should be upon those proposing a new technology to show that it will not harm humanity (or the environment)? Or should we accept a more libertarian approach, one generally supported by the Western tradition, and assume that science unfettered is more likely to bring us to "truth" and a better tomorrow than would attempts to reign in its reach?

Human Cloning and Human Dignity: An Ethical Inquiry

THE PRESIDENT'S COUNCIL ON BIOETHICS

The Ethics of Cloning-to-Produce-Children

The prospect of cloning-to-produce-children raises a host of moral questions, among them the following: Could the first attempts to clone a human child be made without violating accepted moral norms governing experimentation on human subjects? What harms might be inflicted on the cloned child as a consequence of having been made a clone? Is it significant that the cloned child would inherit a genetic identity lived in advance by another—and, in some cases, the genetic identity of the cloned child's rearing parent? Is it significant that cloned children would be the first human beings whose genetic identity was en-

tirely known and selected in advance? How might cloning-to-produce-children affect relationships within the cloning families? More generally, how might it affect the relationship between the generations? How might it affect the way society comes to view children? What other prospects would we be tacitly approving in advance by accepting this practice? What important human goods might be enhanced or sacrificed were we to approve cloning-to-produce-children?

We will begin by formulating the best moral case for cloning-to-produce-children—describing both the specific purposes it might serve and the philosophic and moral arguments made in its favor. From there we will move to the moral case against cloning-to-produce-children. Beginning with the safety objections that have dominated the debate thus far, we will show how these concerns ultimately point beyond themselves toward broader ethical concerns. Chief among these is how cloning-to-produce-children would challenge the basic nature of human procreation and the meaning of having children. We shall also consider cloning's effects on human identity, how it might move procreation toward a form of manufacture or toward eugenics, and how it could distort family relations and affect society as a whole.

. . .

I. The Case for Cloning-to-Produce-Children

A. Purposes

In recent years, in anticipation of cloning-to-produce-children, proponents have articulated a variety of possible uses of a perfected technology: providing a "biologically related child" for an infertile couple; permitting reproduction for single individuals or same-sex couples; avoiding the risk of genetic disease; securing a genetically identical source of organs or tissues perfectly suitable for transplantation; "replacing" a loved spouse or child who is dying or has died; obtaining a child with a genotype of one's own choosing (including one's own genotype); replicating individuals of great genius, talent, or beauty, or individuals possessing traits that are for other reasons attractive to the cloners; and creating sets of genetically identical humans who might have special advantages in highly cooperative ventures in both war and peace. The desire to control or select the genomes of children-to-be through cloning has charmed more than a few prospective users, in the United States and around the world.

Although we appreciate that a perfected technology, once introduced for one purpose, might then be used for any of these purposes, we shall

examine further only those stated purposes that seem to us to merit serious consideration.

1. To Produce Biologically Related Children

Human cloning would allow individuals or couples with fertility problems to have biologically related children. For example, if a man could not produce sperm, cloning would allow him to have a child who is "biologically related" to him. In addition, it would allow married couples with fertility problems to avoid using donor gametes, and therefore avoid raising children with genetic inheritances from outside the marriage.

2. To Avoid Genetic Disease

Human cloning could allow couples at risk of generating children with genetic disease to have healthy children. For example, if both parents carried one copy of a recessive gene for the same heritable disorder, cloning might allow them to ensure that their child does not inherit the known genetic disease (without having to resort to using donor gametes or practicing preimplantation or prenatal genetic diagnosis and elimination of afflicted embryos or fetuses).

3. To Obtain "Rejection-Proof" Transplants

Human cloning could produce ideal transplant donors for people who are sick or dying. For example, if no genetic match could be found for a sick child needing a kidney or bone marrow transplant, and the parents had planned to have another child, cloning could potentially serve the human goods of beginning a new life and saving an existing one.

4. To "Replicate" a Loved One

Human cloning would allow parents to "replicate" a dead or dying child or relative. For example, one can imagine a case in which a family—mother, father, and child—is involved in a terrible car accident in which the father dies instantly and the child is critically injured. The mother, told that her child will soon die, decides that the best way to redeem the tragedy is to clone her dying child. This would allow her to preserve a connection with both her dead husband and her dying child, to create new life as a partial human answer to the grievous misfortune of her child's untimely death, and to continue the name and biological lineage of her deceased husband.

5. To Reproduce Individuals of Great Genius, Talent, or Beauty

Human cloning would allow families or society to reproduce individuals of great genius, talent, or beauty, where these traits are presumed to be based on the individuals' desirable or superior genetic makeups. For example, some admirers of great athletes, musicians, or mathematicians, believing that the admired attributes are the result of a superior genetic endowment, might want to clone these distinguished individuals. Just as the cloning of cattle is being promoted as a means of perpetuating champion milk- or meat-producing cows, so cloning-to-produce-children has been touted as a means of perpetuating certain "superior" human exemplars.

B. Arguments

The purposes or reasons for cloning-to-produce-children are, as they are stated, clearly intelligible on their face. When challenged, the defenders of these purposes often appeal to larger moral and political goods. These typically fall within the following three categories: human freedom, existence, and well-being.

1. The Goodness of Human Freedom

Strictly speaking, the appeal to human freedom is not so much a defense of cloning itself as it is of the *right* to practice it, asserted against those who seek to prohibit it. No one, we suspect, would say that he wanted to clone himself or any one else in order to be free or to vindicate

the goodness of liberty. Nevertheless, human freedom is a defense often heard in support of a "right" to clone.

Those who defend cloning-to-produce-children on the grounds of human freedom make two kinds of arguments. The first is that because individuals in pluralistic societies have different definitions of the good life and of right and wrong, society must protect individual freedom to choose against the possible tyranny of the majority. This means securing and even expanding the rights of individuals to make choices so long as their choices do not directly infringe on the rights (and especially the physical safety) of other rights-bearing citizens. In *Eisenstadt v. Baird* (1972), the United States Supreme Court enunciated what has been called a principle of reproductive freedom: "If the right to privacy means anything, it is the right of the individual, married or single, to be free from unwarranted governmental intrusion into matters so affecting a person as a decision whether to bear or beget a child." Defenders of cloning-to-produce-children argue that, in the event that the physical risks to mother and future child were shown to be ethically acceptable, the use of this new reproductive technology would fall under the protective umbrella of reproductive freedom.

A second defense of human cloning on the grounds of freedom is the claim that human existence is by its very nature "open-ended," "indeterminate," and "unpredictable." Human beings are always remaking themselves, their values, and their ways of interacting with one another. New technologies are central to this open-ended idea of human life, and to shut down such technologies simply because they change the "traditional" ways of doing things is unjustifiable. As constitutional scholar Laurence Tribe has argued in reference to human cloning: "A society that bans acts of human creation that reflect unconventional sex roles or parenting models (surrogate motherhood, in vitro fertilization, artificial insemination, and the like) for no better reason than that such acts dare to defy 'nature' and tradition (and to risk adding to life's complexity) is a society that risks cutting itself off from vital experimentation and risks sterilizing a significant part of its capacity to grow."

2. *The Goodness of Existence*

Like the appeal to freedom, the appeal to the goodness of existence is not an argument *for* cloning, but an argument *against* opponents who speak up in the name of protecting the cloned child-to-be against the harms connected with its risky and strange origins as a clone. This argument asserts that attempts to produce children through cloning, like *any* attempt to produce a child, will directly benefit the cloned child-to-be, since without the act of cloning the child in question would not exist. Existence itself, it is argued, is the first "interest" that makes all other interests—including the interests of safety and well-being—possible. Even taking into account the possibility of serious genetic or developmental disorders, this position holds that a cloned individual, once born, would prefer existence as a clone to no existence at all. There is also a serious corollary about how, in the absence of a principle that values existence *as such*, we will and should regard and treat people born with disabilities or deformities: opponents of cloning might appear in a position of intolerance—of saying to cloned individuals, "Better for us (and for you) had you never existed."

3. *The Goodness of Well-Being*

The third moral argument for cloning-to-produce-children is that it would contribute in certain cases to the fulfillment of human goods that are widely honored and deeply rooted in modern democratic society. These human goods include the health of newborn and existing children, reproductive possibilities for infertile couples, and the possibility of having a biologically related child. In all these circumstances, human cloning could relieve existing suffering and sorrow or prevent them in the future. Those who take this position do not necessarily defend human cloning-to-produce-children as such. Rather, they argue that a moral and practical line can be drawn between cloning-to-produce-children that serves the "therapeutic" aims of health (for the cloned child-to-be, for the infertile couple, or for an existing child) and the "eugenic" aims of producing or mass-producing superior people.

Some people argue more broadly that an existing generation has a responsibility to ensure, to the extent possible, the genetic quality and fitness of the next generation. Human cloning, they argue, offers a new method for human control and self-improvement, by allowing families to have children free of specific genetic diseases or society to reproduce children with superior genetic endowments. It also provides a new means for gaining knowledge about the age-old question of nature versus nurture in contributing to human achievement and human flourishing, and to see how clones of great geniuses measure up against the "originals."

C. Critique and Conclusion

While we as a Council acknowledge merit in some of the arguments made for cloning-to-produce-children, we are generally not persuaded by them. The fundamental weakness of the proponents' case is found in their incomplete view of human procreation and families, and especially the place and well-being of children. Proponents of cloning tend to see procreation primarily as the free exercise of a parental right, namely, a right to satisfy parental desires for self-fulfillment or a right to have a child who is healthy or "superior." Parents seek to overcome obstacles to reproduction, to keep their children free of genetic disease or disorder, and to provide them with the best possible genetic endowment. The principles guiding such prospective parents are freedom (for themselves), control (over their child), and well-being (both for themselves and what they imagine is best for their child). Even taken together, these principles provide at best only a partial understanding of the meaning and entailments of human procreation and child-rearing. In practice, they may prove to undermine the very goods that the proponents of cloning aim to serve, by undermining the unconditional acceptance of one's offspring that is so central to parenthood.

There are a number of objections—or at the very least limitations—to viewing cloning-to-produce-children through the prism of rights. Basic human rights are usually asserted on behalf of the human individual agent: for example, a meaningful right not to be prevented from bearing a child can be asserted for each individual against state-mandated sterilization programs. But the act of procreation is not an act involving a single individual. Indeed, until human cloning arrives, it continues to be impossible for any one person to procreate alone. More important, there is a crucial third party involved: the child, whose centrality to the activity exposes the insufficiency of thinking about procreation in terms of rights.

After all, rights are limited in the following crucial way: they cannot be ethically exercised at the expense of the rights of another. But the "right to reproduce" cannot be ethically exercised without at least considering the child that such exercise will bring into being and who is at risk of harm and injustice from the exercise. This obligation cannot be waived by an appeal to the absolutist argument of the goodness of existence. Yes, existence is a primary good, but that does not diminish the ethical significance of knowingly and willfully putting a child in grave physical danger in the very act of giving that child existence. It is certainly true that a life with even severe disability may well be judged worth living by its bearer: "It is better to have been born as I am than not to be here at all." But if his or her disability was caused by behavior that

could have been avoided by parents (for example, by not drinking or using drugs during pregnancy, or, arguably, by not cloning), many would argue that they should have avoided it. A post-facto affirmation of existence by the harmed child would not retroactively excuse the parental misconduct that caused the child's disability, nor would it justify their failure to think of the child's well-being as they went about exercising their "right to procreate." Indeed, procreation is, by its very nature, a limitation of absolute rights, since it brings into existence another human being toward whom we have responsibilities and duties.

In short, the right to decide *"whether* to bear or beget a child" does not include a right to have a child *by whatever means.* Nor can this right be said to imply a corollary—the right to decide what kind of child one is going to have. There are at least some circumstances where reproductive freedom must be limited to protect the good of the child (as, for instance, with the ban on incest). Our society's commitment to freedom and parental authority by no means implies that all innovative procedures and practices should be allowed or accepted, no matter how bizarre or dangerous.

Proponents of cloning, when they do take into account the interests of the child, sometimes argue that this interest justifies and even requires thoroughgoing parental control over the procreative process. Yet this approach, even when well-intentioned, may undermine the good of the child more than it serves the child's best interests. For one thing, cloning-to-produce-children of a desired or worthy sort overlooks the need to restrain the parental temptation to total mastery over children. It is especially morally dubious for this project to go forward when we know so little about the unforeseen and unintended consequences of exercising such genetic control. In trying by cloning to circumvent the risk of genetic disease or to promote particular traits, it is possible—perhaps likely—that new risks to the cloned child's health and fitness would be inadvertently introduced (including the forgoing of genetic novelty, a known asset in the constant struggle against microbial and parasitic diseases). Parental control is a double-edged sword, and proponents seem not to acknowledge the harms, both physical and psychological, that may befall the child whose genetic identity is selected in advance.

The case for cloning in the name of the child's health and well-being is certainly the strongest and most compelling. The desire that one's child be free from a given genetic disease is a worthy aspiration. We recognize there may be some unusual or extreme cases in which cloning might be the best means to serve this moral good, if other ethical obstacles could somehow be overcome. (A few of us also believe that the desire to give a child "improved" or "superior" genetic equipment is not necessarily to be condemned.) However, such aspirations could endanger the personal, familial, and societal goods supported by the character of human procreation. We are willing to grant that there may be exceptional cases in which cloning-to-produce-children is morally defensible; however, that being said, we would also argue that such cases do not justify the harmful experiments and social problems that might be entailed by engaging in human cloning. Hard cases are said to make bad law. The same would be true for succumbing to the rare, sentimentally appealing case in which cloning seems morally plausible.

Finally, proponents do not adequately face up to the difficulty of how "well-being" is to be defined. Generally, they argue that these matters are to be left up to the free choices of parents and doctors. But this means that the judgments of "proper" and "improper" will be made according to subjective criteria alone, and under such circumstances, it will be almost impossible to rule out certain "improvements" as unacceptable.

. . .

II. The Case against Cloning-to-Produce-Children

A. The Ethics of Human Experimentation

We begin with concerns regarding the safety of the cloning procedure and the health of the participants. We do so for several reasons. First, these concerns are widely, indeed nearly unanimously, shared. Second, they lend themselves readily to familiar modes of ethical analysis—including concerns about harming the innocent, protecting human rights, and ensuring the consent of all research subjects. Finally, if carefully considered, these concerns begin to reveal the important ethical principles that must guide our broader assessment of cloning-to-produce-children. They suggest that human beings, unlike inanimate matter or even animals, are in some way *inviolable*, and therefore challenge us to reflect on what it is *about* human beings that makes them inviolable, and whether cloning-to-produce-children threatens these distinctly human goods.

In initiating this analysis, there is perhaps no better place to start than the long-standing international practice of regulating experiments on human subjects. After all, the cloning of a human being, as well as all the research and trials required before such a procedure could be expected to succeed, would constitute experiments on the individuals involved—the egg donor, the birthing mother, and especially the child-to-be. It therefore makes sense to consider the safety and health concerns that arise from cloning-to-produce-children in light of the widely shared ethical principles that govern experimentation on human subjects.

The ethics of research on human subjects suggest three sorts of problems that would arise in cloning-to-produce-children: (1) problems of safety; (2) a special problem of consent; and (3) problems of exploitation of women and the just distribution of risk. We shall consider each in turn.

1. Problems of Safety

First, cloning-to-produce-children is not now safe. Concerns about the safety of the individuals involved in a cloning procedure are shared by nearly everyone on all sides of the cloning debate. Even most proponents of cloning-to-produce-children generally qualify their support with a caveat about the safety of the procedure. Cloning experiments in other mammals strongly suggest that cloning-to-produce-children is, at least for now, far too risky to attempt. Safety concerns revolve around potential dangers to the cloned child, as well as to the egg donor and the woman who would carry the cloned child to birth.

An Abiding Moral Concern.   Because of these risks, there is widespread agreement that, at least for now, attempts at cloning-to-produce-children would constitute unethical experimentation on human subjects and are therefore impermissible. These safety considerations were alone enough to lead the National Bioethics Advisory Commission in June 1997 to call for a temporary prohibition of human cloning-to-produce-children. Similar concerns, based on almost five more years of animal experimentation, convinced the panel of the National Academy of Sciences in January 2002 that the United States should ban such cloning for at least five years.

Past discussions of this subject have often given the impression that the safety concern is a purely temporary one that can be allayed in the near future, as scientific advances and improvements in technique reduce the risks to an ethically acceptable level. But this impression is mistaken, for considerable safety risks are likely to be enduring, perhaps permanent. If so, there will be abiding ethical difficulties *even with efforts aimed at making human cloning safe.*

The reason is clear: experiments to develop new reproductive technologies are necessarily intergenerational, undertaken to serve the reproductive desires of prospective parents but practiced also and always upon prospective children. Any such experiment unavoidably involves risks to the child-to-be, a being who is both the *product* and also the most vulnerable human *subject* of the research. Exposed to risk during the extremely sensitive life-shaping processes of his or her embryological development, any child-to-be is a singularly vulnerable creature, one maximally deserving of protection against risk of experimental (and other) harm. If experiments to learn how to clone a child are ever to be ethical, the degree of risk to that child-to-be would have to be extremely low, arguably no greater than for children-to-be who are conceived from union of egg and sperm. It is extremely unlikely that this moral burden can be met, not for decades if at all.

Can a highly reduced risk of deformity, disease, and premature death in animal cloning, coupled with the inherently unpredictable risk of moving from animals to humans, ever be low enough to meet the ethically acceptable standard set by reproduction begun with egg and sperm? The answer, as a matter of necessity, can never be better than "Just possibly." Given the severity of the possible harms involved in human cloning, and given that those harms fall on the very vulnerable child-to-be, such an answer would seem to be enduringly inadequate.

Similar arguments, it is worth noting, were made before the first attempts at human in vitro fertilization. People suggested that it would be unethical experimentation even to try to determine whether IVF could be safely done. And then, of course, IVF was accomplished. Eventually, it became a common procedure, and today the moral argument about its safety seems to many people beside the point. Yet the fact of success in that case does not establish precedent in this one, nor does it mean that the first attempts at IVF were not in fact unethical experiments upon the unborn, despite the fortunate results.

It therefore appears to us that, given the dangers involved and the relatively limited goods to be gained from cloning-to-produce-children, conducting experiments in an effort to make cloning-to-produce-children safer would itself be an unacceptable violation of the norms of the ethics of research. *There seems to be no ethical way to try to discover whether cloning-to-produce-children can become safe, now or in the future.*

2. A Special Problem of Consent

A further concern relating to the ethics of human research revolves around the question of consent. Consent from the cloned child-to-be is of course impossible to obtain, and because no one consents to his or her own birth, it may be argued that concerns about consent are misplaced when applied to the unborn. But the issue is not so simple. For reasons having to do both with the safety concerns raised above and with the social, psychological, and moral concerns to be addressed below, an attempt to clone a human being would potentially expose a cloned individual-to-be to great risks of harm, quite distinct from those accompanying other sorts of reproduction. Given the risks, and the fact that consent cannot be obtained, the ethically correct choice may be to avoid the experiment. The fact that those engaged in cloning cannot ask an unconceived child for permission places a burden on the cloners, not on the child. Given that anyone considering creating a cloned child must know that he or she is putting a newly created human life at exceptional risk, the burden on the would-be cloners seems clear: they must make a compelling case why the procedure should not be avoided altogether.

Reflections on the purpose and meaning of seeking consent support this point. Why, after all, does society insist upon consent as an essential principle of the ethics of scientific research? Along with honoring the free will of the subject, we insist on consent to protect the weak and the vulnerable, and in particular to protect them from the powerful. It would therefore be morally questionable, at the very least, to choose to impose potentially grave harm on an individual, especially in the very act of giving that individual life. Giving existence to a human being does not grant one the right to maim or harm that human being in research.

3. Problems of Exploitation of Women and Just Distribution of Risk

Cloning-to-produce-children may also lead to the exploitation of women who would be called upon to donate oocytes. Widespread use of the techniques of cloning-to-produce-children would require large numbers of eggs. Animal models suggest that several hundred eggs may be required before one attempt at cloning can be successful. The required oocytes would have to be donated, and the process of making them available would involve hormonal treatments to induce superovulation. If financial incentives are offered, they might lead poor women especially to place themselves at risk in this way (and might also compromise the voluntariness of their "choice" to make donations). Thus, research on cloning-to-produce-children could impose disproportionate burdens on women, particularly low-income women.

4. Conclusion

These questions of the ethics of research—particularly the issue of physical safety—point clearly to the conclusion that cloning-to-produce-children is unacceptable. In reaching this conclusion, we join the National Bioethics Advisory Commission and the National Academy of Sciences. But we go beyond the findings of those distinguished bodies in also pointing to the dangers that will *always* be inherent in the very process of trying to make cloning-to-produce-children safer. On this ground, we conclude that the problem of safety is not a temporary ethical concern. It is rather an enduring moral concern that might not be surmountable and should thus preclude work toward the development of cloning techniques to produce children. In light of the risks and other ethical concerns raised by this form of human experimentation, *we therefore conclude that cloning-to-produce-children should not be attempted.*

B. The Human Context: Procreation and Child-Rearing

Were it to take place, cloning-to-produce-children would represent a challenge to the nature of human procreation and child-rearing. Cloning is, of course, not only a means of procreation. It is also a technology, a human experiment, and an exercise of freedom, among other things. But cloning would be most unusual, consequential, and most morally important as a new way of bringing children into the world and a new way of viewing their moral significance.

A man and woman give themselves in love to each other, setting their projects aside in order to do just that. Yet a child results, arriving on its own, mysterious, independent, yet the fruit of the embrace. Even were the child wished for, and consciously so, he or she is the issue of their love, not the product of their wills; the man and woman in no way produce or choose a *particular* child, as they might buy a particular car. Procreation can, of course, be assisted by human ingenuity (as with IVF). In such cases, it may become harder to see the child solely as a gift bestowed upon the parents' mutual self-giving and not to some degree as a product of their parental wills. Nonetheless, because it is still sexual reproduction, the children born with the help of IVF begin—as do all other children—with a certain genetic independence of their parents. They replicate neither their fathers nor their mothers, and this is a salutary reminder to parents of the independence they must one day grant their children and for which it is their duty to prepare them.

Gifts and blessings we learn to accept as gratefully as we can. Products of our wills we try to shape in accord with our desires. Procreation as traditionally understood invites acceptance,

rather than reshaping, engineering, or designing the next generation. It invites us to accept limits to our control over the next generation. It invites us even—to put the point most strongly—to think of the child as one who is not simply our own, our possession. Certainly, it invites us to remember that the child does not exist simply for the happiness or fulfillment of the parents.

To be sure, parents do and must try to form and mold their children in various ways as they inure them to the demands of family life, prepare them for adulthood, and initiate them into the human community. But, even then, it is only our sense that these children are not our possessions that makes such parental nurture—which always threatens not to nourish but to stifle the child—safe.

This concern can be expressed not only in language about the relation between the generations but also in the language of equality. The things we make are not just like ourselves; they are the products of our wills, and their point and purpose are ours to determine. But a begotten child comes into the world just as its parents once did, and is therefore their equal in dignity and humanity.

The character of sexual procreation shapes the lives of children as well as parents. By giving rise to genetically new individuals, sexual reproduction imbues all human beings with a sense of individual identity and of occupying a place in this world that has never belonged to another. Our novel genetic identity symbolizes and foreshadows the unique, never-to-be-repeated character of each human life. At the same time, our emergence from the union of two individuals, themselves conceived and generated as we were, locates us immediately in a network of relation and natural affection.

Social identity, like genetic identity, is in significant measure tied to these biological facts. Societies around the world have structured social and economic responsibilities around the relationship between the generations established through sexual procreation, and have developed modes of child-rearing, family responsibility, and kinship behavior that revolve around the natural facts of begetting.

C. Identity, Manufacture, Eugenics, Family, and Society

1. *Problems of Identity and Individuality*

Cloning-to-produce-children could create serious problems of identity and individuality. This would be especially true if it were used to produce multiple "copies" of any single individual, as in one or another of the seemingly far-fetched futuristic scenarios in which cloning is often presented to the popular imagination. Yet questions of identity and individuality could arise even in small-scale cloning, even in the (supposedly) most innocent of cases, such as the production of a single cloned child within an intact family. Personal identity is, we would emphasize, a complex and subtle psychological phenomenon, shaped ultimately by the interaction of many diverse factors. But it does seem reasonably clear that cloning would at the very least present a unique and possibly disabling challenge to the formation of individual identity.

Cloned children may experience concerns about their distinctive identity not only because each will be genetically essentially identical to another human being, but also because they may resemble in appearance younger versions of the person who is their "father" or "mother." Of course, our genetic makeup does not by itself determine our identities. But our genetic uniqueness is an important source of our sense of who we are and how we regard ourselves. It is an emblem of independence and individuality. It endows us with a sense of life as a never-before-enacted possibility. Knowing and feeling that nobody has previously possessed our particular gift of natural characteristics, we go forward as genetically unique individuals into relatively indeterminate futures.

These new and unique genetic identities are rooted in the natural procreative process. A cloned child, by contrast, is at risk of living out a life overshadowed in important ways by the life of the "original"—general appearance being only the most obvious. Indeed, one of the reasons some people are interested in cloning is that the technique promises to produce in each case a particular individual whose traits and characteristics are already known. And however much or little one's genotype *actually* shapes one's natural capacities, it could mean a great deal to an individual's *experience* of life and the expectations that those who cloned him or her might have. The cloned child may be constantly compared to "the original," and may consciously or unconsciously hold himself or herself up to the genetic twin that came before. If the two individuals turned out to lead similar lives, the cloned person's achievements may be seen as derivative. If, as is perhaps more likely, the cloned person departed from the life of his or her progenitor, this very fact could be a source of constant scrutiny, especially in circumstances in which parents produced their cloned child to become something in particular. Living up to parental hopes and expectations is frequently a burden for children; it could be a far greater burden for a cloned individual. The shadow of the cloned child's "original" might be hard for the child to escape, as would parental attitudes that sought in the child's very existence to replicate, imitate, or replace the "original."

It may reasonably be argued that genetic individuality is not an indispensable human good, since identical twins share a common genotype and seem not to be harmed by it. But this argument misses the context and environment into which even a single human clone would be born. Identical twins have as progenitors two biological parents and are born together, before either one has developed and shown what his or her potential—natural or otherwise—may be. Each is largely free of the burden of measuring up to or even knowing in advance the genetic traits of the other, because both begin life together and neither is yet known to the world. But a clone is a genetic near-copy of a person who is already living or has already lived. This might constrain the clone's sense of self in ways that differ in kind from the experience of identical twins. Everything about the predecessor—from physical height and facial appearance, balding patterns and inherited diseases, to temperament and native talents, to shape of life and length of days, and even cause of death—will appear before the expectant eyes of the cloned person, always with at least the nagging concern that there, notwithstanding the grace of God, go I. The crucial matter, again, is not simply the truth regarding the extent to which genetic identity actually shapes us— though it surely does shape us to some extent. What matters is the cloned individual's *perception* of the significance of the "precedent life" and the way that perception cramps and limits a sense of self and independence.

2. Concerns Regarding Manufacture

The likely impact of cloning on identity suggests an additional moral and social concern: the transformation of human procreation into human manufacture, of begetting into making. By using the terms "making" and "manufacture" we are not claiming that cloned children would be artifacts made altogether "by hand" or produced in factories. Rather, we are suggesting that they would, like other human "products," be brought into being in accordance with some preselected genetic pattern or design, and therefore in some sense "made to order" by their producers or progenitors.

Unlike natural procreation—or even most forms of assisted reproduction—cloning-to-produce-children would set out to create a child with a very particular genotype: namely, that of the somatic cell donor. Cloned children would thus be the first human beings whose entire genetic makeup is selected in advance. True, selection from among existing genotypes is not yet design of new ones. But the principle that would be established by human cloning is both far-reaching and completely novel: parents, with the help of science and technology, may determine in advance the genetic endowment of their children. To this point, parents have the right and the power to decide *whether* to have a child. With cloning, parents acquire the power, and presumably the right, to decide *what kind* of a child to have. Cloning would thus extend the power of one generation over the next—and the power of parents over their offspring—in ways that open the door, unintentionally or not, to a future project of genetic manipulation and genetic control.

The problem with cloning-to-produce-children is not that artificial technique is used to assist reproduction. Neither is it that genes are being manipulated. We raise no objection to the use of the coming genetic technologies to treat individuals with genetic diseases, even in utero—though there would be issues regarding the protection of human subjects in research and the need to find boundaries between therapy and so-called enhancement (of this, more below). The problem has to do with the control of the entire genotype and the production of children to selected specifications.

Why does this matter? It matters because human dignity is at stake. In natural procreation, two individuals give life to a new human being whose endowments are not shaped deliberately by human will, whose being remains mysterious, and the open-endedness of whose future is ratified and embraced. Parents beget a child who enters the world exactly as they did—as an unmade gift, not as a product. Children born of this process stand equally beside their progenitors as fellow human beings, not beneath them as made objects. In this way, the uncontrolled beginnings of human procreation endow each new generation and each new individual with the dignity and freedom enjoyed by all who came before.

Most present forms of assisted reproduction imitate this natural process. While they do begin to introduce characteristics of manufacture and industrial technique, placing nascent human life for the first time in human hands, they do not control the final outcome. The end served by IVF is still the same as natural reproduction—the birth of a child from the union of gametes from two progenitors. Reproduction with the aid of such techniques still implicitly expresses a willingness to accept as a gift the product of a process we do not control. In IVF children emerge out of the same mysterious process from which their parents came, and are therefore not mere creatures of their parents.

By contrast, cloning-to-produce-children—and the forms of human manufacture it might make more possible in the future—seems quite different. Here, the process begins with a very specific final product in mind and would be tailored to produce that product. Even were cloning to be used solely to remedy infertility, the decision to clone the (sterile) father would be a decision, willy-nilly, that the child-to-be should be the near-twin of his "father." Anyone who would clone merely to ensure a "biologically related child" would be dictating a very specific form of biological relation: genetic virtual identity. In every case of cloning-to-produce-children, scientists or parents would set out to produce specific individuals for particular reasons. The procreative process could come to be seen increasingly as a means of meeting specific ends, and the resulting children would be products of a designed manufacturing process, products over whom we might think it proper to exercise "quality control." Even if, in any given case, we were to continue to think of the cloned child as a gift, *the act itself teaches a different lesson*, as the child becomes the continuation of a parental project. We would learn to receive the next generation less with gratitude and surprise than with control and mastery.

One possible result would be the industrialization and commercialization of human repro-

duction. Manufactured objects become commodities in the marketplace, and their manufacture comes to be guided by market principles and financial concerns. When the "products" are human beings, the "market" could become a profoundly dehumanizing force. Already there is commerce in egg donation for IVF, with ads offering large sums of money for egg donors with high SAT scores and particular physical features.

The concerns expressed here do not depend on cloning becoming a widespread practice. The introduction of the terms and ideas of production into the realm of human procreation would be troubling regardless of the scale involved; and the adoption of a market mentality in these matters could blind us to the deep moral character of bringing forth new life. Even were cloning children to be rare, the moral harms to a society that accepted it could be serious.

3. Prospect of a New Eugenics

For some of us, cloning-to-produce-children also raises concerns about the prospect of eugenics or, more modestly, about genetic "enhancement." We recognize that the term "eugenics" generally refers to attempts to improve the genetic constitution of a particular political community or of the human race through general policies such as population control, forced sterilization, directed mating, or the like. It does not ordinarily refer to actions of particular individuals attempting to improve the genetic endowment of their own descendants. Yet, although cloning does not in itself point to public policies by which the state would become involved in directing the development of the human gene pool, this might happen in illiberal regimes, like China, where the government already regulates procreation. And, in liberal societies, cloning-to-produce-children could come to be used privately for individualized eugenic or "enhancement" purposes: in attempts to alter (with the aim of improving) the genetic constitution of one's own descendants—and, indirectly, of future generations.

Cloning can serve the ends of individualized enhancement either by avoiding the genetic defects that may arise when human reproduction is left to chance or by preserving and perpetuating outstanding genetic traits. In the future, if techniques of genetic enhancement through more precise genetic engineering became available, cloning could be useful for perpetuating the enhanced traits and for keeping any "superior" manmade genotype free of the flaws that sexual reproduction might otherwise introduce.

"Private eugenics" does not carry with it the dark implications of state despotism or political control of the gene pool that characterized earlier eugenic proposals and the racist eugenic practices of the twentieth century. Nonetheless, it could prove dangerous to our humanity. Besides the dehumanizing prospects of the turn toward manufacture that such programs of enhancement would require, there is the further difficulty of the lack of standards to guide the choices for "improvement." To this point, biomedical technology has been applied to treating diseases in patients and has been governed, on the whole, by a commonsense view of health and disease. To be sure, there are differing views about how to define "health." And certain cosmetic, performance—enhancing, or hedonistic uses of biomedical techniques have already crossed any plausible boundary between therapy and enhancement, between healing the sick and "improving" our powers. Yet, for the most part, it is by some commonsense views of health that we judge who is in need of medical treatment and what sort of treatment might be most appropriate. Even today's practice of a kind of "negative" eugenics—through prenatal genetic diagnosis and abortion of fetuses with certain genetic abnormalities—is informed by the desire to promote health.

The "positive" eugenics that could receive a great boost from human cloning, especially were it to be coupled with techniques of precise genetic modification, would not seek to restore sick human beings to natural health. Instead, it would seek to alter humanity, based upon subjective or arbitrary ideas of excellence. The effort may be guided by apparently good intentions: to improve the next generation and to enhance the quality of life of our descendants. But in the process of altering human nature, we would be abandoning the standard by which to judge the goodness or the wisdom of the particular aims. We would stand to lose the sense of what is and is not human.

The fear of a new eugenics is not, as is sometimes alleged, a concern born of some irrational fear of the future or the unknown. Neither is it born of hostility to technology or nostalgia for some premodern pseudo-golden age of superior naturalness. It is rather born of the rational recognition that once we move beyond therapy into efforts at enhancement, we are in uncharted waters without a map, without a compass, and without a clear destination that can tell us whether we are making improvements or the reverse. The time-honored and time-tested goods of human life, which we know to be good, would be put in jeopardy for the alleged and unknowable goods of a post-human future.

4. Troubled Family Relations

Cloning-to-produce-children could also prove damaging to family relations, despite the best of intentions. We do not assume that cloned children, once produced, would not be accepted, loved, or nurtured by their parents and relatives. On the contrary, we freely admit that, like any child, they might be welcomed into the cloning family. Nevertheless, the cloned child's place in the scheme of family relations might well be uncertain and confused. The usually clear designations of father and brother, mother and sister, would be confounded. A mother could give birth to her own genetic twin, and a father could be genetically virtually identical to his son. The cloned child's relation to his or her grandparents would span one and two generations at once. Every other family relation would be similarly confused. There is, of course, the valid counterargument that holds that the "mother" could easily be defined as the person who gives birth to the child, regardless of the child's genetic origins, and for social purposes that may serve to eliminate some problems. But because of the special nature of cloning-to-produce-children, difficulties may be expected.

The crucial point is not the absence of the natural biological connections between parents and children. The crucial point is, on the contrary, the presence of a unique, one-sided, and replicative biological connection to only one progenitor. As a result, family relations involving cloning would differ from all existing family arrangements, including those formed through adoption or with the aid of IVF. A great many children, after all, are adopted, and live happy lives in loving families, in the absence of any biological connections with their parents. Children conceived by artificial insemination using donor sperm and by various IVF techniques may have unusual relationships with their genetic parents, or no genetic relationships at all. But all of these existing arrangements attempt in important ways to emulate the model of the natural family (at least in its arrangement of the generations), while cloning runs contrary to that model.

What the exact effects of cloning-to-produce-children might be for families is highly speculative, to be sure, but it is still worth flagging certain troubling possibilities and risks. The fact that the cloned child bears a special tie to only one parent may complicate family dynamics. As the child developed, it could not help but be regarded as specially akin to only one of his or her parents. The sins or failings of the father (or mother), if reappearing in the cloned child, might be blamed on the progenitor, adding to the chances of domestic turmoil. The problems of being and rearing an adolescent could become complicated should the teenage clone of the mother "reappear" as the double of the woman the father once fell in love with. Risks of competition, rivalry, jealousy, and parental tension could become heightened.

Even if the child were cloned from someone who is not a member of the family in which the child is raised, the fact would remain that he or she has been produced in the nearly precise genetic image of another and for some particular reason, with some particular design in mind. Should this become known to the child, as most likely it would, a desire to seek out connection to the "original" could complicate his or her relation to the rearing family, as would living consciously "under the reason" for this extra-familial choice of progenitor. Though many people make light of the importance of biological kinship (compared to the bonds formed through rearing and experienced family life), many adopted children and children conceived by artificial insemination or IVF using donor sperm show by their actions that they do not agree. They make great efforts to locate their "biological parents," even where paternity consists in nothing more than the donation of sperm. Where the progenitor is a genetic near-twin, surely the urge of the cloned child to connect with the unknown "parent" would be still greater.

5. Effects on Society

The hazards and costs of cloning-to-produce-children may not be confined to the direct participants. The rest of society may also be at risk. The impact of human cloning on society at large may be the least appreciated, but among the most important, factors to consider in contemplating the morality of this activity.

Cloning is a human activity affecting not only those who are cloned or those who are clones, but also the entire society that allows or supports such activity. For insofar as the society accepts cloning-to-produce-children, to that extent the society may be said to engage in it. A society that allows dehumanizing practices—especially when given an opportunity to try to prevent them—risks becoming an accomplice in those practices. (The same could be said of a society that allowed even a few of its members to practice incest or polygamy.) Thus the question before us is whether cloning-to-produce-children is an activity that we, as a society, should engage in. In addressing this question, we must reach well beyond the rights of individuals and the difficulties or benefits that cloned children or their families might encounter. We must consider what kind of a society we wish to be, and, in particular, what forms of bringing children into the world we want to encourage and what sorts of relations between the generations we want to preserve.

Cloning-to-produce-children could distort the way we raise and view children, by carrying to full expression many regrettable tendencies already present in our culture. We are already liable to regard children largely as vehicles for our own fulfillment and ambitions. The impulse to create "designer children" is present today—as temptation and social practice. The notion of life as a gift, mysterious and limited, is under siege. Cloning-to-produce-children would carry these tendencies and temptations to an extreme expression. It advances the notion that the child is but an object of our sovereign mastery.

A society that clones human beings thinks about human beings (and especially children) differently than does a society that refuses to do so. It could easily be argued that we have already in myriad ways begun to show signs of regarding our children as projects on which we may work our wills. Further, it could be argued that we have been so desensitized by our earlier steps in this direction that we do not recognize this tendency as a corruption. While some people contend that cloning-to-produce-children would not take us much further down a path we have already been traveling, we would emphasize that the precedent of treating children as projects cuts two ways in the moral argument. Instead of using this precedent to justify taking the next step of cloning, the next step might rather serve as a warning and a mirror in which we may discover reasons to reconsider what we are already

doing. Precisely because the stakes are so high, precisely because the new biotechnologies touch not only our bodies and minds but also the very idea of our humanity, we should ask ourselves how we as a society want to approach questions of human dignity and flourishing.

D. Conclusion

Cloning-to-produce-children may represent a forerunner of what will be a growing number of capacities to intervene in and alter the human genetic endowment. No doubt, earlier human actions have produced changes in the human gene pool: to take only one example, the use of insulin to treat diabetics who otherwise would have died before reproducing has increased the genes for diabetes in the population. But different responsibilities accrue when one sets out to make such changes prospectively, directly, and deliberately. To do so without regard for the likelihood of serious unintended and unanticipated consequences would be the height of hubris. Systems of great complexity do not respond well to blunt human intervention, and one can hardly think of a more complex system—both natural and social—than that which surrounds human reproduction and the human genome. Given the enormous importance of what is at stake, we believe that the so-called "precautionary principle" should be our guide in this arena. This principle would suggest that scientists, technologists, and, indeed, all of us should be modest in claiming to understand the many possible consequences of any profound alteration of human procreation, especially where there are not compelling reasons to proceed. Lacking such understanding, no one should take action so drastic as the cloning of a human child. In the absence of the necessary human wisdom, prudence calls upon us to set limits on efforts to control and remake the character of human procreation and human life.

It is not only a matter of prudence. Cloning-to-produce-children would also be an injustice to the cloned child—from the imposition of the chromosomes of someone else, to the intentional deprivation of biological parents, to all of the possible bodily and psychological harms that we have enumerated in this chapter. It is ultimately the claim that the cloned child would be seriously wronged—and not only harmed in body—that would justify government intervention. Members of the Council are in unanimous agreement that cloning-to-produce-children is not only unsafe but also morally unacceptable and ought not to be attempted.

Too Much of a Good Thing
How Splendid Technologies Can Go Wrong

Daniel Callahan

I begin with a brief account of my ordinary workday. Professionally I am engrossed in matters of national health policy, and particularly the growing cost of health care, once again into double digit inflation. Those costs are increasing the number of uninsured, putting great pressure on the federal programs of Medicare and Medicaid, and threatening employer-provided health insurance. What is to be done about that?

To get to my place of work, up the Hudson River, I cross the Tappan Zee Bridge, which is choked with cars, well beyond its original projected capacity, and fed by a highway that features daily traffic jams. What is to be done about that?

The main source of rising health care costs is the emergence of new technologies and the intensified use of old technologies, accounting for some 40 percent of the annual increase. The main source of the traffic problem, here and elsewhere, is simply too many cars, ever increasing in number. Not many people see analogies between health care technologies and automobiles, but there is nothing like sitting in a traffic jam to expand one's imagination. The problems are more alike than anyone might guess.

Both problems raise two familiar questions, now in a new guise. One is ancient: how should we cope with those features of our lives, and thus of our human nature, where what is good gradually turns into something bad, usually inadvertently? Medical technology is an uncommon human benefit, but when its pursuit and deployment begin to create economic fits, public and private, its good begins to turn bad. The automobile increases freedom and mobility, and like medical technology is a source of enormous national economic benefit. But when our air is besmogged, our highways jammed, and our commutes a misery, its good turns bad.

The second question my two illustrative technologies raise is this: is technology simply a neutral reality, neither good nor bad in itself, but to be evaluated solely on the basis of the uses to which it is put—or does it have a life of its own, subtly shaping our values and ways of life whether we choose that to happen or not? As opponents of gun control are fond of saying "Guns don't kill; only people kill." That may be narrowly true, but is it the full truth? Is it irrelevant for our safety how many guns we have in our house? And are we fully free—the autonomous creatures we are alleged to be—to use or not use medical technology as we like, or to drive or not drive an automobile, or does each technology draw us to its use in ways often beyond our control?

While there are some people who cleverly manage to avoid the health care system altogether, putting their faith in prayer or austere living or exotic jungle potions, most of us can't get away with that. When we hurt we go to the doctor, and doctors these days turn to technology to diagnose us and to treat us. We expect no less. And while there are some strange creatures in Manhattan who have never learned to drive, few of us have successfully evaded the American car culture.

In short, medical technology and the automobile are social realities most of us cannot imagine living without. In each case we can preach moderation; in each, moderation has proved hard to come by. In each case, the cumulative social impact of the technologies seems beyond our control, in great part precisely because it is a good that we cannot easily do without and which (of its very nature?) leads us to want more of it than we now have.

The Ends of Technology

Technology responds to some deep and enduring human needs: for survival (agriculture, defense); for increased choice, pleasure, and convenience (telephones, movies, escalators); for economic benefit (computers and software, machine tools, airplanes for export); for liberating visions of human possibility (space travel, instant world-wide communication). Medical technology and the automobile have many if not most of these attractions, and serve most of those needs. And because they serve multiple needs in multiply complex, overlapping ways, their grip on our culture is extraordinarily powerful. Medical technology serves:

- our survival (forestalling death, relieving our morbidities, and softening our disabilities);

- our choice and convenience (with contraception and prenatal diagnosis);
- our economy (jobs, investments, exportable medical equipment and drugs); and
- our dreams of a better, more liberated life (through genetic engineering and psychopharmacology, for example).

No wonder our culture swallows medicine whole. Yet I believe that equity and technological progress are on a profound collision course. The recent rise of health care costs, beginning in the late 1990s, tells the story—depending upon how we look at it. It is tempting to see the problem as strictly technical, solvable by better management, more effective cost control methods, evidence-based medicine, or market solutions that force people to make decisions about what they are willing to pay for. But at base there is a fundamental clash of long-standing values: the golden ideal of unlimited medical and technological progress, at the core of American health care values, versus the social ideal of universal coverage of health care costs, guaranteeing every citizen decent health care at an affordable price. The trajectory of health care costs is rapidly undermining the ideal of affordable, equitable health care, putting universal care in the United States further and further from our grasp.

In thinking about this tension consider a few economic and demographic realities: 40 million uninsured Americans, with the number going up; $1.3 trillion in health care expenditures, the highest in the world and the highest per capita; an increasing array of expensive technologies and drugs; and the likelihood that the new genetic-based drugs will be even more expensive than present drugs; inflationary pressures of 10–20 percent per year in health care costs over the past couple of years, with no prospect of change in that pattern; an aging population and the imminent retirement of the baby boom generation, likely to push costs even higher; and rising public demands for the latest and the best in medical technology—as the technologies improve, the standards of good health care rise in lock step.

If we are tempted to think that our American problem is unique, it is worth glancing at European and Canadian health care. Those countries long ago embraced universal health care, and for a long time were able to afford it. But they are now hanging on by their nails, subject to the same cost pressures we are. Bit by bit, universal health care in other countries is being eroded: the queues get longer, the out-of-pocket payments increase, denials of care less than urgent become more common. Just as we have, they have tried the efficiency, cut-the-fat route, embraced evidence-based medicine, and even toyed with the idea of health maintenance organizations. Those are all worthy and necessary efforts, but as in the United States, they have not worked well to control costs.

Consider now the automobile. While it does not meet our need for physical survival in quite the way medical technology does, it has proved itself necessary for our:

- social existence (getting where we need to go);
- choice and convenience (going where we want to go, when we want to go there);
- economy (long our leading industry); and
- vision of a better life (living and going where we like).

Yet as with health care, the social and economic costs mount. Some eight million autos were manufactured in 1980, and twelve million in 1999. Americans drove one trillion miles annually in the 1970s, and two trillion by 1999. More is spent on transportation and related costs in the United States than on medical care, education, and clothing combined. The poor can hardly exist without a car to find decent work, and enough has been written about the urban sprawl problem, a product of the car, that I will say nothing more about it.

There is no shortage of solutions to the automobile, but they all have problems. Building more roads is likely to attract more automobiles, eventually using up the initial gains. Improving auto mileage runs into industry opposition. Public transportation is expensive and might not lure people from their autos. Tax incentives and disincentives to control driving patterns might help, but probably won't make a dramatic difference. As with health reform efforts, auto reforms are necessary and sensible—but their chance of putting much of a dent in the overall problem is not encouraging.

What ones sees when comparing medical technology and the automobile is that both serve functions other than those most closely related to their formal ends—health for health care and mobility for the automobile. Those other functions include their economic benefits and their capacity to evoke liberating visions. That combination makes them a far more potent force than if their formal function only was at stake. But those formal functions have proved more than sufficient to give both of them a seemingly unstoppable social force.

It appears, in sum, that both technologies have built within them the capacity to endlessly escalate our desires and raise the baseline of acceptability. Where it was once possible to speak of "the family car," an increasing number of families have individual cars for each person; upscale houses now routinely feature three-car garages. Even if decent public transportation is available, people still want automobiles, and more automobiles.

Here one encounters a puzzle. Is the proliferation of automobiles the result of industry pressures and advertising, or would the desire for cars be there even if those pressures were diminished? I don't know, but my guess is that the natural attraction of the automobile—"natural" in the sense that most adults in most countries will want one—is simply enhanced by advertising and by the symbolic role of the automobile as a token of social status.

One can imagine a limit to the number of cars that the United States might have. If every individual over age sixteen already owned an automobile, then, except for population growth, the number of automobiles would surely level off. And traffic problems could grow so horrendous that people would be fearful of using cars. But one can also imagine the automobile surmounting these limits. Families might acquire more cars than household members, and people might simply become habituated to daily traffic jams— treating them much as they treat the weather, where everyone complains but nobody does anything about it. Everything will then get worse, and we will say it is the price we pay for the benefits.

The situation is far worse with health care. There, the need for good health is in principle unlimited. Our bodies are finite—subject to injury, disease, decline, and death. The best that medicine can do is to ward off those evils, prevent some diseases, rescue us from others, rehabilitate us from still others, and put death off for a time. Medicine can take just pride in the thirty-year increase of average life expectancy in the twentieth century and the rapidly growing number of people living into their 90s and 100s. But eventually something or other gets us.

However great the improvement in health, the doctor's office will still be full and the hospital still a going concern. Put another way, however great medical progress has been, it eventually runs out. We may not encounter the frontier of progress, of medical possibilities, until we are 100, but there is an endless frontier.

With medical technology, it is seemingly impossible to envision some ultimate saturation point. In addition to the endless possibilities of lengthening and improving the human life span, medical research and technological innovation themselves stimulate ideas for even greater future improvements; and with those improvements come greater expectations about what counts as a decent level of health. Scientific progress spurs expectation progress, with the bar always set higher once the earlier goals are achieved. The annual cry during appropriation hearings for the annual National Institute of Health is that the research promise and possibilities have never been greater; and that is always, in some sense, true. The more we know, the easier it is to know still more.

Going Too Far

It is easy to understand why we can go too far with the automobile and medical research. In medicine, there is considerable evidence that there is often a "technological imperative" at work, making it hard for physicians, patients, and families to stop treatment with a terminal patient no longer able to benefit from the treatment. So, too, it is possible for individuals to be induced to buy automobiles more expensive than they can afford, or to buy two automobiles when one would do quite nicely.

Medical technology seems to know no boundaries because it is hard to say just what bodily failings and lethal threats we should be willing to accept. The medical research agenda now goes after all lethal diseases, but it also goes after human enhancements and wish fulfillment. Death itself is made to seem an accidental, contingent event. Why do we now die? Not because of the inherent finitude of the human body, as most people thought for most of human history. We die, it is said, because we engage in unhealthy lifestyles, or because research has not yet found a cure for our diseases. And many doctors, when they lose a patient, feel that it is somehow their fault, even if their brain and their colleagues tell them otherwise. For many of our citizens, health has become not simply a necessary means for living a good life, but itself one of the ends of a good life. Medical technology, like the automobile, is imbedded in our culture. It is part of our picture of modern America.

I own a summer house on a small Maine island. When I first went there thirty years ago, there were no more than twenty cars or so. Now there are close to sixty, although the population has not much changed. The island is small and fully walkable; and not long ago everyone did walk, even when they could have driven. The islanders of thirty years ago believed that one of the charms and assets of the island was the absence of cars; and there seems to have been a built-in, culturally transmissible, taboo—a self-imposed limit that kept the cars out. But once the trend toward cars got started, the earlier limits transgressed, little was to stand in their way.

Technology as a Neutral Force

Given the power of medical technology and the automobile to have such a hold on our lives, I find it hard to say that they are merely neutral tools, to be used or not used as we see fit, just lying about. Except for their pejorative connotations, I find technologies to be much like viruses or germs. They are external agents that can invade our bodies and make a great difference in our fate and health.

But that is to speak in a general way. We also know that even in the worst plagues, not everyone perishes. The social context and the character of individual bodies affect the outcome. This is why we often think of viruses as neutral: they do not behave in any wholly independent, context-free way. Of course, common sense dictates that we treat them with care, avoiding them when possible, but no one is guaranteed to get sick from contact with them.

Medical technology and the automobile are similar. Not everyone will, so to speak, invariably be infected by them, though both are hard to avoid. And just as some diseases that are medical threats to individuals also confer some genetic protection, so too medical technology and the automobile have many valuable traits. Our health depends on the e-coli bacteria in our gut; but outside of that setting, let loose in the world, e-coli can be deadly. I once suggested at a meeting at the Centers for Disease Control and Prevention (CDC) that, in light of the national obesity problem, perhaps a Surgeon General's warning should be affixed to every automobile and TV set, warning of their health dangers if used to excess. Everyone laughed except the director of the CDC. He said that he did not think that was a politically promising way to go, and I came away with the impression that even as a joke it was impermissible. Similarly, when I even suggest to most audiences, much less to research advocates, that we might want to rethink and even slow down and redirect innovation in medical technology, I am guaranteed a chilly, shocked reaction.

In sum, if in some literal sense technology is neutral, in the important sense of the way it affects human lives it is anything but neutral. When the technology is ubiquitous, when it serves important human values and ways of life, and when it is all but impossible to avoid using, then it has captured our lives. Most new technologies are introduced not as enslaving tyrants, but as choice-increasing, society-enhancing developments that we are free to take or leave. But as the rise and dominance of the automobile and medical technology show, freedom and choice can be fleeting when the technology takes up a central place in our cultural gut and we require them as much as our private gut requires e-coli.

I will conclude by noting that with both technologies there are alternatives. A few years ago in Prague I was talking with a doctor who often had to spend her weekends at the hospital where she worked. She always took the tram rather than driving the family car. When I pointed out that it was a ten-minute ride by car, with plentiful parking available, but forty-five minutes by tram, she looked at me in an uncomprehending way and said, in effect, that she could not understand why anyone would drive anywhere when public transportation was available.

In the case of medical technology, it is well known that most of the improvements in health status have come from public health measures and improved socioeconomic status. Much more research is needed on the background conditions and determinants of health, but the big research money goes to genetic and other biomedical research, looking into the depths of biology for cures rather than into the breadth of human societies to determine why some people get sick and others do not. This latter approach—often called a population rather than individual perspective—has powerful theoretical support. What it does not have is glamour, an economic lobby, and an intuitive appeal equivalent to the development of new technologies.

The difficulty with these alternative strategies with the automobile and medical technologies is that they have not sunk into our public and private psyche with the power of the technologies. They do not have behind them the overlapping strands of attraction and profit that the technologies do. They do not—to recur to my language above—seem to have the power to change our way of life, to bury themselves so deeply within our way of life that, however much we worry and complain about their harms, we cannot let go of the good and goods they bring.

Could all of that change? Maybe. It may be that the health care cost problem will become so bad that the now well-insured middle class will begin to hurt, and will consider some serious alternatives. It may be that the traffic jams and commutes will grow so long that the public will revolt against the hegemony of the automobile. In other words, for those of us looking for a change, probably the best we can hope for is a nasty crisis that will *force* a change. But it's not likely to happen. As those of us who have longed for universal health care for many decades long ago learned, the capacity of this country to muddle through what in other places would seem a great crisis is formidable.

C. Bioterrorism and Emerging Infections

In the 1960s and 1970s, when bioethics was emerging as a field, many health care practitioners and members of the public believed that the days of mass epidemics of infectious disease were over. The difficult health care problems of the future, at least in the developed world, would involve chronic diseases, the utilization of new technologies, and the cost and equitable distribution of those technologies.

By the 1980s that optimistic vision was fading. Although most Americans and Westerners continued to die from noninfectious chronic diseases[19] and the high cost of treating them remained a top policy problem in the United States, the microbes had returned. In an accelerating pace, new diseases, known as "emerging infections," began to appear.[20] First, there was Legionnaires Disease, named so because it was discovered after an outbreak struck a convention held by the American Legion. Then more dramatically came HIV, a new human pathogen that traveled from the rain forest of Africa to be discovered when young men began to die mysteriously in New York and San Francisco.

HIV has killed more people than any other "new" microbe, but it was not the last one to visit us. In subsequent years, lyme disease, hantavirus, West Nile fever, SARS (sudden acute respiratory syndrome), and even monkeypox have all infected individuals in this hemisphere for the first time. In addition, familiar infections, such as tuberculosis, have become more prevalent and more virulent, as they have become resistant to common antibiotics.

The threats posed by infectious disease have been augmented by the possibility of bioterrorism. The use of infectious agents in warfare is nothing new. During the

Middle Ages, for example, soldiers threw the bodies of plague victims over the walls of enemy cities.[21] This old threat reappeared as a contemporary possibility in the 1990s as the significant bioweapons program of the old Soviet Union came to light.[22] National security specialists began to conduct simulation exercises to shed light on what would happen if a terrorist used a biological weapon, such as smallpox.[23] Unfortunately, the hypothetical use of a biological weapon became only too real in October 2001, when someone (as yet unknown) contaminated the U.S. mail with a processed form of anthrax, leading to several deaths, many more illnesses, and the closing of a congressional office building and several mail facilities for long periods of time.

The anthrax attacks, which were followed within a year and a half by the international outbreak of SARS[24] (which was not believed to be the result of a terrorist attack), placed public health and its efforts to contain and halt infectious diseases back in the forefront of public debate. These concomitant developments also raised significant questions for bioethics and the directions it should be taking in future decades.

First, the reemergence of infectious diseases and the advent of bioterrorism should remind us of the complex etiology of health threats. As we noted in Chapter 2, the scope of bioethics depends, in part, on how we define health and how broadly we conceptualize the causes of illnesses. During much of the twentieth century, when the major causes of illness and premature mortality in the West were due to chronic diseases, it was tempting to see the causes of ill health as rooted in an individual's genes and lifestyle choices. The reemergence of infectious diseases as a major cause of morbidity in the developed world raises a question about those assumptions. Most obviously, in the case of communicable diseases such as SARS and smallpox or animal borne diseases such as West Nile fever, it is difficult to assign individuals responsibility for their condition. The threat to health can only be understood on a population level.

More interestingly, perhaps, the source of these diseases may well arise from broad environmental conditions. According to the Institute of Medicine's Committee on Emerging Microbial Threats to Health, a broad array of societal and environmental conditions, including international travel, human population growth, overuse of antibiotics, agricultural and food handling practices, and many others, give birth to emergent infections.[25] If the Institute is correct in connecting the rise of infectious disease to broad changes in agriculture, development, and health care, what does that mean for the scope of bioethics? Are matters as diverse as the laying of roads in the rain forest and the consolidation of farming now properly within the purview of bioethics? And if so, do the foundational assumptions and principles that have guided the field apply to these very different domains?

The prospect of infectious epidemics has also caused policymakers, lawyers, and ethicists to debate the degree to which individual rights and autonomy may be limited in order to control the spread of a communicable disease. Throughout history, governments have responded to epidemics by limiting travel and isolating or quarantining individuals who have the disease or are thought to harbor it.[26] This practice declined during the twentieth century as antibiotics and vaccinations provided potent tools against infectious disease and as Western governments became more sensitive to individual rights.[27]

Fear of bioterrorism and the appearance of new untreatable infectious diseases such as SARS have served to revive interest in some of the traditional public health measures, such as quarantine. In the fall of 2001, following the anthrax attacks, the Centers for Disease Control and Prevention asked the Center for the Law and the Public Health at Georgetown University Law Center and Johns Hopkins University School of Public Health to draft a model law that would provide state governments with clear authority to impose quarantines and isolation and mandatory treatment on individuals upon the governor's determination that a public health emergency exists.[28]

In *Public Health Law in an Age of Terrorism: Rethinking Individual Rights and Common Goods*, Lawrence O. Gostin, one of the chief drafters of the model act, defends the use of coercive public health powers. He begins with the assertion that "the balance between individual interests and common goods needs to be recalibrated in an age of terrorism." According to Gostin, the model act achieves that new balance by providing the government with clear authority for protecting the common good while safeguarding the rights of individuals by providing for due process protections for individuals whose rights are limited. Gostin argues that while it may be "fashionable" to say that individual rights do not conflict with the common good, "public health officials need to make hard choices, particularly in public health emergencies."

George J. Annas, a lawyer and bioethicist, challenges Gostin in *Bioterrorism, Public Health, and Human Rights*. According to Annas, the model act "unnecessarily ignores basic human rights." To Annas, public health officials can be more effective in protecting the common good when they protect individual rights and "rely not on force but on persuasion, and not on blind trust but on trust based on transparency, accountability, democracy, and human rights." Does Annas provide a sufficient answer to Gostin's point that hard choices need to be made? Or is Gostin too quick to assume that the common good relies upon limitations of individual rights? Does the SARS epidemic, in which governments from China to Canada relied upon quarantines to limit the disease's spread, prove Gostin's point? Or does the fact that most quarantines were "voluntary" and that thousands fled Beijing when rumors spread that the city would be closed support Annas's point about the necessity of trust?[29]

Wendy E. Parmet considers these issues in *Bioterrorism: Public Health Perspectives*. Responding to Gostin's claim that both liberal and communitarian ethics support curtailing civil liberties during public health emergencies,[30] Parmet suggests that the discipline of public health provides its own perspectives and norms that may be useful for evaluating responses to bioterrorism. According to Parmet, this perspective should, in fact, make us very wary of relying upon coercive powers, as they may well be less protective of the public's health than would be policies that rely more on public trust and cooperation. Likewise, Edward P. Richards stresses that bioterrorism is more similar than different to other health threats, particularly those posed by emerging infections. To address all of these problems, Richards claims, we do not need emergency plans or draconian measures, but a reinvestment and recommitment to public health itself. Richards writes that "a better strategy is to focus directly on the real problems and address them in ways other than esoteric reports. . . . Rather than elaborate bioterrorism contingency plans on the shelf at the local health department, educate the public to demand effective public health every day, thus rebuilding the political support necessary for an effective public health infrastructure."[31] Thus just as some bioethicists have stressed the need for examining the day to day and population-wide issues of health care, rather than the dramatic critical cases that have traditionally attracted so much of the attention of bioethicists (see Chapter 1), Richards argues that public health and law must look more to the mundane and be pulled less by remote prospects of the apocalypse.

More fundamentally, Jonathan M. Mann has argued that respect for human rights may serve as an important vehicle for maintaining health. Mann recognized that in the case of HIV/AIDS, health would be better served by respecting human rights than by violating these rights. Coercive and liberty-limiting measures such as the invasions of privacy inherent in, for example, mandatory screening, would only alienate people, perhaps driving them away from the very measures they should turn to in order to control the spread of the disease. Thus respecting human rights was thought to serve the interests of health. The human rights that Mann has in mind are moral rights; they are rights that people have in virtue of their status as human beings. They are also universal in the sense that all human beings have them in virtue of their humanity. They are moral in the sense that they are not, regrettably, at this time legally enforceable.

In *Medicine and Public Health, Ethics and Human Rights,* Mann sets out the connection between public health and human rights. He argues that public health needs to develop and articulate an ethic and medicine needs to explore the possibility of integrating a human rights perspective. Mann points out that health policies can have an effect on human rights. Public health policies may easily discriminate against certain groups or classes of people by targeting some groups and ignoring others. Or, if governments adopt policies that affect people but do not provide the community with the scientific basis of the policy, they deny their right to "receive and impart information and ideas. . .regardless of frontiers."[32] Second, human rights violations can potentially impact health. Torture is a good example of how violations to human rights can harm health. According to Mann, "even for torture only more recently has the extensive, lifelong family and community-wide and transgenerational impact of torture been recognized." Third, Mann states that "promoting and protecting human rights is inextricably linked with promoting and protecting health." So-called reproductive rights, for example, are essential for reproductive health. Moreover, health and human rights have a similar mission: advancing human well-being. As you evaluate these arguments, consider the power the language of human rights confers on public health. Ronald Bayer makes this point when he says, "a moment of careful reflection would suggest that the identification of a powerful idiom capable of inspiring challenges to the status quo makes a unique and special contribution."[33]

Do you find Mann's argument persuasive? Does the possibility of bioterrorism and the reality of emerging infections demonstrate the need to integrate considerations of justice, trust and democratic theory into our ethical analysis of health care? Or do they simply reinforce the importance of focusing on the classic need to balance the rights of the individual versus the good of the many?

Public Health Law in an Age of Terrorism
Rethinking Individual Rights and Common Goods; In Defense of a Model Act that Was Written to Bring Public Health Law into the Modern Age

LAWRENCE O. GOSTIN

Public and scholarly discourse in the late twentieth century became highly oriented toward "rights." The political community stressed the importance of individual freedoms rather than the health, security, and wellbeing of the community. The salience of individualism could be seen on both sides of the political spectrum. The ideological left favored a set of personal interests, principally autonomy, privacy, and liberty. This meant that individuals should be free to make choices, restrict the flow of health information, and have unfettered movement, without regard to the needs and desires of the wider community. The ideological right favored a set of proprietary interests, principally the freedom to contract, conduct business, use and develop property, and pursue a profession. This meant that entrepreneurs should be permitted to engage in free enterprise without the fetters of, for example, occupational health and safety regulations, inspections and products liability, zoning and nuisance abatements, and licenses.

In this civil and property rights society, the tone has been distinctly antigovernment. The State has been perceived as inefficient, bureaucratic, and burdensome. Citizens have opposed taxation and broad health and welfare spending as well as oppressive regulation. From a funding perspective, this has meant that health dollars have been allocated primarily to advanced biotechnology and health care, which serve the needs of individual patients, particularly those who can afford private health insurance. Funding for traditional prevention and population based services represents only a small fraction of health spending, estimated at around 1 percent at the state level and less than 5 percent at the federal level.[1]

As a result of chronic underspending, the public health infrastructure is badly deteriorated.[2] Public health agencies lack the capacity to conduct essential public health services at a level of performance that matches the constantly evolving threats to the health of the public. Critical components of that infrastructure include a well-trained workforce, electronic information and communications systems, rapid disease surveillance and reporting, laboratory capacity, and emergency response capability.[3]

The public health law infrastructure is equally deficient. The law establishes the mission, functions, and powers of public health agencies. Yet public health laws are highly antiquated, after many decades of neglect. Very little consideration has been given to modernizing these laws to reflect advances in public health practice and constitutional law. Reform of public health law is essential to ensure that public health agencies have clear missions and functions, stable sources of financing, adequate powers to avert or manage health threats, and restraints on powers to maintain respect for personal rights and liberties.

The balance between individual interests and common goods needs to be recalibrated in an age of terrorism. The attacks on the World Trade Center and Pentagon on 11 September 2001 and the subsequent dispersal of anthrax spores through the U.S. postal system reawakened the public to the importance of public health, safety, and security.[4] The president's 2003 budget reflects changing priorities, with an influx of funding to prevent and respond to bioterrorism.[5] However, even in this budget, disproportionate funding is devoted to biotechnology rather than to basic prevention and population-based services.[6]

This paper explores the appropriate balance between individual interests and common goods. The current focus on individualism should be seen not as fixed and authoritative, but rather as transient and culturally derived. There is, of course, an alternative philosophical tradition that sees individuals primarily as members of communities. This communitarian tradition views individuals as part of social and political networks, with each individual reliant on the others for health and security.[7] Individuals, according to this tradition, gain value from being a part of a well-regulated society that seeks to prevent common risks.

In legal terms, this communitarian tradition is expressed in the "police power" to protect the health, safety, and security of the population. In fact, the linguistic and historical origins of the concept of "police" demonstrate a close association between government and civilization: *politia* (the state), *polis* (city), and *politeia* (citizenship).[8] The word had a secondary usage as well: cleansing or keeping clean. This use resonates with early twentieth century public health connotations of hygiene and sanitation.

First, this paper explains modern efforts at public health law reform. Even before September 11, the Robert Wood Johnson Foundation's (RWJF's) Turning Point initiative supported comprehensive reform of antiquated public health laws "the Public Health Statute Modernization Collaborative. After the anthrax outbreak, the Centers for Disease Control and Prevention (CDC) asked the Center for Law and the Public's Health (CLPH)

at Georgetown and Johns Hopkins Universities to draft the Model State Emergency Health Powers Act (MSEHPA). Thirty-five states and the District of Columbia have introduced legislative bills or resolutions based in whole or part on this model act. Nineteen states and D.C. have enacted MSEHPA or a version of it.[9]

Next, the paper shows why existing public health laws provide a weak foundation for public health practice. They are obsolete, inconsistent, and inadequate from a public health and civil liberties perspective. State legislation does not facilitate, and may even impede, the critical variables for public health preparedness: planning, coordination, surveillance, management of property, and protection of persons. Finally, the paper offers a systematic defense of MSEHPA. The model act has galvanized the public debate around the appropriate balance between public goods and individual rights. Although it has had success in many state legislatures, it has been criticized by both ends of the political spectrum. Many of the critiques offer a rationale for protecting property and personal rights against state incursions. This defense shows how MSEHPA creates strong public health powers while safeguarding individual freedoms—adopting clearer standards and more rigorous procedures than existing statutes do.

Two National Projects for Public Health Law Reform

The Institute of Medicine (IOM), in its foundational 1988 report, *The Future of Public Health,* acknowledged that law was essential to public health but cast serious doubt on the soundness of public health's legal basis. Concluding that "this nation has lost sight of its public health goals and has allowed the system of public health activities to fall into disarray," the IOM recommended reform of an obsolete and inadequate body of enabling laws and regulations.[10] In its 2002 report, *The Future of the Public's Health in the Twenty-first Century,* the IOM notes that little progress has been made in implementing its 1988 proposal. The committee recommends that "public health law be reformed so that it conforms to modern scientific and legal standards, is more consistent within and among states, and is more uniform in its approach to different health threats."[11] The U.S. Department of Health and Human Services (HHS) in *Healthy People 2010* similarly argued that strong laws are a vital component of the public health infrastructure and recommended that states reform their outdated statutes.[12]

Public Health Statute Modernization Collaborative

In response to a sustained critique of the crumbling public health infrastructure, the RWJF, in partnership with the W.K. Kellogg Foundation, initiated the Turning Point project in 1996: "Collaborating for a New Century in Public Health." Turning Point launched five National Excellence Collaboratives in 2000, including the Public Health Statute Modernization Collaborative. The collaborative's mission was "to transform and strengthen the legal framework for the public health system through a collaborative process to develop a model public health law."

The Public Health Statute Modernization Collaborative is led by a consortium of states, in partnership with federal agencies and national organizations. The collaborative contracted with the author to draft a model public health act under the guidance of a national expert advisory committee. It has published a comprehensive assessment of state public health laws, demonstrating the inadequacies of existing law to support modern public health functions.[13] The objective is to ensure that state public health law is consistent with modern constitutional principles and reflects current scientific and ethical values underlying public health practice. This model public health act will focus on the organization, delivery, and funding of essential public health services and functions. It is scheduled for completion by October 2003, and current drafts are available on the Internet.[14]

Model State Emergency Health Powers Act

The law-reform process took on new urgency after the terrorist attacks of late 2001. In response, the CLPH drafted MSEHPA at the request of the CDC. The act was written in collaboration with members of national organizations representing governors, legislators, public health commissions, and attorneys general.[15] There was also an extensive consultative process involving the major stakeholders such as businesses, public health and civil liberties organizations, scholars, and practitioners. MSEHPA, therefore, was written following a broad dialogue regarding the purpose of emergency public health law, its proper reach, and the protection of civil liberties and private property.

The act is explained in greater detail elsewhere, but the following brief description provides the background for a more sustained defense of the act's approach.[16] MSEHPA is structured to reflect five basic public health functions to be facilitated by law: preparedness, surveillance, management of property, protection of persons, and public information and communication. The preparedness and surveillance functions take effect immediately upon the act's passage. However, the compulsory powers over property and persons take effect only once a state's governor has declared a "public health emergency." A public health emergency is defined as the occurrence of imminent threat of an illness or health condition caused by bioterrorism or a novel or previously controlled or eradicated infectious agent or biological toxin. The health threat must pose a high probability of a large number of deaths or serious disabilities in the population.

The act facilitates systematic planning for a public health emergency. The state Public Health Emergency Plan must include coordination of services; procurement of vaccines and pharmaceuticals; housing, feeding, and caring for affected populations (with appropriate regard for their physical and cultural/social needs); and the proper vaccination and treatment of individuals.

The act provides authority for surveillance of health threats and continuing power to follow a developing public health emergency. For example, it requires prompt reporting by health care providers, pharmacists, veterinarians, and laboratories. It also provides for the exchange of relevant data among lead agencies such as public health, emergency management, and public safety.

MSEHPA provides comprehensive powers to manage property and protect persons, to safeguard the public's health and security. Public health authorities may close, decontaminate, or procure facilities and materials to respond to a public health emergency; safely dispose of infectious waste; and obtain and deploy health care supplies. Similarly, the model act permits public health authorities to physically examine or test individuals as necessary to diagnose or to treat illness; vaccinate or treat individuals to prevent or ameliorate an infectious disease; and isolate or quarantine individuals to prevent or limit the transmission of a contagious disease. The public health authority also may waive licensing requirements for health care professionals and direct them to assist in vaccination, testing, examination, and treatment of patients. Finally, MSEHPA provides for a set of postdeclaration powers and duties to ensure appropriate public information and communication. The public health authority must provide information to the public regarding the emergency, including protective measures to be taken and information regarding access to mental health support.

In summary, MSEHPA requires the development of a comprehensive plan to provide a coordinated, appropriate response in the event of a public health emergency. It facilitates the early detection of a health emergency by authorizing the reporting as well as collection and exchange of data. During a public health emergency, state and local officials are authorized to use and appropriate property as necessary for the care, treatment, and housing of patients and to destroy contaminated facilities or materials. They are also empowered to provide care, testing, treatment, and vaccination to persons who are ill or who have been exposed to a contagious disease and to separate affected individuals from the population at large to interrupt disease transmission. At the same time, the act recognizes that a state's ability to respond to a public health emergency must respect the dignity and rights of persons. Guided by principles of justice, state and local governments have a duty to act with fairness and tolerance toward individuals and groups.

Inadequacy of Existing Public Health Legislation

Before beginning a detailed defense of the model act, it is important to show why current law provides a weak foundation for the effective identification and control of serious health threats. Critics attack MSEHPA as if it were proposed in a regulatory vacuum. Yet public health is practiced under a voluminous set of laws and regulations. The issue is not whether the act provides an ideal solution to perennially complex problems. Rather, the issue is whether the act does a much better job than existing legislation does. As the following discussion demonstrates, existing state law is obsolete, fragmented, and inadequate. Outdated state laws do not support, and even thwart, effective public health surveillance and interventions.[17]

Public health legislation is so old that it tells the story of communicable diseases through time, with new layers of regulation with each page in history from plague and smallpox to tuberculosis and polio, and now HIV/AIDS and West Nile virus. Many laws have not been systematically updated since the early to mid twentieth century.[18] State laws predate modern public health science and practice. Research demonstrates that existing public health law does not conform to modern ideas relating to the mission, functions, and services of public health agencies.[19] Existing state laws also predate advances in constitutional law and civil liberties (such as privacy and antidiscrimination). For example, many public health laws do not provide rigorous procedural due process protections. Existing laws are so obtuse that few public health practitioners, or even legal counsel, fully understand them. Discussion of law reform, therefore, must take account of the obsolescence and complexity of current legislation.

Public health laws are inconsistent both within states and among them. Within states, different rules apply depending on the particular disease in question. Public health officers may legally exercise compulsory powers (screening, vaccination, directly observed therapy, or isolation) for one health threat but not another, and they may have a duty to assure privacy, nondiscrimination, and procedural due process in some cases but not in others. Inconsistencies among the states and territories lead to profound variation in the structure, substance, and procedures for detecting, controlling, and preventing disease. A certain level of consistency is important in public health because infections diseases usually occur regionally or nationally, requiring a coordinated approach to surveillance and control.

Many current laws fail to provide necessary authority for each of the key elements for public health preparedness: planning, coordination, surveillance, management of property, and protection of persons. States have not devised clear methods of planning, communication, and coordination among the various levels of government (federal, tribal, state, and local), responsible agencies (public health, law enforcement, and emergency management), and the private sector (food, transportation, and health care). Indeed, because of privacy concerns, many states actually proscribe the exchange of vital information.[20]

Current statutes also do not facilitate surveillance and may even prevent monitoring. For example, many states do not require timely reporting for Category A agents of bioterrorism.[21] At the same time, states do not require public health agencies to monitor data held by hospitals, managed care organizations, and pharmacies and may even prohibit them from doing so.[22]

Extant laws usually do provide powers over property and persons, but their scope is limited.

Some statutes permit the exercise of certain powers (such as quarantine) but not others (such as directly observed therapy). Other statutes permit the exercise of powers in relation to certain diseases (such as smallpox and tuberculosis) but not others (such as hemorrhagic fevers). There are numerous circumstances that might require management of property in a public health emergency: shortages of vaccines, medicines, hospital beds, or facilities for disposal of corpses. It may even be necessary to close facilities or destroy property that is contaminated or dangerous. There similarly may be a need to exercise powers over individuals to avert a serious threat to the public's health. Vaccination, testing, physical examination, treatment, isolation, and quarantine each may help to contain the spread of communicable diseases.

In summary, existing public health laws introduce two kinds of error that require correction. On the one hand, many statutes fail to provide adequate powers to deal with the full range of health threats. On the other hand, when they do authorize coercion, statutes rarely provide clear standards and fair procedures for decision making.

A Defense of the Model Act

There have been several specific objections to MSEHPA: *federalism:* federal, not state, law is implicated in a health crisis; *emergency declarations:* the scope of a public health emergency is overly broad; *abuse of power:* governors and public health officials will act without sufficient justification; *personal libertarianism:* compulsory powers over nonadherent individuals are rarely, or never, necessary; *economic libertarianism:* regulation of businesses is counterproductive; and *safeguards of property and persons:* MSEHPA fails to provide strong protection of individual and economic freedoms.

Federalism

Critics argue that acts of terrorism are inherently federal matters, so there is no need for expansion of state public health powers. It is certainly true that federal authority is extraordinarily important in responding to catastrophic public health events: Bioterrorism may trigger national security concerns, require investigation of federal offenses, and affect geographic regions or even the entire country. Consequently, the federal government often takes the lead in responding to a public health emergency, as it did in the anthrax outbreaks. Indeed, the federal government, under the national defense or commerce powers of the Constitution, is entitled to act in the context of multistate threats to health and security.

The assertion of federal jurisdiction, of course, does not obviate the need for adequate state and local public health power. States and localities have been the primary bulwark of public health in America. From a historical perspective, local and state public health agencies predated federal agencies. Local boards of health were in operation in the late eighteenth century, and state agencies emerged after the Civil War. Federal health agencies, however, did not develop a major presence until Franklin Roosevelt's New Deal. State and local agencies have played a crucial role in infectious disease control from colonial and revolutionary times, through the industrial revolution, to the modern times.

From a constitutional perspective, states have "plenary" authority to protect the public's health under their reserved powers in the Tenth Amendment. The Supreme Court has made it clear that states have a deep reservoir of public health powers, conceiving of state police powers as "an immense mass of legislation. . . . Inspection laws, quarantine laws, and health laws of every description . . . are components of this mass."[23] The Supreme Court, moreover, regards federal police powers as constitutionally limited and has curtailed the expansion of national public health authority.[24]

From an economic and practical perspective, most public health activities take place at the state and local levels: surveillance, communicable disease control, and food and water safety. States and localities probably would be the first to detect and respond to a health emergency and would have a key role throughout. This requires states to have effective, modern statutory powers that enable them to work alongside federal agencies.

Declaration of a Public Health Emergency

Critics express concern that the model act could be triggered too easily, creating a threat to civil liberties. Community-based organizations objected to the idea that a governor might declare a public health emergency for an endemic disease such as HIV/AIDS or influenza. Although this may have been a problem with the act's initial version, the current version expressly states that a governor may not declare a public health emergency for an endemic disease.

Legal scholars express concerns that a governor could declare an emergency for a theoretical or low-level risk. However, the drafters set demanding conditions for a governor's declaration, clearly specifying the level of risk. A public health emergency may be declared only in the event of bioterrorism or a naturally occurring epidemic that poses a high probability of a large number of deaths or serious disabilities. Indeed, the drafters rejected arguments from high-level federal and state officials to set a lower threshold for triggering a health emergency.

Finally, commentators suggest that governors retain too much discretion to declare a public health emergency. However, the act specifies clear criteria for triggering gubernatorial powers and uses language that fetters the exercise of discretion. The act also allows the legislature and judiciary to intervene if the governor has acted outside the scope of his or her authority. Taken as a whole, the drafters carefully limited the circumstances under which the act's more robust powers can be invoked.

Governmental Abuse of Power

Critics argue that governors and public health authorities would abuse their authority and exercise powers without justification. This kind of generalized argument could be used to refute the exercise of compulsory power in any realm, because executive branch officials may overreach. However, such general objections have never been a reason to deny government the power to avert threats to health, safety, and security. The answer to such general objections is to introduce into the law careful safeguards to prevent officials from acting outside the scope of their authority. The model act builds in effective protection against governmental abuse. It adopts the doctrine of separation of powers, so that no branch wields unchecked authority. These checks and balances offer a classic means of preventing abuse.

MSEHPA creates several hedges against abuse: (1) The governor may declare an emergency only under strict criteria and with careful consultation with public health experts and the community; (2) the legislature, by majority vote, can override the governor's declaration at any time; and (3) the judiciary can terminate the exercise of power if the governor violates the act's standards or procedures or acts unconstitutionally. No law can guarantee that the powers it confers will not be abused. But MSEHPA counterbalances executive power by providing a strong role for the legislature and judiciary. Therefore, it sets clear criteria for the exercise of power, requires a consultative process, and imposes checks and balances. There is little more that any law could do to prevent abuse of power.

Personal Libertarianism

Critics imply that the model act should not confer compulsory power at all. In particular, they object to compulsory powers to vaccinate, test, medically treat, isolate, and quarantine. Commentators reason that services are more important than power; that individuals will comply voluntarily with public health advice; and that tradeoffs between civil rights and public health are not required and even are counterproductive. Certainly the HIV/AIDS epidemic has demonstrated that

public health and civil liberties can be mutually reinforcing—respect for individual freedoms can promote the public's health. Nevertheless, the arguments that law should not confer compulsory power are misplaced.

First, although the provision of services may be more important than the exercise of power, the state undoubtedly needs a certain amount of authority to protect the public's health. Government must have the power to prevent individuals from endangering others. It is only common sense, for example, that a person who has been exposed to an infectious disease should be required to undergo testing or medical examination and, if infectious, to be vaccinated, treated, or isolated.

Second, although most people can be expected to comply willingly with public health measures because it is in their own interests or desirable for the common welfare, not everyone will comply. Individuals may resist loss of autonomy, privacy, or liberty even if their behavior threatens others. Provided that public health powers are hedged with safeguards, individuals should be required to yield some of their interests to protect the health and security of the community.

Finally, although public health and civil liberties may be mutually enhancing in many instances, they sometimes come into conflict. When government acts to preserve the public's health, it can interfere with property rights (for example, freedom of contract, to pursue a profession, or to conduct a business) or personal rights (for example, autonomy, privacy, and liberty). The history of public health is littered with illustrations of tradeoffs between public health and civil liberties.[25] It may be fashionable to argue that there is no tension, but public health officials need to make hard choices, particularly in public health emergencies.

Individuals whose movements pose a serious risk of harm to their communities do not have a "right" to be free of interference necessary to control the threat. There simply is no basis for this argument in constitutional law, and perhaps little more in political philosophy. Even the most liberal scholars accept the harm principle—that government should retain power to prevent individuals from endangering others.[26]

The Supreme Court has been equally clear about the limits of freedom in a constitutional democracy. The rights of liberty and due process are fundamental but not absolute. Justice Harlan in the foundational Supreme Court case of *Jacobson v. Massachusetts* (1905) wrote: "There are manifold restraints to which every person is necessarily subject for the common good. On any other basis organized society could not exist with safety to its members"[27] Critics argue, without support from any judicial authority, that the Supreme Court's landmark decision in *Jacobson,* reiterated by the Court over the past century, is no longer apposite. There is, according to this line of argument, a constitutional right to refuse interventions even if the individual poses a public risk. Yet the courts have consistently upheld compulsory measures to avert a risk, including the power to compulsorily test, report, vaccinate, treat, and isolate, provided there are clear criteria and procedures.[28]

Economic Libertarianism

Civil libertarians have not been the only group to criticize MSEHPA. Businesses, as well as law and economic scholars, have complained that it interferes with free enterprise. Most economic stakeholders, including the food, transportation, pharmaceutical, and health care industries, have lobbied CLPH faculty and legislators. These groups argue that they may have to share data with government, abate nuisances, destroy property, and provide goods and services without their express agreement.[29]

Generally speaking, the model act provides several kinds of powers to regulate businesses: destruction of dangerous or contaminated property, nuisance abatements, and confiscation of property for public purposes. All of these pow-

ers have been exercised historically and comply with constitutional and ethical norms. If businesses have property that poses a public threat, government has always had the power to destroy that property. For example, if a rug were contaminated with anthrax or smallpox, government should have the power to order its destruction. Similarly, if businesses are engaged in an activity that poses a health threat, government has always had the power to abate the nuisance. Businesses must comply with all manner of health and safety regulations that interfere with economic freedoms. Those who believe in the undeterred entrepreneur may not agree with health regulations, but the regulations are necessary to ensure that business activities do not endanger the public. Finally, government has always had the power to confiscate private property for the public good. In the event of bioterrorism, for example, it may be necessary for government to have adequate supplies of vaccines or pharmaceuticals. Similarly, government may need to use health care facilities for medical treatment or quarantine of persons exposed to infection.

Businesses argue that government should not have broad powers to control enterprise and property. If these powers have to be exercised, businesses want to ensure that they are compensated according to market values. The model act follows a classical approach to the issue of property rights. Compensation is provided if there is a "taking"—that is, if the government confiscates private property for public purposes (such as the use of a private infirmary to treat or isolate patients). No compensation would be provided for a "nuisance abatement"—that is, if the government destroys property or closes an establishment that poses a serious health threat. This comports with the extant constitutional "takings" jurisprudence of the Supreme Court.[30] If the government were forced to compensate for all nuisance abatements, it would greatly chill public health regulation.

In American history and constitutional law, private property has always been held subject to the restriction that it not be used in a way that posed a health hazard. As Lemuel Shaw of the Massachusetts Supreme Judicial Court observed as early as 1851: "We think it settled principle, growing out of the nature of well ordered civil society, that every holder of property . . . holds it under the implied liability that it shall not be injurious to the right of the community."[31]

Safeguards of Persons and Property

The real basis for debate over public health legislation should not be that powers are given, because it is clear that power is sometimes necessary. The better question is whether the powers are hedged with appropriate safeguards of personal and economic liberty. The core of the debate over MSEHPA ought to be whether it appropriately protects freedoms by providing clear and demanding criteria for the exercise of power and fair procedures for decision making. It is in this context that the attack on MSEHPA is particularly exasperating, because critics rarely suggest that the act fails to provide crisp standards and procedural due process. Nor do they compare the safeguards in the model act to those in existing public health legislation.

It is important to note that compulsory powers over individuals (testing, physical examination, treatment, and isolation) and businesses (nuisance abatements and seizure or destruction of property) already exist in state public health law. These powers have been exercised since the founding of the Republic. MSEHPA, therefore, does not contain new, radical powers. Most tellingly, the model contains much better safeguards of individual and economic liberty than appear in communicable disease statutes enacted in the early to mid-twentieth century.

Unlike older statutes, MSEHPA provides clear and objective criteria for the exercise of powers, rigorous procedural due process, respect for re-

ligious and cultural differences, and a new set of entitlements for humane treatment. First, the criteria for the exercise of compulsory powers are based on the modern "significant risk" standard enunciated in constitutional law and disability discrimination law. The act also requires public health officials to adopt the "least restrictive alternative." Second, the procedures for intervention are rigorous, following the most stringent requirements set by the Supreme Court, including the right to counsel, presentation and cross-examination of evidence, and reasons for decisions. Third, the act shows tolerance of groups through its requirements to respect cultural and religious differences whenever consistent with the public's health. Finally, the act provides a whole new set of rights to care and treatment of persons subject to isolation or quarantine. These include the right to treatment, clothing, food, communication, and humane conditions.

In summary, MSEHPA provides a modern framework for effective identification of and response to emerging health threats, while demonstrating respect for individuals and tolerance of groups. Indeed, the CLPH agreed to draft the law only because a much more draconian approach might have been taken by the federal government and the states acting on their own and responding to public fears and misapprehensions.

Rethinking the Public Good

Values in the United States at the turn of the twenty-first century could be characterized fairly as individualistic. There was a distinct orientation toward personal and proprietary freedoms and against a substantial government presence in social and economic life. The homeland terrorist attacks in 2001 reawakened the political community to the importance of public health. Historians will look back and ask whether 11 September 2001 was a fleeting scare with temporary solutions or whether it was a transforming event.

There are good reasons for believing that resource allocations, ethical values, and law should transform to reflect the critical importance of the health, security, and well-being of the populace. It is not that individual freedoms are unimportant. To the contrary, personal liberty allows people the right of self-determination, to make judgments about how to live their lives and pursue their dreams. Without a certain level of health, safety, and security, however, people cannot have well being, nor can they meaningfully exercise their autonomy or participate in social and political life.

My purpose is not to assert which are the more fundamental interests: personal liberty or health and security. Rather, my purpose is to illustrate that both sets of interests are important to human flourishing. The Model State Emergency Health Powers Act was designed to defend personal as well as collective interests. But in a country so tied to rights rhetoric on both sides of the political spectrum, any proposal that has the appearance of strengthening governmental authority was bound to travel in tumultuous political waters.

The Center for Law and the Public's Health at Georgetown and Johns Hopkins Universities is supported by Cooperative Agreement no. U50/CCU31911802 from the Centers for Disease Control and Prevention. The author gratefully acknowledges the intellectual contributions of many organizations, notably the National Governors Association, National Conference of State Legislatures, National Association of Attorneys General, Association of State and Territorial Health Officials, and National Association of City and County Health Officials. The contents of this paper are solely the responsibility of the author and do not necessarily represent the official views of the CDC or the organizations providing assistance in the development of the model act. The Alfred P. Sloan Foundation provided funding for the development of MSEHPA. The Reforming States Group, comprising leaders of states' legislative and executive branches, in collaboration with the Milbank Memorial Fund, provided technical assistance to many states. MSEHPA grew out of the work of the Public Health Statute Modernization National Collaborative of the Robert Wood Johnson Foundation (Turning Point). The Public Health Law Program at the CDC offered critical contributions throughout, particularly Richard Goodman and Gene Matthews. The drafting team for the model act included, in addition to the author, Scott Burris, James G. Hodge Jr., Julie Samia Mair, Jason W. Sapsin, Stephen P. Teret, and Jon Vernick.

References

1. K.W. Eilbert et al., *Measuring Expenditures for Essential Public Health Services* (Washington: Public Health Foundation, 1996). For state-level spending, see Centers for Disease Control and Prevention, "Effectiveness in Disease and Injury Prevention Estimated National Spending on Prevention—United States, 1988, *Morbidity and Mortality Weekly Report* 41, no. 29 (1992): 529–536. For federal-level spending, see J.I. Boufford and P.R. Lee, *Health Policies for the Twenty-first Century: Challenges and Recommendations for the U.S. Department of Health and Human Services* (New York: Milbank Memorial Fund, 2001).

2. Institute of Medicine, *The Future of Public Health* (Washington: National Academy Press, 1988).

3. CDC, *Public Health's Infrastructure: A Status Report* (Atlanta: CDC, 2001).

4. L.M. Bush et al., "Index Case of Fatal Inhalational Anthrax Due to Bioterrorism in the United States, *New England Journal of Medicine* (29 November 2001): 1607–1611.

5. Office of Management and Budget, Executive Office of the President of the United States, *Budget of the U.S. Government, Fiscal Year 2003*, 4 February 2002, www.whitehouse.gov/omb/budget/fy2003/pdf/budget.pdf (22 August 2002).

6. M.H. Cooper, "Weapons of Mass Destruction, *Congressional Quarterly* (8 March 2002): 195–215.

7. D.E. Beauchamp and B. Steinbock, eds., *New Ethics for the Public's Health* (New York: Oxford University Press, 1999).

8. *Webster's Third New International Dictionary, Unabridged* (1986).

9. The nineteen states are Arizona, Delaware, Florida, Georgia, Hawaii, Maine, Maryland, Minnesota, Missouri, New Hampshire, New Mexico, Oklahoma, South Carolina, South Dakota, Tennessee, Utah, Vermont, Virginia, and Wisconsin.

10. IOM, *The Future of Public Health.*

11. IOM, *The Future of the Public's Health in the Twenty-first Century* (Washington: National Academy Press, November 2002).

12. Department of Health and Human Services, *Healthy People 2010* (Washington: DHHS, 2000).

13. L.O. Gostin and J.G. Hodge Jr., *State Public Health Law Assessment Report,* April 2002, turningpointprogram.org/Pages/phsc%20statute%20assmt.pdf (22 August 2002).

14. See "Model State Public Health Act, Draft Document as of May 31, 2002, "turningpointprogram.org/Pages/phsc-MSPH%20Act3.pdf (22 August 2002); and Turning Point, "Public Health Statute Modernization National Collaborative," www.hss.state.ak.us/dph/deu/turningpoint/nav.htm (22 August 2002).

15. J. Gillis, "States Weighing Laws to Fight Bioterrorism, *Washington Post,* 19 November 2001.

16. See L.O. Gostin et al., "The Model State Emergency Health Powers Act: Planning for and Response to Bioterrorism and Naturally Occurring Infectious Diseases, *Journal of the American Medical Association* 288, no. 5 (2002): 622–628. Readers should refer to the specific language of the MSEHPA for the most accurate account. Center for Law and the Public's Health, "The Model State Emergency Health Powers Act, as of December 21, 2001," www.publichealthlaw.net/MSEHPA/MSEHPA2.pdf (22 August 2002).

17. L.O. Gostin, "Public Health Law Reform, *American Journal of Public Health* 91, no. 9 (2001): 1365–1368.

18. L.O. Gostin, S. Burris, and Z. Lazzarini, "The Law and the Public's Health: A Study of Infectious Disease Law in the United States, *Columbia Law Review* 99, no. 1 (1999): 59–128.

19. K.M. Gebbie, "State Public Health Laws: An Expression of Constituency Expectations, *Journal of*

Public Health Management Practice 6, no. 2 (2000): 46–54.

20. L.O. Gostin et al., "The Public Health Information Infrastructure: A National Review of the Law on Health Information Privacy, *Journal of the American Medical Association* 275, no. 24 (1996): 1921–1927.

21. H.H. Horton et al., "Critical Biological Agents: Disease Reporting as a Tool for Bioterrorism Preparedness, *Journal of Law, Medicine, and Ethics* 30, no. 2 (2002): 262–266.

22. Gostin et al., "The Public Health Information Infrastructure.

23. *Gibbons v. Ogden,* 22 U.S. (9 Wheat.) 1 (1824).

24. *United States v. Lopez,* 514 U.S. 549 (1995).

25. L.O. Gostin, *Public Health Law: Power, Duty, Restraint* (Berkeley and New York: University of California Press and Milbank Memorial Fund, 2000); and L.O. Gostin, ed., *Public Health Law and Ethics: A Reader* (Berkeley and New York: University of California Press and Milbank Memorial Fund, 2002).

26. J. Feinberg, *The Moral Limits of the Criminal Law,* 4 vols. (New York: Oxford University Press, 1987–1990).

27. *Jacobson v. Massachusetts,* 197 U.S. 11, 26 (1905).

28. On averting risk, see *Washington v. Harper,* 494 U.S. 210, 227 (1990) (upholding forced administration of antipsychotic medication if the inmate is dangerous to himself or others and the treatment is in the inmate's medical interest). On compulsory testing, see *Skinner v. Railway Labor Executives' Ass'n,* 489 U.S. 601 (1989). On compulsory reporting, see *Whalen v. Roe,* 429 U.S. 589 (1977). On compulsory vaccination, see *Zucht v. King,* 260 U.S. 174 (1922). On compulsory treatment, see *McCormick v. Stalder,* 105 F.3d 1059, 1061 (5th Cir. 1997) (finding that the state's compelling interest in reducing the spread of tuberculosis justifies involuntary treatment). On isolation, see *Greene v. Edwards,* 263 S.E.2d 661 (1980).

29. S. Lueck, "States Seek to Strengthen Emergency Powers: Movement Is Raising Privacy and Civil-Liberties Concerns," *Wall Street Journal,* 7 January 2002.

30. *Lucas v. South Carolina Coastal Council,* 505 U.S. 1003 (1992).

31. *Commonwealth v. Alger,* 7 Cush.53, 84–85 (1851).

Bioterrorism, Public Health, and Human Rights

Taking Human Rights Seriously Is Our Best Defense against Terrorism and Fosters Both the Federalization and Globalization of Public Health

GEORGE J. ANNAS

A central lesson from 9/11 is that threats to public health are national and global. Unfortunately, public health as a field has an unappealing tendency to look backward when planning for the future. Even the influential 1988 report of the Institute of Medicine, *The Future of Public Health,* ignored the need for federal public health leadership and financing.[1] Rather than "moving public health into the 21st century [the report tried to] return it to the 19th century," leaving us poorly prepared for bioterrorism.[2] As Lawrence Gostin's paper outlines, the Centers for Disease Control and Prevention's (CDC's) request to develop a state emergency powers act in the wake of the anthrax attacks reflects this regressive tendency. Its exclusive concentration on the state level misses an important opportunity to exercise national public health leadership and instead promotes a return to the paternalistic pre-human rights days of nineteenth-century public health practices such as forced examination and quarantine.

In this brief commentary I make three arguments: (1) Bioterrorism should move us toward a more federalized and globalized public health system, (2) protecting basic human and constitutional rights is essential to effective coordination of medicine and public health, and (3) 9/11 and the suggested act should prompt thoughtful reflection, debate, and action to modernize public health practice.

Federal (and Global) Public Health

State public health laws are often antiquated, but their most antiquated feature is their underlying premise that public health is exclusively a state-level concern. A bioterrorist attack on the United States, for example, is inherently a matter of national security, making it a federal matter. That is why the FBI, not state or local police, took almost immediate control in the wake of the anthrax attacks. State laws regarding bioterrorism should be primarily aimed at preparing state and local authorities for their important job of assisting federal agencies, such as the new U.S. Department of Homeland Security, in the response. Biological attacks are different in kind from nuclear and chemical attacks, and they require specially tailored defenses.[3]

Public health policy should be national, and the addition of national security to federal financing and interstate commerce provides sufficient constitutional authority for Congress to enact legislation giving the federal government the leadership role in public health in the twenty-first century. In response to bioterrorism, in particular, it is imperative that the federal government develop a national plan that individual states can help implement, and that the federal government supply the states with badly needed financial and other resources to improve their public health infrastructure, training, and coordination.

At the outset of the twenty-first century, bioterrorism, although only one threat to public health, can be the catalyst to effectively "federalize" and integrate much of what are now uncoordinated and piecemeal state and local public health programs. This should include a renewed effort for national health insurance; national licensure for physicians, nurses, and allied health professionals; and national patient-safety standards. Federal public health leadership will also help us look outward and recognize that prevention of future bioterrorist attacks and even ordinary epidemics will require international cooperation.[4] In this regard, the threat of bioterrorism joins HIV/AIDS and other epidemics to demonstrate the need to globalize public health.

Public Health and Medicine

A major planning question in responding to a bioterrorist attack is the relationship between medicine and public health. It is almost certain that any attack will first be recognized by physicians working in a hospital emergency room.[5] Therefore, proposals to train emergency room personnel to recognize patients exposed to the most likely bioterrorist agents make perfect sense, as do up-to-date communication systems that can track relevant disease occurrences quickly and accurately (although there is no necessity to report data that identify patients). But who should be in charge after an outbreak has been confirmed?

The suggested act assumes that a state's governor will designate "public health officials" to be in charge and that these officials—who will be issued badges—will be empowered to take over hospitals and order physicians to examine and treat (and quarantine) individuals against their will, even when there is no evidence at all that the individual is either sick or contagious. The act's first draft was even more extreme, making it a crime for any individual to refuse to be examined or treated and a crime for a physician to refuse an order by a public health official to examine or treat a patient.[6] Moreover, should any patient be injured, or even killed, by the treatment (as, for example, immunocompromised individuals could be by smallpox vaccine), the public health officials and state would be immune from lawsuit.

This approach is likely to be counterproductive. Despite its talk about balancing human rights with disease prevention, the suggested act unnecessarily ignores basic human rights. Physicians, on the other hand, have effectively incorporated the doctrine of informed consent into their core medical ethics precepts. Public health still favors legal mandates and government-backed paternalism. Public health should be abandoning paternalism, rather than attempting to use 9/11 to increase it. Public health officials are likely to be much more effective in responding to emergencies if they work with both physicians and the public, rather than trying to exercise arbitrary and unaccountable power over them.

As evidenced by both 9/11 and the anthrax attacks, U.S. hospitals and physicians stand ready to help in any way they can in a mass emergency. The public is also eager—often too eager—to accept medications and line up to seek screening and care at hospitals. The real problem in a bioterrorist event will be supplying medical care, drugs, and vaccines to those who demand them. Nonetheless, the prospect of arbitrary forced treatment and quarantine would rightly engender distrust in government and public health officials and could actually discourage those who might have been exposed from seeking treatment at all—even encourage them to escape to another state. As 9/11 demonstrated, most people want to protect their families first and are likely to avoid public health officials who they believe might arbitrarily separate them from their families. As long as the public trusts its physicians and public health professionals, the problem will not be getting Americans to accept treatment, it will be persuading the worried well that they don't need treatment.

Democracy and Public Health

The suggested act has been criticized by both civil liberties and libertarian groups. But they are hardly alone. As the act's authors note on the cover page of their second (21 December 2001) and apparently final draft, not one of the groups involved in any way with the original draft and the revision, including the authors themselves, have endorsed the proposal as written.[7] The original "model act" has been relabeled as simply a "draft for discussion," prepared "to facilitate and encourage communication," and does "not represent the official policy, endorsement, or views" of the Center for Law and the Public's Health, the CDC, the National Governors Association (NGA), the National Conference of State Legislatures (NCSL), the Association of State and Territorial Health Officials (ASTHO), the National Association of County and City Health Officials (NACCHO), or the National Association of Attorneys General (NAAG), or anyone else.[8]

There is no chance that every state, or even many states, will adopt the suggested act, so if uniformity is seen as necessary, only a federal statute can provide it. So far, only Delaware and South Carolina have embraced the suggested act. More typically, states have ignored it, or like California, have considered it and rejected it outright. Other states, like Minnesota, have adopted some of its provisions but have rewritten them to be consistent with contemporary medical ethics and constitutional rights.

Under the new Minnesota law, for example, even in a public health emergency, "individuals have a fundamental right to refuse medical treatment, testing, physical or mental examination, vaccination, participation in experimental procedures and protocols, collection of specimens and preventive treatment programs."[9] Of course there are extreme circumstances under which isolation or quarantine can be employed. But the Minnesota legislature permits such measures only under much more limited conditions; the right to refuse all interventions continues in isolation and quarantine; and family members are permitted to visit. Most of the other provisions of the suggested act, including the immunity provisions, were referred to the Minnesota commissioner of

health, who was instructed to study them and report back to the legislature, after having solicited public comment on any recommendations.[10] The Minnesota legislature properly recognized that human rights and health are not inherently conflicting goals that must be traded off against each other; they are, as Jonathan Mann and colleagues first articulated in the context of the international HIV/AIDS epidemic, "inextricably linked."[11]

The suggested act was drafted under extreme, albeit self-imposed, time constraints in the immediate aftermath of 9/11 and the anthrax attacks, when fear ruled reason. This is a predictable prescription for disaster. Sensible public health and bioterrorism legislation must be drafted in a calm atmosphere, in a transparent, public process.[12] Most importantly, as Ken Wing has noted, "statute drafting is a technical and instrumental job" one that should follow, not precede the more fundamental task of deciding what the statute ought to say.[13]

Ultimately, public health must rely not on force but on persuasion, and not on blind trust but on trust based on transparency, accountability, democracy, and human rights. There is plenty of time to draft and debate a twenty-first century federal public health law that takes constitutional rights seriously, unites the public with its medical caretakers, treats medicine and public health as true partners, and moves us in the direction of global cooperation.

The author happily acknowledges the value of numerous discussions with members of the New England Coalition for Law and Public Health on the subject of bioterrorism and public health in helping him to formulate his views, which do not necessarily reflect those of all members of the coalition.

References

1. Institute of Medicine, *The Future of Public Health* (Washington: National Academy Press, 1988). But see more recently, IOM, *America's Vital Interest in Global Health: Protecting Our People, Enhancing Our*

Economy, and Advancing Our International Interests (Washington: National Academy Press, 1997).

2. G.J. Annas, L. Glantz, and N.A. Scotch, "Back to the Future: The IOM Report Reconsidered, *American Journal of Public Health* (July 1991): 835–837.

3. M. Hamburg, "Homeland Security Research and Critical Infrastructure, Testimony before the House Energy and Commerce Subcommittee on Oversight and Investigations, 9 July 2002. See also M.T. Osterholm, "Emerging Infections" Another Warning, *New England Journal of Medicine* (27 April 2000): 1280–1281.

4. J. Frenk and O. Gômez-Dantês, "Globalization and the Challenges to Health Systems, *Health Affairs* (May/June 2002): 160–165; D.P. Fidler, "A Globalized Theory of Public Health Law, *Journal of Law, Medicine, and Ethics* (Summer 2002): 150–161; and W. Mariner, "Bioterrorism Act: The Wrong Response, *National Law Journal* (17 December 2001): 18.

5. D.A. Henderson, "Public Health Preparedness, in *Science and Technology in a Vulnerable World,* ed. A. H. Teich, S.D. Nelson, and S.J. Lita (Washington: American Association for the Advancement of Science, 2002), 33–40.

6. G.J. Annas, "Bioterrorism, Public Health, and Civil Liberties, *New England Journal of Medicine* (25 April 2002): 1337–1342.

7. "The Model State Emergency Health Powers Act, as of December 21, 2001," www.publichealthlaw .net/MSEHPA/MSEHPA2.pdf (28 August 2002). Text of the suggested act is also available in the *Journal of Law, Medicine, and Ethics* (Summer 2002): 322–348, although the disclaimer has been moved to the end in this publication.

8. "The Model State Emergency Health Powers Act, as of December 21, 2001."

9. *2002 Minnesota Chapter Law 402* (signed by the governor 22 May 2002).

10. Ibid.

11. J. Mann et al., "Health and Human Rights, *Health and Human Rights* 1, no. 1 (1994): 6–23. And see generally, J. Mann et al., eds., *Health and Human Rights: A Reader* (New York: Routledge, 1999); and G.J. Annas, "Is Privacy the Enemy of Public Health? (Review of *The Limits of Privacy*, by Amitai Etzioni), *Health Affairs* (July/Aug 1999): 197–198.

12. M.T. Osterholm and J. Schwartz, *Living Terrors: What America Needs to Know to Survive the Coming Bioterrorist Catastrophe* (New York: Dell, 2000), 154–155.

13. K. Wing, "The Model Act: Is It the Best Way to Prepare for the Next Public Health Emergency?" *Northwest Public Health* (Spring/Summer 2002): 10–11.

Bioterrorism
Public Health Perspectives

WENDY E. PARMET

Public Health and Bioterrorism

A public health perspective does not provide any definitive analysis of what actions the state ought to take to confront possibilities of bioterrorism. Nor can these perspectives form the sole guideposts for legal analysis, which invariably must take into account a myriad of other considera-

tions, including legal precedent, the norms and modalities of legal reasoning, and the teachings of moral theories. Nevertheless, public health's perspective can contribute, I believe, to our discussion of the issue.

First, to the extent that public health's assertion—that the public's health is an objective good—is accepted, it helps validate the initiative to prevent morbidity or mortality from bioterrorism. From a public health perspective, the value of a population's health is not simply a question of preferences or cultural deliberation. It is an objective value worthy of concern, period.[94] This means that if bioterrorism is a threat to a population's health, it is a legitimate target of concern and intervention, even if the public is not thinking about or caring about it at the moment. This is a view evident in old case law, but less prevalent today as both rights theory and utilitarianism in the guise of neo-classical economics have led judges to question whether health is indeed an important and legally recognizable value.[95]

Second, and more importantly, public health's teaching about both the importance of populations and their interdependencies provides a firm justification for government to take actions in order to prevent populations from being harmed by bioterrorism. As Gostin reminds us, bioterrorism is not something that individuals can protect themselves from (not withstanding the government's advice last winter to purchase and use duct tape).[96] Bioterrorism, like SARS, asthma, and a million and one other threats, affects populations and can be best addressed at the population level. Thus, public health provides a very different and far less skeptical lens on government action than does either liberalism, or potentially communitarianism.[97]

The need and justification for population-based approaches, however, does not necessarily require or sanction the type of coercive interventions contemplated by the MSEHPA. For one thing, the very interdependency of populations that is core to the public health perspective and that justifies population-based interventions, should cast doubt on framing public health problems as a contest between individuals and the public. Ironically, Gostin's discussion of bioterrorism, by focusing on the power of the state over individuals and the way that power can be limited by legal processes, actually derives from a liberal perspective that assumes that the good of the individual exists apart from the good of the population, and the ability of legal processes

to serve as a neutral device, to ensure the impartiality of decisions harmful to the individual.[98] A population perspective, in contrast, may well question not only whether the individual can be viewed as having preferences or rights apart from the population, but whether the focus on limiting those preferences or rights is in fact the best way to address the problem. Gostin does advocate other population-based approaches to address bioterrorism, like the retooling of the public health infrastructure.[99] Still, he remains convinced that when push comes to shove, it comes to the individual versus the state.

Public health's focus on interdependency may also lead us to ask not only whether we can limit individual rights, but the degree to which the application of coercive, and indeed frightening, measures upon individuals will itself be harmful to public health. Thus, we must care not only about the "rights" of the individual subject to quarantine or forced vaccination (as the rights theorist would do), but the impact of those measures on social solidarity and the ability of a community to confront a threat.[100] Here, there is much reason to believe, as Gostin has written elsewhere, that coercive measures may actually be corrosive of population health and respect for individual dignity, and egalitarian approaches may be more supportive of public health.[101] Thus, public health itself may come around to supporting the liberal's concern for human rights and the communitarian's concern for participation and deliberation, not as goods in themselves, but because they may help create a community conducive to health. Certainly, regimes that are repressive and disdainful of human dignity are not often associated with positive public health outcomes. Indeed, while the use of surveillance and rapid isolation has been credited with limiting the spread of SARS, even with that air-borne disease, which posed the strongest case possible for mandatory isolation, the verdict is still out as to whether coercive measures themselves did more harm than good. Certainly there is reason to wonder whether SARS would have spread as rapidly as it did had it first made its appearance in a more open and less repressive a society than China.[102] And we do not know whether the epidemic in Canada would have spread further or been halted earlier if that country had a less secure tradition of protecting individual rights and providing for social welfare. Moreover, the history of past quarantines certainly should give pause before one assumes that they actually benefit the public's health.[103]

Importantly, while I have written elsewhere about my worries and qualms about the MSEHPA,[104] public health's emphasis on empiricism cautions me to conclude with the observation that we really don't know the answer to the questions posed. We do not know the risks of bioterrorism; nor do we know either the risks or benefits of preparing for it, or revising our laws to provide states additional emergency powers. It may well be that if a catastrophe arises, the clarification of legal power will prove useful and a population may be saved. But it is also possible that emergency powers can be abused, that "code oranges" will prove to be misguided,[105] that due process hearings will not provide much protection, and that more harm than good will come from the displacement of energy and resources from common everyday killers to bioterrorism.[106] Indeed, if the history of public health law teaches us anything, it is that we need to be open and skeptical to uncontested claims about what will best promote the population's health. With that claim, I suspect, neither liberals nor communitarians would disagree.

Notes

94. Of course, it is just this axiom with which critics, especially neo-classical economists, are apt to differ.
95. See Richard A. Daynard, Regulating Tobacco: The Need for a Public Health Judicial Decision-Making Canon, 30 *J.L. Med. & Ethics* 281, 281 (2002); Wendy E. Parmet, Legal Rights and Communicable Disease: AIDS, the Police Power, and Individual Liberty, 14 *J. Health Pol., Pol'y & L.* 741, 748–62 (1989).
96. Gostin, . . . at 1160; see also Philip Shenon, Threats and Responses: Precautions; Administration Gives Advice on How to Prepare for a Terrorist Attack, *N.Y. Times*, Feb. 11, 2003, at A16.
97. This is to the extent that communitarianism is understood as stressing reciprocal extralegal relationships, not the formal invocation of state authority.
98. Liberals generally profess a commitment to the rule of law which entails legal recognition of rights and a separation of law from politics. Legal-process theorists are liberals who especially value the neutrality of the law and legal processes. See Gerald B. Wetlaufer, Systems of Belief in Modern American Law: A View from Century's End, 49 *Am. U.L.Rev.* 1, 8–10, 21–34 (1999).
99. See Gostin, . . . at 1128–31.
100. See, e.g., Peter A. Gorski, Caring Relationships: An Investment in Health?, 115 *Pub. Health Rep.* 144, 144–50 (2000); Ichiro Kawachi et al., Long Live Community: Social Capital as Public Health, 8 *Am. Prospect* 56, 56–57 (1997). George Annas made this precise point in his criticism of the MSEHPA. See George J. Annas, Bioterrorism, Public Health, and Human Rights, 21 *Health Aff.* 94, 94–97 (2002).
101. Lawrence O. Gostin & Zita Lazzarini, *Human Rights and Public Health in the AIDS Pandemic* 69 (1997).
102. Marwaan Macan-Markar, Health-East Asia: SARS Outbreak Draws Contrasting Responses, *Inter Press Service*, Apr. 4, 2003.
103. Parmet, . . . at 55–71.
104. See, e.g., Wendy E. Parmet, Quarantine Redux: Bioterrorism, AIDS and the Curtailment of Individual Liberty in the Name of Public Health, 13 *Health Matrix* 85 (2003).
105. Gostin seems to equate a "code orange" state with the "moderate risk" scenario for which he thinks we should accept some government limitations. See Gostin, . . . at 1136. On the problems and confusion associated with the government's declarations of "code orange" and its efforts to determine and warn the public about threat levels, see Anya Sostek, Orange Crash: The Confusion and Cost of Complying with National Terror Alerts are Driving Cities to Question the Whole System, *Governing*, Aug. 2003, at 18.
106. See Parmet, . . . at 110–15.

Medicine and Public Health, Ethics and Human Rights

Jonathan M. Mann

The relationships among medicine, public health, ethics, and human rights are now evolving rapidly, in response to a series of events, experiences, and struggles. These include the shock of the world-wide epidemic of human immunodeficiency virus and AIDS, continuing work on diverse aspects of women's health, and challenges exemplified by the complex humanitarian emergencies of Somalia, Iraq, Bosnia, Rwanda, and now, Zaire.

From among the many impacts of these experiences, three seem particularly salient. First, human rights thinking and action have become much more closely allied to, and even integrated with, public health work. Second, the long-standing absence of an ethics of public health has been highlighted. Third, the human rights-related roles and responsibilities of physicians and other medical workers are receiving increased attention.

Public Health and Medicine

To explore the first of these issues—the connections between human rights and public health—it is essential to review several central elements of modern public health.

Medicine and public health are two complementary and interacting approaches for promoting and protecting health-defined by the World Health Organization (WHO) as a state of physical, mental, and social well-being. Yet medicine and public health can, and also must be differentiated, because in several important ways they are not the same. The fundamental difference involves the population emphasis of public health, which contrasts with the essentially individual focus of medical care. Public health identifies and measures threats to the health of populations, develops governmental policies in response to these concerns, and seeks to assure certain health and related services. In contrast, medical care focuses upon individuals-diagnosis, treatment, relief of suffering, and rehabilitation.

Several specific points follow from this essential difference. For example, different instruments are called for: while public health measures population health status through epidemiological, survey, and other statistically based methods, medicine examines biophysical and psychological status using a combination of techniques, including dialogue, physical examination, and laboratory study of the individual. Public health generally values most highly (or at least is supposed to) primary prevention, that is, preventing the adverse health event in the first place, such as helping to prevent the automobile accident or the lead poisoning from happening at all. In contrast, medicine generally responds to existing health conditions, in the context of either secondary or tertiary prevention. Secondary prevention involves avoiding or delaying the adverse impact of a health condition like hypertension or diabetes. Thus, while the hypertension or insulin deficiency exists, its effects, such as heart disease, kidney failure, or blindness, can be avoided or delayed. So-called tertiary prevention involves those efforts to help sustain maximal functional and psychological capacity despite the presence of both the disease, such as hypertension, and its outcomes, heart disease, stroke, or kidney failure.

Accordingly, the skills and expertise needed in public health include epidemiology, biostatistics, policy analysis, economics, sociology, and other behavioral sciences. In contrast, medical skills and expertise center on the exploration, analysis, and response to the biophysical status of individuals, based principally on an understanding of biology, biochemistry, immunology, pharmacology, pathology, pathophysiology, anatomy, and psychology

Naturally, the settings in which public health and medicine operate also differ: governmental organizations, large-scale public programs, and various fora associated with developing and implementing public policy are inherently part of public health, while private medical offices, clinics, and medical care facilities of varying complexity and sophistication are the settings in which medical care is generally provided. Finally, the relationship between the profession and the people with whom it deals differs: in a sense, public health comes to you, while you go to the doctor. And expectations associated with each domain differ: from medicine, individual care and treatment are sought; from public health, protection against broad health threats like epidemic disease, unsafe water, or chemical pollution is expected.

Therefore, public health and medicine are principally distinguished by their focus on collectivities or on individuals, respectively, with a series of subsidiary differences involving methods of work, systems of analysis and measurement, emphasis on primary versus secondary or tertiary prevention, types of expertise and relevant skill, settings in which work is conducted, and client/public relationships and expectations.

Yet obviously, there is substantial overlap. Public health requires a sound biomedical basis, and involves many medical practitioners, whose services are organized in settings such as maternal and child health clinics, or immunization programs. Also, medical practice operates within a context highly influenced and governed by law and public policy. The potentially fluid relationship between public health and medicine is further suggested by recent proposals in this country that certain traditional public health functions be delegated to the private medical sector.

Despite these many differences, people equate medical care with health. Certainly, this basic confusion has informed the recent discussions of health care in the United States; and coverage of health issues in the popular press around the world reflects this perspective, in which access to medical care and the quality of that care are seen as the principal health needs of individuals and populations.

Medicine and Health

Yet the contribution of medicine to health, while undeniably important (and vital in certain situations), is actually quite limited. For example, it is estimated that only about one-sixth of the years of life expectancy gained in this country during this century can be attributed to the beneficial impact of medicine, medical care, and medical research. And it has been estimated that only about 10 percent of preventable premature deaths are associated with a lack of medical care. Similarly, the World Bank has estimated that a lack of essential clinical services is responsible for between 11 and 24 percent of the global burden of disease. Of course, none of these data, including also the notable decline in diseases like tuberculosis well before antimycobacterial therapy became available, suggest that medical care is irrelevant; rather, they suggest its limits.

In 1988, the United States' Institute of Medicine defined the mission of public health as "ensuring the conditions in which people can be healthy." This profound definition begs the most vital question for public health, namely, what are these essential conditions in which people can best achieve the highest possible level of physical, mental, and social well-being? If not medical care—its availability and quality—then what?

The vast majority of research into the health of populations identifies so-called "societal factors" as the major determinants of health status. Most of the work in this area has focused on socioeconomic status as the key variable, for it is clear, throughout history and in all societies, that the rich live generally longer and healthier lives than the poor. Thus, in the United Kingdom in 1911, the age-adjusted standardized mortality rate among members of the lowest social class was 1.6 times higher than for the highest social class. Interestingly, following creation of the National Health Services to ensure full access to medical care, and despite a dramatic change in major causes of death (from mainly infectious to mainly chronic diseases), in 1981 this societal gradient not only persisted, but increased, to a 2.1-fold higher standardized mortality rate among the lowest compared with the highest social class.

A major question arising from the socioeconomic status-health gradient is why there is a gradient. For example, among over 10,000 British civil servants followed for many years, health status and longevity were better for each successive category of civil servants, from lowest to highest. This raises two issues: first, while we believe we can—at least intuitively—explain poor health among the destitute when compared with the rich, associated with a lack of good food, housing, and with poor sanitary conditions, even the lowest class of British civil servants cannot be considered poor. Secondly, why should the civil servants in the next-to-highest group, living in quite comfortable circumstances, experience poorer health than the highest group?

Beyond these unanswered issues, many recent studies have pointed to the limited explanatory power of socioeconomic status, generally measured in terms of current income, years of education, and job classification. Other measures, such as the extent of socioeconomic inequality within a community, the nature, level, and temporal pattern of unemployment, societal connectedness and the extent of involvement in social networks, marital status, early childhood experiences, and exposure to dignity-denying situations have all been suggested as powerful potential components of a "black box" of societal factors whose dominant role in determining levels of preventable disease, disability, and premature death is beyond dispute.[1]

An Ethics for Public Health

Public health, although it began as a social movement, has—at least in recent years—responded relatively little to this most profound and vital knowledge about the dominant impact of society on health. To illustrate: we all know that certain behaviors have an enormous impact on health, such as cigarette smoking, excess alcohol intake, dietary choices, or levels of exercise and physical fitness. How these behaviors are conceptualized determines how they will be addressed by public health. The basic question is whether and to what extent these behaviors can be considered, and therefore responded to, as isolated individual choices.

The curve represented in Figure 1 (replicable among public health practitioners in at least three countries) reflects a strong belief that important health-related behaviors are substantially

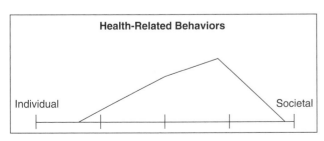

Figure 1   Health-Related Behaviors

influenced by societal factors and context. Yet examining public health programs designed to address the health problems associated with these same behaviors reveals that they generally consist of activities which assume that individuals have essentially complete control over their health-related behaviors. Traditional public health seeks to provide individuals with information and education about risks associated with diet or lack of exercise, along with various clinic-based services such as counseling, or distribution of condoms and other contraceptives. However, while public health may cite, or blame, or otherwise identify the societal-level or contextual issues—which it acknowledges to be of dominant importance, both in influencing individual behavior and for determining health status more broadly—it does not deal directly with these societal factors.

At least three reasons for this paradoxical inaction may be proposed. First, public health has lacked a conceptual framework for identifying and analyzing the essential societal factors that represent the "conditions in which people can be healthy." Second, a related problem: public health lacks a vocabulary with which to speak about and identify commonalities among health problems experienced by very different populations. Third, there is no consensus about the nature or direction of societal change that would be necessary to address the societal conditions involved. Lacking a coherent conceptual framework, a consistent vocabulary, and consensus about societal change, public health assembles and then tries valiantly to assimilate a wide variety of disciplinary perspectives, from economists, political scientists, social and behavioral scientists, health systems analysts, and a range of medical practitioners. Yet while each of these perspectives provides some useful insight, public health becomes thereby a little bit of everything and thus not enough of anything.

With this background in mind, it would be expected that in the domains of public health and medicine, different, yet complementary languages for describing and incorporating values would be developed. For even when values are shared at a higher level of abstraction, the forms in which they are expressed, the settings in which they are evoked, and their practical application may differ widely.

Not surprisingly, medicine has chosen the language of ethics, as ethics has been developed in a context of individual relationships, and is well adapted to the nature, practice, settings, and expectations of medical care. The language of medical ethics has also been applied when medicine seeks to deal with issues such as the organization of medical care or the allocation of societal resources. However, the contribution of medical ethics to these societal issues has been less powerful when compared, for example, with its engagement in the behavior of individual medical practitioners.

Public health, at least in its contemporary form, is struggling to define and articulate its core values. In this context, the usefulness of the language and structure of ethics as we know it today has been questioned. Given its population focus, and its interest in the underlying conditions upon which health is predicated (and that these major determinants of health status are societal in nature), it seems evident that a framework which expresses fundamental values in societal terms, and a vocabulary of values which links directly with societal structure and function, may be better adapted to the work of public health than a more individually oriented ethical framework.

For this reason, modern human rights, precisely because they were initially developed entirely outside the health domain and seek to articulate the societal preconditions for human well-being, seem a far more useful framework, vocabulary, and form of guidance for public health efforts to analyze and respond directly to the societal determinants of health than any inherited from the past biomedical or public health tradition

Public Health and Human Rights

The linkage between public health and human rights can be explored further by considering three relationships. The first focuses on the potential burden on human rights created by public health policies, programs, and practices. As public health generally involves direct or indirect state action, public health officials represent the state power toward which classical human rights concerns are traditionally addressed. Thus, in the modern world, public health officials have, for the first time, two fundamental responsibilities to the public: to protect and promote public health, and to protect and promote human rights. While public health officials may be unlikely to seek deliberately to violate human rights, there is great unawareness of human rights concepts and norms among public health practitioners. In stark contrast to the large number of bioethics courses available in medical educational settings, a recent survey of all twenty-eight accredited schools of public health in the United States and schools of public health in thirty-four other countries identified only seven formal courses in human rights for the presumed future leaders of public health.

Public health practice is heavily burdened by the problem of inadvertent discrimination. For example, outreach activities may "assume" that all populations are reached equally by a single, dominant-language message on television; or analysis "forgets" to include health problems uniquely relevant to certain groups, like breast cancer or sickle cell disease; or a program "ignores" the actual response capability of different population groups, as when lead poisoning warnings are given without concern for financial ability to ensure lead abatement. Indeed, inadvertent discrimination is so prevalent that all public health policies and programs should be considered discriminatory until proven otherwise, placing the burden on public health to affirm and ensure its respect for human rights. In addition, in public

health circles there is often an unspoken sense that public health and human rights concerns are inherently confrontational. At times, this has been true. In the early years of the HIV epidemic, the knee-jerk response of various public health officials to invoke mandatory testing, quarantine, and isolation did create a major clash with protectors of human rights. Even quite recently, an opinion piece in the British Medical Journal purports that excessive respect for human rights crippled public health efforts and is therefore responsible for the intensifying and expanding AIDS epidemic.

However, while modern human rights explicitly acknowledges that public health is a legitimate reason for limiting rights, more recently the underlying complementarity rather than inherent confrontation between public health and human rights has been emphasized. Again in the context of AIDS, public health has learned that discrimination toward HIV-infected people and people with AIDS is counterproductive. Specifically, when people found to be infected were deprived of employment, education, or ability to marry and travel, participation in prevention programs diminished. Thus, recent attention has been directed to a negotiation process for optimizing both the achievement of complementary public health goals and respect for human rights norms.

A second relationship between public health and human rights derives from the observation that human rights violations have health impacts, that is, adverse effects on physical, mental, and social well-being. For some rights, such as the right not to be tortured or imprisoned under inhumane conditions, the health damage seems evident, indeed inherent in the rights violation. However, even for torture, only more recently has the extensive, life-long, family and communitywide, and transgenerational impact of torture been recognized.

For many other rights, such as the right to information, to assembly, or to association, health impacts resulting from violation may not be initially so apparent. The violation of any right has measurable impacts on physical, mental, and social well-being: yet these health effects still remain, in large part, to be discovered and documented. Yet gradually, the connection is being established.

The right to association provides a useful example of this relationship. Public health benefits substantially even requires involvement of people in addressing problems that affect them. Because the ability of people concerned about a health problem to get together, talk, and search for effective solutions is so essential to public health, wherever the right to association is restricted, public health suffers. Taking a positive example from the history of HIV/AIDS: needle exchange—the trading-in of needles used for drug injection for clean needles, so as to avoid needle-sharing with consequent risk of HIV transmission—was invented by a union of drug users in Amsterdam. Needle exchange was a classic example of an innovative, local response to a pressing local problem. Needle exchange was not and would have been highly unlikely to have been developed by academics, government officials, or hired consultants! Yet the creative solution of needle exchange and respect for the right of association are closely linked. Thus, in societies in which people generally, or specific population groups, cannot associate around health, or other issues, such as injection drug users in the United States, or sex workers, or gay and lesbian people in many countries, local solutions are less able to emerge or be applied and public health is correspondingly compromised.

A third relationship between health and human rights has already been suggested; namely, that promoting and protecting human rights is inextricably linked with promoting and protecting health. Once again, this is because human rights offers a societal-level framework for identifying and responding to the underlying-societal-determinants of health. It is important to emphasize that human rights are respected not only for their

instrumental value in contributing to public health goals, but for themselves, as societal goods of pre-eminent importance.

For example, a cluster of rights, including the rights to health, bodily integrity, privacy, information, education, and equal rights in marriage and divorce, have been called "reproductive rights," insofar as their realization (or violation) is now understood to play a major role in determining reproductive health. From an early focus on demographic targets for population control, to an emphasis on ensuring "informed consent" of women to various contraceptive methods, a new paradigm for population policies and reproductive health has recently emerged. Articulated most forcefully at the United Nations Conference on Population and Development in 1994 in Cairo, the focus has shifted to ensuring that women can make and effectuate real and informed choices about reproduction. And in turn, this is widely acknowledged to depend on realization of human rights.

Similarly, in the context of HIV/AIDS, vulnerability to the epidemic has now been associated with the extent of realization of human rights. For as the HIV epidemic matures and evolves within each community and country, it focuses inexorably on those groups who, before HIV/AIDS arrived, were already discriminated against, marginalized, and stigmatized within each society. Thus, in the United States the brunt of the epidemic today is among racial and ethnic minority populations, inner city poor, injection drug users, and, especially women in these communities. In Brazil, an epidemic that started among the jet set of Rio and Sao Paulo with time has become a major epidemic among the slum-dwellers in the favelas of Brazil's cities. The French, with characteristic linguistic precision, identify the major burden of HIV/AIDS to exist among "les exclus," those living at the margins of society. Now that a lack of respect for human rights has been identified as a societal level risk factor for HIV/AIDS vulnerability, HIV prevention efforts—for example, for women—are starting to go beyond traditional educational and service-based efforts to address the rights issues that will be a precondition for greater progress against the epidemic.

Ultimately, ethics and human rights derive from a set of quite similar, if not identical, core values. As with medicine and public health, rather than seeing human rights and ethics as conflicting domains, it seems more appropriate to consider a continuum, in which human rights is a language most useful for guiding societal level analysis and work, while ethics is a language most useful for guiding individual behavior. From this perspective, and precisely because public health must be centrally concerned with the structure and function of society, the language of human rights is extremely useful for expressing, considering, and incorporating values into public health analysis and response.

Thus, public health work requires both ethics applicable to the individual public health practitioner and a human rights framework to guide public health in its societal analysis and response.

These relationships between medicine and public health, and between ethics and human rights, can be provisionally diagrammed as in Figure 2. At the hypothetical extreme of individual medical care, ethics would be the most useful language. However, to the extent that the individual practitioner is cognizant of the societal forces acting upon the individual patient, societal level considerations may also be articulated in human rights terms. At the other extreme of public health, human rights is the most useful language, speaking as it does directly to the societal level determinants of well-being. Nevertheless, the ethical framework remains critical, for public health is carried out by individuals within specific professional roles and competencies. In practice, of course, positions between the hypothetical extremes of medicine and public health are more common, calling for mixtures of human rights and ethical concepts and language.

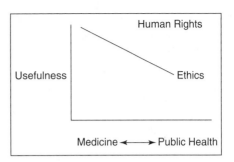

Figure 2 Human Rights

Professional Roles and Responsibilities

The placement of both human rights and ethics and public health and medicine at ends of a continuum suggests also that the interest domains of individuals and organizations can be "mapped" (as in Figure 3), and areas calling for additional attention can be highlighted.

According to this mapping approach, the "French Doctors" movement can be seen as primarily medical, primarily ethics-based, yet with growing involvement in the public health dimensions of health emergencies and in human rights issues raised by these complex humanitarian crises. Similarly, many traditional, medical ethics-based institutes and centers can be placed on this map. At the Harvard School of Public Health, the Francois-Xavier Bagnoud Center for Health and Human Rights, along with several others, is now focusing on the

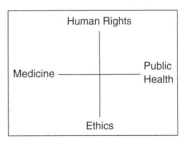

Figure 3 Human Rights

health-human rights territory. This map also suggests two major gaps in current work: on the ethics of public health, and on the relationships between medicine and human rights.

Where are the ethics of public health? In contrast to the important declarations of medical ethics such as the International Code of Medical Ethics of the World Medical Association and the Nuremberg Principles, the world of public health does not have a reasonably explicit set of ethical guidelines. In part, this deficiency may stem from the broad diversity of professional identities within public health. Yet, curiously, many of the occupational groups central to public health (epidemiologists, policy analysts, social scientists, biostatisticians, nutritionists, health system managers) have not yet developed, or are only now developing, widely accepted ethical guidelines or statements of principle for their work in the public health context. Thus, while a public health physician may draw upon medical ethics for guidance, the ethics of a public health physician have yet to be clearly articulated.

The central problem is one of coherence and identity: public health cannot develop an ethics until it has achieved clarity about its own identity; technical expertise and methodology are not substitutes for conceptual coherence. Or, as one student remarked a few years ago, public health spends too much time on the "p" values of biostatistics and not enough time on values.

To have an ethic, a profession needs clarity about central issues, including its major role and responsibilities. Two steps will be essential for public health to reach toward this analytic and definitional clarity.

First, public health must divest itself of its biomedical conceptual foundation. The language of disease, disability, and death is not the language of well-being; the vocabulary of diseases may detract from analysis and response to underlying societal conditions, of which traditional morbidity and mortality are expressions. It is clear that we do not yet know all about the universe of human suffering. Just as in the microbial world, in which new discoveries have become the norm—Ebola virus, hantavirus, toxic shock syndrome, Legionnaires' disease, AIDS—we are explorers in the larger world of human suffering and well-being. And our current maps of this universe, like world maps from sixteenth century Europe, have some very well-defined, familiar coastlines and territories and also contain large blank spaces, which beckon the explorer.

The language of biomedicine is cumbersome and ultimately perhaps of little usefulness in exploring the impacts of violations of dignity on physical, mental, and social well-being. The definition of dignity itself is complex and thus far elusive and unsatisfying. While the Universal Declaration of Human Rights starts by placing dignity first, "all people are born equal in dignity and rights," we do not yet have a vocabulary, or taxonomy, let alone an epidemiology of dignity violations.

Yet it seems we all know when our dignity is violated or impugned. Perform the following experiment: recall, in detail, an incident from your own life in which your dignity was violated, for whatever reason. If you will immerse yourself in the memory, powerful feelings will likely arise—of anger, shame, powerlessness, despair. When you connect with the power of these feelings, it seems intuitively obvious that such feelings, particularly if evoked repetitively, could have deleterious impacts on health. Yet most of us are relatively privileged, we live in a generally dignity-affirming environment, and suffer only the occasional lapse of indignity. However, many people live constantly in a dignity-impugning environment, in which affirmations of dignity may be the exceptional occurrence. An exploration of the meanings of dignity and the forms of its violation—and the impact on physical, mental, and social well-being—may help uncover a new universe of human suffering, for which the biomedical language may be inapt and even inept. After all, the power of naming, describing, and then measuring is truly enormous—child abuse did not exist in meaningful societal terms until it was named and then measured; nor did domestic violence.

A second precondition for developing an ethics of public health is the adoption and application of a human rights framework for analyzing and responding to the societal determinants of health. The human rights framework can provide the coherence and clarity required for public health to identify and work with conscious attention to its roles and responsibilities. At that point, an ethics of public health, rather than the ethics of individual constituent disciplines within public health, can emerge.

Issues of respect for autonomy, beneficence, nonmaleficence, and justice can then be articulated from within the set of goals and responsibilities called for by seeking to improve public health through the combination of traditional approaches and those that strive concretely to promote realization of human rights. This is not to replace health education, information, and clinical service-based activities of public health with an exclusive focus on human rights and dignity. Both are necessary.

For example, the challenges for public health officials in balancing the goals of promoting and protecting public health and ensuring that human rights and dignity are not violated call urgently for ethical analysis. The official nature of much public health work places public health practitioners in a complex environment, in which work to promote rights inevitably challenges the state system within which the official is employed. Ethical dimensions are highly relevant to collecting, disseminating, and acting on information about the health impacts of the entire range of human rights violations. And as public health seeks to "ensure the conditions in which people can be healthy," and as those conditions are societal, to be engaged in public health necessarily involves a commitment to societal transformation. The difficulties in assessing human rights status and in developing useful and appropriate ways to pro-

mote human rights and dignity necessarily engage ethical considerations. For example, beyond accurate diagnosis, beyond efforts to cure, and even beyond the ever-present responsibility for relief of pain, the physician agrees to accompany the patient, to stand by the patient through her suffering, even to the edge of life itself, even when the only thing the physician can offer is the fact of his or her presence. Is this not as relevant to public health? For public health must engage difficult issues even when no cure or effective instruments are yet available, and public health also must accompany, remain with, and not abandon vulnerable populations.

That this work—added to, not substituted for, the current approach of public health—will require major changes in public health reflection, analysis, action, and education, is clear. That it is urgently required, in order to confront the major health challenges of the modern world, is equally clear.

Physicians and Human Rights

Finally, turning to the third issue raised by new challenges to the domains of public health, medicine, ethics, and human rights: what about the human rights role and responsibilities of medicine and the medical professional? To what extent and in what ways are—or might, or should—medicine generally and physicians in particular be involved in human rights issues? Physicians have developed important roles in the context of human rights work. This work generally started from a corporatist interest in the fate of fellow physicians suffering human rights abuses, and then expanded in four directions. First, physicians created the "French Doctors" movement, providing medical assistance to populations in need, across borders. This dramatic and catalyzing work, including the concept of the right to assistance and the duty to intervene, expressed—in medical terms—the same transnational, universalist impulse as the modern human rights movement. Then, groups such as

Physicians for Human Rights applied medical methods and analysis to detect and document torture, executions, and other similar human rights violations. In this manner, credible documentation, necessary also for redress and prosecution, has increasingly been made available. Meanwhile, Amnesty International has been concerned with the participation of physicians in human rights violations, usually in the context of torture and imprisonment under inhumane conditions. Finally, at a global level, physicians have articulated a role in seeking to prevent health catastrophes, exemplified by the Nobel Peace Prize-winning organization, International Physicians for Prevention of Nuclear War.

These historic and often courageous engagements with human rights issues have carried physicians to the frontiers of new challenges, exemplified by complex humanitarian emergencies, efforts to identify the full range of health consequences from human rights violations, and further struggle with societal issues inextricably linked with the health dimensions of conflict, economic consumption, and the degradation of the global environment. Increased physician participation and concern with these issues will inevitably blur pre-existing boundaries between public health and medicine and create new interactive configurations between human rights and ethics.

Yet for individual medical practitioners, how is a human rights perspective relevant? Human rights and dignity will be engaged to the extent that the physician seeks to go beyond the usual, limited boundaries of medical care. Take two examples: a child with asthma, or a woman seeking emergency room care for injuries inflicted by her spouse. In each case, the limited medical perspective is vital. For the precipitating factors for asthma, and the likelihood of seeking early care as asthmatic attacks begin, lead directly to environmental conditions, economic issues, and discrimination. Similarly, domestic violence invokes, necessarily, societal issues in which the human rights framework will be useful, if not es-

sential. Whether considering cancer, heart disease, lead poisoning, asthma, injuries, or infectious diseases, while the medical professional may start from a context dominated by individual relationships, a larger, societal set of issues will inevitably exist. The question then becomes, to what extent is the physician responsible for what happens outside the immediate context and setting of medical care? To what extent is a physician responsible for assuring access to care of marginalized populations in the community or helping the community understand the medical implications of public policy measures, or identifying, responding to, and preventing discrimination occurring within medical institutions?

Where, that is, does the boundary of medicine end? This seems a uniquely rich context for ethical discussion, at the frontiers of human rights and public health.

Of course, for those interested in the human rights dimensions of medicine, many may accuse physicians of "meddling" in societal issues that "go far beyond" their scope or competence. Also, issues of human rights inherently and inevitably represent a challenge to power—and health professionals are often part of, or direct beneficiaries of, the societal or institutional status quo that is challenged by the claims of human rights and dignity

In conclusion, there is more to modern health than new scientific discoveries, or development of new technologies, or emerging or re-emerging diseases, or changes in patterns of morbidity and mortality around the world. For we are living at a time of paradigm shift in thinking about health, and therefore about medicine and public health. Health as well-being, despite the World Health Organization's definition, lacks more than rudimentary definition, especially regarding its mental and societal dimensions. The universe of human suffering and its alleviation is being more fully explored. Awareness of the limits of medicine and medical care, growing recognition of the health impacts of societal structure and function, globalization and consequent interdependence, and the sometimes active, sometimes ineffectual actions of nation-states, all intersect to lead toward a new vision of health.

In the ongoing work on values and their articulation, we must acknowledge the provisional, untidy, and necessarily incomplete character of our understanding of the universe of health. In this context, medicine need not compete with public health, nor ethics with human rights; the search for meaning deserves to draw on all, as new constellations emerge and new relationships evolve.

Yet at such times of profound change, another kind of value becomes all the more vital. To build bridges—between medicine and public health, and between ethics and human rights—the critical underlying question may be, Do we believe that the world can change? Do we believe that the long chains of human suffering can be broken? Do we agree with Martin Luther King that "the arc of history is long, but it bends towards justice?" Bioethical pioneers at the frontier of human history, we affirm that the past does not inexorably determine the future—and that it is precisely through this historic effort to explore and promote values in the world for which we share responsibility, articulated in philosophy and in action—that we express confidence in our own lives, in our community, and in the future of our world.

Reference

1. N. E. Adler et al., "Socioeconomic Status and Health: The Challenges of the Gradient," American Psychologist 49, no. 1 (1994): 15–24.

Notes

1. J. H. Warner, "Book Review, G.L. Geison, The Private Science of Louis Pasteur (Princeton: Princeton University Press, 1995)" *Bulletin of the History of Medicine* 70(4)(1996): 718–720.
2. M. M. Marrus, "The Nuremberg Doctors' Trial in Historical Context," *Bulletin of the History of Medicine* 73(1) (1999): 106–123.
3. Tuskegee Syphilis Study Ad Hoc Advisory Panel, *Final Report of the Tuskegee Syphilis Study Ad Hoc Advisory Panel* (Washington, D.C.: U.S. Government Printing Office, 1973).
4. Allan M. Brandt, "Racism and Research: The Case of the Tuskegee Syphilis Study," *Hastings Center Report* 8 (December 1978): 21–29.
5. 45 C. F. R. Pt. 46.
6. 45 C. F. R. 46.116.
7. 45 C. F. R. 46.108–113.
8. Margot A. Henriksen, "Dr. Strangelove's America: Society and Culture in the Atomic Age" 16 (1996), cited in Willie Curtis, "Symposium: Responding To Rogue Regimes; From Smart Bombs To Smart Sanctions; National Missile Defense: A Retreat from Dr. Strangelove or How I Learn to Stop Worrying and Love MAD," *New England Law Review* 36(2002): 795, 800.
9. George J. Annas, "The Randolph W. Thrower Symposium-Genetics and the Law: Mapping the Human Genome and the Meaning of Monster Mythology," *Emory Law Journal* 39(1990): 629.
10. Ibid.

11. Gina Kolata, "Scientist Reports First Cloning Ever of Adult Mammal," *New York Times,* February 23, 1997, 1.
12. Calvin Simerly et al., "Molecular Correlates of Primate Nuclear Transfer Failures," *Science* 300(2003): 297.
13. National Bioethics Advisory Committee, *Report and Recommendations: Cloning Human Beings, Executive Summary,* June 1997, at http://www.georgetown.edu/research/nrcbl/nbac/pubs/cloning/chapter6.pdf.
14. John Robertson, "Why Human Reproductive Cloning Should Not in all Cases Be Prohibited," *New York University Journal of Legislation and Public Policy* 4(2000/2001): 35, 37–38.
15. George W. Bush, "Stem Cell Science and the Preservation of Life," *New York Times,* August 12, 2001, p. 13.
16. Ibid.
17. Eric Leipoldt, Christopher Newell & Maurice Corcoran, "Christopher Reeve and Bob Carr Dehumanise Disability—Stem Cell Research Not the Best Solution," *On Line Opinion,* January 27, 2003, at http://www.onlineopinion.com.au/2003/Jan03?Leipolt_et_al.htm.
18. George J. Annas, Lori B. Andrews, and Rosario M. Isasi, "Protecting the Endangered Human: Toward an International Treaty Prohibiting Cloning and Inheritable Alterations," *American Journal Law and Medicine* 28(2002): 151, 153.
19. J. Michael McGinnis and William H. Foege, "Actual Causes of Death in the United States," *Journal of the American Medical Association* 270(18) (1993): 2207–2213.
20. Laurie Garrett, *The Coming Plague: Newly Emerging Diseases in a World Out of Balance* (New York: Farrar, Strauss and Girouz, 1994).
21. Judith Miller, Stephen Engelberg, and William Broad, *Germs: Biological Weapons and America's Secret War* (New York: Simon & Schuster, 2001), 37–38.
22. Ibid.
23. Tara O'Toole et al., "Shining Light on Dark Winter," *Clinical Infectious Diseases* 34 (2002): 972.
24. World Health Organization, "Communicable Disease Surveillance & Response (CSR)," http://www.who.int/csr/sars/en/.
25. Committee on Emerging Microbial Threats to Health, Division of Health Sciences Policy, Division of International Health, Institute of Medicine, *Emerging Infections: Microbial Threats to Health in the United States,* Joshua Lederberg, Robert E. Shope, Stanley C. Oaks, eds. (Washington, D.C.: National Academy Press, 1992): 34–12.
26. Wendy E. Parmet, "AIDS and Quarantine: The Revival of an Archaic Doctrine," *Hofstra Law Review* 14(1985): 53.
27. Wendy E. Parmet, "Individual Rights and Communicable Disease: AIDS, The Police Power and Individual Liberty," *Journal of Health Politics, Policy & Law* 14(1989): 741, 749–754.
28. The Center for Law and the Public's Health at Georgetown and Johns Hopkins Universities, *The Model State Emergency Health Powers Act,* Dec. 21, 2001 at http://www.publichealthlaw.net/MSEHPA/MSEHPA2.pdf.

29. Joseph Kahn, "The SARS Epidemic: Health and Politics; Some Chinese Say Government's Response to the Epidemic Has Been Too Heavy-Handed," *New York Times*, May 23, 2003, A8.

30. Lawrence O. Gostin, "When Terrorism Threatens Health: How Far Are Limitations on Personal and Economic Liberties Justified," *Florida Law Review* 55 (2003): 1 105–1169.

31. Edward P. Richards, "Bioterroism and the Use of Fear in Public Health," http://biotech.law.lsu.edu/blaw/bt/epr_bioterror 01.pdf (visited January 3, 2005).

32. Jonathan Mann et al., "Health and Human Rights," in *Health and Human Rights a Reader*, ed. Jonathan Mann et al. (New York: Routledge, 1999): 7–20.

33. Gerald Oppenheimer, Ronald Bayer, and James Colgrove, "Health and Human Rights: Old Wine in New Bottles," *The Journal of Law, Medicine and Ethics* 30:4 (Winter 2002): 522–532.

Recommended Readings

Andrews, Lori. *The Clone Age: Adventures in the New World of Reproductive Technology.* New York: Henry Holt, 1999.

Annas, George. *Informed Consent to Human Experimentation: The Subject's Dilemma.* Cambridge, Mass.: Ballinger Publishing Co., 1997.

Annas, George, and Grodin, Michael. *The Nazi Doctors and the Nuremberg Code: Human Rights in Human Experimentation.* New York: Oxford University Press, 1992.

Attaran, Amir, and Gillespie-White, Lee. "Do Patents for Antiretroviral Drugs Constrain Access to AIDS Treatment in Africa?" *Journal of the American Medical Association* 286(2001): 1886–1892.

Baker, Edward L., and Koplan, Jeffrey P. "Strengthening the Nation's Public Health Infrastructure: Historic Challenge, Unprecedented Opportunity; It Takes a System that Is Competent to Handle Routine Public Health Situations to Handle the Emergencies." *Health Affairs* 21:6 (Nov. 2002–Dec. 2002): 15–27.

Beecher, Henry K. "Ethics and Clinical Research." *New England Journal of Medicine* 274(1966): 1354–1360.

Berry, Michele. "Ethical Considerations of Human Investigation in Developing Countries: The AIDS Dilemma." *New England Journal of Medicine* 319: 16(1988): 1083–1086.

Brock, Dan W. "Human Cloning and Our Sense of Self," *Science* 5566(2002): 314–316.

Burris, Scott, Kawachi, Ichiro, and Sarat, Austin. "Integrating Law and Social Epidemiology." *The Journal of Law, Medicine and Ethics* 30 (4)(2002): 510–521.

Caplan, Arthur. "Twenty Years After: The Legacy of the Tuskegee Syphilis Study, When Evil Intrudes." *Hastings Center Report* 22(1992): 29–32.

Committee on Assessing the System for Protecting Human Research, Institute of Medicine. *Preserving Public Trust: Accreditation and Human Research Participant Protection Programs.* Washington, D.C.: National Academy Press, 2001.

Committee on Assuring the Health of the Public in the 21st Century, Board of Health Promotion and Disease Prevention, Institute of Medicine of the National Academies. *The Future of the Public's Health in the 21st Century.* Washington D.C.: National Academy Press, 2003.

Fukuyama, Francis. *Our Posthuman Future: Consequences of the Biotechnology Revolution.* New York: Farrar, Straus & Giroux, 2002.

Garrett, Laurie. *The Coming Plague: Newly Emerging Diseases in a World Out of Balance.* New York: Farrar, Straus and Giroux, 1994.

Garrett, Laurie. *Betrayal of Trust: The Collapse of Global Public Health.* New York: Hyperion, 2000.

George, Erin P. "The Stem Cell Debate: The Legal, Political and Ethical Issues Surrounding Federal Funding of Scientific Research on Human Embryos." *Albany Law Journal of Science & Technology* 12(2002): 747–808.

Gostin, Lawrence. "The Human Right to Health: A Right to the 'Highest Attainable Standard of Health'." *Hastings Center Report* 31(2001): 29–30.

Gostin, Lawrence O. "When Terrorism Threatens Health: How Far Are Limitations on Personal and Economic Liberties Justified?" *Florida Law Review* 55(2003): 1105–1169.

Hopkins, Patrick D. "Bad Copies: How Popular Media Represent Cloning as an Ethical Problem." *Hastings Center Report* 28(1998.): 6–13.

Hubbard, Ruth, and Newman, Stuart. "Yuppie Eugenics: Creating a World with Genetic Haves and Have-Nots." *Z Magazine* 15(March, 2002): 36–39.

Jonas, Hans. "Philosophical Reflections on Experimenting with Human Beings." *Ethical Aspects of Experimentation with Human Subjects* 98(1969): 1.

Jones, James H. *Bad Blood: The Tuskegee Syphilis Experiment.* New York: Free Press, 1993.

Kass, Leon R. *Life, Liberty and the Defense of Dignity: The Challenge for Bioethics.* San Francisco: Encounter Books, 2002.

Katz, Katheryn D. "The Clonal Child: Procreative Liberty and Asexual Reproduction." *Albany Law Journal of Science & Technology* 8(1997): 1–63.

Kaveny, M. Cathleen. "Cloning and Positive Liberty." *Notre Dame Journal of Law, Ethics and Public Policy* 13(1999): 15–35.

Lurie, Peter, and Wolfe, Sidney. "Unethical Trials of Interventions to Reduce Prenatal Transmission of the Human Immunodeficiency Virus in Developing Countries." *The New England Journal of Medicine* 337(1997): 853–856.

McCartney, James J. "Embryonic Stem Cell Research and Respect for Human Life: Philosophical and Legal Reflections." *Albany Law Review* 65(2002): 597–624.

McKibben, Bill. *Enough: Staying Human in an Engineered Age.* New York: Henry Holt & Co., 2003.

Miller, Judith et al. *Germs: Biological Weapons and America's Secret War.* New York: Simon & Schuster, 2001.

Moreno, Jonathan D., ed. *In the Wake of Terror: Medicine and Morality in a Time of Crisis.* Cambridge, Mass.: Massachusetts Institute of Technology Press, 2003.

Moreno, Jonathan, Caplan, Arthur, and Wolpe, Paul Root. "Updating Protections for Human Subjects Involved in Research." *Journal of the American Medical Association* 280(1998): 1951–1958.

Nathan, Aaron. "The Astonishing Testimony of Doctor Brigitte Boisselier Before a Subcommittee of the United States Congress in March 2001." *Cardozo Studies in Law and Literature* 14(2002): 397–421.

National Bioethics Advisory Commission. *Cloning Human Beings.* Volume I: Report and Recommendations of the National Bioethics Advisory Commission. Rockville, Md.: NBAC, June 1997 (available at http://bioethics.george town.edu/nbac).

National Commission for the Protection of Human Subjects of Biomedical and Behavioral Research. *The Belmont Report: Ethical Principles and Guidelines for the Protection of Human Subjects of Research,* April 18, 1979.

O'Toole, Tara. "Emerging Illness and Bioterrorism: Implications for Public Health." *Journal of Urban Health: Bulletin of the New York Academy of Medicine* 78(2) (2001): 396–402.

Parmet, Wendy E. "Quarantine Redux: Bioterrorism, AIDS and the Curtailment of Individual Liberty in the Name of Public Health." *Health Matrix* 13(2003): 85–115.

Resnik, David B. "The Ethics of HIV Research In Developing Nations." *Bioethics* 12(4)(1998): 287–305.

Resnik, David B., and De Ville, Kenneth A. "Bioterrorism and Patent Rights: 'Compulsory Licensure' and the Case of Cipro." *American Journal of Bioethics* 2:3(2002): 29–39.

Robertson, John. "Why Human Reproductive Cloning Should Not In All Cases Be Prohibited." *New York University Journal of Legislation and Public Policy* 35(2000/2001): 35–43.

Thomasma, David C. "Proposing a New Agenda: Bioethics and International Human Rights." *Cambridge Quarterly of Healthcare Ethics* 10(2001): 299–310.

United States Holocaust Memorial Museum. "Online Exhibitions: The Doctors' Trial, The Medical Case of the Subsequent Nuremberg Proceedings," www.ushmm.org/research/doctors/index/html.

Welsome, Eileen. *The Plutonium Files: America's Secret Medical Experiments in the Cold War.* New York: Dial Press, 1999.

Wright, R. George. "Second Thoughts: How Human Cloning Can Promote Human Dignity." *Valparaiso University Law Review* 35(2000): 1–38.

Yach, Derek, and Bettcher, Douglas. "The Globalization of Public Health, II: The Convergence of Self Interest and Altruism." *American Journal of Public Health* 88 (5)(1998): 738–741.

Credits

Rene Dubos, "Health and Creative Adaptation." From *Human Nature Magazine,* Health and Creative Adaptation, by Dubos, Rene. © 1978. Reprinted with permission of Wadsworth, a division of Thomson Learning: www.thomsonrights.com. Fax 800 730–2215.

Daniel Callahan, "The WHO Definition of Health," *Hastings Center Studies* 1, no. 3 (1973): 77–78. Reproduced by permission. © The Hastings Center.

Geoffrey Rose, "Sick Individuals and Sick Populations," *International Journal of Epidemiology,* 2001, Vol 30, pp. 427–432. By permission of Oxford University Press.

Ichiro Kawachi, Bruce Kennedy, and Kimberly Lochner, "Long Live Community: Social Capital as Public Health." Reprinted with permission from *The American Prospect,*Volume 8, Number 35: November 1, 1997–December 1, 1997. The American Prospect, 5 Broad Street, Boston, MA. 02109. All rights reserved.

John Inglehart, "The American Health Care System—Expenditures," *The New England Journal of Medicine,* vol. 340, Jan. 7, 1999, pp. 70–76. Copyright © 1999 Massachusetts Medical Society. All rights reserved.

Wendy Mariner, "Rationing Health Care and the Need for Credible Scarcity: Why Americans Can't Say No." *American Journal of Public Health* 85, no. 10 (1995): 1439–1445. Reprinted by permission of the American Journal of Public Health.

Gerald Dworkin, "Autonomy and Informed Consent," pp. 100–120 of *The Theory and Practice of Autonomy.* Reprinted with the permission of Cambridge University Press.

David Rothman, "The Origins and Consequences of Patient Autonomy: A 25 Year Retrospective," *HealthCare Analysis* 9 (2001): 255–64. Reprinted by permission of Health Care Analysis.

George J. Annas, " 'Culture of Life' Politics at the Bedside—The Case of Terri Schiavo," *The New England Journal of Medicine,* vol. 352, April 21, 2005, pp. 1710–1715. Copyright © 2005 Massachusetts Medical Society. All rights reserved.

Garrett Hardin, "The Tragedy of the Commons," *Science* 162, no. 3859 (1968): 1243–1248. Reprinted with permission of Science.